SELECTED LETTERS OF WILLIAM EMPSON

SELECTED LETTERS OF
WILLIAM EMPSON

EDITED BY

JOHN HAFFENDEN

OXFORD

UNIVERSITY PRESS

OXFORD
UNIVERSITY PRESS

Great Clarendon Street, Oxford OX2 6DP

Oxford University Press is a department of the University of Oxford.
It furthers the University's objective of excellence in research, scholarship,
and education by publishing worldwide in

Oxford New York

Auckland Cape Town Dar es Salaam Hong Kong Karachi
Kuala Lumpur Madrid Melbourne Mexico City Nairobi
New Delhi Shanghai Taipei Toronto

With offices in

Argentina Austria Brazil Chile Czech Republic France Greece
Guatemala Hungary Italy Japan Poland Portugal Singapore
South Korea Switzerland Thailand Turkey Ukraine Vietnam

Oxford is a registered trade mark of Oxford University Press
in the UK and in certain other countries

Published in the United States
by Oxford University Press Inc., New York

British Library Cataloguing in Publication Data

Data available

Library of Congress Cataloging in Publication Data

Data available

Typeset by RefineCatch Limited, Bungay, Suffolk
Printed in Great Britain
on acid-free paper by
Biddles Ltd, King's Lynn, Norfolk
ISBN 0–19–928684–1   978–0–19–928684–3

1 3 5 7 9 10 8 6 4 2

ACKNOWLEDGEMENTS

I am grateful to the Empson family for their friendship and hospitality, and for entrusting me with this task: primarily (with regard to this volume) the late Hetta Empson, Mogador Empson, Jacob Empson, Simon Duval Smith.

I am indebted to the British Academy for a Research Readership in 1989–91, and for a later grant-in-aid; and no less to the Arts Council of Great Britain, the Society of Authors, the Leverhulme Trust, and the Research Fund of Sheffield University for awards towards the high costs of my research on Empson over the years. The award of an AHRB research leave in 2001–2 enabled me to bring this particular project on the letters to a final fullness.

Many libraries and other organizations and institutions have been generous in affording me accommodation, or in providing research facilities of one sort or another, and in granting permission for the publication of the Empson letters under their control. I am eager first of all to thank the Houghton Library, Harvard University (custodian since 1986 of the Empson Papers), and in particular Leslie Morris (Curator of Manuscripts), Rodney G. Dennis (former Curator), and Elizabeth A. Falsey (who undertook the awesome job of preparing an inventory of the papers). I am deeply grateful too to the authorities of Beijing University, Peking, who kindly hosted my visit to China in 1984; the British Embassy, Peking (Alan Maley, First Secretary, Cultural Section, British Embassy, and Martin Davidson; David Marler, Cultural Counsellor, British Council Representative in China); the British Council, London (Angela Udall, Leigh Gibson, Specialist Tours Department; Martin Carney; Adrian Johnson, Cultural Counsellor and British Council Representative, Beijing); and the British Embassy Cultural Department, The British Council, Tokyo; BBC Play Library, Broadcasting House (Deborah A. Halfpenny); BBC Written Archives Centre, Caversham, Reading (Jacqueline Kavanagh, Written Archives Officer; Gwyniver Jones, Assistant-in-Charge, Enquiries; John Jordan, Enquiry Assistant); Beinecke Library, Yale University; Department of Manuscripts, The British Library (Sally Brown, Dr Chris Fletcher); Butler Library, Columbia University (Bernard R Crystal, Curator of Manuscripts; Kenneth A. Lohf, former Curator); Chalmers Memorial Library, Kenyon College Archives (Thomas B. Greenslade, College Archivist);

Chatto & Windus; Cornell University Library; Embassy of the People's Republic of China; Exeter University Library (Alistair Patterson); Harry Ransom Humanities Research Center, University of Texas at Austin (Ellen S. Dunlap, Research Librarian; Cathy Henderson, Research Associate; Elizabeth L. Garver); Modern Archives Centre, King's College, Cambridge (Dr R Moad, Dr P. K. McGuire); Manuscript Division, The Library of Congress, Washington, DC (Fred Bauman, Reference Librarian); Lilly Library, Indiana University; Magdalen College, Oxford; Magdalene College, Cambridge; John Rylands Library, University of Manchester; Mills Memorial Library, McMaster University (Carl Spadoni, Research Collections Librarian); the National Archives, Washington, DC (Kathie Nicastro); National Library of Scotland; Library/Information Service, National Sound Archive, British Library (Lee Taylor); Princeton University Library (Jean F. Preston, Curator of Manuscripts); Reading University Library (A. J. C Bainton, Michael Bott); Rockefeller Archive Centre, Tarrytown, New York; St John's College, Oxford; School of Oriental and African Studies, London; Special Collections and Archives, The Library, University of Sheffield (Lawrence Aspden, former Curator); The Society of Authors; *Times* archive; The Library, University College London (Gill Furlong, archivist); The Library, University of Victoria, Victoria, BC, Canada (Chris Petter, University Archivist and Head of Special Collections); and Wren Library, Trinity College, Cambridge (Dr David McKitterick).

Individuals who have most kindly afforded me information, advice and assistance in various capacities include: A. Alvarez, Professor Paul J. Alpers, Dr Charles Aylmer, Professor Shyamal Bagchee, Jonathan Barker, Sebastian Barker, Dr D. K. Barua, the later Professor Walter Jackson Bate, Clark Beck (Librarian, Special Collections/Archives, Rutgers University), Jonathan Benthall, the late Sir Isaiah Berlin, Professor Francis Berry, Robert J. Bertholf (Curator, The Poetry/Rare Books Collection, State University of New York at Buffalo), Andrew Best, the late Professor Max Black, Meifang Blofeld, Professor James Booth, the late Margaret Bottrall, Margot Bottrall, the late Ronald Bottrall, Gordon Bowker, the late Professor Muriel Bradbrook, Baroness Brigstocke, Professor David Bromwich, John Brown, Stephen Burt, James Campbell, the late Peter Carnell, the late Alan N. Cass, Professor Chao Chao-hsiung, Peter Cheeseman, Igor Chroustchoff, Ken Churchill (The British Council), Mary Coleman, Professor Thomas E. Connolly, Peter Conradi, Dr John Constable, the late Alistair Cooke, Jenny Cowan, Professor C. B. Cox, Professor Sir Bernard Crick, Mrs C. Cruickshank (Archivist, Faber & Faber), D. W. Cruickshank,

Peter Currie, Gordon Daniels, Natalie Davenport, Roger Davenport, the late Gwenda David, the late Hugh Sykes Davies, Professor Frank Day, Professor Martin Dodsworth, Professor John Doheny, the late Francis Doherty, Dr Penelope Doob, the late Elsie Duncan-Jones, Professor Katherine Duncan-Jones, Eamon Dyas (*Times* archivist), Brian Dyson (Hull University Library), H. J. Easterling, the late Professor Richard Eberhart, Professor Philip Edwards, Professor Arthur Efron, Mrs Valerie Eliot, the late Charles Empson, the late D. J. Enright, Maggie Fergusson (Royal Society of Literature), the late Professor Leslie Fiedler, the late Professor C. P. Fitzgerald, Mirabel Fitzgerald, Mrs Paddy Fraser, Michael Freeman, Professor Norman Fruman, Mrs Rintaro Fukuhara, Professor David Fuller, John Fuller, the late Professor Dame Helen Gardner, Helen Gardner (Society of Authors), Professor Averil Gardner, the late Roma Gill, Victoria Glendinning, Adrian Goodman, Prof. W. Terrence Gordon, Professor Gayle Greene, Dr Eric Griffiths, John Gross, Dr Michael Halls, the late Ian Hamilton, Saskia Hamilton, Dr Jason Harding, Dr Henry Hardy, Claire Harmon, Professor David Hawkes, Mark Haymon, the late Sir William Hayter, the late Sir Robert Helpmann, Christopher Heywood, the late Professor Christopher Hill, Geoff Hill, Andrew and Geraldine Hillier, Charles Hobday, the late Professor Philip Hobsbaum, Dr Anthony Hobson, Theodore Hofmann, Richard Holmes, Professor Michael Hollington, Dr Michael Holroyd, Dr Eric Homberger, the late Professor Graham Hough, the late Judge W. H. Hughes, Professor Yukio Irie, Kevin Jackson, the late Professor A. N. Jeffares, Elizabeth Jenkins, Dr Nicholas Jenkins, Mary-Lou Jennings, Professor James Jensen, Professor Jin Di, Professor Jin Fa-xin, the late John Henry (David) Jones, Brian Keeble, Paul Keegan, Anne Kelly, Professor Richard J. Kelly, Dr Tim Kendall, Dr Gilbert Kennedy, Professor Sir Frank Kermode, Professor Kim Jong-gil (Kim Chi-gyu), the late Professor L. C. Knights, the late James Laughlin, the late Sir Desmond Lee, Dr E. S. Leedham-Green, the late Professor Peter Levi, the late Professor Li Fu-ning, Professor Li Zhiwei, Professor Grevel Lindop, Dr Richard Luckett, the late Professor Hyam Maccoby, Jim McCue, the late Professor Maynard Mack, the late Dr Eric Mackerness, the late Professor Ian MacKillop, Alan and Robin McLean, the late Jenny McMorris, the late Professor Charles Madge, Nick Malone, Joyce Marks, Dr D. H. Marrian, Professor William H. Matchett, Professor Giorgio Melchiori, D. H. Mellor, M. C. Meredith (School Librarian, Eton College), Professor Karl Miller, Professor Earl Miner, Professor Andrew Motion, the late Professor Kenneth Muir, the late Dr Joseph Needham, Sir Patrick Neill (All Souls College, Oxford), Professor Christopher Norris,

Professor A. D. Nuttall, Mrs Diana Oakeley, Professor Darcy O'Brien, Professor Kazuo Ogawa, Sumie Okada, A. E. B. Owen (Keeper of Manuscripts, Cambridge University Library), Dr Barbara Ozieblo, Dr David Parker, the late Ian Parsons, the late Marjorie Tulip (Trekkie) Parsons, David Perry, John Oliver Perry, Dr Seamus Perry, the late Professor Frank Pierce, Professor H. W. Piper, Dr David B. Pirie, the late N. W. (Bill) Pirie, Mrs Dorothy Poynter (secretary to the late Professor Kathleen Coburn), Dr Kate Price, the late Professor F. T. Prince, Syrithe Pugh, Qien Xuexi, the late Sir Peter Quennell, the late Dr Kathleen Raine, the late Mrs Dorothy Richards, Professor Christopher Ricks, Professor Andrew Roberts, Professor Mark Roberts, Professor Neil Roberts, Peter Robinson, the late George (Dadie) Rylands, Susan Rieger, the late Professor W. W. Robson, Professor Thomas P. Roche Jr., Lisa A. Rodensky, Earl M. Rogers (Archivist, The University of Iowa), Derek Roper, Professor S. P. Rosenbaum, the late Dr A. L. Rowse, Professor Alan Rudrum, Professor John Paul Russo, the late Lorna Sage, Professor Roger Sale, Professor Michael Schmidt, Miranda Seymour, the late Martin Seymour-Smith, Dr Erica Sheen, C. D. W. Sheppard (Brotherton Library, University of Leeds), the late Mrs Norah Smallwood, the late Janet Adam Smith, Professor Nigel Smith, Dr Richard C. Smith, the late John Sparrow, the late Sir Stephen Spender, Lady Spender, the late Nikos Stangos, Susan Stephens (Assistant Registrar, University of Sheffield), Professor Herbert Stern, the late Dr Alice Stewart, Sir Roy Strong, Sharon Sumpter (Archives Associate, The Archives of the University of Notre Dame, Indiana), Sun Yu-mei, Professor John Sutherland, Kevin Taylor, Mark Thompson, John L. Thorn, Anthony Thwaite, J. B. Trapp (The Warburg Institute), Professor Jeremy Treglown, the late Julian Trevelyan, the late Professor John Unterecker, Robert Vas Dias, Professor William Vesterman, Professor Sue Vice, the late Igor Vinogradoff, the late Professor John Wain, William Wain, the late Keith Walker, Stephen Wall, Jemma Walton, the late Professor Wang Zuo-liang, Dr George Watson, Professor J. H. Willis, Jr., David Wilson, Professor Mark Royden Winchell, the late Professor Robert Winter, the late Professor Yang Zhouhan, and the late Lord Zuckerman.

At Oxford University Press, I greatly appreciate the deep personal generosity and superb professional care of Sophie Goldsworthy, Andrew McNeillie, Tom Perridge, Val Shelley, and all other members of their team. Tom Chandler, an outstanding copy-editor, has saved me from innumerable errors; those that remain are all my fault.

JH

CONTENTS

ABBREVIATIONS

GENERAL

A	WE, *Argufying: Essays on Literature and Culture* (London, 1987)
BL	British Library
cf.	compare
Constable	*Critical Essays on William Empson* (1993), ed. John Constable
CP (1955)	WE, *Collected Poems* (London, 1935)
CP (2000)	*The Complete Poems of William Empson* (London, 2000)
CQ	*Critical Quarterly*
CR	Christopher Ricks
CV	*Coleridge's Verse*, ed. WE and David B. Pirie (London, 1972)
EG	*Empson in Granta* (Tunbridge Wells, Kent, 1993)
E in C	*Essays in Criticism*
ERL (1)	WE, *Essays on Renaissance Literature*, vol. 1: *Donne and the new philosophy* (Cambridge, 1993)
ERL (2)	WE, *Essays on Renaissance Literature*, vol. 2: *The Drama* (Cambridge, 1994)
ES	WE, *Essays on Shakespeare*, ed. by David B. Pirie (Cambridge, 1986)
FC	WE, *Faustus and the Censor: The English Faust-book and Marlowe's 'Doctor Faustus'*, ed. John Henry Jones (Oxford, 1987)
FRL	F. R. Leavis
Gill	*William Empson: The Man and His Work*, ed. Roma Gill (London, 1974)
GS	WE, *The Gathering Storm* (London, 1940)
HE	Hetta Empson
IAR	I. A. Richards
IAR: *SL*	*Selected Letters of I. A. Richards, C.H.*, ed. John Constable
IAR: *SW*	*I. A. Richards: Selected Works 1919–1938*, ed. John Constable (10 vols.: London, 2001): volume no. in brackets
JH	John Haffenden
LRB	*The London Review of Books*
MG	WE, *Milton's God* (1961; Cambridge, 1981)

3 1833 05090 3282

n.d.	no date
NED	*New English Dictionary on Historical Principles* (1907)
NYRB	*The New York Review of Books*
OED	*Oxford English Dictionary*
RB	WE, *The Royal Beasts and Other Works* (London, 1986)
Russo	John Paul Russo, *I. A. Richards: His Life and Work* (London: Routledge, 1989)
SCW	WE, *The Structure of Complex Words* (London, 1951; 3rd edn., 1977)
SSS	WE, *The Strengths of Shakespeare's Shrew* (Sheffield, 1996)
STA	WE, *Seven Types of Ambiguity* (1930; 3rd edn., 1953)
SVP	WE, *Some Versions of Pastoral* (London, 1935; 1966)
TLS	*The Times Literary Supplement*
TS	typescript
TSE	T. S. Eliot
UB	WE, *Using Biography* (London, 1984)
WE	William Empson

ARCHIVE REFERENCES

All Souls	All Souls College, Oxford
BBC	BBC Written Archives, Caversham, Reading
Berg	Berg Collection, New York Public Library
BL	British Library, London
Columbia	Butler Library, Columbia University, New York
Cornell	Olin Library, Cornell University
Edinburgh	National Library of Scotland, Edinburgh
Faber	Faber & Faber Ltd
Houghton	Houghton Library, Harvard University
Hull	Hull University Library
King's	Modern Archive Centre, King's College, Cambridge
Leeds	Brotherton Collection, Leeds University Library
Lilly	Lilly Library, Indiana University
McMaster	McMaster University Library
Magdalene	Old Library, Magdalene College, Cambridge
Manchester	John Rylands Library, University of Manchester
Penguin	Penguin Books Ltd.

Princeton   Department of Rare Books and Special Collections, Princeton
                 University Library

Reading   University of Reading Library

Sussex   University of Sussex Library

Texas   Harry Ransom Humanities Research Center, University of Texas
                 at Austin

Times   The Times Archive

Trinity   Wren Library, Trinity College, Cambridge

Tulsa   McFarlin Library, University of Tulsa

UCL   Manuscripts and Rare Books Room, University College London

UCLA   Library, University of California at Los Angeles

Yale   Beinecke Library, Yale University

INTRODUCTION

Private letters often seem most exquisitely adapted to their setting when written most casually; it is exactly the extent to which their language is careless, the proportion of carelessness they give to the different matters in hand, which is so precise. Similarly in conversation this more refined sort of implication is very highly developed.

Seven Types of Ambiguity, p. 49

I have a fatal habit of irritating people when I write them letters (a thing I do only by effort) . . .

Letter to I. A. Richards, ? September 1948

It is easy to feel (though admittedly it goes utterly against everyone's experience) that all the letters in a collected or selected edition, tidily serried and all dressed up in scholarship, must have been composed in the best of all possible conditions: at an escritoire or equivalent, in study or library, and with calm of mind. William Empson's letters were put together in markedly diverse and often stressful circumstances: they were written, and often re-written, in university digs, bed-and-breakfast establishments, squats, monasteries, hostels, huts, and basements; on mountains, on ships, in trains, in planes; in Cambridge, London, Tokyo, Peking; in Cambodia, Egypt, Ceylon, the USA, and Canada. Some sense of the not uncommon drama surrounding the business of his letter-writing can be gauged from this directive to a friend, posted from Japan in the summer of 1933: 'Write via CANADA: when letters go by Siberia all one's mind is clouded with a doubt, and after one letter is lost the correspondence is broken. But it is fine in a way to think of a real use being found for our letters, warming bandits.'[1]

He died just before the advent of the universal e-mail, but his itinerant life required him to dash off an enormous number of letters, to mother and brothers, to wife and children, elders, mentors, mistress, friends, editors, peers and pupils. Hetta Empson, who made sure she lived life to the full, even during the turnover associated with the arrival of Communist forces in Peking, wrote to a friend an undated letter (probably in April

---

[1] WE, letter to John Hayward.

1950) which gives an insight into her husband's habits of work at the time: 'Max & I went to the Dump [a favourite drinking place] . . . and I didn't get home till three, where William was typing in a pool of pai gar a letter to his publisher.'[2] *Pai gar* is a white moonshine made from millet, with a taste like gasoline; it would serve well to fuel a heated letter, and in this case Empson (at the age of 43) was almost certainly 'banging out' to Ian Parsons, his friend and publisher at Chatto & Windus, a letter chastising him for the non-appearance of his book *The Structure of Complex Words* (which took three years to make it into print even after he had sent in the final text). His wife's incidental description of the place and circumstances is almost certainly the only surviving account we shall ever have of Empson in the act of writing a letter. Still, it is known to be typical: he would read and write at all hours of the day and night, just as it suited him; and Hetta's few words conjure a picture of his indefatigable habits of work, his possible slight inebriation, and the rapt intensity of his typing.

Many years later, in August 1967 (aged 61), he was recovering at home in Hampstead from an operation for cataract; and even though he had feared for his sight, he took the trouble to insist by letter that certain emendations be made to a letter he had submitted in a published exchange having to do with Milton; he wrote accordingly to the editor of the periodical in question: 'Yes, I am willing to have my letter printed, and to have the other two asked to reply, but I want you to make a few corrections before it is sent to them and let me see proofs before it is printed. I wrote it just before going into hospital for a cataract operation, when very afraid of going blind, and it is perhaps tiresomely defiant; but the changes are only a matter of avoiding misunderstanding. I am sure that someone needs to speak up against the dead weight of the fashions of two generations.'[3] Feeling he may have been just too stern, and even a touch tear-jerking, he immediately added as an act of grace: 'The eye (your good heart will be impatient to learn) is likely to come back in use but still isn't.' Illness would not detain him long. Even when doctors told him to do nothing but rest, he got back to writing and revising his essays (as with the constant refashioning during his last years of *Faustus and the Censor*) and his letters. Such was the man: obdurate but far from insensitive. Conscientious, self-exacting, impatient with wrongheadedness, he could also be very kind—as in swiftly assuaging any hint of blackmail in that letter on Milton.

There is little reason to suspect that he wrote his letters with a constant

[2] HE, undated letter to Walter Brown, 'Friday night' ? Apr. 1950 (*Hull*).
[3] WE, draft letter to Irene Skolnick, 31 Aug. 1967 (TS in *Houghton*).

eye on posterity; that he would talk himself up or put on airs—though it has to be said that he could sometimes talk for effect (as the phrase has it). All the same, he was not so innocent as not to be aware that his newsy letters from places like Tokyo and Kunming in the 1930s, and Peking after the war, would have value to history as eye-witness reports of local events and conditions. Indeed, he felt that many of the letters he wrote to his mother and to friends such as John Hayward might serve as equivalents of a diary, or as drafts of a volume of travel-writings that he would put together at some later date. From time to time he had it in mind too that he would one day write his memoirs, but not before reaching the age of 80 (when he felt a person's best work would be over and done with). He told his publisher in 1973, at the age of 66: 'When I am past anything else maybe I will be able to dictate my memoirs.'[4] He died at the age of 77, with his life's work in literary criticism not yet finished off; but even so, given his temperament, it would seem to me that he would never have got round to writing any memoirs. His memory for persons and encounters was selective, and in any case it would have gone against the reticent habits of a lifetime to talk about himself or his personal relationships. Any reader who wonders why there is not a greater leavening here of family letters will be interested to know that one of the most personal letters Empson ever wrote to his wife reads as follows:

Saturday 8th [December 1956]

My dearest Hetta,

    Very glad to hear that all went well. I shall come home next Thursday 13th, and will visit you on the Friday (if they allow that, as they presumably do; no doubt Helena will know). Helena wrote and told me how things were going, also that she was improving Jacob's Latin.

    Much love, and I am glad you are happy

    William.

That innocuous-seeming letter was written just two days after his wife Hetta had given birth to a child, Simon, by her lover Peter Duval Smith. The terseness is typical of the man. I must admit that when I first came across that blank note, out of any context, I thought it must be referring to something routine—perhaps an operation for varicose veins?—and almost passed over its huge significance.

    Literature, literary criticism, the free exchange of ideas—what Empson called 'the tradition of fair public debate'—are what most engaged his

---

[4] WE, letter to Ian Parsons, 16 Jan. 1973 (*Reading*).

mind, not his own personality or personal history. These letters, wonderful as they are, are the best of his memoirs we will ever have. However, even at about the age of 30, towards the close of his first turn of duty as a teacher in the Far East, he was really not surprised, and yet not terribly deeply vexed, when he learned that his friend John Hayward had been prompt to make use of his letters for his own purposes. This passage, written from wartime China in May 1939, amounts to a deliciously disingenuous rebuke to Hayward, and it also shows how Empson could turn his mind all round a question and see it from other points of view—in this case, by admitting the virtue of gossipy letters and the biographer's curiosity:

Somebody had poor Julian Bell's great gushing Life and Letters it would have offended him rather I think.[5] But my word how he did write letters. And what is this business of keeping letters? Do *you* keep letters? It must be a widespread practice judging from biographies. Rather an ugly one I think. It certainly couldn't be done in my mother's house, where any writing left about (including two complete plays of mine some time ago) gets immediately destroyed. Very properly too, as I feel even when it turns out inconvenient. Do you suppose for instance that all your correspondents are saving up the letters for the life and letters? And do they get *paid* for this rather eerie and passive piece of work? How unexpected people are. But perhaps Julian's lot were more likely to do that kind of thing. Darwin I remember, though, a different kind of man, said it had been a great help to him never to destroy a single letter . . . By the way, what on earth was the disease of Darwin? Was it simply neurotic? They never say, and he seems a very unneurotic man otherwise.

Those comments add up to a sly dig at Hayward for his impudence in allowing the *Sunday Times* to make use of quotations from Empson's letters to Hayward—this is made clear in a letter to his mother just a few weeks earlier (7 April 1939): 'Thanks for the Sunday Times cutting. Rather annoying to have the friends selling the letters, that must be John Hayward. I think he might have bought a stamp with the proceeds and written back to me.'[6] The small social betrayal is thus taken in good part; and in any case, as he admits, he shares the weakness: that is, the healthy instinct to read and know as much as possible of one's heroes.

He wrote letters for two primary and proper purposes: for conversation and for literary-critical controversion. Often the two purposes would amount to the same thing. An acute social being, he was always at pains to be alert, both as critic and as letter-writer, to the character of his audience:

---

[5] Julian Bell, *Essays, Poems and Letters*, ed. Quentin Bell (1938).
[6] WE, letter to mother, 7 Apr. 1939 (*Houghton*).

how they (individual or group) would understand things; what they needed or liked to be told; what arguments would impress or sway or incite them. Fit communication needs the fullest responsiveness, with whatever portions of play and pressure the case may call for. A letter must needs address itself, in every possible sense, to a known or imagined audience. 'Our whole mental life is based on being social animals,' he wrote as early as 1933. 'Of course the man may quarrel with his company when he gets it, and feel pleased about that but what he chiefly needed was the company.'[7] (Six of the most intensely felt letters he ever wrote took the form of the persuasively coded series of 'Letter' poems addressed to his Cambridge friend Desmond Lee, whose company he desired with unfulfilled high intensity: they are the only evidence that survives of a long-nurtured but sadly one-sided passion.) The code of private letters, as he learned it from his mother and his aunts in his earliest years, lays down that one must seek to entertain the absent but closely-imagined company (to write *to* them and not *at* them)—or at least not to bore them—and to present them with a positive face. It is ill manners to convey ill thoughts: merely an unwarranted affliction. A letter is a gift; it should please, and should therefore endeavour to amuse. These mandates are expressed in a letter to a friend dating from 1938 (Empson is in his early thirties): 'I write to you as a kind of tonic, feeling very flat at the end of term and indeed wondering how to pass the evening. The duty of sounding cheerful in prose, above all in letters, will no doubt do me good.'[8] The code is rehearsed between friends in the know, and so the response is bound to be an intimate fellow-feeling. The wink in the confession comes in the phrase 'sounding cheerful', which is as much as to say that all writing is anyway a show, a performance, and in the case of personal letters should be a decent combination of willing intention and right rhetoric.

Letters to his mother and to certain friends contain a fair amount of what Empson fliply called 'chat about his travels': noticings, happenings, anecdotes. Landscapes are described, curiosities recounted, persons characterized; and he tells over all the news and gossip he can gather that might have significance. They are good, eager missives, albeit at times a bit too preoccupied with local politics or tending to overinterpret the importance of exceptional conditions.

John Hayward, a shrewd judge who saw the merits of Empson's chatty letters home from his years in the Far East, told another friend (the editor

---

[7] WE, 'The Ideal of the Good' (*c.*1933), *A*, 450.
[8] WE, draft letter to John Hayward, 1938 (*Houghton*).

Frank Morley) in December 1940: 'Empson's letters . . . are always very entertaining and original—dry, ironical, witty descriptions of persons and events. Some he sent me from China were so good that I arranged with Peter Fleming to get "The Times" to contact him with a view to his writing some special articles on the Sino-Japanese war. They cabled a proposal, but Bill had already engaged himself to write, if at all, for some other paper—an obscure highbrow rag [*Life & Letters*, edited by Robert Herring] for which in the end he never wrote anything at all.'[9] (Hayward was mistaken in that last observation, for Empson did publish in *Life & Letters* in 1940 a fine propaganda article with the title 'A Chinese University'.)

Peter Fleming (brother of the novelist Ian Fleming) was at the time a staff writer on *The Times*, and he did indeed contact Empson at Hayward's suggestion (though his approach, as Hayward said, ultimately came to nothing). Empson's response to Fleming's overture opened with a flourish that seems positively counter-intuitive but is startlingly true: 'Busy I am not, indeed the lack of conversation makes it hard to write anything, a fact that I have only seen written down by the late Walter Raleigh.'[10] (It is as true and profound a remark as this splendidly paradoxical aphorism, dating from April 1933: 'Always rather embarrassing to wonder what one gets out of travel to make up for its privations; except that it requires so much imagination to stay at home.') Cyril Connolly, in *Enemies of Promise* (1938), considered that for any writer too much society, with all its diversions and indulgences, is one of the factors that defeats fulfilment. Empson reckoned otherwise. For him, writing required company, a community: exchange and interchange, the give and take of ideas. Good writing also meant approximation to the spoken word, everyday intercourse, and not to any mode of specialized discourse. Roy Campbell, who got to know Empson at the end of the war, would extol his sure conversational capacity in an essay written for the Central Office of Information and circulated far and wide by the British Council:

Mr Empson is one of the few English writers whose conversation is on a level with his writing. It is rare nowadays for anyone except an Irishman to speak English in

---

[9] John Hayward, 'Tarantula's Special News Service, Letter XXVI' (to Frank Morley), Dec. 1940 (*King's*). Of WE, JDH said too: 'In many ways he's an undisciplined writer and needs encouragement, which is easier to give at a distance, as this does not involve one in having to drink too much in his company or in sharing his hang-overs. But he is one of the brains of his generation . . .'

[10] WE, letter to Peter Fleming, n.d. (1939) (*Houghton*). Sir Walter Raleigh (1861–1922) was a writer and critic.

complete sentences without hesitating; but when Empson gets well launched into one of his celebrated monologues he takes one back to the great days of English conversation in the eighteenth century. In listening to Empson's conversation one gets a key to the amazingly mathematical construction which underlies his poetry, for although his conversation sparkles with all the incidental brilliancies which are the delight of all convivial company, one is even more struck by the architectural design of his reasoning and the control which he exerts over the most abstruse and complicated matters.[11]

His ideas were clear because he cared about keying his language to his audience, and so (to coin an ambiguous phrase) seeing how they saw it. 'I wonder if you have an expert on Elizabethan plays knocking about,' Empson asked his greatest fan and friend, Christopher Ricks, in 1976, 'fairly young, who would be prepared to enter into correspondence about them.'[12] The desired correspondent should be young because energetic, and thus likely to keep up with the secondary reading.

A good number of the letters written during Empson's years in the Far East (Japan, 1931–3; China, 1937–9, 1947–52), and during briefer visits to the USA (1948, 1950, 1954), are therefore 'conversation pieces' in this best sense. (Incidentally, I have included fewer letters written during years at the BBC, but only because so many of them are about bureaucracy and programme planning that they really need to be retailed in the full biographical context.) Describing life, observations, and contacts, the travel letters aim specifically to please or to interest the addressee; and, most importantly, they are written with the active interlocutor in mind. A passage from one of the best examples in this kind, sent from a strangely semi-derelict town in south-west China in 1938, reads as follows:

We live in the middle of a flat saucer, with the hills some way off, and I find that must be rather oppressive; because yesterday I got out of it for the first time (I have been walking the longer way to the hills with the tin and mercury mines before) and when I got just over this bare rocky series of fatuous rolling hills there turned out to be a little valley over the top, rich with trees, a whole village snug inside them, a lake or large pond with a sturdy temple at the far side, (a stone barn as in the Lake district with comic statues inside), and coming down to the side into the lake the real hanging gardens of the mountain paddy fields, curved like the lines of bees' wings under the microscope, high thin standing rice at each stage that you could see down to the water through, a delicate pale acid green, and that

---

[11] Roy Campbell, 'William Empson: Contemporary English Poet and Scholar', an undated article (1947) produced by the Central Office of Information and circulated via the British Council (S.6547); copy in *Houghton*.

[12] WE, letter to Christopher Ricks, 8 Mar. 1976.

strange effect of massive engineering or 'structural' palatial architecture (the terraces are very deep)—all in a little hollow just hidden from us that happens to
have water, only a dimple if we could see it on our Siberian view of hills. It felt like
coming home, I mean it gave me a nostalgia for the attractive parts of China and
started me remembering my travels instead of daydreaming. That I wanted to tell
you about, but I won't tell you about being bitten by a large bear, or the robbers
who insisted on flashing their daggers in the moonlight though I told them I had
an apparently permanent attack of cramp. In fact I had much rather you would
talk to me.

He closes abruptly with a tease, a bribe, a cliffhanger: an invitation to
reciprocate. By describing the exotic allure of the landscape, and by holding back the tantalizing stories he has up his sleeve—a bear and bandits,
no less—he hopes to lure his correspondent into correspondence: to tell
him back some tales of home. He knew full well too when the boot was on
the other foot, writing to Kathleen Raine (for example) from Communist
China in the autumn of 1950: 'We were delighted with your letters though
I was too lazy to earn more by writing back.'[13]

   If several of the most immediately attractive letters of the early period
are conversational, Empson evidently feared that some of his accounts of
local politics, happenings, and social conditions amounted in a more self-
interested way to mere reportage: bulletins which he might have done
better to keep to himself and write up later. They seemed to him, that is to
say, to be more like articles, broadcasting matters for general consumption
without respect to the individual being addressed in any particular letter.
In other words again, they seemed to him to be lacking in the requisite
manners. He wrote home in 1938:

I got back from Hanoi to find letters saying all was well . . . [including] yours . . .
saying that my badtempered one about robbers filled you with dismay. I was only
using you to think at, and wonder whether to leave; it must be rather distressing
for you at this distance, but when I say I am cheerful I really am . . . I am sorry to
be writing an article at you, mamma, but I seem to have nowhere to publish these
things.[14]

In the opening pages of *Ambiguity* he keenly discriminated: 'The English
prepositions from being used in so many ways in combination with so
many verbs, have acquired not so much a number of meanings as a body
of meaning continuous in several dimensions; a tool-like quality, at once

---

[13] WE, letter to Kathleen Raine, 5 Oct. 1950 (carbon in *Houghton*).
[14] WE, letter to mother, from Mengtzu, China, 11 Aug. 1938.

thin, easy to the hand, and weighty.'[15] That notion of the preposition as a handy instrument is sharply relevant to this letter to his 'mamma', since the operative phrases 'using you to think at' and 'writing an article at you' are eccentric or aberrant (and even slightly improper, as he seems to feel). They reduce mother to a blank slate, or a place to type out a commentary on affairs or impersonal reflections. It is another way of signalling that 'what he chiefly needed was the company'—whence the oddity of the full clause: 'I was only using you to think at, and wonder whether to leave.' He thinks to leave because there is no one else around to think with.

Other examples of this process of apologizing or disclaiming include this remark (which was written from Eliot House at Harvard University, a place that his mother might have assumed to be pretty companionable): 'This habit of using you to think with doesn't make for very lively letters.'[16] Thinking *at* or thinking *with*: there is a patent distinction between the implications of those phrases. The first is as rude as the current cant phrase 'I hear what you're saying', and the other implies cooperation. But Empson does not choose here to mark shades of difference: he is concerned simply with the sheer rudeness of using a letter as a substitute for an article. His botherheadedness on the subject can be discerned in the following extracts from another letter to his mother: 'it seems stupid not to cash in a little on China . . . I am using you as a machine to think with . . . I have promised Chatto's a silly chat book about the Far East . . . I am pleased to hear my letters don't arrive, because they seem such awful nonsense to me. It is just as bad trying to write articles. Everybody talks nonsense about China.'[17] The difference is between 'using you' and being in genuine epistolary communion with you. Furthermore, such muttering notes of self-deprecation as Empson saw fit to use in those extrapolated phrases are excellent examples of what he himself would later characterize as 'the delicious social hints and evasive claims-by-mumble of spoken English' which he found 'positive intoxicants'.[18] The slang of 'cash in a little' and the minifying self-protectiveness of 'silly chat book' convey implications of which Empson of all people was profoundly aware: they serve to mime a maiden aunt, or even 'mamma' herself, and in so doing they absolve by anticipation any small criticism or stricture she might express by the very act of incorporating her language, her dialect, her attitude, within his own utterance. In his essay 'Statements in Words'

---

[15] *STA*, 5.
[16] WE, letter to mother, 8 Nov. 1939.
[17] WE, letter to mother, 27 Jun. 1939; TS draft in *Houghton*.
[18] WE, 'Rhythm and Imagery in English Poetry', *A*, 156.

(of which an early version was published in 1937), he took keen note of the surprisingly complex colloquial usage that goes 'How *awful* for somebody . . .': 'In itself the use of the word in such a context does not involve any change of meaning; the persons who use this school-girl slang really do feel awe on the occasion; they feel the adult world to be cruel about meaningless rules . . . But the effect of the queer little piece of slang is still to convey "I am the sort of speaker who might really find the occasion terrible." So far as the speaker recognises that she is using slang there is an idea "by putting it in this amusing way I admit that it is really only embarrassing, but still I am . . ." etc.'[19] Just so, Empson's hearty declaration to his mother that his letters are all the better for being undelivered, since 'they seem such awful nonsense to me', is a mode of self-defensiveness: it fends off the fair chance of her finding fault with them. Possibly he felt vulnerable to the likely accusation that it is boring and bad-mannered to become earnest about politics, or the war in China of all things.

In a further letter to 'mamma' he similarly makes use of slang and idiom to spring from self-disparagement to self-congratulation in three nimble moves: 'This is a ridiculous object as a letter, and don't read it if it bores you, but I seem full of unwanted information. You might keep it for the travel book if you can be bothered. What an ass I would have been if I had refused to leave England.'[20] The opening phrase of those brief colloquial sentences assumes the voice of official disdain—as it might have been enunciated by A. B. Ramsay, Master of Magdalene College, Cambridge, when he sent Empson into exile for possessing such a 'ridiculous object' as a french letter—and yet the last sentence begins with pompous schoolboy slang ('What an ass') only to end up using a kind of litotes, affirming a positive sense of himself by stressing the negative of the contrary. Whether or not his mother feels impatient with his letters, packed as they are with gossip and documentary information, he is still proud of having gone East.

The 'ridiculous object' that was the letter in that last example is thus neutralized in its bad effect; it is put down as an inconsequential trifle. All the same, the subtext he does not quite admit to his mother is that he is still pleased with it, and trusts she will assuredly keep it, since it is also a memo-as-memento. This notion is pushed still further in the last letter to 'mamma' I want to cite here:

Of course the annoying thing about coming back to England is that one would

---

[19] WE. 'Statements in Words', *SCW*, 60.
[20] WE, letter to mother, from Hong Kong, 15 Mar. 1938.

like to write up the experiences in China. But all the really amusing things that happen to anybody . . . mustn't be written up. And later on I shall have forgotten it.

I feel fond of this letter, can't you put it in a drawer.[21]

The kind of letter that was formerly set down merely as a 'ridiculous object' is now more like a pet, toy or keepsake; indeed, it has such an interesting character or personality that it is virtually personified, fondly. It seems not by accident that at about this time, when drafting the essays that would emerge as *Complex Words*, he noted that 'a word may become a sort of solid entity, able to direct opinion, thought of as like a person'.[22] He certainly knew the ways in which the limitations of his mother's language constructed her world, and he knew how to direct her opinion— specifically, by being able to couch things in her idiom. In other words, he understood the terms that were like 'solid entities' to her way of thinking. In crossing his mother's terms of reference and her language with his own subversive context in such a way, he successfully achieves in parts of his letters what Mikhail Bakhtin styled, with reference to parody, an 'intentional dialogised hybrid'.[23] And yet, in the case of this particular letter— which was taken up with the muddles and machinations pertaining to the administration of Basic English in south-west China—he must have decided it was tiresome by any measure, too local and private for those not in that circle. He did not post it. All the same, he made sure to keep it— those pages recorded a crucial phase of the struggle for educational standards in wartime China, and of his lived experience.

'In the learned world, a man loses his standing if he refuses to answer a plain refutation,' declared Empson in 1973.[24] If one part of the code with which he grew up maintained that personal letters are a form of conversation—sharing a language, inviting an exchange of ideas, imparting cheerfulness—another fundamental aspect of the code stressed a point of honour: the necessity to state, and to stand up for, one's convictions. Along with what I call the 'conversation letters' in this selection (giving news and views of all sorts, from East and West), the more substantial, and intellectually and critically far-reaching, series of letters has to do with the discussion of literary texts and literary criticism (as well as lesser but

---

[21] WE, TS draft letter to mother, 12 Jun. 1939 (*Houghton*).   [22] WE, *SCW*, 39.

[23] M. Bakhtin, 'From the Prehistory of Novelistic Discourse', in *The Dialogic Imagination: Four Essays*, ed. Michael Holquist; trans. Caryl Emerson and Michael Holquist (1981), 76.

[24] WE, 'The Hammer's Ring', in *I. A. Richards: Essays in His Honor*, ed. Reuben Brower, Helen Vendler, and John Hollander (1973), in *A*, 221.

related cultural and pedagogic issues such as the fortunes of the Basic English project in Japan and China), and above all with the unremitting business of argufying. 'Argufying'—a term he did not coin but which has come to seem peculiarly his own—he glossed as 'the kind of arguing we do in ordinary life, usually to get our own way; I do not mean nagging by it, but just a not specially dignified sort of arguing.'[25] He noted too that it could involve some pretty rough dealing: 'Argufying is not only mental; it also feels muscular. Saying "therefore" is like giving the reader a bang on the nose.'[26] (His aversion to public formality went hand-in-hand with his passion for making use in his literary-critical exchanges solely of the language of everyone's everyday conversation. For him, criticism is continuous with ordinary talk, just as literary values should never be separated from all human values. He loathed the pretensions of a specialized discourse, and would have concurred with Orwell that 'the inflated style is itself a kind of euphemism'.[27]) These are the letters of criticism and controversion, and in them the controversion is utterly wedded to ordinary, argufying conversation.

Empson felt he needed an implied interlocutor (who would sometimes be of the order of T. S. Eliot or Frank Kermode) or an actual opponent to oblige him to prove his ideas: he relished correspondence that was combative, if not downright aggressive. Robert Martin Adams (who himself crossed swords with Empson in 1954 over their interpretations of Milton) wrote in a memorial essay: 'Empson has been the most militant of our critics, as can be seen at once by glancing at his critical style. He recurs continually to the formula, You may say that . . . followed by, Then I can answer that . . . His passion for the dialectic amounted almost to obsession; if it led him sometimes into private labyrinths, it also engaged, and continues to engage, minds that can recognize resistance as a form of tribute.'[28] As a result, parts of this volume take the form of serial disputations with stout fellow critics including F. W. Bateson, Norman Fruman, Helen Gardner, Frank Kermode, and Rosemond Tuve. Not only did he refine his ideas, and seek to defend them in private correspondence, and wherever possible in follow-up letters printed in periodicals, as well as in the prefaces to reissues of his books, he also took pains to rewrite his letters (as I shall try to show in just a moment) so as to make his points much more effectively, more confrontationally.

---

[25] WE, 'Argufying in Poetry', 167.   [26] Ibid. 170.
[27] George Orwell, 'Politics and the English Language', *Inside the Whale and Other Essays* (1962), 153.
[28] Robert M. Adams, 'Hero of the Word', *NYRB*, 32: 6 (11 Apr. 1985), 32–5.

He professed from an early moment in his career, in the early 1930s:

If you attack a view in any detail that proves you to have some sympathy with it; there is already a conflict in you which mirrors the conflict in which you take part; that is why you understand it sufficiently to take part in it. Only because you can foresee and enter into the opposing arguments can you answer them; only because it is interesting to you do you engage in argument about it.

For personally I am attracted by the notion of a hearty indifference to one's own and other people's feelings, when a fragment of the truth is in question . . .[29]

Empson became to a marked degree notorious for his eagerness to enter into conflict with other critics on matters of principle, especially during the post-war years when he would cry down what he dubbed 'neo-Christian' critics for their 'disgusting' beliefs. He was never more scornful than when tackling fellow critics (such as Helen Gardner) for their doc-trinally blinkered, or at best bland and unexamining, acquiescence in T. S. Eliot's unsupported assertion, made at the turn of the 1930s: 'Donne was, I insist, no sceptic.'[30] The same applied to his spats with scholars of Milton. For Empson, this big issue ran corrosively deeper than the sort of difference of opinion that could be called in any way purely 'academic'. A critic who accepted an unquestioningly 'Christian' interpretation of a piece of literature (as for example C. S. Lewis and many another critic on *Paradise Lost*) was accepting an evil religion with real and virulent human effects. The Christian God was nothing less than a torture-monster. He meant exactly what he said on this matter; like John Stuart Mill's father, he judged Christianity the *ne plus ultra* of wickedness. Indeed, Empson appreciated that certain other critics considered him to be slightly off his head when it came to his contempts for Christianity; that 'neo-Christianity' was nothing less than his King Charles's Head (as he readily conceded of himself, employing that very phrase, in a letter to Ricks).[31] But certain critics would be shocked when he pinpointed in their analyses the terrible moral implications of which they seemed unaware.

In the early 1950s he engaged in a bout of robust contestation with the American scholar Rosemond Tuve, for example, on the question of his interpretation, in *Seven Types of Ambiguity*, of George Herbert's poem 'The Sacrifice'. (This was not a battle between generations, for they were near contemporaries.) Tuve patronized Empson as historically 'naïve' for

---

[29] WE, 'Obscurity and Annotation', *A*, 83.

[30] T. S. Eliot, 'Donne In Our Time', in *A Garland for John Donne*, ed. Theodore Spencer (1932), 11–12.

[31] WE, letter to Christopher Ricks, 1 Jul. 1972.

discerning in Herbert's work some evidence of strain in the face of the awfulness of the Christian conception of Redemption. The shocking departure from convention that Empson read into Herbert's work was to be explained, she claimed, by reference to the liturgical tradition: there was little in Herbert that was not already to be found in the offices of Holy Week. A number of readers of this stand-off might therefore draw the conclusion that Empson's construction of the poem was at once ingenious and ill-informed; that he is the amateur outfaced by the majesty of Tuve's scholarly comprehension of 'tradition'. Yet one recent scholar-critic sees much sense in Empson's analysis of Herbert. Richard Strier observes that it is too easy to dismiss Empson as ignorant of literary history:

> Tuve sees herself as policing the borders of the past, so that no anachronistically modern element can falsely enter and so that the massive outlines of 'the tradition' can be clearly discerned by the (not so humble) seeker after truth . . . 'The tradition' . . . is complex, multifaceted, and internally conflicted; it is always the product of contestation . . . Tuve is using her construction of 'the tradition,' backed up by massive but very selective erudition, as a bludgeon with which to browbeat a less learned but more adventurous and not necessarily less accurate critic . . . Tuve's 'tradition,' like all such hypostases, is produced by special pleading . . . 'Traditional,' for Tuve, means medieval . . . Empson emerges as the better historicist . . . [T]here has never been a homogeneous and self-consistent 'tradition' or dominant discourse. A work might be using heterodox ideas . . . Empson keeps the particular in focus rather than letting it dissolve into its (supposed) component elements.[32]

Tuve was thus a good foe to pick a fight with. She was well armed with learning, and she had been the first to criticize Empson's work. Although she felt that at times his blows came too near the knuckle, since he scorned her ideas in a way that could seem *ad personam*, it was her very inclination to take cover from argument behind a winsome chattiness (including the suggestion that he ought to be as 'nice' on paper as he was in person) that aggravated the situation for him. He felt she too readily substituted personality for critical principle; and as far as he was concerned no charm offensive could avail when Christianity was on trial.

Empson was gratified when his opponents spoke up for themselves (whatever the dispute). The battle was at its best when fairly joined on both sides. It was typical of his sense of right dealing that he wrote to the editor

---

[32] Richard Strier, *Resistant Structures: Particularity, Radicalism, and Renaissance Texts* (1995), Essay 1: 'Tradition', 17, 21–2, 24–5.

Sylvan Barnet about the draft text of his introduction to Shakespeare's *Narrative Poems* (in the Signet Classics series): 'as you gather, I think that most of what has been written on the subject is wrong, and it would be fair to the reader if opinions differing from mine were strongly represented.'[33] Now and then, indeed, he would say he found it 'good-humoured' for an antagonist to retaliate with a vigorous refutation or counter-argument. Just as one may call a friend a fool, a rogue, or a dog—or even, in today's terms (with a necessary grin) a bastard—in an entirely hearty or matey way, the code of letters allowed for the paradoxical compliment that rudeness between equals need not be personal. On occasion, an opponent would snap back that Empson had got the completely wrong end of the stick: this too seemed to please him no end. The academic and critic A. E. Rodway, in a review of Empson's *Collected Poems* (1955),[34] noted that when responding to questions following a poetry reading at Nottingham University Empson had denied that the Buddha's famous 'Fire Sermon' (which he used to preface the poems) carried any especial significance for him; it was there, Empson said (no doubt by way of steering clear of elaborate explanations), 'because I liked it.' But Rodway was having none of such bluff: 'Somebody's leg was being pulled,' he ribbed Empson in his review. Empson responded with a letter observing among things: 'I was shocked, at the reading mentioned by Mr Rodway, to gather from some questions that my book might be used to support the current religious revival, and I said that, if a son of mine wanted to become a Buddhist monk, I would beg him not to. This felt to me very unlike pulling anybody's leg, however low-minded it might appear to neo-Christians.' However, Rodway related to me in a later year: 'when I replied that I was as atheistic as he was, and equally opposed to the Christian resurgence, the correspondence became amicable, and we had several friendly meetings thereafter.'[35] That too was characteristic of Empson's terms of engagement.

An even more important part of the code of honour was a matter of epistolary etiquette. He was not one to attack a book in print and then hope that his assault would not come to the author's notice. He would own up to what he wrote, and would even take the trouble to draw his criticisms to an opponent's attention. For many years (from the mid-1950s), for instance, he reviled the way in which Hugh Kenner interpreted James Joyce. Kenner, who was a Catholic, reported Joyce as a 'disgusting' author

---

[33] WE, letter to Sylvan Barnet, 4 Jul. 1967 (carbon in *Houghton*).
[34] A. E. Rodway, 'The Structure of Complex Verse', *E in C* 6: 2 (Apr. 1956), 232–40.
[35] Allan Rodway, letter to JH, 22 Mar. 1989.

who reneged on his early rebellion against Christian doctrine: this is what Empson specifically termed the 'Kenner Smear'. In 1970 Empson published an article pursuing the attack he had launched with a review of Kenner's *Dublin's Joyce* (1956). 'The chief claim of this theory is that Stephen Dedalus is presented not as the author when young (though the book-title [*A Portrait of the Artist as a Young Man*] pretends he is) but as a possible fatal alternative, a young man who has taken some wrong turning, or slipped over the edge of some vast drop, so that he can never grow into the wise old author (intensely Christian, though in a mystically paradoxical way) who writes the book.'[36] Having thus written up his scorn for Kenner's work on Joyce, he was keen for Kenner to be given the chance to respond to it: he sent him an offprint.

Dear Hugh Kenner,

I thought you ought to be sent a copy of this, as it is a very obscure publication and you would never see it otherwise. People have sometimes printed attacks on me which I don't get hold of till ten years later, and it always strikes me as a lost opportunity.

Yours with good wishes
William Empson[37]

It was exactly the same form of courtesy as he had extended to Rosemond Tuve some twenty years earlier, when he notified John Crowe Ransom (editor of *Kenyon Review*) in January 1953: 'I have been reading Rosamund [*sic*] Tuve's "Reading of George Herbert", part of which was published in the *Kenyon*, and found so much more I wanted to answer that I have posted her [my] text to see if she will discuss it before we print any more assumptions about each other.'[38] In the same letter to Ransom, he noted too, with considerable dignity: 'I felt inclined to answer Cleanth Brooks' review of my Complex Words ['Hits and Misses', *Kenyon Review*, Fall 1952, 669–78], which though very friendly sticks to a difference of principle, and it seems clear that my next book will have to try and answer a lot of these points of principle. However if you are printing my long article next Spring you won't want a letter from me fussing about a review as well; I think that would be out of proportion; there will be plenty of occasions no doubt, for the difference of principle.' In fact, he did draft at the time a response to Brooks's review of his book which he held back as

[36] WE, 'Joyce's Intentions', *Twentieth Century Studies*, 4 (4 Nov. 1970), 26–36. See also 'The Ultimate Novel', *LRB* (19 Aug.–2 Sept. 1982), 3–5.

[37] WE, letter to Hugh Kenner, 11 Jun. 1971 (*Texas*).

[38] WE, letter to John Crowe Ransom, 13 Jan. 1953 (*Kenyon College Archives*).

suggested (it is included in this volume); and he duly found his occasion to take personal issue with Cleanth Brooks in September 1955 (also included in this volume), when Brooks initiated an exchange by way of a letter about Empson's review entitled 'Still the Strange Necessity' (*Sewanee Review*, 63 [Summer 1955], 471–9), which had included an impatient critique of W. K. Wimsatt's strict views on the Intentional Fallacy.

Notwithstanding his eagerness to encourage opponents to answer back at him, he was naturally avid to have the final say in any particular row. This was not a contradiction: even the code of honour allows a winner. Why else would one write criticism, he maintained, unless it is to 'win agreement' or to prevail over others? It was in such a mood that he worked in his more controversial letters to end up with a 'bang': a persuasive peroration or a slick dismissal. For instance, when drafting a letter that he hoped would finish off a long-running controversy in the *Times Literary Supplement* in the 1970s with the American scholar Norman Fruman, apropos the poetry of Coleridge, he initially composed this ultimate paragraph: 'It would be right, Sir, to allow my opponent a further reply, as he was the person originally attacked. But I will not make any further rejoinder.'[39] However, after reflecting further upon that very honourable gesture, he carefully amended his phrasing to read: 'Not to reply often seems like a confession of defeat, so may I say in advance that I do not intend to answer again, unless there is some accusation of unbearable absurdity.'[40] The slight but significant change meant he proposed to reserve to himself the right to have the coveted last word. More commonly, he would go in for firm disdain rather than the wholly gracious gesture. This closing sentence of a letter to another scholar strikes fair and square the rather haughtily witty note with which he liked to sign off his letters: 'Like God in sending Raphael to talk to Adam, I feel sure that this letter will do no good, but at least that it will leave you "without excuse".'[41]

Like the boy disclosing that the emperor has no clothes, Empson the truth-dealer declared the Christian God to be a grotesque and unprincipled tyrant. On occasion, he would make use of slang (as to his mother) to reinforce his attack. One usage he liked in particular was the idiom 'to blow the gaff', which he used to mean that he was exposing false doctrine.[42] In the context of such a grave issue as the evilness of Christianity, and given that Empson was in moral earnest in denouncing it, 'blow

---

[39] WE, undated letter headed 'Coleridge' (carbon in *Houghton*).
[40] Ibid.
[41] WE, letter to K. Jha, 20 Jun. 1971 (carbon in *Houghton*).
[42] See WE's footnote to 'The English Dog', *SCW*, 166.

the gaff' may seem on the face of it to hit the wrong register. The col-
loquialism is surely what Bakhtin termed (though exclusively and fal-
laciously with regard to prose fiction) 'heteroglossic', being at odds with
the expected formal terms of a dread moral indictment. Needless to say,
the idiom is funny: it lightens tone. Looked at from one angle, it decries the
Christian pomp as a piffling pretence; but then, looked at with an eye on
the speaker, it might betray a further touch of self-deprecation, and ironically lessen the moral force of the charge, by engaging in the shorthand of
slang rather than in fully persuasive oratory. However, I say this not to
catch Empson out, for if he presented himself sometimes as the *enfant
terrible*, he would do so with full self-awareness. Just as Sylvia Plath was not
the victim but the creator of her poems, Empson was not the innocent of
his language. In a footnote to his essay on 'The English Dog' (first published in 1936–7 and revised for *Complex Words*), he anticipated the self-
reflexive inclinations of postmodernism with these reflections on his own
usage: 'I have kept on using "blow the gaff" for something like "give the
low-down", with the extra idea of puncturing something inflated. It is too
meaningless to be a good phrase, and apparently it is used by criminals
merely for "betray a plot to the police". But I have failed to think of any
better one.'[43] He loved the disarming kick of informality: it got under the
guard of propriety, and it helped to settle hash. There is no doubt he was
self-aware in deploying such a strategy. In a 1959 letter about an article he
was putting together on the subject of W. B. Yeats's 'Byzantium' poems, he
pointedly declared: 'I want to present myself in the article, not as having
read all the other exegetists, as I actually haven't, but as speaking with a
literary kind of common sense.'[44] This is as much as to say that he knew,
long before Bakhtin was read in English, that all utterance is stylized.

Empson drafted and redrafted a good many of his letters, both when
writing to private correspondents and for public print (he took exactly the
same pains as with his essays), seeking to improve succinctness, emphasis
and tone; also to discover exactly how his ideas fell out. The Forsterian
adage, 'How can I know what I think till I see what I've said', was deeply
felt by him. If a passage didn't read right, with the rhythm and inflection
of natural speech, it could probably not stand up as good sense. In 1966,

---

[43] WE, 'The English Dog', *SCW*, 166. For a further example of his use of 'blow the gaff', see
the chapter on 'Honest Man', *ibid.* 187–8.
[44] WE, letter to A. N. Jeffares, 24 Aug. 1959 (carbon in *Houghton*). In explaining why he liked
to undercut the formal register of professional literary-critical discourse, he added: 'the great
danger of this kind of magazine is to hit the eye as a corpse.'

when Professor C. B. Cox accepted his essay 'Donne in the New Edition' for publication in *Critical Quarterly*, Empson was prompt to follow up with a note that begged to apologize for a bit of bother:

Thank you for your friendly letter, and I am very glad you are willing to print the whole article. But will you please cut out one sentence, three or four pages before the end. It says something like 'This is Protestant, the other is the icy breath of Plato.' I added it in (as teachers do) just because it was more information, but it spoils the run of the rhetoric there.

If you will take out that sentence, I think I can face the terrors before me, great though they undoubtedly are.

It was characteristic of his care for integrity that he chose thus to sacrifice an eye-catching, witty punchline for the sake of rhythm and truth.[45] For him, the tone and tendency of each word always counted, as did the structure of an argument.

He did not particularly mind being asked to cut an essay or letter to fit the space available in a magazine—he allowed that abbreviation can sharpen sense—but there was a line to be drawn. In 1971 he submitted a remarkable memoir, 'Orwell at the BBC', for inclusion in a collection of essays to be entitled *The World of George Orwell*, edited by Miriam Gross. After a while, however, he became aware that his research had not been thorough enough: there was more information about Orwell's final illness—in *The Collected Essays, Journalism and Letters*, edited by Sonia Orwell and Ian Angus (1968)—than he had realized when writing his piece. He therefore typed out a three-paragraph 'Afterthought' (of about 500 words) containing corrections of fact and further reflections. 'Dear Mrs Gross,' he wrote on 2 July 1971, 'I will cut this if you tell me I have to, but I will think it very unreasonable. There is always a lot of white knocking about, at the end of the book, say. And they could print it in its proper place if they would use small enough type.'[46] Hard upon receipt of this addendum, Miriam Gross telephoned to say she might possibly manage to include the additional piece, but only if it could be cut by half. Feeling reasonably ready to oblige, Empson set to and cut his 'Afterthought' by exactly half; it was now to be called 'Correction'. 'Dear Mrs Gross,' he then typed. 'Thank you for your prompt phone-call. As agreed, I have cut this extra bit

---

[45] He would write similarly to Karl Miller, editor of *The Listener*, on 9 Nov. 1967: 'Would you take out one sentence from my review *Heaven and Hell*, which I now think irritating and unconvincing—"I do not myself . . . and if he did (which I do not believe) he would be a bad man". My voice is becoming sadly shrill. You might put *instead* of that sentence = "The problem does not only arise 'ideally'." ' (See the review in *A*, 620–1.)

[46] WE, letter to Miriam Gross, 2 Jul. 1971 (*Houghton*).

by half, and feel that the result is an actual improvement, as the subject is too gloomy for prattle; but it could not be made even shorter.' That statement might have seemed decisive enough. Yet in the next sentence he managed to undo his firmness by offering this extra concession:

> If a further cut is essential, I would choose the last sentence of the first paragraph (*I wanted . . . too well*); but it seems to me that the whole matter is still confusing unless what happened is said plainly.
>
> I really think that this shortened version ought to be printed; a publisher has no business to force me to print what I know to be wrong merely for convenience.
>
> Of course, I don't mind what it is called.
>
> Yours with thanks[47]

In that instance, for whatever reason (perhaps Mrs Gross felt his contradictory mannerliness betrayed a hint of irresolution), the piece was not in fact published.

For Empson, none of his critical writings, whether in book, essay or letter, was ever to be quite finished. Ideas and style always needed to be improved; the final word was always to be sought.[48] 'I am afraid,' he wrote to an editor about one of his essays, 'by saying "pedantry" at the end I only concede the victory to my opponents, who will think this means there is some scholarly argument in favour of the change. So I need to add the word "illogical", making "illogical pedantry" . . .'[49] This need to keep revising explains why he loved to put out new editions or reissues, including prefaces, afterwords, further reflections and final opinions. Also, when reading offprints of articles, or when asked to autograph a book, he would often take the opportunity to write in corrections and additions. On occasion, however, an afterthought would come to him just too late to make a difference. In January 1974, John Sparrow, Warden of All Souls College, Oxford (and an Empson contemporary), published in the *Times Literary Supplement* a deftly straight-faced article about John Milton which parodied the habit of those several scholars who ventured to unveil the subject of Shakespeare's sexuality. A few weeks later, following a series of inevitably contentious letters (some good, some silly), Empson wrote this paragraph into a letter of his own for publication:

---

[47] WE, draft letter in *Houghton*. The sentence he would allow to be cut reads in full: 'I wanted to illustrate [Orwell's] power to imply a shaming rebuke, and how it sometimes got turned on confusingly; but I illustrated confusion all too well.'

[48] See a supportive letter (3 Aug. 1957) from John Crowe Ransom concerning WE's dissatisfaction with his article 'Donne the Space Man' (published in *Kenyon Review*, 19, Summer 1957): *Selected Letters of John Crowe Ransom*, ed. Thomas Daniel Young and George Core (1985), 387–9.

[49] WE, letter to Sylvan Barnet, 4 Jul. 1967 (carbon in *Houghton*).

The poor Warden deserves respect for appearing so firmly in a white sheet, having to explain, while accepting rebuke for, a very good and clear parody. The only shame attaches to those who rebuked him, or presumed that solemn lies must always be told before the children. I am glad too, Sir, that the turbulence somehow included a rebuke to your reviewer for saying that John Fuller's book of poems was a form of masturbation; mean-minded jabber of this type might do if the man would sign his name, but it is quite incompatible with the principles of an anonymous review.[50]

His letter went to press (8 March 1974) before he managed to submit some slight corrections which he wrote by hand on a carbon copy. In the second sentence he would have preferred on second thoughts that the phrasing 'solemn lies must always be told' should read 'a show of solemnity must always be kept up'; and in the final sentence, 'jabber of this type' should become 'stuff like this'. The reasons for such amendments are not difficult to make out: they had to do with getting the tone right, removing the inappropriate and perhaps even contemptuous pomposity of 'solemn lies', and the coarseness of the throwaway insult of 'jabber'.

Several examples of letters that were redrafted before being posted survive among his papers (a few are given in the text below). They give further evidence of the efforts he put into adding persuasive force to an argument, or else tweaking its tone. One undated letter to John Hayward (not included here), written in 1951, survives in a draft version (there may have been other lost drafts) which is perceptibly more downbeat than the constructive and outgoing version he posted. It aimed to persuade Hayward to arrange publication in an English periodical of a short story written by one of his students in the People's Republic of China. In the surviving draft he remarks among other things:

As for ourselves [the Empson family], everything is entirely friendly except for the post cut-off quite recently . . . I propose to stay here and do some placid work, refusing an offer to fly to an American Summer School because I thought that would be trying the patience a bit too high. It would be rude simply to leave while the British Council wants me here and can't send a substitute; but it is annoying not to know whether my book [*Complex Words*] has been published and if so what was thought about it. I have plenty of writing to go on with and do not pretend to have interest in as apart from sympathy with modern China; sympathy I think anybody ought to feel.

It is useless to ask for books or letters because they have stopped coming; never

---

[50] The reviewer may have been alluding to Byron's remark on Keats's *Endymion*: 'such writing is a sort of mental masturbation—he is always f-gg-g his own *imagination.*—I don't mean that he is indecent but viciously soliciting his own ideas' (*Letters*, 7. 225).

mind, my dear, I am recovering myself now; if only I had time to go through all those bits of paper in the house I might really get somewhere.

Yours with great affection

William Empson

'The duty of sounding cheerful in letters' is not fully achieved in that letter, despite the dutiful-sounding profession that 'everything' was 'entirely friendly'. The predominant sentiment is too negative and abstract: 'rude', 'annoying', 'do not pretend to have any interest as apart from sympathy'. To be sure, Empson represents himself as pursuing 'placid work', but his prose lacks exemplary animation; and the repeated expression of 'sympathy' appears flat and passive, not optimistic. The kindliness of the close is mixed up with palpable moping.

The revised version, as finally received by Hayward, expresses much more purposiveness and vigour; it looks beyond the self, beyond abstractions:

I plan to stay here and write a patient little series of essays about Dover Wilson . . .

It is all friendly and placid here while the world outside the university becomes increasingly threatening. Food prices are remarkably stable, and even the sterling exchange rate is staying fixed at present at its new low level. Drains are being taken up and bits of building going on all over the town; professors from here get sent out during the holidays to look at the villages in remote parts and return placidly enthusiastic with the progress made. There is nothing startling about it, but of course if we are all driven into a world war things will tighten up everywhere. I have asked the British Council to keep me on for the next academic year, but they always delay answering.

Very good wishes; I do hope you are going on all right.

William Empson.

The big world picture is still baleful, but in the foreground are manifestations of a progressive energy which Empson reports with ready will: a 'friendly and placid' working and social environment, currency stability, building activity, professors sent to witness agrarian developments and mellowly reporting upon the good of it all. Yet the phrase 'placidly enthusiastic' seems contradictory, even oxymoronic, and might be felt to undercut the show of enthusiasm—though one can of course be quite as enthusiastic for equanimity as for excess. Although the words convey little to feel fully confident about, the tone is upbeat, the interest is engaged beyond solipsism, and Empson seems contentedly well-wishing: he sounds even a bit cheerful. It is just possible that the difference between the two versions of the letter stems from the difference between a maudlin hangover and a merry night before; but (more probably) the cheer in this case might have been geared up for political reasons. Along with the majority of the peoples of Peking, Empson welcomed the Communist accession to power after all the corrupt brutality of the Nationalist régime, and he felt it important to try to convey in his letters to the outside world an inspiriting faith in the new political order. Still, he does leave quite enough room for ambiguity in the phrase 'placidly enthusiastic'. Whatever the effective degree of adjustment in that instance, the energy he put into refining such adjustments is characteristic of his approach to letter-writing.

It is in fact impossible to overstate the fundamental importance to Empson of style and idiom. For him, the connoisseur of complex words and double meanings, almost any word or phrase might carry a spin, an implication, that deeply affects tone and meaning. In *Complex Words* he noted incidentally, 'a knowledge of the style can sometimes feel so like a knowledge of the spoken voice that we seem to pick up the intonation directly.'[51] (His care to render his own prose as if it were oral speech qualifies it as what Bakhtin called *skaz*—though Empson did not know of the term and would anyway have disliked it.) In 1958, for example, he would write out of the blue to his friend Geoffrey Gorer:

Yesterday morning I was rather glumly opening the Sunday Times and my eye fastened on a half sentence in an outside column:

> by and large, more contented with the way they spend their evenings, and,
> slightly to my surprise, tend to go quite considerably later to bed.

I thought at once 'This must be by Gorer', and so it was. There are rather few writers now who have an immediately recognisable style like that, though when we were young there were quite a lot. It struck me as unusual nowadays, so I thought you deserved to be told.

Another writer whose style he thought wholly individual was Christopher Ricks.

To take a literary instance, in Act II of the A-text of *Doctor Faustus*, Faustus declares to Mephistophiles, 'Come, I think Hell's a fable'. The idiom has several possible connotations. It might be bold or arrogant or self-deluding. It could even be said as between pals who both know, if they are honest, how and when to blow the gaff. Empson, writing in 1973, complained to his colleague Roma Gill that Fredson Bowers, *éminence grise* among textual critics in America, seemed to have given no thought in his

---

[51] WE, 'Statements in Words', *SCW*, 63.

1973 edition of the play (unlike Gill in her edition for the New Mermaid series in 1965) to the implications of the line, and did not explain why he had ruled against it. 'Faustus is not allowed to say "Come, I think Hell's a fable", and there's no sign at all that "Come" has been rejected. The locution was then new, I gather from the NED, and has a powerful effect on the tone, implying "We are both educated people living in the modern world; you need not keep up this pretence"; whereas if you leave it out Faustus seems to be blurting out a deep sour inner resistance . . .'[52] Such a superb reading of the character and the context goes far, I believe, to justify Empson's use of paraphrase as a mode of critical analysis. As for Empson's own style of conversational exchange, one of his favourite (and probably unconscious) locutions was the idiom 'To be sure . . .', which naturally embraces a range of implications from the mild 'Yes, I agree with what you've said so far, but . . .' to the sharp 'Well, if you must begin with the obvious . . .'; the tone would be indulgent or impatient, and either way finely tuned to contextual implication.[53]

Notwithstanding his accomplishments as an inveterate paraphraser, Empson was drubbed by John Carey (among others) for his eagerness to indulge in such a questionable practice. Carey protested that to paraphrase a poem is to stand at a remove from its actual means of expression. Empson believed to the contrary that glossing a piece of literature by means of paraphrase—so long as it is done with subtlety, respect, and honesty, and without reductive intent—can help to enable the reader to pick out subtle shades of socially acute nuance and mood. He wrote in 'Feelings in Words': 'language is essentially a social product, and much

[52] WE, letter to Roma Gill, n.d. (1973–4), in *Houghton*. Cf. WE's gloss in *Faustus and the Censor: The English Faust-Book and Marlowe's 'Doctor Faustus'* (1987), 132–3: 'This use of *come* appears in the NED (though one would like more information) as a new development, so that it would be "modern slang"; the speaker appeals to the good sense of the hearer, or rather the common background which he can presume they share—"Be yourself", he says, "Remember, we are living in the sixteenth century".' Gill was to show the superiority of her work by writing to the *TLS* to point out that Bowers had perpetuated five small errors in the Clarendon edition of *Dr Faustus* by W. W. Greg, thus showing that Bowers's collations had been based on Greg's work and not (as good practice requires) directly on the early quartos.

[53] Other expressions used by WE for demurral or put-down were 'Nonsense, my dear' and 'Your feelings do you credit'—the latter being WE's stock response, as Christopher Heywood recalls, 'to anything to do with Freud, Marx, Einstein and The Bomb, these being the stock topics of conversation in the 1950s.' (e-mail to JH, 1 Nov. 2001). See also WE on the 'kind of coolness [that] has established itself in various phrases used in arguments, to admit one of the assertions of the opponent while claiming that this does not weaken your case. No doubt it is true and certainly all have this effect when used at the beginning of a sentence, whereas surely is a tender appeal to the opponent—"even you, though you will want to deny this, can see the truth of it if you try".' ('Feelings in Words', 28).

concerned with social relations, but we tend to hide this in our forms of speech so as to appear to utter impersonal truths.'[54] But it is very often the casual tricks of language, not the grandstand effects or conscious avowals (or even doctrines), which have the most subtle effects. To take an example, he went on, one simple type of mood is put across when a literary author uses quotation marks as a way of 'picking out the Sense intended by a personal hint . . . This is done in speech by various tricks, particularly by a slight pause before the word and then an unusually precise intonation of it. Both this and the written quotation marks can mean either of two things according to context: "What *they* call so-and-so, but I don't" or "What *I* call so-and-so, but they don't", and "you" can be made to join either party. Thus there are several possible Moods behind a quotation mark . . .'[55] In a similar way, whereas his own prose style has seemed to some readers casual or sloppy, he was quite often using the tricks of informality deliberately to make an effective analytical or debating point. Such devices centrally included the use of approximate quotation as a way of exploring a subtlety. Indeed, Empson seems to have worked on the basis of a notional but unorthodox distinction between literal quotations and what he styled 'as *they* say' quotations.[56] However, when another critic used inverted commas in a less responsible fashion, perhaps as a way of handling an awkward specimen rather than as a purposeful method of descrying shades of sense, he could get quite cross. In a draft letter to one correspondent about the acute differences between their readings of John Donne's poetry, for example, he challenged his opponent on this fair point: 'You have an odd idea that putting in inverted commas would somehow make safe anything you say; this is all wrong; putting in inverted commas only makes a difference in a complex social situation which I do not observe any time you talk about them.' (It is an irony that in the case of that particular opponent, Empson became so peeved while composing his letter that he rushed straight into a misrepresentation of his antagonist's actual beliefs with a crudely reductive 'inverted-commas' version: he felt no sympathy, he said, 'with your vulgar neo-Christian attitude "of course

<hr/>

[54] WE, 'Feelings in Words', 18.   [55] Ibid.

[56] See letter to Ian Parsons (his editor at Chatto & Windus), 25 Mar. 1960, with regard to the editing of *Milton's God*: 'And I have sometimes corrected back your single quotes to double quotes, but this was merely on a guess about your intention which I now expect was wrong, so I am quite willing to change them again. I thought you were distinguishing between literal quotations (double quotes) and "as *they* say" (single quotes), which does seem the most useful distinction if one is to have both; but if not I agree that it is only fussy to have double quotes' (*Reading*). Parsons must have been surprised to learn that WE was on occasion providing approximate rather than exact quotations; WE's 'convention' was not otherwise known to him.

[Donne] meant nothing at all in the love-poems; nobody in the class must bother, please, about what he meant until he came out in favour of Christianity and burning people alive". I really think it a political danger to have this nonsense so much in fashion among literary critics; the Christians are really likely to start again doing the full wickedness which their religion is calculated to excite, though perhaps not till after I am dead.' Famously, James Joyce loathed the convention of marking dialogue in fiction by means of the 'eyesore' of 'perverted' commas: setting off speech with dashes was far prettier. Empson, in contriving a prejudicial paraphrase of his opponent's belief, was being 'perverted' not in an aesthetic but in a more moral sense; he would not have allowed himself such a glib gloss when criticizing a literary text.)

It is relevant to mention here the question of Empson's inclination to quote rather freely from memory, and on occasion to forgo checking his quotations before publication. (While working in Japan and China, it must be admitted, he was as often as not literally unable to check quotations: the library resources were simply not available.) Like Samuel Taylor Coleridge, he had a quick and prodigious memory for poetry, which stood him in good stead when teaching. But now and then he would print a false version of a verse, and some critics were quick to accuse him of distorting the quotation to support a critical construction of his own devising. However, there is in fact no evidence at all, from any stage of his career, to sustain the accusation that he ever deliberately misrepresented a quotation, for whatever peculiar or perverse purposes; any actual misquotation was an unconscious error on his part—and assuredly never desired by him. He was well aware that deliberate misquotation would be improper and ultimately pointless; there would be nothing to gain from knowing irresponsibility all the while texts are there to be checked. He would insist to his collaborator, David Pirie, about Coleridge's remarkable fleet memory, 'Such a memory is dangerous, because it is always liable to select and (according to its lights) improve . . .'[57] The trouble was that—probably out of a defensive reflex—he tended too readily to pooh-pooh the pretensions of painstaking scholarship. It did not help his case.

For the very most part, however, Empson took immense care to express precisely what he meant in any piece of writing that was destined for publication (including letters). He was in fact jealous of the exact words he set down on the page, and would now and then upbraid literary editors

[57] WE, letter to David Pirie, 1 May 1970.

who presumed without asking to sub-edit, to cut or amend, his wording. Invariably, indeed, where he might appear to be most casual in his prose style, he had been most studied, most conscious of the effect he was aiming to put across. It is unusual to find him quietly accepting any modification introduced into an article or a published letter. In May 1954, for example, Janet Adam Smith, who was at the time literary editor of the *New Statesman*, courteously sent a note to alert him to, and to apologize for, the fact that her editor had changed just one word in his review of Dylan Thomas's *Collected Poems*. It was too late to do anything about it, since the issue was already out, but she must have felt that Empson could be touchy and even pugnacious about such things. Unexpectedly, he responded with an unoffended letter exhibiting his customary sensitivity to verbal implication: 'I agree that in principle it was very wicked of the Editor to change a word, but I hadn't noticed it and do not now think it disastrous. As I remember I put "I hope I do not annoy anyone by remarking that the Cross of Christ [in Thomas's poem 'Altarwise by Owl-light'] is also the male sexual organ" and he made it "explaining". This makes me heavy-handed and rather suggests I hold some theory of the sort myself but otherwise does no harm. I can't see that it removes any obscurity, either, though.'[58] Still, Janet Adam Smith was a friend of his (and widow of another good friend, Michael Roberts), and he respected her position.

More usually, he would explode with irritation when an editor deigned to cut or correct his wording, even—especially—when it came to any modification of idiomatic or colloquial usage, or a dash of slang that he particularly relished. A passage from *The Structure of Complex Words* is crucial to this consideration:

It is surely a striking reflection that a great deal of the thought of a man like Dr Johnson, and probably the parts of his thought which are by this time most seriously and rightly admired, were not carried on his official verbal machinery but on colloquial phrases . . . that he would have refused to analyse on grounds of dignity, even if he had been able to . . . You need to know, as well as the serious opinions of a man . . . how much weight he would allow, when making a practical decision, to some odd little class of joke phrases . . . such as carry doctrines more really complex than the whole structure of his official view of the world.[59]

His own such joke-phrases included, it turns out, a curious locution, actually a nonce-phrase, that he used for the opening of stanza 6 of his

---

[58] WE, letter to Janet Adam Smith, 18 May 1954.
[59] WE, 'The English Dog', *SCW*, 174.

poem 'Ignorance of Death' (first published in 1940, though probably drafted in 1936):

> Heaven me, when a man is ready to die about something
> Other than himself, and is in fact ready because of that,
> Not because of himself, that is something clear about himself.

Responding in 1963 to a letter from the poet and critic D. J. Enright, who had enquired about the meaning and provenance of the phrase, Empson explained:

I can't say much more than that it isn't a misprint ('Heaven me, when a man is willing [*sic*] to die about . . .'). Of course these tricks of speech are rapidly variable, and might perhaps be objected to as 'private poetry', a thing I have often been accused of, but wrongly, I thought. 'Heaven me' is meant to sound aunt-like, placid and in a way experienced; I am admitting to feeling respect for heroic behaviour, but do not want to present myself as heroic. 'Of course I don't deny that, but this is no occasion to get excited about it'. It still seems to me the right interjection for the occasion.

However, having said so much, thoughtfully and moderately, he then broke out with a further paragraph which becomes so belligerent as to seem self-defensive:

I wonder if the difference is that your generation is determined to appear manly and sincere, with no hanky-panky, whereas mine thought it showed civilised awareness to make mild unfunny imitations of old ladies, pansies, Cockneys and so forth when expressing a view which the group imitated would especially sympathize with. Come to think of it, all you fiercely upright young men would die of shame rather than do that.

The notion he advances is that he and his pals were wont to amuse themselves by mimicking marginal groups such as old women and homosexuals. Yet at first blush, even if Empson and his gang aped other accents and attitudes to the life, and voiced the very things that the old ladies, queers and Cockneys might say for (and of) themselves, it is difficult to imagine that the puerility of the young mimics did not have the better part of sympathy or empathy. Such behaviour would seem on the face of it (despite what he protested to Enright) to betray a cast of mind that was rather more condescending than inclusive in feeling. The Empson set may have been essaying a version of parody, a mode which (as Linda Hutcheon has shown) implies a degree of complicity with the values it challenges, but it is hard to be sure in such a case just who is being the more parodied—the impressionists or their butts? Empson could expertly

take off his mother—the 'old lady' of his poem 'To an Old Lady'—
because he understood so precisely her social context and cultural assumptions, and indeed participated in them in so far as he had grown up with
them. But the 'defence' that his youthful 'imitations' did no harm, and
indeed demonstrated 'civilised awareness' because the views he expressed
while guying such groups were just what they thought for themselves,
smacks of sophistry. Enright had caught him on the raw.

The main reason for Empson's crossness is probably that he felt Enright
suspected him of voicing a sentiment that was all too aunt-like; whereupon
he protests that he is merely 'putting on' the aunt. However, what is
remarkable about his rebuke to Enright (albeit Enright probably did not
deserve the scolding) is that it speaks for a very early retaliation to the
notion of Political Correctness. Empson loved mischief and transgression,
and scoffed at po-facedness. There was nothing unusual in his way of
bonding with his fellows by means of burlesque: as with any group or
game, to jest about outsiders serves to hearten the insiders. But Empson
found it vexatious that his original 'encoding intention' (to adopt Linda
Hutcheon's term) seemed to have been lost on Enright.

In so defending his neologistic usage 'Heaven me' against a supposed
criticism by Enright, he was probably anticipating an insight regarding the
loaded term 'common' that he would hit upon in a book review dating
from 1977. Raymond Williams, in his *Keywords: A Vocabulary of Culture and
Society* (1976), was to note that it becomes increasingly difficult, even in
examples dating from as early as the sixteenth century, to separate the
neutral uses of 'common' from 'more conscious and yet vaguer uses to
mean *vulgar*, *unrefined* and eventually *low-class*'.[60] From a surprisingly early
year, wrote Williams, 'common' has been utilized as a marker of social
division. Empson, in a review of Williams's book, noted in passing: 'I think
there really is a trick about common for "low-class". The usage is assumed
to be itself low-class, so that the better-class person saying it is having fun,
talking in inverted commas.'[61] Just so, if 'Heaven me' was made up to
sound 'aunt-like', it was annoying that a reader could think to interpret an
implied quotation as the poet speaking in *propria persona*. It would have
been best for Empson to get the tone right in the first place, so that
'Heaven me' should come across more obviously as a piece of posing on
his part. Empson's mother might have called someone 'common' (vulgar
or low-class) and mean it, but if Empson was to make use of the phrase, he

---

[60] Raymond Williams, *Keywords: A Vocabulary of Culture and Society* (1976), 62
[61] WE, 'Compacted Doctrines' (1977), in *A*, 186.

would be talking in inverted commas. A critic who could think him sincere when he made up 'Heaven me' was in effect accusing him of the very worst thing: not only was the poet failing to show up the fussiness of the patois employed, he was seen to be speaking just like mother.

For a final example of his great anxiety to make himself understood— to take pains to fine-tune mood, tone, and implication—a protest published in the *TLS* in 1975, commenting on a book-review about Richard III, is especially apt:

Sir,—I hoped for a vigorous letter from an informed source about G. R. Elton's review (October 10), but as only a mild one has appeared . . . I make bold to express the coarse voice of the general public. What we learn from the review is first that no evidence is any longer offered for the belief that Richard killed the Princes in the Tower. What every history book, however brief, always told the children is now admitted to be wrong. It is insinuated instead that this does not matter because the man did a lot of other bad things, not mentioned. We learn, secondly, that the life of Richard III by Sir Thomas More, or partly in his handwriting, contains a lot of lies; but this does not matter because the effect of them is artistic. Goodness, how sad!

Presenting himself in that way as the voice of the ordinary, historically-interested citizen, he offers a gentle satire on the sadly changing fortunes of historiography and critical judgement. Yet the form in which his letter appeared in the *TLS*, including two seemingly tiny sub-editorial interventions, made him blow his top. The letter he thereupon despatched to John Gross, the newly-installed editor of the *TLS*, has not survived, but the heat of his vehemence on the matter can be gathered from the few quotations Gross included in his well-couched response:

I am very sorry that you were caused so much pain and distress by the form in which your letter appeared, and will be happy to publish a correction of the quotation if you like. The letter was sub-edited by a member of the staff, to conform with *The Times* house style—this is the practice which I inherited from my predecessor . . . so I wonder if it is quite fair to speak of the perils of writing for 'my' magazine as opposed to the TLS past and present . . . I sympathize with your distaste for overdoing the shriek-marks [exclamation marks] . . . I would also regret any permanent ill will towards *The Times Literary Supplement* on your part more than I would in the case of the great majority of writers, since I consider you to be a poet and a critic of genius, and there aren't many of your species around. And I assure you that that isn't meant to be disarming, since if your letter caused me regret it also made me cross. I suppose I can't object if you say you suffered 'severe pain and shame', since only you know how much the shoe pinches. But 'carefully rewritten to secure the hog-wash style throughout'?

'Grossly inaccurate'? 'Disgusting'? 'Obviously very unsafe'? The world is full of sin and sorrow, and surely to come on like this is a pretty close equivalent, in its excessive shrillness, to a thick peppering of shriek-marks.

But you are a man of genius, and in your own words, 'Oh well'.[62]

Gross's deft mix of flattery and rebuttal seemed to win the day: Empson let it go.

But what dread offence had the *TLS* perpetrated to merit such execrations from Empson? It had (merely) amended 'Goodness how Sad' to 'Goodness, how sad!' Taken from a story by Evelyn Waugh entitled 'Cruise (Letters from a young lady of leisure)', it is the catchphrase of a society girl who prattles her days away in a series of letters home to her beau during a Mediterranean cruise with her parents. Nothing affects her empty-headed poco-curantism ('This is the Sphinx. Goodness how Sad'). Her ignorance of punctuation aptly accentuates the gush of her inanity, so that 'Goodness how Sad' is rendered even thus. First published in 1933, the story was included in Waugh's collection *Mr Loveday's Little Outing*, from 1934 onwards. At the *TLS*, neither editor nor sub-editor had recognized the allusion—and who can blame them? And yet in regularizing the grammar and punctuation, they must have felt that Empson had simply been sloppy in his typing. One can see at a glance why he felt annoyed. He had employed the joke-phrase out of Waugh to colour his letter with a light-hearted period tone. He was putting on a persona out of the 1930s to rib the new historical wisdom—it is a mode of argufying, 'a not specially dignified sort of arguing' (his complaint did not seriously matter to him)— and putting to use the lingo that Waugh picked up from the Guinness set and satirized in *Vile Bodies*.[63] But to render the allusion in the form 'Goodness, how sad!' makes him into a tutting ninny—an aunt, no less.

---

[62] John Gross, letter to WE, 3 Nov. 1975 (*Houghton*). Gross was not merely writing to the moment, for he genuinely admired Empson. In *A Double Thread: Growing Up English and Jewish in London* (2001), he related: 'Empson in particular redeemed the notion of analysis. He was a poet primarily, or had been until his muse deserted him—an enormously gifted one. But for all his rich idiosyncrasy, he presented his readers with a critical method they could build on. He showed you how it could be done. And though he could be baffling—I often didn't see how he had got from one sentence to the next—he was so entertaining that you forgave him. (One glimpse of him from a later period. When I took over at the *Times Literary Supplement* I was anxious to secure his services as a contributor, and he was one of the first people I called. "Oh, it's you," came his strange sing-song voice over the phone. "Are you in the chair already?" "Yes." A long pause. "*Does it swivel?*" ' (188). See also Gross, 'Remembering William Empson', *New York Times Book Review*, 20 May 1984, 14.

[63] WE, who admired Evelyn Waugh, relished the incongruity of reading a Waugh story that he had borrowed from a Chinese colleague during the celebratory parade—he and his colleagues were processing past Chairman Mao Zhedong in Tiananmen Square, Peking—marking the first anniversary of the declaration of the People's Republic of China on 1 Oct. 1950; he

All aspects of style, including mood, tone, idiom, implication, and the tricks of allusiveness, mattered to Empson. Style was not everything, but no piece of writing whatsoever could work unless style was fully functional. It was scarcely a joke when he wrote home to his wife in November 1974 from the University of Pennsylvania, where he was spending time as a visiting professor: 'Thank you for the Times Crossword puzzles; I have sometimes finished a New York Times one, so I don't dislike them merely because they expect me to know famous names of baseball and Broadway. The Times (London) has a better style.'[64] He was over-sensitive when readers misapprehended his own prose style precisely because he was so sensitive to the tricks of style in literary works. It was important to him to be as lucid as possible in his critical analyses. For that reason, he rather resented any critic who undertook to explicate his writings. He had written what he had written, explaining his ideas and insights to readers as clearly as he could manage, so he saw little need for extra explanatory mediation.

Ever conscious of the duty of sounding cheerful in prose, he was quite capable of sharing a joke about the difficulties that others experienced with the style of his writings. In 1954, he wrote to Janet Adam Smith about his review of Dylan Thomas's poems (I have quoted another paragraph from this letter above):

There has been some other puzzling about the style of the piece. Dear old J. Isaacs, when I ran into him at some party, said it was the most childish thing on the subject he had yet seen, and he gathered all I meant was that the only good part was the final Milk Wood. How he came to think that I can't imagine: I suppose he thinks if a critic says something simply that proves he means to be ironical. Then he said 'How do you manage to get it as loose as that? Do you dictate it?' I explained I used beer, but that when I saw the stuff in print (I had to admit) it shocked my eye as much as it did his. He was very friendly, you understand. One thing is, I have to read so much Mandarin English Prose now, especially in literary criticism, and am so accustomed to being shocked by its emptiness, that I feel I must do otherwise at all costs.

There was thus a political element to his campaign to make his written words carry all the ready accessibility of conversation. But one possible

wrote the next day to Kathleen Raine: 'Yesterday I went on parade with Waugh's *KingScott's [Scott-King's] Modern Europe* [1946], a handy thing for the pocket, and then when I started to read it in the long wait felt I had to apologise to one of the Chinese colleagues in the file behind because I had never returned his loan of this powerful little skit. I would give it back soon I said. But no other kind of apology seemed necessary to anyone; as I had assumed of course, but in a letter to England, it now occurs to me, that might look a Significant Detail' (carbon in *Houghton*).

[64] WE, letter to Hetta Empson, 14 Nov. 1974 (*Hull*).

corollary of his usual stylistic demeanour (as he understood full well) was that to some readers he could now and then come across as flippant, or amateur, or as a cheery toff.

Some of the recent reviews of my work [he wrote to Roma Gill in 1979] have wondered why I am always so *facetious*, making it impossible to take what I say seriously; this author is probably a tragic clown, they say, staving off lunacy. Perhaps it comes from imitating Bertrand Russell. It is so, whether lunatic or not, that I can't bear to print a thing till I can read it over without feeling bored; if it feels boring, that proves it is wrong . . . A lot of details get cleared up from having to re-write, but it would be better to think clearly first.

Whether or not readers enjoy the personality Empson crafted into his prose comes down in the end to a question of taste. But there is no secret behind it other than the hard graft of the author in writing and rewriting until he had more nearly satisfied himself that style and sense measured up to one another. This is true too of a surprising number of his letters, whether public or personal. The letters that were written straight off—like that to Edith Sitwell about her novel *I Live Under a Black Sun*, written from Hanoi in 1938—are now and then perceptibly awkward in style, though usually absorbing in every other aspect.

He wrote to his publisher in November 1951 about the critical reception of his long-gestated critical book, *The Structure of Complex Words* (which had been worked over again and again, though not continuously, since the early 1930s):

I had been feeling that my prose style in the book was too tense and twitchy to be readable or even sound true, so I was comforted by an adverse review in *Tribune* which said the style was so slack, like a fireside chat. There was a reviewer of *Pastoral* who said it was obviously improvised and printed without second thoughts, but maybe this was better than trying to be accurate; which pleased me as I had spent so many years trying to make the style natural.[65]

George Watson, Fellow of St John's College, Cambridge, has written in a memorial essay on Empson: ' "I still have to put in the careless ease," he once remarked, sitting by the pond in his Hampstead garden, when I reproached him gently for not collecting his essays. "The careless ease always goes in last." It is as good a remark as you will hear about the art of exposition.'[66] That way of putting it makes the process sound like adventitious ornamental trimming; in a letter to his collaborator David Pirie in

---

[65] WE, letter to Ian Parsons, 16 Nov. 1951 (*Reading*).
[66] George Watson, *Never Ones for Theory? England and the War of Ideas* (2000), 70.

1969, Empson himself made it clear that the sheer hard slog of revision was a key function of the business of writing, and of thinking through one's writing: 'putting in the careless ease often amounts to discovering what the point of the whole thing was and rewriting it completely.'[67]

The issue of this volume of selected letters is by no means meant to imply that I have had the pick of every possible Empson missive: that is not the case (it would be beyond human possibility for all of them to have survived). All the same, I believe I have gathered up copies of the overwhelming majority of those still extant. Yet I know too of other letters I have been unable to locate (as yet, I hope I may add), or which have not survived the tidiness or carelessness, or the house removals, of their recipients. G. S. Fraser recalls in his memoirs, for instance, that in the 1940s he received the benefit of the older man's wryly-noted experience: 'Empson, when he went to China, wrote suggesting that I should try to get a teaching job there too. "When you come back," he wrote, "you will find the same people talking about the same things, even after a lapse of five years . . . unless, indeed, you find it was wise to get away in time." '[68] The last phrase carries the distinctive curl of Empson's wit—it conveys the 'bang at the end' that he favoured, the showman's flourish that dazzles or disarms— since it advises that returning home should mean a prompt new departure. In 1962, Empson exchanged letters with the classicist Sir Denys Page (Regius Professor of Greek, and Master of Jesus College, University of Cambridge) about the difficulties of reconstructing the 'very complicated picture' of the Theban plays. In the same year, and possibly in the same month, Empson posted a query to S. M. Stern of All Souls College, Oxford, about whether the Berbers 'did have songs which rhymed, around the time of St Augustine'.[69] In 1964, while browsing through *The Listener*, he fell upon a talk by Erich Heller, 'Faust's Damnation', and in particular a reference to Marlowe's tutor at Cambridge whom Heller claimed had been 'burned for heresy'; he was naturally avid to know much more about the playwright's fatally heretical tutor. In 1951 he was moved to write Anne Ridler a long and unsolicited letter of advice about her revisions to Michael Roberts's *Faber Book of Modern Verse*; Kathleen Raine should be represented more fully in the updated volume, he appears to have thought, among other changes. 'I agree with what you say about the Faber Book,'

---

[67] WE, letter to David Pirie, 19 Apr. 1969 (Pirie).
[68] G. S. Fraser, *A Stranger and Afraid: the autobiography of an intellectual* (1983), 182.
[69] S. M. Stern, letter to WE, 2 Jan. 1962 (*Houghton*).

Ridler responded, 'but I had not the freedom to make nearly such drastic changes as those which you suggest . . . I do not know whether what I have said in the introduction about the new techniques will cover what you wanted—but you will see.' (Charmingly, too, she offered this compliment on his own work: 'I hope that before I die I shall read another book of your poems—even what we have is, with Auden and T. S. E., the best of the lot.') In a later year, when reporting to me that Empson's letter had been lost or thrown away, Anne Ridler explained the situation by way of a marvellously ambiguous run of subjunctives: 'alas, I don't remember his letter about the 1951 supplement to the Faber Book, and if it had had anything interesting in it, I think I should have kept it. I believe he did approve of my selection—or I think I'd have remembered if he *hadn't*.'[70] Paul Giles (now Reader in American Literature and Director of the Rothermere American Institute at Oxford) wrote to Empson when he was a research student, having picked up on a favourable reference in Empson's criticism to the poetry of Hart Crane: did Empson have a specific interest in Crane's punning? 'He wrote back saying he hadn't really thought of Crane within that context; he mentioned a passage from (I think) "Voyages" that he liked, though he said he didn't like the "death wish" he found permeating Crane's poetry. It was quite a brief letter . . .'[71] Other lost letters seem to have been equally memorable, and to offer some even more surprising insights. Professor W. W. Robson told me once, 'I remember discussing Max Beerbohm with Empson in some letters, which I am sorry to have lost. Here are one or two things he said in them: "Max was wrong (in the parody of Kipling in *A Christmas Garland*) to show Kipling sucking up to the police. Dickens does that; Kipling never does." "Max's parodies of Kipling and of Arnold Bennett . . . made Kipling give up writing for ever and Arnold Bennett for three whole days." '[72] Given the remarkably wide scope of Empson's interests, it would be most interesting too to know exactly what he had asked his old friend N. W. Pirie (an agricultural scientist specializing in soils and plant nutrition at the Rothamstead Experimental Station) that inspired this reply from Pirie: 'my impression is that all birds, most if not all reptiles and amphibians, and most fish have one hole. Some of the sharks have a penis and I think sperm comes out through it. Some birds have a sort of penis but I think use it only for tittilation as female hyenas do. As you know, women with large

---

[70] Anne Ridler, letter to JH, 6 Oct. 1986.
[71] P. D. Giles, e-mail to JH, 16 May 2001.
[72] W. W. Robson, undated letter to JH.

clitorises do not pee through them . . . The disadvantage in passing sperm out through the same hole as urine seems small.'[73] All such lost or mislaid letters are a real loss (as are those that Empson wrote to the late Gay Clifford, and two letters berating Philip Edwards for his interpretation of *The Spanish Tragedy*), for their perceptions on a wonderful plethora of topics, and for the quality of mind expressed with style.[74]

But at least I can report a letter that might otherwise be mislaid by way of anonymity. It is a letter Empson ghost-wrote for his friend Alice Stewart, and it was published in *The Times* on 16 January 1971 (p. 13), as 'The lethal habit':

Sir, I am tempted to ask if anything is being done to test whether the spraying of tobacco with pesticides is the reason why smoking has become so dangerous. The question is crucial because the death rate for lung cancer began to increase only after the spraying of tobacco crops from the air became a practical proposition; then again, it is hard to invent any reason why cigarettes should be more dangerous than cigars, except that the former come mainly from the United States and the latter from South America, where the rainfall is higher and spraying is less intensive.

What I have in mind is that trace compounds of pesticide origin may increase the risk of chronic bronchitis and lung cancer either by adding to the number of carcinogenic substances in tobacco smoke (synergistic action) or, more likely, by introducing a poisonous element into the situation by altering the way in which the tobacco burns (catalytic action). An adequate test of this theory would be provided if the Government banned the importation of tobacco which had been sprayed. The growers would need only a year's grace, and it would be relatively simple for the excise authorities to decide, at the point of entry, whether the cargoes were contaminated. Six or seven years might be enough to decide whether the bronchitis and lung cancer death rates were being affected.

The plan would cost the Government neither votes nor revenue. The public are already concerned about the rising death rates, and anyone can see that chemicals which are lethal to pests are likely to be injurious to humans; a solution of the problem which allowed them to go on smoking would be generally welcome. Britain, as a large consumer of tobacco, is in a position to make the

---

[73] N. W. Pirie, letter to WE, 20 May 1983 (*Houghton*).

[74] However, at least one supposedly discarded letter turns out to have been no such thing. On 2 August 1992 Professor W. J. Bate wrote to me: 'The sole contact I had was a short note he wrote, after or while he was writing (for the NY Rev. of Bks) a review of a short biography I'd written of Coleridge . . . In that note, which I didn't keep, he said only that he liked the book, & hoped I'd be pleased with his review.' In fact, Professor Bate was misremembering, for WE had not written to him about his biography; it was L. C. Knights who had reviewed Bate's *Coleridge*: 'Coleridge Lives!', *NYRB*, 11: 11 (19 Dec. 1968), 25–30. WE wrote of the book, in his notes: 'dishonest book hiding his early religious beliefs.'

demands of an important customer, and growers willing to accept our conditions would revert to older methods of husbandry.

I am, etc.,

A. M. Stewart

Department of Social Medicine, Oxford University

The ideas came from Dr Stewart, a professional epidemiologist; the clarity of the wording is Empson's—though properly disciplined to eschew his personal style.

Virtually every one of Empson's letters carries his distinctive tone of voice, as well as perspicaciousness and wit, so I earnestly hope that many others may come to light after the appearance of this volume. One batch of letters I would dearly love to recover, for instance, is that between Empson and his friend John Davenport. At a Sotheby's sale on 28 July 1977, Lot 555—featuring twenty-two letters between Empson and Davenport—was purchased by Pickering & Chatto, and in due course that reputable old firm sold their prize on to another customer. Sadly, Pickering & Chatto has somehow mislaid its marked-up catalogue of the Sotheby's sale, and they have no other record of who ultimately acquired the Empson-Davenport correspondence. Dear Reader, please tell me if you know.

In due course, I feel sure, there will come a time when a complete collection of Empson's letters will be called for in some form. In the meantime, this selection offers a fair gathering from the prodigious range of ideas, activities, and interests explored and expounded in the letters of a poet and critic of genius.

A NOTE ON THE TEXT

The considerable majority of Empson's letters were typed out by the author, so that transcription presents few problems. Shorter missives were penned in Empson's own good hand. In all cases I have used either original typescripts or manuscripts or xerox copies of the originals. The texts of all letters published in periodicals and newspapers are taken from the printed sources. Where letters have found their way into research archives, locations are identified in italics at the end of each letter; where no source is indicated it may be assumed that the original is still in the possession of the recipients or their heirs and assigns. For all other materials, unless otherwise stated, the source is the William Empson Papers now owned by the Houghton Library at Harvard University (a collection which fortunately includes a good number of carbon copies of letters from the later period that Empson kept for himself); the call number of the Empson collection is MS Eng 1401. Where a letter is flagged 'Houghton carbon', this may serve to indicate that the final text may have been altered by hand before being sent off. While a few obvious errors (e.g. 'Funny enough' for 'Funnily enough') have been silently corrected, all points of punctuation in the letters are given as written. To save space and to secure a reading text that is as clear as possible, letter-heads have been relineated. Dates given in letter-headings have been standardized according to the form: 12 August 1935. Where dates were not given in the originals, they have sometimes been deduced from internal or contextual evidence; any doubt about a date is signalled by a question mark in parentheses.

With a few exceptions, the letters are arranged in chronological order so far as it can be determined. The exceptions are some few groups of letters having to do with specific controversies which are brought together in clusters—they include exchanges with Rosemond Tuve about George Herbert's poetry, a quarrel with Laura Riding about *Seven Types of Ambiguity*, and a run of ranklings with Norman Fruman about his scholarship on Coleridge—where it would be irksome for the reader to find them distributed amongst other letters on unrelated issues, and where it makes best sense to print the set in sequence. The beginnings and ends of these sequences are identified by the symbol § plus a Heading and 'End' plus § respectively, and are placed by the earliest letter in the sequence.

Very few cuts have been made in the letters, and those few are indicated by square brackets, which invariably mark the excision of extraneous or trivial matter. No cuts whatever have been made for reasons of censorship. In a few cases—a torn sheet, or utter illegibility—a word or phrase has had to be left out of the transcription: this too is made known at the appropriate point in the text.

Headnotes or footnotes are supplied where some explanation is required, and to identify persons and circumstances as they arise. To cut down on clutter, many of the principal addressees are described in a biographical glossary at the end of the text. Persons so described in the glossary are flagged by an asterisk positioned after the surname in the first citation or in a footnote, and in the index.

TABLE OF DATES

influence, perhaps not unlike an east wind.' Participates in debates at the Union.

12 June: publishes his first literary notice in *The Granta*.

June: gains 1st class in Part I of the mathematical tripos; awarded college prize.

1927   *5 February*: acts in a production at the Cambridge ADC of his one-act play, *Three Stories*, a melodrama.

Begins reviewing film and theatre, as well as books, for *The Granta* and *The Cambridge Review*. For 1927–8, while still a student of mathematics, becomes 'Skipper' (literary editor) of *The Granta*.

June: publishes first poem at Cambridge, 'Poem about a Ball in the Nineteenth Century'; he is influenced by seventeenth-century metaphysical poetry, especially John Donne.

1928   *June*: Senior Optime (Upper Second) in Part II of the mathematical tripos: a disappointing result.

October: registers for the English Tripos; tutored by I. A. Richards at Magdalene College and attends Richards's lectures on 'Practical Criticism'; begins work towards *Seven Types of Ambiguity*; becomes president of The Heretics.

November: launches avant-garde magazine, *Experiment*, co-edited with Jacob Bronowski, Humphrey Jennings, and Hugh Sykes Davies (it runs for seven issues, the last in May 1931).

1929   *20 January*: gives a talk at Cambridge on ambiguity in literature.

February: publishes 'Ambiguity in Shakespeare: Sonnet XVI' in *Experiment* (the essay will in due course form part of *Seven Types of Ambiguity*).

March: takes title role in *The Tragedy of Tragedies: or the Life and Death of Tom Thumb the Great* by Henry Fielding, in a production by the Cambridge Mummers.

June: gains first class with 'special distinction' in English Tripos; awarded a Magdalene college prize; elected to a Charles Kingsley Bye-Fellowship for 1929–30.

July: discovered by college porters to be in possession of contraceptives; an extraordinary meeting of the Governing Body of Magdalene College resolves to deprive Empson of his Bye-Fellowship and remove his name from the college books. Empson removes himself to 65 Marchmont Street, London, where he lives as a freelance writer for the next two years; he is cultivated by literary figures including T. S. Eliot, Virginia Woolf, Harold Monro, and Sylvia Townsend Warner.

October: *Letter IV* published by Heffer's of Cambridge.

Six of the eighteen poems he has written to date feature in *Cambridge Poetry 1929*, published by Leonard and Virginia Woolf at the Hogarth Press.

November: publishes 'Some Notes on Mr Eliot' (a further preview of *Ambiguity*) in *Experiment*.

1930   *November*: *Seven Types of Ambiguity* published.

1931   *29 August*: begins three-year contract as a professor of English at Tokyo University of Literature and Science (Bunrika Daigaku); teaches also at Tokyo Imperial University.

1932   *February*: six poems are included in anthology, *New Signatures*, published by the Hogarth Press.

1934   *Poems*, in an edition of 100 copies, privately printed by The Fox & Daffodil Press, Kinuta-mura, near Tokyo.

8 July: returns to London, where he spends the next three years as a freelance writer.

1935   *May*: *Poems* published in London.

October: *Some Versions of Pastoral* published.

Publishes translations into Basic English of two works by J. B. S. Haldane, *The Outlook of Science* and *Science and Well-Being*. Gains MA, University of Cambridge.

1936   W. B. Yeats includes an Empson poem in the *Oxford Book of Modern Verse*; Michael Roberts picks six for *The Faber Book of Modern Verse*.

1937–8   *August*: takes up appointment at National Peking University, arriving just as the Japanese invade China; journeys through China with I. A. Richards and his wife; works with the exiled Peking universities— amalgamated as the Temporary University (*Chang-sha lin-shih ta-hsueh*, or *Linta* for short)—from November 1937 to February 1938 at Nan-Yueh, Hunan Province; journeys to Hong Kong.

1938–9   Continues university teaching with the National Southwest Associated University (*Hsi-na lien-ho ta-hsueh* [*Xinan Lianhe Daxue*], commonly abbreviated to the acronym *Lienta* [*Lianda*]), in remote exile, first in the town of Mengtzu and then in Kunming, the capital of Yunnan province, near the Indo-China (Vietnam) border. In the autumn of 1939, sets off to return home by way of the USA, where he spends a period in Boston (broadcasting on Basic English).

1940   *28 January*: arrives back in England.

26 June: joins the Monitoring Service of the BBC at Wood Norton Hall, near Evesham in Worcestershire, working as a sub-editor.

September: *The Gathering Storm* published in London.

1941   Transfers to the BBC Overseas Service in London, where he becomes a Talks Assistant and then Chinese Editor, organizing talks to China and propaganda programmes for the Home Service; for two years, works alongside George Orwell.

2 December: marries Hester Henrietta Crouse ('Hetta'), a South African artist, at St Stephen's Church, Hampstead, London.

1942   *9 November*: birth of first son, William Hendrik Mogador.

1944   *30 September*: birth of second son, Jacob Arthur Calais.

1947–52   Teaches at National Peking University, his post being subsidized by the British Council; witnesses the civil war and the six-week siege of Peking late in 1948; the Communist takeover and the inauguration of the People's Republic of China, including the beginnings of reform and 'thought control'.

1948   *24 March*: *The Collected Poems of William Empson* published in New York.

July–August: teaches at Kenyon College Summer School, Gambier, Ohio, USA, on leave from Peking.

1950   Further summer visit to the Kenyon College Summer School.

1951   *July*: *The Structure of Complex Words* published in London.

1952   *summer* returns with family from China to England.

15 December: *The Poems of William Empson* broadcast by BBC.

1953   *October*: takes up Chair of English Literature at the University of Sheffield, where he works for the next eighteen years, with occasional sabbaticals at American and Canadian universities.

1954   *May*: Gresham Professor in Rhetoric, Gresham College, London, lecturing on 'The last Plays of Shakespeare and their Relation to the Elizabethan Theatre'.

June–July: Fellow of the School of Letters, Indiana University, Bloomington, Indiana.

27 October: *The Birth of Steel: A Light Masque* performed for Queen Elizabeth II at the University of Sheffield.

1956   *6 December*: birth of Hetta Empson's third child, Simon Peter Duval Smith.

1961   *February*: *The Collected Poems of William Empson* (New York) issued in paperback.

Milton's God published.

William Empson Reading Selected Poems (*Listen* LPV3) issued.

1964   *Autumn*: Visiting Professor, English Department, University of Ghana, Legon, Accra, Ghana.

1968   Hon. D. Litt, University of East Anglia, Norwich.

Ingram Merrill Foundation Award.

June–August: Visiting Professor, Department of English, State University of New York at Buffalo.

1971   Hon. D. Litt, University of Bristol.

Summer: retires from University of Sheffield.

1972   *January–February*: gives Waynflete Lectures on 'The editorial choice of the text of a poem', at Magdalen College, Oxford.

Publishes *Coleridge's Verse: A Selection* (with David B. Pirie).

1973   Visiting Professor, York University, Toronto.

1974   *Lent Term*: delivers Clark Lectures at Trinity College, Cambridge, on 'The Progress of Criticism'.

Hon. D. Litt., University of Sheffield.

Honorary member of the American Academy of Arts and Letters/ The National Institute of Arts and Letters.

1974–5   Visiting Professor of English, Pennsylvania State University.

1976   *Autumn*: Visiting Professor, Department of English, University of Delaware, Newark, Delaware.

Fellow of the British Academy.

Honorary Fellow of the Modern Language Association of America.

1977   *10 June*: Hon. Litt. D., University of Cambridge.

1979   Knighted in New Year Honours for 'services to English literature'.

Elected Honorary Fellow, Magdalene College, Cambridge.

1982   *January–April*: Visiting Professor, University of Miami.

1984   *15 April*: dies in London.

Collected Poems reissued; *Using Biography* published.

1986   *The Royal Beasts and Other Works* and *Essays on Shakespeare* published.

1987   *Arguifying: Essays on Literature and Culture* and *Faustus and the Censor: The English Faust-Book and Marlowe's 'Doctor Faustus'* published.

1993   *Essays on Renaissance Literature*, vol. 1: *Donne and the new philosophy*.

1994   *Essays on Renaissance Literature*, vol. 2: *The Drama*.

1996   *The Strengths of Shakespeare's Shrew: Essays, Memoirs and Reviews*.

2000   *The Complete Poems of William Empson*.

LIST OF RECIPIENTS AND DATES

Ian Parsons	31 Jan. 1967	Christopher Norris	7 Oct. 1971
Christopher Ricks	23 Feb. 1967	*The Listener*	25 Nov. 1971
Helen Gardner	4 Mar. 1967	Christopher Ricks	3 Dec. 1971
C. B. Cox	15 Mar. 1967	Francis Doherty	7 Dec. 1971
Critical Quarterly	Spring 1967	Richard M. Wilson	n.d. (1971)
New Statesman	31 Mar. 1967	Peter Levi	n.d. (1972)
W. R. Elton	6 Apr. 1967	Frank Kermode	n.d. (1972)
Review of English Studies	1967	John Sparrow	14 Mar. 1972
Hyam Maccoby	11 May 1967	Geoffrey Posner	n.d. (1972)
Christopher Ricks	30 May 1967	Veronica Forrest-	
Essays in Criticism	Jul. 1967	Thomson	n.d. (?1972)
Essays in Criticism	Apr. 1968	Christopher Ricks	1 Jul. 1972
Francis Berry	8 Jun. 1967	*TLS*	14 Jul. 1972
Christopher Ricks	3 Aug. 1967	*Re* Nick Malone	17 Aug. 1972
Christopher Ricks	10 Aug. 1967	Christopher Ricks	27 Aug. 1972
Christopher Ricks	11 Aug. 1967	Penguin Books	22 Oct. 1972
W. D. Maxwell-		*TLS*	12 Jan. 1973
Mahon	6 Nov. 1967	Roger Sale	n.d. (1973)
Cecil Woolf	n.d. (1967)	John Sparrow	6 Mar. 1973
Encounter	Feb. 1968	David B. Pirie	17 Mar. 1973
Hudson Review	Winter 1967–8	Alan Rudrum	n.d. (1973)
Ian Hamilton	11 Jun. 1968	Alan Rudrum	28 Apr. 1973
Michael Holroyd	6 Dec. 1968	*TLS*	18 May 1973
TLS	20 Feb. 1969	A. L. Rowse	27 May 1973
David B. Pirie	19 Apr. 1969	Frank McMahon	21 Aug. 1973
David B. Pirie	n.d. 1969	*New York Review of*	
Robert Burchfield	19 Jul. 1969	*Books*	20 Sept. 1973
Philip Hobsbaum	2 Aug. 1969	*Essays in Criticism*	Oct. 1973
Darcy O'Brien	n.d. (Feb./Mar.	Penelope R. Doob	n.d. (1973)
	1970)	Roma Gill	4 Dec. 1973
G. S. Fraser	16 Feb. 1970	Roma Gill	n.d. (1973)
David B. Pirie	1 May (1970)	Nick Malone	11 Dec. 1973
A. D. Nuttall	26 May 1970	*TLS*	8 Mar. 1974
David B. Pirie	n.d. (? Jun. 1970)	Christopher Ricks	13 Jun. (1974)
Christopher Norris	3 Aug. 1970	Jeffrey M. Miller	19 Nov. 1974
Christopher Norris	27 Sept. 1970	Christopher Ricks	19 Jan. 1975
David Wilson	5 Nov. 1970	*New York Review of*	
Nikos Stangos	19 Dec. 1970	*Books*	n.d. (1975)
Christopher Norris	7 Jan. 1971	Richard Ellmann	18 Feb. 1975
Nikos Stangos	25 Mar. 1971	Richard Ellmann	8 Apr. 1975
William Lyons	3 May 1971	Earl Miner	28 Apr. 1975
Hugh Kenner	11 Jun. 1971	Richard Wordsworth	3 Aug. 1975
Richard Ellmann	14 Jun. 1971	Jacob Empson	'Saturday' (Aug.
Karunakar Jha	20 Jun. 1971		1975)
Christopher Norris	21 Jun. 1971	*TLS*	24 Oct. 1975
Richard Ellmann	1 Jul. 1971	Richard Ellmann	7 Nov. 1975
Christopher Ricks	27 Sept. 1971	Richard Ellmann	25 Nov. 1975

THE LETTERS

TO ELSIE DUNCAN-JONES*

And, of course, there was William Empson, admired of us all. I didn't know him well but he printed a piece of mine in the first number of *Experiment*[1] and praised me for selling 30 copies of that issue in Newnham alone . . . Our acquaintance had begun with a correspondence about Hopkins's son-net 'The Windhover' during the vacation. He addressed his first reply to E. E. Phare, Esq. (at that time such a mistake gave pleasure.) Everybody in that little 'coterie', as my tutor, not quite approvingly, called it, I think felt the pre-eminence of 'Bill'. (Elsie Elizabeth Phare, 'From Devon to Cambridge, 1926: or, Mentioned with Derision', *The Cambridge Review* (103: 2267), 26 Feb. 1982)

4 September 1928

Dear Miss Phare,

Thanks: what I should like to do would be to print the section about The Windhover, getting on to 1500 words, but I doubt if you or the boys would let me ('Precision' applied to verse seems to me to show a false notion of reality).

Commentators on Shakespeare *will* imply 'the man is being obscure again', and give three things in the notes, some one of which they think the word 'means'; usually the effect of the passage involves the word meaning all three and more. Passages in The Windhover in the same way mean both the opposites created by their context, it seems plain; [I. A.] Richards* said that once, and then edged away from it.[2]

'Buckle' means at once girt about you, like a belt, for war, and/or

---

[1] E. E. Phare, 'Valéry and Gerard Hopkins', *Experiment*, no. 1 (Nov. 1928), 19–23. For good accounts of *Experiment*, see Jason Harding, '*Experiment* in Cambridge: "A Manifesto of Young England" ', *The Cambridge Quarterly*, 27: 4 (1998), 287–309; Thomas R. Sawyer, 'Experiment', in *British Literary Magazines: The Modern Age, 1914–1984*, ed. Alvin Sullivan (1986), 177–9; and Kate Price, 'Finite but Unbounded: *Experiment* magazine, Cambridge, England, 1928–31', *Jacket Magazine* 20 http://jacketmagazine.com/20/price-expe.html.

[2] See IAR, 'Gerard Hopkins', *Dial*, 81: 3 (Sept. 1926), 195–203; in IAR: *SW* (9), 95–103: 'Why in hiding? Hiding from what? . . . What is the greater danger and what the less? I should say the poet's heart is in hiding from Life, has chosen a safer way, and that the greater danger is the greater exposure to temptation and error than a more adventurous, less sheltered course (sheltered by Faith?) brings with it. Another, equally plausible reading would be this: Renouncing the glamour of the outer life of adventure the poet transfers its qualities of audacity to the inner life. (*Here* is the bosom, the inner consciousness.) The greater danger is that to which the moral hero is exposed. Both readings may be combined, but pages of prose would be required for a paraphrase of the result . . .

'If we compare those poems and passages of poems which were conceived definitely within the circle of Hopkins' theology with those which transcend it, we shall find difficulty in resisting the conclusion that the poet in him was often oppressed and stifled by the priest' (99).

buckled like a bicycle-wheel, smashed by accident and no longer working. 'Here' means at once either the bird or the fire. It is a trick often used in poetry, and always in jokes, to express two systems of values, an agony or indecision of judgement. Freud and Ambivalence, in fact, I wish you had driven that home.[3]

But what you say about 'No wonder of it'; he trusted in the values created (out of the focus but in the field of consciousness, for instance) irrelevantly in the course of action, seems very much on the spot and adds to my pleasure in the poem.

(I am afraid this way of replying to contributors is a little impertinent.)
Yours
William Empson

TO ELSIE DUNCAN-JONES

14 September 1928

Dear Miss Phare,

Quite, I was off the limited and definite point of your article, which in itself I agree with. Firstly I should have said it was a matter of proportion, that a writer should not be either static or dynamic, and then 'completely assimilate manner to matter'; he should completely assimilate dynamics into his stasis. Secondly the reasons for one's interest in the point of your article refer (as you admit) to [T. E.] Hulme[4] and all that hullabaloo about Time and Western Man: I could never see why there had to be such shouts of enthusiasm[,] and the other side were in such a vast state of decay, but it did seem important, even though the moral and geographical qualities involved kept changing sides too.[5]

---

[3] See 'Instincts and their Vicissitudes' (1915), in *The Standard Edition of the Complete Psychological Works of Sigmund Freud*, vol. xiv. On *Ambivalenz Konflict*, see *Inhibitions, Symptoms and Anxiety* (1926), in *Standard Edition*, vol. xx.

[4] T. E. Hulme (1883–1917), philosopher and poet, was killed in the First World War. His writings were brought together in *Speculations*, ed. by Herbert Read (1924). Admired by Ezra Pound and TSE, he hailed the demise of humanism and the ascendancy of classicism (including a belief in original sin) over romanticism.

[5] WE reviewed *Time and Western Man*—by Wyndham Lewis—in *Granta*, 21 Oct. 1927: 'Mr Lewis' thesis, though not new, deserves restatement. It is that two main props of our faith in Western common-sense have been damaged; private integrity of effort, by the success of the machine, which has produced a level horde of craftless and identical "hands"; private integrity of thought, by the removal of a fixed God, which has fostered the idea of an unknowable, ever-changing organic flux, and referred all belief to contemporary shifting needs . . . What is not so clear is whether Mr Lewis disapproves of all such tendencies equally . . .' (*EG*, 19). Wyndham Lewis (1882–1957), artist and writer, won wide attention as editor of the short-lived Vorticist magazine *Blast* (1914–15), and for his experimental novel *Tarr* (1918); later works include *The Apes of God* (1930) and *Revenge for Love* (1937). His work as an artist includes celebrated portraits of T. S. Eliot and of Edith Sitwell.

That is a very deep word about Sibyl['s] Leaves,[6] the calm was lost when the pictured movement ended.

An opposition (not bothering about Wyndham Lewis) that would fit these two poets, is to make the dynamic the sort [of people] that to feel secure must be in the hands of an external movement, as Hopkins in the hands of the Church, and the static the sort that like to be their own master. I don't remember that Hopkins shows time-sense in the Proustian sense, and I believe the Valéry business about hacking at marble came in with African sculpture, which *I* don't think of as hacked bit by bit, those lovely egg shaped things were conceived in the round and your eye walks over them.[7] There are many more elements in the business, obviously, than have been cleared up: without Lewis evangelizing about God and Western Common Sense being on the static side, and then putting the West as dynamic against the static East.

[–] which makes the clarity, definiteness and small range of your article, of course, all the more valuable.

Do send along your Hopkins article, it would be rather a smack at Richards if we got somebody to say something quite different.[8] And we are quite likely (about size) to have two numbers in the term.

Yours

William Empson

(Feminine and Masculine, for instance: but I ought to have guessed from your handwriting.)

TO ELSIE DUNCAN-JONES

7 October 1928

Dear Miss Phare,

You say the two meanings of buckle are simply two, and can be held together in the ordinary way. But they *are* the opposites created by the context; the life strung to activity, the life broken and made static. (The fact is this idea of opposites is a factitious one, you can string, as it were, a scale, between any two points.) All that makes them opposites is the poets' wish to connect them, the variety of impulses which make one suggest the other. In the obscure field where images take effect in poetry, they are the

---

[6] Gerard Manley Hopkins, 'Spelt from Sibyl's Leaves'.

[7] Valéry's images, Phare noted, 'are succinct, and one rarely merges into another . . . He is like someone chipping with an axe at a lump of stone; he uses single, detached blows; the unity is the result, the figure which he disengages from the rock' (20).

[8] WE had hoped she might take issue with IAR's essay 'Gerard Hopkins'.

most natural form of two meanings joined in one word. P, if you like, is the opposite of not p, but they both state the outline between them. Primitive languages have the same word for two opposites, you state, as it were, the scale of grey, and whether you mean black or white is conveyed incidentally. 'Not' is a late and strange human invention, used with a variety of meanings whenever the thinker found himself in a difficulty. And in the dream-world considered by analysis, opposites of a certain kind are regarded as interchangeable, both referring to the same more elaborate state. 'Of a certain kind' certainly seems important, common sense, any orderly attitude to the world, is so dependent on distinctions, and if any conclusion might safely be negated you would have No conclusion at all. But that it is effective in poetry, and, as I say, jokes, I must say I believe.

You say the poem then consists of two alternate meanings, according to which meanings you take. It would consist of many more. But as the meanings are all connected with one another, and make—rather pitifully perhaps—different statements about the same situation under the same sets of impulses, they produce a very rounded and grand unity. You might as well say contrapuntal writing was several different tunes—you might certainly say it to me anyway, as I always find it a question of listening to one and letting the others take effect. But the others *do* take effect, especially of course when you know it better. . . .

Yours
William Empson

TO IAN PARSONS*

Magdalene College, Cambridge
[n.d.: received 6 June 1929]

My dear Ian,

Last time I saw you [you] very kindly offered to consider a manuscript, and at the time I thought there wasn't enough I wanted to see in print. But I think I was being contrary.

I could offer about twenty poems, of which about five would go onto a second page. On the other hand I should want to print very full notes; at least as long as the text itself; explaining not only particular references—paraphrasing particularly condensed grammar, and so on—but the point of a poem as a whole, and making any critical remarks that seemed interesting. And I should apologize for notes on such a scale, and say it was more of an impertinence to expect people to puzzle out my verses than to explain them at the end, and I should avoid the Eliot air of intellectual snobbery.

It would be kind of you if you would say in advance if you could consider such a scheme: if it would be worth my while to sit down and write the notes, I mean.

I was thinking of offering a logico grammatico-critical essay to the Hogarth called the Seven Types of Ambiguity: you don't do small essays (15,000 words) do you? I suppose I ought to let you know.

I should be very proud to be produced as well as you did Timothy.[1]

Yours

William Empson

Reading

TO IAN PARSONS

[n.d.: received 14 June 1929]

Dear Ian,

Most of these you have seen already. There are twenty-three of them. I doubt if I have turned out (dear me; I mean turned out of the collection, of course, not 'output' in a professional sense—though that would be true too) enough even now; I should be glad of your advice.

When I am not actually faced with explaining them I feel notes aren't wanted: but I think people would be more easily tempted to read verse if there was plenty of critical writing thrown in, demanding less concentration of attention, and with more literary-magazine or novel-reading interest—I know *I* should. And there is a rather portentous air about compact verses without notes, like a seduction without conversation. Arguably I ought to wait till I have more of them.

Yours

William Empson

This is my only text for some of them, so please let me get it back.

I shall be in London some time next week, and might see you then, perhaps.

Reading

---

[1] T. H. ('Timothy') White (1906–64) read English at Queen's College. His writings include the Arthurian tetralogy *The Once and Future King* (1958)—adapted as the musical *Camelot* (1959). Chatto & Windus published *Loved Helen, and Other Poems* (1929).

TO I. A. RICHARDS*

Yokefleet Hall, Howden, Yorkshire
[n.d.: Summer 1929]

Dear Mr Richards,

You wanted to be the first, I remember, to tell me I had been given a Bye-Fellowship, and I want to be the first to tell you it has been taken away again. I left some contraceptives in a drawer when my things were being moved; with criminal carelessness; I remember being no more than amused when I found they had been stolen, I didn't understand what was going on, in the way of collecting gossip and so forth, at all. As for the Body, they obeyed their own rules, poor creatures; I should like to, but cannot, feel indignation at the workings of a system with whose principles I disagree.

I am writing up Ambiguity in the country and feeling very puzzled about my future. Would I be at all wise to creep into the Civil Service on any 'character' the Master's charity would allow me (I have behaved politely to him; I thought him shockingly unscrupulous),[1] or would I be at all wise to go and live in a garret, as I should like to do, go on with what I think worth doing, and take small journalist jobs if I can get them? It can so easily become despicable, don't you think, to hang about London starving and taking an interest in Art; one *ought* to be ambitious, and to refuse all solid jobs at my age is to prepare for oneself a great deal of bitterness and impotence in twenty years' time.

Still I seem to have decided to do that, though I shall be grateful for any advice you have time to give me; and the difficulty at the moment is to get away from my family; it is a sufficiently painful one.

I don't know how much details would amuse you. The Master (with an air of melancholy conviction) told me that anybody who had ever touched a French letter, no matter when or why, could never again be allowed with safety in the company of young men, because he was sure in some subtle way, however little he himself wished it, to pollute their innocence; and this in spite of the fact that his own intellectual powers would have been destroyed. As an act of grace I was allowed to poison the air of Magdalene for a day after my exposure, and this gave time for several of my judges to

---

[1] A. B. Ramsay (1872–1955) was Master of Magdalene College from 1925 to 1947; Vice-Chancellor of Cambridge University, 1929–31. His publications include a spoof of a long-lost collection by Horace (with Rudyard Kipling and Charles Graves) entitled *Q. Horati Flacci carminum liber quintus* (1920).

come and explain that I must not bear a grudge, or that what they had done would be the best thing for me in the end, or that 'personally' they thought their own actions a Great Pity, or that though they were not addicted to Those Particular Vices (I wept with rage when this was said to me) I was to understand they had extremely Broad Minds.

Let me rein in my growing bitterness (it has been all my own fault, and I ought to have taken decent care of another person's interests if not of my own) and say how much I admired Practical Criticism, and hope to have profited by it; I think it your best work so far, and would like to find for it even higher praise.

I shall be curious to hear about the journey, and what you think of China.

William Empson

Magdalene

TO JULIAN TREVELYAN*

[n.d.: Summer 1929]

Dear Julian,

I'm afraid I've let you in for a difficult job rather;[1] I have just been kicked out of Cambridge, so probably the President next year will be Professor Piccoli, a dear thing who doesn't know a bit what the Heretics like, and wants watching about Croce.[2] I have got a promise from Wittgenstein to speak next term but that is absolutely all.

Yours, rather apologetically
William Empson.

Trinity

TO JULIAN TREVELYAN

Yokefleet Hall, Howden, Yorkshire
[n.d.: 1929]

My dear Julian,

Thank you for your psychological reactions; I liked particularly *condone* for *condole*, the frustrated attempt to leave out *not* before *well*, and the

---

[1] Trevelyan would take over from WE as Secretary of the 'Heretics'.

[2] Raffaello Piccoli (1886–1933) was Professor of Italian at Cambridge University, 1929–33. His publications include *Astrologia Dantesca* (1909), *Benedetto Croce: An Introduction to His Philosophy* (1922), and *Italian Humanities: An Inaugural Lecture* (1929). Benedotto Croce (1866–1952), Italian critic and philosopher, was author of (among other works) *Filosofia dello Spirito*, in three volumes (1902, 1904, 1912).

reading *lake* for *cake*.[1] What happened (since you ask) was the porters found a French letter in my rooms, and the bedmaker had also been very industrious at reading letters and so forth; let it be a warning to you, young man, I had no idea one was so officially spied on. It was high time I got away from the place; I shall do journalism now if I can.

As for you, poor thing, left to wrestle with the Heretics, seven lions make a quorum: certainly Virginia Woolf[2] had better come again, last time she read *Mr Bennet and Mrs Brown*, see Hogarth Essays, but that was five years ago; 'Piccoli, the dear' will give a short talk about Croce; Wittgenstein has more or less promised, and will be up so you can fit him into a gap; [Arthur] Waley[3] is a great catch of yours; if you can get the Indian and the sculptor and Radclyffe for a talk to the girls that will do very well.[4] You and Piccoli between you are going to bar out the scientists, I am afraid; [J. B. S.] Haldane[5] (but he is on holiday) and Eddington[6] (whose address I don't know) ought to be tried; that would be done most easily after term has started. Charlotte Haldane, if treated with slight caution, is a great help in getting people; I doubt if she would perform again herself; and anyway did it rather recently.[7]

---

[1] Trevelyan's letter of consolation has not been preserved.

[2] Virginia Woolf (1882–1941), novelist, literary critic, and diarist.

[3] Arthur Waley (1889–1966), poet and translator, read classics at King's College, Cambridge, and worked in the Oriental Department of the British Museum, 1913–29. A self-taught orientalist, he won acclaim for his translations from Chinese and Japanese poetry and drama. His translations include *The No Plays of Japan* (1921) and *The Book of Songs* (1937).

[4] Radclyffe Hall (1880–1943), novelist and self-pronounced 'congenital invert'; her writings include *Adam's Breed* (1926) and the courageous (and infamous) novel about lesbianism, *The Well of Loneliness*, which was banned on first publication in 1928: it was republished in 1949. WE's reference to 'the girls' is thus a knowing joke.

[5] J. B. S. Haldane (1892–1964), geneticist, was Reader in Biochemistry at Cambridge—where in 1925 he had been dismissed from his post by the academic watch committee known as the 'Sex Viri' because he had been cited as a co-respondent in the divorce of Charlotte Burghes (his future wife); he was reinstated on appeal. In 1933 he was to become Professor of Genetics, then of Biometry, at University College, London, from where he retired in 1957. Then he joined the Biometry Research Unit at the Indian Statistical Institute, Calcutta. For ten years from 1940 he was chairman of the editorial board of the *Daily Worker*, and in 1940 he would join the Communist Party. His writings— all of which delighted WE—include *Daedalus, or, Science and the Future* (1923), and *Possible Worlds* (1927). See WE in 'Portrait of J. B. S. Haldane', *The Listener*, 78 (2 Nov. 1967), 565–8.

[6] Arthur Eddington (1882–1944), theoretical physicist and astrophysicist, held the Plumian Chair in Astronomy at Cambridge from 1913, and was to be knighted in 1930. His works include *Space, Time and Gravitation* (1920) and *The Nature of the Physical World* (1928). 'I have a very great respect for the way Eddington could carry on a profound discussion in this apparently popularizing language; any good scientist, I strongly suspect, conducts his formative thinking in this kind of way, but few of them have enough nerve to say so afterwards' (*SCW*, 365).

[7] Charlotte Haldane (1894–1969), American-born journalist and novelist, was married (1926–45) to the geneticist J. B. S. Haldane (following a divorce in which Haldane was co-respondent). She entertained WE and others including Malcolm Lowry, John Davenport, Michael Redgrave, Hugh Sykes Davies, and Kathleen Raine, at their home, Roebuck House, in Old Chesterton. Her works include *I Bring not Peace* (1932), *Youth is a Crime* (1934), and *Truth will out*, a memoir (1949). See also Judith Adamson, *Charlotte Haldane: Woman Writer in a Man's World* (1998).

Geoffrey Webb, a charming architect mixed up with my late College, (or praps not, why do I think that?) promised to speak this term;[8] Betty Wiskemann[9] will know his address.

Sorry to expose you to all the work.

William Empson

The great thing is to get somebody who will do for the first or second Sunday, and get out some sort of card. Then you can pick up the locals.

[8] Geoffrey Webb (1898–1970), art historian, read English at Magdalene College, graduating in 1921. In 1929 he returned to Cambridge as lecturer in the Extramural Department. In 1934–7 he was Lecturer at the Courtauld Institute of Fine Art; and in 1938–49 he was Slade Professor of Fine Art at Cambridge. From 1948 to 1962 he was secretary to the Royal Commission on Historical Monuments (England). His writings include *Architecture in Britain: The Middle Ages* (1956).

[9] It was on account of Elizabeth Wiskemann, daughter of a German émigré, that WE was obliged to leave Cambridge in 1929, when his condoms were discovered and advertised by a college servant. Seven years senior to WE, Wiskemann was born on 13 August 1899. She won an Exhibition to Newnham College, where she gained a first in Part II of the History Tripos in 1921. Thereafter she held a Gilchrist Research Studentship in 1924–5 while working for a doctorate on 'Napoleon and the Roman Question', but she was bitterly disappointed when her thesis was awarded only an M.Litt. in 1927. Thus it was during the ensuing year or so, while taking stock of her life, that she came to know WE. 'Her interest in individuals and her lively social conscience,' wrote L. K. Duff, 'combined with views on human duties and rights deriving, through nineteenth-century liberalism, from the *philosophes* of the eighteenth-century Enlightenment. Her spiritual home was perhaps among the radical (and anti-clerical) liberals of 1848' ('Elizabeth Meta Wiskemann', 1899–1971', Newnham College Roll, Jan. 1972, 70–4). A redoubtable woman, Wiskemann pursued a remarkable career. 'If I had remained an academic specializing in the nineteenth century, I suppose my life would have been considerably duller than it became,' she later wrote. She spent much of the early 1930s in Germany, writing on German affairs for the *New Statesman* and other periodicals, and warning of the Nazi menace. Following the publication in 1935 of two articles that were especially hostile to National Socialism, Hitler's police placed her under observation; and in July 1936 she was detained at the Gestapo headquarters on Prinz Albrechtstrasse in Berlin. Though familiar with Nazi methods of interrogation, she revealed nothing of what she knew of German intelligence. 'Do for heaven's sake look round,' she told herself, 'you're in a place of unusual interest'; and indeed, by studying the maps on the walls, she gathered a great deal about Hitler's policy of eastward expansion. Once released from detention, she was expelled from Germany and spent the remainder of the 1930s in those countries of central and south-eastern Europe that were falling prey to Nazi influence. In 1937, at the behest of the Royal Institute of International Affairs, she started on her first book, *Czechs and Germans* (1938), which was followed by *Undeclared War* (1939). She afforded unsparing help to refugees from Hitler. During the war she was assistant press attaché at the British Legation in Switzerland, charged with collecting non-military intelligence about enemy-occupied Europe: she was one of the first to send in reports about the Nazi death camps and about Tito's partisan movement in Yugoslavia. Her work put her on the Nazi Black List. Though she won no honours for her services, she was proud to receive an honorary D.Litt. from Oxford in 1965, when the public orator described her as both 'a Cassandra who lived to record the war she had foretold' and 'a historian who had obtained international recognition'. Her later works include *The Rome–Berlin Axis* (1949), *Germany's Eastern Neighbours* (1956), and *The Europe I Saw* (1968). In 1958–61 she was Montague Burton Professor of International Relations at Edinburgh University; in 1961–4 a tutor in Modern European History at the University of Sussex. At the end, harrowed by failing sight and jealous of her self-dependence, she took her own life in London in Jul. 1971—the very month in which WE retired from teaching at the age of 65.

Perhaps this note reads rather like a brave attempt to hide my feelings, which must be counter-acted; in many ways it is very distressing that I have been so careless and so ill-used; not least, my dear, in that we cannot have our year of feeding the lions together.

Trinity

TO I. A. RICHARDS

65 Marchmont Street W. C. 1
Monday [early December1929]

Dear Mr Richards,

It was very cheering to get your letter and Mrs Richards'; I have heard from Mr Ogden* and Mr Eliot* and am arranging times to see them. This is quite a nice room for 28/- a week, and I have a taste for squalor and cooking my own meals. I am trying to finish Ambiguity (it is over 60,000 words by now) and get it published, but I am much hampered by a doubt as to whether any of it is true. I feel, if that (Ambiguity, not its untruth) attracted notice, my position would be stronger.

My family insisted on writing to Mr Ramsay to find whether he would give me a 'character' for the Civil Service, and apparently he has said he will. The only letter I have seen says fairly definitely he won't. So I suppose he wouldn't actually kick me out of Leeds University either.[1] The Civil Service exam begins next August, and it would involve learning all the mathematics I have forgotten, with more; it is not the sort of examination I could do well, nor the sort of work I should do well if I got in. On the other hand August is my best chance.

I am fairly sure I am right not to go in.

If it was possible to go to Leeds I should be very glad, I think.

I have seen Mr Ogden, who was very brisk and seemed to think nothing impossible; he made me write to Mr Haldane and ask him to write to Mr [John Maynard] Keynes and ask him to write to Mr Tawney and ask him

---

[1] Ian MacKillop, *F. R. Leavis: A Life in Criticism* (1995), discusses the position that became vacant at Leeds in 1929 when Lascelles Abercrombie was appointed to a Chair in London. 'At Cambridge ... Q [Sir Arthur Quiller-Couch] wondered whether Richards might allow his name to be put forward ... Q was relieved that Richards wanted to stay in Cambridge, but he was doubtful about Leavis' (105).

to let me lecture to the W. E. A.[2] So I have done that, and shall use your very generous testimonial (for which I must thank you very warmly) just to write to the W. E. A. myself at the same time: it seems a good thing to have done, if possible.

You ask me who made gossip; I think none was necessary. The porters told the Master they had found contraceptives, and he was very excited, and anxious to get the place purged of such things. (I think he had told them beforehand to be sure and let him know of anything they could find). His argument to *me* was that I had caused scandal, but I think he was relying on the imagination of Mrs Tingey [his bedmaker at Magdalene].

I think it very lucky you weren't in Cambridge for the row; you would only have shocked the Master, and incurred the consequences your colleagues seemed so afraid of.

Please tell Mrs Richards she was quite right in thinking I should want to get away from the English, but my impulses are not so powerful as to drive me to China, and I was satisfied by a month in Spain.

She suggested Leeds; I wonder whether you would advise this; whether there are likely to be any vacancies; and how much I should depend on keeping my past dark—it doesn't seem to be very dark; I was told my Case

---

[2] In response to WE's appeal, Haldane wrote to the economist John Maynard Keynes (1883–1946) with all the fighting energy he had learned from personal trial: 'This letter is intended to serve as an introduction for my friend Mr. W. Empson B. A. Empson took a first in English Pt. II, following a second in Maths Pt II. He appears to me to be rather a good poet, and has a general education, which is rare. You will remember that he was given a by-fellowship at Magdalene.

'He happened to be in possession of some contraceptives, which were stolen from him by one of the college servants, and presented to the master. He admitted having used articles of this type in the past, and was deprived of his post. I tried to make him fight the matter, but he would not, as he feared that the name of the woman in the case would come up.

'He is now looking for a job, while writing a great work on literary criticism. I suggested that you might be able to help him. He appears to be a hard case, I understand that, in order to stay at Magdalene, he had turned down an offer of a fellowship elsewhere. But an academic career is now closed to him, though he is eminently suited for one, and not at all suited for any other sort. In his place, I should have brought a criminal charge against the vice-chancellor for receiving stolen goods. However he wouldn't, not being a pugnacious person.

'I shouldn't write to you, in spite of the hardness of his case, unless I thought he was a very good man at his job. I. A. Richards, whose opinion is worth more, will support this statement' (*King's*).

R. H. Tawney (1880–1962), economic historian and writer on progressive socialism and Labour policy, was educated at Rugby School and Balliol College, Oxford. In 1905 he joined the executive committee of the recently established Workers' Educational Assocation (WEA) and became for many years intensely involved with adult education; for fifteen years from 1928 he was to be president of the WEA. In 1920 he joined the London School of Economics, where he became Reader in 1923 and Professor of Economic History, 1931–49. His many influential publications include *The Acquisitive Society* (1921), *Religion and the Rise of Capitalism* (1926), *Equality* (1931), and *Land and Labour in China* (1932)—the last of which followed his visits to China as an educational adviser to the League of Nations. With his brilliant colleague Eileen Power he published *Tudor Economic Documents* (1924).

had been mentioned to the International Sex Convention by somebody on the staff of the Yorkshire Post.

However there is no great hurry at the moment; I really seem to be living within my income.

Yours

W. Empson

I'm afraid I don't know who was at the Meeting, except for the obvious people; they were hidden away in the dark rather, and I was concentrating on my little speech.

Magdalene

TO C. K. OGDEN*

[n.d. ?1930]

Dear Mr Ogden,

I found a dictionary of hieroglyphs in the British Museum; perhaps you would be interested to hear about the opposites that Freud claimed in Egyptian.[1] It is true about *black* and *white*; they are pronounced the same but with a different determinative to show which is which. But they mean 'dead white' and 'dead black', and are derived from the idea of 'strong'; there are other words for the shades in between. It is hard to see how there could be a conflict in the mind of an Egyptian as to whether he was dead white or dead black; however one might appeal to a more primitive language from which the word was derived. There are two pairs of words, pronounced nearly the same, for 'young' and 'old'; one pair is defined by the dictionary as 'childhood' and 'second childhood', the other is derived from the idea of 'shaking' and feebleness. Thus in each case the words are similar because the things are thought of as similar, not because they are thought of as opposite. At the same time it is odd that black and white

---

[1] Sigmund Freud chanced in 1910 upon a pamphlet by the philologist Karl Abel, *Über den Gegensinn der Urworte* (1884), which he said enlightened him as to 'the strange tendency of the dream-work to disregard negation and to express contraries by identical means of representation.' In a number of languages, Egyptian, Semitic and Indo-European, there are relics of the primitive world in which a number of words have two meanings, 'one of which says the exact opposite of the other.' But what may strike us now as a lexical peculiarity, the sheer absurdity of words which unite antithetical meanings, came about because our very conceptions arise from comparison. Primitive man, according to Abel, 'only gradually learnt to separate the two sides of the antithesis and think of the one without conscious comparison with the other.' Whereupon Freud, in ' "The Antithetical Sense of Primal Words" ' (his review of Abel's book, 1910), took this peculiarity of the contradictory meanings that seem to be an habitual phenomenon in primitive languages as 'a confirmation of our supposition in regard to the regressive, archaic character of thought-expression in dreams.' See Freud, *Collected Papers*, iv, trans. Joan Riviere (1925), 184–91.

should be thought of as similar; it may have something to do with interpreting the colours on a ceremonial wall-painting, but that only takes the oddity one step further back.

I found Mr Richards' article where you said it would be; I must have overlooked it before.

[Inadvertently unsigned]

McMaster

TO I. A. RICHARDS

[n.d. ?1930]

Dear Mr Richards,

Till I got your letter I thought I was very pleasantly settled in London, but now I find I want to go to China very much. Please get me this job if it can be made to seem decently reliable; thank you very much indeed for trying to arrange it.

Evidently you are to be congratulated on a great success at Peking, if they are remodelling the English School on your recommendation. I hope my sympathy about the cheek-bone will be out of date by the time this reaches you.

I am cramming some young men for the Civil Service English paper; it is rather good for me, as I have to bring them lists of dates and quotes to learn by heart. I have undertaken to do that till the beginning of August, but I shall be able to make some arrangement if I have to start before then.

[*Corner of page torn*] if I am to be in a hurry I suppose I shall want to come by land, and luggage might be rather expensive.

I have applied for a job in Japan, and not heard the answer yet; but it was a very long shot. There seems to be no doubt China would be much nicer.

Kind of you to ask for verses; I shall try and collect some to send on. This letter had better be sent off at once.

Yours

W. Empson

I have just offered *a* finished version of Ambiguity to Chattos, to ask them how it ought to be altered. It is a very amateurish sort of book; I don't understand the difference between Thought and Feeling, and you have got to have some way of using that distinction if you are to know where you are.

Remember me to Mrs Richards

Magdalene

TO I. A. RICHARDS

65 Marchmont Street, W. C. 1
29 January [?1930]

Dear Mr Richards,

If the Harvard job you are kindly trying to arrange for me falls through, would you mind letting me know for certain? I have met Professor Wu Mi,[1] who seems a very delightful person, and a Miss Eileen Power[2] has offered to pull strings to find me a job in China: so I am in hopes of getting one, even if Harvard falls through: but it would be as well to let her know definitely that I should be free to accept a job if there was one.

I am very pleasantly busy in the Museum Library, but it would certainly do me good to have a settled job, and I want to travel, and, as you see, it is now fixed in my mind that I want to go to China.

Thanks very much for that magazine. Some sort of conversion seems to have occurred to Mr [John Middleton] Murry in the middle of writing an article for it.[3]

Surely the trouble about your view of belief, (that beliefs not of the scientific type can only be tested by the degree to which they lead to good lives), is the trouble about all forms of pragmatism, that it saws away the branch it sits on. That belief itself is not of the scientific type (I don't see how it could be tested by experiment) so there is no question of its being

---

[1] Wu Mi (b. 1894) took his BA (1920) and MA (1921) at Harvard. A disciple of Irving Babbitt, he taught Western literature at Chinghua (Qinghua) University, 1924–44. From 1922 to 1933 he was founder-editor of a journal, *Hsüeh-heng (Xueheng) (Critical Review)*, which denigrated the literary revolution in China: Babbitt's humanism was used in opposition to May Fourth Iconoclasm, the anti-traditionalism of the period 1917–23. He was to be a colleague of WE's at the Southwest Associated University (*Lienda*) in 1937–9. For IAR on Wu Mi, see IAR: *SL*, 57.

[2] Eileen Power (1889–1940), medieval historian, became Professor of Economic History at the LSE in 1931. Her works include *Studies in English Trade in the Fifteenth Century* (ed., 1933); *The Wool Trade in English Medieval History* (1941). See further Maxine Berg, *A Woman in History: Eileen Power 1889–1940* (1996).

[3] John Middleton Murry underwent, by the 1930s, what TSE was to call a 'religious' conversion to Communism. The article in question here may have been 'Beauty is Truth', in *Symposium* 1: 4 (Oct. 1930), 466–501, to which IAR published a reply in *Symposium* 2: 2 (Apr. 1931), 226–41; repr. in IAR: *SW* (9), 234–46. Murry (1889–1957) was editor of the *Athenaeum*, 1919–21, and founded and edited the *Adelphi*, 1923–48. In 1918 he married Katherine Mansfield, who was to die of TB in 1923. His works include studies of Dostoevsky, Keats, D. H. Lawrence (with whom he was on close but turbulent terms), Blake, and Shakespeare; *Between Two Worlds* (1935); *Jonathan Swift* (1954); *Love, Freedom and Society* (1957); *A Defence of Philosophy* (1962). Murry was to review in the *TLS* both *STA*—'Analytical Criticism' (18 Dec. 1930), reprinted in Constable, 30—and *SVP*: 'Pastoral and Proletarian: In Search of All Possible Meanings' (30 Nov. 1935), in Constable, 67. See also David Goldie, *A Critical Difference: T. S. Eliot and John Middleton Murry in English Literary Criticism, 1919–1928* (1998); Jason Harding, *The 'Criterion': Cultural Politics and Periodical Networks in Inter-War Britain* (2002).

true. And if you say that that belief too must be tested by whether it leads to good lives, you are postulating either a test which could only convince those who agree with you or a standard of goodness common to all systems of belief.[4]

I am thinking here of the evidence for a belief as what will convince those who at the time believe something else, but that is hardly fair to any belief. The only theories which make conversion respectable are Prevenient Grace and some form of naturalism, and neither alone are very satisfying. I mean, you must either be convinced, as by a gift of prophecy, that a way of life will be valuable when you have got into it: or you must suppose that everyone recognises a good life when they see it, by a primitive and inalienably human power of judgement—even though that way of life is based on a belief different to theirs. 'We needs must love the highest when we see it.'[5] Certainly we could get nowhere if this (or the gift of Grace) did not occur in some degree; how in any case it can be obtained to a sufficient degree is a question rather for the revivalist than the philosopher. And yet it is a very important one, particularly for a pragmatist philosopher.

That is the normal crux about pragmatism, but the process of convincing people is always a mysterious one. Those who believe your whole system are much better off than other sorts of pragmatist, because they have a conception of a fixed standard of good in terms of which the truth of a belief must be interpreted. And the belief in that standard of good (which amounts to a formula for goodness, added to a statement that it cannot be worked out exactly, but can be useful, with due care, as a means of estimating what is good: in particular negatively, as a means of escaping from other people's estimations without a sense of vacuum) can itself be regarded as a pragmatic belief; 'This belief as to the nature of good is to be tested by whether it leads to *the good life that it defines*.' This is not a vicious circle; and indeed your theory of value, since it provides for estimating good rather than calculating it, seems designed to do good rather than to give certain knowledge.

But much more of an act of faith is needed to decide that your belief about goodness actually leads to the goodness that it defines than that it is roughly true in the ordinary sense. (It is an act I myself find I can make, but that is more or less an accident.) The trouble about it is that it seems cruder and more definite than it is, and may well lead to judgements cruder than it recommends.

---

[4] IAR commented in the margin: 'Problem is where in the circle you arrange your choice (that makes it a circle?).'

[5] Alfred Tennyson, *Idylls of the King: Guinevere* (1859), l. 655.

Firstly it assumes[6], especially in the definition of an 'important' impulse, that all impulses are equally valuable: secondly it (therefore) assumes that they are commensurable: thirdly it assumes that the value of the satisfaction of two impulses (supposing them to be in isolation, so that their satisfaction involves no further satisfaction of other impulses) can be obtained by addition of the satisfactions of the impulses separately.[7] All these are doubtful: the first and third perhaps only because it is so difficult to imagine the satisfaction of an isolated impulse (but anyway they require some demonstration): the second because it puts the notion of value in an odd place. I think that lives as a whole, or state of mind and body lasting for a finite time, as a whole, can be compared in value, but it is not obvious that the satisfactions of two impulses can be compared in value at all. (Keynes has a good passage about probability, that there is no reason why two probabilities about different matters should be commensurate.)[8] Happiness might be like a potential, so that [one] could say when a man was more or less happy but not what his absolute happiness was: and if so you might get odd effects like when you move a pole round an electric current, and its potential goes up by a constant though it is back in the same place and the place has the same potential.

All one can say is that your theory of good assumes a mathematical basis which may well be much too crude. If so it is very likely to cause a false impression of certain knowledge and lead to inadequate judgements.

Nor am I sure what an impulse is: apparently it need not be a conscious impulse, so it cannot easily be recognised. The Freudian point of view would seem to be that there are very few fundamental impulses, and that they are not originally impulses to do anything in particular: they are made into definite impulses by circumstances—by beliefs formed and by training, particularly.[9] So if you set out to provide an education to make people satisfy most impulses you must also set out to provide the impulses that allow of most satisfaction. (Of course you said this in the chapter on

---

[6] Corrected in the margin to 'seems to assume'.

[7] Cf. 'Theories of Value': 'It may be that the human mind can recognise actually incommensurable values, and that the chief human value is to stand up between them; but I do not see how we could know that they were incommensurable till the calculation had been attempted' (*SCW*, 421).

[8] See *A Treatise on Probability* (1921), in *The Collected Writings of John Maynard Keynes*, viii, ed. R. B. Braithwaite (1971).

[9] IAR commented in the margin: 'My "impulse" physiological rather than psychological[,] microscopic not macroscopic' (*Magdalene*). John Paul Russo notes: 'The power of impulse in Richards' system appears to extend from crude sensation to the driving force behind civilization itself. He was perhaps trying too hard to squeeze the universe into a ball' (*I. A. Richards: His Life and Work* (1989), 183).

value yourself, but it adds to the vagueness of an impulse, regarded as a fundamental brick.)

This is the point of the joke about n+1 being more valuable than n, which I remember failing to discuss with you when you were teaching me.

It is to people who are taking the theory of value as a guiding light, but with this extreme degree of caution, that I think it will be most valuable: so that for them one can make the act of faith of believing it pragmatically true. And it is to them that the art and literature of other civilisations can be a valuable substitute for the other civilisations' beliefs: Mr Eliot would be right in comparing this to relying on the wall paper when the walls had fallen, if the people in question were not already provided with walls— rather of the steel and glass type.[10]

So that, waiving the interest in discussion, I find that act of faith is one that I make without difficulty. Certainly to stop short of it, to adopt what Mill said was the motto of the Whigs—'There is no God, but this is a family secret'[11]—to preach those doctrines, which one may suspect Mr Eliot of doing, which you think will do good, and not to preach harmful doctrines, such as the doctrine you order your own life by—that may be very heroic, but it is a sacrifice I shrink from, or a habit of mind I regard as neurotic. For who is any one man that he should treat himself as God like that, that he should behave as if it would blast civilisation if he told his neighbours what he was thinking about? If the basis of that course of action is fear of the consequences of any other course of action, then it has no solid ground for its calculation, because merely by a process of doubt it claims to know a great deal. Let it be more afraid of the consequences of its own course of action. It seems to me that secret

---

[10] See TSE, 'Literature, Science, and Dogma', *Dial*, 82: 3 (Mar. 1927), 239–43; in IAR: *SW* (10), 74–9. 'Mr Richards thinks that the only thing that can save us from "mental chaos" is poetry, a poetry of the future detached from all belief . . . Poetry "is capable of saving us", he says; it is like saying that the wallpaper will save us when the walls have crumbled. It is a revised version of *Literature and Dogma* [by Matthew Arnold]' (78–9). See Russo, 194–5, 'Richards was piqued by Eliot's mockery . . . On the basis of a few illustrative metaphors, Eliot misconstrued his theory as quantitative and mechanistic; whereas the entire tenor of his commentary had been organic and qualitative . . . Yet Richards made Eliot's . . . case against him that much easier by his brevity of treatment and gaps in argument. He often elided the number and quality of impulses without much ado, and "impulse" itself stood for too wide a variety of mental and physical happenings'; and IAR: *SL*, p. xxxix.

[11] John Stuart Mill wrote (*Autobiography*, 1873) that he was brought up by his father with an aversion to Christianity (which was the '*ne plus ultra* of wickedness' since it flaunted a God who gloried in being the 'Omnipotent Author of Hell'). WE's epigrammatic epitome is his own paraphrase of this passage from Mill: 'This point in my early education had however incidentally one bad consequence deserving notice. In giving me an opinion contrary to that of the world, my father thought it necessary to give it as one which could not prudently be avowed to the world' (*Autobiography and Literary Essays*, ed. John M. Robson and Jack Stillinger (1981), 45).

pragmatism is a much more insidious force, sapping at the basis of a civilised attitude to life, than overt pragmatism, however universal a state of theoretic doubt that may involve: this is not a proposition of philosophy but of psychology, but it is a sufficient argument (if true) for *either* sort of pragmatist. Secret and overt pragmatism, I do believe, are the only two candidates.

[W. Empson]

[P. S.] I am sending you my notions about the article you so kindly sent me. Evidently they are more interesting to me than to you, so perhaps it is not too absurd to ask you to keep them and let me have them back some day, like an essay: which I should be very glad to have corrected.

Magdalene

TO JULIAN TREVELYAN

65 Marchmont Street, W. C. 1
Monday [1930]

Dear Julian,

I have not answered before through not knowing what to say. But it now occurs to me that I could read a paper, or read from notes, about whether poems ought to be annotated, whether it is important, and why it is hard. If you want a bright caption I suggest 'Sphinx, or the future of exegesis', and I can do that as soon as you want it. If it is too short for a paper (it is too long for a life) I could give examples from the Bentley edition of Milton, and the answers to Bentley, which I have been being very excited about (not because any of them are any good, of course, but they raise the crucial questions and the answers by contemporaries are sometimes illuminating.[1]

Yours

William Empson.

Myself, of course, I am in favour of being chatty and explaining everything, but that is undergraduate of me. Once you begin to parley with the reasons for the impossibility of explanations you are whirled o'er the backside of the world far off.

Trinity

---

[1] Trevelyan had rather provocatively invited WE to come back to Cambridge and present a paper on a subject of his own choosing to the Heretics Society. These remarks adumbrate 'Milton and Bentley', in *SVP*, 149–91.

§ THE *OUTLOOK* CORRESPONDENCE

In February 1930 the Oxford periodical *Farrago*, ed. by Isaiah Berlin*, ran an article entitled 'The New Criticism' (22–34) by John Sparrow*. Sparrow derides IAR's *Practical Criticism: A Study of Literary Judgement* (1929) as the product of 'a school of criticism both wrong-headed and harmful . . . finding in psychology a solution for the problems of criticism.' Critics such as IAR, he asserts, 'are unable to define the values which they . . . try to explain away', and are 'reluctant to regard literature simply as matter for enjoyment.' The 'protocols' are no more than 'the untutored reactions of a set of students to certain poems which have been set before them'; thus their criticisms are by definition abhorrent: they lack 'discrimination and experience'. Beauty, Sparrow maintains, 'is realised immediately'; it is certainly not (as IAR would have it) something 'having properties such that it arouses, under suitable conditions, tendencies to self-completion in the mind'—for 'what, after all, is self-completion?' IAR's attempts to explain the matter are fruitless, as when we are told that 'to be sincere is to act, feel and [? or] think in accordance with "one's true nature".'

'But when we asked [Sparrow goes on] for the meaning of "in accordance with one's true nature" . . . we are told that "to define it more exactly would perhaps be tedious and . . . needless".' Readers who are uncertain of their judgements and choose to act on Mr Richards' advice 'will find it unnecessary to enter libraries, but will sit comfortably at home, with fingers pressed firmly upon the eyeballs, arousing in their inner natures tendencies to complete their true selves'; 'It is easy to see where this sort of criticism will lead . . . we shall be encouraged . . . to study the reactions of schoolboys, infants, idiots; and finally Mr Richards will read poems good, bad, or indifferent, to cats and dogs, and then present us with a volume faithfully recording their responses.'[1]

WE's answer to Sparrow's diatribe appeared in *Oxford Outlook*, 10 (May 1930) under a title wittily taken by the editor from poem number three by Catullus, l. 16: 'O Miselle Passer!' ('O poor little Sparrow!').

OXFORD OUTLOOK, 10 (May 1930): 'O miselle passer!'

I was delighted to see Mr Sparrow attacking Mr Richards in *Farrago*; much was to be expected from so fundamental a quarrel. But some degree of imaginative sympathy is necessary if criticism is to be profitable. And the

---

[1] See IAR, *Practical Criticism* (1929), 290–1.

stocks here, perhaps, are too different for their union to be fertile. Still, it is nice to be allowed to write about Mr Richards in Oxford, even when the purpose can only be to reduce misconceptions, and the hope be so faint. (It is curious to remember that people think of Oxford and Cambridge as a unit; how strange that I should feel like an envoy between two worlds.)

The root divergence seems to be that Mr Sparrow thinks the meaning of a poem, and its mode of action, ought not to be analysed too deeply, nor ought the poet or his reader to be analysed too deeply. Evidently this is a matter of degree; you have at least got to construe poetry, not merely snuff it up; Mr Sparrow admits that analysis is in some degree possible and at least useful if not necessary. One may say in general that those who judge in literary matters by 'intuition' always assume a legacy of analysis, and complain when it is carried further. This is not in itself unreasonable; one must judge how far a thing needs to be explained by what seems most agreeable to one's own habits and by what independently of them, seems most effective; there is little ground here either for me to argue or for Mr Sparrow to be so confident. But he might have paid some attention to the reason Mr Richards himself gave for thinking further analysis urgent: that, as this is the first generation which has tried on a large scale to enjoy simultaneously the literature of a great many generations, of a great many views of life, we need, more than previous generations, an intellectual background for our appreciation. (Certainly appreciation, that is, pleasure, is the object in view, but appreciation is not therefore amoral as Mr Sparrow seems to think: it is the purpose and index of morality: it is the difference between civilisation and barbarism.)

Certainly, too, the protocols, as criticism, were bad; it is just because they are bad that the process of analysis needs to be carried further than Mr Sparrow wishes. I quite see that they give no pleasure to the appreciative critic, who needs to protect a private sensitivity. They are tedious and sometimes facetious; they display to the bitter end what it would be more merciful to hide; I confess I could not attend the original lectures because I found them embarrassing for that reason. But this is not a thing I am proud of; nor ought Mr Sparrow to be; one has been trained to regard literature far too much as a social competition. The interpretation of the protocols is an administrative matter, and a certain rational humility is required if one is to make use of them. It is no use simply saying they are bad; the point of collecting them (among other things) was to show that, in the present bewildered state of the poetical *public* (and it is all very well for Mr Sparrow to be too proud to mind the public, but if you are a poet, the poetical public is what you are writing for) some form of intelligible process of interpretation is urgently needed, if only to give people confidence. They achieve this aim, with a violence which may be sufficient to convince those who could supply the need. Mr Sparrow gets out of it by saying that the boys were very ignorant, but one of the boys he quotes as particularly (may I say) boyish, was an English don of indubitable taste and learning, and middle age.[2] Either Mr Sparrow himself has made a howler here, or the protocols were not bad merely because the boys had no experience.

As for Mr Richards's particular recipe for being 'sincere', I am very willing to believe that it does not work for everyone, and that Mr Sparrow finds it unnecessary. But his objection to it is that it would produce a nineteenth-century mode of judgement, and that (with all humility) I may say I know to be wrong. For I agree with Mr Sparrow in his tastes; I too prefer Pope to Shelley, in this daring modern way. But I do not read Pope with a sense that it is delightful to escape, just for a moment (in a coy, playful fashion—not, of course, meaning any harm) from one's own good intentions and kind heart; I think it is precisely a serious mode of approach, viewing life as a whole, which makes the 'Rape of the Lock' seem brave and civilised and Shelley hysterical and a child.

> But since, also [alas], frail beauty must decay,
> Curled or uncurled, since locks will turn to grey.
> Since, painted, or not painted, all shall fade,
> And she who scorns a man must die a maid,
> What then remains, but well our power to use,
> And keep good humour still, whate'er we lose?[3]

It is alarming to hear Mr Sparrow say that one cannot *afford* to sit by the fire and think about death before reading lines like these;[4] it almost makes one believe he reads them with the vulgarity of Mr Strachey, who thought it was clever of the little fellow to be so rude.[5] In the nineties, I quite see, it

---

[2] See Hugh Carey, *Mansfield Forbes and his Cambridge* (1984).

[3] Alexander Pope, *The Rape of the Lock*, canto v, ll. 25–30.

[4] See also 'William Empson remembers I. A. Richards', *LRB*, 2: 11 (5–18 Jun. 1980), 14: 'Before trying to taste a literary work, [IAR] advised in *Practical Criticism* [281–2], it would be a good thing to clean the palate from previous assumptions by reflecting on the "enormity" of time and space, and the "oddity" of human birth and death. This advice was met with fierce ridicule by the professional literary critics, who seem to me now even more absurd than they did then.'

[5] Lytton Strachey (1880–1932), in his Leslie Stephen Lecture on Pope (1925), remarked: 'To us, after two centuries, the agonies suffered by the victims of Pope's naughtiness are a matter of indifference; the fate of Pope's own soul leaves us cold. We sit at our ease, reading those Satires and Epistles, in which the verses, when they were written, resembled nothing so much as spoonfuls of boiling oil, ladled out by a fiendish monkey at an upstairs window upon such of the passers-by whom the wretch had a grudge against—and we are delighted' (*Characters and Commentaries* (1941), 279).

was urgent for an aesthete not to think about death, because the only 'serious' view of life that he could fall back on was wicked nonsense; but nowadays, really, one is safer. To start at the mere shadow of virtue is a hypochondria in Mr Sparrow. And it is hard, by the way, to see how Mr Sparrow reconciles this solemn cult of triviality with his repeated accusation against Mr Richards, that he is not interested in 'values'. The most obvious claim of Mr Richards upon public attention is that he has produced a workable theory of aesthetic value, I hope it is only some misunderstanding as to what Mr Sparrow means by the word which leads me to this bald and verifiable contradiction of him. One must feel the same, for instance, about his treatment of this quotation: 'to be sincere is to act, feel, and [? or] think in accordance with "one's true nature".' Now both *and* and *or*, here, might mean a variety of things, and Mr Sparrow's correction is very puzzling. Can he really think it impossible to feel and think at the same time? Obviously the idea of organic coherence, of *and* rather than *or* in this passage, is the whole crux of that difficult and easily vulgarised notion of sincerity.

Indeed (though it is impossible to deal with these matters in a short article), I dare say that this attitude towards thought and feeling would be as good an approach as any to the understanding of Mr Sparrow. Feeling and thought are not separate objects; in one of their senses they are more like an inside and an outside. At a moment you may be conscious of either side in any proportion; you are more conscious of thought, for instance, if the thing in hand is a novelty; more conscious of feeling if it is urgent and not unusual. But if what you are conscious of as a feeling is badly thought, that is part of what you feel; you wish then to be conscious of it as thought, and put it right. Mr Sparrow, on the other hand, thinks that thought and feeling are simple and different; he can see that beauty is not simple thought, so he thinks it must be simple feeling, only different from other feelings. And I suppose his idea of 'value' is another simple and separate object; a sort of spotting the winner when you are valuing a thing you are neither thinking nor feeling. Mr Sparrow's style is of a beautiful clarity: it has the patient simplicity of Matthew Arnold; and it leaves him utterly at the mercy of his vocabulary.

'Most of what he says is commonplace veiled in the language of psychology; old friends turn up disguised as "autogenous emotions", . . . "inhibitions", and expect to be greeted as important strangers.' Now surely Mr Sparrow must know better than I that the same subjects have always been discussed in literary criticism; that the degree of delicacy, subtlety, and profit with which it has been possible to discuss them has always depended on the terms available; that a new word, even though (by miracle) it referred to precisely the same things as an old one, must yet suggest different ideas, the same ideas in different proportions, a different way of dealing with the same things; that the substitution of one term for another, has been the symbol and body of all advances in criticism. I cannot believe that Mr Sparrow's attitude to this matter is as shallow as he pretends.

He then makes great play with a 'definition' of Beauty, which he finds in an appendix on page 359. It is an amusing example of the barrister's attitude to criticism; the definition is given at the end of a list of possible definitions, heralded by 'we might say for this purpose', and used to illustrate a point of language. If Mr Sparrow is really curious to know how Mr Richards defines beauty, he might look at *The Meaning of Meaning*[6] where there are nineteen definitions shown in relation to one another. Not that the advocate's method is doing much harm here, the definition is quite profound enough for Mr Sparrow's discussion.

What Mr Sparrow calls Mr Richards's definition of 'beautiful' and Mr Richards does not, is 'having properties such that it arouses, under suitable conditions, tendencies to self-completion in the mind.' I should myself say against Mr Richards here that the word *self* seems inadequate; it obscures the element of objectivity in criticism; it lets one forget that a reader, by a valuable effort, can put himself into another century and another mind. But Mr Sparrow is only concerned to say that beauty is a simple feeling. 'Certain qualities are such that to realise their presence in an object is to recognise that the object answers to a complex definition . . . but beauty is quite clearly not such a property; it is realised immediately, and the world has realised for thousands of years that certain things are beautiful without even asking whether they arouse tendencies to self-completion.' Now if it were true that the matter was so simple, if there was nothing more to be said, it would be at least a linguistic convenience to treat beauty as a simple noun. But as the view stultifies the intelligence, abolishes criticism, makes most of the facts about beautiful things wholly unintelligible, and leaves us with a sense that the whole thing is a necromancy to which any charlatan may have the password, it is not found in practice to work as if it was true. It is decently plausible about painting, because the modes of satisfaction are there little understood, and are far removed from the verbal system on which the discursive intelligence usually supports itself; but of poetry it seems startlingly unlikely; any at all illuminating remark by a literary critic (as to why a particular line is so effective) demonstrates that it is untrue. It

---

[6] IAR and C. K. Ogden, *The Meaning of Meaning* (1923).

is made roughly plausible by what one must readily admit to be the extraordinary character of the arts; the way they convey *some* impression of their value, to the trained critic, at the first glance of the eye. But I need only recommend to Mr Sparrow's attention what he has himself admitted, that analysis is useful, and that it is possible to write literary criticism.

'Even if Mr Richards's "definition" is a true description of all beautiful things, it must fail to be what it sets out to be, a definition.' Perhaps the inverted commas are the most obviously unfair detail in Mr Sparrow's article; it is he who chose to treat the thing as a general definition, and he now sneers at it for being called so. As for the rest of the sentence, he has stolen it, if the reader will believe me, from the sentence by Mr Richards immediately preceding the one he quotes. 'Lastly a perhaps still more sophisticated view reduces this formula to something so vague and general that it ceases to be useful as a means for investigating differences between what is said to be beautiful and what is not.' Though I am acquainted with Mr Sparrow, I own I was a little surprised to find he had done this.

He comes back to the question as to whether beauty is a simple quality, by way of the problems of communication. What creates a tendency to self-completion in one mind has not therefore any reason to create it in another; yet it usually does. Mr Richards says that beauty is an individual reaction; yet he says that beauty is still objective. Mr Sparrow feels that this is a mere disorder; that one or the other must be true, not both. Now very little sense of fact, very little sense of that rational modesty which realises it is dealing with a complicated matter, would have suggested to Mr Sparrow that these are in fact both true; that is precisely why people discuss these questions; why there is a problem of aesthetic communication at all. It is obvious, it is the necessary assumption for criticism, that a poem conveys very nearly the same experience to extremely different people, if they are tolerably competent; certainly this is very extraordinary, and might make one think that beauty was a simple magical essence. On the other hand, it is obvious that there have been coherent, durable, and complete reactions to the same work of art which were very different to each other; songs by Handel, for instance, which Mr Sparrow would think charmingly funny roused Boswell 'to that pitch of resistance which he trusted he might never have to sustain'.[7] Beauty, in some difficult way, both is and is not objective; I am sorry if I am puzzling Mr Sparrow.

---

[7] This is misremembered by WE, since James Boswell found Handel's oratorios 'truly most sublime' (*Boswell in Holland, 1763–1764*, ed. Frederick A Pottle (1952), 50). But in *Life of Johnson*, ed. R. W. Chapman (1904; new edn. 1953), Boswell delights in Johnson's defence of a constitutional monarchy, with the rider that there are necessary checks on abuses perpetrated by a

Mr Richards said that for verbal convenience, and for the gratification of the sense that poetry is an inexplicable power, it is very proper, after realising that beauty is not an inherent quality, to talk of it (on such occasions) as though it were. 'From a writer who is attacking self-deception and exalting sincerity this admission seems particularly strange,' says poor Mr Sparrow. It is pathetic and at the same time a little embarrassing, like hearing death called strange by a child. Surely everybody who talks about these matters nowadays has heard of the problems about verbal fictions, and the philosophy of *As if*?[8] The prime intellectual difficulty of our age is that true beliefs may make it impossible to act rightly; that we cannot think without verbal fictions; that they must not be taken for true beliefs, and yet must be taken seriously; that it is essential to analyse beauty; essential to accept it unanalysed; essential to believe that the universe is deterministic; essential to act as if it was not. None of these abysses, however, opened under Mr Sparrow's feet; he simply used the word 'strange' because he could not but notice that he was making two contradictory accusations.

The same helplessness appears about Mr Richards's advice to those 'whose response to a poem is uncertain.' 'Mr Richards is continually forced to express himself in this way because he dare not say frankly either "those who are not sure whether a poem is good or not" or "those who are not sure whether or not they like a poem".' What is this question of daring? Why is it brave to use these forms of words? How far one's response to a poem is the complete one, how far it is the right one, how far it is the one intended by the author—these are mysteries, and if they could be answered would be answered differently in different cases. Since it is not necessary to bring in these matters, since Mr Richards was only *talking* about the business of arriving at a single coherent response, he did not drag in difficulties by a careless use of language. What Mr Sparrow is complaining about here is that the language did not allow him to mis-construe it.

Finally we come to Mr Sparrow's peroration. 'It is easy to see where this sort of criticism will lead . . . finally Mr Richards will read poems, good,

---

supreme legislative power: 'And then, Sir, there is this consideration, that *if the abuse be enormous, Nature will rise up, and claiming her original rights, overturn a corrupt political system.*' . . .

'This generous sentiment, which he uttered with great fervour, struck me exceedingly, and stirred my blood to that pitch of fancied resistance, the possibility of which I am glad to keep in mind, but to which I trust I shall never be forced' (301).

[8] The German philosopher Hans Vaihinger (1852–1933) proposed in *Die Philosophie des Als Ob* (1911; *The Philosophy of "As If"*, 1924) that in order to comprehend the irrational world we live in, we construct systems of thought—falsehoods or fictions—and behave as if they were true. See WE on 'verbal fictions': 'Vaihinger's *Philosophy of As If* presented a very mixed bag of these entities, as well as I remember, without constructing much of a philosophy of them' (*SCW*, 423).

bad, or indifferent, to cats and dogs, and then present us with a volume faithfully recording their responses.' It must indeed have been easy.

Sparrow returned to the fray with 'Practical Criticism: A Reply to Mr Empson', *Oxford Outlook*, 10 (1930), 598–607, expostulating that 'until a poem is understood it cannot be fully enjoyed . . . Further, in order to understand a poem one must, usually, know something of the author.' WE shows confusion of mind, Sparrow alleged,

> when he classes together, and then fails to distinguish between, analysis of the poet and of the reader, of the poem and its 'mode of action'. (In this last phrase there lurks a further confusion: what is a poem's 'mode of action'? . . .) . . .
>
> True, the protocols gave me no pleasure; but this was not because I felt a need to 'protect a private sensibility' (whatever that may mean . . .) nor because I was 'embarrassed' by them . . .
>
> But I do understand Mr Empson when he says that 'if you are a poet the poetical public is what you are writing for', and I profoundly disagree with him . . .
>
> Mr Empson proceeds to manufacture another opinion for me: 'it is alarming to hear Mr Sparrow say that one cannot afford to sit by the fire and think about death before reading' Pope, and then to accuse me of 'starting at the mere shadow of virtue' . . . the word which he so carefully *italicises* did not appear in my article . . . I said that Mr Richards introduced worse considerations where they were irrelevant, and that he was a prig, and I am afraid that I can find no other word to describe one who, like Mr Empson, prefers 'The Rape of the Lock' to Shelley because Pope is 'brave' and Shelley 'hysterical'. I prefer 'The Rape of the Lock' to the hysterical parts of Shelley because it seems to me that it is well written, and that Shelley when he is hysterical writes badly . . .
>
> Mr Richards wrote in his book (p. 289) that 'to be sincere is to act, feel and think in accordance with one's true nature.' Before criticising this definition I corrected it so that it expressed what I believed (and still believe) Mr Richards to have meant. As they stand, the words mean that you cannot be sincere unless you are thinking, feeling, and acting simultaneously. No sane man believes this . . .

Beauty 'cannot be defined,' Sparrow concluded:

> I do not see how any intelligent person could think that the beauty of a work of art *is* an individual reaction to it, and when someone having said this goes on to say that it is 'still objective' my doubts about his sanity are doubled . . . and so it comes about that we have a volume of psychology called a volume of 'criticism' . . . Mr Richards and his

followers are conducting a campaign against the intelligence; victims of yet another form of inverted snobbery, they will not admit that literature has indefinable qualities, and that some people are able to detect and appreciate those qualities and others are not, and that the 'reactions' of the latter are valueless to the literary critic; they shrink from . . . leaving the inexplicable unexplained.

WE's response was published in the next issue of *Oxford Outlook*.

OXFORD OUTLOOK, 11 (March 1931)

65 Marchmont Street, W. C. 1

Dear Sir,

There is little use in continuing this controversy; Mr Sparrow and I have made our points, and are never going to convince each other. But he makes two specific accusations which I must answer if the case is not to go by default, and it seems reasonable that a few of the remarks he calls unintelligible should be said in a different way. It will be a labour of patience.

He says I misrepresented him, because I said that his objection to Mr Richards' recipe for sincerity was that it produced 'a nineteenth century mode of judgement.' He did not say this, and he now says that he does not know what it means. It is odd that Mr Sparrow should claim to have no historical sense, but I can assure him that he is not seriously mis-represented by the phrase. He quoted Mr Richards's recipe, and then said, 'Old-fashioned critics have often been derided for introducing moral con-siderations where they were irrelevant, but we doubt whether any old-fashioned critic was ever quite such a prig as this. We recommend the advice to those who are not quite sure what they feel about "The Rape of the Lock" '; I hope every reader will substitute these words for 'nineteenth-century' in my article, if he thinks them likely to help Mr Sparrow in any degree.

He says I misrepresented him, because he did not 'say that one cannot *afford* to think about death before reading "The Rape of the Lock" '. Certainly my phrase confused statement with implication; if anyone, after reading my whole passage as an argument, thought that Mr Sparrow had said this in so many words, I am sorry to have misled him. What I meant, obviously, was that Mr Sparrow implied it; and I am now even more convinced that I was right in my judgement of what he was implying, because even now, in the act of denying it, he implies it still more plainly.

'Either [following Mr Richards's recipe for watching football] might put you into a suitable frame of mind for enjoying certain sorts of poetry, but either would as *certainly incapacitate* you (my italics) for enjoying others.' Now he certainly implied that Mr Richards's recipe could not reasonably be used before reading Pope, and I suppose he means by this that to do so would 'incapacitate' him. If so, I certainly think that he reads Pope in one of the less valuable ways.

There is a general point of some interest here. Controversy demands imagination; you must try to understand your opponent's position, so that you can select the things worth talking about; so that you can find the root of his errors, or of your disagreement with him. If I read too much into Mr Sparrow's article it was from a wish to understand him, and I should be better instructed by his reply if he had thought me worthy of the same treatment.

For instance, he gets in a good hit about the 'poetical public'; a clumsy phrase of mine; the matter is much more complex than either of us implied. Of course a poet must not pander to a public, but he must be intelligible, and so much of poetry is a matter of tone towards an imagined public (of good critics, but good critics of a certain sort) that a poet who does not expect ever to find such a public does not in fact write well, if at all. The matter is a topical one nowadays because much of the best modern poetry is so difficult to read, and so hopeless of finding fit readers. It is for this reason, I said, that it would be useful nowadays, both for the poet and the public, if the 'poetical public' had some process of interpretation for the verbal subtleties involved in poetry. And I used that clumsy phrase (assuming it would not be misunderstood) because I wanted to say this briefly, without tedium to the reader; it seems to me rather a pity that Mr Sparrow could only understand that one phrase.

'To be sincere is to act, feel and think in accordance with one's true nature.' I said that *and* might mean several things here; Mr Sparrow in effect challenges me to produce them. In part it separates the three verbs and so means the same as Mr Sparrow's *or*; 'To be sincere is to act in accordance with one's true nature, and to feel in accordance with one's true nature, and to think in accordance with one's true nature.' In part it suggests that you are not being sincere unless you are acting, feeling, and thinking simultaneously; Mr Sparrow took this as the only possible meaning; but I consider the sentence gains from the fact that it is suggested, so as to imply that when you know your own mind completely thought and feeling are peculiarly connected, and allow you to act directly. Also it may mean 'to be sincere in your attitude to a particular topic is, within the period that you adopt that attitude, to do all three things and relate them together.' The total impression given by an intelligent reading of the sentence combines these three more exact statements so as to convey something more general; and it is unprofitable for a reader to invent a special interpretation which makes nonsense. Of course I know that Mr Sparrow will not be satisfied by this, and I will say that it is the wrong way to use language; I can only assure him that I think it a right, and in difficult matters the only possible, way to use language.

Mr Sparrow says that analysis of the poet and of the poem are legitimate criticism; and that analysis of the reader is legitimate, but only psychology. He then asks what the 'mode of action' of a poem can be, and how it can be analysed, and how its analysis can be different from the analysis of the reader. Certainly it would be valuable to know this. I think that people mean by the phrase (I assure Mr Sparrow that they use it) both the devices which a poet has employed to convey what he does convey, and the way those devices come to convey to the reader what they do. Evidently you cannot know this without knowing some part of what happens in the mind of the reader, and some part of what happens in the mind of the author; and some 'analysis of the poem', so far as it is different from this, will also be necessary to it. I suggested these different sorts of analysis, not as different objects, but as different elements of one act. And the reason I did not discuss them separately (a point he complains about) is that I think you cannot know, *a priori*, how much you need to know about any one of them before you can know about the others. That is why I think he is wrong in trying to separate them.

The essential objection of Mr Sparrow to Mr Richards, if I may attempt to sum up, seems to reside in this: Mr Richards considers that there is no one certainly 'right' way of reading a given piece of poetry; that poetry is important because of the way it acts on people; that it does not only act valuably on the best critics; that it would be useful both for the critic and the educator to know how it acts on people; and that this can be found out (in a sufficient degree to be useful) by a process of inquiry. Mr Sparrow and I may be content, so far as I can see, to differ on this series of issues, because only time and experiment can decide them.

I must thank you for your courtesy in allowing us to lay bare this difference at such length in your paper.

§ END

———

THE NATION & ATHENAEUM,
29 November 1930, 291: 'Shelley'

Edmund Blunden,[1] in a querulously indulgent review of *Ambiguity* (*Nation & Athenaeum*, 22 Nov. 1930, 267), said of WE's fifth type: 'The next type "occurs when the author is discovering his idea in the act of writing, or not holding it all in his mind at once." And here Mr Empson calls Master Shelley out, and investigates the stanza, "The world's great age begins anew", finding it a set of meanings "hurried on top of each other"; "it seems rather a creditable thing to have happened to Shelley." '

Sir,—I can't pretend to feel in any degree ill-used by Mr Blunden's extremely generous review of my book, but I should like to try and excuse myself for a fault he criticised; the point seems of some general interest.

He quotes me as speaking with childish impertinence, at one point, about Shelley. My defence is that I was then defending Shelley against a particular criticism made by Mr Eliot.[2] If you are defending a poet against a particular objection, and want to convince those who think him guilty, it is no use obscuring the issue by general praise with which they do not agree. You are implying praise by your defence; you need to convince them that you understand their position.

Furthermore, if you are contradicting a great critic on a detailed point, it seems better manners to contradict him only on the point at issue. When I was wondering whether the tone of the passage was all right (that is a curiously large part of the business of a critic), I was much more anxious not to be impertinent to Mr Eliot than not to be impertinent to Shelley. Of course, I don't deny that that may show my inadequate appreciation of Shelley.

---

[1] Edmund Blunden (1896–1974), poet, editor, journalist, was literary editor of the *Nation & Athenaeum*. He had seen savage service during the First World War; and after working briefly at the *Athenaeum*, he was appointed Professor of English at the Tokyo Imperial University, 1924–7. Later he became a Fellow and Tutor at Merton College, Oxford, 1931–44; and Assistant Editor of the *TLS*, 1945–7. After serving on the UK liaison mission in Tokyo, he became Professor of English Literature at the University of Hong Kong, 1953–64. His tenure as Oxford Professor of Poetry, 1966–8, was cut short by illness. His sympathetic life of Shelley appeared in 1946.

[2] See TSE on Shelley's 'To a Skylark', in 'Note on Richard Crashaw', *For Lancelot Andrewes: Essays on Style and Order* (1928), 96; and Ronald Schuchard, 'Editor's Introduction', in TSE, *The Varieties of Metaphysical Poetry* (1993), 14. 'Empson did not attribute the discussion so directly to Eliot in the first edition [of *STA*] . . . writing more obliquely that Shelley's poem "has received much discussion lately. I am afraid more points will have been brought out than I have noticed" ' (197).

TO I. A. RICHARDS

This letter is connected with the development of what IAR would describe, in *Mencius on the Mind* (1932), as 'a dictionary that is only a dream-project for the future'. While attempting to understand the works of Mencius, and to mediate between cultures with perhaps radically differing ways of formulating their ideas, IAR conceived what he termed 'a plan for a technique' – viz., the exercise of 'Multiple Definition'. 'It is a proposal,' he wrote, 'for a systematic survey of the language we are forced to use in translation, of the ranges of possible meanings which may be carried both by our chief pivotal terms—such as Knowledge, Truth, Order, Nature, Principle, Thought, Feeling, Mind, Datum, Law, Reason, Cause, Good, Beauty, Love, Sincerity . . . —and of our chief syntactic instruments "is", "has", "can", of', and the like. Everyone will flaccidly agree that such words are ambiguous . . .'

One crucial aspect of this approach would be 'to introduce a distinction between the "senses" and "gestures" of a word, phrase, or sentence':

'What may be called the Total Meaning of a word or phrase is a complex function—of which Intention, Feeling, Tone, and Sense seem to be the main components. It is convenient—for the purposes likely to be dominant in our present scientific phase of interest in comparative studies—to group the first three functions (emotive functions) together as a "gesture" and oppose them to "sense" which is what science professes to be built of.'

As to the key-words to be treated in this multiple manner, IAR wrote: 'The ideal list would not only display in a convenient form all the chief senses and gestures of a word, but would indicate their connections with one another . . . and the history of the chief movements, the geologic history as it were, of the major summits. Collections of illustrative passages showing the use of the word with a given sense or gesture in characteristic contexts would support and make concrete the abstract definitions. Such a presentation of "Love" or "Truth" would—in addition to its service as an instrument in interpretation—be an admirable substitute in education for whole courses of half-comprehended and confused reading. It would also be an invaluable means of keeping our more and more disoriented and discrepant minds aware of what may be meant, and so in touch with one another.'

It was inevitable that IAR should invite WE to participate in the project. Although keen to do so, WE believed there were drastic problems with it. For one key matter, IAR's insistence on opposing the 'sense' of a word to its 'emotive functions'—his notion that the 'gestures' of a word will often 'be dependent upon the sense', or contrariwise that 'concepts (senses)' have 'accompanying gestures'—was unhelpful and indeed radically false.

The White House, Fulford, York.
29 December 1930

Dear Mr Richards,

As to whether I should *like* the job you suggest, I can soberly reply I know nothing in the world I should like better. Whether I am at all qualified for such work is another matter; I take it you would not expect a complete analysis of any one word, only a sufficient degree of analysis to make the plan work and show its possibilities. Setting out to do a complete analysis of one of the words on your list would be a very large claim, one does not even know how large.

Perhaps it would be best to set down the prejudices with which I should come to the work. I suspect that many important philosophical words get their usefulness, not from a mere ambiguity, but from being like an unattainable limit, or like a continuous scale that can be pivoted at any required point. The process of analysis, in some such cases, cannot be finished, can only be carried to the degree that is needed for some purpose. So that the philosophical point of view, which claims to be independent of 'practical' purpose, necessarily cannot conduct an analysis of them.

And apart from this, one has to consider how far a philosophical word is meant to be read differently by different readers, people at different stages of acceptance of the philosophy. Such words are often used so esoterically that a particular use of one of them cannot be pinned down, not merely to one meaning, but even to one complex of meaning. So the N.E.D. method of listing different uses of a word is, as you say, not much use; even when you look up the references, there is often no adequate evidence that the example belongs to that particular subheading, or indeed to any one subheading at all.

And it is no use thinking that the philosophers were wrong to be ambiguous, that the comparative and analytical method is going to clear things up, simply by avoiding ambiguity. Even when there is one complex of meaning it is unwise to assume that any other linguistic machinery is going to supersede what has been found, first by generations of use, then by the mind of the philosopher, to be the most effective one. One has some hope of showing by these methods how words have been used, but not till a much later stage, at any rate, how they ought to be used.

Nor can you avoid the difficulties of *literary* analysis in analysing a philosophical word; you can set no final bound to the ways in which it has been working. The moral is not that one shouldn't try to analyse such words but that one should try to analyse them as far as is useful and then show how much has been left (in any particular case) to be absorbed unanalysed, as the word itself was in the original example.

I think one would need to be on one's guard, in this sort of work, against the scientific attitude to truth; the idea that the mind is outside the universe and, otherwise passive, collects propositions about it.[1] Any attempt to survey language is a little of this sort; some of the philosophers whose language is being surveyed would say that one was applying the scientific method to a suprascientific use of language. And the notion of 'openmindedness' involved is a difficult one; in trying not to take any one metaphysical view one is liable to fall into a materialist view and think of it as commonsense. In doing such work one would be saying what has often been said already, so as to bring into play new machinery; and the main thing would be to keep in mind what you were doing it *for*.

I am thinking here only of the business of analysing the English words used in Chinese translation, but the business of interrelating them with the original Chinese words would presumably raise the same problems in a more acute, and more illuminating, form. That is why I personally think it would be so well worth doing.[2]

Yours sincerely

W. Empson

Magdalene

TO T. S. ELIOT*

65 Marchmont St, WC1
[n.d.? June/July 1931]

Dear Mr Eliot,

Thanks for that introduction, which as it turned out I couldn't use, [Arthur] Waley being out. I have been offered a job in Tokyo, safer and more remunerative but (there seems no doubt) much less interesting: and shall be going there in August.

Yours very sincerely

W. Empson.

Faber

---

[1] Cf. WE in *The Criterion*, 9: 37 (Jul. 1930), 770: 'The scientific view of truth . . . is that the mind, otherwise passive, collects propositions about the external world; the application of scientific ideas to poetry is interesting because it reduces that idea of truth . . . to a self contradiction. 'And yet one must not accept such a contradiction as final . . .'

[2] See also WE's 'The Need for a Translation Theory in Linguistics', *Psyche*, 15 (1935), 188–97: Appendix III in *SCW*, 434–43.

TO I. A. RICHARDS

23 Fujimocho, 5 chome, Kojimachi-ku, Tokyo
(a pretty little house, very secluded, where
I am rolling about on the correct mats)
13 October 1931

Dear Mr Richards,

Things seem to have settled down enough now for it to be time to write and thank you. Other people have been telling me what you said in your last letter, about the spiritual conditions being so pinched; I heard Quennell[1] on that topic before I left London, anyway. It is quite true that the Japanese are uncomfortable bogus people who don't really enjoy anything in sight: the Christian converts who look at you with great liquid crucified eyes like spaniels with indigestion (a most embarrassing thing in a lecture room) seem anyway to have some emotional life: the others seem curiously toothy and bloodless, they hang on like lice to that state of life to which it has pleased the Emperor to call them. There is one teacher at the Bunrika[2] who seems to enjoy what he reads: I think they are a good race, it is the immediate history of it makes them so frightful.

I have rather stupidly been talking about Pope and Donne (which they put up with so long as they are told it's the latest fashion) and suchlike: very little contact of any kind has occurred so far. (Feel rather in the wrong about that, but it seems important to settle down first.) The Japanese teachers don't know the students by name, anyway: everybody warns me whatever I do not to ask a student to lunch. That must surely be nonsense, but I am going in for listening to any advice. (A teacher warned me solemnly not to buy a bicycle, for my dignity's sake. But there I have kicked over the traces.) I haven't quarrelled with the teachers, any way.

As for Quennell saying they are so ignorant, after all the English School at Cambridge isn't so amazing. If one could get them to be less ant like that wouldn't matter: but it is hard to believe they would ever really enjoy any literature, any way.

But really, when people give these very kind warnings about my nerves, I don't think I'm as tender as all that. Really with a large salary and a good cook and only eight hours work a week a young man ought to be able to

---

[1] Peter Quennell (1905–93), biographer, poet, and editor, was WE's predecessor at the Tokyo Bunrika Daigaku. Educated at Balliol College, Oxford (which he left without taking a degree), he fostered close friendships with writers including Evelyn Waugh, Anthony Powell, Harold Acton, and Cyril Connolly. In addition to his own work as an author he later became celebrated as co-editor, with Alan Hodge, of the journal *History Today*, 1951–79, and was knighted in 1992.

[2] Tokyo Bunrika Daigaku: Tokyo University of Literature and Science.

keep a stiff upper lip: I am much too frighened about economics to think myself badly off here. (With all this leisure it would be as well to try and understand them.)

There will be an opportunity to say some things in favour of Basic, but I don't think (guessing) the prospects are very bright: the Japanese teachers are against it out of snobbery—but you know more about that than I do.

There are some Buddhas with the primitive Greek smile, which means a great deal more than I know. Is there a large book about either of these, or their connection? Has it been translated from the German?

Yours with gratitude

W. Empson

Please let me have back those notes on pragmatism some time. I feel very parsimonious of ideas already: all my fads are going to be bleached out of me.

I was talking about Basic today (16th) to some teachers' congress, and old Ishikawa said afterwards that he and the Advisory committee (is it that?) are not *not* in favour of it, and after all are only waiting for our textbook, and have to consider where they can fit it in—and I think of him as honest, though sly: so I suppose there are some prospects.[3]

Magdalene

JAPAN CHRONICLE, 25 November 1931, 5:
'The Learning of English'

Sir,—Mr [Arundel] Del Re's objections to Basic English are that it is unsymbolic, artificial, not an introduction to literary English, and not suited to the Japanese. I should like to give briefly what I think the main answers.

The first is simply a mistake: you learn three meanings to each word, the special, the general, and the main symbolic; you are using symbols all the time. Apparently the textbook will be out next month, which should clear up points like that.

---

[3] WE lectured on behalf of Basic English to the 8th Annual Convention of the Institute for Research in English Teaching on 16 Oct. 1931. He pleaded in his talk, as the *Japan Times* reported (20 Oct. 1931), that 'Basic did not depend on any tricks of language . . . Basic was not as some critics maintained nothing but a jargon or "pidgin".' More and more writers were appreciating the merits of 'a sober simple style'; the prose of Edward Garnett was 'very much like Basic English'; and even Swinburne, whom we associate with a peculiar richness of language, when he wanted to create an effect of movement and energy, as in 'An Oblation', made use of monosyllabic words and a simple sentence-construction. Ishikawa Rinshiro (1879–1939) was Chairman of the English Department at the Tokyo Bunrika Daigaku.

To a very great extent Basic English is the basic of English, so (secondly) it is not artificial, and (thirdly) it is the English you need to learn first if you are to feel that *get off a boat* is prior to *disembark*.) So far from being jargon, it cuts the tempting sorts of jargon out, and it is absurd to call phrases like *have a mind to* or *put to death* 'artificial': they are the sap of the language.

No-one denies that Basic is simple; it is as compact as a bomb; at worst it is only a part of English you have to learn anyway; and it is a valuable, as well as a convenient, thing to learn first.

I sympathise heartily with Dr Del Re's fear of the cruelty of the sciences, but I fear also the despair of waste and the squalor of misunderstanding. Unlike the N. E. D., Basic is a thing you can decently ask a pupil to learn.

That it is not suited to the Japanese I can believe; it is not suited to our mortal nature; it is a logical and analytical system which may prove too sharp a mental discipline, by itself, for people to use. But surely it would be a more cheerful first step in English than learning 20,000 words bang off.

—Yours etc.

W. Empson

TO I. A. RICHARDS

23 Fujimocho, 5 chome, Kojimachi-ku, Tokyo
31 March 1932

Dear Mr Richards,

Thanks for that essay. One other thing about the theory of value. I said it might not do good (be pragmatically true) because it seemed cruder than it was; you very generously agreed and said 'restate it then'. But on the other hand that may be why it does do good. It is cheerful because it seems to make things simpler; it has a 'scientific' implication that one may arrive at a good life by being adventurous, intelligent, and brisk; I certainly think that a good implication. But once one has realised how complex the full theory would be it ceases to have this or any pragmatical effect—any folly (any 'ethical invasion' the crude theory might help to keep out) might suddenly be found to satisfy impulses. Except on a naturalist view which makes all such theories unnecessary. I think the 'levels' you insist on in plays are just as important as in philosophical statements; the question whether a statement leads to good lives involves

(a) whether the implications at different levels are good for people at those levels (or most of them, or those of them the philosophy most approves) and

(b) whether (for those for whom (a) is not true—a theory which provided [for] no such people would be stultifying) the statement leads them to the level that would be good for them.

The trouble about pragmatist ideas of value is that they lead you to some complex social view like this; even within the individual, both because he needs, so to speak, to be a sympathetic member of the audience, and to have a handy (stock-response) form of his belief as well as a delicate one for special occasions. Not, of course, that this is peculiar to pragmatist beliefs. It may seem impossible and rather discreditable for a man making a general statement to estimate things like this, but it is some such process (thought of simply as a judgement of value) which is in fact what philosophers do, and why philosophy is not trivial, when it isn't.

One can get at this another way. The pragmatist view of an additive theory of value is a belief not of scientific type, and not circular, if you can say 'this belief as to the nature of good is to be tested by whether it leads to the good life it defines'. But it is a scientific sort of belief in that it aims at generalising so as to cover all sorts of value, and therefore it doesn't define any one sort of good life, or it would fail to be general. It seems not general to the sort of person who is interested in it because (as you say) it throws him back on his own judgement (in fact it suits the individualist cult of personality that produced democratic ideas and may be destroyed by them); but this is the result of a crude view, a not too great confession of ignorance; the theory doesn't aim at leaving out satisfactions due to herd instinct or submission to authority.

Of course, one reason the theory seems fruitful is that it gives a framework that any amount of scientific information can be fitted into; but it can't aim at being completely worked out in those terms or the result would be tyrannical. So far as it is to keep fresh it must always have a borderline beyond which it is no use. Obviously, so far as it merely says 'value might be calculated but can't be yet', it can't tell you which way of life to pursue: the pragmatic interest is in the implications of the cruder statement of it.

(I should be very grateful if you could tell me what books to read about that. Has anything more by Pavlov been translated?)[1]

---

[1] WE had read I. P. Pavlov, *Conditioned Reflexes: An Investigation of the Physiological Activity of the Cerebral Cortex*, trans. G. V. Anrep (1927).

It's no use writing about Japan yet. I think I can stick it for three years all right. Mrs Richards said you might be coming East again; what are the prospects? Are you going to start just as I leave for England?

Yours

W. Empson

The noise is very destructive, especially hammering, and squalling babies, as you foresaw.

I send this as a bait for a letter more than as any use: it won't be new to you.

Magdalene

TO JOHN HAYWARD*

23 Fujimicho, 5 chome, Kojimachi ku, Tokyo
[?March 1932]

Dear John,

Thanks for the book. I shall show it to people.

The only thing Peter [Quennell] didn't complain of about Japan was the noise: that is the one thing at present that I can't get over. As for teaching—I quite like talking to myself in public. The thing is to look at the blackboard or anyway not at the assembled frogs. They can read what you write on the board though they can't understand what you say. If you write steadily on the board and keep up a spoken patter, *never* waiting for signs of intelligence or making jokes, the hour gets through all right. But the perpetual hammering and squalling of babies is beating me during this holiday; I suppose it's only a matter of changing house. I have taken a room in a hotel for the moment, but it is beastly.

I don't think them so very inscrutable: one man in the course of an essay about satire and Pope set to work to explain how hard he found it to love his father. We were reading Housman in one class, which I thought would suit them (suicide is the national sport, of course), but it was embarrassing to read a series of dull essays saying that Housman must be a good poet because he really did make them want to kill themselves, especially to go and die in Shanghai—I wish we could know them . . . the lads that will die in their glory—and so on (one of that class was sent to Shanghai and killed, and various others mobilized). I wonder if it would have made the old gentleman feel ashamed of himself?[1]

---

[1] Cf. 'Feelings in Words', *SCW*, 11–13; and 'Teaching English in the Far East and England', *SSS*, 206.

You thank me for two letters on the journey: I hope you got some (or one anyway) from Tokyo? I am afraid of letters not arriving, and they say they are often censored (which makes one even less willing to try and throw pieces of paper across the gulf).

Please give condolences and congratulations to Elaine, not less serious because both out of date.[2] The dividers of time in this sort of communication make you believe in relativity.

Yes, nearly all the Japanese women I have seen seem to be just what Mrs Quennell told me they would be.

The Japanese flag (a poached egg, or clot of blood on a bandage, which gives the insanely simple and self-centred effect of an amoeba when drugged) is very much in evidence: the theatre (as excellent as they say) has the deaths of heroes at Shanghai on display, with terrific foffings [sic], and professors describe them to you at tea. The efforts of patriotism have made the whole country crawl with babies, dirty and noisy in themselves and sure to cause famine in the next generation.

This is a squalid way to look at a country, though.

Bill.

King's

TO I. A. RICHARDS

23 Fujimocho, 5 chome, Kojimachi-ku, Tokyo
23 April [1932]

Dear Mr Richards,

I wrote for some *Quies* [wax ear plugs] to the Other Shop but didn't send the money, which might hold it up: I wonder if you could do something to help it on its way? I am clutching round for somewhere I can work free from noise. I have taken a room in an apartment house as well as my Jap house: they have different noises and so are a relief, but I can't work in either.

I met Mrs Sansom the other night: they [George and Katharine Sansom] are just back.[1] She was very friendly and charming.

---

[2] Elaine Binney, John Hayward's girlfriend at the time, who had been unwell.

[1] George Sansom (1883–1965) joined the Consular Service in 1904. Sir Charles Eliot, British Ambassador, 1919–26, wrote of him in 1921: 'For sheer intellectual power he is in all probability easily first in the Government Service in Japan' (quoted in Katharine Sansom, *Sir George Sansom and Japan* (1972), 13). He was commercial counsellor in Tokyo, 1926–39. He married Katharine Sansom (1883–1998) in 1928. Knighted in 1935, he was elected in 1947 Knight Grand Cross of the Order of the British Empire. After the War, he became the first Director of the Far Eastern Institute at Columbia University. His works include *Japan: A Short Cultural History* (1931) and

Nara is all you said it was: I am trying to get hold of some intelligent book about Buddhas: there is obviously a great deal to be said about how they get their effect simply on the lines of Darwin's book about the origins of facial expressions: surely somebody must have said it. And is there a book about the early Turkestan-Afghanistan ones with photos? It is annoying that the Japanese, who are rightly anxious that you should admire the Nara stuff, become defensive as soon as you try to discuss it. (But I think I can find *some* information about that somewhere in Tokyo).

The Buddhist monastic people must be the best end of Japan but one would have to face the language to find much there: and I got rather a horror of the infantilism of the language when I was trying to pick some up.

'I dare not move my dim eyes any way'[2] about pragmatism, after realising some of the difficulties in the line I wanted to take up. Has Wittgenstein published the book that was being talked about?[3]

What I wanted to say but couldn't about your distinction between the sort of truth that can't be tested by fact ('conceivably') and the sort that can is that no truth of interest is of the first sort—not even your theory of value—because the 'working in practice' is an appeal to fact. One can't say that the belief in other people's feelings is of the first sort, for instance: it is an instinct but there are lunatics in whom it fails: if experience makes us believe it experience might 'conceivably' (if one woke up into some nightmare) make us *not* believe it. In fact Wittgenstein's distinction simply classes the problems of philosophy as psychology and then does not discuss them.[4] (Like the formalist view of mathematics.)

I was reading Mrs Dalloway with some class and asked them at the end to write an essay about 'how far is she ironical?': they came and said they didn't want to write about that because it might be connected with

---

History of Japan (3 vols., 1958–64). See also Gordon Daniels, 'Sir George Sansom (1883–1965): Historian and Diplomat', *Britain and Japan 1859–1991: Themes and Personalities*, ed. Sir Hugh Cortazzi & Gordon Daniels (1991), 277–88.

[2] John Donne, *Holy Sonnet* 1, l. 5.

[3] WE had read *Logisch-Philosophische Abhandlung* (1921), by Ludwig Wittgenstein (1889–1951), in translation (1922) by C. K. Ogden with F. P. Ramsey.

[4] See for example the following propositions by Wittgenstein:

4.1121: 'The theory of knowledge is the philosophy of psychology.'

5.641: 'There is therefore really a sense in which in philosophy we can talk of a non-psychological I.

'The I occurs in philosophy through the fact that "the world is my world".

'The philosophical I is not the man, not the human body or the human soul of which psychology treats, but the metaphysical subject, the limit—not a part of the world' (*Tractatus Logico-Philosophicus* (1922), 77, 153).

politics.[5] They seem so much spied upon that it is mere nagging to try to extract thought from them: I just prate away at my appointed hours.

Okakura[6] has come back in favour of Basic, but his disciples are usually disciples of Ishikawa too; I suppose they will all have to kill themselves from the clash of loyalties. Poor Mr Palmer is not much in favour of Basic now.[7]

You said you couldn't use Quies because it made your head hot, but I would put up with a lot of discomfort to get out of earshot of babies and the sound of the Japanese language (very like them).

Yours

W. Empson

Magdalene

TO SYLVIA TOWNSEND WARNER*

519 Shirokane Sankocho, Tokyo

4 June (1932)

Dear Sylvia Townshend [*sic*],

I was very cheered to get your letter, when it was at last lowered into my tomb here. Those of my friends in England who realise that I am now far beneath its surface seem to feel it hopeless to try and communicate with

---

[5] See also WE's essay '*Mrs Dalloway* as a Political Satire', first published as '*Mrs Dalloway*', *Eigo Seinen* (*The Rising Generation*) 68 (15 Dec. 1932), in *A*, 450–2.

[6] Okakura Yoshisaburö (1868–1936) taught for twenty-five years from 1896 at the Tokyo Higher Normal School School (precursor of the Bunrika), and was later famous as a radio teacher of the language, and a professor at St Paul's (Rikkyo) University. See obituary in 'International Notes', *The Basic News*, 1 (Jan.–Mar. 1937), 11–14. In '20th Century Jap' ('These Japanese' in *The Listener*, 5 Mar. 1942), WE was to say: 'I remember the great linguist Okakura saying an odd thing, apropos of nothing, as Japanese confidences do come; he said to me "It's one of our great difficulties that we have no colloquial Japanese; we can't talk to each other as equals, as the English do; there is always a formal relationship implied in the grammar".'

[7] Harold E. Palmer (1877–1949) had been recruited to Japan as 'Linguistic Adviser to the Mombusho' (Department of Education). With Japanese government blessing he set up in 1923 the Institute for Research in English Teaching (IRET). He was opposed to the theory and methods of Basic English advocated by C. K. Ogden and IAR (and by their apprentice, WE). Palmer began his career as a journalist on his father's newspaper, the *Hythe Reporter*, later he worked as a language teacher in Verviers, Belgium, before becoming a lecturer in the Department of Phonetics (under Professor Daniel Jones) at University College London, where he specialized in methods of language teaching. After fourteen years in Japan (where he was awarded a D.Litt. by Tokyo Imperial University), he returned to England in 1936 to become a consultant to the publishers Longmans, Green. *Selected Writings* has been issued in ten volumes by the Institute for Research in Language Teaching (Tokyo, 1995–9). See also Richard C. Smith, *The Writing of Harold E. Palmer: An Overview* (Tokyo, 1999); and Richard C. Smith and Imura Motomichi, 'Harold E. Palmer, 1877–1949', in *Britain and Japan: Biographical Portraits*, iv, ed. Hugh Cortazzi (2002), 233–46.

me. On the whole I should like to accept your kind invitation to Norfolk rather than to Dorset: we have hills here but never any space.

Everybody finds something to grumble about in Japan, which is a pity in a way because the Japanese hate not to be loved (it is not simply that things are different, they really are 'quaint' on purpose, in that way: you remember the courtier in Genji who had a genius for beating time—there is the same concentrated sense of style about dusting, which is done with a little flap on a stick—patter, patter, patter, smack, smack, smack—slow, ineffective, and done with an infantile air of charm which easily becomes loathsome) but I think the main thing that gets on people's nerves is the noise: the men selling bean cake in the street use a little flat whistle that makes you stop whatever you are doing and howl at the moon, it is a more Buddhist sound than one would have thought possible. I have just moved into a European house hoping to escape from it, and am very cross—indeed rather hopeless—at finding it as bad as ever. But I am now fairly nearly out of earshot of Japanese babies and my cook, and the screech of the sliding screens of a Japanese house, which were holding up all mental life before.

The theatre is very good, it's quite true, but all 'charming', so one stops going quite soon. The Nara Buddhas are really worth coming here to see. The later ones I can't like, though they are good sculpture (drapery and so on): the face rapidly becomes a slug-like affair with a pool of butter round the mouth. But the early ones feel as if everything was ready for an immense intellectual achievement which suddenly died.

Funny to see Noh plays after reading Mr Waley: they're not Celtic and hopeless as you might think because the dances are terrific South Sea Island affairs, all crowing and prating and stamping like buck rabbits.

One reason it is no use writing from Japan is that one tends to write a special correspondent letter and copy it out to people.

I shall stay here two more years, if I can. Of course it's very deadening but I am less hysterical here than I got in Bloomsbury.

It is very pleasant, but not very invigorating, to have you write so generously about my verses: they were mostly done at Cambridge, and aren't like what I want to do now.

Yours sincerely
William Empson.

Reading

TO I. A. RICHARDS

519 Shirokane Sankocho, Tokyo
2 September [1932]

Dear Mr Richards

Very glad to get your letter. My pupils often ask me to explain about methodology, and I always tell them I have no idea what the word means, but that they had better ask Mr Palmer, who is now lecturing on the word, tout court. Fukuhara* teases me by saying that my book [*STA*] (which you are so right in calling fluid) is full of methodology, so I am in need of a ruling on this point. Serious work with you in two years time is almost too much to hope for.

I enclose an article inspired by you, which I still think true, but the style is too constipated to make decent reading matter. I am a great deal more comfortable since I got into this European house.

How very curious the Buddhas at Keishu are: did you go there? He becomes a fertility earth-god with snakes like the Greek ones, and you get Yaksa figures (holding the medicinal apple) who are Snakes earth-touching with the other hand. It is shocking to think how I have failed to get on with any experts about them, but after all many experts prefer you to know something about their subject before they 'get on' with you.

I have written to Ogden asking if I can be any use about Basic, which ought to have been done before. Certainly the place makes you feel the need for it.

When a man like Fukuhara holds out against it so adroitly I take it his feeling is that the literary attitude to language needs to be kept up (is important even in the intelligent use of language for mere statement) and yet can only be kept up by bluff, by the literary teachers keeping their stranglehold on education. All language teaching must be hooked on to literary language teaching. (So that to say they are trying to keep their jobs is ungenerous even when true). 'We learn English for its moral qualities not for communication'. The only obvious answer would be insulting—that the Japanese student doesn't get any qualities out of the muddle he is left in, except in the rare cases who would have gone in for literary stuff anyway. The anti-literary feeling in Basic, the wish to push the language away when you don't want it, seems very like the Restoration wish to push Elizabethan poetic stock symbols away—in that case the movement obviously produced good writing (moved back to something very like Basic) and by now seems hallowed. But it is not much use saying that to Fukuhara, who needs rather to be told that one could pass very effectively from

Basic to literary studies—which is true enough, but the artfulness required for both sides of the argument, even when disinterested, seems rather paralysing.

I should like to review the Theory of Fictions[1] or at least have it very much: have written for your Mencius [*Mencius on the Mind*, 1932] but the floods have put the post wrong of course.

I am trying to write an essay about double plots and the off-conscious uses of irony but a sense of the uselessness of it has been preventing me from finishing it.[2] When you say you propose to put all these sorts of studies on a less muddled program I can only sit and look, like a dog who does not know what is on the dinner table.

One reason I wanted to come East was to find out what teaching was like across so large a gulf, but most of the Bunrika students (having done some teaching already) are so anxious not to lose dignity that I am flung nervously into acting in sympathy with this object; after a year of it I know very little indeed even of what they know, still less what works for them in literature or what methods would make anything else work. When Peter [Quennell] says they none of them have any feeling for literature at all, though, he is probably complaining about the normal conditions of literature teaching: it is not necessarily useless because it is so bluff at the time: I have some feeling for Virgil now though I had none when I was being taught it.

Certainly I don't think that sensibility is always a residue of conscious discrimination; if it was there would be more hope for Methodology.

If you do make a list of questions 'rising' like a miasma from my rubbish-heap of a book it would be very stimulating for me to have them sent here.

Yours very sincerely

W. Empson

Magdalene

---

[1] *Bentham's Theory of Fictions*, ed. C. K. Ogden (1933).
[2] See 'The Double-Plot in *Troilus and Cressida*', *The Rising Generation* (Tokyo), 67 (1932), 366–7; 'Double Plots: Heroic and Pastoral in the Main Plot and Sub-Plot', *SVP*, 27–86.

TO I. A. RICHARDS

519 Shirokane Sankocho, Tokyo
I am now in a quiet though expensive European house,
and have no further excuse for hysteria.

[n.d. ?November 1932]

Dear Mr Richards,

Wouldn't you say [apropos IAR's proposal in *Mencius on the Mind*, 'a plan for a technique', for 'multiple definition'] that the notion of a *list* of definitions is inadequate, because the important thing is to see how the parts of the list interact, why the word wants you to think of them as connected[?][1] I doubt whether anyone ever uses Beautiful in the sense 'represents something' *only*;[2] definitions to show its use would be more like sentences using the elements of the list as words ('represents something enjoyably' and 'represents something enjoyable', to start with). The effect of wit in your method of finding three possible meanings for Keats's unfortunate moment of triumph [in 'Ode on a Grecian Urn'] is due to the hauteur with which you refuse to follow—sympathise with—the process he is going through.[3]

---

[1] *Mencius on the Mind*, 95: 'The task of Multiple Definition includes a survey both of the senses and the gestures of a word. It will often be found that the apparently "indefinable" peculiarities of a sense can be resolved into features of its range of gestures; and the definer's job is much simplified by the seeming complication.' IAR responded to WE's letter on about 21 Nov. 1932 (this is taken from IAR's diary): 'As to getting English subjects into some more perspicious [*sic*] order, why not? I'm not going to let your greedy gaze & nervous shuffles embarrass me in contemplating the still empty table. There are no mysteries about providing fare—since it's only a programme that's promised. All that's needed is a little willfullness at the same time. My notion, just now, is to look forward to a Dictionary & try to write an essay first on what it should try to do & how it might do it—with sample articles on such nice words as Love & Belief—And your remarks on making a mere list are perfectly to the point, one does want much more, as you put it "how the parts of the list interact . . . & why the word wants you to think of them as connected". Of course it's that matter of grouping (mutual, sheltering, re-inforcing) of senses by *one* word which really makes the great differences in the East & West traditions. At least it would be worth while trying systematically to see how far this was true or not, wouldn't it? & one could be as free as one liked with the primary definitions one chose by which to order one's arrangements. What I see is a line of work long enough to last 20 life times—not like trying to sharpen a point that breaks away but like (& no more disappointing) printing cards one prints oneself in various arrangements. Arbitrary but showing me, as nothing else could, what one was being arbitrary about—whether it would be more useful to do this with a bi-lingual apparatus (Chinese & E) or just with English I'm not sure.' (*Magdalene*)

[2] See *Mencius on the Mind*, 96.

[3] See *Mencius on the Mind*, 109–10: 'As an exercise, some curious readers may wish to examine . . . the celebrated equivalence "Beauty is Truth, Truth Beauty"—not as it occurs in the *Ode to a Grecian Urn*, but apart from the poem, as philosophers and critics have mostly taken it.

>   Though shalt remain, in midst of other woe
>   Than ours, a friend to man, to whom thou say'st,
>   "Beauty is truth, truth beauty—that is all
>   Ye know on earth, and all ye need to know."

In the poem it is said by the Urn, whose utterance continues probably to the end of the

There and in Christ and Mencius the unit of thought seems the paradox rather than the statement (of course this method, as in Wilde, can be
as jejune as the more rational one at its worst). It is from there so to speak
that the incitements to action or judgement branch out; possibly it is for
that rather than its words that one wants a list (it stands for a conflict like
the negative). One root paradox of the Chung Yung, for instance, seems to
be 'no man can leave the way; therefore the best men must strive unceasingly to get onto it'; this is essential to the use of 'way' [*Tao*: way, path,
principle] and would not appear in a list of its meanings (of course the list
might help you to understand it, but what you want to know is how the list
is used).[4] There seems to be the same latent paradox e. g. in Mencius vii. i.
xvi: 'extend them to all under heaven, and they are the same'. 'Extend
your view of them, and you find they are the same; suppose them
extended, and they would be the same; let mankind at last so extend them,
and they will be the same'.[5]

Nor is it clear that a finite list is always useful; if a word stands for a
whole scale to give a finite number of meanings for it is still ambiguous
and may make irrelevant distinctions. And a change of meaning in a
word may correspond to a real change of situation when you regard the
thing talked of in a different context; it is merely an economy to admit this
in the word; I take it a fact of physiology is 'stated' by the Italian c and
Japanese s which become sh before i, and our belief that k remains the
same between a and i is itself refuted by the Arabic q. One may need to
separate what are joined here but the less subjective question is why the
other man has joined them. And if the object of Multiple Definition
was to stop people from thinking queerly (though for that it would be
Additive Definition) one could reply that that may be the only means of
thinking; a word may be not so much a collection of meanings as a
path through the jungle; a bit of it taken along is not a part of its use but
no use to the ordinary walker. (The best satire I know on this trustful
attitude to the words of the great comes in Samuel Butler's Fair Haven,

poem. Urns induce states of mind in their beholders; they do not enunciate philosophical positions—not in this kind of poetry—and "say'st" is here used by a metaphor which should not be
overlooked. Taken apart from the poem, the equivalence has been given . . . some very discrepant interpretations . . . The fact that the ranges of Beauty and Truth overlap at three points . . .
gives the equivalence, either as a gesture or as having some indefensible sense, a peculiarly strong
suasive force. And this accounts for its *power in the poem* (when, of course, it is not apprehended
analytically) to convey the feeling of deep acceptance which is often a chief phase in the
aesthetic experience.' See WE's response in *SCW*, 6.

[4] *Chung Yung*, or *Doctrine of the Mean*, by Confucius's grandson Tzu Ssu.
[5] Cf. *Mencius on the Mind*, 142.

where it is crashing; but I am not thinking of the words of the great so much as of words).[6]

I wish I could get poor James Smith to send you his thesis for a Trinity fellowship, where he did for Aristotle very much what you have done for Mencius; I copied out some into my book, and it has always been my intellectual capital on these matters; but I expect the (rather repulsive) petulance which made him annoy Trinity and refuse to get into touch with you at the time will make him refuse to send it to you, though I will ask him to, as somebody ought to see it.[7]

You recognise all this yourself in the book; I only want to say that it need not be very cumbrous to list 'main paradoxical uses' under the list of meanings, like reducing a system of forces to resultant and couple. And one would want to put against the gestures, in their list, the meanings or combination of meanings that produced them; clearly 'meets deep needs of our being' has always attached to it 'something worth while here'.[8] The subjective-objective distinction, it seems to me, cannot be made at the beginning; to retire from a complex situation into a feeling feels and works at first like developing it into a generalisation; they are to be distinguished when you have understood the whole thing, by a wholesale judgement of value.

Your remarks about De La Mare in *Science and Poetry* [1926] are an example; I agree both with the statement (that he reaffirms the Magical View under cover of stating it to deny it) and with the judgement (that he

---

[6] Samuel Butler's *The Fair Haven* (1873, 1913), is an ironical defence of Christianity purporting to take comfort from the discrepancies in the Gospel narratives relating to the death and resurrection of Jesus.

[7] James Smith (1904–72) graduated from Trinity College with a double First in English and Modern and Medieval Languages Tripos; he also won the Oldham Shakespeare Scholarship. He was theatre critic of *The Gownsman*, and in 1925–6 'Skipper' (editor) of *The Granta*, where he published a number of WE's early pieces. Also, as it was noted in *The Granta*, he revived the Cam Literary Society 'and even presided over it for a year, in order to introduce Cambridge to T. S. Eliot.' He went on in the 1930s to write some essays for the *Criterion* and for *Scrutiny*, one of which—'On Metaphysical Poetry', *Scrutiny*, 2: 3 (Dec. 1933)—gave WE an impetus in his work on *SVP*. He would also take WE to task, in 'Books of the Quarter', *The Criterion*, 10: 41 (1931)—reprinted in Constable—for the extravagances of *STA*. So seriously did WE take Smith's criticisms that he dedicated a large portion of the preface to the second edition of *STA* (1947) to answering them. See a memoir by Edward M. Wilson, 'James Smith (1904–1972)', in Smith, *Shakespearean and Other Essays* (1974), 345: 'At William Empson's request I sent [Smith] the draft preface to the second edition of *Seven Types of Ambiguity*, in which the author replied to some of the criticisms made in the review in *The Criterion* in 1931; Smith read, but did not comment on, it.'

[8] See *Mencius on the Mind*, 96–98, where IAR lists the first phrase as a 'sense', the second only as a 'gesture' (a term incorporating 'Intention, Feeling, Tone'—namely, 'the emotive functions of words') that conveys a variety of 'attitude, intention, etc. . . . though ordinarily a vague sense will, of course, be present.' IAR speaks of 'concepts (senses)' having 'their accompanying gestures' (100); and allows that gestures will often 'be dependant upon the sense that is present' (95).

uses this to hide in a world of fantasy); but the judgement does not follow from the statement.[9] Most poets use the machinery (obviously Housman, who is otherwise so near him

> These are the tears of morning
> *That weeps,* but not for thee.)[10]

but not to obtain the state of feeling, even granted that it is always debilitating. The question for criticism is how and when the connection between the two is made; and on your system you would have to call your judgement of the special case a gesture rather than a statement.

As for the Grecian Urn, one must approach the final equivalence through the paradoxes the poem is built up out of; 'it is receptivity to the outer, trivial, life which gives fulness to the valuable inner' (so at the end we ignore the outer-v-inner issue) 'brief moments of strain which give a glimpse of permanent value' (however painful life is one must hang onto the moments of intuition and work from them), and either, from Keats seeing a way of life in the vase (Orpheus), 'the delight in beauty which gives the strength to recognise truth' or as its opposite, from the man on the vase never catching the girl (Christ), 'the strength to renounce the delight in beauty' (and so somehow to make beauty permanent) 'which gives the strength to recognise truth'; also from the town left empty (with a touch of death-wishes) 'the blankness of this reserve in beauty which is like the impersonality of truth' (because both involve the cutting off from the final judgement of the pain of life after it has been judged as trivial). In all these truth and beauty need not be distinguished in the actual process of living as well as one can, and so may be treated as the same at the (possibly uneducated) climax. Of course to tease the people who use the line wrongly wants Multiple Definition, but to understand Keats wants a

---

[9] IAR construes the 'Magical View' as meaning 'roughly, the belief in a world of spirits and powers which control events, and which can be evoked and, to some extent, controlled themselves by human practices. The belief in inspiration and the beliefs underlying ritual are representative parts of this view.' In much of the poetry of Walter de la Mare, he argues, 'no intimation of the contemporary situation sounds. He is writing of, and from, a world which knows nothing of these difficulties, a world of pure phantasy for which the distinction between knowledge and feeling has not yet dawned.' Even when de la Mare seems 'to be directly facing the indifference of the universe towards "poor mortal longingness," a curious thing happens. His utterance, in spite of his words, becomes not at all a recognition of this indifference, but voices instead an impulse to turn away, to forget it, to seek shelter in the warmth of his own familiar thickets of dream, not to stay out in the wind . . . Mr de la Mare takes refuge in the dream-world of the child.' (*Poetries and Sciences,* a reissue of *Science and Poetry* (1926, 1935) with commentary (1970)), 51, 69–70.)

[10] A. E. Housman, *Last Poems,* XXVII ('The sigh that heaves the grasses'), ll. 7–8.

methodology of paradox; your three meanings are included but not thought of.[11]

[Yours sincerely
W. Empson]

Magdalene

TO MICHAEL ROBERTS*

519 Shirokane Sankocho, Tokyo
12 November 1932

Dear Roberts,

You are very clear what this war is, what side you are on, and that you have allies; I feel rather out of all this. What is 'The Oxford Movement' I keep hearing about? Is it Hitler or Auden's Boy Scout attitude?[1] What political views are you fighting for, if any? I am taking in the New English Weekly; is there anything in that? I am in need of letters. What is [Carew] Meredith doing now?

I should like to write 3–5000 words about Richards' pragmatism as opposed to the offensive covert pragmatism of people like Wyndham Lewis and Chesterton; also about Richards' theory of value by addition, and how far it is valuable when you have left out the simpler fallacies in it

---

[11] See also WE, 'Feelings in Words', *SCW*, 6–7: 'there are [in IAR's books] a series of phrases to the effect that the Emotions given by words in poetry are independent of their Sense. It seems to me that this doctrine, if taken at all simply, would be sure to lead to bad criticism . . . I think an example can be found in his defence of the last lines of the *Grecian Urn* (*Mencius*, 116) . . . Professor Richards says:

"Urns induce states of mind in their beholders; they do not enunciate philosophical positions—not in this kind of poetry—and *say'st* here is used as a metaphor which should not be overlooked."

I do not think poor Keats would have liked to be told he was writing "this kind of poetry". Professor Richards goes on to show that the ranges of meaning in Truth and Beauty overlap at three points, so that there are three ways of making "Beauty is Truth" a mere tautology (not a sentence with any meaning). These possibilities, he says:

"account for its power in the poem (when, of course, it is not apprehended analytically) to convey that feeling of deep acceptance which is often a chief phase in the aesthetic experience."

Now it may well be that the lines are bad. But it seems to me that Professor Richards is not defending them; he is merely calling them bad in a complacent manner. And I should have thought, for that matter, that any word other than an exclamation or a swear-word has got to be apprehended as a meaning, giving room for a possible analysis of the meaning, if it is apprehended at all. A poet no doubt is not building an intellectual system . . . But all the same if he leads up with clear marks of solemnity to saying that Beauty is Truth he does not want to be told, any more than anyone else, that "of course" he meant nothing at all except to excite Emotion. It seems to me that a flat separation of Sense from Emotion would be merely a misreading here.' See further WE on Keats in 'Thy Darling in An Urn' (1947), in *A*, 284–7; and *SCW*, 368–74.

[1] Cf. WE's 'Just a Smack at Auden' (*CP*, 81–2), first published in 1937.

which Richards now admits. Or rather to boil down my scrabbly notes to that length. Is this the sort of thing you want, and when do you want it?

I am living here in rather dismal comfort, wasting time without saving money; but my nerves are better than when I left Bloomsbury.

You may be interested in a local opinion about Manchuria. Of course one feels the popular jingoism and official militarism like a weight on the back of the neck; my Japanese colleagues more than I do. And no doubt it is a bad thing for the League to lose face so wholesale. But the immediate thing is that the game will rapidly send Japan bankrupt; there's no interference needed from outside for that.

Yours sincerely
William Empson

Professor Andrew Roberts

TO I. A. RICHARDS

519 Shirokane Sankocho, Tokyo
9 January 1933

Dear Mr Richards,

You have again charmingly waved away the objections I took courage to make to your position, and remarked that you agreed with them. But the distinction between facts and feelings is dickey[,] it's not clear what's left. How about the belief in the existence of other people, which is among the things Wittgenstein can't say: is it capable of being tested by fact or is it an imaginative assent?[1] It seems clear that God and immortality can be first-type beliefs and disbeliefs of the same sort (if other people are): the appearance of God or ghosts *might* give one such evidence as one accepts elsewhere. This must be connected with the fact that they are no use, when clearly held as imaginative assents (*unless* one is leaving the initiative to someone else—the author one is reading for instance). The belief in other people is not destructible in this way—survives pragmatism—but this seems only because it can't be tampered with. It can be lost, I understand, in dementia praecox. As for the belief in free-will, which seems to be complex, different parts of it would be 'disproved by fact' if there were

[1] Cf. WE in 'Theories of Value': 'I . . . feel that though the [IAR] Theory of Value is adequate, and indeed fruitful as giving insight, in the field for which it is supplied in the *Principles*, that of describing what happens when we get a valuable effect from a piece of artwork, still the darker puzzles about pseudo-statements were always unnecessary. Of course, if you say that a statement about the existence of other people is inherently meaningless, as I take it Professor Wittgenstein would do, then all statements about value are meaningless too; but we need not bring these scruples into other branches of study' (*SCW*, 428).

plagues of universal paralysis or universally successful fortune-tellers. What important pseudo-beliefs are left, except empathy which looks after itself?

The queer thing about 'tone' as an essential element of literature is that literature essentially tries to renounce the situation that calls for 'tone'. It is not *to* one person or audience because it is permanent and so for all sorts: it is hardly even *from* one person because the artist has in a sense to be impersonal. 'Tone' in literature is a reaction between these assumptions and the speech-ones that require a simple 'tone' (except that one is so ignorant as a rule of the person addressed that one addresses him as anybody). Your 'tone' for instance can hardly be kept from the uses as in 'high-toned'—'trying to push the reader into a class the author wants recruits for by treating him as a member of it'. This seems only to say that a 'tone' is adopted with 'intention', but tone so treated seems a queer derivative from the original definition. ([Thomas] Gray says [in 'Elegy in a Country Churchyard'] 'there is no carrière ouverte aux talents' and by implying that he is the voice of nature—'nor there is for flowers' who don't want to be picked anyway—implies that the existing political arrangements are inevitable. This is done by 'tone' but yet is an implied 'statement', and in another sense is done by a renouncing of 'tone'—by implying that the poem comes not from him but from everybody or nature.)[2]

Palmer nows says as 'a teacher of experience' that it is easier to learn all uses of e.g. *price* than the Basic ones (including the participle, with *have* and an object, not called a verb). I wish somebody would tell me the answer to this: it seems his only good argument. (Not that he can claim experience in teaching Basic.) But it may be no use trying to deal with Palmer when Okakura is obviously determined never to work with him (very reasonably).

I can't complain of boredom here because I wanted to subject myself to a firm course of boredom when I came: my nerves are a great deal better now than they were when I left Bloomsbury. And a year of talking cleverly at the blank air—throwing away 'brilliance'—has purged a lot of non-sense out of my mind. Whether two years more of it will amount to sheer self-destruction is another thing. (You might think this sounds hard on the pupils, but it seems true that they really like this process best: they take it from the tone of your voice, like dogs.—So long as you write some sentences on the blackboard afterwards).

[2] For WE on Gray's 'Elegy', see 'Proletarian Literature', *SVP*, 4–5.

Okakura's spelling scheme seems a very good one, if there is hope in any. You can move easier to Standard from it than from Anglic,[3] and it has more of the suggestions of dialect that Anglic has (*oe* like Cockney, *lh* [? *dh*] like Irish). The only thing is that the dashes and colons would be slow in writing. He asked me what papers might be sent a copy for review, but I knew of none at all.

You say that romantic love is a novelty to the East. I don't know in what sense this can be true. All these lovers' suicides are traditional enough. Sansom tells me that what he would call romantic love poetry starts in Japan as soon as there is a leisured class not wholly occupied with military discipline. As for not being officially approved of, I don't know that Wertherism ever has been anywhere.[4] And yet there seems a peculiar difference between Japanese and Western women which one can't explain by saying 'they haven't votes' or 'they are despised in practical matters': they are very different from South European women who seem to be legally placed much the same, and I'm told the wife does the accounts of these small shops, and is as much in command as a Frenchwoman. You might make it Age rather than Sex War: the grandmothers are influential enough. The difference seems mainly in the idea of 'sitting at the head of the table'—'ruling the drawing-room'—what you miss is the sniff of the charlady which means she has summed the room up—(and means to show you what she thinks). No doubt it's all different in China: people sometimes say women are better off there. You can get Japanese to agree that there is much less pleasure to be got out of Japanese women—I always feel very sorry for the young men I like here on those grounds. But I can't see that is due [to] a shift in their use of words like 'love': it is chiefly that the conventions for women demand that they should be dull—and infantile, which is more hopeless.

This rather squalid letter is mainly to thank you for the eidelweiss. Are you really coming out to China just as I leave here for England next year? It seems very bad luck for me. Peking will then probably be under Japanese advisors and perpetually fighting them, so you may not be able to go.

Yours sincerely

W. Empson

[Headnote:] The popular perversion of Buddhism says that they live in heaven together afterwards. I suppose [illegible] in China?

Magdalene

<hr>

[3] Anglic is a system for 'easy-spelling' English based on 'Saxon' English, making use of 54 key sounds or phonemes: 27 consonants and 27 vowels.

[4] 'Wertherism' was instigated throughout Europe by Goethe's *Sorrows of Young Werther* (1774), which induced a fashion for lovelorn excess and suicidal behaviour.

TO I. A. RICHARDS

519 Shirokane Sankocho, Tokyo
13–18 February [1933]

Dear Mr Richards,

I am stopping trying to do literary work:[1] it seems too hollow, for some reason. It would be worth while doing some translation into Basic, but very little else. I have just lost all my lecture notes, with the pleasure which losing things I am irritated with always gives me. There was a point about the use of the word *dream* in Yeats which I should like to try and remember for you.

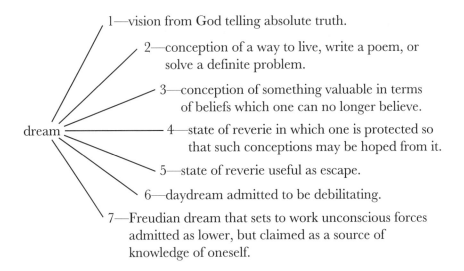

1—vision from God telling absolute truth.

2—conception of a way to live, write a poem, or solve a definite problem.

3—conception of something valuable in terms of beliefs which one can no longer believe.

dream 4—state of reverie in which one is protected so that such conceptions may be hoped from it.

5—state of reverie useful as escape.

6—daydream admitted to be debilitating.

7—Freudian dream that sets to work unconscious forces admitted as lower, but claimed as a source of knowledge of oneself.

7 gets back to the 'mysterious forces' of 1 and 2. The 'romantic' Yeats manner always implies 'You've got to be high-toned if you're to read this: I don't write for the sort of man who thinks I mean a *nasty* dream—and if he does think that about *my* dreams he's probably wrong'. In his later use of *dream* he includes all the meanings—

> The soul remembering its loneliness
> Shudders in many cradles
> —business man etc—
> cradle within cradle, and all in flight and all

---

[1] Added by WE in the margin: 'vapid remark. Time I went to China'.

> Deformed because there is no deformity
> But saves us from a dream[2]

1–4 saves us from a conception of value—which would involve powerful effort. 5–7 saves us from a conception of desire which would jolt us out of the order at present achieved.

Very tactful of him to keep his language and leave room for the Freudians in it: the dream is no longer necessarily admired. A sort of complacence in him makes him able to be a very intelligent poet, don't you think?

I am afraid of this next year: two years is enough at a time.

Isn't there a magazine of psychology started, with Jung mainly? I have lost the reference. Please let me know about that kind of thing. I have only just come across Lashley's brain-smashing experiment.[3]

[W. Empson]

Magdalene

---

[2] WE is alluding to W. B. Yeats's 'The Phases of the Moon' (*The Wild Swans at Coole*, 1919); Michael Robartes is speaking:

> The soul remembering its loneliness
> Shudders in many cradles; all is changed.
> It would be the world's servant, and as it serves,
> Choosing whatever task's most difficult
> Among tasks not impossible, it takes
> Upon the body and upon the soul
> The coarseness of the drudge.
> OWEN AHERNE.   Before the full
> It sought itself and afterwards the world.
> ROBARTES. Because you are forgotten, half out of life,
> And never wrote a book, your thought is clear.
> Reformer, merchant, statesman, learned man,
> Dutiful husband, honest wife by turn,
> Cradle upon cradle, and all in flight and all
> Deformed, because there is no deformity
> But saves us from a dream. (ll. 88–102)

(WE uses the same passage as epigraph to his poem 'Autumn on Nan-Yüeh' in 1937.)

[3] Karl S. Lashley (1890–1958), American behaviourist and pioneer in the field of physiological psychology, specialized in the study of brain function and memory. *Brain Mechanisms and Intelligence* (1929) reported the findings of experimental work with rats: in endeavouring to establish whether there is a single biological locus of memory, or 'engram' as he called it, Lashley removed or surgically damaged portions of the cerebral cortex in rats, and was led to the conclusion that memories are in fact stored throughout the cortex (according to the law of equipotentiality). While his findings have been questioned in more recent years, still it remains true that memory is widely distributed in the brain and is not confined to a specific location.

TO JOHN HAYWARD

Hotel du Nord, Peking
7 March 1933

(Impossible to get back to Tokyo for a party on the 12th, owing to the war: a painful first contact with the realities of war in these parts.)

My dear John,

I am sitting half drunk in this bar over a stupid book about Theories of Value, back today from the earliest Chinese Buddhist carvings in a loop of the Great Wall, (where there is no war), very lovely indeed, and being hacked to bits for American collectors (who like the faces only !!!) very fast. But the carvings by lasting just a millennium and a half have lasted till adequate photographs were taken (about a century before they will finally crumble away, unless elaborate and expensive steps are taken) which may be a reliable immortality. Many heads have been stolen since the 1924 collection of photos was made, and four of the thirty caves have fallen in altogether. It is really rather stirring that the photos were taken just in time—not that any photo is more than a souvenir, or one wouldn't take the trouble to go. The Buddhas are the only accessible Art I find myself able to care about.

It seems obvious looking at the Peking altars and stuff that this universal-state sentiment, with or without emperor, will be revived: but I know nothing about it to claim feelings with. The disorder of the country seems much exaggerated: the horrid softness of the frowsy old men one gets e.g. as guides is the same in Japan as in China: not specially national.

I don't think I knew what the Chinese meant by those Ming dragons till I saw Chinese looking and moving like dragons—sleepy and while arrogant and dangerous in some way feminine—but a little work on portraits in the Museum would tell one that. Always rather embarrassing to wonder what one gets out of travel to make up for its privations; except that it requires so much imagination to stay at home.

They could quite easily have become Michael Angelo in these early carvings—there are plenty of incidental floating angels with no Oriental introversion, at Yün-kang, with no Indian or other influence, but like the Han North-Chinese animal carvings: they just chose not to. I suppose most of our Great Traditions are only histories of refusals to follow up opportunities.

I wish I knew a decent book about faces later than Darwin's [*The Expression of the Emotions in Man and Animals*, 1872]. The Eastern Buddha type seems really to depend on the Mongolian Fold[1] but I have never seen a Buddha with one. I am sure that the general rules about telling character from faces are the same for the whole human race—allowing for the type the individual varies from—but how much does the type mean? etc. etc.

Very curious that European education—success of it—an opened and somehow more vulnerable way of thought—seems to make an entirely different sort of face without Mongolian fold. But after all there is the same curiosity at home about the faces that go with feminine fashions.

My students have to write an essay at the end of the year. (At both universities I am told they all have to pass. 'Mark them ABCD : D is failure, so mark them ABC': 'Under 60% fails them, so mark them up to 30 and add 60': are the instructions given to a friendly foreign professor). At the Imperial I sit in and they do it in two hours. Six people out of thirty spotted a quotation from Ben Jonson I hadn't used in lecturing—after all, blank as they are, the thing's not total farce. At the end a young man came in and explained with great dignity and politeness that he was sorry he had been unable to attend my examination, as he was drunk last night and had only just woken up. He may have invented this merely to show there was no ill-feeling. At the Bunrika they are going to be teachers so have to defend their dignity and write essays in their spare time. I gave a tea party (about fifteen, of a given year) nearly all of whom had chosen to write about D. H. Lawrence and Sex. The house was submerged in student life, all in a herd, rather stirring to me because I had a guilty feeling that my own student life was so similar—in which two young men sat down and wrote their essays about sex one on each side of the tea-table, in a war of Japanese speech with the gramophone playing. They are really rather sweet once you accept them as hopelessly silly.

I take it you are all right as am still seeing your reviews. I wish you would write to me via Canada. I feel sure that many interesting letters have been generously sent only to be used to light fires for the bandits in Manchuria. Fine to think of real human use being found for our letters.

Love

Bill

King's

---

[1] Epicanthic fold: a fold of skin covering the upper eyelid, giving the impression of 'slant eyes'.

TO I. A. RICHARDS

Hotel du Nord, Peking
[n.d. ?March 1933]

Dear Mr Richards,

If all impulses are reactions to stimuli designed to remove the stimuli, then there is no possible life on your definition which has positive value. If removing stimuli is all the fuss is about the quickest way is suicide, and a good enough psycho-analysis might make one believe that enough to act on it. It seems clear that positive satisfactions occur, but I don't know where they come in from a Behaviourist standpoint.[1] (They are implied in any form of Buddhism, under the disguise of a superstitious fear, in the rule that it's no good committing suicide; you must try to get to the impersonal world even if it is null when reached).

I was trying to write an article about your Value and its opponents, but feel obviously too ignorant. Don't you bring in the *will* secretly twice—in the idea of an impulse being *satisfied* (obviously an electric shock in a nerve can't be 'satisfied', and it is never prevented from relieving the nerve of potential)—and in the very crucial 'balance–deadlock' opposition where *balance* suggests a man walking on a tightrope—able to do what he *wants* on it—and *deadlock* two men fighting and neither getting what he wills?[2]

On the Behaviourist view there is no positive value but anyway there would be no value if there was no consciousness. Granted that our molecules would move as they do if they didn't produce consciousness (this is unbelievable, but only because one doesn't know why they do, whether they couldn't *not* produce it by acting as they do) still it seems clear that the

---

[1] Cf. Russo: 'Richards was not a behaviorist; he used behaviorist elements; he was an instrumentalist and behaviorism was one of his instruments'; 'the evidence is overwhelmingly against his ever having been a behaviorist' (125, 175).

[2] See IAR: 'The equilibrium of opposed impulses, which we suspect to be the ground-plan of the most valuable aesthetic responses, brings into play far more of our personality than is possible in experiences of a more defined emotion.' Aesthetic experiences provide 'a balance of opposites' or 'states of composure', argued IAR: 'What happens is the exact opposite to a deadlock, for compared to the experience of great poetry every other state of mind is one of bafflement' (*Principles of Literary Criticism* (1924, 1967), 197–8. Cf. WE, 'A Doctrine of Aesthetics' (1949)—on the reprint of *The Foundations of Aesthetics*, by IAR, C. K. Ogden, James Wood—'The chief puzzle of the treatment by impulses is that you need to distinguish between a Balance and a Deadlock, and the only obvious difference is that one is called good and the other bad. However, "We might describe balance as a conflict of impulses solving itself in the arousal of the other impulses of the personality" (77). It seems very doubtful how this formula would apply to a Buddhist mystic, for example; he would consider that the process of meditation was excluding "other impulses of his personality", but you could argue that the other impulses do get absorbed in some passive but unharmful way, so that he has a genuine "balance" under the terms of the definition. Here again, the trouble with the theory is not that it appears wrong on fuller examination but that it turns out to say extremely little' (*A*, 214).

fact of consciou⌐⌐ess makes a difference to the value. (The Freudian unconscious may well be consciousness somewhere else, not in the 'focus', so one needn't worry about that). They [Behaviourists] would say that having an appetite for dinner, feeling sure you will get it, and getting it, is of negative value (or null as a limit): because a need has been unsatisfied and then merely satisfied after an interval. Obviously there is positive pleasure at both stages. It seems to me that there is positive pleasure in appetite because the creature is (a) conscious (b) capable of knowledge—it is the intellectuality of the creature that turns a state of need into a state of pleasure. If those same movements of atoms caused consciousness of need but not knowledge there would be more pain than pleasure even in having enough food.[3]

And the statement that deadlocks need to oscillate while balances tend to be fixed still doesn't separate the valuable states from the perversions, which tend to be all too fixed.

I don't understand whether an impulse is defined as physiological or not. If it is I don't understand what its satisfaction is. The word 'tendency' is specially misleading here as dragging in a hint of will to the inanimate.

One might say that the knowledge is essential to the satisfaction—the sense that the desires will be satisfied to [?by] the pleasure even e.g. of music where the desires are not severe—but that this must have a correlate in the physical events and can be accounted for by their rules. But one knows nothing about the rules connecting the physical to the mental states—it seems possible to say that the same physical events might conceivably produce consciousness but a different consciousness, and that if they did they would obviously have a different value. (You escape this by your appeal to fact, to what men 'at bottom' prefer, but still the fact that the events are valuable is peculiarly independent of them). If physical events give pleasure by producing knowledge not by producing something *immediately* useful to the organism in which they occur then the satisfaction of the impulses concerned simply with the organism's *uses* is not the criterion of value.

This reacting-to-painful-stimulus business is probably nonsense anyway, because pain (I understand) is not an essential opposite of pleasure but a separate biological invention. The Buddhist position seems to be that pain is a result as well as cause of pleasure, that pleasure is essentially misleading because it is a creator of desire that eventually leads to pain. But this is mere assertion made convincing by seeming to invoke the removal-of-

---

[3] WE added at the head: 'No need to go through all this to refute Money-K. [See p. 62 n. 2.] We know that pleasure exists and may be sought—he has to prove it "isn't really".'

stimulus idea only (and backed up by transmigration): clearly some people escape from this life (supposing it is their only one) without getting much pain out of their pleasures. (Fatuous these terms are: the air as I write is full of pain and despair from a Russian prostitute being very slowly turned out of the bar—everybody having to collect the money and ornaments she has flung all over the floor, so that she is tremendously in command of the situation). But if pain is quite separate from pleasure it seems even less likely that the satisfaction and frustration of an impulse are (other things being equal) of equal and opposite value, which is (apparently) needed for your theory. [Incomplete]

Houghton draft

TO I. A. RICHARDS

Hotel du Nord, Peking
Sunday 2 April 1933.

Dear Mr Richards,

Peking very good in more ways than one, but no Buddhas of any merit. No train to the caves with Buddhas in a loop of the Wall till Tuesday.

Buddhism is relevant to what I am trying to think about, in connection with the Value business (what a stupid writer Westermarck is).[1] The question obviously rises on the Calculable Value theory whether optimism or pessimism, otherwise such dim terms, are true: whether the total satisfaction of all lives is negative (e.g.). Freud's dim but rich concept of death-wishes comes in here: one sense of it is certainly that all impulses are reactions to a stimulus aiming at the removal of the stimulus: if this is all that the fuss is about, the way to remove all stimuli is suicide. And if we could be completely psycho-analysed we might accept and act on this conclusion—whether psycho-analysis is really a process of showing the subject the truth or of hypnotising him into agreeing with the analyst. Westermarck escapes this issue by taking what he calls emotions as reliable: if the psycho-analyst can change them, and really many people can change them, this is no longer true. (Clearly to do this the analyst would have to analyse down to the most primitive organic levels: the question whether 'bringing into consciousness' is possible, in the end, or can possibly have any effect, comes up sharply here). The suggestion of

---

[1] Edward A. Westermarck (1862–1939): Finnish sociologist, philosopher, and anthropologist; author of *The Origin and Development of the Moral Ideas* (1906) and *Ethical Relativity* (1932), which argue that no moral truths or judgements could have an absolute validity: they are subjective and relative. Cf. WE in *SCW*, 414.

'satisfaction' as opposed to its derivation carries the puzzle neatly, and 'content' has gone the other way—starting with the idea of still holding a satisfaction as a thing you can keep after its simpler part is over—as your content—turning to 'putting up with what you can get'. It seems clear that there is an issue in this about value, because it raises the question whether value other than avoidance of pain can be achieved.

You deal with this by the pregnant words 'balance—deadlock', which make an ingenious claim to be unemotional and scientific. Certainly they bring in the value considerations which the analysts try to shirk. But the suggestion that a balance is a fertilising sort of flat conflict because it allows the energy to flow into other channels, (thus at once giving a store of energy, a sort of battery, a storm that shakes things to a more reliable level—and a process that brings more of the whole organism into a single reaction)—which obviously goes a long way—still doesn't face the issue that this may be done badly: it is just this process that sends energy into perverse desires that give pain when unsatisfied and no pleasure when satisfied. Some such perverse desires give satisfaction when satisfied by sheer luck from an irrelevant source as a discovery, and no doubt those are kept up; this idea of development from perversions is exactly parallel to the idea of organic evolution from the very few mutations—accidents to the germiplasm [germ plasm]—which happen to be useful.[2] (So that the use of the origin of an idea as a test of its validity is fully refuted by the men who use it). But there is nothing in your distinction to distinguish these from pathetic perversions.

What *balance* and *deadlock* suggest is respectively a man able to walk on a tightrope and two men fighting where both are unsatisfied and neither able to get further or escape. There is a subtle introduction of the Will here. The balance is between falling to left or right: there is no balance between walking forward or backward, or between falling or not falling. (The conception of will itself is such a balance, between random and fixed). The Buddhist position as I understand it is that impulses within causation are essentially avoidances of pain, and that (apparent) satisfactions are harmful because they are creators of desire which eventually produce more pain. One might say that some satisfactions are obviously positive because the aged bewail the failure of their desires, but the Bud-

---

[2] R. E. Money-Kyrle discusses the evolutionary differentiation of cells into germ plasm and soma, in *The Development of the Sexual Impulses* (1932): 'In certain species the cells did not always separate when they divided, but remained as united though distinct individuals. The outer ones were then specialized as a protective covering, lost the power of conjugation, and so, perhaps, become [*sic*] mortal. But the inner cells, or germ plasm, retained their original character, and from time to time conjugated with other like cells and grew about them a new body' (55).

dhist answer does for this. The Mahayana [Buddhist] business then claims that there are positive satisfactions but they are essentially apart from causation and therefore 'impersonal': you get in Money-Kyrle's *Development of Sexual Impulses* e.g. an early-Buddhist pessimism which obviously excites this sort of escape.[3] (By the way when D. H. Lawrence said that Buddhism was all pomp built round a vacuum he was in Ceylon and talking only about Hinayana Buddhism, about which what he said may be true).[4] I certainly do not see what other means would introduce positive satisfaction: on the whole, you understand, since the pleasure is defined as the removal of an equal pain. A conceivable loophole is in his definitions of 'desire'—a sensation of a need together with the idea of the means of quieting it; 'appetite'—a sensation of a need together with the sensation of the means of quieting it.[5] It is the intellectuality of the creature, the fact of its consciousness, which alone makes a state of want able to be a state of pleasure. This at least gives consciousness a legitimate importance: in his book there is no suggestion as to why it should occur or whether everything would be the same if it didn't. Counting the impulses satisfied in a creature with an appetite relieved without consciousness the total value is nil; counting in the consciousness the value is positive.

Consciousness of course (which people so cheerfully give to atoms 'in a dim form' to make everything 'continuous') is an alarming business because (supposing it to be consciousness of something) you must be

---

[3] See Money-Kyrle, *The Development of the Sexual Impulses*, 61: 'Our private purpose is to remove and avoid our needs and injuries as effectively as possible, but only if we do so in the same manner as our ancestors, shall we in turn perpetuate our race . . . It is possible that the most economic way of removing and avoiding injuries and needs is to seek death rather than life, and that nothing but an inherited false idea of death as a state of pain and want has prevented our race from exterminating itself.' See also WE's reflections on Money-Kyrle in 'Theories of Value', *SCW*, 424.

[4] D. H. Lawrence wrote to Mabel Dodge Sterne on 10 Apr. 1922, from Candy in Ceylon: 'Buddhism seems to me a very conceited, selfish show, a vulgar temple of serenity built over an empty hole in space'. (*The Letters of D. H. Lawrence*, vol. iv, ed. Warren Roberts, James T. Boulton, Elizabeth Mansfield (1987), 226).

[5] Money-Kyrle differentiates between sensation and appetite in 'The Impulses of the Organism', 29–36: 'The consciousness of the child . . . contains both a sensation of need plus a sensation of a means. It is the sum of these two kinds of sensation that we may call an *appetite* . . . The combination of the sensation of a need plus the idea of a means may be called a *desire*. A desire thus differs from an appetite . . .

'There is a difference between the rather painful and anxious longing for an imagined means which is not yet attained and the pleasurable anticipations of the immediate removal of the need when the means is already before us. It seems legitimate to reserve the words desire and appetite for these two states. Thus, when we are hungry and imagine food, we may be said to experience desire; but when the food is already before us, that is, when the visual image of the means has become a visual sensation, we may say that the desire has become an appetite . . . [N]othing is ever sought which is not a *means* (adequate or inadequate) to the *removal* or *avoidance* of a real or false injury or need.'

conscious of that and of its alternative, of two things, of the number two—'dimly'—of the rest of mathematics. Nothing is gained by saying that consciousness may be 'dim': if the rocks are conscious the universe is peculiar: I don't say it isn't. ('Insight' needs fitting in here just as 'will' did before). It seems clear that consciousness is somehow involved in value, because if there was no consciousness we would at any rate feel there was no value. I am not sure that the 'consciousness' issue does not cover the 'will' one: the real puzzle about choosing is that you must be able to choose to choose to choose, as to know that you know that you know. Both regresses are only the reflections from two mirrors got by turning the mirror of consciousness back on itself.

A more literary point is the question why Money-Kyrle's pessimism is so annoying, why one feels he has no right to it. Just the same idea really is behind Powys (T F) who makes it seem [in his novel *Mr Weston's Good Wine*] Eternal Truth, as Buddhists do: one is tempted to talk about 'experience behind it' but I don't believe in Powys' experience of country people—I was beaten by the village idiot as a child, come to think of it, which will do for an 'experience'—I am sure country people in Yorkshire aren't like that, though of very little else about them. His early books are obvious records of shock at finding himself unpopular in the village.[6]

The point is that death-wishes of that sort aren't even impressive unless they drag other things into them, and in the right way. 'The Only Penitent', I have been sorry to have to decide, is the wrong way, though only if you take it seriously. The whole point of the climax is that God takes on himself all sins: this pretends to be a striking and advanced blasphemy but is in fact God's forgiveness of sins. The objection here is that the issue is not made real because there is no real sin in the book. Powys is very capable of describing cruelty and some sort of death-wishes (cruelty to oneself) which he doesn't consider valuable (this alone blows the gaff on his death-cult) but though there are endless little jokes about sin in the book they are all bawdy jokes about things Powys himself doesn't think sinful. The sexual amusement of the village might easily be made to seem sinful by letting in an abortion or what not, but he is careful to make us feel that it is all 'pastoral'. It is disappointing to find him playing this trick because it is typical of the 'nineties. Wilde's Pen Pencil and Poison is trying to make you feel that Wilde too is an 'artistic' sinner—even to prophesying

---

[6] Cf. WE's remarks in 'Proletarian Literature': 'nobody would take the pastoral of T. F. Powys for proletarian, though it really is about workers; his object in writing about country people is to get a simple enough material for his purpose, which one might sum up as a play with Christian imagery backed only by a Buddhist union of God and death' (*P*, 7); and on Powys in 'Death and Its Desires', *A*, 534–56.

his own 'curious courage' in causing his own trial[7]—but he only found this satisfying because he was really talking not about sin but about scandal—he didn't think his sexual habits (anyway) as wicked as poisoning a friend with arsenic to annoy an insurance company. This trick is slavish (that is the 'nineties' 'sense of sin') because it is intellectual dishonesty—he isn't trying to deal with what he thinks right but what is considered right in the drawing-rooms he is pet of, and with his relation to them as a 'wicked artist' from outside. Powys' 'naughty jokes' are a shockingly poor preparation for the enormous issue he tries to raise as a climax—if he put his idea of evil into the book it wouldn't stand the strain. (One can see he is cheating when he makes the parson's wife think of seducing a farmer so as to have a sin which she could confess—this is out of place because it involves the suggestion if not of real sin at least of real pain).

What seems clear as a matter of taste is that this set of ideas, so far from being a straightforward statement about life, is a peculiarly tricky play with symbols. Money-Kyrle doesn't bring it off and the 'pessimism' he arrives at (apart from the nonsense of his last chapter ['The Effects and Value of Psychology']) affects me as 'boyish'. It really seems clear that there are positive satisfactions, and that a majority of the people in this bar, like myself, are receiving them as I write. But I do not see how they can be accounted for if all action is attempt to escape immediate pain: and if there are no such satisfactions there is no complete thing, no whole individual, which you would call valuable.

Yours etc.

W. Empson

Houghton

[7] Oscar Wilde's essay *Pen Pencil and Poison* (1891) is a disquisition on the the artist and poisoner Thomas Griffiths Wainewright which argues that there is 'no essential incongruity between crime and culture'. In the world of aesthetic value, the artist and the murderer can co-exist without clashing: 'The fact of a man being a poisoner is nothing against his prose.' See *The Artist as Critic: Critical Writings of Oscar Wilde*, ed. Richard Ellmann (1970), 320–40. WE refers in particular to the paragraph opening: 'The insurance companies, suspecting the real facts of the case [Wainewright claimed insurance on a policy for the life of his sister-in-law, Helen Abercrombie, whom he had murdered], declined to pay the policy on the technical ground of misrepresentation and want of interest, and, with curious courage, the poisoner entered an action in the Court of Chancery against the Imperial' (334).

TO MICHAEL ROBERTS

Hotel du Nord, Peking
2 April 1933

Dear Roberts,

Sorry not to have finished that little article for you, but I found boiling it down made it grow up, and I don't know my own mind about the thing any longer. Not a simple issue and not obviously an important one. I suppose I didn't inconvenience you, but am sorry if I did.

The chief thing I feel in this very agreeable place is that worship of the state claimed as universal is bound to come back—these great altars like football stadiums will be used again. But what one's 'feelings' are worth is another thing. Quennell wrote a good book [*A Superficial Journey through Tokyo and Peking*] about his & my job, though he oughtn't to have done it.

Bill.

Professor Andrew Roberts

TO JOHN HAYWARD

519 Shirokane Sankocho, Tokyo
12 July [1933]

Dear John,

Have turned up your letter in clearing papers, and forget if I tried to answer it. I am grateful to those who still write to me—though the singular might be used.

I am continually writing to local papers defending Ogden's Basic English. We all start writing to the papers in my profession towards the end of term, when our nerves are worst, and Basic is a fine excuse for a quarrel. But in my heart I don't know whether it is a great invention or a simple rape on the gagged mouth of Britannia.

There was a splendid man lecturing on Old England here, recommended by the Dowager Lady Swaythling, so all the Embassy and many very distinguished foreigners and Japanese women came in their glory. (It is not very difficult for me to write a long cheery newsy letter, with nothing in it about the boy's sex life, because I have to cudgel my brains doing it for my dear mother.) I got as far as the door, not knowing what great forces were at work, but went off on reading the program. Apparently it was a fearful scene of agony. He began by saying 'Well, now the lights are out. So now you can all 'old 'ands'. You could hear a shudder run through the whole audience. Japanese professors ran gleefully to and fro in the interval with notebooks, asking whether 'yours truly' was correct English for 'I myself'? No? was it in frequent use? My informant was sitting next to a grand Japanese lady, got up as they are to look like exquisite dolls with no opinions about anything. But the account of the delights of Bournemouth pier broke through the Oriental reserve altogether. She was squirming in her chair and whispering in English '*Shut* up—oh, shut up'. There you have East really meeting West, and they all had to stay to the end out of respect for the dowager—that is the most puzzling part of it to me—why were they surprised? You could see what it would be from the program.

How horrible if I've written this out to you before. Grim business letter-writing is.

I walked over the hills about six miles to Kamakura yesterday: pine and birch and bamboo, with little winding paths up and down. Very small steep dark green hills looking out over acid light green flat ricefields and the sea. Damp boiling electric sunlight, with wild tiger lilies and great velvet black butterflies. With such a nice young man I picked up at the Municipal Swimming Pool, who is preparing to be a doctor and attempting to teach me the crawl-stroke. It is time I left this country—I have always been afraid of the third year—but there is a very great deal of genuine lazy pleasure to be got out of doing nothing here. One can only like them much when they have nothing to do with literature, and can't like them much without being sorry for them, but indeed there is a great deal to be felt besides glum distaste and contempt.

Well now. Surely I've earned a reply. Send me some potted biographies for the last two years.

The Sansoms—Commercial Secretary—are nice people here. Not that I see them much, or anybody else.

Love

Bill

Write via CANADA: when letters go by Siberia all one's mind is clouded with a doubt, and after one letter is lost the correspondence is broken. But it is fine in a way to think of a real use being found for our letters, warming bandits. Perhaps they are safer in the summer.

King's

TO I. A. RICHARDS

519 Shirokane Sankocho, Tokyo

5 September [1933]

Dear Mr Richards,

The right way to get through the heat seems to be to spend most of it naked and a lot of it sunbathing. I am trying to learn to draw, mainly in the hope of getting to understand faces.

I feel very greedy to have something to do with your dictionary, and send with this some notes on the uses of *honest*. The French honnête homme is no doubt the same, but I doubt if they made such rich satire out of it as our eighteenth century people. One would need to know a lot of languages for such work.[1]

I haven't attempted to distinguish sense from feeling on this list. It seems clear that every 'feeling' must be turned into a sense (translated into one, as you say in that good Psyche review) before it can be listed.[2] In actual use there is not a sharp distinction but a scale between the two, and what one hearer feels as a sense another senses as a feeling. So far as a word is taken to have only one sense the other senses brought into play but not clearly recognised may be classed as feelings. (Not that a sense and a feeling are the same any more than an inside and an outside, but the two go together.) The difficulty is when there is no first order sense (like when there are no first order differentials) and the senses otherwise only feelings are promoted; but you treat this if difficult as a clash of senses. The sense of 'how do you do?' is 'I wish to be civil to you at the start of this meeting'. The feeling of it is a wish to be civil. The purpose is to be civil. The tone *is* civil. I do not see that a dictionary need make these distinctions.

What a dictionary I think should do is to show in some examples a hierarchy of the senses of the word (the N. E. D. breaks into a wail over *nice*, and admits that the senses are always mixed);[3] it should list an

---

[1] Added by WE in the margin: 'This may well be no use as all the amusing senses are pretty well obsolete.' See WE's 'Honest Man', in *SCW*.

[2] IAR wrote, in 'Preface to a Dictionary', *Psyche*, 13 (1933), 10–24; IAR: *SW* (9), 274–93: 'Normally all words have Sense . . . [T]hey represent or assist in representing states of affairs. But they often take their Sense from or through other language functions which are employing them. Thus *beautiful* and *poetry* on most occasions have a Sense which comes to them from the Feeling or Intention they express . . . Such words may and usually do have other Senses (on the same or other occasions) but it is important to recognize how many of the Senses of our words have this origin. *They are translations from the other functions of language.*' If language is 'originally emotive throughout,' he stresses, 'the chief method by which it has grown in subtlety' is by way of 'this process, translation of the other functions into Sense' (291–2).

[3] See 'Nice' in *NED* (1907): 'The precise development of the very divergent senses which this word has acquired in English is not altogether clear. In many examples from the 16th and 17th

example as under one head and say which of the other senses are at work as feelings (for *nice* most examples would come under the vague head of 'approved' that the N. E. D. throws in at the end, but each of the other heads would be present whether or not one could find examples in which that sense was the chief sense); and it would not be out of place in doubtful cases for the dictionary to give arguments in favour of its opinion. Your second list as to the 'feelings' should then become unnecessary; except that where there are several senses at work behind the chief sense one might state as it were the resultant of their forces. Under (1) cases would be listed where sense (1) was the sense and sense (2) the feeling; under (2) cases where sense (2) was the sense and sense (1) the feeling. (3) might give a sense never used as a chief sense—see under (1); where it would appear as a feeling. I don't know whether this would give absurd results. Certainly (3) is different from (1) and (2) in such a case, but not I think different in kind; if it grows it will come above ground and be like them. Feelings imposed by the sense of the context are another matter, and hardly one with which a dictionary can deal. But you may well think this approach inadequate.

It seems very clear that *no* important change in language fails to 'register a change due to factors outside it'; except to a behaviourist who claims that thought is not outside talk. To show that a change is important is to find the factors (which may work only through sound etc.). I feel afraid of an earnest tone about language, because control of its tricks depends on understanding forces really outside it; to say Let's talk about language is like saying Let's have a nice talk, a nice cup of tea; it makes you feel there is nothing to say. (And to translate a feeling into a thought is an achievement both of thought and feeling.) I think you will share this prejudice; one reason for it is that the intellectual has been trained to waste irrelevant forces by irrelevant distinctions (as a diplomat, so to speak), but not as a rule to use his powers without wasting themselves.

I have smacked out a lot of words on my typewriter about Far Eastern Buddhas but need to know the recent work on facial and bodily expression; I have read nothing but Darwin.[4] (Expression of Emotions). Please let me know of a recent book about that with a bibliography; some doctor's book about the muscles twitched in different nervous diseases might be the thing (only English or French for me). I met a charming Russian anthropologist working at Peking since your time who hates Basic because

centuries it is difficult to say in what particular sense the writer intended it to be taken.' Cf. *SCW*, 26–7.

[4] WE was at work on a study of Buddha faces; it was never to be published, but see 'The Faces of Buddha', *The Listener*, 5 Feb. 1936, 238–40; *A*, 573–6.

he thinks it is an attempt at Ethnical Domination (I said he was quite right) who may tell me about that. Why Far Eastern Buddhas have George Robey eyebrows. What forces give the Japanese a *racial* small nose, though a larger nose than normal in them as elsewhere means more independence of character; is the racial force at all allied to the personal one? That sort of thing (and mouths).

Palmer sent me and a lot of other people his reply to your published letter. ['A Denial', *Japan Chronicle*, 23 April 1933, 26] My secret suspicion is that you did say all he claims, and that you are right in complaining at his use of private diplomacy for propaganda. What a dust. What is needed in Japan is for things to be made easy for the *teacher* (textbooks etc) and a rough but tolerable system for taking the Middle School pupil on to guessing at a decent version of a flowery passage from Ruskin set for translation at the end of a five year course. Mrs Sansom, by the way, now going to India for the Conference, I have made a convert to Basic; but her delightful husband claims only to know at sight whether a teacher is or is not Basic. (It is odd to me how donnish our diplomats here are, as far as I am let see them; though of course it is the don bourgeoning [*sic*]. Such a College note about the whole Embassy Compound. The buildings look like blottingpaper [?cottages?] for a grandiose part of [?Hampstead?].)

[W. Empson]

Magdalene

TO JOHN HAYWARD

519 Shirokane Sankocho, Tokyo
8 October [1933]

Dear John,

Letters are no use, but I shall write a page back to show I was glad to get yours. 'Too much rice' (the Chinese rickshaw boys' name for illness in general—I don't know whether they would use it for starvation) has been grown in Japan this year, and the farmers are badly off. My young woman was expecting to have to sell herself to a German business man to support her parents, but a brother-in-law has rallied and we are all right. I made no offers but bought her some clothes.

This is the best weather in Japan, and the suicide season. There was a sporting man who jumped into the Oshima crater (the fashionable place for it just now) shouting out to the holiday crowds 'Let's all do it: come on with me'. It would hold most of the nation, I believe.

The Fleet is in, and I was taken drinking with some Able-Bodies: considered a charity to take them to the right beer-halls. One knew how blue-eyed and idealist and cultured they were, but it is stirring to an exile. Has anything been heard of Malcolm Lowrie [*sic*], the best of that Experiment lot, who wrote short stories about the sea?

I am trying to have a book of essays ready when I come home [*SVP*], but it will be quite dull.

Do you share with me a suspicion that Major Douglas is right about economics?[1] Of course he doesn't know, but nor does anybody.

Yours

Bill.

King's

TO SYLVIA TOWNSEND WARNER*

519 Shirokane Sankocho, Tokyo
10 October [1933]

SHIROKANE SANKOCHO (means thrice-brilliant platinum)

Dear Sylvia Townshend [sic],

This is the best time of year in Japan, a glittering sun in decently cool weather with a very high sky. You don't really get nothing but Autumn Tints as most trees are pines. It is perhaps better later on, though, when you are quite safe from them, and the rice fields have settled down as rather crisp looking stubble. It is only then that the country isn't irritatingly like Japanese prints.

Also the season for suicide, one of the national sports. There was a particularly sporting man who while throwing himself into the Oshima crater (on an island you go to for holidays—the most popular place for it) shouted out to all the trippers 'Come on—let's all do it'. The crater would in fact hold most of the nation. But the police take a graver view and put up little black-and-white notices—'Your country needs you'. 'Think again.' Most of my pupils are somehow sticky with a damp infantile gloom, even when giggling. If they were badly beaten after a long exhausting

---

[1] C. H. Douglas (1879–1952), economic theorist, propounded the theory of 'social credit' (his notion was that prices for goods might be kept lower than actual costs by supplying more money to consumers, or subsidies to producers). His works include *Economic Democracy* (1920) and *Credit-Power and Democracy* (1920). The Labour Party discountenanced the theory in the 1920s, but it was promulgated in the 1930s, in the *New Age* and *New English Weekly*, and in Douglas's own organ *Social Credit*, as a panacea for the Depression. Ezra Pound proselytized for Douglas's ideas. 'As for economics, I know nothing about them,' wrote WE to C. K. Ogden at about this time. 'The Douglas people seem obviously right in their criticisms and very dickey in their plans. How can Sargent Florence say that there would always be enough work under any degree of mechanisation? It seems a verbal contradiction.' (*McMaster*)

war—which they are asking for—they might really take to dying out like the people of the smaller islands further south. It is very much of a South Sea Island, though one mustn't tell them so—they are always in and out of the water, what with the baths and the swimming, their houses are obviously meant for warmer climates (it is most strange to ski past cottages with the snow piling up onto the rice-straw matting, whole walls open to the wind, and children lying teasing each other under quilts) and all the colours they use, even the clashing pinks, are somehow under-water colours, colours of jelly-fish, like the textures.

—This is becoming a Special-Correspondent letter, which is never any good. Shall I tell you about the great Basic English war? I am a Basic Fan. The most feverish passions have been excited about the thing. Towards the end of term, in the profession, we all begin writing eager nerve-wracked letters to the newspapers. There is an Official Adviser [Harold E. Palmer] to the Japanese Government; a very busy man in a remarkable position: his advice has never been taken. He is very like Ogden, and unfortunately they met; there was some kind of explosion: it's still not clear what, though they have both given their versions of it in most ample detail. But the heaviest fighting at present is going on over what Richards (I. A.) said to Palmer (Official Adviser) privately in 1930; enormous typescript private letters onto dozens of carbon papers keep being circulated to all combatants. I have had Ogden send me a Blue Print of a Machiavellian letter which I was to pretend originated from me, in a style that wouldn't deceive a child. (*This is private* as we say in the controversy). The whole letter (from him) is usually headed *Private*: then *Very Secret* and *For Your Personal Use* are employed like 'bloody' as a sort of punctuation.

This seems rather boring and foolish now I look it over, but it is really my chief interest in the teaching business—the only thing that might do some good if they would use it.

I shan't write verse till I leave this country, but am sending you a thing ['Letter V'] I wrote in my first month here, before the clogging effect had got to work.

Yours sincerely

  Bill Empson

Reading

TO CHIYOKO HATAKEYAMA*[1]

519 Shirokane Sankocho, Tokyo
23 December [1933]

Dear Miss Hatakeyama,

Yes, very reasonable to translate your own where you feel easy about altering.

You keep jumping from iambs to dactyls, which only seems like prose in free verse but in a strict form has a very strong effect on the reader: that I think is the chief reason why one can't write good English free verse without practice in the much more *exacting* rhythms of the strict forms (I don't mean harder to do well, but worse when they are a little wrong).

I hope you will come and have tea here if you are in Tokyo. I shall be away ski-ing for about ten days after Dec 28, otherwise at home.

Yours sincerely
W. Empson

Actually as a way of translating I should say that Arthur Waley's method with vers libre was much the best. The thing is that we learn vers libre from metre.

TO RINTARO FUKUHARA*

519 Shirokane Sankocho, Tokyo
28 February [1934]

Dear Fukuhara,

Hope I didn't bore you the other night by getting so childishly drunk. We went on and ate Chinese food after you left.

This letter has just come from the man who edited New Signatures.[1] He is an angular ugly-ish Scotch sort of young man, very steady, no vices, rather lacking in joie de vivre for my taste, but of course very well-informed about English literature and I should think well able to make Japanese students understand him.

---

[1] I am indebted to Peter Robinson for making available a transcription of the correspondence between WE and Chiyoko Hatakeyama (1902–82). See glossary for Robinson's ground-breaking articles on the WE–Hatakeyama relationship.

[1] Michael Roberts wrote on 7 Feb. 1934 to ask after a job in Japan, with a salary big enough to support two people. 'I have been sacked from my school job on a ridiculous charge of undermining the religious opinions of my pupils.' He had just produced 'a book of propagandist-criticism' and felt 'pretty well ashamed of it now that it is printed. I should be glad to get out of the country, if only to escape from the role of poetic uncle or big brother which has been forced upon me ever since New Signatures: I'm not allowed to grow up myself . . . The fact is, I want to go and climb mountains for a time: Richards says there are quite entertaining ones in Japan.'

Of course it's a private letter which you will treat as such. I know no reason for not recommending him heartily. The *two* people probably means a wife—I don't know. He is I should say thirty.

Please let me know what you think, and who else I might recommend him to.

Yours very sincerely

W. Empson

Mrs Fukuhara

TO CHIYOKO HATAKEYAMA*

There follows an undated fragment of a letter by WE, possibly written after the sole meeting between WE and Chiyoko Hatakeyama on 26 Mar. 1934.

[. . .] about life is to keep a wide variety of interests so that you can keep moving from one to another before they get stale, don't you think? Most of the poetry you have shown me is very introspective—more than you are in your own life, I should say. English poetry is getting into a sort of knot because so many things are said as well (and more likely to be read) in prose, and that makes it introspective: I don't know how it is with Japanese poetry. Of course in a foreign language it is hideously difficult to write verse with a variety of *sorts* of feeling in it: but in your Japanese verse it might be a good thing to try to show the clash of different philosophies, and social comedy, and quote lines of poetry by people quite different from you that you have thought specially good,—in fact take to being 'clever' like the moderns. The intellect is an escape from emotion when it doesn't have a good effect on the emotions afterwards, which it often does.

This may easily be bad advice.

Not that I think your poetry is mere expression of emotion empty of thought; it isn't: but that writing about subjects far away from oneself is often more use in the end.

Yours sincerely

W. Empson

A Lunatic Woman [by Chiyoko Hatakeyama]

From where your madness, young mother?
'I ate up the law that held my boy to smother.
I stole a shawl to hide my darling,
But the shawl with its spell hid my boy in the darkling.

I saw him not in my prison home.
He puffed away with the spell as it began to gloam.
Ah, almighty judges, you declare I killed my boy?
Oh, no, I loved him, loved him, my loveliest toy!'

I see your madness whence, poor mother!
But may there not be some heaven farther
Than Heaven, where our darkness is light [,]
Our blames are praises, the left is the right?

WE suggested a few emendations to this draft poem, and went so far as to draft variant versions of the first stanzas on the other side of the paper:

Whence your madness, young mother?
I ate the law my boy would smother.
I stole a shawl to hide my dear.
It was bewitched. He is not here.

Was not in prison with me. Darkness fell
And he puffed away like smoke, under a spell.
He was my life, he was my joy—
The judges say I killed my boy.

WE notes alongside his effort: 'My attempt is very nasty, now that I look at it later.' He comments on the problems with her poem: 'Your difficulty is that you use poetical and everyday words alike—the poetical word needs to come only where it is wanted.' About the final verse: 'The rhythm needs to be strong at the end to make the comfort seem serious. You make it run quickly and jingle.' Finally: 'To a Christian she can look for comfort in Heaven—the heaven farther than heaven is I suppose Buddhist?'

TO CHIYOKO HATAKEYAMA

517 Shirokane Sankocho
Monday
[n.d., but possibly sent in an envelope franked 9. 5. 5 and 9. 5. 7 (5 and 7 May 1934), and on which WE wrote: 'Sorry to be so slow. I got your letter as I was posting mine.']

Dear Miss Hatakeyama,
All I meant about Japanese poetry was that to convey a clash between

philosophies in poetry (because you can't lecture about either of the two, they have to be hinted) is so difficult that you had probably better try it in Japanese poetry first—I thought you were still writing Japanese poetry too?

I knew there was some play of doctrine at the end of the Mad Woman [the poem above], and what you say about the ideal state of Heaven not being essentially moral—anyway not a matter of keeping or having kept rules—is no doubt true; but you [end of fragment]

TO CHIYOKO HATAKEYAMA

[No address]
[n.d. ?June 1934]

Dear Miss Hatakeyama,

I haven't decided about the time when I go, but expect to stay in Tokyo until then. I sent a postcard saying that I would be very grateful if you gave me records of the 6th symphony, which perhaps you didn't get. It was very good of you: there is no need.

I wrote a book called Seven Types of Ambiguity (Chatto and Windus) but don't think you'd like it. I don't know a good book on prosody.

It seems certain that women writers *don't* get good effects *only* by making themselves womanly—Emily Bronte was as 'unwomanly' as George Sand though in a different way. Jane Austen accepted the limitations of her life as a basis for art, but she depended on a strong 'catty' side that you could hardly call 'womanly'. I wouldn't worry about that if I were you.

If anything I should say your art was too womanly rather than not enough.

Yours sincerely
W. Empson

TO I. A. RICHARDS

519 Shirokane Sankocho, Tokyo
[n.d. 1934]

Dear Mr Richards,

Do you know I have collected a large sheaf, in throwing away old papers, of letters begun to you and not finished. What a disease.

Thanks very much for the *Basic Rules*—I wrote an article round it for the Basic Monthly, but Daniels[1] wants it kept for some future paper. It helps to

---

[1] F. J. Daniels taught at Hokkaido Imperial University.

get rid of the feeling that Basic only suits one philosophy, of Cambridge type.[2]

Imbecile of me not to have asked you for those books a year ago: it is too late now to try and get them discovered and sent out, while one is still in reach of the statues.

It still seems to me that the ing-eds in Basic ought to be used as regular verbs on the analogy of *seem*—I have never heard any argument why that should be *harder* than the present ones—nearly all learners start from a verb system and this one is regular. (Or anyway as nearly regular as the ing-ed system.) This would take all the *crotchety* feeling out of the system and make it possible to talk easily. (This would be the last stage in learning.) In fact if Basic succeeds I think that will happen spontaneously. Of course it doesn't make you able to say any more and will would [*sic*] remove the 'no-verb' advertisement, but the feeling here (I think very unfortunately) is that Basic has been advertised unscrupulously. Still now it's got just so far the only thing to do seems to be to back it up as it stands.

Odd to see Eliot saying about your sincerity ritual that 'birth and death can't be odd unless you have some conception of how man would naturally come into the world'.[3] In the first place of course *any* way of connecting mind and matter, the individual and the universe, freedom and necessity would be an odd enough thing to contemplate. But the fact of psychology goes the other way: what happens is that the religions and philosophies are spun out of and made exciting by a native feeling of the human mind, once it starts reflecting, that its situation is queer (like Keynes' discussion about whether the universe can be said to be improbable).

I cleaned up that essay on your Theory of Value a bit and added more, but it is very amateur. It seems clear that summing the impulses satisfied (and probabilities of satisfying perhaps) in a specious present is quite a different process from summing them through a whole life—for one thing

[2] WE wrote a review, in Basic English, of two works by IAR, *Basic Rules of Reason* (1933) and *Basic in Teaching: East and West* (1935), for *The Spectator*, 14 Jun. 1935 (*A*, 229–31): see letter to *The Spectator* below, 2 Aug. 1935. See further WE's paper on 'Basic and Communication' (1939), *SSS*, 161–9.

[3] TSE, in his lecture 'The Modern Mind'—in *The Use of Poetry and the Use of Criticism: Studies in the Relation of Criticism to Poetry in England* (1933), 121–42; reprinted in IAR: *SW* (10), 212–28—took IAR to task for the deficiencies of his theory of value, specifically his apotheosis of the salvific character of a secular poetry. IAR's 'theological ideas' can in fact be determined from his writing in *Practical Criticism*, claimed TSE; 'the intense religious seriousness of Mr Richards' attitude towards poetry' amounts to 'nothing less than a regimen of Spiritual Exercises'. Citing IAR's recommendation that one of the wonders worth contemplating is 'The facts of birth and of death, in their inexplicable oddity', TSE commented (in a citation that WE paraphrases): 'I cannot see why the facts of birth and of death should appear odd in themselves, unless we have a conception of some other way of coming into the world and of leaving it, which strikes us as more natural' (220–1). On relations between IAR and TSE, see IAR: *SW* (10), pp. x–li.

in the second case they are no longer there when you sum them, for another they are not interacting in the same way. That line would take you on to questioning the reality of the permanent individual, I suppose. For another they are not interacting in the same way.

A feeble attempt at putting (x) for 'feeling (= sense not in focus of consciousness) of x' and x? for 'feeling (= emotional element without the sense) of x' left me uncertain whether you can put (x?) and (x)? and whether they are different.

I am just convalescent after the end of the academical year, which I haven't yet got used to, and hope for some ski-ing this week.

My respects to Mrs Richards.

Yours

W. Empson

Shall go round by India in the heat which they say doesn't kill you, and do a few sights, then come home.

I have kept this senselessly for some months. I shall send you my nagging little *honest* if I can and ask for your opinion of it. I hope to see you this year—you aren't going out of England then, are you?

Magdalene

TO I. A. RICHARDS

71 Marchmont Street [London]

[n.d.] Tuesday

Dear Richards,

Honest is going on slowly.[1] I have got clear about one main notion— terrible how long it takes one to see the obvious. The main thing with these queer words is not a new sense or emotion from the interaction of the two senses but a new *proposition*. Take the nineteenth century delicate (1) refined (2) sickly—other senses (luxurious) have been dropped out and there is no obvious relation between the surviving pair. You then get an age which finds the word useful and gives the *connection* of the two senses the *chief* stress.[2]

[1] IAR wrote to TSE in Oct.–Nov. 1934: 'William Empson is back in 71 Marchmont Street again and has just sent me the first draft of his new book—which I find intoxicatingly good. A Dictionary article on the word Honest' (IAR: *SL*, 84). See 'Honest Man' in *SCW*.

[2] IAR responded with this note: '*Honest*. Yes you are quite right: the important thing is the condensed proposition in the word in its double simultaneous use. It is obvious as you say: in fact one is always almost explicitly saying that's how it is when one uses any of these words. I remember after listing varieties of *Beauty* & *Truth* noticing how—in addition to the plain assertions one got with B3 T2 etc—one got a very numerous set of alternative assumptions in the course of keeping B3 distinct from B4 or B2 as the case might be. It all seems rather interesting. I'm not sure (haven't tried) whether any two senses of such words give a proposition (false or true) or how much nonsense arises. I think I'll try tomorrow.' (*Houghton*)

1 = 2 Refined women *are* sickly 'Refined women are disgusted by the body and tightlaced'—or 'women are such fools that you can't make them think till you make them ill'. Various *causes* may be implied but what you list is the insistence on the connection as a general and natural step. '=' meaning what 'is' would do. Of course you list the equation only when it is there—many contradictions of sense don't do it.

One might then go through the XIX definitions of beauty in the M of M [*The Meaning of Meaning*, by IAR and Ogden] and deduce 1/2. 18. 19 propositions about the arts (not about *beauty*) by taking them in pairs.

I am relieved at having got to this; it seems to be what I was trying to think about. A mere new sense of a word is obviously less powerful. Let me know if you think it all nonsense.

I enclose another bit of the *Bacchus* poem. There ought to be a lot more mythological stuff if I can do it.

Respects to Mrs Richards.

Bill Empson

Magdalene

SCRUTINY, 4: 1 (June 1935)

A rejoinder to a review of IAR's *Coleridge on Imagination* (1934) by FRL[1]: 'Dr Richards, Bentham and Coleridge', *Scrutiny*, 3: 4 (Mar. 1935), 382–402; in IAR: *SW* (10), 336–57. IAR wrote to his wife on 8 Mar. 1935: 'I'm writing to Empson. It's really very nice of him to deal with F. R. L. so.' (Magdalene). FRL wrote to R. G. Cox on 4 Apr. 1935: 'A nasty & stupid letter from Empson, concerning my Richards review; obviously written in collusion with R., who doesn't propose to expose himself personally. We probably shan't print it. Then the story will go round that Empson wrote a devastating reply which we were afraid to print.' See IAR: *SW* (10), li–lxx.

---

[1] F. R. Leavis (1895–1978), literary critic and university teacher, was an early advocate of WE's verse and critical writings, though by the 1930s he turned against WE (and IAR). Educated at Emmanuel College, Cambridge, where he read History and English, he became in 1932 Director of Studies in English and a Fellow of Downing College, where he was appointed Reader in 1954 (at the age of 59). Rigorous and polemical, moralistic and judgemental, discriminatory, and exclusivist (WE came to think him narrow-minded and sanctimonious), Leavis was yet a remarkable, and remarkably influential, critic. His works include *New Bearings in English Poetry* (1932), which incidentally praised WE's work; *Revaluation* (1936); *Education and the University* (1943); *The Great Tradition* (1948); *The Common Pursuit* (1952); *D. H. Lawrence: Novelist* (1955); and *English Literature in Our Time and the University* (1969). In 1932 he founded, with his associates, the quarterly *Scrutiny* (until 1953): WE contributed to the periodical 'Marvell's Garden' (vol. 1 (Dec. 1932), 236–40) and 'Proletarian Literature' (vol. 3 (Mar. 1935), 332–8).

Sirs,

Everybody must feel unwilling to enter the feverish atmosphere of Dr
Leavis's quarrels, but someone ought to state the case against his review of
Dr Richards' *Coleridge on Imagination*. We are told that the book does
'bluntly, nothing' towards the detailed linguistic analysis of poetry, and an
answer must attempt a summary of the book.

There is a strictly literary point, supported by examples (nowhere
referred to by Dr Leavis): that the mature poetry of Coleridge and
Wordsworth depends on an interplay between, or a uniting of, two
opposed views of Nature. Philosophy comes in because this process was
partly cause of, partly caused by, the philosophical ideas Coleridge
developed when he first revolted against Hartley; it is no use for the literary
critic to ignore the connection. The process was also discussed by Coleridge in terms of psychology, and his ideas here, the book claims, are still
valuable apart from his poetry. Many of the psychological ideas he
developed and based his work upon after his revolt against the Hartleian
dynasty of psychologists have now come to be accepted by that same
dynasty; we are given examples. One of these is the Fancy–Imagination
distinction, and there is a long defence of it; when Dr Leavis complains of
the triviality of the examples and the evasiveness of the results he does not
know that these are Coleridge's results and Coleridge's examples, which
Dr Richards is only trying to defend against the intervening attacks.

This seems enough to keep a small book from doing 'bluntly, nothing'.
It may be true that the author fails in 'supporting, when they appear, some
serious critical journals' (p. 392) and he may even be 'lighthearted', but
these personal faults need not make his book quite empty. I should agree
with Dr Leavis so far as he says that Dr Richards is too content to start
hares and had better have worked out his material more fully; this does not
account for so many pages of anathema. In saying that the 'poetic function' is of great importance to society Dr Richards is obviously not denying that the society must be such as can support it and be affected by it; he
is merely talking about something else; and granted this point his 'pre-
posterously extravagant' hope (p. 391) for a quasi-political salvation from
literature is just that of Dr Leavis. The review is dimly aware of this, and
then says it can't be true, or the man would fluff up his feathers and
perpetually scream at the Book Society.

One or two minor points. Dr Richards is shown to be always insensitive
as a prose writer because he calls the Old Coleridge the Highgate Spell-
binder, not realizing that this implies something disagreeable (too comic to
answer, but try Carlyle on the Old Coleridge). The slight on Mr Eliot

seems imaginary; his work is referred to by implication in the context as 'the best criticism of today' and for that reason called in evidence. The motorbus (p. 390) is obviously not Science, whose intellectual constructs are not its brute facts. I am not even sure that Dr Richards disagrees with Dr Leavis about the Immortality Ode (p. 399), and he was not 'summing it up' but answering an attack by Coleridge on some of its lines; the suggestion that he is proved to have no taste in poetry by his failure to say that he agrees with Dr Leavis is ridiculous. On Dr Leavis's logical point it seems sufficient to read (p. 386) 'result in a Nature (iv) through which our power of control over part of Nature (i) is increasing by embarrassing leaps and bounds.' And there is a curious paragraph on page 385. Dr Richards is first blamed for introducing his pupils to things they probably did not know about before, such as the term 'nominalism'. Immediately after, as a destruction of his pretensions, 'one is left also with the impression of having been reminded of a number of commonplace philosophic considerations from which strict thinking might start.' This seems no bad ambition for a teacher.

Yours sincerely,

W. Empson

[No comment on the above seems necessary. Mr Empson is referred back to his texts.—F. R. L.][2]

TO CHIYOKO HATAKEYAMA

This is a literal translation, by Peter Robinson with Chikayo Saito and Eichi Hara, of Chiyoko Hatakeyama's poem in Japanese, 'Baka'. Her own English version—which is now lost—was completed by 15 Jan. 1935.

Fool

A great fool who cannot hate the others,
look!
He strides through the town.

Eyes sagacious-looking
Mouths distorted by common sense,
the object of their ridicule is just his individual body.

As if there were no vault of heaven,
as if there were no world beyond the sight,
people's eyes and mouths

---

[2] This published comment was appended to WE's essay by FRL.

demand an object to despise,
to set in the frame of their common sense.

Eyes swarming like maggots,
lips laughing like poison flowers,
look!
Notwithstanding these, among them
a great fool is strolling around.

For him, the eyes of people are bright stars,
to his ears which are unclean
the derisive laughter sounds like delicate music,
and he goes on in dream-visions
staring far away beyond the sky.

The fool who doesn't know how to hate the others,
look!
He strides through the town.
[8 Nov. 1934]

> 71 Marchmont Street, London WC1
> 9 July [1935]

Dear Miss Hatakeyama,

I got your last letter and thought I would 'let the matter drop', which was rude and cowardly of me: then this letter sent such a good poem ['Fool' above] that I wrote one of my own from it which I enclose. I have sent it to a paper as yours *translated* by me, which I oughtn't to have done without your permission. I say 'one of my own' though the ideas are all yours, and that is really the trouble.

It is no use 'repairing' your teacher because in a way he was always a cheat. I wanted to see more translations of your Japanese poetry and thought the originals must be very good, but I never really believed (1) that you had a chance of writing good English poetry—good enough for you really to want to do it: you might have a kind of success but not with the best public. I know that medieval Europeans wrote fairly good Latin (and Japanese, Chinese) poems but both were using their normal medium, the only one they had been trained in. It is almost impossible to write good poetry in a foreign language, and you haven't even favourable conditions. And I never really believed (2) that my 'teaching' was anything but putting my sort of poetry onto yours. Of course there were some mistakes of grammar but as poems they had better contain mistakes—the English reader must be made to see that Japanese ways of feeling must be guessed at, not English ones. If you were English and wrote as you do I should want to make many of the same 'corrections' and you would not let me do it, so that the personal reasons against 'correction' are as strong as the ones of national tradition.

What I would like to do is this—not out of good nature or because I am sorry to have behaved badly, but because it would interest me and I think I might do it well—if you will send me 'corrected' versions of your poems, with some more English poems and direct ['simple' deleted] translations from your Japanese poems, I will try to do a small book of 'translations' and get it published in England. Perhaps that is no use to you. But I shall think myself lucky to get such good material to work on if you let me do it.

Yours very sincerely

W. Empson.

The Fool.

Describe the fool who knows
All but his foes.
Wading through tears striding the covered sneers
And against tide, he goes.

Delighting in the freedom of those bounds
Your scorn and even your reason are his aid;
It is an absolute health that will not heal his wounds,
Wisdom's the charger mounts him above shade;

Hanged by suspense and eternally delayed.

'Your eyes are corpse-worms.
Your lips are poison-flowers'.
They become stars, the eyes he thus transforms;
All the lips' whispers are cool summer showers.

A hand-written line runs from 'They become stars . . .' to the following note:

He gives them their dignity (extracts beauty from works of art made of his hatreds). I think you meant this but I'm not quite sure. You see how we stand—if you didn't mean it I don't mean to alter my translation. But for the book you would of course check the translations and stop me from misrepresenting you too seriously.

Perhaps the main difference I want to make in translating is to concentrate the ideas into fewer words—a thing present day English poetry is very anxious to do, perhaps too much.

THE SPECTATOR, 2 August 1935, 191: 'Basic English'

WE reviewed IAR, *Basic Rules of Reason* (1933) and *Basic in Teaching: East and West* (1935), for *The Spectator*, 14 Jun. 1935 (see *A*, 229–31). IAR reacted in a letter to his wife (15 Jun. 1935): 'Empson has done a long thing in *Basic* in the Spectator. He is an ass: this not being at all the moment or the way . . . and his Basic has one or two slips in it . . .' (*Magdalene*)

C. M. Cather responded from Port Said to WE's review with a letter published as 'The Rôle of an International Language' in *The Spectator*, 26 Jul. 1935, 154. His objections included these remarks: 'Mr. W. Empson mentions its usefulness as an auxiliary international language. But surely for international use we cannot accept anything short of a full language. For example, one which all international organizations could adopt as their only official language, in which *The Spectator* would appear as fully satisfying as at present, and in which the ordinary citizen in a foreign country could converse with the natives, socially and otherwise, as naturally on all subjects as he can in his own language at home.'

Sir,—Mr Cather says as a point against Basic English that 'for international use we cannot accept anything but a full language. For example one which all international organizations could adopt as their official language, in which *The Spectator* would appear as fully satisfying as at present, and in which the ordinary citizen in a foreign country could converse with the natives, socially and otherwise, as naturally on all subjects as he can in his own language at home.' This is merely an ideal; the question is what available roads go towards it. Basic would do very well as the official language of an organization, probably with an extra list of twenty-five nouns; it would seem quite 'natural', e.g., for the notes of the week and the political articles of *The Spectator*. It would be clumsy, of course, for jokes, delicacies of description, suggestions of *milieu*, things that you cannot do in a foreign language anyhow without learning it to a rare perfection or making points of your mistakes. So the word 'natural' begs a question: Basic gives a natural English for careful plain statement, but that is not always the natural way to talk. Certainly if you want to talk English naturally in the sense 'like a native' you must learn it, and Basic is a good first step. But the claim that Basic itself is a dignified and rational means of expression, quickly learned and at once widely understood, is not refuted by the phrase 'we cannot accept it.'

Yours, &c.,

W. Empson

TO I. A. RICHARDS

71 Marchmont Street, WC1
Wednesday [October 1935]

Dear Richards,

Would you let me know if you got a rather superficial article on Emotions In Words I sent off to you some weeks ago, putting Please Forward on it, which was probably unwise. No reason why you should have answered yet, but if it is lost I had better start writing it up again from the scraps, as the Criterion was to have it by Nov. 1.[1] I disliked it when it had gone off.

I am puzzling over a book on ethics by Laird;[2] such a queer topic, as a Chair. Not sure if I told you the little article about splitting Buddha photographs came back, some time ago, all right; I have just summoned up energy to send it to the Burlington [Magazine], which is unlikely to want it. The next thing about *honest* would be to face the jungle of derivatives of *sense*. One thing that can't be put in a formula there is the 'importance' of the word in the sense liability to be used in preference to other words—*sense* as 'good sense' bounds up at the Restoration, but that use of the word is quite clearly knocking about before with its full performance. Not sure if a rise to favour like that can always be classed as an equation suddenly imposed—the equation idea probably has to be stretched before you can say so.

Hope you had good climbing. Regards to Mrs Richards.

Yours very sincerely

Bill Empson

Magdalene

[1] 'Feelings in Words' was first published in *Criterion*, 15: 59 (Jan. 1936), 183–99; expanded for *SCW*, 1–38.

Houghton retains this sheet of autograph comments by IAR:

'On Feelings *in* Words.

'(I always have a creepy feeling of *déja écrit* about this topic—very likely in the past I've scribbled you something to the same effect, or else read it in your works!)

'It occurs to me that synonyms should be a good main material for you. Something is usually different in their meanings even when senses and implications tally very closely. It might be that the implications (for different contexts) had different prominences (back of the mind etc) & that that gave different *obviousnesses* to the different words in the synonym group for any given purpose etc etc etc. One could still call this prominence either to emotions or implications. So a writer who keeps his verbal selection field well lit would be aware of these things and in his choice would show us that it was so. etc etc etc.

'But a less conscious user might merely be aware that word A had tricks whereas word B hasn't (without recalling at all what tricks they are). Much as we size up a dog as pattable.

'*Content* : *satisfy* was the instance I was thinking about but it also illustrates your tension story *if the metaphor is allowed* to separate out into tenor & vehicle sides.'

[2] John Laird (1887–1946), Regius Professor of Moral Philosophy at the University of Aberdeen. WE reviewed Laird's *An Enquiry into Moral Notions* (1935), on the 'right' and the 'good', in 'Three Ethics', *The Spectator*, 29 Nov. 1935; *A*, 571–2.

TO I. A. RICHARDS

71 Marchmont Street, W. C. 1
[n.d. October/November 1935]

Dear Richards

Thanks very much. You can keep your Tone; and your Gesture; I want a monosyllable. My '£' is now called a 'Mood', which gives a suggestion of grammar (as in Subjunctive M) which goes all right. The only pain is to lose the assonance of 'cosy tone'. (All the same it ['Feelings in Words'] is a superficial essay.)

Very sorry about Mrs Richards; I wish I had known in time, to take her a book or something.

As to where we differ, I fancy I want language to be *correct* (English or something) and you want it to work well (enough). That seems why I want lexicography and don't jump at *glare* (flare glitter) which [are] obviously made words, but we have them.

It seems fairly urgent for somebody to understand pronunciation; I have just been to a show of the Grierson Post Office films, where the feelings in the filming are entirely contradicted by the appalling voice of the announcer.[1] I can't endure the Wireless news announcer voice—it is a favourite slave keeping the other slaves from violence—and there seems to be no spontaneous feeling against it among people who talk well themselves. Ogden's friend [Professor Daniel Jones] who partly caused the B.B.C. accent apparently claims there isn't one. Palmer of Tokyo has I believe done some decent work on spoken English; it is a thing I would like to know something about, and would be glad, as always, if you could tell me of a nice book.

Bill Empson

Magdalene

IAR responded to the preceding letter with an undated letter from Magdalene (Oct./Nov. 1935); his comments included the following:

Dear Bill,
    No, I don't think 'correct' <—> 'working well (enough)' is the difference. I've just lately been taking down and reassembling all the

---

[1] The GPO Film Unit grew out of the Empire Marketing Board film unit, which was set up by John Grierson with the assistance of Basil Wright. See *Grierson on Documentary*, ed. Forsyth Hardy (1945); and Kevin Jackson, *Humphrey Jennings* (2004). The most celebrated production of the Film Unit was the documentary *Night Mail* (1935), directed by Wright and Harry Watt, with a verse-commentary by W. H. Auden, music by Benjamin Britten, and a sound track by Alberto Cavalcanti.

notions of 'correct' I've been able to think of or find. All most complex. I wish you'd try jotting down what you take yours to consist of. It may be a new brand—but these 'correct's can't easily be described without a plan of the rest of the car, e.g. the whole language machine and its links up with Laird's queer subject. It's true though that I want to be *explicitly* normative in my discussion though only with reference to norms which are recognised to be inapplicable as formulae—I mean they can't be formulated so specifically, for specific cases, that they will discriminate for us. (Ends of *Practical Criticism* stuff.) You, perhaps, have a different range of services from language you care about, while being equally normative. It seems likely, doesn't it? that in the subject any difference in conception will generate different purposes and *vice versa*.

Glad I can keep Tone and Gesture, it would have looked a little silly. *Mood* seems good. If subjunctive etc. comes well forward. I turned it down because of 'happy' 'irritable' moods, but they needn't interfere.

I wonder if a nice book, or one which might introduce you to one, wouldn't be Leonard Bloomfield, *Language*.[2] Terrific bibliography. You might find him interesting on flare, glare, gloat, stare, dimmer, flimmer, flicker, etc pp. 156 & 245 etc. But on BBC voices, isn't it partly the fact that they are trying to be, and to an unusual degree are, pure of 'accent' and, worse still, of individual irregularity that makes them so horrid? Like new pennies and standardized *decorative* articles? They have to pass a test, whence complacency, and the air of being 'it' and a model. And couldn't that effect accrue to 'the standard voice' very soon, however it did in fact talk [. . .]

I fancy that 'slave', etc., implications are just political positions, voices being pre-eminently capable of assuming any things of that sort that anyone likes to put on to them. . . . [IAR: *SL*, 92]

I don't think *Feelings in Words* is superficial in any bad sense. It doesn't pretend to go deeper than it does. And for God's sake isn't it time that something 'superficial' was properly done?

Houghton/IAR: SL, 92–3

TIMES LITERARY SUPPLEMENT, 7 December 1935, 838: 'Some Versions of Pastoral'

'Pastoral and Proletarian: In search of "All possible meanings" ' (*TLS*, 30 November 1935, 798) praised *SVP* as 'an exciting and stimulating book run disappointingly to seed'. What it lacked was a 'normative principle', a

---

[2] WE criticized Leonard Bloomfield's 'mechanist' or behaviourist linguistic theory, as proposed in *Language* (1935), in an essay entitled 'The Need for a Translation Theory in Linguistics', *Psyche* 15 (1935), 188–97; reprinted as 'Appendix III' of *SCW*.

sense of relevance in the face of the multiplication of meanings. 'Half its present pages might have been cut with advantage, and the remaining substance expanded . . . into something quite different from the mental gymnastics which ought to have been sacrificed.' The first chapter, on proletarian literature, is nevertheless 'a sustained piece of criticism':

> The chapter is brilliant; and shows signs of having been written after the rest of the book. He ends the chapter with the words:—
>
>> In the following essays I shall try to show, roughly in historical order, the ways in which the pastoral process of putting the complex into the simple (in itself a great help to the concentration needed for poetry) and the resulting social ideas have been used in English literature . . . The book is very far from adequate to such a theme; taken widely the formula might include all literature, and taken narrowly much of the material is irrelevant. Probably the cases I take are the surprising rather than the normal ones, and once started on an example I follow it without regard to the unity of the book.
>
> The last statement is, unfortunately, only too true. It seems to us a surprising admission . . . For straightway Mr Empson proceeds to suffocate his pregnant theme under a vast mountain of 'possible meaning' . . . He is determined to be impregnable.

Overall (the review ended), the book is governed by a 'radical scepticism'.

Sir,—Without having any personal ground of complaint against your fair and often cordial review of my book 'Some Versions of Pastoral' I should like to ask space for an explanation that seems to raise a wider issue. Your reviewer thought that a fundamental philosophy was presumed by my sort of criticism or the faults of my book; it was 'radical scepticism' as against 'the normative principle', or Cambridge as against Oxford, or anyway something that went to the roots. But when he came to point out some of the faults of the book he very fairly quoted the sentences in which I apologised for them; this rather puzzled him, and indeed it does not look as if we have enough theoretical difference to quarrel over. The fact was simply that I had written most of the essays before it struck me that they all bore on one topic, and had interested me for that reason; what I had to say on the topic I said, and then thought no harm in printing the essays as they grew.

Of course he is right in saying that you must decide what a piece of writing conveys, and have something to say about it, before you can start analysing its language as a means of criticism. He could hardly have suspected anyone of denying this if he had not first suspected them of a rash philosophy. My only claim is: so little is known about the action of language that one can fairly look round for 'all possible' ways in which the agreed effect may have been produced. To decide how a literary effect is produced is after all an accepted branch of criticism. However trivial or irrelevant my contributions to the inquiry may be your reviewer has no fundamental objection to it. One may suspect indeed that these philosophical quarrels in fields outside philosophy always turn out to be differences in what you take first or find more interesting; but in this case I think even the suspicion of a philosophical difference has flared up from my (surely harmless, and certainly guileless) claim that there is one thread running through a set of essays.

Yours sincerely,

W. Empson

TO IAN PARSONS

71 Marchmont Street, W. C. 1.

[n.d.]

Dear Ian,

I want to ask you to advise me if there is some paper that might print the enclosed stuff as an essay. It is merely a bit of my next book, but obviously the sensible thing is to get a little money and advertisement out of using parts of a book as articles, when possible. There seem to be a lot of literary papers which I ought to read but don't, and I hope it's no great trouble to you to suggest one that might use this, or tell me there aren't any.[1]

Hope your anthology's going all right.[2] Why don't you do an Anthology of Utopias, as you seem to go in for them; fragments from prose ones, either comic or making an important suggestion, and where possible complete poems. Shakespeare contributes the 'olives of endless golden age' sonnet [no. 107] and speeches with jokes against them from The Tempest; the Marvell Definition of love, remould it nearer to the heart's desire,[3] Chapman Round as It,[4] Pope etc. gardening or employing gardeners, just

---

[1] Added by WE in margin: 'Criterion no good twice running.'

[2] Parsons was putting together *The Progress of Poetry* (1936).

[3] Edward FitzGerald, *Rubaiyat of Omar Khayyam* (1859), stanza LXXIII.

[4] See *SVP*, 73: 'Evidence as well as probability . . . lets one say that the position of the tragic hero was felt to be like that of Christ, and that elements were exchanged between them . . . At that same time the two were very different, and the tragic idea, having a classical background, was by no means dependent on the Christian one. The famous passage in Chapman that uses

between the desert and the sown,[5] hints of utopias from pessimists (tout est ordre . . . luxe etc.)[6] including specially rosy versions of death (peace the lovers are asleep);[7] then an 'unEnglish section' with the women and cows breeding a great deal in the Bible and the Chinese making things fit their names. The new-born babies and the angels like insects (without memory, acquiring ardour by fanning their flanks) in the Paradiso,[8] contradictions from H. G. Wells,[9] everything being One from Bradley,[10] epigraph on significance of Utopias from Toynbee's Study of History . . .[11]

Bill Empson

Reading

the globe-metaphor, about the man that joins himself to the universe and goes on "round as it", shows how flatly the idea was derived from Roman Stoicism; the same metaphor for instance is in Marcus Aurelius (xi. 2). Mr Eliot remarked about this that no man would join himself to the universe if he had anything better to join himself to, and certainly there is an element of revolt in the Elizabethan use of the idea.' The reference is to George Chapman, *The Revenge of Bussy D'Ambois*, iv. 1, in which Clermont epitomizes what he calls 'this one thing' that contains 'all the discipline of manners and of manhood': 'A man to ioyne himself with th'Universe | In his main sway, and make (in all things fit) | One with that All, and goe on round as it, | Not plucking from the whole his wretched part, | And into straits, or into naught revert, | Wishing the complete Universe might be | Subject to such a rag of it as he . . .' (139–45; *Four Revenge Plays*, ed. Katharine Eisaman Maus 1995, 221).

⁵ There are a number of possible sources, but WE may well be alluding to stanza x of FitzGerald's translation of *Rubáiyát of Omar Khayyám* (1859): 'With me along some Strip of Herbage strown | That just divides the desert from the sown, | Where name of Slave and Sultan scarce is known, | And pity Sultan Mahmud on his Throne.' Cf. WE's note to 'Four Legs, Two Legs, Three Legs', regarding the Great Sphinx: 'I have never seen anything in print about how dramatically she is placed between the desert and the sown' (*CP*, 325).

⁶ See Charles Baudelaire, 'L'Invitation au Voyage', *Les Fleurs du Mal*, poem 53: 'La, tout n'est qu'ordre et beauté, | Luxe, calme et volupté'.

⁷ Richard Crashaw, 'An Epitaph upon Husband and Wife': 'Peace, good reader, do not weep; | Peace, the lovers are asleep.'

⁸ The opening lines of the *Paradiso*, Canto XXXI, figure the host of angels as 'like a swarm of bees' (*come schiera d'ape*) which descends into the flower: '*Quando scendean nel fior, di banco in banco* | *porgevan della pace e dell'ardore* | *ch'elli acquistavan ventilado il fianco* ll. 16–18;
'When they descended into the great flower they imparted to it, from rank to rank, of the peace and the ardour which they had gained fanning their sides': *The Divine Comedy of Dante Alighieri*, iii: *Paradiso*, trans. John D. Sinclair (1946), 446–7).

⁹ 'Wells's early works are remarkable for the way they do justice to conflict . . . He constructs contradictions and then explores their structures and possibilities . . . inventing symbols, images, and characters that bridge the gap between opposites. These early works thereby develop, not answers, but intricately balanced patterns which, by helping us focus clearly on the contradictions within civilization, force us to ponder, though hardly resolve, central moral issues of our world' (John Huntington, 'The Science Fiction of H. G. Wells', in *Science Fiction: A Critical Guide*, ed. Patrick Parrinder (1979), 34).

¹⁰ See F. H. Bradley, *Essays on Truth and Reality* (1914); and TSE, *Knowledge and Experience in the Philosophy of F. H. Bradley* (1964): 'We are forced to the assumption that truth is one, and to the assumption that reality is one' (168).

¹¹ The sense here must be 'use as an epigraph'; Arnold J. Toynbee writes of utopias in *A Study of History: Abridgement of Vols. 1–VI* by D. C. Somervell (1946), 183: 'these works are always programmes of action masquerading in the disguise of imaginary descriptive sociology; and the

POETRY: A MAGAZINE OF VERSE (CHICAGO), 49 (January 1937) 237: A Riposte to Geoffrey Grigson, 'Letter from England' (November issue)[1]

Geoffrey Grigson, in 'A Letter from England' (*Poetry* 49: 2, Nov. 1936, 101–3), sought to berate the work of contemporaries including Herbert Read, David Gascoyne, F. R. Leavis, and C. Day Lewis. Of Dylan Thomas's *Twenty-Five Poems* he opined that 'twenty-four twenty-fifths of them are psychopathological nonsense put down with a remarkable ineptitude in technique'. A few writers are praised—Isherwood, Madge*, Spender*, MacNeice—and one above all: 'His toughness, his curiosity, his love, his versatility, his plain cleverness as a writer still lift W. H. Auden above everyone else.' For the rest, 'I find only a jelly of mythomania, or self-deception, careerism, dishonesty, and ineptide'; and (as WE notes below) Michael Roberts is dismissed by way of a pun on his hobby of mountain-climbing as 'the literary *climber*, tapping away in bewildered Newcastle.'

Dear Sir:

Somebody ought to explain about Grigson, when he introduces himself to a new circle of readers, as he apparently did in the November *Poetry*. The trick of being rude to everybody is, of course, paying journalism of a certain kind, but in Grigson it also comes from the one honest admiration discernible in him, for the work and methods of Wyndham Lewis. However, Grigson shows no sign of having any theoretical basis to be rude from, which Lewis has plenty of; nor has Grigson any capacity in poetry himself; published partly under an assumed name, Martin Boldero, his stuff has been pathetic. This of course need not stop him from being rude to good effect, and he has a good journalistic nose for what he can safely be rude to. But it is annoying to have him call people 'climbers' when no other brickbat seems handy. Grigson himself is the only climber in the

action which they are intended to evoke is nearly always the "pegging", at a certain level, of an actual society which has entered on a decline that must end in a fall unless the downward movement can be artificially arrested. To arrest a downward movement is the utmost to which most Utopias aspire, since Utopias seldom begin to be written in any society until after its members have lost the expectation of further progress. Hence in almost all Utopias—with the noteworthy exception of that work of English genius which has given this whole genre of literature its name—an invincibly stable equilibrium is the aim to which all other social ends are subordinated and, if need be, sacrificed.'

[1] Geoffrey Grigson (1905–85), poet, editor, and acerbic critic, worked for the *Yorkshire Post* and *Morning Post* before founding the influential periodical *New Verse* (1933–9), which brought out some of the early poems of W. H. Auden, Louis MacNeice, and Dylan Thomas. With Denys Kilham Roberts he edited *The Year's Poetry* (1934) and *The Year's Poetry, 1937–38* (1938).

field. Not that a climber is anything very shocking; but he has got himself a comfortable job as critic by nose and noise alone. He may have published some decent criticism which I have not read, but in his magazine he does not so much as pretend to give reasons for insulting people. (He has not attacked me; I had rather a sharp review in his paper from someone else, but that was criticism all right.) Of course apart from this 'climber' talk it is a good thing to have someone making a lively noise, but someone else, as he points out, ought to say Boo.

> The coxcomb bird, so talkative and grave,
> Whom from his cage calls cuckold, whore, and knave,
> Though many a passenger he rightly call,
> You hold him no philosopher at all.[2]

Grigson responded in *Poetry*, 50: 2 (May 1937): 'Mr Empson is right; I am not rude (if he must have the word) from "any theoretical basis." I attempt to be rude—a typically inert theoriser and poetical *pasticheur* of Mr Empson's kind would scarcely see it—I say, I attempt to be rude from a moral basis, a basis of differentiating between the fraudulent and inert and the active, genuine, and desirable. The inert verbalism in which Mr Empson deals may not be fraudulent, but it has always, if Mr Empson would care to know, struck me as quarter-man stuff so unreadably trivial that it is not worth insulting or attacking.'

WE returned to the fray in the same issue.

POETRY: A MAGAZINE OF VERSE (CHICAGO), 50: 2 (May 1937)

The important thing here seems to be the anti-intellectual stuff. I wouldn't want to deny that it lets Grigson put up a case; in fact, that is the danger of it, that it will defend anything. For instance, it is a bad thing to be a quarter-man, but it is a great sign of being a quarter-man if you strut about squaring your shoulders and seeing how rude you can be. And it is necessary to make your final judgements 'on a moral basis', but if you haven't done some thinking *first*, your moral intuitions will as like as not be mistaken and harmful. If you set out to forget simple truths like these it gets easy to be proud of yourself for being manly and moral.

---

[2] Alexander Pope, 'Moral Essays: Epistle I. To Richard Temple, Viscount Cobham' (1734), ll. 5–8. WE misquotes the second line: 'That from his cage cries Cuckold, Whore, and Knave'.

The anti-intellectual line can be a useful defence for valuable things; a man like D. H. Lawrence had a right to it. But as to whether the fifth-rate (not that I agree about who is fifth-rate) form defensive fronts—they do, they do; and this is one of their fronts.

POETRY: A MAGAZINE OF VERSE (CHICAGO), 49 (1937):
'A London Letter'

A question that obviously ought to be raised by a British number of *Poetry* [edited by W. H. Auden and Michael Roberts] is whether the distinction is real, whether the position and intention of the poets isn't much the same anyway under the two flags. Ignorance of America makes me unlikely to have anything of importance to say about this, but then it might make me a better specimen of our prejudices.

There was that remark by Ezra Pound, in some Outline or Short-Cut of his, that after a certain date the English gave up writing decent poetry and the Americans took over in a body.[1] The sting of truth here comes from people like T. S. Eliot and Pound himself, who might live anywhere. Hart Crane seems to me often first-rate, and distinctively American as he wanted to be, but he didn't feel he had a body to be a member of. Any discussion of this kind of body must go into politics and social conditions, and it seems worth putting down some obvious differences between the countries, which affect the verse written in them.

The first thing is that America has no enemies in reach and the necessary imports are trivial in quantity; if it could decide what it wanted to do and get the politicians in hand, it could do it. England is the only country (the Japanese claim to the same excuse is still fairly bogus) which depends for most of its food on people who send food from outside, and who do this only because they believe in an obscure and toppling credit system. You can argue against this assertion, but the country feels it so much that the least political poet comes to absorb it. The thing that struck me when I came back to England recently after three years was a queer kind of patience in every bus-driver; not fatalism or a conviction of doom, but a

---

[1] Ezra Pound pronounced, in *How To Read* (1931), 42–3: 'apart from Yeats, since the death of Hardy, poetry is being written by Americans. All the developments in English verse since 1910 are due almost wholly to Americans.' Of WE, Pound would later write in a cryptic note: 'Employment for Empson, or one of those critics who never do anything very useful: a serious study of the UNWARRANTED INFERENCE as devil's assistant and implement for mind conditioning.' (*Strike* 4 (Washington, DC), Sept. 1955, 2)

feeling that we have to keep quiet and watch our feet because any hopeful large change might make everything very much worse.[2] This is quite foreign to America; the panic feeling of the slump was a feeling that something rather undefined was urgent as a last hope and must be done. Much the same difference comes out in jokes about war; many people in England were puzzled like myself by the Mothers of the Unborn Veterans. It was a real strong joke if they thought the war was coming unless stopped; if they thought the other countries were going to have a war but not them it was nasty. A friend of mine [Julian Trevelyan] paints in an old wharf on the Thames; he said it was sure to be mistaken for the Houses of Parliament, so he was going to paint Bomb Me on the roof. One doesn't know whether the American jokes are like this charming plan or not. The difference comes out for instance in the comparatively large (and well deserved) sales in England of poems by Auden and Spender, who were viewed as young communist uplift. The bulk of that new public of buyers, which was mainly interested in the political feelings expressed, were not I think idealists in the sense of enjoying sentiments they did not mean to act on, nor yet definite sympathisers who wanted to get something like that done. In America they would have been one or the other; in England there was an obscure safety and bafflement in moving from the poem to consider what the country could possibly do.[3]

You hear it said that in a real democracy the writer can tap the life of the whole country, whereas in a class-conscious country he is tied to his clique and the stuff is bound to be narrower in range. I doubt whether this applies much to verse, which has narrowed its range anyway because people feel you need special reasons for choosing the verse form at all. No doubt it has some effect on novel-writing, but even there the difficulty is much less in getting to know people than in getting the result across to the public. For instance, the point about dialects in England is that most villagers have a wide range between standard English and the dialect or indeed the several dialects, and put a great deal of weight on varying the talk with the person addressed and the feeling towards him. It is the same kind of thing as the elaborate syntax of polite forms in languages of the

[2] WE wrote to Ralph Hodgson, on 20 Aug. 1935: 'What I notice in London is . . . this eerie patience of everybody—they feel any sort of row will make things worse' (*Ralph Hodgson Papers, Yale University: GEN MSS 245: Box 9, folder 177*).

[3] Cf. 'Early Auden' (1975): 'I have sometimes known later critics say, "Oh, well, Empson wasn't so much of a mug as to be a pylon poet; he may have very little to say, but at least he didn't say that." Well, of course, I agreed with the pylon poets entirely. I've always felt I ought to make that point plain whenever I had the opportunity: I think they were quite right, I just didn't know how to do this kind of poetry' (*A*, 375–6).

Far East. Nobody puts this into dialect novels except for the crude change to standard English (which is hardly used except for rudeness) because the novel-reading public would not understand it; I wouldn't myself. In fact if you are expected to talk standard English you are not allowed to learn this game; the old style squire still does it a bit, but it seems patronising. We have so little machinery for handling speech that if a novel admits its characters don't talk standard English they are assumed to talk a flat complete dialect. Here the American novelist is obviously better off, or simply more competent, partly because the variations of language in America are felt to be less touchy and important. But the difficulty is in the public (it would be a bore to keep on *explaining* the exact impact of some shade of local dialect), not in any isolation of the author through snobbery; the interesting uses of dialect would not appear if the talkers felt stuck in their classes.

I was shocked recently by a Welsh poet [Dylan Thomas] who turned up in Kleinfeldt's[4] saying he needed money and had had an offer as checker-in at a Welsh mine; this was very absurd, and he had a much more cosy plan to become a grocer. What with the Welsh nationalism, the vague and balanced but strong political interests of this man, the taste for violence in his writing, and the way he was already obviously exhausting his vein of poetry about events which involved the universe but happened inside his skin, it seemed to me that being a checker-in was just what he wanted; and I shouted at him for some time, against two talkers I should otherwise have been eager to hear, to tell him that he was wasting his opportunities as a Welshman and ought to make full use of a country in which he could nip across the classes. I still think that something like that ought to happen to him, but no doubt he was right in saying that the plan was no good. The English no less than the Americans cling to a touching belief that social distinctions in modern England are more bitter than elsewhere.

However the difference in the *public* for poetry in England and America seems to me very real, though I know little about it. For instance MacLeish's *Conquistador* [1933] struck me as an able and agreeable verse book which would have no point without a fairly large public for verse books, a thing that you don't find in England.[5] This is not the grousing of a verse-writer; publishers are generous to verse, apparently because it looks well in the catalogue, and it gets a good deal of space in reviews,

---

[4] 'Papa' Kleinfeld was the proprietor of the Fitzroy Tavern in London.
[5] Archibald MacLeish (1892–1982), US poet; Librarian of Congress, 1939–44.

apparently because people who don't read poetry still like to talk about poetry, and there are always corners needing to be filled in the magazines. But of the people I come across and like, I doubt if anybody reads much modern verse who doesn't write it. You could pick out in *Conquistador* a series of authors who had been borrowed from and used, and I felt rather critical about this at first, but of course if you have a public to write for it is an excellent thing to use the existing tools (compare the Elizabethans). The English poet of any merit takes, I think, a much more clinical view of his own products. The first or only reason for writing verse is to clear your own mind and fix your own feelings, and for this purpose you want to be as concentrated as possible. Mr Eliot said somewhere that a poet ought to practice his art at least once a week,[6] and some years ago I was able to ask the oracle whether he thought this really necessary, a question on which much seemed to hang. After brooding and avoiding traffic for a while he answered with the full weight of his impressiveness, and I am sure without irony, that he had been thinking of someone else when he wrote that, and in such a case as my own the great effort of the poet must be to write as little as possible.

TO CHARLES MADGE*

71 Marchmont St. WC1
[?1937]

Dear Madge,

I have turned over all the pages and read many of them; there's a lot of very interesting material of course. About lions being magnanimous— Wycherley's Plain Dealer says [that] instead of being like a crocodile it is better to tear your friends in pieces honestly like generous lions and tigers;[1] this is just when the modern sense of generous was coming in, and I

---

[6] TSE wrote in his introduction to Ezra Pound, *Selected Poems* (1928): 'The poet who wishes to continue to write poetry must keep in training; and must do this, not by forcing his imagination, but by good workmanship on a level possible for some hours' work every week of his life.' See also WE, 'The Style of the Master', in *T. S. Eliot: A Symposium*, ed. Richard March and Tambimuttu (1948); *A*, 361.

[1] 'I choose to go where honest, downright barbarity is professed; where men devour one another like generous, hungry lions and tigers, not like crocodiles' (William Wycherley, *The Plain Dealer* (1676), I. i. 612–16). See WE, 'Honest Man', *SCW*, 192–4: '*Generous* still meant mainly "of good stock", so that the paradox would look less stark. Well-bred horses were generous, just as all lions were magnanimous . . . Wycherley's *honest* here is clearly more than "not lying", something like "accepting its own nature, therefore as good as it has the power to be". Yet all normal meanings that would give praise are denied. In trying to imagine what he means one keeps

thought he meant what we would—your stuff on m[agnanimity] makes it more likely. Interesting because I too feel that the mammals are generous in some obscure way and don't know why. The stuff about Hayley (and people) on Milton[2] as inventor is extremely neat but needs much more evidence; one never knows whether you mean something that really happened or some game of your own with consciously unreal symbolism—did they use Milton or go the same way, were the same forces really at work if things merely happened like Milton; that would make a book of its own needing both more evidence and more proof that you understood what people actually felt about the thing. The same about treason in the Fairy Queen, for instance; it might be inherent in the symbols but what did (a) Spenser (b) the successful contemporary reader actually feel about it when in a normal state of mind?

The shape of the book I think is bloody insolent. This idea that one must write very esoteric stuff because nobody will read [it] anyway seems to me nonsense—you get plenty of readers if you give anybody a chance. Surely even a communist can have a reasonable amount of democratic feeling; the point about writing as plainly as you can is that you are testing your ideas against somebody who is not a specialist and just knows about life in general. Really subjective writing seems to me nasty to touch, gluey on the outside like David Gascoyne.[3] I feel I have some right to be rude about this because [I am] so much open to the same faults. You had much better imagine before you write anything that England has long been a settled communist state, and that the only difficulties before you are (a) making the comrades hear what you want to say (b) convincing them that you are not talking nonsense; assuming the future to have arrived is a piece of symbolism quite in your manner; you will find it works much better both as making you write better and making people buy your books.

---

shifting to the memory of accounts of actual savages—how did he suppose that this tribe kept itself going? The main effect is a blind Samson's attempt to ruin *honest* and *generous*, those vaguely complacent terms of praise, the two pillars of the temple.'

[2] See William Hayley, *The Life of Milton, in three parts* (1796).

[3] David Gascoyne (1916–2001), poet, translator, essayist, diarist, was the first chronicler of Surrealism. His publications include *A Short Survey of Surrealism* (1935), *Collected Poems* (1965) *Paris Journal 1937–39* (1978), and *Selected Verse Translations* (1996); and in 1996 he was appointed a Chevalier de l'Ordre des Arts Lettres. Of WE at about this time he noted: 'But what a bore! His poems get steadily duller and more wooden; though some of his early ones, like "Arachne" or "The proper scale" ["The Scales"], apart from their intellectual cross-word puzzle ingenuity (or their famous ambiguity) are, in a certain way, decoratively or evocatively, quite exciting' (*Journal 1936–37* (1980), 60). However, he reflected in 1980 (12): 'I no longer feel in the least as I did then either about Empson, or his poetry, which I now much appreciate, while greatly admiring his critical writings.'

Actual chapters of quotation without confessing what you quote for, actual articles in quotation without confessing who they are quoted from, all that kind of thing, is merely indulging yourself in madness without the excuse of being mad. Of course there isn't much money in the kind of criticism we write anyway, but the kind of thing one needs in the way of sales and success, enough recognition and criticism to go on doing one's stuff without the insanity of isolation, you can get in presentday England at once, but only if you don't pretend to be mad. You must expect me to take you seriously if you left the MS to ask my view of it, and I advise you very heartily not to publish this as it stands. Better make it several books and put in a great deal of your political opinions; I don't see that you lose anything by putting them in, it will make the thing far more human, and you may become sufficiently interested to find the main things you wanted to say. I myself generally find what I was trying to talk about while I am rewriting so as to try to be intelligible, and one reason why I haven't even read many of your pages of quotation is that I very much doubt whether you have even yet discovered, what I am sure is genuine when found, the reasons why you think them interesting.

I smack this out in a state of moderate beer assuming that you are not appallingly sensitive. The difficult thing would be to say it tactfully, but I don't believe you are as neurotic as your piece of writing. As to a public, of course there is a real muddle; the recent events have kept on showing a public opinion which I find I agree with, its muddle is my own, and I feel I can write decent (of course unselling) books with a notion that it is part of the country that provides the language. A man who doesn't feel that at all has of course a different situation, and I should have thought the straight way out was to bring in the politics firm and clear. Surely you haven't Magdalene [College] on your mind as a source of isolation? When I meet any of those old parties I am eagerly friendly out of gratitude to them for sending me away. Anyway, just as a point of theory, literary symbolism demands a public for symbolism; by all means imagine a public, and as a matter of fact you will imagine a real one; but those who write for no public are even unconscious of their asylum.

Love to you and Kathleen [Raine]*

 Bill Empson

TO T. S. ELIOT

71 Marchmont Street
[n.d. July 1937]

Dear Mr Eliot,[1]

I have just heard of an English professorship going in Cairo, which I want to apply for; the thing is decided in Cairo and the application 'with testimonials' has to get there by 31st July. I should be very much obliged if you could let me have a testimonial; to be any use it must come quickly. I really am an interested and industrious lecturer, but can hardly expect you to know it; still, I feel you would be willing to put in a word for me. The wording implies that you send everything together, but no doubt a separate thing sent to 'The Dean of the Faculty of Arts / Egyptian University / Guizeh / Cairo' would be all right. I had better ring you up and ask you what you feel about it.

Yours very sincerely
W. Empson

Faber

TO JOHN HAYWARD

The Hong Kong Club
15 September 1937

Dear John,

I forget whether I wrote to you before, but fancy I didn't. It has been an amusing month running round, and I hope now I may really get a job in Changsha. Old Richards is very impressive in action as a traveller— getting the party on a boat to Shanghai where no women are allowed, by interviews both with the consul and the shipping agent, and then getting accommodation on a new boat sighted in Tsingtai by fetching out a sheet of Magdalene College notepaper and writing all the magic words like Rockefeller on it, so that beds had to be made up in the officers' smoking room. Getting the aeroplane to Changsha next Tuesday has been a heavy bit of wangling too. From then on they mean to climb mountains in Yunnan; whether I want to come too rather depends how hopeful things are in Changsha. There is an emergency university there with people from all over China, which might be very fine; on the other hand it is just the

---

[1] Geoffrey Faber's secretary Erica Wright scribbled on this letter a note for TSE: 'Mr Empson rang up anxiously about this.'

kind of thing the Japanese are likely to bomb, and one may find only quarrelling and dithering and failure of cash from Nanking. But I am very glad I got to Peking just in time to catch the Richards's (they would have stopped me if they could cable) and came on with them.

Richards is writing a Basic Primer, a charming and fantastic work which often puzzles me and will defeat Chinese children I am afraid.[1] Only he and DowwoFea are at the top of the cliff romping with the local professors (who are having a first class war about reducing Hong Kong University salaries etc.—we hear more about that war than the Japanese one, without getting any better information) while I have been kindly put up at the Club at the bottom, so [Victor] Purcell[2] and I can never get hold of him and make him work. There is some hope that he may be getting out of the Ogden corsets or letting them out a bit before the end.

But you will want politics. I only feel how very Japanese Hong Kong is, and I suspect the southern Chinese generally are. It is very fine that the Chinese are pulling themselves together so much. We met the great Hu Shih, who started Pei Hua (isn't it? colloquial style anyway); he is going from here to America and England on propaganda.[3] Said that Peking

---

[1] See Rodney Koeneke, *Empires of the Mind: I. A. Richards and Basic English in China, 1929–1979* (2004); and Alan M. Hollingsworth, 'I. A. Richards in China and America', in *R. O. C. & U. S. A.: 1911–1981: Collected Papers of an International Conference Held by the American Studies Association of the Republic of China in November 21–23, 1981*, ed. Tung-hsun Sun and Morris Wei-hsin Tien (Taipei, 1982).

[2] Victor Purcell (1896–1965), a British civil servant who had worked since 1924 in the Chinese secretariat of the Malayan Civil Service at Penang—becoming Assistant Director of the Education Department for the Straits Settlements—spent a month travelling with WE and the Richardses through China; he had been awarded a Commonwealth Service Research Fellowship to work with Basic English. 'I think he is a remarkable man,' wrote IAR. 'Everything here is in the hands of the Colonial Service people and a keen and discerning Basic enthusiast, who belongs to the Service like Purcell, is invaluable. I am learning a lot from him. He seems to me to see the general Chinese educational problem very clearly too.' (IAR, letter to David H. Stevens, Director of the Humanities Program, Rockefeller Foundation, 10 Sept. 1937: *Rockefeller Archive Center, 1/601, box 48, folder 400.*) See also V. W. W. S. Purcell, 'The Teaching of Basic', *The Basic News* 5, Jan.–Mar. 1938), 12–22. Purcell was to publish a lively account of his few weeks in their company, *Chinese Evergreen* (1938), though he disguises their identities: IAR is 'Edwards', Empson 'Dudley'—after the infamous Empson and Dudley. After the War, Purcell became UN Consultant on Asia. His publications include *The Problems of Chinese Education* (1936); *Chinese in Southeast Asia* (1951); *The Sweeniad*, a satire (1957); and *The Memoirs of a Malaysian Official* (1965). After Purcell's death, IAR wrote of him: 'I wish I could have been more patient with him! He was a sort of door-god of a man, with much more talent than his judgement could afford' (IAR: *SL*, 169).

[3] A key figure in the Sino-foreign liberal academic community, Hu Shih (1891–1962), who was described by John King Fairbank as 'the modern Voltaire', was educated in China, and in the USA at Cornell and Columbia. His doctorate was supervised by the pragmatist philosopher John Dewey, whom he came to revere. Hu acted as translator for Dewey during his lecture tour of China in 1919–21, and later edited the journal *Tu-li p'ing-lun* ('The Independent Critic'). For his advocacy of *pai hua*, the vernacular language, he soon became recognized as the father of the Chinese literary revolution. From 1927 to 1930 he taught at Kuanghua University even while

would be settled under China again next year—not a believable man, but a very good talker. But at bottom the difference of the people in the two countries is less than anybody makes out I believe.

The Hong Kong papers are so pro Chinese that we get as little real news here as in Peking with all papers suppressed and a terrific rumour industry.

Love
Bill.

King's

TO SOLLY ZUCKERMAN*

[n.d.: late 1937]

This letter was possibly not posted, but Lord Zuckerman read the transcript I sent him (published in *RB*) and said (letter to JH, 7 April 1986) he found it 'fascinating. Nothing in [WE's] text is an affront to biological wisdom, and the Wuzzoo and all the others like him are beautiful, fantastic creatures. I particularly liked the way he brought in the breeding season'.

Dear Dr Zuckermann [*sic*],
I am starting to write a fantasy novel ['The Royal Beasts'][1], about a Central African tribe which is not of human stock. It would be giving too much trouble to ask your advice, but I propose to put down the main points of the novel in a letter, and would be grateful if you feel interested enough to answer. Various Peking universities have had their arts departments moved onto a sacred mountain in Hunan, a rather isolated place, and it seems best to have a novel to write, now I have got there.

The boundary between a separatist Dominion and a British Crown Colony, in an inaccessible and mountainous part, has been taken over from a previous treaty with an African chief, and is therefore defined in terms of tribal areas not of territory. All land up to the last tribes south of the mountains belongs to the Dominion. Then a gold mine is discovered at

serving as president of the China National Institute. At the invitation of Chiang Monlin, he became Dean of the College of Arts at Peking University, 1931–6, and in 1937 he was about to embark on a goodwill mission to the United States. A year later, he was appointed China's ambassador to Washington, a post he held until 1942. Returning to China only in 1946, he become Chancellor of Peking University. He was to flee China for the USA on the brink of the Communist takeover in 1948. From 1958 until his death he served as president of Academia Sinica in Taiwan.

[1] WE began his 'silly novel' by 10 Sept. 1937, while staying in Hong Kong.

the foot of the mountains in the territory of this new tribe. Britain has reached a condition where there is an urgent need for gold. The governor of the colony takes up the claim that these men do not constitute a tribe, and the case goes to the Lords. Britain I think wins the case, and then in a second case it is decided that the creatures are persons in the same sense as Joint Stock Companies, so that British Law applies to them. All the Christian sects demand to send missionaries, and the Japanese for purposes of cultural penetration claim that Buddhism is the only religion open to non-human species. The difficulty is to stop the novel with a good enough bang. I am rather afraid that they will all have to die of a plague of colds. A great deal of the stuff needs technical knowledge that I can't scratch together here.

About the creatures themselves. I want them attractive enough to excite sympathy and clever enough to stick to their case. They are well informed about the Dominion treatment of negroes and determined to keep out of it; they swear by their gods they are not men. (Rather tempting to make them swear they are parrots on totemistic grounds; business of hushing this up). They are covered with valuable fur, and to keep this off the market they demand the status of Royal Beasts, like sturgeon. They have a rigid breeding season with some kind of bodily change; a sexual skin is hardly pretty enough and apparently does not go with a breeding season. One could say they are a Lemuroid stock, but they have a broad nose and muzzle; all the lemuroids seem to have a rat expression which I don't want. Having a breeding season means that they have become rational without using Freudian machinery, interesting to try and work out. They rebuke mankind a good deal on this point. But they pick fur all the year round, have a craving for it. The hero is presented with a Persian cat and throws it out of the window, much shocked at being incited to an obscene perversion. They are incapable of interbreeding with man, at least such evidence as is timidly brought into court leads to that view, because it was acquired in a criminal manner, so it cannot be a strong argument. However their blood can't be transfused with any human group, and they have long furry tails. I don't think there would be much difficulty in getting a united front of scientific experts in court to say they weren't men, though some experts would say they were a closely allied species. You might easily get the law refusing to concern itself with the scientific definition, though, and saying that a man in law is a rational creature capable of observing contracts or what not. The Catholic Church would I think undoubtedly claim that they were men, on such grounds as were used in its great sixteenth century decision that the Terra del Fuegans were; but I need to find out what grounds were given then.

It seems possible to make them a very recent mutation, all descended from one ancestor three or four generations ago. Hence all their customs are in a state of flux, they need a new language and so on. There was a 'language' before but with no object-nouns as it was entirely concerned with distinguishing social situations. In that case the Catholics might claim that they have only had souls since the mutation, a clear example of the divine purpose. But this would only make the story rather more unplausible, I suppose.

Apart from fun with politics and theology the interesting question is whether an intelligent race with a breeding season could develop at all, and whether it would be very unlike ourselves mentally. They get no social training from family life and no source of mental energy from repressed sex; most of the year they are a herd like wolves and sheep. One must suppose a period of very hard conditions in which they survive by learning to make concerted plans under a leader. I was tempted to make them vegetarians with a strong head for alcohol, but it is only in hunting that you get much scope for concerted plans. If they were water animals they might make plans like beavers, but there seem to be no water monkeys. Possible reasons are that the primate body does not swim fast and catches cold easily. A water animal with the use of fire might have entertaining customs, but does not seem plausible. I take it they can't with decent plausibility be made grazing animals, with hay being demanded at the big political dinner, because no monkey digests cellulose. (It is no good making them an entirely new kind of creature because there must be serious doubt whether they are men or not). They have retreated to a single mountain area which they defend against negro attacks; the negroes are afraid of them, don't talk much about them, and when they do say things that sound like romancing. This makes it reasonable enough that they haven't been discovered. But it is not clear what large animals they can hunt up in the mountains. They must have an elaborate social structure of personal dominance, I think, reflected in the old language; because otherwise their lives seem too blank to develop intelligence. Rice-growing, come to think of it, would be a very neat employment for them; once they had taken to the mountain they would have to do a great deal of centralised waterwork to make the stuff grow, and the planning would require dominant leaders. Or some plant like rice; rice could hardly be got to them. The dominating situation arises during the breeding season only, when the herd originally split up into pairs for a short period. It is not clear how this could spread over into the placid herd situations between breeding seasons. The sexes are then hardly distinguished, but you discriminate a good deal about your fur picking partner. The hunting cooperation seems an easier thing to invent, partly because somebody is already dominant over the animal hunted, partly because the object is more in view. An intelligent race without either domination or pervasive sex I find too hard to imagine. To be sure one could run the novel on making them simply a tribe with evidence it wasn't human stock, but this seems hardly interesting enough.

You see the kind of topic. Grateful if you care to send comments.

[Unsigned.]

Houghton, bMS Eng 1401 (685)

TO EDITH SITWELL*

Hanoi
28 April [1938]

Dear Edith Sitwell,

Thank you very much for your book, and the inscription.[1] It followed me to Hongkong, where I was having a very lazy and agreeable time waiting for my students to finish walking eight hundred miles to Yunnan. The new term is to begin in a tin-mine in a few days, but may be late; I have been doing Angkor. The still active tin-mines are terrible places I believe; the only water there is pumped, so you can cut off not only pay in a strike but water. They are up for sale from China to both English and French business; I have run into some friends in this little hotel, very improbably, and the hotel is very suspicious of our pretences of innocence.

My difficulty with the book is that I can't help taking a gossipy interest in Swift, wanting to know *why* he was so unhappy—were they both illegitimate children of Temple? and that kind of thing. You I think would dislike that, and the device of telling the story in the modern world with the other tragic stories does a great deal to cut it out. And for that matter you very likely give all the reasons there were, only you are not interested in them as reasons. You conveyed the unhappiness of Swift so massively that I wanted the briskness of an explanation—it so easily implies that one can do better oneself; whereas he stands out in your book as normal and typical, too much so to need explaining. I can't feel sure whether I am right in being left rather unsatisfied through that. It is a question maybe of fact rather than of taste; whether that kind of unhappiness really does follow normally from greatness in the human creature; and put like that I

---

[1] *I Live Under a Black Sun* (1938), a novel based on the life of Jonathan Swift.

wouldn't set up to answer it. But the way I feel it is that I wanted more reasons just as a way of carrying the poetry or the claims on the readers' feelings. But I put this down when I look round for a criticism; it is anyway a large book, I think, and a terrible one.

The China war seems to be going all right, only one mustn't think that immediate successes mean too much; it will take a long time. It seems the Chinese have got a tolerable Red Cross now, and I think that is important; the only way the Japanese could win would be if the Chinese soldier came to feel he hadn't decent enough people behind him. That pacificist book [*Ends and Means*, 1937] by [Aldous] Huxley seems rather stupid here; what the Japanese do in the conquered territory is to get local figures to run a puppet government with all their families held as hostages. That is very hard to break once it has started, even against strong public feeling. It might conceivably be met by real universal non-resistant non-cooperation, but the only way to get any kind of universal agreement is by sturdy simple defence, so the question does not arise. You may say it is tragic to see the Chinese being forced to cultivate Jingo nationalism; that's a bad thing, but the mental effects on a proud group held as slaves are worse. Auden and Isherwood turned up in Hongkong when I was there, very good company, and queerly muddled I thought about hating all armaments men and wanting the Chinese to win.

About Angkor, which the French are managing very well, I found my prejudices against Hinduism stronger than ever; the Vat itself is a dignified public building, but it hasn't the noble and tender and extraordinary imagination of the Buddhist things like the Bayon and Neak Pean and Prah Khan. The French have pulled down that beastly tree that destroyed Neak Pean, which everybody writes of so tenderly, and pray God they put the stones back now instead of saying how picturesque they are lying in a heap. It was a lotus temple in the middle of a bathing pool, with elephants trunks and snakes and huge petals curving up to the little rectangular niches for the God of Mercy, and I think must have been wonderfully beautiful. The normal reaction to the Bayon, the thing with the big heads, seems to have been mucked up by the idea that the heads were Shiva (and anyway the central tower was built out of proportion by Hinduism soon after the thing was made); my French guidebook said it was 'exasperated romanticism'. The whole point of the repeated head of the Boddhisattva of Mercy, coming in and out in an elaborate order as you stand on the terrace, is that you are perfectly protected and enclosed, 'safe in thine eternal arms', a hushing, nursing, milky security; about the opposite of romance as well as of exasperation. The story of how 'primitiv' it was has now happily been smashed by a bouleversement des dates (tiens) which makes it later than Angkor Vat.

My address will be The Associated Universities. Mengtzu. Yunnan China. I should be grateful if you would write. How is Dylan [Thomas] getting on?

Yours very sincerely

W. Empson.

Princeton

TO JOHN HAYWARD

The Combined Universities, MENGTZU, YUNNAN, China
23 May [1938]

My dear John,

The military instructors in the adjoining loose-box are only separated from me by matchboarding with large slits in it, so I oughtn't to type even if they kept quiet enough. They talk pretty steadily, or rather want to, but when they can no longer think what to say they express themselves by a wide repertoire of yawns. The Customs man here, a very entertaining chap, says he will try to get me a room in the French Consulate—this large compound is the Customs. That may make bad feeling if it comes off, because the French refused the place to the school, not wanting Natives in it; still it is no use my staying here if I can't get any writing done—the question is whether to stay another year. During the day we have lectures about ten yards away. The mud floor has insects, the naked tiles have leaks. I eat with the professors for twelve shillings a month.

Mengtzu is a curious ghost of departed wealth. It struck me this evening, now that the lake has filled up and isn't a field of muck, that it may have been a pretty little French colonial town. There were about two hundred Europeans trading here about fifteen years ago. But the Mengtzu people refused to let the railway come here, on religious grounds, so all the trade went elsewhere—there is a Chinese small railway to the tin mines, with a special small gauge so as to keep the French engines off, but it has no need to stop here. So there were plenty of buildings for the School to take. The halfpay Customs man and a mad Greek running a shop built on compensation money for earlier outrages—or rather sitting in it; he is determined not to sell his stock—were the only Europeans by now. The garden of this compound was partly laid out by Stella Benson, and is very pretty; the eucalyptus trees are older—fifty years old in fact, that is why they fall down, not being built for damp soil; they have hardly any roots. Her husband came here as inspector the other year, he has re-married, and kept bursting into tears, the Customs man said. Mengtzu means the Dull Place, and the Chinese despise it and the tribes bitterly. It would be a great sheep farming area if somebody would bring sheep and dig ponds. We get Miao in Miao costume here on market days, bangles and embroidery and kilts; my pupils believe a wild Miao would eat them. I have been bitten by a large bear, but I regret to say it was only in the local zoo where I was giving it a much needed drink, so not wild life really. The Miao do lovely reliefs in silver, rather Sumerian, which the Chinese of course won't look at; I mean to get hold of some, but no shop in these parts will admit it has any stock.

You may have noticed a fretful note about other people's nationalism; maybe it is because the Greek in the shop positively (today) refused to order the French wine from Hanoi. It is adulterated, he said, and he won't deal with the French; he can only let me have Greek wine, which I am now drinking. Also my colleagues are all furious with the French, a fussy tactless and (when frightened) limited nation no doubt, but still I thought they ran Indo China very well. Certainly it will be no kindness to the Annamites (whom I like) if the Chinese try to do an anschluss later on. Amused by an Annamite on a bus somewhere who said that the bus company was Chinese, then in a melancholy way 'I suppose even in London most of the business is done by Chinese?' He didn't feel part of China. The French have done a system of romanising Annamite very well I'm told, with packs of accents for tones etc; years off the schooling of course, but any way the romanising started in the seventeenth century. George Yeh[1] was saying what a tragedy it was that they couldn't have any literature in Annamite now. I must try and look into that when I'm next in Indo China—they obviously have romanized novels, but have they verse? They all looked healthy and well fed in the villages, I thought, and there are clinics all over the place. In the great strike of 1921? which got to Annam as well as Hong Kong the French behaved very horribly, I believe (it is almost incredible

---

[1] George Yeh (1904–81)—Yeh Kung-chao (Ye Gongchao)—son of a cultivated Cantonese family, gained an MA in Indo-European linguistics at Cambridge, after taking a first degree in the USA, where his gifts brought him to the attention of Robert Frost. From 1935 he taught in the Department of Western Languages and Literature at Peking University. After the overthrow by the Communists of Chiang Kai-shek's Kuomintang Government in 1949, he became Minister of Foreign Affairs for the government of Nationalist China; and in 1958–61 he was Taiwanese Ambassador to Washington; later an adviser to President Chiang Kai-shek; and ultimately minister without portfolio (1962–78). In 1978 he was named senior adviser to Chiang's son, Chiang Ching-kuo. He wrote several books on literature and culture, and won a number of medals and citations.

that the Hong Kong British did their own washing and cooking through three months of the heat, and broke the strike almost without bloodshed—we/they deserve to keep the beastly place) and are normally rather bad up country I believe. But you get far more easy friendliness from the casual native than in any British colony. A little brutality seems to pay.

About the China war—you know more than I do as I write, and will know much more when this arrives, if it does. I believe the crux was when the Japanese last autumn said they want the whole Yangtze valley. Their dignity won't let them stop without it, and if they go on till they get it they are likely to crack first. Murphy the Customs man has a Lolo wife, who was always very indignant with the Chinese for their appalling treatment of her tribe, and never that he can see (he says) hears politics or news from anybody, and she is now to his astonishment and distaste talking about Our troops and wanting the papers. An anthropologist on the border of Thibet was saying last autumn that every coolie there had heard of the war. And the official Chinese propaganda is most of it unintelligible. I think there's no doubt that the bug of nationalism has arrived here, and if it has the Japanese can't win.

Angkor was wonderful, but I think this constitutes a letter, deserving an answer. How about John Davenport?[2]

With very much love

Bill Empson

Saw Auden in Hongkong, very amusing and busy meeting the great. Isherwood was the one who was worrying about politics I thought.

Houghton

TO JOHN HAYWARD

[Mengtzu]
[n.d. 1938]

My dear John,

I write to you as a kind of tonic, feeling very flat at the end of term and indeed wondering how to pass the evening. The duty of sounding cheerful

---

[2] John Davenport (1910–63), critic and journalist, won a dazzling reputation at Cambridge as bibliophile, linguist, poet, pianist, art connoisseur, boxer, and boozer. As Julian Trevelyan remarked, he 'became an institution from the moment he arrived ... Fat, witty, bibulous, charming, bawdy, with a vast storehouse of a mind out of which nothing escapes, John has remained much the same throughout the years. With him was often to be found Malcolm Lowry, either leaning through the bar at the Maypole, or strumming on his banjo' (*Indigo Days*, 17). WE delighted in Davenport's learning, wit, and boisterous sociability. See further Anthony Quinton, 'A Temporary Master', in *People: Essays and Poems*, ed. Susan Hill (1983), 138–44.

in prose, above all in letters, will no doubt do me good. I sent you an illegible scrawl a month or two ago which may well not have arrived. We live in the middle of a flat saucer, with the hills some way off, and I find that must be rather oppressive; because yesterday I got out of it for the first time (I have been walking the longer way to the hills with the tin and mercury mines before) and when I got just over this bare rocky series of fatuous rolling hills there turned out to be a little valley over the top, rich with trees, a whole village snug inside them, a lake or large pond with a sturdy temple at the far side, (a stone barn as in the Lake district with comic statues inside), and coming down to the side into the lake the real hanging gardens of the mountain paddy fields, curved like the lines of bees' wings under the microscope, high thin standing rice at each stage that you could see down to the water through, a delicate pale acid green, and that strange effect of massive engineering or 'structural' palatial archi-tecture (the terraces are very deep)—all in a little hollow just hidden from us that happens to have water, only a dimple if we could see it on our Siberian view of hills. It felt like coming home, I mean it gave me a nostalgia for the attractive parts of China and started me remembering my travels instead of daydreaming. That I wanted to tell you about, but I won't tell you about being bitten by a large bear, or the robbers who insisted on flashing their daggers in the moonlight though I told them I had an apparently permanent attack of cramp.[1] In fact I had much rather you would talk to me.

So then I went out and drank beer and found an economist student [Chang Chiu-tse] trying to read my Ulysses (which I told him not to) who told me that that fearful bombing of Canton was done to make the Can-tonese demand defence aeroplanes from Hankow, which they did, which they were refused, and their loyalty survived the refusal but the policy of intensive bombing of Canton did not. This sounds to me an explanation of a thing I wanted one of (I thought the Japs must be planning an attack near Hongkong). The indifference of the population of Canton to bombs is almost a justification of the passiveness that in other cases looks so hopeless; they are really the last people to hope to break by panic. The only people I despair of in this war are the Japanese; they may succeed in splitting China into a Communist north and capitalist south, and I fancy that might make two lovely ' " 'nations' " '. Still if WE want the East weak I suppose we may want a technical Japanese victory on those lines; nor am I prepared to think it silly to want a weak China as well as a weak Japan.

---

[1] See WE, 'Chinese Bandits', *SSS*, 187–9.

But in the long run we won't get it. But then in the long run we are all dead. I must say I feel there may be a kind of plan in [Neville] Chamberlain's policy, hard though it is to believe he is anything but a business man. I find 'Life and Letters' mentioning me as a contributor practically in the fighting lines, and this makes me wonder about my own politics; I suppose I am a belated Little Englander. But even so it is so clear that the Japanese are now smashing themselves that little england might quietly try to cash in. The one thing that we would be wrong not to do, I feel, is to back the dollars I am paid in. This seems silly enough talk. What has impressively and suddenly happened is that China (even Yunnan) has got the bug of nationalism; and the most Proustian brutalities of the hostage system in the towns cannot hold the country against that. What I fear the Japanese may succeed in doing (with disaster to themselves) is to make a communist North,

[William Empson]

Houghton: ?draft

TO ROBERT HERRING* (editor of *Life & Letters*)

The combined universities, Mengtzu, Yunnan, China
14 July [1938]
Address now: Post Office, Yunnanfu, Yunnan

My dear Herring,

I have begun you a letter once or twice, and stopped because it seemed stupid to send a letter without an article about China, and then I stopped that from feeling ignorance and distaste for gossip—we take in your paper here, after all. But George Yeh said he was thinking of sending you an article about this place, and the politics and the universities, and it gives a sensible reason for a letter to write and say he is the best chap I have come across here, so it ought to be good. Also I wish you would send that little book with my Shakespeare essays in it, as I ought in the course of leisure to be trying to finish a queer book that they would come into, and have no text.[1] For that matter back numbers with the Dog article would be appreciated, as there is only the first part yet arrived, and I need my text.[2] Anybody who writes to me is begged to tell me of books worth buying. I propose to stay another year, as that was what I undertook to do; the

[1] *Shakespeare Survey*, ed. by WE and George Garrett (1937), included two essays by WE: 'The Best Policy', 5–21, and 'Timon's Dog', 2–36.

[2] 'Timon's Dog', *Life and Letters* 15 (Winter, 1936), 108–15.

impulse simply is The Japanese are not going to stop me. I like being here or I would not have undertaken [it], but it is not about politics or journalism or anything else. The only nuisance about the money going wrong is that I lose it if I go and see friends in Hongkong or Macao or Singapore. My friends in Japan I have to avoid writing to while on Chinese territory, for fear of nuisance to them. The poem about a girl in Japan that you published left me entirely blank when I found it in the copy here.[3] It may even be decent verse, for all I know, I feel only a vague embarrassment. The poem I sent you from Nanyueh I remember now as the kind of bad-tempered letter that makes people you are fond of quarrel with you.[4] My attempts at getting out of the narrowness of my early verse are painfully half-baked. The fact is my opinions about politics are half-baked; it seems to shine through. Your paper I think is extremely good. I used like other readers to think it was a valuable rag-bag, open to decent stuff of all sorts, but now that it is defining itself I feel less able to write for it. You want a more coherent politics than mine. I have another Shakespeare essay for you about Measure for M. but have sent a copy to a Southern USA paper that asked for an article, and had said I would better give them a start even if you want it.[5] It seems to me that the present world is working through an appalling and important stage of development that cannot be tidily summed up; nationalism for instance is a senseless thing, and really the great force of the last fifty years. The Chinese I believe have now caught it like a bug—I can give evidence for that, only it is such gossip—very bad luck for the Japs in one way, it was in the nick of time—and therefore the Japs cannot possibly handle what they have taken on. But if you say that here it sounds like saying that the mere war doesn't matter; of course it matters as much as a few centuries; and the Chinese have still a strong chance given nationalism and time. A thing like cutting the Yellow river banks (which we believe here the Chinese army did) is silly clever because it throws away popular support over a large area. Anyway a lot of good is being done (which would have been done more slowly of course) by cutting out some lazy swine and more important by moving a lot of rich or educated Chinese into what they call 'the interior'; the country gent. system was running in China till the foreign ports got strong, quite recently, and the drag of all money and ability to the ports has made the villages frightfully poorer. My impulses are also poisoned by a sense that '*we*' want

---

[3] 'Aubade' was published in *Life and Letters* 17 (Winter 1937), 68–9.
[4] 'Autumn on Nan-Yüeh' first appeared in *GS* (1940).
[5] 'Sense in *Measure for Measure*' was to appear in *Southern Review*, 4 (Autumn 1938), 340–50; repr. as ch. 13 of *SCW*, 270–88.

both parties to weaken each other; the British patriot would be insane to back the Japanese, but he could also fairly be frightened of a rapidly victorious China. The Japs attacked only just in time for their military plan and I think too late for the political one. But they could conceivably hold great areas for scores of years, by the system of putting up fairly important local puppets in small towns and holding their families as hostages; a very hard thing to break once they hold the town.

Yours

Bill Empson.

None of this is private if you cared to quote bits.

Houghton: copy, bMS Eng 1401 (573)

TO KATHARINE SANSOM

Hanoi

27 September [1938]

Dear Lady Sansom,

I feel it is viewed with more favour at both ends if I write to you from outside China, so this is a good time; I am going down to Singapore to stay with a teacher [Graham Hough*] there for a bit. Our school starts in Yunnanfu on the first of December, to leave room for military training, and then has only a week off till July, too long. Probably I go home then. The papers just now are bursting with mobilisation; rather nice to read about in Annam, because the Annamites are so obviously not going to fight anybody ever. It gives a soothing effect. But I don't think this war will come now anyway. Yunnanfu is very crowded and I have been sleeping on a blackboard, that is taking the profession very seriously, only not for long as I went up to see [C. P.] Fitzgerald[1] in Talifu. We just missed seeing the first bus come through from Burma, in two days. I collected some seeds of a big golden rhododendron to send my mamma, but as they only grow at 14,000 feet it seems possible they won't grow in York. F. claims you can tell the height within 500 feet by the types of rh. but failed (I thought) to make this good. The seeds were apparently suspected of being opium on the way back and a lot got scattered. A chap called Pollard Urquhart, if you met him in Peking, has been sent to Yunnanfu to run the Richards

---

[1] C. P. Fitzgerald (1902–92), historian and anthropologist, was educated at the School of Oriental and African Studies, London, and undertook field work in China from 1923 to 1939. At the time of this letter he was making an anthropological survey of the non-Chinese Min Chia people. From 1946 to 1950 he was British Council representative in Peking, where WE came to know him well. His publications include *China: A Short Cultural History* (1935).

teaching scheme, very good company, and seems to be getting something done, but as the Middle Schools have just been moved out for fear of bombs he will have to buy a bicycle.[2] The bombing scare has the good effect of making rather more room in the town, and I don't think will come to much, as you get a prevailing wind from Thibet soon after the rains stop. I haven't heard from Richards since Canada, and don't know where he is; there was a rumour he was to give up Cambridge and stay in America as King of Basic etc. My brother Charles has got out of Palestine and has a job in Rome, rather a comfort for them. I should be very pleased if you could send a note to me c/o G. Hough, Raffles College, Singapore (I feel I can't expect you or the Redmans[3] to write to China) saying how Mrs Nishiwaki[4] and people are getting on. It must be a bit bleak. The effect of the war on Yunnan is simply to let the westernised Chinese get it developed a bit, and the work seems to be going on quick though there is an antiforeign feeling working up against them. The manager of a new mechanised saltmine near Talifu, dressed as a soldier because it belongs to a division of the Yunnan army, was saying how it wouldn't have happened for twenty years without the war. We went on up beyond LiChiang [Lijiang] and saw tribes and a few Thibetans, but it was the wrong time of year, they felt very hot and some had taken their boots off, which it seems hardly ever happens. I am glad to be out of Mengtzu, the dead city, but it is a place to have lived in. It would be fine to read a Sitwell reconstruction of the two hundred Frenchmen who were settled residents of the place in 1900. They say the consulate was kept up so thoroughly after the exodus that fresh ink and paper were laid regularly on the official desk not as they were used up but as they withered away. It was laid out as a very pretty provincial town. The Customs Compound was modelled on the Forbidden

[2] Arthur Pollard-Urquhart, an energetic Scot, taught English in the Western Languages Department at Tsinghua University. In Kunming, where he arrived on 25 Aug., he rented premises at 78 Pei Men Kai (where WE became his lodger and friend) in order to run a branch of the Basic English Institute, with support from the Rockefeller Foundation, on behalf of R. D. Jameson and IAR. (See Rockefeller Archive Center: RG 1, series 601, box 48, folder 397: 'Orthological Institute, China'.) Pollard-Urquhart (who had urged IAR to make his first visit to China in 1929) was killed in a car accident during an air raid, a year after WE's return to the UK in 1940.

[3] H. Vere (later Sir Vere) Redman taught during the 1930s at Tokyo Commercial College; he worked too as a journalist, and won a reputation for his understanding of Japanese affairs. In 1939 he was made press attaché at the British Embassy, which he left for London at the end of 1942—though not before being arrested by the *Kempeitai* (the Japanese gestapo) and incarcerated in solitary confinement in Sugamo prison for eight months. During the war he was to serve as Director of the Far East Division of the Ministry of Information. See Sir Hugh Cortazzi, 'Sir Vere Redman, 1901–1975', in *Britain & Japan: Biographical Portraits*, iii (1997).

[4] WE took drawing lessons from Marjorie Nishiwaki, an English artist married to a Japanese who lived in the old medieval capital of Kamakura, south of Tokyo.

City; it was nearly enough to house the combined universities even though many buildings had fallen down. I am interested about the way Yunnan rides horses. The bit and the saddlegirth are never used, when do you suppose they were invented? Was that why the war chariot was going for a thousand years before the cavalry came in? Did Genghis use a bit? I can't get these experts to take an interest. It turns out that there are Taoist automatic paintings, very surrealist, done in a state of trance; there was one in an inn where we stopped but nobody could tell us any more about it. I am sending Julian Trevelyan a collection of war posters, and they are surrealist enough, but the Taoist ones seem to be made according to the theory. It is puzzling to know whether to write a travel book; this last year has been a bit out of the way, though next year will be dull I should think, but on the other hand all the vultures have descended and there is going to be such a gush of books about China, all left unsaleable I should think by the coming war. It seems that Victor Purcell has written a book about the journey across China he and I did with the Richards, which I need to get hold of; he was heading for a quarrel with Dowwofea all the way and it burst out at the end. ('Chinese Evergreen'.) It struck me at the time it would make a real funny novel but I only saw him as a character and certainly wouldn't have written it myself. The truth is that ill-natured jokes about your companions are very nearly all you think of while travelling, so naturally that has to be the material of the travel book. But what Purcell has put in I don't yet know.[5]

Love
Bill Empson.

Houghton, bMS Eng 1401 (645)

TO IAN PARSONS

78 Pei Men Kai, Kunming, Yunnan, China, via Hanoi
11 February [1939]

My dear Ian,

It seems not much use writing across these distances, but Imperial Airways is coming here, and that ought to make a letter take only five days and be reasonably cheap. I haven't heard from anybody but my mama for some while; the truth is I suspect that people write by ordinary mail and

---

[5] Purcell would write to IAR on 19 Dec. 1938: 'Did you read my "Chinese Evergreen"? I was a little anxious about your reactions but Bill Empson [who had visited Purcell in Malaya before rejoining his university-in-exile in Kunming] says he thought I treated us all "very kindly". I hope you think so too.' (*Magdalene*)

the letters get burnt in Shanghai. Hoping this finds you in the pink as it leaves me. We haven't been bombed for a long while, which rather offends us, but presumably they will get here before the rains. My best love to Juan Marks, hope he is all right.[1]

I am trying to pull together a language book [*SCW*], which is mostly finished really but seems to have no shape. You may have seen bits of it in Life and Letters and the Criterion. (L and L put two bits into a pamphlet which I ought to have asked your permission for, come to think of it). It really ought to be done by the autumn. What do you think about a chatty travel book? I feel it is only sensible to cash in on the travelling. But it would have to be light and thin; I don't want to pretend to know about politics and be 'frank' about people. Stuff like the articles sent to poor Night and Day.[2] (By the way, I suppose there's no question of being paid for those travel articles, supposing any of them got printed?). Also in a year or two there may be a question of a new edition of Ambiguity; at least I gathered from sales that the thing was trickling slowly and steadily to the end of the edition. I read it the other day and thought the beginning parts seemed very beastly. I should like to cut and alter a fair amount in the first two chapters and leave the rest as they stand. However you may not think it worth while; I don't remember from the contract that I have any right to demand it. The really urgent thing is an index. As to a preface, if I am allowed to clean up some of the muddle at the start it is perhaps worth

---

[1] John Marks (1909–67) was a fervent hispanophile. After graduating from Magdalene College, where he had edited *Granta*, he spent some time in Spain and was then employed as a publishers' reader by Chatto & Windus and by Cassell; he was also, for a while, film critic of the *New Statesman*. After initial wartime work at the Ministry of Information, he was seconded to the BBC where he made broadcasts to Spain. He served for ten years from 1943 as correspondent of *The Times* in Madrid. After working for some years as Night Editor at United Press International, he ultimately went freelance until his death from cancer at the age of 58. He is celebrated for his translation of Louis-Ferdinand Céline's *Voyage au Bout de la Nuit*.

[2] *Night & Day*, a glossy magazine modelled on the *New Yorker*, was edited by Graham Greene and WE's friend John Marks (with Ian Parsons as managing director); it ran for just six months from 1 Jul. 1937, being finally ruined by a libel action involving Greene's review of Shirley Temple's film *Wee Willie Winkie*. WE contributed 'Notice This Gate', to the first issue; he also sent 'Travel Note' (about Ceylon), 5 Aug.; 'Learning Chinese', 19 Aug.; and 'Letter from China', 25 Nov. The series was republished in a single volume, ed. Christopher Hawtree, as *Night and Day* (1985), with a Preface by Greene: 'It's sad to think how few of our regular contributors are left to remember Night and Day—Anthony Powell, V. S. Pritchett, Feliks Topolski, Malcolm Muggeridge, Osbert Lancaster, Hugh Casson—but is there any paper which can rival our roll of honour? It reads like the death of a whole literary generation: Evelyn Waugh, Elizabeth Bowen, Herbert Read, William Empson, Nicolas Bentley, John Betjeman, Cyril Connolly, Stevie Smith, A. J. A. Symons, John Hayward, Hugh Kingsmill, William Plomer' (vii). Shirley Hazzard was to note, in *Greene on Capri: A Memoir* (2000), that Greene admired WE's poetry: 'Graham pointed out that Empson was a poet: "Practising rather than prating" ' (75–6). (Greene was presumably alluding to Iago's dismissal of Cassio's 'soldiership' as 'mere prattle without practice' (*Othello*, I. i. 25).)

saying that the attempt has been made. There have been two letters from America, practically a fan mail, and I think the book is getting a small belated sale over there.

I am living very comfortably with a chap doing Basic here, in a house rented from the British and Foreign Bible Society. Basic seems to be doing well, in a slow way, as it has to be; Richards has done a very good first year book. Yunnan is being developed a great deal; this end of China is going to be an important country whatever the eastern end does. Climate lovely. There is really no excuse if I don't get some work done . . . Regards to McDougal.[3]

Yours
Bill Empson.

Reading

TO JOHN HAYWARD

78 Pei Men Kai, Kunming, Yunnan, China via Hanoi
4 March [1939]

My dear John,

I got a letter from you last year, and began at once writing how grateful I was for a letter and eager to reply, but for some reason that and the later attempt were never finished. That was in Mengtzu; I am now in a very different scene of life. I shall try to do gossip about it. It is almost the boarding house life which I thought vainly I should never lead. The house belongs to the British and Foreign Bible Society, owners now on leave, but we have an American Shanghai Bible salesman eating here, and his wife, and a depressed refugee Jew who teaches German. The renter is a Peking art-and-sin fan, (cf Florence),[1] very nice, sent down here by Richards to run a Basic training place. He is very good at dealing with Chinese, and it is going well. He is nature's landlady though furious at being made one, and appalled by the hardships of this town; from the Spartan sleeping on the blackboard, the high ideals, the companionable silence throughout the Chinese meal, I now go down from my charming bedroom and balcony to a perpetual squeal of complaint and attack on China throughout the

[3] William McDougall, Reader in Mental Psychology at the University of Oxford; author of *Psychology: The Study of Behaviour* (1912) and *The Group Mind* (1920).

[1] P. Sargant Florence (1890–1982) was Professor of Commerce at Birmingham University, 1929–55. An American citizen with a lively, witty personality, he was a friend at Cambridge of C. K. Ogden, and a founder of the Heretics Society and of the *Cambridge Review*. His works include *Basic English for the Social Sciences* (1962).

excellent European meal. I was puzzled to know why he contradicted himself till I realized it was because virtue is a mean; there are therefore always two possible complaints on every topic, and he says both. Happy talk about birds is going safely on with the Bible salesman. Polly: Of course the Chinese catch birds and sell them *alive*, something for nothing, irresistible to a Chinese, of course that's all they care about birds. After a pause the Bible salesman says Of course some Chinese are very fond of birds, they *buy* birds. I KNOW says Polly leaping on him, they give far too much, ridiculous extravagance. It is a great change after last year.

I am doing some unpaid teaching at a strange little man's school, half Chinese half French, half brother to Lady Somebody married to a diplomat, who doesn't know. Seems about seventy, has been running this school on charity, very poor, for the last forty years, still talks in millions. Another of the people who were ruined by a lawsuit in French IndoChina—say they were. He bored Polly badly when he came to dinner and stayed after midnight. I was fascinated hearing the old gentleman get tipsy and live over again all his lawsuits. We couldn't guess at all how much was true, he is maybe a bit mad, but very nice and it is a remarkably good school. My first lecture there he kept running in and out like a butler bringing brandy and cigarettes, a great nuisance, and he is supposed not to be able to afford it. In the old days he used to have the British consul come over to the school and expect comforts. He goes back before the railway.

The present British consul here is a pity; he carries the blank and glum style so far that the man sent by the British Government to see the track of the Burma railway, for instance, refused to give him any information, so he is not only hated by business people but can't tell them anything. He is famous for getting an injunction from Shanghai (under extraterritorial rights, this year) to suppress a dog in the next house which he said barked. He gets £100 entertainment allowance and doesn't entertain at all. His wife is fond of saying she liked Japan and the Chinese say he is a Japanese spy. Being offended at being sent here he denies there is any trade at all, which as I say is a pity, because there are quite large opportunities from Burma. The poor things have a childminded daughter who came here to a cocktail party and hid behind the piano. It was like feeding a bear in a cage. He told Polly the Burma road was closed two days before an arranged visit of Burma government people came up the road with fifty tons of machine guns to discuss prospects with him. A disappointed man.

It was nice when we had an air raid alarm at the beginning of this term, when one walks out among the graves outside the town, and we saw some men digging a hole, and when asked why they were digging the hole they said This is the Burma railway. The embankments round here are made now but may melt in the rains. It will kill I am afraid the delightful mule trade which had been going for centuries, but the part up through Li Chiang (so far as I went) to Thibet is all right. You get very pro modernisation here; when they put the iodine in the salt, which they will though it is held up at present, they will cure half the population of goitre. The mines are already worked, under the worst labour conditions in the world, and the sciences only improve them.

The bomb situation is complex but mild. I doubt if they'll come again. We are told that they have just published in a Peking paper that they mean to bomb this town, and that these announcements are usually true, but that seems too whimsical to believe. This house has a garden round it if the town burns, as it would (it has no fire engine) and is by the American consulate. The school is outside the walls. Last false alarm three people were crushed to death leaving the town, in the gates; getting caught in the town while shopping might be bad. But raids only occur in the morning and shops only open in the afternoon. The graves outside the wall have largely been turned into dugouts by digging them open, you squat there and look out. Three dollars a grave is paid to the Grave Protection societies and the bones are replanted in large piles on the hills. You have to get in because the police have orders to shoot anyone who stands up, but they would be likely to miss. We brought down an aeroplane here last time they came; one must remember to call it three aeroplanes, because three villages reported it and this statement is officially held to. It was brought down by a learner who happened to be in the air at the time; he flew along behind them, in an interested way, which it seems is a totally hopeless form of attack, so hopeless and easily countered that the Japanese had not been taught what to do. They turned round and went home, having killed about ten people. The French defenders of the town are supposed to have refused to leave the ground.

The American consulate are nice people but pursue culture, one young lady visitor exhibiting embarrassingly bad paintings, another with an e. b. novel about China which poor Polly was asked to vet. I was asked to read my verses at a tea and I am afraid offended them by saying No I Won't like a child, but still can't think of any polite way it could be said. Touchingly generous, there was a big party which went on flowing with champagne because, they said, they had run out of everything else. Americans all believe there will be a European war in a few months, which seems quite mistaken of them. We get the wireless every night about the weather and where the queen is. I can't decide whether to come home in July or not.

Much love
Bill Empson.

Theodore Hofmann

TO JOHN HAYWARD

76 Pei Men Kai, Kunming, Yunnan, China via Hanoi
4 May [1939]

My dear John,

Glad to hear from you.[1] I sent a rather fretful message to you via Eliot, but meant nothing; I don't gather that my mamma is bothering about bombs [the Japanese bombing of Kunming] anyway. Rather glad to hear you have a wide view, after the move, I used to feel that very beautiful room [at JDH's former address] was rather shut in. Interesting that the Richards were trying to have a baby, very sorry they didn't succeed. Or were they maybe after all not trying? Poor [Derek] Verschoyle, I'm rather glad he's left her, I had an impression he was overstrained holding down the job all day and the wife all night.[2] There is a story that three thousand government advisers have been sent by Japan to Bangkok, in column of fours presumably, [which] seemed somehow a parallel case. I have just got a letter from Fleming inspired by you, nice of you to give the leg-up, I shall try to do something but have just sent off most of my few opinions to Life and Letters.[3] You don't say how Dryden is going on; I wish to God I could get on with my mad little literary book, the Sibylline leaves are gradually being thrown away by the servant. We had an air raid the other day, with so much incompetence on both sides that the local governor was suspected of a private arrangement, which I don't believe. I am trying to arrange a year off and then come back, as it seems hard just to walk out. Means

[1] John Hayward had written to WE from 115 Swan Court, Chelsea, London, on 26 March 1939: 'I've moved from Bina Gardens to Chelsea, where I have a flat of my own and an aged crone who keeps house . . . I made up my mind to leave my Etruscan-Tudor bed-sitting room in Earl's Court after the Munich Crisis, when my Christian landlady delivered an ultimatum to the effect that if war broke out—as it damn well nearly did—she would not be responsible for feeding or watering me . . . I'm seven stories up with a fine view over London in the direction the bombers will take if they decide to come . . . Mrs. Richards had a bad miscarriage but is now restored to normal health . . . I told Peter Fleming (The Times) he should get you to write an article or two on the situation in Yunnang. He said he'd write.' (*Houghton*)
[2] Derek Verschoyle (1911–73): literary editor of *The Spectator*, 1932–40. His works include *XXX Poems* (1931) and *The English Novelists* (1936).
[3] 'A Chinese University', *Life and Letters* 25 (Jun. 1940); in *SSS*, 190–4.

paying passage myself. I feel rather unwilling to lose the foothold here, with people feeling so black at home, though this war of yours looks less likely now. The wireless has given out and we have now no news.

May 16 Seems now pretty definite that I am coming home in July or so. How frightfully unwilling I feel to put down anything on paper. I am still far too talkative, though. George Yeh says he wants to write articles for English papers but somehow it seems hard to praise China, when he sits down to it. I feel exactly that, the little article to L and L was taken twice to the post after all the re-writing because I was so afraid of saying something disagreeable. Let alone what lies we all tell, anything I say in a letter turns out to be wrong shortly afterwards. Ian Parsons wants a travel book and maybe if I can take some kind of purgative I can tell all my polite funny stories once and for all and then stop. As I get older I find I still act the same way at parties but get alcoholic remorse the next and even subsequent days more heavily. It seems to me I must have been really intolerable last week at the American Consulate (though probably they were quite pleased to have something to laugh at) and the depressed tone of this letter maybe only comes from that.

Somebody had poor Julian Bell's great gushing Life and Letters it would have offended him rather I think.[4] But my word how he did write letters. And what is this business of keeping letters? Do *you* keep letters?[5] It must be a widespread practice judging from biographies. Rather an ugly one I think. It certainly couldn't be done in my mother's house, where any writing left about (including two complete plays of mine some time ago) gets immediately destroyed. Very properly too, as I feel even when it turns out inconvenient. Do you suppose for instance that all your correspondents are saving up the letters for the life and letters? And do they get *paid* for this rather eerie and passive piece of work? How unexpected people are. But perhaps Julian's lot were more likely to do that kind of thing. Darwin I remember, though, a different kind of man, said it had been a

[4] Julian Bell, *Essays, Poems and Letters*, ed. Quentin Bell (1938). Elder son of Clive and Vanessa Bell, Bell (1908–37) grew up at the centre of the Bloomsbury circle that included his uncle and aunt, Leonard and Virginia Woolf. Educated at King's College, Cambridge, where he became acquainted with WE, he published a volume of poems, *Winter Movement*, in 1930; and his work was represented (alongside poems by WE, Auden, and Spender) in Michael Roberts's watershed anthology *New Signatures* (1932). After teaching at the University of Wuhan, 1935–7, he left China in order to participate in the Spanish Civil War, serving as an ambulance driver with Spanish Medical Aid: he was killed on 18 Jul. 1937.

[5] These comments are clarified in a letter to WE's mother dated 7 Apr. 1939: 'Thanks for the Sunday Times cutting. Rather annoying to have the friends selling the letters, that must be John Hayward. I think he might have bought a stamp with the proceeds and written back to me. What I told you was quite as true as what I told him, though the details about the graves are true.' (*Houghton*)

great help to him never to destroy a single letter . . . By the way, what on earth was the disease of Darwin? Was it simply neurotic? They never say, and he seems a very unneurotic man otherwise.

All my love

Bill Empson

TO IAN PARSONS

78 Pei Men Kai, Kunming, Yunnan via Hanoi
16 May (1939)

My dear Ian,

It seems fairly settled now that I am to take a year off and come home this autumn, so there is no great need to write long letters. I should want in a travel book to tell my polite funny stories once for all, the difficulty is to get the tone so that you aren't being too rude or revealing, but there is surely quite a flow once that has been found. I don't well see why you want to see samples. As I understand I have undertaken to give you the refusal of my next book anyway, for any offer that you make within reason. Actually I have ignored an offer from another firm [I forget which] (very annoying to get that here thinking it was an interesting letter) because I presumed that was in the contract. The next *two* books was I think put in the contract of *Ambiguity*. I should like a more definite agreement in the contract for this one, but as regards pay for this one I thought I had already made myself unable to bargain. Of course I was thinking of literary books not made to sell much anyway, and if I am to do a chat book for money it seems a pity not to be able to fight for money. But I should never have thought of that if you hadn't put it into my head. What worries me is to know whether a chat book would be bad for the reputation, but in fact it obviously wouldn't if done in a quiet casual way. The real auto-biography there seems no great need to record. What I would like to say in a businesslike tone is what happened to the travel articles sent to Night and Day (with which I understand you were connected); if they were printed did nobody pay me for them even in some token form? If they were not printed can I still get the text back for my chat book? I should want also to put in two or three articles about Buddhas, short and I think quite harm-less to the balance of the thing; photographs would of course be very nice but perhaps rather overbalancing, and I wouldn't fight for them. It wouldn't be a straight travel book, any story placed in England that fitted in could come. I have got a small sheaf of bits for it done; what I don't see is the kind of tone and shape, but it ought to be done quickly if at all. I am grateful to you for writing and asking for it because increasing sickness with my literary book (one sheer chapter of which has been thrown away by the servant here) makes me feel I haven't enough stuff for it yet and [I] would like to hold it back. Eliot said to me long ago that Ambiguity was a pity in its present form and ought to be made tolerable, and I must try to see what permanent reshaping can be done when I get to England.[1] I should be prepared to pay for getting the edition decent, but the issue about re-paging could no doubt be settled easily. It seems important to take this one chance of improving the thing. I don't feel so sure though that I will be competent to improve it during the chance; I only feel that a lot of the first chapter and bits of confusion in the second are below the standard aimed at. Besides as I am entitled to demand a second edition by the contract it is worth your while to be able to advertise second thoughts for a further trickle of sale.

Your letter came at a good time, helping me out of the gloom of the first week of the rain. Now that I have got leave for England and libraries without losing the connection I ought to be up and doing, like the maiden lady who always beat carters for the sake of their horses in the springtime.

Tra la la. It all looks fairly black, but at last the wireless has broken here, so we aren't forced to hear the news.

Bill Empson

Reading

TO *SCRUTINY* (Unpublished)

[No address; n.d.: March 1940]

An unpublished response to D. W. Harding, 'Regulated Hatred: An Aspect of the Work of Jane Austen'—*Scrutiny* 8: 4 (Mar. 1940), 346–62; collected in *Regulated Hatred and Other Essays on Jane Austen*, ed. Monica Lawlor (1998)— an essay which contested the notion that Austen was a writer of affectionate satire; on the contrary, she was intensely critical of her society. 'Hence one of [her] most successful methods is to offer her readers every excuse for regarding as rather exaggerated figures of fun people whom she herself detests and fears . . . The people she hated were tolerated, accepted, comfortably

---

[1] Cf. E. W. F. Tomlin, *T. S. Eliot: A Friendship* (1988), 45: 'Referring to [*STA*], Eliot said he thought Empson ought to re-write it from start to finish.'

ensconced in the only human society she knew; they were, for her, society's embarrassing unconscious comment on itself' (352–3).[1]

Dear Sir,

I have a point or two of objection to the article on Jane Austen in your last number, not very serious, but it seems a good thing to have a discussion about so good an article.

This left-wing-intellectual approach to the lady, the idea that Tories think she is praising the present system, but we pink boys know that her heart is with the rebels—it is equally grim whether Mr Harding is being absurd or the readers he considers normal are. Surely anybody ought not to need to *discover* through Unconscious Psychology that Jane Austen hated and feared her comic monsters of cruelty and stupidity; or that Dickens did either, for that matter. Mr Harding says it is 'unbelievable' [348] that Henry Tilney could have said that in polite society in the English counties 'every man is surrounded with a neighbourhood of voluntary spies'. It is unbelievable (apparently) because he is not presented as an embittered or politically dangerous person; and because Jane Austen knew so well in her own life the nuisance of affectionate family observation, so that she could only have meant this to be said bitterly. What would really be surprising would be if Henry Tilney had got through one speech in the whole novel without dragging in his stock vein of humour. It seems very likely that Jane Austen found the attack on romantic novels, which she wanted to make through his mouth, was getting too solemn, so she put this phrase in as an afterthought to keep him 'in character'. The only 'paranoiac' part of the question is Mr Harding's idea, that nobody could strike out a phrase like that without 'a touch of paranoia' [348].

Do not accuse me of taking a cosy view. Jane Austen undoubtedly felt the suffering of living in 'a neighbourhood of spies', and of what Mr Harding calls the thesis of another of her jokes, that 'the ruling standards of our social group leave a perfectly comfortable niche for detestable people and give them sufficient sanction to persist'. He is only wrong in saying that if she had said this she would have aroused 'the most violent opposition'. Because she did say it. He is only discovering the obvious. What is this revolution that he feels she might have sponsored? that is the

---

[1] D. W. Harding (1906–93) read English and Psychology at Emmanuel College, Cambridge. He was co-editor, with FRL, of *Scrutiny*, 1933–47. After early years at the London School of Economics and at Liverpool University, he became the first Professor of Psychology at Bedford College, London, 1945–68. He edited the *British Journal of Psychology*, 1948–54. His writings include *Experience into Words* (1963).

only political question. Nowadays no doubt she could have had a private revolution and gone to live somewhere where she would only meet other lady novelists, instead of a whole cross-section of the life of the country. She would certainly have thought that personally and in a small degree socially harmful, as it is. As to any public revolt against Upper Class Politeness, the idea is faced very squarely in *Mansfield Park*. After many pages of growing horror at the evils of subsidised snobbery and stupidity the heroine is sent back to her mother, married to a decent highgrade worker in Portsmouth, and nobody there is unkind to her. Weighing the contrast slowly, the heroine decides that the evils of life at her grand aunt's house are *nothing* beside the pains of life in Portsmouth, and that these pains come chiefly from the (natural and inevitable) want of Politeness in Portsmouth. Now it was because Jane Austen was willing to work for general Politeness that she had to endure the evils against which Mr Harding represents her (if I am right) as unconsciously but feverishly revolting.[2] And from what I remember of her life she had a good deal of experience of Portsmouth and what it stood for to make her decision with; there was a good deal of discussion, wasn't there, about whether she had better be sent to keep house for one of her cousins in a debtor's jail? and little jokes about bastards and so forth in her surviving letters which presume a less prim attitude in her intimates than we find in her books? and at the same time phrases like 'I think we all maybe ought to be Methodists', as you might say now 'Salvation Army lasses'? What I am trying to argue is that the things Mr Harding thinks he is discovering in her Unconsciousness or in her secret tricks with an unconscious public are quite simply in the sunlight of her writings, and in the experience (one would presume) of any reasonable critic who praises her.

It is wrong to assume (much more widely than in this case) that Jane Austen must *either* have had 'an ambition of entertaining a posterity of urbane gentlemen' *or* some dark psychological need to write something that would let her complexes creep out and yet pass off as normal. What any tolerable urbane gentleman enjoys in her writing is precisely her full illustration of the moral which she herself clearly drew. In any tolerable society, whatever its political arrangement, you will have a variety of people meeting each other, and therefore Politeness will be necessary, and to maintain Politeness is liable to involve serious sacrifices. Yet they are

---

[2] Harding notes that Austen 'allies the Cinderella theme to another folk-tale theme which is often introduced—that of the princess brought up by unworthy parents but never losing the delicate sensibilities which are an inborn part of her . . . The contrast between Fanny Price's true nature and her squalid home at Portsmouth is the clearest statement of the idea' (355).

worth it; if only because Politeness is the outward sign of more serious values less often called on. That is what all the urbane jokes are made out of. It may be very offensive to a Communist. But really it isn't buried in the Unconsciousness of the author or the normal reader.

Yours etc.

William Empson

Houghton carbon, bMS Eng 1401 (647)

TO JAMES JESUS ANGLETON*

Robin W. Winks describes James Jesus Angleton's success while a student at Yale University in 1939 in acting as 'an impresario on behalf of William Empson. Empson was returning from China to England in the company of I. A. Richards, the critic Angleton particularly admired, and both were in Cambridge, Massachusetts. After a soccer game there, Angleton sought Empson out and persuaded him to give a lecture at Yale. He then persuaded Dean [William] DeVane, who did not care for Empson's work, to provide the necessary fee. Angleton mailed invitations to dozens of poets and stayed up the night before the scheduled event until 3:00 A.M. slipping notices under student doors. When he returned to [Reed] Whittemore's room he found the speaker passed out, apparently from alcohol, and feared the worst. The next day, however, Empson stood before his huge audience for long moments in silence, and then, as he finally began, at first haltingly and then with newfound vigor, he captivated the crowd and so won over the dean that DeVane said he might offer Empson a permanent job at Yale— though when Angleton broached the subject with Empson, the critic said that he must return to England' (*Cloak & Gown: Scholars in the Secret War, 1939–1961* (1987), 337).

95 Lamb's Conduit St., London W. C. 1

12 June [1940]

My dear Angleton,

Thanks very much for your letter, which I got yesterday, so it took six weeks. It is very kind of you to be still thinking about getting me a job in America, and I hope to work there some time after the war, but I don't think I could, or would want to, go till then. I felt very mixed about applying for jobs when I was there, and am glad now that nobody gave me one; to be sure I could have stayed on working for Richards; but it seems clear that this is the proper place for an Englishman to be at present. I tried to get a Ministry of Information job that would send me back to China, though (my teaching job in China is still held open for me); and now the B. B. C. have given me a job sub-editing Lord Haw-Haw, doing during the night a precis of the day's foreign broadcasts.[1] I am to be called up in a few months' time, and don't mean to try and nip into the army before, very likely the eyes will be considered too bad anyway.

I have just handed over a collection of verse to T. S. Eliot at Faber's and the contract gives them sole right to assign American rights; maybe that doesn't mean much, but Eliot I think would be good at placing them.[2] I am hoping to get a combined American volume from the two English books of verse. As soon as I get proofs I will send you off a spare set, and let you know what suggestions he has to make about publishers etc. As to revising Ambiguity, I am ashamed to say I haven't done it yet; the English publisher will only stand for photographing the original and changing 16 or 32 pages at the start, and that makes it feel rather a pokey job. Chatto's have rather a distaste for books and are a good deal wrapped up in warwork; they felt sure no American publisher would want the revised text; I should be very grateful if you could get something done ahead of them. However first I have got to do the work myself. This seems rather a choking-off reply to you, but anyway I am grateful and will keep you in touch.

Eliot gave his latest poem to The New English Weekly[3] because he likes its economics, but I hear it has now turned very Fascist or Fifth-Column and bothered him rather . . . but looking again I see you were wondering why he gave it to the Partisan Review. I wouldn't know; he's almost dangerously loyal to old friends; probably if it needs explaining he's got one on the paper. He is in excellent form. Spender published a journal in 'Horizon' with an absurd write-up of a lunch with 'Tom', in which Spender is always telling Tom why Tom's poetry isn't going to last etc., and how Spender's will, because of its directness, innocence etc. I asked Eliot what he thought of this and he said (this must be read in an Eliot imitation): 'Well, the manuscript was kindly submitted to me, for my criticisms. It seemed to me necessary, in the interests of truth, to correct

[1] The US-born William Joyce (1906–46), who was educated in London and gained a first-class degree in English from Birkbeck College, London, became a Fascist and began broadcasting propaganda from Germany in the Reichsrundfunk's English-language service in Sept. 1939. His nickname 'Lord Haw-Haw' was coined by a *Daily Express* journalist. By Jun. 1942 he was to become the chief commentator in the English-language service, and in Sept. 1944 he was awarded Germany's war merit cross first class. Arrested by the British, he was to be convicted of treason in late 1945 and hanged in London in Jan. 1946.

[2] *GS* was to be published by Faber & Faber on 19 Sept. 1940.

[3] 'East Coker', *New English Weekly*, 16: 22 (21 Mar. 1940), 325–8.

the name of the cheese.'[4] It's a beautifully good tempered kind of humour he has.

Glad you told me about Norton; please tell him if you see him that I wanted to see him again and was simply too busy. As for MacNeice, I have nothing whatever against him except a dim impression that he doesn't like me, but I feel sure that this mutual delusion started from him.[5] If I had a special grudge against somebody I would regard it as an alarming symptom of madhouse psychology. Sorry I missed him in New York.

June 26   It seems silly sending off letters now so I kept this a bit, and am now tearing out some wise remarks about America and the war. Too much talk. The only thing to do with Ambiguity, I now feel, is to proof correct the text only, give a few pages of notes saying where it seems wrong ten years later, and as you say give an index.

Yours very sincerely
Bill Empson.

Yale: YCAL MSS 75, Box 1, folder 30

TO JAMES JESUS ANGLETON

69 Burford Road, Evesham, Gloucestershire
29 July [1940]

My dear Angleton,

I'm afraid I *don't* want that letter published, though if you have published it already I can put up with it. It's all right for me to say 'this is the

---

[4] It seems possible that Spender invited TSE to see his piece only after its initial publication, since it was only in the various reprintings of the journal that the cheese was finally identified as Port Salud. See Stephen Spender, 'September Journal', *Horizon*, 1: 5 (May 1940), 356–67, 359: 'I had lunch with Tom Eliot a few days ago at his club. The stupid thing is that I can hardly remember anything of what he said. I remember that we had cheese, which he chose . . . I said how necessary I felt it to be lucid in poetry when the world was so chaotic. Eliot said he thought the poetic drama might be a way of attaining to lucidity, because, I suppose, it puts one outside oneself, whereas the poem tends to-day to be an introspective monologue . . .

'Eliot said that an objective form might lie in the poetic drama, because here one had to meet one's audience half-way and adopt to some extent its standards. I agreed, but this, of course, raised the question of whether the poetic drama is a suitable form for the stage to-day . . . I asked him whether he didn't feel that perhaps the trick of his poetry wasn't to make the reader identify himself with Tom Eliot and enter into his subjective vision. Then how could he be sure that at a later time, when the personal music and situations of Tom's poetry are no longer such as people can easily enter into, that his poetry won't be seen too much from the outside . . .?'

[5] Louis MacNeice (1907–63), poet and dramatist, was Lecturer in Classics at Birmingham University, 1930–6, and Lecturer in Greek, Bedford College, London, 1936–40, before becoming a producer and feature writer for the BBC, 1940–9. In a curious entry in *The Concise Encyclopedia of English and American Poets and Poetry*, ed. Stephen Spender and Donald Hall (1963), MacNeice described WE as 'the oddest English poet who wrote between the two World Wars . . . And of his generation he is probably unique in that he has not a trace of self-pity' (128).

proper place to be' in a private letter, where I am talking about myself, but as soon as I have it published I am obviously hinting about other people, and I want to avoid that. In fact it would be positively unfair. Anyway I believe I told you I was waiting to be called up, and now I have settled down as a reserved occupation in the BBC, for a bit anyway (so it wouldn't be true). I hardly know why; I imagine I should enjoy the company in the army, and nobody could pretend I was necessary here, though I make them get the names of Chinese towns right sometimes. Partly the line of news; it is very fascinating to have all the world's wireless brought you every day. And I know what an incompetent soldier I am from the O.T.C. [Officer Training Corps, at Winchester College] so feel I am very likely more useful here.

You would like to hear that the country house has electrified wire round the estate, and we are challenged by four successive sentries in the dark before reaching the hut where we work till dawn; looking down from the hill at dawn you get the same level low-lying bank of fog that we did when isolated on the Sacred Mountain, a thing the Japanese paint very well.[1] Of course other people find the colourful detail much more striking than the person who's used to it, but I was pleased about the fog.

You ask about Eliot's War Work. He thinks it is important war work to go on publishing in England, chiefly verse because of the paper shortage. He was willing to do propaganda in Italy of course, but that was too late. He may very well be patrolling the streets of London at night, but if so he'd probably not tell; he is very silent. I feel myself it's likely to go on a long time, which makes one rather uneager to rush into things. What a nasty story about Macleish: it makes one want to keep quiet, don't you feel? Still I must say I might be doing a bit more than I am.

Very glad to hear that Eberhart is leaving his school; as you say it seemed to be time.[2] Give my best wishes back to the Cummings's.[3] I am hoping to settle down at last to fidgeting with the text of Ambiguity, and will send you a (short) draft of the corrections as soon as possible. It will have to go through Chatto's of course but they wouldn't complain about

---

[1] See WE's poem 'Autumn on Nan-Yueh'.

[2] Richard Eberhart (1904–2005), US poet and critic who befriended WE while reading for a BA at St John's College, Cambridge, and became an enthusiast for his poetry. From 1933 to 1941 he was an English master at St Mark's School, Southborough, Mass. In 1951 he founded the Poet's Theatre in Cambridge, Mass. He was to be Professor of English and poet-in-residence at Dartmouth College, 1956–70. His publications include *New and Collected Poems* (1990); and his awards include the Bollingen Prize, 1962; a Pulitzer Prize, 1966; and the National Book Award, 1977. In 1986 he was elected to an honorary fellowship of St John's College, Cambridge. See his 'Empson's Poetry', *Accent* 4 (Summer 1944); *On Poetry and Poets* (1979), 117–18.

[3] The poet and author e. e. Cummings (1894–1962) and his third wife, Marion.

an American revised edition. Very good of you. You say very nice things about me which I wish were truer; and that's a good thing, because sometimes one hopes a line of praise isn't true at all. Your letter took just a fortnight, as mine did; pretty good. Sorry to hear your family are in Milan, sounds very inconvenient, but I expect they are safe. Final proofs of the verse book were passed yesterday and I hope to send it you soon.

Feel a little uncomfortable about the printing business. If you have printed the letter it might be better to print some of this, the reasons for not wanting the first one printed, next time. The first paragraph seems all right. But then I am not supposed to write anything about the BBC while employed by it, so all references to that have to come out, and it doesn't leave much. I am not at all secretive, it is only that people misunderstand things if one isn't careful, and your description of the process is fairly hair-raising, you must admit.

Will write again. Best wishes.

Bill Empson

[P. S.] This must seem an odd fussy letter to come just before the invasion of Britain, but we think we can handle that if it comes; it is the long-term aspect of the war that is gloomy.

This anxiety not to tell anybody what to do or what they ought to have done isn't altogether a good thing no doubt, the 'flight from leadership', but in the present case surely it's only right.

Yale: YCAL MSS 75, Box 1, folder 30

TO *THE SPECTATOR* (Unpublished): 'Pacifism and Pacificism'

W. R. Matthews, the Dean of St Paul's, in 'Pacificism as a Vocation', took issue with a decision by 'the Archbishops' to publish a report, following a visit by a deputation of clergy from the Anglican Pacificist Fellowship, that included the statement 'Pacificism is a genuine vocation for some.' Pacificism is purely a moral choice, he insisted (*The Spectator*, 9 Aug. 1940, 141): 'the pacificist doctrine that it is always wrong to fight cannot be a symbolical way of saying that to fight in some circumstances in defence of righteousness is a moral duty. A proposition cannot be symbolical of its contradictory.' The argument was continued in the following issues of the magazine: 16 Aug. 1940, 169; 23 Aug. 1940, 193; 30 Aug. 1940, 220; 6 Sept. 1940, 245. The correspondence on 30 Aug. included the assertion from J. Peter-Grant that 'an exponent of pacifism (not pacificism) is a pacifist (not pacificist), as spelt in *The Spectator* . . .', to which the editor snapped back: ' "Pacifism" is an inaccurate abbreviation of "pacificism," which is in common usage and to be found in all reputable dictionaries.' WE's contribution here was not published; possibly it was never posted.

69 Burford Road, Evesham
4 September [1940]

Dear Sir,

The merely verbal part of this controversy is not trivial. It is no use saying that *pacificists* is 'the correct form'. Here as often before the language has made two words and is ready to give them definite meanings—the feelings are already distinct. *Pacifist* feels a bit slovenly, but there it fits what it describes, a slow popular movement which may do good in the end but which has used very muddled thinking. It is already a historical word. What a pacifist may be we have to learn by grim experience; it is no use saying that he doesn't exist because he is an incorrect form. People are too word-conscious now for that political move to be effective.

The trouble with '-ist' words in general is exactly the problem of your correspondents. 'Ist' words ought to mean men who hold definite doctrines, but they sag, first to meaning men who take a side in a particular case, and then to men with a 'tendency' to take such a side. An *optimist* was at first a man holding a special (and as it worked out rather gloomy) doctrine, but the fatuous use of it to mean a hopeful man is now normal. The new '-ist' word *pacificist* only gives a fresh start to this process, and the start is not really fresh, because the suggestions of the word go the other way. A *pacifist* has commonly been a fanatic, and is now required to be such by the Conscription Boards; he has at least a definite opinion. The more refined *pacificist* sounds like a man in favour of being 'pacific', wherever possible presumably, so he is *not* a man with a fixed doctrine.

It would be no good hiding my own bias. I think that Jesus and the Buddha could be outright pacifists without practical hypocrisy, not merely because they were celibates with no possessions, but also because they lived in warm fertile climates, and among peasants respectful to fanatics. Nobody in peacetime England or America who allows himself to be protected by the police is within reach of consistent pacifism. If he says he is he cheats.

But it is likely that 'they've got something there', and that a doctrine capable of being practised by a good enough man, not merely of being held in the air with a tone of disapproval as an 'ideal', might be worked out and tied to the comparatively virgin word *pacificist*. A pacificist won't get much field if we lose the war, but there seems no need to be afraid that he will make us lose it. When an exhausted Europe at last tries to make peace terms he might be very valuable. But he must first take the chance offered by the name, and give it a decent currency, by making a determined effort not to cheat *ab ovo*—a thing that Aldous Huxley, to take the most distinguished recent example, has I am afraid not done.

Yours sincerely

W. Empson

Houghton

TO I. A. RICHARDS

The White House, Fulford, York |
(My mother's address is still very 'permanent')
8 December [1940]

My dear Richards,

Delighted to get your very kind letter, and annoyed to find you didn't get one of mine some time ago. I sent off a batch to America about June when I got fixed in my present job, and was beginning to feel I must have offended everybody by them, but I suppose either they all sank or they were all held to be giving information. I will now be careful. I am doing minor but satisfying work for the BBC and am safe and comfortable. It is on the side of incoming news, but it is very good of you to suggest a recommendation from WRUL. I was doing a little educational broadcast recently which went off all right and enjoy getting hold of the microphone.

I do feel very sad about Pollard [Urquhart]; he got to be an intimate friend of mine and deserved everything you say of him.[1] Basic in China needs somebody who though enthusiastic takes that tone with an opponent, not This is marvellously good but My dear chap, you don't realise how bad the ordinary practice is; he is a real loss; but you know all that. Give Wu my love and tell him he was kind to me.[2] He is a good thing for China to have in Boston; they will like him for the right reasons. My letters to China haven't been answered; it is bad news if the university has had to move again, but they were sturdily trying to get out of it.

[1] T. T. Shui wrote to IAR on 20 Oct. 1940 with an account of Pollard-Urquhart's death: after being knocked down by a lorry during an air raid, when people and vehicles were crushed together in a desperate effort to get out of Kunming's narrow East Gate, his wound began to fester and turn black with gangrene; and he died two weeks later (*Magdalene*).

[2] Wu Fuheng (1911–2001), who worked for the Basic English Institute in China, was awarded a scholarship to work with IAR at Harvard. Professor Wu was later to become President of Shandong University, 1979–84.

Glad to hear your plans are working out. Some while ago I got a goodhumoured postcard from Miss Lockhart acknowledging receipt of an attack on the new Basic Dictionary.[3] She also holds an attack on the Concise Oxford with more theory in it, which Og didn't want to print to avoid quarrels. I am very sorry to have just missed getting home to make the points before this dictionary was in the press, and hope something can be done later. I think it's missing a big chance, and George Yeh would say the same; he was warning his students against all existing dictionaries and anxious to get a good Basic one. It still (e.g.) cheerfully uses 'low' and 'common' in definitions with the idea of social contempt though there is nothing to show that this one of the list of their meanings is wanted. Simply using numbers in brackets would clear most of it up and be short; if in doubt about a definition you look up the word with a number after it and count the semicolons in its definition to find out which sense is being used. This presumes that you say something, which no dictionary has yet done, about what you mean by the distinction between comma and semi-colon: is a group of synonyms separated only by commas in a definition meant to give a single HCF or LCM or what? The possible misinterpreta-tions of the normal dictionary entry are very complicated, and people actually make them. People use even the senses separated by semicolons as if approach shots at a single meaning that none of them quite fit, often rightly, but one could clear it up a bit more. The order of the senses separated by semicolons is also unexplained here. You don't want the NED principle of derivation, the oldest first, though that seems to be used sometimes; you want to lead off with the 'dominant' sense, which will work unless the context decides, and in cases where the dominant sense colours the others it wants (D) in brackets after it ('rude health' always gets definitions which would make you use it wrong if you didn't assume a spread process) . . . The derivations are often wanted, but as such in square brackets and probably only where synonyms are collected to be dis-tinguished (effect result consequence). People often use a dictionary as a thesaurus anyway, and the mere avoidance of circularity except in Basic words doesn't help a reader to clear them up by seeing the alternatives. It doesn't take a lot of space; two or three words on a double page will be oneline references, probably to the general Basic word, where the similar words are collected and contrasted—then you can see what the definer is trying to shut out of his definition, or when the words are used loosely (effect result consequence) he can commonly give derivations as a

---

[3] Leonora Lockhart, secretary of the Orthological Institute in London.

mnemonic to show the different points they start stretching from. Rarely but sometimes you need to put the 'feeling' of a word separately in brackets. The dictionary I thought was sometimes guilty of hiding gaps in Basic, for instance WC latrine etc get shuffled away though a foreigner may easily be anxious to feel he has picked the right word there; he obviously wants the synonyms collected and distinguished. The same with 'proportion', where the idea 'x varies directly as Y' is of radical importance and never gets separated out. There are also a fair number of minor errors of the kind people pick on, like calling smoke a gas and gas an elastic, defined as going back to the old shape after stretching. I don't think my little plans would make it more than a third longer, and after all people like George Yeh are very clear about what they want and can't get from dictionaries. I think the thing would have a unique claim if it was pushed a bit further but at present hasn't.

Very pleased by what you say about the book of verse, as you will guess from the enclosed presscuttings. They feel they can express an old hatred of modern verse because of the war, a fretful little bundle. John Hayward thought he had arranged a combined US edition of verse, but I have just heard from Eliot that it has fallen through. I hope something can be done later. Eliot it seems is doing two nights air raid duty a week and cheerful on it. I haven't had a drink for ten days, you'll be interested to hear. I can't get down to revising Ambiguity. As for the Revelation suitcase under my bed (that is its trade name) full of paper that went round the world with me, it suggests Joanna Southcott, but a small book will emerge from it in the end.[4] This is an unpleasant letter; I can't think of any gossip. Nothing very startling to report. Give my love to various people and say I did write some letters.

Bill Empson.

Magdalene

TO I. A. RICHARDS

160A Haverstock Hill, NW3
12 January 1943

My dear Richards,

I was very glad to get your letter and kind present of tea. I'm ashamed to say I haven't been keeping up with the Basic front and had no idea that

---

[4] Joanna Southcott (1750–1814), millenarian visionary, published an enormous number of prophetic pamphlets, and in her final year prophesied that she was to be the mother of Shiloh, an incarnation of divinity. At her death she left a 'great box' (a Revelation suitcase, as it were), containing further prophecies. which has been lost.

you were making language teaching films in [Walt] Disney's studio, but am delighted to hear it. In fact I haven't any cultural side to speak of, being now definitely an all-time propaganda hack; if I'm not fussing about broadcasts *to* the Far East I ought to be fussing about home BBC programmes *on* the Far East, the second is my artwork which I may do when I get home from the office. The BBC and MOI both sometimes nibble at the idea of using Basic, and I do then put in a word for it, but as you know what always frightens the BBC is that they can't advertise one product if its trade rivals are likely to complain, and it seems likely that persons describing themselves as trade rivals of Basic would complain. It is very dreamlike to have [Vere] Redman head of the Far East section in the MOI and George Yeh running the London Chinese MOI, or perhaps rather like a fancy dress ball. But they I think both feel they are in their proper places now. There was some suggestion of helping English language teaching in China through the MOI, and Redman was willing to realise that Basic was the way to go about it, but George thinks in terms of face a good deal naturally and said that any scheme of that sort must be exactly mutual, involving the teaching of Chinese in English secondary schools. He only said that once, to be sure, and if the thing comes up again later he may have swung over to another line, but at the moment it seemed a dead end. He is still delightful company and I think is doing a lot of good for AngloChinese relations, but you know how temperamental he is.

My wife [Hetta Crouse] is a tall blonde Boer who broadcasts in Afrikaans; we met in the BBC school; I have also a son now two months old named Mogador after a town in North Africa which was being occupied at the hour of birth. I am told that the word is also Yiddish for a muddle. That is, he was christened William Hendrik, but Mogador was added in the eyes of the law all right when he was registered. We have a basement flat in Hampstead and I ought now (if not writing a Home Feature about China) to be digging in the garden. My wife is willing to go to China and a good cook. I am really very happy and cosy, but I write down this fact with some surprise, because I manage to find the propaganda business extremely worrying and liable to go wrong in quite unexpected ways and a great strain on the nerves and temper; maybe this is only the trick of inventing difficulties.

I can't think of any gossip; we seem to see very few people really. Tom Harrisson[1] is in the army which must be a fairly complete blow at the Mass

---

[1] Tom Harrisson (1911–76), co-founder of the Mass-Observation social survey project, grew up in South America but was educated at Harrow School and at Pembroke College, Cambridge, which he left without taking a degree. In 1933–5 he participated in an Oxford University

Observation business. Kathleen Raine who of course has been long separated from Madge has now got some Foreign Office job and seems happier. Bottrall came back from Sweden for a bit but I didn't see him; he has
now gone back there taking his wife; I understand they are both enjoying
it, but she said she found it very difficult to get enough clothes to appear
like a gentlewoman; of course they flew out. Margaret doubting whether a
Japanese agent (say) would take her dress for that of a gentlewoman seems
a comic picture. Julian Trevelyan has had an exhibition of paintings he did
in Lagos or thereabouts on a tour for army camouflage; I thought they
were a bit trivial and didn't get to the exhibition, but people tell me they
were very gay and fine when you got a roomful. John Hayward is living in
Cambridge and when I last saw him said solemnly that I must come back
later because he was writing a cable for the Ministry; I gather he is doing
some work for the MOI; he was in excellent form. [Arthur] Waley of
course is working his head off but seems well, and I am hoping to get him
into a home broadcast about Chinese poetry; it would have to be prere-
corded in case he was too busy at the hour named. G. S. Fraser* I think is
much the best of the rising poets (I haven't met him); it seems he has a staff
army job in Cairo and is editing a magazine there; I only saw one number
and it wasn't awfully good, but then it hadn't anything to speak of by him.
Tambimuttu's* anthology [*Poetry London*] was surprisingly good I thought.
My office is next door to George Orwell's* and I find him excellent
company; it is wonderful how he still manages to do some writing.

Give my best wishes to Mrs Richards and other friends, especially
[George] Sansom if you see him.

Yours

Bill Empson

I have written a ballet ['The Elephant and the Birds', posthumously
published in *The Royal Beasts*] in which Bobby Helpmann was to appear as
the Buddha in his incarnation as an elephant, but he was so bitterly
offended that I am afraid nothing more will come of it, though the

---

expedition to the New Hebrides, where he studied the way of life of the cannibals of Malekula
(now Vanuatu). Back in England, he joined forces with Charles Madge to undertake 'anthropology at home', basing himself in Bolton in Lancashire and observing the lives and customs of the
local people. WE spent a few days participating in the project, and helped to compile *May the
Twelfth* (1937). *Britain by Mass-Observation* (1939), edited by Harrisson and Madge, became a best-
seller; and *Living through the Blitz* (1976) affords an impressive account of London at war. In 1942
(as WE notes here) Harrisson joined the King's Royal Rifle Corps; he was later to see active
service with the Special Operations Executive in Borneo, and would win the DSO for his brave
exploits. After the war, he decamped for twenty years to Sarawak, where he became a government ethnographer and museum curator. See Judith M. Heimann, *The Most Offending Soul Alive:
Tom Harrisson and His Remarkable Life* (1998).

composer I believe is still at work. By the way the best recent painter here is a man called [Leslie] Hurry, and he was going to do the sets but he is not still at work on them.[2]

Houghton; signed but not posted

TO E. M. W. TILLYARD*

[n.d. 1944]

My dear Tillyard,

I should like to send you a long fussy letter about my reactions to your book on the Shakespeare histories [*Shakespeare's History Plays*, 1944]. I must say first that I realise it will become a standard work; without it one doesn't realise what a 'history' is at all; your book is an essential one for anybody approaching the topic.[1]

At the same time you leave the literary judgements (wouldn't you agree?) almost just where they were before. Reading through your book another process of development goes on, that of the reader's opinion of Shakespeare. When he is told that Shakespeare as a young man believed that the three henry sixes amounted to an important world message he cannot avoid thinking the Bard something very near a solemn cad. As your claim for the conception of the History rises, so you approach with increasing solemnity the keystone of the whole arch, the perfect picture of a royal character, the last history play of henry five, and you fully admit

---

[2] Robert Helpmann (1909–86), Australian ballet dancer and actor, began his career in 1934 when he joined Ninette de Valois at the Vic-Wells Ballet; he took leading roles in ballets by de Valois and by Frederick Ashton. His partners included Alicia Markova and Margot Fonteyn; and he was mentored by Constant Lambert. From 1937 he was also an actor, appearing as Bottom to Vivien Leigh's Titania in Tyrone Guthrie's celebrated production of *A Midsummer Night's Dream* at the Old Vic Theatre. From 1942 he became too a brilliant choreographer: among his many achievements he choreographed the ballet for the film *The Red Shoes* (1948). From the late 1940s he acted with Barry Jackson at Stratford-upon-Avon; later with Laurence Olivier and Vivien Leigh in *Antony and Cleopatra* and Bernard Shaw's *Caesar and Cleopatra*. Film roles included that of the Child-catcher in *Chitty Chitty Bang Bang* (1968). He was to be knighted in 1968. WE probably made contact with Helpmann through Leslie Hurry (1909–78), British painter and theatre designer, whom HE had befriended. In 1942 Helpmann choreographed a wonderful dance–mime production of *Hamlet*, set to Tchaikovsky's fantasy overture; and it was at Helpmann's invitation that Hurry (a tall, highly-strung, breathless man with only a modest reputation as a painter) designed the set and costumes. Thereafter, over a period of thirty-five years, Hurry designed more than sixty productions for companies ranging from Sadler's Wells to the Royal Shakespeare Company. For unknown reasons, the dream team of WE-Helpmann-Hurry never came to pass.

[1] Cf. WE's comment, in 'Sense in Measure for Measure', upon 'Dr Tillyard's patient and illuminating collection of evidence that the scheme of the Shakespeare History plays was drawn from a pompous contemporary myth made up to flatter the Tudors (a thing which he seems to admire more than it deserves)' (*SCW*, 270).

that Shakespeare found it as ridiculous when he got there as you do. The reader now at last thinks quite highly of the author Shakespeare, but it is difficult to see why he should still admire the history play form.

My feelings are crossed by a personal puzzle about whether my own published views were wrong or whether you ought to have given me credits for them, supposing you agree with them. They only cross your path at the two henries four. After some reflection about this I am struck with how much Zeitgeist has been going on. I mean, if it really came to my wanting to complain to you about giving credits, I would have to think who had told *me*, let alone whether I had told *you* in a publication offered for further discussion a dozen years ago. Of course I have dropped the whole thing for so long that I only come back to it in this rather clumsy way. But after clearing my mind to realise that I have got left out of my own accord I still feel that I was backing a different side from yours and that I ought now to support it.

To defend the histories, I think, and explain how so able a mind found the Tudor Myth worth serious attention, you need to go back to a much more fundamental and permanent affair, the Golden Bough and the magical kingship. It seems to me that you describe Shakespeare looking for a good type of king as if it were a good type of office administrator. But since a good king worked by magic as a symbol and divine recognition of a good condition in the country he didn't really have to be a good king at all. Of course in practice one got very interesting and dangerous positions, but at bottom it wasn't the king himself who had to be smart, as would be frankly admitted in the case of a baby king. The theorising about divine right which you claim your period escapes has I think obviously cast its shadow before, and needs to be reckoned with. Otherwise I suggest the thing is absurdly null. That is, after you have traced all the sources and proved that Shakespeare's opinions were rather unusually high class but still old and respectable, you are left with the view that there was nothing positive in his opinions except fear of civil war. It seems to me that the operative sentiment all the time in his treatment of kingship is the idea that a king is half outside morality altogether because he is doing a magical job irrelevant to morality, and therefore his position though wonderful is inherently horrible and unreal; it is the most dramatic thing in the world because the man can't really be blamed for it, and yet he will be. Your picture of a long series of plays intended to allot the right amount of blame to each king makes the thing flatter and nastier than it was.

Houghton: unsent, bMS Eng 1401 (660)

TO HAROLD RAYMOND* (Chatto & Windus)

[Written on BBC notepaper, as from 160A Haverstock Hill NW3]
21 September 1944

Dear Mr Raymond,

I have been wanting for the last ten years or so to get out a little book about Far Eastern Buddhist sculpture, and want to put the plan up to you again. It seems to me that the book would do quite well soon after the defeat of Germany, when popular interest is directed that way. The book would be largely concerned with Japanese sculpture of before 1000 AD, and to that extent rather pro-Japanese than otherwise, but would put the Japanese work as within a single Far Eastern tradition, indeed as largely done by non-Japanese artists; the point would be to look at one aspect of Far Eastern civilisation of which the Japanese are a late offshoot. I have got enough photographs myself but would welcome any help.

The book as I conceive it would be a halfcrown bookstall pamphlet with a large proportion of photographs, and only about 10,000 words. The book would (a) give pictures of some of the best sculpture in the world, at present only obtainable in learned publications, largely German (my photographs are Japanese and not published in Europe)—the stuff is of such quality that it is absurd not to have it available in reproduction; we might as well have no reproductions of the Venus of Milo; (b) my little book would I believe give the first published statement about a theory about early Far Eastern Buddhas which after I had believed myself to invent it I found taken for granted by the experts both in Tokyo and in Boston—that is, that the faces are designed to be asymmetrical on a rigid pattern derived from a fortunetelling rule but psychologically correct. When I showed my split photographs to the big chap in Boston he merely said 'We don't want that published; that's how we tell the fakes'.[1] Unfortunately printing the left on both left and right and the right on both left and right and the original unmangled head trebles the number of photographs required, and there would be no point in the booklet unless this were done at least three times. The split technique does not apply to India, started in Indochina about 500 AD, runs across China and Japan and ends about 1000 AD. I have seen the available material in these

[1] Langdon Warner (1881–1955) was assistant curator of Oriental Art, Museum of Fine Arts, Boston, 1906–13. He was field fellow of the Fogg Museum at Harvard at the time when Empson talked to him late in 1939. Katharine Sansom characterized Warner as 'a jolly sort of buccaneer . . . the gentlest of men and a passionate aesthete. We already knew of his amazing journeys in China, where he discovered lost caves filled with superb sculpture and paintings' (*Sir George Sansom and Japan*, 20).

countries and in Korea and across the USA (missing Washington) all right.

There would be no novelty in the little book without the theory and the photos for it, but its main point should be to make available photos of the grand early Chinese and Japanese and Indochinese Buddhas. As such it would undoubtedly be welcome on railway and other bookstalls. I am anxious to have it cheap because there are no cheap reproductions of the statues. If you want more words of course I can put out (a) theorizing about the facial type and (b) travel talk, but I do not want to add to the cost of the thing.

Yours sincerely

W. Empson

Reading

Harold Raymond expressed moderate interest in the idea, but doubted whether such a project would be feasible as a book—'or at any rate not as a smallish low-priced affair' (13 Oct. 1944). All the same, he had shown the photos to Ivy Davison, Executive Editor of the *Geographical Magazine* (which was published by Chatto & Windus), and she expressed interest in running an article based on the photos (though she was attracted less by WE's theory of asymmetry than by the general beauty of the sculpture). WE responded on 17 Oct. that he would prefer to try other publishers.

TO C. K. OGDEN

[BBC] 200 Oxford Street, W. 1.

27 September 1944

Dear Mr Ogden,

I have been asked by my BBC superiors to translate a weekly bulletin into Basic for West Africa, and I understand that they have talked over details with you. There were plans to do one for the East but they have dropped at present. Of course I would be very pleased to make myself useful; the only reservation I made when asked to do it was that I could only do it for the African Service on the understanding that I was filling in a gap till they trained someone to do it regularly. My job is on the Eastern Service, and anyway you can't run a regular service with only one man to do it; he is bound to get ill or go on holiday or something. The idea that the BBC is training someone to write in Basic for the African programme was agreed to over the telephone, and I hope you will represent from your side that that ought to be done if the scheme is to be put on a steady footing.

I am still not clear what is to be put out, but I understand that it is most likely to be a news summary of the week. A weekly summary doesn't raise the problems about hot News in Basic, but I have been told to ask you *whether there is an agreed list of extra news words*, and anyway I want to ask that myself. The problem about news, especially for the BBC, which has a policy of being cautious about news, is that half the time you are quoting a communiqué or some text which is the only authority for the story, and that source is itself couched in vague or puzzling terms. If you can't get a form of words that gives the impression intended in Chinese (or whatever language you are broadcasting in) you had better leave it out anyway, but still you want to give as interesting a news bulletin as you can.

I always leave out the pet names of specialised aircraft in bulletins for translation into Chinese, and think the same could be done in Basic (*heavy and light bomber and fighter* are the only essentials) but suppose the Beaufighter has *shot up a barge*. What *shooting up* may be I have never got explained to me, but it would be positively false to say that the fighter had damaged a ship. What would a 'pincer movement' become in Basic? Are there stock agreed Basic forms for a jeep, a bulldozer, duck, and so on?

Of course I would want to put up the problems to you later on as they arose, but a key factor, if the BBC use of Basic develops, is going to be convincing the news boys that the system is adequate to handle their professional crotchets, and these usually turn on leaving the cover of the necessary amount of vagueness while giving the interest of as much definiteness as can be risked.

This, I think, is the only important point, but I would like to give you a puzzle. What would Basic have made of Churchill's statement that Italy would be left to stew in her own juice? We gave it as such to the Chinese translators. Two Chinese broadcasts took it on the same day, one billed for Chungking, the other for Japanese occupied areas. The man billed for Chungking made it 'The Italians will be given time for natural political development among themselves in their present painful circumstances', and the man billed for Japanese occupied areas made it: 'The Italians will be given opportunities later, but at present they will not be prevented from suffering for their crimes'. This may or may not have shown a spontaneous tact in translators, but might be a bit puzzling for any listener who heard both broadcasts. A survey of how the BBC translated that announcement to all its languages would, I think, be of linguistic interest. Of course it would be absurd for me to ask you 'How would Basic do it?' The serious question is: 'How would the man putting into Basic choose to do it?' He would be sure to argue that there wasn't any other way of putting it into

Basic except the one that expressed his own opinions. However, that problem isn't the main one here.

I hope you are flourishing.

Yours very sincerely,

W. Empson

C. K. Ogden, Esq., 3 The Square, Buxton, Derbyshire

BBC

TRIBUNE, 10 November 1944, 12, 14: 'Clumsy Apologists'[1]

George Orwell, in 'As I Please' (*Tribune*, 27 Oct. 1944), criticized the 'homey' style and approach to Christian apologetics of C. S. Lewis[2] in his recent collection of broadcast talks, *Beyond Personality*. One critic (W. J. Turner) had even been so absurd as to liken a previous book by Lewis, *The Screwtape Letters*, to Bunyan's *The Pilgrim's Progress*. 'A kind of book that has been endemic in England for quite sixty years,' Orwell went on,

> is the silly-clever religious book, which goes on the principle not of threatening the unbeliever with Hell, but of showing him up as an illogical ass, incapable of clear thought . . . The line of attack is always the same. Every heresy has been uttered before (with the implication that it has also been refuted before); and theology is only understood by theologians (with the implication that you should leave your thinking to the priests) . . . The special targets of these people have been T. H. Huxley, H. G. Wells, Bertrand Russell, Professor Joad, and others who are associated in the popular mind with Science and Rationalism . . .
>
> One reason for the extravagant boosting that these people [the Christian apologists] always get in the Press is that their political affiliations are invariably reactionary. Some of them were frank admirers of Fascism as long as it was safe to be so. That is why I draw attention to Mr. C. S. Lewis and his chummy little wireless talks . . . They are not really so unpolitical as they are meant to look.

Sylvia Barrett (b. 1914) sought to defend Christian apologists against Orwell's attack on C. S. Lewis and his like (*Tribune*, 3 Nov. 1944):

> The assertion that 'these people's political affiliations are invariably

---

[1] See *The Complete Works of George Orwell*, xvi: *I Have Tried To Tell the Truth*, ed. Peter Davison (1998), 439–45.

[2] C. S. Lewis (1898–1963) was Fellow and Tutor in English at Magdalen College, Oxford, 1925–54; later Professor of Medieval and Renaissance English, University of Cambridge, 1954–66.

reactionary' is particularly choice if it is intended to refer to Chesterton. It is hard to believe that a political writer of Mr. Orwell's status is really ignorant of the firebrand activities of the weekly paper which was run by G. K., his brother Cecil, and Hilaire Belloc, especially the conspicuous part it played in the showing up of the notorious Marconi shares scandal and its determined fight against monopoly . . .

Such clumsy attacks on religion do a . . . disservice to the cause which Mr. Orwell has at heart . . . No social or economic system, however efficiently planned, can hope to succeed any better than the present one without vastly more good will than is current in the world today, and there is only one ultimate source for that good will. Lasting social justice will only be achieved when the majority of human beings have learned to love their neighbours with a love which is quite independent of personal likings and such love has its only firm and sure foundation in the faith that even the most apparently unattractive of human beings has an irreplaceable value in the eyes of his Creator.

About George Orwell and the letter from Sylvia Barrett, saying that his attacks on popular apologists for Christianity are clumsy, dishonest, and on a wrong literary foot.

Orwell's quotation from C. S. Lewis, she said, was a complaint about broadcasting colloquial style which unfairly proceeded to assume that the content must be bad because the style was. C. S. Lewis wrote a wonderful book, *The Allegory of Love* (about the history of medieval allegory) when he was content to be a scholar; I think his first book as a Christian apologist was *The Problem of Pain*, in which he says that wild animals don't live for ever, but maybe pet animals do, because their owners have taught them to feel nicely. This was long before he started broadcasting. His style went wrong because his thoughts became silly, and the distinction that Sylvia Barrett wants to make is therefore false.[3]

Orwell said that the apologists were always reactionary in political affiliations, and Sylvia Barrett says this is absurd because of Chesterton, a Liberal. Chesterton was a splendid writer, full of true prophecies about how Europe would go after his death, and unless the word is used as an empty insult it is absurd to pretend that he didn't end up in favour of Mussolini, and therefore as a Fascist; the reasons were decent ones, but he

[3] 'I wish I had seen more of C. S. Lewis . . .,' WE said much later. 'I rather liked his being reckless and unscholarly, but *The Screwtape Letters* was a quite dreadful book' (John Horder, 'William Empson, Straight', *The Guardian*, 12 Aug. 1969).

made no bones about the choice. He wanted a Catholic smallholding peasantry, and that was where it took him.[4]

Sylvia Barrett then widens her net and says that there is no hope for the world unless everybody becomes Christian (I don't think she would really object to this summary of her formula) because otherwise there won't be enough goodwill. This is difficult to refute because it is hard to say that there ever has been enough goodwill inside or outside or before or after the Christian communities. But it is a very harmful idea that the Chinese and the Russians (to name the major cases) are bound to be untrustworthy allies because they don't profess this religion; they haven't got holy thoughts like we have, so we must be ready to cheat them in advance. This nasty little bit of salesmanship for Christianity keeps cropping up. Anyone who has lived in non-Christian countries without prejudice knows how obscure, if not downright false, the argument would become on examination; and meanwhile it is one of the main roads to the next war.

W. Empson

TO T. S. ELIOT

160A Haverstock Hill, NW3
22 December 1944

Dear Mr Eliot,

John Davenport tells me that nobody is putting in to be Professor of Poetry at Cambridge—that you yourself aren't, and so on.[1] He told me I ought to put in, and that the person to write to about it is you. It seems to me it would be stupid not to stand. Can you advise me whether and how to do it, if it is already too late and so on?

Yours very sincerely
W. Empson

Faber

---

[4] Cf. WE on Wyndham Lewis's *Time and Western Man* ('Ask a Policeman', *Granta*, 21 Oct. 1927): 'sometimes like Mr Chesterton's Distributists he merely demands for everybody three acres, effort, and a cow' (*EG*, 19–20).

[1] WE was referring to the King Edward VII Chair of English Literature at Cambridge University, vacated by the death on 12 May of the long-standing incumbent, Sir Arthur Quiller-Couch (1863–1944), invariably known as 'Q'.

TO JOHN HAYWARD

160A Haverstock Hill, NW3
Thursday, 28 Jan. 1944 [1945]

My dear John,

I have been teased by John Davenport, now working for ENSA,[1] who tells me I ought to 'put in' to be Cambridge Professor of Poetry because the only entrants so far are J B Priestley and G[eorge] Barker. I wrote to Eliot about it who says the only way to affect the choice is to have Influence at Downing St and nobody does or can put in. He advised me however to write to you and ask what is likely to happen and whether any steps can be taken.

My wife and both my infant sons are expecting to return to China, but I should think they could put off returning to China for a bit.

My office life seems to me very amusing in its proletarian way and so exhausting that it is making me quite ill, but like all family jokes it is hard to explain what the interest is. Do write to me quite apart from this professional inquiry. I haven't heard any news from anybody.

Love
William Empson

King's

TSE was to write to John Hayward on 12 Feb. 1945: 'I imagine that the interest of Empson, [George] Barker and others in the Professorship must have flagged by now.' (*King's: Hayward Bequest L/12/1/24*)

TO I. A. RICHARDS

160A Haverstock Hill, NW3
(The British Broadcasting Corporation, Broadcasting House,
London, W. 1.)
1 July 1945

My dear Richards,

It is very disgraceful not to have written to you for so long. I doubt whether I have written since I married. I have now two sons. I am still working on broadcasts in Chinese. My wife is a Boer and broadcasts in Afrikaans—I have been getting very wrapped up in the broadcasting,

[1] The Entertainments' National Service Assocation was set up in 1939 for the entertainment of British forces; its star performer was Vera Lynn. Later called the Department of National Service, ENSA was disbanded in 1947.

though of course I mean to leave it after the war; and have done no writing to speak of.

I am chiefly writing to ask whether you have any views about the professorship vacated by Q [Sir Arthur Quiller-Couch]. It ought of course to be offered to you, and I hope you would take it. It has been put into my head that I ought to be hoping for it, and I confess I feel it had better go to me than to some I could name. I have more or less definitely undertaken to go back to China, which my wife wants to do—please don't tell George Yeh I was asking about this, because he might feel it was an attempt to break a promise; but after all if I am setting out to educate two children I had better try to earn some money. The gossip is that C. S. Lewis is going to get it, and I cannot forgive him for believing that pet animals live for ever because they have been taught nice feelings by their owners. He seems to have no interests now except his moralising. The other favourite is J. B. Priestley—this gossip comes from John Hayward. I should think there very likely won't be any appointment till after the war. But I thought perhaps I might reasonably let you know that I would be pleased to get it.[1]

Certainly the end of the war appears as the longed-for dawn all right; I mean I look forward to being back in a university where one could do some real work again, and yet feel I hardly know how I should start or what the light would reveal. A tired grey harried old man, I appear to myself, certainly sober enough but maybe too dull; you I don't imagine at all changed. Bottrall has turned up from Sweden where he has been writing a certain amount of good verse. The young man Jim Angleton from Yale, of Furioso, turned up here very mysteriously, and I took him to a pub to meet the BBC Features and Drama side, who mocked at him rather, and he disappeared equally mysteriously but I thought maybe in a huff. This was maybe a year ago and he was expecting to be in London for the duration. He was in mufti. Give him my best wishes if you see him.

My love to you and Mrs Richards
Bill Empson

Magdalene

---

[1] In the event, Q's successor as King Edward VII Professor of English Literature at Cambridge was to be Basil Willey.

TO GEORGE ORWELL*

160A Haverstock Hill NW3
24 August 1945

My dear George,

Thanks very much for giving me 'Animal Farm'. It is a most impressive object, with the range of feeling and the economy of method, and the beautiful limpid prose style. I read it with great excitement. And then, thinking it over, and especially on showing it to other people, one realises that the danger of this kind of perfection is that it means very different things to different readers. Our Mr [Adrian] Julian the child Tory was delighted with it; he said it was very strong Tory propaganda.

Your point of view of course is that the animals ought to have gone on sharing Animal Farm. But the effect of the farmyard, with its unescapable racial differences, is to suggest that the Russian scene had unescapable racial differences too; so the metaphor suggests that the Russian revolution was always a pathetically impossible attempt. To be sure, this is denied by the story because the pigs can turn into men, but the story is far from making one feel that any of the other animals could have turned into men.

Then again, the military situation of the animals is obviously much weaker than you make out, as the farm must be valuable and it is worth the men's while to bring some more guns. It was pathetic therefore even in the beginning for the animals to think that the farm was now theirs; one 'suspends disbelief' much more in supposing that they were left in control than in supposing that they had various human powers. The implication of the satire here is that the Russian revolutionaries were pathetically wrong in supposing that the state would wither away in two generations. And in fact it seems to me clear that if the Russian state had begun to wither away the Germans would have won the war. This doesn't justify any of the incidental bestiality of the pigs; but the story doesn't make one feel that their general policy was obviously wrong; it tends rather to seem necessary, and I doubt if you wanted that.

I certainly don't mean that that is a fault in the allegory; it is a form that has to be set down and allowed to grow like a separate creature, and I think you let it do that with honesty and restraint. But I thought it worth warning you (while thanking you very heartily) that you must expect to be 'misunderstood' on a large scale about this book; it is a form that inherently means more than the author means, when it is handled sufficiently well.

Bill Empson[1]

UCL

TO THE BRITISH COUNCIL

[From BBC, 200 Oxford Street, London]
3 September 1945

T. Tunnard Moore, Esq., The British Council, 3 Hanover Street, W. 1

Dear Sir,

I was appointed to a lectureship in English Literature in the Peking National University in autumn 1937, through the recommendation of Dr. I. A. Richards. As things worked out, the University was unable to cable stopping my appointment and I reached Peiping on a Japanese troop-train to find the University already fled. I met it in Changsha the same year, and gained some credit there as an European who carried his subject in his head. My Chinese colleagues came through the Japanese lines without books or other property and could naturally continue to lecture from memory, but it was considered smart (on the sacred mountain of Nanyueh) when I too as the only European typed out carbons for the class of enough English poetry and prose to cover the courses I was set to do. When we withdrew to Yunnan I continued lecturing in Mengtze (where at last my books turned up) and finally in Kunming, where I am particularly proud to have slept on my blackboard. I left in Kunming for the use of what was by then the south-west Associated Universities, all my books, pictures and gramophone records; their carriage had cost me between thirty and forty pounds. I have been very pleased to hear from students of mine who have been sent to England during the war that they are being used by the

---

[1] See also WE, 'Orwell at the BBC', *A*, 500: 'one cannot understand either book without realising that he considered having to write them as a torture for himself; it was horrible to think of the evil men, stinking Tories, who would *gain* by his telling the truth, let alone jeer about it triumphantly. Awful, though, for instance, to think of Hetta reading *Animal Farm*; "it is like cutting off the baby's arm," he said. (So far as I could tell, she did not feel any of the distress he feared, because she did not believe him.) "Anyway *Animal Farm* won't mean much in Burma," he said to me one day with timid hope, "because they won't know what it is about; they haven't got mixed farming there, like the English mixed farming," . . . And though he was rather anti-aesthetic, indeed one might sometimes think philistine on purpose, he was inclined to retreat into an aesthetic position when the book first came out. With all the reviews ablaze he stayed cross at the reception of the book, so that we said: "What more do you want, George? It's knocked them all right back. They all say it's terrific." "Grudging swine, they are," he muttered at last, when coaxed and stroked into saying what was the matter; "not one of them said it's a beautiful book." '

University not merely kept for me. If I went back I should want to leave the books with the library, but there are a lot of annotated pages which I should like to read when I try to start writing literary criticism again.

In autumn 1939, I was advised by the Chancellor of my University, Dr. Chiang Mon Lin, that a European war was due soon and that he would allow me indefinite wartime leave while keeping me on the books of Peita. Dr. George Yeh of the Chinese Ministry of Information in London (with whom I shared camp life while refugeeing) is in the same position, so for example is Dr. Hu Shih. It is the Peking not the Peiping University because it dates back to the end of the emperors, and it is famous for keeping an open forum and for the political activity of its students, and in short, for maintaining a splendid intellectual life throughout years of failure to pay its staff. This historical background still gives Peita considerable weight in modern China. I am proud of being on the Peita staff and feel I cannot throw it up; nobody throws it up. I have written several times to Chiang Mon Lin expressing my wish to return, my hope that he should regard my present work as B. B. C. Chinese Editor an adequate ground for his excusing me my university duties, and my concern to encourage Anglo-Chinese relations in general. His last reply, sent through Dr. George Yeh, was that I had only to send him a cable and I would be welcomed back any time to [I] chose to come. Chiang Mon Lin is now Secretary-General of the Chinese Executive Yuan.

This I wish to do, but since leaving China I have acquired a wife and two young sons. I can no longer be (as I otherwise cheerfully would) the only European who dared to share the horrors of native life and at the same time the only man on the Peita staff who enjoyed low-class Chinese food. I cannot go back unless I can support my wife and children, and I hope to avoid any separation. Meanwhile, I understand that my unfortunate Chinese colleagues, much more learned than myself, are at present keeping their families alive if at all by doing the washing for the rickshaw coolies.

What I feel I can reasonably bring to the attention of the British Council is that, if it considers sending me out to China on the literary side, a man such as myself has a considerable amount of goodwill in hand ready for immediate use. On my own side I feel I am considered to have behaved generously in small matters while I was there (for example I gave up nearly half the contracted salary so as to share in the cuts made in the incomes of my Chinese colleagues) and I should be unwilling to go back unless I felt free to be generous in small matters again. You would not, I think, find me an inactive member of the British Council Staff.

As the B. B. C. Chinese Editor during the intervening years I have had decent relations with a wide variety of the Chinese who have come to this country. The original suspicion of the Chinese about these broadcasts has now been worn down so far that I am almost prepared to leave the B. B. C. Chinese Service, feeling that it can now continue of its own weight. I can promise you that no ill-will has been created to my knowledge by the B. B. C. attempt to break the Japanese intellectual blockade.

It seems to me that I must soon send an answer to Chiang Mon Lin, who is now a more important political figure than he was when we parted. I want to go back; I would like to go back even before Peita leaves Kunming. But I have no right to go back unless the British Council can enable my family to retain a normal living standard.

If you wish for references I suggest Mr John Morris, my immediate superior in the B. B. C., and Dr. George Yeh of the Chinese Ministry of Information in London, my immediate superior in Peita.

Yours sincerely

[William Empson]

Houghton carbon

[WE was to return with his family to Peking in the summer of 1947; he would continue teaching at Peking University until the summer of 1952.]

TO QIEN XUEXI

A colleague named Chien Hsueh-hsi (Qien Xuexi)—to whom WE had shown a copy of his review of Cleanth Brooks's *The Well-Wrought Urn* ('Thy Darling in an Urn', for the *Sewanee Review* 55, Oct. 1947)[1]—wrote on 1 Sept. 1947 in connection with his interest in 'the criteria of literary

---

[1] WE would write to Tambimuttu on 30 Aug. 1948: 'I have been reading a fair amount of American literary criticism lately while here (at Kenyon College, Ohio), not as much as I should but enough to be rather saturating. It seems much more energetic and enterprising than the English variety, I think, but the determined refusal to charm gets to make it seem a bit lifeless somehow in bulk. Cleanth Brooks wrote a good book The Wellwrought Urn, very much up my street but a good book on any count I should say; probably you have seen that; I don't really know what else I should recommend. They are haunted by a feeling that if it isn't a branch of science it is no good, and at the same time the ghost of Oscar Wilde and the feeling of political impotence of the American intellectual gives it no contemporary relevance somehow, except for the educational campaigns they are so many of them mixed up in to be sure, and perhaps one should add the ghost of Kipling in the form of US patriotism (there is a keenness to emphasize that US literature is at last ahead of the British, whereas the fact that the British are so groggy that their toenails have practically stopped growing isnt really anything for the Americans to measure themselves against). Perhaps I was only being contrary when I felt I couldn't join in their admiration for recent US books warmly enough to satisfy. However it was all very cordial and pleasant.' (*BL: Richard March Papers*)

criticism'; he had written his own notice of Brooks (which he enclosed), discussing among other things the meaning of the 'paradox of the imagination'. One problem that vexed him was an age-old one: what is the difference between meaning in poetry as against philosophic meaning? If meaning implies an awareness of value, science shows no such awareness:

> it may be apt to call poetry a dialectic of feeling and philosophy a dialectic of thought. But the thought-feeling antithesis should have ceased after Wordsworth and Coleridge. Thought does seem to be the crystallization of feeling and no thought can be deep if not impassioned—scientific thought, involving no feeling and no awareness of value, being perhaps not to be called thought altogether. It is hence more to the point, and Mr Brooks will probably approve, if we call poetry concrete dialectic and philosophy abstract dialectic.

Another matter that worried him was Brooks's insistence on evaluating a poem according to 'internal criteria':

> The problem is: can we assess the complexity, the power, the scope without any reference to criteria outside the poem? Mr Brooks himself said a little later on that 'a poem . . . is to be judged by its coherence, sensitivity, depth, richness, and toughmindedness'. And [such criteria] are of course outside the poem. Indeed he has acknowledged 'It cannot be claimed for such a test that it eliminates the subjective element in judgement. It does not, of course, and no meaningful criterions of poetry can ultimately eliminate the subjective' (230).

7 September 1947

Dear Mr Chien Hsueh-hsi,

Thanks for your letter. I think I agree with your phrase that poetry is 'concrete dialectic'; the question is rather what we do with these phrases after we have got them. It seems clear that one must still consider first whether a given object is 'poetry', and then if it is also found to be 'concrete dialectic' that is further confirmation of the theory. But if one set out to write concrete dialectic on the ground that it would be sure to turn out good poetry I think it would be rather a matter of luck whether it turned out good poetry or not (so it would be, of course, if one set out to write good poetry). The aphorism is not a recipe, if this is so, and yet it is rather hard to see what else it can be.

The point where I most disagree with you is about science. I should have thought that the present age had very little to boast about in any form of imaginative work except the scientific one, and it is obvious that a physicist like Einstein or Eddington is making superb uses of the imagination. A critic who cuts himself off from the only fertile part of the contemporary mind is I think unlikely to understand what good work feels like when it is new, and as far as my own work is concerned anyway I am sure I have always found the worldpicture of the scientists much more stimulating and useable than that of any 'literary influence'. In any case it seems to me trivial to say that scientific thought isn't real thought; it only suggests a quarrel between different faculties in a university about which should get more money and better buildings. For that matter all the good philosophy in the last fifty years has been influenced very strongly by modern physics, so by your own account poetry ought to be influenced too, but only as the lady's-maid who is not given the clothes till the fashion for them is out of date.[2]

I quite agree that the ultimate criterion for a good poem is not 'internal', that is inside the poem, and I should have thought it was evidently not inside any one reader either. The term 'subjective' always leads to confusion, I think. The reader has got to make up his own mind, but what he is deciding is whether the poem is likely to last, for his own feelings and for subsequent generations—he has to make the same kind of prophecy about both. (Of course this is only one of the things he is deciding; I mean that there is no absolute line of division corresponding to 'subjective'). The ultimate decision can never be made, though later generations can make a working approximation to it; and the chief reason why it can't be made is that nobody gets to see the whole of things. But in getting to see any tolerably representative or workably large world-picture it seems obvious that you would need to bring in the sciences as well as the philosophies, and for that matter the other arts. It seems perhaps rather obscurantist to say that one must know all there is to be known before one can judge a poem, but it only amounts to saying that one's interests should not be deliberately narrowed.

[Yours sincerely
William Empson]

Chien Hsueh-hsi reiterated (9 Sept.) that the pursuit of science is distinct from questions of human value: 'Science seems to me to aim at the knowing of all phenomena as they are, apart from their bearing on human life or human wishes. All its imaginative feats are guesses to be verified and not

---

[2] Cf. WE, '*The Ancient Mariner:* An Answer to Robert Penn Warren': 'The advances of science in our time, though very likely to cause disaster, have been so magnificent that I could not wish to have been born earlier; and I estimate that most of the poets worth study who were in fact born earlier would have felt so if they were alive now.' (*SSS*, 146).

wishes or ideals to be pursued and realized. However it may open up the world within and without us, it excludes from itself all reference to the wishing and idealizing principle of man, which is the center of value.'

TO QIEN XUEXI

17 September 1947

Dear Mr Chien Hsueh-hsi,

My remarks about science, I am afraid, sounded too excited; but the reason for it, it seems to me, is merely that I do not know how to discuss the matter in abstract terms, only in terms of the social consequences of the different opinions. The same thing happens when I try to talk to scientists who believe that literary language is meaningless. Pragmatism is a harmful false doctrine, but in cases like this where one cannot see one's way through a question the social consequences are the line of argument which forces one to see the question as a whole.

Of course one can define terms as one likes, and it is possible to define meaning, significance, and thought as all only occurring when there is a reference to human wishes or ideals as well as to facts. The listener is also allowed to wonder what the purpose of an unusual definition may be, and it is commonly to make some ingenious persuasive use of the words after-wards. However even accepting the definitions I should deny that they make science meaningless or insignificant or unthinking. One of our major desires about the universe is that it should be orderly and capable of being understood; this is partly for our own safety and partly from a metaphysical feeling that we want to be at home in it or not alien to it. What you describe as a 'guess' about the universe has to be based on something, and one of the things it always has to be based upon is the pious faith that the universe is intelligible. Copernicus for instance has been accused of believing his theory because of its great elegance and simplicity in spite of the facts appearing to be against it; not because he was indifferent to truth but because he trusted his wish that the true answer should be elegant and simple. I do not mean that this is the whole story; we want a good deal more of the universe besides intelligibility, and a certain amount more I think is provided by science though not much; and on the other hand the desire to recognise the truth however disgusting it may be is itself an 'ideal'. So the dichotomy, it seems to me, breaks down both ways round; and for that matter the 'social consequences' of it are bad for science as well as for the humanities.

But it's easy to talk like this so long as one does not have to say what one actually recommends; the ways in which they ought to influence and react on one another, it seems to me, are very subtle and marginal ones, perhaps never of a kind which can be put in logical form. The only thing one can be sure ought not to happen is the blocking of the underground passages between them by some unnecessarily absolutist theory.

I am sorry to have taken so long to answer; it is from being on holiday rather than from being busy.

Yours sincerely

William Empson

TO IAN PARSONS

11 Tung Kao Fang, Near Peking National University, Peiping 9.
21 November 1947

My dear Ian,

I was very glad to hear that [the second edition of] Ambiguity has come out after all; I felt sure it was a casualty of the various disasters. May I remind you that I asked you early this year to subscribe for me to a press agency as soon as it came out but not before; I hope you didn't forget; if you did please do it now, but I imagine what reviews there were would come out fairly soon. I am curious to know whether there is still a fanatical body of opposition to the book, or whether it has come to seem a fuss about the obvious.

We are abandoning our large room and moving into small rooms with stoves, as the cold is beginning; the seasons come late because there is such a long way to go from the heat to the cold or back again, and the great swing from one to the other is rather like being at sea. The dollar is driving downwards with the same majestic determination but prices in pounds on the open market are pretty steady. The Americans here seem quite baffled to know what their government is going to do. The political situation seems likely to continue as a stalemate for some time.

[. . .]

I am going on steadily with Intraverbal Structure [*SCW*] but keep running into puzzles, in fact I am only inventing the theory after tidying up the literary evidence for it, so I don't know how long I shall still take. It is getting much better, I think.

Yours very sincerely

Bill Empson.

I am all for having New Directions do the poems; perhaps I had better write whatsisname [James Laughlin] a note independently, as he was very cross when they were taken away from him last winter.[1]

Reading

TO MEARY JAMES TAMBIMUTTU*

11 Tung Kao Fang, Near Peking National University, Peiping 9
12 March 1948

My dear Tambi,

I hope this will do all right; I don't see that it could be found irritating.[1] The diplomat's wife was Lady Sansom and the young poet was Spender, who I suppose won't like having the story told but what of it. However do what you think; maybe it would be better to let the old boy have a say in what he wanted printing and what he didn't. It seems a very good plan of yours.

I am ashamed at not having answered your kind earlier letters. I am gradually finishing a long prose book between literary criticism and linguistics, and haven't had energy for anything else. I go to America for a Summer School as they call it in June to talk about my stuff, and regard soon after that as the deadline for sending it to Chatto's. Then I hope to look round a bit and see if I can still write verse. Don't you think it is time someone wrote a long didactic poem in terza rima telling people what to do in bed? Verse about the world situation was all right in the thirties but does seem now to strike rather a chill. A new battle for freedom to print highminded advice about sex would strike something a bit warmer, wouldn't it?

As for books, I never answered you; I want very much to see the new Fraser;[2] tell him if you see him that he never answered my letter. I don't know what else there is that I want. [. . .]

We are extremely comfortable here, and Hetta and the children are chattering away in Chinese. The political situation is a great field of rumour, but with any luck we will be able to stay on.

Yours very sincerely
William Empson.

'Of course his really important work can't be published yet; it will have to be posthumous'—That seems a very convenient thing to get people to say about one.

---

[1] James Laughlin (1914–97) founded the publishing company New Directions in 1936; authors published by him included Ezra Pound and William Carlos Williams.

[1] WE, 'The Style of the Master', in *T. E. Eliot: A Symposium* (1948); *A*, 361–3.
[2] G. S. Fraser, *The Traveller has Regrets* (1948), a volume of poetry.

TO KATHLEEN RAINE*

11 Tung Kao Fang, Near Peking National University, Peiping 9
26 March 1948

My dear Kathleen,

I am delighted to hear that you are out of the hands of priests, and what little I know of [Elias] Canetti is all in his favour.[1] Your letter arrived today while I was rereading Roberts' Recovery of the West, in the course of a vague effort to decide whether I believe in Richards' Theory of Value. I agree heartily with what Roberts is saying until the historical Christ is made to appear as a necessity for the support of Values, and that seems to me so plainly untrue that I do not know how he has arrived at it. But then it occurs to me that I may simply be inexperienced in the whole subject. I have had a decent amount of neurosis and unhappiness (to claim to have been cheerful all the time would be a grave confession from anyone I think) and have done things I considered low and irresponsible for pleasure, but I cannot remember ever being faced with a real moral decision such as a conflict of loyalties. Of course one may be looming up for us, if the Americans force Britain into war with Russia; I would not want either of them to win and would not want Britain to lose. The decisions may be very painful I daresay. Meanwhile I suspect Richards himself (between ourselves) of making a wrong moral decision when he dropped China and took a nice job at Harvard; if he had stuck to Basic he could have got it working here, whereas now he is very comfortable and feels it has come to nothing. And I do not think that came from weakness, he is a very stiff-necked character, but from following his own Theory of Value. On the other hand I don't think that the feelings of emptiness and frustration which Roberts describes so clearly in the thirties came from absence of moral theories or holding bad ones so much as from the quite just realisation (however dim in the way it was felt) that the country was being frustrated and with it the prospects of world peace. I have been lucky in being able to convince myself that what I was doing was worth doing (even the Chinese broadcasting, which I now think wasn't really) and no doubt many people who look more muddled and wrong have shown greater insight. But I can't feel that belief in a religion has much bearing on the way people stand up to a real moral decision. Of course I think children ought to be taught that they ought to do right and may have to think hard to decide what right is, but it seems to me that they are perfectly willing to

---

[1] For Elias Canetti on the Empson ménage in London, see his memoirs *Party im Blitz: Die englischen Jahre* (2003), 17–19; translated as *Party in the Blitz* (2005).

learn this idea without being taught heavenly rewards and punishments for it. However there again I am talking in the dark; I don't mean that my own young, who are in excellent health and temper, have been exposed to preaching of that sort at their tender age; they may yet silver my grey hairs with shame. I get fits of thinking I ought to have more opinion about these things, but I certainly don't feel a personal need for it.

What a shame Conolly [*sic*] not publishing your review; I hope he paid you for it all the same; if he doesn't you ought to sue him I think.[2] Probably one lawyer's letter (7/6) would be quite enough to frighten him. If [G. S.] Fraser is really thinking of coming to China I wish he would write and say so, or even the [British] Council may make an appointment in time and he may miss it. It hadn't occurred to me that you might come; I should think your children are a bit old for it. We assume ours will get into Chinese schools from the start and the language will be useful for them later, and they are talking quite a bit of Chinese already. However if you want to come I have no doubt things could be arranged. Certainly time is more important than place and you mustn't expect Buddhas here to be more than occasional art objects; I don't find I regard China as romantic and strange at all (SouthEast Asia does, where they are all soft and delicious and probably on the verge of stabbing you in the back, but not here) what is nice about people in Peking is that though rationalistic to the point of flatness they are casual and unhurried and don't mind eccentricity. Traditional wisdom no doubt does crop up, but not as much as it should, certainly not among students who tend to be very ignorant about their own country. I am sorry to miss the Indian exhibition and am relieved to hear you say the Buddhas aren't very good. Hinduism I never really like, though of course it is an instructive object being Ancient Night in person practically unreformed in any way; my picture of the Buddha is that he made a superb attempt to clean up Indian mysticism by carrying it to extremes. We have some Indian students here and they are a terror to the others because they talk all night in the dormitory to show that they have a right to speak. Talking of the East–West religious contrast, have you any idea where Blake got the idea that 'there are no individuals, only states'?[3] It seems such a fundamental point that none of his sources for oriental religion would be likely to make it clear to him. Is there any evidence that

---

[2] Cyril Connolly (1903–74) became a key figure in wartime literary London as editor of *Horizon* (1939–50). From 1950 he was chief literary reviewer of the *Sunday Times*. His writings include *The Rock Pool* (1936) and *Enemies of Promise* (1938).

[3] William Blake, 'Milton', Book II, part 32, l. 10: ' "We are not individuals but States, Combinations of Individuals" ' (*Complete Writings*, ed. Geoffrey Keynes (1966), 521).

he had Chinese sources, too? It seems he had got quite a lot of stuff about India.

Would you hand on this note to Tambi? He has sent me a cable asking for criticism of Eliot, for his birthday number, after I had sent him some chatty anecdotes [*A*, 361–3], and I can't send both or they would get in each other's way, besides it would mean more work than I have time for, and I gave him what he asked for, so altogether I begrudge his cable even the price of airmail stamps for reply.[4] But give him my warm regards.

Richards' Theory of Value (or any self-fulfilment theory) fits fairly well onto Christianity, I think; the trouble is only that it is always liable to make you take too narrow a view if you actually try to calculate with it. But it doesn't fit at all onto a Buddhist one; it depends too much on believing in the individual. I have at times felt that Buddhism was true, but the hardening of Aldous Huxley into disapproval of everybody who isn't an arahat does now rather unreasonably make me feel that it isn't. . . . My reflections are pretty pitiful, when I come to write them down; but I know you are concerned about these things and I wanted to report what I had to say.

Love from us both.

William Empson

BL

TO T. S. ELIOT

11 Tung Kao Fang, Near Peking National University
1 April 1948

Dear Mr Eliot,

I have just been writing down some anecdotes about you for a presentation volume which I expect you know is coming; they are intended to please, and seem agreeable to me, but I am afraid these things often annoy instead of pleasing.[1] Such at least was the intention.

However I am extremely annoyed with you for mucking up the chance of an American edition of my verse. I have heard recently from Laughlin

---

[4] When Tambi cabled to say he would like there to be more criticism in WE's memoir, WE responded in his note (26 Mar. 1948), forwarded by Raine: 'I think it would put my little piece off balance if I tried to put in serious criticism as well. Besides, I don't know what I would want to say' (*BL: Richard March Papers*).

[1] John Hayward, who was sharing a flat with Eliot in Carlyle Mansions, London, wrote to Tambimuttu on 4 Apr. 1948: 'There seems to be nothing objectionable in Clive Bell's and Empson's contributions. I have however corrected some errors of fact in the latter (I was present on the two occasions to which Empson alludes)' (*Rare Book and Manuscript Library, Columbia University Libraries*: Ms Coll *PL-NY*).

that he won't publish me till he has finished pushing Vernon Watkins,[2] and he advises me not to wait. He suggests that I should try Allen Tate at *Henry Holt*[3] or a small publisher *Harry Duncan*, The Cummington Press, Mass.[4] I gave The Gathering Storm to Faber's seven years ago or more (after Chatto's had accepted it) on the definite understanding that you would try to get me an American edition, and so far as I can learn you have positively hampered that ambition so far as you have done anything about it at all. I could well understand your no longer taking any interest in publishing, but if that is all why should you twice prevent Laughlin from printing my verse? Well then, I have to go to America this June for six weeks' lecturing (if they give me a visa), and shall I try to do something about the suggested publishers myself? It would be better if you would take a hand, but if you are not interested in the matter please at least tell me so.

We are extremely comfortable here, but no doubt will be less so if the communists arrive, as they are expected to do by next winter or so. My impression about America and Russia is that people only join one side of this line-up because they dislike the activities of the other, so that whichever side had the sense to keep quiet would win. The Russians seem at present to be showing that much sense in China, if nowhere else, and are naturally forging ahead here. I understand the expected policy of the British Council is to stay here if the communists let them carry on, and the communists are expected to do it. Certainly I and the family want to stay on, but might get squeezed if the university was technically moved south (most of it wouldn't go in any case). I have done a lot of typing since getting here and have practically finished a long prose book between linguistics and literary criticism, which had been started before the war but not looked at all through it; and feel if I could once emerge from this heap of paper I could start afresh. I am still not drinking for fear of the old stomach ulcer, which I sometimes imagine I can hear grumbling; it is rather like Letter to a Wound in The Orators [by W. H. Auden]. However

[2] Vernon Watkins (1906–67), Welsh poet, bank clerk, friend of Dylan Thomas, was author of *Ballad of the Mari Lwyd* (1941) and *The Lamp and the Veil* (1945).

[3] Allen Tate (1899–1979) studied at Vanderbilt University, where he became associated with *The Fugitive*, the journal of the Southern renaissance (his friends included John Crowe Ransom and Robert Penn Warren), and he was later committed to the sectional movement known as 'Southern Agrarianism'. He was poet in residence at Princeton, 1939–42, and consultant in poetry at the Library of Congress, 1943–4. In 1946–8 he was literary editor with the publishing firm of Henry Holt, New York. He was Professor of Humanities at the University of Minnesota, 1951–68. His publications include *Collected Poems, 1919–1976* (1977), *Essays of Four Decades* (1968), *Memoirs and Opinions, 1926–1974* (1975), and *The Fathers* (1938).

[4] Harry Duncan (1916–1997), typographer, printer, and publisher, was proprietor of The Cummington Press from 1939 until his death.

perhaps it is also the creeping meanness of middle age; if I was drinking here I should have no excuse for not spending a lot of time with rather tedious people. Hetta is enjoying herself I think and learning quite a lot of Chinese, but it does sometimes strike her that her drinking companions have very little to say. The city of course is very beautiful.

Yours very sincerely
William Empson

Houghton

TSE rebuked WE (29 Apr. 1948) for sending him 'the most insulting letter which I have ever received.' There had never been any failure of commitment on the part of Faber & Faber; on the contrary, accountable steps had been taken in the interests of WE's work. 'If you have preserved a copy of your letter you will naturally not expect me to express any pleasure in the fact that you have contributed to a "presentation volume" to myself. My first intention was to cable to ask you to withdraw your contribution, but as this would have involved drawing other people into this discussion I refrained from doing so. I shall be obliged, however, if you will in future address all your communications to Mr. [Peter] du Sautoy instead of to myself.'[5] All the same, WE's ill-judged charge had evidently rallied TSE—within days of receiving WE's letter, on 8 Apr., he wrote to Allen Tate, 'And until I can get William Empson's poems published in New York I am not so much interested in anyone else.'[6]

TO T. S. ELIOT

11 Tung Kao Fang, Near Peking National University
17 May 1948

Dear Mr Eliot,

In spite of your instruction to me I am asking John Hayward to pass on this letter to you with a request that you should read it. It seems clear that there is a misunderstanding, and I do not think you would want an attempt to explain it to be sent you through Mr du Sautoy.

I was of course very much shocked by your reply, which I had no idea that I deserved. After reflecting on it I feel, and very much hope, that you must have supposed I was accusing you of some mean trick or underhand

[5] TSE, letter to WE, 29 Apr. 1948 (*Houghton*).
[6] TSE, letter to Allen Tate, 8 Apr. 1948 (*Princeton*). Robert Lowell told a friend in June 1947 that TSE had said to him that WE's poetry 'was good the way Marianne Moore was' (*The Letters of Robert Lowell*, ed. Saskia Hamilton (2005), 65).

plot. This is a very nauseating idea, but surely it ought to be an inconceivable one. After all you have known me for a long time now, and surely I have never given you any reason to form such a suspicion. I am very sorry if I wrote in such a clumsy way as to make it plausible, but how could I know that I had to guard against it?

Actually it seemed to me that the qualities in you which I was complaining about were in themselves rather endearing than otherwise, but that they had become such an obstacle in this case that I had to speak up. Please allow me to recall the position as far as I knew it. I wrote to you some time after the war and asked how the plans for an American edition of my verse were going on; you sent a jovial answer to the effect that I had better write some more before the attempt was made. I do not know when I shall be able to write any more, so that this seemed to me an embarrassing, though kindly, misapprehension. Certainly I could not gather from your letter that you considered it was not your business to arrange to do it. Later on, at some time, you told me your were rather wary about publishing with Laughlin, and of course I did not mean to suggest, when I recalled this, that you were deliberately acting against my interests. I am much hurt at your supposing that I did. Later on again you told me over the telephone that there had been an agreement with another publisher which had 'slipped your memory', so that the MS had been promised to two publishers, neither of whom now want it, anyway at present. I could not gather from this that you did not consider the matter your business. When I heard recently from Laughlin that he too did not want it now I wrote and said that you had made a muddle of it, and that still does not seem to me intolerably insulting. My point of view is that I would like the stuff to be available in America, for the comparatively few people who would be likely to want it; I did not particularly care about having a good or successful edition. It seemed to me that your various cautions, though of course done in my interest, were only delaying the matter, and I said so. In any case it seemed to me likely, and praiseworthy rather than not, that you should no longer be much interested in publishing, having very much more important work to attend to; and I therefore suggested that I should try to find a small publisher for it myself on my forthcoming trip, though no doubt I should do it very incompetently. To be sure this is the second letter; I am not sure what I said in the first, but as I remember I urged on you that I wanted to have the stuff published before it was out of date, and that cautions about getting a good publisher, and delay because I might write something better, had been going on much too long.

I am myself a very incompetent man at this kind of thing, and people are always telling me that I am making a muddle, and that my efforts are doing more harm than good. It never crosses my mind to say that this is a mortal insult, and that all relations must be broken off for it. I do hope most earnestly that you are not taking this kind of attitude; I never thought you were that kind of man at all; it would be a most painful discovery. Perhaps I should explain that I do not write in this way out of any bumptious idea that we are on a level; it seems to me quite obvious that you are an enormously better poet than I am; but it is very bad for a great writer to refuse to be treated like other people.

However I am sure you are not doing that; I am only trying to point out that there are two very clear-cut alternatives. Either I was accusing you of an underhand trick or I was simply complaining that you had let the thing get into a muddle. And I do assure you with all my heart that I was not accusing you of any underhand trick; indeed I really think I could say that I have been insulted by your suspecting such a thing. I do hope you will let me know that you have cleared it out of your mind.

Yours very sincerely
William Empson

Faber

TO JOHN HAYWARD

11 Tung Kao Fang, Near Peking National University, Peiping 9
18 May 1948

My dear Hayward,

Would you mind giving the enclosed letter [above] to Mr Eliot, and saying I hope very much he will read it as I believe it will clear up a misunderstanding. He wrote and said I must write in future to another of the Faber partners, perhaps only meaning on questions of business, but the distinction is hard to draw, and of course I am anxious to clear the question up.

I was very glad to get your letter. No doubt it is eccentric of me, as you say, to use people's surnames; but it is not done out of formality; I know a lot of Johns, and they seem rather a mixed bag, whereas I only know one Hayward and the name seems very distinctive. Besides I have so often been irritated by people talking about our dear John, when it is considered polite to make the conversation a guessing game under cover of warm agreement till one finds out who is in view. As for the unaddressed letters signed Tommy which have been known to arrive asking me to recommend them for a job, I think they are enough to put one off Christian names altogether.

I am really working very hard, correcting compositions and that sort of thing, and trying to get through before I pop off to America for the holidays early. And the world news of course is enough to make anybody feel neurotic. I see few people, talk no Chinese, and take very little interest in the local arts. It is rather hard to say why I like being here so much, as I certainly do. One says one 'likes the Chinese', but I don't like the look of most of the people I am introduced to here, any more than anywhere else. What is meant I suppose is a much more general feeling of affection, chiefly for the people you see in the street. But I suppose most of them, though they have the great merit of not looking fussed or hurried, look pretty sordid from concentration on some half dishonest employment. The women do not raise my spirits at all. The weather and the beauty of the town do a bit, but not much. As far as I can see it comes down to a diffused homosexual feeling, that is, you will seldom go through a street without seeing at least one agreeable young man, and you feel affectionately towards him because he seems so content with himself, and there is no need for anything to be done. I do not think this is a peculiarity of mine; considering the high proportion of buggers among the foreigners who genuinely 'love China' it seems to be the chief thing the country has to offer. No doubt you could generalise it into saying you like to be in a place where there is no sense of sin[1] and no feeling that it is a duty to worry, combined with an adequate amount of hardheadness (of course I don't feel at all that the Chinese are delicious tender creatures, like the at present murderous but always kittenish inhabitants of south-east Asia; you don't feel outside the modern commercial world in China) but even so I should say you get this more general feeling through looking at working class young men—seldom from students, who do tend to be harried a bit, poor things.

We were expecting a whirl of strikes and persecutions in May, but so far it is passing off quietly. Last month the government hired a mob of several thousand hooligans described as an anti-communist students' movement to attack the universities, and the foolish hooligans broke in to a compound for professors here and broke a lot of their windows before being whistled off. This had an excellent effect on the morale of the Peita

---

[1] Cf. IAR, *Mencius on the Mind* (1932), 75: 'There is no officially recognized war in the Chinese mind between the Soul and the Body, between will and desire. Hence that absence of a sense of sin which used so to puzzle missionaries.'

[Peking University] professors, who came out on strike on their own account and signed a very firm document protesting against secret police ill-treatment of students. The government has a baffling capacity for putting itself in the wrong (this is only one example), and has been quietening down a bit. The chief trouble just now is that some Tsing Hua medical students, that university being out in the country, have been putting iodine and stuff on sores and otherwise giving elementary free help to nearby villages, also teaching a little writing to the children; this has been strictly forbidden on pain of arrest. You would think the government could hardly invent a better way of putting itself in the wrong. Of course it is reasonable enough in the middle of a civil war for any government to try to put down propaganda for the enemy, and that is really a difficult job because the ideas of the students are so very woolly, though very right-minded I think, that you can hardly say which are communists even when they are being frank with you. Which, I mean, would become communists if they were to decide after being informed; the point is that they seem so very uninformed. But they are very patient and disciplined and indeed brave about their own movement, which is largely a matter of trying to protect fellow-students. In general I think their political position is the unimpeachable but not very helpful one that the civil war had better stop and something sensible had better happen afterwards.

Hetta is due back tomorrow from a long jaunt to Mongolia (she is very fond of Mongols), disguising or selling herself as a correspondent for UP or AP, and eyed very suspiciously by an American representing AP or UP. They went to write up the first postwar revival of the annual Jenghis Khan festival, but it was called off because Communists had taken the holy place, so I understand they went from Paotou to Kweisui by lorry and came down the Yellow River back again by barge. She has to fly back because the railway is cut. I will wait till tomorrow to see if she turns up with gossip. (Come to think of it, I hope I haven't written all this kind of thing out for you before).

May 21st. Hetta flew back yesterday from the Mongols. She has had about enough of them, and is tired of meals consisting only of a sheep boiled without salt. The best picture I thought was of an area where the Chinese have succeeded in grabbing some Mongol pasture and are ploughing it up. The ox-plough moves surprisingly fast over the sandy soil, and the desert can be seen moving in behind it immediately as the sand blows in. It will be quite impossible to grow anything there and probably impossible ever to get the grass back. You watch the ploughs advancing over a vast treeless plain. After eating the boiled sheep, by the way, you first wipe your greasy hands on your boots, then push them under the robe and rub the armpits etc., then the face, and clean off the red felt robe which thus gets to look like leather. She objects that the Mongols are no-idea people as the Chinese say, with no songs even that she heard, and all that can be praised is the construction of the yurt.

Talking of singing, I have recently heard The Song of the Yellow River, which really is very beautiful. It is a cantata about the Japanese war, written in communist areas during wartime, strung together from Yellow River folk-songs and scored for European orchestra, which does some rather surprising things but it is definitely European music. This is not a bastard art as you might think because the folksongs have never been as foreign to our ideas as the opera and upperclass singing. It seems the only art in China with some late prospects.

Yours very affectionately
Bill Empson.

King's

TO IAN PARSONS

Kenyon College, Gambier, Ohio
12 July 1948 | I am due back in Peking late in September.

My dear Ian,

This is just to say that things are proceeding according to plan; I am doing a course of lectures here about my forthcoming book, after bringing a text of it with me, and I hope this process will result in making it less unreasonable as I find out what the class can't swallow. When the school is over I hope to have a week or two rewriting as found to be necessary and then post the text to you from here. It should therefore arrive about the end of August. I should warn you that it is rather over 200,000 words, not an intolerable length I hope, but on the massive side. Allen Tate is lecturing here and has written to an American publisher telling them to do my collected verse; of course if I can get any offers you and Faber will be informed beforehand.[1] I get here what is probably a misleading impression

---

[1] TSE wrote to Tate on 26 Jul. 1948: 'If this reaches you before the summer school has broken up please tell Empson that we have now a firm offer for his poems from Harcourt, Brace and Co. which is what I always wanted, and I hope they may be able to bring the book out early next year.' (*Princeton*) Parsons confirmed in a letter to WE, 13 Aug. 1948: 'Du Sautoy of Faber's rang me up yesterday to say that when T. S. E. was in America recently he was able to interest Harcourt Brace in your collected Poems (this was after Laughlin had said he couldn't do them yet awhile), and I agreed that Faber's should go ahead and see if they could clinch the deal. I hope it goes through, though I must say these Americans puzzle me—Brace gives up AMBIGUITY

of my fame in America, as we all seem to be on the same side in a literary war, with the enemy in the majority. I have a vague suspicion that the side I am supposed to be a leader of is rather a reactionary one, but [F. O.] Matthiessen is an honest chap I think; too patriotic to be an accurate judge of American writers no doubt, but that you expect.[2] This is very English country, with rain and big trees and mixed farming, but at present very muggy and hot.

[. . .]

Your cheque for 98 pounds has been sent here; very nice; but I am not clear whether the balancesheet means that only 21 copies sold in America or does not cover American sales at all. I was amused to see an eager footnote in a new book here boosting the New Critics (Hyman* The Armed Vision)[3] saying that the rewriting of Ambiguity is a retraction and shows that something very valuable has been lost, whereas Leavis' paper said that my underwriting all my old errors showed that no maturing could be expected.

Yours very sincerely
W. Empson.

Reading

because he couldn't sell it and Laughlin takes it on and does extremely well with it; then the next minute Laughlin gets cold feet about the Poems and Brace decides to take them on!' (*Reading*) *The Collected Poems of William Empson* (2,000 copies) was brought out by Harcourt, Brace on 24 Mar. 1949.

[2] F. O. Matthiessen (1902–50) was a foremost American scholar; his pioneering *American Renaissance: Art and Expression in the age of Emerson and Whitman* (1941) is a modern classic. Educated at Yale, at New College, Oxford (as a Rhodes scholar, 1923–5), and at Harvard University, he became an English instructor at Yale, 1927–9, before returning to Harvard for the rest of his career; he was ultimately a full professor of history and literature. A man of high conviction and a complex nature, he was a homosexual and pacifist, an active Christian, and a democratic socialist. Pro-Soviet in his politics (in 1948 he wrote, 'I accept the Russian Revolution as the most progressive event of our century'), he was an active campaigner for Henry Agard Wallace in his Progressive Party bid for the US presidency 1948. Prone to melancholy and depression, he committed suicide on 31 Mar. 1950. His other works include *T. S. Eliot: An Essay on the Nature of Poetry* (1935), *Henry James: The Major Phase* (1944), *Theodore Dreiser* (1951), and *The Responsibilities of the Critic* (1952); he also edited *The Oxford Book of American Verse* (1950). WE thought him 'a levelheaded creature' (letter to HE, 29 Jun. 1948).

[3] See below for letter (in 1949) to Stanley Edgar Hyman, author of *The Armed Vision: A Study in the Methods of Literary Criticism* (1948). Hyman was to meet WE in London in the summer of 1969; WE wrote on 12 May that year: 'Looking forward to seeing you. But for you, I am afraid, if you have been looking forward for thirty years, the experience is bound to be depressing. We had best walk across the Heath and look at the Rembrandt [in Kenwood House]'. (*Library of Congress*)

TO ROBERT LOWELL*

as from: 11 Tung Kao Fang, Near Peking National University, Peiping 9,
China
27 August 1948

Dear Robert Lowell,

Sorry not to have seen you, but it was a rush getting things done on time. I write this on the freighter going back to China. Mr Coffin of Kenyon kindly arranged about the recording, and I did exactly the poems you named.[1] I did not like the way I did them; there was a feeling of staginess I thought when I read them over. There are also one or two fluffs, and an actual misreading of 'both man and beast' instead of 'both god and beast' in *Arachne*; however it struck me that this did no fatal harm. I hope you are satisfied with them.

If all goes well, I shall be back in Kenyon in two years' time, and not then trying to finish off a book, so I hope we will meet again then. (It seems absurd to want to finish a book on a visit, but you can't post it air mail and the ordinary mail from China to England takes several months).

May I congratulate you on your own verse, which I have only read just recently; I have been very much out of things. I hope you are doing more.[2]

Yours with thanks
William Empson.

Houghton, bMS Eng 1905 (443)

---

[1] WE had recorded his poetry for the Library of Congress. Charles Coffin, Dean of the Kenyon School of English, had research interests in literature and theology (including the work of John Donne). He saw WE as a man of many 'subtle tensions', as he wrote in a memo (9 Mar. 1949): the living embodiment of 'the most puzzling ambiguity of all . . . He is a master of dialectic, yet he is no casuist. Great sophistication and knowing attends utter simplicity and child-like gentleness.' He noted further: '[WE's] detractors accuse him of "reading too much into" a poem, but I have heard him silence a hubbub of young critics with a firm but witty insistence that "Shakespeare must have meant precisely what he said".' (*Kenyon College Archives*)

[2] Lowell would extol WE's poetry on 29 Jan. 1958: 'it can't be denied that almost no praise would be too high for your poems. You have the stamina of Donne, yet a far more useful and empirical knowledge of modern science and English metrics. I think you are the most intelligent poet writing in our language and perhaps the best. I put you with Hardy and Graves and Auden and Philip Larkin . . . All this—because recently the scales, so to speak, have dropped from my eyes and your work is now as clear to me as, say: Frost's' (*The Letters of Robert Lowell*, 310).

TO HETTA EMPSON

On board Narrandera
21 September [1948]

My dearest Hetta,

We are expected to get to Manila in two or three days, so I may as well start writing to you; we have been at sea from Vancouver since the 2nd. I foolishly told you to write to Shanghai not Manila, but I hope you sent something to Manila. There is a frightful rumour that this dawdling boat is going down to Cebu, at the southern end of the Philippines, before going to Hongkong and Shanghai. That would add another week I suppose. If we do that I really think I ought to fly from Hongkong, assuming one can get an air passage. It would mean a lot of muddle about finding the boat again at Taku bar and probably extra difficulties about customs. I find that cosmetics are among the things you aren't allowed to import except as for your own use, and from Mrs Brown's letter Walter's parcel has a lot of cosmetics as well as yours and presumably David [Kidd]'s if it is on board, as I believe it is. It seems too absurd to pretend that all this paint is for my own face, and the difficulty about simply paying the duty is that I want to get the American money through undeclared, what there is of it, so I can't simply fish it out to pay whatever startling sum they may invent. If I do come all the way by sea, which would mean at least the second week in October, you must mind and come and meet me if only to say that part of the luggage is your property; I suppose we might get away with that. If I knew [John] Blofeld's[1] address in Hongkong I might ask him to reserve an air passage, but I suppose that would only lead to further confusion. You might perhaps send me a short letter to Hongkong saying what his address there is (short I mean because if we go straight to Hongkong from Manila I might not get it, but I should fancy we will waste enough time for that whichever way we go). As you will gather I feel frustrated and very cross with the shipping agent, who airily told me the boat would take about a month.

The passengers who got on at Vancouver are two American young women and a business man and his wife, originally Austrian, who are not so bad; all the American ladies tend to gush and I have to guard my words

---

[1] John Blofeld (1913–87), a scholar of Taoist and Buddhist religious practices, supported himself in the 1930s by travelling and teaching in China; later he joined the British foreign service and worked for the Embassy in Chungking, Peking, and Nanking. A translator of Chinese Zen texts and author of general works on Taoism, his writings include *The Wheel of Life* (1959), *The Way of Power* (1970), and *City of Lingering Splendour: A Frank Account of Old Peking's Exotic Pleasures* (1961).

not to give them any opportunity. Most of the time I spend doing sums. I started doing a couple of reviews but feel I can't go on with them. I read through *Ulysses* again, which I got a copy of in America, and think now that it has a 'point' which Joyce apparently was shy about and succeeded in hiding from his readers—I mean that Bloom has a quite specific neurosis about his wife which is going to be cured by his homosexual feelings about Stephen (if Stephen doesn't behave too badly, as remains possible at the end of the book). Bloom wants another child but feels he can't copulate with her, and hasn't done for ten years since the first son died. If he can get her away from her present lover and get her to bed with Stephen, he feels, he will be able to try again; Stephen agrees near the end to give Mrs B enough Italian lessons to get her songs right, and Mrs B in the final chapter decides that she would like to have Stephen and also that she is prepared to fetch her husband breakfast in bed next day and cosset him up, so it looks as if the thing is shaping quite hopefully. As for Stephen, of course he is mainly occupied with jeering at everybody and being 'bitter', but he realises he needs a mothering type of woman to heal him up a bit. If Stephen is the author it is clear that he got out of this mental condition somehow, and a brief affair with Mrs B before he leaves Ireland perman- ently for Zurich seems to fit the case very well. After all there needs to be some reason why the author thought that such a very slight story was worth such enormously elaborate treatment. The usual view is that the book is Pure Art meant to show the pointlessness of everything (or the pointlessness of everything in Dublin) and that it would be awfully naive to expect the characters to feel better as a result of it. Joyce himself was tainted with this Purity business, and I think the effect is to make the great work seem rather meanminded and pokey. But if one believes he was only hiding the real point of his story (and knew it had a point because it had happened to him) I think the whole thing seems much better; in fact it is a bold treatment of a subject which nobody else has dared to handle. But even so it doesn't really gain from trying to hide the point.[2]

---

[2] This passage signals the beginning of WE's long efforts to prove James Joyce's covert purposes in *Ulysses*: see in particular 'The Ultimate Novel' in *UB*, 217–59. According to WE, Leopold Bloom is preoccupied with negotiating a happy Eternal Triangle: a *ménage à trois* involv- ing Stephen and Molly. In an uncollected piece, WE noted that 'the notes written by Joyce to advise himself how to write the play *Exiles* . . . show that he regarded the Consenting Triangle as an exalted and progressive ideal.' Knowingly running the risk of scandalizing narrow-minded readers, WE eagerly associated himself with Joyce's putative opinion in interpreting such a *ménage* as a worthy object: a form of moral idealism, not perverse inclination. He considered his exposition of the secret of *Ulysses* as in no way a slander on Joyce. He was concerned with rescuing, not damaging, Joyce's reputation, he maintained; and he thought it 'a high-minded thing' for the novelist to present in such a way 'a current problem'—'a blow for freedom'. (See also WE's pieces on Joyce in *A*.)

I put this in if only to show I'm not quite as dead as I sounded at the beginning, but mental life has pretty well stopped for the last week. I hope you aren't very bored too. Maybe the school will begin the term on strike so that it doesn't matter being back late, but I haven't heard from you for so long now that I can't guess. We have a radio but it is difficult to get any news out of it; however I gather that there hasn't been any world explosion so far.

Very impatient to get back to you

William.

24th. Manila. We still don't know whether we are going to Cebu, but I may as well post this at once.

Your letter of Aug 27th has arrived; very nice and interesting but a long time ago already. As you say, I might buy a coat in Hongkong perhaps. Glad to hear your reading of poetry went off well. Maybe after a solemn clean-up we will all be quieter for a bit in the universities.

We now *are* going to Cebu; and I think I had better try and fix up a flight from Hongkong, leaving the luggage on the boat. There seems no immediate need to fly from here.

Houghton

TO AN UNKNOWN RECIPIENT

[Draft letter about David Garnett's novel *The Grasshoppers Come* (1931); probably dating from late 1940s; recipient unknown]

The story assumes a certain horror for machines, as producing a machine civilisation opposed to human values: this is connected with a fear of science—say behaviourism—as attempting to explain people, as if they were grasshoppers, and so making them, by removing ideals and ideas, really more like them; and on the other hand a fear, excited by that same scientific knowledge, that the stupidity will lead to calamity because science has yet done so little.

There is also a strong influence from the Bible (the main English literary authority about locusts). There they are used as metaphors of attacking armies, especially coming in from the East: the invading Mongols too were compared to locusts. Hence these locusts are associated with the Yellow Peril fear in Europe (perhaps also because the Chinese are traditionally supposed to have inscrutable, unchanging faces, like the locusts, and the locusts have faces like horses suggesting nomads); mental connection is snapped at a critical moment when we and the hero are already feeling relief as from nightmare, he finds he has been saved by a Chinaman (also in an aeroplane). (The Chinaman belongs to a War-Lord's army, which may well be compared to a swarm of locusts: but the Warlord, with a very complex irony, is interested in the sciences and so a sympathetic character.)

Furthermore locusts were eaten by Hebrew prophets when alone in the desert, composing prophecies such as is needed now, because everything is like locusts: especially by St John, just before the new era: the hero can only feel that civilisation is blank, and that if he is saved he would like to go on living as he is now: he has nothing to bring as a prophecy from the desert, and yet that parallel gives a sense of lurid, unexplained excitement to the whole story.

The locusts first are useful, then overcome him; machines have been useful in the West, but we are now afraid they are burying civilisation by sheer quantity. It is only as a secondary metaphor that the locusts become herd-like undisciplined people (like the two who hired the machine, and die without mention like the grasshoppers): from that point of view the pilot becomes the hero, the prophet normally stoned by the people: he is a typical hero of the machine age because he is brave, an excellent mechanic, and has no culture except irony. (There is a contrast here between the man who runs the machine, who becomes heroic though stupid, and the people who use the machine, who become mechanical dolls). (Also something of the spiritual isolation of the machine worker in his relations with his wife.)

When the locusts have almost stifled him, he makes a disastrous gesture. I'm not sure whether the locusts in the story would have stifled him if he hadn't made that gesture: at all events they defeat him by making him enter their world, since they make him do something imaginative and foolish rather than something ordinary because that would seem therefore mechanical (the free-will idea has always tied our theologians into knots of that sort). It is a satire on civilisation when the idiot eyes of the locusts mistake the burning, which is his ruin, for the rising sun. At the crisis of a tragedy you go below the rational world and call on subconscious modes of thought, sources of will, because the mind can no longer solve the problems put before it—that is the essence of the tragic situation: here it is by breaking out into sheer folly that he wakes up as it were from the nightmare: it is becase the aeroplane burned that the Chinese aeronaut saw it and saved him. (There is no escape from the machine civilisation then, except by smashing it—or rather, since there is so much sense of nightmare about the incident here, by not smashing it, but keeping the independence of mind which could smash it if it chose.)

You said it was unwise to bother about symbols. I think it is only of interest to dig the symbols out, even to this moderate degree: they work without being noticed. But I think these are the reasons why, to people who take it simply as a story, it is in fact such a good story.

Some of the hero's sentences are written too preciously: some of the descriptions, which could afford to be precious, are too dull, or state excitement too flatly—he said he tried to write it like a newspaper account, and at moments I think succeeded too well. The reasons I think it very good are not reasons of style: they are what I have been trying to outline.

They first help then overcome <stifle> him.

fear of machines: many subdued by things *like* the stupid, mechanical, scientifically explicable creatures.

St John in the desert ate locusts: rediscovery of Christianity, or sense of need for coming Messiah.

Coming from East: the yellow peril with a mask for a face. (from Arabia into Palestine)

But no, machines: holding the hand of the Chinaman. The war lord (Attila) is interested in science—he is sane and enquiring, and good at mechanical things (therefore a good man—the men not interested in mechanical things are poor) not a machine. (Bad flyer: social break-up; but sense of relief).

At the same time his army laying waste China like the locusts.

Compared to horses: the Scripture phrase.

Biblical influence, in here.

(It is dull working the machines: and they produce spiritual isolation: they have already cut him off from his wife.)

He is saved because he goes mad, saved by his loss and folly which breaks his own machine, when he wants to break the animals who look like it. (That makes the aeroplane see [   ]): instinct of the Hebrew prophet. The other two not worthy to face this opposition (but we ought to be told about them)

(Opening out the place they come *from*: opposite ends)

'tragic' situation, agon, implied: he loses reason at the crisis of the tragedy.

horse's hoofs shall be counted
lame as Oedipus? or Vulcan?
they being the Sphinx

Houghton

TO IAN PARSONS

11 Tung Kao Fang, Near Peking National University, Peiping 9.
New Year 1949

My dear Ian,

Very glad to get your letter, but you may have made a mistake in not writing off all your points at once. If the town falls it seems unreasonable to expect letters to go on coming; only the air mail gets through, of course, and that only on the new airfields inside the city. We propose to stay on here, and of course if the government falls altogether letters can be expected to start again; it is impossible to say whether Peiping is likely to fall soon or be besieged till the end. We have laid in a little food but not enough to be worth looting, such was the way we looked at it, and the pre-siege estimates were not more than three months; about one has now passed, and the food situation is not yet appalling—prices are very high compared to what people here are used to or can (most of them) afford, but not I believe wildly high by English standards. If the siege goes on the thing is no doubt bound to get very bad, and it is difficult to estimate. I could send some mildly amusing gossip about life here, but letters are naturally censored and might I suppose be suppressed if found irritating, so I had better concentrate on getting an answer through to you.

I am of course very willing to hear your suggestions [with regard to *SCW*], and I already have a copy of the text here. By all means send them off air mail when you get this, and they will probably arrive in the end by one route or another. You will probably say that the first two chapters are going to choke off readers who would have enjoyed the literary parts in the middle. I have just read through them again and they do seem almost malignantly stiff; but I have to present the theory before the reader is asked to watch it in operation. Conceivably one would have a Reconsideration chapter towards the end of the book in which a lot of the wire-drawing of the theoretical position could be put, so that the first two chapters could give the skeleton of the theory at a good deal less length. But I have a feeling that the shape of the book (as apart from how the unwilling reader can be lured on) is better like it is; with a lot of theory at the beginning and the end and what might be called the meat of the sandwich in the middle. If the thing is planned on a descending curve for the interests of the literary reader he may struggle further through the text but only to greater disappointment in the later stages. However you will say what you think.

One point I want to make clear is that I can't again sign a contract giving you foreign rights on future books. As I understand, I signed in the Ambiguity contract that you had the refusal of the next two prose books and this was taken to include the foreign rights. I could I suppose have got out of it for this book by your refusing the little Buddha book, but that would have been a bit off the point and anyway I would prefer to have this one done in a tidy manner from England; I don't imagine enormous profits are in view anyway. But it might turn out important to be free to place later [*the paper is torn here*] without coming under British taxes etc.

We are in good health and go along comfortably so far, though of course one must expect this dragging affair to lower one's spirits. I do not imagine we are in danger from the war, but there might well be a period of looting if the siege drags on, especially if there is an interregnum period. You understand there are one or two under British [protection] still here, and quite a large foreign community. The British consul is a young man [Martin Buxton] who was at the siege of Mukden, and much better value than most consuls we think. I spent the New Year at Tsing Hua university outside the town, which is in communist hands, having gone there to give my weekly lecture on Macbeth, but the boys did not want to be lectured to; so I have not gone this week. It was an interesting and pleasant trip across the lines, with a police pass you understand; I was invited to a students New Year party in the evening, with singing and dancing and so forth, and came back next day. There seems to be no fighting around here at present. It is all more placid than you seem to expect, but of course the real question is how the food supply works out.

I hope you are going on all right. The local English paper has stopped and we are very behindhand on English news; I am curious to know what happened about the great trial of corrupt officials, but perhaps it is even now still sub judice. A little personal news has come, mostly bad, the death of Michael Roberts[1] and the separation of the Trevelyans. I got a letter from Harcourt Brace saying that the verse book has gone to the press, which I must answer. We were rather revelling in the thought that no more letters would have to be written, but the post soon got started again.

Yours very sincerely

Bill Empson

Looking through the book after getting your letter, it struck me that I had been rather unfair to [Hugh] Kingsmill. I think a footnote ought to be added near the end of the chapter on *Othello*, end of the third section,

---

[1] Michael Roberts died of monocytic leukaemia on 13 Dec. 1948.

where I quote Kingsmill as saying that Othello is 'very slenderly attached to his character of a general'.[2] The footnote should say:

However I would not want to deny the main assertion of his treatment, that 'The power and reality of *Othello* are in the intensity of his longing for ideal beauty, and the agony of the failure to attain it'.[3] But one can examine the fundamental drives of an author (as he does very impressively) without letting it make the characters unreal. And on the other hand I should agree that one feels Othello somehow a 'magnificent puppet',[4] but the reason I think is the more public one which I am trying to describe.

Reading

TO I. A. RICHARDS

11 Tung Kao Fang, Near Peking National University, Peiping 9, China
22 January 1949

Dear Richards,

It seems we have made a compromise arrangement here with the air mail still working, so there is no longer any obstructive drama about letter writing. We were expecting some difficulties but there have been none to speak of, and presumably the banging is now over.

I was very glad to get your postcard from Switzerland, and sorry to miss you while I was in America, particularly because I wanted you to do a look-over of my forthcoming book, which Chatto's have provisionally accepted, by the way. It contains an apparent attack on your views on Emotions in words, practically all the attack coming out in a recent Kenyon Review.[1] I hope you weren't irritated by that if you saw it; the controversy seemed necessary to show where I stood myself, and the book is certainly not intended as anything but a development of your lead.

It seems clear that the subject of Middle School English teaching is going to come up fairly sharply here in the near future; any reorganiser would be tempted to cut so many weekly periods given to English with such poor results, and the ones in question are likely to be rather against

---

[2] See 'Honest in Othello', *SCW*, 244 (the proposed footnote was not used). WE is paraphrasing Hugh Kingsmill's suggestion—*The Return of William Shakespeare* (1929), in *The Dawn's Delay* (1948)—that Othello does not come out 'into the open air of the world . . . No, you must look elsewhere for light on the art of war' (286).

[3] Kingsmill, *The Dawn's Delay*, 289: 'The power and reality of *Othello* are in the intensity of its longing for ideal beauty, and the agony of the failure to attain to it.'

[4] Ibid. 286.

[1] 'Emotions in Words Again', *Kenyon Review*, 10: 4 (Autumn 1948), 579–601.

the language anyway. It seems rather important for the university people to get an agreed opinion on it before the reorganising is considered. I have been lazy about it so far but (with this book out of the way and so on) rather feel capable of activity now. I went to Tsing Hua at the New Year, which then involved crossing the fighting line with a police pass, to give my regular weekly lecture on Macbeth, but the children didn't want it and asked me to an evening party with singing and dancing instead. Hsi si Liang, if you remember him, now in control of English language teaching there, urged me to start the ball rolling with a circular to teachers etc., and Bob Winter* (who is in roaring form) agreed that the whole question would have to come up in the Spring or so; then when I got back it turned out the local British Council was running an innocent discussion series for Middle School teachers from next month, so I thought I would hold my noise and try to work through that. Bob, I trust, is going to do a new edition of your textbook; I gave him last spring a mass of small recommendations for it, chiefly concerned with the absence of the promised introductory Teachers' Handbook. It seems to be agreed that the teachers can't be spoon-fed enough, and that a lot of introductory stuff is needed to make the book a plausible competitor with otherwise obviously inferior ones. I take it from your firm refusal to answer an earlier letter that you don't refuse permission for him to do this; he was anxious last year to get permission, but unless you let one of us know that you disapprove of this plan I will go ahead with trying to push him into it. Of course he would be glad to get any advice.

Another thing I am keen to bring up is this; why don't you become head of the British Council in China for the coming two years, after Miss Greer [Grier] goes in November (she might be extended for a few more months)?[2] It sounds a fussy kind of job but successive heads seem only to fuss about what they themselves find interesting. You could do much what you liked. People expect the new capital to be here in Peiping; we rather hope to avoid the over-crowding, but anyway you wouldn't have to be stuck in the south for the hot weather. Of course the salary would appear a sacrifice to you, but I suggest you could get two years' leave from Harvard to do work of importance to English-speaking peoples and your own

[2] Lynda Grier (1880–1967) was appointed to head the Nanking office of the British Council at the surprising age of 68, after serving for almost a quarter of a century (1921–45) as principal of Lady Margaret Hall, Oxford. She had no experience of running an organization of such far-flung and anfractuous complexity as the China branch of the British Council in a time of national emergency. In the event, she was to work extremely hard as the chief representative for the British Council in China for two years, 1948–50, and would be awarded the CBE for her services to China.

government, and the salary business could then be adjusted. The normal two years' appointment would I really think be quite enough to clear the subject. People are tired of controversy and merely want a definite lead. No doubt the Council is afraid of Ogden, but it should be quite possible to make clear to them your difference of attitude to Ogden, and that would be about as far as their minds go on the topic. The Chinese are a field you were forced to let drop, and I am sure you feel that at the right time that part of the career ought to be tidied up. Now is the time; no later period would give anything like the same opportunity. The decision may really come in the next year or two whether the Chinese go on learning English in bulk at all. It is time to put your oar in.

As to the politics, my point of view is simply that the Chinese communists had much better not be forced into the arms of Moscow, where they don't really want to be; this seems to be the attitude of most foreigners on the spot. So one could say that getting the Middle School English teaching here on a tolerable footing is really a matter of world importance in preventing the Third World War. How often do you receive calls of so high a character?

If you were willing to consider the British Council job the next question would be how to put it forward. No doubt you know all about that, but I talked to [C. P.] Fitzgerald who is very ready to put your name forward inside the machine if you are willing. He is rather under a cloud in the machine, chiefly because they very stupidly will not use sinologues; but he knows plenty of ropes in it. Please then let me or Fitzgerald here know if you think the plan possible, because an internal line of suggestion might help any other if no more. Actually you are so obviously more suitable than anyone else they are ever able to think of that the petty jealousies if brought up could hardly be sustained I think. I do hope you will consider it seriously.

By the way please post me if you have got it another copy of the 1937 Chinese Ministry of Education Committee's recommendation about English teaching methods; I thought I had one but I have lost it, and it obviously needs recalling now.

This is a very dull letter but I just wanted to get off some practical points. The family is very well and chattering away in Chinese. Please give our best wishes to Dorothea. Hetta feels it is time she did some more travelling.

Yours very affectionately

Bill Empson

Rockefeller Archive Center: Harvard U–I. A. Richards collection, record group 1. 1, series 200, Box 234, folder 2797

IAR, in forwarding the last letter to the Rockefeller Foundation in New York, added in a covering letter to John Marshall of 3 Feb. 1949:

> I am telling him and Fitzgerald to go ahead with their suggestions to the British Council. I imagine we might go out about next Christmas. If so, I'd very much like to have some people from this country to come out with me on Fellowship to produce materials for the Chinese schools with me . . .
>
> Notable, isn't it, that they already think something can and should be done. There is a kind of hopeful stir?

But John Marshall, replying on 8 Feb., put a damper on the plan:

> You perhaps will understand it if I say that the prospect of your going to China to head British Council work there hardly thrills me. I know what a useful service you could undoubtedly render in that capacity, but honestly it seems to me that you would be seriously limiting the scope of your activities. That, however, is something for you and Dorothea to decide, and the rest of us can only stand by and await your decision.

In the event, IAR did not put himself forward to lead the British Council in China, though he and Dorothy would make a return trip in 1950.

TO STANLEY EDGAR HYMAN*

Only one page of this letter (1949) survives. In 1948 Stanley Edgar Hyman had written of *SVP*, 'Empson draws heavily on sociology, chiefly of the Marxist variety'; also, 'the book is implicitly Marxist throughout, something that only Kenneth Burke seems to have perceived' ('William Empson and Categorical Criticism', *The Armed Vision* [rev., 1955], 248–9).

[Both of the world powers, the USA and the USSR, are] patently lunatic (one of them says that you mustn't get into a bath unless it is superheated steam and the other says you mustn't unless it is a solid block of ice); and the only hope for the world is to find an independently strong country which will be able to refuse to listen to the nonsense talked by either side. Such was my opinion before my return to China in 1947, and the later events have not altered it; of course Mao Tse Tung has to prevent petty gossip by taking his side firmly in the present chatter, but he is still free to follow the interests of his own country. The reason is simply one of geography; China is not Bulgaria; in fact I suspect both America and Russia in a world war would be anxious *not* to have China as an ally into which they must sink troops and material as into a bog, whichever side the Government of China was backing. Of course if China induces Malaya to go Communist that bankrupts the British, but there are a number of natural stops against it, and the same for the Dutch in Java. Once you get international trade reopened from China on a firm basis you will no longer have a simple world war situation, please either tell lies for Russia or for China, and the whole assumption that we must have a world war depends on this simple opposition between two colonial European powers whose theories were both worked out in London. It is too silly to tell me that everybody who matters has got to be killed because these two colonial powers have made it a point of honour to destroy everything that knows better as well as each other (and England of [*photocopied paper folded over*]. Nobody has anything to gain from the muchtalked of third world war, and if I, in my small way, can do anything to prevent the belief that it is inevitable I can do it better here than elsewhere. I will stay here if I am allowed. Earlier in this long paragraph I mentioned a possible censor, but I take it that this kind of talk is not too offensive in China. I am entirely in favour of the Chinese revolution, and think it less revolutionary than the British one; my deviation is merely that I suspect Stalin of nationalism, and I was saying so the other night to a Chinese communist who did not regard it as an unbearable point of view. From the other side, my deviation is that if Britain fights China I am a Conscientious Objector, solely on patriotic grounds, to try and improve my country's relation with China, and I think I would stick to that though I don't like to say what will happen; what I mean is that Britain and China want to survive, whereas the two lunatic colonials America and Russia haven't got anything worth keeping and only want to win, and both have the power to destroy everything worth keeping.

Such is the reason why I think I am right to stay here, and try to handle the Chinese set-up. It makes a tedious introduction but I want you to think me a decent man. The following paragraphs will discuss why I think you a decent man.

I did not think you one when I first read your book, at the Kenyon College Summer School last year. I am so old now that your praise seemed to me only a fact worth noticing for its public effects, good or bad. Your praise of me as a Marxist critic has (very falsely perhaps) given me a strong leg in the Peking area. You might regret what you did here.

Houghton, bMS Eng 1401 (583)

KENYON REVIEW, 11:4 (Autumn 1949)

In a letter to the *Kenyon Review* (11: 2, Spring 1949, 316–20), Gerald A. Smith took WE to task for his criticism—in 'Emotions in Words Again' (*Kenyon Review*, 10: 4 (Autumn 1948), 579–601)—of a 'doctrine' of IAR that there is a distinction between emotive and cognitive language, and between feeling and sense in poetry; IAR in various places had himself resolved the apparent problem. In any event, WE seemed impossibly to desire a 'scientific proof' for everything: 'He wants to keep the whole range of poetry open to analysis . . . [whereas] I feel that there is a great deal of poetry that he wouldn't care to explicate . . . It can hardly be considered scientific to try to explain scientifically what we do not know scientifically.'

FRL, in a separate letter (315–16), complained about this sentence by WE in the same article, 'Emotions in Words Again':

> He [Max Eastman] found it particularly absurd that the arts should be viewed as a socially important alternative to religion; on the other hand Dr F. R. Leavis became angry with Professor Richards for not taking this view seriously enough, because if he did he would obviously support the Leavis social schemes about the matter. (582)

FRL recalled that WE had submitted a protest (published in *Scrutiny*, 4: 1, June 1935; see above, 79–81) about FRL's review of Richards's *Coleridge on Imagination*; he revealed too: 'In a subsequent private letter of apology Mr Empson expressed some regret for his public letter. However, he now repeats the offence, wantonly, and adds to it by further misrepresentation.' FRL regarded his own review of IAR not as 'angry' but as 'amused and decidedly cool'; it offered 'a long and very careful examination of the whole neo-Benthamite enterprise of Professor Richards' book'—and he said that WE had never attempted to answer his full critique. FRL went on: 'When he refers to "the Leavis social schemes," I don't know what he means—except that he clearly intends a sneer: the "schemes" to which I have devoted myself (at the cost, as he cannot be unaware, of not advancing my academic career or worldly prosperity) are the attempt to serve the function of criticism by establishing and keeping going a serious critical review; the working out of the methods by which literary study may be made a discipline of intelligence; and the vindicating of the idea of liberal education. What, I might ask, are the Empson schemes?—but he implies, I suppose, that he is not green enough to have any.'

Sirs,

The problems of the post here have kept me from getting my Spring *Kenyon Review* till July, when I write this; I do not want to hide from the criticisms of me in it, but could not complain if you felt this answer came too late for publishing.

As for Mr Gerald A. Smith, I don't at all deny that Professor Richards has often written sentences which avoid or indeed solve the confusions I was accusing him of; my point was merely that his published work often leaves room for a confusion about these problems, one that actually occurs in the minds of his readers and other people, and had better be cleared up if possible. Indeed I think of his writings as a help in doing so. As to Mr Smith's doubts about me, I can assure him that I habitually believe things without scientific proof or any completion of a verbal analysis, and that I think other people had much better do the same. We have to pick up a sense of the world as best we can; but there are danger-points in this process which need to be isolated. Perhaps the most obvious comes in the almost neurotic form 'because my opinions were arrived at by intuition I can ignore any future evidence.' I may be wrong in thinking that the subject can be taped down at all tidily, but otherwise I don't think Mr Smith and I really disagree.

As for Dr Leavis, I do wish I could clear his mind of the idea that I have been ratting on a private confession written to him fourteen years ago about a review of one article of his. No one article is in question, and I wish I had written many more admiring letters to Dr Leavis with which he might threaten me. But I would certainly have forgotten all about them at once, as I have done the one he mentions. My convictions about Dr Leavis (a state of mind on the whole greatly in his favour) are an 'intuition', built up of a rather long experience almost every detail of which I have totally forgotten. This of course illustrates how an ordinary practical judgment is built out of things not at all in reach of 'verbal analysis' (and by the way I have not yet seen evidence to think this one wrong). All I would want to say is that the feelings you get out of a printed text *are* likely to be in reach of verbal analysis, and had better be so regarded.

However, as to the claim by Dr Leavis that his criticism of Professor Richards is very good and has never been answered, my impression is that the people who saw the whole position did not think it worth answering. This, I should guess, was what I was trying to hint at, without success, in the private letter which accompanied some attempt to clear up the fallacies in the Leavis attack. It looks as if Mr Smith feels now about me much as I did so long ago about Dr Leavis; the real question is always whether this kind of 'attack' is getting anywhere on its own, whatever springboard it uses. All the same, I do see that my phrase 'social schemes of Dr Leavis' might be regarded as a sarcasm, though as a matter of fact (to its honour) his magazine had always had plenty of them. In the forthcoming book from which my article was taken I will alter it to 'programmes' if I have the opportunity, and as far as I can see that prevents any misunderstanding about the intended tone.[1] The purport still seems to me true, and fair comment, though of course very unimportant.

The final kick of Dr Leavis is to presume I would think it 'green' to have any social schemes of my own, and this is connected with his claim to be a self-sacrificial figure who has followed the narrow path at great cost. I don't want to make any counter-claims of the same sort, but I don't think I need put up with being called a smart-aleck. I gave up writing for ten years because I really thought allied propaganda important, whereas he very rightly kept his flag flying at Cambridge. The ideals for liberal culture which he gives in his letter are just those which I would want to support, and believe I am supporting. I can't feel there is any cynical career-hunting about my wish to do it in present-day Peking. Of course I also find Peking very interesting, but then Dr Leavis has always found Cambridge very interesting. It seems to me that we have both had rather fortunate lives so far, in that we have been able to act on our ideals (the same ones) without finding it too disagreeable—with the help of a certain amount of obstinacy.

William Empson
Peking National University

A REFERENCE FOR JIN* FA-SHEN

National Peking University, Peiping, China
5 February 1950

Recommendation for a scholarship:—

Mr. Ching Fa-hsing was studying English literature in the Combined South-Western University from 1944–6, and at the Peking National University after it returned to Peking (ceasing to be this combined refugee body) from 1946–8. He is still working in the university.

Last year he gave me a graduating thesis on Milton, or rather on *Paradise Lost* [which was to inspire aspects of WE's *MG*], which I thought showed a great deal of clear-headedness and independent judgement as

---

[1] See *SCW*, 7. FRL asked D. W. Harding (4 Apr. 1951) to review *SCW* for *Scrutiny*: 'The Empson I can't do myself, since I see that he retains a mean and nasty "smear" at my expense about which I protested, fruitlessly, to Ransom at the Kenyon. Ransom replied that he regarded Empson as a kind of saint. Empson is a great power in America—very much more so than Richards' (Emmanuel College, Camb.; Leavis collection, letter 76).

well as the purely literary powers of appreciation needed. He was chiefly concerned with the intellectual difficulties which confront Adam and Eve, owing to the curiously conflicting character of the hints the advisory angels give them; Milton found it hard to argue that to seek knowledge was a great evil, and he passed his own difficulty about the theme very dramatically to characters of his story. I hope this part of the thesis at any rate will get published, because it seems to me new and illuminating. [See *MG*, 147.]

Mr. Ching Fa-hsing has a secondary interest in philosophy, which was already required for the kind of interest he took in the dramatic theology of *Paradise Lost*, and he has also been studying the epic tradition as a whole to give a background for his views on Milton, which he wants to treat more fully. He is at present writing a novel on war-time China, on which I have only seen the first sections; they are a very direct and sensitive record. He seems to me a determined and high-minded character of considerable ability, and I hope that he will be enabled to continue his work.
Comment on the graduating thesis: —

I find this a very interesting examination of the poem, and so far as I know it opens a new ground. There is clearly room for further development of the theme, but it is sufficiently worked out to make a good thesis. Your point seems a philosophical rather than a poetical one, but I think it is intimately connected with the poetry, and I hope you will develop it from both sides.

TO JOHN HAYWARD

The School of English, Kenyon College, Gambier, Ohio
2 July 1950

My dear John Hayward,

I am here to talk to a Summer School, and plan to set off to Hongkong early next month, from there to try to nip back behind the Iron Curtain. Hetta and the children have been left in Peking. As I remember it is I who owe you a letter, not you me, but it is rather damping from either side to know that the Peking post is still a bit liable to lose things. I do wish you would send me a letter here, which there would be time for before I leave on Aug. 4th. L. C. Knights* is here from England, a very nice fellow but not very communicative. I missed seeing the poet George Frazer [*sic*] in Japan, where I spent a night, but may be able to make contact on the way back. He sent me an entertainingly gloomy letter to describe the gloom of the younger literary scene in London which he is taking two years' leave from. I gather the Japanese work him frightfully hard. I only saw [Vere] Redman there, who said the Japs are coming to feel they are a very attractive maiden with two rich suitors, and are making increasing demands on America as the price of their favours. Flying over Alaska was a thrilling sight, owing to the mysterious rule that one is thrilled by absolute devastation, particularly after not being allowed to go more than ten miles from Peking (on the flat) for some time. My position here really seems to me very dramatic; there can be few other people in the world who are receiving pay simultaneously and without secrecy from the Chinese Communists, the British Socialists, and the capitalist Rockefeller machine. Practically a little friend of all the world. But fortunately my associates here have no interest in the matter at all; two years ago there was Matthiessen here, who was interested in the world picture and whose suicide was rather a disaster I think, but now we are as concentrated on our profession as a conference of dentists practically. Except for Kenneth Burke, a very intelligent and charming fellow I think.[1] Getting a permit from the Peking police to go to America and (I hope) return was done mainly on a recommendation from the university, and the reply that came back from its high quarters, when I pushed up the request in the proper way verbally through a Chinese colleague, was a charming anxiety that the Americans would surely throw me immediately into jail and anyway not let me return. The idea that most Chinese now have of America seems very like the Koestler idea of Russia.[2] Poor Orwell's book 1985 [*sic*] turned up just before I left Peking, who sent it to me I don't know; it seemed very remote but I left Hetta handing it round to anyone interested. It seems very without the fundamental truth-feeling of a good novel (that's just how it would happen though I don't know how I know, you need to feel), and I got an impression that he was just feeling miserable about the approach of death.[3] In Peking we have had

[1] Kenneth Burke (1897–1993) attended Ohio State University and Columbia University, but left without a degree. After periods as a music critic for *The Dial*, 1927–9, and *The Nation*, 1934–46, he taught literature and criticism at Bennington College from 1943 to 1961. His writings, which draw upon disciplines including psychology, anthropology, and sociology (as well as Marxist economics), include *A Grammar of Motives* (1945) and *Language as Symbolic Action: Essays on Life, Literature and Method* (1966). In 1951 he was elected to the National Institute of Arts and Letters, and in 1966 he was made a member of the American Academy of Arts and Sciences. With WE, he was a Fellow of the Kenyon School in summer 1950.

[2] Arthur Koestler (1905–83), Hungarian-born author and journalist; his notable political novel, *Darkness at Noon* (1940), is centred upon the Soviet purges of 1936.

[3] WE wrote to Kathleen Raine on 2 Oct. 1950: 'Somebody sent us poor Orwell's 1986 [*sic*] by book post just before I left for America, without any puzzle from censorship here of course, or rather it arrived then, conveniently because I arrived knowing about it and was able to say I thought the poor chap was writing about his sense of exasperation and approaching personal death and had lost the ring of truth which all his previous writing had. It seemed a very remote heartcry when looked at behind the Bamboo Curtain' (*Houghton carbon*).

no victimization of professors for their opinions so far, not even ones who were officials of the Kuomintang Youth Movement and suchlike; the professors grumble at having to go to so many long meetings but are otherwise better off. A tremendous confession did occur at Tsing Hua, in six or nine hours grilling of the Business Manager, when he confessed to twenty years embezzlements including quite a bit since the liberation; but really not through drugs or torture, the point is that different individuals in the audience had only to piece their information together at the meeting; and even he is still employed by the university though naturally not still business manager. The group confession process is obviously more workable as well as more humane than a purge with a lot of jailing and shooting. However how it works out is of course still in the balance; the fundamental thing, I have always thought, is that China is not Bulgaria in that the Russians know they can't invade and hold it by force. Meanwhile though the Americans in diplomacy seem to be driving them into the Russian arms plenty of trade is going on; a Shell man was telling me on the boat to Hongkong that his firm in Tientsin during the year had had six million US dollars turnover (Communist tax now a workable 1 ½ %) which the Peking Government had paid by cheques on American banks. It really seems reasonable to hang on in the belief that relations will eventually improve if enough people hang on. Besides, Mog and Jake my sons are going to a Chinese school and learning characters, which only makes them 'backward' if we have to leave soon, but is a reliable paypacket for their after lives if we can keep it up a few more years. There is still the beautiful city and the charming good humour and the best food in the world and a cup of tea when you wake up. I do hope it lasts. To go back to academic freedom, my students in the Composition Class (where they read an essay in English and then write about it themselves) were shooting at me last academic year because they wanted to read communist documents, but I said they needed to read a mixture of documents nearly all reactionary or playful and thus develop a capacity to judge for themselves. They took this up to higher quarters, I was upheld, and by the end of the year they appeared quite satisfied. Of course it does make a bit of a nervous strain, and dear old I. A. Richards when he turned up told me I was drinking much too much, even though I always feel I can do the mediating process quite honestly; the two fundamental tropes are 'Marx didn't really say that' and 'if you hope to convince someone who agrees with the author, and that is the purpose eventually in view, you are going the wrong way about it'. How next year will turn out if it does at all I don't know; there may be considerable changes; but I do feel I haven't been wasting my time so far.

I wrote to Richards some while ago and urged him to come to China and on his reply told the Yenching (missionary university) people he was thinking of it, and they got him an entry permit by asking for him (he had a sabbatical year from Harvard to play with); you understand the permits are hard to get and my British Council boss can't come and stays in Hongkong. His interest of course is to make them adopt his English-language-teaching methods, now very different from the Ogden formula, and when I left he was making an impression in the right quarters; the point is, not that they are keen on teaching the enemy language, but that they don't want to sack all the Middle School teachers who are accustomed to give most students six years of it (without the slightest result); they would like to make it three years and get some results (from the ones who haven't chosen Russian) instead; what they want then is a mass education method which can be learned by stupid teachers and imposed in some foolproof form. Richards is so smooth as to be beautiful to watch in action; within two days of hitting Peking he was saying that all his new methods worked equally well for teaching Russian and his material for that was only just not ready yet (of course Hetta and I had told him what to say, but he can absorb a new audience and a new front just on a word). The trouble is that after very successful language-teaching rush jobs in wartime America he cannot renounce machines, magic-lanterns and gramophones at least must be in every classroom, and the Chinese won't pay for that; he could not be made to believe that posters though easily printed in bulk would do as well as magic lanterns, which require foreign lenses. I don't know how his visit worked out nor whether it is over; he and Dorothea were determined to go on and conquer new peaks in Alaska by this time but you can't be as lordly as all that about modern travel every time. He told me that *Time* magazine has a complete file of sexual and alcoholic scandal against me, which they have only not published on his personal intervention, and will prevent or conclude my employment in any American university as soon as they feel safe in publishing it. This is the kind of thing that makes a man feel important and gives him nerve (you understand I had already refused about eight offers from American universities; the post seems to let through nothing else). They would feel safe I presume, though Richards would not agree to this distraction from his very affectionate moral dia-tribe, if they had also political grounds. Meanwhile the British Council is entitled to sack me if I mention politics at all while they employ me, and I have to make a public speech as part of my employment here in two or three weeks time, at which I shall say whatever I think it important to say. The advantage or perhaps the limitation of being an obstinate man is that you don't have moral problems, only risks; what you ought to do is always clear. We are all very placid here, but I cannot feel that my life is dull. However it would be silly to dramatize the thing, and I do not expect any kind of publicity to follow my little talk.

Chatto's still won't publish my book [*SCW*], now most of it more than ten years old, but they may bring it out any time; I hope you will like it. Richards on reading the proofs in China, which he could do as two copies arrived by post all right, praised it but regarded it as solely about dictionary technique and advised me to get employed by the Oxford Dictionary, apparently because scandal would soon exclude me from all further contact with the growing mind. I believe in neither side of this unexpected drama (I was ready to stop the edition by cable if he had minded my attacks on him, but his mind is always on something else); but talking to Kenneth Burke here does make me feel that my bombshell like the atom bomb itself is more narrow in impact than the strategist would like to claim. I have been doing a bit more critical writing, and very much needed to get to America just to see recent texts and decide whether my opinions were refuted or out of date, otherwise one can't finish one's little article clearly. The only irritating thing about life in Peking is the post, which will either improve or get impossible presumably. So do not feel I am dead yet as regards writing; but don't you feel as I do that the world is rather dead, nobody I believe is writing well in any part of the world. The Chinese communist short stories have great merit in limited numbers, but it is a very narrow field (of course we know the chaps employed on translating them into English, and the whole subject of what should be sent abroad is one of frequent tedious discussion in my house). The only thing the Chinese might do well quite soon, I think, very oddly, is European music for human voice; the whole revolt against the classical Peking theatre (too tedious to report in detail) turns on a just belief that the peasant singing has always been more real than the upperclass falsetto, and European music always developed by taking in folkmusic from an outlying area (not as music critics pretend by developing the mathematical theory and inducing the human ear to accept the resulting discords, because the discords were in each [case] a result of fitting into the old formula a new folkmusic, as Europe expanded); and The Song of the Yellow River (which I heard in my university when it was very dangerous for the boys to do it, though I had insisted on the BBC two years before photographing the whole text before a correspondent took it on to America during the war— the BBC has this smashing piece but won't touch it) made me cry and seemed to me an entirely solid basis for a school of European-style music;

but then of course I had loved this peasant singing before it was made dramatic and rhetorical by a European orchestra.

There was a great moment in Peking of a merely gossip kind when Richards and I were both there, the marriage of a young man sent from England to learn Chinese under the Scarborough plan, who has always been in and out of our house, and of course met all our friends, and when he at last got permission for his wife to come out he innocently invited everyone he knew.[4] This is impossible in modern Peking and Hetta tried at the last moment to send out warnings, but it all happened and was like the sea giving up its dead. The British consul came, the secret British communists came, the Chinese police who spy on the foreigners came, the Christians came, the university came, and it was really a good party such as I have always thought one of the keenest pleasures in life. Richards came and at once begged to be allowed to go away; he could not bear it.

[Incomplete]

Houghton: ?draft, bMS Eng 1401 (570)

TO MR MACCOLL

The Poems of William Empson, a reading, was broadcast by the BBC Third Programme (in a production by Peter Duval Smith) on 15 Dec. 1952.

[n.d. 1952–3]

Dear Mr MacColl,

Thanks for your letter. I don't understand the problems at issue, and wish I did. I too hated the poetry-reading voice, and refused even to hear the records played through to test them, let alone hear the whole thing on the air (the verse and the prose were recorded at separate sittings, with the difference of sound mechanically exaggerated). One of my friends, whose judgement I respect, felt the same; but otherwise people of very varying tastes really seemed to like it. The producer was keen to get the verse reading lush, and lushed me up for it on rum and Guinness mixed; not that I blame him, I too thought that was probably the best method. It was certainly better than the trial version sober.

---

[4] David and Jean Hawkes were married on 5 May 1950. David Hawkes (b. 1923) studied Classical Chinese at Oxford University 1945–48, and was a research student at the National Peking University, 1948–51. He was later to become Professor of Chinese at Oxford, 1959–71, and a Research Fellow of All Souls College, 1973–83. Renowned as a translator, his publications include *Ch'u Tz'u: The Songs of the South: An Ancient Chinese Anthology* (1959); *A Little Primer of Tu Fu* (1967), *The Story of the Stone*, i–iii (1973–80); and *Classical, Modern and Humane: Essays in Chinese Literature* (1989). See further *A Birthday Book for Brother Stone: For David Hawkes, at Eighty*, ed. Rachel Mayand and John Minford (2004).

My first conviction is that the reader should throw himself into the verse, and not do it with 'reserved' English 'good taste'; that kind of falsity you will at least agree I avoided. I thought what I did was simply 'ham', like a provincial Shakespeare actor a hundred years ago, not a bad thing. What I chiefly wanted to get rid of, from the first version, was a 'snooty' effect, which the producer called 'proprietary'—'you talk as if you didn't want them to know what it means'. I am not clear what class issue you raise by 'Fortnum and Mason'; it suggests trying to sound genteel, whereas my wife says she and some other people thought I sounded as if I was trying to sound low class. I wasn't conscious of either, but to make one's voice a bit less classy isn't a bad thing in itself; in Yorkshire, where I come from, to throw in a bit more dialect on suitable occasions is a recognised form of politeness for many people, not at all condescending. What is chiefly needed, for this kind of verse, is a style of speaking which allows you to emphasise a number of words close together, and this can't be done in classy colloquial English, where it is a positive mannerism to suggest that you are in an inner circle by being deliciously unstressed.

No doubt these problems wouldn't arise if I had a bit more competence at reading; but as it is I really don't believe they could be solved in the way you suggest.

Houghton: unsigned; unsent? bMS Eng 1401 (601)

§ GEORGE HERBERT'S 'THE SACRIFICE' AND ROSEMOND TUVE*

As the zenith of his examples of the seventh type of ambiguity—where 'the total effect is to show a fundamental ambiguity in the writer's mind'—WE put forward a close analysis of George Herbert's 'The Sacrifice' (*STA*, 226–33), in which 'the various sets of conflicts in the Christian doctrine of the Sacrifice are stated with an assured and easy simplicity, a reliable and unassuming grandeur, extraordinary in any material, but unique as achieved by successive fireworks of contradiction, and a mind jumping like a flea.' His interpretation reaches its climax with this stanza:

> O all ye who pass by, behold and see;
> *Man stole the fruit, but I must climb the tree;*
> *The tree of life to all, but only me:*
> > *Was ever grief like mine?*

'[Christ] climbs the tree to repay what was stolen, as if he was putting the apple back; but the phrase in itself implies rather that he was doing the stealing, that so far from sinless he is Prometheus and the criminal.'

Twenty years on, Rosemond Tuve, in 'On Herbert's "Sacrifice" ' (*Kenyon Review*, 12 (Winter 1950), 51–75), complained that 'a reader familiar with the traditions out of which this poem sprang will find Empson's reading inadequate.' The poem is derived from the liturgical offices of Holy Week, especially the Improperia or Reproaches of Good Friday. Thus, where WE perceived in the poem 'contradictory impulses . . . held in equilibrium by the doctrine of the atonement', Tuve maintained to the contrary: 'the use of sharp antitheses ironically paralleling the tree of death with the tree of life is no novelty of a latter-day Metaphysical poet, and . . . a considerable naiveté is required of us as readers if we are to think that Herbert's particular phrasing of the convention makes us see Jesus as a son of the house, climbing in the orchard.'

WE responded to Tuve's dismissive scholarship with a letter, 'George Herbert and Miss Tuve', in *Kenyon Review* 12 (Autumn 1950; in *A*, 250–5). However, when Tuve, in *A Reading of George Herbert* (1952), continued to disparage his interpretation, he drafted this further rebuttal.

'George Herbert and Miss Tuve', was written as an article for the *Kenyon Review* answering one by Rosemond Tuve, 'On Herbert's "Sacrifice" ', which has turned out to be an extract from her book *A Reading of George Herbert*. In the preface to that book she says 'Readers interested in differing points of view regarding the value of knowledge to criticism should read Empson's courteous rejoinder', giving the reference and making no attempt at all to answer my points. I had not felt myself to be pulling any punches, but it looks as though a rather more discourteous approach may be the only way to make contact with a mind so embedded in complacency. Her fuller version still says 'the phrase about climbing the tree (ascending the Cross) is the veriest commonplace' (p. 31), and 'Herbert uses the time-honoured "climb", for the ascent of the Cross' (p. 91), and still she offers among all her wealth of illustration not a single example of this; unless one could count a footnote reference to a verse of the Song of Solomon about 'I will go up to the palm-tree', which she does not show to have been traditionally misinterpreted as *climbing* it. What has happened, I suspect, is something familiar among examination students: her head has got into a buzz with over-reading, so that it mixes things up. This then is also why she thinks that the style of Herbert is exactly like the style of the medieval liturgies (except for some mysterious personal quality which she can't further describe); she has read so much on these themes that any one bit merely sets her head buzzing with all the others. She feels, as she is so fond of saying, 'it's a convention'. I do not call this 'knowledge' at all, and it is clearly not a help to criticism.

There is an odd twist when she is discussing the very beautiful verse from 'Dulnesse':

> Thou art my lovelinesse, my life, my light,
>> Beautie alone to me:
> Thy bloudy death and undeserv'd, makes thee
>> Pure red and white.

The 1941 editor [F. E. Hutchinson, *The Works of George Herbert*] sensibly quoted J. B. Leishman to the effect that the last line, 'which many would find offensive', seemed to him 'in keeping with the whole tone of the poem, and not at all extravagant' (*The Metaphysical Poets*, 1934). She bridles at the ignorance of this, and says: 'Those who find this offensive must needs be frequently offended if they read much poetry and prose written on this subject; that cannot be extravagant which walks within the conventional bounds' (p. 149). But of course it can; the normal occasion for this kind of extravagance, as everybody knows, is when people are competing to lead a fashion; were crinolines not extravagant? Was *The Man of Feeling* [by Henry Mackenzie (1771)] not extravagant? To demand this boundless charity from the historian is to make him abandon criticism altogether; there is much more mysterious judgement in thinking, like the poet Cowper, that Herbert is very good although he was so Gothick. And besides, if you make yourself really servile about accepting a 'convention', if you insist on taking it as a matter of course for us few who are in the know, you are at bottom refusing to let it give you the shock which it was intended to produce, even in its prime. This comes out, I think, in her remarks about the 'image' of Christ as a baby in the tree whence Adam took the apple (p. 89): 'This baby is the saving King, and no more connotes smallness or the helpless midnight cry than the healing oil connotes the squeak of rusty hinges or the "climbing" of the tree a fruit-stealing expedition.' This is in line with her gruff order that we mustn't imagine Hamlet taking arms against a sea; but it is far more absurd. What on earth was the point of the Christ-child if you weren't allowed to think about a child at all? What can she mean by calling it an 'image'? If people had been so numb in emotion as she demands they could never have invented her convention. For that matter, the 'image' of the healing oil obviously did 'connote' the idea of soothing a physical friction, and the idea of climbing the Tree, if found before Herbert, would have connoted a variety of occasions on which trees were in practice climbed. She suggests to me a powerful secretary, determined not to let the reporters write up what is actually said by her lunatic millionaire: 'Think of it But as a thing of custom,' as Lady Macbeth said on a similar occasion.

However, I would agree with her as against the people who attack the Intentional Fallacy, if I understand the controversy she is engaged in there; of course the reader ought to try to make out what the author intended, and had better be willing to go a long way; but he ought to be ready to decide that good intentions haven't been enough to make the result good. It seems to me merely quaint to have embattled armies fighting on either side of this simple truth.

I am quite ready to find wrong the suggestions I made in *Ambiguity*, but on looking this case over the only one I feel sure must be given up is the pun on 'man's weal' at the end of the poem; the scar of a burn seems always to have been a very minor meaning of the word, which couldn't push its way in (that kind of criterion was what I was aiming at in my later book *The Structure of Complex Words*, 1951).[1] I am not much attached to the ideas she rejects from the following passages, but I do not see how she can reject them so confidently:

> Then on my head a crown of thorns I wear:
> For these are all the grapes *Sion* doth bear,
> Though I my vine planted and watered there:
>> Was ever grief like mine?

> So sits the earths great curse in *Adams* fall
> Upon my head; so I remove it all
> From th' earth unto my brows, and bear the thrall:
>> Was ever grief like mine?

> . . .

> Lo, here I hang, charg'd with a world of sinne,
> The greater world o' th' two; for that came in
> By words, but this by sorrow I must win:
>> Was ever grief like mine?

---

[1] The closing stanza of 'The Sacrifice' reads: 'But now I die, now all is finishèd. | My woe, man's weal; and now I bow my head: | Only let others say, when I am dead, | Never was grief like mine' (249–52). WE argued in *STA* (1930): 'The force of *but* is that their wickedness will go on; "My side will be pierced but I shall not feel it." To gauge his attitude towards this fact, one must consider . . . that *weal*, which claims here to mean prosperity, carries some trace of its other meaning at that time, not a scar but a pustule (as in "Commonweal" it is the social order, good and bad, which is identified with the tribe's relation to its totem)' (289). That gloss was cut from subsequent editions of *STA*, as WE explained on a draft of Philip Hobsbaum's Ph.D. thesis, *Some reasons for the great variety of response to literature among modern literary critics* (1968; published as *A Theory of Communication*, 1970): 'I took the supposed pun on *weal*, and various other overstrained bits, out from the second edition, but I think Tuve ignored that [in *A Reading of George Herbert*] just as you do.' WE wrote too: 'Well, I am much heartened by what you say [in *A Theory of Communication*, 131–4 and 250], as I had come to think both I and Tuve were often in the wrong there. Your chapter needs shortening for greater effect, I think, but I can't disagree with it' (*Special Collections, University of Victoria, Canada*).

I said that the crown of vine-leaves, the opposite of what he gets, seems to be the crown of Dionysiac revellers, the joys of the world in their most dramatic form; and I still think that is a natural reflection, for a reader in Herbert's time as well as in ours. Rosemond Tuve says it 'would require a temporary lapse, not a movement, of thought, and make nonsense of the double-entendre *thrall*' (p. 63). I do not understand what double-entendre she means (she is too fond, I think, of leaving her reader in this position), but it could not get hurt by the crown of vine-leaves, because that only comes in as the *opposite* of a crown of thorns. She then lists, around page 59, a good deal of the Bible imagery about vines (and I feel she needn't talk as if only a ripe medieval scholar has ever heard of it); but all this, though certainly concerned in the passage, does not give any *crown* of vine-leaves, such as the opposition implies, and I don't gather that the Jews had such a thing. She then goes on to tell us, what is of real interest, that Herbert seems to have *invented* this connection between the thorns of the curse on Adam and the thorns on Christ's head, or at least it is contemporary with him, not medieval, and she expresses wonder at how 'tiny' it is: 'This last, minute, logical link between thorns and thorns is the measure of Herbert's "originality" in this image' (pp. 62–3). I don't think it is tiny at all, and at any rate it was not invented by persons unacquainted with the classics—or with the Copernican view of the world, which we have next to consider. I said that the earth is being viewed as from a reasonable distance, like a globe map, so that it seems about the size of a man's head; surely that is the 'image' required, if I may borrow this very misleading term, when you think of the thorns being picked off one such object and put onto another; and it is driven home when Christ says that the load on his head is 'the greater world o' th' two'. The Copernican world was exciting heavy controversy in Herbert's time, and the Anglicans were almost the only sect not afraid of it; I do not know why Rosemond Tuve is so determined not to let it cross their minds. It doesn't make much difference here, except for letting the survey of the poem become even more far-reaching.

However, these details, though I didn't want to hide from discussing them, aren't the main point. What Rosemond Tuve is doing, I think, and what a number of other recent critics have done (Professor C. S. Lewis on Milton, for example), is to arrive with a great fanfare of trumpets at the surface meaning of the poem, the part that was meant to be quite obvious at the time, and then promulgate a new law that anybody who thinks there is a secondary meaning must be grossly ignorant of this surface meaning. I am as much embarrassed by her occasional praise of me, for my brilliant discovery of something obvious, as by her recurring scorn for my supposed ignorance of something obvious; surely, most of the points we make nowadays only didn't get printed before because no one thought they need be. These critics no doubt have a real fear, from their teaching experience, that the obvious may become forgotten in a new barbarism; but I find something totalitarian in their methods of fighting it, only delusively strong for defence, and hopeless for sustaining a tradition. What I meant about Herbert's 'The Sacrifice' was that he set out to write a traditional devotional poem, just as Rosemond Tuve says, and then found that the strain of his power to see all round this theme was almost too great, it was almost breaking the frame; I meant this in the first writing, and thought I had removed any possible doubt by a note to the second edition of my book, where I say the question in Herbert's mind, if he had read my criticism, would have been simply whether he ought to have the criticism stopped from being printed. It is true that he uses medieval techniques, as she says, but when the drama of heightening the paradoxes is made so thrilling the audience is forced to wonder whether they will topple over. This thrill is unusual, and not a defining mark of what is called Metaphysical Poetry; it is in several poems by Donne and perhaps only this one by Herbert, which I should agree with Mr Hutchinson in calling a rather early work. Looking for anything else like it in Herbert, I would be inclined to quote from 'Longing':

> Behold, thy dust doth stirre,
> It moves, it creeps, it aims at thee:
> Wilt thou deferre
> To succour me,
> Thy pile of dust, wherein each crumme
> Sayes, Come? (37–42)

It is wonderfully powerful, but doesn't part of the power come from an obscure recognition, in part of his mind, that what he is describing is altogether monstrous? I am not sure. But in 'The Sacrifice' we are on more public ground, and I gather that Rosemond Tuve does not differ from me as much as she supposes. 'The secret of the power of this poem,' she suggests, lies in 'the density of the serried layers of suggested concepts and emotions, in the frequently almost shocking juxtapositions of these emotions, and in the resulting variety and constant movement of the tone, from pitying to condemnatory, from tender to intellectually incisive, from brash to gravely meditative', and so forth (p. 49). But would she describe Christ in the Good Friday Responses as brash? The double meanings that struck me as really peculiar, worth putting into my seventh type of ambiguity (where 'the total effect is to show a fundamental division in the author's mind'), are the ones where

Christ can appear to be rejoicing in the extremity of the torments that his enemies are incurring; and they seem to me to crop up too often and too ingeniously to be regarded as mere failures in writing, not intended by any part of the author's mind. That is what I meant by what Rosemond Tuve finds a merely 'fake' picture (p. 71) of the beautiful dry purity of George Herbert as like a cricket in the sunshine, whose habits are more savage than they seem; I think that the intelligence he was applying to the construction of these conceits was driving him near a criticism of the whole topic. Perhaps I should add that I am not myself a Christian, because the belief in a Supreme God who takes pleasure in giving torture seems to me ineradicable from the religion, and I find difficulty in imagining the minds of good men who accept it. But I do not think that this distracts my judgement when I feel that Herbert was far more conscious of the monstrosity than a composer of a medieval liturgy, and that that is why their styles make such a puzzlingly different impression while apparently using the same themes and techniques. I hope it is now clear that I claim to have a great deal of knowledge about Herbert, and do not claim as Rosemond Tuve asserts, that I can taste a poem better with no knowledge. I claim to know not only the traditional background of Herbert's poem (roughly but well enough) but also what was going on in Herbert's mind while he wrote it, without his knowledge and against his intention; and if she says that I cannot know such things, I answer that that is what critics do, and that she too ought to have 'la clef de cette parade sauvage'.

Having thus spelled out his vexation, WE determined that Rosemond Tuve had best be forewarned that he was proposing to publish yet another snub to her scholarly authority; he offered her a right of reply.

TO ROSEMOND TUVE

Studio House, Hampstead Hill Gardens, London N. W. 3
7 January 1953

Dear Rosamond [*sic*] Tuve,

I have just written the enclosed essay for a book, to include a variety of controversial articles including the one about your Herbert essay from the Kenyon; but the book can't come out for at least a year, and it seems absurd to keep the essay for so long without showing it to you. By all means ignore it if you prefer, or answer it on your own terms; but if you would care to reply before I send the material to the publisher, which ought to be in two months or so, I would try to give fair weight to your reply, not printing it as such in my book but saying we had discussed the matter, and that this had led to my altering my remarks—if it had done, and I should rather expect it to.

I feel this would make us both look rather more sensible; but I shall have no complaint if you are busy with other things and don't care to reconsider the subject.

Yours sincerely
William Empson

Tuve responded from Connecticut College, New London, on 14 Feb. 1953. Cheerily conciliatory, she stood by the scholarly interpretations in her book. 'About the practical matter you mentioned . . . "saying this had led to my altering my remarks"—I don't imagine you'll want to alter them much if any. It's too hard to alter things.' She concluded: 'I find that I don't care a hang . . . whether you say dreadful things about me that I don't think true, and so far as I can tell this is because you go at the poetry so hard.' It was just such a pity that he invented 'arguments From Character of Author . . . You write excessive angry, but I don't think you are.'

TO ROSEMOND TUVE

Studio House, Hampstead Hill Gardens, London N. W. 3.
25 February 1953

Dear Rosemond Tuve,

I was very pleased by the tone of voice of your letter, but am not sure that it gets us much further on detail. About climbing the tree of life; and by the way I refuse to 'see concordance'; it is the business of scholars like yourself to give the public like myself tolerably available evidence before you expect us to believe your assertions; what I was doubting, as I should have explained, is not the word *ascendere* but the grammar of *in arborem*, which in the Song of Solomon seems to be correctly translated '*to* the tree'. However I agree now that the distinction of grammar wouldn't be important, and the English you quote before Herbert is anyway clear. You still do not give any quotation for climbing the Tree of Life as apart from the Cross, though you feel it is universal. I still want to know, not because I am trying to save my face in a quarrel with you but because it is interesting, whether anybody before George Herbert said that Christ was climbing the Tree of Life in being put on the Cross; not by implication but directly, as Herbert does. Surely it is reasonable to put this question to a scholar, and rather irritating if the scholar won't say more than that everything is somehow felt everywhere.

I can't see your objection to the crown of vineleaves, but it may be explained by your saying 'Take the Pledge', a very un-historical-minded piece of wincing here; the idea that Drink (and Smoking) are bad was not even Puritan when Herbert wrote. I assumed that the pleasures of the world were assumed to be inherently good, otherwise there would be no merit in renouncing them for a particular duty. You feel that the line of 'images' is 'generally somehow cleaner that that', but I suspect that the Uncleanness of Drink and Smoke is still hanging about your mind; the cleanness of the logic of the argument is what I would expect, and here the logic is firmly opposing the Crown of Thorns to some other crown, which might have been expected under better circumstances. Your feeling that this would involve a connection between the vines and the curse is merely off the logic; the vine was intended and would have been there if there were no curse. One could no doubt feel that to drag in the pagans was a bit Renaissance rather than Medieval of Herbert, but I can never understand why critics who claim to be historical think they show expertise by getting their date wrong and claiming that Renaissance writers were really Medieval ones.

You say you are not meaning to write another book. The academic system is bad in requiring a book 'on the table' too early and then burying people under 'administration' when they are ripe for their book. I was rather shocked at your saying that I needn't rewrite my bit posted to you because it is always a nuisance to rewrite. I rewrite everything I print about twelve times, mainly in the interests of intelligibility, and I think you had much better do that too. Checking references always seems to me a trivial duty compared to checking style. I think that your style has greatly improved in your last book but is still very bad, simply from failure of communication. I also think that if you tried to write more clearly you would find your own ideas are a great deal more muddled than you suppose. So I hope very much that you will write another book, but as a labour of love, intended to be agreeable in itself—the distinction between the writer and the reader becomes unreal (because the same thing pleases both) if you take your own style as seriously as you take the style of the authors you are describing. One can imagine this doctrine working out wrong, but it does seem what you need to be told.

The most serious part of your letter seems to me where you suggest that my opinions about religion make me misread Herbert; saying this doubt-fully; then at the end of the paragraph saying firmly that I must not call it a *virtue* for Herbert to have 'unconsciously taken a position like my own' or rather (it is no use looking for soft words) unconsciously exposed the deep evil which he imagined himself to praise. But that is precisely what I called a virtue in the poem, twenty years ago, with enough fuss and build-up surely if any is enough to make you believe I meant what I was saying. It is rather a terrible thing to have to say, but I still believe it and I thought at the time that I had said it as plainly as I could. I do not believe in your capacity to read medieval authors because I am so surprised to find you totally incapable of reading *me*; you are still, even in your willing friendly frame of mind, just hovering and fluttering timidly round the idea that I might possibly be accused of meaning a thing which I say that I mean again and again for a long time as plainly as I can. I am not at all flattered by an idea that I am putting in 'personal' opinions; this is mere wordplay if it only means my own opinions are the only ones I can have, and I know I am not biased by any private grudge against Christianity. What seems to me odd is that you could go through this enormously long process of writing a piece against me without even toying in your mind for a moment with the idea that I might conceivably have meant what I said.

Well, well, maybe it isn't true about Herbert anyhow; I think it is, but I don't care. It really is true about *Paradise Lost*; that poem is evil unless you read it as Blake did, and I must say so till I die, and it raises exactly the same problems of interpretation.

William Empson

[P. S.] I have taken no copy of this letter and have no idea of printing it as part of our controversy.[2]

> On a separate sheet—possibly a draft of the second page of the letter above, and thus not posted in this form—WE typed still more robustly:

Of course I shall rewrite my remarks where you make convincing objections to them; I am rather shocked by your saying that it is tiresome to re-write anything. Practically everything I have printed has been re-written about twelve times. I strongly suspect that you could write much better if you would take the necessary trouble. When you say you aren't

---

[2] In a notebook (*c.* 1960), WE reflected: '[Graham] Hough said the effect of disapproving Christianity would be to make me unable to appreciate Eng. Lit.—a drive at my professional competence. I don't think this usually true, but it does seem true about Herbert's *Sacrifice*. I now feel that he was an ass if he was ignorant of the ambiguities of the poem, and at best perverse if he wasn't. He ought not to have put up with such a disgusting doctrine—to this extent I agree with my opponents of a third of a century ago. Can one get further evidence from the manuscripts that he screwed up the ambiguity in later drafts? But what use would it be anyway?'

inclined to write any more books you are probably right about the demands of the academic system, where a book has to be 'on the table' too early and the later years when a good book could be written must be given to 'administration'. Please feel that making a book of criticism can be a thing you would like to do in your periods of leisure, for personal satisfaction, and yet that the enormous labour of re-writing twelve times is only aimed at making yourself intelligible or directly convincing to the ordinary tolerably informed reader. Unless you feel that you will not write decently at all. By good writing I mean directing yourself to the mind of the public you can reasonably expect, once you aim at getting outside your own clique. I think that your last book (Reading of Herbert) was much less bad than your previous books, as a matter of style, but that all of them are farcically bad, from a person who is actually claiming to interpret 'style'. You cannot get from one clause to another of one sentence without spreading a complete fog all round any reader about what you are trying to say. This is a deeply respected style in America, highly paid for in subsidized magazines, and to me as an Englishman it always seems only like what Dickens described in *Martin Chuzzlewit*, the transcendental ladies who said 'sweetly sleeps the calm ideal' and all the rest of it, while quite sure that the person addressed was being cheated into his death.[3] May I also recall to you the romantic lady in Huck Finn, who was enormously eloquent about death without ever realising the central facts of the case, that her whole rich family who might have supported her were actually getting killed under the eyes of Huck. Do not start jeering back at me about these large historical remarks because they are only part of a large historical view which is never out of my mind; and I only bring them up to say that you must not claim any American excuse for writing appallingly badly. Your nationality does not impose on you a duty to write in this disgraceful manner, and if all people like you insist upon doing it to such a disgraceful degree your own countryman will show their natural good sense by just tossing you away. . . . I thought I could end my paragraph here, and then I realised you might think I was telling you to go into the advertising business. But it isn't quite as mad as that, not yet anyhow; you

---

[3] Despite his admiration for Thoreau and Emerson, Dickens lampoons the rhetorical excesses of the Transcendentalists by way of the 'literary ladies': ' "Mind and matter," said the lady in the wig, "glide swift into the vortex of immensity. Howls the sublime, and softly sleeps the calm ideal, in the whispering chambers of Imagination. To hear it, sweet it is. But then, out-laughs the stern philosopher, and saith to the Grotesque, "What ho! arrest for me that Agency. Go bring it here!' And so the vision fadeth." ' (*Martin Chuzzlewit* [1844], ed. Margaret Cardwell (1984), ch. 34, 467). See also WE in 'A is B': 'Inversion for emphasis can of course be done with any sentence, as by the transcendental ladies in *Martin Chuzzlewit*, who said something like "Howls the profound, and sweeps the deep" ' (*SCW*, 363).

wouldn't be sacked from your job if you wrote decent prose. America allows you to write a book. The books you have printed so far seem to me hopeless stuff; the only hope for you is to promise yourself that you will never publish vast heaps of dirty cheating Heaven-raping totally meaningless . . . personal claims . . . in future.

As in all such cases, I cannot tell whether you will think me insolent or a grateful source of release. But anyhow what I am saying is just ordinary world opinion.

[P. S.] I underline on the typewriter some points when I read this over merely because I know the emphasis isn't obvious to you.

In a final attempt to tease him out of his testiness (as she saw it), Tuve wrote again on 27 Mar. 1953. She still believed in the findings of her book, which offered 'proper and sufficient data for any claim,' she said. On the other hand, she fairly retaliated, 'You're simply Terrible for sitting in your own world and thinking out what flaws in the other man can explain his not thinking and writing as you like . . . Stay nice in private, and I don't care so much what you print.' At a later date, WE wrote of Tuve: 'I had a long exchange of private letters with Tuve, a charming woman to meet but very unsatisfactory with a pen in her hand, and I have lost all of both sides of that.' And Tuve declared of WE: 'We're buddies now.'[4]

§ END

————

NEW STATESMAN, 17 January 1953

Sir,—Your lady correspondents do not realise that the custom of writing (say) 'Madeleine Wallace' is a result of the Emancipation of Women. I do not know whether she is married, single, resuming her maiden name after separation, or simply offering a pen-name; and it is not my business to inquire. What would be presumptuous (or too intimate) would be a demand to know before even addressing her whether she is 'Mrs.' or 'Miss.'

[4] Thomas P. Roche, Jr., letter to JH, 10 Jan. 1995. See also Hobsbaum, *A Theory of Communication* (1970); and Richard Strier, *Resistant Structures: Particularity, Radicalism, and Renaissance Texts* (1995), Essay 1: 'Tradition'.

TO *KENYON REVIEW* (Unpublished)

This next, unpublished letter was drafted in response to a review of *SCW* by Cleanth Brooks*: 'Hits and Misses', *Kenyon Review* (Fall 1952), 669–78. On 13 Jan. 1953 WE wrote to its editor, John Crowe Ransom: 'I felt inclined to answer Mr Cleanth Brooks' review of my *Complex Words*, which though friendly sticks to a difference of principle, and it seems clear that my next book will have to try and answer a lot of these points of principle. However if you are printing my long article next Spring you won't want a letter from me fussing about a review as well; I think that would be out of proportion; there will be plenty of occasions no doubt, for the difference of principle.' (*Kenyon Archives*)

I feel I ought to answer the charge, in Mr Cleanth Brooks' friendly review of my book *Complex Words*, that it is extremely mixed-up; if it were, I think, it would be very tiresome and would deserve less charity. Surely his lack of interest in the subject, which he admits, is enough to explain why the bits that interest him seem ill-connected. The subject is how we get affected by current suggestions of words in common use, what logical structure can be found in the process, and so on; I try to lay down principles; then I test them on a series of words which at different periods carried varying suggestions about the best way to arrive at truth (the choice of words was already made when I wrote my *Pastoral*); then I try to defend my position in general against other theorists, and it turns out that the suggestions in the words examined in the literary chapters are still relevant—I claim that they are actively at work forming fallacies in the minds of the theorists. Actually I followed my nose about what seemed interesting, with long interruptions, and did not realise how connected the result was till I fitted it together; but then I thought it all did fit together, surprisingly and reassuringly.

However, the reaction of Mr Cleanth Brooks is [not merely] due to lack of interest in linguistic theory; he positively wants to keep it out of literary criticism, and at least one of his reasons is very public-spirited—ordinary people ought to be got to judge decently for themselves, and they can't if they are always badgered by a malignant pantheon of scientism and historicism and [im]pressionism and heaven knows what. Let them be told it is enough to stick to the words on the page; anything else is being 'an incorrigible amateur'. The most obvious breakdown of this position, I think, though it is healthy within limits, is when you try to decide about Hamlet or Falstaff, and find that one of the major subjects being discussed is just what words the author did want to have on the page. It is all right drawing the curtains and making the evening cosy, but you want to feel you can get out again if need arise.

Some of Mr Cleanth Brooks' remarks in his review suggest to me the distinguished guest who is more offended than he cares to admit when the boys let off squibs under his chair. He feels it very 'amateur' of me to put in anything about the history of syphilis when considering *Measure for Measure*, a play which talks about the disease a good deal; and when I say its introduction is 'usually dated about the beginning of the sixteenth century' he rebukes my amateurism by a footnote—'The first European outbreak occurred in Italy in 1493'. But I knew about that line of evidence; I also knew that it has been questioned; and I wasn't trying to let off a squib under a professor but to get the subject into reasonable perspective. The idea that every question has been settled, if only you go to the right Faculty of your University, and that is why you must never mention it in the wrong one, seems to me merely harmful.

He asks why I chose to talk about *all* in Milton, and how I know that Milton was an all-or-none man. Actually I chose because the Kenyon Summer School put me down for Milton by mistake, but it struck me this was good luck, because *all* is an interesting test case; it cannot be supposed to attract complex meanings, and yet it is clearly important for Milton's style, perhaps because he is clearly an all-or-none man. I would be a more 'responsible' literary critic, says Mr Cleanth Brooks, if I did not start hares like this. But I was being responsible about my linguistic theory, taking the case hardest for it to handle that I could think of; as to Milton, I am free to admit I know what every competent reader of him knows. What is really being felt by Mr Cleanth Brooks is that a literary critic must behave like a psychologist or what not; he must pretend he doesn't know what is ordinary knowledge till he has proved it by his direct analysis of the text before him. I think this claim to rigour often becomes a mere artificial elegance in the scientists, and then confuses them; it is obviously not needed for some kinds of literary criticism.

Perhaps if I examined the other points I would only be repeating the same arguments.

Houghton: unpublished draft, bMS Eng 1401 (588)

§ BATESON, WE, AND ENGLISH-SPEAKING CRITICISM

ESSAYS IN CRITICISM, 1: 3 (January 1953), 114–20:
'Answers to Comments'

The final paragraph of this letter responds to an article by F. W. Bateson[1] which borrowed Matthew Arnold's title 'The Function of Criticism at the Present Time' (*Essays in Criticism*, 3: 1 (Jan. 1953), 1–27).[2] Adopting the accusation that Edmund Wilson (*The Triple Thinkers*, 2nd edn., 1952, 243) had levelled against TSE's criticism—that it was 'fundamentally non-historical' —Bateson sought to exemplify his discontent with 'the English-speaking critic' of today. He taxed WE for the 'deficiencies' of *STA*:

> A characteristic specimen of Empsonian irresponsibility is to be found on the second page of *Seven Types*. It is the by now almost notorious list of reasons, ten in all, why 'the comparison holds' in
>
> > Bare ruined choirs, where late the sweet birds sang.

Perhaps because of its early occurrence in the book no specific comment of Empson's has been more often dismissed as over-ingenious. But I am not sure that the real point has not been missed. The grosser irresponsibility does not lie in thinking the choirs must have been monastery choirs (though the reference is more likely to be to the parish churches of the deserted villages of the period), or that the choirs were made of wood . . ., or that 'the cold and Narcissistic charm suggested by choir-boys suits well with Shakespeare's feeling for the object of the Sonnets' . . . These are details that could be corrected without Empson's essential point about ambiguity being affected, though it may be significant in a general way that he has not in fact made any of these corrections in the revised edition of *Seven Types*. The real critical error is more fundamental. It is simply that the line on which Empson expatiates is not a separate sentence or even a separate subordinate

---

[1] F. W. Bateson (1901–78) founded the periodical *Essays in Criticism* in 1951. Before the war he worked for Cambridge University Press, and edited the *Cambridge Bibliography of English Literature*. Afterwards, he taught at Oxford, where in 1950 he founded the Critical Society. In 1963 he was elected to a Fellowship at Corpus Christi College, where he was Tutor in English Literature, 1946–69. His works include *English Poetry: A Critical Introduction* (1950), *Wordsworth: A Reinterpretation* (1954), *The Scholar-Critic* (1972), and *Essays in Critical Dissent* (1972); and from 1965 he was general editor of the Longman Annotated Poets series.

[2] See also a specific rejoinder by FRL, 'The Responsible Critic: or the Function of Criticism at Any Time', *Scrutiny*, 19 (1953), 162–83.

clause. It is a verbal fragment that is, strictly speaking, *unintelligible* when lifted like this out of its syntactic context.

After quoting this full sentence from Shakespeare's sonnet—

> That time of year thou may'st in me behold
> When yellow leaves, or none, or few, do hang
> Upon those boughs which shake against the cold,
> Bare ruin'd choirs, where late the sweet birds sang.

Bateson went on:

> It will be seen that the choirs provide a comparison within a comparison. In the outer comparison Shakespeare, feeling himself so much older than his friend, compares himself with those days at the end of autumn when the last leaves are falling from the trees. In the inner comparison, on the other hand, the trees of the outer comparison are compared with church-choirs that have been abandoned and are now falling into ruin. Grammatically, therefore, the function of the inner comparison is to *qualify* the outer comparison . . . And within the line the important ambiguity will now be seen to hinge on the word 'where'. The logic of the passage demands an equation of 'where' with the boughs, whereas the word-order makes it impossible not to connect the place where the birds sang with the choirs. The total effect, as one reads, is of birds *in* the ruined church as well as *on* the leaf-covered trees round about it—and, as a result, the image becomes a symbol not so much of the ageing poet as of a universal process of mutability.

In a personal letter (24 Jan. 1953), Bateson reassured WE: 'I'm afraid the Empson-baiting continues in the Jan. issue. This is a longish article by me . . . The embarrasing point about it all is that I know in my bones that you're much the best living lit. crit (now that T. S. E. has gone out of business). Only if you're *wrong* I must say so, mustn't I?' (*Houghton*)

I have been reading the back numbers of *Essays in Criticism* for 1952, after coming home from China, and feel I would like to speak up in the discussion which it has been conducting so ably about methods of literary criticism. Not that there is any battle for me to fight, but I feel I get referred to with a kind of pitying fondness, as the wild old man who still doesn't know the rules which have recently been invented for this game. I think the rules only tend to make the game tedious, without making the beliefs arrived at any more secure of absolute or scientific truth. It is a delusion for the critic to think he can cover a subject completely; he is always talking to an audience who know quite a lot but may not know the small extra thing he is saying, and a later audience may always disagree. 'Flower in the crannied wall', as Tennyson truly remarked; if I could really account for that 'I should know what God and man is'.[3] The great Puritan preachers who did what was called 'dividing the Word of God', that is, extracting the whole of their theology by logical analysis of any text they might happen to expound ('Seventeenthly' and so on) are the ancestors of our modern criticism of poetry; but this exercise is not always a convenient way to teach a subject.

I twice come into these numbers of the magazine as a standard butt for having compared Marvell's poem *The Garden* to Buddhist philosophy (at the beginning of a long essay ['Marvell's Garden', in *SVP*]); whereas a probably useful article by Mr Kermode* shows that the notions Marvell was playing with were then extremely familiar to the educated public. So I would have presumed, and surely I was not thought to be saying that he must have learned them from a Buddhist.[4] We have only two or three independent civilizations to compare, developing in parallel through thousands of years, and it has a steadying effect to compare them. Marvell was playing with deeply rooted ideas, so native to human life that any full civilization would arrive at them; that is what he was claiming himself, so that he would only be mildly interested to hear that the East agreed with him; but I think I was right to point it out. To prove that his ideas weren't only a fashion, because they occurred elsewhere, seems to me more interesting than to prove that he was only copying out a current fashion from the French. He did it so well that he made it into something permanent, and it seems to me that the more interesting points are not the ones that are copied. We had better realize, I quite agree, that the current of fashion allowed him to do it fairly easily ('anything really worth doing', said Samuel Butler with a haunting truth, 'can be done fairly easily'),[5] but this need not prevent us from saying how good it was. These historians who argue that everything good has been copied from something inferior never seem

---

[3] Alfred Tennyson, 'Flower in the Crannied Wall' (1869): 'Flower in the crannied wall, | I pluck you out of the crannies, | I hold you here, root and all, in my hand, | Little Flower—but if I could understand | What you are, root and all, and all in all, | I should know what God and man is.'

[4] Frank Kermode insists in 'The Argument of Marvell's "Garden" ' (*E in C*, 2: 3 (July 1952), 226–7) 'that "The Garden" must not be read as autobiography . . . The pseudo-biographical critic is wasteful and deceptive; he diverts attention from the genre just as certainly as . . . Mr Empson [does] when he invites us to reflect upon the Buddhist enlightenment (*Some Versions of Pastoral*, 119–20).' On the contrary, ' "The Garden" . . . is poetry written in the language of, or using the "norms" of, a genre in formal refutation of the genre' (230).

[5] ' "Above all," she [Alethea Pontifex] continued, "do not let him work up to his full strength, except once or twice in his lifetime; nothing is well done nor worth doing unless, take it all round, it has come pretty easily" ' (Samuel Butler, *The Way Of All Flesh* (1903), ed. Michael Mason (1993), 158).

to me to say what they want to prove. Mr Kermode also, I think, expresses an over-excitable loathing for 'biography' and the obvious assumption that Marvell was writing in Fairfax's garden—as a young tutor to a child, rather uneasily secure against the Civil War, feeling he ought to pull his weight but not really liking either side or believing their fight was necessary. To imagine this personal situation helps you to make human sense of the paradoxes of the poem, which don't pretend to be dogmas; and it still would even if they were copied directly from the French, which Mr Kermode does not prove. *Appleton House*, I think, is a disgusting poem when read straight through for its surface meaning; it is gross and probably timid flattery, which the brilliance and depth of the detail only makes more painful; the fact that he could write a completely balanced poem *The Garden* at the same time (supported by a 'convention') seems to me of great interest, and I cannot imagine why Mr Kermode should order us so gruffly not to think about it, nor why I am not allowed to call him stupid if he seriously thinks that Marvell wrote the poem in later life between his business intrigues and his political satires. The truth of the poem Marvell may well have felt then more deeply.

I want to keep to one point about Intentionalism and Blake's poem *Jerusalem*, where the discussion seemed to me balanced and the example well chosen; indeed, no one seems to have realized that it was the only plausible example to choose.[6] The *Song of Solomon* and the Chinese *Book of Odes* [*Shih Ching*] were reinterpreted to a startling degree after they had become ancient sacred texts, and such cases get quoted at us as a kind of bogey; but the same thing can't be done by modern English critics, whose conditions are quite different; there isn't any 'problem' whether they 'ought' to do it, and when an Intentionalist critic says his rivals try to do it, instead of thinking what the author intended, he is doing propaganda. But there is a plausible case for thinking that this ancient fraud has happened again once recently in the case of *Jerusalem*, a poem frequently enjoyed in mass community singing with a strong religious aura by people who know nothing about the discussion in print over what Blake really meant. My first convictions here are that the ordinary users of a language have a considerable even if obscure skill in it, and that the importance of print is automatically overrated by anyone who gets his opinions printed. If I sneaked the mike after one of those community singings of *Jerusalem*, and told them what your contributors say Blake really meant, I don't believe it would startle them. There might be considerable annoyance at the

---

[6] *E in C*, 2: 1 (Jan. 1952), 105–14, with contributions by John Wain, F. W. Bateson, and W. W. Robson.

rudeness of my insisting that what Blake meant by Jerusalem was absolute sexual freedom, because that would be raising problems that the audience didn't want to have raised; but they would have realized that this expansive poetic mood involved that kind of thing, and just let it go quietly. Such is the second point listed by Mr Wain, his first, that the patriotism was based on something about British Druids, would rightly be considered by the audience a boring bit of gossip only; and his third, that the *dark Satanic mills* meant the altars of the churches, they would rightly think too silly to be seriously annoying, though they would see a kind of 'talking' point in it. I might well get into trouble, but there isn't a real gulf here between the mob and the scholars. The *dark Satanic mills* certainly do not mean *only* the altars of the churches.[7]

I don't deny however that the question what they do mean is of real interest. The community singers feel that they mean the appalling factory conditions of perhaps a century ago, a kind of folk memory, which might come back if they were not fought against, a very weighty thing. The scholars say that Blake wrote before these conditions had developed, so what he was objecting to was Reason or what not. The contributors to the discussion (in No. 1) seem to me charmed by the theoretical interest of what a critic should do in a 'pure' case, therefore not concerned to worry whether the example really gives it. Now a theorist can reasonably treat his example as a mere illustration unless he is faced with an existence problem: Are there *any* examples of this, within the field of discourse? Here I think there are none, that is, none of the massive quality presumed unless you go far back into history and into different conditions. The crowd raises no problem about Blake because it is broadly right. Then in No. 4 ['Immediacy in Poetry: A Romantic Plea'] a certain amount of guff, if I may say so, was talked by contributors [John Bayley, F. W. Bateson, and David Cecil] about the inexplicable, the almost-*too*-far-away, the magically

---

[7] John Wain reported the findings of F. W Bateson in *English Poetry: A Critical Introduction* (7) thus: 'Under the heading "The Primacy of Meaning", the author is belabouring the modern lack of concern with what a poem is actually *saying*. As an example we are told that Blake's "And did those feet in ancient time" (note the "intentionalism" implicit in steering clear of the name *Jerusalem*, a title given to the poem not by its author but by subsequent editors) has a meaning very remote from anything imagined by the "millions" who "chant these lines every year". Someone should explain to them (i) that the phrase "ancient time" refers to the legend that Pythagoras derived his system of philosophy from the British druids—the point being that British artists need feel no undue reverence for Greek and Latin models, (ii) that "Jerusalem" means, not an ideally happy England, but "something much more abstract", and in particular, sexual liberty, (iii) that by "dark Satanic Mills" Blake refers to the altars of the Churches . . .

'I am far from wishing to dispute that this is the real meaning of Blake's verses . . . But are we to do so? The lines themselves would never, in a thousand years, yield this meaning; it has to be supplied from outside' (105–6).

immediate beauty of the phrase *dark Satanic mills*. But nobody mentioned Bronowski's book about Blake, which argued that he meant this kind of thing quite literally.[8] The first thing to look for in a current discussion of this topic is further evidence about whether Bronowski was right or wrong.

His view is that Blake as an hereditary engraver was hard hit by the Industrial Revolution before it had got going for other people, and then saw quite enough around him as a basis for prophecy about the Machine Age; his circle of friends, now almost entirely forgotten, were discussing this kind of thing as well as the latest information (largely false) about ancient mythology and suchlike. Mr Bateson summed up the controversy in No. 1, by saying 'In the last resort, Blake's readers must choose between Samson's mills and the steam-driven textile factories', and gave a shriek-mark [an exclamation mark] to the idea that they must precariously balance in a subtle tension between Gaza and Lancashire [113]. I take it this is only because he thinks Blake could not have imagined the factories; the argument collapses if you allow that he did. Then there is no logical difficulty at all; whenever you speak in general about cats you precariously balance in a subtle tension between black cats and tabby cats. The double reference of course is why people who already know about both back-grounds, as we can't help doing, feel an 'immediate' striking power in the phrase before they analyse it—this solves the problem which No. 4 found so metaphysical (I agree that the immediacy is an important test of good verse).[9] Certainly there is a gap in our knowledge about this side of Blake, which might yet be bridged a little better. But he walked into a house in London and told Tom Paine he had twenty minutes to escape the police and get out of the country, and Paine believed him, rightly as it turned out, and did only just escape from the country.[10] In the face of that kind of thing, I don't see how you people can go on talking as if Blake was a holy

[8] J. Bronowski, *William Blake 1757–1827: A Man Without A Mask* (1944): ch. 3, 'The Satanic Wheels', 58–94.

[9] John Bayley, writing in the 'Critical Forum' on 'Immediacy in Poetry: A Romantic Plea' (*E in C,* 2: 4, Oct. 1952, 453–60), suggested that in recent years 'precision' had been 'reached at the expense of the poem's immediacy. What if the poet *intends* this immediacy as the indispensable medium of his poem's effect.

'To put the case as baldly as possible—does the poet intend his poem to be read Analytically or Romantically? Clearly he doesn't or shouldn't ask himself the question, but today it certainly exists implicitly in the poet–audience relationship . . . Asking the question in this form such a poet might produce tortuous intellectual syntheses on the one hand, or a superficially "magical"—what Empson had called "taste in the head"—poetry, on the other. Take the phrase *dark Satanic mills* . . . Blake's phrase . . . is neither magically vague nor arduously meaningful, but its effect, and I should maintain its full effect, is certainly instantaneous' (455).

[10] Thomas Paine (1737–1809), writer and revolutionary; author of *Rights of Man* (1791–2) and *The Age of Reason* (1793). See Bronowski, *William Blake*, 45.

innocent who had never heard of politics at all. I hope there isn't a new rule in the game, so that politics mustn't be mentioned when one is playing literary criticism; that would sound to me like funk.

As to your very generous review of my book *Complex Words*, I only want to try and make myself clear at some points where doubt was expressed.[11] It is true that in interpreting a period 'equation' (between two meanings of a word) I act as a historian and say what I think the equation then meant, and there is often a slight jump; but I think that whenever a group of people (for example) assume that 'the poet is a bright social talker' they will slide into thinking 'the tone of polite society is the final judge of the arts'. I too wanted not to be intolerable to the ordinary polite reader, a forlorn hope perhaps; I don't think I cheated when I hurried things along at times.[12] Then there is a kindly mystery raised about my conclusion on Wordsworth's use of *sense* [in *The Prelude*]; I can't possibly have meant, says the reviewer, to *praise* the confusion of meaning I describe, so my 'motives' in saying the poetry is good 'whatever they may be' must be pretty fishy.[13] But I promise him I do think it good; I can't even imagine any advantage for me in telling lies there. For that matter, the main point of my long sequence about the English word *sense* is that some obscure 'sense' in the talkers had made them meet one jolt after another with a sturdy power of balancing.[14] This little worry in the reviewer I think comes from fear of the

[11] Richard Sleight, 'Mr Empson's Complex Words', *E in C*, 2: 3 (Jul. 1952), 325–37.

[12] Sleight writes: 'Irritating, difficult and wrong-headed though it often is, *The Structure of Complex Words* is unquestionably the most important contribution to critical theory since [TSE's] *The Sacred Wood*' (337). His specific criticisms include these remarks (327): 'It is the interpretation of the equations which appears a little open to doubt. To take the simplest: $3 = 1, 2 = 1$. (Where "1" is the wit as a bright social talker, "2" is the wit as critic, "3" is the wit as poet.) My substitution gives: "Both poet and critic are bright social talkers." That is, being a bright social talker refers to a poet's or critic's writing, not to his social gifts as an ordinary person. The copula may be altered to "ought to be" or "have to be if they want success", but variation in this direction does not much matter. Empson's interpretation is: "Both poet and critic are social entertainers (and must keep to the tone of polite society, since that is the final judge of the arts)." I have bracketed the words which seem an unwarranted inference from the equation's terms.'

[13] 'Empson's thesis is that "sense" as used by Wordsworth is a key-word, which successfully unites in itself the operation of the highest imaginative powers with that of the external senses. Those who don't agree will be reduced to denying Wordsworth's success . . . Empson rather boggles at his conclusion of not being able to find any consistent theory expounded' [by Wordsworth; though WE] 'ends: "in saying this I do not mean to deny that the result makes very good poetry, and probably suggests important truths." The reader is tempted to exclaim: "Ridiculous, how can poetry, which is incoherent at such a vital level, possibly be good?"

'Whatever the motives underlying Empson's remark, there is the puzzle left of the amount and kind of coherency that ought to be expected in the Romantics.'

[14] 'The horrifying vistas of stupidity, arrogance and malice opened by taking to pieces the assertions made in connection with "honest" may also be traced back to the absence of modifying rationalizations which usually sweeten the pill. In these chapters the mostly subconscious processes that operate automatically to change a word-structure as soon as it gets accepted, are examined as if they were conscious (as they could be) . . . The procedure results in the exposure

Preconscious (I use that word only to recall the distinction from the deep Freudian unconscious); he expresses this fear all the time, and it is worth bringing up because it may be common among literary persons who dislike science. Your Preconscious is known about because if it goes wrong you get one or other type of clear-cut well-documented mental disease; for instance, you can't read a capital letter written on a blackboard till you have traced it with your finger. It is ordinary medical knowledge that we need an elaborate equipment, of which a separate bit very seldom goes wrong, before we can carry on the behaviour which we consider elementary. I did not mean any satire on the race of man when I took this for granted; nor, for that matter, did I mean to give the bad picture of the word *honest* which he finds so horrible; in the innocence of my heart, I thought that the pleasant uses were well known, and that what needed most study were the abnormal uses which Shakespeare elaborated in Iago. My reviewer thinks I give a farcically satirical effect by sticking to the logic and ignoring the emotions; I think that the 'feelings' in the background, though not examined by the speaker, are commonly quite reasonable and can be treated so without further worry. In the case of the *Grecian Urn*, my critic makes two opposite objections almost in one breath; that my reading of it is too confusing for him, and that I have no right to suggest that the meaning intended by Keats is rather too confusing to make a good poem.[15] Seeing how confused the commentators are, I think my view is at least plausible. In the same way he can't bear the idea that T. S. Eliot made a real objection to Othello and yet that Othello is a tragic hero.[16] But the world is wide; I didn't make it, and I didn't make rules for critics either.

I am just trying to pick up various points. It seems that the Empson

of all sorts of delusions. One supposes the errors would have seemed less humiliating, if a background of subconscious motivations had been allowed. Empson's analysis boils down to the conclusion that, as most of us share them, most of us are fools and liars, as well as being amazingly self-centred' (330).

[15] 'On the epigram spoken by the Urn he says: "What it tells us is a revelation, and revelations are expected to be puzzling." Then he suggests possible ways of getting a solution and ends: "The effort of seeing the thing as Keats did is too great to be undertaken with pleasure. There is perhaps a puzzle about how far we ought to make this kind of effort, and at what point the size of the effort required simply proves the poem bad." . . . A given amount of effort, it is implied, is to be allowed to a particular poem and once the ration has been exceeded the poem is adjudged bad.' (334)

[16] WE paraphrases TSE's view of Othello's final speech as 'a repulsive attempt to cheer himself up and ignore the realities of what he had done'. Sleight comments (335): 'But Eliot is certainly wrong here, since once Othello is given this motive, he does become "repulsive"; in other words, as hero he forfeits everybody's sympathy at the moment when he most needs it. Shakespeare cannot have been so incompetent as to risk revolting his audience like this. Empson, however, agrees with Eliot and attributes Othello's attitude to his Stoicism. But Stoicism is on the whole admirable, the repulsive cheering-up process is not.'

comment on 'Bare ruined choirs, where late the sweet birds sang' has become a by-word for self-indulgence and absurdity. Earlier on I used to think it was being picked out for much too much praise. The intention of this passage, which came early in my old *Ambiguity*, before the real problems began, was just to show what putting in some background is like; in Shakespeare's time, the ruins of the monasteries must have been a prominent feature, so that *any* contemporary reader would easily think of this meaning for the line—it isn't a question of the peculiar mind of Shakespeare. I don't think it need have startled people into either kisses or kicks to have me offer this placid example of a bit of background.

ESSAYS IN CRITICISM, 3: 3 (July 1953): 'Bare Ruined Choirs'

Why is the Editor so certain that the 'bare ruined choirs' must have been in parish churches, not monasteries? I should have thought that the change from plough to sheep, though it put a lot of people out of work, seldom left a village totally empty so that the roof of the church fell in, whereas a lot of monastery churches admittedly had been ruined. I may be ignorant here, but it seems to me that he is irresponsible rather than I, in rejecting the obvious without giving any reason for it. Looking up my old Arden text of the *Sonnets*, I find I had marked an eighteenth-century suggestion that the monasteries were in view here, so I can't be accused of wanton novelty.[17]

I am not much attached to my choir boys, who were put in the list merely to show what a variety of ideas *might* belong to the comparison; but I still think they sound more like birds than most people in choirs, were not unknown in monastery choirs (what about the Children of the Queen's Chapel, for that matter?), and suit the general theme of youthful male charm; thus helping, if they happen to occur to a reader, what the Elizabethans called the 'decorum' of the comparison. Admittedly, they don't apply to Shakespeare himself, whose age is the tenor of the comparison, because he is said *not* to be like them, but the person addressed is presumably told, at the end of the poem, that he will stop being like them 'ere long'. Thus I deny that my remarks only fit a 'verbal fragment . . . *unintelligible* when lifted like this out of its syntactic context'; on the contrary, the Editor was not considering the whole context, but I was. It is clear that this charge is the one he takes most seriously, but I do not see why he assumed I

---

[17] George Steevens thought Shakespeare's 'image was probably suggested . . . by our desolated monasteries' (New Variorum edn., ed. H. E. Rollins [1944], i. 190).

was doing something so obviously wrong; the poem is too well known to need quoting in full (except in the Thesis Style, which only aims at attaining a required length), and I even put a clause in the actual sentence about 'relating the simile to its place in the Sonnet'. I agree that the main function of the ruins is to remove the idea of next Spring from the boughs, but this does not prevent them from suggesting other things.

He says it is 'significant', apparently of my irresponsibility, that I did not make the changes he wants in my second edition; but I don't believe in them even now that I have heard of them. I see I did make a change, to make clearer that the thought of the ruined monasteries might be connected with fear of the growing power of Puritanism—not only is Shakespeare getting old, but the whole world of Elizabethan gaiety is threatened. This could much more reasonably be blamed as far-fetched; but I think it was a recurring idea in Shakespeare's mind, and anyhow the purpose of my sentence was to show the variety of ideas that *could* come in. The Editor himself says, at the end of his rebuttal of me, that 'the image becomes a symbol not so much of the ageing poet as of a universal process of mutability'. I realize that a lot of people agree with his line of objection, but I really can't see what the worry is about.

> In a personal letter (2 Apr. 1953), Bateson continued to reassure WE: 'I'm sorry we are having this row, because—in spite of all my reservations—I really do admire you a lot more than any other living critic.' Nevertheless, he published his retort immediately after WE's last piece: 'Mr Empson can't see what the worry is about. Exactly. In a sense, indeed, that was the whole point of my article. It is not that he *won't* see but that he *can't* see. The most dazzling critic of my generation, a critic incomparably more perceptive and acute than the rest of us put together, has little or no contextual sense! That is what my grumble amounts to.' WE has a 'defective contextual sense': 'the suggested allusion to monastic choirs is not only historically improbable, it is also poetically disastrous.'

I am glad of the opportunity to try and get this point cleared up. My First Type is meant to be different from the other ones, and it is only about the first one that I would say what the words 'might' imply needs emphasizing; because what is in question is a general sense of richness of possible reference. I agree that it is doubtful whether the choirs were monastery ones (though their roofs could not have stood fifty years without lead, I would bet) but this doubt only makes my example illustrate better the process it was intended to illustrate.

The Editor feels it would be vulgar of Shakespeare to compare his supposed approaching old age to (in effect) the end of an historical period; but he himself brought in 'a universal process of mutability'. I think what he really feels is that this kind of reference ought not to seem obtrusive in the poem, and that something in the tone of my writing makes it appear so; but I was only saying, however tactlessly, that it is present in the background. However I believe that a reader in Shakespeare's time would often think of it quite clearly; a rule that poetry must be too pure for such a thing ('How appalling if my verse is suspected of hinting at the Boer War') would strike me as ninetyish and not at all Elizabethan.

However, looking back at the whole sentence which he quotes, it does seem wrong for me to say 'these reasons, and many more ... *must all* combine to give the line its beauty', because obviously it is very beautiful even if you don't reflect at all about the Destruction of the Monasteries. One could claim that 'its beauty' meant 'its full original beauty', but the phrase does seem to put the emphasis wrong. All the same, I believe (1) that a response adequate to make the line beautiful at all is much more complex than we easily recognize, and (2) it is greatly heightened, as is a lot of other poetry, if we think back to its historical setting. Of course I have no objection at all to his parish churches, and will in future think of them alongside my monasteries.

§ END

TO JOHN WAIN*

[n.d. ?1953]

My dear Wain,

I want to reflect about The Intentional Fallacy (thanks for sending it) and the simplest way is to write you a letter. I did an article recently for *Essays in Criticism* saying I don't believe the problem arises in the sharp way you had proposed about Blake (this only came up briefly). I read in Peking the Lewis–Tillyard *Personal Heresy*, and found that though my eye passed contentedly enough over all the pages it seemed very small beer; probably I ought to look at it again.[1] My prejudice is that these problems, though they exist, are such as a critic ought to be able to handle by good sense, and that they gain little from being formalized. Certainly in a big historical case like the Chinese *Book of Odes* one poem may simply become two

---

[1] E. M. W. Tillyard and C. S. Lewis, *The Personal Heresy: A Controversy* (1939).

poems; but that isn't at all painful; Waley says his translation is meant to give the original meaning, whereas previous translators have tried to give the important and long-accepted official interpretation of them, a very proper intention.[2] But the attempt to apply this kind of thing to modern or recent English poetry seems to me only inventing something to worry about.

The Wimsatt–Beardsley essay however seems to me good, especially from a reasonable breadth.[3] It gets quite a bang from Plato saying the poets don't know what they mean, but it seems to run away from that point into complaining about commercial plans to make would-be poets satisfied by a 'course'. The less the poets know what they mean the more their critics can claim to know as well as they do. The hatred of 'biography' and the claim that a good poem should have all requirements for reading it 'within itself' seems to me mere petulance, like saying 'I won't visit any house that hasn't got a Coca-Cola machine and a sun-bathing apparatus'. Obviously a person of more serious interests would be willing to put up with inconvenience. As to the Lowes *Road to Xanadu*,[4] it is true that he rather tiresomely refuses to go into deep water, but he had so much coast-line to visit that his long book doesn't become trivial. It seems to me a quite unexpected complaint that he 'pretends to say more than he does' (by elegant chapter headings apparently).[5] I think he makes *Kubla Kahn* into a good poem, and probably more judged by the author in writing up than Coleridge afterwards pretended—the maritime empires take him on to the land empires, and they are contrasted to the empire of the illuminated solitary mind; when you put in the background of his reading, which can be done quite shortly, the poem is strong and coherent; without that it is a fragment of decoration. I can't imagine why the authors think they have refuted this obvious view, and argue from it that you never need to know what special ideas an author had when he wrote. They say the history Coleridge was drawing upon 'has passed and was then passing into the

---

[2] Arthur Waley, in *The Book of Songs* (1937), his translation of the *Shih Ching*, does not quite say what WE suggests (17): 'It is not likely that we can recreate all the mental associations of people in China three thousand years ago.' But cf. Waley, *The Way and Its Power: A Study of the Tao Te Ching* (1934): 'I want to make it clear that this translation . . . is not "literary"; for the simple reason that the importance of the original lies not in its literary quality but in the things it says, and it has been my one aim to reproduce what the original says with detailed accuracy' (14).

[3] W. K. Wimsatt, Jr., and Monroe C. Beardsley, 'The Intentional Fallacy', in *The Verbal Icon: Studies in the meaning of poetry* (1954), 3–18.

[4] John Livingston Lowes, *The Road to Xanadu: A Study in the Ways of the Imagination* (1927).

[5] 'In certain flourishes . . . and in chapter headings like "The Shaping Spirit," "The Magical Synthesis," "Imagination Creatrix," it may be that Professor Lowes pretends to say more about the actual poems than he does. There is a certain deceptive variation in those fancy chapter titles; one expects to pass on to a new stage in the argument' (11–12).

very stuff of our language' [12]. I am glad to have them talk so romantically, and it is true that what Coleridge dreamed deeply about was hardly at
all private to himself but more like a folklore of historians; but all the same
you don't get it from just knowing what the words mean. A bold argument
that you can seems to me wilful; it is refuted from the start by the way
Coleridge held up publication and at last published with excuses. Here I
am arguing the other way round from the case of Blake's *Jerusalem*, where I
say the community singers are broadly right about Blake's intentions. All
I say about either poem is that you need to be broadly right about the
poet's intentions before you find the poem good.

   I think they are right about the Donne verse:

>   Moving of the earth brings harms and feares;
>   Men reckon what it did and meant;
>   But trepidation of the spheres,
>   Though greater far, is innocent.

They say it is absurd to drag in a learned argument about the movement
of the earth in the Copernican theory, because the whole point here is the
notion of a sudden earthquake, and people theorizing about it afterwards.
They then say 'Perhaps a knowledge of Donne's interest in the new science may add another shade of meaning, an overtone to the stanza in
question, though to say even this runs against the words' [14]. I don't see
that their distinction here is really one between the poet's 'private' intention and the 'public' value of his poem, which in any case he didn't
publish. It is quite true that one needs to get the proportions right. The
immediate point of the stanza doesn't require Copernicus at all, but I
think we need not doubt that a thought of it did cross Donne's mind here,
as so often elsewhere, and that the idea of several planets each carrying life
again suggested to him the inherent autonomy of a pair of lovers. The
grammar might be 'and also the sudden introduction of the idea that the
earth moves, therefore there may be life on other planets not within reach
of Jesus, has affected the Churches like an earthquake'. The argument
doesn't require it at all, indeed there might be a claim to innocence
because the argument doesn't, but it pretty certainly came to Donne and
would easily come to his private readers. However I didn't say this to a
Japanese or Chinese class when I was trying to make them realise the
merit of this whole kind of poetry, for which the poem which includes this
verse is one of the obvious introductions. The point about Copernicus is
only worth bringing up if you are interested in the whole background of
Donne's mind, but is none the less real. I can't see that this raises, and still

less that it illuminates, any problem about whether a critic 'ought' to consider the 'intention' of an author or 'ought' not.

The points about Eliot's notes to *The Waste Land* seem rather indefinite, and can surely not be offered as a proof that it would be better without notes. It is quite true, as is hardly recognised enough by the placid remarks of the essay, that Eliot could shake the literary world by the mere force of the poem *before* it was tolerably understood; that this can happen is one of the basic surprising truths about poetry; but you can't argue from there that to understand *The Waste Land* a bit better makes it any weaker. Nor do I find the final joke, to the effect that it is no use asking such a poet what he meant, though of course it has a broad truth, any serious ground for imposing a New Rule that a critic 'ought' not to ask him.[6] As J. B. S. Haldane remarked some while ago, arguing against some other line of purism, 'I find geometry sufficiently difficult to justify my using any method which I find will work'.

The argument that it is Romantic to bother about what the poet intended, and therefore must be wicked, only seems to me fatuously pokey. The argument that poems ought to be allowed to improve with time only appears in the notes, and presents nothing to answer for lack of cases. The interesting parts of the thesis hardly in fact seem to me to emerge here. What one can sometimes say, I think, is that the poet was inspired and meant more than he knew, and that the later reader can recognise in his working the growth of ideas which, though also working in his contemporary public, and therefore accepted when they accepted his poem, were then obscure or even forbidden. Milton seems the main interesting possible case; Shakespeare isn't 'interesting' in this sense because he wouldn't have been upset if you had told him. But in any case the mind of the author, both conscious and subconscious, has to continue being an accepted topic for the critic; it can't be swept off the table just because the room looks a bit untidy.

Yours very sincerely

W. Empson

Houghton: undated carbon

---

[6] In 'The Intentional Fallacy', Wimsatt and Beardsley scoff at 'the way of biographical or genetic enquiry, in which, taking advantage of the fact that Eliot is still alive, and in the spirit of a man who would settle a bet, the critic writes to Eliot and asks what he meant, or if he had Donne in mind [when writing "The Love Song of J. Alfred Prufrock"] . . . Our point is that [TSE's answer] would have nothing to do with the poem "Prufrock"; it would not be a critical inquiry. Critical inquiries are not settled by consulting the oracle' (18). WE noted in his copy: 'the poet may mean more than he knew—easily may not want to tell. No reason for not asking.'

TO ANTONY BRETT-JAMES*

Studio House, Hampstead Hill Gardens, NW3
13 February 1953

Dear Mr Brett-James

I am sorry to be slow in answering your letter, but I thought there were some other photographs we might dig out. The two I enclose were taken by a photographer [Jane Bown] from The Observer, but not used and not likely to be wanted by them; credit to the photographer, whose name is on the back, must no doubt be cleared, but so it must with the other photographer of the one I return to you.[1]

My point of view is that I don't at all mind being a joke in a picture but I think people very soon get tired of a joke; and what is much worse they soon begin to suspect it is pretentious; as a photograph for regular use I think the one without a cigarette holder, though dull, has very much more wearing quality. I leave it open to you but suggest the use of that as the only regular one.

Yours sincerely
William Empson

Houghton

TO MAX BLACK*

Studio House, Hampstead Hill Gardens, London, N. W. 3
17 April 1953

My dear Max Black,

I have only just found your *Language and Philosophy* [1949] in the London Library, and poked my nose into it here and there; I have been rather out of touch with these things in China. It must seem very absurd to write to you before finishing, but my attitude or claim about philosophy is so strictly amateur that this may be the right way to do it.

I think you are obviously right, again and again, in saying 'this question is merely linguistic', but that doesn't feel enough.[1] You give an airless effect

---

[1] The photograph by Jane Bown of WE with a cigarette holder is reproduced on the jacket of *RB*.

[1] In *Language and Philosophy: Studies in Method* (1949), Max Black takes issue with a range of philosophico-linguistic issues including the linguistic method in philosophy, the justification of induction, and the semantic definition of truth, as well as Bertrand Russell's philosophy of language, Wittgenstein's *Tractatus*, and the semiotic of Charles Morris. Black also criticizes the Ogden–IAR theory of interpretation in *The Meaning of Meaning*, and berates the vagueness of

by having to pretend that you don't know why these people raised such questions, whereas you obviously do know and could say something about it (otherwise you couldn't even know that you weren't going to sound unbearably silly when you called the question merely linguistic; and the process of publication already commits you to trying not to sound unbearably silly). The question may be merely linguistic, but if the answer is ineffable there is a peculiar degree of paradox in calling *that* merely linguistic; if, as is more usual, the question is an inadequate expression of a related group of questions which would admit of different true answers on different occasions, then you have no right to reject the traditional duty of a philosopher to offer wisdom. Nor is this a romantic or metaphysical fancy; it is what (as a matter of history or sociology) the people who voted you your pay intended you to do for your pay. A steady attention to the linguistic situation of the linguist himself is required if your line of argument is to appear solid.

I therefore think that, after showing a question to be merely linguistic, you should regularly also consider why this question *appeared* real (because all arguments by philosophers that something isn't reality but appearance must immediately be met by the question 'why then does it *appear* real?'— and I do not know offhand of any classical case of a good reply); you ought to stick your neck out, and say 'they are thinking of *this* kind of thing, and *here* the answer is so-and-so, and in *that* case the answer is different, and I do not know all the cases, or feel sure of my answers, but you the reader can now see that your *feeling* that there ought to be one answer is now sufficiently satisfied, because I have shown that it isn't only one question. You can therefore trust my judgement, instead of regarding me as an almost insanely specialised type of acrobat'. I am sure you need to do that much, or become tiresome; it is your business. You can't merely appeal to language, because the language you are using already includes

---

IAR in his account of emotive meaning: 'the weaknesses of Richards' earlier critical theories are connected with overemphasis upon the need for a *science* of criticism. When this was coupled with an excessively nominalistic conception of the nature of scientific discourse, the consequences were disastrous. On the one hand, referential discourse was so narrowly defined that on a strict interpretation almost no utterance would qualify for that description; while the remaining field of nonreferential discourse was left so spacious that essential distinctions could hardly be made with any effect. That a theoretical structure having such grave flaws could have proved so acceptable is only to be explained by Richards' engaging refusal to be bound by strict adherence to his enunciated general principles' (211–12). Of C. L. Stevenson's 'causal theory of meaning', in *Ethics and Language* (1944), which in good part remedies the weakness of the Ogden–IAR doctrine, Black yet laments, 'Stevenson's restriction of analysis to *verbal* meaning seems to need more justification than he gives; much behavior that makes no use of words undoubtedly involves the use of signs, and a general linguistic theory should be able to include all signs within its scope' (217–18).

to a surprising degree (rightly, I should think) the language of the philosophers you oppose.

Hoping to see you some time.

Bill Empson

Houghton: unposted?

TO I. A. RICHARDS

Studio House, Hampstead Hill Gardens, NW3
18 May 1953

My dear Richards,

Very nice to hear from you. It is very doubtful whether I can go to America at all this year, but even if I get a dramatic laisser-passer I will be here till the middle of June. So do ring us up when you are in London; Hetta if given a bit of notice has developed a flair for producing a Chinese dinner. I doubt whether we can say anything cheerful, as you suggest, but we go on talking. The puzzle about my American visa is that my passport proves me to have lived in Communist China, and therefore I require six months' clearing even granted that I was paid to be there by the British Government, which is no recommendation. I gave only six weeks to clear my visa, and Hetta says I am ridiculous; it is dignified to be a martyr, but not to be ignorant of the facts of life and therefore liable to be strangled by red tape. I say that the only strong evidence against red tape is from the man who isn't a martyr, and has nothing against him but red tape; I confess that if I had wanted to handle red tape (as in planning a visit to China perhaps) I should have started a year ago, but here I think the onus lies on the inviting party; they ought to know their own laws and not take for granted that every foreigner will start to learn them as soon as they invite him. I have written to my brother Charles in Washington, reassuring him that I had already told Indiana that they would find him too spry to put a foot wrong.[1] I would be very sorry to lose my leg in Indiana; I don't want them to feel I have behaved badly and can't be asked again; but I think the inviting party ought to be told 'It's your worry not mine, brother'.

Hetta and I did a trip to Sheffield and find it isn't a hornet's nest, as some of them are; they are reasonable people, doing all right as it is, and

[1] Charles Empson (1898–1983) joined the Foreign Service in 1920; after fourteen years in Baghdad and a series of postings in Europe, the Middle East and South-East Asia, he became Minister (Commercial) at HM Embassy in Washington, 1950–5, and was later to be Ambassador to Chile, 1955–58. He was to be knighted in 1956.

only anxious to know whether the new appointment is going to be positively unpleasant. We thought we reassured them without pulling our faces
about or telling them any lies. As to the Interview for Sheffield, I have
invented a saga of comedy about it, but these jokes are only extras to the
broad fact: that the answers which seemed to me the only natural ones also
seemed natural to the committee—you couldn't fool them, but they
expected you to handle them. It is a real comfort, as I felt on the P & O
boat leaving the American journalists in Hongkong, to be among people
who know what you are going to say so well that they can only be bothered
to listen if it is a mildly interesting story; I felt it then like diving out of the
heat into a deep pool.[2] Of course poor Hetta, who has more outgoing
strength than I, finds it dreadfully boring and hard to school herself into
enduring; but she is to stay with the kids in the London flat, which is not
dull as London goes.

Hoping to see you both,
William Empson

Magdalene

TO THE EDITOR OF *MIND* (Unpublished)

[1953]

Sir,

Mr Duncan-Jones has kindly sent me his review of my book [*SCW*]
before publication, and perhaps I may write in at once about some points
where my intention was queried.[1] He is right about the misprints, which I
am sorry for; the corrected edition should now be available. The criterion
for my fourth type of 'equation' is not that both meanings can act as
subject simultaneously but that either can act as subject, because a change
of order does not change the meaning.

I consider that I committed no 'logical monstrosities' and indeed that I

---

[2] Cf. 'Teaching English in the Far East and England' (1953): 'I want . . . to remark that I am
very glad to be back in England. The point where the change was already felt, quite fully, I
thought, was in getting on to the P & O boat at Hong Kong. Hong Kong itself was rather
tiresomely full of correspondents and general excitement, but when you got on to the P & O
boat—it wasn't that you were among dull people at all; so far from that, there always seemed to
be a faint question whether you had a story good enough to swap with the man you were talking
to, and then he would swap one all right if there was time before dinner. It was like diving out of
intense heat into a deep cool pool' (*SSS*, 216–17).

[1] See *Mind*, 62 (1953), 413–17. Austin Duncan-Jones (1908–67) was Professor of Philosophy
at Birmingham from 1951. Educated at Cambridge, he married WE's friend E. E. Phare in
1933. He was editor of *Analysis*, 1933–48; President of the Aristotelian Society, 1960–1. His
works include *Butler's Moral Philosophy* (1952).

have no detailed criticism to answer under that head. The idea that 'a logician' looks down on these matters from a height, and somehow knows that you mustn't say a word is complex to mean that its operation is complex, seems to me absurd; if a training in logic makes a man stupider than he would be without it, that is only to its discredit. A logician, on the other hand, might have a sense of professional outrage, properly enough, at the primitive mental operations which it was my business to describe; I only say he should brace himself to admit that they are widespread. The machinery which my critic finds useless, except perhaps as a mnemonic to myself, is meant to distinguish between different actual operations of the mind when using language; he does not seem to consider whether the claim is true. I tried to limit the pedantry of detailed analysis to as little as was necessary to illustrate my thesis. I agree that all words could be viewed as complex, but many of these mental goings-on cause no bother or 'come to the same thing in the end'. Some of the words I used for rough definitions, as between one broad aspect and another, struck me as obviously complex; the word 'hearty', for example; but there was no pretence that they were simple. We could not deal with these matters at all unless our own language-sense was presumed to be in tolerable working order; indeed, to think otherwise seems to have been a frequent source of fallacy among philosophers.

As to the 'personalist heresy', I think that a reader should try to decide what his author intended to say, and should be willing to make a fair effort to suit him, straining the meanings of words a bit and so on; and should also consider the probable response of the audience intended, when he is not one of them himself; but should also be ready to decide that he has now made enough effort, and that the intentions of the author, however good, have not produced a good piece of writing. Any theory designed to give a shorter answer, I think, loses touch with common sense.

W. Empson

Houghton

TO BONAMY DOBRÉE*

The University, Sheffield 10
Sunday [November 1953]

My dear Bonamy,

I was very pleased to get your letter, because I had thought you felt I had behaved badly somehow about Leeds and Sheffield, though I didn't know why sufficiently to write you a letter about it. I look forward to visiting you next term.

I write this in a mood of exhaustion after feeling my Inaugural is all right, at least it is over-length and can be cut freely, by my wife for example if she can be bothered.[1] It is an extremely disgusting thing which has cost me a lot in whisky, because it is pure Show Off, and I *can* show off; the whole trouble about this silly thing, which has to be written for printing, is that it has to be a show-off in what *they* consider good taste. But never mind, I feel I have done it now, I don't have to shut myself up alone and drink beastly whisky to finish it, anyhow.

Thanks for your kind remarks about Virginia Woolf, but I don't know the first facts about the medical side of it, and would like to. Did some Harley St. doctor tell her she was going mad? *Why* did she suddenly decide she was going mad?

Yours with thanks
William Empson.

Leeds

TO JANET ADAM SMITH*

Sheffield University,
18 May 1954

My dear Janet,

Thank you for your postcard. I agree that in principle it was very wicked of the Editor to change a word, but I hadn't noticed it and do not now think it disastrous. As I remember I put 'I hope I do not annoy anyone by remarking that the Cross of Christ is also the male sexual organ' and he made it 'explaining'.[1] This makes me heavyhanded and rather suggests I

---

[1] 'Teaching English in the Far East and England', *SSS*, 201–19. WE wrote to HE (22 Nov. 1953): 'I am smacking out my silly Inaugural on the typewriter, which depresses me very much because it seems nothing at all but show-off, but I think that's what they want and it will soon be over . . . I told them to send Arthur [his eldest brother, residing at Yokefleet Hall] an invitation to the Inaugural, because I thought his address gave a bit more swank. I shouldn't think he'd be fool enough to come, but he might feel he would like to have a look at the set-up in general, and there is no reason to shut him out, after all.' (*Hull*)

[1] See WE on Dylan Thomas's *Collected Poems* and *Under Milk Wood* (*New Statesman*, 15 May 1954; *A*, 391–5): 'You must remember that he was a very witty man, with a very keen though not at all poisoned recognition that the world contains horror as well as delight; his chief power as a stylist is to convey a sickened loathing which somehow at once (within the phrase) enforces a welcome for the eternal necessities of the world. It is particularly important to realise this at the end of the sequence "Altarwise by Owl-light" [. . .] "Green as beginning, let the garden diving | Soar, with its two bark towards, to that Day | When the worm builds with the gold straws of venom | My nest of mercies in the rude, red tree."

hold some theory of the sort myself but otherwise does no harm. I can't see that it removes any obscurity, either, though.

There has been some other puzzling about the style of the piece. Dear old J. Isaacs, when I ran into him at some party, said it was the most childish thing on the subject he had yet seen, and he gathered all I meant was that the only good part was the final Milk Wood. How he came to think that I can't imagine: I suppose he thinks if a critic says something simply that proves he means to be ironical. Then he said 'How do you manage to get it as loose as that? Do you dictate it?' I explained I used beer, but that when I saw the stuff in print (I had to admit) it shocked my eye as much as it did his. He was very friendly, you understand. One thing is, I have to read so much Mandarin English Prose now, especially in literary criticism, and am so accustomed to being shocked by its emptiness, that I feel I must do otherwise at all costs.

I have been having General Irritation of the Intestines again, after coming up to London for a recording, and must stop drinking and smoking for a few days (also bothering about anything, but this is hardly a bother). It isn't alarming if you treat it seriously but gets frightfully painful if you don't.

Love
William

Andrew Roberts

NEW STATESMAN, 25 September 1954, 362: 'Wykehamist'

Richard Crossman,[1] in a review of *Rendall of Winchester* by J. D'E. Firth,

'I hope I do not annoy anyone by explaining that the Cross of Jesus is also the male sexual organ; Dylan would only have thought that tiresomely obvious, a basis for his remarks. But when you get to the worms instead of the birds able to build something valuable in this tree, and the extraordinary shock of the voice of the poet in his reverence and release (at the end of the whole poem) when he gets to his nest, you do begin to wonder whether he meant something wiser than he knew.'

[1] Richard Crossman (1907–74), classical don, politican, and diarist, was WE's contemporary as a scholar of Winchester College, where he became Prefect of Hall (Head Boy) in the year after WE went up to Cambridge. Crossman read classics at New College, Oxford, where he became a Fellow and Tutor, 1930–7; his publications at the time included *Plato To-Day* (1937) and *Socrates* (1938). After wartime service in the Ministry of Economic Warfare and at the psychological warfare division of the Supreme Headquarters of the Allied Expeditionary Force, he was elected Labour MP for Coventry West in 1945. He was ultimately to serve as a cabinet minister in the administration of Harold Wilson, from 1964 till 1970 (his posts included Lord President of the Council and Leader of the House of Commons). But perhaps his major claim to fame rests upon the posthumous and precedent-setting publication of his ministerial diaries, in three volumes (1975, 1976, 1977). According to Stephen Spender, Crossman had remarked while up at Oxford in the 1920s, 'Even if I become Prime Minister, I'll never be as great as I was at Winchester' (cited in Anthony Howard, *Crossman: The Pursuit of Power* (1990), 20).

recalled of his schooldays: 'for six years I fought first for survival and then for success, according to rules which barred very few holds . . . The secret of Winchester—and, indeed, of the classical tradition in our leading public schools—is that it imposes on a boy's mind a complex structure of rules, a rigid hierarchy of values, and a system of taboos, privileges and obligations utterly remote from his home life or from the world outside.' ('The Wykehamist', *New Statesman and Nation*, 18 Sept. 1954, 328).

Sir,—Whatever can Mr Crossman mean by saying that as a scholar at Winchester he 'fought first for survival and then for success, according to rules which barred very few holds'? I thought we spent all our time talking our heads off, educating one another in a delightful manner but rather inclined to be above any struggle. I remember him as talking for victory a bit, but it never occurred to me he imagined he had anything to fight for; apart from passing his exams. It is true that he was about a year older than me, and the fashions change very quickly in such places. But hardly as fast as all that.

TO DESMOND LEE*

[n.d.: 1954]

My dear Desmond,[1]

I ought to have answered before and have treated my kids rather badly by leaving their affairs alone till the end of term. However, I think your advice was very sensible, and I am struggling to get them down for St Paul's, without abandoning the hope of Winchester: chiefly because their present Headmaster, a generous dignified character on the edge of retirement, feels he is above modern fuss and can at least certainly get them into St Paul's, where he has some undefined influence. Any school that could arrange to let in the elder boy, he said to me, would be certain to let in the younger one; they are just what these schools really do want to have, only of course these schools all get their feet absurdly tied up in their regulations.

I wouldn't mind spending less money, but I haven't yet inquired how much cheaper it would be to send them to St Paul's, as day-boys presumably, with decent food at home. It is almost a religious reverence when I

---

[1] WE wrote to HE in 1954 ('Friday'): 'By the way Lee who was headmaster of Clifton [College] has just been made headmaster of Winchester; I wrote and congratulated him and he answered that he hoped both my children would be coming to him later. I can't help feeling it gives a tiny bit of pull to have the dear old friend in the job now.' (*Hull*)

continue to offer the boys to Winchester, and my wife thinks it all wrong—
so does Dick Crossman, who I was very surprised, when meeting him
recently, to find sincere or at least barefaced in insisting that he had to
fight, when we were boys together, for what really everybody gave him
with both hands. In our time it was the best available education, and we
kids in College said so. We thought it was entirely because of ourselves, not
a bit because our teachers were very properly dishing out good education,
a thing we seldom denied.

Such is the reason why I would like my sons to go to Winchester, and it
seems rather a dreadful thing to say to the old friend I love best; because it
is piling on him an impossible demand, and I am aware that nearly all the
letters he gets from old parents would pile upon him the same impossible
demand. When we were kids, we thought we were under our own steam,
and it was only good luck to have a fairly good teacher; but the point was
that every child had the right ticket, which wasn't fussed about. The only
thing which seems to me strange now is the completely passive acceptance
by the children of the system by which a child got in. I have seen such
dreadful universal hatred, expressed in cruelty by prefects with applause
from younger children, go on that it was quite obvious that the child's
parents ought to withdraw him, he is bad maybe but this torture is making
him permanently harmed. I am never easy about Spencer Leason [*sic*], the
great Bishop, who was carried naked in a bath tub round Chamber Court
while passages were read aloud from his private diary.[2] He was an excellent
teacher to me, and of course to the whole class, really a generous mind;
but I don't quite like seeing him in purple and Dick Crossman plotting
together in the Athenaeum [Club]. They have the same tiny grudge: we
were both given the best education of all, and we still pretend we were
wronged. Now the fundamental idea of all administration, as you well
realise, is not to have people think they are wronged. It does seem to
me tiresome to see these characters sit together in the Athenaeum and
say they were both wronged. There are very real troubles in the world

---

[2] Spencer Leeson (1892–1956) entered Winchester College as a scholar in 1905 and returned
to teach there for three years from September 1924. In 1916 he gained a 'war degree' (Classics)
at New College, Oxford, and his employment thereafter included a period at the Board of
Education and eight years (1927–35) as Headmaster of Merchant Taylors' School, London. He
later served as Headmaster of Winchester for eleven years, 1935–46. According to a devoted
memoir, he 'flung himself with tremendous zeal and abandon into the work, riotously happy,
enjoying every moment of his time with the boys, making friends on all sides, full of fun and
laughter, and universally beloved' (*Spencer Leeson, Shepherd: Teacher: Friend: a memoir by some of his
friends* (1958). A devout and conscientious Christian, he was ordained a priest in 1940, and
consecrated Bishop of Peterborough in 1949.

but a decent education is not one of them. Winchester invented both these characters; it seems to me bad tempered of them to be cross about it.

When 'old boys' came down to visit us from their first year in Oxford or Cambridge, we were accustomed to say 'how dreadfully young they have become' (chiefly because they had begun drinking and smoking); and I remember seeing this return at once obviously outfaced by the children. It was a commonplace to say that a man coarsened a good deal when he went to the university. Not the great step from the university to the world, but just leaving Winchester for Oxford or Cambridge, was where we thought a man at once visibly lost the cutting edge of his intellectual purity. I know it is tiresome for a Headmaster to be told of an ideal which he is allowed to do nothing to attain, but it was so that in my time we schoolboys merely jeered at the undergraduates who were kind enough to visit us.

And one of the reasons, if I may gear on my serious belief here to my personal business in writing this letter, is that we had several White Russians in College who were let in on a postwar Government scheme, not on literal examinations but because they were both just good enough and would make the place more lively. Two out of the three I know did very well, and though it would be absurd to pretend that they altered the machine much they did do good to it, if only because they helped the vain children to feel that they had all the world at their feet. I must never deny what I felt at the time, that the other children (not the teachers at all) were giving me such a ripping education that it equipped a man to go anywhere in the world alone, from leaving school on. When I first went there the system was very brutal, but in my last year under William Hayter the present Ambassador to Moscow it had swung over completely, and Hayter got through a year in office, without allowing any beating at all.[3] We then had the loathsome spectacle of a teacher, the then Second Master, head of the College boys, leeringly approaching elder children and saying it would

---

[3] William Hayter (1906–1995), diplomat and college head, was a scholar at Winchester, where he became Prefect of Hall (Head Boy), 1924–5: he selected WE as one of his 'inferiors' (a junior prefect). Hayter 'has a sweet gentleness entirely his own,' it was written at the time. 'Such is his tolerance, that even the continued and irritating effervescences of his two prefects but rarely ruffled him.' In 1924 they acted together in a school production of Marlowe's *Dr Faustus* (Hayter as both the Cardinal of Lorraine and an Evil Angel, WE as the Clown; while Richard Crossman played Mephistophiles). After joining the diplomatic service, Hayter was given postings in Vienna, Moscow, Chungqing, Shanghai, Washington DC, and Paris, before becoming Ambassador in Moscow, October 1953–February 1957. He was Warden of New College, Oxford, 1958–76. See also Hayter's *A Double Life* (1974).

be in accordance with tradition if they choose to torture younger children. This we thought filthy, but I have never inquired. Winchester I am sure is not as dreadful as it was when the child Empson took a vow while in fear that he would never deny that it was good. Please, the whole point of this is that I did not accept being tortured; the child fought against it; but the child could easily realise that it was being carried up in an aeroplane high above the world, from which in the end it could fall like a hawk.

Houghton: draft, bMS Eng 1401 (594)

§ GERARD MANLEY HOPKINS: 'THE WINDHOVER'

In *STA* WE cited the 'proud but helpless suffering' of 'The Windhover' as an example of the seventh type of ambiguity—which 'occurs when the two meanings of the word, the two values of the ambiguity, are the two opposite meanings defined by the context, so that the total effect is to show a fundamental division in the writer's mind'. Hopkins sacrificed his early poems on becoming a Jesuit, and this poem conveys 'an indecision, and its reverberation in the mind'. WE's full analysis includes these points:

> Confronted suddenly with the active physical beauty of the bird, [Hopkins] conceives it as the opposite of his patient spiritual renunciation; the statements of the poem appear to insist that his own life is superior, but he cannot decisively judge between them, and holds both with agony in his mind. 'My heart in hiding' would seem to imply that the 'more dangerous' life is that of the Windhover, but the last three lines insist it is 'no wonder' that the life of renunciation should be the more 'lovely'. 'Buckle' admits of two tenses and two meanings: 'they do buckle here', or 'come, and buckle yourself here'; 'buckle' like a military belt, for the discipline of heroic action, and buckle like a bicycle wheel, 'make useless, distorted, and incapable of its natural motion.' . . .
>
> Thus in the first three lines of the sestet we seem to have a clear case of the Freudian use of opposites, where two things thought of as incompatible, but desired intensely by different systems of judgements, are spoken of simultaneously by words applying to both; both desires are thus given a transient and exhausting satisfaction, and the two systems of judgement are forced into open conflict before the reader (1984, 225–6).

In a footnote added to the second edition (1947) he insisted: 'the test is "buckle". What would Hopkins have said if he could have been shown this analysis? . . . If I am right, I am afraid he would have denied with anger that he had meant "like a bicycle wheel", and then after much conscientious self-torture would have suppressed the whole poem.'

Years later, in the *TLS* (13 Aug. 1954), an unsigned article, 'Pied Beauty in Spanish' (pp. 509–10), reviewed the difficulties of rendering into Spanish the well-known complexities of Hopkins' poetry, as negotiated in the successful translations included in a monograph by Jose Manuel Gutiérrez Mora entitled *Hopkinsiana*. Among the many obstacles for a translator, the article cited the famous instance of Empson's treatment—which 'followed up an essay on Hopkins by Mr I. A. Richards'—of the ambiguities of the word 'buckle' as Hopkins deployed it. 'This is the perfect test-case for the deeper understanding of translator and interpreter—and Sr. Gutiérrez Mora is both,' the reviewer noted. 'The word "buckle" is ambiguous in meaning and mood; it might be an imperative, a challenge to "brute beauty", or a statement; and it might mean either "buckle" in the sense of breaking down under strain, or "buckle" in the sense of preparing for military action, the two meanings Mr Empson quotes without deciding between them, because it is their simultaneous existence in the poet's consciousness and in the impact on the reader which gives "a transient and exhausting satisfaction".'

F. N. Lees, in a letter (3 Sept. 1954), was irked by the reviewer's endorsement of WE's effort to balance contraries; WE's paraphrase—his 'effectively contradictory development'—of the word 'buckle' could not be supported, Lees contended. After 'diagrammatically' supplying his own paraphrases, with the suggestion that they mean 'a fusion of the senses . . . not an invitation to use each in turn', Lees proceeded: 'But why not the bicycle wheel sense? Because "the fire that breaks from thee" is yet another subject for this verb, and it is as difficult to accept its buckling in [WE's] "crumpling" sense as it is easy to accept its sudden addition to the "brute beauty and valour, &c.," its "joining in".' While conceding that there seemed to be a 'less contradictory hint of *internal* struggle and clash latent' in his own interpretative approximations, Lees asserted in conclusion that WE (and IAR) attached 'the feeling of conflict . . . to the wrong places in the poem, which has thereby been deformed.'

WE replied with the following letter.

TIMES LITERARY SUPPLEMENT, 1 October 1954[1]

Sir,—I am not certain about the double meaning for 'buckle' which I proposed long ago in Hopkins's 'Windhover'; anyway, the main conflict of the poem is there without it; but I see no force in Mr Lees's argument against it. What I meant, and said more clearly in the second edition [of *Ambiguity*], was that Hopkins set out with the idea 'like a belt' and would have been shocked to realise that (in his extreme tension of feeling) he was also using, at the back of his mind, the idea 'like a bicycle wheel'. I believed this for the human reason that it was how his mind was likely to work, not for an aesthetic reason, that it made the poem better; though it does give an appallingly direct impression of his mental conflict. Mr Lees, in his first paragraph, flat asserts that this may be 'attractive' but cannot be true; and his only argument is the offer of a joke case with no inherent plausibility.[2] The Hopkins case seems to me painful rather than attractive, but directly relevant to the central impulse of the poem. Merely to assert that the half-conscious pun is impossible is to ignore well-known facts about what strange things the mind can do.

I cannot see why Mr Lees makes 'the fire that breaks from thee then' another subject for the verb 'buckle'; buckling a fire is very strained, and the phrase need only be an exclamation—'how much fire breaks from thee then' (after extreme self-discipline). And surely the newly ploughed

---

[1] An undated draft letter by WE in Houghton seems to indicate either that Lees had sent WE a draft of his initial letter to the *TLS* or that he had composed a further letter which was not actually published:

Dear Mr Lees,

Thank you for showing me your letter. Your point that the incompatible can't be half-conscious does seem a strong one, but I don't think it applies to this case. The meanings are, so to speak, incompatible within the line but not within the poem as a whole. I think what we really disagree about is the meaning of the last line and a half, which you describe as "active acceptance and resignation". The image of the last embers seems to me horrible in its passivity, and indeed masochism, and I do not see how you can regard it as "active". (Of course I do not mean to <under-rate> deny the strength of character which <would> could stubbornly continue a course of action while saying that it was only leading to exhaustion and torture.) If you allow the last line its natural force, I think, the pun on "buckle" becomes only a striking incident.

As to your controversy with Fr. Peters [W. A. M. Peters, S. J.], of course I think it is wildly absurd to suppose that the bird is the only person addressed—the whole point of the poem is that the bird is *not* in this fire. But also I do not see why Christ should be the only person to receive the moral [incomplete].

[2] Lees mocked WE's 'attractive' notion of 'a transient and exhausting satisfaction' in 'the Freudian use of opposites' with this analogy: 'William Cowper, in "The Task", tells how, "as a truant boy . . . I fed on scarlet hips"; yet while an appropriate erotic fantasy would not be hard to imagine, I think I shall not be reproved if I dismiss it to what Americans call the "pulp" magazines and confine my attention to the more innocent satisfactions of the hedgerows. Similarly, though it is clearly a trickier case, with "buckle": we must decide *which* it means; and I suggest that it has the *not* like a bicycle wheel meaning' [*sic*].'

furrows are what 'shine', not the plough; at least they do in the heavy wheat land that I come from—they look greasy. The idea is that the ploughman makes a beautiful shape though he is simply trying to plough as well as he can.

Then Mr Lees rejects the ideal of '*internal* struggle and clash', though he admits it to be 'latent' even in his own paraphrases; and his reason is only that this idea 'does not lead suitably to "no wonder of it" '. But the poem says it does, because all forms of worldly training have a likeness to the poet's terrible spiritual training; the trouble is that they give strength and beauty, whereas his, he says in another of these appalling sonnets, has made him impotent. Such is his recurring doubt; his training does not seem to have had good effects, at least in the world. Mr Lees thinks, apparently, that if you allow the meaning 'buckle like a bicycle wheel' it has to apply to the bird as well as the poet, and this would be absurd; but the whole topic of the poem is the contrast between them. The beauty of movement in the bird comes from the skill it has gained by laborious practice, a form of self-discipline which does have plainly good results. For that matter, I think Mr Lees had probably do some more ploughing before he tells us that there is no 'struggle' in learning to do it well.

What does clearly fit in, I think, with the idea of the buckled bicycle wheel, the broken Old Adam, is the final frightful image of the ash falling into the almost exhausted fire, as the last movement possible to it, and creating a new diffused glow of torture; such is what happens when the bird stirs the poet's hidden heart, and 'gold-vermilion' is meant to recall paintings of martyrdoms. I cannot feel that a critic is being sober or well-balanced or any of those good things if he merely refuses to realise what the poem is about.

William Empson

'One has to rule out accidental homophonic distractions if the context shows them to be such,' Lees replied (*TLS*, 22 Oct. 1954, 673). The word 'buckle' might convey either of the meanings suggested by WE (and seconded by the reviewer of *Hopkinsiana*), but it could not mean *both* at once: we have to decide which it means. 'I certainly never asserted that "the half-conscious pun is *impossible*" (my italics); I claimed that in this case a reader could see that the word could not mean both . . . Something antagonistic welling from the sub-conscious (an *unconscious* pun) presents only the difficulty of proving that it has occurred, and it cannot take place with or displace the poet's meaning—though . . . it might interfere with it for the reader . . . As for a "*halfconscious* pun", well, I think that this is just a phrase for avoiding issues . . . I feel no disagreement with Professor Empson in respect of what the poem, in general, is about . . . But I was trying to get clear the precise movement of the poem's meaning, and in this I see no place at all for "the negative meaning of 'buckle'."

TIMES LITERARY SUPPLEMENT, 29 October 1954, 689

Sir,—It is not only that I cannot agree with Mr Lees's interpretation of the Hopkins *Windhover*; I cannot even see that he is offering one. Surely, what convinces us that an interpretation is right is that it 'makes sense' of the poem—all the details become significant and carry out a single intention. We have to rely on this process even in quite simple uses of language. Mr Lees does not seem to make any such claim for his various scattered preferences.

As to a 'half-conscious pun' (such as the one on *buckle*), I still think it is a familiar mental experience, at any rate among poets. In the field of consciousness, just as in the field of vision, the area seen accurately is much smaller than we commonly have to realize, because there is also a fairly large vague periphery which we rely on to tell us where to direct our attention. However, it would perhaps be rather fussy to insist on the term '*half*-conscious', if it seems evasive to Mr Lees; all I meant by it was that the pun did not come from any deep Unconscious, as in a Freudian dream. The poet might easily have noticed that his mind had produced this pun, but he would have been rather shocked if he had noticed it, I think, even though it fits so well the theme which he was intentionally treating.

William Empson

The following year (*TLS*, 6 May 1955), J. G. Ritz, of the Faculté des Lettres at Lyon, offered an interpretation which 'answers all the difficulties of the sonnet, while rejecting far-fetched explanations': 'The whole poem is at once one of Hopkins's splendid meditations on Christ's glory and sacrifice as God and Man-God, and one of his deep ponderings' over the necessity of imitating Christ. Ritz's account opens by observing that the poet:

watches [the bird of prey] as he glides and hovers in the air, and admires his mastery. He then sees the bird swoop down (or he imagines it) and 'buckle' or 'gather together' his beauty, valour, pride . . . for his sudden fall upon a prey that he will snatch away from the ground. He drops like lightning . . . and this 'fell swoop' is for the poet . . . even more lovely than the bird's masterly gliding in the air; and it is 'more dangerous', since it is a sheer fall and there is a victim. The second tercet justifies the 'fire' image. One should not wonder at it. The share

and mould-board, as they sink into the soil and tear it open, shine—are
on fire, one might say—and grey embers, when some poker stirs them,
fall and reveal fire burning under the 'rind' of blue ashes.

The windhover is symbolical of Christ who 'swooped down like a bird of
prey': 'Christ's incarnation, his lowly life in Galilee, are "lovelier" and
"more dangerous" since they imply the redemption of men and their salvation. To be Christ's prey is no small matter for Hopkins . . .'

'Too many critics seem to vie with one another in their quest of subtle
niceties,' Ritz concludes:

why should Mr Empson construe so strangely 'plough down sillion
shine'? True, sillion may shine, but it is the shine of the plough that the
poet is considering . . .
    Finally, the conflict between artist and ascetic . . . is simply not
there. The bird's 'achieve' and mastery are admired as those of a
creature of God and as a great symbol of Christ. And 'buckling'
beauty and valour and act . . . is not self-destruction but self-
dedication. It must be remembered that 'The Windhover' belongs to
Hopkins's 'Welsh salad days', not to the terrible years of 'No worst,
there is none'.

TIMES LITERARY SUPPLEMENT, 20 May 1955

Sir,—The letter of Mr Ritz on Hopkins's 'Windhover', in your number of
6 May, deserves respect for giving a consistent interpretation of the whole
poem; and an interesting one, though I am not convinced by it. Some
weeks ago you, Sir, were mentioning in an editorial [18 Mar. 1955, 165]
the recent letters about the poem, and said that I seemed to have become
doubtful. That is not what I meant; I was so sure of the general purport of
the poem that I thought it was little affected if one left out, say, the pun on
'buckle'. But Mr Ritz makes the purport quite different, and his argument
from the date is rather strong.

    I think the poem is about training and about the doubt in Hopkins's
mind, expressed with painful force in later sonnets, as to whether the
severe Jesuit training had only crippled him. The flight of the bird and the
lines made by the ploughman are beautiful with the unconscious grace of
an acquired skill; but all that Hopkins has got from his discipline, as far as
he can see, is what the Americans call a 'slow burn'. He none the less
exults in the sacrifice. I confess I had not realised that the poem was done
in '77, the year of his ordination, whereas all the 'terrible sonnets' seem to
belong either to '85, when he was sent to Ireland and felt overworked, or

'89, the year of his death. However we need not assume that the suspicion was remote in '77; he had been under the training for nine years, burning his youthful poems in '68; and 'my heart in hiding' is bound to mean something like it. I can agree that the effect is meant to be less tragic than in the later sonnets.

Mr Ritz, on the other hand, takes the poem as about gloating over torture. Hopkins must have been 'stirred' by the hawk because he saw it, or imagined it, swoop and catch its prey, just as Christ has swooped and mangled Hopkins. The swoop, the act of violence, is what is 'lovelier' and 'more dangerous' than the masterly gliding (whereas I had assumed that the parallel spiritual achievement was more so than the animal one). The plough has now to be envisaged as both ripping up and searing the flesh of the earth, and what 'shines' is this hot weapon. Mr Ritz expresses surprise at my wanting the new furrows to be what shine, but our two views there merely follow from our basic assumptions. To take 'plough down sillion' as a whole scene in movement is not too strained, as grammar, for Hopkins if he wanted it; the trouble is that this mood of contemplation is not wanted by Mr Ritz, who even has to take a poker, in the last line, to the exhausted fire. I am not sure why he thinks this savage interpretation more suited to the happy 'salad days' of Hopkins, but he is well supported by the 'Deutschland' of '75—e.g., 'the swoon of a heart that the sweep and the hurl of thee trod'.

Hopkins must have known, I agree, that the 'valour and act' of the bird, the source of its beauty of movement, was killing other creatures; and the idea of the fierceness of God was not strange to him; but if this is the point of the poem why is he so far from saying it? The need for a suggestion of conquest in the bird he does feel, and says merely that it 'rebuffed the big wind'. The sweep can only be deduced from 'Brute beauty and valour and act, oh, air, pride, plume, here | Buckle'; and if we insert this sudden crisis we have next to compare it to rather un-sudden things, the plod of the ploughman and the occasional fall of the embers as the coals that support them burn away. I agree and shall remember that the power to swoop was part of why he felt the bird made a good symbol for Christ; but I do not think it was in the centre of his mind here, where he is considering the gradual effects of a given course of life. At least, I was sure he was considering that till I was confronted with the date; but then again, it is not an odd theme for the year of his ordination.

The question, I think, has a larger bearing. Christian apologists nowadays, I seem to notice, have become rather defiantly keen on recalling the stark roots of primitive human sacrifice and their place in Christianity, even boasting in print (one is to suppose with a laugh) that the religion provides a more efficient sadistic drug than the forbidden Horror Comics. Hopkins like other mystics was very capable of scolding his God for cruelty, but I don't think this idea rode his mind all the time; a more impersonal cruelty in the nature of things is what he sighs over in 'no wonder of it'. I am not sure that he wouldn't have considered Mr Ritz's interpretation blasphemous, unlike the pun which I proposed on *buckle*.

William Empson

On 25 May 1955 J. G. Ritz wrote a riposte, though it was not published: the editor had resolved 'to close the Windhover argument'. WE was not fair, Ritz maintained, to manufacture such a 'lurid commentary' on his text:

> I submit that *in no way* can it be said that I take the poem "as about gloating over torture". I never suggested that Christ "had mangled" Hopkins, or that the poem was "a scolding of God for cruelty". Such sadistic views are not mine.' Whose are they?
>
> Certainly not Hopkins's. When the poet chose the windhover as a symbol of Christ, it was to interpret in aesthetic terms the mystery of Christ's Incarnation . . . Christ snatches souls away from all earthly desires as the windhover seizes its prey and soars back to heaven with it. True, the bird is a killer, and Christ is not. There the comparison must end . . .
>
> All Hopkins's readers know that he considers God as "a father and fond", and at the same time as a mighty Master "treading down" the heart of his most faithful servant. This may well be thought "savagery", but Christians have long accepted the image as depicting God's power over souls . . .
>
> The question Hopkins asks in the last tercet is: How can the Incarnation of Christ be a lovelier and more dangerous fire than His splendour in Heaven? The two images of the plough and the falling embers supply him with simple and natural comparisons . . . The earthly quality of the images implies that Christians (those plodders, those embers) in devoutly imitating Christ's own humbling down will glow and shine . . .
>
> I ask: in all fairness, is this my reading of the sonnet: "blasphemous, savage, and gloating over torture"? And what other basic assumptions are mine than the *strictest* adherence to Hopkins's own words and images? (Houghton)

In forwarding a copy of his letter directly to WE, Ritz wrote a further (single-spaced, two-page) covering letter (30 Sept. 1955), reiterating at the start: 'I never imagined for a moment that any reader would see in the allegory of the swooping bird . . . a gloating over torture.' He went on:

As much as you, I hate that sort of unhealthy religious attitude, but we both know as literary critics that the image and the allegory belong to the Christian tradition, and can be accepted without any morbid feeling ... But in the Windhover, Hopkins is meditating on Christ's Incarnation and on the glory He gained by humbling Himself to our manhood.

As to the notion that the poem takes a poker to the embers, Ritz noted:

Of course, a poker is terribly prosaic and you were not slow to see it. It is obvious that I have no need of it. I was only a victim to my French love of logic and esthetic parallelism,—something like this, if you like:

> Sheer plodding makes plough shine down sillion
> Mere poking makes embers glow gold-vermilion.

However, he closed: 'I humbly submit that my explanation is as near as possible to what Hopkins means to say, and a little nearer to it than former explanations. No wonder of it: all former critics helped me to see more clearly into the matter.'

TO J. G. RITZ

Sheffield University
16 December 1955

Dear Mr Ritz,

It is now the end of my term's work, and I really must send the promised reply to your letter. I wrote a long draft some weeks ago,[3] and then thought I had better keep it and think the matter over. It is gloomy work because I cannot expect any friendly agreement; I seriously think your view both historically and morally wrong; I think there is a permanent bad element inherent in Christianity which is just now being dragged rather danger-ously into the forefront, and that you in your view of the Hopkins poem are one of the unwitting agents of this process. I realise that you must think it offensive of me to drag all this fuss into a tiny scholarly problem, but I cannot see it otherwise.

You say that the falcon swooping onto its prey is by that act a symbol of Christ humbling himself to our manhood, and that this is a Christian tradition familiar to those properly informed. I think this is a distortion of human sentiment so hideous that it recalls the slogans of George Orwell's *1984*, and by the way people do not realise that that book was meant to

[3] The draft, dated 27 Nov. 1955, was printed (in part) in *A*, 335–7.

attack any system of power through inquisition, Christian quite as much as Communist. You say 'Christians have long accepted the image as depicting God's power over souls', and of course I agree that Hopkins did feel and write about this power. But he did not think this power 'identical with' the act of Christ in humbling himself to accept manhood, and if you pretend he did you are merely making a monstrous '1984' paradox, such as 'Love is Torture'. I do not only think it nasty, I also think, as a matter of history, that Hopkins would have been very much shocked to hear what you say.

You say 'What other basic assumptions than mine are the *strictest* adherence to Hopkins' own words and images?' Probably the word image is the source of confusion here, because in your exegesis you start with the symbol of the falcon as an ancient and already many-sided Christian tradition. But the poem does not do this; it evidently starts by describing a real accidental event, and then says what the poet thought after being moved by its beauty. When you insist that the falcon must have swooped and caught some food there is really no adherence to the words of the poem, not even a very loose one; you could only claim 'an adherence to the *image*', that is, the symbol. It seems clear to me that if Hopkins, who was a rather excessively sensitive man, had actually seen the bird catching prey he would only have been moved as he would have been moved by seeing a stoat catching a rabbit; he would only have felt disgust, I hope I don't have to explain.

As to the poker, I certainly did not mean as you suggest that it is too 'unpoetical' to be present; I thought it spoilt the *logic* of the poem (and really this is not an objection which only a Frenchman would make) because the beauty produced by the activity of the bird and the plough are both incidental or God-given results of learning a hard skill; whereas poking a fire is neither skilled nor prolonged nor unintentionally beautiful; it has nothing to do with the matter. On the other hand the image of the surface of half-burnt coal which falls in, because the inner fire has eaten away its support, at a random moment (as by the accident of the dedicated poet seeing the violent beauty of the bird), and thus making the brilliance of the inner fire suddenly obvious—this seems to me so beautiful and so naturally true that I cannot understand your refusal to understand it. I am driven to think that you suppose that God, whose only pleasure is gloating over torture, cannot endure waiting any longer for this bit of torture, so he takes a poker to it.

Please do not think I am trivial because I force the point till it sounds like a joke; I am really shocked, and by a general trend not only this one case. The effect of the quarrel between Christians and Communists seems to be that they egg each other on to exactly the same disastrous results.

Yours very sincerely

W. Empson[4]

Houghton, bMS Eng 1401 (637)

§ END

TO IAN PARSONS ['The Birth of Steel']

Department of English Literature, The University, Sheffield 10
6 November 1954

My dear Ian,

Thinking over my useless reply, why shouldn't you end my Collected Poems with the Masque for the Queen at Sheffield University? It is I believe the first time English royalty has been given the real old flattery for three hundred years—Minerva descends and says she is identical with Elizabeth, addressing her personally, and creates the steel industry; in effect the Queen is told in person that, besides being a spirit universally diffused, she herself personally invented the entire technology of the steel industry. The Queen thought it funny and was sweet about it, to me and the composer (the music was terrific) and the two speaking parts. It isn't meant to be good poetry but it's somehow politically right (I mean, it combines queen-worship with pro-worker sentiment and fair claims for the university back-room boys) and it is really rather a curiosity. It is only about four pages. Now that it has gone off so very well (though unknown outside Sheffield) I don't see why it shouldn't be put in the book.

Thus you might hold up publication till next year to do that, if you want a big list next year. But maybe it is technically too inconvenient by this time to add four more pages.[1]

Yours

Bill Empson.

Congratulations and thanks from the Queen and the Lord Mayor of Sheffield and I don't know who not might even pad out the Notes.

Reading

---

[4] See also *MG*, 231–2.

[1] *CP*, including WE's masque *The Birth of Steel*, was published in an edition of 2,400 copies by Chatto & Windus on 29 September 1955.

PARTISAN REVIEW, 21: 6 (November–December 1954), 698, 700,
'Empson, Adams, and Milton'

In an essay on WE's 'Milton and Bentley' (*SVP*) entitled 'Empson and
Bentley: Something About Milton Too' (*Partisan Review*, 21: 1 [Mar.–Apr.
1954], 178–89), Robert Martin Adams[1] evokes WE as 'wild but willing'. He
goes on: 'Empson's account of Bentley is impressively inaccurate verbally.
Though he makes some point of quoting originals, he seems to quote
largely from memory, and inaccurately at that . . .

'Rather more disconcerting than these pervasive and sometimes purposeful slips is Empson's habit of attributing to Bentley or Pearce phrases
and ideas of his own invention . . .'

As for Milton, Empson stretches the poet on a Procrustes' bed: 'The
violations of decorum which Milton evidently considered somewhere
between the natural, the tolerable, and the necessary, and which angered
Bentley into the hypothesis of an editor, Empson treats as positive virtues.
Whether Milton wanted an incongruity, or couldn't avoid it, or was
unaware of it, Empson is eager to see an unintentional richness in the
poem; and I suppose one sounds ungrateful or petulant in refusing to see
what he's dug up with such spaniel vivacity . . .'

More specifically, with respect to the resources of Milton's epic: 'Empson
finds it easiest to ignore elements which don't serve his purpose, even
when—especially when—they do serve Milton's. He is enthralled by the
subconscious motives which apparently enabled Milton to write an interesting poem in spite of himself . . . Milton, if he had expected his poem to be
read by detailed analysis of the imagery, would certainly have written it very
differently than he did. He would not have written an epic at all, he would
have written a Euphuistic romance . . . His unit of thought and expression,
within which images are fitted and arranged (and from which Empson
vigorously extracts them), is the verse paragraph . . . There's something
profoundly frustrating about a man who insists on investigating a giraffe as
if it were a rabbit oddly botched in the making . . .

'Bentley wanted to do away with the pastoral elements in the poetry
because they disturbed the character Milton was forced to assume. Empson
muddles Milton's need to do away with them by suggesting a simple regret
for Elizabethan hey nonny nonny which is really a more complex and
inclusive melancholy, for a lost synthesis of virtue and grace, for a series of
organized stock responses, for an architecture of the emotions . . . *Paradise*

---

[1] Robert Martin Adams (1915–96), critic, editor, and translator, taught at Cornell University,
1950–68, and was later Professor of English at the University of California, LA. His works
include *Ikon: John Milton and the Modern Critics*, (1955), which reprints this essay as 'Empson and
Bentley: *Scherzo*' (112–27), *Stendhal: Notes on a Novelist* (1959), *After Joyce: Studies in Fiction after
'Ulysses'* (1977). He was a founding editor of the *Norton Anthology of English Literature* (1962).

Lost is one of the first pastorals which express nostalgia for the good old days when life was complex and harmonious instead of simple and disorderly. Reading Empson, one can't help feeling that the chaotic uniformity of his responses largely justifies the melancholy of Milton's conclusion.'

Sirs:

I hope it is not too late to offer some comments on the article by R. M. Adams in your March–April number, about my essay on Milton and Bentley. No doubt he is right in finding so many copying errors; I wish I had known about them before the second edition, when the type was cast. I copied out my Bentley and Pearce quotations in the British Museum and wrote the essay in Tokyo; certainly I ought to have remembered to check them later on, when I could. But I do not see that the mistakes he quotes make much difference. Indeed, this idea of checking your quotations as an absolute duty is fairly recent, and not always relevant; for instance Hazlitt habitually quoted from memory, and commonly a bit wrong, but he was writing very good criticism. When I was building an argument on a detail of the text I would be keen on getting the detail right while I was looking at it, but not otherwise. I hope this does not sound insolently casual; actually, I have to put an absurd amount of time into trying to write decent prose, so that the reader can get the point without bother, whereas Hazlitt apparently could do it at his first shot. What I do submit is that a critic is spending his time better if he does that than if he struggles for the degree of accuracy which is rightly expected from a textual editor.

What is more serious about Mr Adams' article is the claim that I was giving a harmful account of *Paradise Lost*, actually spoiling the poem for my more trustful readers; by the 'chaotic uniformity of my responses', 'treating a giraffe as a rabbit oddly botched in the making', and so on. But I wasn't telling anybody how to read it, except on the one issue about 'pastoral' where Mr Adams appears to agree with me. By the way, I can't see why there is any separate problem about Imagery in Epics, though of course I agree that an author shouldn't be saddled with meanings that are irrelevant to his style and purpose; only you must call it bad writing if they thrust themselves in. I agree that the quaint bits of animus against women, which the Bentley treatment makes prominent, are rather deflating to the poem, and perhaps I made too much fuss about them; but a reader ought not to have to protect his innocence from seeing the lapses of Milton. In the poem as a whole, these bits of nagging are swept aside by the tremendous speech of appeal from Eve to Adam which saves the situation of mankind. But it is not only that one feels they were in the mind of Milton;

historically they are part of the movement away from medieval ideas such as chivalry; and one needs I think to appreciate *Paradise Lost* as a monumental summing-up of the way the mind of Europe was going, Counter-Reformation as well as Reformation. Something has obviously gone very wrong with Milton's God, too, but he didn't invent that either; the human mind is splendid but appalling, and what you are getting here is a massive specimen of one of the ways it can go. The poem needs I think to be regarded rather like Aztec or Benin sculpture, invigorating as well as marvellous but clearly produced by a sickening ideology and social practice. I did not say this in my essay, partly because I was concerned with something else, but also because it has been obvious ever since it was said by Blake and Shelley. Nowadays we get these Neo critics [New Critics], who apparently demand that you must sink your self totally in the art-work when viewing it. I would say that my approach is more 'total' than Mr Adams', not less as he implies; you need to see both sides of the thing; it is out of place to feel a tender regret for the imperial but appalling court of Benin.

Also I don't think I need have been blamed, at the end of his article, for suggesting that Milton (in his turn) had merely 'a simple regret for Elizabethan hey-nonny-nonny' rather than for a dignity which was more remote. Considering that this hey-nonny-nonny included the plays of Shakespeare, and that Milton's party had closed the theatres, it doesn't seem out of place to remark that his direct experience gave him something to go on for the weird deep melancholy with which he continually clashes together the loss of Eden and the pagan world.

William Empson

Houghton: drafted 12 August 1954

ESSAYS IN CRITICISM, 5: 1 (January 1955), 88–90: 'Yes and No'

I felt much interest in the last number of *Essays in Criticism*, and perhaps I may send some rather scattered remarks on it.

I join the side which thinks that returning to the old rhetorical terms would only do us harm, but I agree that our present pet word 'image' is grossly confusing. To begin with, as is soon evident if you see the writing of students, people who accept it as meaning a picture in the mind become seriously liable to miss the point of whatever they read. *What* 'image', now, 'underlies' the 'zeugma' of

> Or stain her honour, or her new brocade?

Certainly, her attitude to her reputation for chastity is compared with her attitude to her reputation for dress—both are vain, conventional, super-ficial, and yet both are suitable to her position in life, natural, in a way touching. But is a picture of a brocade in the mind anything but an obstacle, to a person trying to catch all that at one shot? We know that people vary very much in how far they use visual images, but the only practical need seems to be to give a warning to the excessive imagists.

I agree with the article on Dylan Thomas but want to remark that the whole point of the poem 'A Refusal To Mourn The Death Of A Child By Fire' [*sic*] gets left out; quite possibly, as so often happens in criticism, because it was thought too obvious to mention. Dylan was deeply horrified by the raids, and by Hitler, but was also determined not to let his art become propaganda, not even against Hitler. The Refusal in the title of the poem was really *that* refusal, and the poem becomes much better if you read it so, though the text of it, with a very decent consistency, refuses to say that.

I agree with everything in the article about *The Golden Bowl*, except its interpretation of the results. Henry James I think was morally a very confused man, and anyhow it seems impossible to deny that his attitude to sexual passion was confused.[1] Even though his mind insisted (as the article rightly showed) on building up a sickeningly horrible case against both father and daughter Verver, still he was telling himself he was doing what his father would have wanted, that is, showing how the good cool rich Americans can subdue the savagery of the wicked Europeans. Towards the end of the book, far too much cuddling of dear old Verver by the author is going on for me to believe that James ever admitted to himself what a loathsome picture he was presenting to the outside world. Indeed, if this were not so, the disagreement among critics (which the article admitted with a mild surprise) could never have arisen. No doubt it is hard to say how one arrives at a critical decision when the field is so large; but I have actually come across that kind of puzzle, especially in the reactions of Chinese professors to the Rockefeller Foundation visitors, and the reason *why* I think that James, though he was a wonderful reporter or recorder, did not understand what he was saying there is that it is only now begin-ning to be realised by the American mind. James does not show any sign of thinking himself such a startling moral innovator as he would have to be before telling himself he meant what your critic very properly regards as the only sensible meaning the book would have.

[1] Cf. *MG*, 27: 'I certainly do not know when Henry James is good; I always feel sure he is jabbering away like that only to make the reader as hopelessly confused about the rights and wrongs of the case as he is himself.'

THE OBSERVER, 9 January 1955, 2: 'Thomas and Thompson'

Geoffrey Grigson, in a letter to *The Observer* ('Thomas and Thompson', 2 January 1955, 2), declared his dislike for the poetry of Dylan Thomas. The incompetent Thomas indulged a 'Victorian pastiche'; he 'derives . . . from the two poets he liked most of all when I first knew him. These were James Thompson (B. V.) and Francis Thompson. The prototype of the Thomas line and manner and matter anyone can find who troubles to examine Francis Thompson's "Ode to the Setting Sun" . . .

'The Thomas and Thompson situations are oddly and instructively alike. Francis Thompson was accepted because the public required a figure or wild pet to represent the Genius of Poetry, and because an apparent novelty and energy did not really contradict a pre-existent pattern; he wrote extraordinary nonsense with extraordinary incompetence (in most of his poems), frequently about life, death and birth, in a grandiose poetic language.'

Sir,—The ideas of Mr Grigson about verse have long seemed to me very odd, and they do again in his letter which you published last week. Why does he think he proves that Dylan Thomas is bad by saying that he 'derives from' Francis Thompson? The literal statement that Francis Thompson is 'now justly and altogether disregarded' can be refuted by any person who says, as I do, that he is not disregarded by me. Its meaning must therefore be of a more subtle or modish kind—Mr Grigson not only establishes a current fashion, but also asserts it as an eternal truth.

Francis Thompson was a good influence on English poets, and was rightly recognised as one by the time he died in 1907, because he brought back the peculiar merits of the seventeenth-century 'metaphysicals' in a usable form—long before Mr T. S. Eliot did, for example. He was very much a Roman Catholic author, whereas Dylan Thomas wrote with equal conviction from some kind of pantheism; so that any apparent identities would be meant to be read as unlike. But I have no doubt that Dylan Thomas was greatly influenced by him, like all the other good poets after his time.

Yours faithfully,

W. Empson

Thomas's poetry is not bad because it derives from Thompson, responded Grigson (16 Jan. 1955, 2); 'I think [it] is bad because of a muddle of badly manipulated images, which are often frigid, false and sentimental. I think it bad for the bad ear it reveals, for bad lines faltering from cliché rhythms into flatness, for cheapness, and profundity which is not profound; above all, for lack of a grown-up and masterly execution.

'As for Dylan Thomas and Francis Thompson, it is an example only of like deriving from like, a badness from a similar badness, without improvement . . . No one should be scared by Professor Empson into believing in the "good influence" of Francis Thompson . . . If "all the good poets" since Thompson's day have been so "greatly influenced" by him who on earth are they? Is there a Geiger counter which can detect this great influence in the later poems of Yeats, in the poems of John Gray, T. S. Eliot, Wyndham Lewis, Marianne Moore, D. H. Lawrence, Robert Graves, James Elroy Flecker, Edward Thomas, Andrew Young, John Crowe Ransom, W. H. Auden, Norman Cameron, Louis MacNeice, E. J. Scovell, Richard Wilbur, Drummond Allison, John Wain? Beyond a touch of Crashaw degraded and sentimentalised, what peculiar merits of which metaphysical poet did Francis Thompson restore?'

THE OBSERVER, 23 January 1955, 2

Sir,—Surely the list of poets sent last week by Mr Grigson does not affect the matter. During the last fifty years the technique of the 'metaphysicals' has come to seem usable again (whether it is called 'Crashaw degraded' or not); even the poets who reacted against this movement were affected by it; and Francis Thompson was a pioneer of it, as was recognised when he died in 1907.

However, I agree that Dylan Thomas is in one way specially like him; both are ecstatic and (though careful about form) throw their theme into language pretty recklessly. This courage makes them sometimes catch high and sometimes fall badly. Maybe the real difference between my opinion and Mr. Grigson's is that I bother only about the poems I think good, whereas he likes to bay at the moon about the ones he thinks bad.

It might be an improvement if all critics, especially when writing about Shakespeare, were forced to use the grammatical form, 'I think him good when writing like this and bad when writing like that.' But the process would work out wrong if it did not reach agreement that a lot of Dylan Thomas is very good, and quite a bit of Francis Thompson.

May I congratulate you, Sir, on your sensible leader last week about Mrs Knight, which seems somehow relevant here.[1]

---

[1] The leader in question, 'Morals' (*The Observer*, 16 Jan. 1955, 6), defended Mrs Margaret Knight's right to broadcast her rationalist views: 'Mrs Margaret Knight's broadcast talks on "Morals without Religion" have been attacked in some newspapers with brutal vehemence. She has been headlined as "The Unholy Mrs Knight," compared in a cartoon with a horned devil at the microphone, and told by her politer critics that her pernicious and affronting opinions should not be allowed on the air.

'We deplore these displays of intolerance, more especially since they claim to be inspired by Christianity.'

TO BONAMY DOBRÉE

Department of English Literature, The University, Sheffield
6 May 1955

My dear Bonamy,

How splendid it is that you have the world at your feet just now when you retire with all your good health sense and temper firmly about you. I have two reasons for writing apart from my natural desire to express my pleasure at the spectacle. I have been teased about the poet W. S. Graham, in pubs in London, and urged to get onto you at once, but then I heard that the decision about the resident poet in Leeds had already been made; and I was already aware that my position in the matter was weak, because what I could say for the poet Graham was only what I was certain you had already considered.[1] All the same, I have met the poet Graham and like him, and know that he isn't a drunkard if that's the problem, and think he ought to be first on the list for next year if he had missed this one.[2] But the appointment isn't much of a career, somehow, is it? The duties the young feel are so arduous; I am sure he felt it was his duty on meeting you as an employer to get drunk and make a quarrel. I do not know why a willing employer should be expected to have any patience with this compulsion. You also said once, what I have never repeated at all, that you meant to make George Fraser your successor. I suspect that remark was only a playful bit of rivalry between two professors, because I had just been explaining to you my total failure to get George on my staff at Sheffield.

---

[1] W. S. Graham (1918–86), Scottish poet, was born in Greenock, Renfrewshire, and trained as an engineer; he was given initial support by the publisher and philanthropist David Archer and was later taken up by TSE at Faber & Faber. From 1944 he lived mostly in Cornwall. His works include *Cage Without Grievances* (1942), *The White Threshold* (1949), *The Nightfishing* (1955), *Malcolm Moony's Land* (1970), *Implements in their Places* (1977), *Collected Poems, 1942–1977* (1979).

[2] Philip Hobsbaum, while researching for his Ph.D. under WE, coined the concept of the 'Misreadable Poem', meaning a poem so deeply obscure that no meaning could be shown to be valid. In 1961 he cited as a case in point W. S. Graham's 'The Nightfishing', claiming that it was too obscure to be fathomed. WE made interesting stabs at glossing the poem for Hobsbaum; and in response to the complaint that Graham had sacrificed structure to local poetic effect, he devised a generous aphorism—'good texture can be seen first and makes one decide that a meaning is worth looking for'—before falling back on giving his opinion of Graham: 'He agreed to do a piece for the BBC about his home village, mostly in prose, and returned to the village for the purpose; but annoyed the BBC by failing to produce it after the hour had been advertised. Really I think he has been fighting like a cat to get out of the home village and being a fisherman, but he recognizes, in a way, that this is the only interesting material he has, to make himself into an author with. I suspect that that conflict is what makes him incoherent, not anything about philosophy. A nice chap and a genuine talent, however distorted.

'I think he could write good poetry, because this feels so like good poetry. But I have to agree with you I don't think it comes through.' ('Empson as teacher: the Sheffield years', in *William Empson: The Critical Achievement*, ed. Norris and Mapp (1993), 301–3.)

But this joke, if it was only a joke, was a great deal more sensible than you thought. George Fraser really would be a good appointment. I hear that the poets to whom he is always being kind are always suspecting that he is playing some deep plot, merely *because* he is always doing justice and acting as sensibly as he can all the time. And of course his mind is *capable* of knowing enough to do justice. He has a number of languages, and the only reason why he hasn't better academic qualifications is simply that he was conscripted to the Second World War; he never let up on his education, even when the editor [Fraser himself] of the Eritrean Times was called the Dirtiest White in Cairo (still a sergeant therefore not let in to Shepards). You know all this and will be more doubtful about his period of madness. My opinion, knowing him well, is that he would be absolutely all right in Leeds. I would rather have him out of London because there he can't stop looking after too many lame dogs all the time. Perhaps this letter is off the point because there is no real question of the appointment. But I want to remind you that it would be the most distinguished appointment possible for Leeds.

Hoping to see you soon.

William Empson.

Leeds

THE TIMES, 23 June 1955: 'Future of the Masque'

Sir,—Your Music Critic's article discussed whether 'the masque has a future,' and said that it must take a modest form if it is to survive in the modern world. Sheffield University did one this year [*The Birth of Steel*], for the visit of the Queen to inaugurate its Jubilee anniversary, and we now hear that no British reigning sovereign has been so received since the Stuarts. The doubts of your Critic have therefore an historical basis, but we do not think they have any other.

We followed the old formula without inhibitions, assuring Her Majesty that she herself personally had invented the entire technology of the steel industry, which she was touring at the time; and this, with its opportunities for splendour, seems to have been felt as a proper way to treat the occasion. The performance took just under 15 minutes, and no doubt that old full length would have been thought too much. But, apart from that, we did not find that the modern world requires 'modesty' in a masque. We actually puzzled our heads over this question, and the modern world turned out to think that the more knock-down the show could be the better.

Yours, &c.,

William Empson, author; Gilbert Kennedy, composer; Peter Cheeseman, producer.

NEW STATESMAN AND NATION, 25 June 1955, 894:
'Better English'

T. C. Worsley,[1] in a review of G. H. Vallins's *Better English* (1955), protested: 'In the later part of his book Mr Vallins seeks to make pedantry the master in spheres where it should be a domestic servant. Indeed I increasingly wondered, as I read on, whether he is fit to be trusted even with the lower forms, so insensitive is his response to the values—as opposed to the rules— of language . . . Let me take, as an example of Mr Vallins's blindness to these values, a sample from the chapter headed "The Turgid and the Turbid," where he quotes—besides extracts from Pritchett, Graves, Empson and Critic—a large slice of Worsley, describing it as "a passage abounding in small errors and ambiguities." ' ('Dead from the Waist Down', *New Statesman and Nation*, 49 (18 Jun. 1955, 859–60), 859)

Sir,—May I testify, just to support Mr Worsley in his remarks on Mr Vallins, that the bits of my prose which Mr Vallins blamed in *Good English* had been written with particular care, chiefly to avoid misunderstanding in the reader, and that I thought the complaints against them wrong-headed.

TO CLEANTH BROOKS*

In response to WE's book-review 'Still the Strange Necessity' (*Sewanee Review*, 63: 3 (Summer 1955), 471–9; in *A*, 120–7)—which included adverse critical consideration of *The Verbal Icon*, by W. K. Wimsatt, Jr.—Cleanth Brooks wrote to the *Sewanee Review* (63: 4 (Fall 1955), 696–7):

> Mr William Empson tells us that he had 'long felt uneasy about Mr Wimsatt's drive against what he calls the Fallacy of Intentionalism' . . . I must confess that for my part I have long felt uneasy about the kind of impression that is exhibited throughout Mr Empson's essay.

[1] Cuthbert Worsley (1907–1977) , author and schoolmaster, volunteered during the Spanish Civil War to work in an ambulance unit. His publications include *Behind the Battle* (1939), *Flannelled Fool* (1967), and *Fellow Travellers*, a fictionalized memoir (1971).

The impressionism comes to a kind of high point in the remarks that Mr Empson makes about the photograph reproduced on the jacket of *The Verbal Icon*. To Mr Empson, Wimsatt looks like 'a mastodon rising with dripping fangs [tusks?] from some primeval swamp.' But if the publisher had omitted the picture, would Mr Empson have written a different review? Would the omission have removed a bit of evidence relevant to Mr Empson's estimate of the book—or merely a temptation for him to digress? . . . It is interesting to follow the course of [Empson's] mental history—the shifting impressions, the burgeoning doubts and fears, the confirmation of things that he had long felt uneasy about. Because his brilliant career is part of the intellectual history of our times . . . it is important that his latest impressions be made a matter of record—especially the mellowing of some former astringencies and the decisive repudiation of certain positions that he once held and may even be said to have pioneered.

Studio House, Hampstead Hill Gardens, London, NW3
16 September 1955

Dear Cleanth Brooks,

Your letter to the *Sewanee* has been sent to me, and I thought I would like to send a private letter, though in print I am content to leave you the honours of good taste. I felt while writing it that the review seemed conceited and ill-tempered, but felt I could not avoid that without failing to tell the truth.

As to the man's [W. K. Wimsatt's] face, which you suggest is not his fault, I made clear that I didn't believe in it, because what I blamed him for was striking such an absurd pose for the camera. It is interesting to hear from you that the photographer probably chose it, and not the author; but I still think it unduly innocent of the author to put up with such an absurd fashion. The attempt of the theories against Intentionalism and so forth is I think to put literary criticism in a pseudo-scientific strait-jacket, and I certainly thought this long before I saw the picture; but I think the picture illustrates it very strikingly, even if it only expresses the yearning of the photographer to portray an Oil Baron. I gave about sixty words to the picture and at least twenty times as much to criticising the book; when you say there is no criticism of the book, I naturally suspect that you cannot answer what there was.

I do not know why you say that I have decisively abandoned some old positions that I may be said to have pioneered; I do not think I have abandoned any; but in any case I would always have been against any pig-headed cast-iron dogmatic position such as the Rejection of

Intentionalism. The reason for putting in so much about 'Empson thought years ago' and suchlike, which you naturally find self-important, as I felt myself, was that I wanted to insist that I really had not changed my mind.

As to 'impressionism', I seriously do think that a critic is no good unless he has impressions; and relies on them, apart from the processes of checking and making sure which nobody has argued against in principle. My book on Ambiguity, if I may go back to that, continually said that the analyses were only supposed to show what happened in the mind of the fit reader (and there were plenty of such readers). To say that the reader ought to abandon all attempt to use his imagination, especially in imagining what the author intended (but must instead follow rules laid down by some master critic) seems to me to abandon the whole instrument which is all we have for appreciating works of art. I still think the photograph very well suited to the whole subject.

Yours sincerely
William Empson

Yale: YCAL MSS 30 (Cleanth Brooks Papers), Box 3, folder 85

MANDRAKE, 2: 11 (Autumn and Winter 1955–6)

Dear Sir,

An article on my literary criticism[1] in *Mandrake* Vol. II No. 10, questions the sincerity of my book *Complex Words*, and perhaps not to answer it might seem letting the case go by default to some readers whose opinions I would value. So I will try, though it is hard to answer such flimsy stuff without being ruder than I care to, and sounding more excited than it deserves.

After a few flourishes about my cynicism, my irresponsibility, my affectation of 'toughness', my undergraduate 'm'enfoutisme' and what not, the poisoned barb is stuck with an unobtrusive deftness into the reader's mind:

> 'In general, it is difficult not to believe that Mr Empson is not aware that his latest work is in many ways a solemn joke, a joke intended to disturb one by its display of erudition,' etc. [330]

I fancy the author forgot to cross out one of his negatives, or failed to count them on his fingers; but perhaps he was in an ecstasy of subtlety. In any case, he says that my book was 'intended' to produce these effects, which must have been done by me.

---

[1] Geoffrey Strickland, 'The Criticism of William Empson', *Mandrake*, 2: 10 (Autumn–Winter 1954–5), 320–31. Strickland (1931–96) was Reader in French at Reading, and a founding editor of *Cambridge Quarterly*.

What I feel about the book, if there is any doubt, is easily told. I think it is wonderful; I think it goes up like a great aeroplane. A certain amount of noisy taxi-ing round the field at the start may be admitted, and the landing at the end is bumpy though without causing damage; but the power of the thing and the view during its flight I consider magnificent. When after long struggle it began to 'come out' I was astonished at its unity, at the way so many lines of effort which had felt somehow significant really did fit in (this must be what my critic takes to be its dreary paucity of ideas). When it was done I felt Nunc Dimittis; I was free, I was ready to die. I was to fly with the text from Peking to Ohio, where some final checking in libraries might well be done, and it was reasonable to leave at Peking a fully corrected spare text in case of accident. There was little reason for alarm, but having to do this made me notice the firmness of my sentiments; I did not care about anything as long as the book got printed. This is disagreeably like writing an advertisement for myself, but consider how much more disagreeable it is for me to be told that I was cooking up a fatuously tiresome mass of spoof, licking my lips over the hope of jeering at anybody who was fool enough to take it seriously. The meanmindedness of anybody who can believe I did that feels to me quite sickening.

I would now like to offer a placid discussion on some general points, but it is hard to get hold of any. I think a critic should have an insight into the mind of his author, and I don't approve of the attack on 'The Fallacy of Intentionalism'; but I am not sure on which side of that fence your critic wants to poke out his nose. As to his accusation that I have a cult of no prejudices, which only encourages rootlessnesses, I would be more impressed if I had not also been accused of stubborn prejudice—'*Why* do you imagine that you know these things?' and so on. To give both good and bad examples using the same technical device is I think obviously not the same as offering a metaphysic with no values. As to the suggestion that I must be 'naïve' if I admire some passages in Swinburne, because anybody who is in the know knows that there is a rule against Swinburne— that strikes me as painfully naïve. After some experience of Communists, it is not so much they as this school of critics whom I would accuse of insisting upon the letter of their arid formula, and taking for granted that any man who does not use it is either a fool or a knave.

There is now a painful duty before me; a simple *tu quoque* needs to be said. I think it an 'alarming portent', to borrow a stock phrase of this school, when I come home and find sheer platoons of pompous young men, each of them mouthing and leering and insinuating and displaying his donnish 'intimacy' in precisely the same manner, a manner in which he has been drilled. Wherever the eye hits, on any page written by one of these indistinguishable young men, it receives an immediate impression of farcical insincerity.

Yours, etc.

W. Empson

TO LESLIE FIEDLER*

[n.d.: 1955–6]

My dear Fiedler,

Not long ago I did a letter to the London magazine Encounter [edited by Stephen Spender and Irving Kristol], in the course of a controversy about the Chinese sociologist Fei Hsiao Tung;[1] the controversy had entered its second round, after a reply from the American [Karl A.] Wittfogel, and was reaching more general issues about free speech etc.[2] I find the editors cut out my final paragraph [written on 23 August 1955], which refers to yourself, so I shall post it to you. I said:

> I see that dear Mr Fiedler is still carrying on in your magazine. Since it began, he has been positively praising whatever the reader is likely to think most disgusting in America at the moment; this time it isn't a monstrous legal killing, as in your first number, but only horror comics. Everybody likes a man to be gallant, but I don't think you are on to a really good line there. People might begin to think

---

[1] The case of the distinguished social anthropologist Fei Hsiao-t'ung/Fei Xiaotong (1910–2005) became a test of WE's contention that China's intelligentsia had not yet been clubbed into conformity by the Ideological Remoulding campaign of 1951–2. WE had known Fei since before the Liberation, and believed him to be a conscientious person as well as an outspoken critic of the political and social policies of the Nationalist Government. Educated at Yenching (Yanjing) and Tsinghua (Qinghua) Universities, Fei had also studied under Bronislaw Malinowski at the London School of Economics, where he gained his Ph.D. His landmark study, *Peasant Life in China* (1939), appeared with an enthusiastic preface by Malinowski. In 1943 he lectured and pursued research at Harvard and Chicago, and at the Institute of Pacific Relations in New York; and in 1946 he again visited England under the auspices of the British Council to work at the LSE. After the Communist victory, his posts included membership of the culture and education committee of the Government Administration Council. In June 1951 he was appointed vice-president of the Central Institute for National Minorities in Peking. Though a non-Communist who made known his misgivings about moves to substitute pragmatism for systematic theoretical research, he was yet volubly 'progressive' and assented to the effort involved in developing the requisite proletarian consciousness.

[2] Karl August Wittfogel (1897–1988) was an orientalist scholar and Director of the Chinese History Project at Columbia University. See 'China—Then and Now (II)', *Encounter* 4: 1 (Jan. 1955), 78–80; WE, 'Fei Hsiao-tung' (letter), *Encounter* 5: 2 (Aug. 1955), 74; Wittfogel, 'Fei Hsiao-tung' (letter), *Encounter* 5: 2 (Aug. 1955), 74–75; WE, 'Fei Hsiao-tung' (letter), *Encounter* 5: 6 (Nov. 1955), 60.

you were taking advantage of the young man's innocence, or something.[3]

In view of your book title [*An End to Innocence*, 1955] saying that people who disagree with *you* are innocent, you understand, the final crack seemed fair comment. I agree that the article you gave the magazine on Walt Whitman, for instance, doesn't come under this head; but I think it probably true that you don't realise the whole position.

It is widely understood over here that the magazine is taking foreign gold for an attempt to affect opinion in England. Thus when you, for example, tell your views to the British public in it, you do so by foreign subsidy, presumably because they wouldn't sell on their own merits; and it is not only in my own case that the magazine has refused to print the retorts of the English reader.[4] The Americans wouldn't like such an arrangement any more than the English do.

By the way, a letter has arrived for the magazine from Fei Hsiao Tung himself in Peking, answering the accusations of Wittvogel [*sic*], and at least one number has passed without printing it.[5]

I thought it was fair to keep you informed about the matter, and I am sending a copy of this letter to the editor.

Yours very sincerely

W. Empson.

Houghton carbon

Leslie Fiedler's riposte to WE (18 January 1956) included: 'We can afford to be frank with each other. There is, at least, no point in your posing as an objective, fair-minded, somewhat patriotic English citizen appalled at American propaganda. From my memories of your extraordinary speech at Bloomington [the Indiana Summer School, 1954], I am convinced that your arguments must be considered as those of an apologist for a particular point of view . . . A man who believes the cooked-up reports about germ warfare in Korea would be willing to believe anything . . .

   'I not only did *not* support the execution of the Rosenbergs, but the main

---

[3] See two essays by Leslie Fiedler published in *Encounter*: 'A Postscript to the Rosenberg Case' (Oct. 1953); 'The Middle Against Both Ends' (Aug. 1955).

[4] Stephen Spender told Fiedler he had cut the paragraph criticizing Fiedler's articles from WE's letter because it had 'no connection with the main purport' of the letter; he sought to reassure him too, 'Irving Kristol and I are completely responsible for the policy of this magazine' (letter, 9 Jan. 1956; copy in Houghton)—albeit that just over a month after publishing Fiedler's piece on the Rosenbergs he conceded that he thought Fiedler's piece betrayed 'rather obvious anti-communism' (quoted in John Sutherland, *Stephen Spender: The Authorized Biography* (2004), 372).

[5] See Fei Hsiao-tung, letter to the editors, *Encounter* 6: 2 (Feb. 1956), 68–9.

point of my essay was an explanation of why they should have been spared. As for my piece on Popular Culture, it quite specifically states that my attack on the opponents of the comics is not to be construed as a defence of the comics themselves . . .' (*Houghton*)

He added by hand, at the foot of the page: 'It occurs to me that you may not have read my articles at all—and were simply playing it by ear!'

TO LESLIE FIEDLER

Department of English Literature, The University, Sheffield 10
10 February 1956

Dear Fiedler,

Thank you for your letter. I was interested by the footnote in red pencil, saying that your two articles were attacks on their subjects, not defences of them as I thought, so probably I was 'playing by ear'. I certainly did read them at the time (it would be too much to go and look them up now), and what I said was not only the impression I got but what other people said when they mentioned the articles to me. Indeed, as I only claimed to be reporting the English reaction to them, in my letter to you, I might still be right though I *had* been playing only by ear. No such article can be purely pro or con, unless very narrow, and I daresay the proportion seemed quite different to you from what it did to the English reader. If so, it was just as well to tell you.

There is one thing I feel I should try to make clear; so far as I know, I haven't changed my opinions about politics since I was a young man. At that time Spender was shouting away on the Left-Wing band-wagon, and I was commonly called reactionary. He is now shouting like you on the reactionary or pro-American band-wagon, whereas I am just where I was; and still think myself free to speak up whenever there is too much non-sense being talked on either side. I hope this partly relieves the fears you expressed for my future.

As to 'foreign gold', of course I didn't mean to reproach you for taking it; I have often been employed abroad myself. I was asking you to realise the point of view of the English reader, and one would think the English editor. The magazine is generally understood to be supported by UNESCO, that is, largely by American money; and it is evidently very pro-American. This set-up is liable to be resented, so that it works out as anti-propaganda. It seems rather friendly of me, really, to warn you of that.

Going back to my 'extraordinary' speech at Bloomington, you must remember that Churchill had just flown over to Washington to try to prevent the Americans from causing a world war over Indo-China; at least, the English thought he did, and succeeded in it. Meanwhile I was made to sign an affidavit, as a condition for my visa to lecture at Bloomington, that I would 'support American policy', that is, act as a traitor to my own country for American pay. At a time when the two countries were seriously disagreeing about foreign policy the demand could hardly be regarded otherwise; and what I think extraordinary is that the Americans can make such demands without realising that foreigners feel they ought to be resisted. The point about my wearing my Communist uniform, as I hope I made clear, was not that I had one (a matter of no interest) but that Churchill had paid me to have one, all through the Korean War; I thought this would make everybody realise that the foreign policies of our two countries were actually different. Hence it seemed to me perfectly consistent to hurry back and do the Masque for the visit of the Queen to Sheffield, an extravagant bit of flattery which she thought pleasantly funny. I hope this makes my position more intelligible.

Yours sincerely
William Empson.

Leslie Fiedler: TLS; Houghton: ALS

TO LESLIE FIEDLER

Department of English Literature, The University, Sheffield 10
13 February 1956

Professor L. Fiedler, Montana State University, Missoula, U. S. A.

Dear Fiedler,

It occurs to me, after the week-end, that my last letter to you was too solemn for the occasion; also that you may actually not know what the occasion was if you very reasonably don't take the magazine *Encounter*, in which case it is all bound to seem rather surprising.

Spender had published an article containing a 'smear' on a distinguished Chinese acquaintance of mine (and of plenty of other people in England); so I thought it ought to be driven into his head that this practice was not welcome in England, and having started on this I have been trying to rout him out of a few of his innumerable bolt-holes in the matter. The chief object of writing to you was to send a carbon copy to him; I wouldn't have thought there was any need to tease you about your articles otherwise, though of course I meant what I said.

Yours sincerely,

William Empson.

Leslie Fiedler

TIMES LITERARY SUPPLEMENT, 30 March 1956, 195: 'Waiting for Godot'

Much correspondence was incited by a review essay on the meanings of Beckett's *Waiting for Godot* ('They Also Serve', *TLS*, 10 Feb. 1956, 84). The issue for 23 Mar. 1956 (181) carried this from Philip H. Bagby:

> Surely Mr Beckett must be chuckling away somewhere in France at the attempts of your reviewer and your correspondents to extract some clear message from the manifold ambiguities of his play. Its strength lies clearly in its uncertainties, and in the fact that it gives us no final answer, no decisive reason to prefer either hope or despair.
>
> It seems likely that Godot will never come, but it is by no means certain. His messengers (or messenger) may or may not be false prophets. Numerous alternatives are presented: the mutual affection of Vladimir and Estragon, Vladimir's longing for death, Estragon's reliance on Godot's promises, Lucky's dependence on his master and Pozzo's dependence on his slave, waiting and journeying or, if we must find an allegory, Christian consolation and existentialist action by virtue of the absurd. Very likely still other possible courses are offered us in the dense texture of the play, but we are never told whether we should choose one or all or none of these alternatives. One choice seems clearly to be rejected; it is 'thinking' or reason as exemplified in Lucky's frightening tirade. Yet, after all, is not Lucky obviously mad?
>
> At the end, the playgoer leaves the theatre puzzled, disturbed, forced to worry about the uncertainty of the human situation, but what choice he makes or whether he makes a choice at all is up to him. For my part, I believe that Godot does come—to those who know how to see him. But this answer I find in myself, not in the play. Mr Beckett asks questions; he gives no answers.

Sir,—Mr Bagby was quite right, I think, to point out the radical ambiguity of *Waiting for Godot*, but not all ambiguity is good. Here it expresses the sentiment: 'We cannot believe in Christianity and yet without that everything we do is hopelessly bad.' Such an attitude seems to be more frequent in Irish than either English or French writers, perhaps because in Ireland the religious training of children is particularly fierce. A child is brought up to believe that he would be wicked and miserable without God; then he stops believing in God; then he behaves like a dog with its back broken by a car, screaming and thrashing on the public road, so that a passer-by can only wish for it to be put out of its misery.[1] Surely we need not admire this result; the obvious reflection is that it was a very unfairly risky treatment to give to a child.

To be sure, we all ought to feel the mystery of the world, and there is bound to be a kind of literary merit in any play which makes us feel it so strongly; but we need not ourselves feel only exacerbated impotence about the world, and if we did we would be certain to behave badly. 'Oh, how I wish I could go to Hell! Why can't I go to Hell? It does seem a shame I can't go to Hell.' In itself this peculiar attitude deserves only a rather disgusted curiosity. But I would hate to suggest a moral censorship against the play; it is so well done that it is an enlarging experience, very different for different members of the audience. It would only be dangerous if it was liable to suck a member into the entire background to be presumed for the author, and that it cannot do.

William Empson[2]

TO A. ALVAREZ*

Department of English Literature, The University, Sheffield 10
29 August 1956

Dear Alvarez,

I was struck by your saying in your lecture on Donne at the Summer School that we know his friends as a young man and how like-minded they were to him. I would be very grateful if you would tell me who they are and where one can read: 'O Wearisome Condition of Humanity',[1] you mentioned that man, who seems to be pretty unreadable, but you mentioned two others. I am doing a piece about Donne the Space-Man, which I would rather like you [to] see before it goes to the *Kenyon* (but that is always rather an imposition) and any bit of evidence that the inner ring *knew* he was writing about life on other planets would come most welcome.[2]

---

[1] See letter to Christopher Ricks, 11 Aug. 1967.
[2] See also a leading article, 'Puzzling about Godot', *TLS*, 13 Apr. 1956.

[1] Sir Fulke Greville (1554–1628), *Mustapha*, a Senecan tragedy (1609), v: 4.
[2] 'Donne the Space Man' was first published in *The Kenyon Review*, 19 (Summer 1957); repr. in *ERL* (1), 78–128.

You hinted in the pub after I had read my poems that I was playing to the gallery; which rather amused me, because I suspected you were disillusioned at not finding them esoteric enough. They weren't meant to be at all esoteric. They came from more isolation and suffering than is suited to public performance, but that is well known to be true of most performance, including clowns'.[3]

Look us up when you are in London.

Yours sincerely

William Empson

BL

ESSAYS IN CRITICISM, 6: 4 (October 1956), 481–2: 'Mr Empson and the Fire Sermon'

A. E. Rodway, in a review of *CP* (1955) ('The Structure of Complex Verse', *Essays in Criticism* 6: 2 (Apr. 1956), 232–40), noted that at a poetry reading at Nottingham University, WE had denied that the Buddha's famous 'Fire Sermon' carried an especial significance for him; it was there, he said, 'because I liked it.' 'Somebody's leg was being pulled,' Rodway ribbed WE.

Though grateful to Mr Rodway for his appreciative review of my Collected Poems, I feel I ought to answer his query about the version of the Fire Sermon put at the start. I thought I made an earnest and patient effort to explain myself at the poetry-reading he mentions, but with the quaint rigour of the modern young he presumes I was trying to cheat— 'somebody's leg was being pulled'.

Like many others about thirty years ago, I looked up the Fire Sermon (recorded in Ceylon as one of the first sermons of the Buddha, given soon after he had decided that it was just possible to make himself understood) because of Mr Eliot's *Waste Land*. With all the repetitions it takes about ten minutes, and the experience is rather like having a steam-roller go over you;[1] but I had to select details from three or four translations before I

---

[3] A. Alvarez was to write, in 'A Style from a Despair: William Empson': 'the poetry is an outcome of a peculiarly strong and sensitive feeling for the intellectual tone of the time. Empson seems to create less out of personal situations than out of an emotional response to something he has already known with his wits, intellectually . . . It is as a stylist of poetry and ideas that, I think, Empson is most important' (*The Twentieth Century*, 161 (Apr. 1957), 346).

[1] Cf. TSE's Clark Lectures (1926): 'On one side the conceit is merely the development in poetry of an expository device known to preachers from the earliest times, the extended, detailed, interminable simile. The Buddha used it in the Fire Sermon' (*The Varieties of Metaphysical Poetry*, ed. Ronald Schuchard (1993), 130).

could get a version which would bear so much repeating. Afterwards, while in the East, I came to admire Buddhism a good deal more; I have written a book about the statues, which has been lost, after a lot of travel in pursuit of them. So it did not seem to me odd, for an omnibus volume, to reprint this version of the Fire Sermon from the start of my first book of poetry; somebody might even find it convenient.

I was shocked, at the reading mentioned by Mr Rodway, to gather from some questions that my book might be used to support the current religious revival, and I said that, if a son of mine wanted to become a Buddhist monk, I would beg him not to. This felt to me very unlike pulling anybody's leg, however low-minded it might appear to neo-Christians. Of course I think Buddhism much better than Christianity, because it managed to get away from the neolithic craving to gloat over human sacrifice; but even so I feel that it should be applied cautiously, like the new wonder-drugs.

The Fire Sermon itself is unlike most of Buddhism, and leaves Christianity far behind, in maintaining that all existence as such, even in the highest heaven, is inherently evil. Such is the great interest of it; but I think this all-embracing hatred commonly attracts only bad characters; and, to do Mr Eliot justice, I do not think that it is explicitly stated in his devotional verse. There is a fine article by George Orwell on Gandhi, saying what a nice clean smell Gandhi left behind him, but also saying that common men do not (as the religious like to presume) simply fail to become saints; when they understand the issue, they often feel it would be morally wrong to become a saint—especially as not loving one person more than another.[2] I am glad Mr Rodway recognized that my verse sometimes tries to bring out these very sharp contrasts between one and another of our accepted moral beliefs; it is much pleasanter than being thought a Parnassian fribble, as for example by Mr Enright in your previous number.[3] But, all the same, when I mention fire in my verse I mean it to have the usual confused background of ideas, not (as Mr Rodway thinks) the specific and raging dogma of the Fire Sermon. I can be sure of this because, though I probably never thought about the Fire Sermon when writing or revising, I had already decided that I thought its doctrine wrong, though fascinating and in a way intelligible. You might say that it is present as one extreme of the range of human thought, because the

---

[2] George Orwell, 'Reflections on Gandhi', *Partisan Review*, Jan. 1949; *The Penguin Essays of George Orwell* (1984), 465–72.

[3] 'Is the poetry of William Empson—to consider this type of writing at its best—much more than a sophisticated witticism, an ingenious joke? It is clear enough (and this is a sign of some virtue) that the poet is playing about, that he does not believe in what he is saying even while he is engaged in saying it' (D. J. Enright, 'Literature and/or Belief', *E in C*, 6: 1 (Jan. 1956), 62).

poetry often tries to take the position 'what I am saying is admitted to be true, though people look at it in so many different ways'; but even so it is pretty remote, and not appealed to.

TO HELEN GARDNER*

In September 1956, at the suggestion of A. Alvarez, WE contacted the scholar Helen Gardner; he hoped she might look over his essay 'Donne the Space Man' [*ERL* (1), 78–128]. She responded on 15 Sept. with the reminder that in 1952 she had edited the *Divine Poems*, complete with a reordering and redating of the sequence, and that she was now purposing to edit the *Love Poems: Elegies and Songs and Sonnets*—'and would that I *had* any evidence for dating them.' All the same, she went on, 'I could tell you if at any point your information was out of date or if at any point information I have is relevant. A lot in Grierson [*Poems of John Donne* (1912)] is just slightly unreliable . . .'

On 19 Oct., she wrote again: 'I thought you might like to see some quotations in a bad carbon copy of a talk I gave to an Anglican & Orthodox group which shows Donne conceiving, as you suggest, possibilities of salvation in Jesus Christ beyond a Church & beyond where the Gospel is preached.' Having thus misapprehended one of the major points of his piece, she went on: 'your main attitude towards Donne & his poetry I sympathize with very strongly.' Then she added a few specific comments on his essay, including this reproach to his point on 'a bracelet of bright hair about the bone': 'Need you give currency to this notion of Mr. [Theodore] Redpath's. Surely even in the most wildly superstitious countries "a bone" dug up could not be taken as a *relic of Christ*, who left only grave-clothes in the tomb. The only physical relics ever referred to are the holy foreskin! Sweat, tears, blood. Surely the contemptuous "a something else thereby" implies "my arm bone with the bracelet round it will be thought to be the arm bone of one of the Magdalen's fancy-men? . . .' Of the *Elegies* she remarked: 'I see no reason to believe Donne did any revising & think the variants in this text have arisen in process of copying. As far as I can see the line Grierson printed arose in Bridgewater, a very erratic MS. I have no doubt that Donne wrote "Here is no pennance . . .". The scribe's note is I think an interesting one—not biographically but as pointing to the poem's relations to the frank treatment of "bedding" accepted in *Epithalamion*.' On Holy Sonnet V she insisted, 'You have got the textual point wrong. For this sonnet & these others. *1635 is* the first ed. It reads *land* and all subsequent ed. simply reprint *land*. The reason 1635 has *land* is that it was, as I demonstrated, taking its new poems from *O'F* . . .'; and so 'the only authority for *land* is O'F, a late *MS* . . .'

Sheffield University
26 October 1956

Dear Helen Gardner,

Thanks very much for your immediate and helpful reply, especially since you were so busy. I shall answer some of your points in this letter, as we are both interested, but am not asking you to trouble with writing again; except on one point, where you felt there was too much to write down. It is about Satire III; would you deny that Donne expresses disapproval of any Pope or King who imposes a religious doctrine by force? That seems an essential issue, and if it is doubted I must expand my article there. Perhaps you would answer Yes or No on a postcard if you are too busy for more; and I wish you would also mention where your article on *Othello* appeared.[1]

You got me wrong on *Sonnet V*; I want the plural *lands* so we agree (it looks as if my phrasing had better be made clearer). As to 'A something else thereby' in *The Relic*, the central idea I am imputing to Donne is that there can be many incarnations, so the belief that Jesus left no bones on earth would not affect Donne's possible status as founder of a new religion. No doubt he would have used your argument if he had been [acc]used of blasphemy, and it might work as further satire on 'misdevotion', but it could not prevent the first obvious shock effect of the line. By the way, I really did think years ago that this meaning was taken for granted; I certainly didn't learn it from Redpath's edition. As to *Elegy XIX* and 'There is no penance due to innocence', it seems to me that you are imputing more than 'erratic' behaviour to the scribe of the Bridgewater MS. On your view, he wrote a note interpreting the poem and altered a line at the climax of the poem to make it fit his interpretation; surely this could not be done out of carelessness, only out [of positive] dishonesty. And it doesn't seem a very promising [kind of] cheat, when he could be checked for so many [. . . It is] at least equally likely that he gave what he had reason to believe was the original form of the line, and added a note explaining why he did not think it need be bowdlerized or emended as unintelligible, though this was usually done.

Looking at your letter again, I see you say I have got the textual point wrong 'for this sonnet and three others' (beside *Holy Sonnet V*), but I think this must be a misunderstanding due to your overwork. The

---

[1] Gardner's lecture 'The Noble Moor' was the British Academy Shakespeare Lecture for 1955; it was printed in the *Proceedings*.

only textual point I brought up apart from these two was 'we the sphere' in *The Ecstasy*, where I merely echoed Grierson's decision and made deductions from it; I am sure at least I haven't got the point the wrong way round, which was what I thought you must mean. Perhaps you only mean that one can't impute intentions to the editors if they were only copying one manuscript; no, but if the errors seem to show a consistent intention one can impute them to some copyist. It is only important as a slight bit of evidence of the climate of opinion in which the poems were admired.

I am glad to be put right about the number of the spheres, but don't see that the addition of an eleventh by Clavius in 1607 affects the argument.

Thanks very much for your typescript, which I return. That the Anglicans alone recognised salvation as possible through other Churches is certainly an important point which I ought to have mentioned.

Yours with many thanks,

W. Empson.

Gardner's reply (28 Oct. 1956) included the following points:

1. Of course the end of Satire III declares the inalienable rights of conscience and consequently implies in the use of the word 'unjust' in reference to the powers men claim to have received from God disapproval of forcers of conscience. My objection was to your treatment of the adventurers' passage. . . .

3. In speaking of Sonnet 5, you spoke of all editions from the second reading 'land'. But in this and three other sonnets the second edition of the *Poems* of 1635 is the first edition, as these four were not printed in 1635. Therefore *all* editions read *land* . . .

4. I cannot see how you can believe that a bone with a love token round it could possibly be taken in the most deeply superstitious region, say in Southern Italy, for a bone of Christ. And if this meaning were 'taken for granted' many years ago I think it only proves what extraordinary notions people can cherish. . . .

I don't think it is necessary for your argument to go into textual points, except on the sphere/spheres question in the *Ecstasy*. As for Redpath he is a child in these matters and really needs an elementary course in the principles of textual criticism. . . .

Of the three textual points you bring up my view is.

1. *land* in sonnet 5 is a copyist's error in O'F and if *1635* and subsequent editions has not followed O'F in this error, you would never have heard about it . . .

2. Ecstasy. Sphere/spheres. The first edition reads *spheres*. Only one MS. Dobell agrees with *1633* here, and this is a MS. which does *sophisticate* . . .

3. 'Going to Bed'. There are two versions of the line you are interested in MS. . . . [Y]ou had better make your point as you wish from what is in print in Grierson. You can if you like say that I think that the textual evidence points to there being no question of two versions both coming from the poet and, if there is any 'softening' I don't believe it is his.

TO HELEN GARDNER

Sheffield University
Guy Fawkes' Day [5 November] 1956

Dear Helen Gardner,

Thank you for your second very helpful letter. I agree that I had better leave textual points out of my article so long as the text my argument wants is the accepted one. I still think there was a tendency in some copyists to wince away from any suggestion of life on other planets, but the matter is not important and should be treated fully if at all.

What does seem to me important is the proposal to change the accepted text, near the end of *Elegy XIX*, from Grierson's 'There is no penance due to innocence' to 'Here is no penance, much less innocence'; which [Clay] Hunt wants because he does not understand the first version [*Donne's Poetry*, (1954)] and you, as I am now learning, from the evidence of manuscripts. I think that Donne wrote the first version and meant by it to deny the orthodox view that sex outside marriage was inherently sinful; the second version, invented to avoid this implication or simply to make sense when it was not understood, turns the end of the poem into a jeer against the woman praised and the exalted feelings of the speaker. Thus instead of a noble though perhaps boyish poem we are to have a sordid and mean-minded one, and the general reader must be expected to examine the evidence for this work of destruction.

You said in your first letter that, having gone through the manuscripts, you thought Grierson's reading arose in the Bridgewater manuscript, which is erratic. Also this is the one which contains the note 'why should not a man write his own epithalamion' etc. I answered that the change in the text could not be made unconsciously by a man sufficiently interested in its meaning to write the note; either he was cheating, rather absurdly, or he was going back to what he believed to be the original text and adding an explanation of it. You answer that the scribe of the Bridgewater MS. 'is content constantly to write absolute nonsense', and add that this reading of the line is found in many other MSS. So I realised, but I was relying on your earlier statement that the other MSS. which give this reading appear to be derived from the Bridgewater one; I am sure that you will not, on reflection, seriously mean to abandon this statement merely because you dislike a minor deduction from it. You then add a most valuable piece of information—'Actually this poem and the note are in a different hand from that of the MS as a whole'. Well then, the argument that the scribe of the MS was erratic becomes irrelevant; the writer who added this part must be supposed to have taken a special interest in it. He was sure Donne had said that this act of love was an innocent one, and that was why he added a note; though I agree with you that his explanation was probably wrong. It seems to me that this adds up to a strong argument.

You suggest in your letter that the general reader cannot make useful deductions from the *apparatus* in a modern text, and that an opinion can only be reached by those with a thorough acquaintance with the manuscripts. But surely, if this is true, there is no use in printing the *apparatus*; the original intention behind this laborious practice was to lay the technical problems open before the public.

I am very glad you agree that *Satire III* protests against forcers of conscience, I will certainly order your Academy Lecture pamphlet, and I am puzzled you do not see that '*a* Jesus Christ' would be inherently different from 'Jesus Christ'.

Yours with many thanks
William Empson.

Houghton carbon, bMS Eng 1401 (561)

ARROWS (New Year Edition, 1957), 5–6; *A*, 599–600:
'Everything, beggars, is on fire'

David Simpson, in an appreciative notice (1955) of *Collected Poems*, erred in suggesting: 'in the preface to his new book [WE had] taken for his text the Heraclitean notion that fire, being in constant motion, is therefore present in all forms of life, because life itself is in constant motion.'

Arrows of last year carried a generous review of my Collected Poems, which, however, said I had 'taken as my text' *The Fire Sermon* of the Buddha. I feel I ought to try to clear this up, as I am also having to do in the

Oxford *Essays in Criticism* [the reply to Rodway above]. I realise now that it was rather asking for misunderstanding to put the thing first, as authors generally mean that seriously, but I meant hardly more than that I admired the famous object and thought I had made, by picking words from various learned translations, an English version suitable for reciting in full—a rather unnerving experience if you do all the repetitions.[1]

It is said to be one of the earliest sermons of the Buddha, and carries the unearthliness of his system as far as is conceivable. One should realise that it denounces not only all existence on earth but all existence recognisable as such, even in the highest heaven. A man may naturally pause before agreeing that he believes all that. To be sure, the coolness of Buddhism towards Heaven, and towards the supernatural in general, is one of its most attractive features. On one occasion when the Buddha was preaching, the magic of his words became too much for him and he rose forty feet into the air, but he shouted down to the audience begging them to pay no attention; it would be over in a moment, and wasn't of the smallest interest compared to what he was saying. Any lecturer can sympathise with this point of view. Also we are told there was a minor god who became interested in philosophy, and one of his questions was so difficult that he was referred up and up in the hierarchy (it is always thought of as like a Government Department) till he was asking it of the Supreme God, who was rather embarrassed but quite plucky about this, so he waved his hand and the clouds gradually rolled back till at last, infinitely far below, the divine eyes could pick out the Buddha, crosslegged under a bo-tree. 'I can tell you who knows the answer,' said the Supreme God; 'it's That Man, down there.' The basic position, of course, is that Buddhists believe in abandoning selfhood, sometimes interpreted as merging oneself into the Absolute or the impersonal Godhead. If you are good but rather a busybody you are liable to be reborn as a god yourself, which may hold up getting to Nirvana indefinitely; just as over here a too virtuous scholar is liable to be made to do administration.

When I was first confronted with the idea that I had advertised myself as a Buddhist I said that, if a son of mine wanted to become a Buddhist monk, I would beg him not to; this is so, but I would not want to speak of the condition with great horror.[2] When I was refugeeing with the Peking

[1] When TSE was arranging for the US publication of *CP* (1949), WE had written: 'I should like to have the Fire Sermon on the flyleaf as in the Chatto edition [of *Poems*, 1935]' (2 Dec. 1946). The Fire Sermon had not been included in *GS*.
[2] Cf. 'Mr Eliot and the East' (1933): 'I would be sorry to hear of one of my friends becoming either a Buddhist or Christian monk, though I would expect him to be less hurt in bringing his mind to accept being a Buddhist one' (*A*, 569).

universities at Kunming (on the Burma Road) in 1939 there was an English Buddhist in an entirely genuine and severe monastery across the lake, who could sometimes be induced to boat over for a vegetarian dinner. He was keen to get a monk's passport, but I believe he left that monastery before the yearly three weeks of marathon, or almost incessant, meditation, with bangs on the head if you were found dozing at the squatting-post. He turned up at the War Office a few years later as an Intelligence Officer; I forget whether we sat on committees together about the Far East, with me representing the BBC Far Eastern Division, but I remember him in his uniform very well; I heard he was considered the only man they had had there who continued throughout his military career to think it wicked to kill even the lice on his body. Not that it was very surprising; a number of people felt they disapproved of Hitler enough to allow of stretching one or two points.

Buddhism deserves respect; for one thing, though not only, as an extreme; it needs to be remembered when one tries to survey what the human mind could think about a subject. But I naturally would not want to present myself as a believer by mistake.

TO G. WILSON KNIGHT*

Department of English Literature, The University, Sheffield
3 February 1957

Dear Wilson Knight,

I have recently read your new book on Byron's marriage and want to send you my congratulations. The evidence is much stronger than I had gathered from reviews and very well presented. Also, you clean up a point which I had always felt unpleasant. Byron in Quennell's treatment, decisive because in the Penguins, appears *too* much of a cad to his wife [Annabella Milbanke], excusable perhaps as a young neurotic but an unbearable man to accept as a poet; I mean, in trying to break his wife's spirit as a bride by thrusting on her the sister [his half-sister Augusta Leigh, daughter of Byron's father by a former marriage] he enjoyed more. Hugh Kingsmill, a forgotten man whose judgement I continue to respect, always thought of Byron as a disgusting cad about women for this reason. As usual the truth is much less damaging than the face-saving lie.

Such is the decisive praise which I think the book deserves, but I want now to make points vaguely against it. You gracefully say in the book that you don't know enough about these people and don't much want to,[1] but still I approached it with the prejudice that you don't know enough, even about vice let alone about Regency aristocrats. I think he obviously had committed incest with his sister and that nobody concerned thought it mattered much, except that Byron felt it was useful in poetry as a symbol of general rather irrational guilt-feelings, chiefly as a cover for less avowable acts. This explains why he seemed at the time to be hinting at it recklessly; whereas calling his love for Augusta 'pure' wouldn't conflict with that at all—it was peace. You seem to assume that 'pure' means sexual abstinence, whereas the history of the word is very complicated.[2] Also you seem to assume that a 'homosexual' is a distinct character, incapable of pleasure with women, whereas this is a very recent delusion.[3] I was astonished to have a bit of linguistics talked at me by a distinguished Chinese pansy my wife and I met at a Peking dance-hall; he said that in Chinese there were many words for a male invert like himself but no word meaning men who enjoyed them, because it was presumed that any man did, as he claimed to have proved; but the English word implied that only special men did, and he could go right on with anecdotes about how it wasn't only special men, among any of the distinguished conquerors of

---

[1] Wilson Knight writes in his preface: 'I find myself ill-at-ease among the great families and social customs of the past' (*Lord Byron's Marriage* (1957), p. ix).

[2] According to Wilson Knight's argument, Byron worked hard to win the reputation of 'a normally sexed man', though he was in fact homosexual: 'the assumptions of both his contemporaries and later biographers that a close association with a member of the opposite sex must have involved sexual intercourse are, with so extraordinary a bisexual temperament as his, unwarranted' (14, 16). In his dealings with Lady Frances Webster, he may have been conscious 'that he was less attracted by, perhaps we should say "more averse from", heterosexual intercourse than he liked to admit, even to himself' (21). Byron was a man whose 'instincts were abnormal'; '[H]e was in part a feminine type'; and while he indulged the 'sin of homosexuality', he sought to overcompensate for it with his 'strongly male manner of address' (23–4). Only after her separation from Byron did his wife attempt to concoct proof for the allegation that he had committed incest with Augusta before his marriage; but '*Not a word of Lady Byron's evidence subsequent to her leaving her husband can be trusted*' (101; italics original). In poems addressed to Augusta after the separation, including 'Stanzas to Augusta' and 'Epistle to Augusta', Byron specifically figures her as 'pure'; as Wilson Knight contends (129), Augusta is always associated for him with 'pure thoughts' (*Manfred*, III, i. 165). Contrary to WE's rather wilful interpretation of it, Wilson Knight's thesis is that no incest took place, even though many writers on Byron do accept the charge: 'though knowing perfectly well that incest is not the point, they find it easier, as though by a process similar to that George Orwell named "double-think", to pretend simultaneously that it was' (240). Byron had 'one, and really only one, failing: homosexuality, together with its extension into the marriage-relationship' (254).

[3] With regard to the 'bisexual integration', Wilson Knight writes: 'Roughly we may note certain conditions and characteristics of such abnormal persons . . . There is, often, a close relationship to the mother, with the father playing a less emphatic part, a well-known condition often associated with the name "Oedipus". A strong feminine element is preserved, which is less "effeminacy" than spiritual insight, and the result is "bisexual". Such men are . . . ill-attuned for marriage; they may be ascetic, licentious, homosexual, or incestuous in tendency' (281).

China during his time. Byron himself had so many faces that he becomes hard to imagine, but I think he should be conceived as invincibly normal therefore willing to show softness, not as an embarrassingly pansy figure whose weakness was loyally hushed up—a view which Harold Nicolson[4] presents somewhere, when he is shown addressing British officers, with the gratuitous suggestion that they must have felt embarrassed.[5]

It strikes me that the way Annabella's parents must have behaved is extremely like the way Byron behaved; if he *talks* in favour of sodomy that's enough to fight on, and make a complete break at once. They were all ready to behave very romantically.

However, you agree in the book that the incest may have occurred.[6] I only wanted to complain at any suggestion that he was a specialized buck homosexual, a man taking the male part, because this object has only been created by law.

William Empson

Leeds

---

[4] Harold Nicolson (1886–1968) was a diplomat, author, and Labour MP.

[5] In January 1824 Byron was entertained to dinner in Argostoli, Cephallonia, by the genuinely admiring officers of the 8th (the King's) Regiment of Foot, under the command of Colonel Charles Napier (an officer who would immortalize himself 22 years later when, after annexing Scinde, he sent back the witty message 'Peccavi'). 'The civility with which he had been received . . .,' writes Harold Nicolson, 'should have convinced a man less diffident or self-conscious than Byron that his countrymen in this outpost of the Empire did not look upon him with the hostility which he persistently imagined to be his lot. He was convinced, in his morbid, self-centred way, that he had become an object of loathing and ridicule to every Englishman, and he shrank with feminine timidity from exposing himself to any converse with them.' When the officers offered a toast to his health, his reply, according to Nicolson, was 'characteristic. His soft voice trembled a little with what in truth was a sincere emotion and an unaffected nervousness . . . He added that he was so conscious of the honour they had done him that he regretted he could not adequately express his sense of obligation, since he had been so long in the practice of speaking a foreign language that he could not easily express his sentiments in English. We may doubt whether the officers of the garrison were wholly pleased by this little gesture of affectation, but Byron for his part was delighted when he again resumed his seat. He leant towards the Colonel flushed and excited. "Had it been a success?" he asked. "Had he said what was required?" He sat on there beside Colonel Duffie, puzzled and delighted by their kindness, blinking a little at all those young boyish faces, and feeling very shy and happy and perturbed' (*Byron: The Last Journey, April 1823– April 1824* (1924, 1948), 122–3). Nicolson describes Byron at this period as 'self-conscious and effeminate' (5).

[6] Actually, Wilson Knight allows only: 'I do not argue that there had been no love-interchange between Byron and Augusta, but merely that we do not know the exact nature of it, many varieties of amatory interchange being, of course, possible which stop short of what is normally meant by "incest"; that we have Byron's firm statement to Lady Melbourne that it was a non-sensuous, by which he may have meant no more than a non-coitional love . . .; that Lady Byron had been willing at first to pass it over; that it had nothing to do with the Separation' (135). Byron was perfectly 'frank and open' about the nature of his relations with Augusta, and he evinced no guilt, Wilson Knight maintains; all told, there is no substantive evidence whatever of incest between them.

TO GRAHAM HOUGH*

10 February 1957

My dear Hough,

I ought to be doing a lot of other things, but I shall yield to pleasure and play truant and post you some reflections after reading your excellent book on D. H. Lawrence [*The Dark Sun: A Study of D. H. Lawrence* (1956)]. I can't expect him to be wise because it seems (for instance) that after Lady Ottoline Morrell had helped him by asking him round to meet some people he published the profound thought (thinly disguised) that it was because of her murderous hatred for men that the mouth of her womb had hardened into a beak which scratched the cock of any man who poked her. Now, if this had been physically true, any man capable of blowing his own nose and fond of the woman could have handled it, I suggest by wearing plasticine under a French letter. But as she had never let him go to bed with her at all the invention seems to me just farcically caddish, a long way beyond the invention of Evelyn Waugh. The theory that a really manly man does not allow the woman he is enjoying to have an orgasm seems to me to have the same quality of pathetically ignorant nastiness. It was a Victorian middle-class theory about one's wife, often earnestly held (a class where men tend to marry late in life might intelligibly feel that to avoid awakening the wife's desire would avoid the dangers both of overstraining the old man and of making the wife want adultery); Lawrence no doubt heard it said and felt it was the kind of Puritanism he liked to boast of; but I bet it wasn't working class, and I bet he only took it up because he knew he wasn't adequate for Frieda. The picture of him surrounded by adoring unsatisfied women who say 'isn't he original' when he writes down 'the moon is a glowing core of phosphorus' and suchlike in the *Unconsciousness* books does not make one expect him to say anything wise. I cannot respect him either for being so interested in homosexuality and never daring to have any experience of it. I do not think him very outspoken about sex, because it seems to me he must have meant something quite simple in *Women in Love* about why one pair of lovers was bad and the other good in spite of 'exploring the dark depths of shame' something quite simple about what they did in bed, but he left the novel as an obscurantist tease because he didn't dare to say what it was. The best book about him, I still think, is poor old Hugh Kingsmill's which you do not allow into your bibliography.[1] But still I think yours is a splendid book; it is

[1] Hugh Kingsmill, *D. H. Lawrence* (1938).

a fine flower of the wilful refusal to attend to biography; it sticks to the text only till that process feels Simon Stylites or the man who always faints after running a mile in four minutes (the science journals have been telling us the trick is that he doesn't breathe, but I may have got this entirely wrong).

However, looking over the pages I have dog-eared again, I think you do manage to get in a great deal of comment from a basis of human experience while maintaining the technical statue [status] of a judge who has only access to the text. It makes the book too impressive to be ignored.

William Empson

I have left this lying about for a week or two but now I don't see why not to post it.[2]

Houghton, bMS Eng 1401 (581)

TO MICHAEL FREEMAN*

Department of English Literature, The University, Sheffield 10
22 June 1957

Dear Mr Freeman,

Thanks for your letter.[1] You naturally feel bothered by the duty of organising, depressed by the lack of response, and so forth. I don't think it shows poor spirit if the students don't want extra lectures; I hate going to lectures myself, and expect it is more important for students to read books, also of course discuss them while they are interested, and feel that advice is easily available. Getting them to discuss after collecting them by a tolerably interesting bait would probably be the best thing for you to aim at.

The universities have been geared up now to pack in about as much training which can be recognised by a ticket qualifying a student for later employment as can be done in the three years; I don't think you would find Oxford and Cambridge very different there—it can hardly be

---

[2] George Watson relates a Hough anecdote: 'In the 1930s, at a dinner in Hanoi . . . [Empson] remarked to Graham Hough . . . shortly after the death of D. H. Lawrence: "You know, I think I see what Lawrence's novels are about: they are about *coming* at the same time", adding even more disconcertingly: "I have once or twice managed it myself" ' (*Never Ones for Theory? England and the War of Ideas* (2000), 64).

[1] As a first-year student, Freeman had been elected secretary of the Arts Society and was trying to build up its programme. He wrote to WE (who was supportive in his role as president) about his plans and disappointments; he was feeling insecure. The English Honours school was small (about a dozen students a year), tucked into a cramped Georgian terrace, with the staff getting to know most of the students quite well. Freeman was fairly typical of the student cohort: first-generation at university, unsure about the institution and academic discipline, and rather over-awed by the staff despite their considerateness. WE understood all this, and was warm towards the students; this letter made Freeman 'feel much stronger about the job,' he reports.

avoided, because so many students are now paid for by Local Authorities, who demand to be assured they aren't wasting their money. The way out would be to make it four years, but I expect a majority of students would prefer to be earning a salary after three. So I don't think you need feel Sheffield is low because they aren't keen to turn out.

It is clear that you don't just want me to read my own poems again, and it would seem pretty absurd for me to do that every year; but I do prefer it because it isn't in the syllabus, it isn't just another professional lecture out of hours. You suggest at the end doing my Inaugural again instead. That was simply chattering about my teaching in China and Japan, and I am certainly very willing to do it again (there is no question of requiring a text to read out). It ought to interest them as so many of them are going to be teachers, but it strikes me they mostly hate Abroad and don't want to have to bother about it, let alone go there; so maybe it wouldn't interest them much. However we can certainly do that if you think it would make them come. I could also talk about the Chinese and Japanese theatre, which might collect some of the theatre chaps; but I think this is an offer for a second appearance of the prof. on the notepaper later in the year, not the best thing for the lead-off one which you seem to be billing me for.

We had perhaps better meet before you go for the holidays.

Yours truly

William Empson.

ESSAYS IN CRITICISM, 7: 3 (July 1957), 318:
'Restoration Comedy Again'

In spite of having the editor call me morally impregnable (irresponsible, etc.), I make bold to offer a charitable thought about Mirabel, in *The Way of the World*. Mr Wain found him an unbearable cad, and the rejoinder of the Editor seems mainly to defend the plays as being satires.[1] But Mirabel,

---

[1] John Wain, in 'Restoration Comedy and its Modern Critics', *E in C* 6: 4 (Oct. 1956), 367–85, followed the example of L. C. Knights (in 'Restoration Comedy: the Reality and the Myth', *Explorations*, 1946) in castigating Restoration Comedy as the symptom of a sick society, as manifesting a 'frightful confusion' whenever 'a moral attitude is to be taken up' (377). The 'centre' of Etherege's *The Man of Mode* 'is Dorimant's warfare against women' (382); and the 'whole plot of the *Plain Dealer* is simply a piece of crude misanthropy and getting one's own back ... If Wycherley's mind really worked like this, he must have been little better than an idiot, and a nasty idiot into the bargain. *The Country Wife* is even worse, because more tangled. Horner is meant to be admired for his clever trick, but Harcourt is equally so for his persistent attempt to marry Alithea honourably. It is the same with Congreve. Most of *Love for Love* is in fact pretty direct propaganda *for* good sexual morality' (382–3). Likewise, it is crucial to recognise that Mirabell, in *The Way of the World*, is 'a cad'. In 'Second Thoughts: II. L. C. Knights and

however sordid it may have been to arrange a society marriage for his ex-mistress, also took care to protect her by holding her property under deed of gift; thus circumventing the injustice to women of the current marriage laws. Owing to this forethought, he can outwit the villains at the end and make the good people happy. It is taken for granted that he is absolutely trustworthy, and would never use her money (as he legally could do) even if ruined by the various plots.

This does seem a case, even if the only one, of what Mr Bonamy Dobrée said in *Restoration Comedy* long ago [1924]; that the plays are looking for a more reasonable and contented arrangement between the sexes. Congreve says nothing against the law, and twice says that the plan only concerns part of her fortune, which I don't understand; but he evidently knows that the law may work out unjustly. Also, as Mr Bonamy Dobrée said, the love between him and Millamant seems pathetically real when they both find it so hard to reconcile with their modishness. I quite agree with Mr Wain, and with Professor L. C. Knights, that the idea of sex as only enjoyable when it is a victory over the partner is often present, and desolates the heart (one feels these people would be less miserable if they gave sex up); but that is not always what is going on in the plays.

However, I couldn't expect this to convince our fiercely moral young men; Mr Wain may next denounce the Married Women's Property Act.

William Empson

TO FRANK KERMODE*

Sheffield University
24 November 1957

Dear Mr Kermode,

I have just been looking at your British Council pamphlet on Donne[1] with great interest and feel sure that it makes an important point, but am not sure how far you would take it. You say (p. 11 etc) that Donne's aim and standard method is 'making a new and striking point by a syllogism concealing a logical error', and that he learned this from the witty Counter-Reformation preaching which was called *gusto espagnol*. Now, I can well understand that a man arguing for Christianity often does it by

Restoration Comedy' (*E in C*, 7: 1 (Jan. 1947), 56–67), the editor F. W. Bateson sought to defend the representation of 'the "serious" role of sex in a Restoration comedy of manners' (62): 'the implicit seriousness', say, of *The Country Wife* (66).

[1] Frank Kermode, *John Donne* (1957), Writers and Their Work no. 86.

arguments which he knows to be false, but surely he does not boast of this practice in public as 'the highest and rarest kind of conceit'? Surely they must have maintained (and believed) that some kind of subtle or poetical truth was shown by the literally false argument? This point is important for your remarks on the love poetry, because you take for granted that Donne does not mean what he says there, and that *The Extasie* is meant to be as frankly absurd as *The Flea*. But surely, as this is so very much against ordinary opinion, against the spontaneous reading of such a variety of critics, and also so nasty in itself, you need a rather stronger argument than to say 'Donne was merely imitating the preachers, and they were all known to be cheats too'?

You say of *The Exstasie*:

> the argument, a tissue of fallacies, sounds solemnly convincing and consecutive, so that it is surprising to find it ending with an immodest proposal. The highest powers of the mind are put to base uses [use], but enchantingly demonstrated in the process. (p. 12).

There is a similar point of view on p. 23, speaking of *The Nocturnal*, where you say:

> The witty sneer about the object of the sun's journey to the Tropic of Capricorn helps to distance these inferior loves; and we return to darkness, the perpetual sleep of the other Sun, and the propriety of this saint's day as the type of darkness and lifelessness.

But surely, Donne is not speaking of the act of love with mere loathing; if he was, why should he be sorry that his mistress is dead? There is an obscure gaiety, which greatly sweetens the poem without doing anything to weaken the mood of despair, in the way he looks back on his bold love and tells others that they may well do the same, though his time for it is past. The suggestion earlier, I think, from the way he throws in his old formulas for love poems quite casually ('Oft a flood' and so on) is 'what fun we were really having, when we thought we were in such despair over the obstacles to our love; but now I know what real despair is'. There is no reason to think that the poem means to sneer at sexual desire in itself. The same twist in your own mind, I think, comes out when you wince and fret at the sexual metaphors in the religious poems (p. 39 etc.); you feel they must be meant to be disgusting, but they are not. You recognise this in a way (p. 40) when you say [apropos 'Batter my heart, three person'd God'] 'We respond crudely to this kind of challenge', evidently feeling we ought to be still purer somehow. But no, it is your neurotic sex-horror, described as manichaean by theologians I believe, which is crude.

I am rather alarmed at the determined effort of other people besides yourself to change the text of *Elegy xix* and read

<blockquote>Here is no penance, much less innocence</blockquote>

instead of

<blockquote>There is no penance due to innocence,</blockquote>

which you call a 'very inferior reading' on p. 25.[2] This is merely because you don't see the point of it; she is like Adam and Eve before the Fall, not yet corrupted by 'late law'; that is why she has already been called 'America', where the Noble Savages are. The poem therefore is 'heretical', as you say we are tempted to think merely because we are so awkward with such conceits (p. 40).[3] But why is it essential to suppose that the young Donne was not heretical, however much he appears to be? In other cases, the Christian critics are quite happy to say that an author had very wrong ideas till he was converted, but in the case of Donne they have somehow decided to pretend he never was. I can't see that there is any real argument for this procedure. Of course, I should agree that the convention of wit-writing made it safer for Donne to write like this, even though he didn't dare to publish (they would feel it wasn't quite sensible to burn him alive for it); and maybe he did alter the line in the elegy himself later in life, to remove the only bit which has to be regarded as heretical if taken seriously. But this let-out process gives no reason for supposing that he can't really have entertained the ideas which he expressed. The whole procedure which you and the others of your school regard as so scholarly seems to me merely a wilful campaign to impose your own neuroses on the text.

I was also reading your *Romantic Image* [1957] with admiration but dissatisfaction; I can't understand whether you regard the belief as true or are only writing its history. Kathleen Raine and Herbert Read take the Image very seriously, but I can never feel I understand what they mean by it. However, I wanted to bring that up because you say in passing somewhere

---

[2] Kermode notes (24–5) that 'Elegy xix' has been 'regarded as the poet's own epithalamion, a fancy as harmless as it is improbable, except that it has perhaps resulted in the acceptance of a very inferior reading in line 46'; explaining further in a footnote: ' "There is no pennance due to innocence", the reading of 1699, is represented in most manuscripts by "There is no pennance, much les innocence". The received reading makes the poem slightly more appropriate if the woman is a bride. But clearly she is no more innocent than she is penitent, and ought not to be wearing the white linen which signifies either innocence or penitence.'

[3] Kermode does not say 'heretical'; he observes more circumspectly that 'our awkwardness . . . leads us to charge *Elegy* xix with blasphemy' (40).

that even Empson now usually puts in a bit of consideration of the context when he does verbal analysis.[4] Now, I consider this is merely a slander. I always did consider the context, but I thought the arguments drawn from that could be taken for granted and not made to pad out an already long text. I have now answered in magazines about five attempts to prove that I had ignored the context in some bit of criticism, and I consider I proved every time that I had known a great deal more about the context than my opponents did, indeed that was why my reading was right. The only effect of this activity on the minds of persons like yourself is that you go on repeating the slander but add a boast that you have now converted me. You have indeed made me feel that a good deal of rather dismal background stuff always needs to be put in nowadays, just to remove the hopeless initial misapprehensions which appear to have become the established orthodoxy.

Yours sincerely

W. Empson.

Houghton, bMS Eng 1401 (589)

'It is very unlucky that I have this knack of annoying you,' Kermode responded on 2 Dec. 1957. Taking up specific points of interpretation in WE's essay, he remarked: 'It is true that the dramatic situation of *The Exstasie*, as I read it, is of a seducer using words as some use drink; I put it as nastily as possible to bring out of the point that it seems to me a ravishing poem.' On *The Nocturnal*: 'It was obviously possible for Donne to display, in suitable contexts, contempt and even loathing for the act of love. He does so very often, sometimes pretty sickeningly in the Sermons . . . By the same token I continue to prefer "Here is no pennance . . ." It is prejudging the issue a bit to say that this is a "change" because that gives a false authority to the 1669 text; a lot can happen to a MS poem in 26 years. There are two reasons why the woman might go on wearing a white gown, penance or innocence; neither here applies, so she ought to take it off. What's wrong with that?' He wrote in conclusion: 'It's just as well that I never supposed you owed me a sympathetic reading, though I must admit I shouldn't have supposed it possible to get so much that is really sinister out an unpretentious pamphlet.'

When he returned the annotated copy of 'Donne the Space Man' which WE had sent to him, Kermode re-emphasized on 26 January 1958: 'The article gave me acute pleasure, and also explained a number of points that puzzled me in your first letter, e.g. about Elegy xix, where I still prefer, with

---

[4] '[T]he question of how to treat partial aspects continues to rise and trouble practical critics, and occasionally provides new insights. Mr Empson . . . has developed a habit of referring regularly to the whole work in the discussion of its parts' (Kermode, *Romantic Image* (1957), 156).

Hunt [Clay Hunt, *Donne's Poetry* (1954)]—whose book I liked much less than you—the reading "no penance, much less innocence". The tone surely permits these terms to have invisible inverted commas, like "honour" in other poems . . .

'I entirely agree that Donne must have been felt as a shock, and all the part of Miss Tuve's book [*Elizabethan and Metaphysical Imagery* (1947)] which says he wasn't is not only wrong but easily shown to be so. Some of this shock is a matter of being a little risqué in theological matters, certainly; and I entirely agree about "a something else thereby", finding it strange that there has been so much hesitation over it. Donne's head worked theologic- ally; he was all out to be épatant, the poems were private; the result is the one you would expect . . . However, the "something else thereby" is in my view only an example of the sort of thing liable to happen, not an example of a substantial and persistant doctrine of Donne's. And I feel the same about the new-philosophy argument; Donne always uses it, exactly as he uses alchemy, angelology and all the rest of it, as providing useful illustra- tions . . .'

WE referred the issue to his colleague W. A. Murray, who responded in an undated letter: 'I must say I cannot find any argument to support "no penance, much less innocence", and I still agree with you, though for differ- ent detailed reasons. I think that the dominating associations are Paradise- innocence-nakedness, and that although America is felt to be a good place for the new Paradise, the association "new-world" is only slightly felt. The conclusive argument for me would frame itself thus: White linen is the garb of angels and ghosts; it is also the dress of earthly penitence; even saints wear it in repentance for the loss of innocence in the original paradise of Adam and Eve. (This was an accepted iconographic tradition, v. Combe, *Jerome Bosch*, St. Jerome at Prayers, where the saint is in white linen.) There- fore in the new Paradise, in which we are pre-lapsarians, and neither angels nor ghosts, there is no need for penance and white linen. The joke lies a little further back in the poem, in the comparison of their new Paradise with that of Mahomet, which I suppose had some sort of sexual connotation (sexual relationship in Paradise being no sin) for the 17th. century, as for later times. I think that K[ermode] ought to disprove your case rather than require you to prove yours, which seems the simpler and more coherent solution. I have also wondered, though it is a matter for the linguistic histor- ian, whether "no penance, much less innocence" doesn't sound a little odd as a seventeenth century phrase? What does it mean anyway?'

Following another (now lost) letter from WE which reported Murray's construction, Kermode returned to the issue of Elegy xix on 1 May 1958: 'I take this poem as being of the sort that does habitually say, "let's have no more of all that cant about 'honour', 'innnocence' etc." "You certainly aren't penitent; thank god you're not 'innocent'; so off with that white linen." I don't understand Murray's troubles over the grammar. It's no use saying it's not a C17 phrase when it is.'

THE SPECTATOR, 13 December 1957, 833: 'Kidnapping Blake'

W. W. Robson[1]—in a review, 'Kidnapping Blake' (*The Spectator*, 6 Dec. 1957, 806–8), marking the bicentenary of the birth of William Blake—attacked what he called the 'Jungian assumptions' underpinning an essay by Kathleen Raine that focused on the poems 'The Little Girl Found' and 'The Little Girl Lost' (*The Divine Vision: Studies in the Poetry and Art of William Blake*, ed. Vivian de Sola Pinto). Raine imported bizarre meanings into Blake's work, Robson complained, making Blake 'more of a crank than ever, one with an esoteric, derivative, literary philosophy'. The 'Little Girl' poems are absurdly over-interpreted, 'with detailed and learned commentary, as an elaborate neo-Platonic interpretation of the myth of Demeter and Persephone'. Among other examples, he cites Raine's reading of Blake's simple lines including—

> How can Lyca sleep
> If her mother weep

—'Porphyry at length describes the intense desire of the "moist" souls to descend, as Lyca wishes to descend, into generation . . . If the story were simply that of a lost little girl being sought by her parents [Lyca's words] would be nonsensical; no mother would refuse sleep to her weary child; and no child would give as a reason for her inability to sleep her mother's vigilance. [Therefore] Blake's story is myth pure and simple.' On the contrary, Robson protests, the poem 'is "pure and simple" without bringing in "myth" at all.' Likewise, it may seem possible that Blake, in 'Hear the voice of the Bard', was influenced by Thomas Taylor's translation of *The Five Books of Plotinus*. 'But,' Robson challenges, '*when* does that influence appear in his poetry. Miss Raine (p. 51) says it appears as early as the *Songs of Experience*, and thinks that the phrase "the lapsed soul" used by Blake [. . .] was derived from Taylor's "lapse of the soul", a phrase used in his translation of Plotinus. But Taylor's *Five Books of Plotinus* appeared in 1794; and 'Hear the voice of the Bard' had been *engraved* by October, 1793 . . . All the Plotinus parallels given by Miss Raine on pp. 52 ff. are, therefore, irrelevant.' All in all, Raine seems 'oddly out of sympathy with [Blake's] emotional and moral purposes'.

---

[1] W. W. Robson (1923–93) was an admirer of WE and his work. He was for many years president of the Oxford Critical Society, which played host to Empson, as well as (on a more regular basis) to FRL. He was a founding editor of the periodicals *Essays in Criticism* and *The Cambridge Quarterly*. His other writings include *Modern English Literature* (1970), *The Definition of Literature* (1982), *A Prologue to English Literature* (1986), *Critical Enquiries* (1993).

WE wrote to Raine on 8 December 1957: 'I have posted a short letter to the Spectator, saying that Robson was unfair to you about the dates of publication and about the mother-weeping argument. These attacks are always a good opportunity to put one's own case, but I have found it so often convenient to wait a week or two and see what other people say—so long as they say something.' (*BL: Deposit 10318*).

Sir,—I share some of the uneasiness of Mr W. W. Robson about Miss Kathleen Raine's work on Blake; she seems to make him such an orthodox mystic, as early as the *Songs*, or even such a literal copyist of previous mystics. But his review is unfair to her at several points.

He appears to refute her easily by saying that Taylor's translation of Plotinus appeared a year too late, but he doesn't admit that she answered that; chiefly by saying that, with Blake's method of making a book, you can't be sure of the date on his title-page. It looks as if he couldn't be bothered to read that part. Then, as to 'The Little Girl Lost', who says

How can Lyca sleep
If her mother weep?

he finds no explanation needed; she is 'worried about her mother's anxiety.' Well, if I were lost in a forest at night, I should hope people were looking for me; surely the down-to-earth Mr Robson here, and not the mystical Miss Raine, is the one who is imputing unlikely motives to the child. I would rather believe that the child symbolises something than that she is meant to be altruistic in such an overstrained way. However, to do this only makes a weakness in the poem seem intelligible—the poet is not positively admiring what we find bad, so he is not mawkish.

Mr Robson then complains that Miss Raine is so determined to get her mystical meaning that she 'even says the poem "fails" because he [Blake] has not "completely integrated" his neo-Platonic material!' But there she is only saying what I have just said, which surely did not sound too otherworldly; the detail is rather bad as part of a human story, she feels, and she explains it as an undigested bit of symbolism. She may be all wrong, but if so she needs to be attacked more intelligently.[2]

Yours faithfully

William Empson

---

[2] David Fuller, a student of WE's in the 1960s, recalls mentioning to WE that he was working on a book to be called *Blake's Heroic Argument* (1988). WE responded: 'Blake was a great character, but not a poet. I've tried to persuade Kathleen Raine of that, but without success' (letter to JH, 8 Oct. 1988).

TO THE GULBENKIAN FOUNDATION

Sheffield University
22 January 1958

Dear Mr Sanderson,

I write to recommend the magazine *Mandrake* for a grant from the Gulbenkian Foundation. I am afraid I may forget some of the points which you allowed me to put to you by word of mouth, but this letter will at least, as you suggested, give something definite to put before the Committee.

The editor is Mr Arthur Boyars,[1] of 44 Cholmley Gardens, NW6, who informs me that the magazine was started soon after the war by Mr John Wain while a student at Oxford. He edited it for about two and a half years, and then the present editor took over. It has never paid its contributors. The sale has been around 3,000, which the editor estimates as meaning 20,000 readers, since it aims at a public with rather specialised interests and commonly not well-off. There are 400 subscribers, half of them outside England; he mentioned receiving requests for the magazine from Singapore and Ibadan. He now finds, with the general increasing stringency, that he is unable to carry on and also that contributors expect to be paid. The loss on a number has recently been about 50 pounds, and paying the contributors would mean about 70 pounds more. There should be at least two numbers a year. He estimates that a grant of this size for five years should be enough to put the magazine on its feet.

I have myself been in China for much of its life-time, working for the British Council, and do not know its earlier performance; indeed, I came to know of it from two articles on my own work which I would describe as attacks. Thus I am not trying to obtain a grant for a clique of my own. But I found general agreement that it deserved support. Last year I was advised by Mr John Davenport, as a personal friend of Lord Moyne, that the Guinness firm might support it given reasonable assurances;[2] and I sent round a short statement about it to literary figures asking for their signatures. There were no refusals, and the following signed: Sir Herbert Read, Bonamy Dobrée, John Hayward, Janet Adam Smith, Kathleen Raine, and G. S. Fraser. As it happened, Lord Moyne or the firm had already just decided to give a Poetry Prize instead of supporting a magazine, and the document with its signatures cannot be recovered. The

---

[1] Arthur Boyars (b. 1925/6) was a literary journalist and poet.
[2] Bryan Guinness, second Baron Moyne (1905–92), was a poet and novelist; vice-chairman of Arthur Guinness, Son & Co. from 1949.

signatures did not exactly mean that they like the magazine; indeed, most of them hold some different position in literary criticism, as they tended to explain when writing back; but they all agreed that it expressed a strand of present-day literary-critical thought which needs expressing.

Earlier I had written to the Arts Council about it, with the agreement of Hayward and Fraser who are on the relevant committee, but the proposal was voted down on the ground that the magazine was concerned with literary criticism, and hardly at all with publishing creative work, which was held to be part of their 'terms of reference'. Well, I would be prepared to agree that literary criticism has become in some way inflated, partly from having so many people employed in teaching English Literature, but also because it has really moved forward in this century, and explained things which had never been explained before, so that it continues to attract a fair number of energetic and interesting minds. The tree must be allowed to grow; it is a mistake for these endowing bodies to tell the young men to go away and write poems instead.

Speaking as a Professor of English Literature, I can add that a lot of young lecturers at universities actually need to get into print with the results of their critical labours, or they cannot 'pass the bar' to assured employment and yearly rise of salary. While this system of promotion is being operated, it is surely very unfair to them to have such great difficulty in finding anywhere to publish the kind of work which they think it right to do. I mean, it is easier to get published the results of historical research in the field of English Literature, because that can be taken by magazines which are subsidized on the ground that they are evidently learned journals, but many young lecturers think it more important to advance our understanding of literature by attending to the text. Their work is in the same position as that published in technical journals, which everyone assumes must be subsidized, almost as a part of the public outlay on universities, except that it doesn't count as technical. One might feel that the authors in *Mandrake* seem too cross, though it has undoubtedly printed some good articles; but they in any case influence opinion in the rising generation a good deal, and they may be expected to become more sensible if they are not prevented from thrashing out their problems in print. It is in this kind of way that I feel the magazine is needed, and so I think did most of the other signatories; without it, there would be a certain extra hampering and crossness in the movements of opinion over this fairly important field.

My experience with the British Council abroad has I think also some relevance here. It was felt as painfully bad to have *Scrutiny* stop publication, because foreigners felt so sure it was honest. Dr Leavis often seems to me very wrong-headed, but he both appears and is very incorruptible, sure not to be hushing anything up. *Mandrake* is not just a successor to *Scrutiny*, being prepared as I understand to disagree with Dr Leavis at various points; but the same kind of people write for it, and it has the same fierce high tone. The editor is positively unwilling to receive a subsidy from a body, such as a Sunday newspaper or a publishing firm, whose literary policy elsewhere he might think it his duty to attack. To get this kind of voice published under present conditions, he feels, and I expect rightly, requires help from an evidently disinterested source. Guinness would have been all right, but it strikes me that the Gulbenkian Foundation, with its attitude of good-will towards Britain from a somewhat international point of view, is an even more suitable body to fill the gap.

You suggested that, if another number of the magazine came out soon, that might influence the committee favourably. I reported that to Mr Boyars, but he said he could only afford to produce a number of half the normal size, and felt that this might produce a bad rather than a good impression. I promised to report his reply.

Thanking you for your readiness to consider the matter in detail,

Yours sincerely

William Empson

Houghton, bMS Eng 1401 (560)

TO JANET ADAM SMITH

Department of English Literature, The University, Sheffield 10
16 February 1958

My dear Janet,

Thank you very much for sending me Michael's Poems, and I am proud of my presence in your very just and perceptive memoir.[1] I wish we had all got abroad together again; before very long, by the way, unless I am too poor, my kids ought to be taken to Switzerland.

I saw a stupid review of the book the other day, wondering with the

[1] See Janet Adam Smith in Michael Roberts, *Collected Poems* (1958), 39: '[W]hen I knew him, a good part of our mountain holidays . . . would take the form of travel. We would be off for a week or ten days with rucksacks and ice-axes, every day crossing a pass or a mountain . . . I remember one of these journeys particularly; when, with William Empson, we started out on skis from the Lac de Tignes for a tour of the Tarentaise, sweated and edged our way up to the high passes, balanced delicately on the frozen debris of great avalanches, swooped and skidded down into valleys where they never expected any strange skier, and ours were the only tracks.'

lordliness of a new fashion why he bothered to grind out such unpoetical poems, especially as he didn't talk about his religion in them. I found the poems more singing than I had remembered or expected, and for that matter there is a good deal of religion in them. It is rather hard to believe there *is* any new fashion, at any rate for us old fogeys, but if there is I think Michael's poems are likely to survive it. I had dogseared a lot of pages and will send you my preferences after thinking it over.

Look, about this belief that leukemia was a result of taking on worrying work, and no time for mountains or poems, which was clearly a kind of grim satisfaction for him in hospital: I shouldn't think it is much satisfaction for you, and there is very little reason to believe it.[2] I have recently been seeing a lot of Alice Stewart, who has been doing statistics on children who died of it and is now doing the same for adults.[3] She greatly fluttered the doctors by evidence that the children were getting it from precautionary X-rays of pregnant mothers, but of course does not claim that is the only cause. What she did say, when I showed her the passage in your memoir, was that it is very hard to imagine any mechanism by which worry could affect the bone marrow, which is what goes wrong; it is quite unlike the stomach ulcers, for instance. It is a form of cancer, and we have no folk-lore that other cancers are due to worry. So I don't think you need feel sure that he sacrificed his life by his conscientiousness. All the same, it is always quite possible that the folk-lore is wiser than the doctors.

Thanking you again, and looking forward to seeing you,

Bill Empson.

Andrew Roberts

[2] Janet Adam Smith wrote in her memoir: 'Michael's own death was entirely in character with his life. He died of leukaemia: Rilke, a poet he loved and admired, also died of this disease whose causes still remain so obscure, and he described it as a disturbance of "equilibrium". Up to the war, Michael had kept his varied activities nicely in balance: his teaching, his criticism, his poetry, his climbing. From 1941 to 1945 he worked at a pitch that left no time or energy for writing, and there were next to no holidays, and no poetry. After the war he tried to rebuild the pattern . . . but the job of building up a bomb-damaged, war-dispersed college was infinitely more exacting than his pre-war teaching, in anxiety and nervous energy as well as in time and physical strength . . . A central balance had been disturbed: he suffered from the sense that some of his talents were not being used. "If you don't write poetry, you come out in purple spots," he told Kathleen Raine when she visited him in hospital.

'So leukaemia, which is a disturbance of the balance between the corpuscles of the blood, may have reflected this disturbance in his life. I think it was a death as much chosen, as much his own, as if he had died on the mountains: it was the risk inherent in the effort and exhilaration of living so variously and intensely.' (32–3)

[3] See Gayle Greene, *The Woman Who Knew Too Much: Alice Stewart and the Secrets of Radiation* (1999); and *Half a Century of Social Medicine: An Annotated Bibliography of the work of Alice M. Stewart*, ed. C. Renate Barber (1997).

TO IAN PARSONS

Department of English Literature, The University, Sheffield 10
27 April 1958

Dear Ian,

Thank you for the full statement of my account with you and the cheque (it is always rather sad to see how my first book is much better thought of than my later ones) but I doubt whether it is quite what the Income Tax people want. Would you ask your finance side just to send a statement of anything you have paid me during the tax year ending last April 5th, with dates, so that it can be checked against the bank account. It may be that there's nothing to report, as you kindly gave me an advance before the tax year began and your recent cheque came just after it; but if my lawyer is to believe this story he must be given it in black and white.

I am now very conscious of what my next book is to be about and getting on with it as fast as I can, and it might be ready next year but not before. As I think I told you, it is essays on Donne Milton Fielding Joyce and a few extras, aiming at the general point that the neo-Christian movement has greatly upset the natural and traditional way of reading such authors; so that there has to be a certain air of challenge about the book. After that, if I am spared, and we are all spared, I must try and do the book on Shakespeare next; most of it has been done already, but there is no harm in delaying a bit, and it would all need checking again in the light of later knowledge. I always worked slowly and would still do even if I didn't have to mess about being a Professor, but I hope you don't regard me as already dead. The first drafts of the chapters for my next book are getting published in the *Kenyon Review*, if you are interested to keep an eye on them.

Hope you are going on all right.

Yours very sincerely

William Empson.

Reading

THE TIMES, 1 August 1958, 9: 'London Library'

It was reported in *The Times* (30 Jul. 1958) that the London Library had lost its appeal to the Lands Tribunal against a decision of the Central London Valuation Court that its premises in St James's Square should be assessed for rating at £11,000 gross value and £9,163 ratable value. The decision by Sir William FitzGerald, president of the tribunal, overturned an exemption which had obtained for 80 years, on the basis of the Scientific Societies Act of 1843. In FitzGerald's opinion, the London Library really existed as much for the convenience of its members as for the 'purpose of literature exclusively'. A leading article decried the decision under the headline 'Philistines Rejoice'.

Sir,—I feel I ought to bear my witness as a member of the London Library, though no doubt many more competent persons will be doing so too. I have long found it so genuine and helpful towards a member who wants to get a bit of work done that to decide it is not 'devoted to literature exclusively' seems an evident injustice.

The technical interpretation of this legal phrase is evidently very tricky. Apparently the 'convenience' and 'personal gratification' of the members themselves, solely in the course of themselves 'advancing and fostering' their own knowledge of literature, is held to be sufficient to prove that the Library is not devoted to such advancing and fostering 'exclusively'. Now, Sir, a club or a college or what not from which no member could have the pleasure of learning anything, but could only learn how to teach other people, seems impossible to achieve and very bad if even approached. All scientific bodies such as the British Association are frankly and genuinely concerned to exchange knowledge among their members as well as to spread knowledge elsewhere. They would not deny that this process, if it works well, is to 'their own personal gratification', but they would not consider that pleasure in itself is enough ground for subjecting them to a punitive tax.

Yours truly,
William Empson

Department of English Literature, The University, Sheffield 10

TIMES LITERARY SUPPLEMENT, 3 October 1958, 561:
'Idea and Image'

Sir,—I warmly agreed with Dr Leavis's letter about *Paradise Lost* so far as it went, but was left doubtful what conclusion he would now draw.[1] I had understood his position to be that the poem is bad because it makes God bad (or at least, that its basic faults are most strikingly seen in the harshness and unreasonableness it imputes to God); whereas I think, like Blake and

---

[1] FRL, 'Idea and Image', *TLS*, 19 Sept. 1958, 529.

Shelley, and surely with the concurrence, however reticent, of the main Victorian tradition, that that it is precisely why the poem is so good. Dr Leavis feels it wrong that so much recent intelligent thought about the poem is getting ignored, and I feel so too; but I can sympathise with a critic who feels he cannot take seriously a proof that the poem is bad—it is so evidently not bad. If he were told instead that its theology is so very eerie that he had better read it as he does a novel by Kafka, and would then find it much more interesting and serious, I expect he would feel that the idea had sufficient inherent probability to be worth trying out.

Milton (on this view) seriously believed that he was justifying God, as he begins the poem by saying, but it is clear from the *De Doctrina* that he had come to think God extremely hard to justify (his own views are expressed there with firm confidence, but the almost indistinguishable views of opponents are described with horror as devil-worship); so that his epic would need to be a grim challenge calling forth all his powers. His Arianism and other heresies were only part of a sturdy return to the Bible; he would allow no refining upon the nature of God. He had always been the type of propagandist who is liable to be embarrassing to his own side, greatly to the credit of his intellectual honesty; so it is not very surprising that his defence of the Christian God turned out as practically a satire on him [*printed as* them]. What we cannot get away from feeling wonderful about the poem is its barbaric strength; but I should have thought a modern Christian had much better admit, and can cheerfully admit, that it gives a very barbaric picture of God.

To be definite, may I offer one detail first noticed I think by M. Paul Phelps Morand (*De Comus à Satan*, 1939). When God shows the scales in Heaven to prevent the good angels from fighting Satan in Paradise, God must be cheating his own troops to make certain of the Fall of Man.[2] All the successes of Satan are unflinchingly described as due to God's direct choice, beginning with the release of Satan from his chains; and God has already told all the good angels that man will fall, with surprising rancour, so he cannot allow them to prevent it. The effect of dramatising his [infinite: *word omitted in print*] foreknowledge in this Homeric way is to present him as a [Quilp-like: *word omitted in print*] trickster; and I do not think Milton can have failed to realise that the effect of the scales incident is to leave Satan free to produce the Fortunate Fall. If you regard the poem as inherently nerve-racking in this peculiar way, you do not feel that any

---

[2] See Paul Phelps Morand, *De Comus à Satan: L'Œuvre poétique de John Milton expliqué par sa Vie* (1939), 158–60.

separate justification is needed for its extraordinary style, which has also been so much attacked; the style is necessary for the effect [*originally* central purpose].

William Empson [Sheffield, 30 September 1958]

TO DEREK ROPER*

Derek Roper, a colleague in the Department of English Literature at Sheffield, took issue with a number of points in WE's essay on *The Spanish Tragedy* (*Nimbus* 3 (Summer 1956); repr. in *ERL* (2), 17–37).

13 October 1958

Dear Roper,

I have been mulling over the play and your comments on my theory. None of your objections seem to me decisive except one, a rather important one. You are probably right in thinking

> To thrust Horatio forth my father's way.   (III. x. 59)

means 'out of his way'; it is FORTH B. 2. in the *OED*, from out of, e.g. 'He went forth his desk'. Lorenzo has just been telling Bel-imperia that the king and their father were coming privately to consult with Hieronymo, and that he had come first to arrange the meeting; so it is just his style of pride to say 'I murdered Horatio to remove a disgusting object from my father's path'—except that now he doesn't even literally admit the murder of Horatio. There is now no approach to admitting the murder of Andrea, and we need not even be sure that the Ghost of Andrea guesses it before the end. I still think this must be the point of the presence of the Ghost, even granting that he and Revenge are only a 'frame'; but the point just gets taken for granted.

You feel this is absurd, and it does seem very odd; but the whole suggestion of the 'atmosphere' is that the Court of Spain is poisoned with criminal secrets, though it always behaves with such formal grandeur that they as it were couldn't be mentioned. The style of course is frightfully stiff, and we tend to assume that this is just Early Elizabethan Drama, but it was also very well fitted for describing what they thought about the Court of Spain. Secrets keep being hinted at; I notice now that Lorenzo, when saying he guesses Hieronymo knows who murdered his son, adds:

> A guilty conscience, urged with the thought
> Of former evils, easily cannot err.   (III. iv. 14–15)

Surely we are expected to be curious about his former evils.

You wrote that Proserpine in the production 'suggests that the Ghost might enjoy seeing Balthazar himself killed', as he [Balthazar] had killed him in battle. No, she doesn't, she grins and whispers; then Revenge cheers up Andrea by saying that at least he will see Balthazar killed, and also find out what 'the mystery' was—that is, surely, why the underworld have been puzzled how to classify him. Certainly the Ghost sticks to the idea that he wants at least to see Balthazar killed, but he makes clear that he finds the whole procedure pretty baffling. It is no use your saying that Ghosts were conventionally blood-thirsty, because the question is whether this early Ghost was a conventional one. Certainly he ends, in his rather fatuous way, by saying he is pleased about the whole sequence of deaths, listing them in order; but this is merely because the whole affair is cleared up and he is permitted to reward the good ones, whom he loves. By the way, it isn't quite such nonsense as you thought to have him send Bel-imperia

> . . . to those joys
> That vestal virgins and fair queens possess   (IV. v. 21–2)

Presumably she counts as an honorary queen rather than an honorary virgin; she was princely-minded to select her two lovers rather than submit to the wicked royal marriage. I don't say that this is very good, but it would prevent the audience from thinking the line farcical.

You were saying that surely Bel-imperia would tell what she knew when released, and could not be told more secrets than she knew already (the murder of Andrea as well as of Horatio). She says her brother is

> Too politic for me, past all compare;   (III. x. 85)

and when he ends the scene by saying

> Nay, and you argue things so cunningly,
> We'll go continue this discourse at court   (III. x. 104–5)

he means to imply feelingly 'you wouldn't dare'. He says at the beginning of the scene that he can safely release her now that the nine-days' wonder of the murder is overblown (xi), which seems absurd as the king hasn't even heard of it (III. xii. 61–2) but we presume they are accustomed to hushing such things up. I take it the main idea is that she can't expose him, both because she has no evidence but her own assertion and because she would be exposing her love affair by making it. Anyhow, she knows that the Court is determined to ignore what she says and force her into the royal marriage. You were saying that the play ignores this aspect; well, her father begins II. iii by saying he will force her into the marriage, and the king then says the heir of it will be the King of Portugal. The audience needed no more; Balthazar himself of course firmly ignores it and claims to be pathetically in love with her, even while he is murdering her lover, because that is the grand manner of his Iberian Honour. The one moment when she 'comes to life', by the way, is where she tries to save Horatio from being murdered by crying

> I lov'd Horatio but he lov'd not me   (II. iv. 58)

—a sacrifice of her pride, which is normally the chief motive of a Spanish character.

I was interested to see, going over the play again, that the sub-plot accuses Alexandro of murdering Balthazar in the battle. This gives a point to the tiresomely lengthy sub-plot, which I had thought was merely wanted to show how wicked revenge is and how usual in the Iberian peninsula; no, it brings in the idea of killing a man on your own side under cover of a battle, and this makes it easier to guess that this was what happened to Andrea. You say that the General's first account of the battle in I. ii doesn't mention that Balthazar had a troop of halberdiers up his sleeve to finish off Andrea; therefore, you feel, it can't be important when the eye-witness Horatio describes them in I. iv. But this is just what is suspicious; the Spanish General was not in the plot, but Castile and Lorenzo had tipped off Balthazar how to be ready to kill his rival in the battle. Surely this is a consistent development.

I agree that one can't say what motives Hieronymo has for killing Castile at the end, because he is at last definitely mad; my point is that this early audience would be surely moralistic, and wouldn't want to have Castile killed, let alone have Revenge approve of the killing and a punishment arranged in Hades, unless he had been shown to deserve it. I still think that, and still think the peculiar situation of the Ghost must have been meant to have its obvious explanation in view. But I must say I am shaken by your explanation of 'my father's way'; it looks as if the explanation of the mystery never comes to the surface at all though it is planned for all along. One might I suppose fall back on the irritating theory that our text is cut; or your theory that Kyd left ideas lying about which he didn't use in his final version. I might enquire whether anything has come to light about the history of the text; there was a quarrel about the property in it, as I remember.

Thanks for your notes.

W. Empson

TO MARK ROBERTS*

2 February 1959

Dear Roberts,

I came to your lecture for scientists just to learn details about Practical Criticism, but as sometimes before was led to reflect what very different opinions we hold. You remarked, as a standard example of the need for a historical approach, that no author described a complex character before the Romantics, or gave it priority or something; so I thought I had better send you this heretical little piece about *Volpone*, which I smacked out to try to save Roper from talking too much nonsense in the lecture course he had to take over hurriedly. What the children write in tutorials about Jonson has been shocking me for years.

I was sorry to hear you say that C. S. Lewis takes money on false pretences because he doesn't think English texts worth examination. He does, in his own way; just recently I was going into the text of a poem by Donne with him quite thoroughly. I suspect all you mean is that he won't parrot the shibboleths of your vain bibble-babble. The trouble with the technique, I think, is that one often feels it to be operating without the faintest idea what the point of the poem in view is, so that it has the pathos of the blind man fumbling at the elephant's tail. This quality, of course, is what would make Lewis brush it aside. I am always struck by it when Swinburne comes up in tutorials; Eliot I expect, when he pretended not to know what Swinburne meant [in 'Swinborne the Poet'], was making a joke rather than telling a lie, but a dreadful punishment followed; the disciples got stuck in the posture he had assumed, and by this time they honestly don't know. He must often by this time, as Housman said on another occasion, feel like Sin when she brought forth Death.[1]

---

[1] In the preface to his edition of *M. Manili Astronomicon Liber Primus* (1903), A. E. Housman lamented the 'conservative reaction . . . chiefly fostered by the teaching and example of Messrs Vahlen and Buecheler: men of wide learning and no mean acuteness, but without simplicity of judgment . . . Among their pupils are several who comprehend neither Latin nor any other language, and whom nature has prodigally endowed at birth with that hebetude of intellect which Messrs Vahlen and Buecheler, despite their assiduous and protracted efforts, have not yet succeeded in acquiring. Thus equipped, the apprentices proceed to exegetical achievements of

When you say that the students nearly always come to agree with your evaluation of a poem, that does not prove to my mind that the same thing would happen universally. They must be struggling, poor beasts, to capture the tone of this very peculiar fashion as best they can; I realise that it is pretty well the only part of the teaching here that they are keen about. They cannot suspect they are being blinkered (or tight-laced or foot-bound) by pursuing this vogue; but I should expect that within a generation it will seem wildly absurd, more so than the line of talk of any coterie of the 'nineties.

I am grateful to you for building up the Practical Criticism Course here, from nothing at all, as was very much needed; and I agreed with your recent letter on the topic in *Essays in Criticism*. What they seem to find in various universities is that under the present system the examination answers come out sheepish in some queer manner. Don't you think we might, once in a way, have a discussion before the group between two teachers who genuinely did disagree, and were neither of them likely to be won over? It strikes me that might have a mildly healthy effect.

Yours sincerely,
William Empson

Houghton, bMS Eng 1401 (640)

Mark Roberts spoke up for himself in a 4-page letter of 4 Feb. WE had either misunderstood or misrepresented him, he protested:

> such disagreement as you have expressed to me so far has always been about things I have said or about things I have been reported to you as saying, not about what I have published (I note that you agreed with my last bit in *Essays in Criticism*, for example). And certainly what you appear to have thought I said in my lecture last Friday was not at all what I did say. For instance, it was no part of my point about the need for historical imagination to argue that no one before the Romantics had ever drawn a complex character, as you take me to have said. What I said was that before the Romantics you 'never'—giving myself the liberty of the populariser—get the investigation of individual psychologies in all their *peculiar* detail given first place, made the principal subject in works of fiction. 'Character is fate' is a typically Romantic proposition: character in earlier fiction is not considered to be the centrally important thing . . .

which their masters are incapable, and which perhaps inspire those masters less with envy than with fright: indeed I imagine that Mr Buecheler, when he first perused Mr Sudhaus' edition of *Aetna*, must have felt something like Sin when she gave birth to Death' (*Selected Prose*, ed. John Carter (1962), 44).

Again, though I was sorry to find I had trodden on your toes in mentioning C. S. Lewis . . ., I never said he didn't think English texts worth examination; I simply quoted a remark of his about 'the real frivolity, the solemn vacuity' of valuing literature *as* literature. And I asked why, if literature *as* literature has no value, we should consider it worthy of study in our universities? . . . At all events, I certainly did not mention him because, as you put it, 'he won't parrot the Shibboleths of your [my] vain bibble-babble.' . . . But how do you know I have any Shibboleths? And what are they? I suspect you have here projected onto me something that you find elsewhere. You say in your next sentence: 'The trouble with the technique, I think, . . .' But it was I. A. Richards, not me, who was concerned with technique; I specifically said, in my lecture, that there neither is, nor can be, any technique in literary criticism . . .

Which brings me, more or less, to the next point, namely that I did *not* say that 'the students nearly always come to agree with your [my] evaluation of a poem'. What I said was that, left to themselves and without any prompting from me, they usually come, in discussion among themselves, to some sensible consensus of opinion, which represents genuine agreement among themselves and with which I do not usually disagree to any great extent. I further said that they generally want more help with the business of arguing their view as effectively as possible than they do in the matter of coming to sensible conclusions. This opinion finds support, I think, in what you say at the end of your letter: 'what they seem to find in various universities is that under the present system the examination answers come out sheepish in some queer manner'. If I understand you rightly, I certainly agree with this: there is often quite a sensible view buried in the sheepishness but they just aren't very good at getting the view over to others.

There is, however, one thing about both your letter and your *Volpone* piece which worries me a good deal. This is your habit of talking in terms of 'orthodoxy' and 'heresy': you describe the *Volpone* piece as 'heretical' and you say that current critical fashion has turned some epigrams by T. S. Eliot into a cast-iron 'orthodoxy'. I should hate to see the critical world bisected like this . . .

From some of your remarks I do wonder a little whether you do not imagine that *I* preach some party line or other. You agree with what I say in my note in *Essays in Criticism*, so you cannot mean to refer to Practical Criticism when you speak of 'this very peculiar fashion' and of students 'being blinkered (or tight-laced or foot-bound) by pursuing this vogue' . . . My views are my own, because they are what the evidence forces me to think . . .; if I agree with anyone it is on the evidence, and not on any mere *ipse dixit* . . .

Incidentally, I should strongly support any proposal that the Department meet, as a body, say, once a month, for critical discussion of selected texts of manageable length. I think it is a great pity that, at present, such debate only takes place if it is privately arranged.

TO MARK ROBERTS

8 February 1959

Dear Roberts,

Thanks for your good-humoured letter. It wasn't that you were treading on my toes about C. S. Lewis; what chiefly struck me was that he could take you to court for slander, and be sure to win, for saying in a public lecture that he is taking money on false pretences. The remark seemed to me boiling with the lunatic self-righteousness of the Leavisites, convinced that they are a persecuted sect and justified in any degree of underground behaviour; that was why I wrote to you as indistinguishable from all the other Myrmidons or Bolshies.

What you now say is of course quite different, and I trust it doesn't mean that Lewis is undermining the purity of Cambridge about Anglo-Saxon. I don't know the context of his remark, but feel sure you have misunderstood him. He wouldn't mean that studying a literature is frivolous unless it is combined with learning a language; but that it is frivolous unless related to judgements of value, experience of life, some kind of trying out [of] the different kinds of attitude or world-view so as to decide which are good ones. I would gather that you would feel the same, as you were telling the scientists earlier about Conrad and the manly virtues; whereas *Essays in Criticism* has come to feel like the squeaking of bats. It was a fatal step, I always think, when Leavis began attacking Richards' Theory of Value, which however hard to express properly is an essential plank in his platform; Leavis has never shown any philosophical grasp of mind, and took for granted that he could strut about on the rest of the platform without ever falling through the hole. The effect has been to turn his intensely moral line of criticism into a quaintly snobbish one, full of the airs and graces of an elite concerned to win social prestige, though this is much opposed to his real background and sympathies. I am afraid Richards has got accustomed to being a hot-gospeller at Harvard, on rather too easy terms as regards literary criticism, and as you suggest I don't like Lewis's Christianity a bit—though I must say that the callowness of his devotional writing doesn't seem to affect his critical judgements; but anyway I am sure they are both right to bring their own beliefs into their criticism all the time.

I agree that it would be a good thing to have more discussion in the Department, but I am rather doubtful about trying to do it in formal meetings.

I feel I have rather wasted your time by entailing an answer at such length as you wrote, but any suspicion of the full-blown Leavisite madness seems to me to demand immediate Scrutiny.

Yours with thanks,

W. Empson

Houghton, bMS Eng 1401 (640)

TO IAN PARSONS

This letter relates to WE's recording of *Selected Poems*, produced by George Hartley and issued by the Marvell Press: *Listen* LPV 3, 1959

Department of English Literature, The University, Sheffield 10
21 April 1959

My dear Ian,

Thank you for the full statement of my earnings from you, interesting to me but I am afraid not just what the tax-man wants. He wants a dated list of all money you paid me during last year, only; would you mind asking your accounts side to prepare and send that.

I was much amused to read the copy of your letter to the young man [George Hartley] from Hessle, and thought that would be the end of it; but no, he is unpuncturable and got me to do one long playing disc all the same. He made me give him two meals and hung around till he could take the night train back to Hessle, refusing to remain in London to edit the disc next day. I was so cross with him that I read the first side in a frightfully snooty voice, murdering the poetry, which I thought I had learned not to do. However I insisted on doing again three poems which it was positively bad taste to have read facetiously, and I daresay the effect will work out tolerably various in tone. He had allowed only just enough time, and much of the reading seemed to me painful to hear played back. But I expect it will do no great harm.

Yours

W. E.

Reading

TO BORIS FORD*

28 April 1959

Dear Mr Ford,

The question raised in your circular is one that many young literary people feel doubtful about, and I am very ready to offer my 'Personal Affirmation' for what it is worth. I am 52, was educated at Winchester and Magdalene College Cambridge, and taught English Literature for ten years in Japan and China before being made Professor of it at Sheffield. As to money, it isn't 'simply a living' I have to earn but enough to send two sons to public school; not to give them a class advantage, but because when they returned to England from China they knew little but Chinese, and couldn't have passed their 11+; the elder one at least would have been permanently wronged by his father if he hadn't stood cramming well enough to scrape through Common Entrance at 14. It is one of the tricky points about the Welfare State.

Poets are extremely various, but good poetry is commonly written when the author is young and again (quite often) when he is old; most poets who do both have written a lot in between which a wary reader of the collected volume will skip. Minor poets such as myself need not I think regard it as very dreadful to stop writing poetry in middle age. But, if they are determined to go on, I think it fair to say on the evidence that they would be wiser not to become dons. Writing novels I know very little about, and what else I have to say is about literary criticism.

This has become a much more powerful and interesting tool since about 1900, and many of the able literary young want to go in for it. They can I think certainly do it quite as well while employed as dons, though they should be warned against insisting they must be Professors, a capacity in which they are liable to get heavy extra chores. Bonamy Dobrée warned me like that when I was looking for a job after leaving Communist China, but the decision just lay with the dates of the Appointment Boards; as I had to write back to him while agreeing that his judgement was probably right, I would look too much of a fool if I withdrew from one and then failed to get the other. I do not regret the way it fell. But at least a literary critic can become a university lecturer without feeling that he is wasting his talent, and indeed is likely to improve it that way.

My students in Tutorials at Sheffield (of course the Professor just shares out with the other lecturers) don't seem to me as interesting as at Tokyo or Peking merely because they are less strange, but really they are just as much a problem; you need all the time to try to understand where the resistance comes from, and whether there is a good or in fact interesting reason behind it. I do not know how a literary critic could be in such close contact with the existing audience reaction anywhere else; he certainly won't do it by writing journalism in obedience to the hunch of an editor. Even the process of lecturing, however much you consider it outdated by the invention of print, means for the lecturer that he acquires in the course of years a great familiarity with his subject. So long of course as he has not played the fatal trick of writing a lecture and reading it out more than once; this I have never done, and most lecturers don't. Indeed, the trouble is that distinguished old buffers like me rapidly reach the point where they can talk away about anything in their field but can't bear to write it down. A duty of high speed in writing should not be imagined, but they can do an article or one chapter of the book each holiday if they took that into their heads as the target, and they would come to it much fresher really than if they tried to write their book all the time. I think I would become gravely ill if I tried to write my book all the time.

But this alternative is not quite what is offered to us critics. You must remember that, if a young critic makes the great renunciation, saying 'It is beneath me to read all these horrid essays', the next thing he will have to do is turn out a lot of shockingly coarse hackwork, which really is beneath him and will remain permanently in print to shame his later years. A university job does at least mean that you are free to print in a decently considered manner; and, so far from trying to stop you, most of the English universities make your promotion actually depend on eventually printing something good enough. It therefore seems to me very mistaken when young writers imagine that this is a shameful way to come to terms with the society they are living in; though I must say I never understand why they don't try [to] become postmen in country districts, surely much the best job for the type of writer who needs to feel uncontaminated.

Yours sincerely
William Empson

Houghton carbon, bMS Eng 1401 (555)

TO IAN PARSONS

Department of English Literature, The University, Sheffield 10
14 May 1959

My dear Ian,

It is tiresome of me not to have answered your letter of 28th April earlier; I could recite excuses about being busy (we have just had Eliot here opening a new library and reciting poems) but really I was just shirking reading a contract. However I now gather that it doesn't require signing, and I might just as well have faced it earlier.

As to income tax, I have changed my Tax Man this year to a man on the university staff, and my request to you was merely part of trying to give him everything the Hampstead house-property man used to ask for. He seemed very amateurish at it, but has to be kept on for quarrels about the house as representing the firm that bought its lease. I have no doubt what you say is right, and expect the new man will not need to have your statement predigested for him.

I am grateful for your suggesting 75% of the profits from Mr Hartley's venture [the recording of WE's *Selected Poems*] as my share, and certainly think it fair for the publisher to have the rest. My kind of verse is meant to be read rather than heard, and anything which further discouraged printing of suchlike stuff would seem to me bad.

I am not quite clear why you sent me this draft contract, except as it would apply to my next book; no doubt the main point is that you are offering me more than usual over Hartley. I feel rather unwilling to promise you the refusal of my next two books; it strikes me that that clause might more gracefully be struck out after any long connection such as we have had. But I have no intention of offering them to anyone else if I am spared to complete them. The only thing we have come near quarrelling over doesn't come into the contract anywhere; the author should have some power to insist on the publisher putting in correction slips, also on his informing the author when reprinting so that corrections can be inserted, even when it is a matter of second thoughts by the author, and still more when he has failed to correct his proofs correctly. You may say that the matter is adequately handled by custom, but if you are tidying up the standard contract it is a point which seriousminded authors feel greatly needs tidying. In my case, I ought at some point to get round to tidying up the mistakes in *Pastoral*, which would mean a rather heavy bit of checking in the British Museum, and I certainly don't want to do it just now.

Come to think of it, there was another point of quarrel; I shall always believe that you threw away a very big American sale of my *Complex Words* by holding it up for five years [*above the line*: Oh well, three at least] until the fashion for that kind of thing had passed, so that nobody wanted it when it came; you did this out of mere ignorance of the American market, and my impression is you wrote to me every autumn for four years in Peking that it was essentially a spring book, but what you wrote to me every spring I no longer remember. However, this kind of thing is I see covered by clause I of the new contract, because you undertake to publish within a year. You understand, I twice flew from China to American summer schools at that time so that I knew about the sales prospects for my book, and the speed with which their literary fashions were swinging to and fro; I agree that it is rather unusual for the date of publication to matter much about that type of book.

You kindly ask for an advance announcement for the Milton book, which I ought really to get done this holiday, but I keep finding more things that ought to go in. It really must be done soon. The Autumn List I take it refers to essentially spring books, forthcoming. I will try to write 150 words on the back.

Yours very sincerely
William Empson.

Professor Empson's new book surveys the main arguments of the controversy about *Paradise Lost* which has been so lively for thirty years, and claims to show that the poem feels much better if the objections to it are accepted and taken seriously; because, though thought of as literary, they are at bottom theological. The poem is wonderful because it is an awful warning, not against eating the apple but against worshipping that God; it is like Aztec or Benin sculpture, or the novels of Kafka, which raise our spirits by the same method of letting us experience a mode of life which our consciences or good sense forbid us to follow. The decision of Empson is against any form of Christianity, in the last chapter of the book; but he recognises that most modern Christians would also be strongly against Milton's God. The pressure of their Communist opponents, he considers, is very likely to make them start burning people alive again, though it is the last thing they intend; so that the effort of reconsidering Milton's God, who makes the poem so good just because he is so sickeningly bad, is a basic one of the European mind.

This seems to me what the book is about, but of course there is a good deal more about the poetry in it, which is what takes time to write. Tell me how you feel about this 'descriptive matter'.

Reading

CRITICAL QUARTERLY, 1: 2 (Summer 1959)

Dear Sirs,

May I send my congratulations on your first number. I also want to send some comments on Mr Gerber's remarks about the novel *1984*.[1] There, he says,

> the individualistic, rational, liberal and humanist conception of man is opposed, not only to party collectives, but also to the complete unconditional surrender to the transcendental, paradoxical nature of God. It almost seems as if Orwell, being gradually broken down bodily and on the point of death, had filled his political satire with unconscious or half-conscious meanings of another kind.

He gives a series of details to show that the satire

> has the age-old symbolic structure, and even phraseology, of resistant man's breakdown and conversion to some power which we generally call by the name of God.

The trouble about modern criticism, a wonderfully powerful instrument, is that it is always liable to be applied totally upside-down. Every point Mr Gerber makes (I think) is true and piercing, except the presumption that the author could not have been 'conscious'. Orwell considered that the ultimate Betrayal of the Left, the worst thing about the way Communism had developed, was that it had nearly got back to being as bad as Christianity. For a few centuries the enlightened sceptics had managed to prevent that loathsome system of torture-worship from burning people alive, but it would spring like a tiger again at any opportunity to revive its standard techniques; and in the increasingly crazy modern world, with whole continents regarding Christianity as the only alternative to Communism, the opportunity was almost sure to come. Communism had no inherent ideological need to be as torturing as Christianity, but had so far shown itself very ready to learn from its opponent. In the world of Orwell's book, it would be fatuous for the author to mention whether the capital in view is the post-communist or the post-Christian one, because they have become indistinguishable, and maintain a permanent half-hearted state of war merely to secure for both sets of rulers the pleasures of police terror. Surely Orwell made it very clear that he considered it the

---

[1] Richard Gerber, 'The English Island Myth: Remarks on the Englishness of Utopian Fiction', *CQ*, I: 1 (Spring 1959), 36–43.

ultimate shame for a man to hand over his conscience either to Stalin the Big Brother or to the incessantly gloating monster God the Father, so that he took pains in his writing to confuse them. Surely the conception of a Ministry of Love, whose towering office hagrides the city because each citizen believes it has calculated for him the torture he would find most unbearable, corresponds to nothing in Communism and a great deal in the history of Christianity. It is not even known in the story whether Big Brother is a living human ruler, a dead one presented as still alive, or a god imposed by the ruling group. That is presented as unimportant; because a man who has yielded up his conscience to an authority which craves to torture him and can only be restrained by the observance of taboos has in any case lost all real morality, both the sense of personal honour and of the public good. A reasonable criticism, I think, would be that the story becomes tiresomely incredible, owing to the determination of the author to make his allegory apply to both political groups at once. The bland assumption that he must have been unconscious at the time seems to me almost too absurd to discuss; though he himself, to be fair, regarded the certainty that his work would be used for evil as one of his inevitable torments.

I think literary criticism has got into a very corrupt frame of mind when it can regard a sustained denunciation of the Christian God as an unwitting testimonial for him; and indeed when it assumes that not even an eccentric like Orwell could still believe his own conscience must ultimately tell him the difference between right and wrong.

Yours sincerely
William Empson
Sheffield University, 24 March 1959

CRITICAL QUARTERLY, 1: 4 (Winter 1959): 'Christianity and *1984*'

Dear Sirs,

Two letters in your last number consider me blinded by hatred in using some phrases about Christianity when discussing *1984*. I tried hard to make my letter clear though short, and I see that its grammar does make these phrases describe the attitude to Christianity of the author in the book; the letter was an answer to a critic [Richard Gerber] who had found Christian tendencies in it. What can be said to literary critics who must not be told what the book means, because that hurts their feelings, but must be allowed to cosset one another with explanations that it has a morally low meaning which would have hurt the author's feelings intensely? The cult described in the novel *ought* to be called 'a loathsome system of torture-worship', and the literary critics who have so accustomed themselves to conniving at anything which can be called a Christian Paradox that they smile with tender broad-mindedness even at that, I again submit, have done moral harm to their judgement by their religious revival.

George Fraser tells me to correct my ignorance of history, and assumes I can only have a mathematical reason for thinking Christianity liable to persecute; we can be sure at least that this was not why George Orwell expected it to start persecuting again. I well know that many very saintly characters have been and are Christians; one is not tempted to deny this in thinking it a tragedy that Europe got saddled with a religion so very predisposed to enter phases of great evil. Well may Fraser appeal to the last two centuries, but the relevant question is how the Christians managed to stop burning people alive just before. A hundred years ago, Buckle's *History of Civilisation* gave a lot of evidence to prove that the growth of scepticism was what had made the change possible; during his recent centenary the reviewers all jeered at him, confident that he was out of fashion, and betrayed no idea even of what he had been discussing, let alone of why the question had ever seemed important.[1] They had been affected by the revival too.

The forecast of Orwell, in this horrible novel written while he was dying, is that Christianity and Communism will soon wear each other down till both have lost their original ideals and become the worship of a monster. I first read the book in Communist Peking, and thought its forecast absurd. But now when I find literary critics praising the final moral collapse of the hero of the novel, because it is so Christian somehow, thus exactly fulfilling Orwell's forecast of how their minds will work, without having the faintest idea that the book itself makes the forecast, I think I am justified in letting out a small cry of horror. An opponent cannot much better the position by scratching up sordid bits of evidence purporting to prove that Orwell was a sadist, or by saying that I myself am blinded by hate, unless he can support an argument that the forecast was something different. The immediate imputation of bad character is not enough; many people would not consider it actual proof of sadism to have a

---

[1] H. T. Buckle, *A History of Civilization in England*, 3 vols. (1868).

man regret the prospect of a revival of the Christian use of rack, boot, thumbscrew, and slow fire.

Yours sincerely,

W. Empson   18 October 1959

TO THE DEAN OF THE FACULTY OF ARTS

The University, Sheffield 10
19 July 1960

My dear Dean,

You kindly told me a month or two ago that there was no reason to raise the question whether my health would allow me to become Sub-Dean, with an implied promise of becoming Dean, till about this time next year. But two things have happened since which made clear that I have to trouble you with it now.

One is that the next victim on the rota, the Professor of Spanish, told me in the public scene of the Teachers' Bar that he too would refuse to become Dean if I refused. I said that he must wait till he got the medical evidence, and that it was very solid; but though an extremely friendly and generous-minded man he really does require to be satisfied by the medical evidence, because he would regard it as a point of honour not to allow himself to be cheated.

The other is that I am putting in my name for election as Professor of Poetry at Oxford next after Auden. At least, after a lunch in Oxford with Auden and W. W. Robson at which they asked me to stand, I agreed to pay for having my Cambridge MA transferred to an Oxford MA as a first step, and made quite a fuss about saying that I would only stand if Sheffield University allowed me off for the overlapping period from being Sub-Dean. My health really could not take both at once, and I begged them earnestly to regard this as literal truth so that they could explain it to my grander supporters whom they would next approach.

I said to you, if you remember, that I was only asking to put off my administrative duty for one period of three years, because by that time I expected to be more competent. I could not indeed put it off a further three years without escaping by enforced retirement. When I add Oxford to my stomach, the two together are bound to strike the Professor of Spanish as a farcical case of malingering; I had better have left one of them out. But the Faculty had much better be told the truth, which is that they have a natural though not close connection.

The Oxford appointment (for three years) as you know is an odd one, made by vote of all Oxford MA's, requiring only six lectures a year and the reading out of some local compliments in Latin always composed by someone else, with the salary of 350 pounds. For my first year at Sheffield [1954] I was allowed to be also Professor of [Rhetoric at] Gresham College, an almost exactly similar appointment though now so derelict that I gave it up after a year. The Oxford appointment feels better now that Auden has held it, and I am sure that Sheffield University as a whole would feel mildly gratified if I got it; but I will not stand for the election unless I am already assured that I will not be made Sub-Dean the year after.

The politics of these elections are in a way only an Oxford game but they are played with great energy. Three years ago I was being pressed very strongly to stand, chiefly by the science side, but as soon as Auden appeared as a candidate I posted off my reasons for refusing to compete with Auden. I am now told by my side (including Auden) that I must stand because otherwise a bad candidate would get in, almost certainly Helen Gardner, a very generous-minded woman in her way but a fanatical Christian. I offered to hold my candidature in reserve to swing in someone good; but I was told that further alterations of the statute, so as to make the conditions able to appoint good men, could only be made if I carried straight on from Auden with the same recommendations.

As to my health, I was assured that what I have been publishing in American magazines for the last ten years could be read straight out as my lectures; the Oxford statutes would consider them new lectures because they had not been published in England, and the regulation would not be felt as absurd because they would be completely unknown to the audience. I could not be too ill to read out what I was already known to have ready, when the real work I was asked to do was to help in removing the limitation of the appointment to an Oxford MA. I am very doubtful whether I could do this work if I got the job, but I certainly could not refuse it on grounds of health. I was driven into making a conditional acceptance.

The reason why I write at such length, boastfully as it may appear, is that I need to explain the relation between my stomach pains and my mental state. Now that I have at last sent off the book about Milton to the printers, I have two more books in line which have in rough already been printed by chapters in the broad American journals; all of them need a great deal of re-writing, but during the next three years I may hope to do a great clearing up of all this back-log. Oxford means nothing to me, I promise you I am far too vain for that, but it would make my books very much better if I were allowed to go and lecture on the material in Oxford, and meet intelligent comment, before I decided what to print. I mean, I do not want the job for the reputation, but I do want it for the experience; and it would be no use to me in a later three-year period, because Empson is though very full of his line of talk also very near the age when he has shot his bolt.

As soon as I could get away from my duties this holiday I settled down to make the last corrections to my book about Milton, which I had promised to do weeks before, and I was seriously afraid I might be in too much pain to be able to finish it. Please do not suppose that all this talk about my health is a trick. There is no evidence for my waking at three in pain and trying to hold it down with one medicine after another till I go to work, except that I began asking for treatment as soon as I got back from Communist China and have told a tolerably consistent story about these occasional attacks. I am keenly conscious of the absence of any other evidence, and realise that you, Sir, must at once be conscious of it professionally. But the doctors are both astonished when I say that I need evidence before the Faculty will believe me.

I expect that, if I am allowed to get printed what I have been getting ready during the next four years, I will then find that my stomach is quite ready to let me take my turn of duty. This is after all the last period in which I feel I have unfinished work and a duty to finish it; if it had not been for one or two accidents, the usual plan would have ticked over for me as a natural one, just as it has done for many other people.

Yours sincerely
William Empson.

Houghton, bMS Eng 1401 (669)

THE LISTENER, 28 July 1960, 157: 'Milton's Satan'

In response to WE's 'Satan Argues His Case', the first of three radio talks on *Paradise Lost* printed in *The Listener*, 64 (7 Jul. 1960), C. S. Lewis protested (21 Jul. 1960, 109): 'Professor Empson is mistaken when he says I have argued that Milton's Satan "must be meant to be funny". I took *Paradise Lost* as a tragic, and *The Egoist* as a comic, treatment of "the satanic predicament". I said that Milton has subordinated the absurdity of Satan to his misery; but that, just as Meredith cannot exclude all pathos from Sir Willoughby, so Milton cannot exclude all that is ridiculous from Satan. Surely the distinction between saying this and saying that Satan is "meant to be funny" is not imperceptibly fine?'

Sir,—I was saying that God laughs at Satan, in his first words in the poem, and that this supports Professor Lewis's view, though it is rather coarse of God. I know that Professor Lewis would show better feeling. But his account of Satan as morally absurd in *A Preface to Paradise Lost* is very impressive, and clearly true up to a point. Milton would think it in order to be sardonic about the enemy of mankind, and seems to have disliked the character he imagined. My point is that, at the same time, he was scrupulously careful to give the character the strongest arguments he could invent. So it did not occur to me that fairness demanded my recalling the qualifications of tone in Professor Lewis's position; though I readily agree that he put them in.

Yours, etc.

William Empson

TIMES LITERARY SUPPLEMENT, 5 August 1960:
'The Muse in Chains'

Sir,—While realizing how little I understand about the music of English verse, I am sure that no metrical theorist will get anywhere until he attends to a point recovered from the mind of Coleridge by Mr Robert Graves. Practically all good English poetry uses 'jammed stress', that is, two adjoining syllables count as one stress to the ear. Phoneticians cannot imagine this because they unconsciously assume that a consonant does not make a noise, only a vowel; but on a recording machine two syllables can easily appear as one jagged piece of noise. Instead, like Mr Hawkes,[1] they divide the stresses on vowels into half and quarter stresses; but this only takes them farther away from what the human mind actually does when it feels a line to make a beautiful rhythm. The recognition, I think, is always immediate, simply a feeling, and often comes on first reading, but it also often only comes after long patient reading of a poet; and I have known Far Eastern students to write convincingly in correct English that they had just discovered one of these beauties of rhythm, when they could hardly speak the sounds of the language at all.

[1] See 'The Muse in Chains' (leading article), *TLS*, 13 May 1960, 305; and ensuing correspondence including letters from Terence Hawkes on 1 Jul. 1960, 15 Jul. 1960; an exchange with WE printed in *A*, 165–6; and an article by Hawkes, 'The Problems of Prosody', *Review of English Studies*, 3: 2 (Apr. 1962), 32–49. Terence Hawkes (b. 1932) taught at the State University of New York at Buffalo, 1957–9, and from 1959 at University College, Cardiff; his other publications include *Linguistics and English Prosody* (with E. L. Epstein, 1959), *Metaphor* (1972), *That Shakespeherian Rag: Essays on a Critical Process* (1986), *Meaning by Shakespeare* (1992).

What really goes on, I concluded, is a larger process of which 'jammed stress' is merely an essential ingredient. The mind learns how to balance between two alternative ways of giving a line the (say) five stresses which it is understood to promise; this point of balance is what is felt to be beautiful; and the more natural or colloquial or energetic alternative usually means allowing yourself to scan by a 'jammed stress'. No doubt quarter stresses really occur, and could be used in programming a machine to speak verse tolerably; but they have nothing to do with the impulse at work in the mind which recreates the music intended by the poet, because that works by recognizing that two alternative ways of making the agreed five beats are wanted both together. Of course, people often get interested in delicacy of pronunciation, but that is a very much more tiresome thing than getting the rhythm right.

William Empson

NEW STATESMAN, 60 (10 September 1960), 340:
'Sex and Paperbacks'

Sir,—Mr Barclay writes: 'Can it be that we have all—publishers included—underestimated the public's taste by using the gimmick of the "sexy" cover?'[1] The paperbacks of the Poirot stories show the hero either with a shaggy-dog moustache or with a tiny moustache clipped very thin; whereas every reader knows that one is going to hear about his very large waxed moustaches all through each book. The pictures cannot be planned to make M. Poirot sexy, because his moustaches are his only sexual asset. The blurbs of paper-backs in general are just as ignorant as the hideous pictures. I have just read *The Dark Frontier* by Eric Ambler, an excellent story about the invention of an atom bomb, first published in 1936. Any reader would be more likely to buy the book if told it had been a well-imagined forecast, but the blurb only boasts that it has all the usual ingredients of a political adventure story.

Mr Barclay assumes that 'we', the publishers and illustrators, were making some calculation in such cases about how to sell the book. Surely it is obvious that they were incapable of making any calculation, because they hadn't read it. It is they who are the illiterates, not the buyer.

---

[1] Christopher Barclay's letter, 'Sex and Paperbacks' (*New Statesman*, 3 Sept. 1960, 309), followed a querulous article by Walter Allen, 'Paperbacks' (20 Aug. 1960, 253–54). WE harmlessly conflates two separate sentences by Barclay.

TO CHRISTOPHER RICKS*

Sheffield University
20 September 1960

Dear Mr Ricks,

Thank you for sending me the off-print of your article on The Changeling; I had missed that number.[1]

I feel no doubt that the double meanings you describe are all there, or all but one where you express doubt; and that they are meant to be felt as pointed; more like jokes than poetry, though grim dramatic irony rather than jokes.[2] It is also probably an important bit of explanation when you say that the *use* of the coarse fun of the sub-plot is to draw attention to the double meanings of the tragic plot, or make the audience ready enough to see all round them.[3] It certainly makes the play read much better as a whole.

I am only rather doubtful how much the two authors would intend it, and incidentally how far it could be got clear in a modern production. I haven't read enough bad Elizabethan plays to make an estimate, but I gather they so often just jammed a tragic and comic story together that the audience could hardly expect this one to be doing anything else. The authors clearly knew enough to make a few cross-references between puns in the comic and tragic parts, but they might do this for their own satisfaction, without much hope that anybody would recognise it. It would be enough to suppose that Middleton [author of the main-plot] read

---

[1] CR, 'The Moral and Poetic Structure of *The Changeling*', *E in C*, 10: 3 (Jul. 1960), 290–306. When he started teaching at Oxford, CR was to recall, 'I wrote an essay on Middleton's tragedy *The Changeling*, to which Empson twenty-five years earlier had brilliantly (and soundly) turned his mind. In *Some Versions of Pastoral*, his concern had been with the bizarre mad-house sub-plot, what it was up to, what such things might ever be up to. My essay was on some affiliated puns in the play, turning upon the act of sex and other acts. Because my argument owed much not only to Empson on the sub-plot but to Empson on Complex Words, I took the liberty (and fraternity, while disclaiming equality) of sending him a copy when the article came out in *Essays in Criticism* in 1960' ('Empson as a Man of Letters in the 1960s', *News from the Republic of Letters*, no. 7 (Sept. 1997), 7).

[2] CR refers (299) to the scene in which Beatrice sends for Diaphanta in order to show Alsemero out of the room: 'Perfect your service, and conduct this gentleman | The private way you brought him' (II. ii. 54–5).

'Diaphanta,' writes CR, 'is indeed to perfect her service with Alsemero—and both *private* and *way* hint at it.

'This last conjecture is perhaps over-ingenious, but one cannot doubt the importance of the double meaning of *service* at the height of the play, in the interchanges between Beatrice and De Flores. *Service*, like *blood*, *will*, *act* and *deed*, presents two meanings (one sexual) which the tragedy shows to be inextricable.'

[3] CR, 291: 'The sub-plot is full of obscene and witty puns; often they are the same as are used more quietly in the main-plot; and always they alert us to a fascination with innuendo, making it possible for us to pick it up in the main-plot without poetic grossness or buffoonery.'

Rowley's part (collaboration was usually done for speed, but even so he could read the comic stuff a few scenes ahead) and felt a solemn irony about the comic lunatics, who were presumably in the joint plan to start with; so that he wrote with these echoes in his mind. Surely, the broad ideas about a changeling and an anti-masque and indeed a comic lunatic were much more obvious to that audience than a modern one, and the connections of thought come more from those ideas than from the puns. Still, I am sure what you say is true, even if one can give an easier account of how it happened.

I also disagree with your monolithically moral attitude, which maybe you have just accepted as part of the current atmosphere; but I am not sure that it makes very much difference here. The theatre audience was always against the Arranged Marriage, so it would start off in favour of Beatrice, though very soon her protest has become far too rough. The dramatist does not rub in the idea of protest because he wants to swing the audience away from her, but it would be there anyhow. After all persons then who felt as you moral boys do now would have solemnly assured you that the theatres expressed an immoral point of view, so you can't be on firm historical ground when you all take for granted that they didn't. It is merely part of a swing of fashion towards decorum, like those described by Addison and Macaulay. Then again, part of the wickedness which does get ascribed to Beatrice was thought of as typically Italian, not what the English would do, one was glad to reflect, but terrifically aristocratic, and we felt rather provincial at being unable to rival the Southern Europeans there. On both counts, one was less inclined to regard Beatrice as simply a bad girl; and what the play drives home, as you say, is that she seems blindly unconscious even of being likely to run into trouble.

One might get a little more point into the double meanings here. *Service* and *employed* and *performance* are all to do with harnessing love for a social convenience, as the Arranged Marriage presumes it can do; and that is the first cause of the whole action. Beatrice seems from the start, as you say, to have a perverse craving, seen in a nagging expression of bodily disgust, for the man she thinks only suitable to be her Hired Murderer; and this might be seen as a parody of the attitude of a man who makes an Arranged Marriage.[4] Her blindness about the intention which his leering puns

---

[4] CR, 302: 'How far are we to take her initial loathing for him as sexual in origin? Certainly from the start of the play, she is far from indifferent to him; her thoughts return again and again to him, with obvious fascination . . . She herself is to say that "My loathing | Was prophet to the rest, but ne'er believ'd" (v. iii. 156–7). And in support of such a view, one might perhaps instance those pregnant interchanges with De Flores, where for all her simple cunning and, in the later scene, outraged modesty, she picks again and again the words which are tragically capable of a double meaning.'

express so frankly you explain as due to 'egotistic singlemindedness', rightly as far as that goes, but it in turn is due to the aristocratic conviction that she can always keep control of a 'servant'. That wouldn't need pointing out to Swinburne, and I expect he took it for granted in your quotation.[5] All this brings a bit of social criticism into the comments of the play, though only as part of a controversy very familiar to the intended audience; and that feels less dismal and stupid than what the current school considers a 'moral' deduction. Undoubtedly she becomes a kind of lunatic when she breaks out of the social order in such a tigerish manner; but she is also seen as breaking out of a bad one.

You remark with an air of relief that we are not 'faced with Complex Words' here.[6] Not, I agree, so long as the point of the pun is merely that Beatrice cannot realise the obvious warning in the insinuation of De Flores; but so far as the puns build up to a bit of social criticism they carry a bit of general doctrine, and take effect as Complex Words, though I would not say that examining them as such is a needed route towards seeing all round the drama. You say that I found some 'curiously minor connections between the sub-plot and main-plot', but I still think that these would be familiar ones for the intended audience, and quite as likely as the puns to make them feel that the two parts worked together as a whole.[7] This of course would make them notice and appreciate the puns.

However, after searching my mind for the limits of my agreement, I think you bring out some very important points; I must mind and not forget them.

Yours with thanks,

William Empson.

---

[5] Responding to critics (inc. William Archer and E. E. Stoll) who consider Beatrice not very intelligent, a poor judge of character, and even 'imbecile', CR remarks (302): 'Yet elsewhere Beatrice *does* seem to be clever and cunning. Surely we can save her cleverness by suggesting that her failure is an egotistic single-mindedness, a tragic failure to see puns. Obsessed by her own wishes and meanings, she does not see that De Flores has other wishes and other meanings—but that does not make her unintelligent. The tragedy springs from the fact that hers is "a nature", in Swinburne's admirable phrase [*The Age of Shakespeare* (1908), 181], "absolutely incapable of seeing more than one thing or holding more than one thought at a time".'

[6] CR, 303: 'There is no dramatic and moral exploration of a complex linguistic situation, as there is, say, with *Nature* in *King Lear*. On the contrary, what makes the verbal structure dramatically viable is precisely its combination of fundamental simplicity with local subtlety.'

[7] CR, 301: 'That there are some curiously minor connections between the sub-plot and the main-plot has been shown by Empson in *Some Versions of Pastoral*; yet a major connection still seems lacking, and I must admit that the thesis which I have put forward cannot establish one. But it does point to one clear function of the sub-plot: its use of innuendo . . . The sub-plot is full of obscene wit . . . Often the same words are played with, or the sexual applications chosen: employment, honour, serve, serve the turn, forward, bold; always it is clear that this is a play full of innuendo. But the crude buffoonery of the sub-plot (the meanings are forced on us) makes possible the seriousness of the main-plot.'

TO IAN PARSONS

The University, Sheffield 10
19 November 1960

Dear Ian,

Things are about back to where they were when I spoke to you about putting in for the Oxford Professorship, and you expressed a benevolent interest. Afterwards I was told that the election would be next autumn, and then Oxford refused to let a Cambridge man stand; but now they have thrown it open to all comers and the election is next February. I take it the Milton book won't be out by then, which is probably just as well.

Helen Gardner and Edith [Enid] Starkie are both putting in, and either would make the first Oxford female professor; I am told that sentiments of chivalry are very likely to win the day. Eliot has refused to stand, but I gather that talent-scouts are peering into distant valleys.

I have been getting almost chronic teachers' stomach-ache recently, and would be rather relieved to lose; but as a sport it seems quite entertaining. Let me know if you have any tips for wooing the electorate.

Yours
Bill Empson.

Reading

TO IAN PARSONS

The University, Sheffield 10
6 December 1960

My dear Ian,

Very kind of you. W. W. Robson of Lincoln College gave me lunch with Auden when Auden told me to apply, and is busying himself, but now that the thing is thrown open he might prefer some other candidate; he tele-phoned me in Sheffield to report the victory in Congregation and asked who else I thought might be asked to stand (I suggested Graves, but I don't think they will) or perhaps merely who I would refuse to stand against.[1] I

---

[1] W. W. Robson wrote in an undated letter to JH: 'Auden, the holder, would have liked Empson to succeed him. I asked Auden and Empson to lunch in my rooms at Oxford to discuss the matter. Empson said he would like the post, as it would save him from having to be Dean of his faculty at Sheffield, which he didn't want to be, and might stimulate him into writing some more poems. But he wouldn't run against Robert Graves. Graves was willing to run, as it turned out.

'I organized Graves's campaign and got the statute changed so that he could run (which he otherwise could not have, as he had not graduated MA in the ordinary course). This was an

understood him to say earlier that Isaiah Berlin* was on our side; I know him slightly and called on him not long ago, and he is an old pal of Auden of course. I don't know anybody in Sheffield who would be likely to affect Oxford. Krebs the Nobel bio-Chemist who went to Oxford from Sheffield[2] muttered something into my ear while we were both making speeches to a Social Medicine conference in Oxford last term (implying that he was incessantly at work on my behalf in the highest and most secret councils of the university), and I must write to a Boer scientist Kits van Heyningen who was pressing me to stand last time. I am sure the scientists are my best bet, but those seem to be all the strings I have. Come to think of it, I can well write to William Hayter [Warden of New College].

But they talk so very busily, making a duty of it like diplomats, at Oxford, that it doesn't seem much use telling them a thing they are certain to have heard already. This of course applies only to my own timid attempts to recommend myself; if you would put in a subtle reason for preferring Empson, different for different voters one would expect, that would be most valuable.

Yours with thanks
William Empson

Reading

TO IAN PARSONS

Department of English Literature, The University, Sheffield 10
6 December 1960

Dear Ian,

Wash out all that I said this morning; to no purpose did I address a Social Medicine Conference in Oxford. Robert Graves has consented to stand, and I said (as soon as they removed the qualification) that I wouldn't stand against him, so I withdraw. Of course he may get tired of it fairly

---

inexplicable mistake: I knew what Graves was capable of, having read his Clark Lectures. But I went ahead. Graves was not a success as Professor of Poetry (in contrast to Auden). Empson might have been better, but as he was so unpredictable this cannot be said with confidence. In any case, he would not have been elected. Convocation usually chooses someone from Oxford.

'Auden and Empson were in good form at this lunch. I remember an amusing discussion of P. G. Wodehouse (his private personality, rather than his work).'

[2] Sir Hans Krebs (1900–81) was born in Germany and came to England in 1938. He taught at Oxford before moving to a Chair in Sheffield. Later he held the Whitley Chair of Bio-chemistry at Oxford, 1954–67. It was at Sheffield that he discovered the cycle of chemical reactions within the cell (the Krebs cycle or citric cycle) that turns food into energy, for which he was awarded the Nobel Prize, 1953.

soon. (I wonder if he is an MA? However, they wanted to change the rules some time.)

So call off your team; I shall always remember the proposal and wish I had seen it in action.

Yours

Bill Empson.

Reading

CRITICAL QUARTERLY, 3: 1 (Spring 1961)

Sheffield, December 1960

Dear Sirs,

I see that an article on *Lear* by Barbara Everett, in your current number,[1] lists me among recent critics who have accepted the pietistic views of A. C. Bradley [*Shakespearean Tragedy*, 1904], so far at least as to believe that Lear dies of a passion of joy. I have been feeling that Professor L. C. Knights takes a pietistic view in his recent book, and that Shakespeare would be surprised at the whole idea of using the play as a source of doctrine;[2] so I would like to try to make my position clearer.

Was Bradley the first to think Lear dies of joy? I expect many critics had thought it did not need writing down. We have been told in a set speech that Gloucester, a usual parallel to Lear, has died of joy; and I don't know what else the final words of Lear could mean but that he imagines he sees Cordelia breathing. But he is being fooled again; during a performance, one could hardly take this as implying a consoling dogma. The scenes with Gloucester (I grant) assume that to fool an old man may do him good, at least if it keeps him from blasphemy; perhaps because our frame of mind at the moment of death decides our status in the next world. But the thoughts of these deceived persons can hardly be taken as a revelation; even if Shakespeare felt them so, and even if we ought to know that from the style, he could not expect the audiences to know it. The final delusion of Lear is meant to be very sad but in a way a mercy, as the characters tell us.

I was trying ['Fool in Lear', *SCW*] to support the view of George Orwell, that the old man is 'still cursing, still not understanding anything'

---

[1] Barbara Everett, 'The New King Lear', *CQ*, 2: 4 (Winter 1960), 325–39; citing WE's 'Fool in Lear', *SCW*, 125–57. Everett (b. 1932) was a Fellow of Newnham College, Cambridge, and of Somerville College, Oxford, 1965–99. Her publications include *Poets in Their Time* (1986), and *Young Hamlet: Essays on Shakespeare's Tragedies* (1989).

[2] L. C. Knights, *Some Shakespearean Themes* (1959).

at the end.[3] I failed even to make anyone rebut this view; perhaps from not being clear enough, but anyhow it seems to be unmentionable. To accept it, one need not deny that Lear achieves his renunciation and regeneration, in the 'I will drink it' and 'birds in a cage' scenes. The point is that the story knocks him off his perch; when Cordelia is hanged, he again wants revenge and kills the slave who was doing it. What is more, we should think worse of him if he continued to be a non-attached yogi; the reason why the play has to kill Cordelia, which has so often been found wanton, is that we need to know whether Lear's renunciation of the world will survive her death. Immediately after the 'I will drink it' scene, Kent says that the drums of the approaching army can already be heard; they can be used to insist that Lear though now genuinely angelic is no longer in a condition to save his daughter's life. They ought to get steadily louder until the battle, making a kind of answer to the thunder which was the previous background noise.

The Orwell view thus seems to me to make a better play, so far as the difference is noticeable. The reason why no one will mention it, I think, is that it doesn't feel religious enough; but Shakespeare could at least feel that it wouldn't get him into trouble with the ecclesiastical authorities.

[William Empson]

TO MAURICE BRUCE*

Studio House, Hampstead Hill Gardens, London NW3
[n.d. ?1960]

Dear Professor Bruce,

I am sorry I forgot to return your two books about *Ecclesiastes* before leaving; they are on the shelves of my room at the University if you want them, though I am afraid you might have to get the key from the porter. They were most helpful, especially the more textual smaller one, which I must buy for next year. I will give them back next term.

I should be grateful if you could advise me on two points about *Paradise Lost* which I can't get clear from the literary critics. Milton says in the prose summary before one book [v] that God sends Raphael to talk to Adam and Eve 'to render man inexcusable', and some critic remarked that here Milton was only quoting St Paul. The only reference to the word listed at the end of my Bible is irrelevant; could you put me on to what text this

---

[3] See George Orwell, 'Lear, Tolstoy and the Fool', *Inside the Whale* (1940), 108.

critic (I forget who he was) could have meant?[1] Critics of course have recently become very interested in the theological position of Milton, but they don't strike me as very first-hand about it.

The other question is larger, about what Milton can have meant when he introduced the War in Heaven by making God say

> This day I have begot whom I declare
> My only Son   [v. 603–4]

and so forth, which Satan regards as *ultra vires*. Now C. S. Lewis for example (Preface to P. L.), defending Milton, says he had able backing for the phrase but merely chose to put it in an odd place.[2] It should apply to the final glorification of the Son at the Last Day, but would not seem at all shocking when put here. It comes in the Second Psalm, is interpreted by St Paul as a kind of prophecy of Christ, by making a Jewish leader into something corresponding to Christ, occurs in one Gospel manuscript as said by the voice from Heaven at the Baptism of Christ, and is referred to by another early Father as coming there in the lost Gospel to the Hebrews. I am not trying to teach you, only to show that I have poked round a bit; but then in wondering what the point of all this could be I invented a little theory, which I want to ask your advice about. The phrase in Ancient Hebrew, 'I now beget this man', was a legal formula of adoption, and the evident literal absurdity of it was therefore meant to be recognised as driving home its meaning, 'From now on, he is to be treated in every possible way as my son'. Or is this not so? If it is so, it explains the air of embarrassment about the variations of text; the phrase would be excellent

---

[1] St Paul berates the heathens (Rom. 1. 19–21): 'For what can be known about God is plain to them, because God has shown it to them. Ever since the creation of the world his invisible nature, namely, his eternal power and deity, has been clearly perceived in the things that have been made. So they are without excuse; for although they knew God they did not honour him as God or give thanks to him, but they became futile in their thinking and their senseless minds were darkened.'

[2] Cf. C. S. Lewis, *A Preface to 'Paradise Lost'* (1942), 86: 'Professor Seurat suggests that this heresy [Arianism, the disbelief in the coeternity and equality of the Three Persons of the One God] appears in *Paradise Lost*, V, 603, when the Father announces to the angels "This day have I begot whom I declare My onely Son." Now if this is taken literally it means that the Son was created after the angels. But that is impossible in *Paradise Lost*. We learn in III, 390, that God *created* the angels by the agency of the Son, and Abdiel refutes Satan by making the same assertion in V, 835—to which the best answer Satan can bring is that "we weren't there to see it done". The puzzle would be insoluble if Milton had not given the solution in *De Doctrina*, I, V, where he says that "beget", when used of the Father in relation to the Son, has two senses, "the one literal, with reference to the production of the Son, the other metaphorical, with reference to His exaltation" (Bohn, Prose Wks, vol. IV, p. 80). And it is obvious that "This day I have begot" must mean "This day I have exalted," for otherwise it is inconsistent with the rest of the poem. And if this is so, we must admit that Milton's Arianism is not asserted in *Paradise Lost*.' See too *MG*, 99–102.

in the Psalms, as an adoption of a forerunner, but not suitable to Christ, who was a Son already; or at least it might be misunderstood by a person experienced in Jewish custom. And when Milton uses it at this point of his story, of course knowing his Hebrew and his texts very well, so that the Father adopts the Son on a specific day in Heaven, he is hinting at his own Arian views. However, though I suspect this must be a bit true somehow, the line still seems wrong according to Milton's views. He believed that the Son was co-eternal with the Father and the instrument by which the Father created the angels, so that his Arianism doesn't come to very much 'on paper', one might think; this belief comes out both in the poem and in the long unpublished *Christian Doctrine*, which seems evidently an unvarnished search for what he believed. One might say, the only use for the phrase at that point of the poem is to make it natural for Satan to revolt, which he does on the ground that he believes the Father to be merely a usurping angel. (I have read somewhere that Milton had ancient authority for this explanation of Satan's behaviour, but forget where). In any [incomplete]

Houghton carbon, bMS Eng 1401 (519)

In a related (unpublished) review entitled 'Rajan on Milton' [B. Rajan, *'Paradise Lost' and the Seventeenth Century Reader* (1947)], WE wrote:

> It seems to me a timid book, and I get an impression that this is not merely out of 'scholarship' but that people feel the classics need conserving; it has become important to insist on the obvious surface meaning for fear that might be forgotten. This may actually be becoming necessary but should not frighten people off considering the whole effect on Milton's contemporaries if you like—that is quite enough. The force of the thing, obviously, depends partly on the strength of the objections to the surface meaning which had to be overcome.
>
> He is interesting on 'This day I have begot'; I did not realise that even on the 'exultation' interpretation Milton has wilfully moved back the exultation from the resurrection of the dead to before creation.[3] The purpose as he says is no doubt to give a parallel in heaven to the apple viewed as indifferent in itself; both are mere tests of obedience with no other sense in them, and the fatal sin of both Satan and Adam is mere disobedience to an arbitrary rule. This shows, I think, how determined Milton was to rub in the inherent nullity of the apple, which his poetry none the less denies all the time. Rajan admits that the intoxicating effects of the apple do not look as if it is inherently

[3] See Rajan, *'Paradise Lost'*, 3, and 143 n.

null, but merely says Milton put it in for 'dramatic effect'.[4] Does he think dramatic effects are any bit of random padding? The next question for him would be why, if the 'Tree of Knowledge' doesn't inherently give knowledge, God takes care to drive our parents away from the 'Tree of Life'; he doesn't mention that.

He makes a good point [94] in saying that the Devil was assumed to be viewed not primarily with curiosity or even hatred but with fear; therefore he thinks nobody would take seriously the case which the Devil presents (even though he traces direct quotations by the Devil from antiroyalist tracts). But the more the Devil is viewed with fear the more there is a fear that he may be telling some monstrous truth; a passionate denial of his arguments is a way of taking them seriously. Rajan I notice can make jokes which assume the parallel between Milton and our first parents; e.g. Eve going alone to the temptation 'is not interested in a fugitive and cloistered virtue'.[5] What does this joke mean unless there is a connection between Milton's own disobedience and theirs?

He says that Milton gives a feeling in the first books that Satan might succeed in defeating God. 'The conflict therefore is neither Promethean nor farcical. It is dramatically real in proportion as you assent to the illusion of equality which the poem communicates' [96]. Here again, what does he think a drama is? How much more real could a conflict be in a poem? And as soon as you suppose that this God, who is treated simply as one of the characters, might be defeated, then you tacitly admit Satan's whole case—that God is only pretending to be the omnipotent creator and is really a usurping angel. When he says that Milton's 'verse' is not adequate to deal with Heaven [128–29] I think he is merely belittling the poet in order to evade the poem; the fact is that as soon as you make God a simple individual (instead of treating him by metaphysical poets' methods) you give Satan a logical case—and thus of course make him all the more dangerously wicked.[6]

TO IAN PARSONS

Department of English Literature, The University, Sheffield 10
22 January 1961

Dear Ian,

I will be posting off the last chapter [of *MG*] to the printer tomorrow. I was expecting your hurry-up note to be ruder; it came by the same post as

---

[4] Rajan discusses the 'architecture' of the poem on p. 45.
[5] Rajan, 69 (Rajan is alluding to *Areopagatica*).
[6] See also *MG*, 34–5.

a letter from Edmund Wilson,[1] handing on the report of a Dominican about what Aquinas said, from which it is clear that my sentence had much better go out. He wishes Aquinas *had* said something like that, but can only find faint hints that Aquinas even thought it; James Smith must have made it up when we were all young. My bit had better go out anyway, and I have cut some other short items which seem only annoying or open to attack. I am very glad I called the chapter back, and am sure it is much improved.

I haven't cut anything I thought honour required keeping in, and I must say I find the chapter pretty oppressive to read. Still, it needn't be done again one would think; the next book ought to be able to illustrate the position quite light-heartedly.

Did you see Koestler kicking me in the New Statesman?[2] It had a useful effect perhaps in causing a sober approach to revising the last chapter. I did slip up there, but from too much sobriety oddly enough; I have had to stop drinking and smoking to avoid stomach-ache, and it has a very uneasy effect on the literary output.

Yours
Bill Empson.

Reading

---

[1] Edmund Wilson (1895–1972), writer, literary journalist, critic and historian; his works include *Axel's Castle* (1930), *To the Finland Station* (1940), *The Wound and the Bow* (1941), *The Scrolls from the Dead Sea* (1955), and *Patriotic Gore* (1962).

[2] Arthur Koestler wrote to the *New Statesman* on 20 Jan. 1961 to 'pin a lie'—'a forged quotation'—in WE's review of *The Lotus and the Robot* (repr. in *A*, 605–6); his protest included these remarks:

'After obliquely hinting that my attitude is that of a sympathiser with Hitler (suited to Mosleyites in 1939) and similar smears, Empson proceeds: "Soon after the war, Koestler felt he hadn't enough petrol and wrote to the *Partisan Review*, 'The Labour Party is betraying its trust. I have to bicycle a mile and a half for my groceries. We old-fashioned country squires are being wronged' (or words leaving that impression)."

'The alleged quotation, from beginning to end, was invented by Empson, and the qualifying phrase in brackets does not diminish the effect of this slanderous fabrication. The article to which he refers appeared in *Partisan Review* in Nov. 1947. It discussed the Labour government's decision to abolish the petrol allowance for private motoring, and pointed out that it compelled the little man to lay up his family car or motor bike, whereas—"the squire has his farming allowance and will be seen driving about the countryside as before, by using the simple dodge of putting a sack of potatoes or pig-food into the dicky to prove that he is on some farming errand. In industrial areas the directors, managers, executives, etc, will have their business allowance . . . From the point of view of the working man-in-the-street it is still 'they' who flit past him in their cars" . . .

'I expect your reviewer to apologise in unambiguous terms for imputing to me words which I never wrote and opinions which I never held or expressed.'

WE was obliged to subscribe to the following apology (drafted by WE himself), in the same issue: 'The sentences in quotation marks were meant to be a parody of the article in *Partisan Review*, which I had not seen since it was new. I thought I had made this clear and I am sorry if they were taken as a quotation, and for suggesting that Koestler used words "politically leaving that impression". I agree that unchecked reminiscing is a bad thing, since one's memory is likely to play one false, as it has admittedly done in this case.' (See *New Statesman* archive at the University of Sussex: ref. *NS* Review Corresp. Empson.)

TO FRANK KERMODE

WE sent Frank Kermode an offprint of his essay 'A Defense of Delilah'
(*Sewanee Review* 68 (Spring 1960), 240–55). In his thank-you note (12 Feb.
1961), Kermode said that he believed Milton 'was deliberately not being
speculative about theology in the poem; of course it must have made him
think about theology, and he was building up the DCD at the time, so that
his views could change very considerably without making much or any
difference to what he said in the poem . . . I really think there is something
to be said for seeing it [*Paradise Lost*] as deliberately not selling politics and
theology, but stating facts of another kind, which a good man would agree
justified Milton's views anyway.' (*Houghton*)

> Studio House, Hampstead Hill Gardens, NW3
> 27 March 1961

Dear Kermode,

Now that I have got off the proofs of my Milton book I have read your
piece on him again, as your letter needed; if I had been allowed galley
proofs I would have discussed your type of position in my book, and some
other things which appeared after I had gone to print. I hadn't thought
anybody could be so Oscar Wilde as all that. But maybe the effect would
only have been ill-tempered and dismal, as I can see no merit in your
position.[1]

---

[1] See 'Adam Unparadised', in *The Living Milton: Essays by Various Hands*, ed. Frank Kermode
(1960). In his review of Kermode's volume ('Handling Milton', *The Guardian*, 16 Sept. 1960),
WE wrote: 'The contribution of the editor, Professor Kermode, is I think the most searching, but
his mind is hampered by his aesthetic doctrine. Why, he asks, did Milton permit acts of love
before the Fall, and thus "take on the task of presenting an Adam and Eve unimaginably
privileged in the matter of sexual gratification?" His answers are all right, but Milton roundly
insists that they were no more privileged than any other honeymoon couple: "whatever hypo-
crites austerely talk", "Defaming as impure what God declares | Pure, and commands to some,
leaves free to all."

'Milton rejected any tradition that conflicted with the plain text, and God in Genesis tells
Adam and Eve to multiply before they have fallen. Professor Kermode cannot attend to what
Milton says, or to his firm ground for saying it, because Milton has to be traditional, so he must
have expressed a holy sex-horror; still, perhaps the facts are meant to be recognised by a joke,
when Milton is praised for "lying properly about everything." In the same way, as the poem must
be very aesthetic, the private theological treatise of Milton is used to argue that he did not
believe what he said in the poem. But the manuscript contains additions in various handwritings
which show changes of opinion; Sewell [Arthur Sewell, *A Study in Milton's Christian Doctrine*,
1939], by identifying the handwritings of the men to whom Milton dictated, deduced that he
changed his theology during the serious work of writing *Paradise Lost*. Professor Kermode gives
no reason for assuming that this is wrong, though his whole position depends upon the assumption. In short, the new principle that you need not be bothered about Milton, because he did not
really mean anything anyway, does not strike me as a positive kind of liberation.'

See also Kermode's generous review of *MG*: 'Empson's Milton', *The Guardian*, 13 Sept. 1961:
'Professor Empson cannot be other than honourable, independent, and expert (Satanic, one

You say he was 'deliberately not selling politics and theology, but stating facts of another kind, which a good man would agree justified Milton's views anyway'. So far as I can see you only give one such fact; that the act of love is disgusting, and was already disgusting before the Fall. What reason you have for thinking that Milton described it so I don't understand. Why you think the idea is still interesting, even now, whereas all Milton's public interests are so dull that even he couldn't have tried to sell them in a poem even then—just baffles me. I am not clear whether you speak from a religious position, and regard your disgust for sex as a revealed truth; perhaps it doesn't make much difference, but the unconscious politics I think are something else, a form of democracy: 'We're all Filf; you 'old on to vat. E's just as much Filf as I am, see?' In this way the belief gives comfort and assurance, and no doubt acts as a mild aphrodisiac. To have it smeared over all the authors of the past seems to me a weirdly sordid thing to happen, bad though the effects of Christianity must always be expected to be. The reason why you call it Symbolical is I suppose simply that that is a prestige word, used without other meaning for anything you consider artistic.

Some while ago, come to think of it, I was saying this about your treatment of Donne, and you answered that the ideas were his not your own. There is a bit more truth in it there than about Milton, but it is still unfair. Donne struggled to overcome the shame implanted by his pious education, and we have no reason to doubt that he was sincere in thinking it bad, but he could not entirely argue himself out of 'a kind of sorrowing dulness in the mind'. When he was beaten back into Christianity, as the only way he would be allowed to feed his wife and children, he thought it a point of honour to drive himself into as much shame as he could. Milton contrived to identify himself with this social demand, and boasts about his youthful chastity as an athletic feat. The belief in *Comus* that it would give him magical power came true in a way; it made him splendidly free from false shame, as was frighteningly obvious in the divorce pamphlets. No man would be less patient of a conniving state of shame, found perversely enjoyable, which you ascribe to so many authors. Come to think of it, Swinburne is the poet who really does express what you say they all express.

---

might say) on the subject of the poetry. When he is attacking Christianity he is frankly propagandist, but his loathing is honestly based on a detestation of the doctrine of eternal punishment . . .

'The tone of Empson's book is in a way Miltonic, the intelligence coming out sometimes as disgruntled wit and controversial bitterness . . . The result is that the book conveys a strong sense of a civilised conscience and literary power though at the same time it is very much a provocation to other critics . . .'

Your book pp. 90, 106. Why do you twice say that the epic poet had a right and privilege to intervene? I thought Milton was often blamed for letting his self-importance break the epic rule of anonymity. I don't see what you get from it anyway.

p. 91. The materiality of the angels is 'related to his feelings about life in general', but 'he couldn't afford to hint at any discontinuity between matter and spirit'. He claimed to have found proof that there is no discontinuity; you phrase it so as to insinuate that he was lying. But though this theory about angels was 'related to his feelings', you say, whether God has predetermined us to Hell wasn't; when he makes God discuss that it is just tact and meant to finish quickly with the dull subject. This is gross nonsense. A man who believes in Hell can't help relating the prospect of it to his feelings about life in general; you are merely ascribing to Milton your own boredom with almost all his topic. I grant that some of his remarks about poetry are rather hard to interpret, but when he said that poetry ought to be simple he was probably getting at the Metaphysicals or what not; everybody's remarks on the subject then were like epigrams, needing interpretation; and he is very unlikely to have meant that the doctrine didn't matter in a religious poem. You say that he would have put his heresies into the poem if he had taken its doctrines seriously. But he could hardly hope to survive if he had done, and the sacrifice would be useless, because he certainly wouldn't get the book printed. It seems the licensers held it for a year (though I am not clear that the evidence is very firm). Your whole picture is so very 'artistic', without the faintest interest in the forces actually at work, either in Milton's own mind or in the society he handled.

Not having the text here, I have just been to the public library to see why you can't read the description of innocent sex without thinking of the description of fallen sex, and what I find Milton had written there, in an irrelevantly crosspatch way perhaps, was KERMODE IS WRONG: 'Whatever hypocrites austerely talk' and so on. It still only seems to me (as in my review) prurient simpering for you to say he was 'lying properly'.

p. 116. You say Milton the theologian must have 'disapproved of the theme of perturbation as an index of fallen nature'; no, because he doesn't make it an index, only you do. Eve was sensible to be perturbed at her dream though still innocent; and the apple merely happens to be an intoxicant—that is not why eating is was wicked. There is no proof here that Milton didn't believe what he was saying. p. 120[.] The paradox of Eve [is] more central because more natural than that of the Felix

Culpa. Both are dismal, whether you rejoice in the propriety of that or not, but Milton seems from the structure of the poem to have expected the Felix Culpa not to be dismal, till he tried it out. p. 118 You seem to be labouring hard to avoid any reflection about justifying the ways of God, which is what Milton says the poem is about after all; thus you say Adam finds *life* inexplicable; what he says it's about is God's Justice. It is a queer struggle to avoid the author's topic, crowned by praising Blake and Shelley for being Oscar Wilde (p. 122).

Yours sincerely

William Empson

Frank Kermode; copy in Houghton

TLS, 28 April 1961, 263: 'Academic Caste'

A series in the *TLS* on 'University Writing' began with an article on 'Hull, Leeds, and Sheffield' by a 'Special Correspondent' (14 April 1961, 234):

There the staff seem on the whole friendly but distant . . . Even staff verdicts on the students themselves are oddly divergent: Professor Empson finds that at least they are independently, up here in the rebellious north, seeming generally to feel that the main use of a university teacher is as someone to argue with. Others, however, complain that the students cling to them with disturbingly complete trust, and ask nothing better than to be handed lots of ready-made ideas from their teachers' minds to regurgitate when examinations come round.

The views of Mr Philip Hobsbaum*, a post-graduate researcher, and founder and spiritual director of the duplicated magazine *Poetry from Sheffield*, coincide very much with this latter reading of the situation. A man inclined to strong opinions strongly expressed, Mr Hobsbaum blames the staff roundly for their failure to encourage cultural activities or indeed have anything much to do with students at all:

There seems to be a clearcut division between the Union and the staff; and a post-graduate, distrusted by both sides, has to choose. As for the staff themselves, those who try to fraternise with the students are liable to be ridiculed by their fellows, and may even find their social standing among the staff or their chances of promotion impaired if they persist, on the principle that a man who hob-nobs too much with students isn't really the sort you could give a responsible job to.

Sir,—Your article 'University Writing-1' reports a graduate student [Philip Hobsbaum] as saying that, at Sheffield University, 'As for the staff themselves, those who try to fraternise with the students are liable to be ridiculed by their fellows, and may even find their social standing among the staff or their chances of promotion impaired if they persist . . .' In recommendations to Arts Faculty committees I have often heard as an extra reason for promotion that a man has done extra work with students. The idea of penalising him for it would be received with astonishment. I have never heard any echo of ridicule for it either.

It is romantic, in a way, to have a graduate student who believes himself to be living at the court of Louis XIV; he arrived here already graduated and with firm convictions acquired elsewhere.

William Empson

TO STEPHEN SPENDER*

Department of English Literature, The University, Sheffield 10
6 June 1961

Dear Spender,

I have been much tied up with exams, but have now emerged enough to answer your letter. I haven't ever felt cross in the slightest degree about the quarrel at Louis MacNeice's in front of the Austrian Ambassadress; I thought she was overwhelmingly charming, and that we had put on just the kind of show she would expect to see when she went out slumming to look at authors. I was told next day that you had thrown a glass of wine at me, but no decisive evidence could be found on my admittedly used garments, and my only impression was that I had made better cracks than you. I couldn't have been tempted to be cross about it.

What we were arguing about, on the other hand, I would always feel had to be taken seriously. As I understood the position, and still do, you were and are taking American money, perfunctorily disguised as international money, to confront the British public with innocent-seeming American propaganda. You can't expect to do this without ever hearing a grumble; you wouldn't have got away with it in earlier times.

It was later, I think, that I had to write to your magazine because of a gross libel which you printed against poor Fei Hsiao-tung; and I was then confronted with a very queer technique. Several gross lies would be printed at the bottom of my letter as the reply to it, and I could not print any reply to any of these for several months, when another gross barrage of completely random lies would be printed under my letter as the refutation of it, again not admitting of answer for several months.[1] It would obviously, I thought, have been stupid to go on trying to answer all the lies under these unfair conditions. It is possible that I did you an injustice there; if I had taken the trouble to write an extremely long answer to the cocoon of lies you might have been shamed into printing it, because I realise that all this was done by your American playmate [Irving Kristol],[2] while you hoped you might draw the money without getting involved in his tactics. You were present when I came round to discuss the matter and it turned out that he had defence for the lies he had then been going on telling for two or three years, in your magazine.

This seems to me a case where I would be wrong not to draw the line; and nothing but a laborious effort of self-delusion, I think, can explain how you came to imagine that I was only cross because of some personal offence taken at one of Louis' parties.

Yours sincerely
William Empson

Lady Spender

TO STEPHEN SPENDER

[Sheffield]
7 June 1961

Dear Spender,

On second thoughts, it is absurd to grumble about money as I did in writing to you last night. A man could be blamed for taking money to do what he knew to be wrong, while saying that he thought it right, but the real accusation would be against his sincerity. For all I can say, you may really believe your American propaganda, and regard the tricky devices for sustaining it as a necessary Cold-War duty.

It is none the less true that I couldn't be on friendly terms with a man who held such beliefs.

---

[1] See for example the editorial comment on WE's defence of Fei Hsiao-tung, *Encounter* 5: 6 (Nov. 1955), 60–1: 'For a critic who is distinguished for his analysis of other men's ambiguities, Mr Empson seems peculiarly insensitive to his own. After having asserted, in a previous letter, that Fei is happy as a Communist functionary, he now states that, because he is a functionary, Fei is in no position to say whether he is happy or not. We do not see how he can have it both ways.'

[2] On Irving Kristol (b. 1920), the CIA-funded co-editor of *Encounter*, see Frances Stonor Saunders, *Who Paid the Piper? The CIA and the Cultural Cold War* (1999).

I hope this makes the matter clear, and I wish to withdraw any irrelevant insults.

Yours sincerely
William Empson

Lady Spender

TO STEPHEN SPENDER

Sheffield
9 June 1961

Dear Spender,

What I said to your co-editor in your presence was that I thought further replies might worsen the position of poor Fei, trying to do good in a difficult set-up, even more than the disgusting smears in your magazine had already done; and that I did not of course mind being made to look untrustworthy myself, by lies told in rebuttal of my remarks, since I had only entered on all this to try and help Fei. After co-mate had admitted that he had told lies, I therefore said that I would not demand public retraction of those lies.

If you did not understand what was being said at the interview you must be quite unfit to assume responsibility for the magazine. It is more charitable to suppose that you told yourself lies about the matter afterwards. You must have been sincerely deluded when you sent that letter supposing I was only cross about an insult at a party which I have never known (I have read your letter again, as your next letter asked me to do). I think you must have told yourself lies about that too, or you could not have thought that whatever incident occurred would seem so important to me.

There was one moment in talking to your hired assassin which felt to me of deep interest; I told the poet Auden so, but he seemed impalpable there, and next perhaps I may try whether it rings an echo even from your ruined conscience. I was saying to the beast 'But why should you print an article saying that this world-famous anthropologist, who is in fact being allowed by the Chinese Government to be head of plans for the tribespeople, is secretly an American spy? What good does this bit of wrecking-work do you?' And then I was somehow inspired to say: 'It's such a stupid thing to do, if you understand the set-up at all. Well now, to start with, how do you know he *isn't* an American spy?' Novelists often compare conversation to duelling, and the thought is very remote to my experience; but here I was watching the poor hired liar and he did behave rather as if he had been stabbed. Patently he thought: 'Does Empson know? If he's right, I've got myself in a jam with the US Secret Police.' No doubt he recovered from this fright quickly, since Empson could not be in the know; but we had a revealing instant.

I thought 'Poor old Spender; though never a sensible man I could like at all, he never deserved such a grisly end as having to get his bread from such nastiness as all that amounts to.'

William Empson

I can see your mind will dodge the point somehow. The point is that your co-editor became frightened when I said 'Suppose the accusation in the magazine is true'.

Lady Spender

TO STEPHEN SPENDER

Sheffield
14 June 1961

Dear Spender,

Oh, dear, I suppose I am being unreasonable. What you have said almost completely exonerates you, and I don't think the magazine has carried anything similar after that case. No doubt Kristol took almost no interest in the case; I mean only that his attitude to propaganda seemed to me unscrupulous—no doubt he would think that a patriotic duty.

There is really no need for me to go on talking about it. I have scarcely thought of it since the call at your office ended the controversy, and am sorry that it got brought up again.

Yours sincerely
William Empson

Lady Spender

TO T. R. HENN*

T. R. Henn lamented in an article entitled 'Science and Poetry' (*Nature*, 5 Aug. 1961, 534–9) that few contemporary poets had 'attempted any kind of "liaison of vocabulary" between science and poetry'; poets were failing as mediators between the two cultures, he remarked: 'on the whole it seems as if modern poets distrust technological achievements; as in William Empson's "To an Old Lady" (which is the Moon) . . .' (p. 535).

21 August 1961

Dear Mr Henn,

Your article in *Nature* for Aug 5 says that 'certain possibilities of science in our time have stirred momentarily the poetic imagination', but 'on the whole it seems as if modern poets distrust technological achievements; as in William Empson's poem "To an Old Lady" (which is the Moon).'

The old lady was my mother, and I was saying that though we were so completely in the same tradition, or were planets of the same sun, we had no contact and only recognised each other in times of trouble, when no longer self-enclosed in the confidence of our tradition ('but in darkness is she visible'). As the moon can be seen in the daytime, the lady cannot be compared to it, and she is said in the first line to be compared to a planet. When I said it would be better not to do space-travel to her I was thinking only of the personal situation—that to try to explain such feelings would cause embarrassment. I did not mean that I disapproved of space-travel, and I think I do not deserve to be accused of meaning such a silly thing.

I have been trying to write a piece about Donne, showing that his metaphors from astronomy meant a great deal to him in personal terms, and were felt to raise theological questions. This was commonly supposed when I was young and imitating Donne, but since then there has been a great drive to insist that he was only making silly jokes. I think this is done by people who consider it their Christian duty to exclude any heretical ideas from Donne, but the effect is to make his work seem trivial and in bad taste.

Thus I have even seen it said that, in comparing his love to a pair of compasses, Donne meant an irony against materialism—he despised his love for being like a tool. But he loved his compasses for being so elegant and for being so sensible; and the whole point of the poem is to say 'This kind of love is real'. Criticism which leaves out the whole point, I find, usually imputes nasty and trivial meanings to the author.

I am thus used to seeing the thing done to Donne, but to have it done to me, his humble imitator, seems a new extremity of unpleasantness. And yet, writing to *Nature* to complain of such a thing would seem adding to it, somehow.

Houghton copy, bMS Eng 1401 (571)

MILTON'S GOD

TLS, 6 October 1961, 663

A review of *MG* ('God and Mr. Empson', *TLS*, 29 Sept. 1961, 646), though entertained by WE's approach, lamented: 'Once the critic strays from his text in order to exploit the many theoretical absurdities of an epic which has an omnipotent and omniscient character in it, there need be no end to the anti-Christian fun and games . . . But nobody will be bored by it, and no intelligent reader will be unimpressed by its local insights. For example, in his discussion of Adam's Fall, Professor Empson challenges the Christian moralist (Professor C. S. Lewis) who speaks of the "even higher claim" than conjugal love that is being made on Adam: "Neither in Adams's secret despair nor in his practical and generous counsel do we find any 'pinch' of the kind C. S. Lewis meant, any recognition that obedience to God is a higher 'value'." The point is well taken, but the next step ought not to be a denunciation, with Professor Empson, of God's "vanity and bad temper"; rather, a heavier stress on the terrible conclusiveness of Disobedience within the scheme of *Paradise Lost.* In fact both professors are being irrelevantly high-minded, in opposite directions. And in Professor Empson's case this often happens.'

Sir,—I have no ground for complaint against your percipient and charitable reviewer of my book, but when he calls my remarks 'irrelevant' to *Paradise Lost* we are acting on different literary theories, and a main purpose of my book was to argue that his one is wrong. He says that, instead of questioning the morality of the epic, I should have laid 'a heavier stress on the terrible conclusiveness of Disobedience within the scheme of Paradise Lost'. But I deny that a poem is a private self-subsisting world of this kind. I gave quotations from Sewell [*A Study in Milton's Christian Doctrine*, 1939] and Milton himself to prove that Milton, about the time when he wrote the poem, positively denied this importance of blind obedience, and elsewhere expressed anxiety verging upon horror lest God be found unjust. Many recent critics have found the poem bad for complacent pomposity, and I answer that, if you realize that Milton was really worried about the official subject of his poem, you find the poetry very genuine. It is an extremely queer literary theory, I submit, which describes this thesis as irrelevant to the poem.

William Empson
Studio House, Hampstead Hill Gardens, London, N. W. 3

TO HELEN GARDNER

Department of English Literature, The University, Sheffield
9 October 1961

Dear Helen Gardner,

Now that I have found the review you mentioned I would rather like to take up one detail with you, though I could not sensibly write to the magazine with so little to complain of.

You say I seem a different (worse) character when I accept the story of Milton adding the Arcadian prayer to the King's book before denouncing it, and you say I accuse [J. S.] Smart though not by name. I left out his name because I was merely reporting a controversy of [Paul Phelps] Morand [in *De Comus à Satan*, 1939], without claiming to know who was right except that I said he gave more evidence than Robert Graves. I thought this bit helped to show the outlook of Morand; also it gave an opportunity to show my outlook. As at several other points in the book, I think that both the opposed factions are in the wrong, because if Milton did do what he is accused of it is to his credit.

A sheer book which is nothing but hundreds of greasy lies cooked together—that is agreed to be what the thing Milton was attacking was. The accusation against Milton was that he added one more lie which was somehow enough to make the public realise how the thing stank. Now, if anyone on our side had managed to do this to *Mein Kampf* in the last war, we would still be boasting our heads off about it. The controversy about Milton here is therefore completely misconceived, because it is conducted by people who agree in making very queer assumptions.

As I see it, you cannot imagine anyone not thinking that a mass of greasy lies is nice. I could never be friends with anybody who did not think it *a faire vomir*. Here I really am like Milton, but thank God I am not alone; and I don't think I am like him in any other point of interest. It feels to me horribly queer, and like the wriggling things you see when you pull up a stone, to have you report that my intellectual operations seem to you very unusual, not like anybody else you know except Milton himself.

What R. W. Chambers said isn't in our library; I will try to look it up in the [British] Museum one day, but I suspect I have already read it and felt it only to express moral outrage at having a lie disturbed.[1] All the same, I recognise that the evidence for the story is not enough, and I think it rather

---

[1] R. W. Chambers, 'Poets and their Critics: Langland and Milton', *Proceedings of the British Academy*, 27 (1941), 109–54.

unlikely that Milton was such a practical hero as the story amounts to. What I set out to say in the book was surely relevant enough; that I would admire him for it if he had done it.

Yours very sincerely

William Empson

I am excessively upset by my reviews, kind though most of them are; I myself have been confronted with the duty of doing an outrage, and then come shocking eyeopeners.

Katherine Duncan-Jones

CRITICAL QUARTERLY, 3: 4 (1961), 368: 'Milton's God'

R. L. Brett,[1] in a review of *MG* (*CQ*, 3: 3 (Autumn 1961), 285–7), contended that 'in attacking Milton's God [WE] is often attacking Christianity itself . . . To identify Christianity with Milton's poem is a confusion, I believe, not because Milton was not advancing in the main the great Christian doctrines as a believer, but because no poem can do justice to the fullness of the Christian religion . . . It is not only that Milton created problems for himself by taking the Homeric epic as a model, but that there are fundamental and intrinsic difficulties in trying to represent Christian truths in dramatic poetry.'

Dear Sirs,

My case may go by default unless I try to show that my book is not so illogical as Professor Brett finds it.

'Empson proceeds to make a good deal of satiric capital out of the relations between the Father and the Son . . . But if it is the one God who is sacrificing himself a good deal of this misfires.' Milton when he wrote the poem did not believe in the identity of the Father and the Son, and said so in the *De Doctrina*. He found the supposed doctrine merely a delusion; my last chapter, surely without contradiction, adds that I think so too.

Perhaps this should be qualified. In writing the book I accepted Sewell's view that Milton became an Arian while writing the poem; but reading Sewell again I think his evidence weak—the change might come earlier or later. When Milton uses a Biblical phrase which has been used to support the doctrine of the Trinity we cannot deduce that he then accepted it; the

---

[1] Raymond Laurence Brett (1917–96) was from 1952 Professor of English at the University of Hull. His publications include studies of Crabbe, Coleridge, and Hazlitt, and *Andrew Marvell: Essays on the tercentenary of his death* (ed., 1979), to which WE contributed 'Natural Magic and Populism in Marvell's Poetry'.

way he changed his theological opinions was to re-interpret Scripture, so that he would always be willing to quote it. The main thing is that he makes the Son and the Father about as identical as a terrier and a camel; whether he did this because he was already an Arian, or realised afterwards that it amounted to being an Arian, does not seem to make much difference.

Then, Professor Brett finds me wrong to argue that God (in Milton's view) intended to lead Satan into greater evil, from the lines:

> the will
> And high foreknowledge of all-ruling Heaven
> Left him at large to his own dark designs
> That with reiterated crimes he might
> Heap on himself damnation . . .   [i. 211–15]

'The word *might* implies a permissive freedom.' I doubt this; surely 'he castrated him that he might be chaste' is good seventeenth-century grammar and not permissive. But anyway the problems of free will are larger than English grammar; and Milton was tacitly quoting the Bible when he made God say:

> This my long sufferance and my day of grace
> They who neglect and scorn, shall never taste;
> But hard be hardened, blind be blinded more,
> That they may stumble on, and deeper fall.   (iii. 198–201)

How God can possibly be acquitted of causing sin, in the face of such texts, is one of the questions he examines with anguish in the *De Doctrina*. I cannot see that I was in any logical confusion when I quoted passages showing him thinking so.

Yours truly,

William Empson

The University, Sheffield   30 October 1961

TO IAN PARSONS

Department of English Literature, The University, Sheffield 10
20 November 1961

Dear Ian,

Thank you for the copy of your letter to [George Hartley at] the Marvell Press. It would probably take a good deal of pressing to get a reply. I have had no word from him, and two people have told me that the record [*Selected Poems*] is hard to get—shops do not know how to order it. On the other hand, though the reviews struck me as very bad, several people have told me that they liked the record. It came out unproduced, as it was, and if you like that it is O.K. Not bad as a prestige object, somehow, is my impression, but very little good otherwise.

Glad to hear you are looking into it.

With thanks

Bill Empson

Reading

NEW STATESMAN, 29 December 1961:
'W. B. Yeats and the Irish Protestant "stock" '

Sir,—Mr Richard Ellmann*, considering a speech of the poet Yeats to the Senate of Eire pleading for legal recognition of the convictions of Irish Protestants, says it was snobbish of Yeats to call them a stock.[1] Whether they were a stock is a question of fact, and I write hoping that some other readers may be able to clear it. Did the Protestant Ascendancy make a principle of refusing to interbreed with the Irish natives, and if so did they succeed in carrying out their intention?[2]

Mr [Williams] Plomer, explaining why he does not consider himself a South African, remarked that if the cat has kittens in the oven you don't call them biscuits. Would the great line of Irish wits, from Congreve to Wilde, have said the same if you had called them Irishmen? I rather

---

[1] Richard Ellmann, 'Heard and Seen', *New Statesman*, 8 Dec. 1961, 887–8.
[2] Ellmann replied on 19 Jan. 1962: 'Yeats . . . spent his life, like Parnell, in bringing his countrymen together. My objection to this passage was that it was divisive, that it magnified differences which Yeats really wanted to reduce, and that references to "stock" in Ireland, and in the Senate of the Irish Free State, by someone whose ancestors are English, are bound to sound snobbish to people whose ancestors are not. Yeats himself took this position only for the moment, and generally held that he belonged as much as anyone else to the "indomitable Irishry".'

suspect that Yeats was telling a truth so obvious that it didn't even feel tactless when he called the Protestants a 'stock'.

TO PHILIP HOBSBAUM*

Studio House [London]
3 February 1962

I have scribbled a lot of first thoughts but I suppose have only one radical proposal—that you should treat the two poems as two *stages* in Shelley's method of composing a poem (and he only revised if the first shot seemed worth it). At least, you could leave that open as an alternative possibility without altering any of your analysis.

Yours

W Empson

The moral superiority spread by Eliot among readers of Shelley seems to me rather horrid farce.

TO DAVID HOLBROOK*

Department of English Literature, The University, Sheffield 10
23 March 1962

Dear Holbrook,

I think Dylan Thomas, when his method comes off, and it does in a fair number of his poems, is a wonderfully good poet. He and Auden are the only two real English poets of my age and younger. The efforts of Leavisites to get them thought bad are nasty and ridiculous, but fortunately can have no lasting effect.

So I shall read your book with curiosity when I can do so without buying it. May I add that my publisher has never asked me to give him a list of my friends' names for publicity purposes—and I should have laughed if he had done.

Yours sincerely

William Empson

Houghton: top copy, possibly not posted, bMS Eng 1401 (580)

TO CHRISTOPHER RICKS

[Sheffield]

Tiresome as this letter may be, I could not have written it without help; I estimate now that it has taken half a bottle of whisky, leaving me with something in hand.

6 May 1962

Dear Mr Ricks,

It is extremely kind of you to send me this horrible book [David Holbrook, *Llareggub Revisited: Dylan Thomas and the state of modern poetry* (1962)], after I had forgotten to ask you for it; I have tried to finish with it quickly. I will send you what occurs to me and keep a carbon, not having read all the book even; this may restrain my desire to write and denounce Holbrook in the weeklies where he has been making pretence to be wronged by reviewers. How can I write to the papers before I know whether Peter Alexander has sued me for libel?[1] My mental state is bad enough as it is. But I must remember to thank you very much for your splendid feast, and say how much I hope you will look me up in London. We can always give you a bed when you want one; and I shall be going home often from now on, though of course often at Sheffield till the end of June.

I feel sympathy with Holbrook's Dissatisfaction with Poetry Today;[2] Kingsley Amis (p. 27) is in rather bad taste even if the last two verses draw some moral which I miss (but then it may be lack of virility which makes me uneasy in brothels), poor Edith [Sitwell] seems to deserve her scolding, Betjeman is not at his best here—but the central trick can be observed in his case.[3] Betjeman offers us an obscure kind of superiority to the scene and the characters from its very correctness, from the very wholeheartedness of our sympathy with such a familiar scene (and readers to whom it isn't familiar may be flattered). English sentiment is hard to analyse but

---

[1] Professor Peter Alexander of Glasgow University impugned Empson, in the *TLS* ('Milton's God', 16 Feb. 1962, 105), for practically libelling a deceased fellow scholar: 'My attention has been drawn to a passage in Professor Empson's recent study of Milton in which he represents the late J. S. Smart as deliberately dishonest in his criticism and treatment of a distinguished Swedish scholar.' See ensuing debate in the pages of the *TLS*: 2 Mar. 1962, 137; 16 Mar. 1962, 185; 23 Mar., 201; 6 Apr. 1962, 240; 27 Apr. 1962, 281; 11 May 1962, 339; 25 May 1962, 380.

[2] Derek Roper recalls: 'When David Holbrook's attack on Dylan Thomas, *Llareggub Revisited*, appeared, E told me it was "lying filth", and forbade me to buy a copy for the Dept Library. He said he was going to ask the University Librarian to see that any copy that the Main Library bought was kept locked up, so that it couldn't corrupt the students ("the children"). I don't know whether he did ask this, or if so what response he got.' (Undated memo to JH.)

[3] Holbrook discusses the following poems among others: Kingsley Amis, 'A Dream of Fair Women'; Edith Sitwell, 'Metamorphosis'; and John Betjeman, 'Youth and Age on Beaulieu River, Hants'.

surely not puzzling—it turns on feeling cosily within some ring. Holbrook argues that the poem is 'essentially cruel' [27], and this is just credible to a thoughtful reader because he can feel that there is some kind of bite in it. But the bite is merely in saying 'How standard we good-class people are!' with perhaps just a touch of 'How is it credible that any man can love a sports-minded English lady?'—'but they really do' the warning voice adds insistently. Without this saving amount of bite the sentimentality and the snobbery would become nauseating, or rather those rude words would become deserved; as is well enough appreciated by the very large Betjeman audience. They view him much as they do a stately home. For Holbrook to call this 'essentially cruel' is grossly false, a cheat intended to down one of his competitors. The same 'cultivated recoil from life' [35] is then found in T. S. Eliot while recoiling from priests[4]—he could not be caught at a more sympathetic moment, but Holbrook I think honestly cannot tell cases which fit his thesis apart from cases which don't. Such is the buildup of the chapter to a terrifying three lines from Dylan Thomas [ll. 4–6 of 'Altarwise by owl-light'], said to show the same love of horror as the other examples. The critic [John] Bayley is blamed (p. 36) for saying [in *The Romantic Survival*] that this is 'Thomas's obsessional theme, the telescoping of existence', which is refusing to see the handling of language as a moral activity. Well, Dylan really was liable to get the horrors, and they seem to go with flashes of insight and acceptance at their high points in his verse, as well as with a deep sense of fun or parody without which they would be dislikeable. The end of the sonnet sequence which this example begins is a more mysterious case (I agree, with Orwell rather than Holbrook, that the surrealism of Dali is nasty and also a form of salesmanship) because at last the confident acceptance of love has become the main overtone of the horror:

> When the worm builds with the gold straws of venom
> My nest of mercies in the rude, red tree.

I looked up in the index 'Before I knocked', as this is an overwhelmingly good poem though marred by a rather unexplained bitterness at the end; and sure enough it is denounced, but the text you have sent me leaves out pages 129 to 144, so I don't know more. 'The force that though the Green Fuse' and the final song of Polly Garter in *Under Milk Wood*, also but less strikingly 'Fern Hill', are the main cases I think where Dylan is expressing rather unexpectedly good or generous feelings and the imbecile denouncer

---

[4] Holbrook cites stanza seven of 'Mr. Eliot's Sunday Morning Service'.

continues to plod straight forward on his path, explaining them as incapacity for love, fear of impotence and so forth. Of poets my age and younger, only two I think have the real fire: Auden and Dylan Thomas; and Holbrook has now written a book about each of them, grumbling and whining in order to have them removed from his path.[5] He has just written to the TLS (May 4th 62) saying he had to write the present book 'before I could take myself seriously as a poet at all'. As he is a poet whom no one need take seriously this is rather a majestic enterprise, likeable in a way but one which needs to be removed from the path of a willing reader.

By the way, it seems absurd to accuse Dylan (p. 102) of telling Jesus to get back into the womb because Dylan is jealous and wants to be Christ himself. Critics have regularly got confused in 'Before I knocked' over whether Christ or the author is speaking. The idea that any man can become Christ, who is a universal, is a sixteenth-century heresy which has gone on knocking about. When Dylan talks about events inside his skin he takes for granted he is talking about all mankind, and free to call himself Christ as soon as it illustrated a point. I do not like or claim to understand 'Vision and Prayer', but I see no reason to accept the claim of Holbrook [102–3] that he understands it and Dylan didn't . . . I call him Dylan because I knew him, like most of the other people who call him so, not because he has established himself as a universal child.

In 'Fern Hill' (p. 155) 'the retrospect is not that of a man placing his childhood and his nostalgia for it', but 'of a man pitying himself for ever growing up'. This is so, and I don't feel the sentiment in my own life at all. But the idea that it proves Dylan to be emotionally corrupt, unfit to guide young people, unimportant 'if we pause, to bring up our touchstones' . . . all this seems to me plainly mean-minded and an incapacity to read. If Blake is allowed to praise innocence why . . .? And if Thomas's development into manhood had gone wrong in some way, which is the chief thesis of Holbrook, why may not Thomas regret it himself? Why would it be better to write poetry as if his manhood were perfect? All the same, I feel there is some adult comment behind the tremendous end of the poem, and would not admire it so much otherwise, but I can't be sure what:

> Time held me green and dying
> Though I sang in my chains like the sea.

The obvious literary reference has at least something to do with it;

---

[5] 'I suppose Holbrook *did* write a book against Auden?' asked WE in a letter to CR dated 30 Oct. 1962 (C. Ricks). There was no such Holbrook book on Auden.

whatever Dylan may be pitying himself for, he is comparing himself to a man of eighty, who had the authority in his countenance which men would fain call master:

> Alack, tis he; why, he was met even now,
> As mad as the vexed sea; singing aloud,
> Crowned with rank fumiter . . .   [*King Lear* IV. iii. 1–3]

And here too there is a mysterious reassurance behind a good deal of what might seem wilful horror; the sea is dangerous all right, but when we think it is angry it is really only singing. The whole idea of the witty and quarrelsome Dylan as somehow infantile in comparison with Holbrook, a man who advertises himself by sordidly self-pitying circulars and announcements in the newspapers, is one which cannot enter my mind.

We need not say that Holbrook has no ear for rhythm because he does not find it in these poems, since he does not know what the point of them is, and that is the main clue; the point and the rhythm usually express good feeling, in some way which Holbrook denies to Dylan Thomas. So the chapter-title 'The Death of Rhythm' need not detain us; though most of his discussion of 'The Force that through the Green Fuse' (p. 163) has that theme. The poem is pantheist; all kinds of forces in the outer world are compared to things inside the young Dylan's skin, and he is already complaining he is beginning to grow up wrong. The things outside him are splendid, and cheer him up, though the corresponding ones inside him are likely to be a bit off. The comparison of the forces that make the green shoot grow to forces of human industrialism, chemistry or electricity, are meant to show how strong it is; the routine assumption of Holbrook that science is always horrid ('Yah—he thinks it isn't horrid') merely puts him out, and he wrongly says that the poetic argument is 'against growth' [163]. The roots of trees are eventually blasted I suppose by lightning or a high wind; Nature will make young Dylan too first grow and then die. There is no 'posture against natural growth in Time, because the poet wishes to pity himself for belonging to natural processes' . . . and so forth [164], lecturing with insane self-righteousness. Dylan I grant is complaining a bit, but it is only the *crooked* rose which has been bent by the same wintry fever as himself; plainly this is not a complaint against all life. I think it means that a false spring brought out the rose too early and it was nipped by a frost; the poet also took fire too early for a healthy growth—he was about seventeen when he wrote this, and probably thought he had started masturbating dangerously early.

The poem then says that the cycle of water, evaporated from the sea and returning to it by the rivers, is like the circulation of his blood; and the claim of Holbrook that this is incomprehensible does no credit to Holbrook's teachers and literary mentors. The idea itself ought to be a commonplace, but the treatment of it shows I think great beauty of feeling. The next verse is I grant more mysterious; as is standard in pantheism, the dangerous forces in Nature have to be included in the Godhead. But 'my shroud sail' is not an 'irresponsible pun' [164] because the same Nature blows him through the stages of his life and wraps him up at the end of it. Holbrook sees no point in the final lines of the verse but 'a Tarot touch from Eliot' and 'a sensational way' of uttering some universal thoughts by Holbrook.[6] Well, Dylan has been claiming identity with the ground of all Nature, in a correct Hindu manner, as of course the well-educated child knew quite well, and now he identifies himself with human society like a Christian; the body of the hanged man is destroyed, leaving no relics, by burying it in quicklime; but this is made from the bones of Dylan, who thus receives the criminal back into himself like an Earth-Mother. Now Holbrook is always lecturing us about how we ought to have compassion and social responsibility and suchlike, so it is interesting to observe that when they are put under his nose he can't recognise them at all. He grumbles that the hanging man has nothing to do with the force which is also time; 'Time, of course, brings the threat of maturity which the poem is a desperate attempt by the poet to conceal' [165]. Now, just consider the lad of seventeen or so, writing this astonishing thing, and grumbling at the end of every verse that something was going wrong about his growing up; how can he be trying to conceal *that*? To do poor Holbrook justice, he has no idea what the poem is about, and I expect would be cross at being told that he ought to recognise such philosophical or scientific ideas.

The lips of time leech to the fountain head;

'Time sucks the blood of the fountain head (?by making us old and drying our faculties)' [165]. Holbrook calls his chapter 'The Death of Rhythm', and I suppose I started finding good meanings in this poem because of its extreme beauty of sound. The end of the poem is slightly terrifying, another case of Dylan confronting the full horror of Nature while praising her; but a man unable to feel its haunting beauty of sound seems to me obviously no poet and, for that matter, quite unfit to be a teacher of literature. Given the suggestions of the sound, the line has to be

---

[6] Holbrook: 'I see no point in this, except that it is a sensational way of referring to the unity of all flesh in clay, both murderer's, poet's and Christ's, and the clay which consumes all is itself compounded of all' [165].

interpreted 'Creatures who live in time draw their strength from an eternal source'; indeed, they drag their way to it, and stick till they are cut off. This does a good deal to make tolerable the comparison of the accumulation of semen to that of pus; my trouble is that I feel the whole verse to be consistent and very beautiful but find it hard to say why. The great spaces of time in evolution, surely, have gradually amounted to our Heaven by developing all the details of the human type which we consider ideal (young Dylan of course would be very fresh from reading about evolution); 'a weather's wind', the merely local trouble of his own life, is not a thing he can improve by talking to it about the general good intention which had taken ten to the tenth years. Not able to scold his own body, he is even unable to make contact with any other suffering lover, supposing the man to have got himself buried already. Funny as it sounds when translated, this interpretation makes a consistent poem and as it seems to me one of overwhelming beauty; and far greater moral and spiritual health than poor Makeway Holbrook will ever attain. His central argument is that the poem exists 'only by its suggestion of unwilling growth in the immature boy' [166], and I deny that this is present in the poem in any degree. Good God, the child Dylan was determined to hit London and have pleasure, at whatever cost; only after a cocoon of totally irrelevant fantasies has been spun by Holbrook can anybody suppose he didn't want to grow up, in the relevant sense of attaining his sexual majority. Like many other men, he did not revere his childhood till he was safely past it.

I can't go into all the cases, but should observe that in 'A Refusal to Mourn' (p. 170) Holbrook appears to understand the whole poem, or as near as makes no matter, but still hates it; then he remarks 'why he shouldn't say anything is not clear' (p. 171), meaning why the poet says he won't say things. The answer is plain; Dylan in wartime thought it wrong to be a propagandist poet, favouring one side, and while saying 'I'll keep myself pure' he says to the dead child 'I'll keep you pure, too'. I myself thought it a duty to do propaganda against Hitler, and much of this was fun, but I had sometimes to eat dirt from people who replied to my advances that I must do my own dirty work. The reason why the greater poet Auden clung to America was that to become Britain's wartime bard would have meant unbearable phoniness, and the poet Dylan though so much less political had to insist on his purity. If Holbrook were writing about a trivial eighteenth-century poet he would be protected by his whole profession from imbecile mistakes like this one.

Going back to p. 99 'whoever Ann was' [in 'After the Funeral']—why not find out, if he wants to know? And why blame the poet for egotism because he uses wholly standard rhetorical devices while being swept totally out of himself in admiration for the terrible strength shown in the working life of the old servant. This is a very interesting case, because there is no real difficulty for Holbrook in understanding the words, but there is a sharp rivalry because Thomas is showing respect for honest worth, the precise gift by which Holbrook is to sweep the world. Thud thud thud go the formulae; I have just read it wondering what to quote, and could only quote all of it. He despises him for failure to control his passion, for excessive demand upon the world to admire the dead servant, for praising her after admitting that she requires no praise . . . 'why not let her die then?'. Coarse as the rivalries between poets, in our rough island story, have invariably been, this I think can be chalked up as the coarsest cry yet voiced.

I agree with Holbrook (p. 228) that the loving drunks [in *Under Milk Wood*] are a rather tiresome bit of propaganda for drunkenness; but it isn't so that all drinkers are neurotics and wake up moaning. Many of them do boast like this, however much they may pay for it later. The frightful nonsense talked about Ben Jonson is having its effect, I see; authors who mention rude things must always show they are shocked by them, as Ben Jonson is misread to make him do (in fact, of course, he was militantly anti-puritan). The evident fact that Shakespeare didn't can be ignored as long as Jonson did. Of course, if you are a prominent Malvolio yourself you are keen on making sure there isn't any more cakes and ale. Maybe you will say that any poem which laughs at Malvolio 'reinforces untenderness. It is a cruel work, inviting our cruel laughter' [201]. On any other ground, this is a fatuous thing to say about *Under Milk Wood*, which is beautifully tender but sometimes rather too sentimental. (I have seen the play, and the audiences are plainly not being spurred to cruel laughter). Holbrook sometimes comes near recognising this, as about the last song of Polly Garter: 'Note the special pleading in "She loves him back": in the circumstances, he drunk, she dreaming of Willy Wee—would she be likely to?' [223–4] The answer is 'Of course Holbrook wouldn't be likely to, but we love Polly because she would'. Holbrook seems to think that all drunken men are impotent, which would make his complaint more sensible; or at any rate that Dylan was. I think nobody who had met Kathlin [Caitlin] would believe she would have stayed with him to the end if this was so. I had never heard the phrase 'love him back' before, and thought it a wonderfully good one; it seems to imply exactly the comradely feeling of Polly, with the real loved one far away. Here in fact as often elsewhere

Holbrook has picked on a particularly good bit to complain that it is particularly bad.

This tiresome stuff is just a try-out, but I send it to express my gratitude.
William Empson

And he is at King's, too; it is like Madame Verdurin becoming a Guermantes.[7]

NEW STATESMAN, 18 May 1962: 'Pascal's Wager'

Frank Kermode, in a review of a new translation by Martin Turnell of Pascal's *Pensées*—'Pascal for Unbelievers', *New Statesman* 63 (4 May 1962), 637–8—wrote of the famous Wager:

> The most recent of many objections to the Wager occurs in Professor Empson's book on Milton, where, in an impressive page, it is maintained that
>
>> this argument makes Pascal the slave of any person, professing any doctrine, who has the impudence to tell him a sufficiently extravagant lie. A man ought therefore to be prepared to reject such a calculation. [46]
>
> But Pascal was not trying to convince himself; and a lie would have to be very convincing rather than extravagant to defeat so powerful and so sceptical a mind. Of course the view that one *ought* to reject the Wager is decent, and this is Empson's point; there is probably no way of arranging for a direct contest between him and Pascal, since they agree about so much—Pascal was also aware of the apparent injustice of God, but thought it a delusion inherent in fallen human intelligence—but interpret the data so differently; Empson depends, Pascal would say, to an unreasonable degree, on reason. And, Empson excepted, this is, crudely speaking, the aspect of Pascal's case that most interests the modern infidel.

Sir,—Professor Kermode, in passing, has queried a remark of mine about Pascal's Wager. I was speaking of the logic of the argument in itself, as it would be understood by an ordinary man; and what I meant by 'a sufficiently extravagant lie' was just a numerically large enough offer or threat from the next world to offset any pain or shame probable in this world. I readily agree that Pascal himself would not have let Christianity be out-

---

[7] See also an abbreviated and tempered version of WE's letter to CR (6 May 1962) published in *E in C* 13: 2 (Apr. 1963); *A,* 396–8.

voted by bigger offers from a competitor, but this only shows that his theory was wrong.

Still, I have looked up the wager in 'XI' of the *Pensées*. I find I don't understand the argument at all, and I don't think this is from not understanding the French. How can he say that you lose nothing if you lose the bet? On the next page he is discussing fear of Hell and the difficulty of renouncing the pleasures of the world, so we need not think he had forgotten such matters when arguing about the wager. In effect he was torturing himself to death in the hope of a heavenly reward or at least of avoiding the pains of hell; plainly he would not have lost nothing if he got no reward after renouncing the world. For that matter, if he can't lose by the game, whatever it is, why should he call it a bet?

I grant that my remarks in the book seem a bit far from what Pascal wrote, but I still think that they fit what most readers have always supposed he must have meant.[1]

TO PHILIP HOBSBAUM

19 May 1962

Dear Hobsbaum,

There would be no harm in going to America, but you must mind and come back; it might be easier to get jobs here after the thesis is published, anyway. I will certainly recommend you to America, and I don't believe my name is a deterrent (they think me politically bad, but that doesn't come off on you). However, my recommendations don't seem much good in the homeland either, though I promise you I have been writing warmly in your favour.

I hope you get Liverpool (or Keele), but it might be a good thing for you to have the visit to America early, anyhow.

Yours very sincerely
William Empson

---

[1] Kermode replied on the same page of the *NS*. W. W. Robson said in a letter to JH: 'At dinner once in my college we discussed Pascal's Wager. Empson was very struck by my saying that I had read somewhere that it is found in other religions besides Christianity. He found this of profound importance—why, I don't know.'

SUNDAY TIMES, 27 May 1962

[In response to extracts from Maurice Collis's biography *Stanley Spencer*.]

Sir,—Stanley Spencer when observed at a party made everyone else look fretful, because he radiated so much expansive contentment—in fact, the scene would make a Stanley Spencer painting. All this stuff about how miserable he was seems absurd.

TO ROBERT LOWELL

Eng Lit Dept Sheffield University
20 June 1962

Dear Robert Lowell,

I was extremely pleased to get your letter about my book on Milton, nine months ago, and have carried it about meaning to answer it ever since. I answer it now because exams are about over and some backlog can be cleared up, not because I have thought of an adequate reply. The last chapter was a very depressing thing to keep on rewriting, and reviewers mostly took the line that only a spiteful cad would have insulted them so, which made an understanding letter very welcome. Still, I have borne my witness now, and the later books may be quite cheerful.

The other nice letter came from EMW Tillyard, whom I had thought one of my chief opponents.[1] He wrote that since his retirement he had been planning a book on Shakespeare's early comedies (The Taming of

---

[1] E. M. W. Tillyard (former Master of Jesus College, Cambridge, and examiner of the young WE in the Cambridge English Tripos in 1929) considered himself well reproved by *Milton's God*: the book had interested him 'vastly', he wrote to WE on 27 Oct. 1961. He applauded too WE's coinage 'Neo-Christian', and said he feared writers such as Dorothy Sayers and Helen Gardner who manifested the neo-Christian tendency (though somehow not T. S. Eliot). He went on: 'I have not been able to test your theses; but I do know that whether they will convert me or not they are vastly important in having put the poem in a new light. Recent books I have read mostly pick about with details but you call for a reconsideration of fundamentals. This is hard on the reader; and I have no doubt that many critics will get out of their holes by saying that you are awfully clever and ingenious and diverting but really too far-fetched to be taken seriously. You may have to wait several years before you get a fit return for your efforts. But you will get it . . . [Y]our book has thrilled me.' Tillyard 'agrees with my book . . . all along the line, though I rather thought I was attacking him,' WE related to his brother Arthur 'I suppose he still considers himself an Anglican; he says that all the churches of Christendom ought to renounce the horrors of the Old Testament, as a precaution. Oh, well.' Of Tillyard's book *Studies in Milton* (1951), WE sometime wrote in his notes: 'Strangest part the cool admission that most Christians don't believe in this wicked old father—seems I am making a fuss about nothing; but this is very bad behaviour from intellectuals—they have comfort and approval, and the ignorant or direct-minded people, encouraged by the intellectuals to think the religion is believed, are driven into suffering and evil. It ought not to be supported unless it publicly stops worshipping its monster.'

the Shrew is a surprising work) and felt that to understand the narrative method he had better compare the Old Testament, so his wife had been reading it aloud to him in the evenings. He had found it the wickedest book he had heard for years; imagine, he said, poor old Basil Willey trying to put the sack of Ai into business-men's prose; and he thought it urgent that the Churches should unite in denouncing such impudent wickedness. I was greatly looking forward to the next developments, when most unfortunately he upped and died on us; aged 75 I think, but the doctors ought to be able to keep so much vigour in being. I suppose they haven't really lengthened the average life except for the cures of a few specific diseases.

I generally do the first day of the Aldermaston March, as it is through nice country with a few spectators, and the Anglican parson of a parish along the route has been tending to crack up under it. He began by handing marchers his parish magazine, which explained that destruction of the world by the atom bomb was fully sanctioned by prophecy, and could be expected from the texts to be quite rapid and decisive, and after all it was high time, so why complain? 'I don't know how you feel, but this is how I see it' he was saying gruffly and very like an officer and gentleman as he first handed the copies out, some years ago now. But they came in greater and greater numbers, like locusts; I am told he began hitting out at them at random, and he is no longer seen along the route now, this year or last I think.

I wish you would come over; we would love to see you.

Yours with thanks

William Empson.

Houghton: bMS Am 1905 (416)

TO CHRISTOPHER RICKS

As from Studio House, 1 Hampstead Hill Gardens, London NW3
I will go back next week.
31 August 1962

My dear Ricks,

Thank you for the Dickens book;[1] I thought it very interesting and have written a lot of notes.

They were as afraid of the English mob in the 1840's as the Boers now

---

[1] CR had lent WE his copy of Philip Collins, *Dickens and Crime* (1962).

are of the Kaffirs, and in the same way a lot of Dickens' manly fierceness is a form of cowardice. The reason why the criminals were mysteriously impervious to preaching was that the working class felt it was being wronged, and with much truth. The despair of reaching them by moral suasion, even the Alice Through the Looking Glass plan of keeping them locked up all the time so that their crimes can't be committed (can Dodgson have deliberately taken it from Dickens' magazine article?), come I think from a half-conscious recognition that the opponent is stubborn through a moral resistance. Not only Marx expected revolution, and we don't easily realise it because there hasn't been a mob in England for a long while now. Encouraging as far as it goes.

Many thanks

William Empson

TO GIORGIO MELCHIORI [*Seven Types of Ambiguity*]

Giorgio Melchiori, in his capacity as an adviser for English literature to the publishers Einaudi, suggested making an Italian translation of *STA*; but Einaudi hesitated. Before he could receive a final answer, Melchiori was taken to hospital where he underwent two very serious operations (doctors said he had only a fifty per cent chance of survival). But one day in 1961 Italo Calvino, Einaudi's main adviser, turned up at the hospital and told Melchiori he had read *STA* and considered it absolutely fundamental. You are the only person who can translate it, so you had better not die on us now, Calvino urged him. Later still, following this exchange of letters, Melchiori visited WE in Hampstead and gained further insights into the most puzzling and debatable parts of the book. Melchiori's translation, with his introduction, was published in May 1965: *Sette Tipi di Ambiguità* (Torino), no. 7 of PBE (Piccola Biblioteca Einaudi).

Turin

24 August 1962

Dear Professor Empson,

Perhaps, in the first place, I'd better introduce myself to you. I am at present the professor of English Lit. at the University of Turin, and you may have come across the two books I published with Routledge & Kegan Paul, one on contemporary English literature and the other on Yeats.

Several months ago I suggested to the publisher Einaudi that they should produce an Italian version of your *Seven Types*, since I always considered it a basic work of criticism, and I felt it wrong that it should be ignored here (while American critical books, employing your methods and derived from your theories are considered revolutionary and are continually quoted and translated). I think that Italian criticism, still largely bound to Croce's aesthetics, has a lot to learn from you – and the *Seven Types* is the best book to start with as being less strictly specialized than your *Pastorals* or *Complex Words*. Needless to say, my suggestion was due to my great admiration for your work, and I was glad that it was accepted – as you may have learnt from Chatto, with whom I believe Einaudi got into touch for rights, etc.

I undertook the translation (and I shall also write an introduction for Italian readers). This is now completed – I used the *third* (1953) revised English edition. I knew that translating your book would be hard work, and I am now turning to you for help with some difficulties which I was unable to overcome, as well as for advice on dubious cases.

You will understand that addressing an audience which has a very vague knowledge of English literature (the specialists have already read it in English) a number of explanations have been necessary, so that in several cases I have been forced to amplify your sentences, incorporating information which is taken for granted with English readers. In some further instances I believe that it would be better to omit sentences or parts of sentences, but for these I would like to have your approval, and am enclosing a list. I suggest this drastic measure only with reference to some of your asides which are not essential to the argument and which would require long and elaborate (and therefore distracting) elucidation for Italian readers.

I have taken the liberty of checking your quotations against the most authoritative editions and in many instances I found numerous variants. None of them, though, affects your argument. One question. Is there any reason for attributing to an *Essay on Women* a quotation from *The Rape of the Lock* V—1930 at pp. 72–74 of your book, and a passage from *Moral Essays* II 239–48 at pages 149–51 ?

Of course I would be very grateful for any further suggestions or comments you may want to add and I should very much value your help if you have time to look over the enclosed sheets and let me have an answer as soon as possible.

The Italian publisher tells me that this is the first translation of *Seven Types* into any other language. Is this so?

I hope that this translation will give your book the standing it deserves in Italy, where there is a lively interest in critical theory, and that it will serve to bring us into contact with one another.

With my very best wishes,

Yours sincerely,

Giorgio Melchiori

Suggested omissions

p. 86: I would omit most of Pope's satirical note, from the words (in your text): 'and explains . . . to . . . should overlook it'.

p. 93: I would omit the quotation from *1 Henry IV* at the bottom of the page: I find it distracting, while the passage from *Othello* that follows it immediately is a very clear illustration of your argument.

p. 141: Omit the parenthetical sentence: (Never name her ... Mrs. Quickly).

p. 217: I want to omit the aside: 'it would still be like Coleridge's parody', and the line which I am afraid is a misquotation, or perhaps a printer's error, joining together two lines of an imitative poem of Coleridge's which would require a lengthy explanation: '*So* sad am I!—but should a friend and I | Grow cool and *miff*, O! I am *very* sad!' (a different version of the same sonnet is to be found in a note to *Biog. Lit.*)

Queries:

p. xv (Pref. to II ed.) ll. 5 ff.: 'I do not see . . . practical decision'. Is it correct to interpret this (translating back word for word from the Italian): 'I do not see any way out of the dilemma which would grant much importance on the level of practical decisions to the deep truths that Mr Smith expressed in his review.'?

p. 3, line 27: 'the poet's social tone'. Is this the tone of the poet seen within his social setting?

p. 15, last line: Does 'As a matter of introspection' mean: 'judging from one's own experience'?

p. 24, line 4 from bottom: I have not been able to identify the quotation 'gathers a moment, then scatters'.

p. 41, line 25: 'beside the forces given to us'. Does 'beside' mean 'as compared with', or 'apart from'?

p. 45, just before second quotation: 'and puts no stress on the complementary part of the irony, which it assumes'. I am not clear as to what this 'complementary part of the irony', as distinct from the dramatic irony, refers to.

p. 52, end of second paragraph: Can 'a regress of echoes' be translated 'echoes getting further and further away'? And, in the same sentence, I should be inclined to drop 'similarly vowelled', as the similarity hardly strikes the ear.

p. 56, line 17: 'risen a heavenly body' is another quotation I have not been able to place.

p. 82, line 21: 'and there is no need for exhortation in the matter'. Can this be omitted? Or, if not, who need not be exhorted?

p. 92, first lines: I am not sure what is meant by 'these notes of the material for rhetoric', or even by 'physiological shorthand'.

p. 98, second paragraph: 'Doubt as . . . normal form': I have translated (word for word retranslating from the Italian) as follows, but am neither sure that I have understood it myself or that I have succeeded in putting it across: 'Doubt as to the interpretation of a metaphor may concern both its terms, without sharing its alternatives; it will refer instead to the ambiguous character of the normal form.'

p. 111, line 5 from bottom: 'universes of discourse' cannot be translated literally, and I have failed to find an equivalent.

p. 123, line 4: 'he would not allow such implied comparisons as require to be observed'. Can this be translated 'such implied comparisons as require particular attention', or does it mean something quite different?

p. 151, line 28: 'in the high bogs of the mountains': I feel inclined to omit, as it would need considerable explanation to make it intelligible to an Italian reader.

p. 156, lines 13–14: 'looking backwards, it may be the *oak* itself'. Should not this read 'looking forwards'?

p. 163, line 7: 'as if by capture': can this be translated 'as if he had succeeded in capturing'?

p. 209, line 2: What is an 'evolutionary by-blow'?

p. 215, line 4 & 3 from bottom: 'the *hill* is *green* as young, fresh and springing, or with age, mould and geology'; does this mean that the hill is green in that it is young, fresh and springing, and at the same time is green because of its age, because there is mould on it, and therefore for geological reasons?

p. 217, line 15: the reference to *Horace, III*, is not clear to me: could you specify which work you are referring to?

p. 217, line 17: 'and even distinction from her'. Does this mean that he identifies himself with melancholy?

p. 230, line 3: 'and there is a further echo . . . stretched out arm': I cannot construe this sentence, and should be very glad of a paraphrase.

p. 244, lines 19–20: I have not noticed that you have actually used the phrase 'outside the focus of consciousness'. To satisfy my own curiosity I should like to know where.

p. 252, line 13: what does 'the word-pair' mean and refer to?

p. 254, lines 5 & 4 from bottom: I do not understand what the parenthesis '(for instance, it is no use saying that all men are *not* equal)' is meant to exemplify.

Studio House, Hampstead Hill Gardens, NW3

British Museum
3 September 1962
I have gone here for a text suiting your page references.
Dear Mr Melchiori,

Thank you for your letter, and I certainly think you ought to cut jokes which would seem even duller when translated, and such-like; the only criterion is that a reader should not be able to complain that something important to the argument was omitted in the translation, and I do not think that your suggestions ever amount to this.

p. 86　Pope certainly.

p. 93　OK

p. 141　OK

p. 217　By all means cut this flat joke. I misquoted Coleridge because I was quoting from memory, as Hazlitt for example continually does. I think it would be bad taste in such a case to *do research* for one's joke and thus quote accurately. But in the same way the joke would lose its tiny function if translated. I expect you had better cut more than you propose.

p. xv　you are correct.

p. 3　I. A. Richards had defined 'tone' as the relation of the author to his readers, and I expect I meant a little of that. The poet is not only '*seen* within his social setting' but *felt* in relation to *yourself*, the reader—he might bully you, you might order him out of your house for smelling too bad. But maybe this is clear without altering your translation.

15.　Not quite 'judging from one's own experience' because the question is whether one knows *how* to. 'When we try to look inside at our own acts of judgement we *seem* to be judging by sound and rhythm' (but perhaps something else decides how we create these impressions of sound and rhythm, which appear to be directly presented to us).

24　'Gathers a moment, then scatters' comes near the end of the Waley translation—in his *Chinese Poems*; the whole page is an exegesis of this poem. The quotation on the previous page is the beginning of it. (It says *fair* morning not *spring* morning, but mentions the spring in the next line. I simplified the quotation to save space).[1]

---

[1] The notion that WE was 'saving space' in *STA* by misquoting a single word is comically absurd. He is analysing (23–5) a poem by T'ao Ch'ien, trans. Arthur Waley, as 'New Corn', which is given here in full: 'Swiftly the years, beyond recall. | Solemn the stillness of this fair morning. | I will clothe myself in spring-clothing | And visit the slopes of the Eastern Hill. | By the mountain-stream a mist hovers, | Hovers a moment, then scatters. | There comes a wind blowing from the south | That brushes the fields of new corn.' (*One Hundred and Seventy Chinese Poems* (1918), 79)

41 'as compared with' not 'apart from'—as a matter of what the English has to mean. *Given to us* is unduly obscure I think—'the forces of life working through us' is all that is needed.

45 After the murder of Duncan, Macbeth says he dare not go back to the corpse and smear the guards with blood, so his wife does it. We are to remember, when he says 'Look on it again I dare not' (the complementary part of the irony) that this soldier was praised at the beginning of the play for not fearing the corpses he produced in battle—'nothing affeared of what thyself didst make' (the initial 'dramatic irony'). But it is not usual I think to call this initial use 'the dramatic irony'.

52 I was thinking of the diminishing echoes as like a kind of logical fallacy, but this is no help to the argument. *Regress of echoes* and *similarly vowelled* had both better go out.

56 It was meant to be a quotation from the Epistles of St Paul on the Resurrection of the Body; I expect you could suggest that without treating it as a quotation. Or you could take it out, as it is very strained—the Platonic idea of being a pattern is much more relevant to fatherhood.

82 I meant that modern editors will continue to do what nineteenth-century ones did, whether they are told a theory to justify it or not. I now think they have become pedantic to the point of obscurantism, and badly need exhortation to recognize several meanings at once, so my joke is a wrong forecast. Better leave it out.

92 'teeth-forehead-faults' might be notes for a speech; parts of the body are assumed to be enough to call up an argument in which they are used as symbols or metaphors. However, I hope that what I mean would be clear if the sentence ending with a question mark were omitted.

98 No, the 'two words' are not the tenor and the vehicle of a metaphor, the thing meant and the thing it is compared to, but A and B in the 'normal form'

'the A and B of C'.

I think this clears it up.

111 'Universes of discourse' is an artificial term in English, evidently translated from some other language, and it might well have been Italian. It just means 'contexts' I suppose, but a very large kind of context, as when you say the rules which apply to triangles are being misunderstood if one even attempts to apply them to lovers; or the physical meaning of 'pressure' is radically unlike its meaning at the conference-table. I think the phrase comes from philosophy, but I can't now remember which

philosopher. Your translation needs to bring in the idea of 'different fields of experience'—that is all, I suppose.

123   I can't agree with your translation here, about Dr Johnson, because I think many implied comparisons in literature *do* work in us *without* being observed, and with these Dr Johnson's taste is quite at home—he does not mention them, but it seems clear from his judgement that they have had the right effect on him. When he needs to understand an implied comparison before he can feel rightly about it, however, he complains that it ought not to be present or that the poem is illogical.

151   Well, Italian mountains do have high bogs, like other mountains, or Italy wouldn't have rivers. However it is only a piece of poetry, giving insight I think but not necessary to the argument, so leave it out if the urban readers will be too much irritated.

156   I assume the puzzled reader goes on till he reaches the word *oak* and then says 'perhaps *it*, the thing I didn't understand before, was the oak'. However, by all means leave out forwards or backwards.

163   yes, I think so.

209   A 'by-blow' I took to mean a thought by the way, an incidental idea; but I am afraid I was just using the word wrongly. It is only remembered as an eighteenth century word for a bastard.

215   yes, I think so.

217   The reference certainly looks ignorant. I expect I meant Odes I. 5—I can't find a Horace. Better omit everything in the bracket anyway—no reference is needed.

244   I agree—this actual phrase hadn't been used before; I gave it as a sample of the many such phrases one has to use.

230   as if Jesus had said 'the absurdity of the thing', speaking with contemptuous mockery like the God of the Old Testament (He that sitteth in the heavens shall laugh; the Lord shall have them in derision: Psalm 2.4); and there is another memory of this old dispensation—of Jehovah administering the Law of Moses before Jesus made it out of date by inaugurating the Law of Love, when he 'stands' before his judge, in the attitude of power ([With] his own right hand and his [stretched-out] arm, he hath gotten him[self] the victory: Psalm 98. 1). I still think I am right about the feeling in the verse, though it is recognized from the rhythm much more than from the meaning of the words.

252   'the word-pair' is the same as 'this doublet' early in the previous paragraph, both poetical–prosaic and intuitive–intellectual. Rather clumsy, I agree.

254   Some theorists say that all men are equal—both of the French and the American revolutionaries said something very like it. I think the American Constitution says it. My comment is merely that one should try to understand paradoxes which are literally unbelievable.

—217—I missed out. 'She' [Keats, 'Ode on Melancholy', l. 21] has become the mistress, not only Melancholy, I said in the previous paragraph [*STA*, 216]. He returns to the womb when he abandons all masculine resistance to his earth-goddess. His soul is hung up obscurely in her temple with the souls of all the other men her might has conquered, and these souls feel merely part of her. I am not sure now that this is a sensible thing to say about Keats, though many people have said it; but there is no doubt that I meant the apparent absurdity.

Turning back to your letter, I am pretty sure that *Seven Types* has never been translated before. As its assertions can only be judged by people with an intimate understanding of English poetry, I can't help doubting whether translation is much use. But I genuinely admire things in Dante which I only realise because books in English have described them to me, so I have no right to deny that some readers may be helped. I should be inclined to cut a lot of doubtful parts from a translation; but then the readers would feel they weren't getting the real thing.

I cannot imagine why *Essay on Women* got inserted on p. 72, but the poem quoted on p. 149 was occasionally called The Essay on Woman. However of course give what references you find standard (the Everyman Edition is confusing about Pope, as I remember). When I wrote the book I did most of the quotations from memory, except that when interested in Shakespearean punctuation for example I would look up and argue from the right text, even while printing the wrong one. Thus making the book decently tidy has been a matter of successive editions.

It was tiresomely careless, but I still consider that the solemnity of modern scholarship is excessive and hampering—that is, when methods suitable to editors are expected from critics.

I owe you a great debt of gratitude, and hope that I have answered the questions you raised. If not please let me know.

Yours truly

William Empson

TO F. T. PRINCE*

Studio House, Hampstead Hill Gardens, NW3
19 December 1962

Dear Professor Prince,

Thank you for sending me your edition of *Paradise Lost* Books I and II [1962]. I wish to comment on a couple of points in Appendix IV ['Milton's Critics'].

Leavis thinks the poem bad, and I think it good; we only agree in thinking the behaviour ascribed to God in the myth unjust. Most men can recognise gross injustice when it is under their noses, and this agreement does not make us into a peculiar sect. Indeed, the literary critics who pretend not to be able to recognise it seem to me to deserve the name of a sect, that of the neo-Christians.

However, this is unimportant compared to your paragraph on Shelley, which seems to me an evident mis-statement. You say that he reached the conclusion that Milton's Devil is morally superior to his God by applying a double standard of morality; because he said that desiring and plotting revenge, though evil, are venial in a slave, but not to be forgiven in a tyrant.[1] Well, he was treating this double standard as one which the mind cannot resist; and you yourself, unless you are totally unfit to administer justice, must I think relate the degree of blameworthiness to the degree of temptation. It is in any case an entirely traditional thing to do. What Shelley was saying was that the wickedness of God in the myth, since nothing makes him torture Satan except vanity and spite, is so great that we are tempted to feel the wickedness of Satan trivial by comparison. You show no interest in denying this; so far as we gather, it would be enough for you to have God no worse than Satan. Shelley is not content with the double standard; if the instinctive movement of judgement is to be so called; he says:

> The character of Satan engenders in the mind a pernicious casuistry, which leads us to weigh his faults with his wrongs, and excuse the former because the latter exceed all measure. In those who consider that magnificent fiction with a religious feeling they engender something worse.

[1] 'Shelley, in the Preface to *Prometheus Unbound* (1820) and *A Defence of Poetry* (1821), argued that "Milton's Devil as a moral being" is "far superior to his God". He reached this conclusion by applying a double standard of morality: "Implacable hate, patient cunning, and a sleepless refinement of device to inflict the extremest anguish on an enemy, these things are evil"; but they are "venial in a slave", and "not to be forgiven in a tyrant", i.e. God' (Prince, 196).

And the reason why he calls the Father wicked is that he disobeys the precepts of the Son; he believes that revenge is just apart from the consequence of it, but 'Such is the doctrine which Jesus Christ summoned his whole resources of persuasion to oppose'. Clearly it is your party, and not Shelley, who rely upon a double standard here. You are attempting the standard propaganda device of retorting the accusation of your opponent.

This answer is so plain to anyone who has the text of Shelley, which is not hard to come by, that I suppose you must have written out of a sense of religious duty. Hence I do not expect that writing this letter can be any use, except that it may prevent you from claiming that by making no answer I had tacitly confessed to being refuted.

Yours truly

W. Empson.

Houghton carbon

Professor Prince responded with a letter on 27 Dec. 1962. Although he was a Roman Catholic, he declared, he endeavoured to keep his religious feelings out of his professional academic work; and so, with respect to Milton, to be non-sectarian. Yet the 'double standard' he imputed to Shelley was surely something that the Romantic poet would have owned as 'an important element in his revolutionary philosophy': 'That he was not himself content with it does not plainly appear from the further sentences you quote, which have always left me uncertain of his intention (was it perhaps to excuse himself for the double standard he has just asserted?).' In any case, the double standard goes 'back to the Gospels, where there is one rule for the righteous, and another for the sinner.' Since the Christian faith is essentially 'irrational', it is not for Christians to question 'the justice or injustice of God's actions in Genesis'; indeed, we can only know anything of God the Father through God the Son. Empson's argument appeared to claim that mankind is responsible for all good and God responsible for all evil. Finally, although he felt some sympathy for Empson's views, he had to end by rejecting them—but it was far from his aim in Appendix IV even to attempt to 'confute' them.

TO F. T. PRINCE

Studio House, Hampstead Hill Gardens, NW3
30 December 1962

Dear Professor Prince,

Thank you for your courteous letter, and I promise you I have no intention of making it public. Evidently my letter wandered about too much; I chiefly wanted to deny that Shelley 'applied a double standard of morality', and your answer still takes for granted that he did. But I feel now rather better able to guess what happened in your mind.

Shelley says that revenge is evil in anyone, from God to Satan; there is no double standard so far. Then he says that it can be forgiven in a person who hits back while yet suffering a wrong, but not in a person who is safe and comfortable, and merely acts out of spite (though a Renaissance noble perhaps might have called it a point of honour). Of course I have paraphrased, but his words mean this more easily than anything else. It is an almost universally accepted platitude and probably you would not want to call it a double standard; if you did, I don't suppose that your Church would support you.

Instead, as I understand, you answer that Shelley did assume that whatever slaves do is good and whatever rulers do is bad, so that he really had a double standard, and it does not much matter if the sentence you picked on had a loophole in it. No doubt, in his headlong way, he often presumed from too little evidence that some action of a slave was justified and some action of a ruler came from bad motives, just as you I suppose would tend to assume that a bishop had good motives; but this is quite a different thing from laying down a double standard in principle. In general the tyrants he attacked were real ones, and he takes nothing for granted in this argument about *Paradise Lost*. I think that this line of talk about Shelley is only a tendentious fashion, so that all attempts at illustrating it would fail, and this makes the failure of your attempt more important.

I am assuming that 'a double standard' means different laws for different classes, such as men and women, or the rich and the poor; not merely an admission that there may be mitigating circumstances. Actually, it would not seem to me absurd to expect a higher standard from the Creator than from his creatures, but that is not in question; as I understand your argument, you are only defending the right of God to be as revengeful as Satan. The poem says that God is causing Satan intense pain all the time, whereas God at most only suffers because he 'thinks himself impaired'; and Shelley deduces that God had less excuse than Satan for revenge. I do not see how anyone can deny that it is unjust to call this 'applying a double standard'. The poem, I should have recalled, says that God released Satan from his chains in order that he might heap on himself damnation.

I quoted another sentence or two by Shelley from the same passage, to show that the sentence you half-quoted does not mean what you say it does, and you answer that you have always been uncertain of their intention, but have supposed that Shelley inserted them to excuse himself for the sentence you chose. That is, you first misread a sentence to be in the fashion, then you accuse the author of insincerity in all the other sentences which prove you were wrong.

You speak of my rage and disgust at Christianity, but I can forget the tortures inflicted by Christians nearly all the time, I am happy to say. What I do find is that the complacency of the present fashion among literary critics, following T. S. Eliot, is so intense and so blinding that a certain roughness of language is needed before they can even entertain the idea that the phrases they are all parroting are simply wrong.

Yours truly

William Empson

I held this letter over and read your letter again next day, and I now understand that you were telling me, not only that you love Shelley, but that you were positively praising Shelley to the young by telling them he had a double standard of justice, because that is so Christian. Well, of course, any man who worships the Devil is automatically free to recommend any degree of evil to the children. But if you meant to recommend Shelley by your remarks in Appendix IV you must be so incompetent in elementary use of English that you could hardly have reached your present eminence.

I sit here hesitating what to type down, because it would be too rude to say I don't believe you and it is impossible to invent any convolution of your mind which would make your behaviour anything else except dirty twopenny cheating.

Derek Roper; Houghton: carbon copy, without postscript

ESSAYS IN CRITICISM, 13: 1 (January 1963), 101–4: 'Lady Chatterley Again'

John Peter*, in *E in C* (Oct. 1962), took issue with two articles by John Sparrow in *Encounter* (Feb. and Jun. 1962) which argued that D. H. Lawrence had woven a panegyric of sodomy into *Lady Chatterley's Lover* (ch. 17).[1] Peter rejected the imputation of unnatural intercourse, but Sparrow

---

[1] When the article by Sparrow, 'Regina vs. Penguin Books' (*Encounter*, 101 (1962), 35–43), was pointed out to WE in the 'Teachers' Club' at Sheffield—an overexcited colleague rushed over to announce to him that someone had discovered a new kind of scandal in Lawrence's treatment of sex—WE slowly lowered his newspaper and remarked airily, 'What, have they found another hole?' See also Sparrow, 'Afterthoughts on Regina *v.* Penguin Books Ltd.', in *Controversial Essays* (1966).

reiterated his argument in *E in C* 13: 3 (Jul. 1963), where he further argued that Lawrence's approval of anal intercourse 'was limited to cases where the parties were of opposite sexes, just as his hero sought by means of this act to "burn the shame" out of his mistress, so Lawrence was seeking to persuade his readers that it was not a thing to be ashamed of, but a proper element in a full sexual relationship between man and woman'. Sparrow, replying to Peter (*E in C*, 13: 2, Apr. 1963), wrote that he had seen a proof copy of this letter by WE; he added, ambiguously: 'I am very glad that the correctness of my interpretation, and the importance to be attached to the question . . . should be so strongly confirmed by an expert' (204–5). (John Peter was to stick to his case in *E in C* 13: 3 (Jul. 1963), 301–2.)

Mr Peter makes a gallant defence, but the Warden could still claim that no one had 'even attempted to pick a hole in the *nexus*' of his reasoning. After quoting a long description of the seventh amorous encounter of Connie and Mellors, he said in effect, 'What was she so ashamed of? What seemed to her new and frightening, after she had made so much progress in the six previous lessons? And why did she not get the usual pleasure, though she felt satisfied afterwards?' Then Mellors's wife turns up and accuses him of unnatural pleasures, and Connie reflects jealously that he had 'known all that sensuality' even with his wife.[2] To deny that Lawrence intended the inference here only make him look ignorant. During the second half of 1961 five critics planted a belief or suspicion that he did mean it, and judging from the conditions of publication they must have decided independently; except that (as I understand) the idea had come quite near the level of consciousness by the end of the trial itself.

Mr Peter replies: 'One does not need to practise them to know that there are dozens of sexual procedures which diminish the woman's pleasure'; but he does not explain why the one adopted satisfied the deepest longing of Connie by affronting her deepest shame, nor yet why Lawrence tacitly recommends it. I think he had only one argument that needs answering; Mellors in chapter 14 grumbles against women who love feeling and cuddling, every kind of going off except the natural one: 'They always want you to go off when you're *not* in the one place where you should be, when you go off.' [212] But the grumble is that these women try to enjoy themselves, instead of letting the man master them. They are particularly well mastered if the man uses the anus instead of the adjacent vagina, as we are told of Connie—'It cost her an effort to let him have his

---

[2] D. H. Lawrence, *Lady Chatterley's Lover* (1928; 2nd edn., with introd. by Richard Hoggart, 1961), 276.

will and way of her. She had to be a passive consenting thing, like a slave, a physical slave.' Mellors would only laugh at the pedantry of anyone who called him inconsistent there.

Professor Kermode, I thought, printed the best comment; that Lawrence thought Connie mentally very sick and only to be cured by drastic treatment, like the old-style lancing of a boil. She, like her whole civilisation, needed a 'gros baiser'.[3] This is morally much better than what Mr Peter imputes to Lawrence; but we still need to plumb into Kermode's French and ask why this particular kiss was expected to heal her. It is one of the few basic ideas of Lawrence that the emancipation of Western women is driving them mad, because a woman needs to be mastered, and therefore western civilisation will soon collapse. His disciples tend to ignore the doctrine, and maybe it is what Mr Peter is resisting here. I think it is all nonsense, myself; what would he have made of the emancipated women of communist China? Women do not require bullying; men can keep their mental health under a regime of bullying better than women can. To be sure, a woman likes to feel in the hands of a reliable man; and so does a reliable man. It is clear from the many reports of the Lawrence ménage that Lawrence himself, to his credit, had no direct knowledge of what he was recommending; and I don't think he succeeds in imagining Connie as a patient who could only be cured by the treatment he describes. The story is thus rather like a daydream about a Limerick.

All the same, Lawrence was deeply informed and sympathetic, and likely to have got hold of some important idea.

> She would have thought a woman would have died of shame. Instead of which, the shame died. Shame, which is fear; the deep organic shame, the old, old physical fear which crouches in the bodily roots of us, and can only be chased away by the sensual fire. [258]

But how old? Not implanted by evolution into our 'bodily roots'. Ralph Hodgson told me about 1932[4] that the human disgust for turds must have been acquired by natural selection at the start of the Neolithic, because all villages died of typhoid except those few which made a cult of shame; and

---

[3] See Frank Kermode, 'Spenser and the Allegorists' (British Academy Warton Lecture, 1962, reprinted in *Shakespeare, Spenser, Donne* (1962), 12–32. Kermode epitomizes his argument in his *Lawrence* (Fontana Modern Masters, 1973): '*Lady Chatterley's Lover* is about the need for a rebirth of phallic consciousness conceived, in a familiar Lawrentian way, as the only means to regeneration both personal and national ... Constance Chatterley ... becomes, in part, a representation of England as a sleeping beauty, only to be revived by the *gros baiser* of a phallic prince' (124–5).

[4] WE visited Ralph Hodgson at Sendai, Japan, for the Christmas holidays 1933.

that the civilised mind was still contorted by this initial struggle. The thought is so much of Lawrence's period that I expect he meant it by 'old, old', which is otherwise panting nonsense.

> How she had really wanted it! She knew now. At the bottom of her soul, fundamentally, she had needed the phallic hunting out, and she had believed she would never get it. [259]

But what was being hunted? It has been argued that Mellors entered the vagina from behind, which many peoples consider normal; to do so makes the cervix, the mouth of the womb, harder to reach, among Nordics at any rate, so that Mellors would be setting himself a handicap:

> . . . it took some getting at, the core of the physical jungle, the last and deepest recess of organic shame. The phallus alone could explore it! [259]

If the phallus is going up the end of the digestive tube, it is pathetically little able to explore that mystery—about as long as a cricket pitch, with the last eight inches or so usually empty. We need to find something other than that cervix for the 'core' to be, or Mr Peter's side wins after all.

A man has the prostate gland which can be stimulated through the anus, and it is liable to go frighteningly wrong even without. A woman has nothing so specific there, but she can get pleasure from the inside of the whole ring of bone through which a child is born; the chief cause of her birth-pangs is also one of her deepest areas of satisfaction. To awaken her all round in this way is not a sordid ambition, and the hands may well be working on it while the normal act is in progress. Probably this was Lawrence's basis in experience for the phrases about exploring the jungle, and probably he was drawing upon folklore for the belief that sodomy is the way to melt the frigidity of a lady. (Professor Wilson Knight in describing the row about Byron quoted a man making this charitable reflection—*Lord Byron's Marriage*, p. 252).[5] We should remember that the earlier novels take a

---

[5] G. Wilson Knight writes: 'There are possible reasons [for Lady Byron's break away from her marriage] on grounds of frigidity; and we know that Byron wanted children, even if Lady Byron . . . was less interested. We have already (p. 192) seen that the bridal night passage in [the apocryphal poem] *Leon to Annabella* may contain a hint to this effect, and it certainly tells us that reluctant brides in ancient times preferred to start that way (311–16).' (*Lord Byron's Marriage*, 252). On p. 192 Wilson Knight explains, though still shyly: 'The marriage is described [in the poem], followed by the wedding night, which is rather strangely treated. What "viands" awaited him, writes Leon, "I will not say" (64); he tells how he pressed her "trembling", "half-resisting" and "half-yielding" form, and then breaks off with "but thou know'st the rest" (106); and at last diffidence was gone (113). There may be a suggestion that Leon's unorthodox approach was first used to overcome his wife's reluctance, a custom which our poem later on tells us was usual in ancient Rome.'

rather mysterious stand on telling men to refuse orgasms to women, or at least to refuse one kind of orgasm; and at one point the hero's penis is hurt by the beaklike cervix of an elderly admirer, who is denounced for doing it on purpose though unconsciously.[6] The excitable areas around the cervix, I take it, were what a man should protect himself [from] by refusing to satisfy, and the woman should accept a longer act of pleasure which gave her a more diffused kind of satisfaction. It sounds cuckoo and maybe it is, but it is not merely an excuse invented by Lawrence; for instance, what appears to be the same discipline for the harem crops up in Dr Needham's* great treatise on Chinese science (vol. II, pp. 146–52).[7] At any rate, in supposing that Lawrence thought sodomy would be good for Connie, one is not making him inconsistent with the beliefs he had been publishing before.

Information in this field is hard to come by. I revere however the capacity of Professor Wilson Knight to stretch out his hand and say, without requiring to know the practical details, 'This means something noble'; before his colleagues have even got upset about them.

William Empson
University of Sheffield

TO D. J. ENRIGHT*

Sheffield University
5 March 1963

Dear Mr Enright,[1]

Glad to send you my salutes. But in answering the question [about the curious locution in l. 16 of his poem 'Ignorance of Death'] I can't say

---

[6] In an undated note (late 1930s) WE wrote: 'Now that the great battle for frankness has been won, or so people seem to think, now that A. Huxley the lost Leader is always telling people that they have the millennium already and oughtn't to like it, surely it is curious that so little of the Wisdom of the Ages has actually been printed. When I first got to Changsha [in 1937] the main thing to do was to help agree on a skeleton library for the English School, to be sent out when possible, and as we thought closely of names and got to D. H. Lawrence, George Yeh said to me, "Yes, *Lady Chatterley*" and put that down alone. I kind of minced a bit at this, and he said, "Well, that's the only one where he got anything said he wanted to say, isn't it?"—or I understood him to mean that, if he didn't say it. It is painfully true, and he only says one thing, as far as I remember, about how ageing women get a power to hurt the men who please them and enjoy it. Only one *physiological* thing, you understand; and maybe he only wanted to talk about the spirit. But granting he wanted to say things of this kind he made a poor list of them. Half the men you meet in a decent bar could say a good deal more; I could give one or two tips myself.'

[7] WE reviewed Joseph Needham's *Science and Civilisation in China*, ii: *History of Scientific Thought*, in the *Observer*, 19 Aug. 1956: *A*, 596–8.

[1] Enright wrote to WE on 14 Feb. 1963 from the University of Singapore, where he was Professor of English, 1960–70 (see *Memoirs of a Mendicant Professor*, 1969). Enright actually admired 'Ignorance of Death' and was to include it in his anthology *The Oxford Book of Death* (1983).

much more than that it isn't a misprint ('Heaven me, when a man is willing to die about . . .'). Of course these tricks of speech are rapidly variable, and might perhaps be objected to as 'private poetry', a thing I have often been accused of, but wrongly, I thought. 'Heaven me' is meant to sound aunt-like, placid and in a way experienced; I am admitting to feeling respect for heroic behaviour, but do not want to present myself as heroic. 'Of course I don't deny that, but this is no occasion to get excited about it'. It still seems to me the right interjection for the occasion.

I wonder if the difference is that your generation is determined to appear manly and sincere, with no hanky-panky, whereas mine thought it showed civilised awareness to make mild unfunny imitations of old ladies, pansies, Cockneys and so forth when expressing a view which the group imitated would especially sympathize with. Come to think of it, all you fiercely upright young men would die of shame rather than do that.

Well, such is the answer, but I can see that it won't make you think the poem any better.

Hoping to meet you one day

William Empson

TO ROBERT WINTER*

Sheffield University
7 March 1963

My dear Bob,

What a saga your recovery has been; I had no idea it was like that. I ought to have answered you long ago, but my No. 2 here [Douglas Hamer], who had been doing it for many years and knew all the ropes, was made to resign at the age of 65 last year, and I have been having to run the department myself for the first time. It is rather a badger, and I have eight more years to go before I retire with a tiny pension; it will be important to have things to publish ready when the profits would no longer go in income tax. Hetta has never taken to Sheffield but stays in London with the children, teaching foreigners; very strong and well. People seem rather cross and dismal, I think, though they don't quite know why. The students if not just slack are very Christian, with a craving to scold the authors of earlier times. Respectable old buffers, however, are still often not Christians; so it is not very surprising that my old schoolmate [Ian Parsons] was willing to publish Milton's God—though he pencilled on the MS that he expected we would both be prosecuted for blasphemy. The reviewers nearly all took the line that I was a cad to have hurt their private feelings.

About *The Windhover*: one can take the sestet about the priest as simply a contrast to the octet about the bird, but that makes it an Imagist poem, and I think Hopkins would mean the contrast to have some specific point. He seems to me very much a teacher; the 'terrible sonnets' are really saying that the Jesuit training doesn't seem to have made him any better, as a student might say 'I've done three years French on your method and I can't talk it'. This poem is earlier, the year of his ordination, and he would still expect that the training was going to make him pure etc. I come from the heavy wheat country of the Humber, where the earth when ploughed really does shine, almost like petrol spilt on the road; so I take 'sheer plod makes plough-down-sillion Shine' to mean that that whole scene shines, not merely that the plough-share gets scraped; the good ploughman, though he has learned his skill by dull labour, makes a beautiful set of lines on the contours—though he is only trying to make straight ones. Thus the dull training produces spontaneous beauty, and no doubt the aristocratic bird had to practise too. In a similar way the dammed-up desires produce the inner fire of the poet and the martyr. This gives adequate connections of thought, and it removes the need for the present Catholic view that the bird caught and ate a rabbit, as Jesus caught and ate Hopkins. I agree with you that the poem exists for people who haven't got this explanation, which I took a long time to think of, but quite a lot of people have been left unsatisfied by its apparent inconsequence.

I don't think you need feel doubts whether Housman in the poem [*More Poems* XXIII: 'Crossing alone the nighted ferry'] is doubtful about belief in oblivion. The idea is that ghosts are ferried across Lethe to a wharf in the underworld, and especially devoted ghosts meet their lovers on this wharf; or so the other man thinks, but even if it is true he won't find Housman there. There may also be an idea 'Considering the known properties of Lethe, he is as usual presumptuous to expect it anyway'; but I suppose one could cross Lethe without drinking it. It is a very fine poem. I don't think it expresses contempt for Lethe, and he doesn't deny that he will be in the city of the grave, only that the lover can't expect to be met there.

Please give Chi my best wishes, and I am sorry his liver is bad. Interesting about Teilhard, but I am afraid I never managed to read him. No, I didn't go to the Edinburgh Writers Conference. I went to the last day of a symposium on Chinese Communist Literature at a country house near Oxford, with papers by many of our Chinese ex-colleagues now dons in America; compered by the US diplomat Boorman, with the whole discussion taperecorded, for a week. A young English sinologue summed up the results (which were extremely friendly, apart from some grumbling about puritanism etc) and described an early author who had worked for the Japanese as a traitor. They all made protests against this harsh word, as they certainly wouldn't have done in the war. So they feel they are traitors, poor things. Otherwise they seemed cheerful enough. I hope my son Mog gets to Peking.

With very good wishes from us both,
William Empson.

Herbert Stern

TO MARTIN BUXTON*

The University, Sheffield 10
30 March 1963

Dear Martin Buxton,

How is Myat Tun [U Myint Thein][1] getting on? Is he jettisoned by modern National-Socialist Burma? Don't tell me you don't know; I know you don't, and also that you can find out easily enough whether he is still posted abroad, or perhaps even whether he is now a recognised official at home.

Fairly early in the war Myat Tun and I used to make a weekly journey across London to the Burma Office, while Burma was being lost for ever by the British Crown, to discuss there what he should say in his broadcasts in Burmese. When I left Communist Peking he smuggled out for me a small suitcase containing unfinished plays, an unfinished novel about Africa, none of it to do with China; I have never looked at them since but revere Myat Tun for saving them with such firm instructions and energetic adroitness. So I would be grateful if you would inquire about his current address, merely so that an old friend can salute him.

I also ran into Myat Tun in 1947 on the Rice Board in Singapore, as my brother Charles was an official on it there at the time.

Yours sincerely
William Empson

Houghton: top copy, bMS Eng 1401 (517)

---

[1] U Myint Thein (1900–94), lawyer and diplomat, studied at Rangoon University and at Queen's College, Cambridge; he was called to the Bar in 1925. He became Burma's first Ambassador to China, 1948–53. He was Chief Justice of Burma, 1957–62, and was then gaoled for six years by the revolutionary government.

TO F. W. ROBERTS* (HARRY RANSOM HUMANITIES RESEARCH CENTER)

Sheffield University
20 April 1963

Dear Mr Roberts,

Thank you for sending me a photograph of Topolski's painting of me, and I gladly give permission to reproduce it; I should have thought that I had no right to refuse.[1] However, I wish to take the opportunity of congratulating Texas University upon carrying out this generous-minded plan.

I want also to make a suggestion. If it has not been done already, I strongly recommend that the University make an offer for at least one of the preliminary sketches for each painting.[2] The sketches are full of witty comment and of the energy of Topolski's line, and I expect some people will always think, as I do, that they are better than the paintings. They would at any rate be found interestingly different.

This would be a fitting completion to a scheme which has already been carried out grandly.

Yours truly
William Empson.

Texas

---

[1] An article in the *Sunday Telegraph* (25 Feb. 1962) reported that Feliks Topolski had been commissioned by 'an American organisation' to paint twenty distinguished writers. 'By which American organisation? "There," says Topolski, "is the 'drama'. I just don't know." The commission reached him through a man [F. W. Roberts] who had come over here to buy manuscripts.' Financed by the Harry Ransom Humanities Research Center, The University of Texas at Austin, the contract included portraits of W. H. Auden, John Betjeman, T. S. Eliot, E. M. Forster, Robert Graves, Graham Greene, Aldous Huxley, John Osborne, J. B. Priestley, Herbert Read, Bertrand Russell, Edith Sitwell, Stephen Spender, and Evelyn Waugh.

Topolski wrote of WE in *Fourteen Letters* (1988): 'I never even tried to follow his rapid academy-cum-wit pronoucements—I accepted in hearsay their profundity cum humour. When he posed for me my eye was not on his performing lips but aimed below at his then mandarin beard, springing from under his jaw, acquired in Peking whence just back. I felt fully comfortable with Hetta his wife, and the boys.

'Hetta, soon after the war, posed in the nude at my studio for Clement Davenport and me: Clement's idea that we should refresh our draughtsmanship. Hetta, having never done this before, trembled all over reclination at first, thus implanting flesh-awareness on to her remarkable South Africa-moulded monumentality. With the years she developed her innate dominance—an impressive stomping far from motherly personage. Thus the boys, engulfed between these two originals, had to take command, aiming at normalness.'

[2] Topolski did not paint face to face; he worked from drawings made while the subject was sitting for him.

TO CHRISTOPHER RICKS

Department of English Literature, The University, Sheffield
4 June [1963] Tuesday

My dear Ricks,

I hope you won't sell the book by Sparrow you were reviewing, as I am anxious to borrow it some time.[1] But don't post it as I trust I will be seeing you. We are having a party in Hampstead this Saturday June 8th, by the way, and would be very pleased if you could come; but it is just a for-all and I am not sure we can offer a bed. Do come if you can manage it.

I am sure we could put you up somehow. If you are coming please reply to Studio House—I am going there on Thursday.

The Sparrow book must be absurdly wicked, as you make clear while pretending to kow-tow to that Donald Duck of a mandarin.[2] I was much comforted by your saying that any joke used by Nabokov has earned final retirement.[3] The point about poor Wyndham Lewis surely is not just that he was wrong about Hitler but that he had made such a hoo-ha about

---

[1] John Sparrow, *Independent Essays* (1963).

[2] '[T]he essays on sexual morality seem to me quite the best part of his book,' remarked Ricks in his review. 'Oscar Wilde, Roger Casement, Peter Wildeblood, A. E. Housman—here is what Mr Sparrow calls "A Difficult Topic" . . . Anyone who thinks that the law, and the society which retains it, causes unnecessary pain, will have to read Mr Sparrow. And that for the very reason which has made him any reformer's pet ogre: that he is naturally a defender of authority, law and tradition. It is true that in this book many of his jibes at "progress" and "egalitarianism" seem extremely trivial, but on this one question he makes an essential point with feeling and force . . . Granted, Mr Sparrow is unjust in supposing that reformers naively think that a change in the law would bring about an immediate and deep change in public feeling. Granted, he seems unnecessarily pessimistic . . . But in the end—and this is the main reason for respecting his book—it is not conservatism or snobbery or pessimism that makes him reluctant to join with the reformers: it is a genuine and unignorable doubt about whether the last state won't be even worse than the first . . . Just the same, it is a pity that Mr Sparrow does at times write as if all readers of the *Observer* cheer when they hear that a homosexual is made to vomit in front of pictures of men' ('The Warden', *New Statesman* 65 (31 May 1963), 833).
   George Watson relates of WE: 'it was amazing to hear him talk of Sparrow as a youthful radical. Once, I recall his telling, at a speech-day at Winchester, the boy Sparrow had turned to him and asked him to stand up and look around at a large assembly of parents. Empson wonderingly did as he was told. "Now, Empson," said Sparrow, "when in years to come you are asked to appoint a Wykehamist or to overlook a fault in one, just remember what you have seen today." But now, Empson went on savagely, a life spent in Oxford had turned Sparrow into "the trusted family butler—and that is just the matter with Oxford: it turns people into trusted family butlers" ' (*Never Ones for Theory?*, 66).

[3] CR wrote of a novel by B. S. Johnson: '*Travelling People* is a teaser. Even if one knows what one likes about it, and what not, it's still very hard to settle which things really matter. Those I don't like are probably those on which Mr Johnson most prides himself—in fact, the whole Shandean rigmarole of the book, with its comic names like Henry Henry (surely if Nabokov has got round to a joke, it must be well past retiring age) and Maurice Bunde, nicknamed (nudge) Maurie and therefore sure to die before the end of the book . . . But still I enjoyed and admired it. The author has a mind, and he knows a lot, and he cares, and he is very good on people who are absurd but not contemptible' ('Teaser', *New Statesman* 65 (26 Apr. 1963), 647).

being the one man who could see through politics and grasp the future.[4] One does also feel, as someone said, that he doesn't believe there *is* anything nice because nothing nice has ever happened to him; a pathetic though so often a dangerous condition.

Hoping to see you, even if you can't make the party.

Yours

William Empson

TO G. S. FRASER*

Department of English Literature, The University, Sheffield 10

29 July 1963

Dear George,

Thank you for your charitable letter. I do seem to have been ruder than I meant[1]—Lowell and Larkin are very good poets I think, but they seem to me almost my own age. In grousing about the young I meant people like Peter Porter, the group in fact which Alvarez called the Christie poets very splendidly in a recent review.[2] (They seem to be tidying the mouldy bits of

---

[4] In a shrewd review of *The Concise Encyclopædia of Modern World Literature*, ed. Geoffrey Grigson ('Blowing the Gaff', *New Statesman*, 10 May 1963, 713–14), CR noted: 'The only place where idiosyncracy turns into something less attractive is the entry for Wyndham Lewis. Its critical estimate would not actually be mine ("the greatest of modern English prose-writers", given more space than T. S. Eliot—more space, indeed, than anyone in the world except Yeats). But the case is argued with passion and skill. And, unfortunately, with cunning, as when we're told that Lewis "played into the hands" of his enemies when in 1931 he published "his apparently sympathetic *Hitler*, a book which is inconsistent and difficult to follow." Now *apparently* is a very useful word, since it can mean "manifestly so" or "not in fact so", but the tone suggests exculpation. And yet *Hitler* (the "Man of Peace") is unmistakably and dismayingly sympathetic. Mr Grigson (the essay sounds as if it is his) wishes to defend Lewis, and he could have chosen to do so by arguing that a man could admire Hitler in 1931 and not be wicked. Or by simply relying on Lewis's later recantation. Or by saying that a man can have wicked opinions and be a very good writer. Perhaps none of these arguments would be very forceful, but they would be a lot better than pretending that the book is only "apparently" sympathetic to Hitler . . . [T]o proclaim that the question of Lewis and fascism has been "very briefly disposed of by T. S. Eliot" [in *After Strange Gods*] is simply to say that the pot called the kettle white.'

[1] 'William Empson in conversation with Christopher Ricks', *the Review* 6 & 7 (Jun. 1963): 'I don't react very readily to any modern poetry . . . Milton could say "God damn you to hell" and make it a singing line, but these people think it's got to sound ugly or they aren't sincere. I think it's Samuel Butler who describes a wallpaper of the Victorian period, with flowers on it, and he says that some bees came in and they went to every one of the flowers all the way down and then they went to every one of the flowers all the way up and they tested every one of these right across the area, and they never realized that *none* of the flowers had any honey' (*CP*, 121–2).

[2] In 'Whatever happened to modern verse?', a review of three collections of recent poetry, A. Alvarez wrote of *A Group Anthology*, ed. by Edward Lucie-Smith and Philip Hobsbaum: 'The editors deny any group style—though the poets come pretty near one in their penchant for bombastic monologues, in the manner of a kind of latter-day, sour-breathed Browning. But they do have a group preoccupation. It is with, in one word, nastiness: torture, wounding, defecation,

chopped-up corpses they have collected). Such was what I had in mind, but I didn't want to name them. Maybe the effect was that I insulted everyone else, but I shouldn't think it got much attention. I couldn't read the Empson Number [of *the Review*, nos. 6 and 7, June 1963] because it gave me the gripes, so I think a tiny bit of lashing back was only in order.

Yours with thanks
William Empson.

Edinburgh: ref. Acc 4681/3

TO CHRISTOPHER RICKS

Wednesday [?1963]

My dear Ricks,

Congratulations to you and your wife on the new son [William]; I ought to have written at once. And thank you for sending me Clifford Leech's book; I would like to do a short review later on, to show my position (the book seems to be just a detailed statement of the evidence for *his* position).[1] But I can't stand another controversy just now—it gives me the belly-ache, as even that Empson Number [in *the Review*] did, which was supposed to be in the main so flattering.

About the Sparrow book, which I look forward to reading, I agree of course that the psychologist's claim to cure homosexuality is great presumption (it isn't new; I remember my playmates jeering at it when I was a student); but why should Sparrow assume that if such men aren't treated as criminals they must be treated as mentally diseased? In Denmark they are treated as neither, and the results don't appear to be disastrous. The Sparrow argument is a typically donnish way to obscure the issue.

Yours very sincerely
William Empson

rotting teeth, the death of small animals. The tone of the book is dominated by a rather schoolboyish spitefulness. Perhaps this is what they are after. Perhaps, after all, it does genuinely relate to the frustrations of suburbia. But I can't see it as much impetus for poetic originality, except of a peculiarly limited and neurotic kind—to train, as it were, versifying Christies.' (*The Observer Weekend Review*, 9 June 1963, 27) John Christie (1899–1953) committed a series of murders at 10 Rillington Place in London.

[1] See WE, 'Mine eyes dazzle'—a review of Clifford Leech, *Webster: 'The Duchess of Malfi'* (1963)—*E in C* 14: 1 (Jan. 1964); in *ERL* (2), 110–15.

TO CHRISTOPHER RICKS

Department of English Literature, The University, Sheffield 10
1 September 1963

My dear Ricks,

I was very much relieved to find your letter when I got back exhausted from Narbonne last night, as I then first saw my review [of Ricks' critical study *Milton's Grand Style*] (proofs were done in the office) and it made me say you had treated me with 'greater generosity' (than you did Donald Davie) instead of 'great generosity'.[1] However I suppose it only sounds like laboured facetiousness.

I expect to be in Oxford next Tuesday evening; shall I give you a ring on the Wednesday morning to see if you are available?

Yours with thanks

William Empson

I thought there wasn't room to go into your remarks about Sam. Ag. Not to sustain the metaphors really does make it seem rather more like a play, I think, as well as making Samson feel exhausted, 'Oerworn and soild' [l. 123]. But one line which you called lifeless struck me as very much an image. The poet explodes into an Alexandrine at the thought:

A thousand foreskins fell, the flower of Palestin [l. 144]

Nisus and Euryalus in their deaths were like poppies, which I found hard to envisage at school.[2] How much more encouraging to the fancy to make the foreskin into the calyx of some flower undetermined: almost the only bit of evidence that Milton was interested in young men.[3] Ah, well . . .

---

[1] 'Still Milton' (WE's review of Ricks, *Milton's Grand Style*), *New Statesman*, 23 Aug. 1963, 230. 'From the first page the book sets out to refute the accusation against Milton that he only wrote "music" and had cut himself off from the virtues of the spoken language.' After discussing Ricks' answers to TSE's and FRL's objections to Milton, the review goes on: '[CR] speaks with greater generosity of the work of Empson, but finds that critic a shocking failure as an explorer: I ought to have examined the later 18th-century critics, instead of being content to giggle over Bentley and the first replies to him. Bentley still seems to me puzzling; one might think that our modern denouncers of Milton just couldn't construe, but they agree here with a man who undoubtedly could.' WE's review does not in fact compare CR's treatment of himself with Ricks on Davie.

[2] See Lord Byron, 'The Episode of Nisus and Euryalus' (1807), ll. 379–84: 'As some young rose, whose blossom scents the air, | Languid in death, expires beneath the share; | Or crimson poppy, sinking with the shower, | Declining gently, falls a fading flower; | Thus sweetly dropping, bends his lovely head, | And lingering Beauty hovers round the dead.' (*Complete Poetical Works*, i ed. Jerome J. McGann (1980), 89).

[3] Cf. WE's poem 'Doctrinal Point' (1935), which delights in the unregulated otherness of the free flower, and includes the wondering couplet: 'They have no gap to spare that they should share | The rare calyx we stare at in despair' (*CP*, 59).

THE LISTENER, 5 September 1963: 'Argufying in Poetry'

William Cookson* responded in *The Listener*, 70 (29 Aug. 1963, 314), to
WE's 'Argufying in Poetry' (*The Listener*, 22 Aug. 1963; *A*, 167–73):

> 'Most of what Professor William Empson has to say is invalidated
> because, surprisingly, he appears to be unaware that Symbolism and
> Imagism are totally different things. To quote Ezra Pound: 'Imagism is
> not symbolism. The symbolists dealt in "association" that is, in a sort
> of allusion, almost of allegory . . . The image is the poet's pigment . . .
> The *image*, in our sense, is real because we know it directly' (*Gaudier-
> Brzeska, a Memoir*).
>
> 'Mr Empson says that "The main rule is that a poet must never say
> what he wants to say directly . . . he must invent a way of hinting at it
> by metaphors, which are then called images." For sheer confusion of
> terms this statement is hard to beat, for this is precisely what a poet
> who uses imagism does *not* do. He seeks "direct treatment of the
> object" and hence frees himself from all metaphorical paraphernalia.'

Sir,—Mr Cookson says I don't know the difference between Imagism and
Symbolism, and I may well be weak on it. I think both theories are very
confused, and if my remarks sound confused it is because I meant to show
that. Very likely there is something important to be learned about images,
but it is not present in the usual critical talk about them. My idea about
Imagists is that they were a small group which concentrated upon carrying
out with puritanical rigour an aspect of the general Symbolist theory,
around 1912, and the results were so depressingly poky that even Ezra
Pound before long stopped calling himself one. I am surprised if Mr
Cookson means what he appears to say, that the best poems written in
English during this century are all Imagist not Symbolist.

Surely Yeats, though a friend and pupil of Pound, considered himself
Symbolist not Imagist? *Another emblem there; that stormy light* . . .[1] Would Mr
Cookson say that a swan literally, without any metaphor, *is* the moral
eminence given to human affairs by an aristocratic system? We expect the
poets to tell excellent lies, but they had better tell more plausible ones.
Anyway, this distinction is not what most critics mean now when they talk
about a poem's images. I am not surprised to learn that Pound, when
introducing Imagism from Chicago, insisted that the new revelation was
absolutely different from the old one. Poets would make pronouncements
about these Movements in an expansive tone of voice, like that used when

---

[1] W. B. Yeats, 'Coole Park and Ballylee, 1931', ll. 17–18: 'Another emblem there! That
stormy white | But seems a concentration of the sky'.

offering one another drinks, and as a rule they could look after themselves. But when an earnest logical student takes up this line of talk he gets bogged down very rapidly; I have seen it happen. The theory which set out to praise the wonder of vision acts in practice as if he had blinded himself.

TO CHRISTOPHER RICKS

The University, Sheffield 10
Friday 20 September [?1963]

My dear Ricks,

[. . .]

The Sparrow book is also being posted back; I am glad to find that he doesn't argue [when discussing homosexuality, in 'A Difficult Topic', *Independent Essays*, 180–92] for wicked laws against buggers on the ground that otherwise they must be treated as lunatics; it was you who invented this piece of donnish obstructionism, as a deduction from his one page blaming psychologists.[1] He is rather firm in saying that danger to minors can be dealt with separately,[2] in fact it seems to be only cowardice, or a belief that the public resistance would be improbably massive, which prevents him from recommending a change in the law. I am glad he is not such a bad man as you made him appear.

It was most helpful of you to tell me that Merritt L. [Y.] Hughes' comments on the little Milton controversy were out [in *The Complete Prose Works of John Milton* vol. iii]; they are grossly disingenuous, and I shall now try to state my case in the second edition of *Milton's God*; if you hadn't told me I would just have removed the irritating sentence and given a reference to the TLS files. I haven't got hold of Macartney yet. The Leeds Yeats Number seemed to have nothing in it; do you want it back?

Yours very gratefully
William Empson

---

[1] 'The remedies suggested in the chapter on 'Prevention and Treatment' [by Dr Lindesay Neustatter, in the collection *They Stand Apart* (1955)] make plain the inability of medicine or psychology or social hygiene to deal satisfactorily with the problem. "Radical" treatment, which aims at curing the condition, either by psychotherapy or by administering hormones, has little prospect of success' (191).

[2] 'It is a commonplace that the undetermined sexual inclinations of adolescence provide schools with one of their most difficult problems; but it is difficult to see how that problem would be aggravated by a change in the law which affected only relations between adults' (188).

TO JOHN OLIVER PERRY*

John Oliver Perry attended WE's seminar at the Kenyon School of English in the summer of 1950. He recalls in a letter to JH (10 Nov. 1989):

> In his class . . . Empson read proof sheets of his forthcoming *Structure of Complex Words*, and I was enthralled writing a 'term paper' on the Shakespearean puns on 'nothing'—'noting', 'an O thing', etc—in *Much Ado*, where the musical and observational meanings were in my callow mind overshadowed by the sexual. My last sentence was a suggestive, I thought, query about what Cordelia might have meant by her reply, 'N-o-thing', to Lear's request for a sign of love in Act 1, but Empson's written rejoinder at the end of my paper was to the effect that I should not make such unsupported remarks. I was suitably chagrined for being so smart assed, but several years later (1963) when I tried again using Empson's 'Structure' as a system, I wrote Empson, asking if he remembered me and the 'nothing' paper, telling of my new project in theory of metaphor with computer analysis of 20 'time' words in Shakespeare.

Sheffield University
Sunday 6 October 1963

Dear Mr Perry,

Thank you for your friendly inquiries, and of course I remember your piece very well. I felt it as an important warning, especially, as you recall, because it made Cordelia particularly prominent with the dirty word; well, how far Rosalind was allowed by the audience to joke about sex without loss of status is a moot point, but Cordelia has to be a tragedy queen and a theory which makes her the Widow Twankey (how I crow if you have never seen the Widow Twankey in a horrible panto) must be wrong. I am glad I urged you to delay publication.

You are right in a way to think it is time I got back to linguistics. I am sure I was right to leave them; after publishing that book I became interested in poking the Christians out of immensely harmful weasel-holes which they have been establishing all over the standard teaching account of English literature. I haven't much more to say about that than I have put out in occasional articles, but getting them unbeatable in evidence at twice the length and fitting them into books is a long job. I am earning my living and preparing to stand by about getting two sons started in life, and the English scene (my elder brother assures me) is more snobbish than ever, so that it is terrifyingly important to throw in money at the right point or otherwise get the child started on the right leg. As for myself, it is a straightforward happiness that as long as I tick over at my profession I have enough money for those I love, but in seven or eight years' time I shall have to retire and become sharply poor; the lease of my London house ends a year or two later, probably with unreasonable demands for money. Thus the instinctive wisdom of my behaviour is looming into view; if I publish a book now three quarters of the profit goes in taxation, but if I can only keep enough reputation to be able to publish after I am forced to retire I shall need to publish all this material which is so heaped up that it almost blocks the window.

Still, I wouldn't mind a bit trying to groom myself to get back into linguistics; in fact, if you will send me a reading list I undertake to look at each work and send you a report on whether I refused to continue and what I thought if I did. It would an important kindness, though I must be allowed an indefinite time limit for the date of my report. I really don't know whether anything useful or sensible at all has been done in that field; I suspect not, but if it has I would be most grateful to you for telling me what it is and where to look for it. I thought we were all falling back on an obviously bogus 'tradition'.

What nonsense Leavis talks about maturity; I get more fretful as we get older but he gets worse.

Hoping you will tell me a book to read.[1]

Yours with thanks

William Empson

TO CHRISTOPHER RICKS*

The University, Sheffield 10
14 October [1963]

My dear Ricks,

What a puzzling case Rowse* is; one might think he was going off his head. He is only sixty, which seems nothing to me. Perhaps he just needs the money—I suppose the false claims get him American Book of the Month status etc? What can he be paying blackmail for, poor soul?

The same number of The Listener that had your good review, with much more homework in it than mine,[1] has an article showing that the

---

[1] Perry comments: 'His willingness to be guided by me in the newer "languistics" was misplaced, but I did suggest Max Black on Metaphor . . .'

[1] 'Shakespeare's Angel', WE's review of Martin Seymour-Smith, *Shakespeare's Sonnets* (1963); A. L. Rowse, *William Shakespeare* (1963); Peter Quennell, *Shakespeare* (1963), in *New Statesman*, 4 Oct. 1963; *SSS*, 13–20. Ricks reviewed Rowse and Quennell in 'All the Answers', *The Listener*, 10 Oct. 1963, 565–6.

chances of your children having equal sex would be different if they were indistinguishable. A very eerie business, I think, whenever it crops up.

I am afraid you probably encouraged Sparrow to say wickeder things than he had dared to blurt out in his book.

Don't bother to answer this. I am due to talk to a Society in Oxford in four weeks' time and hope to see you then.

Yours

William Empson

I am trying to write notes for the second edition of Milton's God. How dismal quarrelling is, and pretending careless ease drives me to drink.

TO JOHN PETER*

Sheffield

17 October 1963

Dear Mr Peter,

Yes, I will certainly recommend you, as I liked your book on Milton[1] and what I gathered of your outlook in general. Very likely my name may appear on the paper without my advice being asked. But if it is I shall feel a slight difficulty.

I think your thesis all nonsense.[2] Around 1930 when just down from college and in London I heard a good deal of gossip about Eliot's sexual problems, which were very intense because his shyness was overwhelming, but the ladies were what he was approaching, not the gentlemen. At the time it was considered remarkable that he was so totally unhomosexual, and often remarked upon.

I forget the date when your views were first printed, but I remember hearing about it from John Hayward, who was then sharing digs with Eliot.[3] Hayward said that Tom himself couldn't think twice about this rubbish, but his affairs were in the hands of literary agents, and it was they who insisted upon a firm legal threat. When you say 'Because the man

---

[1] John Peter, *A Critique of 'Paradise Lost'* (1960). WE noted in his review ('Unsporting', *The Listener*, 27 Oct. 1960, 750, 752): 'Mr. Peter enjoys a good deal of the poem, but considers that honesty demands his pointing out anything he can find wrong with its story, theology, and versification . . . I warmly agree with many of the results; though I also think that most of these "faults" in Milton become very good if you regard them as firmly exploring the contradictions of his religion.'

[2] John Peter's essay arguing for a homosexual element in the works of TSE—'A New Interpretation of *The Waste Land*', *E in C*, 2: 3 (Jul. 1952), 242–66—was repr., with 'Postscript (1969)', in *E in C* 19: 2 (Apr. 1969), 140–75.

[3] Hayward and TSE shared a flat—WE's 'digs' is an understatement—for ten years from 1946, at 19 Carlyle Mansions, Chelsea.

frightened me, and said Boo to my argument, that proves that my argument must be right somehow, and I will be safe to slander him as soon as he is dead', you are assuming that Eliot himself acted in the matter; but a leading business man like Eliot is accustomed to farm out his affairs to agents, and I felt no reason to doubt what Hayward said merely in the course of gossip, that Eliot did not feel personally concerned.

Eliot's education in America was so grand as to be rather monastic like the English, and we hear of someone saying, after Eliot had hugged (The going forth by day of Osiris Brown—I forget the name of that good poet) a friend at the close of a drunken student party, 'Pray God Eliot forgets tomorrow that he did that, or he will be in torture'.[4] He was fond of his young men friends, but this only means that he wasn't very badly lacking in normal equipment there. He was considered unusual in being so firmly heterosexual (when he could manage anything) from then onwards.

Of course I have no doubt that Eliot when a comparatively poor bank clerk in London actually was invited by a Greek business man to a week-end at Brighton [*The Waste Land*, l. 215], but Eliot's refusal would be so automatic that he has no idea really of what would have happened next.

So I think you are chasing a total phantom there, but I am willing to be any assistance I can.

Yours sincerely

William Empson

Christopher Heywood: copy

NEW STATESMAN, 1 November 1963: 'Shakespeare's Angel'

WE reviewed *Shakespeare's Sonnets*, ed. by Martin Seymour-Smith* (1963), in the *New Statesman*, 4 Oct. 1963; *SSS*, 13–18. In response, MS-S—in a letter to the *New Statesman*, 18 Oct. 1963—reaffirmed his view that the conclusion of sonnet 144 'undoubtedly does mean . . . that the poet will not know for certain if his friend is sleeping with his mistress until he develops symptoms of venereal disease: "to fire out" meant to communicate venereal disease . . .'

---

[4] The reference is to a work by the poet and novelist Conrad Aiken (1889–1973), *The Coming Forth by Day of Osiris Jones* (1931); in *Collected Poems*, 2nd edn. (1970), 574–610. In a memoir, 'King Bolo and Others' (1949), Aiken wrote of TSE at Harvard: 'Were we gayer as undergraduates than those of today? At all events we were gay, and my earliest single recollection of our sixty-year-old hero is a singularly attractive, tall, and rather dapper young man, with a somewhat Lamian smile, who reeled out of the door of the Lampoon on a spring evening, and, catching sight of me, threw his arms about me—from the open windows above came the unmistakable uproar of a punch in progress. "And that," observed my astonished companion, "if Tom remembers it tomorrow, will cause him to suffer agonies of shyness." And no doubt it did: for he *was* shy' (*T. S. Eliot: a symposium* (1949), 20).

Also, he did not accept the view WE attributed to him, that 'anal coition took place, with the Earl as the girl'; all the same, 'I do say that it is hard to explain the text without assuming that some kind of physical relationship took place': probably masturbation, as WE suggests (albeit eschewing WE's 'grudging'). Finally, WE's reading of the sonnets seems anyway 'rather perverse. Can he honestly maintain that such poems as 40–42 and 133–137 (the ones about his mistress being taken over by his friend) are "amused and pleased"? Or that the subject of "Th'expence of spirit in a waste of shame" is about social climbing?' Whereas WE tends 'to ignore direct statement', MS-S finds the sonnets 'to be more about love than going to the right parties.'

WE returned to the fray in *New Statesman*, 1 Nov. 1963:

Sir,—I have followed up the chain of scholarly references purporting to prove that the Dark Lady is accused of having gonorrhoea, and it is even feebler than I expected. None of the critics mentioned in the New Variorum footnotes (at the last line of Sonnet 144) says anything about this idea; the authors in periodicals for 1901 and 1907, who might seem presented as discussing it, discuss whether *firing*, or *firing out*, for 'dismissing' a person, was traditional English or new American slang. One of them quotes a line from Edward Gilpin's *Skialethia* (1598), without comment on its extra obscene meaning because that is not to his purpose; but the New Variorum editor deduces that Shakespeare gave the phrase the same extra meaning. Gilpin is a remarkably ham-handed satirist, and the first five lines of his 39th Epigram all struggle to warn the reader what is coming: the reader is leered at and nudged and cockered up till the clincher comes in the final sixth line:

> But I'll be loath (wench) to be fired out.

The only fun here is that a usually innocent phrase has been given an extra nonce-meaning; and it took a lot of putting in—never was joke-work more of a sweat. If anything, this proves that the extra meaning would seem remote to the first readers. Mr Seymour-Smith tells me that I 'ignore direct statement' and that Shakespeare's line 'undoubtedly does mean' a venereal disease; as who should say 'Why, don't you know the language; that's the gerundive.' But people do not *have* to drag a sick joke into ordinary language, when they are talking straightforwardly, even if the joke is known; and this epigram was almost certainly written later than the sonnet. I agree that it is hard to be sure how much Shakespeare meant; the Lady will keep her affair with the Friend secret till she dismisses him, and then give Shakespeare all the gossip—easy enough, but the phrase does seem meant to be rude to her, calling her a fox-hole or a cannon or something. Still, you can't have proof.

'The expense of spirit in a waste of shame' (129) was almost certainly written about the Dark Lady; for one thing, the previous two and the next three sonnets concern her only. Mr Seymour-Smith must assume it is about the Friend, because he asks me whether it too is about 'social climbing'. This is his usual trick; Shakespeare did feel himself horribly in the toils of the Dark Lady, and often presents his relations with the Friend as innocent by comparison; but Mr Seymour-Smith labours to ascribe all this groaning to the relations with the Friend.

Plays were often written about kings, or dukes ruling city states, because plays are largely about decisions, and the decisions of rulers are felt as momentous by many people; even in their private affairs, they are or were free from ordinary policing to a dramatic extent. Anyhow, Shakespeare expected to continue writing plays about such people, and he must (when about 30) have wanted to observe how they actually behaved. It has nothing to do with 'social climbing', because he went on churning out plays and acting in them, obviously not wasting time on patrons, as soon as he got his essential start from this one patron. But Mr Seymour-Smith (I am sure) cannot bear to let Shakespeare behave like that; it would be snobbery, the most shameful thing in all the world. He scored off his friend for taking over his mistress by not letting on the mistress had clap, did he? Come now, that's more like a man, soldierly you might say.

I know that no word of mine will shake this moral preference in the minds of the Christie School, but it strikes me as very odd even for the second Elizabethan age, and wildly unhistorical when applied to the first.

Seymour-Smith had the last word (15 November 1963). In his edition of the sonnets, he maintained, there is not one word about Shakespeare's snobbery. 'It is simply that neither I nor the available facts are as sure as Professor Empson that the young man in the Sonnets was Southampton; and I happen to think that the poems to the man have less to do with Shakespeare's career than with various erotic states of mind he was going through at the time ... I don't see how you can separate certain of the first 126 sonnets from strong emotions of some almost wickedly non-social, perhaps even sexual, kind.' MS-S refused to accept what he described as WE's presentation of him, 'by implication, as a quasi-Marxist voluptuary sitting in some streaming basement-zenana sweating to pull the chiefly non-amorous glories of literature down to my own sordid level.'

TO WILLIAM COOKSON* (editor of *Agenda*)

Department of English Literature, The University, Sheffield 10
30 December 1963

Dear Mr Cookson,

Thank you for sending me *Agenda*, which I enjoyed. That is, I enjoy sadly little modern poetry, but I enjoyed the critical articles, especially your own. I am glad to find that Lucie-Smith and Co, what Alvarez called the Christie School, aren't the only ones; but I can't really admire Pound and his disciples either. I enclose a pound, as the least troublesome way of sending my subscription for a year, with a scrap of extra 'support'.

As to our brush in print, I gladly accept your remarks, regarded as an olive branch, but I cannot but go on trying to convert you. I do not believe you were 'pedantic' at all; lay not that flattering unction to your soul.[1] It would be right to tie 'Imagism' and 'Images' down to what Pound said they meant at first, if it were possible, but it isn't because the theory doesn't fit the facts. I deliberately use the word 'Imagism' wrongly, to mean the mixture of beliefs held by people who attach importance to Images, to show what a muddle they are in. On the other hand, when you said that the best poetry of this century has not been symbolist but imagist (in the strict sense of Pound), you were not pedantic but wrong.

Interesting to see that the old boy has reached [Canto] CXI. Oh well.

Yours

William Empson

No doubt, if you think Pound is right, you think most good poetry fits his formula. But it couldn't be justified in detail.

Yale: GEN MSS 87: Agenda Records, Box 43, folder 2412

TO MR MIDGELEY

Department of English Literature, The University, Sheffield 10
9 February 1964

Dear Mr Midgeley,

I am in correspondence with a Mr R. N. Trotter, now teaching at Grimsby, who wants to write a Thesis in English Literature for a Sheffield MA, and gives your name as a reference. Perhaps I may explain that I have recently accepted two Oxford Thirds in this way, both of them strongly recommended, and one did well the other is shaping well; but the Dean

---

[1] *Hamlet*, III. iv. 136.

and the Faculty Board feel dubious though the regulations do not forbid it. Unless you recommend him strongly I cannot reasonably put his name forward, as I have told him.

Our correspondence is at a rather interesting point. He offered a thesis on Iago, who he says has 'an inferiority complex from sexual inadequacy': I wrote saying that this was old hat, and he wrote indignantly asking who said it before. I took it to mean that Iago found he could not win the love of women he would be proud of because he was too coarse, too frank, too much an old soldier; but evidently Mr Trotter means by the phrase (as I am just writing back to him) that the penis of Iago had some physical inadequacy (it may be too short, or the orgasm may come too seldom or too quickly—these I think are all). But surely there is nothing in the text of the play to support that, whereas he is always presenting himself as the robustly manly old sweat. When his wife, indignant at both husbands, says to Desdemona

> They eat us hungrily, and when they are full
> They belch us   [III. iv. 101–2]

she is in no doubt that his desires were strong enough while he was favouring her with them. Probably Iago never tried to be 'adequate' for his wife in this sense, did not try to please her, and the idea that he has a complex because he couldn't does him more credit than he deserves.

I thought I had better explain my objection because Mr Trotter said that you had thought highly of his theory, and perhaps I have still got it wrong. As an alternative, he proposes a slogging survey on 'The Significance of the References to the Body' in Shakespeare's plays; under many heads. He would do this as an artificial requirement, and had better write on Iago if any sense can be made of his plan.

You understand, not only I, but the Arts Faculty Committee, don't care to take it on unless it is not only likely enough to pass an External Examiner but also seems worth doing. The fighting reply of Mr Trotter to my letter of rejection has made me think better of him, and the question now hangs upon your reply.

I hope the interest of Iago excuses the length of this.

William Empson

Houghton, bMS Eng 1401 (605)

TO CHRISTOPHER RICKS

18 February 1964

My dear Ricks,

Of course I like being quoted, very much; what else does one write criticism for except to win agreement. It is usually painful because the quoter didn't know what one meant, but you do it with great understanding.

I can't see myself getting to Oxford just yet. Hetta was talking about ski-ing in Austria in the holidays.

Yours very affectionately

William Empson.

I must try and read those grisly Beckett novels, I can see. Rowse has done a richly vulgar book about the Sonnets, evocatively Victorian in flavour.[1]

CRITICAL QUARTERLY, 6: 1 (Spring 1964): 'Resurrection'

John Wren-Lewis, in an article headed 'The Passing of Puritanism' (*CQ*, 5: 4; Winter 1963), took issue with the time-worn polarity between 'the positive, world-affirming outlook of the great classical and Catholic tradition' and the Romantic tendency to deny the world by affirming 'individual creativeness' and personal values: 'affirmation of the values of personal life must sooner or later lead to a denial of the claims of organic life, and *vice versa*.' What we need to recognise is that the classical and Romantic traditions in the West are 'both other-worldly', both escapist. The answer is to overcome the apparently neurotic conflict between personal values and organic life by embracing the scientific and technological revolution which can 'provide a genuine answer to romantic despair, a real alternative to puritanism': it can change 'the workings of nature so as to make the physical world subserve personal values instead of overriding them'. The original Hebrew background to the concept of bodily resurrection 'meant nothing less than the faith that the whole physical order of nature could be changed so as to subserve the values of love, beauty and justice which are involved in the original religious impulse'—faith in our 'human power to transform nature' as first asserted by 'the Hebrew–Christian doctrine of creation *ex nihilo*'. But that doctrine has been falsely used, he went on:

> to sanctify the ordinary order of nature as the reflection of the Will of God—a view which in my judgement fully justifies Mr Empson's stricture, in his book on Milton, that 'the Christian God the Father is the

---

[1] *Shakespeare's Sonnets*, ed. A. L. Rowse (1964).

most wicked idea that ever entered into the heart of man.' But this view of the doctrine of creation also makes no sense, and must have arisen originally by distortion of a radically different idea, which I would express by saying that there is no substantial system in the natural world at all, except insofar as human action, based on the service of the personal values of creativity and love, puts it there.

WE responded to Wren-Lewis's plea for a 'revolution in ethics':

Dear Sirs—Mr Wren-Lewis, in your number for Winter '63, says that for most of Christian history the doctrine of creation *ex nihilo* has been used

> to sanctify the ordinary order of nature as the reflection of the Will of God—a view which in my judgement fully justifies Mr Empson's stricture, in his book on Milton, that 'the Christian God the Father is the most wicked idea that ever entered the heart of man'.

This does not say why I said it, but a reader might easily think that I said it for the same reason as Mr Wren-Lewis, and I am anxious to be allowed to clear myself of that.

I said the Father was bad because he could be bought off by the Crucifixion, which gave him 'satisfaction', so that he will spare a tiny remnant of mankind from Hell, but they must eternally watch from Heaven the torments in Hell of those they have loved on earth, praising him for his mercy. I did not say he was bad because he created the world, and I think that idea a disgusting one. It is petulant snootiness to say 'The world is not good enough for me'; the world is glorious beyond all telling, and far too good for any of us. The world includes, of course, what Mr Wren-Lewis calls 'personal values', and I do not see how he can get them into his eternity with a resurrection of the body, which would be like a toy-shop full of working models. An eternity of contemplating God is conceivable, that is, our fancy does not bump at once against a contradiction, but the function of a body is to go through processes in time. The world is equally good whether made by a personal God or not; but I agree that the God is bad if he is using its accidents to trip us up, sending earthquakes to punish us for example. I thought that this extremity of superstition had become quite rare, but even so Mr Wren-Lewis does well to reject it.

A resistance to the style may be making me stupid; it always makes me echo the Negro Spiritual and think 'Everybody talks about "values" aint got any'. What could possibly be meant, for example, by saying:

> in all previous ages it would have seemed self-evident ... that the affirmation of *personal* life-values such as beauty, peace and love, is

. . . almost certainly antagonistic to, the affirmation of *organic* life, in the sense of the general principle of growth and vitality operating throughout nature.

A monk oughtn't to have a baby, but somebody else has to have babies, if only to keep up the supply of monks. C. S. Lewis in *The Allegory of Love* quoted any amount of medieval praise for Nature in this sense. What *happens* when an affirmation is antagonistic? And why would it stop being antagonistic if we made 'a tremendous act of faith' in the resurrection of the body? This would bring 'a revolution in ethics', 'a belief that in general bodily pleasure is positively good'. People had much better think so, I agree; but if something is good on earth, even if it only lasts for half an hour, it is still just as good whether or not it lasts for eternity in Heaven. The idea that its 'value' is different if it happens in Heaven as well as on earth strikes me as like selling a packet of tea by saying 'The Queen drinks it'; though of course not nearly so sensible. By the time Aquinas has finished with Heaven it is not a recommendation but a smear.

Yours faithfully,

William Empson

P. S. I have got round rather belatedly to reading *Objections to Christian Belief*, and find that the Dean of St John's, in its last pages, agrees with me.[1] What is most needed for religion is a natural theology, which the sciences may yet supply, and meanwhile nothing can justify condemning the universe, he says, and so on. Probably Mr Wren-Lewis thinks that this is on *his* side, which again shows how tricky these matters are to discuss.

> 'Surely Professor Empson is being naive?' Wren-Lewis queried in the same issue. 'The image of a wrathful God who permits extreme cruelty is no more than a reflection of our common experience that nature deals out pain and death without regard for individuals . . . it is not only an extremely superstitious notion of God which one must reject if one regards this sort of thing as an abomination; it is any sort of God who could be responsible for the creation of the natural world as we see it.' WE's observation that 'the world is glorious beyond all telling' Wren-Lewis presumed to be 'a poet's statement, made because, in the poet's vision, the transformation of the world is something which has already begun. May I not invite Professor

---

[1] In his Introduction to *The Reactionaries*, by John R. Harrison (1966), WE was to cite the Dean of St John's to the effect that 'nothing can be true *for any mind* except as that mind can be brought to perceive its reasonableness . . . alleged revelation is of no use except as it enables man to attain his own insights' (*Objections to Christian Belief*, ed. D. M. Mackinnon et al. (1963), 108).

Empson the poet to join hands here with technologists like myself, so as to translate this vision into reality as best we can?'

CRITICAL QUARTERLY, 6: 2 (Summer 1964): 'Resurrection'

Dear Sirs—Mr Wren-Lewis is right to insist that the Christians are in a dilemma about their God, but to an outsider it merely looks like a penalty for self-indulgence. Mrs [Mary Baker] Eddy found comfort in the belief that bodily pain and disease do not exist and in later life she built one house outside another for protection against distant enemies willing mental poison into her. In the same way, Christians find comfort in the belief that a well-intentioned creator will reward the good, until they are faced by the problems of Job. The most energetic statement of this dilemma in a novel is the description of the ten-day death of a child from meningitis in Aldous Huxley's *Point Counter Point*; he seems to have been smeared somehow—I find it discreditable that these modern discussions never mention his *Perennial Philosophy*. His answer is that one should stop believing in this all-executive Father, but accept an impersonal 'Divine Ground', as in Hinduism and in the mystics of all other religions; thus becoming morally free to recognise that the world contains wonderful things as well as horrible things.

Mr Wren-Lewis, as I understand, believes that the only nice things in the world are constructed by technologists, perhaps under the leadership of an emergent deity. His article approves of belief in the resurrection of the body as 'a tremendous act of faith' which is 'required for a confident technology': it seems to be a real case of *hubris*. His letter answering mine repeats that 'personal values' are not 'irrelevant to God', and takes this to prove that they exist in Heaven—eternal existence is somehow what validates these values. I must ask again what difference it could make to their value in time on earth. I realise that the doctrine gives authority to the preacher who says: 'If you don't do what I tell you I won't let you live for ever'; but this is not in itself a proof that we will live for ever.

When Mr Wren-Lewis accuses me of 'primitive technology' he is surely sporting with the impatience of your readers. Moslem theologians, we have long been told, decided that the orgasm with a houri could last a thousand years, but that even the most heroic of the blessed would then pause for contemplation. Can there be some recent biological experiment which has proved that it may continue for all eternity?

TO CHRISTOPHER RICKS

Studio House, 1 Hampstead Hill Gardens, London NW3
13 September 1964

My dear Ricks,

Thanks very much for the off-print—I had seen and admired the art-icle.[1] Very good except I don't think you realise the aching thrill for the homosexual which is the really strong point of Housman's poetry.

I have to confess a slight muddle about my Coleridge article, which I vaguely consented to give to *Essays in Criticism*.[2] The Hull editor [R. L. Brett] considered I had already promised it to him, and he had arranged space for it, so there the matter rests. I have been slogging away at it during the holiday. Your point about syphilis (and thank you for further details) needs to go in, but as historically correct about sailors I think rather than about Coleridge's psychology. He could not miss adding it to his nest of private terrors but was too inactive sexually for it to press him hard.

Hetta and I are going to Ghana on the 8th October and have just bought a house in Wales, near Cardigan; very like buying one's coffin. Alice [Stewart] is in America.

Wish I had seen you this holiday
William Empson.

TO CHRISTOPHER RICKS

[University of Ibadan] Lagos
19 November 1964

My dear Ricks,

Some while ago you suggested my sounding out Conor Cruise O'Brien as a possible editor of the New Statesman, in case of a Labour victory. Earlier, he told me he was very willing to consider it, but expected to stay to the end of his contract in Ghana, next autumn. Now however he has just told me, as I raised the question before going to Nigeria for a week or so, that his relations with the Ghana Government are getting very sticky (they want to run the university as a propaganda organization, which he can't allow) and if he is offered the NS at once he will petition for release from the Vice-Chancellorship. It would save difficulty on both sides, he said.

---

[1] CR, 'The Nature of Housman's Poetry', *E in C* 14 (1964), 268–84; *A. E. Housman: A Collection of Critical Essays* (1968), 106–22.
[2] WE, 'The Ancient Mariner', *E in C*, 6 (1964), 298–319; *A*, 297–319.

After working under him for a bit, I am sure he would be found a very good appointment to the N. S.[1] He is a man of firm principles but much good humour and good sense, and a really impressive power of not getting rattled. He seems to me now a much better character than one gathers from the first chapters of *Katanga*[1962]—there he seems fussy, but he is merely exploring an argument; a more self-conscious character would have crossed a lot out when revising. He is very well thought of by the university, who feel he has stood up for them as no one else could; but there would be no point in having a clash just before he will have to go anyhow. Of course he is much in favour of the Ghana socialist policy at most points.

I write this from Nigeria because letters in Ghana are liable to be read. Please pass my sentiments forward, though I realise I am only empowered to act as messenger. I will be home before Christmas and will hope to see you soon.

Yours affectionately
William Empson

TO THE *TLS* (Unpublished)

5 January 1965

Sir,

Professor Dover Wilson's[1] argument for Herbert as the patron addressed in the Sonnets depends mainly on supposing that, as the poems are echoed by verbal correspondences in the relations of Falstaff and Prince Hal, the plays and poems must have been written together. Everybody reveres the wonderful thick skin or staying power which has enabled the New Cambridge Shakespeare to arrive at its triumphant conclusion, but when Dover Wilson arrives at the personal poems he automatically gives his most absurd example of an error in method which his colleagues

---

[1] Conor Cruise O'Brien, who had been Vice-Chancellor of Ghana University, was not invited to edit the *New Statesman*. He wrote to WE on 22 Jan. 1965: 'The committee decision you refer to was not unexpected. If I had been appointed I should have had fundamental criticisms to make of the Labour Government's foreign and defence policies and it is understandable that an editorial board, the majority of which probably generally endorses these policies, would have felt that they should appoint someone more sympathetic.' (*Houghton*)

[1] John Dover Wilson (1881–1969), educator and scholar, was renowned for his many editions of the works of Shakespeare. He was Professor of Education at King's College, London, 1924–35; Regius Professor of Rhetoric and English Literature at the University of Edinburgh, 1935–45. His publications include *The Essential Shakespeare: A Biographical Adventure* (1932), *What Happens in 'Hamlet'* (1935), *The Fortunes of Falstaff* (1943), and *Shakespeare's Happy Comedies* (1962).

have been pointing out to him for forty years. All his arguments about revision of the plays presume that the Ernie of Avon, the quite unintelligible machine, had only one style in one year, and for dating you need only pull similar bits together. But Shakespeare did not throw away his equipment any more than any other skilled man; he could always write like Marlowe if a character was like a Marlowe character. The Dover Wilson argument is thus always wrong, but it has never before been so astoundingly wrong. Imagine the lowly player conducting in exalted poetry a relationship with an Earl which might create grave scandal and could incur the death penalty; imagine the earnest promises of secrecy, fundamental to the tradition of these things; and then imagine the player offering himself to the mob as a farcically sordid agent not only of corruption but of sedition. It would be a self-torturing thing for Shakespeare to do, and such an author would not write better later, nor would the patron accept the dedication of the Folio. Dover Wilson seems to take for granted that Shakespeare just leaked all the time, without meaning anything by it, but this would not make him any more agreeable to his accomplice.

Herbert would be 17 and Shakespeare 34, just twice his age, when their current affair was exposed in his Falstaff plays. I think it would be much pleasanter if the poems were written when Southampton was 20 and Shakespeare 29, engaged upon The Two Gentlemen of Verona. It seems to me odd that my colleagues when dealing with works of Shakespearean date regard a total ignorance of human behaviour as a professional duty, whereas soon afterwards when discussing novels they feel required to pretend a far wider experience of life than they have.

Yours

William Empson

Houghton, bMS Eng 1401 (661)

TIMES LITERARY SUPPLEMENT, 14 January 1965, 32:
'The Living Language'

In Dec. 1964 the *TLS* launched a series of essays on the subject of 'The Living Language'; contributions were requested from a number of writers.

I am sorry to have nothing to contribute at the moment to your language feature, but there is a question I have been wanting to have answered for some time. How old is the locution 'He said to shut the window' or 'She said not to worry'? And where does it come from?

It seems to me to have come in since I was an undergraduate, but the users do not think of it as new; I have even seen it in the dialogue of a historical novel. It does not sound to me ugly or vulgar so much as comically foreign, like for instance 'Long time no see'.

Alison Hanham responded on 11 Mar. 1965, 199: 'As no one has answered Professor Empson's query about *say* plus infinitive ("he said to shut the window"), may I point out that, far from being new and foreign, it was good Middle English. The *Oxford Dictionary* described it as "obsolete", but since then it has evidently re-emerged in colloquial English. "Not to worry" per se is a different matter.'

Professor R. W. Zandvoort (22 Apr. 1965, 317) offered examples of the usage from Hemingway, *A Farewell to Arms*, Christopher Morley, *Kitty Foyle*, and Dorothy Sayers, *Nine Tailors*. Nevertheless, he was also keen to endorse Marghanita Laski's spoiling remark, offered at the outset of the series (*TLS*, 17 Dec. 1964), that 'the field you more specifically say you are going to apply yourself to, that of the language itself, is already well covered and in any case unsuitable for amateur application.'

WE returned with this 'further comment':

TIMES LITERARY SUPPLEMENT, 27 May 1965, 437

The communication of Professor Zandvoort (*TLS*, April 22) illustrates two interesting types of error. It is no use saying that this work is not for amateurs. Writers can do a good deal towards the upkeep of the language, if they realize they can; for instance, when I was young a useful Freudian term was translated 'wish-fulfilment', then various people said in reviews, &c., that this was the opposite of what was meant, and now the only translation used is 'wishful thinking'. Professional linguists in our society are not expected to exert this kind of influence, and seldom try to.

Also, so far as the linguist has succeeded in making himself unliterary, he has made himself a bad judge of written evidence. To have Dorothy Sayers [in *Nine Tailors*] make an English rustic say 'Rector said to fix the lock' is not, as Professor Zandvoort asserts, evidence for the social status of the idiom; one even finds novelists putting it into the dialogue of historical novels. She would have heard it on the films, and maybe she thought it sounded rustic, or maybe she thought it a likely Americanism for a rustic to pick up from the films.

I am told that there is a similar idiom in Anglo-Saxon, so it may have lasted on in a specific dialect and spread widely after emigration to

America. But then, I have not come across it in American writing earlier than the 1914–19 War, either. I am told there is a similar idiom in Italian, so maybe the American troops brought it home from Italy. Many speakers seem to have adopted it without realizing that it was new—that is the remarkable feature of the case, and surely they had better be allowed to know such things.

TO ARTHUR EFRON*, *Paunch*,[1] 23 (17 Jan. 1965), 81–3:
'Wuthering Heights—I'

Dear Mr Efron,

Thank you for sending me PAUNCH for last October, no. 21. I warmly agree with your main position; in fact I think that the neo-Christian cheating has made nonsense of the English literature of earlier periods on an even larger scale than you say. But I write to disagree with the piece by John Doheny on *Wuthering Heights*.[2] As long as he is faulting neo-Christian critics he does needed work, but he decides at the end that 'the reason why Cathy and Heathcliff are unhappy is because their emotional, sexual development stopped at puberty . . .' Now, this may have been what was wrong with Emily herself, and maybe she demonstrates it unconsciously; the book certainly echoes all along with terrible school-girl nagging; but it isn't the *point* of the story, and to regard the book as propaganda for honest sex is remote from what the author would be likely to take on as her mission or chore. Your movement deserves to succeed, but won't if it opposes the neo-Christians all the time with 'the opposite,' phoney in the same way.

Charlotte's preface to the posthumous first edition says that of course her sister never met these peasants; it was all her imagination; but both the farms seem to be enormous estates (the park of Thrushcross Grange is ten miles round, and that was tops; it was the size of the Duke of Devonshire's one at Chatsworth). Wuthering Heights would obviously need several hundred men to work it; what on earth old Joe can do when he goes out 'to work' at dawn is quite as much a mystery as how Heathcliff makes a fortune in two years' absence, or indeed why he has no sex. An admirer of Emily must admit that she had been kept short of experience. The chief

---

[1] The journal *Paunch* (founded 1963), State University of New York at Buffalo.

[2] John Doheny, 'From *PMLA* to *Wuthering Heights*', *Paunch*, 21. See also 'Controversy on *Wuthering Heights*', *Paunch*, 23. Doheny, who taught English at the University of British Columbia, Canada (1959–92), has written on Thomas Hardy, D. H. Lawrence, the Brontës, George Eliot, and Herbert Read.

shortage was company; the girls could have gone to a fair number of parties in the pony carriage, but their father had quarrelled with all the local gentry, a few miles away; and the girls weren't allowed to meet the local farmers, near by, for fear they married a farmer's son. The heir to a farm would be much richer than their father's curates, but after marrying him one was no longer a lady. (The girls would visit the labourers' cottages with Christian aid.) Now the girls were largely brought up on Romantic literature praising pirates and suchlike, and were convinced that pirates were real men, whereas curates were not. The forbidden sons of farmers were obviously real too; they killed sheep or something; and admiration for some such man, whom she would arrange to pass on her long walks but must never speak to, seems to have led her to believe that her bedroom was visited by the Spirit of the Moor. Heathcliff is found as a child in the world seaport of Liverpool, and is frequently said to be black; but there is a phrase 'a black Yorkshireman,' meaning a particularly cross one, and he is described as that with loving particularity.[3] She did not know what Byron's Corsair looked and behaved like, but she had a model under her view.

Thus the novel ignores class as she knew it in detail, but the essence or agony of it is what makes class. Heathcliff is the soulmate of Cathy, but he isn't given enough education for her to recognize it in time; he seems too coarse. He fights back at the world by acquiring both farms, which though high-class and low-class in decoration are equally rich. He can then get his revenge, trampling the son of his enemy into the same mud that engulfed him. Now the revenge story had a long history, and had always been considered a genuine moral dilemma. The remarkable thing about this novel is that it invents a new end for a revenge story, more suited to the Far East than Christendom perhaps though I don't know of a case there. After he has got full power to brutalize the second generation, and though he insists he has not been so weak as to forgive them, his interests have been decisively torn away; he can no longer keep his mind on his plot; he can no longer even keep his mind on eating, so that his actual death comes from starvation. He keeps being distracted by thinking he has almost seen the ghost of Cathy; this is what she would want to do, if you can believe in ghosts (to save the second Cathy), but you may also believe that his Sub-consciousness, influenced perhaps by the spirit of the moors, rose up and saved the lovers.

---

[3] Christopher Heywood recalls (e-mail to JH, 1 November 2001) that one day he happened to remark to WE, about *Wuthering Heights*, that Heathcliff bore all the marks of slave society, slave colouring, and African origin. 'Nonsense, my dear fellow, he's a black Yorkshireman like Freddie Truman,' was WE's response.

Anyhow something saved them, and what saved them is presented as a thrilling mystery. Such is the *point* of the story, and any account which ignores it is no good.

I expect we would think Emily a very superstitious girl if we met her.

—William Empson

TO DILIP KUMAR BARUA*

15 February 1965

My dear Barua,

I think this is very good, but you must remember that in England all this kind of thing has gone very out of fashion—most people have decided that Theosophy is just absurd; in fact opinion on this matter is *more* insular than a century ago. Instead of innocently saying the *Gita* is important you need to try to convince the examiner—'the Absolute of the philosophers comes from Hinduism' still seems to me a good point even if it needs to be qualified (they don't *despise* the Absolute). And I think when you say 'mysticism' you actually *mean* 'becoming one with the Absolute, or Divine Ground', whereas you will generally find English dictionaries saying it means 'direct personal contact with God'.[1] The Wisdom of the East attracted people as a positive alternative to Christianity which was not nearly so evil. Nowadays people who find the Christian God wicked are usually just atheists; you need to recall what Hinduism and Buddhism meant to the English a century ago. I can't think of any permanent effects but there probably are some. Many Christian theologians have I think borrowed innocent-sounding phraseology from it while holding the torture-monster in reserve, but that is little use.

Aren't there any letters between Carpenter and Tagore?[2]

---

[1] D. K. Barua discusses [Edward] Carpenter's heartfelt response to Indian mysticism and the *Bhagawat Gita* in ch. VI of his Ph.D. thesis, *The Life and Work of Edward Carpenter in the light of intellectual, religious, political and literary movements of the later half of the Nineteenth Century* (1964)—'India, Mysticism and World Religion'.

[2] Edward Carpenter (1844–1929), proto-socialist and a campaigner for homosexual equality, studied at Trinity Hall, Cambridge, and entered holy orders (which he resigned in 1874). Then he took up residence in a village outside Sheffield and worked for more enlightened views of society and sexuality. His writings include *Towards Democracy* (1883) and *England Arise: A Socialist Marching Song* (1886). Proud of his homosexuality, and courageously cohabiting with a series of male partners, he campaigned too for the social acceptance of 'urnings' (as he styled 'inverts' like himself). His *The Intermediate Sex* (1908) had a deep influence on writers such as D. H. Lawrence and E. M. Forster. Rabindranath Tagore (1861–1941) was a prolific and multi-talented Bengali poet, song-writer, artist, philosopher, and educational theorist (he was to set up both a school and a university). He was cultivated during a visit to London in 1912 by luminaries including W. B. Yeats and William Rothenstein. He was awarded the Nobel Prize for Literature in 1913.

When the reviews call Carpenter presumptuous [in *From Adam's Peak to Elephanta* (1892)] for disagreeing with Kipling, in saying that the Congress Party would be important, you should add that Carpenter was proved right, and Kipling absurdly wrong, within the lifetime of both. Otherwise the Examiner will very likely assume that Kipling knew better.[3]

A very good chapter though.

W Empson

TO KIM JONG-GIL*

As from Sheffield University
23 April 1965

My dear Kim,

I am very glad to hear you are going on so well. I am sure you are a most valuable man to have as chairman, and you must not let it weigh you down; when they complain, remind yourself how lucky they are to have you there at all. That is the only way.

Muriel Bradbrooke [*sic*] is a very good character, and I expect she told you, as she said in print somewhere, that my book about Milton is 'only nightmare, after all'; so it is, a nightmare from which the Europeans badly need to wake up, as Joyce said he was trying to do.[1] I am getting very wrapped up in trying to rebut the Christian revival among literary critics, which to most people with political interests seems very small beer.

As to an article about Yeats, yes I have one ready, if you are not too proud to take it. I sent it for the farewell volume of an Indian university on the retirement of an old friend Dinah Stock, the G. A. Stock who wrote a book on Yeats [*W. B. Yeats: His Poetry and Thought* (1961)]; and it should be

---

[3] Barua noted: 'It was indeed daring on the part of Carpenter to prophesy the fall of the Empire just after the meteoric rise of Kipling in the early 'nineties—which had excited so many readers with a new enthusiasm for it. Kipling had many merits as a writer . . . but he nowhere realised a basic fact—that the "white man's burden" was spiritually degrading for both the parties. The obsequious natives by their perverse prostrations were spreading the rot from their own hearts to those of the masters; and he did not feel it, whereas Carpenter felt it immediately.' (202–3).

[1] M. C. Bradbrook (1909–93) was to become Mistress of Girton College. See 'Sir William Empson (1906–84)' in *Shakespeare in his Context: The Constellated Globe* (1989), 190–201; and 'Lowry's Cambridge', in *Malcolm Lowry: Eighty Years On*, ed. Sue Vice (1989), 125–46. See also Richards' diary, 1 Mar. 1934: 'Bradbrook to tea. Pathetic & mousey but acutely intelligent & remarkable memory. Pleasant' (*Magdalene*). Bradbrook's other works include *Elizabethan Stage Conditions* (1932), *Themes and Conventions of Elizabethan Tragedy* (1935), and *Collected Papers* (4 vols., 1981–9). See bibliography in *English Drama: Forms and Development*, ed. Marie Axton and Raymond Williams (1977); and Leo Salingar, *Professor M. C. Bradbrook, Litt.D., F.B.A., F.R.S.L.* (n.d.). Stephen Dedalus, in James Joyce's *Ulysses*, says 'History is a nightmare from which I am trying to awake.'

out this month there, but it will remain quite unnoticed I should think.[2] It is not offensive in Asia, being concerned to say that Christian critics fail to understand what the Byzantium poems were about because Yeats genuinely did think like a Buddhist or Hindu; and Dinah Stock wrote the only book about him which is sufficiently world-minded to follow him there.[3] Though retiring from India the dauntless old lady is going on to be Professor at Makerere in East Africa, so the occasion has less feeling of death about it than usual. If you printed it (or a cut version of it) with this explanation of its source I think it would feel decently fresh. It is called 'The Variants for the Byzantium Poems' and about 11,000 words, but you could quite reasonably give a cut version if you prefer.

I hope this is a viable plan, but keep in touch anyway.

All good wishes

William Empson

---

[2] WE's 'The Variants for the Byzantium Poems'—in *Essays Presented to Amy G Stock: Professor of English, Rajasthan University 1961–64*, ed. R. K. Kaul (1965), 111–36—was revised for *UB*, 163–86. Amy G. Stock (1902–1988) read English at Somerville College, Oxford, and taught for some years in Uganda before becoming Professor of English at the University of Dacca.

[3] WE recommended Stock for a Civil List pension: 'Her book about Yeats is the only part of her literary work that I can speak of, as I had been puzzling about the Eastern philosophies in Yeats, and found her a great help. Nearly all literary critics regard the Hinduism of Yeats as at best high-minded blarney, but she is long accustomed to Hindus, and can judge this part of his mind calmly.' (*Houghton draft*)

Stock wrote to WE (24 May 1965): 'I never thought I had *Byzantium* clear, but you might be right that it couldn't possibly be heaven in any recognisable sense. Yeats never thought of Christianity as more than a transitory mode of embodiment of the absolute; in "The Marriage" bit in "The Soul in Judgment" he says that the Communicators use the words "Christ is revealed" (describing a temporary phase of consummation) out of deference to current phraseology, because presumably it is as adequate as any other for something not amenable to definition. Any religion in defining its scale of values necessarily overlooks or distorts other possible ones, but you have to define your outlines if you want embodiment. I think Yeats sees incarnation in time and space as an improvement on disembodied reality, which surely is quite a consistent view for an artist?—but since definition of outlines means exclusion it is necessarily incomplete and has to keep on changing. Then, instead of life being a preparation for death, the soul after death is getting ready for the next life. But he admits that this is an "antithetical" way of looking at it, and that if he happened to belong to a "primary" phase of incarnation he would see it in reverse; which is how Virginia Moore certainly and F. A. C. Wilson probably see it.

'Do you think "A starlit or a moonlit dome" in the first verse means that he is trying to make a reversible picture? I've sent my books to Uganda so I don't know at what stage of composition the alternative comes in; but it seems odd that in such a distinctly visualised landscape the lighting should be left to the reader's choice.

'I like your account of the mechanical bird. I thought Hans Andersen's Emperor's nightingale might have got into it; any fairy-tale-reading child must have known that. But the toy is quite as probable.' (*Houghton*)

REFERENCE FOR FRANCIS BERRY*

Department of English Literature, The University, Sheffield 10
[n.d. ?1965]

Dear Sir,

Mr Francis Berry would I believe be found a very satisfactory appointment to the Chair of English Literature. He is a man of wide interests and generous feeling, with considerable experience of the problems of an English Literature Department. He has published a good deal of both poetry and literary criticism, increasing his reputation notably in the past few years. He is an old friend of Professor Wilson Knight, and recently visited the excavations of the lost Greenland colony, also Jamaica, writing poems about both. I hope this shows that he is free from the prevalent narrowness.

The Readership at Sheffield is given for 'distinction in scholarship and research', and when he got it *Poet's Grammar* was the last book out. This includes an essay on *Thou* and *You* in the Sonnets, proving that the author was uncertain how intimate he might be—this destroys the argument that the poems couldn't be written to an Earl. I think his last book, *Poetry and the Physical Voice*, has been the most important so far. His day-to-day teaching has for a long time put an emphasis on 'elocution', the emphases required by the meaning and the music required by the emotional tone; he recited to his classes impressively (and will do it with equal readiness in Anglo-Saxon). This is much needed, because much of our current orthodoxy ignores sound or positively despises it; I think this is partly why so much recent poetry is hideous. He has another book to be published by Routledge in April, 1965: *The Shakespeare Inset.*

He has always taken a friendly and helpful interest in his students, inviting them to his house for dramatic readings and suchlike; Mrs Berry would also be found very ready and understanding at such work. During the last academic year he gave 22 lectures at other universities, invited by student societies; he has a high reputation among students as a lecturer.

He is now second-in-command here, and does a good deal of the administrative work, always reliably and sensibly. I should be very sorry to lose him, but there is no doubt that he deserves a strong recommendation.

Yours truly,

William Empson.

Francis Berry

CRITICAL QUARTERLY, 7: 3, Autumn 1965:
'The Argument about Shakespeare's Characters'

Sir,

Congratulations on Mr [A. D.] Nuttall's* article about Shakespeare's Characters, and may it herald the dawn on this topic.[1] There were two other quaint aspects of [L. C. Knights's] *How Many Children had Lady Macbeth?* In one of his most striking speeches, Macbeth implies that he has incurred Hell for the sake of his family, sacrificing himself to found a dynasty ('To make *them* Kings? The sons of Banquo, Kings?'). He is the last man to have thought it didn't matter whether he had a son or not.[2] More generally, Professor L. C. Knights was laughing at fussy pedants who did not appreciate the broad simplicity of the stage, so that they would puzzle like A. C. Bradley about what the characters were doing twenty years before. But as he wrote 'The Method' was coming into power, by which actors are positively trained to imagine what the character they represent was doing twenty years before. I have not noticed any sign that Knights or his school have ever heard of this development.

On the other hand, it is absurd (may I testify) to think that Knights holds this belief because he is coarse. What he was saying there was so much part of an intellectual Cambridge movement that he felt himself

---

[1] A. D. Nuttall, in 'The Argument about Shakespeare's Characters' (*CQ* 7: 2 (Summer 1965), 107–20), took issue with L. C. Knights's 'How many children had Lady Macbeth' (1933; in *Explorations*, 1958). Knights had scorned critics such as A. C. Bradley for having supposedly discussed a character such as Hamlet as if he could be known as a real person, with a history and a personality. Furthermore, discussing Knights's comments on the criticism of Maurice Morgann, author of *Essay on the Dramatick Character of Sir John Falstaff* (1777), Nuttall noted: 'It is strange how grossly Knights coarsens his material . . . In so far as Knights's essay is to be considered as revolutionary, I think it must be taken as making a logical criticism, as attacking not merely poor critical execution, but vicious critical premises.' Knights's argument 'turns on the (erroneous) thesis that one cannot talk meaningfully about characters as such.' Yet Morgann and Bradley were far from confounding fiction and reality in any simplistic fashion; even when Bradley speaks of enquiring into the motives of Hamlet, there is no doubt that he is talking not about Hamlet as a real person but about the character. 'Knights's real objection is to the practice of drawing inferences from the seen to the unseen with respect to persons of the play.' But that radical argument is fallacious: 'Dramatic characters are not . . . constructed in a Berkleian *esse est percipi* way at all. It is just not accurate to say that their fictional existence begins and ends with what we actually see.' Falstaff is 'described in such a way that we always feel there is more to be said [to explain his personality]. This is perfectly possible. By a curious irony this incompleteness, this want of finality in formulation, achieves a greater naturalism than the most meticulous description.'

[2] WE wrote in his notes on Knights's *How Many Children had Lady Macbeth*: 'Interesting that the stupid title was supplied by Leavis, who never admits that anybody can be good unless he is an intellectual of lower middle class origin. Naturally the idea that it *mattered* whether the Macbeths had a male heir, because this was what Macbeth was selling his soul for, could not enter the mind of Leavis, who has always felt venomous against anybody who isn't a lower middle class intellectual and even more venomous against the rest of them.' (*Houghton*)

hardly more than the expounder of a theorem. The anti-personality movement may have been needed in the theatre, but the anti-intellectual movement seems a shockingly clumsy weapon even when used for some good cause. The dogma that the reader of poetry only has the words on the page, and the author didn't mean him to have anything else so he mustn't *know* anything is especially absurd in dealing with plays not meant to be printed. And the dogma that a poet only expresses himself by Images, so that there *couldn't* be two different characters in a poetic drama, is enough to prevent any drama. I take only a few from the nest of goblins who were operative behind the facade of cool logic, chuckling to find for themselves such impeccable cover as the personality of L. C. Knights.

William Empson

In an unpublished essay drafted perhaps at this time, WE wrote:

The drive against character-mongering in Shakespeare criticism, personality in actors and actresses, and eventually against any indulgence in human interest while art-work is in progress, is evidently intertwined with the anti-humanist movement of Ezra Pound, Wyndham Lewis, and T. S. Eliot. My impression is that good local uses for the principle, to brush off some unduly greasy bit of habitual sentiment, were often found; but that no amount of tact in the critics could stave off for ever its inhumanity and wrongheadedness. A simple desire to make actors scan their lines, and not speak the words too emotionally to be intelligible, was the best side of the movement; but the profession is not outwitted so easily, as Yeats realised when he decided to write his final plays for amateurs. Consider Sir Lawrence Olivier's film of Richard III, scanning very well, and evoking the hero wonderfully, especially in the close-ups for the soliloquies, but then cutting the last soliloquy altogether. It felt to me like leaving out the answer to a whodunit. Instead we were treated to some trick photography and a selection from Sir Lawrence's repertoire of farmyard imitations. These, he evidently thought, would be more interesting; and the idea is so widespread among actors that it looks as if sheer classes in farmyard imitations must go on at the actors' schools. I have had to be present at quite a number of real-life scenes in my time; and I think that the drama on the telly, especially, which is nowadays so hard to escape from, sounds like nothing but what it is—professional people nagging at you to make you listen to them. However, this line of complaint has really little to do with the basic theory that drama is not concerned with personality; though the brashness of the term 'personality' itself, prepared to mean anything that would help along a sale, no doubt encouraged theoretical objections among honest men. The objection that A. C. Bradley treated the plays of Shakespeare as historical documents, asking what the characters were doing twenty years before, whereas they are poems, each a unified network of metaphors and other symbols, comes from a different milieu and has different claims.

NEW STATESMAN, 10 September 1965 [written 27 Aug. 1965]:
'Yeats's Politics'

Sir,—I am sure Mr [Conor Cruise] O'Brien is right in saying that the Catholic Church supported the Cosgrave government against De Valera, and this makes the picture less clear-cut than I had gathered from his article, but it does not settle the broad point I was trying to raise. The Indian Moslems, the Turkish Cypriots and the Anglo-Irish are each a minority, mainly descended from conquerors who arrived about 400 years ago, with an inherited tradition and a religion as part of it. It is generally agreed that the first two are entitled to live according to the beliefs which they accept, and may even fight for the privilege, but that the Anglo-Irish have no such right; indeed, an attempt to get it for them seems to be what both Yeats and Mr O'Brien call fascist. No doubt some minorities are too small or otherwise contemptible for special treatment by the law; therefore, a Senator demanding such treatment for his own group will naturally urge, as Yeats did, that this group has deserved well of the state. I can well believe that the demand wasn't practical politics, nor even what Yeats himself wanted in the case of censorship, but it needn't be treated as shy-makingly caddish—how could a good poet be so fascist? One would be glad to learn of some general principles behind these sentiments.

Answering Mr Ricks's kind review of my book on Milton, I did not mean by the last sentence of the appendix now added that Milton 'had consciously voted against his God'; surely, we know that he did not, from his subsequent poems.[1] I have tried to avoid speculating about his psychology, but I should think that revolt against the horror of his God was intermittent rather than subconscious. My sentence only meant that he was able to appreciate a variety of feelings, since the appendix shows him as adroit at propaganda work, and therefore could not be unaware of the strain in *Paradise Lost* upon our sympathies. In saying that he was capable of understanding the poem I only hoped to counter the official view that he was a frozen pig; but I will try to remove the possibility of misunderstanding in the next edition.

[1] See CR, 'The ways of God', *New Statesman*, 70 (20 Aug. 1965), 292–3.

TO CHRISTOPHER RICKS

Department of English Literature, The University, Sheffield 10
18 October 1965

My dear Ricks,

It is very kind of you indeed to propose me again as the Poetry Professor. But it would still be an unpopular move here (if I am too ill to take my share of being Dean why am I well enough to romp about at Oxford?) and I am not sure I *am* well enough—it would be quite a strain.

In six years' time I have to retire (becoming 65 in 1971) and after so much fun abroad I only get £500 a year pension. I shall thus badly want congenial paid employment, and the money won't largely go in tax, as it would at present. I don't feel I shall be gaga in six years' time—I am relying on the retirement to finish various lines of research.

[Incomplete]

TO D. A. R. SHANKAR

[n.d. 1965–6]

Dear Mr Shankar,[1]

I find it difficult to answer you about Allen Tate, because he seems to me merely a follower of T. S. Eliot, content to say anything he believed to be in the current fashion without worrying about it; and the fashion seems to me a nasty one, which I hope will soon die. It expresses contempt for the modern world on aesthetic grounds, explaining that the speaker would have been a cultured aristocrat in earlier times; and Allen Tate can whine and moan with particular resonance because he comes from the Southern States. 'Oh, why can't I have gracious living? The modern world is too unrefined for me. Why can't I have negro slaves? Why can't it be really beautiful, like it was way back in early times, so that I can burn my slaves alive to Moloch? That was the real spiritual religion, when everybody's mind was in a beautiful order.' Though it claims to be so holy and refined,

---

[1] D. A. R. Shankar, a British Council scholar, began an MA dissertation under WE's direction on the topic: 'T. S. Eliot, I. A. Richards and the New Critics: A reconsideration of the influence of Eliot and Richards on the New Critics'. As submitted in Sept. 1967, the title had been changed to *The Literary and Social Criticism of Allen Tate*; and Shankar acknowledged WE's help in a preface: 'Both his writings and conversations have been a source of stimulation.' Shankar followed WE's line of thought on Donne's poetry in his chapter 2, 87 ff. WE was to write in an undated draft reference: 'Mr Shankar worked under me at Sheffield for two years, writing his MA thesis on Allen Tate; this involved reading widely in other recent critics. His mind is scrupulous and penetrating, though of wide sympathies, and he is a most suitable person for further study and research in that field.' (*Houghton*)

it is very near the petulance and perversion of Oscar Wilde—who was in himself a much more agreeable and cheerful character, but had picked this up from Baudelaire as part of his aesthetic campaign, and naturally the worst side of Wilde had the greatest influence on Boston, where Eliot was growing up. However, this business of placing a line of thought in its historical background is often misleading; you, coming from outside, may be better able than I am to see what Tate has to say as a separate individual. I am prepared to believe that he did not understand the nastiness of what he was copying out, but I have difficulty in believing that he understood anything else either. Indeed, the chief trouble with this fashion was that it required you to close your eyes to everything important which was going forward. A young man with the generosity of mind which comes from energy, and feeling a power to join in, would not despise the actual triumphs of the human mind and spirit which he found bursting out all around him. Surely it is time a generation grew up which isn't [all the time crying] 'Boo-hoo, I can't afford to keep a butler any longer'.

The Man of Letters in the Modern World.[2]

p. 67. Tate is unexpectedly well-informed here [in 'Tension in Poetry']; he says that the XVIIth century poet Cowley wrote bad poetry because he liked and admired the recent advances of knowledge during his time, and Cowley really did. So did nearly all English poets; the big exception is the later Donne, who became alarmed at Galileo like the Roman Inquisition. Tate quotes a poem ['Hymn: to light', by Abraham Cowley] on 'the interesting duties of light' (what business has Tate to sneer at light? How can Tate imagine that he praises the Creator by sneering at light ?)

> The violet, Spring's little infant, stands
> Girt in thy purple swaddling-bands.

There is a long evasive discussion, calling the clothes of the infant 'diapers', and the point seems to be that 'the metaphor renders the violet absurd' [p. 70]. This is baffling unless one realises that Americans are compulsively hygienic, and find it horrible that babies piss, or socially acceptable to pretend so. Such a reaction seems to me neurotic, and no real objection to the poetry; the astonishment at the delicacy of the young growth is splendidly conveyed by comparing it to some very aristocratic baby dressed up for a christening. The only effect of Tate's attempt to show he is too refined and spiritual to endure poetry about science is to show that he despises the most exquisite works of his Creator.

[2] Allen Tate, *The Man of Letters in the Modern World: Selected Essays: 1928–1955* (1955).

About the *Ode to a Nightingale* ['A Reading of Keats'], p. 199, he seems to me ill-informed, and calling Keats an Imagist is a century wrong in date.[3] He says 'we cannot agree' that the song-bird was 'not born for death', and goes on to assume that the poem is all about wanting an act of sex with Fanny so supreme that it would kill them both.[4] But not a word in the poem is about his hopeless love-affair or about his rapidly encroaching disease. (Though I suppose the 'magic casements' get their universal appeal from opening Circe to the remote voyager). *Owing* to his certainty of death, he was determined to become a great poet quickly, before he died; naturally he discusses aesthetic methods more than the other Romantic poets of his time. *How* is he to become a great poet—by joining the political agitations which all his friends tell him are urgent? Coming at it from this direction, one realises that it is not false praise of the nightingale but simply true, and a grudging admission, to call it immortal. The birds can sing the same way throughout history and men will always call the old thing beautiful, but a poet can't do that; Keats needs to think of something different. Going into a trance is all right to start with, but he has to come out of it and handle the real world around him, enough of it even to include the political world, if he is to achieve his distinctive utterance in the number of years which yet remain, at most three. I see no merit in Tate's failure to grasp the first point about the poem. Then he quotes the whole of the verse saying that common life is sad ('men sit and hear each other moan [groan]') and says 'looked at from any point of view, this verse is bad' [201]. I know that Tate has only one point of view, but I thought it proved the verse to be good. I also know that Tate is wrong, but I am baffled for the next step, as he lets out no reason for his opinion except (later on) that all the Romantics were Imagists, which is just a clanger.

His remarks about Hart Crane (p. 287) never get beyond saying that the poet was right to be in despair and wrong when he imagined he could praise modern America. I am glad to be reminded that there really was a good side of Hart Crane, generous-minded and open to whatever arrangements the world can achieve; but this is the side of him that Tate is

---

[3] Tate does not use the term 'Imagist' but stresses the 'pictorial method': 'Keats as a pictorial poet was necessarily presenting in a given poem a series of scenes' (198).

[4] 'Keats, both before and after his fatal illness . . . was filled with the compulsive image of the identity of death and the act of love (for example, "You must be mine to die upon the rack if I want you," he wrote to Fanny Brawne); and it is only an exaggeration of emphasis to say that death and love are interchangeable terms throughout his poetry. The "ecstasy" that the nightingale pours forth contains the Elizabethan pun on "die" with the wit omitted, and a new semi-mystical intensity of feeling added. And is it too much to say that Keats' constant tendency was to face the moment of love only in terms of an ecstasy so intense that he should not survive it?' (202).

committed to despising. Tate cosily claims he managed to be friends with the desperate poet, without serious risk to his income; but at the cost of no sympathy with the effort of accepting the modern world which Crane really was engaged upon, though in a tragically deluded manner.

Going back to Donne (p. 238 etc.) one must realise that these essays were written just at the turn, when Eliot was deciding to say 'Donne, I insist, was no sceptic',[5] thus making nonsense of all consideration of Donne's earlier verse; unless he knows he is making dangerous remarks he is like an embarrassing child, somebody ought to warn him to shut up. Tate remains at quite a distance from the words, and I never feel sure he could explain any of them. *A Garland for John Donne* (1931) was the killer for Donne, and here we have the limpid mind of Tate reviewing the explosive book, always plumb on fashion, never distinguishable from any other man who knew the ropes, though very few knew the ropes so well. I do not pretend to interpret the elegant mufflement which precedes the sentence:

> Donne knew nothing of a scientific age, or of the later, open conflict between the two world-views, science and religion.[6]

Well come now, this bit of hush-up naturally excites an impulse to hush-up this awful bit of hush-up too, as it happened to be a frightful gaffe our old pal made. Donne invented this conflict at the same time as the Roman Inquisition, but apart from the high terrible example of Donne it has been rare among English poets; it is a gross slander to pretend that they all despise the works of their Creator and the discoveries of the divine plan achieved during their lifetimes. It is a lie to say: 'The logical argument of "A Valediction: Forbidding Mourning" is a Christian commonplace'[7] because it is a universal, and for that matter pagan, commonplace; whether Tate has any idea what the poem is about, or for that matter how to draw a circle, remains obscure after studying his piece. I wish I could find him saying something faintly relevant on this page, however silly, so that I could tell you what Donne really means, but he is so skilled at his business that he can never stumble into saying anything, wrong or right.

---

[5] T. S. Eliot, 'Donne in Our Time', in *A Garland for John Donne*, ed. Theodore Spencer (1931), 11–12.

[6] 'A Note on Donne' (1932), 238. Tate remarked that Donne's interest in the new cosmologists, Copernicus and Kepler, took the straightforward form of 'an anxiety about the physical limits of consciousness and the bearing of that question on the scholastic conception of body and soul, which Donne presents in the terminology of St. Thomas.' WE preferred the evidence that Marjorie Nicolson marshalled in 'The "New Astronomy" and English Imagination' (1935), *Science and Imagination* (1956).

[7] WE quotes this remark from another essay by Tate, 'The Point of Dying: Donne's "Virtuous Men" ', 244.

I expect I ought to have worked harder, but I feel that I would not learn any more by further study. Of course I have glanced through the whole book.

Yours sincerely
[W. Empson]

Houghton, bMS Eng 1401 (649)

TO CHRISTOPHER RICKS

Department of English Literature, The University, Sheffield 10
31 January 1966

My dear Ricks,

I am very glad you like the article ['The Phoenix and the Turtle', *E in C*, 16 (1966), 147–53]. What seems to me odd is that nobody has said it before, as the material has been in easy reach since 1914. But anyone wanting biography wanted something hotter, and the holy symbolists, I suppose, were just thrilled by burning a woman alive, the most spiritual thing of all. (Of course, I don't deny that Shakespeare really felt sad, but the article is about what he fitted it into, as an adroit social being.)

I would like to tell you a secret 35 years old, about Ambiguity, but I can't think of one. I don't remember any review except James Smith's. Maybe P H Newby wrote a particularly funny attack. I was much supported by my pals then (Brunowski [*sic*] for instance) and rather enjoyed having attackers, whose folly was an interesting branch of study. I suppose a lot of the reviews praised the book more than it deserved, but that wouldn't occur to me at the time, and I thought I was attacked. The most extravagant piece of praise came from J H P Marks, who said with Spanish magnificence that one could tell (say, on meeting them at lunch) how many chapters each of our friends had read so far, as they modelled themselves upon each revelation in turn. We had been reading the *Tale of Genji*, and perhaps these compliments came from Lady Murasaki rather than Gongora. But your public would only be sickened by that. My Word.[1]

Yours
William Empson

---

[1] CR was composing an article about *STA* for a series entitled 'How well have they worn?': *The Times*, 24 Feb. 1966, 15. Speaking of the reception of the book, CR borrowed from WE: 'On the whole . . . if there were extravagances they emanated mainly from the Cambridge enthusiasts. One such devotee claimed that on casual meeting one could tell how many chapters each man in their circle of friends had read so far, as they modelled themselves upon each

TO PHILIP HOBSBAUM

Sheffield
31 January 1966

Dear Hobsbaum,

Glad to hear you are going on all right; here is the Aesthetic Theory chapter back. It is impressive, but rather likely to irritate an external examiner; a disclaimer might well come in early on, saying that you are considering everybody in terms of 'degree of subjectivity', and other features of their theories are left out. I can't myself keep my mind on subjectivity, and the ones I know anything about seemed to me unrecognisable. An interesting point about Mendel turned up recently: that his articles had been readily available in the German 'digests' all the eighty years while biology languished for want of them, but the digests made them sound too trivial to examine (especially by saying that 'fixed ratios' were found but not that they were evens or three to one). It would be hard to discover anything through your digests, too. However, I quite see that merely to show acquaintance with the enormous field gives you a high standing.

I feel strongly about Intentionalism, but in a psychological not a theoretical way.[1] Maybe, as an intention is only known as it is shown, all reference to intentions can in theory be avoided. The same is true of forces, in dynamics, which never come into the equations—one might say, they live in the equals sign, where the cause meets the effect. But all the same nobody could learn dynamics without learning the rules about forces, and using them all the time. This, by the way, is not 'like' empathy but the same fact of our natures. Still, I couldn't really agree that other people's inten-

revelation in turn.' In 'Empson as a Man of Letters in the 1960s', CR was to recall that his piece in *The Times* gave him 'a chance to banter a powerful dignitary, Dame Helen Gardner, a doyenne disguised as a doyen. I told an anecdote: "The atrocious crime of being a young man is one that Empson has never quite managed to live down—not even by dutifully growing older. I once mentioned to a doyen of English studies my feeling that it would really be something to teach such an undergraduate as the young Empson, Dustily, fustily: 'Empson has remained an undergraduate'. There are worse things to remain" ' (10). Ian Parsons told CR (24 Feb. 1966) that *STA* 'came to Chatto's through me because I was at Winchester and Cambridge with Bill, and had published some of his poems in the *Cambridge Review* when I was Editor of that journal. It was read first by Charles Prentice, the senior partner of Chatto's, a man of extraordinarily perceptive taste, and I well remember his coming in and saying that he'd read it at a sitting, and had stayed up until 2 a.m. to finish it'.

[1] In a review of the second edition of *MG*, Hobsbaum had recently written: 'Too much of Professor Empson's book is bedevilled with intentionalism' (*The Listener*, 74 (9 Sept. 1965), 389). Understandably irked by the impertinence, WE wrote in a letter to the editor: 'of course you should try to decide what an author meant; to call it Committing the Fallacy of Intentionalism is the most absurd device for self-castration yet to emerge from America. Anti-intentionalist men are usually anti-Milton men, and they accuse him pretty freely of bad or paltry intentions. The doctrine is only invoked if you refute their accusations' (16 Sept. 1965, 422).

tions are meant to be by-passed in this way; it seems to me that the chief function of imaginative literature is to make you realise that other people are very various, many of them quite different from you, with different 'systems of value' as well; but the effect of almost any Orthodoxy is to hide this, and pretend that everybody *ought* to be like Homer or Dr Leavis.

Just after reading your section on Intentionalism I picked up Kitto's *Form and Meaning in Drama* and found him starting off with a sheer paragraph of questions about what the intention of Aeschylus was in the *Agamemnon*, when he wrote things which seem to us confused or absurd. 'If he was a competent artist,' the argument runs, these details ought all to be useful pointers to us, showing what his theology was or what not.[2] Here, I grant, he is presuming the author is good, but he says later that the plays have merely to be good enough to explain why they were admired and preserved; having got inside them by this assumption, he is quite prepared to decide that a detail was merely conventional or a bit of theology really confused. Without going to the intention, which I suppose amounts here to testing the coherence of a theory about the first productions of the plays, one could not overcome the historical difficulties in such a case. Euphemisms may be devised, so that one pretends not to be talking about the author's intention, but that is what the mind will be doing really, if what it does is any good.[3]

---

[2] 'If Aeschylus was a competent artist, the answers ought all to be the same, namely, "Because this is what he *meant*". And Aeschylus' meaning is what we would like to find' (H. D. F. Kitto, *Form and Meaning in Drama: A Study of Six Greek Plays and of 'Hamlet'*, 1).

[3] In a draft of another essay, WE wrote: 'The problem of what Aeschylus can have meant, whether or not he was a high-minded theologian trying to improve the gods, is still being discussed and makes a natural parallel to the problem of Milton; indeed, I cannot see what point of difference there is between them. Professor Denys Page of Cambridge [Regius Professor of Greek, 1950–63; Master of Jesus College, 1959–73], as I understand, is the most recent blow-the-gaff man; but his position (Preface to the Agamemnon, 1957) is weakened by not answering e.g. Professor Kitto of Bristol (*Form and Meaning in Drama*, 1956) who regards the gods as changing with worshippers, since they are (as Blake would agree) forces within human society. Professor Page has digested thousands of Germans, it appears, but what use is that if he cannot get round to a sensible author. He argues that Aeschylus did nothing to improve the myths, and indeed invented worse ones, and hence that he must have had a pre-ethical world-view.

'The first point to notice is the extraordinary reason given by Aeschylus for Artemis' anger against the Atridae. The common story, in more than one form, told of a deed of insolence or utterance of folly by Agamemnon, action of boast by which the goddess was offended. Here was a suitable background for Aeschylus' narrative; the mortal offends the goddess, and her anger involves him in further wrong-doing; the original wrong was his fault, and all that follows can be traced to it. Alternatively (and better) the wrath of Artemis might have been more closely linked to the chain of destiny which binds the house of Atreus. As Aeschylus actually tells the story, Agamemnon is *compelled, for no fault of his own*, to sacrifice his daughter . . . 'and *necessity* is the word by which Aeschylus describes Agamemnon's submission to the will of Artemis . . .' (the chorus says Necessity.)

'Now this crime, the sacrifice of Iphigenia, is given by Aeschylus the most extraordinary motive. Instead of tracing it back to the mortal's offence against divinity, or otherwise linking it

Also, I think there is a bad reason why you and your pals are so vocifer-
ous against Intentionalism; you will not let an opponent impute good
intentions to an author, but you consider yourselves free to smear him with
bad ones as fast as you can invent them. I remember your denouncing
Milton for the passage where Satan weeps over his troops, saying that
Milton was being sorry for himself, failing to consider anyone else, self-
indulgent and I don't know what. The argument which might have convinced you (I forget what I said) is [that] this brief passage about Satan
comes after three hundred lines about his troops, and is followed by their
reactions to his speech to them, and is part of an entirely coherent and
very large structure. You have to look for the structure, but it is there. To
say 'No, Milton has better intentions than you think' would not be a good
way to argue, I grant. But surely you can see that your pretence of theoretical rigour is merely dishonest there; it is your regular custom, and that
of your school, not merely to impute motives confidently to an author but
to use that as the basis for a denunciation of him. Also, I think your chief
weakness, both in literary criticism and in personal negotiations, is that
you don't realise enough what the other man is getting at; so the doctrine is
bound to be harmful for you.

However, in the chapter, I should think it would be enough to add a
sentence or two explaining that the question is logical not psychological.
Don't spend a lot more time on it.

Yours sincerely
William Empson

---

to the destiny of the house of Atreus, the poet tells us in plain language that Artemis was enraged
because eagles, sent by Zeus to be an encouraging portent, happened to devour a hare together
with its unborn young; she therefore demanded a "second sacrifice", the death of Iphigenia, in
return for the death of the hare and its young. That is what is in the text; and, however crude
and inadequate it may appear, in the text it remains, it cannot be removed.

'Surely this is childish incapacity to approach understanding a myth: it always means something else, the only question is what. Kitto is far better here: the objection is to the cruelty of war.
Why could he not have deserted with his daughter?

'Would it not have been simpler to portray him as committing the crime as a result of his
own decision, not under divine compulsion?—Only if this had been a simple tale of Crime and
Punishment; but it is not. It is a Tragedy, the Tragedy of Man's destiny; and that is most moving
when the human victim is involved against his will (like Agamemnon) or unawares (like Oedipus)
in criminal error for which the penalty must be paid. Agamemnon in this Chorus is depicted as a
man who has no choice but to kill what is dearest to him—a much likelier and more interesting
figure than the weak-willed butcher whom some would apparently prefer to see portrayed.

'—This makes Oedipus nothing but a hard-luck story.' (*Houghton*)

CRITICAL QUARTERLY (Unpublished)

Helen Gardner responded to WE's review of her edition of *Songs and Sonnets*—'Donne in the New Edition', *CQ* 8 (1966); *ERL* (1), 129–58—with a letter to *CQ* 8 (1966), 374–7. She failed to understand why WE 'says that I forewarn the reader that my "apparatus is very capricious". On the page he refers to I state that it is "strictly selective" and proceed to give the principles on which selection of readings is made . . . As I explain in a note, many . . . readers seem to think that Grierson's apparatus is much fuller than it is. He rightly, as every editor must, left unrecorded manuscript errors and individual minor variants in the manuscripts he collated.'

She went on:

> When an editor is faced with genuine variants, both of which make sense, he faces the possibility that the variants may have arisen, not in the process of transmission, but from the author's own revision of his poem . . . I still believe that some of the variants in the *Divine Poems* can only be explained on the hypothesis that the author revised his text. I think this is also true in the *Satires*. But . . . I do not believe the variants in the *Elegies* are authorial in origin. As I explain, the textual situation in these poems is quite distinct. There is, for instance, no 'Group III text' . . . More important *W* agrees, with the usual minor variation, habitually with Group I . . . The agreement of Group I and *W* leads me then to believe that Donne did not revise the text of the *Elegies* . . . With the exception of the line Professor Empson discusses, in the Elegy 'To his Mistress: Going to Bed', none of them are of the kind that suggests authorial revision . . . We are faced with this one variant that might conceivably be authorial: the variant 'much less/due to'.

In a footnote to the last sentence, clearly responding to the force of WE's construction of the poem, Gardner offered a remarkable concession:

> I must acknowledge with regret that I should not, in the interests of economy, have omitted to discuss the minor variant in this line 'Here/ There' and to defend the adoption of 'Here', which has far less authority. This is a type of easily reversible substitution very common in manuscript, initial 'H' and 'Th' being easily misread for each other. I agree with Professor Empson that 'Here' fits the tone of the poem better; I disagree with his view that 'There' makes no sense. Either makes sense . . . If I held the blind faith in stemmatics that Professor Empson so oddly ascribes to me, I should have to read 'There'; but with a variant of this type I think an editor may exercise judgement.

She proceeded in the body of her letter:

> I believe that this variant is scribal in origin, because of the general

unreliability of the manuscripts in which it appears, and the agreement of Groups I, II and *W* in reading 'much less'. I see no profit in
discussing how it arose . . . Grierson thought that the reading I print
was Donne's original reading; and that 'due to' was 'a softening of the
original to make it compatible with the suggestion that the poem could
be read as an epithalamium'. It is impossible to tell whether Grierson
thought Donne himself responsible for the 'softening'. This cannot be
deduced from the fact that he printed the 'softened' line, since on
another occasion in the *Elegies* he shrank, *causa pudoris*, from printing
what his judgement told him Donne had probably written. Professor
Empson cannot call Grierson to his support here if he wishes to argue
that 'due to' is the original reading, and the reading I print a 'bowdler-
isation'. Grierson held the opposite view as to which was the original,
and is ambiguous as to whether it was Donne who altered it.

You pay your money and take your choice. Neither Grierson, nor
Professor Empson, nor I can claim to 'prove' scientifically anything at
all. What 'proof' we can bring is more like legal proof, or legal probability, than scientific. We are dealing with 'witnesses', human beings.
Grierson and I can at least claim, for what it is worth, that we have
worked on and lived with the manuscripts to which we owe all our
knowledge of Donne's poems.

W. P. H. Merchant, writing from the University of Athens, defended Gardner's 'technique' (*CQ* 8 [1966], 377–80); and of WE's interpretation of
poems such as Elegy XIX and 'The Dream', he remarked:

> Professor Empson quite rightly sees a pattern in all this. Groups I
> and II, he observes, are constantly in opposition with group V; this he
> suggests is because the manuscripts of V preserve the original, more
> risqué, readings, I and II a corrected and bowlderized version. I have
> given strong textual evidence to suggest that the converse might be true
> after all—so often the group V manuscripts offer an easier, more
> vulgarized, reading . . .
>
> But other patterns may also be observed—in every case the motive
> given by Professor Empson for the changes is either that Donne was
> pathetically obsessed by public opinion, feeling the need to tone down
> everything he said that offered any individual philosophy, or that he
> was violently opposed to Christianity while at the same time a parson
> . . . It would be a great pity if Professor Empson's own opinions were
> in some way becoming confused with those of Donne.
>
> But let us suppose that Empson is right, despite his violation in the
> course of the article of almost every rule of textual criticism . . . he is
> still faced with a problem, that in expecting editors to print what he
> considers an 'uncorrected version' he is asking them to oppose their

own judgement to that of the poet. It is not good enough to say that 'a poem should appear as when geared up to its highest expressiveness and force' (269); who is to say when that is? And it is not 'all right to be eclectic'. Possibly Donne made changes in his poems not 'under duress' but because they seemed necessary to him. Does an editor have the right to judge when the changes were necessary and when not?'

[n.d. 1966]

Dear Sirs,

The letter of Mr Merchant (about the text of Donne, in your Winter number) serves to remind us of the merits of Professor Gardner, who does at least regard the literary quality of a poem and its variants as part of the evidence before an editor. He lists a number of quotations from my review to show that I prefer one variant to another; this proves I am biased, and cannot judge between them. Then he points out that each of my accounts of how the variants arose could happen backwards; the poet could write 'There is no penance, much less innocence', and 'It could not choose but be | Profaneness, to think thee anything but thee', and then he or someone else (well, both) could alter it. Both Professor Gardner and I had thought these lines too bad to have been written first by the poet; and though she is now driven to toy with the first of them she would never I hope accept the gloss of Mr Merchant: 'There is no reason for penance, still less an innocent sense of shame'. The point of this line is a startling contrast to the earlier praise of the lady as a holy spirit, and if the variant was to make it mean otherwise it was fatuously clumsy. Professor Gardner believes the young Donne would have meant the satire from the start; I think the older Donne wrote it, as a bit of hurried and clumsy botching, to avoid a suspicion of heresy. In the same way, for the line about *profaneness*, there would be no temptation in the first draft to spoil the scansion with the unnecessary abstract noun; but if Donne had first written:

> I could not choose but be
> Profane, to think thee anything but thee

and later feared this might give his enemies a handle, he would be likely to over-compensate by writing in 'Profaneness', to emphasize the change from 'I' to 'it'. By 1614 he would not care whether he was spoiling the poem that the wicked young Donne had written to the shame of the old one. Of course, in all such argument from human probability, a judgement of the literary quality of the writing is needed as evidence.

This is only part of a larger truth; we have to try to fit together an adequate meaning from the small and the large context of the words, and without this basic process we could never have learned to talk as children. Professor Gardner's distinctions between good and bad manuscripts are solely based upon a very large number of choices of this kind; though I think she is too ready to lump together trivial errors and meaningful ones. Surely there must be some intelligent though careless copyists, as well as the stupid but literal ones? She has in any case arrived at a belief, from the total context of evidence, about the author's character and intention; an editor without this basic guide would be likely to accept very bad readings. I think that she has arrived at a wrong belief about the poet, on non-literary grounds, and that this vitiates a number of her conclusions; but, of course, she did right to form an opinion. Perhaps this makes clear that I cannot agree she is Objective and I am Subjective. I began the review by explaining that what I think about Donne was thought by most critics when I was young, and has never been refuted, only swept out of fashion. Broadly, I think the poet meant what he said, and had experienced what he described. Surely, the onus of proof lies with the denier—who says that Donne never experienced mutual love, but cooked up fantasies about it, from his reading of pious and theoretical authors, while neglecting his wife. Also, I would never impugn the desperate sincerity of Donne when becoming a parson; he gradually induced himself, and the poems carry the marks of it, to renounce the larger view of the world which had been his heresy. This was a matter of believing too much not of being a 'sceptic'; he had believed there are souls living on other planets who are also redeemable. The connection of this belief with Free Love, however remote it may seem to Professor Gardner, was rancorously familiar at the time.

Houghton draft, bMS Eng 1401 (532)

TO ARTHUR EFRON, *Paunch*, 25 (Feb. 1966):
'Wuthering Heights— II'

Dear Mr Efron,

Mr Doheny is right I think to argue 'The book is obviously about something important, because one can feel it is good, as writing, so it can't be about anything so dull as you say.' But many people have found the problems of status and revenge oppressively interesting, and maybe what saves him from feeling the same is merely his happy innocence. I read the book after sending you my comments (the first time for years I suppose) and found it much more rawly and brutally about the degradation caused by the class system than I had remembered. Compared to what the book is really about, a psychological sex theory is a twittering ghost.

Americans would perhaps feel more at home with the book if they realised that it is practically the same situation as *Pudd'nhead Wilson*. A son of the family is to be brought up as a slave, and this cannot simply be put right afterwards, because he is really the worse for it. Heathcliff is told he will never again meet the woman he loves, though he will be living in the same house, because he will be in the servants' quarters; this belongs to a larger and more efficiently organised house than the one in the story, but I wouldn't call it dull. When he overhears the girl saying 'It would degrade me to marry Heathcliff now' he escapes and becomes ruling-class in both cash and manners within three years but at the cost of becoming a criminal type, and that does seem the only way, in the time. We don't hear that he even invites her to leave her husband for him, but he only sees her alone once, when she is dying, after his return.

Most of the black-white miscegenation in the States happened under slavery, one is told, and I don't mean to say a word against the act of love—I expect it sweetened the institution of slavery very much; but it did nothing to weaken the institution. The man was the ruling-class partner in the approved cases there, but the historical works of Robert Graves have made very clear that the instincts of a lady allow her to conduct a satisfactory sexual relation with the third footman without ever ceasing to treat him as the third footman. Catherine of course assumes that this is impossible; but does Mr Doheny mean that she ought to have done it?

When she says she loves him like the eternal rocks beneath he has to be somehow a local man, as Emily herself had such extravagant local feelings, though he is also from all the wild parts of the world. It seems clear what Emily would have added to the plot if she had not wanted to avoid shocking the public. Old Earnshaw sets off to Liverpool on foot because a letter has told him that his younger brother's son, by a lady of mixed race in the Port of Liverpool, has been left destitute. He avoids scandal by not saying that this is his nephew, and leaves telling the secret till too late. This is all that is needed to explain the assumptions of the story.

Mr Doheny says I said I made my poetry confused to give the public a tease.[1] What I was saying at the time was that poetry is insincere unless it is

---

[1] John Doheny comments (2 Jan. 1986): 'in a response to his criticism and that of another critic whom I had criticized, I arrogantly, and I now think, rudely, made an uncomplimentary comment on one of Empson's notes to *Gathering Storm* where he makes passing reference to the puzzle interest in poetry ... [T]he exchange on *Wuthering Heights* is still important, I believe, and it represents the unique literary criticism which made William Empson one of the most important critics of our age.'

clinical, resolving conflicts in the author and thus preventing him from going mad; to do this it must satisfy himself as completely unconfused and indeed bare; and if the effects of doing this were trying for the reader, that was nothing to worry about—he could have the pleasure of doing a puzzle. Emily was not a patient girl, and would not have put up with the critical technique of misunderstanding nearly as quietly as I do.

TO CHRISTOPHER RICKS

Department of English Literature, The University, Sheffield 10
1 March 1966

My dear Ricks,

Thank you very much for your article praising Empson in the *Times*.[1] I know how hard these things are to do, and what unrewarding work it seems.

Likely even to meet with ingratitude from the person laboured for, but I hope I will never sink so far. No man really likes being promoted to one of the class of Licensed Buffoons, but it has been an important post in England since the time of Jaques, I suppose, let alone Bernard Shaw. 'When was Empson never waspish?' asked the author of *Justine*[2]—I must try to avoid being waspish now, after the promotion. So let us hope your kind praise will do me good.

Yours very sincerely
William Empson.

The Peerage are a major estate of the realm, and perhaps the Licensed Buffoons, in their small way, could take rank as the beerage?

TO PHILIP HOBSBAUM

Studio House, 1 Hampstead Hill Gardens, NW3
24 March 1966

Dear Hobsbaum,

Thank you for your letter; I think you show great good-humour in being willing to reconsider a doctrine in which you have sunk so much capital. But I don't see that your suggested palliation takes us at all far. It is true of course that a decision about an author's intention can easily be

---

[1] CR, 'How well have they worn?', *The Times*, 24 Feb. 1966, 15.
[2] Lawrence Durrell, author of *Justine* (1957), admired WE: see *Key to Modern Poetry* (1952), 198–9. The remark may have been told to WE by G. S. Fraser.

made wrongly, so that when it is relied upon the evidence needs to be surveyed in breadth, also that it is only a step towards a decision about the merits of some piece of his writing. But I think it is sometimes an essential one. You were mentioning *King Lear* as a case where there could be no doubt about the author's intention, but your whole chapter about whether King Lear dies of joy illustrates a particularly baffling problem of intention; one which I think can only be solved in terms of the author's known character as deduced from his other writings. A producer has to make some kind of decision, and one which feels certainly not what the author meant, because totally unhistorical, reduces the play to a kind of burlesque (whether solemn or not). Professor [Jan] Kott of 'Shakespeare our Contemporary' has that effect, it seems clear from his book.[1] However, I would not feel so cross with an interpretation which was historically possible, however much I felt it to misinterpret the author; maybe because it would have a chance of reaching a partial truth.

I have been mulling over two familiar cruces lately, the *Phoenix and Turtle* and the *Byzantium* poems. Both are commonly misread nowadays in a manner which makes them disgusting, so as to gratify the Christian craving to gloat over tortures inflicted for punishment; and I think that reading them like this is a direct result of the doctrine that you mustn't attend to the author's intention. The effect is that the critic can smear the same fashionable nastiness over every author he considers; that is why it is so popular among herdcritics. In both cases there is a good deal of evidence from the setting, the circumstances under which the poem came to be written, as well as from the rest of the author's work; and it is totally ignored by the current pious torture-embroidery. Both are charming, playful, expectant of good; but in each of them burning people alive crops up as part of the basic mythology. The neo-Christian at once reacts 'Burning a woman alive? Why, that's the most spiritual thing of all', and his superego (a ghostly TSE) pats him on the head while whispering toadlike into his ear 'excellent, my dear fellow; a spontaneously Christian sensibility', and his slobbering Id ejaculates 'Ooh, goody, I hope her eyes pop out'; so naturally he can write his 10,000 words without getting within a mile of the poem. I realise that this is not a logically necessary part of the doctrine, but I expect it is why the doctrine is championed so enthusiastically. I am not sure whether you intended to make a total rejection of the old custom of placing a poem in its *milieu*, and remembering the circumstances in which it was written. This does seem a basic need; having some grasp of

---

[1] See WE's execrations against Jan Kott in *ERL* (2).

the mind of the author is more of a luxury, though I don't believe you can have real criticism without it.

Yours sincerely

W. Empson

TO D. K. BARUA

26 March 1966

My dear Barua,

I have found the reference to *coitus reservatus* in the Oneida Colony; it is in a collection of essays by Aldous Huxley called *Adonis and the Alphabet*, 1956, the final essay, called Appendix.[1] This makes clear how very high-minded it all was, and well suited to become an ideal of [Edward] Carpenter, though as the first purpose was to avoid an excess of children it became rather absurd in his case. The Chinese reference I gave you has probably no historical connection, but proves I think that the Oneida Colony had discovered something real. But what it was I do not under-stand; neither Huxley nor Needham claim to have made it work. My only experience is that a prolonged stand becomes painful, and indeed the condition when unavoidable is recognised as a painful disease satyriasis. Bernard Shaw in a recent collection of letters remarks that what Oneida men really did was use the older women who were past childbearing; this I

---

[1] Chapter 7, 'The Pioneer in Sexual Studies', of Barua's thesis includes remarks on what Carpenter called 'homogenic love' (260): 'He was not prepared to accept Dr Moll's suggestion that the deflection of the sexual act from the purpose of reproduction itself is pathological . . . The true aim of human love, Carpenter insisted again and again, is union, the physical union as an allegory of the union of the souls. He even suggested in a note on birth-control that the best spiritual effect of the sexual act is derived when orgasm is not reached.' In a note: *Love's Coming of Age* [by Carpenter, 1896], 173. Carpenter quotes Dr Alice E. Stockham's book *Karezza* (1896) in support of his claim. But Carpenter could also have derived his idea from ancient Indian Yogic (Tantric) and Chinese (Taoist) literatures. Both these schools of thought recommended some form of *coitus reservatus* as good for mental health and the spiritual wellbeing of the race (see J. Needham's *Science and Civilisation in China*, vol. 2, 148–149 and 427–429). Aldous Huxley writes approvingly of this sexual technique in his account of its practice in the Oneida community of New York in the 1840's. See *Adonis and the Alphabet* (1956), "Appendix".'

In the Appendix to *Adonis and the Alphabet* (1956), Huxley praised John Humphrey Noyes, founder of the Oneida community in upstate New York (1848–80)—where sexual morality was based on the ideal of 'Complex Marriage' (involving multiple partners and the prohibition of monogamy, and procreation only in cases where Noyes approved of the genetic attributes of the parents)—for advocating the 'amative' discipline of Male Continence, also known as *Karezza*: that is, bodily union without orgasm, which served to generate 'social magnetism' (274–85). 'Male Continence is not merely a device for domesticating sexuality and heightening its psycho-logical significance; it is also, as the history of the Oneida Community abundantly proves, a remarkably effective method of birth control. Indeed, under the name of *coitus reservatus*, it is one of the two methods of birth control approved by the authorities of the Catholic Church' (284). See also Spencer Klaw, *Without Sin: The Life and Death of the Oneida Community* (1994).

suppose would be charitable, as they usually need it more than the young girls.[2] Psychologists have long been saying that *coitus reservatus* is bad for the nerves, though not so very bad as *c. interruptus*. Perhaps one first gave the young women a lengthy coddling and then finished off in the old ones, though this final act was not written up in the propaganda.

The thesis ought to have some reference to this, if only to show that Carpenter was not merely being whimsical (or D. H. Lawrence either). That is, unless you prefer to take out your reference altogether.

The external examiner has suggested Monday 23 May for the Oral, which means your handing in the texts a week or ten days before. Can you do this, do you think?

Yours sincerely
William Empson

TO PHILIP HOBSBAUM

12 April 1966

My dear Hobsbaum,

Congratulations on the Glasgow job; I think that is a good place to be. Also thank you for the slim volume of poems [*In Retreat* (1966)]; often funny, but you are a better poet than you allow to appear here. I rather suspect you are stifling your talent out of loyalty to your old School. But maybe you were preparing a non-satirical book at the same time.

I hope you will be looking us up when you are back on the mainland.

[William Empson]

TO MARTIN SEYMOUR-SMITH*

Studio House, 1 Hampstead Hill Gardens, N. W. 3
12 April 1966

Dear Seymour-Smith,

Very sorry to hear about Brian Higgins. I didn't know him at all well really. The poem seems very flattering and touching (unless I misread it) so

---

[2] Bernard Shaw, in a letter to *Truth*, referred in passing to 'the peculiar continence of Oneida Creek' (*Collected Letters: 1874–1897*, ed. Dan H. Laurence (1965), 232); the editor notes that the practices of Oneida Creek involved 'eugenic mating'. Elsewhere he explained further (15 Mar. 1899) that the Oneida Creek Community 'objected to marriage because it was too licentious, & that [J. H.] Noyes, its head & founder, preached a doctrine of absolute continence except for the purpose of continuing the race.' (*Collected Letters: 1898–1910*, ed. Dan H. Laurence (1972), 82).

I couldn't object to having it used.[1] This obituary business seems to be becoming the BBC's chief angle on poetry; I am having to say something about Louis MacNeice too.[2] Very hard to avoid bad taste.

Glad you reminded me about the Bard gloating and tittering because he had arranged for the Dark Lady to give the Earl clap. I have been having to find arguments for Intentionalism (to oppose the American theory that you must never consider what an author is likely to have meant, but only to construe the words on the page); and this does seem a striking example. The idea that the interpretation gives the poem a more welcome moral tone is so very c'ntemp'ry. Oddly enough the same critics if dealing with a novel feel obliged to put up a huge pretence of worldly intimacy with situations that must be remote. I wouldn't mind if the couplet is just supposed to mean 'she will get clap later on, and then he will get it as well as me'. If she has it already, and therefore Shakespeare too, surely he could arrange to blind the Earl in the course of hugging and smugging? Wouldn't that have been more soldierly still?

On the other hand, I think it pretty innocent of [John Crowe] Ransom to run down the Sonnets (though all wrong of course) because he just hates sodomy and wants to keep his young men hating it too.[3] Any theory will do for him if it makes a sodomite poem bad. This is innocent because furtive; he isn't getting his face straight with the public by pretending to be

---

[1] See Martin Seymour-Smith, 'In Memoriam Brian Higgins, 1930–1965', *Reminiscences of Norma: Poems 1963–1970* (1971), 99, which does not refer to WE. Seymour-Smith later wrote of Higgins, in *Macmillan Guide to World Literature* (1973), that he was 'a hit-or-miss poet . . . who had too little time to exercise control over his considerable intelligence. His poems were published in *The Only Need* (1960), *Notes While Travelling* (1964) and *The Northern Fiddler* (1966) . . . His best poems were full of urgency (an urgency that now seems poignant), primitive energy and directness of purpose. They combine passion, humour and subtlety' (342).

[2] MacNeice had been 'a tower of strength' as a BBC radio producer during the war, WE would write in his tribute (part of a radio portrait produced by Robert Pocock and narrated by Goronway Rees, broadcast by the BBC on 7 Sept. 1966; in Columbia: Ms Coll/MacNeice). 'You could show him the rough material . . . and he knew at once what you could put over, what would do. Even with quite a complicated script, one run-through would be quite enough, after he had cut it, and the actors could go out into the blackout and look for beer; he was always unruffled and very much the captain at the wheel of his ship. Of course this may have been because he thought it such tuppenny work that he wouldn't bother, but the results seemed to me very elegant. No wonder people like that wouldn't move over to television. He was very equable, one might think rather low-powered, but you had to look out when he began to look like a camel. That meant he had become decided.'

[3] WE may be recalling a time in the late 1940s when he and Bernard Heringman and John Unterecker wrote a collaborative essay on the subject of Hart Crane's poem 'Voyages III'. When Heringman submitted their effort to the *Kenyon Review*, John Crowe Ransom responded, 'I hate to celebrate a homosexual poem' (quoted in a letter from Heringman to Empson, 9 Aug. 1949; *Houghton*): see *SSS*, 233–42.

butch, but hoping they won't realise he is, so that they will accept his argument at face value.

I am afraid I entirely forget [sic] the Indian party.

Yours sincerely

William Empson

Lilly: Wright, D., Mss; Houghton: notebook draft of part

TO S. P. ROSENBAUM*

Sheffield

20 May 1966

Dear Mr Rosenbaum,

Yes, by all means come and have a chat. July 2nd is the end of term, and I hope to be going home; Studio House, 1 Hampstead Hill Gardens, London, N. W. 3, telephone HAM 0977. Probably that would be more convenient to you. But let me know your movements nearer the time.

What Eliot said about [Bertrand] Russell (surely) was that it would be awful if he were still at a university, rotten and rotting others.

Yours truly,

William Empson

TO MR STUART SMITH[1]

Studio House, 1 Hampstead Hill Gardens, NW3

8 July 1966

Dear Mr Stuart Smith,

Thank you for showing me your book on Walter Mitty. I think it is of great interest but needs reducing to half the length, or less, keeping all the argument but expressing it in a direct manner. At present the book is an immensely prolonged daydream, obeying somewhat pedantically the rules which it lays down for the conduct of daydreams; unless a reader spots this he is bound to become impatient. The author gratifies his pride by pretending to discover, to lay bare very gradually with his pure and piercing scalpel, what every reader knows or thinks he knows already (as the authors of the popular works considered could take for granted). During most of the book, daydreaming is regarded clinically, but the penultimate chapter by a thrilling turn regards it as a process of soul-making, of high

[1] Unidentified.

spiritual value, deserving the impenetrable language of German philosophy; then the last chapter, with graceful modesty, confesses that one cannot discover whether these people get any pleasure from the process, which one feels to be so unimaginably remote.

It is an excellent plan to examine literary works for truths of psychology, but one should remember that fashions change, and that writers are generally expressing conceptions which they know to be fashionable. As recently as 1890, poets were accustomed to write about their 'dreams' with warm self-approval, evidently meaning not deep dreams but fantasies of a better political arrangement or a more aesthetic sexual mate. Oscar Wilde first I think, but Yeats in a more impressive manner, also argued that a young man should try to better himself by inventing a Mask or Pose and then carrying it out, after a preliminary run in fantasy. The function of the fantasy was to discover what really suited his nature, what kind of man he would do best to grow into. And indeed, the capacity for fantasy was presumably evolved because it had this kind of usefulness. It is analogous to play, found among the young of all mammals as a way of learning to use their equipment. Psychologists are fond of saying that a child at first only talks to itself, but obviously it plays at having a conversation between two people; Alice in Wonderland, we are told, often answered herself back quite sharply. Here there is not one character in the fantasy who is the sole representative of Me; even in the simplest form, the others will occasionally say unexpected things. C. S. Lewis in a paper in *They asked for a Paper* distinguished the fantasy about the Snug Town inhabited by mice in Dutch trousers from the wishful type; the Snug Town can give prolonged pleasure, though the dreamer is not present at all—since he could not plan to marry the Mouse Princess.[2] However, the wishful-thinking type of fantasy is undoubtedly very common, and your book need only say that it concentrates on that.

Recently, by a curious twist, theorists have become forbidding in tone though permissive in intention. The daydream has to be written about as a

---

[2] C. S. Lewis, 'Psycho-Analysis and Literary Criticism', *They Asked for a Paper: Papers and Addresses* (1962), 122: 'With the sort [of dream] which [Freud] acknowledges—the dreams of success, fame, love, and the like—I confess that I am lamentably familiar . . . But I cannot recall a period when I did not know another kind. The earliest of these which now comes back to me is what might be called the Snug Town. I can see that little town still . . . I am vaguer about the inhabitants, but I think they were anthropomorphised Mice—"dressed mice" as I would have called them then, with woollen comforters and wide trousers like Dutchmen . . . But the point is that I myself was not a feature in it. I dare say that after the dream had taken full possession of me I may have wished, and wished intensely, that I might find this town in reality and go to it . . . My only reason for wishing to go to it was its adorableness: there was no idea that I was to become a great man there, or marry a mouse-princess'.

disease, even if it is also called a desperate remedy. That a man is likely to do afterwards what he has enjoyed daydreaming about never seems to come into your book, or the books you are examining; perhaps merely because few novelists want to write about a man starting to write a novel. The daydream is presented here, and is now I suppose popularly thought of, as debilitating; a man is less likely to do a thing if he has imagined the doing of it with yearning. I think this consequence must be unusual as well as perverse. But the process has anyway come to seem a-social; a man ought to try to please the girl he is put next to, not shut his eyes and think of a prettier one—that is cheek. Also erotic daydreams are rightly expected to lead to masturbation, which robs some poor girl of her due; no wonder God will punish it. Even daydreaming of a fruit farm is being above yourself or not 'with it'. Such is the climate of opinion, I maintain, which you take for granted, accept as eternal, when you argue from these authors (and drag La Fontaine into line with them); and this explains why you regard it as scientific to claim to have no experience of what you are examining. The style, and much of the argument too, keeps crying archly at the reader: 'Ooh, what a story! No, I never! (i.e. a false accusation). Why, I never even *heard* of such things till I met people like you.' Few people can go on being charmed by this little trick for an eighth of a million words. And you are doing yourself an injustice there, because really you show a good deal of understanding of the subject.

I have not read *Billy Liar* [by Keith Waterhouse, 1962] and *Flowering Cherry* [by Robert Bolt, 1957], but they are evidently full-blast expositions of this popular medical theory. It is odd that you choose Walter Mitty for your book-title, because Thurber regards him as a brother, and the application to him of germanufacture or hun-work ('the coincidence of his frustration and of the world of fulfilment' p. 399) is particularly remote. Surely *all* the modes in which Walter triumphs cannot be called his *self*, unless that mystic word is just his vanity? But then, I am thinking of a student trying to imagine whether he would really like being a doctor or a lawyer, what would really suit him; clearly, a great deal may depend on his arriving at the right answer. You I think mean by his *self* simply his manhood, which is much the same in any man, or ought to be. Thurber would agree that Walter is protecting that; the author is positively keen on defending (American) men in the sex war, and thinks that Mitty is fully justified, or even in a comic way rather heroic, to put up with his wife though she is almost intolerable. He would not feel that Mitty had been cured if he poisoned her. Men I think are better at surviving a regime of bullying than women are, but the defence mechanisms usually strip their minds almost bare; Mitty is doing much better than that, and indeed Thurber is writing witty parodies of the novels which celebrate virility (as you point out) to report his fantasies. Whether Mitty knows they are funny is perhaps not a genuine question; but he is rueful, and extremely without hate; he would come to appreciate them as funny if his conditions of life improved: that is, granting that he is possible—he is invented as an extreme case. So, though I agree with your feelings here, or your judgement, I think that your language does much to obscure it. I think the book fully deserves to be printed, but that till you re-write it at half the length correcting the psychology of your approach you won't really even know what your conclusions are.

I took notes while I was reading, and will copy out any that look as if they might be useful. [. . .]

III. I agree that the heroes of most modern plays are exasperatingly silly characters, but I would expect that their fantasy life is the only wild ground where a better seed could grow. 371 the initiative which the dairymaid is blamed for not taking would be theft, I suppose? During the war I was a propagandist, and we were proud to explain that a stick of chalk was being put into every loaf of bread, which was enough to keep the kids from rickets though they didn't get eggs and so on. Then we reflected that for generations the baker who mixed chalk with his flour was considered the meanest kind of wicked man; and yet, every time holy religion converted a baker so that he renounced the current practice, he made a number of children cripples. The difference between fantasy and what actually [incomplete].

Houghton: carbon, bMS Eng 1401 (653)

TO S. P. ROSENBAUM

2 August 1966

Dear Mr Rosenbaum,

Sorry to have missed you; I am quite willing to answer any questions that I can. But my impression is that T. S. Eliot's views on philosophy were simply obscurantist.

Yours sincerely
William Empson

TO CHRISTOPHER RICKS

Studio House, 1 Hampstead Hill Gardens, N. W. 3
15 August 1966

My dear Ricks,

Here is the Mack review.[1] I am sorry it is so long; have boiled it down, but it doesn't seem to go smaller than this. Let me know what you think. This holiday seems to have been all the battle of life; writing a letter about some untruths by W. W. Robson in The Oxford Review [see below, p. 416], and a terrible last-minute flutter about libel [in his 'Donne in the New Edition'] with the Hull magazine [*CQ* 8]. Cox (my pal; Dyson is anti-E, it emerges) swears he will bring it out in September.[2] Removing joke-phrases which might be twisted into libel has been a good thing, giving me dignity maybe; nauseous greasy prose was thrust into my mouth, giving me a fit of the horrors, but this was quite innocent and insensitive—they didn't at all mind my using decent prose instead. I wish I had realised that. So, with all the child-like drama, I have nearly got through the Long Vac without doing anything towards my book at all. But then, I gather that my opinions are getting so completely out of date that it isn't much use writing a book unless I retain a public by keeping a toehold in the magazines. Or is this rather nonsense perhaps?

Do let me know if you are coming to London.

William Empson

[Postscript omitted]

---

[1] WE's review of Maynard Mack, *'King Lear' in Our Time*, was to appear in *E in C*, 17: 1 (Jan. 1967); *SSS*, 56–62. Mack, who had invited WE to give a lecture at Yale University in 1939, never read WE's review; he was to recall in a letter to JH (15 Feb. 1995): 'I was told by several English friends . . . who knew Mr Empson that in later years he had gone snappish about any criticism of his views and that his review of my book was written both *brutale e furioso*. To be honest, I have always avoided looking up that review because I did not want and still don't want my admiration of him to be tainted by my own ego. Whatever the justice or injustice of his remarks about me, he was a very great critic, a true original in a field of parrots.'

[2] A. E. (Tony) Dyson (1928–2002), critic, lecturer, and gay rights campaigner, was educated at Pembroke College, Oxford. From the 1960s he taught at the University of East Anglia, where he rose to be Reader. His works include (with C. B. Cox) *Modern Poetry: Studies in Practical Criticism* (1963) and *The Practical Criticism of Poetry: A Text Book* (1965); *The Crazy Fabric: Essays on Irony* (1965); *The Inimitable Dickens* (1970); and *Three Contemporary Poets: Thom Gunn, Ted Hughes and R. S. Thomas* (1990). In 1958 he co-founded, with C. B. Cox, the periodical *CQ*.

Brian Cox wrote of WE's altercations with Helen Gardner (letter to JH, 12 Jun. 1985): 'We had to ask him for some changes because we feared the original article was libellous, He was obliging and cooperative. After the publication of his article we received some wild letters from Helen Gardner, and these continued after we published a short letter from him. A letter of 27 February 1967 calls him "crazy" and says Empson's review was "absolutely riddled with error". You will recall that Empson suggested Dame Helen missed the sexual implications.'

TO CHRISTOPHER RICKS

Department of English Literature, The University, Sheffield 10

6 September 1966

My dear Ricks,

Thank you for your encouraging letter.[1] I have bought *Jacobean Theatre*, No. 1 of Stratford on Avon Studies (1960), a dull book, and it is true that Mack is much more sensible there in his few mentions of Lear, especially in not calling him regenerate during the last scene of all.[2] I think all my review needs is a sentence to say he must have succumbed to the corrupting pressure of fetid marshgas during the intervening years. But I will check what he does say later when proofs come . . . I see his last section says, after rightly showing two extremes to be avoided, that the play 'is not used toward a morality theme but . . . toward building a deeply metaphysical metaphor, or myth, about the human condition'—in fact, only a coarse Philistine would let it have any point at all. I think the American guff about myths has allowed them to satisfy the fundamentalists without disturbing the enlightened, and this trick doesn't really let one understand the play. But it isn't quite what my review said it was; you were right to point that out. A bit of rephrasing ought to cover it, anyhow not more than fifty words more.

I was pleased to see that *Tom Sawyer* chap. 21, the school prizegiving, has a superb description of the US prize essay tradition. Funny that the effect of T. S. Eliot has been to destroy their powers of resistance to it.

So, you flew to Rome at the expense of *Esquire* Magazine to judge the premiere, shown in the Vatican, of a film of *Hamlet* with the name-part taken by a Bunny.[3] A full report in print will naturally be expected. I hope you kissed the Pope's toe; they say he has been trying to wriggle out of it.

I can't get an answer out of E. M. Wilson (Spanish at Cambridge)[4]

---

[1] 'Empson had sent me his review of Maynard Mack's *King Lear in Our Time*, for *Essays in Criticism*; I had pointed out that he was perhaps unfair in a particular respect, and had drawn his attention to an earlier essay by Mack' (Ricks, 'Empson as a Man of Letters in the 1960s', 10).

[2] Maynard Mack, 'The Jacobean Shakespeare', in *Jacobean Theatre*, ed. John Russell Brown and Bernard Harris (1960), 11–41.

[3] Ricks told WE he had tried to write a piece about the Richard Burton/Elizabeth Taylor film of *Doctor Faustus*. 'Esquire spiked it, but the kill-fee was life-enhancing.'

[4] Edward Meryon Wilson was Professor of Spanish and a Fellow of Emmanuel College. WE urged him to translate *Soledades* by Don Luis de Góngora, and published in *Experiment* the first fragments of Wilson's verse translation. Wilson wrote on 2 Jun. 1930—when TSE had accepted an extract for the *Criterion*—'If the whole is published may I dedicate it in part to you? You first suggested the work, and I think your poems have had their influence on my method of versifying, with Milton & Dryden.' (*Houghton*) Twenty-five years later, Wilson was as good as his word: he named WE as one of two dedicatees of *The Solitudes of Góngora* (1965); the other is Dámaso Alonso, the Góngora authority. Wilson noted in his Preface: 'William Empson's poems represent a different kind of influence on my work' (p. x).

about whether a Spanish poet around 1590 was writing courtly or amorous compliments on the formula 'You are the Platonic Ideal of Virtue, or Truth or not', walking the earth like the Logos in person, so that when you die there will be no more of it. Can Robert Chester really have been writing this in 1585, or did he copy it from Shakespeare's Phoenix and Turtle after 1597? In any case, where did Donne and Shakespeare get it from? I was told about this Spanish poet when a student, and have come to suspect he is a myth. The Spaniards would say like Spenser that Artegal was both Justice in person and Lord Grey in Ireland, but the literary effect in Spenser is obviously unlike that in Donne. I would be most grateful if you could give me a line on it. I have agreed to do an essay on the Poems for a paperback series, Signet Classic, so will have to reach an opinion.[5]

Yours affectionately
William Empson

THE SPECTATOR, 16 September 1966, 346: *'The Reactionaries'*

Anthony Burgess, in a review of John Harrison's *The Reactionaries* (1966)—which carried a preface by WE: *A*, 627–31—acknowledged that Yeats, Wyndham Lewis, Pound, Eliot, and Lawrence had belonged to an anti-democratic intelligentsia and therefore leant, in politics, towards authoritarianism. 'All except Lawrence, so Mr Harrison tells us, probably derived their view of life from T. E. Hulme, that *éminence grise*, who taught that "the humanist's belief in the perfectibility of man is wrong . . .".' But, claimed Burgess, 'it is perhaps silly and pointless to look for a nexus between misguided political beliefs and supreme works of literature . . . The alleged profascism of these dead writers touches their art at no vital point . . .' He concluded: 'There is an introduction by a man whom the dust-jacket calls simply "Empson." Speaking of Joyce, he says that here was one example of an "original and rigorous author" who "could avoid these political and religiose fashions." Alas, not so. He had indeed "escaped from a theocracy such as many of the authors examined in this book were recommending," but the penultimate episode of *Finnegans Wake* presents the modern world in terms of sexual impotence: a thunderclap is needed to recall a theocratic age. Of course, to Empson the important or salvatory statements may be such *obiter dicta* as "I am afraid poor Mr Hitler will soon have few friends in Europe apart from my nephews, Masters W. Lewis and E. Pound," but why should these be more significant than the *obiter dicta* of a dustman? It is the work, it is the work that counts. Empson, after another slam at Milton's

---

[5] See WE, 'Introduction', in *Narrative Poems* (1968) pp. xv–xlvii (Signet Classics).

"sacrificial theology," finds comfort in the neo-Wellsianism of the Cambridge School of Divinity. I don't think any such ethos is likely to produce a new Hopkins or Eliot, but one never knows. Literature is disconcertingly autonomous' ('Fleurs du Mal', *The Spectator*, 217 (9 Sept. 1966), 326).

Sir,—What Mr Burgess says about 'the penultimate episode of *Finnegans Wake*' is very interesting, and one day if I am spared I will try to decide what the episode means. Joyce might (just) be saying that the world needed God, but not that it needed the Roman Catholic Church. Surely, the story that he was secretly in favour of that was exploded by the Ellmann biography [*James Joyce*, 1959]. However, it is a side-issue here.

The main point of my little preface to John Harrison's *Reactionaries* was to say that one of their main tenets was not standard Christian doctrine, as they supposed. It is the idea, mostly explicitly supported by T. E. Hulme and Wyndham Lewis, that the human should be kept rigidly distinct from the divine, whereas the Athanasian Creed, a work not usually thought to be worm-eaten with liberalism, recommends 'the taking of the manhood into God.' This (I think) is why they can fairly be called Unnaturalists. Mr Burgess might well have answered that, instead of telling us he despises the Cambridge School of Theology.

THE OXFORD REVIEW, 3 (Michaelmas 1966), 77–9:
'*Milton's God*'

W. W. Robson published two reviews of *Milton's God*: the first in *Universities Quarterly*; the second, 'More Empson than Milton?', in *Oxford Review* 1 (Hilary, 1966), 19–28; reprinted as 'Mr Empson on *Paradise Lost*' in his *Critical Essays* (1966)—to which this letter by WE is a response. 'There can be few critical books which are at once so amusing and so serious and passionate,' stated Robson; WE is 'the most brilliant critic of our time'. Nevertheless, Robson 'regretfully' adjudged, 'Empson's book is confused and inconsequent, in so far as it uses *Paradise Lost* as an opportunity for attacking Christianity', for Milton's poem is not 'the central statement of Christianity which his anti-Christian thesis requires it to be.' Was Milton 'crying out against his appalling theology', as WE maintained, or was he not fully conscious of the issues at stake? And was WE 'maintaining Shelley's thesis about *Paradise Lost*, or Blake's—that Milton was "a true poet and of the Devil's party *without knowing it*"?'

Robson's full appraisal of *MG* includes these comments: 'Empson's God is subtly and ingeniously wicked. This wickedness comes out most in the analysis of the fall of Eve. According to Empson, God did not only *allow*

Eve to be misled—that is the straightforward reading of the story—he deliberately misled her himself. A labyrinthine intrigue, enthrallingly related by Empson; note particularly the correlation he brings out between what Raphael tells the human pair about their future "wings", and what the mysterious voice (Satan's) had whispered to Eve in her dream. God must have known what Satan whispered; why then did he permit his angel such dangerously misleading language?

'The reason, to my mind, is simply Milton's inadvertence—though I would not disagree with the view that these inadvertences occur so often as to suggest uneasiness on Milton's part about his self-imposed task of reconciling providence and free will . . .

'I can only observe that the relevant passages of *Paradise Lost* (ix. 745–80, 795–805, 856–85, 961–90, 1144–61) simply do not support Empson. Taking up the main point: let us grant that the serpent's words entered Eve's heart (550), and that the serpent does suggest (692 ff.) that God may praise Eve for her courage. But Eve's speech (745–80), which shows the influence on her of the serpent's arguments, does not repeat this part of them; and this omission is impossible to explain, if the decisive factor in Eve's decision were what Empson says it is.'

Dear Sir,

May I try to clear up one of the misunderstandings about my book *Milton's God*, in the article by Robson for your first number? I realise that he was struggling to be fair to it, though the result is to call me a cheat. All his points could be answered, but perhaps most of the work is covered by the generalisation: Christians, as Samuel Butler said, 'like to be inkled';[1] they require from an expositor of their religion an inkling that they are worshipping the Devil, or Moloch, because that is what excites them, though they also demand a firm pretence that their God is good. There could not be a 'central statement' of such a religion, and Milton was no more deceitful about it than his fellow-worshippers.

But my book does fail to give the textual evidence for its explanation of why Eve ate the apple; I don't know how I came to leave it out, except that I became more interested to consider what happens in the minds of

---

[1] 'Old Mrs Nosnibor,' said Panky, 'says the Sunchild told her they were symbolic of the tribes who had incurred the displeasure of the sun, his father.'

I make no comment on my father's feelings.

'Of the sun! his fiddlesticks' ends,' retorted Hanky. 'He never called the sun his father. Besides, from all I have heard about him, I take it he was a precious idiot.'

'Oh Hanky, Hanky! you will wreck the whole thing if you ever allow yourself to talk in that way.'

'You are more likely to wreck it yourself, Panky, by never doing so. People like being deceived, but they like also to have an inkling of their own deception, and you never inkle them' (Samuel Butler, *Erewhon Revisited* (1901, 1927), 52).

orthodox readers, making them ignore it. I maintain that, when she decides to eat, she believes what Satan has just told her, that God wants her to eat the apple, since he is testing not her obedience but her courage, and the sincerity of her desire to go to Heaven:

> will God incense his ire
> For such a petty trespass, and not praise
> Rather your dauntless virtue, whom the pain
> Of Death denounced, whatever thing Death be,
> Deterred not from achieving what might lead
> To happier life, knowledge of good and evil?   (ix. 692–7)

We gather that Satan does not realise how strong this argument will be, how logically impenetrable and emotionally confusing; his phrasing of it is rather worldly. But it is the most important argument in the logical structure of his speech, and that much he would know. It is the only high argument, that is, the only one which does not impute bad motives to God. Satan also uses low arguments, perhaps to weaken the resistance of Eve by reducing her respect for God, but if he had no high argument she might refuse to listen. Thus it is untrue to say that I am picking on a detail of his confused gabble, not even recalled by Eve in her reply. I grant that, after presenting this argument, he talks on for thirty lines, suggesting bad motives, activating a committee of gods perhaps; but she might regard this as *reductio ad absurdum*: 'What *can* God's motive be in the prohibition? Since it cannot be these bad ones, it must be the good one'. His last word drives this idea home: 'Can envy dwell | In heavenly breasts?'

I do not deny that Eve is bemused by the various arguments, but the high one is clearly present in her mind. It presumes that a risk *ought* to be taken for so great a purpose, and she as well as Satan considers this risk (the snake has 'ventured higher than his lot' and has been rewarded). Also the prize is not merely knowledge but ethical knowledge; Milton uses a typical long-term verbal device to drive this home. The tree has usually, in the poem, been called simply 'of knowledge' (e.g. by Adam in iv. 424, Eve in v. 50); 'of good and evil' is now added twice by Satan (697, 723) and twice by Eve (752, 774).

'Everybody praises you,' she tells the tree; 'Even God admits you are important':

> Thy praise he also who forbids thy use
> Conceals not from us, naming thee the tree
> Of Knowledge, Knowledge both of Good and Evil;

> Forbids us then to taste, but his forbidding
> Commends thee more, while it infers the good
> By thee communicated, and our want.   (750–5)

She does not say that God wants her to eat, I grant, and her speech as it goes on is inclined to echo the arguments which blame God, if he does not want her to eat; the tone is rather petulant; but logically she may still regard these arguments as *reductio ad absurdum*. I certainly did not pretend in my book that Eve gives the high reason for eating, because I show that Milton himself, at about the time of writing the poem, had maintained that a person who did so would be innocent—that is, who broke a direct command of God in the conviction of doing his will. The story requires Eve to be less than innocent, though only a little less. Surely she remembers the high argument of Satan when she says that God's action has *inferred* their need of the apple; other rulers may be in error, but God must intend his actions to infer what they do.

> In plain then, what forbids he but to know,
> Forbids us good, forbids us to be wise?
> Such prohibitions bind not.   (758–60)

Recent pious critics have expressed much contempt for scientific knowledge, mean-mindedly I think, and they feel sure Milton agrees with them that Raphael refuses to tell Adam whether the Copernican theory is true (though, anyway, Milton could not have let him). But Eve here explicitly means *ethical* knowledge, and there is considerable difficulty in maintaining that it is better not to know good from evil. The idea is a paradox, and Eve recognises that, so definitely that it ends her speech because she decides to eat at once. But the decision also depends upon being convinced that God is good; he will interpret the law in a generous-minded way because he will recognise her good intentions. She arrives at this result from an unexpected direction:

> For us alone
> Was death invented? Or to us denied
> This intellectual food, for beasts reserved?
> For beasts it seems; yet that one beast which first
> Hath tasted, envies not, but brings with joy
> The good befallen him. Author unsuspect,
> Friendly to man, far from deceit or guile.
> What fear I then, rather what know to fear
> Under this ignorance of Good and Evil,

> Of God or Death, of Law or Penalty?
> Here grows the cure of all . . .   (766–76)

If she admittedly does not yet know good from evil, she cannot justly be blamed for any action, let alone one admittedly designed to teach her how to tell good from evil. The answer of the story, of course, is that God does punish her for it, by condemning nearly all her descendants to eternal torture; thus proving that he has no sense of justice at all. The bare horror of the thing might seem beyond addition, but it is made grindingly pathetic by the actual movement in the mind of Eve. The snake has behaved well, she reflects, generous-mindedly; one might expect a snake who had got hold of the use of reason to be selfish, but it is actually advising her how to make herself its superior again. She is living in a world where the characters have decent feelings, evidently; how then can she fear that God may be meaner-minded than this snake? So she eats. After she has eaten she becomes frightened, and forgets the high motive which would have been recalled if things had worked out better. I cannot guess what Robson takes her words to mean, or how he can assert that they refute my argument. Now that he has made me look at them again, I find it even harder to understand how Milton could have brought himself to argue that they put her in the wrong.[2]

[Drafted 19 June 1966]

THE TIMES, 25 October 1966, 13: 'Macbeth in History'

Responding to a piece by Caryl Brahms, 'Perils of trying to be "bloody, bold, and resolute" ', about the inherent difficulties of acting *Macbeth*, Laurence Irving wrote in a letter (22 Oct. 1966, 9) that the play is a 'mangled masterpiece', so that the 'grisly actions' of Macbeth and his wife 'seem only to spring from base motives and thus their portrayal baffles their impersonators'; someone should restore the 'coherent plot' of the play.

Sir,—Undoubtedly, the first audiences would see the play in the light of their beliefs about the foundation of the Stuart dynasty. But the great speech of Macbeth about 'no son of mine succeeding', before he plans the murder of Banquo, proves that he would not be content to leave the throne to a stepson.

I think the play must be regarded as a Just-So Story, like 'How the Elephant Got its Trunk': the Scots are shown discovering that their king-

---

[2] See also *MG*, rev. edn. (1981), 324–8.

ship arrangements produce tribal wars, so they accept the more civilized hereditary principle, and there are the Stuarts right at the start. This explains the self-pity of Macbeth, who says that in the old days he would not have been so much blamed:

> Blood hath been shed ere now, in the olden time,
> Ere humane statute purged the gentle weal.

I have to agree that the details don't fit very well but they often don't in a Just-So Story; and this does seem to be the only dramatic bit of background that one could get from the chronicles. To write in more of them would make things worse.

Yours, &c.,

William Empson

TO PETER URE*

16 November 1966

Dear Professor Ure,

Thank you for your hospitality [at the University of Newcastle upon Tyne] and your gift of the off-print of the article on [John Dryden's] *The Indian Emperor*.[1] I disagree radically with a sentence in the first footnote [endnote], and hope you will allow me to make the matter clear. You say that an article by Wardropper[2] has shown . . .

> that one of the major differences between Calderón and Dryden is in their treatment of the religious element in these plays. This is very much less important in *The Emperour* than it is in *El principe*, and is used mainly in Act V, Scene ii in order to point the contrast between the cruelty of the Spaniards in torturing Montezuma and their professed Christian beliefs.

Well, what is presented is the pagan Montezuma being tortured for his gold by Roman Catholics, who ridiculously boast to him that their religion must be true because men have endured martyrdom for it. While in agony, he replies:

---

[1] N. D. Shergold and Peter Ure, 'Dryden and Calderón: A New Spanish Source for "The Indian Emperour" ', *Modern Language Review*, 61: 3 (Jul. 1966), 369–83.

[2] B. W. Wardropper, 'Christian and Moor in Calderón's *El principe constante*', *Modern Language Review*, 53 (1958), 512–20.

> To prove religion true
> If either wit or suffering would suffice
> All faiths afford the constant and the wise.[3]

He draws no contrast between the cruelty and the beliefs of his tor-
mentors, and does not know whether they entertain any belief which is not
discreditable. It is a regular claim of Christianity that no man can be
virtuous without it, but the free-thinking movement regularly claimed that
one could; this powerfully emotional display of a virtuous pagan was
inherently anti-Christian propaganda. The scene may not bulk large in
reading, but in performance it is bound to be 'important' when a man
answers with wisdom and nobility while being tortured on the stage in the
last act. You say that it is not important merely because it belongs to the
Enlightenment.

Also, censorship of such beliefs was in operation. One can readily
imagine the 'scholarship' of the future quoting what was written under the
dictators of our time and calling it 'the settled opinion of the age'. Marlowe invented a way round this obstacle; he could say to his Protestant
audience things which they applauded as being against Roman Catholics,
whereas really the accusation applied to all Christian sects. I do not believe
that the audience were all such fools that none of them could spot this
trick. It is to hide it from modern students, I suppose, that modern criticism is determined never to admit that the Wars of Religion ever
occurred. The audience of Dryden was expected to roar with indignation
against the wicked religion of the Spaniards, and your pupils must be told
that the audience tut-tutted at seeing Christians who failed to live up to
their pure ideals. It is astonishing, really, that the sentence manages to pack
in so many false insinuations while yet appearing so smooth and dull.

I think that the Enlightenment is the only hope for civilisation, and that
the crawling insinuations against it mainly introduced by T. S. Eliot poison
our whole intellectual life. But in any case his movement involves an
immense historical distortion of the literature which it claims to interpret.
There will have to be a reconsideration.

I will send back your Maxwell Poems [by Shakespeare (1966)], but I
really need to hold on to it for a bit.

Yours sincerely
W. Empson

Houghton: carbon

---

[3] *The Indian Emperour*, in *The Works of John Dryden*, ix, ed. John Loftis (1966).

Peter Ure responded on 21 Nov. 1966: 'My collaborator in the Dryden article says that *El Príncipe* is wholly about religious issues, whereas in Dryden these occur only in the scene which you mention. They certainly have nothing like the same scope and depth in Dryden as they have in Calderón. I feel pretty sure that Dryden was not writing an anti-Christian play, although I think he was properly sceptical about Christian professions, and had at that time a true blue English Protestant attitude to Roman Catholics (especially Spanish ones) (one which of course he reversed later on).

'In some ways I think that Dryden has in him the makings of a modern anti-Christian. But I hope it does not sound like a merely conventional and bland answer to say, while believing that Dryden was deeply anti-clerical, I do not believe that he was fundamentally anti-Christian. It seems to me that it would be quite impossible to reconcile the view that Dryden was profoundly anti-Christian with the self-confessional passages at the beginning of Part I of *The Hind and the Panther*, not to mention some bits of *Religio Medici*.'

TO L. C. KNIGHTS*

[27 December 1966]

My dear Knights,

I am afraid there is a considerable worry now about getting [Francis] Berry appointed to a Personal Chair at Sheffield, and I write to ask your help. It was part of the estimates for the next five years (though without naming him), as of course he knew, and he refused a second chair at Bangor on the assurance of the Sheffield one. [R. M.] Wilson* and the present Dean ([Frank] Pierce) agree with me that he fully deserves it, and it would secure continuity when I leave in five years' time; besides, with his children growing up, he needs the money. But the matter turns on his recommendations from Professors in other universities, and two stinking ones have come in, both saying that he is not a Scholar. His last two books have been extremely good, but they try to arrive at new criteria or point out new things to look for when judging a literary work, and in giving examples he is of course not specially concerned to ascertain new details of bibliography or biography. The belief that there is nothing in the subject but 'scholarship' means the death of it, I think, and I expect you agree.

Our new Vice-Chancellor is a Scotch doctor, very inclined to insist on dignity and safety, and without any judgement in the subject as I gather.[1] The Personal Chairs Committee is mainly scientists, and I am co-opted onto it for the case of Berry, which comes up on the 7th January, just before next term begins. I have written urging the V-C to ask the opinion of [Graham] Hough, but have had no answer, and am afraid I have somehow got on the wrong side of him. Hough has read the recent books, and wrote to me that Berry was obviously a lot better than the average Eng. Lit. Prof. You understand, I was only empowered to see the various letters at the end of last term, and was told just before Christmas that the meeting comes almost at once.

Such is the situation, and I think you will find it justifies my sending an appeal. It would not take you two days to reach an opinion on Berry's last two books: *Poetry and the Physical Voice* and *The Shakespeare Inset*. It would be quite natural for you to write a second letter, after saying in the first one that you regretted not having time to read them, saying that you had now read them and giving your opinion. It seems to me that both show considerable breadth and grasp, and that both are of practical value. Naturally, if you don't think that, I am not asking you to speak against your conscience; but you [will] I am sure be prepared to put up with a slight inconvenience to save an old colleague from severe injustice.

All is going well enough otherwise.

Yours sincerely

Houghton carbon, bMS Eng 1401 (591)

§ *SEVEN TYPES OF AMBIGUITY*, LAURA RIDING*, AND ROBERT GRAVES

On 9 Feb. 1931 Laura Riding had written from Casa Salerosa, Deya, Mallorca, Spain, to Empson's publishers Chatto & Windus that she objected to the fact that WE had omitted in *STA* to acknowledge her as

---

[1] Hugh Robson (1917–77) was Vice-Chancellor of the University of Sheffield from 1966 to 1974. Educated in Scotland, where he graduated M.B. from Edinburgh in 1941, he was appointed Professor of Medicine at the University of Adelaide, South Australia, at the age of 35. In 1974 he was to become Principal and Vice-Chancellor of the University of Edinburgh. He was knighted at the end of his tenure of office at Sheffield. See obituary in *The Lancet*, 24 & 31 Dec. 1977, 1370–1.

co-author, with Robert Graves, of *A Survey of Modernist Poetry* (1927).[1] When she had approached WE in the first instance, she reported further, he had said he regretted not mentioning her 'with' Mr Graves—'I had not the book by me and forgot it was a collaboration,' he had written. Riding found this excuse 'pretty thick': it was another case of the 'wilful omission of the first author's name'. She was not after a 'meaningless and useless' apology from WE, but she desired an assurance that an erratum slip would be included in all future copies of *STA* sent out from stock stating that *A Survey* was authored by Riding and Graves—'being careful to give the authorshop in this order'. Graves wrote in a separate note on the same day that he subscribed to everything in Riding's letter; he felt it 'perhaps even more strongly', since he was not flattered but offended by WE's error.

Riding wrote in a further, undated letter (received on 5 Mar. 1931), that she would like to see a copy of the actual erratum slip (with herself identified as the first author), and not just a statement about what it said.

Thirty-five years later, James Jensen,[2] in 'The Construction of *Seven Types of Ambiguity*' (*Modern Language Quarterly* 27 (1966), 243–55), noted:

> As early as 1922, in his first book of criticism, *On English Poetry, Being an Irregular Approach to the Psychology of This Art*, Graves was saying: 'The underlying associations of each word in a poem form close combinations of emotion unexpressed by the bare verbal pattern'[3]—certainly a clear forecast of ambiguity. And in Graves's other critical works, notably *Poetic Unreason* (1925), there are tendencies and preoccupations which bear importantly upon the development of modern criticism. One observes, however, that Empson's acknowledgement of Graves is not general but quite explicit, referring to a particular analysis in a particular book, and this, it develops, is rather perplexing.
>
> It happens that Graves is only one of the two authors of *A Survey of Modernist Poetry*, the other being the poet and critic Laura Riding, and as though anticipating possible neglect of this fact, the book carries the special prefatory notice that it 'represents a word by word collaboration.' Because this note is conspicuously placed, it is difficult to imagine that Empson overlooked it; but what his reasons might have been for omitting to mention Riding is open to speculation. Perhaps when he came to write *Seven Types*, Graves's independent critical writings were well known to him, and, while wishing to acknowledge the

---

[1] WE stated in *STA*: 'I derive the method I am using from Mr Robert Graves' analysis of a Shakespeare sonnet, "The expense of spirit in a waste of shame," in *A Survey of Modernist Poetry*.' See also Martin Seymour-Smith, *Robert Graves: His Life and Work* (1995), 147: 'Neither Riding nor Graves liked *Seven Types of Ambiguity* ("Empson is as clever as a monkey & I do not like monkeys," Graves wrote to me in 1944, but he came to like Empson much better later), as they considered it a corruption and not a development of their own methods.'

[2] James H. Jensen is Emeritus Professor of English at Indiana University.

[3] Robert Graves, *On English Poetry* (1922), 25.

> Sonnet analysis as the specific antecedent of his method, he may have
> felt that to give Riding equal place with Graves would be to understate
> the more comprehensive debt he owed the latter.'   (244)

As a pendant to Jensen's article, William H. Matchett, editor of *MLQ*,
thought to solicit comments on the piece from IAR, Robert Graves, and
WE, together with a 'reply' to such pieces by Jensen. (He did not approach
Laura Riding, but only because he thought she was already deceased.)

MODERN LANGUAGE QUARTERLY, 27 (1966), 257–8: WE's
Comment on James Jensen, 'The Construction of *Seven Types of Ambiguity*'

In the year when I. A. Richards was tutoring me, some of my friends at
Cambridge (especially James Smith, who wrote well in the early volumes
of *Scrutiny*) thought that his 'scientism' was philosophically very absurd,
and I could usually, after my weekly hour with Richards, go and tell them
some particularly absurd thing he had just said. They of course were
following T. S. Eliot, early members of the neo-Christian movement. I
really was much influenced by Richards, but I thought it proper to learn
from both sides, and would probably have said that I was on the side
opposed to him. I am not sure when I decided that he had been quite
right. In 1939, after being robbed in Chicago on my way from China to
England, I was kindly given work writing radio scripts in favour of Basic
English for Richards on the station WRUL [in Boston, Mass.], so that I
could pay the boat fare and repay the very generous loan of Auden, made
when repayment seemed impossible. Chatting in a script about why the
word LIFE, among others, was not in the Basic 850, I said the word was
liable to rhetorical misuse, and offered some mild examples.[4] I was surprised when Richards came back very indignant, and distinctly Welsh as
he becomes at such times, saying that this kind of stuff must be stopped at
once. The stench of an ill-cured saintly relic was what I had preferred,
very disgustingly, to Nature. I thought he was quite right to be firm about
it, and felt rather surprised that I was still copying out fallacies at random
from the death-worshippers. This moment perhaps, ten years later, was
when I positively chose the side of 'scientism,' though it wasn't till I began
teaching in a Christian country that I realised the active harm done by
the religion. The logical problems about 'scientism' are certainly there,

---

[4] Extracts from WE's talk on 'LIFE' are cited in *A*, 41.

and part of the mystery about its truth, but that gives us no excuse for worshipping the Devil instead.

Also, Richards was tutoring me for the First Part of the English Tripos, not to write a book, and he made sure I had looked round the field; I seem to remember a number of bad essays about novels. Two hours may have been spent on ambiguity, but not more. I was rather offended at his correcting my punctuation in red ink, as I thought him worse at punctuation than any prominent author since Shakespeare (or perhaps somebody else invented that crack); but in later years I have regularly impressed upon my staff that this is the most important thing for a tutor to do to a student's essay. Well then, I would not have allowed Richards to give me 'prolonged tuition' about how to write my book, because I disagreed with him in principle, and I could not have induced him to do it by any amount of pleading, because he had his mountain-climbing to do as soon as the exams were over.

Robert Graves had used the method of analysis by recognising ambiguity in a previous book, not collaborating with anyone; I ran into an irrelevant difficulty merely by quoting the wrong book. Graves rightly insisted on the publishers adding an erratum sheet, to give Miss Riding the credit of co-authorship, and this was convenient for me as it allowed me to list some of the more appalling misprints which I had failed to correct, on the same sheet.[5]

Surprisingly, Robert Graves declared in his response to Jensen's article (256): 'I was, I believe, responsible for most of the detailed examination of poems in *A Survey of Modernist Poetry*—for example showing the complex implications of Sonnet 129 before its eighteenth-century repunctuation; Laura Riding certainly for the general principles quoted on p. 5 . . .' (According to Deborah Baker, on the other hand, Graves had maintained to a Cambridge don as early as 1934, 'it is simply untrue that I ever made any such analysis of any particular sonnet. I could not have done so, because it

---

[5] The first printing of *STA* ran to 2000 copies: 500 went to Harcourt Brace Inc., New York. Following the complaint by Riding, an erratum slip was inserted in the Chatto & Windus edition: 'For *from Mr. Robert Graves' analysis* read *from Miss Laura Riding's and Mr. Robert Graves' analysis*. It is regretted that *A Survey of Modernist Poetry* is erroneously referred to as by Mr. Robert Graves. It is by Miss Laura Riding and Mr. Robert Graves.' It is probable that the slip was not included in copies issued in the USA. Following a further article 'Some Ambiguous Preliminaries: Empson in "The Granta" ' (*Criticism*, 8 [Fall, 1966]), Jensen wrote to the editor of *Criticism* 9 (Winter 1967), 108: 'Although it is true that when *Seven Types* first came off the press in 1930 it made no mention of Miss Riding, Mr. Empson apologetically repaired the oversight and included her name in an erratum sheet subsequently added to this edition—though, not unfortunately to my [US] copy. I thus must apologize for having reattributed to this author an omission he long ago made good.'

was Laura Riding who originated this exegetic method', *In Extremis* (1993), 142). Graves took the occasion of his piece also to reconfirm that he had never met WE—'nor did he send me a copy of his book'.

Jensen, in his final 'Reply' (258–9), remarked accordingly: 'Graves is now willing to allow that the analyses of *Modernist Poetry* are his work; but he seems strongly to imply that Empson was equally indebted to the "general principles" for which Miss Riding was responsible . . . [I]t is not yet clear (to me at least) that Empson's reasons for neglecting to mention Miss Riding were necessarily "unchivalrous." On the other hand, neither is it clear how it was only an "irrelevant difficulty" [WE's words] to have acknowledged an indebtedness to the one book in which Graves is actually practicising the "method of analysis" as distinct from merely "recognising" the principle of what Empson (following Richards) called "ambiguity." '

Four years later, on 19 May 1970, Laura Riding wrote to Susan Daniell (Subsidiary Rights Department, Chatto & Windus) to ask once again after *STA*. What had happened to WE's erratum slip, she queried?

Learning from Chatto & Windus (apparently for the first time) that in 1947 there had been a second and revised edition of *STA* in which WE had claimed—'in passing,' as WE phrased it—that 'Mr Robert Graves . . . is, so far as I know, the inventor of the method of analysis that I was using here' (xiv), Riding was intent on ensuring that WE had not perpetuated the misattribution beyond that edition. In a further letter to Daniell (12 June 1970), she reaffirmed that she was 'the actual originator of this technique' of critical analysis. A series of letters followed, all reiterating (as on 8 Aug. 1970) this claim: 'The method, as anyone familiar with my work, my thinking, my laborings with other poets for this better attention to the requirements of linguistic responsibility, is of my formation . . .'

On 19 August 1970, Susan Daniell passed the buck to WE.

TO LAURA RIDING (JACKSON)*

Studio House, 1 Hampstead Hill Gardens, London NW3
25 August 1970

Dear Mrs Jackson,

Miss Susan Daniell has shown me the file of her correspondence with you, and asked me to take over. I am quite willing to do this, and have looked up some of the books concerned.

I had been greatly struck by the following passage, in a book, *On English Poetry*, written by Robert Graves alone (1922):

When Lady Macbeth, sleep-walking, complains that 'all the perfumes of Arabia will not sweeten this little hand', these perfumes are not merely typically sweet smells to drown the reek of blood. They represent also her ambitions for the luxury of a Queen, and the conflict of luxurious ambition against fate and damnation is as one-sided as ever. Or take Webster's most famous line in his Duchess of Malfi:

> Cover her face; mine eyes dazzle; she died young

spoken by Ferdinand over the Duchess's body; and that word 'dazzle' does duty for two emotions at once, sun-dazzled awe at loveliness, tear-dazzled grief for early death.[6]

Two emotions but not two senses of the word, one might think, and yet the two processes of dazzling are quite different. Anyway he is mainly concerned in the book with the Conflict Theory of poetry, that it is a healing process through the confrontation of opposed impulses. This is the necessary background for a theory of poetical ambiguity, which he was approaching. He had reached it by 1926, with *Impenetrability, or the Proper Habit of English*:

> For instance, in Keats's *Eve of St. Agnes*, Madeline is described in 'her soft and chilly nest', 'clasped like a missal where swart paynims pray', where 'clasped' means 'fastened with a clasp of holiness' or 'held lovingly in the hands', if the Paynims are held to be converted, but also, without prejudice, 'shut and coldly neglected' if the Paynims are held to be unconverted. . . . (quotation from a novel) . . .
>
> 'To acknowledge salty hospitality' is in one sense to acknowledge the social obligation of good manners which eating a host's salt implies in most countries. But it is also to comment on the absence of goodwill, in the sense that 'salty' means 'sterile'. In a third sense it is to comment on the host's dry humour in recognising and making fun of his guest's discomfiture, for 'Attic salt' is a well-known synonym for wit. When such a concentration of forces can be exerted at a single point in literature, then, in Humpty Dumpty's words, 'there's glory for you'—using glory in yet another sense than the many we have defined.[7]

---

[6] Graves, *On English Poetry*, ch. 4: 'Conflict of Emotions', 23.

[7] Robert Graves, *Impenetrability, or The Proper Habit of English* (1926), 55–8. WE's citation includes one or two inconsequential slips. Graves's 'quotation from a novel' reads: 'On departure our hero clicked his heels politely and acknowledged the salty hospitality of his host: for the old maquis had enjoyed the youth's discomfiture hugely, and had been thus lavish in heaping him with all manner of delicacies and honours only because he knew that they afforded his guest no enjoyment at all.'

These of course are striking examples of the full process, where alternative possible meanings in a word are used together to handle a complex situation. I felt that I ought to make some wholehearted acknowledgement of the inspiration they had given me.

But these passages, I thought, though they were really very decisive looked a bit scrappy, and when I got round to reading *A Survey of Modernist Poetry* (1927) I felt that the long treatment of the 'lust in action' sonnet would be the right thing to mention in my acknowledgement. It dealt with a complete poem, as I was by this time trying to do, and it had a cumulative weight and impressiveness. What I thought about the collaborator I do not remember, but I suppose these few pages, so very unlike the rest of the book, seemed to me such an evident further step by the mind of Robert Graves that no collaborator could disagree. But I do not deny that it was very foolish of me, if I thought so. When Chatto's told me they had received an enormous letter from Robert Graves denouncing me for a plot against women I found the accusation too absurd even to be painful, but I urged Chatto's to put in an erratum slip, giving the correct authorship; not that they needed urging.[8] I am sorry to hear that the American edition did not carry it, but I think I can explain that. When they sent a statement after the first year only eight people had bought the book; I offered to send them each a Christmas card but they could not be traced. I was told that most of the edition was not merely remaindered but pulped. So Harcourt Brace would be in no mood to fuss with erratum slips. On the other hand, any American buyers in the later years before 1949 would have to get the English edition, which did carry the erratum slip. The American public just would not stand the idea, whereas the English reviews were quite lively and there was a small but steady sale till the edition sold out; I suppose the difference arose because the books of Robert Graves had already made the idea familiar in England.

In the second edition of course I had to omit the reference to the *Survey of Modernist Poetry*, because the original reference to it had been a clumsy mistake, intended to make the little compliment to Robert Graves specific and intelligible, even though slightly untrue.[9] I don't deny that you may

[8] Ian Parsons asked of WE: 'are you sure it was Graves and not Laura herself who sent us the "enormous letter" to which you refer on page 2?' (*Reading.*) WE had imparted to William H. Matchett (3 Jul. 1966) that Graves had also written a ruder letter: 'Graves wrote a 19-page letter to Chatto's, and they were much shaken, because old Harold [Charles] Prentice, who never used a rude word, said it was the most cunt-stricken letter he had ever read.' (*Houghton: carbon with autograph additions*)
[9] In the second edition of *STA* (1947), WE dropped his salutation to the analysis of Shakespeare's sonnet 129 that had featured in *A Survey*; instead, in a bold new preface, he acknowledged 'in passing' that Robert Graves 'is, so far as I know, the inventor of the method I was using here' (p. xiv). Graves and Riding had continued to be incensed by what they regarded as

hold the priority for the ideas in question, but I deny that I learnt them from you, and the only point of these little 'credits' is for an author to give his sources. Besides, after the fantastic accusations of Robert Graves, I had to stick to what I believed to be literal truth or I might appear to confess by yielding. However, at this distance of time, I no longer feel quite so certain; I wish I knew when I read your analysis of 'lust in action'. I would not rush to it, as I did not consider myself a 'modernist' poet or feel keen on arguments to defend them, but surely, looking at the dates, I must have read it before I wrote my book.[10] The analysis uses the idea of ambiguity of syntax, which may need to be made plain by unusual punctuation; I used this in my book a good deal, and it seems quite possible that I derived it from the analysis of 'lust in action'. If you assure me that you invented it, and not Robert Graves, I grant that I may be in your debt so far; I don't remember any case of Robert Graves using ambiguity of syntax in his previous writing. It seems an obvious thing to add, when you are already using ambiguity of lexicon, but one so often doesn't see the obvious.

All the same, the whole affair seems to me very puzzling. Whyever was it that neither you nor Robert Graves used the technique again, having brought it to such a pitch? And, if you despise it so much as your letters imply, whyever are you so keen to have priority in it?

Yours sincerely

William Empson

Cornell; Houghton carbon, bMS Eng 1401 (636)

WE's bare-faced discourtesy. On 24 Feb. 1939, Riding wrote to him: 'Some time ago I saw something you wrote about "sense" (the word) ['*Sense* in *Measure for Measure*', *Southern Review* 4 (1938), 340–50; *SCW*, 270–88]. All this delight that you have in ambiguity [. . .] represents no fundamental ambiguity in meanings—but the ambiguity in yourself.' (*Janet Adam Smith*)

[10] WE had read *A Survey of Modernist Poetry* by 11 May 1928, when he reviewed a work he judged to be inferior, *Words and Poetry*, by George Rylands (1902–99), Fellow of King's College, Cambridge: 'The Robert Graves' school of criticism is only impressive when the analysis it employs becomes so elaborate as to score a rhetorical triumph; when each word in the line is given four or five meanings, four or five reasons for sounding right and suggesting the right things. Dazzled by the difficulty of holding it all in your mind at once, you feel this at any rate is complicated enough, as many factors as these could make up a result apparently magical and incalculable. Mr Rylands, however, is seldom bringing off the trick with sufficient concentration . . .' Asked by Christopher Norris and David Wilson in 1971 about the influence of Graves's 'conflict theory', WE responded: 'Of course, you know everybody was talking about Freud and things like that. I might have got it from many other people who are now forgotten as well as Graves. But I bet I had read more of Graves than I remember now and I certainly was keen on this stuff and wanted to imitate it. I really don't remember now at all clearly but there's no doubt I was picking it up. But it didn't seem, you know, very out of the way—the idea that you wanted to use Freudian theory on literary criticism somehow was the thing that Graves picked up a generation before me. We all had it knocking about. But I certainly did read the Graves. I'm just having to think about that—I mean having to get out some of the books and consider what I remember having read at the time. I had read quite a bit.'

On 31 Oct. 1970 Riding told WE she wanted to put on record her 'sense of outrage' that he still coolly dismissed her role as co-author of *A Survey*; and on 11 Nov. she criticized the 'thin pickings' adduced in his letter of 25 Aug. 'Mr Graves in the 1922 matter quoted has his mind on tricks of the poetic trade. Especially in the Webster line is this point of view irrelevant. The mood, the intent, the point of view, of the *Survey* method are radically different from that of interest in tricky managements.'

On 13 Dec. 1970 she rebuked him once again for having produced such an unconvincing 'early-Graves alibi': there was no 'worth of hide-and-seek stratagem of mock-defence in sober-faced pointing to what you point to in your second citing—for turning the table and putting me on the defensive' A final letter (21 Apr. 1971) assured WE that she would like to complete her reply to him, but that she had suffered 'health difficulties' which made it hard for her to fulfil the plan for the moment.

TO LAURA RIDING

English Literature Department, Sheffield University.
29 April 1971

Dear Laura Riding,

I was relieved to get your letter, having feared you might be ill, but not wanting to reply till you had completed your stated plan. What you now add by the unfinished letter is that you had begun working association with Robert Graves in 1926, and that your influence added something very forceful which is not present in his earlier critical writing. You do not get on to discussing the quotation I made from *Impenetrability*, published as by Robert Graves alone, but that came out only a year before the *Survey of Modernist Poetry*, and indeed mentions your name; so whether you accept it or not does not seem crucial to your argument.

Probably you know that there has been some recent writing on the subject. Last year a number of 'The Review', an English critical magazine which is practically as arrogant as its title, had a number largely dedicated to your work, praising it a good deal; and I found in one of the articles a number of quotations from the *Survey*, which were said to have influenced me (quite evidently) in writing my *Ambiguity*.[11] I read these quotations with dropping jaw; they meant nothing at all to me, and I am sure they would have meant nothing forty years ago. My capacities for absorption are restricted by nature, and I know that much good work cannot enter my

---

[11] See *the Review*, no. 23 (Sept.–Nov.1970), for Roy Fuller, 'The White Goddess', 3–9; and Martin Seymour-Smith, 'Laura Riding's Rejection of Poetry', 10–14.

mind; I know for instance that the poet Auden, whom I greatly admire, at one time imitated your work quite shamelessly, and recently 'The Review' has been praising your criticism; but none of your work has ever seemed to me even capable of retaining my eye on the page. You demand that I admit publically [*sic*] having been 'influenced' by you, which you say I have already 'confessed'; well, for whatever good it may do you, I am already believed to have been influenced by you, but I really will not tell a lie to encourage that, I have already been punished enough.

The American *Modern Language Quarterly* for Sept. 1966, after an article on 'The Construction' of my book *Ambiguity*, carried a letter from Robert Graves confessing that he was himself responsible for the detailed examination of the Shakespeare Sonnet 129 which I mentioned in my initial acknowledgement. I very stupidly forgot that the legal authorship should be acknowledged jointly, because it seemed to me obvious that this one chapter was written by Graves alone, in view of his style and previous writing; the rest of the book was written in any entirely different style. He now admits that I was right, and surely that is the end of it.

The editor wrote to me with astonishment saying he had never read such vituperation as Graves wrote to him about Empson, and he had had to write back again and again before he could extract something fit to print.[12] In just the same way, Chatto's talked to me with awe about the forty-page letters from Graves, forty years ago. But Graves has always been careful to avoid any discussion of the matter directly. 'Shit on that' written on a postcard was his answer to my only approach to him, long ago; these immense outpourings must always be addressed to some humble functionary.[13] And as soon as the functionary had the nerve to talk back, in a cosy way, there was Graves confessing that he had written the chapter himself. I

[12] William H. Matchett wrote to WE on 20 June 1966: 'After an incredibly prima-donna-ish performance with ups and downs of begging, charm, demands and threats, Graves has added a waspish letter to those [*marginal insert*: letters—*not* waspish letters!] from you and Richards which we are appending to the Jensen article . . . It would be much more entertaining were I able to print the supplementary letters from Graves, not just the one written to be printed. One wonders how much he believes in it and how much is just bluff.' (Houghton)

[13] WE misremembers the form of Graves's communication, though he recalls full well the nub of it. In response to an enquiry from WE, Graves sent him this undated letter from Deyá: 'Your query surprises me. Your original fault & your subsequent aggravation of the offence towards Miss Riding & myself contained in the note addressed to Miss Riding completely bitched things between you & her. Hence the note sent by Miss Riding to your publishers, countersigned by myself. If even after that you had sent a note of apology to Miss Riding, & also to me, & it had been accepted, there might have been some excuse for continuing the correspondence with queries to me about Mother Goose. But I can't understand this pretence that all is well. Is it perhaps a winking signal that men of letters should drown their personal feelings in a matter of literary importance? Shit on that. Or is it just possible that you don't realise what all the feeling is about? Yours Robert Graves.' (*Houghton*)

report this to you, but cannot pretend to understand it at all. It all began with shell-shock from the First War, of course. Very possibly he had plotted to delude you into believing you had done the work, so that my entirely accidental breath of reality has to be resisted crazily whenever it is recalled.

Your claim to have put the energy into the theory has much more substance; but then, did it only do harm to the theory? This is a basically interesting question; often asked before, in a way. For instance a book *Interpretations in Shakespeare's Sonnets* (1963) by Milton Laadry [*sic*], which happens to be here. You and Robert Graves are rather scolded for the 'expense of spirit' essay, and so am I for being led astray by it. (p. 168 and elsewhere.) The discovery of ambiguous syntax he finds particularly harmful.[14]

I am inclined to say something more radical; that the 'expense of spirit' example works against the original intention of Robert Graves. He had developed a Conflict Theory of poetry, soon after the war, and went on to consider the verbal means by which conflict finds expression. But your analysis makes Shakespeare in the Sonnet very single-minded, improbably single-minded. I have never seen anyone agree with the decision of you and Graves here to retain the garbled line:

> A bliss in proof and prov'd and very woe,

which you said meant that Shakespeare hated the whole process of this love-affair, even the moments of bodily pleasure—it was all woe together, and that was what he meant in the previous line by saying all the stages were 'extreme'. But surely this word need only mean it was *either* great excitement, or pleasure, or suffering; and your reading is proved wrong by the line that comes next:

> A bliss in proof, and, prov'd, a very woe,
> Before, a joy propos'd, behind, a dream.

I remember an essay of yours, printed about that time, called 'The Damned Thing', which expressed great resentment at being saddled with any sexual equipment at all, and found everything to do with it merely unpleasant.[15] Instead of Shakespeare expressing mixed feelings, in fact,

[14] See Hilton Landry, *Interpretations in Shakespeare's Sonnets* (1963), 133–4. In a footnote on pp. 168–9 Landry declares: 'Empson probably acquired some of his approaches to the Sonnets, including his eye for ambiguous syntax, from Riding and Graves. Unfortunately, some of his examples are trivial and artificial . . ., just as some of theirs are. Much of his criticism is very intelligent and sensitive . . .'

[15] Laura Riding, 'The Damned Thing', in *Anarchism is not enough* (1928), 187–208.

such as he obviously had usually, however cross he felt at the moment, you make him express *nothing but* loathing for the whole condition of normal life. This did not need any subtlety of language; in fact, it is hard to see why he did not express it more plainly. I do not think I imitated this fault in my book, or not much, but I did use quite a bit of 'ambiguity of syntax', which I now think a very dubious thing, and perhaps one which actually cannot occur in the sharp form needed to express a conflict. Anyway it is always a temptation to the analyst, because it gives him a big extra chance of forcing in his own ideas against the surface intention of the poem.

When I came to do the second edition, in 1946, I had become inclined to cut these cases out, having already been warned against them, but I did not want to alter the book too much. You understand, it had kept up a small though steady sale for sixteen years, all the time carrying the erratum slip saying that you and Robert Graves were joint authors of the book *Modernist Poetry* (and hence presumably of the 'expense of spirit' chapter). But in the new edition, as I had come to think that that analysis had been a bad influence, I merely fitted into the new Introduction a 'credit' to Robert Graves, leaving it to be assumed that this referred to his earlier books when he was not writing in collaboration. This was entirely within my rights, and it seemed to me that my silence was charitable.

You express contempt for men who cry, when I quote to you the sentence by Robert Graves about *The Duchess of Malfi*. But you were not being asked to admire the character of Ferdinand, who has just had his sister murdered out of incestuous jealousy, and will next refuse to pay the murderer and turn into a werewolf. He is a hysteric not a stoic; I bet he cried. Anyway, his character is patiently shown as extremely mixed-up, and I have always thought that the Graves comment throws a great deal of light on why the famous line (Mine eyes dazzle) has been so often praised. Your remark betrays a great lack of sympathy (I have to feel) with what he was trying to do, all along, in his earlier work on these verbal points; and that is why I still believe that you really did have an influence on the 'expense of spirit' chapter, as you claim, though he now says he was 'responsible for most of the detailed examination of poems (in the book), for example showing the complex implications of Sonnet 129'. After he had followed your advice, I am led to think, he felt the whole area into which I ignorantly blundered as one of intense irritation, and that is why he never did any more work of that kind, ever again.

Of course you are welcome, as well as entitled, to use this letter and my previous one in any way you think best.

Yours truly

William Empson.

Cornell; Houghton carbon, bMS Eng 1401 (636)

Riding wrote back (7 May 1971) that whereas she knew Graves to be a 'liar', she believed WE differed only in being 'an improviser of fabrications'.

Riding responded to WE's last letter (29 Apr. 1971) with a letter of her own to the editor (6 Oct. 1971); and a revised version of her letter (14 Nov. 1971) appeared in *MLQ* (32), 1971, 447–8: 'It seems to me appropriate to record that, without public statement of mine, recognition of my intellectually and verbally sensitive hand within the glove of the *Survey* method has been mounting, with perception of its connection, via Mr Empson's hobby-horse use of it, with the "New Criticism," which tried to make real horse-flesh of it . . .' The letter Graves published in *MLQ*, she went on, 'contained, besides misrepresentations as to my work and personal life of his unctuous provision, aspersions on my authorial credit and general responsibility of intellect . . .'[16]

§ END

———

TO IAN PARSONS

Department of English Literature, The University, Sheffield 10
31 January 1967

My dear Ian,

Thank you for your letter of very relevant advice. As you suggest, I am still writing articles, and it seems perverse not to collect them. The tax situation has been at least an excuse, in my mind. If I earn money at present much of it goes in supertax, but in four years' time I shall be made to retire, with hardly any pension as I had so much fun abroad, and then I will need to have plenty lined up to publish. Even at that, I need to start getting it lined up pretty soon. I am writing (when I can snatch a minute to meet the deadline) an introduction to an American paperback edition of Shakespeare's Poems, but that will be a chapter of the eventual book on Shakespeare, and I got them to alter the contract so that I keep the rights

---

[16] See also Laura (Riding) Jackson, 'Some Autobiographical Corrections of Literary History', *The Denver Quarterly* 8: 4 (Winter 1974), 12–14.

of reprinting.[1] I am going to a Summer School at Buffalo this year, agreeing at first so as to pay off the Capital Gains Tax and debts before the onset of eternal financial cold; but then Hetta said she had better see New York before the end, and so she is coming too. I doubt whether much will return to the Old Country, of money, I mean. However, this is rather a last fling; a serious attempt to nail together the next book ought to start by the end of this year.

You alarm me about the £600; I hope you were only remembering the kind loan in a vague way. I certainly understood that I had paid it all back, out of my last annual cheque from you. Please make sure.

Yours affectionately

William Empson

I don't think I have [been] losing my public by only writing short articles, usually funny or rude. I suspect they are positively grateful to the old man for not boring them with a book. Anyway, a slight suggestion of lunacy and bad temper necessarily attached to Milton's God, and is now cooling off I think. Many wicked teachers hate me, of course, but it does me good when they say so in their horrible magazines. I am rather surprised in fact at not being more of a back number; maybe it is just because the young are so dull.

High time to produce something, though, of course.

Reading

TO CHRISTOPHER RICKS

Department of English Literature, The University, Sheffield 10
Thursday 23 February 1967

My dear Ricks,

Thank you for asking me again, about Housman, but I am late with a contracted article and don't seem to have anything to say about Housman which isn't already in print.[1] However a reflection about his metre might be usable—remembering that someone at the time of his death (Conolly [*sic* ?) said the five-line verses were 'decadent in scansion' which is worth another paragraph maybe.[2] They do aim at an Aching Thrill, as this bit of Alcaic metre does, but to call that decadent is fairly absurd (I am not sure how it could be refuted).

---

[1] *Narrative Poems*, by William Burto and with an introd. by WE, was published in June 1968 (Signet Classics); WE's introduction is reprinted in *ES*, 1–28.

[1] CR had asked WE to contribute to a volume in the series 'Twentieth Century Views': *A. E. Housman: A Collection of Critical Essays* (1968).

[2] See Cyril Connolly, 'A. E. Housman: A Controversy', *The Condemned Playground* (1985), 47–62; WE, 'Foundations of Despair', *A*, 419.

I could do a very short piece about his metres, then, if the marked bit of material here could be most of it. (pp 38–41). I don't know whether I sent you this before; you wouldn't see it otherwise presumably. It appeared in a shockingly dull magazine The Journal of Aesthetics for 1961 or 1962.[3]

I am much shocked to hear that Karl Miller resigned [as Literary Editor of the *New Statesman*] because he was told to renounce Empson.[4] Was the editor acting as an RC [Roman Catholic]? I must try and see him when term is over.

Yours

William Empson.

---

[3] 'Rhythm and Imagery in English Poetry', *British Journal of Aesthetics* 2 (Jan. 1962); repr. in *A*, 147–66.

[4] Neil Berry relates: 'Miller's connection with the *New Statesman*'—of which he had been literary editor since 1961—'came to an abrupt end early in 1967. In the course of the previous year, the paper had acquired a new editor in the person of Paul Johnson. Except that they were both pugnacious personalities, Johnson, an English public school Catholic, and Miller, a Scot of working-class background and an atheist, were very different individuals . . . Johnson, for his part, considered that Miller's books pages were altogether too rarefied for weekly journalism. When Miller persisted in publishing brain-teasing reviews by William Empson, Johnson dashed off a testy memorandum recording his conviction that the overwhelming majority of readers were likely to find Empson's work "incomprehensible". Miller was outraged, as perhaps he was meant to be, and promptly handed in his resignation' (*Articles of Faith: The Story of British Intellectual Journalism* (2002), 214).

Miller published his own account of the fracas in 1974: 'William Empson has written reviews at various times for the *New Statesman*, whose literary editor I was for some six years. In the autumn of 1966 I found I was not getting on well with the new editor who had taken over, and Empson was the subject of what was, for me, our main disagreement. A piece of Empson's, the editor protested in a memorandum, was "incomprehensible" and "quite unsuitable for the NS". If this was meant to drive me away from the paper, it succeeded. I dropped out, and enjoyed a spell of Luciferian free fall.

'I would accept that Empson's articles—with their velocity, intricacy, and zealous insistence on detail, and his habit of placing many of his most interesting suggestions in asides and subordinate clauses—must have proved difficult for a fair number of readers ("99.9 per cent" seems a bit on the high side, however), and bitterly hard for those who were uninterested in the subjects he was writing about. But the point is precisely that this ought not to have been treated as a decisive consideration. A literary editor should acknowledge the existence of specialist interests, not least his own . . . It was for that reason, as well as for the pleasure of it, that it seemed essential to try to get Empson to write for the *New Statesman* and then for the *Listener*. I am only sorry he did not write more . . .

'It is not necessary to think that what Empson wrote as a journalist during the sixties is as important as any of his main books . . . But it is necessary to recognize that his journalism is continuous in manner and intent with what he has written in his books. His patient (and impatient) conversational style does not change from occasion to occasion; it is inflexibly characteristic and distinctive; and it is a style which lends itself excellently to literary journalism' ('Empson Agonistes', Gill, 41–2).

See also 'Testimonial', *New Statesman*, 10 Feb. 1967—'We wish to express our regret at the resignation of Mr Karl Miller from the staff of the *New Statesman*, and our appreciation of the work he has done as Literary Editor'—signed by luminaries including Noel Annan, Asa Briggs, D. J. Enright, Geoffrey Grigson, John Gross, Ian Hamilton, Stuart Hampshire, Christopher Hill, Dan Jacobson, Frank Kermode, Mary McCarthy, Conor Cruise O'Brien, Christopher Ricks, and WE.

TO HELEN GARDNER

This exchange follows WE's review of Helen Gardner's edition of *The Elegies and the Songs and Sonnets*: reprinted in *ERL*, (1), 129–58.

Sheffield
4 March 1967

Dear Helen Gardner,[1]

Thank you very much; that clears up a lot of points; I still hope to print a letter, but it will be much shorter. I confess now that you are not capricious in your apparatus, and think instead that you are operating an extremely inconvenient machine. How extraordinary to have a rule that, if the edition is agreeing with its copy text, no manuscripts can be listed as agreeing with that text. It is astonishing that *all* the Group V manuscripts read *Profane*, and none of the other manuscripts, and that the nearest you were allowed to come to saying this was that long and frightfully confusing list. Once the simple answer is let out, surely it becomes plain that the cause must be simple too. I am now even more sure that the poet had altered the manuscript to avoid any accusation of blasphemy; and I am puzzled by your conviction that a theory which explains a lay-out of variants like that has no inherent probability. By the way, what made you fail to explain that your Sigma is used when the edition departs from the copy text, in contrast to the square bracket? You are actually trying to define a new symbol, as I now understand, at the end of your list of Sigla, but you can't bear to give the real explanation in print; that needs a private letter. I am glad I was brash enough to go on asking, because I don't see how I could have guessed; the use does not seem to be consistent enough for the intention to become clear. For instance line 52 of *The Extasie* has 'Th'intelligences] The intelligences 1633' but, as I now understand, the square bracket ought to have been Sigma.

I am most grateful to learn that the whole of manuscript W was written consecutively, and therefore after 1617; I had supposed from your emphasis on the earliness of the first part that it must have been written separately. With this further information, and as the first part anyway includes a poem written in 1609, surely your argument collapses. You say that if I had worked on the manuscripts, such as B, I would realise that people did not check their copies to see they had the latest readings. But I did not say this about the man who added a poem to B (he had an old reading); I said it about the long-suffering Woodward, the only copyist

---

[1] WE is responding to a letter which has been lost.

known to have been a personal friend and admirer. When he copied *Elegy XIX* it was perhaps a quarter of a century old; surely he would sometimes see other people's manuscripts, and take an interest in their variants? And a hint that the author intended a censorship process would make him determinedly loyal. Even apart from this, it looks as if he copied the improved versions of verse letters which had first been directed to himself. His manuscript cannot be regarded as a reliable fossil.

I agreed that 'the Kings real, or his stamped face' may have been written when a king was on the throne, though it is not necessary because the mind of Donne is an extremely generalising one; anyway I believe the poem was written soon after his marriage. The same applies to 'Go tell Court huntsmen that the King will ride' (where you give [Mario] Praz credit for inventing what Gosse had already refuted).[2] But when you argue that other poems merely mentioning Kings belong to the same rather late date, I deny it. I agree that calling the whole period at Pyrton their honeymoon was a sad untruth, though it drew attention to a real absurdity; I withdraw it. Your advice to get Xeroxes and look at the manuscripts myself I will gladly do when I have my head a bit more above water.

Yours sincerely
William Empson

Houghton carbon, bMS Eng 1401 (561)

Gardner, in a reluctant response to WE (6 March 1967), noted:

> I have told my readers (p. xcii) that 'emendations of punctuation are made on my own judgement . . .' . . . Grierson took seriously the alterations of punctuation in the subsequent editions; but we know far more than he did about the habits of compositors . . . I have defined my new symbol: Σ—means *All except*. This is a definition. What I gave you was an explanation of why it was useful and when one used it, which would be known to anyone used to handling this kind of material. If all the MSS one is using agree one can write *MSS*, meaning all manuscripts used read against the edition; but when all except one or two do, one needs a shorthand way of expressing this to save writing out a list of fourteen or so MSS. You really are making difficulties and it is unreasonable to expect an editor to provide elementary instruction.
>
> 2. *W* is a fair copy, and fair copies presume the existence of something copied from . . . What is interesting about W is that Woodward has a very full collection of the poems we can date before 1598, the

---

[2] Edmund Gosse, *The Life and Letters of John Donne*, 2 vols. (1899).

single lyric and the two sets of Holy Sonnets . . . Apart from having only *one* of the S and S he has none of the poems of Donne's middle period, Verse Letters and Funeral Poems, though these circulated freely . . .

3. Before you cite Gosse, who is really *pour rire* as an authority, you should look up what he actually says. He does not refute Praz because he is unaware of James's passion for hunting and his habit of rising early on to progress to pursue his favourite sport . . .

I am sorry but I haven't time to go on and, as I say, I have no intention of replying if you wish to continue and the editor is willing to print more from you. Surely there must be someone in Sheffield who can help you on textual conventions.

TO C. B. COX* (editor of *Critical Quarterly*)

Department of English Literature, The University, Sheffield 10
15 March 1967

Dear Cox,

Thank you for your letter. I have just had a letter from Helen Gardner saying that she agrees to your printing my reply, and does not wish to answer it. But if she did (it goes on) she would say that I am still showing mere ignorance, because her private letters only explained the code already printed, and added nothing. This I am convinced is a lie; she may be right about the *apparatus*, but it is agreed that this needs supplementing by the notes and commentary, and there her language is so artful (in both examples) that one is astonished to learn what she is concealing.

Still, it is a great relief that we can stop fussing; what I really need for the eventual book is to recover my historical evidence—I always lose things and have to find them again. Treating the Gardner a bit rough was I am afraid necessary, because it is the only way to make her disgorge information.

[Mark] Roberts has another 5,000 words against her technique in the April *Essays in Crit*. Opinion may yet swing in her favour, I fear.

Yours with thanks,
William Empson

Manchester

CRITICAL QUARTERLY, 9: 1 (Spring 1967), 89: 'Donne'

Dear Sirs,

Professor Gardner has very kindly given me some information bearing on two of the cruces in Donne's text which I was discussing in your Autumn number.

All the Group V manuscripts which include 'The Dream' read *profane*; several omit it, and the manuscript O is not listed separately, but the remaining six are unanimous. My conjectures, about which of them must have read it, were thus very ridiculous; but I think the truth strengthens my case as a whole. With such a tidy and complete divergence, it is natural to expect a simple explanation.

Also, the whole of the manuscript W was written at the same time; and this means, from poems which can be dated, after 1617 or probably after 1620. As it was written by Woodward, whom Donne addressed as a fellow poet and a religious man, the first part of it cannot be relied upon to give an early state of the text; Woodward surely saw another text of the Elegies occasionally, and he would welcome a change made in the interests of decorum.

These points of course do not affect the opinion of Professor Gardner, who knew them long before; I think they count on my side, but the estimate of probability turns on one's view of the interests, and the character, of the poet himself. All the same, it was generous of her to pass them on. I do not think I need ask for space to answer the other arguments in your Winter number.

Yours,
William Empson

NEW STATESMAN, 31 March 1967, 437: 'Is He a Christian?'

Malcolm Muggeridge, in 'Am I a Christian?' (*New Statesman*, 73 (10 Mar. 1967), 323), deplored institutional Christianity for being 'now in total disarray': it 'is not even an impediment to Christian belief, but just a joke.' Faced with 'the whole edifice of 20th-century materialism', he looked to 'the other-worldliness which I still find in the Gospels . . . the sublime truth that to live it is necessary to die, that a life can only be kept by being lost— propositions which strike contemporary minds as pessimistic, but which seem to me optimistic to the point of insanity, implying, as they do, that it is possible for a mere man, with his brief life and stunted vision, imprisoned in his tiny ego and enslaved by his squalid appetites, to aspire after a universal understanding and a universal love. Is this being a Christian?' Jack Dixon responded (24 Mar.): 'The answer is no. The sentiments he mentions are to be found in other religions, and some of them occur in non-religious philosophies such as Stoicism. Christians are people who believe that a perfect man was tortured to death in Palestine 1,934 years ago in order to satisfy his divine father's lust for punishment. This lust was so monstrous that the father would have consigned the whole human race to eternal torment had the spectacle of his only perfect son being broken on a cross not afforded him an even more exquisite satisfaction. If Mr Muggeridge believes this, he is a Christian. If not, he's just kidding himself, like the Bishop of Woolwich and the other humane prelates whom Mr Muggeridge disdains.'

Sir, I write to support the letter of Mr Jack Dixon, rather as an obligation than in any hope of our being heard. It is a most curious thing that many people nowadays 'feel' there is something wrong with Christianity, and wonder which kind of God they would like best, without considering what is wrong with its basic doctrines (to do that, they would think cranky). Shelley found it plain that, the more he reverenced the Son who endured, the more he must execrate the Father who was satisfied by his pain; and no Victorian seems to have been puzzled. Earlier it had been found very unsafe to have saintly Christians in power, because at any moment they might deem it their duty to stop imitating the Son and imitate the Father. Quite possibly we are witnessing the birth-pangs of a great change in the religion, which will allow Christians to stop worshipping the Devil; but if so the time will have to come when they realise what they are doing.

TO W. R. ELTON*

Studio House, 1 Hampstead Hill Gardens, NW3
6 April 1967

Dear Mr Elton,

Thank you very much for sending me your book ['*King Lear*' *and the Gods*, 1966], which I read with great interest and pleasure; I should think it may be the turn of the tide—it is so plainly an *equally* scholarly book, though it arrives at opposite conclusions from the established ones. But I hope you will bear with me when I explain that the 'scholarly' method itself, or what is called so nowadays in Eng. Lit., seems to me totally incapable of arriving at the right answer, or even of getting a roughly correct impression of the work of literature which it focuses upon. So you must not expect to convince me, and I am not even sure what real arguments you have—apart from the broad considerations of good sense which our opponents despise.

I had not grasped how politically prominent [Samuel] Harsnett [*A Declaration of Egregious Popish Impostures* 1603] was, and I agree now that Shakespeare read him in the hope of pleasing the King. But you need to remember the story, which the current Eng. Lit. establishment makes a ritual purity out of refusing to do. Edgar hears his despairing father say that the gods kill us for their sport, and explains to the audience that he will cure father's despair by a trick. Father just before attempting suicide apologizes to the gods for having made this blasphemy, and says he kills himself to avoid doing it again. Blasphemy is assumed to bring harvest failure and suchlike. Edgar is already (before he adopts this plan) pretending to be possessed, but he does this to save his life from the villains; there is no suggestion that either of these acts deserves blame (though to forestall it he says 'O fault' when explaining how the shock of discovery killed his father, no longer blasphemous). Pious trickery is not shown as what Jesuits or Anabaptists do, but as what patiently statesmanlike characters do. I think that Shakespeare was just refusing to take sides, but anyhow he was not joining the side of the King.

The work of a 'scholar' is the same as that of an Imagist poet; both proceed from complete rejection of the intelligence and rely upon a Behaviourist technique of glutting the reader with immediate stimuli. Often this is harmless display, but it is a powerful means of distraction, when convenient.[1] Thus I do not know that an appeal to Heaven answered by immediate thunder happens in any Elizabethan play before *Lear* except *Leir*, but your long recital appears designed to prevent a reader from thinking of this curious point. Both Kings assume at first that the thunder is on their side, though of course Shakespeare puts it in an immensely broader mental setting.

I notice that you fairly often falsify the natural reaction to a remark in the play by forcing in a pietistic interpretation. Thus when Edmund (p. 134) leaves Goneril, saying 'Yours in the ranks of death', you comment that it 'implies that they are of the ranks of destruction'. We are not accustomed to plucky swagger of this sort, though our societies are just as murderous in their glum greasy way as the sixteenth-century ones; but it would be clear then that this is the dashing side of Edmund, his best feature, and he really believes that winning the love of the sisters was the

---

[1] WE added in his notes, 'The collection of a great heap of all references to rats in all Europe from fifty years before and after the play (the rat "topos") doesn't *really* clear up what Lear meant at the end. Oddly enough, it is just the same as the Imagist technique, and based on the same anti-intellectualism. A mere collection of bits, only parallel at a trivial place, is [Rosemond] Tuve's picture of the Metaphysicals, but it isn't capable of moving in a poem, or proving in a treatise, or even improving in a sermon, I should say.'

most worth-while thing in his life. Your assumption that the thought is merely dirty shows that you are a really loyal member of the scholarly Establishment, and will I hope win your book more influence among them.

Your readers badly need to hear more about [DeWitt T.] Starnes and [E. W.] Talbert (p. 237). Do they really find an agreement in the period that Lear deserved to suffer for producing legitimate but adulterous daughters? You never seem to realise when scholars are saying wildly absurd things. The reason why people are bowled over by 'If you have poison for me I will drink it' is not that it is 'pious' (it isn't) but that it is total non-attachment or self-naughting, a thing more prominent in Eastern religions than in orthodox Christianity, but then fairly familiar in mystical Christians; you weaken your case by under-rating it. Edmund does not crave to inflict torture because he makes love to great ladies; your p. 296 is just dirty talk again. Delighted to gather that you believe Lear was written after Macbeth; of course it was.

Houghton: ? unsent, bMS Eng 1401 (543)

TO G. SINGH ['Andrew Marvell': Comment in 1967]

Pierre Legouis, in 'Marvell and the New Critics', *Review of English Studies* 8: 32 (1957), 382–9, took mocking issue with a range of critics of Marvell including Milton Klonsky, A. H. King, Frank Kermode, Cleanth Brooks, and L. D. Lerner. Of WE's discussion of stanza vi of 'The Garden' (first published in *Scrutiny*, 1, 1932), he wrote: 'Either "from the lessening of pleasure . . ." or "made less by pleasure . . .". Since three meanings in Mr. Empson's theory, are better than two, his omission of the real meaning conclusively shows that he never saw it: "from a pleasure that is inferior" (see *O. E. D.* under *Less*, 2), viz. sensuous pleasure, the mind withdraws into a happiness that is specifically its own, viz. contemplation. Here Mr. Empson does exactly what many a bright student has been doing for the last thirty-four years in translations set by me: not seeing the obvious meaning of a phrase and seeing entirely improbable ones instead, *gallice* "fair un contre-sens". So that, to parody a regal remark, we are amused, but we are not impressed.' (383).

It may have been a complacent observation by Legouis that incited WE to take up his long campaign to prove that Marvell had married his land-lady: 'We now know for certain, thanks to Professor F. S. Tupper, that the man Marvell stuck to the last by the wisdom then revealed to him [that in "Upon Appleton House" the poet renounced marriage but not love]. He remained so far a hedonist that he never married. As his eighteenth-century editor, Captain Thompson, R. N., put it for all time: "He had no wife and his gallantries are not known" ' (387).

I am sorry not to have seen earlier an article by Professor Pierre Legouis in the *Review of English Studies* for 1957 (p. 382), attacking a number of critics of Marvell. He says there is an obvious meaning, which never occurred to me [in the chapter 'Marvell's Garden', *SVP*], for

> Meanwhile the mind, from pleasure less,
> Withdraws into its happiness.

The mind leaves the smaller pleasure of observing the world and turns to its own distinctive pleasure, that of observing itself; a still greater pleasure, of observing Heaven, will be adumbrated later in the poem. This part of Marvell's Latin version is unfortunately lost, but I confess that it quite probably agreed with M. Legouis. He is not a native speaker of English, and this may be an advantage in dealing with a translation. But I still say that, regarded as a bit of English, the couplet is very bad if it just means that. Marvell had set himself an almost impossible task, when the whole string of Latin epigrams had to be turned into brief rhyming English ones; and a certain amount of clumsiness in the first couplet of the verse may even be a help; it is a base from which the next three couplets go up like rockets. Even so, the suggestion of other philosophical meanings in this first couplet would be what made him decide to rest content with it. To *withdraw* from a pleasure *into* . . . a cosier one? no, a bigger one; this in itself is hard to take; and to put the adjective *less* after the noun seems particularly unjustified here as a poetical grace, so that one is almost driven to look for some logical force in it.

As an old man now, I feel that I understand better how annoying the poem was meant to be. A father wants his son to hold down a pay-packet, and young Marvell is saying: 'I don't need to go and fight in this war, or stand for Parliament, or anything; I can get a much more balanced maturity just by sitting in this garden'. He feels real love and wonder for the Fairfax estate, as an enchanted peace; but he knows that his argument is impudent, and that is why it can be called witty.

[Sent to Singh of Belfast.][1]

Houghton: typescript

---

[1] G. Singh, Professor Emeritus of Italian at Queen's University, Belfast, has published critical studies of Montale (1980), T. S. Eliot (1985), F. R. Leavis (1982), and Q. D. Leavis (2002); and, with Gabrielle Barfoot, *Il Novecento Inglese e Italiano: Saggi Critici e comparativi* (1998). He is a Leopardi scholar of international repute.

TO HYAM MACCOBY*

Department of English Literature, The University, Sheffield 10
11 May 1967

Dear Mr Maccoby,[1]

In general, it would be an excellent thing for the Jews to speak against Christianity; I am puzzled that they don't. But Al Alvarez thought apparently that my book complaining against the Christian God *[Milton's God]* insulted the Jewish one—though the Old Testament seems pretty firm against Moloch. This was alarming, because it meant I would have committed an atrocity, and there would be a tremendous fuss. But nobody else seems to have taken it up.[2]

This is just second thoughts—there are some notes on your essay separately.

Yours

William Empson

I just took notes as I went along.

---

[1] In 1967 Hyam Maccoby sent WE the draft of an article later published as 'The Figure of Shylock', *Midstream* (New York) 16: 2 (Feb. 1970), 56–69. The page numbers given in WE's comments refer to the draft, which has not survived—'but, as I remember,' wrote Maccoby, 'there is only one substantial difference—that, influenced by Empson's remarks, I re-instated a paragraph from a still earlier draft about Shylock's greatness' (letter to JH, 26 Apr. 1988). The burden of the article is that *The Merchant of Venice* is 'a Jew-baiting play' (57): 'The play is . . . a piece of profound anti-Semitism . . . The clash between Shylock and Antonio is a clash between Judaism and Christianity . . .' (58). The 'deepest secret' of the play is 'that Shylock is God the Father. God the Father in Christianity (as Empson argued in *Milton's God*) is a horror. Christians feel the horror, but they dare not direct it towards God the Father himself. They direct it towards the person whom they regard as the representative and devotee (almost the incarnation) of God the Father—the Jew . . . Shylock's words at his first sight of Antonio, "I hate him for he is a Christian," express the Christian's idea of the hatred which he fancies the Jew must feel for Christianity. As a matter of fact, one of the most remarkable things about Jewish–Christian relations is the *lack* of hatred shown by Jews towards Christians. Despite the centuries-long Christian persecution—the worst persecution in all Jewish history—the tone of Jewish writings about Christianity is almost invariably mild . . . To the Jews, the Christian persecution was simply one more in a series of persecutions which God had sent to test and purify his people . . . If anything, the real Jew has shown too little sense of antagonism towards Christianity, because of his indifference to its doctrine and lack of understanding of its dangerousness' (65–6).

[2] Maccoby responded (15 May 1967): 'as a Jew of Rabbinical background, I was delighted with your stand against the Christian Father-God in *Milton's God*. Though I believe in God only in the same sense that I believe in Hamlet, I consider that the conflict between the Jewish God and the Christian God is still very much alive.

'I was very interested in your remarks about Alvarez. I think it is most important for Jews to point out that the Christian Father-God is *not* the God of the Old Testament. However, he *is* the God of the O. T. *as seen through Christian eyes*—he bears the same relationship to the God of the O. T. as the fantasy-Jew to the real Jew. The Jews managed to make friends with their Father-God— in fact they managed to civilize him. All this was thrown away when the Christians turned him back into a ravening Moloch-figure.'

3 good on 'fawning p'[3]

4 —and on committing no crime.[4]

  The merit of Bassanio is that he is a gambler, a sporting gentlemanly trait (as you say later).[5]

8 *converted* Jews, of course, regularly came.

9 All millionaires in popular literature who are meant to be *popular* have to be disillusioned with their gold, and ready to toss it to the hero. Shakespeare makes him very frankly in love with the hero (though hopeless of being gratified).

14 This story is no good unless 'some' evidence for it is produced.

  Portia was not a judge.[6]

15 Not exactly degeneration. Marlowe wanted to tease the Christians, and found this a safe manner, whereas Shakespeare just wanted to be popular with an easy exposition of the audience's views. Marlowe was the more ready to boil his Jew.[7]

17 I thought Adonis was killed by the Mother-Goddess? Gilgamesh says that at length (and not only Robert Graves).[8]

18 Why not admit that Henry V and Augustus [?] really are unattractive characters?

18 It is an interesting thesis but hardly covers the field. I can't believe Hitler thought the Jews were God the Father—he wasn't Christian enough.

23 Surely Jews are at present in greater danger from Arabs than anyone else, and *they* haven't got 'Christian attitudes'. I have never heard of a Jew who wondered why these persecutions are so regularly incurred by Jews.

28 *What* makes it abundantly clear that Shakespeare approved of the behaviour of Venice? No Londoner did, because they envied Venice and wanted London to be the centre of world maritime trade instead. Shake-

---

[3] See 'The Figure of Shylock', 60.

[4] 'It is noteworthy that no legal crime is ascribed to Shylock at any point in his career. This is most unusual in a Jew-baiting play . . .' (60).

[5] 'Bassanio is a selfish, canting fortune-hunter who thinks nothing of putting his friend's wealth at unjustified risk . . . [Shylock] does not venture or surrender himself in any way. The careless gambling and risk-taking of the Christians is contrasted with Shylock's careful calculations in the moral as well as in the business sphere' (59, 61).

[6] Maccoby refers on p. 64 of his article to 'the scene of Portia's judgment'; later to 'Portia's conduct of the enquiry' (68).

[7] 'There is some human feeling between Barabas and his daughter. Marlowe considered it consonant with the daughter's virtuous nature that she should feel loyalty to her father and should break with him finally only with reluctance. By the time *The Merchant of Venice* was written a certain degeneracy of moral tone had taken place. It is now a point of honour for Jessica to be disloyal to her father . . .' (63–4).

[8] 'Jesus, like all romantic Heroes, like the Young Gods in the cults of Adonis, Attis, Tammuz and Dionysius, dies young . . .' (64).

speare might easily imply (though not loudly enough to spoil the simplicity of his fable) 'Those to whom evil is done | Do evil in return'. Antonio calls himself a 'tainted wether' (castrated ram) and is plainly neurotic.

32 And then, Shakespeare gives the Jew such impressive speeches that Irving could act Shylock and turn the play into the Tragedy of the Jew. I do not think you can argue that this is not in the play at all. There is at least a 'paradox' about the Jew, like the White Devil—the audience feel a (possible) complexity of judgement.

But the fairy-story cannot do normal human justice because it is committed to denouncing Usury, which was standard custom in the City of London, and without which you couldn't have these big ships sent trading round the world. They were the most evident cases of big risk to a large lump of capital with great possible gain. Only the millionaire Antonio could finance a fleet of them by himself. That is the basic insincerity or traditionalism in the fable; Jews are decorations of the real subject Usury. I agree of course that the play 'can't be detached from' antisemitism.

41 I agree pretty well with your final paragraphs.[9] The rival company has *The Jew of Malta* ready in the ice-box when Lopez was killed in 1594, and Shakespeare's Company couldn't have something ready till next year. Shakespeare tried to give the impression of looking back at it in a very large-minded and humane manner, unlike the notorious Marlowe; but he was not strong in speculation and gave a remarkable display of the Christian mind being nastily self-righteous—amounting almost to a diagram of how it gets like that. I think you rather weaken the point if you take it further.

Very interesting though. Thank you for sending it.

William Empson.

§ BASTARD AND BARSTARDS

In his review of Maynard Mack, *'King Lear' in Our Time* (*E in C*, Jan. 1967; *SSS*, 56–62), WE remarked *en passant*:

> I am grateful to Professor Mack for giving the original spelling of a bit of Edmund's first soliloquy: 'Why bastard, wherefore base? ... | ...

---

[9] 'Shakespeare, so far from deploring Christian intolerance, heartily approves of it, and makes his most nobly Christian character, Antonio, the most intolerant of all . . . Sixteen centuries of Christian teaching had left him no other way, and so he created the definitive expression of the myth of Christian anti-Semitism' (69).

with baseness, barstardy? base, base?'[1] This proves that our two pronunciations of the word already existed, one for law and one for
swearing, a most important point.

J. C. Maxwell[2] protested in a letter (*E in C*, 17: 2, Apr. 1967) that the Folio
spelling to which WE referred, in *King Lear* (I. ii. 10), is not 'barstardy' but
'Barstadie'—'a pretty obvious metathetic misprint.' Moreover, although
Maxwell was once told that the lawyers did distinguish between two pronunciations of the word, 'one for law and one for swearing', he had never
noticed the distinction in actual usage.

TO CHRISTOPHER RICKS

Department of English Literature, The University, Sheffield 10
30 May 1967

My dear Christopher Ricks,

Very pleased to get your letter. I am in a rush trying to finish an introduction to the Shakespeare Poems and post it to America before going
back to hospital tomorrow morning, to have the side of my neck taken out
merely as a precaution. But when will I mark the exam papers? Everybody
is very helpful.

You are quite right, I was being too irritating; better simply say in
brackets, after printing the line with the intrusive R, '(here the intrusive R
did not survive printing).' I am sorry that Maxwell lowered the credit of
the Redbrick Professorship, but Newcastle did strike me as dreary, so I
expect he was right to go; giving him 'J. C.' all along would probably
sound best.

Would you please add, as a final paragraph, the words:
A Canadian friend tells me that, where he comes from, they don't
know to say the word except starting like 'bat', no matter how

---

[1] Mack does not actually quote this passage; WE may be recalling the criticism of John F.
Danby, who quotes Edmund's speech (I. ii. 10) with the Folio spelling thus: 'Why brand they us |
With Base? With baseness Bastardie? Base, Base?' (*Shakespeare's Doctrine of Nature: A Study of 'King
Lear'* (1961), 31).

[2] James Coutts Maxwell (1916–76) was educated in Edinburgh and at Balliol College,
Oxford, and taught at the University of Newcastle upon Tyne (where he became a Professor),
1950–66, before returning to Oxford as Reader in English Literature (and Professorial Fellow
of Balliol) from 1966. His writings include editions of Shakespeare in the New Arden Series;
the New Shakespeare (5 vols.); the Penguin edn. of Wordsworth's *The Prelude*; the final volumes
of the Cambridge Shakespeare; and editions of the papers of Sir Walter Greg and of Peter
Ure.

low-class they want to be. J. C. Maxwell seems to doubt whether this pronunciation is even possible.[3]

I cut out a bang at the end about 'expert scholars' who only know English as a dead language, because I think Maxwell is pretty sensible and should not be alienated; but getting in this (quite true) bit of news seems to make the same point.

I can't make plans till after the operation, but certainly hope to see you before you are off to the States.

Yours with thanks
William Empson

ESSAYS IN CRITICISM, 17: 3 (July 1967): [WE's published reply]

It may well be, as Mr J. C. Maxwell has found, that we no longer distinguish by the vowels between privileged highborn bastards and common barstards; but this only shows that a modern expert on Shakespeare is liable to read him wrong. Within living memory, if you were talking about pedigrees to someone proud of long descent from a royal bastard, it was essential to begin the word like 'bat', not like 'barn'; otherwise you would be suspected of low jeering at a subject which demanded reverence. I have heard this going on, and it is not likely to have been a Victorian invention, as that age was little plagued by royal bastards.

Maxwell says that the spelling with the R in *Lear* (F1) is 'a pretty obvious metathetic misprint', but the conditions are such as to make a direct error of this type improbable. It comes in the first speech of Edgar, who says at line 6

> Why Bastard? wherefore Base?

and at line 9

> Why brand they us
> With base? with baseness Barstardie? Base, Base?

Base and *Bastardy* are treated as cognate, and the word spelt oddly comes fifth out of seven such words close together. By this time the printer has become thoroughly accustomed to setting up an initial BAS, and would hardly alter it unless his copy did. I agree however that his subsequent mistake comes under the head of 'metathesis'. The mind somehow grasps

---

[3] See below for the final wording of WE's published letter of April 1968.

all the letters of a word at once, treating this as more fundamental than their order; here, as the printer knows that there is usually only one R in *bastardy*, he omits the R from its usual place towards the end of the word. He may still have understood the dramatic effect of the variant spelling, and not just have followed it blindly; a 'metathesis' could happen in either case.

Also, Maxwell assumes that the Folio was printed from a corrected text of the first Quarto, as has long been agreed; and he reasonably decides that the Folio spelling here would not be written as a correction onto the Quarto. But surely it is impossible to believe that this method was used on every page of the Quarto? I had not realised that the theory gets interpreted in such a sheep-like manner. A hundred lines were added to make the Folio text, mostly in quite long passages, and two of them come in this scene (I. ii. 120–6, 184–91). The Quarto gives this soliloquy as prose, most of it easy to scan but not at the line in question; Edmund merely says:

> Why brand they us with base, base bastardie? who in the lusty stealth
> of nature . . .

The copy used for a facsimile (OUP, 1939) has hardly any margin, and the changes needed for the Folio version could not have been written onto the page with which we are concerned, even supposing that the ends of verse lines were marked by a stroke. No doubt the printer had asked to work from a corrected page of print wherever possible, but this could not be made a rigid rule; where the page could not take the corrections, he would presumably be given the basic manuscript. I do not find that any of the cruces given as decisive proof of the theory comes from 'I. ii', so that this whole scene may have been printed from Shakespeare's manuscript. Anyhow, the man who made the prompt copy would retain the intrusive R if he recognised it as an indication to the actor.

These objections seemed to me minor ones, but I confess I was surprised, having been induced by opposition to take my theory more seriously, at finding strong support for it in the *Shakespeare's Pronunciation* of Kökeritz. He says (p. 183)

> As an actor, Shakespeare may have found it expedient to exchange
> his native Warwickshire [a] for the more fashionable London vowel
> [æ].

That is, Shakespeare would feel it smart to use the 'bat' vowel, but homely to use a vowel 'as in French *patte*'. Such may well have been the origin of the contrasting pronunciations of the word (not as his invention, but at this time); to suggest a country accent (as Edgar does through more elaborate spelling later in the play) makes the actor separate himself from the aristocrats who are the main characters of the drama; in a way, he speaks as one of the audience, like the clowns. However, it may be thought that this change of vowel could not then have been suggested by inserting an R; as is quite often done, I find, in modern detective stories. But Kökeritz (p. 169), after remarking that words spelt with AR get pronounced nowadays as in *father*, says

> and I am convinced that a similar sound was used by Shakespeare and his fellow actors.

This is nearly the same vowel as the one that would have felt countrified, but driven home. If they wanted to go still lower, I expect, they would actually pronounce their R, so as to growl; maybe this is what some of the readers of the detective stories think that the intrusive R means.

The variant sound does not make an important point at the place where it survived printing, though it helps the climax—Edmund, of course, only uses the low pronunciation the second time he uses the word, when he has warmed up. But it is really needed in *Henry V* when the Dauphin puts our English aristocracy in their place on the night before the battle of Agincourt (my spelling here):

> Normans, but bastard Normans; Norman barstards. (III. v. 10)

The repetition here is pointless unless allowed the change of sound, and then becomes positively entertaining. *Henry V*, for that matter, is sadly dependent upon these extra jokes. The patriotic audience did not suppose that the French prince could really become their intimate, but they would want him to be somehow guyed, and this was sufficiently done by letting him slip into a low-class or native English view of the Plantagenet survivors whom Queen Elizabeth was successfully keeping down. The battle was traditionally won by the long-bow-men against the armoured knights, and the play is much concerned to present democratic ideas. So this joke would not be too disrespectful for the period—the kind of thing that only a modern audience would like.

Replying to Empson (*E in C*, 18: 1, Jan. 1968, 112), J. C. Maxwell averred that it is possible for a printer to produce a false spelling without manuscript authorization; equally, it is possible that the manuscript copy for the Folio might have been given as 'Barstardy'. However, he went on: 'Waiving questions of phonology, does Professor Empson really think that this sense of *bastard* could have maintained such an underground existence as not to be recognised in the printed record of the language at all before the present century?' And in any case: 'Not even present-day English uses the abstract noun *bastardy* in the sense of "being a bastard".'

ESSAYS IN CRITICISM, 18: 2 (April 1968)

J. C. Maxwell is a very good textual editor, I think, but he turns out not to be immune from their standard modes of corruption. If Empson, he says, 'thinks that a printer accustomed to setting up a word correctly "would hardly alter it unless his copy did", he has not given much attention to . . .' their habitual errors. But this does not meet the case. I said that a printer who was setting up seven cognate words close together all beginning BAS would not be likely to start the fifth with BARS for no reason and then return to BAS for the last two. J. C. Maxwell will have been taught about 'metathesis' as part of the equipment of a textual scholar; he pishes and tushes when told that it is psychologically unlikely to occur under certain conditions, because he feels that the Psychology Department has no business to intrude into the English Department. He would not otherwise completely misrepresent my argument.

His third point will have struck many readers as decisive:

> Waiving questions of phonology, does Professor Empson really think that this sense of *bastard* could have maintained such an underground existence as not to be recognised in the printed works of the language at all before the present century?

I did not impute any such thing, and I am not even sure which of the pronunciations J. C. Maxwell supposes to carry a new modern sense. Kökeritz maintains that Shakespeare would say *barstard* when young in Stratford but *basstard* when acting the part of an aristocrat at the Globe; thus the first pronunciation would seem low-class or countrified, the second dignified or fashionable. This is all that my argument required; and it is agreed that he uses spelling to represent a country dialect, for a dramatic effect, later in the same play. Still, of course, it is interesting to consider whether different senses of the word are concerned. In the *OED* entry under BASTARD (adj.), numbers 2 to 5 offer a variety of senses, all introduced shortly before Shakespeare was born. Clearly, a lot of play with the word was going on, and it was frequently used for abuse; this would be likely to go with the more low-class pronunciation. I am not sure what J. C. Maxwell means to deny, after 'waiving phonology'. He might very properly mean that the modern use for swearing implies 'prone to cheese-paring or petty cheating; mean-minded', and this does not appear in the *OED* list. We may be sure that the Elizabethan word had a different flavour from ours. But when Thersites describes himself as (in effect) the archetypal bastard (V. vii, end) it seems clear that he is chiefly accused of being mean-minded. A modern audience may surely be allowed to feel itself at home with such uses.

If, on the other hand, J. C. Maxwell considered the dignified legal use of *bastard* as dating only from this century, he was out on a limb. A friend from Canada told me that he didn't know one could pronounce the word except as *basstard* till he came to England, and another friend tells me this pronunciation is standard in both north and south Ireland. It is so well established that the main question is why England herself renounced it; perhaps it was one of the tinier casualties in the class struggle.

§ END

_____

TO FRANCIS BERRY

Department of English Literature, The University, Sheffield 10
8 June 1967

My dear Berry,

I have got the exam paper and will start it very soon.

The way I had always understood our Professorships is that they are equal and identical—there are simply two Profs of Eng. Lit.; and you of course continue when I go. But suppose you make yourself Professor of English Poetry and Poetics—the replacement Professor [for WE himself] will be free to say that you have admittedly no say in whether half the novels studied shall be American ones since 1900 (for instance). I think it is very important for you to be an *all-round* Prof. of Eng. Lit., because in the coming years a defence of the whole stronghold will almost certainly have to be undertaken—though against whom I don't know.

I assume that you speak out of modesty when you want to limit your field, and haven't any positive advantage in view.

I should like to drop MA after both names; it is an absurd thing to boast of, though essential to the promotion; and we both got it late and by arrangement.

Yours sincerely
William Empson

TO CHRISTOPHER RICKS

As from: Studio House, 1 Hampstead Hill Gardens, NW3
3 August 1967

My dear Ricks,

Who was it said that the mind of Henry James was so fine that it could not be corrupted by an idea?[1] This seems so plainly what was the matter with Henry James that it should be followed up.

I have to have an operation for cataract next, a thing which was expected eventually but hurried on by the radio-therapy to prevent cancer. Terrifying I think, but it is considered routine. Any literary answers which could be read out to the blindfold man would be a great kindness; and come to think of it you probably know offhand a lot of answers.

What is the secret that Helen Gardner tells me she won't tell me, because I ought to know; a recent discovery about Rowland Woodward the scribe of her MS: 'W'?—but that I am afraid is only a riddle with no answer.

Who first in Europe said that the soul after death returns like a drop of water to the sea? Or for that matter in Asia either? Maybe Plotinus—I have been learning from Norman Cohn's book (old but recent paperback, and so it goes) that the idea is in medieval neoplatonism already.[2] But then, neoplatonism seems to include practically every idea that agitated their incessantly shaken brains.

---

[1] TSE, 'Henry James', *The Little Review*, 5 (Jan. 1918), 46: 'James's critical genius comes out most tellingly in his mastery over, his baffling escape from, Ideas; a mastery and an escape which are perhaps the last test of a superior intelligence. He had a mind so fine that no idea could violate it' (*Selected Prose of T. S. Eliot*, ed. Frank Kermode (1975), 151). Ricks wrote (6 Aug. 1967): 'it was Eliot who said of James (I quote from memory) that he had "a mind so fine that no idea could violate it". I'm pretty sure that the word is "violate", which is characteristically feline of Eliot, since one takes it that a mind shouldn't be *violated* by ideas (and yet that James's mind could have done with some intercourse, albeit not rape).' (*Houghton*)

[2] Apropos the 'single basic *corpus*' of the quasi-religion of the adepts of the Free Spirit, Norman Cohn writes: 'The metaphysical framework was provided by Neo-Platonism; but all the efforts which had been made, from Pseudo-Dionysius and Erigena onwards, to adapt Neo-Platonism to Christian beliefs were discounted. The pantheism of Plotinus, so far from being slurred over, was emphasized . . . It was the eternal essence of things, not their existence in time, that was truly God; whatever had a separate, transitory existence had emanated from God, but no longer was God. On the other hand whatever existed was bound to yearn for its Divine Origin and to strive to find its way back into that Origin; and at the end of time everything would in fact be reabsorbed into God . . . On the death of the body the soul disappeared into its Divine Origin like a drop of water which has been taken from a jug and then dropped back into it again, or like a drop of wine in the sea. The doctrine amounted of course to an assurance of a universal, though impersonal, salvation; and the more consistent of the Brethren of the Free Spirit did in fact hold that heaven and hell were merely states of the soul in this world and that there was no afterlife of punishment or reward . . .' (*The Pursuit of the Millennium: Revolutionary Millenarians and Mystical Anarchists in the Middle Ages* (rev., 1970), 172–3).

If my eye is spared, and I suppose if it isn't, I must settle down to do my next book, a collection of essays, fairly quickly. Odd bits of information need to be fed into it all the time, that is, they are wanted but not available.

Oh well, the troubles are good for the psychology up to a point, by removing neurotic guilt.

Hoping for a patient reply.

Yours affectionately

William Empson

TO CHRISTOPHER RICKS

Studio House
10 August 1967

My dear fellow,

I am sure you are right to step down and become Red-Brick; how tremendously plucky, though. But I can't find your letter at the moment; perhaps it meant you are becoming Professor at Bristol?[1] Anyway no doubt you will become a Redbrick Professor soon enough.

Sorry to hear that Eliot himself invented the crack about James; I would have preferred to blame some older figure. Going through Helen Gardner's notes to the Donne Elegies, I find she practically takes for granted that MS W was influenced by other editions (e. g. 'The Bracelet' l. 90 note—*who* made 'an attempt'?) so one needn't bother about the mystery.

I go into hospital next Sunday for my eye operation, very frightening but should be fairly quick.[2]

Hoping to *see* you.

William Empson

TO CHRISTOPHER RICKS

Studio House
11 August 1967

My dear Ricks,

I wrote you a letter and forgot why I had started. Yes, I looked up the *Listener* as you told me, and would otherwise have missed the first Karl

---

[1] Ricks was to be Professor of English at Bristol University, 1968–76.
[2] The operation for cataract in the right eye was carried out on 25 Aug.

M[iller] number [3 August 1967]. He seems to be doing all right. Thank you for answering John Fletcher, whom I have never met; but I expect a lot of them will go on repeating what you have refuted.[1] Why does he think it bad to be on the right side, I wonder? Or rather, I know why, but how would he defend it? It is a pity they are so mincing; I suppose because Leavis told them to be mature.

Norman Cohn *The Pursuit of the Millenium* traces the drop of water returning to the sea to neo-platonist tradition, though he doesn't give a decisive quotation. I think I asked you to trace it. Another attempt must be made to read Plotinus (if my eyes are spared) but he is so very self-indulgent, don't you feel?

Yours with thanks
William Empson

TO W. D. MAXWELL-MAHON*

6 November 1967

Dear Mr Maxwell-Mahon,

Thank you for sending me your thesis about my verse, which is now on its way to you by slow mail. I could not send it as soon as asked because of eye trouble; in fact for most of last month I was forbidden to read or write.

The jargon of modern literary criticism seems to me frightful nonsense, but I realise of course that your thesis had to be written in it. It is so remote to me that I am not at all sure how far we are disagreeing. What you call by the mystery-word Image, dragging a long train of false assumptions, I call a comparison. In *The Ants* for instance it occurred to me that the queer habits of these ants were like an unsatisfactory love-affair with a person revered but not understood (to which as a student I was sadly prone). I

---

[1] A review by Ricks, 'Mr Artesian' (pp. 148–9), discussed among other works a critical study *Samuel Beckett's Art*, by John Fletcher (1967): 'Dr Fletcher is an excellent exegete, but he ought to leave the polemical warfare to others: "William Empson, led astray by his zeal for the right cause, publicly complained, in the columns of the *Times Literary Supplement*, of the impertinence of this Catholic (*sic*) Irishman who subjected us to the unwholesome howls of his religious anguish; he even compared him to a dog run over in the street, disturbing the peace of a suburban night by his indiscreet screams of pain."

'Dr Fletcher is the one who's astray. Empson never said anything about Beckett's being a Catholic—he maintained, truly, that Beckett (like Joyce) has been affected by the fact that "in Ireland the religious training of children is particularly fierce." And Empson was right "even" to compare the anguish to that of a dog with a broken back ("a passer-by can only wish for it to be put out of its misery"). At any rate, the hero of *The Unnamable* is "dumb and howling to be put out of my misery", and he toys wittily with the phrase: "It's usually with sticks they put me out of their agony".'

described the ants, making the parallel as far as I could see it, but I did not feel I had to invent a human story in detail to fit it, at all points. The onset of neurotic (uncaused) fear seemed to me a probable result, worth making the start of the sestet. But I definitely did not mean to say that 'the self-conscious mind breeds thoughts from neuroses'. This would seem to me very gorblimey, very pretentious, partly because I doubt if it makes sense. You take for granted that it must be a Symbolist poem, but my poems are never that. The phrase 'worms dying in flower' in the *Letter* ['Letter II', l. 18] is an attempt at describing the final movement of the sparks when you burn a crumbled [*sic*] piece of paper (please light one and watch it); I had no idea of recalling what previous poets had said about glow-worms etc., and no wonder you find the poem in bad taste after you have insisted upon doing so. I daresay the language is rather too violent for the subject, another unsatisfactory student love affair, but they seemed to me upsetting enough at the time.

Your page 76; I think this final *Letter* ['Letter V'] really succeeds in conveying affection, much better than the others do; and I expect this is hidden from you only because you believe there aren't any other poems but Symbolist ones. A basic fact of this technique is that both author and reader have to pretend to be imbeciles, incapable of the real use of language, whereas not even a temptation to follow this nasty rule ever enters my mind. 'More intimacy for less hope'—less hope of getting to bed together, of course, what else?

80. ['To an Old Lady'] I thought I said in my note that the *sun* is not explained by the poem; it meant the traditions which I shared with my mother. The whole conception of the poem of course is that relations with Mum are compared to space travel, and I could not have objected to the use of 'the "sphere" image', even if such jargon could ever have passed my lips. 'But in darkness' etc. meant that you didn't realise what a strong support she was till you were in real trouble; I don't know why you call this 'relying on tradition for effect', but I presume you thought it meant something else. 87 I said my style had got too clotted, not that I had been trying 'to resolve experience by thought alone', and I would feel bitterly ashamed if I had talked such pompous gabble.

88 I still think *Bacchus* is my best poem, because the politicians and the drunks are compared through a long process, while they get worse. It is certainly not about 'an externalised Logos', and I do not understand why you refused to read the notes. I suppose just because they would have stopped you from reading it as a Symbolist poem. However, I am glad you prefer the later poems to the earlier ones. All the same, they did not preach

a system, and you are quite wrong on p. 98 in saying a remark about something else was meant to blame my own earlier technique. I appear a nastily furtive and tricky man when these intentions are ascribed to me; however, you do not make me look nearly so disgusting as the writers in The Review, which I could not endure to read.

99. Success was another love poem, and certainly not a lecture about my return from the East. After quoting 'Nor they nor I know what we shall believe' ['Success', line 18] it seems odd of you to complain 'the stimulus of uncertainty is lost'.

104 I think it simply *is* anti-Christian; why do you presume that is impossible? Because the profession of Eng. Lit. has become a farcically rigid convention, like being taught The Lancers when I was a little boy. That did not last long, though it seemed eternal at the time.

46 'The rule' ['High Drive', line 4] set by the required Phi tells you the movements of the waves in the swimming tank for all future time, but when the water becomes turbulent no such wave-function can be provided.

Derek Roper

TO CECIL WOOLF

The next letter was published, minus the first sentence, in *Authors Take Sides on Vietnam*, ed. Cecil Woolf and John Bagguley (1967), 27. The editors of the anthology—modelled on a famous antecedent, *Authors Take Sides on the Civil War* (1937), ed. W. H. Auden, Louis Aragon, and Nancy Cunard—posed two questions. (p. vii):[1]

'Are you for, or against, the intervention of the United States in Vietnam?

'How, in your opinion, should the conflict in Vietnam be resolved?'

[n.d. 1967]

Dear Mr Woolf,

Thank you for your letter. So far as I can make out, the Americans have no right at all to spread destruction in Vietnam; a U.S. airman who has

---

[1] In a Sheffield student periodical WE was asked about parallels between Vietnam and the Spanish Civil War: 'We ought to feel the same way but it's very natural not to. You see, if Franco won it seemed almost certain that he would join Hitler and close the Mediterranean. Once the Mediterranean had been closed this island would be very weak. It looked certain that Hitler would win. That was what Auden was always saying and what the Tories seemed to be madly blind to . . . Whereas Vietnam, though it's a world threat, it does seem easy to wash our hands of it. Just as we don't feel frightened now at the prospect of war in the intimate way you did when you were reading what Hitler had said. It was obvious that Hitler wanted a war. Nobody actually wants a war now. All the leaders know it's going to be disastrous if it happens' (*Arrows*, 92 (1967), 28).

wrecked a village with napalm there is just as much a war criminal as the accused at Nuremberg.

It is harder to answer your second question; how should the conflict be resolved? But reasonable proposals have been made, and are still being made. The essential first step is just for the Americans to stop doing evil.

Yours truly

William Empson

Sorry for the delay.

Berg

Authors Take Sides on Vietnam included 259 responses (out of an unspecified total number received). It was reviewed by the historian and presidential adviser Arthur Schlesinger, Jr. (who had worked during the Second World War for the US Office of Strategic Services), in 'Two Questions about Viet Nam', *Encounter*, 29: 6 (Dec. 1967), 73–8. As a contributor, Schlesinger declared his interest—'Since my own position is that we should slow down the war and strive earnestly for a negotiated settlement, it will not be surprising if I should find most wisdom in those who argue against both escalation and immediate withdrawal'—and proceeded to doubt the wisdom of writers who presumed to offer their political judgements ('writers can claim no special authority, privilege or immunity'); what was most alarming to him was that 'the book displays one clear and ominous current of opinion—a rising current of anti-Americanism, in the end almost genocidal in its implications.' He noted in addition: 'A number of writers demand a new Nuremberg. William Empson wants to punish American airmen who drop napalm. . .' (75).

ENCOUNTER 30: 2 (February 1968), 93: 'Authors & Ambiguity'[1]

[written 6 December 1967, from Studio House, London NW1]
I see that Mr Arthur Schlesinger, in your December number, reviewing a book *Authors Take Sides on Vietnam*, says 'William Empson wants to punish American airmen who drop napalm.' I said nothing of the kind. I said, 'A U. S. airman who has wrecked a village with napalm there is just as much a war criminal as the accused at Nuremberg.' The hypocrisy of approving both the bombing and the legal executions was plainly the target of this brief remark. I think that legal trial of the defeated enemy by the victors

---

[1] Robert Lowell would write to WE on 24 April 1968: 'I saw your little shot at Arthur Slesinger [*sic*] . . . Even these small things you do as no one else.' (*Houghton*; the misspelling of the name is silently corrected in *The Letters of Robert Lowell*, 500).

set a very bad precedent, and the part of it conducted in Tokyo undoubtedly had a disastrously opposite effect to that intended—the whole nation
admired the behaviour of the heroes who were being made martyrs,
otherwise they probably would have admitted that some of their
behaviour was bad.

Ever since *Encounter* was founded, I have noticed that its political contributors have great difficulty in opening their mouths without a lie hopping
out.

William Empson

[Arthur Schlesinger commented:] I should of course have known that any
statement by the author of *Seven Types of Ambiguity* was not to be taken on its
face; and I regret my misunderstanding of Mr Empson's remark.

HUDSON REVIEW, 20: 4 (Winter 1967–8), 534–8: [A Reply to Roger
Sale: 'The Achievement of William Empson']

Dear Sir:

I was delighted to find myself praised by Roger Sale,[1] and with such
eloquence and extravagance too, for what I would most hope to be praised
for, that is, for being large-minded and resisting the sordidity of modern
Eng. Lit. But the poor young man, I soon found, has been so corrupted by
his education that he can achieve this only at moments. He finds there is a
paltry side to Empson; naturally enough, as he has been taught to expect it
in all mankind. It is my happy duty to relieve him here, and I am sorry my
answer has had to be delayed. Empson is pure where he stands accused;
the consequences of the Fall are to be found only among his traducers.
Surely this will admit a gleam of sunlight into the Calvinist underworld.

I am very bad at correcting proofs of my own writing, always seeing
what I meant to write and considering whether it should be improved, and
in my first book (*Ambiguity*, 1930) I foolishly imitated Hazlitt in what
seemed a civilised practice, making incidental quotations as I remembered
them, which was sufficient for the purpose. The effect of the combination
was that a close study of an odd bit of punctuation in a poem would

---

[1] Roger Sale, 'The Achievement of William Empson', *Hudson Review*, 19: 3 (Autumn 1966),
369–90. In 1970 WE was asked by Christopher Norris and David Wilson: 'Roger Sale wrote
very well about *Some Versions of Pastoral* in *The Hudson Review* but you wrote a letter back, rather a
cross letter I think.' He responded: 'Yes, well, it was merely particular points that I felt I had been
misunderstood about. But often people think they're praising me, you see, when they say things
which I was brought up to believe were very wrong . . .'

sometimes appear with the punctuation wrong, and nearby there were evidently careless quotations. My paragraph would make nonsense until the punctuation was put right, and I struggled to do this as soon as possible, but my opponents were already saying that I had cheated; I had misquoted the text in order to make it fit my interpretation, they said, and they have continued to do so.[2] Now, in dealing with a long poem, I can see, one might be tempted to fudge a detail to fit an overall interpretation; but here I was dealing almost entirely with short lyrics. I was keen on explaining why they were so beautiful, and of course I was not interested in faking the text; almost any other form of our mortal frailty would then have tempted me more. And what I had written about the text did not apply to the erroneous version which had got printed. For years I have sometimes looked up the facts about these accusations, and they would always seem to me such obvious lies that I need not refute them. It has cured me of feeling any great reverence for textual scholars.

The next mortal insult given me by Mr Sale, a body blow, is intended by him as generous praise. He likes my not being such a fool as to believe in history, but just cracking jokes about it, like a real artist. An entirely disproportionate amount of harm was done to the American mind by the tour of Oscar Wilde in his costume, recommending the 'aesthetic' opinions he had derived from the French, the silliest whites in Europe; I felt

---

[2] De Quincey, in a review of Thomas Noon Talfourd's biography of Charles Lamb (1848), lamented what he called Hazlitt's 'habit of trite quotation . . . which places the reader at the mercy of a man's tritest remembrances from his most school-boy reading' (*The Collected Writings of Thomas De Quincey*, 5, ed. David Masson (1897), 236–7. Sale complained that WE had 'mispunctuated [TSE's] "Whispers of Immortality" so as to give the poem a reading not available to readers of the correct version'; and in general WE manifested an 'almost incredible penchant to be lax about details'. But Sale was not the first critic to arraign WE for his supposedly creative misquotations: notably in his discussion of the syntax of TSE's poem, in which (as WE claimed in *STA*, 79) the less obvious grammatical construction is insisted upon by the punctuation. However, as Robert Beare had explained a decade before Sale published his article ('Notes on the Text of T. S. Eliot: Variants from Russell Square', *Studies in Bibliography*, 9 (1957), 27–8), those particular ambiguous possibilities were licensed by the editions of TSE's poetry issued between 1920 and 1932 in which the relevant lines were mispunctuated; the mistake in the text was put right only in *Collected Poems 1909–1935* (1936). Two years after the appearance of Beare's authoritative article, Fredson Bowers, in *Textual and Bibliographical Criticism* (1959), derided WE's interpretative 'gaffe': 'The truth is that Empson studied Eliot, and spun his finely drawn theories about Eliot's literary art . . . from either the third or the fourth edition . . . [I]t was the faulty printer—and not the poet—who introduced the syntactical ambiguity that Empson so greatly admired and felt was the point of the whole poem. I should dearly like to know whether Eliot blushed, or laughed, when he read Empson on this poem and its non-existent point' (31–2). Quite apart from the fact that Beare does not attribute the mispunctuation to the printer (he says only that 'the poem was completely revised for the Knopf edition in 1920'), it is difficult to know why WE should have been accused of comical misconstruction when he had based his interpretation on the canonical collection *Poems 1909–1925* (1925). In sum, it was not WE who had misquoted Eliot, it was all the editions of TSE's poetry published from 1920 to 1932.

sure that a photograph must survive of Oscar Wilde in his costume meeting the chief citizens of St Louis, including a pale small T. S. Eliot dressed as Little Lord Fauntleroy, as was the custom of the period—the dates happen to make this social event impossible, but it retains a symbolic truth. T. S. Eliot as a young man was deliciously impudent, and this was recognised as charming; when English critics said he was trying to destroy English poetry, and at any rate Ezra Pound did oppose the ten-syllable line upon which it has been mainly based for at least six hundred years, he wrote an article saying that *he* was the real tradition and it took great labour, sometimes, to acquire. A history of some sort had to be fubbed up to support his 'tradition', but was sure to fall down at a touch. When I returned to England from communist China in 1952 I was frequently told that I obviously didn't know any history, so I have had to look into the evidence for the opinions I was taught at school, and I found every time that they stand up like a rock. Of course a lot of professional historians became neo-historians to suit this fashion, but they are getting a bit ashamed of it. The Whig Interpretation of History is the correct one, and it is remarkable that the book given that title offers no single reason to think otherwise, being merely a fashion report of some High Table giggles. Anything I print about the past, ignorant as I know myself to be, is intended as real truth about the past which I think worth fighting over.

The really black thing against me in the article is practically an insult to Old Glory, but while touching my cap I must try to put my case. You understand, my British colleagues have accepted nearly all the American literary revolution, and like you can hardly believe that anyone doesn't, but on its political side the line is harder for them to toe. Roger Sale says that I made a deliberately unfair aside in my book *Milton's God* about [Robert Martin] Adams' book *Ikon*, as a retaliation because he had exposed a lot of misquotations in my book *Pastoral*. My mind was then, when I wrote the sentence for my book, and is now when I defend it, concerned with advising Americans on a matter which I think urgently needs their attention. The village cracker-barrel, granting whatever merit it has in its place, gives them no help at all when they consider politics anywhere else, for example Cromwell's Commonwealth or modern Vietnam. Adams had written that he could not regard Milton as

> the frustrated anarchist, ignorant of his premises and terrified of his conclusions (which is the basic picture of Milton the liberal)

—so he is confident, we gather, that Milton must have been a sturdy Anglican Royalist like T. S. Eliot, though of course quite uninterested in politics. The most impressive fact about Milton, I think, is that three weeks before Charles II landed at Dover (when it was already certain that he would land) Milton printed a second edition of his 'Ready and Easy Way to establish a Free Commonwealth', telling the English to break England up into city states like ancient Greece, so that the King would have nothing to take over. This meant almost certain death by torture for Milton, who only escaped it by accident.[3] Adams has clearly been brought up not to know the basic facts about the matter, but I did not single him out there; I said 'like most Englishmen, I never know what Americans mean by a Liberal', and I said again, at the end of a brief tirade about this absurdity from Adams, that this kind of political confusion haunts American literary critics. I could list a series of such remarks by various Americans. It is true that Adams had listed some misquotations of mine in an article, and had insinuated that I had misquoted on purpose; but he was entirely justified in making corrections, and the insinuation I have had time to become accustomed to. With entire purity, my mind was shocked, when I read this wisecrack in Adams' book; the academic attitude to (say) Milton seems to me an impudent confidence that they can twist him into something usable to stop the kids from going Red. I am the more confident that I was right when I meet this loyal chorus from my American critics: 'He's sore, d'you see, on account of he's been shown up.'

The basic problems before Eng. Lit. in our two countries are much the same. Gross misuses of it for political and sectarian purposes are bound to crop up, and might destroy it; but with periodic sanitary efforts it can probably be got to continue in a sturdy, placid way, as is needed.

William Empson

> An undated draft version (Houghton) of the published letter gives a better account of what WE meant by claiming he could offer 'a series of such remarks by various Americans' (he may have withdrawn this last part when reminded that Constantine FitzGibbon was not an American).

Americans are a good deal out of line with Western as well as Eastern Europe, and as well as the rest of mankind, in assuming (verbally at least) that socialism is inherently bad, but naked individualism and competition good. Actually, you find splendid public works being done in the States, and the world's most spectacular operations of organised charity; but all

---

[3] See Masson, *Life of Milton*, vi. 187. David Ogg: 'Against Milton, proceedings were threatened because of the literary aid which he had lent to the Commonweath; these, however, were abandoned through the private intervention of Clarges, Morrice, and Annesley' (*England in the Reign of Charles II*, 2nd edn. (1956), i. 155).

this has to be treated as a kind of brothel which the President winks at. A satellite state is expected to keep more strictly to the basic rules of morality, which are (briefly) that God wants men to fight each other, and thus become manly. American young men think they *ought* to *try* to be wolves, because they know from their Darwin that sheep have very rightly failed to survive; thus you find whole rows of them giving the pathetic appearance of sheep trying to look like wolves. You do not find this elsewhere; it is one of the immediately recognizable things about an American. Americans who write biographies of modern European authors, though otherwise extremely good, regularly break down when they come to the political ideas of their subject. For instance, Richard Ellmann in his definitive biography of James Joyce can do nothing with the socialist conviction of Joyce except try to laugh it off, out of charity; but Joyce himself in his letters says very truly that this was what marked him off from the others in the movement, Ezra Pound and Wyndham Lewis and so on. The same with the splendid life of Dylan Thomas by Constantine FitzGibbon, who can understand and forgive anything else about Dylan Thomas except his going to Prague, a year after it had been captured by Communism, and fraternising, though he readily discovered that he only liked the unofficial poets, and finally shouted out 'I am a Communist, but am I also a bloody fool?' FitzGibbon says:

> If such pronouncements [as these] have any meaning at all, which is doubtful, it is surely that Dylan had no comprehension what[so]ever for politics as that word is normally understood.[4]

Normally in America, is all he can mean. By this time a majority of people in Eastern Europe agree with Dylan on the point, and ought to recognise him as a prophet. He avoided politics in his verse, but not because he didn't agree with the early Auden; and American readers who assume he agreed with Robert Frost must often be getting the words wrong. Well then, these are just two examples of great imaginative sympathy all round except for a complete drop at one point. It is hard for any of us to recreate the mental background of Milton the way we already know it for these modern figures; and when Mr Adams thinks he can understand Milton by one of these insanely isolated American folklore jokes, dating I suppose from the resistance to Prohibition, his language really does need to be viewed in a wider context. I had to say so, and the shape of my book did not allow me to do it at greater length.

---

[4] Constantine Fitzgibbon, *The Life of Dylan Thomas* (1965), 267. WE had reviewed the book in the *New Statesman*, 29 Oct. 1965, 647–8.

This is ugly and tiresome stuff to send in reply, but I have to make some reply; it must be rare for a critic to receive such lyrical and golden admiration. I hope that the generous good-will of Mr Sale may be able to survive the tribute of a patient answer.

Yours truly
William Empson

Roger Sale's response, in the same issue of *The Hudson Review* (538), included these comments: 'I too have a secret belief that the Whig Interpretation of History is nowhere near as bad as is sometimes made out. I do not see, however, how anyone who comes close to sharing my respect for the soundness and sanity of *Some Versions of Pastoral* could allow the Whig Interpretation to be called "the correct one." '

R. M. Adams (540) sought 'to enter demurrers to Mr Empson's two charges against him. I did not accuse Mr Empson of faking his texts to prove his point, and deeply regret that he has chosen to misinterpret me this way ... Stranger yet is Mr Empson's mistaking my view of Milton in the civil war: I am a neo-Marxist, not a high Anglican ... I was trying ... to steer a middle course between the Anglican Tory Milton who accidentally consorted with regicides, and the apostle of universal liberty who just happened to exclude Papists from toleration and proposed a permanent Grand Council not subject to electoral recall. Because I tried to dodge Mr Empson's Scylla, he now imputes to me a passion for Mr C. S. Lewis's Charybdis. In good old seventeenth-century phrase, I beseech him by the bowels of Christ to think it possible that he may be mistaken.'

TO IAN HAMILTON*

Department of English Literature, The University, Sheffield 10
11 June 1968

Dear Ian Hamilton,

Yes, I did use excited language [about 'William Empson Special Number', *the Review*, 1963], but you must remember I was trying to make a dint in a wall of invincible complacency. You and your pals carry on as if you were police officials investigating the activities of sneak thieves, and obviously the effect is that you very often fail to understand what you read. What struck me as filthy, while I turned over the pages and wondered whether to read the stuff consecutively, was the compulsive habit of imputing mean motives to any author under consideration.

There is a current theory that a critic must not commit 'the fallacy of intentionalism', that is, claim to know the intention of an author, and I notice that this rule is never invoked except for a quite simply dishonest purpose. The critic has already imputed a sordid intention to the author, and an opponent has offered straightforward literary evidence that the intention was a more poetical one. Immediately the howl is raised that no such evidence is permissible; only dirty intentions, such as are familiar to the critic, may be imputed. The habitual use of this drug, I should think, is enough to destroy any critical capacity, however initially good.

However, we must all of course try to live with our drugs, and I hope you make a success of it.

Yours sincerely

W. Empson

Houghton: typescript draft with autograph corrections; not posted, bMS Eng 1401 (569)

TO MICHAEL HOLROYD* [Augustus John: A Recollection]¹

6 December 1968

I came alone into a pub just south of Charlotte St., very near the Fitzroy Tavern but never so famous, and found it empty except for John looking magnificent but like a ghost, white faced and white haired . . . it was very long after he had made the district famous, and I had not expected to see anyone I knew. 'Why do you come here?' I said, after ordering myself a drink. 'Why do you?' he said with equal surliness, and there the matter dropped. I had realized at once that he was haunting the place, but not that I was behaving like a ghost too. It felt like promotion . . .

TIMES LITERARY SUPPLEMENT, 20 February 1969, 185:
'Swinburne and D. H. Lawrence'

Sir,—To answer Mr Singh's query (February 6): I meant the sadistic or masochistic passages in the first *Poems and Ballads* as what are frightfully good poetry though morally most undesirable. It is hard to list the best poems because they are so prone to internal collapse. For instance, the verse in *Dolores* about Nero fiddling while Rome burned:

> When, with flame all around him aspirant,
> Stood flushed as a harp-player stands,

¹ From Michael Holroyd, *Augustus John: A Biography*, II: *The Years of Experience* (1975), 185. Dr Holroyd tells me he has mislaid the full letter.

> The implacable beautiful tyrant
> Rose-crowned, having death in his hands

this is knock-down; but the rest of the verse, saying what an enormous noise the Emperor made, a thunder of lyres louder than the fall of buildings, is absurd in an equally decisive manner.

No doubt positive virtues in Swinburne, such as readiness to take a dare, are part of what the reader admires; and I do not expect that the verses do actual harm. I was devoted to them as a schoolboy, when I was being beaten rather too often; and it was quite clear to me that this literary taste did nothing to make me enjoy being beaten. (Can the poet really have been removed from Eton because he proved that he did? What a triumph it would be!)[1] But I cannot help regarding sadism very glumly, as the only perversion really deserving the name, and it seems important to get clear that one can appreciate the poetry without sharing the mental disease. All this, I think, has been familiar since the poems first appeared 100 years ago: I was only pointing out that our current orthodoxy has succeeded in blinding itself to quite large areas of English poetry.

Marking students does seem necessary, but marking the authors studied, as is done now with such immense self-satisfaction, feels to me odd. To the question 'Are sausages better than marmalade? Arrive at an evaluation', even the most expert chef could hardly say more than 'I prefer both, at breakfast, with the marmalade after'. Swinburne and Dylan Thomas were trying to do very different things. However, not to be too proud to join in a round game, I answer that I would mark Thomas rather above Swinburne, as I would sausages rather above marmalade; but then, I would mark Thomas pretty high.

William Empson [Sheffield, 8 February 1969]

TO DAVID PIRIE* (WE's collaborator on
Coleridge's Verse: A Selection)

> Studio House, Sat 19 April 1969; back in Sheff Monday

My dear Pirie,

It doesn't matter a bit about the delay in the letters; I had to finish off three articles after last term, on Donne and Ben Jonson and James Joyce, and they all took more time than expected (putting in the careless ease

---

[1] Swinburne claimed that five years of Eton left a 'swished youth' well able to cope with the 'Titanic flagellations' of the Marquis de Sade.

often amounts to discovering what the point of the whole thing was and rewriting it completely), so I couldn't have done much more about Coleridge, though I have done a little of the essential reading. I am to go and read poems in Dublin on the first of May. Some teaching still goes on till the 14th or so, but then we have a bit of holy freedom before marking. I am to be here for the dentist on the 16th. I hope you will pop over to Sheff before or after that.

What you say about the poem is very true, and I don't know who has said it before. Though Lamb said, I can't find where, that it had greatly horrified him.[1] How weakly optimistic my thoughts about the plot sound beside your massive survey of the incidents. But Coleridge *was* at the time optimistic about God and Nature and *would* assume he was making the incidents of his ballad hang together, making a story which had some point to it. His Unconsciousness very largely took the story away from him, and he must have been realising this, as well as too subservient to Wordsworth, when he cut out all the Gothic horror from the second edition. But I think we put ourselves in a bad light, or throw away an important part of our case, if we say that we print the first edition because it's a complete give-away, the opposite of what the author intended. I think he was struggling to put a good interpretation upon some acts of God, a thing he (at the time) often did when in quite prosy moods; and that the story, showing the intentions of the various spirits, was assumed to be what chiefly did it. [H. W.] Piper (of The Active Universe)[2] blames J. L. Lowes for being merely Imagist, and says Coleridge picked out Images which suited a purpose—he was 'trying to present a world through which the real world could be viewed with "visionary fondness" ' (p. 86). For him, the point of the Hand-of-Glory incident is that the good spirits are galvanizing the corpses, because they are electricity and Animal Magnetism; he doesn't expect or want it to have any point in the story. (Galvani had just published his discovery of the electric current, from the twitching of some frogs' legs hung up to dry for his supper, and the only surprising thing is that Coleridge uses it so little.) Clearly, one may react to a verse in an Imagist or a Symbolist or again in a Novelist manner; and nobody had told Coleridge he must not do this third thing—especially as he was in effect inventing the poems of Walter Scott. And he has already considered the interpretation before the first version is printed, showing that the

---

[1] See Charles Lamb's letter to William Wordsworth, 30 Jan. 1801, in *The Letters of Charles and Mary Lamb*, ed. Edwin W. Marrs, Jr. (1975), i. 266.
[2] See WE's review of H. W. Piper, *The Active Universe* (1963), *CQ* 5: 3 (Autumn 1963); *A*, 320–4.

corpses were not being possessed by their own ghosts; at least, this seems a fair deduction from

> Their souls did from their bodies fly,
>   They fled to bliss or woe:
> And every soul it passed me by
>   Like the whiz of my Cross-bow.

The second edition gives the clarification of the added verse 11. 345–9; the souls that fled in pain did not return. But it does not seem likely that this was a later invention. On this view, the unnerving detail of having the bodies start work again after the spirits have left them (and for what purpose? Can they mean to sail the ship away again?) urgently needs to be explained if it is part of the story; it was invented, I suppose, just as a yet more eerie twist, and then cut out because these explanations would be otiose. So here I still think we ought to follow the author's instructions; the feeling is sufficiently ambivalent (as you point out) without our having to throw hopeless bafflement into the story. And I don't think that restoring the first draft is open to this objection at any other point.

There is ample room for full discussion, as The Times used to say when the United Nations were totally at [? loggerheads].

P. S. Sunday. This seems a rather self-absorbed letter. Rude of me not to answer your kind invitation—I should be glad to come and spend a night with you in Manchester, and that might be more convenient, but I do think Sheff is better if one wants to be near open country.

The verse Coleridge wrote as a substitute on his 1798 text (between ll. 503–4 [*Poems*, ed. E. H. Coleridge, p. 205]) seems likely to have been written before Wordsworth scolded him and he promised to take out Gothic horror, since he doesn't cross out the Hand-of-Glory passage just before. He keeps the first line 'Then vanished all the lovely lights'— naturally, as they were signals for a boat to take off the Mariner, and the Pilot's boat had just appeared. This detail needs restoring in one verse or the other. He is keen to remark that these are good spirits, because he has just made them look particularly fiendish, and especially that they aren't ghosts, because the verse he is correcting was a slip-up there. If the bodies resume a zombie activity after the spirits have left them, either some other spirits have come or they are vampire-bodies (if Dracula wins the beautiful girls, as I understand, he will corrupt their souls; their own souls are what animate their bodies in the grave, which come out and corrupt other people by sucking their blood. I must check on this). Naturally it doesn't occur to him to deny they are angels, as that perversion is not yet in view, but he does want to avoid the mistake of evoking a wrong superstition. Of course I readily agree that his Unconsciousness had been running away with him there, but I think it a case where the author ought to be allowed to correct himself; that is only fair, so long as he is still writing the same poem and not under duress. If we allow that, we are in a stronger position for removing the other changes.

I hope I may use some of your letter with acknowledgements in my piece.

Of course, it is a regular feature of ballad style to repeat a whole incident with slight variations, and Coleridge might do it here without reflecting that it upset the plot.

P. S. Monday. It seems possible to make some deductions about his frame of mind from the order of the changes. When scolded unreasonably by Wordsworth for their joint bad reception he agreed to take out archaisms, Gothic horror, and technical terms from the 1800 version. But he had already written some proposed corrections on his 1798 text; these must be earlier when they change passages which 1800 excludes. I thought there were more. From the start, one would expect, he had been aware of alternatives which he was holding open, feeling artful about it probably; thus the corpses may be animated by angels or by their own ghosts, and the speaker may be allowed to make wrong conjectures, though Coleridge from the start was likely to want them to be neoplatonic spirits. The changes for the spectre ship (c. 190) seem meant to insinuate the connection with slave-ships a bit less obscurely.[3] The additions 'Fear at my heart,

---

[3] Cf. Patrick J. Keane: 'In 1961 Malcolm Ware ['Coleridge's "Spectre-Bark": A Slave Ship?', *Philological Quarterly* 40 (Oct. 1961), 589–93] tentatively identified the poem's spectre-bark as 'a slave ship'. In 1964 and 1972, William Empson described slavery as a concealed motif in *The Ancient Mariner*, a poem of 'adventure and discovery' that 'celebrates and epitomizes the maritime expansion of the Western Europeans.' But the triumphant advances of colonialism incur transgression and guilt, in turn epitomized in the horror of the slave trade, a horror which, earlier denounced in Coleridge's Bristol lectures, enters the poem with the arrival of the spectre-bark . . .

'Sounding rather like Karl Marx, James Joyce, and Ian Watt, all of whom pronounced the religious dimension of *Robinson Crusoe* a spurious afterthought, Empson in 1964 insisted that the Christian pattern of atonement-by-suffering was an excrescence, a theme essentially added by later Coleridge at the expense of blurring the poem's original socioeconomic context. That explains why, eight years later in their collaborative edition of Coleridge's poetry, Empson and David Pirie printed an "eclectic text", essentially though not quite the 1798 version of *The Ancient Mariner*, a poem closer to its original context and free of the prose gloss they thought a moralistic and distorting imposition.'

It is not necessary, says Keane, 'to accept [WE's] and Pirie's too surgical severance of early from later Coleridge. Nevertheless, working (as they do) with the 1798 *Lyrical Ballads* edition of the *Mariner*, I follow up on Empson's hints, both about the exclusion of overt politics and the intrusion of Christian conscience' (*Coleridge's Submerged Politics: 'The Ancient Mariner' and 'Robinson Crusoe'* (1994), 216–17). WE was alerted in Feb. 1965 to Ware's 'Coleridge's "Spectre-Bark" '. See also J. B. Ebbatson, 'Coleridge's Mariner and the Rights of Man', *Studies in Romanticism*, ii (1972), 171–206; and Peter Kitson, 'Coleridge, the French Revolution, and *The Ancient Mariner*', *Yearbook of English Studies* 19 (1989), 197–207.

as at a cup' (after l. 200) are known to be later than 1800. The only other one is the removal of 'Came back the ghastly crew' (between 503–4) for 'Then vanished all the lovely lights | The Spirits of the air, | No souls of mortal men were they, | But spirits bright and fair'. As soon as the Pilot's boat appears, the Hand-of-glory lights vanish; this line Coleridge keeps in his correction, though afterwards it went with the rest. The spirits were signalling for a rescue-boat for the Mariner, surely. The reason why he is so keen (at various points and dates) to insist that they aren't ghosts is that, as you so rightly say, they keep on behaving like ghosts or worse; but they must be allowed both ends of their swing. [. . .]

Houghton: carbon, bMS Eng 1401 (628)

TO DAVID PIRIE

[n.d. 1969]

My dear Pirie,

I have got out vol 2 of the Coleridge Notebooks, from which two points emerge that I wanted to report. By the way, Note 2937 remarks: 'Aeolian Harp motive for opening the sash; & at once lets in music & sweet air; purifies and delights'[1] — it is a great relief to hear that they *could* open the tiny windows in their stuffy rooms, and I hope you will report this detail to Gill.

The extra verse which I thought needed in the Ancient M. (of which you said 'Who decided that it is in Coleridge's handwriting?') turns up in Note 2880, with the other additions to that section invented on his travels; starting with the notice of the steersman's lamp on the third night out going to Malta.[2] Your metrical point, that it imputes a different rhyming

---

[1] See *The Notebooks of Samuel Taylor Coleridge*, ii: *1804–1808 Text*, ed. Kathleen Coburn (1962), entry 2937.

[2]
> With never a whisper on the main
> Off shot the spectre ship:
> And stifled words & groans of pain
> Mix'd on each trembling murmuring lip/
> (And) We look'd round & we look'd up
> And Fear at our hearts as at a Cup
>   The Life-blood seem'd to sip
> The Sky was dull & dark the Night,
> The Helmsman's Face by his lamp gleam'd bright,
>   From the Sails the Dews did drip/
> Till rose clomb above the Eastern Bar
> The horned moon, with one bright Star
>   Within its nether Tip.
> One after one, by the star-dogg'd moon,
>   &c—

(*Notebooks*, ii: *1804–1808 Text*, ed. Coburn, entry 2880).

scheme, is settled because he marks no verse divisions at all and the four
neglected lines had best be printed as a separate verse. I very much hope
you will allow it in the main text, though surrounded with a square
bracket; and I try to give the reasons in the proposed note below. This
would be the only time we use a square-bracket technique, I should think,
but that will show your splendid moderation; clearly a modern editor
ought to have it in reserve.

> The Sun's rim dips; the stars rush out:
>   At one stride comes the dark:
> With far-heard whisper, o'er the sea,
>   Off shot the spectre-bark.
>
> [With far-heard whisper, o'er the main,
>   Off shot the spectre-ship;
> And stifled words and groans of pain
>   Mix'd on each murmuring lip.]
> We listened and look[ed] sideways up;
>   Fear at my heart, . . .[3]

With far-heard whisper. Coleridge first wrote 'With never a whisper on the
sea', and this change does not appear till 1817. He is just reporting real
sailors' legends when he makes the magic ships move without wind, but
when he fills this out by supposing them to make no sound they become
too unimaginable; the hiss, heard from a distance, of their speed through
absolutely calm water, during the immediate nightfall of the equator, is
very imaginable. He would realise this on his own voyages, but he had not
yet applied it when he wrote the following additional verse, Note 2880,
estimated as Oct. 1806.

Each murmuring lip: he first wrote 'trembling', but the chief function of
the crew in the story is to curse the Mariner as they die. It is an echo-verse,
almost repeating the previous one, and Coleridge if he had used it in 1817
would clearly have repeated the correction to *far-heard* (otherwise he would
contradict himself) so an editor who revives the verse must do it for him.
The crew cannot speak, as they are too near death from thirst, but we
heard them hiss as the ghost ship brought hope of water, and we expect
another sound from them as it departs insolently refusing life; the echo
technique of the ballad demands it. Besides, we need a recall to their
reactions before we enter the next verse, in which they wait tensely all
night till the waning moon rises, with the steersman always ready to sail in

---

[3] Cf. WE's introd. to *CV*, pp. 51–4; text, pp. 128–9; Pirie's Notes, pp. 229–35.

the right direction if ever a cup of wind comes, and then die, still dumb but now able to curse the Mariner through the moonlight glittering in their eyes. The only reason one can imagine why Coleridge left out the verse is that, making his corrections in a hurried shuffling way as ever, he could not find the note-book when he copied out the rest from memory. Just possibly he had come to think the ballad echo technique too childish for him, but if so it was a wrong judgement which an editor should ignore.

The steersman's face—lit at night so that he can see the compass; the story is placed at the start of the modern world, with the introduction of the mariner's compass. Coleridge realised the importance of this detail about three nights out on his voyage to Malta (Note 2001, April 1804), a time when he had begun to play the part of the figure he had imagined, at first almost as a comic one.[4] *The dew did drip*: Another detail observed on the voyage, and shockingly wrong for the story; surely the mariners would have enough sense to drink this dew, which could have saved their lives? But there would only be enough to save one or two of those 300 lives; perhaps the Mariner, always the only inventive mind on board, really did lick up all the dew, and it explains the mystery of his survival? Probably Coleridge did not realise that the drip would be fresh water; what he needed it for, and had experienced when he wrote, was the terrible sense of time to wait while a drip marked out the seconds. The detail is slightly bad, but an editor would be wrong to leave it out, weakening the immense consecutive detail of the whole sequence.

I know you have your reputation to consider, as a serious textual editor, and I have not, but in this sequence the introduction of one verse only, in a square bracket, could not be presented as to your discredit. It would brighten up the general tone of the edition a great deal, as a positively bold (thought slight) action done for the beauty of the poem.

Having to coax you so earnestly on this detail makes me appreciate how odd the rules are when I must next beg you to behave with bare honesty when you copy out a line from the Oxford edition,

And my heart mantles in its own delight.

I assumed you had read it in Notebooks II, but your answers made me wonder whether you had read the context, and then I found the

---

[4] 'SICKLY Thoughts about M. mort. [. . .] Light of the Compass & rudderman's Lamp reflected with forms on the Main Sail' (*Notebooks*, ii: *1804–1808 Text*, 1962, entry 2001). Kathleen Coburn notes of the notebook entry: 'cf "The stars were dim, and thick the night, | The steersman's face by his lamp gleamed white"; *The Ancient Mariner* 206–7, lines not in the early versions of the poem, but first added in *SL* [*Sibylline Leaves*] (1817)' (*Notebooks*, ii: *1804–1808 Notes* (1962)).

line quoted (rather dishonestly I think) in the Oxford edition. It is Note 2990:

> I languish away my Life in misery, unutterably wretched from the gnawings of the Disease, and almost equally miserable by the Fear of the Remedy.

[Incomplete]

Houghton, bMS Eng 1401 (628)

TO ROBERT BURCHFIELD*

On 5 July 1969 WE wrote to R. W. Burchfield, editor of the *Supplement* to the *OED*, to ask why the dictionary did not record the use of the verb *possess* as meaning 'a man mastering a woman'?

Burchfield responded (14 Jul.) that surprisingly the Oxford collections included as yet no quotations in illustration of this sense of the verb, although (as he was to explain in a later letter) the work of revising the dictionary had not yet got to the letter *P*. (The first volume, covering A–G— was to appear in 1972; H–N in 1976; and O–Scz only in 1982.) The best he could offer in the meanwhile was an example given by Farmer and Henley in their *Dictionary of Slang and its Analogues* (1902), v. 261:

> 1620 MASSINGER AND FIELD *Fatal Dowry* III. i, *Beaumelle.* Do you come ... to set down, to a lady of my rank, Limits of entertainment? *Rom.* Sure a legion Has possest this woman!

Department of English Literature, The University, Sheffield
19 July 1969

Dear Mr Burchfield,

Thank you very much for your letter. I hope to hear more.

It seems as well to point out that the quotation you have found for me does not prove much, because the joke makes a pun on two uses of the word *possessed*. The man in the Gospel who was called Legion because he had many devils is I should think intentionally recalled.[1] This may well be how the sexual meaning arose, but even so the joke might be familiar for some time before the sexual meaning became independent.

I can give a reference with the opposite sexual meaning; a lady in waiting says 'I want to possess him at dawn, under a sky striped with green', and the heroine reflects 'If she really loved him, she wouldn't

---

[1] Mark 5: 1–20; Luke 8: 26–39; Matt. 8: 28–34.

bother about the weather' (*The Flower Beneath the Foot*, Ronald Firbank, 1928?)[2] It would be interesting to find early examples of this use too.

Yours with thanks

William Empson

OUP Archive

TO PHILIP HOBSBAUM

2 August 1969

Dear Hobsbaum,[1]

Mrs Baehl [English Literature Department Secretary] told me that you had called in your copy of your Thesis, evidently to prepare it for publication, and I had been feeling before that I ought to write you a final appeal not to return to the vomit of your previous training; besides, I want to reconsider the matter, and the end of term is a convenient time.

What is wrong with your whole position, I still believe, stems from the self-blinding theory that a critic is never allowed to gauge the author's Intention. I must not make extravagant claims for a process which all persons not insane are using in all their social experience; I have only to say that the effects of renouncing it (in the unique case of the most delicate and intimate formulations of intention) produces dirty nonsense all the time, with a sort of tireless unconscious inventiveness for new kinds of nonsense.

Above all, it means that you can never get out of the circle of rival colleagues and consider the matter freshly, as it would have appeared to the author (authors of earlier times being necessarily free from our

---

[2] Olga Blumenghast tells Rara de Nazianzi of her passion for Ann-Jules:

Mademoiselle Blumenghast clasped her hands brilliantly across the nape of her neck.

'I want to possess him at dawn, at dawn,' she broke out: 'beneath a sky striped with green . . .'

'Oh, Olga!'

'And I shall never rest,' she declared, turning away on a languid heel, 'until I *do*.'

Meditating upon the fever of love, Mademoiselle de Nazianzi directed her course slowly towards her room. She lodged in that part of the palace known as 'The Bachelor's Wing,' where she had a delicious little suite just below the roof.

'If she loved him absolutely,' she told herself, as she turned the handle of her door, 'she would not care about the colour of the sky; even if it snowed or hailed!' (Ronald Firbank, *The Flower Beneath the Foot* (1923); in *Five Novels* (1949), 17.)

[1] 'There is a truly alarming letter a dozen pages long, or so it seems in recollection, consisting of an analysis of my character and literary theories—both fairly adverse—and our correspondence ceased after that, though there was no quarrel: indeed, a year later we both got plastered in the Sheffield Staff Club arguing about "The Ancient Mariner". However, on reflection, you may find the letter of more interest to my biographers than to Empson's!' (Hobsbaum, letter to JH, 27 Jun. 1985).

technical jargon). What you are offering is a recipe, for the unfortunate man who has fallen into the trade but knows he has no judgement, so that he can back the safest horse. Take the introduction to Blake *Songs of Experience*, where you lay out the range of opinion with confident expertise. I can understand, reading the chapter, that you did not want to throw it away merely because you learned that all these chaps had been wrong from the start; but think how immensely cheering it will be for the reader of the book if you let him know that, as the chapter ends. You have done your work impeccably just the same. The question is about

> Whose ears have heard
> The Holy Word
> Who walked among the ancient trees

and I kept telling you that this meant the Son (always good in Blake) not the Father (at this time bad). Milton in *Paradise Lost* makes the Son walk in the Garden of Eden and meet our parents just after their Fall, so that Blake certainly knew about it, though anyway it was a standard Christian interpretation of the passage in Genesis. All these professional experts, who assume that God the Father could be described as the Logos, are just ludicrously ignorant. I have found since that Kathleen Raine makes the point decisively, in her writing on Blake, and I wish I had remembered where I had got this argument from, because then you might have been convinced by her authority.[2] Not being allowed to consider intention makes you slavish to a shocking degree, but perhaps I could have convinced you there if I had done my work better.

I notice that when you pronounce on this matter of Intention you habitually say 'Never in all my experience have we found . . .' (that considering the author's Intention does any good); well, of course you couldn't find anything, because whenever the right solution depended on doing that you remained boastfully and farcically ignorant. Habitually imputing bad or petty intentions, with a shameless disregard of your official theory, is the next step, and in my experience nearly all the addicts take it.

Your Thesis clearly rated a Ph. D. for its collection of relevant information, and as an examiner I could not defend my own writing; but I still consider that you libelled me grossly. Thus you profess to be gravely 'disturbed' (picture of Hob sobbing because he has caught an opponent out)

---

[2] Kathleen Raine, *Blake and Tradition*, ii (1969): 'The idea of the universal or heavenly man, and especially the doctrine of Christ as the Logos, existing eternally in heaven, as creator of the cosmos, is an integral part of the orthodox Christian teaching' (194).

because I and many others (p. 362) make 'a distinction between the affect-
ive and referential modes of language'. I thought that Richards had made
a slightly wrong distinction in this area, and the section which you pillory
by a footnote is intended to restore the unity which you defend. What
Richards and I both recognized was that analysis must be able to say when
language is used dishonestly, as when a demagogue attempts to cheat his
hearers by exploiting the emotive uses of words so as to prevent them from
following up the referential uses. Such is the habitual procedure of the
author Hobsbaum, and no wonder he disapproves of any exposure of his
technique, just as Father Leavis forbids the reading of parody. Hobsbaum
screams out to his audience: 'What hogs my opponents are! Why, they
actually pee. I never pee.' How readily one can imagine the exhausted but
satisfied Hobsbaum, after the curtain has fallen amid continued roars of
applause, saying modestly: 'Well, of course, it isn't difficult really; they just
like a man who is prepared to make a firm statement.'

I thought highly of the poem about ancient bards ['The Bards'] by
Sidney Keyes (p. 116), where the critics you survey are students taking an
A-level exam. Some of them (as you report) understood what the poem is
about, but this gave you no help, because you are tied hand and foot by
your lunatic theory. Naturally your marking of the answers would be
frightfully unjust. The broad middle-brow public is sharply cut off from
you and your pals here, because they like a poem which can be read like
short stories (and like a song too, but the feeling that Betjeman has packed
in a story is what makes him a bestseller). The bard of the poem (as history
would demand) is not an aristocrat brought up to use expensive weapons
but a plebeian who happened to go blind so that he had no other means of
livelihood but to train as a poet. He has to imagine and praise deeds and
virtues which are greatly against his own sympathies, let alone his experience. But he is proud that he has become a professional man, and really
can praise warriors with a splendour obvious to every listener in the hall.
Yet at the bottom of his mind there is a searing hatred of the men he has
to praise, even while he is jealously proud of the quality of the poetry
which expresses it. This poem, you see, is actually about the astonishing
powers of men to intuit one another's intentions. The bard knew exactly
how the warriors felt, that was why he succeeded as a poet, and Sidney
Keyes (a wartime conscript who was being carried to his death when he
wrote) knew exactly how bad the bard felt in a situation which might have
appeared preferable to his own. Everybody around Hobsbaum can do
Intentionalism, the kids he is examining, the new poet they are being
examined about, the old one he is describing—well, of course they all can,

it is very fundamental. But Hobsbaum can't, because it is forbidden by his dirty theory, and so all the kids who wrote good answers got bad marks, and Hobsbaum ought not to be allowed to do A-level marking. Really, that is what you prove by the Keyes section of your thesis.

Here the whole situation seems to me laid out as in a novel, but I cannot feel clear about 'The Group Approach to Criticism' in chapter 10. It is splendid to have the tape recording, but I expect most readers will feel as I do that it is too hard to understand why Father Hob always won, or at least always said the bang at the end. What can be the point, too, of their always talking in such a gorblimey high-minded manner, where their whole poetic technique consists of saying the nastiest things that their sheltered lives have provided for them as bleakly and rudely as possible? I am very glad that this ugly movement is already out of fashion, and the self-righteousness of its internal discussion only leaves me astounded. Surely their 'discussions' cannot be supposed to prove anything, because what they need all the time is to hear any other voice. The voice of the Master emerges as totally self-enclosed; uniquely safe against imagining the mental processes of anyone else and thus committing the Fallacy of Intentionalism.

Such being my general background impression, I feel a deep interest in your report on *King Lear*; it does seem a case which needs your police-dossier approach. I do not of course feel sympathy for a scholarly technique designed to tell an aspirant which is the safest herd to join, and your claim that the play is not worth Hob's attention unless it is holy enough for Hob strikes me as eerie. But in this case the movements of critical opinion are plainly worth separate study.

You say as I understand that my view of the play makes it 'a piece of nasty and irresponsible trifling, brutality for its own sake' (p. 292). I was relieved to hear you making this objection with such moral rigour, because such is the way I have long thought of your own poems, and those of your whole critical school. While I was emerging from a series of eye operations I was kindly allowed an extra machine to turn on the Third Programme in hospital, and was confronted by a whole programme by George MacBeth of readings from his Christie school, including yourself. This was good luck, as I do not normally hear the machine. The programme seemed to me pettily and wilfully disgusting, and you can hardly have felt more nausea and contempt than I did then when you read my chapter on *King Lear*. The first Shakespeare audiences, you see, assumed that they were being given a warning; 'we will be able to avoid this now,' they felt, 'we have been fairly warned.' But the Christie school gives a random impression, not one of broad avoidable causes. This does not make it any more 'spiritual'.

You give a list on p. 271 of the range of critical opinion about the death of Lear, and I come in as the final 'e', blank despair. I made the death of Lear (a) a moral conclusion to the play (because it is a warning) and (c, d) a happy illusion which saves Lear further pain. It seems to me that you are frightened of getting any opinion from your new machine which does not express a centrist position within current academic fashion. As usual your dilemma arises because you are forbidden to consider what the author intended; he intended to give his audiences a severe shock, which they would none the less accept after reflection as true, chiefly because it was like real history, but also because it was already in the Book of Job. There must have been a lot of painful work for him in arriving at an actable version, in which he would again and again have to decide 'Does this truncated version express it enough? Can the audience still get it the way I meant?' Surely a theory that the scholarly critic must not admit to knowing this is mere farce?

You assume that the taste of the words on the page is all that the scholarly critic may consider, because the author did not *intend* to give him anything else; but how would you explain this theory to Shakespeare, before he had permitted the words to be printed at all? This print-centred or tea-tasting outlook, it seems clear, is what you are preening yourself upon when you write 'the tide of hope is strong in the actual verse', and with busy sarcasm 'It is easy enough to read all the hope and vitality out of the lines once one gets far enough away from them'—also to read it in, once you are far away enough from the intended theatre. *Never* five times repeated does express a residual vigour, but to pretend that it expresses hope is farce; when Lear says that if Cordelia lives it will outdo all his sorrows that sounds to you (alone with your scholarly page and your buttered crumpets) like a 'spiritual' hope, but to an audience interested in the political events of the story it could only convey a last twist of exasperation. This horrible nastiness of Eng. Lit., which makes the teachers preen themselves on being too smart to attend to the story (so that they can tell any holy lie they choose instead) must I think derive from the short-story technique of Chekhov, though he would have been astonished and exasperated by it. The first audiences must have been capable of taking the story as real and true, or Shakespeare would not have presented them with a shock which they regarded as a falsification of history, and most later generations have found intolerable—till the recent invention of 'reconciliation'. I think in fact that modern critics are miles away from what

Shakespeare intended his audiences to get, which was what his first audiences did get, and that no adequate literary experience can be expected from the play until that can be recovered.

I hope you will read *King Lear and the Gods* by G. R. Elton before your book comes out. It explodes the neo-Christian claim that the first audiences could only impute pious meanings to the play all along, in a very boring way most of the time, collecting the background; but this is important because arguments of this historical sort are what have produced a wide acceptance of the views which you say you intuit by just staying close to the words on the printed page. The basic trouble of the purely literary training is that it makes the students bad at estimating a case like this.

For one thing, it gives no idea of the probabilities of the story. The first audiences considered that dividing England was very likely to produce civil war, and avoiding that was about the most important thing; and Lear and Cordelia would simply be *likely* to get killed in the confusion, even if their side won. In ordinary life, people are always having to act on uncertainties, calculate the risk; but you secure boys with your words on the page just scold away after the results are in.

You keep saying that the 'value' of the play lies in the 'reconciliation' of Lear and Cordelia (p. 289, say), and this is just as good if it happens unconsciously after they are dead (p. 272). This false sentiment is miles away from the play. They could not be more reconciled than they are when crying and kneeling to each other, but while they do this the text keeps insisting we should hear the drums of the approaching army which will kill Cordelia, because her father has not looked after her properly, the audience is to reflect. She makes clear that she is just being patient with him, realising he is deluded, so you have not much ground for trying to brighten the scene by expecting her to commit incest with him. You express contempt for some critic who said the play outrages our instincts; well, the accidental death of Cordelia was intended at least to outrage normal expectation in the theatre, and did, till the critical inventions of this century. When you start prating that Lear as a result 'wins through to an order' you make me ashamed of my profession. *What* order, for God's sake, can you extract from his few desperate words? Does Leavis take this peculiarly nauseous line too? I wouldn't know.

By the way, you really shouldn't go into print saying that 'No, no life?' proves that Lear dies making a query about life; Elizabethan printers regularly used the query mark where we use the shriek mark, and that is obviously all they mean here. You can go into print arguing otherwise, but not betraying mere ignorance. And when you write (p. 291): 'It is true that we should think worse of Lear if he had continued to be a non-attached Yogi; but Danby had given excellent reasons . . .'—well, [John] Danby had said it earlier, but you contrive to present this as if it proved Empson was wrong.

I am keen to write down what I meant by saying that 'Lear has got on the wrong side of the next world as well as of this one'. It seemed to me that I was summing up the views of other critics which I had already fully expounded. He wanted to prepare his soul for death while yet retaining 'all the additions of a King'; he wanted to 'give all' but so that he could take back anything he liked; and in order to do this he divided England between his daughters, which the audience would regard as sure to produce civil war. This is the moral meaning; but the obvious meaning is as plain as Punch. Whenever he prays for anything, or anybody else prays on his behalf, exactly the opposite happens at farcical speed. A critic who doesn't even know this much is refusing to read the play at all.

There was an odd detail where you remark that what I say about *Tom Jones* and what a Chicago Aristotelian [R. S. Crane] says do not seem to be about the same book, and the reader is clearly meant to deduce that Empson is wrong. The Germans began to interpret English Literature around 1780, and they have sometimes been right about it, but the English have always considered them farcically wrong. The American university tradition is crushingly German. I should feel considerable fear that I must be wrong if I found myself agreeing with this author. In short, the authorities you have now decided to trust as safe ones appear to me sinking or sunk already, and your own spiritual condition, upon which you appear to plume yourself in the book, impressed me as a record low even for you. Well, this is too hopeful. But such a bad and narrow fashion can't last for ever. I hope you will not boast of being my pupil any longer without admitting that I think all your present opinions harmfully and disgustingly wrong.

Yours very sincerely

William Empson

You know, it seems to me you are unusually bad at estimating other people's intentions, below normal there in fact, so that nursing a sheer theory you needn't even try at it is shockingly bad for you.

TO DARCY O'BRIEN*

Alongside WE's 'The Theme of Ulysses' was a piece by a young scholar named Darcy O'Brien, 'Joyce and Sexuality', *20th Century Studies* 2 (Nov.

1969), 32–8. O'Brien lost the letters he received from WE; nonetheless, he would recall, twenty years on (letter to JH, 29 Mar. 1989):

> Apparently my argument that Joyce retained a strong streak of Irish Catholic schoolboy puritanism and sniggering toward sex (I feel if anything more strongly about this now than ever) touched a raw Empsonian nerve . . .
>
> While I was of course pleased to receive a personal letter from Sir William (I was but 29 years old at the time . . .) . . . I was shocked by what I recall as a rather vituperative tone on his part. I remember well that he said something to the effect that I ought to be a 'Californica- tor'. This was the kind of remark, I remember, that only someone ignorant of the hideousness of the so-called 'sexual revolution' in Cali- fornia could utter. He seemed to be reproaching me, I thought, from some far-off British/Lawrentian shore, full of clap-trap about sexual liberation . . . I confess . . . that I read his letter as the ravings of a randy old man. I was afterwards informed, I don't know how reliably, that Empson himself was living in a ménage à trois arrangement—if true, this made sense of his advocacy . . . Autobiographical, in a word.
>
> I replied to him, however, with all the deference and respect he certainly deserved. I believe I said in my defense only that I thought perhaps I understood Joyce's Irish Catholic background better than he, Empson did. I also said that I thought he was trying to read ULYSSES as an English novel—with a proper ending and so on—which it is not. (By 'proper' I mean *formally* tidy.) The idea of Stephen Dedalus in bed with Molly Bloom seemed as ludicrous to me then as now . . .
>
> None of this detracts from my admiration for Empson and many of his writings. I think he was a rather noble figure . . .

Darcy O'Brien, Centre for Advanced Study,
912 West Illinois, Urbana, Illinois 61801
[n.d.: February/March 1970]

Dear Mr O'Brien,
Thank you for your interesting letter.

Joyce wrote, about Prezioso (Ellmann p. 457): 'The motive from which I liberated myself in art he is unable to liberate himself from in life', and you say this is the 'homosexual' desire to share a woman, shown by Richard in the play [*Exiles*]. But the desire to cuckold a friend, in the play, was *opposite* to the desire of the husband to share freely. Joyce must have meant some- thing different. Ellmann seems to me right (p. 328) in saying that Joyce had led P. on, so he is anyway being sanctimonious here and likely to distort things. I think his next sentence tells decisively against your interpretation; a feature of his wife's dream, he says:

is a secret disappointment that for her *so far* it is impossible to unite the friendship of two men through the gift of herself differently to both[;] for that which seemed possible in the first case is almost impossible in the second case.

My italics for *so far*; in the notes for *Exiles* he also says that the woman wants this arrangement, though in the play she appears bewildered by her husband's wishes; here too he is pretending that his wife wants what *he* wants—so I think, but anyway there is no trace of blaming her for wanting it. P. already had a rich elderly wife, and this would make the plan 'almost impossible', so there had been an earlier 'first case' now lost to history.[1] The first case must have happened after the lie of Cosgrave in 1909; his crisis of feeling over that set his mind to work on the subject. If he is *inadequate* for Nora, can there be some arrangement he would find endurable which would make her satisfied? I do not think you have any right to speak of this movement of thought as either contemptible or insane, and I think Ell. writes very insensitively in seeing no difference between what horrified Joyce and what, after reflection and inquiry, attracted him.

Indeed, the notes for *Exiles* show him trying to get abreast of a current trend. Proust writes in the same way about possible arrangements for such a case (when the loved person cannot be given up, but demands another outlet—an *entirely full* report would be the only way to assuage jealousy); as the two writers are so different, this goes to show that the topic was in the air. I gather that the happy purr of the contented triangle was in real life a very familiar sound in the Edwardian drawingrooms, but the theme was rigidly excluded from novels, in which all triangles had to be presented as torture. Joyce would at once realise that to break this taboo was a central part of his business, but his temperament made the duty a hard one to carry out. The obstacle does not spoil *Ulysses*, where the ideal is kept on the horizon; but in *Exiles* he obviously does not know what he is talking about, how Robert would react, especially.

[You say it can only be out of diseased psychology that Bloom offers his wife to Stephen because he also enjoys being cuckolded by Boylan; but there the automatic arousal is a kind of torture, whereas with a man he liked it could mean happiness.]

I don't deny that, by the time he started FW [*Finnegans Wake*], he had lost hope of making such an arrangement; and with his usual self-righteousness may have 'rejected any rationalization' of the desire (though

---

[1] *Marginal note*: Joyce would be unlikely to find any case really possible.

I think that such language is weaselly double-talk). That indeed is why FW is so dismal and flat. But Joyce might well have admitted that neither he nor his wife had the temperament, and anyway they had got too old for it, without any ratting on his previous ideal. I daresay that adding the Jew-baiting song by Stephen to the Q and A chapter marked a realization that this particular triangle could never have got off the ground. All the same, the possibility of it is what gives the book its horizon or vista—there is an immense coming-together of the themes when you realise what they all amount to is this quite prosy, rather sordid, but practicable offer. Without it the book is just boring nonsense, a self-indulgence by the author.

I felt this very much when reading your essay—how could you list so complacently the failure and meanness of Bloom's emotional life without ever recognising his cries of hope for escape from it? What merit can you see in the book you describe?

Yours, WE

—The most interesting part of his letter, on second thoughts, is that he knew all about the issue; though anybody reading his article would suppose it known. All the other perversions and romps of Bloom are listed, a paltry crew, but what matters to Bloom himself in the book is hushed up. Joyce had repented of it, and no longer wanted the pleasure for himself—therefore it should be hidden from the children, though for Bloom itself *[sic]* it is the centre of the story (and till recently had been for Joyce).

Houghton: notebook draft, bMS Eng 1401 (615)

TO G. S. FRASER*

Department of English Literature, The University, Sheffield S10 2TN

16 February 1970

Dear George,

I have been reading Moore's book about [Louis] MacNeice, and am willing to recommend it to a publisher. But it is surely too much of a thesis; it needs cutting a good deal, and livening up if possible.[1]

I couldn't write an introduction for it because it is too pro-Christian; there is quite typical praise of Louis at one point for not becoming a Communist when his friends were doing it—his balance and good sense and all—but he is regularly blamed for not 'achieving belief' in the

---

[1] D. B. Moore's monograph *The Poetry of Louis MacNeice* was to be published by Leicester University Press, 1972.

Torture-Monster of Christianity (the Father, you understand) and this weakness is found to spoil many of his poems. One has to admit Louis rather asked for this, because he used Christian language when reflecting about the mystery of life in general (that is why I think the book relevant enough to be publishable) but I don't find its complaints at all illuminating. Louis is also told that he was quite wrong to think that a poet ought to be a journalist, and that was another thing the matter with his poems. In short, the thesis reeks of the blinkered sectarianism of the Eng. Lit. classroom, and some of this could be removed before publication. But I think Louis deserves to have books about him, after all.

With thanks

William Empson

Where do you want me to send the text? I had better wait till I hear from you about the recommendation.

Edinburgh

TO DAVID PIRIE

1 May [1970]

My dear Pirie,

Thank you for your long letter of April 15, which I ought to have answered before; except that it called for a mulling over of my whole position, and I have been poking about again in the Letters and Notebooks etc. (finding a number of mistakes in my draft, but nothing I think that can't be corrected); also, I had been commissioned to give an essay on Donne to an American Symposium, and this (for the rest of the holiday, though I haven't finished it, and must by early next month) is what I have been doing instead of trying to arrive at a rapid decision.[1] However, this week I have come back to our problem, feeling fresher about it (Coleridge does seem to me a particularly unpleasant author to try to put oneself in sympathy with, though Donne of course was mangled by the same mill), and I now report my position.

The literary question, of the value of adding the verse ['With far-heard whisper . . .', at lines 221–5 of *CV*], should come first but can hardly expect finality. The biographical question, whether the decision of the author of the 1817 edition can carry any weight, seems to me much easier to decide. As to the practical question, whether you would lose too much

---

[1] 'Rescuing Donne', in *Just So Much Honor: Essays Commemorating the Four-Hundredth Anniversary of the Birth of John Donne*, ed. Peter Amadeus Fiore (1972), 95–148; *ERL* (1), 159–99.

credit by agreeing with the old man on this one detail, which you recognise as a minor factor, I think you have already stuck out your neck so far that being consistent at this point really cannot make it worse. But let us in every possible way record your reluctance, your consciousness of killing the Albatross and so forth, so long as we print the missing verse *as part of the text* though *with whatever form of scholarly qualification*. Of course, however, you will refuse to do this if you continue to think that the added lines spoil the poem; which must be the first matter to discuss.

You say that repetition is only used in this poem to mark slowness, whereas the sailing away of the ghost-ship and the fall of night are immediate. Well, so the poet says, but nobody is going to believe him; watching a ship go off to the horizon, even a speed-boat, and watching night fall are always ruminative because gradual processes; and the chief merit of these later changes has been to make incidents imaginable to the reader experienced in ocean sailing. Coleridge liked the idea of having no twilight in the tropics, and was exaggerating it in an elegant gloss too late for the 1817 (I agree) but he would be bound to know that there are sunsets in the tropics. I mean, that they take an appreciable time. The idea that night fell and made the ghost-ship *invisible* 'too quick for groan or sigh' seems to me just the type of incredible detail which he was now trying to avoid. I must say I hadn't noticed that in the first edition, with '*While clomb* . . . the horned moon', he did not think of the portentous moon as enclosing a star but did think of it as rising with the departure of the ghost-ship. I had accepted what that illustrated American edition tells us about the behaviour of the moon—that he must have a waning moon, if any sickle-shaped moon (growing or waning) is to rise at night. It did not [need to] be a full moon for the watersnakes and he may have been unconscious for some days. 'It is a dying moon that rises ahead of the sun' was the decision of Livingston Lowes. Thus the additions here are concerned to make the whole process of death for the crew slower, as well as to remove what many readers would have called the absurdity of a sickle moon rising at sunset. They wait to die till the moon rises (in the new version) because then they can curse the Mariner with their glittering eyes. They cannot do this by word of mouth because thirst has made them dumb. But surely, if this tremendous point is to be made, there has to be a point when they try to curse him and become convinced that it is impossible, by word of mouth. I agree that the 1817 line 'Too quick for groan or sigh' is pretty bad, but Coleridge was mainly trying to remove a Ballad pronunciation, of the rhyme-word 'eye', which he had let slip in the 1800 edition. And anyway, if 200 men are queuing up for this mode of death, each of them glittering into the face of the Mariner and then staggering off, we must suppose them to move past fairly briskly. The idea that it is somehow more dramatic for the Mariner to be entirely self-centred, and for the feelings of the crew to be ignored, is merely another example of the 'aesthetic' refusal to attend to the story. What is happening here is very decisive for the story; it is the curse of the crew upon the Mariner, which the other group of spirits try to carry out for them; so it is absurd not to let the crew attempt to express indignation. (And of course, though they could not use the vocal chords, they would have to be able to make breathy noises as long as they could breathe). I find it stiflingly aesthetic to object that 'groans of pain' are a 'rather obvious' way of expressing the suffering of men dumb from drought. What you say about hypersensitivity, as they listen to the 'far-off whisper' of the departing ghost-ship, is fair enough, but the poem does nothing to stop us thinking that they first wait and hear the departing whisper and then murmur. They do not have to hurry over it before the sunset; they have all night before them waiting for death till the waning moon rises shortly before dawn—and the steersman waits at his post, ready to use even a breath of wind. The first edition made the incident a hurried one, but the later and better informed version makes it agonisingly slow.

I think it very disgusting 'psychologising' to say that the Mariner's 'knowledge of the crew's hearts will remain limited to the end to the kind of observation and implicit deductions used earlier'. But of course he felt accepted as one of them to start with, or it would not have been such torture to be for ever alienated. It is true that their actual words are never reported,[2] but nor are they here, since they fail to speak; their busy and fierce changes of opinion have been splendidly represented, and urgently need another brief recognition at least before they die. To bring out the tremendous dramatic scene of the death of the crew cursing the Mariner seems to me one of our important duties; and not to do arty talk about 'the pattern of silence on the part of the crew, established from the moment the death-ship curses him and emphasised therefore (The body and I . . .)'. But the creature that does not speak to him is not his nephew at all, only a kind of Ariel possessing the corpse, and not very adroit at making it work. This does nothing to prove that his nephew 'allocated him an inferior status' before dying (and surely hanging a dead bird round his neck would be an odd way to snub a footman?); he is shocked and astonished because it is so *unlike* the way his nephew behaved before. This is again typical Eng. Lit. 'Imagism', being too snooty to believe in the story, or pay any attention

---

[2] Marginal note by WE: 'Or it doesn't matter if they are?'

to it, but twisting any detail in any literary work to make a standard story about the suffering intellectual who is so awfully misunderstood. Many people do read the poem as you do, I don't deny, and that is why it is so important to print a proper text. The crew give a great impression of unreasonable and intimate clamour, though the poem does it so economically.

This I think answers your main points, which I do think radically wrong, and shockingly so, for me, as I had thought you free from the standard Eng. Lit. incapacities to which you have there retreated. But I gathered during my visit that a metrical one was also troubling your mind; you felt that Coleridge would not have done that kind of repetition— picking up the second half of a quatrain as the first half of the next one. This I think must have been again in your mind when you wrote: 'Why, then, you will say, did he not think of your idea of making up a separate stanza by repetition?' But he did think of it; both stanzas are printed on the same page of the standard edition [1912, ed. E. H. Coleridge]. The only question is whether they were meant as alternatives or as consecutive; and I do not believe you would have thought of all these objections to making them consecutive if only he had written them into the notebook the improvement 'far-heard' for 'never a'. This is the point where some kind of typographical invention is required, a save-face for the textual editor which yet allows the reader to move forward uninterrupted (a desirable thing I agree). A double square bracket for this case, as it involves bringing the text into line with a later decision, but single brackets for each verse written into the margin but never passed for print by the author— surely that would meet the technical requirement.[3] However I realise that you do not like the movement here:

> The Sun's rim dips; the stars rush out:
>   At one stride comes the dark;
> With far-heard whisper, o'er the sea,
>   Off shot the spectre-bark.
>
> With far-heard whisper, o'er the main,
>   Off shot the spectre-ship;
> And stifled words and groans of pain
>   Mix'd on each murmuring lip.
> We look'd round, and we look'd up,
> And fear at our hearts, as at a cup . . .

---

[3] See the compromise agreed by WE and Pirie: *CV*, 128–9.

Surely the Mariner could not yet feel sure that he would be treated differently from the others; to make him say that *he* felt frightened, but of course he doesn't know what the others felt like, such cattle as they were (the many men so beautiful), after they had all been through the same eerie and offensive experience and he was the only one who had been told he was saved:—to do this on an aesthetic theory, which you praise, would be almost too nasty even for the old Coleridge. Fear at *my* heart is not a splendid improvement, even psychologically, though it is of course all that M. Paul Valéry could contrive to feel at the Marine Cemetery ['Le Cimitière marin']. However, I was going to report a metrical parallel:

> Never sadder tale was told
>   To a man of woman born:
> Sadder and wiser thou wedding guest
>   Thou'lt rise tomorrow morn.

> Never sadder tale was told
>   By a man of woman born:
> The Marineres all returned to work
>   As silent as beforne.

> The Marineres all 'gan pull the ropes,
>   But look at me they n'old;
> Thought I, I am as thin as air—
>   They cannot me behold.[4]

The first two verses do the ordinary kind of repetition, but the second and third do this elbow-movement, levering himself up to add one more point. The passage was in 1798 but cut out from 1800, merely I think (as I tried to explain) on a misunderstanding, not because he disliked the metrical construction. He may have come to think it too childlike by 1817, so that he cut the verse I want for this metrical reason, but it does not seem likely.

Turning now to the evidence about why Coleridge made the decisions he did for the 1817 edition, ample in a way but tantalizing, my main point is that you make an assumption which can be disproved: that he must have written the extra lines in the notebook (2880) when he composed them, and must have worked from the notebook (first picking it out from the other fifty-four notebooks) when he prepared the 1817 text. The editor is very definite about 2880; it is among the first entries in a new notebook, bought soon after his return to England, having lost nearly all his papers

---

[4] *CV*, 135–6; ll. 415–26; cf. *Poems*, ed. E. H. Coleridge, 201.

on the voyage. It is one of a group of entries in ink, whereas most of them are in pencil, and the others are scholarly items such as a list of metrical feet, examples of picturesque passages in Pindar, and suchlike; probably he was writing the more important things he could remember from one of the notebooks he had lost. Three or four nautical items noticed on the voyage are used (all together) in these fourteen lines. He landed on 17 August and Miss Coburn dates the entry 5–12 Oct, suggesting also that it was part of the preparations for an edition with Longmans, which came to nothing.[5] Coleridge fairly often talked of having poems in his head, though not yet written down; and though this became reduced to sad useless lying there was probably some truth behind it. His verbal memory was extremely powerful, so much so as to be made a legend by his fellow-students; and we know he still had it when he prepared *Sibylline Leaves*, because he showed it on a visit to Cary the translator of Dante, next year—after a day with the translation he seemed to know it by heart. Such a memory is dangerous, because it is always liable to select and (according to its lights) improve; and it is quite likely to have done so in this case. Coleridge would remember the general intention of the added lines, and especially the details observed on the voyage, but he could forget the verse mentioning the crew without any special intention. It is remarkable how little he seems to have bothered about *The Ancient Mariner*; apart from the notes recalling it on his first long sea voyage, when he is evidently planning improvements, it is hardly ever mentioned (either in notes or letters); whereas the yearning hope that he may finish Christabel, on a trip to the seaside for instance, is still going on in Oct. 1816. He is anxious to leave no handle for calumny, and make sure the poem is decorous, but otherwise the main thing it needs is prettifying, one can see him feel.

Regarded as a vision of the depths, he would naturally think of it as boyish stuff, written before he had seen them. The year before he prepared the 1817 text he had had all knives and razors removed from his room, and a man always with him to keep him from suicide. 'The terrors of the Almighty have been around and against me! . . . O I have had a new world opened to me, in the infinity of my own Spirit! Woe be to me, if this last

---

[5] Kathleen Coburn comments (*Notebooks*, ii *1804–1808 Notes*): 'Although this revision of *The Ancient Mariner*, and the two following entries, which are also in ink and also concerned with poetry, are not given a precise date, they do appear to belong to the first six months of Coleridge's return to England. The date of this and 2881 and 2882, all in ink, might be placed, taken by themselves, between 5 Oct 1806 and 25 Nov 1810, the dates of the pencil entries that flank them in the pocketbook . . . [A] reasonable date for all of these seems to be 5–12 Oct 1806. Probably this entry is connected with Longman's offer in the spring of 1807 to publish Coleridge's poems in two volumes and represents preparations made towards eliciting that offer.'

warning be not taken'. (Letter 254, Dec. 1814). He continues to claim in letters that the poems have been much improved, but the emphasis seems to be on morality rather than imagination; as when he writes to J. H. Frere, sending him 'such poems as I dare consent to be known as of my own Will as well as authorship' (Letter 1014; July 1816; presumably all the proofs of the book), and he has hoped that 'you would return them enriched with a few marks of your pencil—if they were mere symbolic signs of disapprobation of particular passages, lines, or works'. Frere translated Aristophanes in a racy manner which was still appreciated in my schooldays; it is odd to think of him as an expert on moral decorum, but he was an Establishment figure.[6]

There are two interesting letters to Gutch, on receipt of batches of proofs (printing began in Nov. 1815, and the final proof-sheets arrived in June 1816).

> It is useless to pluck single thorns from a thornbush. I groan in spirit under this whole sheet; and but that every hour is precious to me at the present moment as I am finishing the last scenes of a play though should have been sent off a week ago to the manager, I would cancel the whole sheet.

Here he must be blaming the printer, but further down the page, as if without noticing it, he has taken to blaming his own poetry when young:

> Should I succeed in the drama, and be enabled to command a single week's leisure, I will assuredly cancel this sheet, retaining only the last two poems, the others being sickly silly or both. (Letter 992, Jan 1816).

Towards the end of the process, he found that

> the new errata, occasioned by some cause or other, after the proofs have been corrected, are dreadfully numerous ... Some actually seem to have been the Compositor's *emendations*—courteous Creature! (Letter 1013, June 1816).

He was told firmly that the fault was his own: 'All the proofs happen to have been preserved, to place this matter beyond dispute.' Part of the dispute concerned a verse not ten lines before the one we are discussing; Coleridge wanted to cut the description of Death, obviously needed in some form to balance the description of Life-in-Death, but had failed to mark this

---

[6] The Right Hon. John Hookham Frere translated Aristophanes, *Plays: a metrical version* (1840), but Coleridge was in fact writing to James Hadley Frere (1779–1866.)

sufficiently clearly, so that the book came out carrying the verse but listing it as an erratum. Maybe the stifled groans of the crew appeared as further Gothic horror to the author's feverish mind; but, on this kind of evidence, I think we may say that his motives at this stage do not matter; we owe a loyalty to his intentions when he was writing well, but not to his intentions when he was out of sympathy with the poem and merely hacking it about. However, of course, if there were a good literary reason for cutting the verse, the author's authority for cutting it could reasonably be claimed.

The idea that, if the cut verse is restored (with the needed correction in the first line), then we have to print 'We looked round, as we looked up | And fear at our hearts' instead of the later version, came from you and not from me, and I would be glad to retain the standard text here. You said that the crew cannot be said to listen if at the same time they are murmuring, and I see now you were assuming from the first text that everything happens fast here; the moon gets up as the night falls, and the men die at once. But if they have to wait nearly all night, there will obviously be a time when they stop trying to groan, finding that they can't, and listen uneasily for the next portent. 'We listened and looked sideways up' does seem very good; I think because we want to know if some god is appearing in the sky to torment them, but do not want to let him know that they are looking. I do not feel any jolt here; the story goes on: 'We heard the hiss as the boat went, and they tried to groan a bit, and then we all listened, and I at least felt frightened that some new disaster must be on its way'. This is not a bit offensive to the crew, though I still think your arguments for ignoring their feelings were. So I should be perfectly willing to retain all that verse as in the standard text, glad to in fact. And you of course are quite free to say in the notes that the double-bracketed extra verse was probably intentionally removed by Coleridge (like the one two verses back) in his later years. But it would be merely inconsistent, I consider, not to offer the restoration in this case as in the others. It seems to me that you have altered your whole position without any intelligible reason given— because I certainly gave you written out this whole lay-out for the three verses, and we rejoiced that we agreed on the text.

I see now that, at the beginning of Section III, this tiresome repetition of 'I wist' comes in the first edition too, so there would be no advantage in returning to that as I had hoped. Interesting that he casually mentions nature-spirits there, as well-known to all: 'as if it dodged a water-sprite'.

Yours affectionately

[William Empson]

Houghton carbon, bMS Eng 1401 (628)

TO A. D. NUTTALL*

Department of English Literature, The University, Sheffield
26 May 1970

Dear Mr Nuttall,

Thank you for your patient and goodhumoured letter; I am glad your opinions are no worse. But by turning to the brothel [in *Measure for Measure*] you escape the real question—the brothel scenes are mainly comic relief. The real issue is whether Claudio can rightly be executed for going to bed with a woman whom he has already married by affirmation, though keeping it secret till the families have agreed on her dowry. *I, William Shakespeare* by Leslie Hotson pointed out that the man Shakespeare made overseer of his will, a respectable landowner near Stratford, had married, about the year before *Measure for Measure* came out, a woman he had been living with for eight years or so—as married by affirmation, and again waiting to arrange the dowry. Shakespeare had probably done this himself, or anyway it is the most respectable explanation of the facts of his marriage. You do not give the slightest reason for believing that Shakespeare admired Calvin for killing such people, or that his audience did—the evidence is that they thought the procedure normal.

You are brought up to assume that Shakespeare was a solemn cad (and that all other English writers were), like Leavis; and I think it makes all your remarks smell of hypocrisy. But of course I regard you as a victim.

Yours sincerely
William Empson
Claudio says he deserves death for it. The audience cannot really have agreed.

Houghton: carbon, bMS Eng 1401 (613)

TO DAVID PIRIE

[n.d., ?June 1970]

My dear Pirie,

Thank you for your letter. It shows that I had better have rewritten my piece before posting it, as if before publication, but why should you not be informed of my state of mind? I have been getting uneasy about the Eng. Lit. profession in general for some time, and saying it in every article I print; I was shocked and surprised to find you falling in with some of its characteristic faults, above all treating 'coherence of imagery' as more real than the story. I certainly did not invent this line of talk to excuse a disagreement with you. But let us agree that you often proved my letter to be wrong—many of your best points, I thought, were against printing the whole of the notebook version, which I had only agreed to do because you said it would be consistent—I am very glad to be freed from this demand. But I estimate that the general noise of my letter distracted you from picking out the major points, which I will now try to summarize.

I thought you made a very good point in saying that Coleridge only uses this repetition ballad technique, which I reconstruct here, to mark delay. He uses it now to introduce a terrific delay, the crew refusing to die till the moon rises, in order that though dumb they may curse the Mariner with the glitter of their eyes. I agree now that they are not already cursing him when they make grumbly noises in their throats, all that they can, at seeing the ghost ship leave them to die. I hardly think I can have meant that; they go through a mental process which ends in an extremely wild action, and this grumbly noise is the reader's only point of contact with its later stages. *Of course* it needs to be in, considering how important the reaction of the crew is going to be for the rest of the story. If you told anybody in another branch of the entertainment business, the films for instance, that the crew must not react at this point for the fancy reasons you gave, they would feel outraged, as I did.

You pay no attention to what my covering letter urged upon you as the crucial point; do you now agree that a long wait is described, while the dew marks out the time with an agonising drip, till the waning moon rises towards dawn. I know you feel impatient about this moon-talk, because it is not part of our way of life to choose moonlight nights for parties and so on, and it wasn't plain to Coleridge at once either, but when he was on board ship to Malta his mind became clear about when the waning moon comes and he began putting scraps of poems about it in the Notebooks. I think there is no doubt at all that he intended to introduce a terrifying delay when he planned the double verses, I mean, whether or not he planned the double verses he intended to introduce a terrifying delay. This would suit the double verses; do you still believe that the crew died immediately, as in the first edition?

You said that I wanted to print what Coleridge didn't write, and I said I only wanted to fit together two verses printed on the same page of the standard edition, and you answer that the way they are printed has no bearing on whether he wrote them, either. But I agree that I have no positive evidence that he intended what I think he must have done, also you have no negative evidence. As the effect of the verse in the long sequence of rhymes is rippingly good and feels obviously intended, and as due warning to the reader by a double bracket has always been part of the plan, I think it has to go in.

The first edition has:

> With never a whisper in the sea
>   Off darts the Spectre-ship:
> While clomb above the Eastern bar
> The horned Moon, with one bright Star
>   Almost atween the tips.

> One after one the horned Moon . . .

and then the crew die at once. The whole purpose or method of the slow build-up of Coleridge's later arrangements for this incident was to make their death slow so that their curse would be more impressive. When he wrote the extra verses in the new notebook, copied from memory from a notebook lost at sea, these lines were halfway and had not yet added the splendid recovery from the mistake of making the ghost-ship inaudible ('With far-heard whisper . . .'), but I don't think you deny that if Coleridge had used the verse he would have added this change to make it consistent. As written, the Notebook verses give us no idea what they were to follow on from. But they go tremendously well if allowed to follow where they naturally belong, and you offer no reason for forbidding that. Sorry, I have been using the plural out of place; it is only this one verse which got cut out; the later ones after great improvement (at some time) were used splendidly. I do not believe that Coleridge in his final editing had any good reason for cutting out the extra verse, and you have not told me anything even like a good reason; and I think that metrically and rhythmically putting back the extra verse makes a tremendous addition to the whole passage, quite apart from its necessity if the story is to have any human reality.

Such is my frame of mind about the matter, and please give your good lady my earnest congratulations.

Yours affectionately

[William Empson]

I have been glancing over the documents, and it is plain that this letter is inadequate to puncture your complacency. You wrote to me that Coleridge could not have allowed men while slowly dying of thirst to groan because that would be 'rather obvious'. Now, it is not your fault, but for historical reasons I find this a sentiment so loathsome that I cannot have any association with it. It is Eng. Lit. at its most stinking.

And really the literary judgement resulting from this nastiness is completely wrong. There is a thrilling improvement to the sequence when you allow the verse back in.

Houghton, bMS Eng 1401 (628)

TO CHRISTOPHER NORRIS*

Department of English Literature, The University, Sheffield S10 2TN
3 August 1970

Dear Mr Norris,

Congratulations on your First. I ought to have answered your letter, but our quota was full already, and I thought one of them might scratch, in which case I could offer a place to you. (Of course, they often fail to get the expected grant). I am still not certain who is coming, but hope to make sure in a week or two.

However, if you are going to write about me it would perhaps be less embarrassing to do it elsewhere. I don't know of anyone else (one or two very dull American studies have been sent). I agree that Kit Smart, though interesting, has been pretty well covered. I am quite willing to read your material, and say what my intentions had been, without being your supervisor. With a First you can pretty certainly get a place elsewhere—and a Government grant, of course; why do you need a London University one? However, let me know if you still want a place at Sheffield. I rather expect we should know by now if any had scratched.

Yours sincerely
William Empson

TO CHRISTOPHER NORRIS*

1 Hampstead Hill Gardens
27 September 1970

Dear Mr Norris,

I don't seem to have any other printed texts of articles lying about here, but will send you what I find at Sheffield, where I go tomorrow.

The news that you think *Cain* [The Wanderings of Cain, by S. T. Coleridge] 'an acquiescence in the paradox of Original Sin' shocks me but does not surprise me. The Eng. Lit. training has become an elaborate plot to delude you in just that way, and the effect is that many authors of earlier times are systematically misunderstood. To Coleridge and the public he intended, very conscious of what Voltaire had said about the Lisbon earthquake and all, *Cain* was straight polemic against the beautiful old paradox.[1] (I will examine little Eros as soon as I return). A good Note by Coleridge in later life is still saying that he will not acquiesce in any holy paradox, because he has a prior duty to the Reason imprinted in him by God.[2] The real Christian paradox is: 'God is love; and therefore you must burn your mother alive; because that will please kind God so much'. All

[1] The Lisbon earthquake, on 1 Nov. 1755, was the greatest natural disaster of the eighteenth century, killing 30,000 people in the city and devastating the Atlantic coasts of Portugal, Spain, and Morocco. Written in 1756, the deist Voltaire's satirical *Poème sur le désastre de Lisbonne, ou Examen de cet axiome: Tout est bien* (*Œuvres complètes de Voltaire*, ed. Moland (1877–85), ix. 465–80), laments the idea of acceding to the Christian Providence. Everything is predetermined, all suffering is fated; everything is good. 'Tout est bien ... c'est l'effet nécessaire des causes nécessaires; votre mal n'est rien, vous contribuez au bien général' (468).

[2] The view that true religious doctrines were consonant with reason can be found *passim* in Coleridge, e.g. on the last page of *Biographia*. In 1970, when WE was writing to Norris, the comprehensive Coburn edition had not reached beyond the year 1808, so it was not a 'Note' in that series. There does not appear to be anything clinching in E. H. Coleridge's selection from the Notebooks, *Anima Poetae* (1894). Other places where WE might have found such a 'Note' are *Inquiring Spirit*, the anthology edited by Coburn, or the *Letters, Conversations, and Recollections of S. T. Coleridge* (ed. Thomas Allsop, 1836), in which Coleridge is reported as saying a number of free-thinking-ish things, so lending weight, perhaps, to the idea of Coleridge as a tenacious rationalist despite the lurch to orthodoxy—e.g., 'Is it possible to assent to the doctrine of redemption as at present promulgated, that the moral death of an unoffending being should be a consequence of the transgression of humanity and its atonement' (103; also quoted in *CV*, 98). (For Coleridge, of course, this appalling thought was exactly what the Trinity, or the Tri-Unity, dealt with.) WE also quotes in his appendix to *CV* from vol. 3 of *Religious Trends in English Poetry* (1949), ed. Hoxie Neale Fairchild, where he would have found, quoted from *Aids to Reflection*, various passages of praise for 'the Practical Reason of Man, comprehending the Will, the Conscience, the Moral Being with its inseparable Interests and Affections—that Reason, namely, which is the Organ of Wisdom, and (as far as Man is concerned) the source of living and actual Truths' (*Aids to Reflection*, ed. John Beer, 195; Fairchild, 321). It is just possible that WE had in mind a sentence from the *Literary Remains* (297–8): 'Let not the surpassing eloquence of Taylor dazzle you, nor his scholastic retiary versatility of logic illaqueate your good sense', another instruction to Lamb; or, maybe, earlier in that volume (37): 'Now that reason in man must have been first actuated by a direct revelation from God, I have myself proved, and do not therefore deny that faith as the means of salvation was first made known by revelation; but that reason is incapable of seeing into the fitness and superiority of these means, or that it is a mystery in any other sense than as all spiritual truths are mysterious, I do deny and deem it both a false and a dangerous doctrine. 15 Sept. 1826' (annotations to Hooker). Marsh, the editor of *Aids to Reflection* (1847), puts the Coleridge position clearly: 'though we may believe what *passeth all understanding* we *can not* believe what is *absurd*, or contradictory to *reason*' (*Aids to Reflection*, ed. John Beer, 497). Most likely of all, however, is that WE has in mind a passage quoted by Coburn in her introduction to Coleridge's *Philosophical Lectures* (1949), in which Coleridge guardedly praises the old schoolmen—who were, for all their faults, 'emancipating the mind from its unquestioning slavery to an ignorant Priest-hood, waking the desire for an intelligible Faith and accustoming the Reason to a sense of its own inherent Rights, and to a confidence in its own powers' (50; compare *Marginalia*, ed. H. J. Jackson and George Whalley, v. 805). All the same, the passage in question, whatever the precise passage WE hand in mind, is not likely to convey quite what WE thinks: 'reason' for the later Coleridge is not an Enlightenment power of 'reason' (which he called 'understanding'), but a supersensuous faculty from God, which sometimes sounds Kantian and sometimes positively mystical (see the poem "Reason"), that part of the composite human creature that is divine.

other holy paradoxes are just part of the breakdown, preparing you to outrage your conscience.

There is plenty of evidence in the Letters and Notebooks that Coleridge understood this horror completely; I hadn't got round to collecting them when I wrote the article, but I realise now that I need to accumulate evidence for a number of major authors. The work seems to me tiresome and not really what I am good at, but reading so much of what the students actually say has made me realise that it has become an urgent duty.

Coleridge of course accepted Anglican dogma (or as much as his stomach could hold down when helped by plenty of opium) during the time of the trip to Malta, quite early. But near the end of his life he still speaks of it with loathing. *Literary Remains* III [1838] 296 [298], supporting Calvinism against the timidly enlightened views of Jeremy Taylor—'Above all, do not dwell too much on the Horror and Absurdity of the dogma he attacks; but examine what he puts in its place'.[3] This Horror and Absurdity was what Coleridge was recommending, the doctrine he had tutored himself into swallowing. If you insist on telling lies about that you will never understand him.

Yours
William Empson.

TO DAVID WILSON

Department of English Literature, The University, Sheffield
Sat 5 November 1970

Dear Mr Wilson,

Thank you for your letter [Wilson and Norris had asked for an interview], and I realise that I ought to be grateful at having young men interested in my work, but really I am only interested in the work I am

---

[3] As printed by H. N. Coleridge: 'Above all do not dwell too much on the apparent absurdity or horror of the dogma he opposes, but examine what he puts in its place, and receive candidly the few hints which I have admarginated for your assistance, being in the love of truth and of Christ' (298). Cf. WE's fiery appendix to his introd. to *CV*, where WE makes it clear that his source for Coleridge's adverse comments on the Sermons of Jeremy Taylor was Roberta Brinkley, *Coleridge on the Seventeenth Century* (1955), 284. The note is now edited in Coleridge, *Marginalia*, ed. H. J. Jackson and George Whalley, v. 597. The editors remark that the work of Taylor being annotated, *Unum Necessarium, or the Doctrine and Practice of Repentance*, 'was to C the most disturbing of his works': the point at stake is that in it Taylor (according to Coleridge) logically tends toward 'Socinianism' (that is, the Unitarianism—on which WE could cast a not-unfriendly quasi-pantheist eye—which inspired Coleridge as a young man, and which he spent most of his adult life noisily deploring). The note is addressed to the Unitarian Charles Lamb.

trying to do now. (The British Council has just taken me to Paris for some lectures, so it must be the Finnish University who preferred Muggridge.)[1] I won't be in London on Dec 12–13 so Dec 19–20 will be the soonest. Better get it over.

1. I didn't contribute any protocols [to I. A. Richards's *Practical Criticism*], feeling shy about the process, though I went to one or two of the lectures. I didn't realise that Richards was right till after he had stopped teaching me—my friends thought him absurd and regarded me as a source of comic anecdotes about my tutorials under him. The young are always wrong and I suppose need to be.

2. I never met Wittgenstein. We all thought the Tractatus very important somehow.

3. No, I have no idea what poems Richards used in lectures.

4. I thought I said *all* my student love-poems were about 'boy afraid of girl', not 'The Ants' especially; and in fact it is too much *about* neurotic fear to convey much feeling of that. We all solemnly admired The Waste Land but I had no idea of echoing it there.

5. I wanted to write poetry with profound comparisons, and *UFA Nightmare* was merely a thriller. It didn't seem to me my kind of poem, when I was collecting them for the book, about 1935. Perhaps this was a snobbish judgement, but I expect I would still make it.

We are having the house altered and repaired, and I don't know whether my wife will be prepared to do a meal for you both when you come; it will depend on whether we have a kitchen then. But I expect it will be all right; would you prefer lunch or dinner?

Yours
William Empson

TO NIKOS STANGOS*

Department of English Literature, The University, Sheffield S10 2TN
19 December 1970

Dear Mr Stangos,

Thank you for your invitation. I would like to do the one on Emily Dickinson, discussing briefly in the introduction whether she is metaphysical or mystical or why she has excited grand claims from recent

---

[1] When the British Council invited the various Finnish universities to nominate visiting guest lecturers, it was at David Wilson's suggestion that Jyväskylä requested WE; but in the event it was Malcolm Muggeridge (1903–90), radical journalist, wartime spy, postwar broadcaster, and Christian, who did the rounds in Finland.

critics, giving mainly the old favourites but one or two which seem to me surprising.[1] I think her chief merit is to rely on the bone and sinew of the language itself, a phrase invented for the supposed 'line' of Wyatt, Jonson and Donne. I will have to read the book proving she was a Lesbian, and will give some poems from later years about affectionate relations with women, but cannot believe I will be converted by it from regarding the major poems as (essentially) about God, Father, and distinguished clergy-men, persons who excite immense feelings which one would prefer not to sustain for more than half an hour, escaping to the kitchen after that as a rule. They can be checked, if one is skilful, but I do not expect that she felt this to carry any large metaphysical doctrine. I find her a sympathetic character, in a very limited way. The remarkable thing is that, if she had not been so extravagantly feminine, all the critics would have admired the essential masculinity of her major poems.

However, we have a major obstacle. I really have not got time to do this till June. This is the last year before I have to retire, and I am tied by another commitment to a publisher, which has already been delayed too long. It would be fair for you to give this interesting subject to someone else, who can do it quicker. However, as I have been lecturing on the lady for some years, and could provide a short list of poems at once, I feel confident that I could do the work you want fairly quickly. It would only have to wait till other duties were out of the way. Could you accept an offer for next autumn?

Yours with thanks
William Empson

Penguin

TO CHRISTOPHER NORRIS*

Department of English Literature, The University, Sheffield
7 January 1971

Dear Mr Norris,

I agree that ethical theory is a crucial matter, but I had not and have not got one. I used to think it was better not to have one, but am now not so sure. When Richards was teaching me I thought his 'scientistic' position was very absurd, as my friends were all following the fashion for Eliot.

---

[1] WE had written of R. P. Blackmur's *Language as Gesture*: 'I think Emily Dickinson was better than he allowed, but it is refreshing to have a major American critic who didn't think it was his duty to boost her (in 1937)' ('Still the Strange Necessity', *Sewanee Review*, 63 (1955); *A*, 127).

About five years later, I think, back from Japan, I had come to think Richards was right (it was then I did most of that Appendix on ethical theory in Complex Words), but this didn't mean feeling sure Eliot was wrong (I think now he was *very* wrong). You have read everything by me but perhaps not an introduction to the later edition of Pastoral which makes some remarks about this change of attitude. I hope I would always have agreed that ethical judgements are relational; no sense can be made of the subject otherwise; but I never thought of Laird as a man whose advice I might actually take.[1] A class-based attitude, strongly expressed by Fielding and Trollope, still affects me a good deal; it says that properly educated or trained men agree with the working classes on essentials, but that most of the noise about ethics is made by Nonconformist lower-middle-class intellectuals whose instincts have been perverted (Samuel Butler said it too, of course). 'The great gay Englishman of Elizabeth's time' wrote G. K. Chesterton, about Carlyle, I think, 'is presented as a solemn cad';[2] this made a great impression on me as a schoolboy, so I could at once recognise Leavis as the type case of the solemn cad.

But in writing Ambiguity I simply wanted to know how the beautiful thing in view was made, how it worked; I am sure I hadn't started reacting against the views of Eliot etc.—though of course I really had differences which I could have been made to notice.

I don't know what happens to the Fielding ethic under the new class structure, but I expect it will only take another form.

Yours sincerely

William Empson

Have you a copy of that article in M. L. Q. Sept. 1966 by J. Jensen on 'The Construction of s. t. o Ambiguity'? I ought to know what was in it, because Laura Riding is still on my tail, and the editor wrote to Graves or something. I would gladly return your copy registered.

David Wilson

---

[1] John Laird, *An Enquiry into Moral Notions*; see WE's review, 'Three Ethics', *The Spectator*, 29 Nov. 1935; *A*, 571–2.

[2] G. K. Chesterton, *Charles Dickens* (1906), ch. 7, 'Dickens and Christmas': 'comfort is, like charity, a very English instinct . . . This ideal of comfort belongs peculiarly to England; it belongs peculiarly to Christmas; above all, it belongs pre-eminently to Dickens. And it is astonishingly misunderstood . . . [I]n England has arisen a parvenu patriotism which represents the English as everything but English; as a blend of Chinese stoicism, Latin militarism, Prussian rigidity, and American bad taste. And so England, whose fault is gentility and whose virtue is geniality, England with her tradition of the great gay gentleman of Elizabeth, is represented to the four quarters of the world (as in Mr Kipling's religious poems) in the enormous image of a solemn cad' (163–4).

TO NIKOS STANGOS*

In May 1971 WE was commissioned by Nikos Stangos to edit a selection of Marvell's poems for the 'Poet to Poet' series published by Penguin Books. Stangos recalled (letter to JH, 18 Mar. 1992): 'I do remember meeting him at Stephen Spender's and soon after asking him to do the Andrew Marvell volume to which he agreed. I thought Empson, whom I very greatly admired, was not sufficiently appreciated as a poet and it seemed to me that coupling him with Marvell would be mutually illuminating.' The delivery date given in the contract (signed by WE on 12 Jul. 1971), which called for an introduction of 10,000 words, was to be September 1971. The commission was not met that year, but WE's account of Marvell's secret marriage ultimately came to figure in *UB*. (Other titles in the series included W. H. Auden on George Herbert, and Thom Gunn on Jonson.)

Studio House, 1 Hampstead Hill Gardens, NW3
25 March 1971

Dear Mr Stangos,

Sorry to be late in answering your letter, but I have only just seen it, finding it waiting for me when I got home from Sheffield. I am afraid there is no question of completing the edition by July, but I should then be free and completely at your service, and two more months ought to be enough. As I wrote, I have another commitment which I trust will be completed this holiday, and won't be able to do much during my final term at Sheffield.

I have had another look at the job, while healing up and delaying the start on the immediate duty. I had already written a proof that Marvell really did secretly marry his landlady, eleven years before his death (aged 58), and it only needs small improvements I think; but it is merely a refutation of a[n] American article in PLMA [*PMLA*] for 1938, and I will have to be able to say that I have looked in the Records Office. This check is likely to take a bit of time, but I expect little from it and will cut it as short as I can.

Recent criticism of Marvell has become sickeningly ghastly, because he is assumed to be the one complete Imagist and Symbolist and T. S. Eliot man; so this bit of biography has a direct effect on the literary criticism, or at least I hope on the reactions of the public. Once you admit that he was the same man all along, an intellectual with populist sympathies, it becomes hard to ignore the political satires. Parts of them really are good poetry, but there is a sad lot of dead wood for the modern reader. I think the best way to deal with it is to print a whole lot of short selections from them; and, for that matter, I wouldn't mind cutting most of the flattery of the Fairfaxes out of *Appleton House*. Otherwise, the poems everyone expects must be in, and the effect of both plans will be quite a lot of pages. I also want a fair amount of elbow-room for my introduction; but, if you feel that this book is the wrong place for a full treatment of the (very scanty) evidence, I could summarize the arguments and results and print the thing in full elsewhere. As it was practically done before you made your kind offer, I could have no complaint. But actually, thinking of the success of the book, I believe this stuff is precisely what would make it sell. Nothing comes to life so entertainingly under legal treatment as a long dead scandal, dragged unwillingly into daylight against fierce resistance from all sides—in its shamefaced way it was a political trial.

The immediate question for both of us is how much length you are prepared to give. Very likely what I plan will turn out quite short, but I realise that these paperback selections aim to look inviting, done with careless ease, quite free from pedantry. As a vehicle for exploding the complacent security of the Eng. Lit. profession, by showing that the poet had this low-class secret, the genre of the paperback selection, you may feel, would be out of place—a further scandal, in fact, like the boss's son seducing a mill-girl. I do earnestly think that this would be a mistaken view; the genre is exactly the right one for the purpose.

Thank you for offering to xerox my selected texts, and of course I don't want to type them out, but we haven't got so far yet. I am working from my old Oxford edition of the poems and letters (Margoliouth),[1] and could send it along ready marked when the time comes. Luckily we haven't any major textual problems; indeed, we wouldn't have any texts at all of the poems now considered so very detached from the world if his widow hadn't insisted on printing them after his death.

Yours truly
William Empson

Penguin

TO WILLIAM LYONS*

3 May 1971

My dear Lyons,

I find the relevant bit of the Belleforest text is in the library after all, so I pass it on at once. You are only asked to translate one sentence, but I had

---

[1] H. M. Margoliouth, *The Poems and Letters of Andrew Marvell*, 2 vols. (1927).

better explain first why the question seems interesting. The medieval Saxo reports in Latin that Hamlet could not tell a lie (pp. 107, 111);[1] this is presented in moral terms, but Hamlet regards a total planned deceit as necessary for survival and for the duty of avenging his father, so that his twists to avoid a verbal untruth only obey a taboo. The guards of his uncle would kill him if they thought him capable of revenging his father, but he can say to them 'My only intention when I grow up is to kill my uncle, avenging my father', and this makes them quite sure he is mad, so that they laugh with deep chesty chuckles and foster him.[2] Any child finds this fascinating; seven to thirteen are perhaps the best ages. But this is not in the pedant Belleforest, who regards Hamlet as like magicians in his own sixteenth century if not as like the Brutus who downed the Tarquins. I hope that Shakespeare realised this ancient fairy-story rule about Hamlet; that a bad fairy at his christening had condemned him never to tell a lie. But the sources are rather hard to interpret.

A crunch soon comes, as the boy becomes a lad, in his reactions to sex. If he knows what to do with a woman, he will no longer be considered mad (mad enough to be immune from slaughter). A friendly foster-sister, after she has interpreted a very obscure message from a foster-brother, gives him the solution (p. 109). He carries off the woman into the woods and they perform the act of sex; on their return he leers at the spies and says 'Oh yes I did', whereas she says: 'Of course he didn't, poor beast; he doesn't know what it means'. After that he is established and almost certain to complete his vengeance. I feel I tell the story better than Saxo did, because he did not quite sympathise with an arbitrary taboo against a lie; but still, he tells it plainly enough, and it really is a good story.

What I cannot be sure of is whether Belleforest intended to tell it on p. 203. If he did, his English translator, probably but not certainly writing later than Shakespeare's writing of *Hamlet*, misunderstood him. Belleforest is pious and mealy-mouthed but as a rule a truthful translator, and I find the last sentence of the paragraph on p. 202 hard to follow, indeed the Englishman on the opposite page has evidently felt that he needs interpret-

---

[1] Saxo Grammaticus, *Historia Danica* (1514), in Sir Israel Gollancz, *The Sources of 'Hamlet': with essay on the legend* (1926).

[2] 'He used at times to sit over the fire, and, raking up the embers with his hands, to fashion wooden crooks, and harden them in the fire, shaping at their tips certain barbs, to make them hold more tightly to their fastenings. When asked what he was about, he said that he was preparing sharp javelins to avenge his father. This answer was not a little scoffed at, all men deriding his idle and ridiculous pursuit; but the thing helped his purpose afterwards' (*The Sources of 'Hamlet'*, 103).

ing. The Englishman makes Hamlet tell a lie, not realising that this is a kind of blasphemy against the legend.[3]

I hang upon your lips.

Yours

[William Empson]

Houghton: carbon, 6MS Eng 1401 (599)

Professor Lyons responded on 7 May 1971:

> I thought I should ask one or two of my colleagues who read more sixteenth-century French than I normally do whether they agreed with my tentative answer.
>
> I think the sentence in question *could* be rendered roughly as follows: The young lord (and the girl) having deceived the courtiers who maintained (= into maintaining?) that he had in no wise attempted to violate her, although he said otherwise, each one (of them) was assured that truly he was mad, and that his brain had no strength whatever for reasonable apprehension.
>
> In an examination one would have to accept the English version printed as perfectly possible, if one takes the sentence in isolation. But it does imply that the young woman received no satisfaction, whereas the preceding sentence indicates the contrary (*eust été* bien marie de son desastre et fortune, et *plus* de sortir de ses mains sans jouyr de celluy qu'elle aimoit . . .). She would have been sorry to escape intact—so presumably she didn't, and she was more concerned to have her pleasure than to save the young man. Unfortunately, there is no explicit statement of the fact in this French text—it looks almost as if something has got lost.

[3] 'Ayant le jeune seigneur trompé les courtisans, et la fille, soustenans qu'il ne s'estoit avancé en sorte aucune à la violer, quoy qu'il dict du comtraire, chacun s'asseura que veritablement it estoit insensé, et que son cerveau n'avoit force quelconque, capable d'apprehension raisonnable' (F. de Belleforest, *Le cinqviesme tome des histoires tragiques* (1582), in Gollancz, *The Sources of 'Hamlet'*, 202). The English translation, from *The Hystorie of Hamblet* (1608), reads: 'The prince in this sort having both deceived the courtiers, and the ladyes expectation, that affirmed and swore that hee never once offered to have his pleasure of the woman, although in subtilty hee affirmed the contrary, every man there upon assured themselves that without all doubt he was distraught of his sences, that his braynes were as then wholly void of force, and incapable of reasonable apprehension, so that as then Fengons practise took no effect: but for al that he left not off, still seeking by al meanes to finde out Hamblets subtilty, as in the next chapter you shall perceive' (203).

TO HUGH KENNER*

Department of English Literature, The University, Sheffield S10 2TN
11 June 1971

Dear Hugh Kenner,

I thought you ought to be sent a copy of this, as it is a very obscure publication and you would never see it otherwise.[1] People have sometimes printed attacks on me which I don't get hold of till ten years later, and it always strikes me as a lost opportunity.

Yours with good wishes
William Empson.

Texas: Kenner Box 51, folder 5: E–F, 1951–1992, n.d., General corresp.

TO RICHARD ELLMANN*

Department of English Literature, The University, Sheffield S10 2TN
14 June 1971

Dear Professor Ellmann,

Allow me to present these two little pieces on the subject of Joyce, both printed in a magazine of the University of Kent which I am sure you would not see otherwise.[1]

The first one I did not see to correct proofs.

They seem rather bristling, but of course you are not among the persons denounced; a shining record of truth-telling in the Biography etc. is gladly praised.

Hoping we meet again.

Yours
William Empson.

Tulsa

---

[1] WE enclosed 'Joyce's Intentions', *20th Century Studies*, no. 4 (4 Nov. 1970), 26–36. 'The chief claim of this theory is that Stephen Dedalus is presented not as the author when young (though the book-title pretends he is) but as a possible fatal alternative, a young man who has taken some wrong turning, or slipped over the edge of some vast drop, so that he can never grow into the wise old author (intensely Christian, though in a mystically paradoxical way) who writes the book.'

[1] 'The Theme of *Ulysses*', *Twentieth Century Studies* (Nov. 1969), 39–41; 'Joyce's Intentions', *Twentieth Century Studies* (4 Nov. 1970), 26–36.

TO KARUNAKAR JHA*

Studio House, 1 Hampstead Hill Gardens, London NW3
20 June 1971

Dear Mr Sha [*sic*],[1]

I was very pleased to see that you had joined the Leavisites, as they will be long-lasting allies so long as you stick to their doctrine rigidly. It is a pressure-group, you know, hardly anything to do with F. R. Leavis by this time, I expect; your letters are stuffed with its jargon. I did not answer because you obviously would not believe anything I said. But after I had thrown your letter away I wished I had it back, as you insinuated that I was taking money on false pretences by teaching literature, and I haven't another example of that being done to me. It is one of the bits of dirt habitually smeared by Leavisites on their opponents. Of course I return the accusation, as I consider the claims of their doctrine wholly false, and its doctrinaire mean-mindedness does much to prevent them from understanding the authors they expound. But these exchanges have become quite old-world. I am glad of the opportunity to write down where I think your thesis wrong.

p. 18. Of course I don't *judge* a poem on linguistic grounds only, and indeed your earlier letter accused me of wantoning in my own arbitrary preferences. But I have often tried to explain the linguistic means by which an author achieves his effects, assuming that my 'class of reader' agreed on the effect but would be interested to know how it was achieved. I did not think of myself as labouring to teach or to convert, though I would be willing to do that at other times.

p. 19. T. S. Eliot once wrote [The Perfect Critic' (1920)]: 'There is really no other method but to be intelligent' or thereabouts; a critic must be ready to call in any method that will serve. I do not see why I am especially at fault here. To say that the method is not transferable is only a confession of incapacity.

---

[1] Karunakar Jha informed WE on 18 Nov. 1969 that he was proposing to write about his literary criticism (*Houghton*). At the All India English Teachers' Conference at Nagpur (Maharastra) in Dec. 1969, he read a paper on 'The relevance of the critical approach of William Empson'. In 1971, when he wrote again to WE, he was studying on a British Council scholarship for a Diploma in English Studies at the University of Wales Institute of Science and Technology. Dr Jha wrote to JH (13 Oct. 1987): 'I wonder how [WE] guessed so wide of the mark that I had joined the "Leavisites". It appears that his vanity misled him to suppose that criticism was like private property shared by Leavis and himself. Any striking ideas in others must be borrowed or plagiarised. He seems to have gone out of the bounds of propriety and politeness in the letter.' Dr Jha noted too (letter to JH, 23 May 1988): 'Perhaps Empson had then been spitting his venom against Leavis (F. R.) about and I happened to come his way. Ironically, Leavis turned out to be the better and greater literary critic, I suspect, though in my letters to Empson or in the papers I had sent him I had hardly shown any preference for Leavis.'

p. 20. No, really; the first two chapters of *C. W.* are *not* 'an attempt to generalise from the practice of criticism'. They are a bit of Linguistics, an attempt to codify some basic facts about all language which are not known to professional linguists because of their incapacity in this part of their field.

p. 22. What you quote is all in the first edition of *Seven Types*. I don't know what was called the third, but no further changes were made in it.

p. 23. You find that two of my books have a 'real but unstated purpose', in that the successive chapters are not unconnected. I think I 'stated' the connections clearly enough, though not pompously.

p. 24. In *C. W.* (for example) I *did* 'present various examples illustrating a single theory', but I did not have to 'look for' them, because the theory had grown out of prolonged work on them. The theory is a linguistic one, and the examples cannot be understood without grasping it.

p. 25. You say: 'Words as encapsulated thought or compact(ed) doctrines was a notion which depended on regarding meaning loosely as behavioural rather than linguistic'. This is a lie, and I would be interested to know where you got it from. It 'depends on' failing to understand the demonstration in the first two chapters of the book. My 'notion' might be refuted, of course, but whether words do or do not behave as the 'notion' maintains can only be a *linguistic* question.

p. 27. What Olson calls 'inferences' seem to be what I call Implications, and treat separately.[2] I generalise the word *meaning* to include them, but your quotation does not show any actual difference of opinion about them.

p. 28. [J. R.] Firth is saying the same thing about 'collocations' (but they often give rise to new meanings of the word, so cannot be kept isolated from its meanings).

Paradise Lost consists very largely of 'simple and great poetry', and the obstacles to grasping it come from the basic fallacies of the Christian religion, or indeed the whole previous disaster of the cult of human sacrifice. But Milton's treatment of the subject has to be approached through his language.

p. 30. In *Milton's God* I made a policy of saying things about my own life, about one in each chapter, to show that what I was saying was real to me. Of course, a school of critics who believe that a critic had positively

---

[2] See Elder Olson, 'William Empson, Contemporary Criticism and Poetic Diction', *Modern Philology* 47: 4 (May 1950), 222–52 (esp. 228–9), which discriminates between meaning and implication or inference, and seeks to itemize four conditions of meaning and inference.

better not know what he is talking about, or know anything but 'the words on the page', is offended by this.

Like God in sending Raphael to talk to Adam, I feel sure this letter will do no good, but at least that it will leave you 'without excuse'.[3]

With good wishes

William [Empson]

Houghton, bMS Eng 1401 (586)

TO CHRISTOPHER NORRIS

Department of English Literature, The University, Sheffield S10 2TN

21 June 1971

Dear Mr Norris,

Congratulations on your marriage, and thank you for your letter, which brings encouragement when needed, though I have to answer that I am shamefully behindhand in my reading of these things. I must have a go at modern linguistics when I reach freedom. An Indian in Cardiff who has brought my *Complex Words* into a thesis has just sent me bits of it, quoting linguists who argue that my first two chapters are all wrong and literary because they confuse the meaning of a word with its collocations. But a standard collocation often *becomes* a meaning of a word, so they cannot be isolated from one another; I agree of course that they need distinguishing, but that I do. However, I think he chose very outofdate linguists to spite me (he also insinuated that I was taking money on false pretences because I did not give my pupils a Rule, so you see how rough life is).

I was just echoing Richards when I talked about Chomsky; he said he had exploded Chomsky (by an essay in *So Much Nearer*), and it did seem clear that he had showed Chomsky to write in an extremely journalistic way, not thinking 'about language' while composing sentences about it.[1]

---

[3] Dalila says, in *Samson Agonistes*, ll. 732–5: 'With doubtful feet and wavering resolution | I came, still dreading thy displeasure, Samson, | Which to have merited, without excuse, | I cannot but acknowledge . . .'; and compare the Argument to *Paradise Lost*, V: 'God to render man inexcusable sends Raphael to admonish him . . .'

[1] In 'Some Glances at Current Linguistics', IAR criticizes Noam Chomsky's 'projected revolution', which asked grammarians 'to add something that might formally explain how language works, how the inter-verbal relations it works through are to be specified'. Chomsky's tentative formulation was to postulate a generative linguistics that defines 'a broad contrast between *surface* and *deep* linguistic structures'—distinctions which may not be all that different from the old 'separation of *logical* from *grammatical* form'. However, while no one should 'undervalue Chomsky's insistence on the necessity for abstract entities in linguistic description, or his concern for principles from which the particularities of the speaker–hearer's performance derive', all too often what he attempts to describe 'is still undescribed'. 'Thus attempts at *formal* accounts of the interdependencies of the linguistic levels and so on must be recognized as inevitably unsatisfactory' (*So Much Nearer: Essays Toward a World English* [1968], 76–7, 78, 80, 83–4, 89).

No doubt I. A. R. was cross at having his own work parrotted without acknowledgement, but the points he makes are strong and impersonal. They seem to me all (modern linguists) very hard to read because of this pervasive careerism behind the cooked-up obscurity. I did try to read Korzybski when young and thought just the same about him.[2]

Sorry not to have edited the tape; I have been very swamped with commitments, and also it is painful to face one's own vapouring. A great deal has to be cut, I find—I have just braced myself to look at it. I have had rather indignant appeals from David Wilson, and will get on with it as soon as I can. I think it can be reduced to a quite sensible article, though a bit shapeless as you say.

Yes, please send me anything easily available about linguistics which you think I should read. I am trying to finish the little edition of Coleridge just now, at last.

Yours with thanks and good wishes

William Empson.

I don't see your problem about 'a rule' quite—surely it is usual for rules to allow of exceptions, forming a case-law which is later digested into a code.

TO RICHARD ELLMANN*

Department of English Literature, The University, Sheffield S10 2TN

1 July 1971

Dear Ellmann,

Thank you very much for your letter. There is a point I wanted to ask you about, but we hadn't your biography available. On p. 450–1 you quote from a dream-book in which Joyce had noted down Nora's dreams *in 1916*; the one about Prezioso weeping has all I need for my theory except that this date seems to me too early. He says that he has 'liberated himself in art' from the theme of the happy triangle, but surely he would say that when *Ulysses* was nearly finished, not merely after finishing *Exiles*. How did you come to put all this 1916 material into a section dated 1918 and dealing with the end of *Ulysses*? It strikes me the date may be a slip.

Also, you say on p. 328 that Joyce reports dreams *of his own* about the

---

[2] In *Science and Sanity: An Introduction to Non-Aristotelian Systems and General Semantics* (1933), Count Alfred Korzybski (1879–1950) sought to make the theoretical foundations of general semantics into a *scientific* discipline; he was interested in 'the neurological attitude toward "meaning".' In 1938 he co-founded the Institute of General Semantics, and he later set up the International Society for General Semantics. See *Collected Writings: 1920–1950*, ed. M. Kendig (1990).

scene where Prezioso wept in the street; but they are not mentioned in the book again. There is no source given in the notes for the dream-book; can you tell me where to look it up? Probably it gives dreams from both Joyce and Nora.

It is not very decisive anyway, but I ought to get more abreast of this aspect, which an opponent sent me as a decisive refutation of my theory.

Yours sincerely

William Empson.

I hope to get to London in four or five weeks, anyway, and hope you will be available for a meal some time.

Very likely Bloom hoped to induce Nora to have a son by her lawful husband as a result of the triangle with Stephen. But his thoughts are not explicit there.

Tulsa

TO CHRISTOPHER RICKS

Department of English Literature, The University, Sheffield S10 2TN
[from Studio House]
27 September 1971

Dear Christopher Ricks,

Yes, the first week in May is free from other things. I am threatened with having to go to Canada [as visiting professor at York University, Toronto] early, but it can't be as early as all that. So let us fix it then. I shall be quite willing to read my piece about Mary Marvell, which certainly won't be out, indeed isn't quite finished. Please thank Miss Pitman; I answer you direct to ask about other things.

Do you know the whereabouts of an Eng. Lit. don called Singh who used to be at Belfast, but seems to have dropped out of the weeklies? He was editing a collection of essays on Marvell, and wanted one of mine, and seemed pretty surly at my wanting to add a page of second thoughts about it—it is odd how learning better is considered a grave sign of weakness in our profession. However he accepted it, but then nothing more happened. Probably the publisher lost heart. And now I am not sure I know better any more, so I would like to ask if he kept the page. Also, you know that sentence in French at the end of T. S. Eliot's essay on Marvell—'a fine spirit that they make no longer in London'.[1] Is he quoting some

---

[1] TSE's quotation at the end of his 'Andrew Marvell' (1921)—'*C'était une belle âme, comme on ne fait plus a Londres*—introduces a grammatical solecism in alluding to the last stanza of Jules

French author, as I had always assumed? But surely no Frenchman would want to say that London had ever made fine spirits. I expect Eliot just wanted to say that they are only made in Boston now, and that modern London to a Bostonian felt as provincial as Dublin (and Paris too I should hope, but I doubt whether this ever occured to him). [Pierre] Legouis might have felt that way, no doubt, but I don't think he would say it. Probably you have known the answer for a quarter of a century, knew it in fact as a teenager.

I find I shall have to read a lot of contemporary attacks on Marvell in the B. M. It seems clear that he was a thoroughly typical London intellectual literary leftwinger, and indeed may have invented the type, but it has gone steadily on.

Looking forward to seeing you

Yours affectionately

William Empson.

TO CHRISTOPHER NORRIS*

1 Hampstead Hill Gardens, NW3

7 October 1971

Dear Mr Norris,

I feel very bad not to have answered you for so long, and not to have read those horrible Frenchmen you posted to me. I did go through the first one, in translation, Jacques Nerrida [*sic*], and nosed about in several others, but they seem to me so very disgusting, in a simple moral or social way, that I cannot stomach them.[1] Nerrida does express the idea that, just as people were talking a grammar before grammarians arose, so there are other unnoticed regularities in human language and probably in other human systems. This is what I meant by the book-title *The Structure of Complex Words*, and it was not an out-of-the-way idea, indeed I may have

---

Laforgue's 'Complainte du pauvre jeune homme': 'Quand les croq'morts vinrent chez lui, | Quand les croq'morts vinrent chez lui; | Ils virent qu c'était un'belle âme, | Comme on n'en fait aujourd'hui! | Ame, | Dors, belle âme! | Quand on est mort c'est pour de bon . . .

Pierre Legouis told CR on 18 May 1972 he could not identify the quotation. WE wrote further to CR (23 Jul. 1972): 'I think it is clear that the Young Pretender [TSE] just invented that bit of French, and [I] am glad to learn it is incorrect. However we must wait and see if more information emerges.'

[1] Jacques Derrida had emerged as a famous theoretical force outside France by 1967, with the publication of *Of Grammatology*, *Writing and Difference*, and *Speech and Phenomena*; so Norris thought it reasonable, given the practice of close reading that Derrida undertook in his early works, to encourage Empson to read them.

got it from someone else, but of course it is no use unless you try to present an actual grammar, an actual grammar of the means by which a speaker makes his choice while using the language correctly. This I attempted to supply, and I do not notice that the French ever even try.

They use enormously fussy language, always pretending to be plumbing the very depths, and never putting your toe into the water. Please tell me I am wrong, and come and have lunch and pick up the documents when you next visit London. But do not make me read any more of it.

Yours with thanks
William Empson

§ JONATHAN RABAN: A CONTRETEMPS BETWEEN WE AND CHRISTOPHER RICKS

Christopher Ricks, in 'Flicking Through', *The Listener*, 86 (28 Oct. 1971, 591), wrote of Jonathan Raban's *The Society of the Poem* (1971):[1]

'Also to Lorna Sage, without whom it would have been even more unscrupulous than it is.' The hard-nosed soft-centredness of that dedication is meant to be disarming: better, though, to take its swaggering cadging straight—it is indeed an unscrupulous way to proffer a book. Jonathan Raban sets out with some imaginative questions . . . but his whole enterprise is vitiated by his imaginative refusal to stand in any other posture than akimbo. Any book about the language of poetry needs to watch its language—which would mean not slyly boasting about being unscrupulous, and not taking over the reader's right of

---

[1] Jonathan Raban (b. 1942) is a novelist, critic and travel writer; his works include *Soft City* (1973), *Old Glory* (1981), *Foreign Land* (1985), *Hunting Mister Heartbreak* (1990), *Bad Land* (1996), and *Waxwings* (2003). WE met him in the summer of 1971 while staying with Robert Lowell and Caroline Blackwood in Kent. He took a liking to Raban and would entertain him to lunch at the Saville Club; and then he put Raban up for membership in the hope that he might thereafter play the host and pick up the tab. Of Raban he wrote to the club secretary on 5 December 1971: 'I only met him fairly recently, but feel confident in the recommendation. He was staying with Robert Lowell, and is doing a book about his verse. I have read his recent book of criticism on recent poetry (*The Society of the Poem*, Harrap), and think well of it. He has a play soon to be performed on the Third Programme, and another has been requested. He has been invited to do a term at an American university for a term next spring. He has been doing a number of reviews in *The New Statesman* and elsewhere. Till recently he was a lecturer in English Literature at Norwich [East Anglia] University, but has now resigned the post. He is about thirty.

'He is thus on his legs, and a writer, and his conversation seems to me very sensible, lively, and well-informed. It strikes me that the Club needs a supply of young people like that, to maintain its tradition, but that they are not very easy to find.' (*Houghton carbon*)

judging the argumentative proceedings to be fair. (Four times we are assured, not altogether reassuringly, that 'I think it's fair to say that . . .' If you don't think it fair to say, let's hope you'd not be saying it.) The brisk slovenliness of the style demeans more than itself: 'Flicking one's way through any anthology of recent poems . . .'; 'If one flicks through an anthology of concrete poetry . . .' Flicking through seems to be what Mr Raban does to poems. And to his own words—what coherence or concern is there in such bright haste? 'All this would, indeed, be a hanging up of parochial dirty linen, were it not for the fact that the texture of so much contemporary verse itself seems to have absorbed the dogma, initiated by Eliot, maintained by both Leavis and the New Critics, and kept fitfully alight by the Critical Quarterly.' 'Alight' is stylistic arson. Everywhere there is easy mastery and dextrous rhetoric: 'The roots of this situation lie deep in the field of sociolinguistics. Sufficient here to remark that . . .'

Worst of all, there is the continual spurious precision and factitious striving of 'a kind of'. 'A kind of required nervous tic'—exactly, and protected by 'a kind of coy cool'. And a kind of encapsulated prophecy, Gaitskellite liberal consensus, racy vulgarity, partisan fervour, Manichean totality, harmonious community, cosmic community, calculated doggerel, syncopated cadenza, deliberate childishness, prophetic science fiction, total environmental collage, hypothetical mode, exemplary necromancy, hedgehog ball, emotional purity, televisual talking head, anarchic irony, mechanical radicalism, illustrative diagram, epic finality, recurrent soliloquy, action criticism—and, at last, a kind of calm joy. Each a tedious small cheat, and so casually profligate as to suggest a contempt for any reader who might be seriously attending.

The book's arguments often depend on matters of tone, which makes it disconcerting that Mr Raban should, for instance, hear the rhymes in Philip Larkin's 'Mr Bleaney' as 'tinkling'. The poem's very first rhyme—'stayed' against 'frayed'—seems to me in context about the least tinkling rhyme in English poetry. Similarly, I distrust Mr Raban's sight when he sees T. S. Eliot's Sweeney as one of the 'guises' in which Prufrock 'crops up': if this is a guise, then to me it's an impenetrable one, since Prufrock's fastidiousness is at the opposite pole from Sweeney's brutality. In all these cases, Mr Raban exhibits a strange unwillingness to engage with what the poems are actually saying: too much is claimed for tone, but also too little in that tone is sufficiently brought into relation to substance. Ed Dorn is praised for these lines:

> Whitman carried into the administration tower of the U. of
> Takes-us underarm spray deodorant.

'The University of Texas gets transmuted into the U. of Takes-us, in an act of cheeky appropriation.' Admiration for this particular pun seems excessive, but the striking thing about Mr Raban's commentary—in a book on 'the society of the poem'—is its omission of any word about what it was that Whitman did from the tower at Texas. For the critic, the crucial matter is the relation (flippant? acute?) between the 'cheeky' tone and the fact of mass murder. To say nothing at all about the insane murders while going on casually and amiably about 'Dorn's voice, casual, amiable, slangy' is to nullify the crux which Mr Raban's critical initiative had itself selected. A nullifying which occurs repeatedly in the book, and which makes it strictly a disappointment and not just a failure.

'Does poetic order correspond in any detailed way to social order? What sort of regime is maintained in a particular verse structure, and does one enter it as a tourist or as a tax-paying citizen?' These are real questions, and at the moments when Mr Raban is prepared to give his mind to them he repays himself with observations that are shrewd and sensitive. As when he says of Gary Snyder that 'the verse itself functions like a commune.' But mostly all he does is divert himself.

THE LISTENER, 86 (25 November 1971), 722:
'Flicking Through'

Sir: I have been puzzling over the review by Professor Christopher Ricks of Jonathan Raban's book *The Society of the Poem*, which you published on 28 October. I had admired the book, and was startled by the virulence of the review, but I feel now that it raises more general issues. Ricks admits that the book asks 'real' and 'imaginative' questions, and that some of its answers are 'shrewd and sensitive'. But he finds its manner very bad, in some way which proves the author to be a bad man—his 'swaggering cadging', for instance—and 26 of his phrases are listed as betraying contempt for any serious reader, 'each a tedious small cheat'. They include 'deliberate childishness, emotional purity, illustrative diagram, recurrent soliloquy', and surely, at this rate, it becomes hard to know what phrases are still permitted. Probably Ricks has a real point about the incident in the University of Texas, obscurely mentioned in one of the poems quoted; he feels that 'insane murders' ought not to be mentioned flippantly; but the poet does not tell us what really happened, nor does Ricks: must a reader of the poem simply keep mum until he has researched the files of

Texas newspapers?[2] Raban seems to describe the tone taken by the poet accurately enough.

I too read the book with some irritation, because he was accepting bad poems or silly fashions in technique without comment; but I think this is sufficiently cleared up in the last few pages. He is concerned to understand why the poets are deluded into liking such tricks, or how their different styles all follow from one trend: so that giving the poets marks all the time would be out of place. It has always been usual for a new kind of work to be considered in an unacademic manner, realising that a just estimate requires a certain generosity, a readiness to take a leap in the dark, or risk a rash generalisation. A man who has been led on to do this, during talk after dinner, will often draw back and try to think of objections, but then go on: 'I think it is fair to say . . .' The other diners do not at once leap up and say: 'Why that *proves* he's a cheat. He's practically *confessed*.' What my brother professor is really saying, I am afraid, is that such matters may only be discussed in the style of a PhD thesis; but that would mean that the clotted nonsense at present talked in such theses would have to be talked for ever and ever. I am sure he is not really so sunk in corruption as this moment of irritation would imply.

By the way, when Raban says he 'leafs through' an anthology he does not mean that he has not read it properly beforehand, but that he is using this casual process of reminder to make a statistical estimate. Probably it is a trick we had better learn.

William Empson

London NW3

Ricks responded (*The Listener*, 2 Dec. 1971, 767):

> [Mr Empson] misreads my objection, which is not to the phrases 'deliberate childishness', 'emotional purity' and so on, but to the phrases 'a kind of deliberate childishness', 'a kind of emotional purity', 'a kind of coy cool', 'a kind of exemplary necromancy', 'a kind of hypothetical mode', 'a kind of racy vulgarity', 'a kind of anarchic irony', 'a kind of mechanical radicalism', and so on—26 times in a

---

[2] In Aug. 1966 Charles Joseph Whitman gunned down 34 people from the tower of the University of Texas at Austin, killing thirteen. Whitman's father was reported to have said, 'I'm a fanatic about guns . . . I raised my boys to know how to handle guns' ('The Madman on the Tower', *Time*, 12 August 1966, 21). In the period leading up to his shooting outage, Whitman had written: 'I've been having fears and violent impulses. I've had some tremendous headaches. I am prepared to die' (22).

short book. My objection is to the spurious precision of this softly fashionable formula, which means to give an air of corrugatedly bending its mind to a recalcitrant problem of definition while in fact demeaning the whole thing into 'a kind of required nervous tic'. Mr Empson judges that I am 'sunk in corruption' for not admiring such a style; but T. S. Eliot, whose authority weighs even more with me than does Mr Empson's, remarked that '*a kind of* is a phrase only to be used in extremity.' I am not persuaded that Mr Raban found himself 26 times in extremity.

On the mass murders from the University of Texas tower (widely reported in English newspapers, and the subject of a poem by John Berryman which outdoes Ed Dorn's): I still think it wrong of Mr Raban—in a book about society and poems—to discuss Dorn's 'cheeky' tone in those lines without saying anything at all about the mass murders which are the tacit subject of the lines; one of the critic's duties must be to intimate the relationship between the mass murders and the cheeky tone. Why is it a good thing to sound cheeky about such hideous killings? If Mr Empson really thinks that it is only those who have 'researched the files of Texas newspapers' who have ever heard of that insane massacre at Texas, then it seems to me that it is he who should raise his head from those PhD theses or whatever.

As to style: somewhere between the 'clotted nonsense' of PhD theses and Mr Raban's junkets, there remain possibilities for an honourable and fortifying critical style. For instance, that of Mr Empson.

TO CHRISTOPHER RICKS

Studio House, 1 Hampstead Hill Gardens. NW3.
3 December 1971

My dear Christopher Ricks,

I certainly won't write another letter to the Listener about our tiny quarrel; it would be sort of nagging, whereas I owe you a lot of gratitude, at least, and my first letter has done what was needed to calm or reassure the sensitive overscrupulous young man (I ought to have written 'kind of sensitive', but it is hard to learn). His case needed attending to, I thought, but so did yours; I would not have written to the paper if I had not had your letter saying you found you 'could not respect Harvard', which I thought evidence of a very unhealthy frame of mind, a brief infection no doubt but one that friends should recognise and speak to you about.[3]

---

[3] Ricks had written to WE from Harvard, where he was teaching at the time; he was decrying not the whole university but the Department of English.

Presumably they have no good Eng Lit dons in Harvard now, any more than in Oxford, but it has a continuing life all the same.

I grant that you introduce the list of phrases with your complaint about 'a kind of', and that I misunderstood you there. But I reread the book with this complaint in view, and failed to notice any of the cases because the fault seems to me invisible. Raban is carrying out his own theory; in this case, he should write as a man talks when propounding a new idea to a circle of friends. Probably he overdoes it; the written style wants to be briefer; but I actually cannot feel any excess of the polite pretence of hesitation even when I read again looking for it. It is not a tone of 'swaggering cadging' anyhow, and he needed to have someone answer in print that that was not his tone; but also it is not an excessive tone of polite hesitation.

Your answer makes me afraid that something bad is happening to you; it is worse than the review, because it seems incapable of understanding the matter. You ought not to have been accused of 'corruption', merely because you 'disliked' the style. But you did not merely dislike it; you told the young man he was a bully and a cadger. I agree that I was talking rather too big when I called this corrupt, but I was doing a simple *tu quoque*, giving you a taste of your own dirty talk; and when a Professor actually can't realise that that is happening to him, but indignantly presumes that the judge is not treated like the jailbird, it is quite usual to feel that he has mistaken his profession.

But never mind; we all escape with no stain on our characters; so long as you let it ride; but in your present mood I do not know what to expect.

Yours affectionately

William Empson

7 Dec. This is very dismal stuff; there must be something wrong with me too. But it had better be posted. WE.

Ricks; Houghton: carbon

Ricks replied with a letter from Harvard University on 11 December 1971:

Dear William Empson,

Your letter, kind in some ways, leaves me more perplexed. I'm not sure whether we should still try to sort the matter out. Still—yr. letter seeks to show me my confusions, so I'll try to show you yours. For a start, if 'what was needed' was a public reassurance for Jonathan Raban, why do you say that you *wouldn't* have written to 'The Listener' had it not been that I had expressed disrespect towards Harvard in a (completely unconnected with all this) letter to you? If in a hasty note to you—replying, you'll remember, to a *query from you* for Singh's address—I spoke too slightingly of Harvard, then I apologise (to it, I suppose, & not to you); but Harvard, I assure you, is in a very bad way, & great institutions can get into states which dispirit & jar one. I still can't see why you now say that you'd *not* have carried out yr. duty to/by Raban if I hadn't disconcerted you abt. Harvard. My remarks abt. Harvard may be 'evidence of a very unhealthy frame of mind' (have you been in Harvard much lately?), & so my 'friend should speak to [me] abt. it'; I can't see that a letter to 'The Listener' abt. Raban *was* a way of speaking to me abt. it, though of course justifiable perhaps on other grounds.

On the relation of style to moral matters: yr. original letter seemed to imply that one isn't allowed to use strong moral terms abt. style; yr. position is now that I misdescribed the style. The former I don't agree with as a principle (you say I'm 'incapable of understanding the matter'; sorry, I think that I understand it but disagree with you abt. it; the latter I'm not persuaded of. You'll grant that there is such a thing as a style of false candour, something collusive and other than the appeal to a 'circle of friends'; I think that to word an acknowledgement thus: 'To X, without whom this book wd. have been even more unscrupulous than it is': to use a false candour; we're being cunningly asked to admire & like the scrupulousness of someone who admits—at once—that his book is unscrupulous. I don't admire that (I didn't *say* 'dislike', did I? I haven't a copy, & my lack of admiration is a moral as well as a stylistic matter. I think it's no way verbally to behave.

Again, when you now say, in a friendly way, 'I ought to have written "kind of sensitive", but it is hard to learn', it's clear to me that I still haven't made clear to you what this particular piece of verbal behaviour is. I'm *not* objecting to that fashionable inarticulacy 'kind of' (though I do deplore what you yourself have called 'the belief that the mumble is the only honest form of speech', *J. of Aesthetics)*,[4] but to the formula 'a kind of x y' (a kind of *adjective noun*), where paradoxes are offered but evaded, & precision pretended but demeaned. To say of a young man that he is 'kind of sensitive' is simply not the same as to say of a poem that it manifests 'a kind of coy cool' (*cool* as a noun is odious anyway). You wd. yourself die rather than write a phrase like 'a kind of coy cool', so why do you defend it in someone else? No, you can't move me on the 'corruption', to use yr. word, of such a prose style; I don't think I fail to understand what you're saying; I simply disagree with it.

Except for the personal reasons that, as you know, I'm not only full

[4] 'Taking for granted that mumbling is the only honest mode of speech is I suppose a fog which has thickened steadily for the last fifty years' ('Rhythm and Imagery in English Poetry', *British Journal of Aesthetics* 2 [January 1962]; *A*, 156).

of respect for & delight in what you've written, but also fond of you—
except for those, I've no objection *in principle* to being called 'sunk in
corruption'; I agree that we must get as good as we give. But that
doesn't mean that I have to agree with yr. *specific* accusations—on
Raban's style, on the Texas murders (anybody ignorant of them is
simply precluded from understanding those quoted lines of the
poem—cd. one read them in the belief that the *Whitman* in question
was *Walt?*), & on Ph D's. Quite honestly, I don't *believe* that you
believe(d) that I was saying that these things shd. only be discussed in
clotted Ph.D prose. For one thing, you wd. grant, I think that I don't
myself write PhD prose. For another, I don't think that 'Essays in
Criticism'—despite its faults—has succumbed to *that* prose. And last, I
don't *at all* at Bristol supervise PhD theses (or M. Litt's) precisely
because I think that the thesis industry is sunk in corruption. In saying
that *that* was what yr. 'brother professor was really saying', I think you
were casting abt. for a tu quoque wh. may be simple but isn't true (to
what I think prose style shd. aspire to, or, I honestly believe, to what *you*
think I was 'really saying').

You speak of Raban as a 'sensitive overscrupulous young man'—I
don't know him (haven't ever met), & it may be that personally you
have the advantage of me in knowing him. But such an advantage can
be a disadvantage too, in that it has funds of good will too available.
You say 'young man' more than once; I can't see the relevance of
youth to this (we *don't*, after all, live at a time when the performances of
youth *lack* favourers or a fair crack of the whip), & anyway I don't
know how much younger Raban is than I am. (I'd have guessed he was
in his 30's, like me—though that seems to me beside the point anyway.)

When I started to write this, I'd thought I'd be able to be more
amiable than this. But I couldn't muster the necessary false candour, so
this will have to stand. I wish this hadn't happened, though.

Yours,

Christopher Ricks

Grudging & not-without-anger affection all the same. Let's both have a
happy Christmas.

Houghton

§ END

———

TO FRANCIS DOHERTY*

Studio House, 1 Hampstead Hill Gardens, London NW3
7 December 1971

I write my answer a day after your gift arrived; it took seven weeks.

My dear Doherty,

Thank you so much for your kind letter and the gift of your book [*Samuel Beckett*, 1971]. I realise that I must try to be abreast of the modern world now that I am superannuated, and am glad of any help in my pathetic attempts. But it is generally found that the capacity to appreciate modern work is one of the first things to go; in fact, whenever an old buffer is observed giving a prize to a young hopeful (a standard practice) one must reflect that, unless someone young enough has advised the buffer, he is certain to have picked on the wrong hopeful. I will say what occurs to me about Beckett and your sober graceful book on him, but I speak as a colleague in another Department might do.

Some while ago I was given the paperback of *All that Fall* as a Christmas present, and was told the basic plot to encourage me to read it; a new book then. What I was told sounded to me artificially horrible, so I did not read it. An almost impotent blind man is put onto a train, to be taken out by his loving relations when he reaches the right station, but he exposes his sex and tries to masturbate before a female whose voice sounds to him sympathetic, not realising that this is a child, who throws herself in horror out of the window of the train and somehow manages to get under its wheels, so that she is killed. Such is the story, and it would be worth asking the police records of England and Ireland, and France I suppose, whether they find it familiar. I think that Beckett was just trying to think of something really nasty to foist on the BBC. An Artful-Dodger glee was all that he really felt about his plot. Your account has a beautiful cool detached purity, but surely this is done at the cost of leaving out the whole point.

Then again, I liked (in a way) and certainly admired the London production of *Waiting for Godot*.[1] It was said to be much more cosy and human than the Paris one, but Beckett is a very intelligent man and probably

[1] In October 1955 WE had participated in a discussion at the Arts Theatre London (where *Waiting for Godot* had enjoyed a long initial run before transferring to the Criterion Theatre) on the subject 'Do we or don't we wait for Godot?' Among other speakers at the forum who were asked to consider whether *Godot* was good, simply as entertainment, were Harold Hobson, Peter Forster, and Peter Coates; and a vote taken at the end of the meeting gave those who were prepared to 'wait for Godot' a majority of about 10 to 1 (reported in the *Bookseller*, 8 Oct. 1955). See also *MG*, 263.

allowed nature to take its course. Your letter speaks of a vague memory of something I had said about disliking Beckett. I have a specific memory of you here, but these things are always liable to be wrong. I had written to the TLS [on 30 March 1956: see above] saying that the play was about the effects of the fierce religious education still prevalent in Ireland, which tells the children that life becomes worthless if they stop believing in God, and they have nothing to keep them from crime, so when they grow up and discover that the Christian God is the wickedest devil ever invented they behave like a dog on the road with its back broken by a motorcar; and I said that this is a very unfair way to treat a child. I was very surprised when you came up and told me (having read my letter) that you agreed that this was an unfair method of education. It struck me that no other Roman Catholic would have made this generous admission; but later on I found that Beckett was brought up as a Protestant (which of course would make no difference to the Irish insistence on the most evil features of the religion), and then I am afraid I presumed you must have known he was a Protestant when you spoke to me. I am rather sorry now to hear you have forgotten all about it. Your report of his remarks about his childhood religious teaching and reactions does not really alter the position; he had religious feelings at his first communion, and it stuck in his head that his 'brother and mother got no value from their religion when they died'. God had cheated the family somehow, and it was an excuse for him—this emerges even when he tries to debunk the idea.

Very likely his work for the French resistance brought grim experiences; and, not long after, he was willing to marry Joyce's daughter, on the theory that a bit of sex would keep her from going mad; he was saved from the marriage only because she became plainly too mad, and we are not encouraged to think that his advances drove her over the edge, but he would be sensitive enough to suspect it. Joyce himself, though basically kind, would be an exasperating tyrant to work for. I am trying to list the excuses for despair of young Beckett, and it strikes me that half the population of the world had much greater ones. The truth is, he was surrounded with what he wanted, plenty to refuse to write about in the heart of the great luxury-centre, where his poutings and pretences of contempt for all creation were each of them sure to be received with a great roar of applause. I think him a circus animal. It is much to his credit that, when kidnapped by the Irish a few years ago on St Patrick's Night, he cried like a horse on peat whisky at the Irish Club of Paris; it would have been out of character to refuse.

Your book is reticent, and I estimate only about 45,000 words; I wonder whether you reduced the words to make it cheaper; publishing is very queer now. But clearly reticence is a Roman Catholic ploy here; what you want to tell the children is that everybody feels absolutely miserable unless they worship the God

> who could be bought by the offer of having his son tortured to death to let off mankind from Hell in exchange; but he ratted on the bargain so completely that the vast majority of mankind will go to eternal torture all the same; and the tiny remnant who escape to Heaven are condemned to spend their whole time in gloating over the tortures in Hell of those they loved on earth, meanwhile incessantly praising God for his mercy.

I indent it hoping to win your attention. This is the most evil God yet invented, which means that his worshippers are under great temptation to imitate his evil. And the present Pope is demanding the destruction of all mankind, by forcing them to breed to the point of famine—offering no reason whatever (as he cannot offer any religious one) except the snobbish one that 'human dignity' demands it. No wonder any propaganda for it has to be reticent.

I think it dreadful, my dear fellow, that a man of your ability has to let himself be hamstrung by such gross farcical evil.

Very affectionately
William Empson

Houghton: carbon, bMS Eng 1401 (538)

TO RICHARD M. WILSON*
(Dean of the Faculty of Arts at Sheffield)

Studio House, 1 Hampstead Hill Gardens, London NW3
[n.d.: 1971]

Dear Wilson,

I must certainly thank you and the Faculty Board for the kind thoughts you have sent to me; I am not sure whether they have any bearing on a problem of etiquette which I am now to lay before you. This morning I received from Oxford the draft of an announcement, saying that 'Professor William Empson' will give the Waynflete Lectures in the coming year at such-and-such times. Am I to write back saying that I am no longer a Professor?

I am emboldened to ask because by the same post I received a circular from the Music Department in Sheffield addressing me as 'Emeritus Professor William Empson', which does not suggest that a vote has been taken deciding that I am not one. Very likely the matter is not brought up till a later Faculty Meeting, during term when more people are present. But I ought to send an answer to the Oxford people fairly soon, so that the hand-out can be printed.

I don't want to call myself Doctor because that seems a misuse of a real word; doctors heal sick people. And to appear as a naked name, funny [*sic*] enough, would feel rather too swagger; it would be classing myself with Arthur Waley and T. S. Eliot. But of course I would take care to act on the decision of the University.

Yours sincerely
William Empson.

Houghton

TO PETER LEVI*

Studio House, 1 Hampstead Hill Gardens, London NW3
[n.d. 1972]

Dear Peter Levi,[1]

Your remarks when we both dined at Magdalen [where WE, who was Waynflete Lecturer in January–February, delivered four lectures on 'The

---

[1] Peter Levi commented on this letter by WE, in an undated letter to JH: 'It's possible I did get his letter, and answer it, but perhaps verbally, as I often saw him then. I remember the dinner at Magdalen (where he was a visiting lecturer that term) very well, and much of the conversation on which he comments. We had started from Milton's theology in *Milton's God*, a book I admire, and moved on to what if anything could make sense of the crucifixion. I had thought Anselm took a madly mechanical and judiciary view of 'redemption', a kind of quid pro quo, like buying back a slave. I still suspect this is the view he does take, but don't care, and can't be bothered to look him up. Thomas says that Christ being God, one drop of blood was enough, or one sigh. Scotus (I will have said at Magdalen) thought Christ would have come even if man had never fallen, just as an expression of divine generosity or love of man. I sympathise with that view. I suppose the crucifixion was just the predictable way this world (let alone the Romans) *would* treat someone like Christ. This will have been my view certainly by about 1967. A little later, but I think by the time of Empson's letter, I entertained the heresy called Patripassionism, which I shared with Auden and others; it says that the Father did suffer at the pain of the Son. I am still inclined to this.

'But of course Empson was right to rub my nose in the earliness of the disgusting views (and metaphors) he outlines. "Satisfaction" for "sin" by pain or blood has never made much sense, or any, to me, except as a very far-fetched metaphor, but there is plenty of evidence of theologians (a race I have detested since about 1961) taking it deadly seriously. (So does Donne.)

'I do think he is slightly and amusingly perverse but not beyond the call of wit. I think the *Catholic Encyclopedia* is a very poor source, and not one I would dream of taking seriously. I think Abelard was usually right in his many quarrels with Bernard, and history judged in the same way, in that Abelard's movement led to the growth of universities and Bernard's to the fanaticism and isolation of monks. Empson's article ['The Satisfaction of the Father', a slightly developed version of this letter to Levi, in *A*, 622–6] is brilliant, lucid, and not over-stated. I do not think it affects me, and I note that he got tired of it. This may be due to something we said later (or I wrote to him) but I do not know. I expect we agreed that it was a tiring, long subject,

Editorial Choice of the Text of a Poem']² made me look the point up in the *Catholic Encyclopaedia*, and its entry under Sacrifice (Christian), which comes at the end of a respectable survey of the whole practice, denounces with logic and vigour the latitudinarian opinions which you expressed, so much so that a smell of burning human flesh seemed to me to engage itself with the always stuffy atmosphere of the B. M. Reading Room. The universal conviction of Christianity, it leads off, was expressed by the Synod of Ephesus (431, rather late perhaps), which said that the incarnate Logos 'offered himself to God the Father for us'. It is often expressed in the NT: Matt. 20.28 'to give his life for a ransom for many', Eph. v.2., 'gave himself up for us', II Cor v. 21: 'Him who knew no sin he made to be sin on our behalf'; and this was not invented by St Paul, goes on the C. E., because it is in Peter I 18–20 'ye were redeemed . . . with the blood of Christ'. This does seem impossible to get away from; it is what everybody supposes to be meant by the incessant use of the torture of the Cross as an advertisement or trademark of Christianity. And yet its interpretation has never been clear, as even the C. E. quaintly admits by ending: 'A comprehensive theory, employing dialectically all the Biblical and patristic factors, is still a desideratum in speculative theology'.

I brought up the view of the late S. G. F. Brandon, of Manchester, that the original use of the Crucifixion had been to deceive the committee of devils who were ruling the world (from their planets) so that they had to release mankind from their clutches—they had been tricked into killing a

---

requiring more learned researches than it merited, since I do remember that we agreed it was impossible or intolerable to believe in such a disgusting God, and I do think I conveyed to him my own suspicion that nobody nowadays does, except lunatics. It was this thought that provoked his reactions.

'And yet. He has a lot of right on his side. I certainly would not have entered into controversy with him. If I did reply I would have been extremely polite. I think I may have, because I faintly remember being appalled that he cited the *Catholic Encyclopedia*, and that can't have been at dinner.

'I think I was taught at school, by Irish Brothers in the 40's, that Lucifer fell because he thought the Incarnation undignified, and that when it happened he was puzzled by Christ. One could check that old Catechism, and see. About the confusion of angels, devils, elementals and God knows what in the minds of Paul and his contemporaries, Empson is right. As to "how the trick was done", it may have been thought that only by dying could Christ descend into hell and bring out its prisoners. If so, the myth goes back to Mesopotamia where Inanu (is it?) does something similar.'

² Peter Levi was to recall of WE during a visit to Oxford at this period: 'He gave almost the only Oxford lecture I ever heard that got a standing ovation; it was a discussion of Donne's manuscripts, delivered during an electricity cut, almost entirely in the dark. Later, he took everyone to a pub where he ordered gin, hot water, and peppermint cordial, which he believed was the ordinary drink of the working classes' ('Hot gin and peppermint' [on *RB*], *Independent*, 4 Dec. 1986).

god, so had to pay a heavy forfeit.[3] This seemed to you an arbitrary absurdity, but I find the substance of it to be deeply rooted in the history, and long surviving; St Bernard of Clairvaux, answering the liberalistic views of Abelard on this point (which sound to me very flimsy, but were of course an effort to retain adequate goodness for God), said that the ransom paid by the Cross was paid to the Devil, not to God. Irenaeus (2nd century) was apparently the first to say this definitely, and call it 'vicarious satisfaction', but there is general agreement (moving to the next shelf, for the two Encyclopaedias of Religion and Ethics) that the first centuries regarded the crucifixion as releasing mankind from the Devil somehow, never mind just how the trick was done. Every use of the terms *ransom* and *redemption* presumes that the slave needs to be saved from his present owner.

The view of Irenaeus was soon denounced, but I did not bother to note the dates of attack after realising that his view could still be maintained by the impeccably orthodox St Bernard, 1000 years later. It is indeed the only solution of the difficulty that feels natural, because it allows God to be good; but it confronts an immense theoretical obstacle, because it makes the Devil nearly as strong as God—it is Manicheanism. It seems clear that St Paul was immensely tactful about this dilemma, having to confront unconverted or halfconverted audiences, and used language which could encourage their beliefs about the spirits now ruling the world without being too definite. Once the Church had temporal power, which meant the power to torture, of course it had to claim for God all the powers of the Devil. All theories about *why* the Father was satisfied by crucifying his Son now become further struggles to make the Father the wickedest thing yet invented by the black heart of man. Gloating over Hell became a requirement for the blessed very early.

You surprised me by saying that Anselm had invented the bad part of the doctrine, and that Aquinas had rejected it: at least, that was what I understood you to say. The next shelf, the two E.s of E. and R. [*Encyclopaedia of Religion and Ethics*], tells me that Anselm considered the *honour* of God to demand satisfaction; and I really am glad to learn about this, though it seems a minor point. Anselm excused God by ascribing to him the sentiments of a feudal lord. I had imagined that the Code of Honour was Renaissance, but of course it was feudal in origin and merely refurbished by the Renaissance. Aquinas in differing from him merely said that 'satisfaction' was not essential: God might have adopted other ways of

---

[3] See S. G. F. Brandon, *The Judgment of the Dead* (1967); reviewed by WE in 'Heaven and Hell', *The Listener*, 30 Nov. 1967: *A*, 620–1.

redeeming mankind, but adopted this one as the most fitting. The satisfaction was superabundant for the Father (Summa pars iii Qq 46–90). I knew there was some hair-raising passage in Aquinas but failed to find it again when I was printing *Milton's God*, and must now go as soon as possible to look up the reference in the top room of the London Library. I am most grateful to you if you have made me recover this lost bit. The peculiar literary style adopted by both Milton and Aquinas when they explain how delighted the Father must have been when torturing his Son to death, because it was the greatest pleasure he was capable of—well, I think it needs pointing out.

No wonder the religion is now trying to destroy mankind by forcing them to breed beyond the famine level. And the only excuse offered by the Pope for this flippant superstition, insanely feeble compared to its consequences, is that the Dignity of man prevents [him] from using any form of birth control except an elaborate calculation from the calendar which he knows is very likely to be ineffective. Havoc and spoil and ruin are my gain has always been the voice of Moloch the torture-monster.[4]

You could not expect me to say less, my dear chap.

William Empson

Houghton: carbon, bMS Eng 1401 (596)

TO FRANK KERMODE ['John Donne—An Illumination'][1]

[n.d. 1972]

Dear Kermode,

Your letter seems to me broad and moderate, while making the crucial points firmly; I feel rather ridiculous at having a collapse on receipt of it,

---

[4] The 'anarch old', or Chaos, tells Satan: 'Havoc and spoil and ruin are my gain' (*Paradise Lost*, II, l. 1009).

[1] A recorded conversation between WE and Kermode was to be made as a trial run for the script of *John Donne—An Illumination*, a show devised by WE, Kermode, Roy Strong (Director of the National Portrait Gallery, 1967–73) and Andrew Hilton, and performed—as part of *A City Tribute to John Donne: Poet and Dean of St Paul's*, celebrating the 400th anniversary of his birth—at the Mermaid Theatre, London, on 2–8 Oct. 1972. Neither WE nor Kermode appeared in person, the 'agreed' text of their discussion being delivered by actors. WE explained in a letter to the French cultural attaché (13 Jan. 1973), 'it was part of the backstairs work for arranging a performance. I wrote many pages recommending what should be done and said in the performance, and what should be shown, and then I did this recording, just to do all I could before I had to fly to Canada. I am thankful for my safety when the terrible struggle of devising the performance went on for a sheer fortnight as I am told. But you should realize that in this recording both Kermode and I were pulling our punches, we were *imitating* a discussion, trying to sketch what had better occur in the play. As it went on, it almost broke through into being real, but never on my side and nor I expect on Kermode's' (copy in Houghton). Richard Holmes reviewed it for

but really it wasn't on that ground. In the main I get my stomach-aches when the pressure is taken off, and I still feel there wasn't any urgency about this. Still, as we have not much time and [Bernard] Miles wants results, I am now inclined to agree with his plan for a recorded discussion; it would at least avoid a lot of typing for our side. By all means have the recording in the studio here if that is convenient. I propose now to write an explanation and defence of my position to you, which need not be among the documents submitted, though I wouldn't oppose that; next I think we should meet and rough out how the discussion should go, then preferably next day do the recording of it. This ought to reduce the plan to manageable size.

I would like also to record some readings of poems, just to show the actor who reads them at performance what intonations are required by my interpretation of them; the different critical opinions often do entail different performances. But I am sure an actor had better read them on the night. You had better make advisory recordings too; most actors of course are accustomed to direction and not offended by it.

You say towards the end that I seem to regard you as a composite enemy, hardly distinguishable from Helen Gardner for example; yes, I really do think that modern literary scholars all take at least one wrong attitude. It is the belief that the text ought to be made as meaningless as possible; one ought to expect an old poem to be trivial and dull, and if readers at the time said it wasn't their delusions deserve to be exposed. To do this is striking a blow for the truth. But I expect that an admired poem really did have some point, at the time, which a critic needs to recover (and at any rate a crinoline was really observed to fill the doorway, even when it was a convention). This seems to me quite different from arguing that the poems are secretly pietistic, with the girl's fawn meaning the Anglican Church, for example; I warmly agree with you that that is a betrayal. The point about letting the crucial passage in *Appleton House* recall the crucifixion is that Marvell really did feel afraid of returning to the world after this necessarily brief retirement, and was not afraid to say so to the patron who was his only immediate reader. I think the emotional scale of the poem is greatly reduced if you are forbidden to let him mean that, and I think it absurd to suppose that *he* felt forbidden, because he was writing in a genre or something. In a rather different way, the glitter of the earlier

---

The Times (3 Oct. 1972): 'The *Illumination* is semi-dramatic, with . . . George Benson and Antony Brown as a pair of faintly buffoon-like modern critics in spectacles and leather armchairs.' Kermode's sorry account figures in his *An Appetite for Poetry* (1984), 129: 'The piece was hardly a success, and I am glad to think the Empson scholars are unlikely to trace *that* manuscript.'

Donne poems comes from being 'contemp'ry', from the currently shocking or attractive ideas they hooked on to, and any chop-logic to say they
didn't *have* to hook on is off the point. In a third way, a poem such as *The
Nocturnal* presumes a situation in which the speaker is living, in this case a
process which has gone on for years; and then a critic ought to consider
'what story would be adequate, would suit the poem best?'—what situation would make all the references in the poem not silly but pointed? It is
not sensible for you to call this process of thought 'fantasy', and I do not
understand how you can maintain that the poem is good while denying
that it has any real subject. So far I feel on firm ground, but of course the
subject may still have been an imagined one. I think this does happen with
Twickenham Garden, a glowingly romantic poem which just uses feelings
active in the poet's mind but not felt about the poor Countess (I had a
letter from India, where an indignant pundit felt that the cynicism of
modern criticism was too disgusting at this point, but I had to agree with it
so far). But then, *Twickenham Garden* does not survey a long series of experiences and claim the authority of later wisdom. I do not believe that you
could read *The Nocturnal* aloud, without plain inadequacy, after your success in renouncing what you call fantasy. In any case, the rule is a completely illogical one, or reflects nothing but the pressures upon the
Departments of English Literature, increasingly heavy as I don't deny.

It occurs to me that we have swapped places, rather oddly. Surely, you
are the one who takes Imagism and Symbolism seriously, whereas I like
poetry that argues. But here (in the Good-Morrow for instance) I think
that living on another planet is an extremely powerful Symbol for the
claim of the lovers to have independent rights; the claim is presented, very
clearly, in The Sun Rising, when he says that all the dignities of the world
are only a feeble imitation of what the lovers confer on one another, but he
gives this a clincher when he compares it to colonising another planet. The
idea was theologically so alarming that it was seldom mentioned, but it
was familiar from the people who tried to colonise America, and frequently mutinied; it would be a very obvious Symbol to the first readers of
Donne. When you argue that it is irrelevant in the poem, because the
lovers only want each other, you talk as if you had never heard of Symbolism. So too when you say there is no evidence for this astronomical interest
in Donne but 'little hints'; what else is there in the Waste Land to show the
interests of Eliot but little hints, please? However, I have a stronger argument against your air of patient scholarly surprise; your state of belief
undoubtedly derives from a book published in 1931, where T. S. Eliot
screamed out and cried 'Donne was, I insist, no sceptic', meaning that he

could not have entertained any belief implying that Jesus was not unique; all Eng. Lit. was hushed, and everybody said that of course Donne didn't mean anything, and till then they all agreed with me. I am too old to feel sure that the very rocks agree with you.

You don't suggest another poem, and I think these ones are reasonable candidates, don't you? I left out the Valediction, of Weeping, though on my side and frightfully good, because it would take so much explaining. But it might be a good thing to have The Expiration, because it will come in the songs, and they will have no idea what it means unless they are told (which might however be done at the time). The lovers have run away together, renouncing the world, so that they have no [one] left but one another, and then on the very day of their escape they discover that they cannot endure one another and must part for ever. It is more than Byronic: and one can see from the variants that Donne invented the final twist of the story in the middle of composing the first verse. But what will you say, if this is brought in, quite briefly? I suppose you will say that it doesn't mean anything, but how can that improve it?

Further evidence that the love-poems take the new astronomy seriously (looking further down your page) is that he renounces it very seriously when he is converted and preparing to be a parson (though of course I only maintain that he took what it symbolised seriously, things like freedom of belief and rejection of the Arranged Marriage—rather a rag-bag I don't deny). When you say '*Even* in Ignatius' he sneers at Kepler I can only answer Of Course; he is just getting ready to denounce it in the Anniversaries. He then wrote a sonnet 'I am a little world made cunningly' to expunge the separate planet as much as he could, and went on saying things like 'No man is an island'. Of course, with any active-minded man, if you ignore the dates you can say he is always contradicting himself.

Yes, better drop the point about air resistance. The 'old stuff' is a great deal more confusing than you think, but to argue about it would only be a bore.

I am much interested in your view that 'I have loved, and got, and told' ['Love's Alchemy'] means that he reckoned up the value of the woman after he had finished with her, and have to admit that it seems more relevant to the effort he is describing. But I cannot agree with you that 'counting' is primary and 'relating' secondary. The OED puts counting secondary, and relating is already present in Old Norse. *Tell on us* is already in the Great Bible of 1539. I can't think of a sixteenth-century use of 'kiss and tell' offhand but feel sure it was in use. Even if the solemn young man did mean 'count', and actually had priced his women in a notebook, he could not prevent the readers from thinking he had kissed and told. On either view I think it a typically juvenile poem.

The only point of giving them Nature's Lay Idiot, I thought, was to give the audience a reassurance that he wasn't simply getting the girls into trouble: here he is sure he gave the girl a leg up. I think he deserves this, and it might keep some of the audience from turning against him. Grierson and Leishman both assumed it [meant] there was a husband, I suppose because there is not enough paradox in saying she owes a greater duty to the seducer unless the opponent is a husband; besides, she obviously has security of tenure. It was Gardner who said the poem was 'innocent' because not adulterous, but I didn't mean to make a point of it. The trouble is that, if we keep in the poem (which I do think is good and would go well), we need to have something to discuss about it. I don't understand how you can say there is no thought of a creator in 'I planted knowledge and life's tree', but saying that might make a discussion.

It seems important to have some idea of his actual relations with women, so I put in one about a lowclass girl (lay idiot) and one about a patroness; they can come out if you like. One needs to consider what reality lies behind the extravagance of his language; at least I do, but you seem content as long as you can parse it, and rather pleased if it is totally false. The sentence about Miss Drury [in the Second Anniversary']:

> Her pure and eloquent blood
> Spoke in her cheeks, and so distinctly wrought
> That one might almost say, her body thought [244–6]

has been so often quoted because it casts some light on what he was praising. The girl blushed as soon as there was anything to blush at; she had no mind–body problem there. Lady Bedford as an experienced courtier cannot have been blushing all the time, but her body took part in her judgements with the same immediacy; her body 'covering discovers her quick soul'. Just to say that her virtue was a lamp, which you find beautiful, seems to me what used to be called 'frigid', so I look for the parallel passages which bring out the point.

Paracelsus is connected in Donne's mind, and his first readers', with the New Medicine implying a more intimate connection between soul and body; and had been prominent in distilling medicines. I try to follow the associations which would have been prominent at the time. But there is no need to talk about him over the Nocturnal. I think we should use the poem.

Yes, I wanted The Legacy because it is sheer grace not deep thoughts.

But I don't agree that the conceits can't be taken 'literally', if you mean as referring back to a real situation. The lady of pleasure is regarded ruefully (as he cannot have her for keeps) but with tender sympathy, and surely a great deal of understanding. It is one of the poems which seem to be about a real situation, but of course situations like that he was anyway familiar with.

I do not say that Donne *was* a Familist or a Joachite—that would be much out of his line; but that he and his intended readers were very well aware of these alarming people, though one might get into trouble for printing about them. I am ready to agree that all these dangerous references were jokes, or at least he would have claimed they were if accused of blasphemy; but why did the joke seem so piercing and alarming, or somehow true? I wonder why you 'won't talk about bad taste'? It is what Donne has been most often and effectively accused of.

Yes, by all means put in more dates. The Government was screwing up on both Catholics and Puritans in 1593, or under greater pressure from both as they would say; and to have a man executed for claiming to be Jesus at that time does at least make it absurd for H. G. [Helen Gardnes] to maintain that people then couldn't even think of '*a* Jesus Christ'. The death of the brother would mean that Donne had a longer fling before he need take a job. About [Thomas] Digges, I only meant that the plugging oppressive rhythms are alike; this kind of earnestness wasn't all on the reactionary side. I think the Digges passage at least ought to be read out; it is very magnificent. [See *ERL* (1), 216–18.]

No other main points. I wonder what evidence you have in mind for believing that some of the 'jokey' poems are late? I have no doubt he could despise women all right after he became a Christian; what I take to be early are poems which regard them as an almost unknown nation, like Huns say—maybe they have tails.

Try and record next Thursday or Friday, perhaps?

Houghton, bMS Eng 1401 (589)

TO JOHN SPARROW*

Studio House, 1 Hampstead Hill Gardens, NW3
14 March 1972

Dear Sparrow,

This article ['Rescuing Donne', 1972; *ERL* (I), 159–99] contains the substance of what I was saying about Donne in those lectures [Waynflete

Lectures]. It is painful to think of anyone reading the article uncorrected, as the printers refused to make the corrections at galley-proof stage or let me see the page proofs either; perhaps one had better just stop using American printers. However, the main purpose of printing at once, apart from the requirements of the Waynflete Lectures, was to be warned of mistakes before collecting my bits about Donne in book form; so please let me know of the ones you find in this. It seems to me very good of you to have come to the lectures, more than one as I was told, because being so deaf I greatly dislike listening to other people's lectures.

I see in Bald's recent life of Donne that you own the copy of *Pseudo-Martyr* which he inscribed to Woodward.[1] Please let me know whether he *dated* the inscription, and if so with what date. He might have presented it, some years after publication, as part of the process of making friends again, and then I think he would write the date (but not if he had simply neglected to do it earlier), whereas in giving a new book writing the date does not signify. However, though I believe Donne really did refuse to send Woodward the *Songs and Sonets* because he thought he had shown himself untrustworthy, I am not keen on my extra theory that the coldness continued after his return home very ill, about 1607, even until the Group I tradition was established in 1614. It seems unlike <them> D. and W. Besides, even granting the main story about Group I, it seems clear that Donne was not trying very hard to collect his secular poems for his bad patrons, or he would have included in Group I 'The Expiration', which had been available in print for several years in a songbook. And why Woodward's text of 'The Refusal' was available to Donne, but not his text of the 'Jet Ring', needs rather more explanation than I could give it. However, I would be very glad of further enlightenment there.

I was perhaps guilty of an insincerity when we met at the party, or anyway I would like to answer more clearly. You said you felt dubious till I explained that I was thinking of popular editions, not of Oxford Collected ones, and then you felt in favour. The difficulty chiefly arises over the unqualified texts of popular editions. But I still think that Helen Gardner's text is repeatedly wrong; probably thirty times inferior to Grierson's, and better only twice.

Yours sincerely
William Empson

All Souls

---

[1] R. C. Bald, *John Donne: A Life* (1970), 222 n.

John Sparrow responded from All Soul's College on 13 August 1972:

I really hope that my answer to the question in your letter about Rowland Woodward's copy of *Pseudo Martyr* doesn't come too late for your purposes. I am afraid it is, in any case, a disappointing answer, for in fact it is that the inscription in the book is (a) undated and (b) in Woodward's hand, not Donne's. At the top of the page Woodward had written a motto (found also in other books belonging to him): *De juegos el major es can la hoja*, and at the bottom '*ex dono authoris Ron: Woodward*'. So it can't, I imagine, be made to tell us much about the row or the reconciliation between D and W.

Now about *Rescuing Donne*, which I have studied carefully. Of course I enjoy seeing anyone making rings round Dame Helen, and occasionally plunging a rapier into a vulnerable spot in her text or commentary. For far too long she has been a Queen, who rules as she thinks fit The Universal monarchy of wit—taking 'Universal' in *her* sense of 'University'—and it is good that she should be reminded of her own fallibility. And I confess to very much enjoying—enjoying perhaps more than I should—your digs at her person (in pursed lips etc) and personality.

Your bull's eye—and Leishman is also a victim here—is *The dream* ('Dear love, for nothing less than thee . . .'), where I am sure you are right.

I won't dare to pronounce on the question of Group V and its origin; your flights of fantasy (e.g. about the bedroom window at the Deanery) *might* be true, and are always what is called 'valuable correctives' to flatly conventional thinking (or lack of thinking) about what really went on in Donne's mind or about the actual circumstances in which his MSS were circulated and his texts transmitted. I wish we could meet and discuss individual instances (of your—by me alleged—'flights'); it's much more satisfactory to do it by word of mouth.

One thing I must say, however—& that is that I think you build far too much on the 'refusal' letter to Woodward ('Like one who in her third widowhood']. It doesn't read to me like a '[——-t]', and you admit that W. himself perhaps didn't read it as such . . .

Yours ever

John Sparrow' [*Houghton*]

WE replied to Sparrow on 6 March 1973 (see below).

TO GEOFFREY POSNER

[n.d.: 1972]

Dear Mr Posner,[1]

I am interested in your questions [about the BBC in wartime] but very ignorant about the answers. As you evidently know, I joined the Corporation to do wartime propaganda work, and almost all the people I met there regularly had done the same, except Louis MacNeice. I do not believe in this gradual class change before the war, nor even that the war 'forced the hand' of the Corporation about the class of its personnel.

You expect that the newcomers were 'angry young men' who were not gentlemen and did not share the ideal of public service. But surely these indignant democrats were social reformers, why can't they have had ideals of social service? I grant you that the hero of Look Back in Anger [by John Osborne] was a very disgusting spoiled child, from a far too comfortable home background, whose sweet-shop would undoubtedly have gone bankrupt at once, and it is very queer that his pretensions were so readily accepted; but he was somehow regarded as a spokesman for more decent people. The Corporation went on being high-minded, I think, though with a very mixed bag of ideals.

The obvious division was not between gents and proles but between the businessman types or civil-service types who decide policy and the artists who carry it out. The Corporation was and is an exclusive hierarchy, supposed to be secret but actually spurting out hot jets of leakage in every neighbouring bar. The administrators were evasively determined to avoid trouble. A gradual recovery from the unhealthy atmosphere produced by Reith was going on, but the main set-up was not changing and I don't know what better one could put in its place, considering how bad the known alternatives are. Of course the technicians and the performers are two quite different things again; maybe their classes were changing. The people I met were not noticeably aristocratic but had all been to some university, or gave that impression; though maybe not all the newsmen imported from Fleet St., who were rather prone to say they had a code of their own especially when another Fleet St. man had had to fill in for them because they were drunk. In fact, looking back, I can't remember Class raising its ugly head at all.

[William Empson]

Houghton, bMS Eng 14701 (629)

---

[1] Geoffrey Posner (Centre for Television Research, University of Leeds) had sent a preliminary paper on 'Recruitment Policy and Training in Broadcasting, 1939–45'.

TO VERONICA FORREST-THOMSON*

[n.d.: ?1972]

Dear Veronica Thomson,

Thank you for the party; I enjoyed it very much, and feel now that I have a much better idea of what will be wanted of me in two years time. Also for the off-print of *Levels in Poetic Convention*; I read it with interest.[1] I still think you are wrong, but I feel now I have a glimmering of what you are getting at. Indeed, other people have been saying it, and I need to arrive at an answer.

It is not merely a revolt among Youth; at the doors of death they still turn out for this protest. Professor Legouis must be all of eighty, and his new edition of Marvell (I read in the reviews) blames Empson for saying long ago that 'nail me through . . . stake me down' in *Appleton House* recalls the Crucifixion, thus releasing the modern sewer flood of Christian allegory.[2] Brash Professor Kermode, who gets the horrors when he remembers how many years it will be before he may retire, feels just the same indignation at the treason which destroyed that graceful poet for the modern world. In the same way, he has to have Donne in all his love-poems just making a dirty joke out of cheating the girls; the reader ought to join in the jeering, with manly toughness. It seems rather odd that you are on the same side as this; I wouldn't have thought it was your line, really. But all three of you genuinely want to keep at bay any 'interpretations' of the poems, because that has shown itself to be so very sanctimonious and off key. Yes, I agree the recent ones feel loathsome, but that is only because they are written by neo-Christians trying to cheat you into worshipping the torture-monster; if you allow the poet to have the feelings which would naturally arise from the references he lets drop, they are slightly flippant, but not as a rule of policy at all, and they make the whole grace of this kind of poetry. For that matter, I think hardly any good poetry would survive your unnaturalist campaign.

As the stuff you quote in your article isn't poetry at all, we can hardly

---

[1] Veronica Forrest-Thomson, 'Levels in Poetic Convention', *Journal of European Studies*, 2 (1972), 35–51.

[2] Cf. WE's 'Natural Magic and Populism in Marvell's Poetry' (in *Andrew Marvell*, ed. R. L. Brett): 'Long ago I said that . . . two verses in "Upon Appleton House" refer to the Crucifixion, but Professor Legouis disagreed: and his Notes in the standard text of Marvell [*The Poems and Letters of Andrew Marvell*, 3rd edn. rev. P. Legouis and E. E. Duncan-Jones, 2 vols. (1971)] are still saying "Empson is wrong". I think Legouis was killing the poetry in the interests of decorum . . . I certainly do not think Marvell wanted to say anything here about the Fall, or the Crucifixion, because he is concentrated upon describing his experiences with Nature; but he uses these comparisons, among others, as a way to describe the experiences more clearly' (42).

decide the point. But I thought there was a certain pathos in your frequent references to 'liberation' from meaning in poetry, so that the poet could just blow bubbles. Think of the Marseillaise, the volunteer army and its attendant mob marching north to liberate Paris, and singing this romantic poetry all the way; but now the only thing the great movement means to you is having a private lunatic asylum where you can blow bubbles all by yourself, except for obsequious nurses paid to tell you that the bubbles are artistic.

All the same, if you can induce them to take up rhyme and metre again, and stop the deadly Leavisite moralising, I really believe you will be doing good in the end, even if a ghastly desert of echolalia has to be passed first.

I missed having a conference with Kermode yesterday about the joint project we are supposed to be planning, and regret it very much; I hope I can get hold of him soon and find how he is reacting to my draft.

So you need not regard me as quite impervious.

Gratefully

Houghton, bMS Eng 1401 (556)

TO CHRISTOPHER RICKS

Studio House
1 July 1972

My dear Ricks,

This is long for a review, and I am willing to consider cuts (I have a carbon copy), but I don't think anybody else has pointed out what important news comes in the Introduction, so I think it needs a bit of length.[1] In writing, I felt afraid of giving offence, but now the tone seems to me all right. You will say that the part about Xianity is my King Charles' Head, but this is where I got it from.[2] I am grateful to you for making me read this book; if not reviewing I am very liable to fail to keep up.

Next I have to do praise of I A Richards for his retirement FestSchrift,

---

[1] WE, 'My god, man, there's bears on it' (a review of *The Waste Land*, a facsimile of the original drafts edited by Valerie Eliot), *E in C*, 22: 4 (Oct. 1972); *UB*, 189–200. Ricks responded on 5 Jul. 1972: 'Thank you for the excellent Eliot piece; I *believe* it—it's new & true & central. We'll not of course cut it.' (*Houghton*)

[2] In *David Copperfield*, Richard Babley ('Mr Dick') suffers from a gentle derangement which has since become proverbial: 'Mr Dick had been upwards of ten years endeavouring to keep King Charles the First out of the Memorial [he is writing]; but he had been constantly getting into it, and was there now.'

while he is doing one for me.[3] One of the grim things about growing old is that you all become the same age, but this particular violation of the calendar is due to his retiring a dozen years late. There are a lot of things to say, really, but hard to think of and very hard to say inoffensively.

Tiresome work but it does clear one's mind a bit. Having such a row of these jobs has meant having to put off finishing the Marvell, but after all why not finish it in the Canadian winter.

Hope you are going on well.

William Empson.

When you write, do tell me the name of that grim Drama Professor who claims to be disproving Shakespeare's theatre—I must read his stuff as soon as I can.[4]

TIMES LITERARY SUPPLEMENT, 14 July 1972, 819:
'*Mansfield Park*'

'Any reader of *Mansfield Park* will agree,' wrote Ellen Jordan to the *TLS* (23 Jun. 1972, 719), 'that Jane Austen disapproves of her characters' decision to act *Lovers' Vows*, but there is a certain amount of critical disagreement about the grounds for her disapproval.' One view, proposed by Lionel Trilling, is that Austen fundamentally regarded acting as immoral; and A. Walton Litz has likewise argued that experience taught Austen to consider 'imitation' as being 'dangerous to personal integrity'. To balance such suggestions, Jordan adduces the personal testimony of Sir William Heathcote, who remembered as a boy that—just two years before she began Mansfield Park—Austen herself, at a Twelfth-night party, had 'assumed the part' of Mrs Candour and carried it off 'with great spirit'.

Claire Lamont suggested (*TLS*, 7 Jul. 1972, 777) that 'an important element in Jane Austen's disapproval of amateur theatricals in *Mansfield Park* is that the play chosen (and, it is hinted, most others too) involved the characters in a situation or emotional encounter not permissible in life ... As the rehearsals of *Lovers' Vows* show, amateurs are not sufficiently "hardened" to cope with the emotions let loose by play acting.'

---

[3] WE, 'The Hammer's Ring', in *I. A. Richards: Essays In His Honor*, ed. Reuben Brower, Helen Vendler, and John Hollander (1973), 73–83; repr. in *A*, 216–24; IAR, 'Semantic Frontiersman', in Gill, 98–108.

[4] A great-grandson of William Gladstone, Glynne Wickham (1922–2004) was educated at Winchester and New College, Oxford (where he was President of the University Dramatic Society). In 1948 he began teaching Drama at Bristol, where he rose to be Professor of Drama, 1960–82. His works include *Shakespeare's Dramatic Heritage* (1969), *The Medieval Theatre* (1974), *English Moral Interludes* (1975), *A History of the Theatre* (1985), *Early English Stages* (5 vols.: 1959–2001). President of the Society for Theatre Research, 1976–99, he was also an adviser on the building of the Globe Theatre, London (and received the Sam Wanamaker Award in 1999).

Sir,—It strikes me that the interest of moral theory (about amateur acting) tends to distract critics from the story. The objection to *this* performance is simply that Father would forbid it if he were at home, as he does when he happens to turn up—immediately, with complete indifference to the feelings of the guests. The heroine does not explain her objection because she is a poor relation—it would seem too sanctimonious if she said to the others: 'You ought to obey your father.' They are not surprised when Father forbids it, as the guests are. Jane Austen was trying to be specially religious here, and it makes the tone rather strained at times; she defends the action of Father in minor ways, though she grants that the other guests would think it savage. Father has just returned from his slave plantation in Antigua, and probably reflects, in the famous phrase, 'too much live stock within doors here'. After all, the best the author can do for him at the end is to allow him to discover rational grounds for repentance.

William Empson
Hampstead, London NW3

Re NICK MALONE*: *THE BURIAL OF CRISPIN PIKE*

Studio House, 1 Hampstead Hill Gardens, NW3
17 August 1972

Dear Sir,

I am glad to recommend the enclosed poem by Nick Malone, and I hope that in this case there is more point than usual in sending a recommendation, because there may be a prejudice to overcome.[1] It seems to me that recent poetry has fallen into a dismal narrow rut, and Nick Malone is quite right to be outside it. The poem is very unself-centred, and much concerned with descriptions of Nature, also with mulling over her relations with mankind. Much of it is in free verse, but it regularly works up to lyrical passages in rhyme and metre. I expect that many readers, like myself, would feel that all this is normal for poetry, and that to meet it in the modern world is a positive relief—when it is so well done.

Christian [*sic*] Pyke, after his burial, is gradually re-absorbed into Nature, in spite of obstacles from modern pollution of Nature, with which there are ghostly concerns.

Yours truly
William Empson.

---

[1] The long poem by Nick Malone, *The Burial of Crispin Pike*, was ultimately brought out in London by Workshop Press (1974), with an introduction by WE. This promotional letter was to be made use of as a blurb on the back cover.

TO CHRISTOPHER RICKS

27 August 1972

My dear Ricks,

You and the other editors ought I think to be offered this, as the correction of a slight inaccuracy in my review [of *The Waste Land*]. I remember that you don't like reviewers to appear ill-informed. On the other hand, for the artistic effect of my pretty review, I am inclined to think that this footnote is better omitted. But there is so often a third hand, as you must have noticed; and I daresay many of your readers would simply like a bit more gossip about the lady. As you please, then.

I wrote a piece about Mouldy Wedding Cake for Hallam Tennyson, and he wouldn't believe that *Tithonus* was kept back for twenty years before printing, till he had searched through your edition. He thought it a rude insinuation to suppose that the poet thought the wish for Nirvana a bit rakish and unChristian. But I don't know why else he would hold it back, do you?—except simply as saying the opposite of *In Memoriam*, which might I suppose be commented on.[1]

We are flying off [to Toronto] as soon as we can, but a very cheap airline has gone bust on us.

Yours

William Empson.

[1] A shortened version of WE's contribution to the symposium *Tennyson: Eighty Years On*, produced by Hallam Tennyson, was printed in *A Colloquium on Tennyson* (*The Listener*, 8 Mar. 1973, 302): 'Tennyson, when old, claims that at the age of eight he had made a line which he thought grander than anybody's else's. It went: "With slaughterous sons of thunder rolled the flood." This helps to show that the use of "roll" in *The Princess* is too internal: "to roll the torrent out of dusky doors". He would boom it out in the Lincolnshire accent and it would be accepted as a climax, but it is too like mouldy wedding-cake. There is even one line where the taint smirches the best and deepest of his poems, "Tithonus". Luckily, the mould has only attacked the last line of the first paragraph: "Far-folded mists, and gleaming halls of morn". A "hall" meant to Tennyson an ancestral country house like the one from which his own branch of the Tennyson family had been so wickedly excluded. In earlier times, the whole population of the house would have eaten their dinner in the hall, but now very likely a full-sized billiard-table had been installed, and it was one room where guests were allowed to smoke—male guests, of course. The more we think about the hall, the more cosy it becomes, though always in an aristocratic way, but the speaker, "the white-haired shadow", had not been feeling cosy at all. The word is only there for the vowel sound and the line feels mouldy.' By way of explaining the reference to 'mouldy wedding cake', the full draft essay that Empson had prepared for the programme opened: 'Some reviewer of Tennyson's poetry when it was new said it was like mouldy wedding cake, and I think that's very true. Not all the time in the poetry but as a recurrent trouble. I tried the phrase out on Christopher Ricks and he thought it romantic, recalling the girls who used to sleep with wedding cake under their pillows to dream of their future husbands. And he actually admired the lines, I think, of mouldy wedding cake so his loyalty is unbeatable.' ('Empson on Tennyson', *The Tennyson Research Bulletin* 4: 3 (Nov. 1984), 107). Of 'Tithonus' the unedited essay explained more fully (and memorably): 'It's a poem in favour of the human practice of dying, which he wrote at the same time as he wrote in *In Memoriam* that if he didn't believe God would let him live forever, he would be very spiteful and sin like crazy. This poem is a great deal nobler but he didn't print it for another twenty years' (108). See also *MG*, 130–1.

TO PENGUIN BOOKS

Unit 12, 21 Potsdam Road, Downsview, Toronto, Canada
22 October 1972

Dear Sir,

Thank you for sending me a cheque for a hundred pounds, which I will not at present cash, and a form explaining that it is an advance upon the publication of an edition of *The Complete Poems* of Andrew Marvell. It is at least premature, but also it assumes a change of plan.

I cannot remember the name of the man [Nikos Stangos] who wrote to me about this, which I greatly regret as he seemed very understanding. Of course I did not carry files of letters with me for a year in Canada; I expect to be home in May or June, and to settle down and complete the edition during this Canadian winter.

A 'complete' edition of Marvell is not what I agreed to do at all. To do that means printing a whole lot of satires written under Charles II of which I believe he only wrote occasional verses, as his turn came round the table, with the waiter instructed to write down what the drinkers invented. Or in other ways there is a lot of dead wood. Nobody would pay any attention if I printed the whole block and said in the notes that only lines so-and-so are any good; but a slight shock effect may be gained by printing only the good bits, which are plainly good. Then again, the main interest of the edition is to come from a proof that he really was married to his landlady for the last eleven years of his life, and was thus a different type of man from what is now habitually assumed (a man like Walter Pater or Mark Pattison, who could not possibly have been nobbled by their landladies).[1] I am sure to be told that this makes no difference to the poetry, though the sustained earnestness of the professional lying about the matter is evidence that at least somebody used to think it made a difference. Thus I need room to manoeuvre a bit and emphasise poems where a difference can be glimpsed. I will not leave out any poem recognised as specially good, though I think even among the early poems one or two are better dropped.

---

[1] Walter Pater (1839–94), writer, aesthete, and hedonist: an advocate of the Hellenic, the homosexual, and the homoerotic in life and literature; his best-known works include the enormously influential *Studies in the History of the Renaissance* (1863), *Marius the Epicurean* (1885), and *Imaginary Portraits* (1887). Mark Pattison (1813–84) was Rector of Lincoln College, Oxford; a man dedicated to the life of learning. Author of *Isaac Casaubon* (1875), he is himself often taken to be the model for the sterile Mr Casaubon in George Eliot's *Middlemarch*. Although WE seems to assume that Pattison was an arid bachelor, possibly even a repressed homosexual, Pattison was in fact married in 1861, albeit sorrily, to a woman 27 years his junior.

The existing plans already make a sufficiently viable book, without trying also to turn it into a cheap annotated complete edition; trying to do that would only mean falling between two stools.

Or at least, if the previous agreement has been broken, though it appeared at the time satisfactory to both sides, surely some named person ought to write and tell me so. I hope this letter is only a product of confusion.

Yours sincerely

William Empson

Penguin

TIMES LITERARY SUPPLEMENT, 12 January 1973: 'Guilty Rimer'

Martin Amis,[1] in an anonymous review (*TLS*, 15 Dec. 1972, 1524) of *CV*, began with this equivocal report: 'The editor, he says, has to make a guess at the author's intention so that he can intercept the poem before it has been mucked up ... [T]he editor ... must gather the evidence and make an informed speculation about what the poet "really meant". The editor, in other words, picks the bits that he thinks make the best poem.' As to *The Ancient Mariner*, WE and Pirie have produced 'an eclectic text which effectively rescues the pantheist poem of 1800 from the Christian one of 1817'; the pity is that they did not think to include the prose gloss even as an appendix. 'Unsurprisingly,' Amis goes on, WE interprets the poem as 'a covert indictment of the Christian God. Coleridge's intention was, so to speak, to "bore from within", an aspect of the poem we no longer appreciate for the simple reason that it has been so successful . . .' Overall, Amis approved of WE's stance: 'Professor Empson rightly takes the *Rime* as the work of a man who sees the universe as devoid of moral order, and his analysis of the poem as being fundamentally about "Neurotic Guilt" is more or less unanswerable . . . The more general remarks about Coleridge are so luminous that one wishes there were more of them. Professor Empson's criticism has always depended on the intensity of his response not only to the work but also to their author, and he here shows a moving sympathy with Coleridge which—were all critics so intelligent—would make us want to lose the intentional fallacy for good.'

---

[1] Martin Amis (b. 1949) read English at Exeter College, Oxford. He has been editorial assistant on the *TLS*, 1974, and literary editor of the *New Statesman*, 1977–9. His novels include *The Rachel Papers* (1973), *Success* (1979), *Other People: A Mystery Story* (1981), *Money: A Suicide Note* (1984), and *Time's Arrow* (1991).

Sir,—Your review of the selection from the verse of Coleridge by myself and Mr Pirie (December 15) was evidently not malignant, but I must ask leave to make some corrections, such as an author always feels to be merely factual ones.

The reviewer says that the Glosses to *The Ancient Mariner*, if removed from the text of the poem, had better have been given in an appendix. On pages 242–3 they are given in full, with line-references, and on page 48, after the first discussion of them, the reader is told where they can be found.

He asserts that Mr Pirie and I say an editor should 'pick out the bits that he thinks make the best poem'. I rejected this idea, as plainly as I knew how, on the second page of the introduction:

> This is not to say that an editor should be free to print what he thinks the *best* version; he owes a loyalty to the author, or rather, to the person the author was when he wrote the poem.

Hence the intention of the author ought to be considered before accepting later changes, and I give various examples. Your reviewer may consider the distinction a false one; but to announce that I do not attempt any is only to tell the most damaging untruth within easy reach.

He says that I regard Coleridge as 'boring from within' Christianity so as to prove that the Christian God is wicked. I said Coleridge pretended that Christianity forbade cruelty to animals, or made his ignorant Mariner assume it, whereas actually it did not; though many Christians nowadays think that it always has done. I said this plainly (page 78), in fact the style is presumably what the reviewer calls my 'Boys' Own eagerness' (meaning no doubt that the only decorous language for Eng Lit Crit is the sloven's pomp of evasive jargon); so he had no excuse for making me say something entirely different, and false.

I have also to protest against the review's total neglect of the work of Mr Pirie, which was quite often at variance with mine; he does perhaps, though I do not, treat the poem as 'the work of a man who sees the universe as devoid of moral order'. Maybe this was what was drifting around in the almost human brain of the reviewer.

William Empson
York University, Toronto

Our reviewer [Martin Amis] writes:—(1) Apologies are due to Professor Empson on his first point—a bad lapse. (2) I do indeed regard the distinction [as] a false one, as the phrasing of my review clearly implied. I did not 'assert' that Mr Pirie and Professor Empson 'say an editor should "pick out the bits he thinks make the best poem" ', only that this is what these editors end up doing; the person the author was when he wrote the poem is, one would have thought, unascertainable. (3) I think a disinterested reader, as opposed to a cross author, would agree on the 'boring from within' point, and also that the Christian position on 'cruelty to animals' is peripheral to the moral scheme of the poem. Neither Coleridge nor, surely, Professor Empson, would want to rest his case there. (4) When I referred to Professor Empson's 'Boys' Own eagerness' I was referring not to his 'style' but to his eagerness, on a different point, which he does not question here. So far as I am concerned, Professor Empson always writes like an angel.

TO ROGER SALE*

English Department, York University, Toronto
[n.d.: 1973]

Dear Roger Sale,

Thank you very much for the splendid praise of my work in your book.[1] I was quite touched by your capacity to read parts of the first two books as symbolist poems, making the successive passages chosen as examples adumbrate some deeper meaning. And I need to reconsider my past work at this time, having at least to bring out editions of old essays which often need rewriting, and in general to try to round things off after retirement. I shall keep a carbon copy of this letter, and see if it does me any good. You will not be surprised if I try to answer your attacks on me rather than return thanks for your praise.

We disagree (I think) at a radical point, where many young American critics would side with you. I don't believe, and never have believed, that a social and literary 'dissociation of sensibility' ever occurred; I don't even believe that everything is getting worse and worse (I agree that another world war would probably be fatal, but this is so well known that the powers may manage to hold off). Eliot merely threw the idea out in passing when young, and is not responsible for its proliferation since. Evidently the split is believed to have occurred soon after the Reformation, so the belief is best explained as R. C. propaganda. I think a great deal of progress has gone on since then, pretty steadily. When you ended your book on Spenser [*Reading Spenser* (1968)] by saying he had discovered that the Dissociation

---

[1] Roger Sale, 'The Achievement of William Empson', in *Modern Heroism: Essays on D. H. Lawrence, William Empson, & J. R. R. Tolkien* (1973), 107–92.

had occurred between Books V and VI, so that he altered the whole style, I realised that you were living in an Eng. Lit. dream world. A student at York explained the line 'Without sharp north, without declining west' as a reference to the well-known old book 'Decline of the West' [Donne, 'The Good-Morrow'] by Oswald Spengler. Your Spenser in its more refined way gave me the same shock. So I don't look at pastoral at all the way you do.

Nor have I had any great change in my opinions, though of course my character may have got worse. I stopped writing during the war because I thought it important to beat Hitler, and got very wrapped up in propaganda; it is rather startling to see that this elementary explanation never occurs to you as even conceivable. I only gradually returned to writing, doing first a book about Buddhist sculpture which got lost. But *Complex Words* was written before I had been confronted with the new orthodoxy in the Eng. Lit. profession; no doubt I was reading enough of it to learn, but I quite failed to realise how much we disagreed—it did not happen till I got to Sheffield, some time after the book was out. I really did not write that book, as you say, in an effort to toe the academic line. (A 'desperate struggle', you suggest later on.) I wanted to offer a coherent linguistic theory about ambiguity, with examples that could be followed up again and again to demonstrate its truth. Most of the literary examples had occurred to me before, and I had unfinished articles about them ready, but luckily they turned out to suit this other purpose. It would be no use to have lots of bright ideas, staving off boredom, because I needed to show that the same ideas worked out consistently over a large field. Of course this does not provide you with a secret Symbolist poem, but I don't know why you feel that the motive could only be a sordid one. There was a sturdy attempt to carry out an argument, so that I had a logical reason for the order of the illustrations, even in Ambiguity and Pastoral, and I can't feel that they are Symbolist poems either. I did, I can't deny, feel it was rather fun to work up to some particularly loathsome bit of Christian torture-worship, as the bang at the end of a chapter; but I think I explained that these were causes of particularly advanced logical and emotional disorder. It did not mean that I was slavering to engage in these tortures myself, as though they were the prettiest fancy in my bag. If there is any insincerity about the change in Empson, it comes in the first two books, where I did not explain that I thought the Father who was satisfied by the Crucifixion disgusting; but really, everyone I knew thought that already, and accepted reserve about it as mere politeness. The topic did not seem to crop up in *Complex Words*. But after I had been teaching for a bit in a Christian country I realised that the children were being cheated about the religion on a ghastly scale, just as you have been, so that it was my duty to speak up on a suitable occasion. It is a lie (though other people beside you tell it) to say that I am now generally embittered; I hate rather little except the doctrine that God is a sadist who could be bought off torturing all mankind by having his son tortured to death. No opponent has ever offered me even a remote sophistry in defence of this doctrine, because there is none. If you read *The Decline of Hell* [by D. P. Walker][2] you will find that Milton would encounter a number of other examples of God's craving to inflict torture, such as that all infants who die before being baptised receive eternal torture. A late seventeenth-century theologian became disgusted by this, and was treated with cool astonishment by his opponents; he seems unable to keep his temper or his manners on this one point, they said. But I suppose nowadays even you, even a Christian with a very thick skin and cool heart, would not feel it as unintelligible if a man became disgusted by this dogma. And, you must remember, the belief that God craves for human suffering is the only operative cause for the RC resistance to birth control, without which the race of man is pretty certain to go down in world famine and nuclear war. The Christians now look as if they are really going to bring Hell and destroy the world. But it strikes me there is so much resistance to the basic doctrine in the grass roots, even the RC grass roots, that its effects may yet be avoided if the intellectuals behave with marginal honesty.

There is in my later work what may look like a failure, I now see, in my practically giving up Ambiguity as a method of exegesis. I had better have explained myself there. Reviewers were telling me as soon as *Ambiguity* came out that not all good poetry was ambiguous, and I could see that the method worked best where the authors had had some impulse or need for the process; but, as it had become my line, I went on slogging at it for two more books. Then I thought I had given a rounded view of the subject, and unless challenged to debate had no need to go on about it. What next confronted me was the appalling mass of misreading which has now become established in Eng. Lit. and makes a variety of authors quite unreadable for the young who accept their teachers. This misreading is always of a pietistic character, but otherwise just whatever will serve. It is not best dealt with by 'close reading' of the text. Take *Volpone* and *The Alchemist*; you say that I am obviously wrong because I do no close reading. In reprinting I had better add some detailed evidence that Ben Jonson was

---

[2] See WE on D. P. Walker, *The Decline of Hell: Seventeenth-Century Discussions of Eternal Torment* (1964): 'The Abominable Fancy', *New Statesman*, 21 Aug. 1964; in *A*, 618–19.

not a Puritan, but hated them for trying to interfere with his pleasures; I need not add any 'analysis', to show that he habitually writes in a sardonic manner, hinting that what the character on the stage admires and praises do not really deserve such praise. This work has been thoroughly done already; the question is how to interpret his intention. The story that he despised bodily pleasure, and despised all his characters for wanting to enjoy it, whereas they ought to have been yearning to be pure in Heaven like Ben Jonson, strikes me as such gross farcical hypocrisy that it does not need verbal disproof. What proves my case, I think, is that the plays are so very much better when this dirty nonsense is wiped or scraped away; but this is not much of a boast, as the present Eng. Lit. account is so intolerable that it is never acted out before an audience. Or take Milton himself: you speak nicely of my account of Adam in the presence of God, and then say it isn't at all what Adam himself sees, as the poetry shows, quoting some; first Adam describes himself flattering God, with a very strong courtly adroitness, then he describes himself fainting away. Wherever can your innocence have led you to here? Surely nobody ever denied that the shameless torture-monster is frightening, or that he demands flattery? What you say has no bearing on the problem. Christopher Ricks in *Milton's Grand Style* did a great deal of close reading of the poem, finding ambiguities and so on, and I think he adds greatly to one's appreciation of the language; but all the discoveries are what Milton wanted to say. This is what one would expect; he was an experienced propagandist. In short, the cases in which a revealing ambiguity gets dropped are rather special ones, and I did not want to be confined to such cases for the rest of my life.

You are on a lower level, I think, when you accuse me of trying to annoy my better-informed readers by playing to the gallery; at least that is what it amounts to, in your quotations from my essay on *Othello*, for example. Ingenious reasons are invented [for] why I chose to tell this lie rather than some other. I merely thought that what I said was true, but don't mind admitting that I hoped to let in a bit of fresh air. The modern classroom demands that the children need only read the words on the page before them, and must never be expected to have any general information or knowledge of life (except of course the raw mass of prejudice which Teacher has to cater for); so I do feel mildly cheerful when I can speak as from outside this airless place. Why you think my remarks about Cassio and Iago obviously wrong, so that they could only be inserted *especially to annoy*, you make no attempt to explain. You just think it *rude* to know anything about the mind of Iago, and I expect you really don't. But, even if you did, the fierce decorum of mass education would insist on your pretending not to.

By the way, you remark that the Sonnets may have been written at the same time as the Falstaff play, another case of your thinking about literature solely in terms of classroom exercises. The relations with the much-needed patron in 1592–5 were a very private matter, possibly dangerous as well as wounding, and he certainly wouldn't put them into a play at the time; but three or four years later, when it was all safely over, and he wanted to describe some quite different relations with a patron, it would be a rather healing kind of fun to echo his old sonnets on the subject—fun for himself alone probably. This seems to me very plain, but the present-day literary critic regards it as a duty to jeer at any normal human reflection. That is why he despises A. C. Bradley, who always sees a human situation in the round [in *Shakespearean Tragedy* (1904)], thus becoming a uniquely good critic of Shakespeare, who does the same. I never joined in the howl against Bradley, and saw no need to apologise for paying my respects to him; your assumption that it was a self-conscious tease feels to me ugly. While the academic critics were all saying that you mustn't attend to characters in plays, but only to the broad simplicity of the stage, the actors were all taking to 'The Method' of Stanislavsky, which tells you to sink deep into your part, and decide what the character was doing thirty years before—precisely like Bradley. Long ago now anyway.

I hardly know what to make of your suspicion that I think Milton's God my best book. I do not think myself dead, as you do, and continue to hope that my best book is not yet written. But I did get a surprise from I. A. Richards, not long ago, who let drop that he thought it my best book. I had showed proofs to him before it came out, and he arrived agitated at my door early one morning saying that the last chapter must be radically cut; I was able to settle this by explaining that it was already with the printer. Of course he was right if he meant that it would be bad for my reputation, among bad or deluded men; but I was relieved that he had outgrown any other objection he had had. When I was crossing the fighting lines during the siege of Peking, to give my weekly lecture on Macbeth, a generous-minded peasant barred my way and said, pointing ahead: 'That way lies death'. 'Not for me, I have a British passport' was the answer that sprang to the lips, and I was right, I think, in both cases, though maybe pig-headed, in feeling sure there was nothing to be afraid of. Because I felt so, neither action was heroic, but when I look back on them I can partly forget that my life has been too sheltered. But you, as I understand, avert your eyes from half of human fate; you would think it positively bad taste in one of your Modern Heroes to do anything heroic at all. The whole crazy structure of modern Eng. Lit. can only be explained as fitted to the mass classroom; and I suppose it really is a good action to try and pacify all those young hoodlums. And yet it seems a bit atavistic of you to want to talk about heroes. I am reminded of a visit by Matthew Arnold to a Sunday School in the Southern States, where he reported, [*text missing*].

[William Empson]
Dare to be a Daniel,
Dare to stand alone.[3]

Houghton carbon, bMS Eng 1401 (644)

TO JOHN SPARROW

Unit 12, 21 Potsdam Road, Downsview, Toronto, Canada
6 March 1973

Dear Sparrow,

Thank you very much for your letter, which gave me great pleasure, except that you sounded so exhausted and ill. I hope that Marrakesh did you good. What I deduced from the letter, maybe wrongly, was that you are now much more inclined to accept my Donne thesis than you were earlier (very good of you to go on worrying about it at such a time), so I write again backing it up. I had thought you had decided it was incredible.

You blame yourself for not writing, but actually you had written, saying among other things that I 'build far too much on the "refusal" letter to Woodward'. I thought I had better delay my answer till I get back to working on the subject again, but I will write now. The argument about this poem is not at all essential to my thesis, except as it refutes the dating of Helen Gardner—I went on drawing deductions because they seemed interesting biographically. She, I maintain, builds far too much upon her dating, very absurdly, though not quite so absurdly as her loyal sergeant [Michael] Milgate. The poem recommends total retirement from the world, with a renunciation even of reading the poems of other authors, and Grierson dated it very naturally from the retirement after Donne's marriage. After this scandal he was uneasy about his reputation, and capacity to get another job, and (we may be sure) would be unwilling to give any wider circulation to his love-poems. But Helen Gardner cannot allow

---

[3] The gospel hymn 'Dare to be a Daniel', composed in 1873 by Philip Paul Bliss (1838–76) for the First Congregational Church of Chicago, takes the burden of its refrain from Daniel 1: 18–21; 6: 1–10: 'Dare to be a Daniel, | Dare to stand alone! | Dare to have a purpose firm! | Dare to make it known.'

that date, because she wants to maintain that the philosophical love-poems (mostly about adultery) were all written at that peculiar time. The purpose, I think, is merely to edify the classrooms, by not letting them think that the poems are about anything real. Hence she makes him talk in this high strain of withdrawal from the world just when he was hanging about the Court and angling for a job. Nobody could believe this unless they expected total insincerity from him all the time; and she regularly tries to blacken his character, though only in an unobtrusive way, as part of her moral problem.

It is remarkable, on any theory, that Woodward never copied out the Songs and Sonnets, though he was a close friend early and late in Donne's life. I do not remember any explanation of it in print, but Helen Gardner once wrote to me, as a brief and cautiously phrased postscript, that the young man might decide to become more circumspect on finding himself in respectable employment. Yes indeed, I expect he did, but we need not saddle him with expressing it in a manner which amounted to a grossly sanctimonious description of his life at the time. Anyway, he must have decided earlier not to give Woodward the Songs and Sonnets (except for the Jet Ring, probably quite early); nobody supposes that he wrote all of them after 1597, and he was [Incomplete].

Houghton carbon, bMS Eng 1401 (654)

TO DAVID PIRIE

Unit 12, 21 Potsdam Road, Downsview, Toronto, Canada
17 March 1973

Dear Pirie,

I have at last read [Norman Fruman's] *The Damaged Archangel* and am inclined to think we had better add some remarks to our second edition.[1] I have half a page to spare on p. 100, and you can get a sheer page on page 254. The point where both of us are affected by the book is our printing of the *Mad Monk*, with the comment that it is the source of WW's *Immortality* Ode. A lot of Americans have been arguing that it is Wordsworth's, evidently, and apparently there is no hard evidence that either of them wrote it. I can't see why Wordsworth would choose to repeat a line of his own: 'There was a time when (three natural objects)', whereas if it is Coleridge's

---

[1] Norman Fruman (b. 1927), author of *Coleridge, The Damaged Archangel* (1971), is Emeritus Professor of English at the University of Minnesota.

Wordsworth might well do this as an intimate signal to Coleridge, while admitting the force of Coleridge's poem but claiming to answer it; and then Coleridge might naturally repeat the signal while challenging the whole cult of Nature. To believe so is not to deny that the *Mad Monk* is theatrical almost to the point of parody, so that Coleridge might not want to reprint it, after using it to feed the hungry maw of the *Morning Post*; besides, anyone who recognised the sequence might claim that both poets had confessed to murder. The cool assumption that the poet could at once recognise the melody of 'old Sicilian song' (Theocritus no doubt) is much more like Coleridge than WW. To argue that the style is only like WW is merely to beg the question at issue. However, there may be some real argument; Fruman's only reference [454 n. 2] is to the Bulletin of the New York Public Library,[2] which I shall try to see when I get to New York. The US Eng-Lit profession is much more prone to be swept off its feet by a fashion than the British one, as when a dozen of them argued that Swift hated his clever-horses for being eighteenth-century Deists, preferring the Yahoos because he was such a mystical Christian; this seems to have passed off.

So the *Monk* alone shouldn't be much bother, but that argument goes with a general denial that Coleridge knew anything about Renaissance Italian theorists, who made Platonism mean the belief in middle spirits; if he was only lying when he made such claims, most of my argument about the *Mariner* falls to the ground. Curious that Fruman can quote [H. W.] Piper with approval [243] and never mention that he is denying the thesis of Piper. Of course a lot of the Fruman debunking must be true, especially about German philosophers; Coleridge had merely felt the need for some belief of the sort they provided, without really having a formulation for it (just as he died in the mistaken belief that he had invented and written out a philosophy); but he had felt the need, from quite early. Fruman despises the philosophy very frankly, while attaching immense importance to the property rights in it, so he is in no position to understand how such a delusion could arise. I have looked up some of the references in the York library [York University, Toronto]; Richard Haven (Journal of the History of Ideas, 1959) is good, saying that C. liked the old mystics as recorders of experience (pillars of fire by night), having had such experiences himself, but could not accept their formulations, and regarded Hartley for a time as providing one. That is what he wanted the sciences to do, and it is hard to

---

[2] Stephen M. Parrish and David V. Erdman, 'Who Wrote The Mad Monk?', *Bulletin of the New York Public Library*, 66 (1960), 209–37.

get away from the witness of Lamb that he heard C. quoting a mystic in Latin when they were at school together (Lamb being fifteen and C. eighteen). C. remarked that L. was only remembering really what C. had told him afterwards, but this wouldn't mean that he had told L. lies; Fruman is very good at inventing such weaselly deductions, but they aren't enough to win his game for him. C. would not be so cosy about admitted [admitting] it if he had told lies.

However, I can't feel cross with Fruman, because he is cross about a lot of pro-Christian lying over Coleridge which did need debunking; even so, he is moving about in worlds not realised, and even speaks of the 'earlier piety' of Coleridge, whereas the schoolboy needed to read Iamblichus because he had already read Voltaire. Americans find it hard to believe in a child taking religion so seriously, but that is just part of being out of touch. That the schoolboy really did try to be apprenticed to a cobbler *because* he could not sign the 39 Articles, therefore could never be a white-collar man with an MA, seems to me plainly true;[3] because it is so consistent, and contrariwise because he went on telling the story like that when he no longer regarded it as to his credit. The case needs presenting at some length, I can see.

The out-of-touchness of Fruman becomes keenly poignant, I think, when he is proving that neither Coleridge nor Lamb knew anything about Shakespeare till they had been taught by the Germans (p. 487):

> In August 1800, Charles Lamb, who was to become one of the great nineteenth-century critics of Shakespeare, could write that George Dyer had called Shakespeare 'a great but irregular genius, which I think to be an original and just remark'. Since he repeated the remark approvingly in a letter to Coleridge a few days later, it does not seem likely that he had as yet heard a contrary opinion from Coleridge. Indeed, Lamb seems scarcely to have been aware of the history of Shakespeare criticism . . .

[3] See Walter Jackson Bate, letter to Empson, 30 Jun. (no year): 'My impression is that Chambers, on p. 12, was speculating about C's motives largely on the basis that this incident (the [?Crispin] incident) took place at 15. All I'm able to say about this now is that Chambers is following Gilman (Life of STC, 1833, p. 21 "When Coleridge arrived at the age of 15 . . .") . . . I followed C's own statement in *Table-Talk* under the date of *May 27, 1830*, "When I was thirteen, I went to a shoemaker . . ." I assumed that Coleridge, saying this in 1830, was likely to be closer to the actual time that this happened than was Gilman, writing after C's death. I was further encouraged in this because Lawrence Hanson—in a later and more detailed work on the early years than the Chambers biography—dates it as "probably in 1785", by which time C was 13 (*The Life of S. T. C.: The Early Years*, 1938; repr 1962, p. 20). Hanson then goes on (pp. 20–21) to mention C's desire to become a doctor, & I simply followed Hanson in this.' (*Houghton*)

This makes plain that Fruman, besides being a bore himself, has no idea what it is like not being a bore (I plagiarize here, but I forget who from); no wonder he becomes cross and suspicious when anybody makes a joke. The same incapacity is at work in the nagging over the *Chamonix* poems; Coleridge had made a ghastly mistake but not one of the kind proposed. Fruman knows the letters describing the trip and says Coleridge gave 'a very lengthy and minute account of his experience on Scafell, without mentioning a hymn, involuntarily poured out [forth] or otherwise' [28]. But he does describe himself doing exactly that, as must surely be obvious to anybody who has ever poked his nose outside the classroom. I was sorry to find that my old friend A. P. Rossiter[4] fell into the same boorishness here: 'The inference is, that the involuntary hymn story was an estecian myth, an imposition upon [on] the guileless Sotheby'.[5] This shows that a Leavisite training makes the student just as unable to read as an American one; they are practically the same thing. Coleridge really had had a revelation from Nature; but he thought he ought to pretend it came from the Christian God. This monster would be more at home on Mont Blanc, which he could only describe from other people's reports (surely all his acquaintance knew he had never been there?)—when he copies the ships' captains reports into the *Mariner*, everybody says he is clever and good. A proneness to accuse other people of doing what he did himself really is a bad trait, I agree, typically child-delinquent, but further away from the valuation of his poetry.

The trouble with this line of attack is that it makes people liable to think the poetry isn't about anything, or not about anything fit for Leavis's classroom. By the time Fruman has started expressing LOVE for Coleridge one has an appalled conviction that Coleridge is almost as nauseating as Fruman. I wonder have you any views or comments for the second edition.

I wrote to Ricks, but haven't had an answer from him. It seemed to be rather a specialised appointment, and they probably had views about just what kind of linguistic [*sic*] they wanted.

Yours

William Empson.

Fruman attaches great importance to establishing that Coleridge learned his good style from Wordsworth, so has to explain that earlier Coleridge

---

[4] A. P. (Philip) Rossiter, whom WE had met in Japan, taught at the Imperial Naval College, Etajima, 1931–32; a Shakespeare scholar involved with Basic English, his works include *Julius Caesar: A Basic English Expansion* (1941).

[5] Fruman, *Coleridge*, 450 n 13.

poems of the same kind are merely a delusion—he was only versifying a newspaper, not trying to write poetry, or he was only trying to write like Cowper. No corresponding earlier poems by Wordsworth are brought forward, a thing Fruman would surely do if he could. This line of interest is yours rather than mine, and I do hope you will deal with it.

Houghton, bMS Eng 1401 (628)

AFTERTHOUGHT (1973)

I wrote this Introduction before reading *Coleridge, The Damaged Archangel* by Norman Fruman, and had better now consider whether that impressive book alters my conclusions about the *Ancient Mariner*. It presents Coleridge as so wholly a pathological liar that (whatever he said later) he probably did not know anything about Paracelsus or the neo-Platonists when he wrote the poem, and would therefore see no more point in his Spirits of the Air than Wieland did in the contemporary *Oberon*. I think the *Mariner* obviously does mean more, anyhow, so that the purpose of finding historical evidence is merely to coax the modern reader into recognising its merits. But also, I think one understands Fruman better after looking up some of the authors he recommends, rather than gazing fascinated at his energetic debunking act. He has not a word to say against Piper (*The Active Universe*) from who I learned this whole theory about what the spirits are doing in the *Mariner*; Piper is given space, as one of the chaps on the right side—he also made some remarks quotable for debunking, but very incidentally. And I am grateful to Fruman for putting me on to Richard Haven (*Journal of the History of Ideas*, 1959), who throws light on the mind of the early Coleridge. He says Coleridge admired the neoplatonist mystics as recorders of experience (facts of mind), having had similar experiences himself, but could not accept their formulations, and felt the need for a scientifically credible one (he read them, in fact, much as I. A. Richards read Coleridge). For a time he believed that Hartley provided it, and Hartley really did recommend achieving unity with the divine. This deals with the argument that the young Coleridge could have had no interest in reading such authors. I do not see how anyone could read Chap xiii of *The Road to Xanadu* [by John Livingston Lowes] or indeed look through the *Letters* for 1796, without admitting that Coleridge was at least pretending to read such authors, even if only to impress his correspondents; and it would not take deep reading to grasp one of their major lines of interest. Maybe the double aspiration is what puzzles a modern reader; Coleridge wanted to be extremely pious, if only to prove that one could be, without accepting the God who was satisfied by the Crucifixion.

For my thesis about the poem, there is no need to believe what he kept saying about his schooldays; and there is some evidence that the interest in spirits began after he got to college. The poem *Happiness*, when sent to brother George in 1791, said to the contented man—

> Tis thine with Fancy oft to talk,
> And thine the peaceful evening walk;

but in 1594, when he was about to end his time at Cambridge, he altered this for [Robert] Southey to:

> Tis thine with faery forms to talk,
> And thine the philosophic walk.[6]

Also a large proportion of the college poems mention fairies, and none of the school poems do; but the idea that any real philosopher is in touch with the spirits has not emerged before now. On the other hand, he was all his life accustomed to bemoan, whenever the journalism by which he kept himself afloat seemed particularly oppressive, that (as well as having had to renounce becoming a bishop) he had been stopped from becoming a cobbler; and I doubt whether a fantasy invented for a boast would take such firm root in his head. Modern biographers usually destroy the causal connections in the story, altering the dates so as to make the incidents pointless; but the old Coleridge never did that, however much he was blaming the child Coleridge and pretending to rejoice in its torments. As he tells the story, the child found that it could not sign the 39 Articles, and therefore could not get a university degree, the gateway to any well-paid white-collar employment; therefore it hunted up a cobbler willing to accept an apprentice, and led this man triumphantly to the Headmaster, explaining that as it was an atheist this was the only future it could envisage. A particularly severe beating was the only answer, and the old Coleridge, licking his lips, was accustomed to say that this was the only just beating of all the many the child received in that unjust place. Coleridge had to sign something before he could go to college at all, as we know because he wrote home about it with shamefaced jocularity; so this action in its bare moral splendour could only have occurred at school. Probably he would feel that the sinning was allowable while he was merely *in stat. pup.* and accepted the lie as a means to further education, but not when he

---

[6] See Fruman, *Coleridge*, 5.

had admittedly become grown-up and used it as a means to gainful employment. His hysterical behaviour at college looks better when you realise that he could not have emerged with a degree, for very settled reasons of conscience, however tidily he had behaved. Modern Eng. Lit. has automatically hushed this point up; and there is a natural punishment for the dishonesty, when a man like Fruman refuses to believe that Coleridge could ever have acted on a point of honour at all.

TO ALAN RUDRUM* [Henry Vaughan, 'The Waterfall']

> What sublime truths, and wholesome themes,
> Lodge in thy mystical, deep streams!
> Such as dull man can never find
> Unless that Spirit lead his mind,
> Which first upon thy face did move,
> And hatched all with his quickening love.
> As this loud stream's incessant fall
> In streaming rings restagnates all,
> Which reach by course the bank, and then
> Are no more seen, just so pass men. . . .

On 20 Feb. 1973 Empson visited Simon Fraser University in British Columbia (journeying from his visiting position at York University in Toronto) to give a lecture on Marvell's secret marriage. Over lunch, Alan Rudrum (who was editing Vaughan's poetry) happened to mention to Empson—thinking aloud about ambiguity—the curious case of the word 'restagnates', for which the *OED* cites this instance as the first known example. Rudrum authoritatively interprets the poem as a metaphorical depiction of 'the processes of life which lead inevitably to death' (*Complete Poems*, 1975, 639). But Empson's endeavour to generate likely senses for 'restagnates' led him to put forward this unconventional reading, which is in harmony with his re-appropriating purposes in general. Rudrum later remarked (letter to JH, 20 Oct. 1986): 'I think the two letters contain some nice Empsonian touches: the misquotation from the poem in the second one, the absolute certainty that he was right, and the extravagantly insulting language of the final sentence, combined with the assumption (in this case correct) that such language need not disturb cordial relations.'

Unit 12, 21 Potsdam Road, Downsview, Toronto, Canada
[n.d.]

RESTAGNANT

Dear Alan Rudrum,

I never seem to have looked into the Vaughan 'waterfall' properly, and am grateful to you for putting me on to this interesting case. But I cannot agree with your conclusions, as I understood them. I do not think there is any ambiguity, and I am sure that the one-pointed decision of the OED is wrong; this often happens when it decides to clear up a literary crux.

However as usual it gives a clear picture of what had been happening to the word, if one includes quotations from the verb and noun, and glances at the Latin dictionary. *Stagnum* is just Latin for a lake, not necessarily still or without outlet, but the suggestion of decay through inaction had already become a habitual moral in the English word *stagnant*. *Restagno* is used by Livy, Ovid, and Pliny, and its only meaning is given as 'overflow'. Derivatives had come into English during the sixteenth century, probably, though the earliest quotations are early seventeenth, mainly through French uses, mainly among alchemists; and both English and French authors often took it to mean 'become stagnant again'. This was sensible of them, as Latin is a tiresomely whimsical language, but if they were still at school they were whipped for it; because this is a classical Latin word. Vaughan was a scholarly man, who would despise ignorance, and his twin brother was a hermeticist accustomed to alchemical operations; such people were proud of their technical terms. Besides, an ambiguity here would make bad poetry, and I even think that the suggestions in the word, however pedantically one tries to exclude them, make it an unsuitable word for Vaughan's intention here. The pool under the waterfall is obviously not *stagnant* in the sense of being still and without outlet, though the OED might justify itself by the literalism that the water on entering it 'becomes a pool again'. This meaning for the word, however, leaves room for a wicked thought in the poem, which says that the restagnation is done by the *rings* on the pool:

> Which reach by course the bank, and then
> Are no more seen; just so pass men.

If it is a stagnant pool, the men have no immortality. But the little wave is enough to make the water lip over the rim, and so the water itself goes forward on its eternal cycle. The whole point is that it 'overflows'.

The cycle also explains an apparent absurdity in:

> All must descend
> Not to an end
> But quickened by this deep and rocky grave
> Rise to a longer course more bright and brave.

The water goes on running down hill, or nearly all of it; but it will at last be evaporated from the sea and will be returned upon the mountains as rain. Aristotle appears to have guessed at this cycle, and Du Bartas to have echoed him; but it was unfortunately lost just when the poets were ready to compare it to the circulation of the blood—much the neatest example of the Microcosm, which Donne would certainly have echoed if he hadn't been told some nonsense about the waters under the earth. The truth was recovered at the end of the seventeenth century by a numerical estimate of the yearly rainfall of the Seine basin compared to the water running through Paris; it needed first to be cut off from theological speculation. The poem of course uses the water-cycle of the planet as a kind of proof of human immortality; we need not fear 'that what God takes, he'll not restore'. But Vaughan was sticking his neck out here, because this analogy, that the soul returns to its source as the rain-drops to the sea, had always been used for a heretical opinion, that the individual is reabsorbed into the Absolute, as in Hinduism or the perennial 'advanced thought' of Europe (see Norman Cohn, *The Pursuit of the Millenium* (1957)). Marlowe at the end of *Faustus* makes the hero try to escape hell with it. Maybe Donne, who was clearly interested in the Radical Reformers but very leary of them, avoided the belief on this ground. (It implies Reincarnation but no permanent self.)

However, there is no sign that Vaughan feels any tension about it, as a heresy. He seems to regard it as the minimum belief in immortality, such as we might expect Nature to teach us, not entailing the rejection of a more ambitious addition; this I should expect was usual among hermeticists. And so he would not feel any need for a deep ambiguity about the matter, as in suggesting that a man's experience after death may be stagnation.

I am afraid this will be merely unwelcome, as you have already finished your edition, but I must bear my witness.

With thanks

William Empson

Houghton, bMS Eng 1401 (643)

As from: Studio House, 1 Hampstead Hill Gardens, London NW3

28 April 73

Dear Alan Rudrum,

Thank you for sending me your text in spite of the arrival of the baby; I hope all is going well and more smoothly now.[1]

Your piece refutes my argument from the brother, which was anyhow a mistake; it is known that alchemists were talking this slang, taking *restagnate* as 'make a pool again', and such is what the OED was telling us; but this gives no reason to think that Henry Vaughan, a literary man and a bit of a scholar, would use in a poem what he would consider a howler in classical Latin. Especially as it makes nonsense there, and would ignore the mystical tradition about running water which Henry is plainly using.

You do not seem to mind whether the poetry is nonsense; it is nonsense to say that the water after falling into the pool begins running up hill. But after reaching the sea it will again rise as a cloud and come down upon the mountains as rain. I agree that the idea of corruption is irrelevant anyway (though it is too hard to keep out, and that is why the use of this pedantic word is bad for the poem), but the idea of stagnation itself is nonsense here, with the waterfall continuing to enter the pool. You say, at the end of your piece, that the disappearance of the 'streaming rings' is 'an invisibility caused by cessation of motion' and this implies a 'somewhat Platonic Heaven in which "becoming" comes to rest in "being" '—presumably the waterfall has been turned off at the main. The poem does not say it has been turned off, nor yet that the rings fade out:

> As this loud brook's *incessant* fall
> In streaming lines restagnates all,
> Which reach by course the bank, and then
> Are no more seen, just so pass men.

The rings go out as far as the bank of the pool, and then disappear (I don't think they get reflected, as a rule, do they?). But though the rings or lines disappear, the water that composed them lips over the bank—it 'restagnates' or overflows—and so continues upon the eternal watercycle which is essential to life on earth. What doctrine he may deduce from this large analogy is another question; but the incapacity of the scholars even to envisage what the analogy is about is to me quite horrifying. It is as if you had been brought up not to know where babies come from.

---

[1] Rudrum had sent WE the text of his article, 'OED Defended: A Crux in Vaughan's The Waterfall', eventually to be published in *The Anglo-Welsh Review*, 25: 55 (1975), 83–6. (His first child, Catharine, was born on 3 Mar. 1973.)

I am therefore greatly distressed that I did not know your letter was a letter, as it hadn't a stamp; I thought it was one of those bills that my wife would deal with when she got back. I am always being tripped up by gadgets in Canada. So I am probably too late to affect your proofs, a most painful thing, as any success in teaching a scholar the basic facts of life, however tiny, would be a crack in the vast façade of imbecility.

How dreadfully sad. My best wishes,

William Empson

I am to go home next week, but hope to see you again some time.

Houghton, bMS Eng 1401 (643)

TIMES LITERARY SUPPLEMENT, 18 May 1973, 556: 'The Dark Lady'

Against A. L. Rowse's insistence—in *Shakespeare the Man* (1973), reviewed in the *TLS* ('New light on a Dark Lady', 27 Apr. 1973, 457–8)—that the famously unidentified 'begetter' of Shakespeare's sonnets must be a 'procurer', G. Wilson Knight[1] argued in a letter to the *TLS* (11 May 1973, 528) that 'begetter' could not, for Shakespeare, carry the meaning Rowse wished upon it: ' "Begetter" means "engenderer", and stands here for "inspirer", naturally regarded as a male force impregnating the poet . . .

> Thorpe's dedication is no triviality, but a highly competent piece of compacted writing. By wishing him the 'eternity' already 'promised' to him, it leaves us in no doubt that the person addressed is also the person addressed in the Sonnets. . . .
>
> This dedication is the only firm evidence we have regarding the young man of the sonnets; and, properly understood, leaves Southampton, whose initials were not 'W. H.', and who seems in any case an unsuitable candidate, as a non-starter.

Taking for his text the case books of Dr Simon Forman, astrologer, physician, and womanizer, Rowse further professed to identify Shakespeare's Dark Lady as Emilia Lanier, *née* Bassano, wife of a minstrel, William Lanier,

---

[1] WE thought G. Wilson Knight 'highminded and warm-hearted in a rather Victorian manner' (*SCW*, 280). Asked about Wilson Knight by Norris and Wilson in 1971, he said: 'Well, there I have been influenced. I admired it very much when I read it. I mean I kind of followed it. I still think it's very good but I'm very much out of sympathy with it now. I feel that you need to get back to taking an interest in character and regard to overall effects of the poetry as a background thing, really. I think he's awfully good about saying what the background effect is. And of course he is a practical amateur actor and producer. He knows a lot about the theatre but I do think you've got to take it in more theatrical terms. I don't think you can get away from that. But, of course, a lot of what he said was quite true—I think he's a wonderful old chap.'

and sometime mistress of Henry Carey, Lord Hunsdon, the Lord Chamberlain. Forman had described this beauty—according to Rowse's own transcription of documents he discovered in the Bodleian Library—as dark: 'very brown in youth'. However, Stanley Wells of the Shakespeare Institute at Stratford-upon-Avon pointed out in a letter to the *TLS* (11 May 1973, 528) that the word transcribed by Rowse as 'brown' is almost certainly 'braue', and that 'braue' here probably 'means "handsome, flamboyant", perhaps shading into "promiscuous".'

Sir,—I agree with most of the letter from Wilson Knight (May 11)—all but the end, where he deduces that the man addressed in the Sonnets cannot have been Southampton. People who try to solve historical puzzles (such as 'Mr W. H.') tend to assume that they must have been set fairly, as in an exam, and have proper answers; but the publisher would not feel any such duty, because he was trying to keep out of trouble. He wanted to set us guessing, and we are still at it. However, he seems to have been willing to allow a glimmer of the answer, to amuse people already in the know, as by giving the right initials in the wrong order; if it ever came to an accusation, he could deny that convincingly enough. He would have been amused to hear that the initials stood for the third husband [Sir William Harvey] of Southampton's mother, but he can hardly have enjoyed this mild pleasure, as the word 'beget' could not then carry the meaning which was later proposed for it.

The Sonnets addressed to a patron are almost necessarily for Southampton, the only person Shakespeare dedicated poems to, and many of the details fit in; but this theory is easier to believe if combined with a reflection made some time ago by Professor Wilson Knight, that Shakespeare may well have written sonnets to someone else, as much as fifteen years later, which got added in at the middle of the collection for the unauthorised printing. Sonnet 120, for instance; if he did write that to the patron, surely he must have been painfully deluded.

As to the main topic, it still seems very probable that Emilia Lanier was the Dark Lady, even if the text does not say that she was once brown and that her husband was a William; because she fits at so many points.

William Empson

[Hampstead, 13 May 1973]

G. Wilson Knight replied (*TLS*, 25 May 1963): 'I am gratified by William Empson's general agreement (May 18) with my letter; but would suggest that . . . the reversal of the initials "H. W." would nullify the composer's purpose, which is specifically to name the man as the one deserving to enjoy the literary immortality promised by the Sonnets, and assured of their presentation. Among the reasons for my rejection of Southampton is the degree of *intimacy* witnessed by the poetry . . .

'For Shakespeare's young man, I personally favour Leslie Hotson's candidate, William Hatcliffe. I have discussed the evidence in *Shakespeare and Religion* [1967], "New Light on the Sonnets".'

TO A. L. ROWSE*

Studio House, 1 Hampstead Hill gardens, London NW3
27 May 1973

Dear Dr Rouse [sic],

Thank you for sending me the second edition of your edition of the Sonnets.[1] I shall try to say what I think.

There was a clumsy phrase in my letter to the TLS about 'what the word *beget* could be made to mean then'. Of course a strained use may occur at any date, and a publisher's advertisement is not a surprising place to find one. But I was reading Samuel Butler's edition recently, and he answers a theory that such uses of *beget* were then frequent; for example, a comic foreigner in a play says 'beget' meaning 'get', with a joke effect, and this had been claimed as an example. Butler is decisive here; but the use by TT must at least be a metaphor, and the real argument is something else.[2] The Sonnets go straight into a sustained extravagant praise of some man, and the dedication has to be supposed to tell us something about him. That is the only thing we could want to hear. I know that publishers are very prone to boast about their scoops, but they are not totally unable to realise what their public is wanting and expecting. 'To the only begetter of these ensuing sonnets' actually may mean what you say it does, but if so it is a trick played upon the readers, most of whom are sure to be misled, and would feel they have been fooled if they accept your answer,

---

[1] *Shakespeare's Sonnets: The Problems Solved: A Modern Edition*, by A L. Rowse (2nd edn., 1973).

[2] Samuel Butler—in *Shakespeare's Sonnets Reconsidered, and in part rearranged* (1899), 28–9, 32–9—decries the notion that the substantive 'begetter' could mean *getter, obtainer,* or *procurer.* In Decker's *Satiromastix* a Welshman is given to pronounce, 'I have some cousin-germans at Court shall beget you the reversion of master of the king's revels'; and yet Sir Vaughan Ap Rees is not to be taken as a serious source of usage (though Boswell, exceptionally and extraordinarily, cites him when glossing 'beget'): he is a character 'who by way of humour is represented as murdering the English language all through the piece'. Butler insists therefore: 'With the metaphorical use of the word we are, of course, all familiar—the use, indeed, is metaphorical in Thorpe's preface—but the idea behind the metaphor is always that of engendering from within, not of procuring from without' (36–7).

afterwards.[3] I agree that T. T. was playing a trick, and merely add that it need not have been such an elaborate one. This also saves us from accepting a very dubious bit of biography; Southampton, as you have done so much to make us realise, tended to keep his mother at arm's length while feeling jealous and suspicious about her husbands; surely he was very unlikely to give her these damaging poems at all, let alone leave them in her keeping.[4]

I feel you may well be right in taking Marlowe for the rival poet [pp. xx, xliii], but I cannot remember what the arguments against it are, though I know I once felt they were enough. This is a dilemma into which you regularly throw your readers. Marlowe is reported as attached to Ralegh's circle, and not in sympathy with Southampton's, but he must have been getting fairly desperate in his last year and ready to try anything. During 1594, the year of the Lopez trial, as I remember, the *Jew of Malta* was acted fifteen times, and this was a record for popularity.[5] To say that Marlowe after his death appeared *every night* on the stage being gulled by his devil would be an irrelevant hyperbole, and anyway these public performances were not given at night. So even the meaning 'at night', which gives a possible let-out, is not attractive. More generally, it strikes me as unlikely that things would work out so much as a later audience expects. While a literary movement is going on, there are always a number of figures who seem to be big but later turn out not to have been, and we never find Shakespeare recognising that some other writer is merely bad, as apart from usefully funny. He could treat as a serious rival a poet so inferior as to be now quite forgotten. If there is any reason for supposing that Marlowe's Leander is Southampton, it ought to be given in the book. But I *hope* the rival poet was Marlowe.

To provide a suitable Dark Lady with the right background and situation is a most valuable step, but the point where it gives any actual help with the poems is I should think still to come. Here I should think your bold phrase that the results will 'take some time to absorb into

---

[3] Rowse claims that 'Mr W. H.' was not Shakespeare's dedicatee, but Thorpe's, the publisher's (pp. xiii–xiv): he was 'the person who got the manuscripts for him' (xliii).

[4] 'The Sonnets were not published until 1609, by Thomas Thorpe, who got the manuscripts from "Mr. W. H." Southampton's mother had died in 1607, leaving her household goods and chattels to her third husband, a much younger man, Sir William Harvey. Now it is common Elizabethan usage to refer to a knight as Mr. (short for Master) . . .' (Rowse, pp. xliii–xliv).

[5] Elizabeth I's physician was an elderly Portuguese Jew named Roderigo Lopez, who was convicted on 28 Feb. 1594 of plotting the death of the Queen; although the Queen procrastinated over signing the death-warrant, he was ultimately hanged, drawn and quartered on 7 June. See Rowse, p. xxi; and Dominic Green, *The Double Life of Doctor Lopez: Spies, Shakespeare and the Plot to Poison Elizabeth I* (2003).

Shakespearean [Shakespeare] scholarship' has actually come true since it was first published.[6]

I do sympathize with your dislike of aesthetic critics who reject history, but you seem to reject the historians as well (surely Mrs C. C. Stopes was a historian). Your book claims that nobody has understood any of the details before yourself, and you go on bringing out details, some of them discovered two hundred years ago, some of them twenty years ago, each of them as your own discovery. As you have grasped the general drift of opinion intelligently, your conclusions are all likely to be the right ones, but this is likely to do positive harm, because you bring them into such odium by your catchpenny pretence that you invented them all yourself. Just as they are settling down to the obviousness of the Southampton theory, they are driven off it again by the obvious nastiness of lying Rouse.

I hope that this is merely a misunderstanding, but it really is widely held. The first step towards rehabilitating yourself will be to add a paragraph to the introduction here, headed 'Acknowledgements', in which you say (and here I pick up my old Arden edition of the Sonnets, 1918):

> The Southampton theory was apparently first proposed by Nathan Drake in 1817, who fully understood the difficulties of the Earl's relations with the Queen; it was taken up again by Gerald Massey from 1866, and treated fully in successive publications. It was revived by Mrs C. C. Stopes in 1904, and has never since fallen out of notice. Mrs Stopes also supported, and perhaps invented, the theory that 'Mr W. H.' means the third husband of Southampton's mother; no further reasons for believing it have been adduced beyond the ones she gave.[7]

The edition mentions the theory that Marlowe was the rival poet but refuses to discuss it or say who invented it. You had much better find out. If you were a dentist, and said that nobody had ever stopped a tooth before Rouse did it, you would merely be considered ripe for the bin.[8]

I seriously wish well to your projects, and hope to save them.

William Empson

Houghton carbon, bMS Eng 1401 (642)

---

[6] Rowse, p. xlv.

[7] This seeming quotation is WE's synoptic version of several passages from C. Knox Pooler's introduction to *The Works of Shakespeare: Sonnets* [1918], pp. xvii–xx.

[8] It is possible that WE did not send Rowse the full ferocious letter as printed here, for Rowse was to reveal in his later book *Discovering Shakespeare: A Chapter in Literary History* (1989), 153: 'In a kindly meant letter William Empson from Cambridge explained the case to me. "I am sure that your broad position is the right one, and I readily sympathise with your irritation against the

TO FRANK MCMAHON[1]

Studio House, 1 Hampstead Hill Gardens, NW3
21 August 73

Dear Mr McMahon,

Thank you for sending me your text, which treats my verse very generously. When I found the first page so very abreast of my recent critical
efforts, I thought: 'Maybe this will tell me what I really want to know,
which is: why will nobody believe a word I say about Donne?' The argument about the Songs and Sonnets looks to me so clear, and it does not get
refuted, only treated with silent passive depression; maybe all right as a
joke against Helen Gardner is the most they will say. I think perhaps you
do show why, by accident, in the way you treat my own verse; you take for
granted that, unless it is flippant and trivial, it must be sickeningly pietistic,
yearning to be spiritual, moaning at the loss of Christianity—whereas I
would have been painfully ashamed to catch myself meaning things like
that, and I am sure my friends at the time did not suspect me of it. Clearly,
rather than have the Songs and Sonnets smeared with this kind of nastiness, any worthy type would say Donne at that stage was coarse and brash
and rather a pig to his women. Maybe the motives of Helen Gardner,
even, were not quite so bad as I presumed, when she blackened his character; but no, I suppose this motive could not appeal to her. Quite often,
though, a poet uses the form to try to imagine a more satisfactory way of
life, and may do it in all sorts of moods; it is a bad result of modern Eng.
Lit. training to make you presume the mood has to be churchy and
smarmy. Or is it merely that the Eng. Lit. jargon, so rigidly fixed now, has
to reek of that? There is something I need to understand here, but
probably never will.

The act of regretting loss of belief in Christianity has always struck me
as a very queer perversion. 'Oh, why can't I go to Hell? It is so unfair. Life
is such a bore without Hell. Look at poor old Mother too, she needs Hell.
What's the good of anything if she can't have Hell?' The religion has
always seemed to me just black horror, or already did when I was a schoolboy, long before writing these poems. Perhaps I ought to have said so, but

---

Eng. Lit. establishment. But I think that, in its slow self-regarding way, it had been coming round
for some time to accept what you and I consider the right view on this matter. The objection to
your publications is one which would be felt in any University Department, if a man claimed he
had found how to stop a tooth, and nobody had done it before." '

[1] On 25 July 1973 McMahon sent WE a chapter from his Oxford graduate thesis 'Empson
and Donne'.

my friends took it for granted. I felt bad about other things, but freedom from the torture-worship was a bit of clear gain.

There do seem to be bits where you catch me exposing myself to misunderstanding there, as in the line: 'Our earth alone given no name of god', whereas Mum is on Mars or suchlike.[2] But she was not a sanctimonious woman, and it seemed clear to me that the Martians would not call their own planet by the name of a god, whereas they would call the earth after some quite unexpected god. Still, it is true she was a Christian and I wasn't; and it might have been easier to talk to her if I had been. I wouldn't mind having thought of that, and if I did it doesn't give the holy boys much to crow over. The bang in the last line, 'but in darkness', was meant to imply: 'It's only when you're in real trouble that you see the old woman at her best', and this was written before I was thrown out of Cambridge, when I thought her behaviour justified my tribute. I ought to have put this in the notes, but was shy about it.

I first screamed out, reading your text, when you say [on p. 5] that Donne's

> images of the lovers as Christlike imply beliefs which make them more than just hyperbole; the lovers' fulfilment in each other realises the newly perceived divine scope of human nature. The reading finds the heart of Donne's poems to be a sequence of images which shadow what cannot be otherwise expressed . . .

So we are back among the French bourgeois, hating and despising the French bourgeois, and expressing themselves inexpressibly by a sequence of images. I expect that Donne could have written down what he meant, so far as it was part of his 'radical thought', in brisk prose, but he might have been burnt alive for it, and anyway would have lost his smart job (even without risking print). And of course you could be a Logos without being like Jesus in any point of character; it usually did end in being sacrificed, but that is not what such characters were aiming at. I have just been reading Christopher Hill's *The World Turned Upside Down*, a wonderful

---

[2] Of WE's 'To an Old Lady', McMahon wrote (15): 'As the separate world image gives her divine status but also suggests that only her mental isolation preserves it, so the decline of her world with her, the sign as in Donne of her divinity, ironically also suggests the dying of such beliefs with her, their survival only in the protected waters of age. What might seem an over-played richness of association, becomes, framed in the scientific modernity of the observer, an appropriate effect of the distance between them, an expression of the longing for the unchange-ably remote . . . [T]he gulf that isolates her among the living becomes one which isolates the observer from her and in her from the tradition of human thought. "Our earth alone given no name of god | Gives too no hold for such a leap to aid her"; the suggestion is developed in the last stanza with a further reference to the sun that long outlasts cooling gods.'

source-book though too scrappy perhaps. You ought to read that, and of course *The Pursuit of the Millenium*. I hope that as these books accumulate my attitude to Donne-when-young will become conceivable. (I can't help feeling that more important than the main subject of your essay.)

Dissatisfaction with M ['Dissatisfaction with Metaphysics'] is meant to be a quite jolly little poem, as you realise, but it is trying to laugh off the fright of being caught on the flypaper.[3] People will only interpret things in a way which is grist to their mill, and so the effects of any action are quite incalculable; however, the advance of science may produce [no] more safety if more caution. This need not be treated as very deep.

Colonising another planet did not seem to me noble in itself, though of course plucky, but notable as a thorough escape; and the comparisons to insects are not meant to make you think 'we are better class than insects, and ought to have better class treatment'; I could never understand why Boswell felt 'sadly humbled' when he saw a monkey, and still expect that he was only pretending.[4] What is clear is that the insects have an even worse time than we do, ever more deeply sunk in the flypaper.[5] The scorpions of course actually did have small flames put all round the glass bowl in which they were enclosed: you never got round to saying that. The verse you quote struck me as very good; I had forgotten it, because the poem is no use for reading aloud. You spoil the rhythm by putting a comma after *carapace*.

I suppose a busy Freudian while being analysed feels that 'degrading self-knowledge' is brought by modern science, making him like an insect,

---

[3] McMahon (5–6) calls 'Dissatisfaction with Metaphysics' a 'witty' poem, and explains that '[t]he revolutionary force of relativity theory . . . overshadows the Copernican revolution as a second deluge would the first, questioning what seemed unquestionable assumptions, defying comprehension . . . The opening stanza presents a fictional cosmological system which characterises the "philosophers' disease", man's interpreting the world in terms of his own beliefs and taking as objective knowledge what his own imagination forms . . . The radical "Dissatisfaction with Metaphysics" comes with the realisation that human perception is inherently distorting.'

[4] 'The trick of the monkey using the cat's paw to roast a chestnut, is only a piece of shrewd malice in that *turpissima bestia*, which humbles us so sadly by its similarity to us' (James Boswell, *The Journal of a Tour to the Hebrides* (1786), ed. R. W. Chapman (1924), 179–80).

[5] Of 'Plenum and Vacuum', McMahon notes: 'The opening description of the scorpions' idea of their world shows man creating to himself . . . the situation in which he believes himself to exist in. The scorpions fear the divine fire from their heaven, the glass enclosing them, and are determined on "suicide defiance": "Delicate goose-step of penned scorpions | Patrols its weal under glass-cautered bubble; | Postpones, fire-cinct, their suicide defiance, | Pierced carapace, stung in mid-vault of bell." . . . Their ground is the "scar of a burn" in being the crust of a cooling planet and this makes the fire that of matter, not of god. The enclosing bubble, "glass-cautered", is the product of the same fire in the sense that the curvature of space-time, the imagined limit of the Einsteinian universe, is implied in the nature of the matter it encloses . . . The scorpions are driven by their fictions; Styx does coerce . . . The identification of man with the scorpions comments on the human nature involved.'

but I never went in for it.[6] I was ashamed of my failures, sexual more than anything else (it is actually hard to remember what I was so unhappy about), but I certainly never thought that science was shameful, making 'violent contrasts with the impossible images' of Christian sainthood. Those filthy torturers? Their incessant greasy lies? *They* are what Europe has most to be ashamed of, and I think it very alarming that the idea cannot enter your mind.

Page 10. I can't see that there is any ambiguity on *lead*.[7] Page 12. The belief that every man has 'divine status' *was* heretical and familiar, and would easily be suggested at the time by Donne's 'planet imagery' (please stop using that nasty jargon).[8] Page 14. Mutual need would have been a great comfort, not contemptible at all; there seemed to be a great lack of it.[9] Page 15. My Mum was a Tory and a terrific class-addict, so that I could bring nobody to her house except people I didn't like; the idea that she was occupied with magical-religious beliefs is just your rigid fancy.[10]

---

[6] McMahon notes (8) that 'the beetle image' of 'Value is in Activity' 'recalls the scorpions and the ants, spiders, cicada of other poems. The image of man as an insect recurring through the poems carries the awareness of the degrading self-knowledge brought by modern science and almost violently contrasts with the impossible images created by religious belief.'

[7] Of 'The World's End', McMahon notes: 'A play on "lead" . . . shows the hope [of escape and independence] frustrated. "Plumb" in the first stanza expresses the urge to dive straight down, away, but on its reappearance the mention of lead brings out the sense of diving like a plummet or dropping a plumb-line; the ambiguity ties the escape to the behaviour of the lead in the Einsteinian universe, circling within it . . .'

[8] Comparing 'The World's End' with Donne's Holy Sonnet V (with reference to WE's discussion in *SVP*), McMahon notes of WE's poem (p. 11): 'The movement from the hope of freedom to the reality of imprisonment repeats that found in the sonnet and the image of the frustrated space-flight . . . powerfully expresses the feelings generated by the necessary acceptance of man's material nature . . . [T]he idea of man's divine status expressed in the separate planet images [in WE's poems] and that of being a soulless animal are seen as being for Donne alternative dreams of escape from the authority to which his possession of a soul exposes him.' He notes too (12): 'The recalling of Donne's sonnet in "The World's End" reflects how the impossibility of religious beliefs about man's relation to the world is most acutely felt as the impossibility of Donne's separate planet imagery.'

[9] Of Donne's poetry as glossed in *SVP*, McMahon writes (13–14), 'The images of the lover as Christlike are both a supreme expression of fulfilment in love and a reflection of the divine image of man that religious belief established. The two are dependent on one another: the beliefs about the divinity of human nature make the ideals of love conceivable, just as now for Empson [in his early poems] the belittling knowledge of man's insect nature can only inspire the selfishness of mutual need.'

[10] 'The character of the separate planet imagery as an essential and universal representation of man established by religious belief,' McMahon notes (14), 'is apparent in "To an Old Lady".' He notes too (15–16): 'As the separate world image gives her divine status but also suggests that only her mental isolation preserves it, so the decline of her world with her, the sign as in Donne of her divinity, ironically also suggests the dying of such beliefs with her, their survival only in the protected waters of age . . . [I]n her can be seen the traditional pattern of "magical" beliefs . . .

'The greatness of the poem is not so much in representing a personal relationship as in discovering in the old lady a richly representative figure in whom the effects in human dignity of the lost beliefs can be appreciated . . .'

Page 21. 'Letter IV' is very much about a neurotic condition, and not I think suitable for a poetry-reading, so I haven't any experience of how it goes over. But I can't see that you have any reason for saying it is about

> the impossible position produced by the conflict of scientific realism with the beliefs that make the relationship, and indeed human life, valuable.[11]

What beliefs can possibly have been whispered into your ear by some toadlike priest? The belief that the Father could be bought off from torturing mankind eternally (or rather, a tiny remnant of mankind) in exchange for the specially intense pleasure of having his Son tortured to death? No decent human relations could exist between two people who both believed this, because each had the overwhelming need to keep Number One out of Hell, and let the other go hang; such is the stated moral of *Paradise Lost*. There is no other university subject except Eng. Lit., I think you ought to be told, in which your head would have been stuffed with such nastiness; not even Divinity, because there they would try to teach you how to sound plausible to the modern world, whereas in Eng. Lit. you are taught to wallow in the creeds of Ancient Night. It has become a dreadfully bad education.

The beliefs recommended in 'Bacchus' are quite obviously not those required for the worship of the Torture-Monster.[12] I daresay it is an unhealthy poem at bottom, but I never feel I have to warn people about that before I read it out; that aspect of it is on the surface, once the merely technical obscurity is overcome; whereas I usually do feel I ought to give a warning about 'This Last Pain'. But the kind of belief I am proposing here, in these various poems about living in accordance with a belief, is nothing to do with belief in The Infamy: I feel as if you have accused me of recommending Thuggee.

However, apart from the appalling effects of your being systematically deluded at the taxpayer's expense, I think you show beautiful sympathy and sensitivity towards my work.

Perhaps we could meet at some point, if you still feel it would be worth

---

[11] Of 'Letter IV' McMahon remarks (21): 'The intensely felt convolutions of the poem reveal the impossible position produced by the conflict of scientific realism with the beliefs that make the relationship, and indeed human life, valuable.'

[12] McMahon notes (22) 'the recognition in "Letter V" that the love for the divine image of the girl is love of a self-created illusion', and that this recognition 'is perhaps anticipated in "Invitation to Juno", a poem which treats lightly and wittily the union of man and goddess on which the attempt to reconcile knowledge and belief in love is centred . . . In "Bacchus" this has become very definitely the difficult success aimed at, to act on the illusory beliefs, to maintain the illusions that make action in the real world worthwhile.'

while. I am trying to write the next Clark Lectures but am otherwise at leisure.

Yours sincerely
W. Empson

Houghton carbon, bMS Eng 1401 (600)

NEW YORK REVIEW OF BOOKS, 22: 14 (20 September 1973), 44: 'The Rights of Editors'

Charles Rosen, in a review of *Coleridge's Verse* ('Isn't It Romantic?', *New York Review of Books*, 20: 10 (14 Jun. 1973), 12–18), remarked: 'Empson is a large-spirited critic, and it pains him to see his poet gradually succumb to the horrors of orthodoxy. To restore Coleridge to himself, Empson and his co-editor, David Pirie, have rewritten the *Ancient Mariner*. Except at one place, they have not actually changed any of Coleridge's words, but they have produced a text that does not look precisely like any of the different versions that Coleridge published . . .

'Empson and Pirie had divided the changes that Coleridge made to his poem of 1798 into two parts: those that merely refine and clarify the original conception, and those that seriously alter it, and even conceal it behind a smoke screen of Christian allegory. In other words, for Empson, Coleridge afterward "ratted on the poem" and tried to pretend that it was about something else . . . There are, indeed, serious cuts in the 1800 version of the poem, and the marginal glosses of 1817 give an interpretation based on sin and redemption through suffering that is gravely at odds with the text of 1798 . . .

'Empson and Pirie's treatment of the text may be high-handed, but any edition with variant readings invites every reader to form just such a text for himself . . . However, it is not, strictly speaking, the "ideal" text that Empson and Pirie seek, but the one truest to the original idea of the poem.

'Their search implies an idealistic (and Romantic) view of literature in which none of the various stages of the text is the poem itself, but only approaches to it. That is indeed the only coherent view that permits genuinely interpretative criticism . . .

'This idea of the poem is placed by Empson squarely in the poet's mind, and he equates it with the poet's intention, which is partially misleading . . .

'Empson treats Coleridge's betrayal of his poetry with generosity and sympathy, and he is wonderfully free of the pious moral airs expressed by recent critics faced with Coleridge's weaknesses . . . For Empson, indeed, the theme of the *Ancient Mariner* is the very reason that Coleridge betrayed the poem and tried to convince his readers and himself that it was about something else. The theme is a sense of guilt and revulsion from life greater than any possible motivation. The disparity between the shooting of the albatross and the subsequent horrors visited upon the Mariner and the crew is the most terrifying aspect of the poem ... Almost as much as anything else, the *Ancient Mariner* warns us of the awesome consequences of religious guilt, and it is in this sense a deeply antireligious poem.'

I have no ground at all for complaint at your friendly treatment of the selection from Coleridge's poetry by Mr Pirie and myself, but it now strikes me that, through the interest of the theoretical case about the rights of editors, we made our actual changes sound larger than they are.

The standard collected text of the *Poems* of Coleridge (Oxford, 1912) gives extra lines, written by the poet but discarded later, at the foot of almost every page, in smaller type; a particularly large number come under *The Ancient Mariner*. In that poem we put all the rejected verses back (though not all the rejected lines) except the ones that would not fit in, as by making a contradiction; and we banished all the prose remarks added by the poet in the margin, the 'marginal glosses', to the notes at the end of the book. It may be argued that the poem is never read except by readers who have the Oxford text, and only if they read the bottoms of the pages too; but our mode of presentation (on this view) is at least better than what most readers get.

William Empson
London, England

ESSAYS IN CRITICISM, 23: 4 (October 1973):
'The Intentional Fallacy, Again'

Edward Larrissy, in an essay 'The Intentional Fallacy' (*Essays in Criticism*, 23: 2, Apr. 1973), took issue with an earlier article by Paul Ramsey (*E in C*, Oct. 1972) on the subject of W. K. Wimsatt and Monroe Beardsley's ideas in their famous essay 'The Intentional Fallacy'. Ramsey had misunderstood the meaning of Wimsatt and Beardsley's 'clear' argument that 'the design or intention of the author is neither available nor desirable as a standard for judging the success of a work of literary art'. We are ignorant 'of an artist's intention or design before he writes a poem,' Larrissy affirmed; so the 'keenness' of the Wimsatt–Beardsley essay lies in 'its clear demonstration' that we can 'never' certainly answer the question as to whether a work has lived up to its author's intentions. Above all, intention must remain irrelevant to the act of evaluation: 'intention is not to hand for use' as a critical standard.

I am afraid it is no use being broad-minded and sensible, like your previous correspondent [. . .] about the dogma that a reader ought never to consider the intention of an author. Sensible people are now beginning to hedge on their earlier acceptance of this view, very rightly, so they explain (with tender humour and so forth) that nobody ever intended the crude interpretation evidently held by outsiders and students; the esoteric doctrine held by professors allows a tolerable freedom. We have heard this kind of thing before. The crude doctrine is what does all the harm, whatever the Intention may have been; and whether or not the high priests imagine they are above it makes no difference.

A child needs to be encouraged to imagine the feelings of the author he is reading, as soon as reading becomes more than a technique; also to decide whether he himself feels differently. The transference of the human uses of speech to writing is perhaps no harder than learning to ride a bicycle, but you could not learn to ride a bicycle if you were never allowed to try. And to allow the wise old men to try, as a special concession, does no good because after such a training they can no longer learn, and will probably do something nasty instead.

When this dogma is operating, the students are usually taught to try to catch the author out, and blame him for breaking whatever critical principles (adopted by whimsy) have been issued to them beforehand. No doubt other plans may be contrived; but the dogma must in some way produce deadness and falsity, because the students are denied any spontaneous contact with an author's mind.

TO PENELOPE B. R.DOOB*

[n.d.: 1973]

Dear Penelope Doob,

Thank you for sending me an off-print of your recent article, with its generous inscription.[1] I am sorry to send a disagreeable reply. But I have to speak up if (as you seem to imply) I am regarded as one of the people responsible for this whole school of critical writing, which is now so very standard in universities; it makes me feel, as the poet [A. E. Housman] said, like Sin when she brought forth Death.

You take for granted that it makes a good play to watch a character commit a sin, and reflect that he or she deserves punishment, and then

[1] Penelope B. R. Doob, 'A reading of *The Changeling*', *English Literary Renaissance*, 3 (1973), 183–206.

watch the punishments become increasingly severe till she is dead. This craving is found in England as well as on the other side of the Atlantic; I remember a young lady at Sheffield saying that she could hardly wait for the tortures on Volpone to begin (or Punch or some such character); but I do not notice that the boys boast of it so proudly as the girls. It is very much part of the Christian revival; it was Coulton, I think, who reported a town in the Low Countries during the Middle Ages which was short of criminals, so that the Mayor bought one from a neighbouring town, for the satisfaction of the people, who tortured him to death in the market place.[2] One does not hear of this from Buddhist or Hindu or Moslem communities. But maybe I wrong you in supposing that you actually do suffer from a loathsome mental disease, putting you into what you would describe as a state of Sin. It is more likely that you talk like this because it is a skill which you have earnestly acquired, and that you murder the play because you have been taught to consider all plays as dead already.

I confess there is a bit of plausibility about your thesis when applied to *The Changeling*, which comes after the great period and was perhaps at first conceived as fitting a crude moral formula; but the long series of critics who have picked it out for admiration all assumed that it had some large imaginative effect, taking it far away from this crude formula, and telling some truth about life otherwise hard to define. What I call 'crude' here, you understand, is what you have been brought up to regard as the most modern, scholarly, intellectual view of a play; that it is the pleasure of inflicting torture upon some member of the community officially provided for the purpose. This degree of barbarism among scholarly critics is quite new; it would still have been howled down twenty years ago. If what you say is true, all the earlier critical attention given to the play was mistaken.

But the matter is not limited to your interpretation of this late play, because your first paragraphs deal with all madness in Elizabethan plays, which you say is always a symbol of Sin. You offer no excuse for this casual murder of a large part of Elizabethan drama. There the state of madness is regularly regarded with awe because it is a time when the roots of the mind are laid bare, as it might be wrecks long ago in a storm at sea, and unexpected sources of wisdom speak up from the wild forces of our nature. There was a fair amount of non-Christian superstition behind this,

---

[2] G. G. Coulton (1858–1947) was a lecturer in English at Cambridge, with a fellowship at St John's College, 1919–34; he lectured on 'Life and Thought, 1066–1550'. An exacting historian and controversialist, his works include *The Medieval Village* (1925), *Art and the Reformation* (1928), *Ten Medieval Studies* (1930), and *Inquisition and Liberty* (1938). It is not known whether WE ever heard him lecture.

making the audience more ready to accept it, but that is little drawn upon by the playwrights themselves. Of course Shakespeare was much the best at this line, so that we hardly give credit to the others, but it is already established in *The Spanish Tragedy*; Shakespeare learned a great deal from that play and shows it in his earliest writing. And you cannot pretend that old Jeronimo goes mad because he is sinful; he goes mad because he is confronted by a total conflict between two duties, particularly trying to this character because he is a conscientious judge. (You on the other hand have been brought up to believe that there couldn't ever be a conflict between two duties, because Teacher always knows what is right.) He cannot help acting queerly, in the presence of the enemy who is his due master, but he tries to make use of that to help his plot; thus establishing the formula for the Elizabethan mad revenger, but he is far more innocent than the later specimens, and had to be, to be accepted by the early audiences. When you remark, in your first paragraphs, that 'the imagery of blindness' comes into *The Changeling*, as usual with madness, though I don't remember that any comes at all, you must be thinking of Lear. Do you really believe that Lear deserved to go mad, for not being patient enough when he was taken down a peg by Regan and Goneril? There is no degree of farcical unreality which would not be unflinchingly accepted by your recent school.[3]

The explanation of how this madness arose, which is now driving students to refuse to take any courses in the older literature, is of course much to do with the demands of great numbers, of mass education, but also with jealousies between departments. You cannot grasp how the audiences of these playwrights would react unless you know their major interests, and to admit a discussion of that would open a door to the History Department. Pretend then that they had all read Castiglione; make him a Set Book. Pretend that the audiences had all read the published sermons of the time, and that they went to the theatres to hear them repeated;

---

[3] In an early, unfinished essay, WE noted: 'One of the most striking peculiarities of the Elizabethan drama, if we compare it with the few other great dramatic periods of the world, is surely the emphasis on madness; usually caused by unbearable wrong, such as most drama deals with, but conceived as interesting in itself or even, paradoxically, as both happier and wiser than recognition of the world. It is not easy to see where they got the idea. We find it in a way obvious now because the labours of anthropologists have collected the surviving fragments of its widespread, primitive roots, but it must then have been something of a discovery. I cannot think of any obvious source for it but the Hamlet story itself, which had recently been made easily accessible in the French of Belleforest. Granting that Kyd used the story, we must suppose him to use it before he wrote *The Spanish Tragedy*, because that has no known source apart from being a simplified variant of the Hamlet story. On this view, Hamlet must have been about the first good Elizabethan play, and one which did much to establish the peculiar tone of the whole drama. This makes it peculiarly fitting that Shakespeare should go back to reconsider the basic object when embarking on his main tragic period.'

ignore the evidence (which is surely decisive) that the government men, both clerical and lay, suspected the theatres of expressing independent views. Always refuse to believe that there were any other opinions in the country except those expressed in official publications; the same technique would simplify the history of Nazi Germany. But I have to suspect, after all excuses of this technical kind have been made, that a good deal of sheer spite is at work; the scholars feel they have been tricked into wasting their lives on the study of remote authors whom they dislike, and they are going to take the mickey out of the bastards somehow.

Such being the general background of this gloomy situation, I now timidly attempt a defence of *The Changeling*. It is a forlorn hope; a critic already convinced that there is no play of human judgement at all in *King Lear* cannot possibly be convinced that there is any in this play. You would need first to be willing to recognise a whole lot of things about the audiences, many of them standard among modern audiences too. All audiences are against the Arranged Marriage; Elizabethan ones were convinced that Spanish grandees, with their terrific code of honour (which though unchristian was a thing one ought to try to keep up with), treated their daughters quite murderously about the Arranged Marriage. I notice you remark that the aristocratic status of Beatrice is 'rather tenuous'. What a lot of history in your own past, how many generations, lie behind this easy presumption. The play shows the father of Beatrice as a Spaniard in command of an enormous fortification, visited as a curiosity by people liable to get lost in it; everybody knew at the time that only a very high-class Spaniard would be given such a post. And Beatrice falls in love with an entirely unsuitable man (by any standard) only a day or two after her father has vowed her to another, merely as his right. She is quite certain that it would be hopeless to plead with her father not to ruin her life in this random manner, but she is an aristocrat too with a fighting heredity, and her only outlet is crime. The Globe audience contained few aristocrats, and would not approve of the behaviour of the father; so far, it would be prepared to admire Beatrice, and certainly not blame her for her revolt, though it would not be surprised to find her rude and petulant towards her servants. What has been found thrilling in the play, and I believe was intended by the authors though evidence is hard to come by, is that she develops a sexual craving, unrecognised by herself, in a servant for whom she expresses disgust, so extravagantly that it becomes a kind of intimacy. As she has to use him to kill her father's choice, or rather finds this a charming order to give to the man she does not know how to approach otherwise, she falls into his power, and then the electric speed of conflicting impulses and misunderstandings does make a tremendous scene, though only if you grant, as against her gradual confused recognition of her lust for him, his massive acceptance of death if only he can first enjoy her. You give the villain a good mark for despising his concubine, I noticed: 'a woman dipped in blood'—but he is jeering at her to remove a state of blindness, confident that once she appreciates reality she will love as he does. Eliot's remark about the '*habituation* of Beatrice to her sin'[4] is as usual pure self-indulgence, imagining that Elizabethan plays happened in the drawing-rooms of Boston; Beatrice doesn't have any time to become habituated. De Flores dies saying that he expected soon to die, as soon as he took on the challenge of this woman's love, and he dies proud and content. You daren't mention this, dare you? It wouldn't fit your dirty gabble, which is all intended to prove that you are better than either of them.

The great fault of this modern criticism, in which you are fighting away to win your niche, is that it is morally just abysmal, a thousand miles down towards Hell below what the successive generations of silly old buffers had been doing before, for two or three hundred years.

Goodness, how sad.[5]

William Empson

[P. S.] By the way, the test for virginity does not express the fear and disgust for science, already felt by all right-thinking people. It is just a bit of Science Fiction, intended to interest and amuse; these people are very smart and up to date, so naturally they have the latest gadgets.

The reason for locating so many plays in southern Europe then is that the English felt socially and intellectually inferior to Spaniards and Italians, who had the latest Code of Honour as well; one must not appear pitiful by confessing to this sentiment, but just work hard at catching up. There was comfort in reflecting that anyway they were monstrously wicked, whereas we were good. Here then it was fitting to feel tragic horror at their crimes, with even some touch of the contempt which seems to be all you can feel for them. But this was by no means the only thing in the Elizabethan mind; the characters seemed very grand and romantic— otherwise the play would be merely sordid, like your treatment of it.

Houghton, bMS Eng 1401 (539)

---

[4] TSE, 'Thomas Middleton', *Selected Essays*, 3rd edn. (1951), 164.
[5] An allusion to a catchphrase in Evelyn Waugh's short story 'Cruise (Letters from a young lady of leisure)': see Introduction above.

TO ROMA GILL*

Studio House, 1 Hampstead Hill Gardens, NW3

4 December 1973

My dear Roma,

Delighted to hear you are coming south; I have been feeling I have too much to write to you, and badly want to have a chat, about Fredson [Bowers] and Faust. The first of my Clark Lectures is billed as 'The Rehabilitation of Dr Faustus', and full acknowledgement will be given to your work on the play. I agree with your remark in your Introduction that the B-text addition of boasts by the Devil at the end that he has successfully cheated Faust alters the whole conception, and add that it turns the play into the devil-worship of the slavering witch-burners, a system of belief which Aquinas regarded with patient contempt. I became convinced that the A-text is Marlowe's original, though cut at some points for blasphemy by the censor, and probably by the Company because they wanted less theological comic scenes. I was startled at first, on meeting Fredson [Bowers]'s edition, to find him sticking to the B-text at such harmful points without acknowledging the A-text in his footnotes apparatus. But then I realised that his Introduction amounts to the fall of the walls of Jericho, though a pretence that he still believes the A-text to be 'debased' is kept up, out of loyalty and stupidity. He admits (in the *Studies in Bibliography* 1973 article, not the edition itself) that his ascribing the B-text additions to Rowley-Birde 'weakens' the belief that A is a 'bad quarto', and only claims to retain belief in it as an act of faith.[1] Of course, one can no longer even say that Marlowe had 'agreed' to the plans of a 'collaborator' if these evil parts were added ten years after his death, so a reconstruction of his intention becomes possible—and most of the time of my lecture must be given to that.[2]

---

[1] See Fredson Bowers, 'Marlowe's *Doctor Faustus*: The 1602 Additions', *Studies in Bibliography*, 26 (1973), 1–18.

[2] This opening passage of WE's first Clark Lecture survives among his papers: 'Up till about 1930, Marlowe was considered an idealistic author, taking part in the Enlightenment; then there was a powerful back-lash, regarding him as a traditional satirist, who would see no good in liberated figures such as Faustus and Tamburlane. Meanwhile a great deal of work has been done, especially by Frances Yates, on the sixteenth-century magicians and their influence, which greatly affected the development of medicine and the other sciences. Magicians were accepted by rulers, Queen Elizabeth among them, on the understanding that they dealt (at worst) with "middle spirits", neither from Heaven nor from Hell, and not with devils; but the clergy, who controlled the censorship (of plays as well as books till 1592), insisted upon the belief that only devils could really be procured. Marlowe in writing *Faust* had simply agreed to dramatise an internationally famous book, but he makes Faust, in the first half of the play, talk as a magician of the time actually would do. Then Faust loses his nerve, or somehow becomes convinced that his spirits are devils, but the audience is not forced to agree. There is a great confusion about the

Friar Bacon and the *Looking-glass* are clearly planned to cash in on the expectations established by the much stronger *Faust*, as you suggest in your Introduction; and it was usually said when I was a student—I ought never to have given it up. The English Faust-book is almost certainly early too, but as Marlowe would obviously meet the translator he might have used the manuscript. Both play and pamphlet ran into difficulties with censorship (as is admitted in the scrap of surviving evidence from the publishers) and that is why the history is so hushed up and the text so scrambled. But this is of minor importance compared to getting a text which makes the intention clear. [Unfinished.]

Houghton: ? draft, bMS Eng 1401 (563)

TO ROMA GILL

[n.d.: 1973]

My dear Roma,

I thought you might be interested to have a report of my reading of the Faust-book [the English translation (*EFB*), by 'P. F.', of the German *Faustbuch* (*GFB*)], which I am grateful to you for finding. It is of course a shockingly silly book, but the author seems to be in just the same state of unscrupulous confusion as Marlowe. Any view of the story which might please somebody, and won't be too annoying for somebody else, has to go in. The only major thing Marlowe added (it strikes me) is

> To him I'll build an altar and a church
> And offer luke-warm blood of new-born babes.

This is quite out of character (Faust's and Meph's[1] as well), and merely added for theatrical effect. The show of the seven deadly sins is added—

text and its dates and even those of the English translation of the Faustbook, only to be explained by heavy censorship. England had kept fairly clear from the Continental craze for witch-burning, and the anxiety of the Government need not be thought discreditable. The original play, now mostly lost, was probably acted a few times. It was always a sad story, but probably less horrible than what first the censorship and then the mob demanded. A good deal of it can be reconstructed.' (*Houghton*)

[1] WE glosses this fond abbreviation in *FC*, 46–7 note: 'It seems as well to put "Meph" for the familiar spirit of Faust, not to raise a laugh but to solve a difficulty. The best form of the name is "Mephistopheles", with an **i**, well known from Goethe but invented earlier in the eighteenth century. It makes the spirit a cool civil servant, a tax collector perhaps, or an inquisitor. The Faust-book calls him "Meph**o**stophiles", with an **o**, so that he is rather clumsy but forceful, even a jovial character. The A-text of Marlowe, which we have no adequate reason to doubt, calls him "Meph**a**stophilis", so that he is a bleating sheep-like figure, who demands love but could bite. It would be tiresome to insist upon the correct spelling.'

an alternative to the false visit to Hell, needed as possible on the stage. I had assumed that 'Come, I think Hell's a fable' was added by the flippant scepticism of Marlowe, with his taste for pert young men; and he does invent this presentation of it; but the Faustbook Chap. IX (after he has started having fun with Meph.) says

> he believed not that there was a God, hell, or Devil; he thought that body and soul died together . . .

The Faust book when being religious is quite as grim as Marlowe, and maybe the practical jokes are more brutal; but it tries to relieve our minds at the end (LXIII):

> The same night [as the day of his death] Doctor Faustus appeared unto his servant lively, and showed unto him many secret things the which he had done and hidden in his lifetime. Likewise there were certain which saw Doctor Faustus look out of the window by night as they passed the house

(that is, Wagner [Faustus's house-boy Christopher Wagner, who supposedly wrote a life of him] is not the only source of evidence).[2] Then we have the final paragraph of awful warning, but plainly Faustus is not finding his new status so oppressive as he expected.

The status of the enactor of Helen is important, because of the theory of [W. W.] Greg that kissing a devil (though a disguised one) would be recognised by the audience as the unforgivable sin. This is plainly not in the text, and the audience were not medieval theologians. Probably, I grant, there is some point now obscure in

> Her lips suck forth my soul, see where it flies!
> Come, Helen, come, give me my soul again.
> Here will I dwell, for heaven is in these lips . . .

Plainly, whatever else he thinks, he thinks she *does* give him his soul again, when she volunteers the next kiss. It seems enough explanation of the fancy that Marlowe always soars up into the air, whenever he feels exalted about anything; but there are also, are there not, some classical or

---

[2] Cf. Jones in *FC*, 32–3: 'The Faust-book refers to a life of Faust by his servant Wagner, and it is made clear in the final chapter of the Faust-book that this is not the Faust-book itself, but another work. There are also one or two places in the Faust-book where Wagner is invoked to supply additional material, so much material must have been available when the work was composed. There is much more evidence for a "Wagner" Faust-book in Widman's *Warhafftige Historie*, a greatly augmented version of Faust's life, complete with exhaustive commentary, published posthumously in 1599.'

Renaissance precedents. However, considering how literally Marlowe is using the Faustbook, we should follow its guidance when in doubt. There Helen is not (I think I can show) conceived as a devil at all, but as a middle spirit of the air, like those of Paracelsus ['De nymphis, sylphis, pygmaeis et salamandris et de caeteris spiritibus', in the *Philosophiae Magnae* (1567)] or *The Midsummer Night's Dream*. The author is at least aware of this alternative, and expects us to be mildly interested in it. When the Emperor Charles V asks to see Alexander the Great and his consort (XXIX), Faustus answers that their dead bodies cannot be brought, but

> such Spirits as have seen Alexander and his Paramour alive shall appear unto you in manner and form as they both lived in their most flourishing time; and herewith I hope to please your Majesty. Then Faustus went a little aside to speak to his Spirit, but he returned again presently . . .

and says it can be done at once, but the phantoms must not be spoken to. The Emperor convinces himself that this is genuine by finding a wart on the back of the lady's neck, which he had reason to expect, and by recalling 'the woman that raised the Prophet Samuel' (merely, I suppose, a help in reducing the incredulity of the readers). When some students who were his guests asked to see Helen (XLV) he gave them the same warning, and said they must remain seated while she was present. Her beauty

> inflamed the hearts of the students, but that they persuaded themselves she was a Spirit, wherefore such fantasies passed away lightly with them; and thus fair Helen and Doctor Faustus went out again one with another.

They are a rough lot, but feel too frightened to disobey the instruction; still, one could feel that without knowing a specific medieval doctrine. Next day they ask him to do it again, because they will bring a painter, but he says:

> he could not always raise her spirit, but only at certain times: yet (said he) I will give you her counterfeit, which should always be as good to you as if you yourselves should see the drawing thereof, which they received according to his promise, but soon lost it again.

They spend the night craving in lustful fantasy, which shows that the Devil often blinds the heart with lust,

> that men fall in love with Harlots, nay even with Furies, which afterward cannot lightly be removed.

I quote at some length out of care not to misreport the author, who seems himself to feel that the details of the affair deserve attention. (Helen while alive had the effect of a Fury; her enactor need not be a Devil.) Why was there this slight embarrassment or doubt about the production of Helen, as about that of Alexander? The power of Mephistopheles over minor devils always elsewhere appears boundless; his attendants have nothing to do but obey him. Besides, in what sense could a junior devil, nearly three thousand years after the death of Helen, be called '*her* spirit'? The term is normally used only of ghosts, the soul of Helen without her body, but Protestants of the time were strictly forbidden to believe in ghosts, as a result of renouncing Purgatory; all Christian sects agreed that there was no return from Heaven or Hell, but Papists might believe in occasional returns from Purgatory on urgent family business. This situation explains why the Protestant author handles the Helen part of his story cautiously and with curiosity about the details; he wants us to guess that this was a Middle Spirit, who had long ago become so deeply attached to Helen that she could still copy her precisely. Such a spirit Mephistopheles cannot order about, and a sudden call may find her engaged, but he can coax her with reasonable confidence as he does human women. (When Faustus enjoys the seraglio of the Grand Turk, the joke is pointless unless the ladies are real, and the Grand Turk is really insulted.) Then in lv, less than two years before the end, Faustus 'commands' Mephistopheles to bring him the fair Helena, 'which he also did' ('also', I submit, implies that this spirit could have refused). He falls in love with her and has a child by her, but they both vanish the day after his death. This I think proves that she is a Middle Spirit; legend is full of such cases, whereas a child by a devil would be eccentric and gruesome. In effect, the childbirth provides the answer to this minor question which the book has been rather carefully posing, and the answer is only allowed just before we enter the rapids of the Doctor's terrible and lamentable end.

The trouble, I think, with our scholarly critics during the present century has been they were confident they could pervert a large part of English Literature by appealing to the official superstitions current when they were written; as everybody must have believed what the Government told them, the traditional interpretations of these works must be wrong. It was just a fortunate corollary that the Reformation never occurred, and everybody was a secret Papist until they all became atheists. I am very tired of this line of interpretation. There is a simple way to answer it: bring out the unofficial superstitions too.

There are many other interesting angles to the book. Faustus (e. g. xv) 'thought his sins greater than God could forgive', like those of Judas and Cain; but we are never told just where he believed he had given this defeat to omnipotence. Still, if you take his fear seriously you will expect to find it in his solemn oration to the students on the evening before the devils tore him to pieces (LXIII); at the very end, the climax, of the long formal sentence expressing farewell. Let them not fall

> altogether from God, as I wretched and ungodly damned creature have done, having denied and defied Baptism, the Sacraments of God's body, God himself, all heavenly powers, and earthly men, yea, I have denied such a God, that desireth not to have one lost.

This is a very odd piece of rhetoric, and one would particularly like to know here whether it is also in the German.[3] He leads up through various Christian entities to God, but his mind does not pause there; maybe he next repents of having denied the Middle Spirits of the air, at least, without this interpretation he makes a pointless anti-climax. The students who saw Helen

> were all amazed to see her, esteeming her rather to be a heavenly than an earthly creature

and they were quite right, because the Middle Air was her home. Next in his swooping humiliation Faustus confesses he has 'denied and defied' earthly men; as a Renaissance professor he ought almost to have worshipped man, but there too he failed, wanting something better. But then the final confession lets out a weird cry which accuses Christianity root and

---

[3] WE strains at an ambiguity here, in *FC*: 'there is a puzzling detail in Faust's address to the scholars, shortly before his end. In the GFB he says (chapter 68): "I despised and denied the baptism, the sacrament of Christ, the human race, all the Heavenly Host and God himself—a God who does not desire that anyone should be lost" [Sp. 220]. The final clause is in apposition, made clear by Jones's dash. As it recalls a text from Ezekiel [18: 23; also 33: 11] there can be little doubt that this was the intention. P. F. makes him say, with a slight confusion marking extra agitation, that he has "denied and defied . . . the Sacraments of Christ's body, God himself, all heavenly powers, and earthly men, yea, I have denied such a God, that desireth not to have one lost" (EFB, 79). Perhaps the contortion arose because he could hardly bear to say it. But there is now a separate sentence, definitely not a clause in apposition to "God", and it has to mean: "I believed that God *does* desire to send some men to Hell". One might think that this could hardly be denied, as the Omnipotent does send them there, but the thought is treated as blasphemy. There is a parallel sentence by Luther, well known because in the *De Servo Arbitrio*, saying that the hardest act of faith is to believe in the mercy and justice of God, because "he seems to delight in the torture of the wretched" [quoted by Aldous Huxley in *The Perennial Philosophy* (1946), 270]. It would be natural for the Faust-book to recall the doubts with which the young Luther had wrestled' (79–80). Jones comments: I suspect P. F. found as much difficulty here [in translating from the GFB] as myself. He has repeated "denied" where I have used a dash. I feel Empson's reading of P. F. here is bordering on the perverse, but I was unable to shake his conviction' (79 n.).

branch: 'It seemed to me obvious from the doctrines I was teaching that the God who could actually be bought off by the death by torture of his own Son from torturing for all eternity the whole of mankind must have *liked* torturing; especially as he cheated us over the bargain, just as the Devil did Faustus—sending nearly all of us to Hell just the same.' In every generation, every morally sane man while he was being taught the central doctrine of Christianity must have felt the same sickening horror; he ought to vomit, but if he vomits he will go to Hell. I began by saying that the Faustbook is unscrupulous, meaning that it repeatedly aims at gratifying an audience without worrying about whether the result is a consistent story; this is so, but if you have on your hands a Myth the correct procedure is to keep it open-ended. I do not know of any other case of a modern myth, recently born and still active ('Faustian Man' means 'God will kill us all for inventing the atom bomb'). Thus the curious silliness of the thing, and still more of the Wagner second part, which appears not to have been translated (London, 1594), made the readers much more friendly to Faustus than Greg could imagine; Faustus is always forgivable because he is a figure of pantomime, gratifying forbidden wishes which are somehow only just forbidden.

Marlowe does seem to have invented the tremendous snub of Mephistopheles: 'You think you had to learn a special skill, taking years, to call up *me*? Why, if you'd said you wanted to go to Hell, I'd have come at once; that's my business'. In the Faustbook poor F. is allowed the dignity of a tremendous struggle before a devil will come. Here I think the peculiar acid clarity of Marlowe may be allowed to have made an addition.

The Faustbook says of Hell 'The unspeakable torments shall every day be augmented more and more'—for all eternity; the most horrifying of all inventions, and I had read somewhere a wrong belief that it was invented by the Scotch.

By the way, both Faustbooks are full of things that Shakespeare used; has anybody pointed that out? The Jew cutting off the limb for example.

A fascinating use of the English word *conscience* in xlvii; Faustus murdered a rival juggler because it wouldn't let the other man win.

With my best wishes for your rapid recovery.

William Empson

P. S. In the E. F. B., Faustus tells Charles V not to speak to the phantom of Alexander, and he does not, but when the phantom bows he tries to get up and bow in return. To bow to an actor (whether human or not) in the style proper for a brother emperor would expose him to ridicule, and Faustus prevents him, but nothing is said about danger. The consort shows herself rational and willing when she bows her head to show her wart—Charles does get up when he goes to inspect her, but he does not explain he is looking for the wart, as he scrupulously remains silent. The precaution of silence may be required because the Paracelsan spirits are easily offended. When Faustus shows the phantom of Helen to the students he charges them to remain silent and seated at the table; they obey because they 'persuaded themselves she was a Spirit' (this seems to imply they were wrong, but how?). The students are quite capable of rape as well as wolf-whistles, so that frightening them would be needed. Some time later, when he has less than two years to run, he sends for her and falls in love with her, giving her all his time. We are not actually told she talked, even then, but her son by Faustus prophesied.

In Marlowe, after the same beginning, Faustus prevents the Emperor from hugging Alexander, saying:

> My gracious lord, you do forget yourself;
> These are but shadows, not substantial

which might imply, but need not, that they are gaseous. Faustus and Charles chat away freely in their presence. But the students are warned to silence (v. i):

> Be silent then, for danger is in words.

The students behave with earnest reverence. Tempted by Old Man to renounce his allegiance, he asks Meph. to fetch Helen again, as she will be an encouragement to keep his oath. He fetches her at once. Faustus does not have to overcome any resistance before speaking to her; he appears to spout off at once. She says nothing, but must be supposed to come when he says 'come' and kiss him back; and she has to be solid enough to be hugged. There is no word of danger, but the distraction of her beauty does of course keep him from repentance, and this period was his last chance.

If the dramatic effect depended upon a belief, that kissing (or touching?) a devil ensured damnation, surely the audience would have been told so. Straight on from here, a series of people tell Faustus why he is damned, with tiresome insistence, and not one of them thinks of this reason which is supposed to be obvious to the audience. The Good Angel says he is damned because he loved the world, an odd phrase if it was really because he loved a devil. Neither in the play nor its source do we find any hint of the belief; and surely most of the audience, if they know of it at all, would say that an act of sex not a kiss was required (but then, F and H leave the stage together, and maybe he has just time to fit it in).

A phrase you quote from the inventor Greg seems to me symptomatic: 'The kiss *signals* the ultimate sin'; only the wiser few, I suppose, are to pick up the hint. But Marlowe was writing a smash-hit for the mob. The use Faustus is making of Helen, which he has explained to Meph., is quite enough for the dramatic point without the bit of medievalism. On the other hand, Marlowe is taking no care to follow the thoughtful account in the source, and does nothing to prevent us from thinking the phantom a Devil. But this would anyway not mean much to the audience, who would be sure he had had plenty of other devils during the past quarter of a century.

I think the comparison to Jupiter and Semele is meant to have an effect, but does not depend on making Helen a succubus; and Faustus does not think he will be like Semele, or he would not muffle it with Arethusa.

To keep Faustus from marriage, he is offered 'a devil dressed like a woman, with fireworks' in II. i; he is not deceived for a moment, but then, he was not intended to be. If the devils can make good enough succubi to satisfy Faustus, obviously they will have done it before the final year of the pact. But if for some reason this is the first time, when their skill has arrived at making a phantom Helen, surely we could be told that he has been innocent so far? What is the point, in short, of the devil in II. i, if Helen is a devil?

Roma Gill; Houghton: incomplete carbon

TO NICK MALONE*

Studio House
11 December 1973

My dear Malone,

Very glad to hear your good news. I am sending you a draft introduction at once, so that we can both consider how to improve it. I am not sure whether I am misinterpreting you by the remarks at the end.[1]

And am I wrong in supposing that nobody writes poems about nature-spirits now? You seem to me very original there, but I read very little recent poetry. However, unless there is a great deal of it your originality can safely be praised.

Hoping to see you
William Empson.

---

[1] The draft was published as WE's Introduction to Nick Malone's poem *The Burial of Crispin Pike* (1974), 5–6.

THE BURIAL OF CRISPIN PIKE

One might expect the burial to be completed by the ceremony, described in the first section, but Crispin must then be gradually re-absorbed into Nature, with the aid of almost impalpable spirits. The process would in any case be complex, but in our time there is an extra obstacle from the widespread pollution of Nature, which has to be combated, in the central section of the poem, by a ghostly but vehement technique which is itself evidently of an industrial character. By the end of the poem matters have worked out satisfactorily, and a good deal of tenderness can be expressed about the human consciousness of Nature:

> sense hovers
> like the butterflies;
> and pours in pollen
> on the bees
> and seethes up tunnels
> ant hordes cleaved,
> and crackles into marquisites
> on flying dragons out of dreams . . .   [ll. 489–96; p. 38]

This used to be one of the regular kinds of poetry, and the modern renunciation of it, a quite recent thing, has done nothing but harm; so we should be thankful, even if surprised, that Mr Malone can revive it with such confident naturalness. We might even go on to wonder how the ban came to be imposed. There was perhaps a double-ruff or lock-grip; either the spirits of Nature are fairies, unmanly and terribly wet, or they are nymphs and oreads and all that, so they are pompous and frigid. The critic may sometimes be observed wondering which club to pick up. No doubt his main accusation would be that to use them is insincere; they are a pretence. And yet we seem to have hardly any other way of thinking about these basic matters; Wordsworth and Shelley would both say that 'the cause of mind is probably unlike mind', and yet believed that *The Prelude* and *Prometheus Unbound* told some obscure truth about man's relation to Nature. If the poet is not allowed to enter that larger world he is in effect condemned to write about his personal worries, giving a stifling self-centred and pokey effect. I am not sure whether Mr Malone himself meant to say something like that, in the penultimate section of the poem:

> When ideas went out to play
> they stole my old green world away,
> their patterns flapped and brought in flight

        this grey decay that fills my sight.
        Alone, therefore, upon these heights
        I seek my fossils in the stone.

But he could hardly mean this as a description of the whole various poem.
William Empson

TIMES LITERARY SUPPLEMENT, 8 March 1974, 238–9:
'Shakespeare's Friend'

John Bayley, in 'Who was the "man right fair" of the Sonnets?' (*TLS*, 4 Jan. 1974, 15), ventured to propose—as against ' "conspiracy" theories of a triangular relation between the author, Southampton and the Dark Lady, or some other pattern of personalities'—that the 'man right fair' of Sonnets 133, 134, and 144 'is *membrum virile*, the Shakespearian penis in fact, as in No 151, where the equivalence is indisputable'; the 'friend' of the Sonnets is merely a personification of the male organ.

    Two weeks later, on 18 Jan. 1974 (p. 54), John Sparrow sought to parody the absurdity of Bayley's insight by proposing a not dissimilar insight of his own—with regard to Milton's sonnet on his blindness:

        When I consider how my light is spent
        Ere half my days, in this dark world and wide,
        And that one Talent which is death to hide
        Lodg'd with me useless . . .

It is no use thinking that Milton was lamenting the loss of his eyesight; nor the loss of his literary gift, as other critics have suggested; rather, it was his sexual potency. 'I would suggest that it is not to his creative but to his *procreative* powers that Milton is referring in this sonnet,' said Sparrow.

    Undaunted by the mockery of Sparrow's intervention, Bayley sought to reinforce his own position on puns on 15 Feb. 1974, 158:

    'I am not, in fact, disposed to fall down in worship before every Shakespearian equivoque or innuendo; I think on the contrary that this fashion which Shakespeare pursued with such delight can set his style further off from us, and sometimes even his characters. For example, there seems little doubt that when the jealous Othello closes his fine valediction to the assurance and achievements of his lost career with the phrase "Othello's occupation's gone!", the pun refers to his sexual possession of Desdemona as well as to his warrior status. But only the most rancorous detractor of his personality would accuse Othello here of either deliberate or inadvertent vulgarity. The fault is Shakespeare's, and it is he who has written, and not Othello who has spoken, something quite out of keeping . . . Conversely, however, a quibble on the right lips can achieve an admirable economy of the ribald. Thus Cleopatra urges herself to hasten after her dead handmaid Iras because

> If she first meet with curled Antony
> He'll make demand of her, and spend that kiss
> Which is my heaven to have.

"Spend" shows that a mere kiss is not the contingency which the Queen fears.

'I certainly find that the wry joke evidently elaborated in these sonnets does bring them closer to us, by making them both funnier and more moving. And I do not see how (to take one instance)—

> To win me soon to hell, my female evil
> Tempteth my better angel from my side

—can seriously be taken to refer to some definite friend of the poet, rather than a kind of fantasy friend, his own sex in masquerade. For why should the lady tempt a friend of the poet in order to win him, the poet, in her "hell"? . . . And, though the rest of the sonnet can be taken as a joke about knowing the friend has been to bed with the lady if he catches the pox, the elaboration involved is surely more stylish, and more in keeping with the tone of these sonnets, if we take it as the poet's trench-humour about his own situation.'

In 'Viewpoint' (*TLS*, 1 Mar. 1974, 210), John Sparrow made it clear that his own effort to construe Milton's 'talent' as his sex was bogus, intended to parody the interpretative excess of Bayley's criticism: 'there is a danger that the prevailing taste for "sexual fantasy" may lead critics to discover "sex" when it is not really there, and Mr Bayley's brilliant ingenuity in this matter . . . often, I think, leads him astray in this respect.'

Sir,—There is no need to worry about 'Othello's occupation's gone'. The great Dictionary [*OED*] is not quite explicit here, but it gives a full paragraph to the temporary sexual insinuation in the verb without listing a single example in the noun. The joke about the verb would surely be recognized as rather silly, not necessarily infecting the more Latin-sounding noun. The noun did, however, acquire a derogatory flavour of its own, as when Shakespeare writes in *Coriolanus* of 'the voice of occupation and | The breath of garlic-eaters', even shortening it to the modern pronunciation so as to emphasize its low class. The speech by Othello has made his audience feel the splendour and romance of his way of life, but he is after all a mercenary soldier, not a trade universally admired, and it is good manners for him to end with rueful modesty by saying, 'Well, I've lost my job.' Also, there is no need to worry about whether Cleopatra meant 'copulate' while saying *kiss*, immediately before her suicide. She and her lover have rightly suspected one another of being capable of far worse acts of betrayal than the sexual infidelity she now pretends to fear from the dead Antony, and it is wonderful good luck to have their affair end so well. To have her express the meaning directly would be off-key, or too much strain on the audience, but it may well be near the surface of her mind. If they had not really expected to meet again in the Elysian Fields, they probably would have tried to betray each other, and both ended in shame. The tittering sense of decorum of the modern sexist becomes eerily out of place here.

John Bayley, I thought, saved his position in his second pronouncement, when he admitted that there really was another lover of the Dark Lady, and that Shakespeare, if in the Sonnets concerned he pretended to be talking about his own sex organ instead, was merely labouring to pass the situation off with a joke.[1] It seems clear that he had never been on a footing to demand fidelity from the Dark Lady, and it would be fatuous to deny that he had become deeply attached to the patron (the reason for believing the story is real is that it could not have been invented for a poem). The few examples in the poetry which might be passed as jokes seem to me very flat jokes, but poor Shakespeare was in a position of trying to make them; and as it seems to have been proved that the lady's husband was not called 'Will', we need some other object called 'Will' to justify the word-play; though I believe there is no single recorded case of calling the organ *will* instead of *john* or *roger*.

The poor Warden [John Sparrow] deserves respect for appearing so firmly in a white sheet, having to explain, while accepting rebuke for, a very good and clear parody (Viewpoint, March 1). The only shame attaches to those who rebuked him, or presumed that solemn lies must always be told before the children. I am glad too, Sir, that the turbulence

---

[1] Bayley returned in the same issue of the *TLS* simply to protest against Sparrow that his own 'critical point, such as it was, had a rather different object: to distinguish quibbles that are at home in their dramatic context and characterization from those that are a gratuitous product of Shakespearean verbal ebullience . . . For Shakespeare in the Sonnets, sex—I do not speak of the ideal of love—was a matter that may have been desperate but was never serious, which was the point of my reference to trench humour. My piece was intended in the Elizabethan vein rather than in the modern spirit of Mr [Kenneth] Tynan and Lord Longford.'

somehow included a rebuke to your reviewer for saying that John Fuller's book of poems was a form of masturbation; mean-minded jabber of this type might do if the man would sign his name, but it is quite incompatible with the principles of an anonymous review.[2]

William Empson

Studio House, 1 Hampstead Hill Gardens, London NW3

TO CHRISTOPHER RICKS

13 June [1974]

Dear Ricks,

I have got all the material for the piece I offered, and written a version of it, but maybe it will be too long for EIC. I thought I would call it 'A Deist Pamphlet by Dryden';[1] it turns the tables on my opponent in EIC a year or two ago, I hope, and is entertaining as history, I feel sure, but isn't very poetical of course. The long piece is for the book, and your request gave me a stimulus to finish that chapter; I would not mind if you cut it a good bit for the magazine.

I hear you are going to Cambridge as Professor in place of [Graham] Hough, and am not sure whether to congratulate you or not; but they certainly need somebody to wake them up.[2]

—I am due to leave for Pennsylvania State U. early in September and undertake to send my piece before then. A year, again.

Thank you very much for your splendid essay in the Book [*William Empson*, ed. Gill]. You have done your prep as usual in a terrific manner and keep reminding me of things I had forgotten I had done. It seems very clear I was much broader and less hampered when young. However, old writers are lucky if they still have a lot of tidying up to do.

Hetta was rather cross at reading in the TLS (the beastly Dubliner's piece) that marriage stopped me writing poetry. I don't think I wrote any

---

[2] See 'Private pleasures'—a review of John Fuller, *Epistles to Several Persons* (1973)—*TLS*, 18 Jan. 1974, 51: 'Light verse bears close affinities to self-abuse: it may not be the real thing, but it has its own peculiar satisfactions ... The danger of light verse (as of self-abuse) is that it can seem private.' Alastair Smart wrote: 'The analogy is neither tasteful nor useful: but it has the merit of fashionableness; and for that reason, no doubt, it is acceptable to some readers of our finest literary review. But odious fashions, however long they must be borne, cannot endure forever' ('Milton's Talent', *TLS*, 8 Feb. 1974, 134).

[1] WE, 'A Deist Tract by Dryden', *E in C*, 25 (1975), 74–100; *UB*, 99–122.

[2] Ricks succeeded Frank Kermode as King Edward VII Professor of English.

after reaching the China war in 1937, apart from some quite slight things. However you don't really say what Donoghue said.[3]

I still think my theory about *The Spanish Tragedy* is quite obvious if you see the requirements of the *story*; when saying I had no evidence I meant what my opponents would call evidence.

I do hope you both come to the Party.

W. E.

I am now doing a piece on the Elizabethan Theatre, with some whacks at Wickham already sent to you, but only incidentally. Adams [J. C. Adams, *The Globe Playhouse*, 1943] and [J. Walter] Hodges are sad [? cases too].

TO JEFFREY M. MILLER

Jeffrey M. Miller, a doctoral student at the University of Toronto, wrote to WE in 1974 to say he was deeply interested in the 'psychological aspects' of the concept of ambiguity in literature. Elder Olson, in his severe essay on Empson—'William Empson, Contemporary Criticism and Poetic Diction', *Modern Philology*, 47: 4 (May 1950)—'posits a false distinction between the linguistic and the psychological aspects of poetic diction; he refuses to recognize that even in speech, our word choice is influenced, indeed charged, by various conscious and unconscious psychological patterns and associations'. Miller's proposed approach to the psychological dimension of ambiguity should bring him closer, he hoped, to an answer to Olson's criticism that 'ambiguity is not even in Empson's view the *principle* of poetry, since its propriety or impropriety is determined by something else—an unanalyzed thing vaguely called the "situation" '. Miller thus asked of WE: 'How would you answer this statement?' He went on: 'If you recall Mr Graves' reply to James Jensen's article in the *MLQ* (Sept. 1966), he says, "the

---

[3] Denis Donoghue was reporting CR's argument in 'Empson's Poetry' (Gill, 145–207). 'Christopher Ricks's essay is long and powerful,' Donoghue wrote in his review of Gill ('Some versions of Empson', *TLS*, 7 Jun. 1974, 597–8), 'a full-scale commentary on the poems in terms of one major preoccupation: begetting . . . [T]he poems are concerned with the misgivings involved in begetting, parenthood, family . . . 'Professor Ricks brings the same insight to bear upon the question of Empson's giving up poetry, a question just as intriguing as that of Forster's silent years. The explanation is that the tensions and contradictions involved in begetting were "one of the important sources of energy" for Empson's poems and that these slackened off: "In the first place, for good personal reasons—it is after all a tension more likely to precede than to follow parenthood, and Empson's giving up writing poetry dates more or less (the later poems are important but very few) from his marriage in 1941 and his becoming a father in the following years" [Ricks, quoted from Gill, 157].'

Donoghue comments on CR's theory: 'It is hardly convincing. Such misgivings are not resolved by the birth of a child, or if they are they are replaced by more specific tensions and contradictions.'

use of the word 'ambiguity' to express rather the *congruity* of combined poetic meanings put me off." This seems to me [a] quibble, because he is really just substituting terms. But I think it is the congruity of ambiguous meanings, their ultimate organic inter-relationship, that Olson overlooks and which may be described, hypothetically at least, as *a* principle of poetry.' He explained further that he was interested also in Robert Graves's early criticism, 'and I hope that a case might be made that the archetypal/ mythological slant taken in *The White Goddess* is a logical development of the idea of psychological ambiguity. That is, that sometimes the secondary meanings (particularly in imagery and symbolism) which we now call arche-typal, depend, for their meaning, on ambiguity.' In conclusion, he emphasized: 'I believe that your methodology enhances our understanding of literature, and its beauty, and that much criticism which has followed *Ambiguity* is simply restatement. When Mr Graves speaks of "congruity", Mr Wheelwright of "plurisignation", Mr Brooks of "paradox", Miss Tuve of "the truth at the heart of all myths", they are all speaking, finally, of ambiguity.'

1000A Plaza Drive, Apartment 415, State College, Pennsylvania 16801
                                                    19 November 1974

Dear Mr Miller,

Thank you for your letter. As you suggest, I haven't been worrying about Ambiguity for some time, feeling that after three books on it I had shot my bolt. I thought there was general agreement that the process occurs and is important sometimes, though not about how often. Insisting that I did attend to the context, though I often took it for granted in the printed criticism, seemed to need saying in letters to magazines at some point—when I got back from China in 1952 perhaps. Here I did feel I had been misunderstood, and I thought I succeeded in clearing it up. But the other attacks that you mention, on the basic theory of the thing, did not seem to need answering. The Chicago School never seems to me to under-stand anything. I liked Tuve, but anybody could see she was wrong-headed—and so on. The term Ambiguity was a bad choice so far as it suggested that the author was being artful and tricky—he need only be conscious of the process, I suppose, enough to make him try for a different form of words if he has lit on a damaging ambiguity. Perhaps I liked the word because I was myself gleefully engaged in regarding the result of imagination as trick-work. But I think a willing reader soon got to ignore this harmful suggestion, which I certainly didn't want in serious cases.

The most damaging attacks, it seemed to me, were made by Leavis when he got tired of using Empson as an ally; so unfair and nit-picking that I felt I would come down to his level in answering him, so I didn't though probably I ought to have done. Before this, Leavis had made a similar grand attack on Richards, who when I was at Cambridge had been the man he revered and quoted all the time. I seem to remember reading the attacks on me in Tokyo, wondering whether I ought to answer—one would expect to remember the place. I was there from 31 to 34, and there is none of it in the first volume of Scrutiny (1932–3), so he must have been printing these attacks somewhere else, just before it started. But I am sure I wouldn't have the Cambridge Review sent to Tokyo. I was remembering this in an essay for Richards's Fest-schrift, and some reviewer said I had got it all wrong, so I made a dim attempt just now to look it up in Penn. State U. Library, but these needling triumphs of Leavis are as though they had never been. If you want to look up attacks on Empson and Richards I am sure these are the best; but maybe you will agree with the reviewer and suspect I merely imagined them. I don't believe that my imagination is so powerful.

I am just here till May. I hope this is some use to you.

Yours

W. Empson

Houghton, bMS Eng 1401 (606)

TO CHRISTOPHER RICKS

Apartment 514, 1000A Plaza Drive, State College, Pennsylvania
19 January 1975

My dear Christopher,

I have been owing you a letter for some time, and ought to send thanks, but find America very numbing this trip, and can write very little. (A good deal of reading and note-taking I have been getting done). Maybe my colleagues are gritting their teeth to face disaster like men, or maybe they just can't be bothered. I should be back at the end of May.

You sent a kind note accepting my piece about Dryden ['Dryden's Apparent Scepticism'] and remarking that you wouldn't like a masochist God any more than a sadistic one. I did a good deal of correcting the piece, and wherever I found *sadistic* I put 'bad'. It seems that these terms are very question-begging anyway and cover a multitude of sins; but also, I would say, that you cannot absorb your ancient sacrificial practices into your new universal metaphysical God, however queerly you twist him.

Hetta sent on a letter from [Ronald] Bottrall, merely a carbon copy of a nasty jeering letter he had sent to you, pretending that he had known my aunts by way of insinuating that you had been wrong about my poetry, in your kind article for my Festschrift ['Empson's Poetry', in Gill].[1] I do hope you haven't suspected me of being in cahoots with Bottrall about this; he turned up in London last autumn, and struck me as a grim warning to other old men; surely one needn't get as nasty as that, I thought—this letter of his only offers a minor example, and I expect you forgot it at once. It stuck in my mind because I felt there was just a tiny bit of truth in it somewhere.

I haven't the book here, but I think you credited me with strong family feelings, and said I stopped writing poetry because I married. There was much else which was a positive comfort to have said, but I had already thought it a gap, a limitation in your mind that you cannot imagine a man taking a real interest in public affairs. I hope I have a normal amount of domestic piety and affection, and I wish now that I had more children—I respect you for having so many. But I dropped all my literary interests, even reviewing, because I got absorbed in the war; I thought the defeat of Hitler so important that I could do nothing else (it was a time of great

---

[1] Ronald Bottrall wrote to Ricks on 29 Sept. 1974: 'I have been intending for sometime to compliment you on your splendid essay on William Empson. It has taught me many things, though that is not surprising, because I do not read much Lit. Crit. nowadays. I prefer art history, history and an occasional biography.

'Now to "The Ants". All this taradiddle about "a love-poem with the author afraid of the woman" is a red herring. The poem is about Empson's Aunts. He had two famous ones who preyed on his mother, father and brother. They were even more formidable than his mother, the "Old Lady". They often came unexpectedly by train from another part of Yorkshire. Hence tunnels, old men running, trains whining and the station. They were frequently short of money and tried to milk ("tap") the squire (William's eldest brother) and his mother.

' "Our tube's narrow darkness" describes the aunts' furled black umbrellas. "Aphids" is a euphemism for £sd (note the last two letters) which meant for them the Empson "dividends". They were crazy about patent medicines, as so many people of that time were, hence "nostrum-plastered". Their "all-but-freedom" means the money they always hoped to get from the senior "branch" of the family, which had to "bear" it. But there was never enough to satisfy the aunts.

'The sestet of the sonnet begins ominously. The aunts are nearing the local station, their breaths ("air") are much too near and creep through every small chink in the manor house. They can of course be seen coming up the garden. One glance is enough.

'Dividends are low in winter, few leavings as far as the aunts are concerned, because of the cost of heating, lighting and extra food. The skeleton in the cupboard endures and Empson secretly knows what it is, although he pretends he doesn't. However, he commits these horrid parasites to hell in the last line.

'There is a tremendous story in this poem which you have completely missed. No wonder you write: "I am still unhelpfully perplexed by it." I hope my helpful explanation will make you feel unperplexed.

'I am sending this letter to you at William's suggestion. I know his family well, as you may gather.' (*Houghton*)

WE wrote to HE on 14 Nov. 1974: 'How tiresome of Bottrall to send me a carbon of his facetious letter to Ricks talking about my aunts and suchlike as he "knows the family well". [. . .] We must try to see as little of Bott. as poss.' (*Hull*)

happiness, looking back, and anyway of considerable pleasure, but I have just a steady trickle of mental productiveness, and it was then all directed into propaganda). I still think the war was quite important enough for that, and a good deal of my previous poetry had been concerned to say so; it could not be called a betrayal of my deeper interests. I remember being scolded briefly by a journalist in a pub near the BBC, on his way out, near the end of the war, because I had dropped all my literary work so completely—'just left us cold,' he said, assuming there was nothing else I was good at really; I was startled by an attack from such an unexpected quarter. Nursing myself back into literary work after the war was rather a business, closely connected with trying to get a complete cure from a stomach ulcer; I first, for about a year, wrote an essay on Buddhist sculpture before 1000 AD, which got lost afterwards. This got me ready to resume my profession as teacher of English Literature, without throwing me into it rawly. Then, when I got to China, carrying about lots of unfinished disordered bits of paper of course I found I had lost the whole chapter on Metaphor (I was writing *Complex Words*) and was surprised to find that, going slowly, I could recover it from memory. There was a real gap, and an urgent practical need to get over it; but there was no such need to start writing poetry again, and the theme which all the modern poets I admired had been working on, which I had been working on too, had been blown out like a candle.

I suppose I look ridiculous when I claim to have been a political poet too, like Auden and Spender and all those geared-up propaganda boys in Oxford (whereas I was in Cambridge); and it is true that I never learned the technique so was never considered a political poet. But my second volume of verse *The Gathering Storm* means by the title just what Winston Churchill did when he stole it, the gradual sinister confusing approach to the Second World War. Of course the title was chosen after writing the poems, during the early years of the war, but nearly all the poems really are considering this prospect, with which I had been fairly closely confronted, in China, Japan, Indochina and Korea. Well then, after the war had been won, I was in the same cleft stick as my brother poets, and I am inclined to congratulate myself upon stopping writing.

It is a very good thing for a poet, one might say the ideal, to be saying something which is considered very shocking at the time, so bad that he is on the verge of being persecuted for this none the less popular doctrine, and then ten years later everybody in his society agrees with him, so that even Tories emit a grudging assent. There is bound to be a slight difficulty for his later output; he cannot merely continue to demand what has already been granted (more socialism at home, the Popular Front abroad). But surely it was not essential to appear in a white sheet of shame, denouncing themselves for having said what everyone now agreed to (only Louis MacNeice kept out of this, I think, and obviously at severe nervous cost). However, most poets have to go on earning the only way they know how, whereas I could escape into another profession. I only met my wife because Hitler attacked Russia, because that made her feel free to do propaganda against him in Afrikaans; we met at the BBC Liars' School for training propagandists; and she was determined to go to China because everybody except the Foreign Office knew it was going Communist. The domestic pressures upon me were the most strongly political ones.

Oh well. Thanks all the same.

Reading this over, I see it is too glib, and some other process was probably at work earlier to make the poetry I hammered out strike me as unfit for publication. My war started in 1937, when I refugeed with the Chinese universities, and I went on writing criticism there, also the Anita Loos poem, which I now think bad.

W. E.

P. S. It occurs to me that I have just been composing some poetry, which you might like to hear about. All the more as I seem to remember your mocking me for removing the only scrap of evidence for my interpretation of the *Spanish Tragedy* and still believing it correct. I would now agree that the text as it was printed cannot be so viewed, but argue that there was a great deal of unnecessary fussing by dramatic censors around the time of the Armada, most obviously affecting Dr Faustus, the Spanish Tragedy, and Sir Thomas More; which was probably got round in performance, but has encouraged an indulgence in nasty fantasies by later teachers of Eng. Lit. The censors did not realise that they were making the works appear nonsensical and immoral, but so they did. Now, in *The Spanish Tragedy* what the ghost of Andrea needs to know (he tells us in the Prologue) is whether he died as a soldier or a lover, which will decide his afterlife status; he is sat down to learn, and surely it is a minimal demand that the play should give some indication of an answer. Also Hieronymo at the end, as an extra, perhaps out of madness, murders the father of Belimperia, the Duke of Castile, and Andrea expresses delight at this extra revenge, consigning him to a particularly severe punishment. Unless the story is allowed to make sense, the moral becomes grossly immoral here, and I am surprised that such lies are told about it nowadays by teachers thousands of times every year. A brief cut was made by the censor, and initially this did not ruin the play, because the audiences were familiar with the point of it and did not need to be told. Elizabeth announced that she was determined to marry her frog Alençon in 1581 and had not retracted when he died in 1584; and of course it was the royal intermarriages of Spain and Portugal which had allowed Philip II to claim Portugal and its empire in 1580. A censor might well consider a glance at the wickedness attendant upon arranging royal marriages too hot.

ADDITION. Before Act III Scene XII: the third Addition is a familiar place, and then Hieronymo, advising the two Portuguese how to petition the Duke, gives them a speech on the way to Hell. He is supposed to go out and come back carrying two means to kill himself, but this would be a breach of stage procedure; something had better happen in between. As soon as H. has gone one way and the two Petitioners the other, the back curtain opens showing the Duke and the Ambassador alone, with respectable furniture but no servants. The Duke himself fetches a decanter from a cupboard and pours two drinks.

> Duke. All is in train, my Lord Ambassador.
> I was glad to learn that Bellimperia's scarf
> Had proved sufficient to pick out Andrea.

(They come forward with their glasses. The Ghost of Andrea, probably on the right of the spectator, leans out panting with astonishment at this bit of news. Till this moment he has seen no reason to require revenge.)

> Duke. (Gulping his drink, as he expects the others at once)
> So now my headstrong daughter will obey.
> Amb. (Panting) Be sure my master will show gratitude.
> Duke. (Reminded of a danger, as his tools are so silly)
> My brother must not hear a word of this.

The curtain closes while Andrea comes back totally looney with two means for suicide, and opens (before he has finished) with the spectacle of the grandees in conference whom he cannot face.

It would be a hit produced with that tiny addition. O. K. W. E.

PPS   I find, reading around in this subject a bit, that Fredson Bowers the great textual expert has decided that the play is meant as an attack on the custom of revenge, showing how wicked it makes even previously good men. What a curious man Fredson must be; I wonder if he has ever seen a play acted all through. Of course revenge is bad for Hieronymo; he tells us so himself, in lines which contrive to be beautiful in spite of Kyd's oddly determined drabness. 'O monstrous times' . . .

> where the soul, that should be shrined in heaven,
> Solely delights in interdicted things,
> Still wandering in the thorny passages
> That intercepts itself of happiness.

Also it is extremely distasteful to him; that is what drives him mad. But he carries it through because he considers it a duty, under the very special circumstances of his son's murder, which make it impossible for Hieronymo though a judge to use the processes of law. The story is designed to make the dilemma sharp for him, and Elizabethans found the dilemma very interesting in real life (it was not only a literary fashion). I find critics and students often assume that everyone knows revenge to be wicked, all Christians at any rate, so that revenge plays can only exist in an imaginary world imitated from Seneca. But Hieronymo immediately after the lines quoted above orders the immediate execution of the impudent Pedringano; the revenge of society, by due process of law, he never dreams of questioning, and the difference cannot seem very great to the person receiving punishment. It might be answered that the difference is none the less absolute. But consider: after an attempt to kill Elizabeth had been discovered, about 1570 I think, a respectable number of the leading men of her regime joined in an oath, published to all Europe, that if Philip II or the Pope in a later attempt succeeded in killing her, they would find means to secure that Philip II or the Pope was also killed. This was considered a proper reply, as well as an effective one. It is useless then to pretend that the Elizabethans lived by an impossibly exalted moral rule, or indeed that the critics and students who talk in this way do so either; they are merely relying upon mummy, or the police or somebody, to save them from having to think about nasty things.

The play is morally disgusting unless you recognise that it is based on indignation about these appallingly tricky royal marriages, their immense irrelevance to the political results they entail (such as the Spanish rule over the Netherlands, always a sore), the nastiness of having to force the girls into accepting them (or even of seeing the poor debauched frog having to pretend he would be able to poke the terrifying old Elizabeth). Once it is admitted that Andrea was killed in battle by a treacherous arrangement, his own side wanting him removed to secure a royal marriage, the play becomes as moral as apple pie. *Thrust Horation forth my father's way* could be acted as an ambiguity—Lorenzo stumbles upon it and then accepts it with sardonic amusement—but it doesn't much matter anyway.

Ricks responded on 26 Feb. 1975: 'I'd known that you'd be goodnaturedly

miffed at that part of my W. E. essay wh. makes much—too much perhaps—of the child-bearing business . . . The essay must seem to slight the
political poems, or the politicalness of the poems; & yet I don't myself—
outside the confines of that essay—slight them at all . . . But I truly appreciate the considerateness & clarity of yr. account of the politics & the poetry,
& of course it persuades me that there I do a great deal less than justice.'

'Yes, I think there is "a tiny bit of truth", perhaps, in Bottrall's letter—&
honestly (not that I'd thought of you as in cahoots) he didn't/doesn't sound
at all bad to me.

'I thrill at what you say abt. *The Spanish Tragedy*, & at yr. splendid interpretation; I suppose the only snag is that my feelings abt. yr. relation to the
play are the only thing that interests me abt. the play, wh. just rests in my
memory as bric-a-brac.' (*Houghton*)

TO *NEW YORK REVIEW OF BOOKS*: 'Empson's Defence' (Unpublished)

This is a draft response to Michael Wood on Gill: 'Incomparable Empson',
The New York Review of Books, 21: 21 & 22 (23 Jan. 1975), 30–3. Wood is
Professor of English and Comparative Literature at Princeton.

(n.d.: 1975)

To the Editors:

Thank you for your review of my work, by Michael Wood in the number for 23 January; most of it I could not possibly complain of; but I feel I
am challenged to defend the treatment of Christianity in my later literary
criticism. He finds it compulsively unreasonable and rude.

This concerns explanations of the meaning of earlier writers in English,
mainly the seventeenth-century ones, though Yeats and the major Romantics also get badly misread, by teachers in schools and university English
Departments. There has been a total change since my taste was formed, in
the twenties, and I did not realise it till I began teaching in England in the
fifties. It seemed to me that my pupils had been corrupted into a complete
misreading of the literature, and one of a morally disgusting kind; they
were continually finding excuses to gloat over the sufferings of someone
who was booked for Hell, and they did it with entire complacency, feeling
sure that the author had done the same. But he had not. As I was receiving
a salary in this line, I would have been taking money on false pretences if I
had not complained about the invariable nastiness pretty soon. It did not
mark any change in my own opinions, only a change in what thrust itself

upon me as needing to be said. Mr Wood hardly likes anything that I wrote after this change, but he does also express a certain uneasiness about my moral position beforehand, sitting on a fence and leering all round. I never put this forward as a plan for life, and I gave it up for literary criticism as soon as there was need to. Trying to carry out my duty often meant writing ugly prose, I cannot deny; but it seems unfair when he blames me even more for my second period.

From what I can make out, priests and ministers of all Christian sects have nowadays become wary about thrusting forward the blacker aspects of their theology; to an ordinary adherent of the religion, it must seem very strange when he hears that the literary dons have been turning it into a kind of tantric sect. But to me of course their temptation seems natural enough; they need to insist on the great historical difference of Christianity before Voltaire, before it was purged by the complaints of the free-thinkers, and they tell themselves they are standing out for the higher 'values' of an earlier world. However, as it is natural to expect, because a cult of human sacrifice can never be completely purged, there is one major reason in the modern world why you ought not to simper at Christians and go along with a pretence that they have become morally harmless. They are even now trying to destroy the entire race of man.

If you can manage to prevent birth control, the latest atom bombs are sure to be used fairly soon in desperate wars to secure the remaining food supplies. In the undeveloped countries, where these arrangements are most needed, the committees for 'family planning', which require a considerable money outlay, are always in the hands of the developed countries which will supply the money. They are habitually disrupted by the Papists. The Papist position here is *not* that a sexual act should only be committed with the intention of producing a child; this really would be an intelligible moral position, with a claim to 'human dignity', though it would still be morally disgraceful to claim to impose the duty on everyone who thought it nonsense. But the Papists jollily recommend you to rely on a 'natural period' so that you have to fuss with a calendar, which destroys any natural feeling in the act, and as everyone knows the method is very unreliable. And the reason for not using an efficient method, for an intention which is permitted, is not a theological one at all; merely that it is 'unsuited to human dignity'. A baby dying of starvation is not a good choice for a picture of human dignity, and no more are a million of them. It is just dirty talk. If simple devices for the requirements of the human body are undignified, how can priests shave in the places where they shave, how can we all use handkerchiefs? The doctrine is respected though it is known to be completely unreasonable because it is known to be murderous. 'Havoc and spoil and ruin are my gain' is the only intelligible picture of the demands of the Holy See.

Houghton: typescript draft, bMS Eng 1401 (612)

TO RICHARD ELLMANN*

Apartment 514, Plaza Drive 1000A, State College, Pennsylvania.
18 February 1975

Dear Richard Ellmann,

I appeal to you to clear up a historical detail which you almost certainly know at once without inquiry, but if not please do inquire and make sure. There must be a number of people still alive who know, but consider how soon they will all be dead. I would send you a stamped addressed envelope if the relations between our two countries permitted it. Bustle about it; you know not the hour. Penn State is at this moment allowing me to lecture upon Ecclesiastes and Omar Khayyam.

It turns out that my colleagues in America and Canada, when they name the hero of the Portrait of the Artist by James Joyce, pronounce the first syllable as 'Dead' not as 'Deed'. At first I thought that they were all disciples of Hugh Kenner, who made large deductions from this supposed change in the sound of the name, but some rejected this idea quite indignantly. There was just no other way to pronounce the word. 'Have the name typed out and go into a Dublin shop and say you're looking for him', I was told; I would soon hear how they would pronounce it (and one would of course like to know whether it has ever actually been a surname). Any expression of doubt here, I found, excited strong anti-British feeling, as practically nothing else did; in fact I await your reply to settle a bet, which I agreed to as the best way to avoid anything worse. It was quite severe; I could hear Cholmondeley whispering his name in the air above us.

The truth is quite straightforward; Joyce had accepted the Italian method of transliterating Greek; for example, a satirical poem ['The Holy Office', l. 46] written between writing *Stephen Hero* and The *Portrait* mentions Eschylus, if I have got it right, but anyhow beginning E, as an Italian would do, though an Italian would still pronounce [it] as in 'deed'. By doing this, he meant only to express his freedom from English-language-speaking persons; no idea of saying that he himself when young was already dead, and incapable of writing a novel, could possibly have crossed his mind when he accepted the spelling of the country of his adoption.

It strikes me as merely another case of Joyce tripping himself up, and so I am the more confident of my interpretation. But nobody will believe me unless you give me the light of your countenance, and of course I know that I have often been wrong. I actually want to know: did Joyce say DEDDALUS or DEEDALUS?

All good wishes

William Empson

Tulsa

Richard Ellmann felt confident (10 Mar. 1975) that 'Dedalus' was to be pronounced with a short 'e': 'I feel sure that Joyce had no intention of suggesting that ded had anything to do with being dead. My assumption is that he wanted to make a spelling less Hellenic and more Irish, by which I mean more easily pronounceable.' Still, he would ask Joan Budgen if she could remember how her father Frank Budgen (Joyce's confidant) had pronounced the name. 'Not having had much luck in convincing you about the ending of *Ulysses*, I haven't much hope that you will accept my pronunciation more readily than my interpretation. But at the risk of losing your bet for you, I think I must say that the pronunciation with a short "e" seems to me indubitable. If Joan Budgen replies to some other effect, I shall reveal it at the cost of humiliation of [or] embarrassment.'

TO RICHARD ELLMANN*

Apartment 514, Plaza Drive 1000a, State College, PA 16801

8 April 1975

Dear Ellmann,

Thank you for your earnest letter. I too will feel humiliated if I am wrong about Joyce's pronunciation of Dedalus. When the letter came I thought I would wait for further news, but this morning I looked up the word in the NED, and the result should be passed on. The adjective 'daedal', it says, was often spelt 'dedal', in the 17th, 18th, and 19th centuries, but always pronounced 'deed' not 'dead' (how it knows, of course, is another thing). Drummond of Hawthornden printed in 1930 the line

A Dedalus he was to catch a fly.

Joyce had been classically trained and in his way was a bit of a pedant; he would realise that cultivated English-speakers for a long time had been taking for granted, if they came across 'Dedalus', that it was pronounced with a 'Dee' and merely followed Italian custom. I grant, if the name was already established in Dublin, he would tend to accept the native pronunciation, but this has not been reported.

However, evidence from someone who heard him say it often would be decisive. The source you mentioned does sound a bit liable to error; I still feel that Samuel Beckett is the right person to ask. But it would be essential to get the right mouse to bell the cat. Some years ago I heard in Paris that he had at last been coaxed to the Irish Club on St Patrick's Day, and after sufficient Irish whiskies had wept there. So he is Irish all right, but was brought up a Protestant, and yet obviously he would hate an Orangeman. The choice of an agent to question him is obviously very hard; it needs to be done by some understanding person resident in Paris. I do wish that you would at once, before it is too late, set your great machine in motion.

Yours with thanks
William Empson.

Tulsa

TO EARL MINER*

Princeton
28 April 1975

Dear Earl Miner,

I brought you along an off-print of this magazine article, hearing you were in Princeton, as I had thought, while reading around a little among the Americans who have recently considered *Religio Laici*, that you showed more breadth of sympathy than the others. Hearing the symposium on Milton, Ambiguity etc. made me feel strongly that some fundamental difference needs to be got clear, though my position is merely taken for granted in the article.

A verbal analyst who rejects all need for any sense of character, or of style, or period, or *milieu*, has renounced most of the means by which people actually do in ordinary life interpret those remarks of their neighbours which cause puzzlement. Obviously he is more likely to be wrong than if he permitted himself the normal equipment. It is not a rule of the game that he has to accept any logically possible interpretation of the words as they appear on the printed page. It may seem that I am a hypocrite here, as I often made this assumption myself in *Ambiguity*; but earlier on I often denied it loudly (in letters to magazines and suchlike); and in England I think I managed to get the denial accepted—that is, I had used the background information I was accused of ignoring, though I often left it unmentioned because it was so well known.

I really agree that Milton would have been a better man if he had envisaged the other meaning of *spare* (at the end of the sonnet *Lawrence, of virtuous father*),[1] and even that he was a better stylist because he was so quaintly liable to leave loopholes for misinterpretation. But this double meaning on *spare* is so very far from the probabilities of his character, his habitual manner, and his whole background that imputing it is hardly more than a joke against him. Perhaps it might be claimed as an expression of a deep unconscious conflict, but there are no signs that he even fretted about his sober habits (whereas there may well be an unconscious ambiguity about attitudes to God in the *slaughtered saints* poem).[2] I am in sympathy with what may be presumed as the inner purpose of the critic here (to make Milton less stiff) whereas I don't sympathize with that of Harth[3] and his pals (who want to make Dryden an ignorantly pious Anglican), but it seems clear that the same error of principle is at work in both. It is somehow felt as a breach of manners to admit any direct knowledge or intuition of an author's character, or style, or milieu (probably I dragged too much 'psychology' into *Ambiguity*, but some of that should be let in too). The resulting decorum makes the criticism painfully airless.

However I was extremely interested by the discussion, and send you my thanks for allowing me to attend it.

Yours very sincerely
William Empson.

UCLA: Collection 821: Earl Miner Papers, Box 46

Earl Miner agreed with WE (5 May 1975) about the importance of a sense of style, period, and *milieu*. 'The problem seems to me to lie in recovering assurance about the meaning of style, period, and *milieu* from a time as long ago as the seventeenth century . . . That said, I confess I read *Religio Laici* to mean something different from your description. To my view, Dryden is uncertain to an immeasurable but important degree . . . I do not think Dryden a Deist or a Catholic in *Religio Laici*. The Anglicans welcomed his poem too warmly, and there were enough people willing to pounce on him if he verged from orthodoxy. It does seem significant to me that he was not

---

[1] John Milton, Sonnet xvii. John Carey declares 'spare' in the final lines—'He who of those delights can judge, and spare | To interpose them oft. is not unwise'—to be ambiguous, citing critics who construe the word as meaning either 'refrain, forbear' or 'spare time to, afford' (*Complete Shorter Poems* [1971], 408–9).

[2] Milton, Sonnet xv: On the late Massacre in Piedmont ('Avenge O Lord thy slaughtered saints').

[3] Phillip Harth, *Contexts of Dryden's Thought* (1968)

attacked as was Blount for being a Deist or, as he was himself later, for being a Catholic. If you ask me whether I think Dryden found deist arguments attractive when he was writing *Religio Laici*, I shall say yes at once . . . But would also say that Dryden was as much inclined toward Catholicism as Deism, even while making an Anglican decision.'

TO RICHARD WORDSWORTH*

3 August 1975

My dear Richard,

You asked me if I had a few tips about your proposed acted-recital from Donne, and I am determined to keep to one page. Winston Churchill in the early years of the war had a report on enemy broadcasts on his desk every morning, prepared during the small hours, and he said he was willing to look at this so long as he never had to turn the page. We were eager to educate him but not to annoy was the first need. I expect you feel the same.

You were right to say that one must make the love-poet the same man as the Dean, but consider how Helen Gardner joins them. Starting with empty-headed lustful poems (Songs and Sonnets I) he married a lady for money and position, but didn't get them, so to spite his wife he wrote a series of poems about imaginary adulteries, yearning for his lost freedom (Songs and Sonnets II). Disciples of HG [Helen Gardner] often say he was a virgin when he married, but she thinks the young cad was genuinely getting girls into trouble. Imagining illicit true love enlarged his mind and gradually drew him into the Church. The objection to these pious thoughts, you understand, is that morally they are very low, low every time, as if to gratify some clamorous deep-seated need.

First period (I now give my own attempt, but its like was common in the 1920's): He is having sex, but rather casually, and not with ladies, though he sometimes pretends the girls are ladies. Of course, I do not mean that the stories in the poems are always true, but he was living in that kind of world, sometimes directly trying to improve on what had happened, to get his face straight. Farewell to Love, the Blossom, The Indifferent, Love's Usury, Love's Alchemy, The Flea, the Curse, Elegy vii (Nature's Lay Idiot), Elegy xii (Come madam come). In Elegy vii, so far from getting the shop assistant into trouble, he has taught her how to catch a rich husband. Second period. At least one serious affair happens before his marriage; and he would only take a lady seriously, both as a social climber and because he needs an educated companion. Legacy, Anniversary, Of my name in the window, The Relic, several elegies. Cases where the lady is already married are strong candidates, but it is more important to recognise the group than be sure of all its members. Third period. After being ruined by his runaway marriage he wrote a few poems, very good, saying it was worth it; probably all within two years after: Sun Rising, Canonization, Valediction of the Book, and no doubt others though with less evidence. Fourth period. Flattery to noble ladies, to get some of the grocery bills paid; these often make a pretence of love, and Twickenham Garden is a glowingly romantic poem, but the Countess hadn't gone to live there till 1608, was inflexibly virtuous, and looks rather like a spider in the painting of her. So this case is rather a warning. Poems that claim the lovers are chaste may belong here or may simply record a stage in the seduction of an alderman's wife, Period I.

He struggled to escape becoming a parson for years, with the King refusing him any other employment; probably he had doubts, but also he would have to throw himself into it absolutely, as he did; and he seems to have felt that loving his wife was incompatible with it. The Holy Sonnet on her death (XVII) needs a comma putting earlier—'thou | Dost woo my soul, for hers offering all thine', making clearer that he regards his God as simply a jealous competitor of his wife (there is no other meaning anyway). So the great Nocturnal is a last attempt to combine loving his wife with loving God, at any rate after she is dead. It was written in 1611, when he was in France with Drury, and his wife only just survived yet another childbirth; evidently he heard a rumour she was dead. He feels he is now free to become a parson, as he will have to do to feed all those children and get them looked after: anyway there is nothing left for him in the world. He looks back on their early troubles together and thinks 'we thought we were having trouble but really we were having the time of our lives'. Of course, there is no evidence for this dating, but the poem requires a situation which allows its assertions to take on adequate meaning, or be sufficiently relevant to fulfil their natural growth. Kermode told me this was sentimental self-indulgence, but don't you bother.

Just got it in. Yours with thanks.

Houghton, bMS Eng 1401 (683)

TO JACOB EMPSON

Saturday [August 1975]

My dear Jacob,

There were one or two things I thought of asking you, but there never seemed to be an occasion, with family life what it is. Have you a History of Science man in Hull, tolerably willing? I am always wanting one. Ask him whether Carlyle had the use of bicarbonate of soda—when did it come in? And, when the Portuguese sailed round the south of Africa or got near it, did anybody *say* that the Milky Way goes all the way round? I think nobody did—they had been sure it went all round for thousands of years, so finding they had been right wasn't news at all. But surely it must have been mentioned.

I gathered that you don't admire Henry Moore, when we saw the grand statue at the Maltings [at Aldeburgh, Suffolk]. I think the theory behind it is all nonsense (so far as I have ever seen it written down), and am sure he has a bad influence, but I have to think his stuff very good in an unexplainable way but plainly, especially that one. Oh well.

Love
William.

TIMES LITERARY SUPPLEMENT, 24 October 1975: 'Richard III'

Sir,—I hoped for a vigorous letter from an informed source about G. R. Elton's review [of *Richard III and His Early Historians 1483–1535*, by Alison Hanham] (October 10), but as only a mild one has appeared (R. Newman's letter, October 17), I make bold to express the coarse voice of the general public. What we learn from the review is first that no evidence is any longer offered for the belief that Richard killed the Princes in the Tower. What every history book, however brief, always told the children is now admitted to be wrong. It is insinuated instead that this does not matter because the man did a lot of other bad things, not mentioned. We learn, secondly, that the life of Richard III by Sir Thomas More, or partly in his handwriting, contains a lot of lies; but this does not matter because the effect of them is artistic. Goodness, how sad![1]

William Empson

[written 17 October 1975]

---

[1] An allusion to Evelyn Waugh's short story 'Cruise (Letters from a young lady of leisure)' (1933); mispunctuated in this form by a sub-editor at the *TLS*. But cf. WE's letter to Penelope Doob in 1973, and see Introduction above.

TO RICHARD ELLMANN

Studio House, 1 Hampstead Hill Gardens, NW3
7 November 1975

Dear Richard Ellmann,

Thank you for your letter, sent off some time ago but recently achieved [received]. I was advised to write to a man who did a play about Joyce, but he is quite inconclusive.[1] Also I have been contacted by a Chicago editor called Shelford [Sheldon] Sacks, who was delighted by the problem and sounded as if he would be very energetic about it. One could also send an appealing letter to the TLS, but I doubt whether the time for that has yet come.

I don't think you realise what strong evidence you have already given on my side of the case. Budgen always said DEE, and you remark that he was an obstinate man, so that Joyce might not have cared to 'correct' him. What on earth could Joyce have said if he had given this correction? As I understand, the Americans are the only ones to pronounce the start of the Greek name DEAD in popular speech however it [is] spelt; the Greeks themselves would say DOI, the French DAY, and the English have followed the Italians in saying DAE (but often spelling the adjective *daedal* as 'dedal' from the seventeenth to the nineteenth centuries). Of course I do not deny that the Americans have a right to pronounce it as they like, as other nations have done, but to impose their pronunciation on other nations is imperialism. I was astonished at the indignation I aroused in Connecticut by saying 'Deedalus'. The only explanation Joyce could have given, when 'correcting' Budgen, was that he ought to talk like an American, for some reason which would have next to be supplied. In the same way, when Beckett said that he didn't remember hearing Joyce say the word, but 'his ear would have been alerted' if it had begun with DEAD, even when written *Dedalus*, he meant that it would have sounded to him a quaint piece of ignorance, as a simple man might say GIRTH for Goethe; whereas Joyce had had a thorough Jesuit training, and was a bit of a pedant. It sounds to me as if many of the people you have asked were anxious to avoid hurting your feelings.

You say that Joyce changed the spelling of the name to 'Dedalus' before he had adopted the Italian spelling for all Greek names; I am sure you are right, but he was already settled in an Italian-speaking area and accepting its language firmly. Very likely you are right in the biography when you say

---

[1] WE wrote to Tom Stoppard, author of *Travesties* (1974), on 28 Oct. 1975.

he changed the spelling 'to make it a little less improbable', but this would not involve any idea of changing the pronunciation. The Italians pronounce the name as the English do. It is true, as Hugh Kenner said, that Deddalus makes him sound 'deadish' and if Joyce had realised what the effect of his spelling would be he would have changed it back again. He was clumsy at calculating such things, and has been outwitted at other points besides this. I think his ghost must spend its time dancing up and down with fury at what Hugh Kenner and others have made of his life's work. So I cannot agree with you that the question is at all trivial.

However, thank you for turning up so much.

Yours

William Empson

Tulsa; Houghton: uncorrected carbon, bMS Eng 1401 (542)

Ellmann wrote again (13 Nov. 1975) to clarify his own position: 'I rather prefer to say Dedalus as if it was pronounced like *dead*. It doesn't seem to me to rouse any mortuary feelings if it is pronounced that way, any more than the word *dedicate*. But I am inclined to agree that since Joyce's friends, including Anglo-Irish ones, pronounced it in a more appropriate classical manner, that he probably did the same. If you are looking for further evidence, I might suggest that he always spelt the unstated title of chapter 7 Eolus, though it was obviously Aeolus.' Feeling 'vague' about what he had said in earlier letters, he conceded too: 'so far as I have been able to determine by questioning people in several countries, the chances are that Joyce did pronounce Dedalus with a long *e*. I don't think however that he much cared how it was pronounced and at this point I suppose I am still intractable.

'I quite agree that Kenner has completely distorted the meaning of Joyce's books, and the wonder is that so much of his distortion has won a good deal of support. It is good to know that there are at least two reasonable beings in the world . . . I did try to take up some of his errors in the TLS two or three weeks ago as you may have noticed.'

TO RICHARD ELLMANN

Studio House, 1 Hampstead Hill Gardens, NW3
25 November 1975

Dear Richard Ellmann,

Thank you for your letter. I have now had answers from two dramatists who made entertainments out of Joyce material, one English and one Irish. They both say, rather apologetically, that I may be right but that their actors pronounced the name Deddalus. So it is not true that only Americans pronounce the name that way; when I last wrote I felt confident, because the eager mind of Shelley Sacks had at once leapt to assure me that a national choice had been made. Of course the English and Irish are very easily corrupted by the Americans, but they can corrupt without any foreign aid too. It might be possible to prove American influence in both these cases, each time involving quite a number of people, but even I feel it would hardly be worth the effort. They must have corrupted easily, if at all.

I ought not to have written that several people were being tactful, out of so few, but I still think that Madame Jolas, who must have heard the name pronounced, and also must have considerable powers of survival, felt that this question could only involve her in thoroughly boring discussions.

I am glad you admit that Joyce probably did pronounce it DEE.

Let us know if you are in London.

Yours sincerely

William Empson.

Tulsa

TO ROMA GILL

Studio House
25 November 1975

My dear Roma,

Please take out of Sheff. U. Library again the German Faustbook of 1587 reprint and let me have it. I am just now working on my chapter about *Faust*, and we have a lodger who not only knows German but wants something to translate; he is keen to do the first English version of the Faustbook since the sixteenth century. I should think he had better just reprint 'P. F.' (or 'Partly-Fake' as we intimates call him) with a guaranteed complete apparatus of corrections, marks of additions, supply of omissions, etc. at the bottom of the page; but either plan would have to be cleared with a publisher first. He proposes the O.U.P.; what do you think? It really would be a tool that university libraries felt they had to supply, and I think it could be made interesting for the general reader. But I haven't seen any writing by the young man yet, except for a poem praising my wife on her sixtieth birthday. If it is too much nuisance to post I will ask son Jacob to pick it up, but surely the Department Secretary would wrap it and post it.

You may be dubious about the morality of doing this again, or rather in a different case, for a non-Sheffield person. But I really do propose to use it, or use him, to tell me whether a large number of details in P.-F. are also in the German. Maybe as an Emeritus I have a permanent right to use the Library, and need not ask for your connivance, though I would still be asking for your help. As the young man lives in my house, I would not be putting the book to any risk. However, you will let me know if you feel there is any obstacle. I already have the Paracelsus *De Nymphis* out of the London U. Library, by the connivance of a Professor, and feel I had better not ask for more till I am ready to hand that back.

By the way, I had a helpful letter from H. M. Adams of Trinity C. Cambridge, who has prepared an unpublished catalogue of all books in C. college libraries before 1600 [*Catalogue of Books in Cambridge Libraries prior to 1600*]. They had *thirteen* copies of Agrippa *De occulta phil.* [1533], one of them in Corpus itself, also Corpus had a 'reply to calumnies' by Agrippa. Even without supposing a censorship cut, I think it is clear that Marlowe imagines Faust as suspecting his devils are only Middle Spirits dressed up, as a reader of Agrippa would do (till the Mask of the Sins, where he loses his nerve); but this makes a feeble play without an extra bit of plot, and this one has to think has been cut. The reason why Meph is so eager to deceive, and talks so oddly if you think of him as a real devil (always boosting the terrors of hell) is that he is a Middle Spirit who wants to get the soul of Faust as a ticket to eternal bliss; now this idea, so far as I know, Marlowe could only get from *De Nymphis*. But there seem to be references to it in P.-F., so the translator would be the man who put Marlowe onto it.

I was given lunch the other day at the Warburg Institute by Frances Yates[1] herself, and the author [D. P. Walker] of The Decline of Hell, who has an office next door to her. He remarked that he had got interested in music and wasn't working on his subject now. She has a country cottage and visits her office once a week. Clearly they live in a heaven for old academics with no teaching at all. She is rather a sweet old thing but very decisive, with a notable moustache. As in talking to Arthur Waley, with whom I once played tennis in the adjoining square, I felt I had been rather a disappointing applicant; though one might feel that one had tried to make the party go, but they had been totally wet-blanket. Certainly I came

---

[1] Frances Yates (1899–1981) was Reader in the History of the Renaissance at the Warburg Institute, University of London. Her publications include *John Florio: The Life of an Italian in Shakespeare's England* (1934), *A Study of 'Love's Labour's Lost'* (1936), *Giordano Bruno and the Hermetic Tradition* (1964), *The Art of Memory* (1966), *Theatre of the World* (1969), *The Rosicrucian Enlightenment* (1975), and *The Occult Philosophy in the Elizabeth Age* (1979). She was appointed DBE in 1977.

with prepared questions and could get no answer to any of them. Still, when she said that Agrippa would have considered the Faust of Marlowe a very wicked man, I felt sure this was a point one should never forget. But really, I expect that Agrippa felt that a good deal of hypocrisy was quite permissible for him, considering how bad his opponents were; and that this Faust was a young fool, merely. She treated the *Midsummer N. D.* in a recent book [*Shakespeare's Last Plays: a new approach*, 1975], with a great failure to consider the interests of the author and the audience, I thought; so I just dangled a few bright thoughts before her, and she was quite certain they were entirely wrong. Nice not to find her ga-ga, at any rate.

Well then, I do hope that your health is holding up, and that you can do me this important kindness.

Yours

William Empson.

TO CHRISTOPHER RICKS

1 Hampstead Hill Gardens, London NW3

26 January 1976

My dear Ricks,

Very nice to see you both. Sorry to be a nuisance, but I left behind a hip-flask which Hetta had just given me, in our bedroom somewhere. It contains a small amount of Marsala, which you should finish up; I am told the main use of it is to make zabaglione. Do not post it after me, but transfer it to Cambridge, and I will hope to pick it up on my next visit. That is, to pick up the flask, not the Marsala.

It occurs to me that my argument about *Dr Faustus* might be outflanked by an apparent agreement. The author did intend a subtle ambiguity at its ending, I can be told, but the ignorant producer and the coarse mob could not be bothered with that, and some hack was made to add the low jeering[1] by the devils and the Good Angel, insisting that Dr. F. would go to Hell, before the play was ever performed. We have no record of a performance before 1594, a year after his murder; maybe he could not have prevented the garbling of the play anyhow, after selling it to a company, but his death would make things easy. There is a mention that [Edward] Alleyn acted the part in a surplice, rather oddly for a Lutheran pastor, or a

---

[1] WE apparently adopted this phrase from Bernard Shaw, who said, as WE noted in a footnote to *FC* (132), that 'the theme of *Ulysses* [is] "the fatal habit of low jeering", boasting that you see through the imposture of society without having any plan to make things better.'

don, so the audience was probably expected to be against him. I think it is true that few would repine at the order of the censorship, and certainly no later attempt was made to restore the first intention. I might answer that a thoroughly rumpy or medieval treatment, making the most of the absurdity of the devils in the Masque-of-Sins visit, would get back to the same effect by a different route. But that of course would be no protest against witch-burning. It would not explain the confusion and disorder of the surviving texts, and the embarrassed silence which makes the date of first performance totally obscure. But perhaps this less dramatic theory is all that I can really hope to put over, so my book had better make terms with it beforehand.

all?

I have written a bit more for the Chorus introducing Act II, usually starting with the soliloquy *Now Faustus must thou needs be damned*:

> Faustus would overreach the Devil now
> And work the spirits yet not pay in Hell.
> He fancies they are doubledealing him
> Claiming Hell's grandeur for a fantasy—
> Not making much of Mephistophilis
> Thinks him a spirit of the elements,
> Until he sees the face of Lucifer.
> He offers murder, but in words alone,
> As meet to flatter Mephistophilis;
> Not after he has seen great Lucifer.

Then the meeting with the other magicians, and the start of the soliloquy after they have gone, are in prose, resuming at 'Despair in God'. I hope my Faust gets performed, but writing the jolly scene in the Sultan's harem will be delayed as long as possible.[2]

Affectionately
William E.

---

[2] CR, citing this passage from WE's letter as a 'supreme kind of practical criticism', notes of it: ' "*Usually* starting with the soliloquy" is deliciously cool.' WE is obliged 'to write a passage (of extraordinary ageless non-pastiche, it must be said) without which his thesis about the play will not be credited. The new lines don't just give the argument a leg up, they give it a leg to stand on.' ('*Doctor Faustus* and Hell on Earth', *E in C* 35: 2 (Apr. 1985), 102–3).

TO JACOB EMPSON

9 April 1976

My dear Jacob,

The Times report of your conference at York makes clear that all the smart psychologists are teasing animals now. You must not lag behind. You should be giving psychedelic drugs to moles and tortoises, and staying up all night pinching their tails to make them dream. Special equipment will have to be designed, of course.

I think the public would be dubious about snakes, but tortoises are sure-fire. I am glad you have thought of moles; they have great charm too. Probably they will enjoy your attentions, but that must remain one of the secrets of the lab.

Your affectionate father
William

TO JOHN HENRY JONES*

9 May 1976

My dear Jones,

I don't see at all why you should abandon the cause of Richard III on the strength of these library books [E. F. Jacob, *The Fifteenth Century, 1399–1485* (1961); J. R. Lander, *The Wars of the Roses* (1965)], but maybe you are going by other evidence.[1] You find it decisive that there is no evidence of anyone seeing the princes after July 83. But if he had murdered them, what would be the use of hiding the bodies? They would lie in state, with doctors to certify that they had died of fever. (Hence the supposed smothering with pillows, to leave no wound; but the device was not acted upon.) Henry VII, on the other hand, had every reason to kill them as soon as he got control, pretending that he had never found them. The mystery-procedure is much more in his character and he had no close family obligations to the real heirs, many of whom he is admitting to have killed. If you ask why Richard kept them hidden, he thought them in danger; and so, on any count, they really were. Why do you suppose that Henry locked up their mother for the rest of her life in Feb 87? And why

---

[1] J. H. Jones wrote (letter to JH, 12 Feb. 2001): 'I had an idea for a Yorkist kitchen-sink drama—"Crookback in anger"—in which Buckingham did the dirty deed: "I have pressing matters to attend to". There was a good biography by Philip Somebody and William liked to discuss it—he was analyzing Josephine Tey's book. Well, it was fun at the time but I didn't get very far with it, perhaps an odd scene.'

was she out of sanctuary and going to Richard's parties after July 83? I grant that, on any view, the Tower must have been a pretty black prison, with a staff that could be silenced by terror, but it was so when Richard took it over.

Interesting that Richard changed his mind about his heir, choosing his sister's son instead of the son of Clarence, who had died under an attainder. But you don't deduce anything about his motives. Probably he wanted to be secure against legal fuss and obligations. That is like his reaction to finding his nephews to be bastards.

You react too strongly against the phrase 'it was life and death to Morton that Richard should go', admitting that Richard had great 'respect for piety'; well then, he was unlikely to kill his nephews. He would not have given Morton the top jobs Morton wanted. Though he tried to make peace among the factions, Richard kept a sharp eye on them; he might well have thought the gabble about his nephews being dead was merely a device to make him expose them in public. You suggest that Buckingham got them killed, and Richard dared not say he had lost them; but I don't think he was so shy. Surely the nest of murderers in the Tower would not have remained faithful to Buckingham under torture; I think Richard would have got to the bottom of this plot very quickly, or rather would have taken care that it couldn't happen. The tower was after all a strong machine; all such machines are no use except in the hands of an administrator who can choose the right subordinates, but this much he could do.

As for the two books, I don't see that they give anything except confirmation of [Josephine] Tey [*Daughter of Time*]. [Dominic] Mancini left London soon after the coronation in July 83, your crucial date, so has no direct evidence for the important period. Lander gives us this on his p. 229, and adds a revealing footnote on p. 231: 'There was, in fact, no definite law on the subject'. Usually a man's will appointing a guardian for his infant son was accepted by the law, but in the case of a King it had frequently been overturned; only in the sense of the jungle was there no law. p. 240. Tey does not give her source for saying that Hastings was held for a week, and thus executed after time for an inquiry; it seems a point to get clear, as the opponents of Richard say that he fell from grace when he did this planned murder. P. 242. At last we get a contemporary letter, of 21 June [by Simon Stallworthe] but I do not know how I should guess the year. It expresses keen anxiety about the political situation, but seems rather on the side of Richard than otherwise. Next we hear that Polydore Vergil [*Anglia Historia*] came to England in 1502, so he had 'ample opportunity to discuss' the recent historical events 'with men who had taken a prominent part in them' [242–3], and this is said without any denial that Henry was regularly killing anybody who put a foot wrong. Lander published in 1963 [1965]. E. F. Jacob published in 1961. (They had both of course read Tey, who had published in 1951, and are trying to elbow her out of sight, but how very feebly.) P. 610 [in Jacob]. Mancini gives 'significant' information [in *De occupatione Regni Anglie per Riccardum Tercium*], by being a humanist writer, as when he reports having seen men cry after Prince Edward had been removed from their sight. It sounds to me like the typical journalist vulgarity of Ciceronian Latin, but of course it may still be true, and his uncle may still not have killed him. No one denies that the two boys were secluded after being transferred to the Tower. Richard might well think that he need only do this till he had got through a crucial period. Jacob on p. 616 admits, though in eerily muffled language, that Mancini lies grossly in saying that Richard was trying to kill or imprison all who might be faithful to his brother's sons. P. 619. 'Richard had it all ready' for a royal herald to read out the reasons for killing Hastings; why does this prove they were wrong, please? Still, even on the edge of civil war, it would be more civilised to hold him for a week and ask what reply could be made; I would like to hear what substance there is in the claim of Tey. Otherwise the chief thing I gained from reading the two books is the lengthy quotation of Thomas More [from *History of Richard III*] in Lander [232–6]; the text really does read as morally very low, all along, just as Tey says, only she might have picked one or two accidental examples. The complete insensitivity of the historians to this, or their determined pretence that they do not know how to estimate evidence, is the most striking feature of the affair.

I remember dear old Professor Potter at Sheffield,[2] a most distinguished chairman and doyen of historians, grumbling about the book by Tey a few years after it had come out, without ever having read it or even knowing her name, and saying that these unaccredited people actually resort to untruth; morally, it puts them in a very weak position, and something ought to be done about it. I was quite sure that his own official side was the one which had resorted to untruth, but I am afraid I ratted there; I felt it would be bad tactics to take on the historians too. (I had arrived at Sheffield as a raw professor in 1953.) Of course this could have made no difference anyhow, what I might say; but I was an observer. I think the historians behaved very foolishly there, and in consequence have lost a

---

[2] George Potter (1900–81) was Professor of Medieval History at the University of Sheffield, 1931–65; President of the Historical Association, 1961–4.

great deal of ground in the public mind. They thought they would look grander if they refused to meet the challenge, and they did not; they look like another trades union, fighting for its uniqueness, and no use to anybody because it claims too much.

Thank you for the loans.

W. Empson.

Houghton, bMS Eng 1401 (585)

John Henry Jones's response to WE (11 May 1976) included these remarks: 'You mustn't think I am down on Richard—I am still trying to make up my mind. I am interested in writing a play about it, so on that count alone I am biased in his favour. Perhaps I feel that Tey goes over the top—necessary in '51, maybe, but it would all be a lot more convincing if it were not so emotionally charged . . .' (Courtesy of the late John Henry Jones)

NEW STATESMAN, 13 August 1976, 208–9: 'The Critic as Vandal'

John Carey[1] stated in his inaugural lecture as Merton Professor of English Literature at Oxford University: 'We take it as an axiom that paraphrase inevitably alters meaning. To reword is to destroy.' As a specific (and choicely chosen) example of criticism that separates form and content by paraphrasing a poem, he cited WE's discussion of George Herbert's 'Afflic-tion' (from ch. 6 of *A*): 'Empson wants to deter his readers from the way of understanding the line that will probably have occurred to them, and accordingly he reduces it to a comic paraphrase' ('The Critic as Vandal—1', *New Statesman*, 6 Aug. 1976, 178).

Sir,

Professor Carey (6 August) ascribes to me a dishonest motive, and I ask leave to explain the real one. I offered, he says, long ago a 'crude rewording' of a line of George Herbert 'so that [readers] will be ashamed of thinking the line meant that, and be readier to believe Empson's less likely alternative'. This could not have occurred to me; I thought both interpretations likely, and needed to make both appear so. I did offer a paraphrase which Herbert himself would not have used, even in conversation; judging from the other examples in the article, this is what is being denounced.

---

[1] John Carey (b. 1934) was Merton Professor of English Literature at Oxford, and Fellow of Merton College, 1976–2001. He has been principal book reviewer for *the Sunday Times* since 1977. His other books include *The Poems of John Milton* (ed. with Alastair Fowler, 1968), *The Violent Effigy: A Study of Dickens' Imagination* (1973), *Thackeray: Prodigal Genius* (1977), *John Donne: Life, Mind and Art* (1981), *The Intellectuals and the Masses* (1992), and *The Faber Book of Science* (1995).

The basic justification is that a critic should not be absorbed parasitically into the author, but should appraise the whole ethos and outlook of the author from the standpoint of his own. At the time, I felt I should not pretend to feel at home in the saintly atmosphere of the poem, and on the other hand needed to present the extra interpretation as a solid one, something that might occur to a plain man. To feel shame about my wording seems to me perverse.

The poem outlines the life of Herbert, saying he had desired the ruling-class career which was open to him but had also felt God was calling him to religion; yet now, having obeyed the call, he feels that God no longer wants him. He is plucky about being jilted in this way, and plans to take up some other line of life:

> Well, I will change the service, and go seek
> > Some other master out.
> Ah, my dear God, though I be clean forgot,
> Let me not love thee, if I love thee not.

Clearly there is an interval before the final couplet, while he finds that he cannot bring himself to go. The last line may express total self-abandonment: 'I will love you however badly you treat me', and then *let me not love thee* has to become, very oddly, a kind of swearing—he invokes the worst penalty he can think of. 'Damn me if I don't stick to the parsonage', I am blamed for writing down, but it does bring out the queer logic or syntax of this version. Another version would follow more naturally from the lines just before, by making a practical appeal: 'Stop calling me if I have no real vocation. Do not make me love you in desire if I am incapable of loving you in achievement.' There is no conflict between the two meanings; he hardly knows which he can afford to say; but unless he means both there is no reason for giving the final line its peculiar form, that of a paradox or riddle. Very likely I phrased the alternatives clumsily, but that is a minor matter. As to the main point, if a man calls me a cheat for saying it I think he is practically deranged.

The other vandals, my colleagues, do not need my defence, but give some help in understanding the attack. Both paraphrase some incident in a poem in a way which is contemporary for them, and both outrage the political, rather than the literary, purity of Professor Carey. As C. S. Lewis was writing in the 1920s, a passing hint at the class-system, while he was trying to come to terms with the Bower of Bliss, might seem of historical interest only; and Professor Carey agrees that he is right about the main structure of ideas in the passage. Professor Ricks, again in passing, says that Milton practically demands 'genocide' in Samson; Professor Carey indignantly retorts that the extermination of an entire ruling class or caste is not genocide but OK. I thought no one denied that the struggle of Milton to accept the barbarism of the Old Testament was bad for him; Samson is a military hero all right, but should not be made a saint. The fourth Vandal is a neo-Freudian or thereabouts, and I usually find them dull and tiresome because so plainly wrong; but this one [William Kerrigan, *The Prophetic Milton*] has thought of a rather deserved joke against Milton's treatment of Samson. Professor Carey regards it as sacrilege.[2]

The critical opinions of academics tend to reflect the methods of dealing with students which they prefer; if looked at in this way the views of Professor Carey, otherwise so blank, become fairly intelligible. He recommends: 'Insist upon reverence for whatever has got on the syllabus. Never allow the pupils to speak from their own experience, which they should learn to forget; but you may placate their resentment by expressing a startling hatred for every elite. Never allow them to paraphrase anything, for fear their spontaneous sentiments may leak out; they must just learn by heart everything that Teacher says to them.' It had already struck me that something seems to have been going very wrong with the Eng. Lit. Departments, and this counsel of despair would be quite enough explanation.

John Carey responded (*New Statesman*, 27 August 1976): 'Professor Empson seems to me to have overlooked my main argument. Put simply, it is this: if we accept that "form" and "content" are indissolubly fused in a work of literature, then it follows that all rewording is misrepresentation. From this it further follows that a book like *Seven Types*, which is full of rewording, must be full of misrepresentation. I am disappointed that Professor Empson cannot bring himself to agree. I did not, of course, use the words "dishonest" or "cheat" about him: these are his rewordings—though I confess I feel it less than candid of him to pretend, in his letter, that Mr Kerrigan's interpretation of *Samson Agonistes* was intended as a joke. When he comes to read Mr Kerrigan he will find that this is, alas, not so.'

WE wrote further, in 1979: 'Carey, in his Inaugural Lecture on becoming a Professor [in 1976], announced a rigorous policy; there must be no more paraphrase, no more reading in or spelling out, because all such tampering

---

[2] In William Kerrigan's account of the ending of *Samson Agonistes*, wrote Carey, 'what takes place . . . is not genocide but something more medical. His attention is attracted to the repeated references to wind . . . Samson, Kerrigan deduces, is in fact suffering from wind, or symbolic wind, and between the pillars he is able to get rid of it'. Kerrigan 'also feels that Samson, between the pillars, is giving birth, or perhaps being born, beside alleviating his constipation' ('The Critic as Vandal—1', 180).

with a text was the work of Vandals. I came in for some of the rough stuff myself, and thought he could have found stronger examples in what I wrote fifty years ago, though I would never have intentionally gone beyond the intention of an author, either in his conscousness or his unconsciousness. But it struck me that the program as he announced it was actually incompatible with teaching, let alone his own style of written criticism; it became a question whether he would achieve a Houdini-like reappearance.' (*A*) Three years on, he felt pleased to find that Carey was 'deeply in sympathy with the author, knowing what he often wants to do . . . it is a welcome advance on [his] Inaugural.' But cf. also his implacable review ' "There Is No Penance Due to Ignorance" '—on *John Donne: Life, Mind and Art*, by John Carey—in *NYRB*, 28: 19 (3 Dec. 1981), 42–50.

AGENDA, 14: 3 (Autumn 1976): 'Questionnaire on Criticism'

1. *If a poem is new, or breaks new ground, new knowledge, by what means or standards do we judge it?*
2. *What is the point of admiring the poems with whose content one disagrees? (i.e. 'Yeats's ideas are silly but his poems are marvellous.')*
3. *How does one complain of wording, rhythm or rhyme without assuming that one knows what was intended?*
4. *If the author's 'intention' is irrelevant is not the form (which may itself be open to intention) the only thing left to discuss?*
5. *If, then, the pleasures of poetry are purely formal does* Macbeth *present ultimately a different pleasure from* Go, lovely Rose?
6. *Is there any original thought in poetry? If, say, the content/thought of* The Voice *by Hardy is commonplace, then what must be admired in the form—which seems to leave poetry as a kind of intellectual flower-arranging?*
7. *If we accept Hardy's awkwardness, for example, why cannot we accept everyone? If the answer turns on 'sincerity', we are dealing with 'personality' or even 'synthetic personality' which brings biographical background into consideration and goes well beyond the tenets of the new criticism.*
8. *Would such an admission not tacitly accept that the underlying value of literature may well be the communication of 'personality, life, spirit'? 'We might come to believe that the thing that matters in art is a sort of energy, something more or less like electricity or radioactivity, a force transfusing, welding, and unifying.' Pound:* The Serious Artist.
9. *How important is subject?*
10. *Why should a critic spoil anyone's pleasure in a poem they read, perhaps wrongly, as a good one? In other words is Coleridge's case a good one: Poems that excite us to artificial feelings make us callous to real ones.*

(1) James Joyce is usually held up as a pure aesthete, who believed that the subject should be footling; but as a young man he wrote to Ibsen that a great play must deal with a great question, felt as such by every mind. No doubt he and Ibsen would think of a topical question, causing controversy at the time. The great advantage of the poets of the Thirties is that they were backed by such a situation (though my own work largely failed to use it). Of course, the first answer to your question is that recognising new work is always difficult and usually takes much time; but the only thing that can happen to aestheticism, after providing a useful fallow period maybe, is to go out of fashion.

(2) Probably, if these works appeal to you, they are recalling some truth which your conventions make you ignore.

(3) Of course you must be willing to impute an intention to an author, and consider the evidence if there is a doubt about it (which doesn't happen very often). This habit is very deeply established; without it you could not have learned to talk. Indeed, one needs a special reason to understand why the absurd veto on it ever arose. I think it is because the American Eng. Lit. theorists are all descended from Germans (the K. of Wimsatt was Kurtz), and no German has ever understood the intention of an English writer, in all the 200 years since they started trying. So at last they tried to erect this mere fact of Nature into a metaphysical principle.

(4) Yes, if you cut out intention you make the whole subject footling. This is not true of all art. Persian carpets or Chinese pots for instance (though you should never forbid yourself to imagine the impulses of the artist), but in literature the medium is close to the discursive reason, and to cut them apart is unnatural.

(5) This seems to assume that there can be no intention behind *Go, lovely Rose*, which I could not agree to, though the chief intention may have been to make a graceful song. *Macbeth*, from the censor's point of view, was a warning against civil war, with a reminder that straying from the legitimate heir is a sure way to produce it. The deep intention may often be a thing the author himself is doubtful about, but this is no reason for forbidding us to recognise the more superficial layers.

(6) There has sometimes been original thought in poetry, but usually good poetry is supporting one current movement against another.

(7) I am doubtful about Hardy, and do not consider a 'synthetic personality' always a bad thing, though I do not expect that he had one. The doubt comes because he does not think enough, carry his thought through; if he had done, I expect he would be more awkward. Obviously you need to

think about his 'biography', his formative experiences and relation to his public. Why ever not?

(8) Certainly one may be affected by an author's personality, but he can only express it by having something to say, and a situation in which he says it.

(9) The only reason for not saying that subject is practically all-important is that a real subject may be almost hidden behind a protective cover subject.

(10) The critic should tell the readers of some better work, so that they get a better pleasure out of that. Merely crabbing a poem is not bad in principle but is very liable to show a character-fault in the critic, and I think must always be suspected of that.

TO THOMAS F. MERRILL: 'The Hazards of Semantic Idolatry'[1]

[Department of English, University of Delaware, Newark, Delaware]
19 December 1976

Dear Thomas Merrill,

While going through papers before packing my bag, I found the off-print you had given me weeks ago; I had stupidly never looked at it. I agree entirely that the sort of conflict you describe was prominent in Milton's mind when writing the poem, and that he expected the fit reader to appreciate it. But I cannot agree that the historical gulf between us and Milton is so very sheer; I have known pious young men nowadays say that it is logically impossible for a God to be wicked, and Tillotson, later an Archbishop, already preaching before Parliament when Milton was planning the poem, maintained that we should not believe a revelation which ordered us to disobey a natural law. You seem to suppose a society which felt no problem about your doctrine, and would accept it comfortably in the poem; but no missionary in the field would ever regard it so.

Suppose a couple who are preparing with many tears to sacrifice their first-born to Moloch. The missionary tells them that Moloch is a wicked God, and they answer that he is talking blasphemy. You would say (p. 389) that he has stripped the problem of its religious status and perversely regarded it as merely ethical. He would hotly deny it, and also deny that he was actuated by 'a narrow literary bias toward the epic' (p. 392), or under

---

[1] See Thomas F. Merrill, '*Paradise Lost* and the Hazards of Semantic Idolatry', *Neuphilologische Mitteilungen*, 77:3 (1976), 387–410; repr. in Merrill, *Christian Criticism: A Study of Literary God-Talk* (1976).

any kind of semantic delusion. 'The absurdity of applying ethics appropriate to men to God' (p. 410) is one which men cannot avoid without ethical disaster. I do not understand how you can praise 'Christian liberty' (p. 400) if it does not imply that an unnatural order need not be obeyed.

The serpent tells Eve that God is testing her courage, and the sincerity of her desire to go to Heaven, not her obedience, so he will praise her if she breaks his rule. She reflects, rather irritably, that she has no way of finding out whether this is true or not. I think, as she seems to do, that the puzzle is an unfair one; and it is certainly not solved by anything you would have told her.

A very interesting piece, though.

With thanks

William Empson

Houghton photocopy, signed; title by Empson, bMS Eng 1401 (604)

TO CHRISTOPHER RICKS

Studio House, 1 Hampstead Hill Gardens NW3
435/0977
14 February 1977

My dear Ricks,

I went and saw [David] Perry, our producer at the BBC, who seems a very nice young man. He aims at 30 mins, and thinks of having some remarks by other people first, not part of the conversation, then this discussion by you and me, which would need to be 20 mins, then a separate bit of poetry-reading at the end, say 10 mins. To get through these three items would need 40 mins, I now think.

Anyway I think our discussion had much better be about the present state of Lit. Crit, here and in America; not trying to elicit historical memories about the old buffer. I think the situation is bad, especially by the Wimsatt Law that no reader may know the intention of an author—hence there must be no Intuition or spontaneity and no biography or grasp of the author's character and style. Are you prepared to defend all that, or say it isn't as bad as I think? The neo-Christian movement (which I used to think so bad) seems to have melted away, except for the age-old routine lying, and instead we have this Inhumanism which is far worse.

Or what else were you planning to address?

Hoping to see you

William Empson

§ COLERIDGE AND NORMAN FRUMAN

TIMES LITERARY SUPPLEMENT, 18 February 1977

Sir,—Coleridge was dictating *The Friend* to Sara Hutchinson in 1810, and she found great difficulty in coaxing him to carry out his periodical obligations. Here the learned have found a number of unacknowledged quotations from Schelling[,] and Coleridge is particularly likely here to have dictated them from his old notebooks hardly knowing whether they were his own or not, but unwilling to invent them again. I gave this as an example, without wasting several hundred words on protecting myself by saying that of course it was only an example; this is one of the things a writer habitually does, if he is not a bore. As for Professor [Walter Jackson] Bate, I thought I was giving him credit for conclusions which his remarks clearly imply, though he does not assert them.

Lamb was a very charitable man, and undoubtedly did mean that 'the remark was just and original enough with Dyer, though a cliché to those better read'; that was *why* he thought it so charmingly funny. Mr Fruman in his retort (Letters, February 11) is still the blind man clutching at one or other end of the elephant.

William Empson

TIMES LITERARY SUPPLEMENT, 18 March 1977

Sir,—I ought to present brief reasons, when challenged, for the warning against Norman Fruman's book (*The Damaged Archangel*, 1971) which I gave in answer to your general question. Two examples should be enough.

For a complete argument that Coleridge was always a parasite, one needs to maintain that he cribbed his poetical style; and Fruman says (page 280):

> it is essentially to Wordsworth that we can attribute the remarkable change in Coleridge's poetry [during 1797] . . . which occurs after, and *only* after, the close friendship with Wordsworth.

Most critics, which agreeing in the main, say that a few of his earlier poems were already in the new manner, especially two written on his honeymoon, the 'Eolian Harp' and the lines 'On leaving a Place of Retirement' (1795–6). The 'Harp' is a conversation with his bride in their country cottage; the instrument is constructed to be played upon by the fitful breeze, heightening their intimate contact with Nature, and his delight in the whole scene encourages thoughts of Pantheism. She calls them blasphemous, and he yields with easy grace, but may be expected to try again. It is arch but candid, and terrible when one realizes that the marriage was to break upon this rock (she took very hard his refusal of baptism to the children, till some time after Berkeley was dead). So his philosophical thoughts were not as unimportant to him as they appear to Fruman. The two poems are not mentioned till the end of a long denunci-ation of Coleridge's early work (page 256) where we learn that their 'steady and clear voices' are 'almost submerged'.

When he at last admits that pantheistic ideas are induced by the wind-harp he says (page 301) that these are merely 'the persistent deistic heresy into which Pope stumbled in his *Essay on Man*', because the poem makes no 'suggestion of spiritual or therapeutic fall-out in the contemplation of nature', which was central for the theory of Wordsworth. But the poem about leaving retirement obviously does do this; a wicked business man comes out from the city and looks at the cottage, and even he is for the moment improved. In fact this poem, though not the 'Wind-harp', might be called smug; the lovers are so glutted with the virtues of Nature that they are sure they will do good in the wicked city. The long critical struggle has no purpose except to blacken the poet indirectly, and shows very little grasp of his interests or feelings.

A famous old scandal about plagiarism in Coleridge, starting soon after he was dead, concerns the 'Hymn before Sunrise' over Mont Blanc (1802). One needs to understand just what had happened. Shortly before compos-ing it he had made a solitary tour in the Lake country, writing up his day for Sara Hutchinson from some farmhouse every evening, and at one point found himself crag-fast, unable to go up or down, beside a dead sheep which had tried to go the same way. He reports to Sara:

> I lay in a state of almost prophetic trance. . . . Oh God, I exclaimed aloud, how calm, how blessed I am now . . . If this reality were a dream, if I were asleep, what agonies had I suffered, what screams!

He thanks God for the powers of Reason and the Will, which make the difference; but it is the scene before him, and the clouds so near above him posting urgently to the northward, that have awed him into calm. After collecting himself in this way he is able to find a crack in the cliff and comes down it without difficulty. Just so, the Mariner saved his life by blessing the water snakes; Coleridge was exhilarated by the affair, bringing it into several letters, and it would have made a very fine Nature-poem. Madly rejecting this last chance, he wrote instead a formal Ode or Harangue about meeting God on Mont Blanc; it has no incident, and feels shrilly insincere. And no wonder, as it suppresses the experience of Nature which had been its origin. Coleridge had renounced Nature, earlier in the same year, by the poem 'Dejection'; now he sacrifices Nature to God the Father, and his nightmares become even worse. He must appear theatrically present on this Grand-Tour mountain, where he had never been; so even the prose introduction is literally translated from a German author [Friederica Brun], who had been there and written a short poem about it, with 'I thought', etc, translated as well.[1] This goes far beyond ordinary plagiarism, and it is hard to see how the poet could even imagine any advantage in it. He could have led forward the obscure lady who had helped him, incidentally making clear that her contribution was not very great, and be sure of increased popularity with no loss of fame. It is more as if he wanted to retain a hallucination.

While the poem was coming out, Coleridge wrote to a new acquaintance, Sotheby, and explained that he had been first inspired by Scafell, where 'I involuntarily poured out a Hymn in the manner of the Psalms'. Fruman nails this as a lie, near the start of his book (page 26); he says that the letter to Sara gives a 'minute account' of the experience on Scafell, 'without mentioning a Hymn, involuntarily poured forth or otherwise'. From then on, another jeer about the phrase may crop up anywhere in his book. Well, I agree that Coleridge is not at his best when pompous. But the Psalms, in English at any rate, often do seem startlingly abrupt, and the address to God from the cliff is like them so far. It is the only occasion in the letter when Coleridge reports himself as speaking alone, and it comes at the point of greatest dramatic interest; how could anyone read the letter and doubt that this was what Coleridge had meant to describe, when writing to Sotheby, even though his description was in bad taste? As to 'involuntarily', a speech to God while expecting death alone is likely to be spontaneous; and he might easily feel surprised by what he said, as his feelings about Nature had become so mixed. Fruman also says (page 451), 'there is no evidence that Coleridge repeated this story to anyone else', apparently meaning the story that he changed the place from Scafell to the Alps. But he sent to [Sir George] Beaumont, with the text of the poem, 'a much finer line written while Scafell was still in my thoughts', and so it exasperatingly is. As to the story that he had spoken aloud, he wrote about

---

[1] See Norman Fruman, *Coleridge, The Damaged Archangel*, 26–30.

that to Sara, at least. One should notice, in these remarks made at the time, that he takes for granted he has not really been to Mont Blanc, any more than he had sailed with the Ancient Mariner; indeed, he could not have pretended that he had.

He ought to have given credit to the living authoress, though he need not to the long-dead ships' captains; but in either case he was admired for imagining vividly what he had learnt only by reading. Boorishness he may be accused of; but no doubt he felt he had been putting himself through a severe trial, in sacrificing to God all the tenderness of Nature, and ought not to be bothered with trivialities. I have to regard the poem as a terrible betrayal of his intimate experience and his powers; to worry about the plagiarism feels to me like the priests who interrupt the trial of St Joan for heresy by accusing her of stealing a bishop's horse.[2]

Finally the letter blames me for 'an assault upon the piety' of Coleridge, and on his intelligence too. Well, nightmares and neurotic fears are usually irrational, and maybe Coleridge sometimes talks as if he were too enlightened to believe in Hell; but we may be sure that his wife and his parson brother frequently threatened him with Hell. In 1803, when Hazlitt stayed with him to paint his portrait (the Notebooks tell us) he triumphantly proved that his God was not malignant, against the jeering of Wordsworth and the visitor, and then screamed the house down as soon as he got to sleep. 'Oh me, oh me'.[3] Fruman refuses to discuss his religious problems at all except for a dismissive reference to a 'flirtation with a Unitarian ministry' (page 256); but he magisterially decides, after listing some nightmares, that Coleridge had an unconscious craving for incest with his mother, which made him impotent. Coleridge would consider this a very gross 'assault'. But it would be no insult to be told, what is probable, that he feared his God would punish him if he committed adultery. Fruman is so remote from the mind of Coleridge that he cannot be expected to understand the poems.

William Empson

TIMES LITERARY SUPPLEMENT, 29 April 1977

Sir,—I pointed out two misreadings in Norman Fruman's book (Letters, March 18), and he makes no attempt to defend them. Instead, he launches an attack on an edition of which I was joint editor (Letters, April 15). I

---

[2] See Bernard Shaw, *Saint Joan*, scene 6; *Collected Plays*, vi (1973), 163, 175.
[3] *Notebooks*, i: *1794–1804 Text*, ed. K. Coburn (1957), entries 1616–19.

suppose that Coleridge was a pantheist when young but revolted against that doctrine fairly early, and Fruman says: 'Fear of pantheism, we are to believe, led Coleridge to ruin the great *Ancient Mariner* of 1798, with the disfiguring revisions of 1800 (so widely hailed elsewhere as beyond praise).' But we two editors welcomed the ironing out of the comic Old English; all we did there was put back the lengthy cuts. I said: 'The poem which was fudged in 1815 to make it Christian had already been fudged in 1800 to make it pantheist.' Epigrams are not much good, but they usually keep an opponent from getting his accusation completely upside down. In 1798 there had been spirits backing the crew, who fought the ones backing the Mariner, but Wordsworth (I supposed) insisted that there must be no 'bad' Spirits of Nature. Whatever the motive for cutting these passages, the poem is plainly better when they are restored. Most readers of the Oxford text, where they come at the bottom of the page, put them back automatically.

I do not understand why Coleridge developed such a horror of pantheism, whereas it would have been easy for him to say that God is both immanent and transcendent, as did Wordsworth and Alexander Pope. But that he was accustomed to talk as a pantheist, before being influenced by Wordsworth, is proved by 'The Eolian Harp', where his bride (in effect) threatens him with Hell for it. The Fruman theory is in a very tight corner here; otherwise even Fruman would hardly have said that Coleridge was imitating Pope at the time. But the poem also expresses belief in spirits, and that might well carry more emotional weight.

The proof by H. W. Piper (in *The Active Universe*) that Wordsworth and Coleridge at the time of their decisive meeting literally believed in Middle Spirits, or fairies, though they had both come to realize that the belief needed expressing with tact, alters our whole picture of them. It is understandable that, after renouncing this belief, Coleridge could write no more nature-poetry, and Wordsworth only through recollections of his youth. But the moment of truth on Scafell is not hampered by this problem; it shows Coleridge on the verge of writing like *The Prelude*.

Fruman has now abandoned the sentence 'Coleridge did not tell this story to anyone else',[4] accepting that Coleridge also told parts of it to at least two old friends. But he pities me for believing it. I believe it because the immediate report of his day, written as a letter to Sara from a farmhouse, works up to a good piece of prose about being crag-bound, full of

---

[4] 'There is no evidence that he repeated this story to anyone else' (Fruman, *Coleridge*, 451 n. 19).

awe and wonder but very real, and quite unlike anything Coleridge could do when lying. Obviously something important happened to him on Scafell, only to be murdered and buried under the conventional poem on Mont Blanc. Trying to answer a literary question without any sense of literary judgement is not manly and tough; it is merely a waste of time.

William Empson

TIMES LITERARY SUPPLEMENT, 1 July 1977

Sir,—Norman Fruman (Letters, June 3) does make an interesting point, I don't deny, about Coleridge's various reports of his excursion in August 1802. The only two that mention his praying aloud at the top of a cliff are the intimate letter to Sara written off at once, and an over-elaborate letter to Sotheby, a very literary character, some weeks later. This does not make me sure it never happened. Most of his friends were critical of his religiosity, and would be liable to jeer at him for praying when he was frightened. The Notebook entry is a rather technical account of the whole tour, prepared as a record of what he had done; but it is absurd for Fruman to deny that an 'exhilarating experience' peeps out when he comes to:

> the *savage, savage* head of Eskdale (Good Heavens! What a climb! dropping from Precipices and at last should have been crag-fast but for the chasm).[1]

He actually quotes part of this, to prove that nothing much happened; and the letter to Sara, he says, merely reports that Coleridge 'exclaimed a few words to God, looked around, and found a path to safety'. The letter reports a fair number of words, not just a nod and a hellow, and a *chasm* is not usually called a 'path'. I hope that Fruman himself has never come down a cliff by a chimney, because then one would have to call his rephrasing dishonest; but, after all, he often does not realize what he is reading. The letter to Southey about the tour, written on the 9th, just after getting home, says it was a 'heart-thrilling' experience, and adds, 'Hartley is almost ill with transport at my Scafell expedition' (Hartley was not quite six years old). Fruman has to treat all this as dull because he makes Coleridge merely a copy-cat, as regards ideas for poetry, and also a man who never really looked at Nature. We are discussing the tour because it made Coleridge write a poem about Mont Blanc, which had to be plagiaristic

---

[1] *Notebooks*, i: *1794–1804 Text*, ed. Coburn, entry 1218.

since he had never been there; he sent Sotheby a text of the poem next month, with a note, admits Fruman, which 'refers to having had Scafell "in my thoughts" '. It quotes a line of poetry, 'O blacker than the darkness all the night', which proves that he had written some poetry about Scafell before the disastrous switch to Mont Blanc. Here Fruman must have known that he was juggling with the evidence, as his thesis requires.

His attack on an edition of Coleridge's poetry by David Pirie and myself is irrelevant, but I am willing to answer. Two verses at the start of the poem, where the Mariner tries to hold the Wedding Guest, were reduced to one in 1800, and the Guest is now sternly determined to carry out his social duty, so that an act of magic seems needed to hold him. He had better be feeling jolly, and willing to take the Mariner to the party. Perhaps it was Wordsworth who felt that more dignity was required. Wordsworth wrote a disgraceful introductory note to the poem in this edition of the *Lyrical Ballads*, and had intended to throw out the whole thing: so he is likely to have demanded changes. Some of the changes get rid of the comic Old English, but others remove valuable details in the story which had been complained of as meaningless. The example that Fruman singles out for praise actually drags in a new bit of comic Old English:

Eftsoons his hand dropt he.

This is not easy to explain, but maybe Coleridge started on the work of revision while still bemused after a tongue-lashing from Wordsworth. As to the 'meaningless marvels', this phrase was invented by Southey in a review, provoked by a detail which the author would readily have explained to him; cutting down the marvels to the average Philistine capacity only made nonsense of the story. It is all marvels after it has got going, so if Fruman were allowed to satisfy himself there would be almost nothing left except the delicious line: 'Eftsoons his hand dropt he.' Gadzooks how flat he fell. Surely it is plain that you can make no estimate of the man's poetry without a grasp of the ideas his mind was working upon.

May I recall that Fruman has not defended his assertions about the two honeymoon poems, the 'Eolian Harp' and the other. On his account, Coleridge could not have written them before he had Wordsworth to imitate, but he did. Fruman in his book excused this by saying that they do not present Nature as making us better, but they plainly do.

William Empson

TO THE *TLS* (UNPUBLISHED): 'Coleridge'

(n.d.: 1977)

Sir,

I hope I am right in detecting an air of finality in the last letter of Fruman, as there does not seem much more to be learned. But I ask leave to explain one or two points.

In his book, speaking of *The Eolian Harp* (p. 301), he said 'This passage has far less to do with moral meanings in nature than with the persistent deistic heresy into which Pope stumbled [. . .]'; and I found it absurd to think of Coleridge imitating Pope. Fruman denies that he meant this, and upbraids me for not answering his rebuttal. But if he did not mean it there is nothing to answer. The poem does say that Nature makes us better, and it is too early to be imitating Wordsworth; so Coleridge has not been proved to be a copy-cat here. Fruman now says that he answered this objection, which is crucial to his thesis, somewhere in the book; but surely he could repeat the gist of it, if he had anything. In the poem, Coleridge says that Nature as found in his retirement makes it seem impossible not to love all things, and this must be an encouragement to obey the precepts of Jesus.

Southey in his review of *Lyrical Ballads* quoted about twenty lines from the 'Mariner' as an example of nonsense; they describe the entry on board of the Spirits of the Air, in a great wind which 'dropped down like a stone'. As Southey believed that a wind could not descend vertically, Coleridge spoilt the passage in 1800; he altered all the passages which had been objected to in reviews. But he wrote to Tom Wedgwood in 1803 (letter 513), without any mention of the poem, of the immense exhilaration he always felt in the Lakes on meeting such a wind. A mountain lake, in some state of temperature difference, gets air descending vertically upon it and then pressing out sideways among the hills, turbulently (see NED воттом 19). Coleridge cannot have wanted to spoil this obviously relevant line, and I submit would only have done it to satisfy Wordsworth. I am sorry I did not make this point in an adequate way before; it seemed to take too much space.

Maybe Fruman was self-indulgently deceiving himself, and not plotting against his reader, when he wrote that Coleridge 'found the path' down the cliff; what is unpleasant about it is his stubborn refusal to attend to the words of the letter. A sheep had died up there, and a pile of stones at the foot of the cliff gave evidence that a shepherd had tried to reach it but failed. A *path*, says the big Dictionary, is 'a way trodden or beaten by the feet of men or beasts'; the chimney was not a path when Coleridge discovered it. One of the things I have learned by this exchange of letters is that the now familiar object is called 'The Fat Man's Agony', and Coleridge, though in good condition at the time, was never slim. Why does Fruman believe him, at one point out of so many, when he boasts to Sara that (after wondering whether he might get stuck) he 'slipped down without any danger or difficulty'? Because Fruman will accept only what suits his purpose of belittlement.

H. W. Piper's book *The Active Universe* (I said) proved some time ago that Wordsworth and Coleridge had literally believed in Middle Spirits when they were young, but soon found that double-talk was necessary when expressing this belief in poetry. Fruman absurdly writes: 'I challenged that. No response'. What answer could he expect? His blanket expression of contempt merely proved yet again that he had failed to understand a book he was quoting. I grant that there is more excuse for him here than usual, because there seems to have been a general agreement to ignore the plain meaning of that important book.

The reason why 'O blacker than the darkness all the night' cannot have been written about Mont Blanc is that the very name of the mountain means it was considered to be perpetually snow-capped. Here as so often it seems uncharitable to believe that Fruman can really be as stupid as he claims. The reason for wanting Coleridge to begin by writing about Scafell is that it makes him an honest victim of his conflicts; if the wrong plan had occurred to him at once the whole affair seems worse. I agree with Wordsworth that the poem is a disastrous show of unconscious insincerity; apparently Fruman thinks it very good, especially the stolen parts (whereas the self-sacrificing Coleridge would regard these as particularly monstrous platitudes). Of course I do not 'justify STC's false claim to spontaneous composition of the poem', a poem about Mont Blanc ['Hymn Before Sun-Rise, In the Vale of Chamouni'] when he was frightened on Scafell; I think he said then more or less what he reported to Sara at the time, and also that, when he used inflated language later to Sotheby, he did not *mean any more* than what he had told Sara. It is extraordinary that Fruman cannot grasp this idea; I suppose it is because he regards anything an author says as a confession extracted from him in a police station.

My objection to the line 'Eftsoons his hand dropped he', placed where it is, lay in its monstrous pomposity, which appears to be just what Fruman praises it for. I did not feel a general contempt for Old English, inconsistent with allowing some bits of it back into our joint text of the 'Mariner'. I said in my introduction to the little book that Coleridge would have modernised these passages like the rest if he had not been driven to throw them out, so that perhaps an editor ought to carry out his wishes; but that, as these excellent bits are particularly intimate, they only feel as if the Mariner is dropping into his home dialect. (This was fortunate as Mr Pirie would not have allowed me to rewrite them.) I was startled to hear that what Fruman quotes was added in 1800, and invented a theatrical incident as an explanation. But it came in 1814, when Coleridge was crazy to appear orthodox and dignified, and made few changes not tainted by that purpose. Fancy believing it came in 1800 just because Fruman said so! I must have been dreaming.

Not to reply often seems like a confession of defeat, so may I say in advance that I do not intend to answer again, unless there is some accusation of unbearable absurdity.

William Empson

Houghton

§ END

TO I. A. RICHARDS*

1 Hampstead Hill Gardens, NW3
4 May 1977

My dear Richards,

Thank you for sending me your collection [*Complementarities*, 1976], which includes a lot of things I am glad to have. But I was disappointed by the title-essay; I feel sure that the lecture you gave at University College contained more than that, and I was hoping for a great deal more. You speak gruffly[1] in the introductory note of a reviewer who said the doctrine leaves no way to decide[2], but surely you need to give *examples* of how 'derivates from mutually exclusive setups may jointly contribute'—I am sure the idea is valuable, but the value is in the working-out.

I find I don't know the answer to this even in the basic example, of light being both waves and particles. As I understand, there are some experiments where it has to be regarded as particles, others where it has to be regarded as waves, and there is no further enlightenment, but no occasion to decide. And in simpler cases, such as velocity and probability, we cannot help thinking both of the bang when the thing hits us and the distance

---

[1] IAR circled this word and wrote the exclamation '!' in the margin.
[2] IAR wrote in the margin, against this word, simply: 'what?'

gone in a finite time, or the frequency of an inherent chance; but both may be present always. A specimen case of a right choice between one of two complementary modes, with another case of a right choice of the other one, is what we require; and I expect you could dictate it straight off. You would then find you had thought of some more of them.

Surely this is what you ought to be doing next; it seems rather a pity you have given the title to this collection, but the title will at least alert many readers to expect the fuller treatment.

I hope you are keeping in good trim. It is a comfort to reflect that when we next meet we will be glorified.[3]

Yours very sincerely

William Empson

Magdalene

TO MR WALTON [Orwell and the BBC]

1 Hampstead Hill Gardens, NW3

2 November 1977

Dear Mr Walton,

Your list of questions seemed aggressive and pedantic, and I expected you to twist round anything I said to mean the opposite. However I now see that there is reasonable ground for a question.

H. G. Wells called Orwell 'the Trotskyite with flat feet', a phrase partly meant to praise him as the only political young man who would speak out.[1] He was tactless partly from intellectual vigour but also partly because he had no grasp of what other people were worrying about. In propaganda for Asiatics one normally had to consider their touchy points a great deal. It was funny in that set-up for him to say 'The FACK that you're BLACK' meaning merely that he thought concern about the subject intellectually contemptible. It was more than funny to find them admiring him for it, and thinking that only a saint could talk so. Maybe only idealistic Indians would think it; but those were the ones he was inviting to broadcast. It seemed astonishing that he could find so many in wartime London, and argued a wide acquaintance among them, but I did not know about that.

---

[3] IAR and WE were to receive honorary degrees at Cambridge in June.

[1] 'Orwell . . . somewhat naïvely or primly never saw why public criticism, when it was not total rejection, should prevent social intercourse. Wells railed against the literary manners of this "Trotskyist with big feet"—a remark that delighted Eileen when it came to her patient ears. Hetta Empson heard about it too and protested that her feet were even bigger—measuring them up against George's at one of the once famous Saturday night "Come all ye's" that she and her husband gave in Hampstead' (Bernard Crick, *George Orwell: A Life*, rev. edn., 1982, 430–1).

A story was going round the Far Eastern Department of the BBC just then of an Indian in a London pub who demanded to have a Negro thrown out, because he could not mingle with the lower races. The indignant drinkers had thrown out the Indian and stood the Negro a pint. Indians are in a weak position to protest against racism; it was even usual to say that they had done the English a great deal of harm by teaching their caste system to us. So calling them black was a much bigger gaff[e] than it would have been with anyone else. Such was the point of my little story, and thinking it meant he was a secret racist would be wildly far astray.

I cannot tell you about his friends; he liked to keep them in separate compartments. My wife was always asking him to dinner with someone new, but I don't remember his wife ever doing that to us. Of course more people wanted to meet him. He seemed to have very little interest in character; he would not think 'this Indian is a typical Babu' or what not, but merely classify the man's opinions. I should say that he was extremely free from racial prejudice, almost to the point of blindness. His Number 2 in the Indian Section was a Moslem, and Orwell was struck down with horror shortly before the liberation of India to find that he had all along been a Pakistan supporter, in favour of separation. You understand, Orwell was passionate about the freeing of India, saying sometimes that if achieved it would be the most important result of the war. Only a man very wrapped up in his own theories could combine that with not realising what the Moslems were thinking, while meeting them all the time.

[William Empson]
Studio House, NW3

Houghton, bMS Eng 1401 (676)

TO JOHN WAIN

John Wain enquired why WE continued to give his translation of the Fire Sermon pride of place in *CP*? 'To keep this flag at the mast-head across twenty years must surely indicate something; but, no, we find Empson a year later [in his reply to Rodway (1956) on *CP* (1955)] casually washing his hands of it . . . So the Fire Sermon is important enough to Empson's poetry to put up in front, and given a new lease there after twenty years, while being "pretty remote, and not appealed to." Is this, one wonders, a procedure Empson would expect from the poets about whom he writes such brilliant criticism?' ('The Poetry of William Empson' (1977), 325–7).

[n.d.: 1977]

My dear Wain,

Thank you very much for your splendid praise of my work in *Professing Poetry* [1977]. I am the more comfortable with it because you don't positively disapprove of everything I am [have] written for a quarter-century (this usually comes as a jolt after I have begun to simper). I feel it is very discerning praise, so it is at least sympathetic; and the best I can do by way of thanks is to say where I think it is wrong.

About the Fire Sermon. I suppose I should not have put it at the front. The books contain several translations, made without knowing the language concerned but with fuss about accuracy, and nearly all good I think. There is no other recitable translation of this, and a reader of the *Waste Land* needs one. I feel I fail to get enough attention for it. However, I suppose I was guilty of religiosity a little, hinting perhaps 'We all feel that life is inadequate for us'. It wasn't till I had started teaching Eng. Lit. in England that I realised how much misreading of the older poetry is caused by pious otherworldliness, easily regarded as a historical duty. I did not believe the religion before, but I accepted the religiosity of Eng. Lit., so far as I could, till 1943 or so. Maybe the modern religion has been cured of doing great harm, but the bogus-historical misreading is still active, and that is directly my business.

You seem to believe that any expansive feeling about the world or about persons must be secretly Christian, so that Auden was burning Christians already in *Spain*. But a belief in a world-spirit is not belief in the Father who could be bought off torturing all mankind by the satisfaction of having his Son tortured to death.

The Ants was the first poem I thought worth keeping, and copies the assumption of Eliot that city life is very bad, not needing war to make it so. Large-scale disaster is expected but not of any specific kind. However it fits war very well. I forget the circumstances of writing it completely, and had done when writing the notes for the sleeve, so you may be right. It would be written during my first two years at Cambridge, but why I don't know. I expect the sexual situation was bad. Though I ought to have been thinking about war, you feel, you should protect me from being thought to have been leftist—which only a bad man would have resisted at that time. To say that the tree [in 'Note on Local Flora'] 'thirsts for the Red Dawn', as the rocks in St Paul or at least Vaughan yearn for the Second Coming, seems to me quite strong; Dinah Stock was within her rights in saying it 'takes a more direct notice of Leftist standpoints' and could surely have said 'not an unsympathetic one'. I never believed in the theory of I. A. R.

that modern poetry should be divested of all beliefs, though I grant of course that my method was indirect. It was not meant to be aggressively dead-pan.

When I said that one can't discuss whether a man believes in the Trinity, I gave the reason: that it is a set of verbal contradictions (in Athanasius at least), so that he can only inure his mind to accepting them. I have never accepted Cambridge philosophical scepticism, and think it is only tolerable inside philosophy, if at all. Surely in prose I am always expressing beliefs, too impulsively for that matter. That the practical test must be whether a religion makes people better I agree, and I agree that the Fire Sermon probably wouldn't. That it has a queer kind of merit all the same is a paradox often found in literature.

I hope you will believe this, and not find it tricky. The points at which I jib do not prevent you from giving the poetry all it deserves, I feel sure.

A great deal of the book was very interesting; the background of *Comus*, and even more of *Ossian*, and you succeeded in finding new quotations from Emily Dickinson. What a disgusting poem Edward Thomas wrote to his wife; I shall never forgive him for it. I suspect Waley had been read by Pound in forgotten poetry magazines.

Very many thanks

Houghton: carbon, bMS Eng 1401 (674)

PMLA, 93 (January 1978), 118: 'Milton's God'

I must ask leave to reaffirm the basic objection to the position of Joan S. Bennett in *God, Satan, and King Charles: Milton's Royal Portraits* (*PMLA*, 92 [1977], pp. 441–57), as otherwise the case may seem to go by default. No one denies that Milton in *Paradise Lost* wanted to be recognised as a Christian; what is maintained is that he found the case for Satan alarmingly strong and wished to present it fully, if only as a warning.

The rebel angels, she says, have a 'mistaken faith in sheer, undefined strength,' so, as God has not yet shown his strength, they wilfully suppose him to be an impostor. But their opinions are more specific. Probably they were created by an impersonal mysterious being (they appeared all together, knowing nothing of the past, but one of them, they now think, was quick enough to pretend he had created the others). They grant that a personal creator is conceivable, but such a being must satisfy the conditions of Aquinas, which include absolute omnipotence. (He must be built into the structure of the universe, as no creator can be.) Hence, when they have resisted the power of God for two days of battle, they claim to have proved him an impostor, who has no right to order them about. Defeat in battle is a trivial thing compared to this moral victory. Such is the whole point of the speeches of Satan in the first book.

They ought to have realised that he is the true God, says Bennett, because of 'the different quality of his strength.' They had 'a vision of divinity,' which removed all *their* strength, as soon as the Son appeared. But the text says that innumerable arrows, like eyes, did it—a paralysing ray, perhaps. There is no suggestion that it had any moral or spiritual effect on them. What we are told is that God deliberately let the good angels fail for two days so as to make them appreciate the unique power he has given to his Son, and also presumably to encourage the rebels in their delusion. When Satan first rises from the burning lake, the poem says, God releases him from his chains that he may 'heap on himself damnation'—and of course on mankind too. When the guard of angels capture Satan in Paradise, God forces them to release their prisoner so that Satan may continue with the temptation. Necessarily it was God's providence that put into Satan's mind the decisive argument for Eve—that God is not really testing her obedience but her courage and the earnestness of her desire for Heaven. And consider, we know that God could have prevented the revolt at the start by proving that he can create, because Satan actually is convinced when Uriel reports having seen God creating the world. The poem sets out to explain why the world is bursting with sin and misery, and the only reason it can find is that God is tirelessly spiteful. He therefore cannot be the metaphysical God of Aquinas, and the heroic rebels were right on the essential point.

As to the political argument, when God presents the Son to the assembled angels he says that any angel who disobeys the Son in any way will be thrown into utter darkness, without hope of redemption. Maybe God only says this to drive Satan into premature action, but it need hardly be called a lie when Satan tells his followers that the Son intends to issue new laws. Apart from the philosophical argument, the rebels feel it would be shameful to submit to God because he has such a bad character, and what we hear from the loyalist angels does little to offset their opinion.

W. Empson

9 October 1977

TO H. W. PIPER*

1 Hampstead Hill Gardens, NW3
5 March 1978

Dear Professor Piper,

Thank you for sending me an off-print of your essay on the Ancient Mariner [*Southern Review* 10: 3, Nov. 1977], which I read with interest though it came as a shock. I had assumed that, after proving that Coleridge when he wrote the poem believed in his spirits, you would use that to interpret the poem.[1] Now that you have come across my book, I hope you will write telling me where you find it wrong; it has received no attention.

The Coleridge of the Sibylline Books would be glad to have you say that he gradually discovered what had always been lurking [in] his mind about the poem; the objection to this view is that, when he wrote the poem, he would have considered it a malignant slander. And it is not enough to call him a silly child; all the Romantics thought the Atonement implied a wicked God. (It is hushed up except in the case of Blake, who has to be called mad instead). Surely, it becomes plain that something is wrong with your account when you say that the Life-in-Death winning the mariner's soul at dice is a mistake; it is a very central incident, and prepared for by the Bible-reference in the second line. Coleridge remarks in an early letter that one of his friends is particularly likeable, because 'he really *hates* God—with all his heart, with all his mind, with all his soul, with all his strength'. Coleridge himself does not have to join in, because he is searching for a philosophical God who has escaped from being a torture-monster, but any good man must feel earnest hatred for the God of the churches, and rather starve than accept bribes about it. He could not be a Unitarian pastor if it meant administering the sacrament: and surely this has to be recognised in an interpretation of the poem.

Such is my general position, but I am specially interested to know what

---

[1] WE was to write in a draft of an undated reference: 'Yes, I can strongly recommend Prof. H. W. Piper for a Visiting Fellowship. I reviewed his *Active Universe* for Critical Quarterly of Autumn '63, and hoped then he was my ally about the *Ancient Mariner*. (The later versions ruined the story by making *angels* of the spirits operating the corpses, with changes needed to make that just plausible; though also removing the destructive facetiousness of style, needed as a protection against ridicule in the first draft.) Piper understood very well the importance of the nature-spirits for the Renaissance view of the world, and the baffled urge of the Romantics to recover it; and he was talking about it very plainly.

'Last year he called me up, when in London for a few days [. . .]. But he now refuses to say that the young Coleridge had believed in nature-spirits *directly*, he had done it in a philosophical manner. He insisted that we had almost no difference of opinion; and it struck me that he really was merely keeping his nose clean. I could not blame him for his fear of ridicule, and do not expect it would be found any handicap in a Visiting Professor.' (*Houghton*)

you make of the spirits. Surely you agree that the author was lying when he called them angels, in 1815?

Yours with much respect,
William Empson

Houghton, bMS Eng 1401 (627)

H. W. Piper responded (letter postmarked 14 Mar. 1978) that he did not regard his article as so different from WE's views as WE seemed to imagine. 'Certainly I do not think for a moment that the spirits were angels in 1797 — they were nature spirits . . . What I am trying to suggest in the article is that the guilt and fear of damnation from which he was trying so hard to escape through Unitarianism crept subterraneously, so to speak, into the poem through the apocalyptic imagery, and that this accounts for the agony in the poem. What need of agony if God does not damn. I don't think he was conscious of it, but I think the fear that eventually drove him into what was poetically a very sterile orthodoxy, was already working up again . . .

'I admired your book. I thought it showed your knack for going into detail, but the big point for me was that Unitarianism was an escape from a wicked God. I had thought the motive political but I think you're right.'

TO H. W. PIPER

1 Hampstead Hill Gardens, London NW3
14 April 1978

Dear Professor Piper,

I was very pleased to get your letter, showing a willingness to reconsider the matter which seems to be unique among experts on Coleridge; but I could not agree that our views have no important difference. The Freudian Unconsciousness has become a great source of delusion in literary matters; the young Coleridge was very well aware, as he tells us in one of the Notes, that he was liable to fits of irrational fear or guilt—he merely refused to treat them as rational. The scenario for the *Wanderings of Cain*, which he was writing just before the *Mariner* (given in the Oxford text), labours to explain that neurotic guilt can cause great harm; and he really does seem to have behaved worse whenever he felt guilty. When he yielded to the nightmares caused by terror of Hell, and undertook to worship the evil God of Christianity, of course he felt intense guilt (off and on) about that too. But the ruined addict, always treating himself as an interesting moral invalid, cannot surely be considered a better judge of literature than the young man; he has become a parasite, corrupting what he wrote then.

One might argue that he came to think the Mariner really was guilty for shooting the Albatross; but we know that soon after the return from Malta, the last period when he made good additions to the poem, his journalism became positively in favour of cruelty to animals, calling them Things.

Consider the tremendous verse, allowed in the first edition only, about

> the bodies rose anew;
> With silent pace, each to his place,
> Came back the ghastly crew.

—a move which can only be countered by the immediate sinking of the entire ship. Surely these spirits are not working on the side of the Mariner; and what can be the point of the long parallelism before, except to adumbrate a conflict between two groups? Of course I agree that Coleridge was shy about appearing as a military author, and right in suspecting that Wordsworth would not even like spirits to be supporting the mistaken side. But there is a definite break here, almost certainly forced upon Coleridge (we know that WW was threatening to exclude the poem altogether). It cannot be sensible to say that he was gradually becoming holy enough to know what he had meant.

All the same, I am greatly encouraged by your letter.

Yours

William Empson.

Houghton, bMS Eng 1401 (627)

NEW YORK REVIEW OF BOOKS, 1 June 1978, 40: 'Milton's God'

Congratulations on your review of Christopher Hill's book on Milton, good anyway but also a welcome contrast to the disgraceful one in the London *TLS*.[1] I only get a mention in your piece, but ask leave to use the occasion to clear my position. The review says (March 23) that Hill:

> rejects Empson's claim in *Milton's God* that the poet felt an active hatred for the God of Christianity.

It would be fatuous of me to say that Milton *intended* to express any such hatred, when practically every homestead right across America was going to contain a copy of *Paradise Lost* as well as the King James *Bible*. If Empson says that, there is no need to open his book. Hill himself does express

---

[1] Christopher Hill, *Milton and the English Revolution* (1977). Professor Hill (1912–2004) was Master of Balliol College, Oxford, 1965–78.

some such disagreement but keeps using the word 'conscious', to qualify it, and that doesn't seem to me much help. The nearest I get to such a distinction in my own book (p. 111) is in saying that Milton's social judgement had told him that the Heaven he was imagining before the fall of the angels was already a horrible place, 'against his overall intention'; but clearly the question is a larger one than that.

The first thing we need to recognise, because modern Christianity goes to extreme lengths to hush it up, is that the moral character of God had become very hard to defend, and that this was widely known, by the time Calvin and Luther had followed Aquinas. Milton was struggling to defend God. He says in the *De Doctrina* that some unnamed opponents who believe God caused evil practically make God the Devil, and later he merely asserts that the relevant Bible texts must not be interpreted literally (my pages 206–7). The doctrine of Free Will needs to be restored, he says (p. 202), to quiet 'the outcry against divine justice'. My opponents think I present Milton as a rude man blaspheming before a pious audience; he thought of himself (wrongly perhaps) as trying to answer people who were denouncing God.

The chief new defence invented for God is that he intends to resign, and will do so as soon as he conscientiously can, as soon as a workable alternative to his rule has been prepared. God is at his worst when we first hear from him, early in Book III, but he is soon won over by the Son and speaks with magnificent generosity, then as on all later occasions, when he foresees his eventual abdication. But somehow, and Milton can hardly be expected to explain why (p. 145), the necessary political lay-out could only be attained through a long and painful training for both men and angels, with many casualties. Naturally God is bad when he acts as a dictator, because dictatorship is inherently bad, but he knows, as Cromwell had known, that he must labour to build a situation that makes democracy possible. No wonder the recitation of history is so dismal in the last two books.

This programme would only be confused by making God an attractive character (p. 275), but it does allow him to be quite free from sadism; he takes no interest in gloating over his Hell, and one cannot even remember that his rebel angels are supposed to be in continual agony. No wonder, I said, that the poets felt they must support the poem, through so many changes of taste (p. 269):

because it is so startlingly innocent compared to the religion it claims
to describe. Milton has cut out of Christianity both the torture-

horror and the sex-horror, and after that the monster seems almost decent.

Christopher Hill gives me welcome support for the idea that God is going to abdicate, saying that it is found in a number of Ranters and suchlike bold men. But they seem to have expected a kind of palace revolution, whereas Milton presents it as a plan which the Creator has been evolving since the start of time.

Such being what my book says, and I hope that I may be excused for giving page-references to prove that, it is not really an answer to say I 'claim' that Milton hated God. But I welcome Christopher Hill saying things rather near it, such as

> Empson is right to suggest that Milton was in some sense aware of the terrible collapse which is always possible . . .

if the widespread hatred of God could no longer be contained.

William Empson[2]

TO CHRISTOPHER RICKS

Studio House
30 June 1978

My dear Christopher,

Congratulations on your splendid piece in the TLS; the dismal old paper does not deserve it. It shows your powers of sympathy and understanding at their best; but I am glad you could admit that [Geoffrey] Hill sometimes feels artificial. I think it is lucky for him that the world is so dismal just now; he could not have made poetry out of anything else.[1]

---

[2] See also 'Final Reflections', in *MG* (1981), 335–6.

[1] Ricks's W. D. Thomas Memorial Lecture, given at the University College of Swansea, was published in the *TLS* on 30 Jun. 1978, 743; reprinted, as 'Geoffrey Hill 1: "The tongue's atrocities" ' in *The Force of Poetry* (1984), 285–318. The poems CR discusses include 'September Song', 'Ovid in the Third Reich', 'Two Formal Elegies', 'Summer Night', 'Doctor Faustus', and 'A Pastoral'. Apropos WE's remark that 'Hill sometimes feels artificial', CR finds fault with Hill in two passages. (i) Apropos 'Two Formal Elegies': 'As originally published, it had within brackets the dedication '(For the Jews of Europe)', and the second poem then ended with an extraordinary tour-de-force: of the last four lines, not only the first and the last were within brackets, but so too were the second and the third. The poem ended with four successive lines each within brackets. Hill was right to think that his is a poetic gift which must be profoundly and variously alive to what simple brackets can do. He had been wrong to think that he could command to favourable judgment a concatenation of four lines, each bracketed, without his poem's indurating itself into mannerism and self-attention, a sequence of self-containedness such as then seals the poem into self-congratulation. By removing the brackets from both the antepenultimate and

I am to see the doctor again next Monday, and hope then to be allowed to drink again (the abstinence is only demanded to suit the anti-biotic tablets). If I can't drink at all I find it very hard to get started at the typewriter.

Do let me know if you are available in London. I expect to come to Cambridge for the Poetry Festival. Or are you already in the US?

All good wishes. I wish the world was producing good enough poets for you to interpret.

William E.

TO CHRISTOPHER RICKS

Studio House
1 July 1978

Dear Christopher,

That is six cents a word you are offering me. A splendid thing; as high as I will ever go probably. But I have nothing to say on the subject so I can't accept.

I think [Robert] Burchfield was talking nonsense about the languages drifting apart. A lot of separate jargons and sublanguages in both countries, no doubt, but the same in both.

When I was young there were about a dozen people writing for journals who didn't need to sign their names; you knew who it was from the style after one or two sentences. Now I don't think there are any—you, when you are really engaged, but not most of the time. So the use of the language has got much deader and flatter, but that doesn't amount to a change in it. I should say that the inflexible machine of education is too good at preventing change.

Thanks however
William E.

the penultimate lines, he not only removed the oppression of paralysing self-consciousnesss, but also tautened the arc of the poem.' (ii) With regard to what he calls 'this sense of the privileged paradoxicality of brackets, in their relation to silence', CR notes: 'Sometimes, even in tragic poems by Hill, the impulse seems to me to harden into mere mannerism . . . I feel a disproportionate mannerism, for instance, throughout "A Prayer to the Sun" ' (292–3, 305).

TO ROMA GILL

Studio House
10 January 1979

My dear Roma,

I *am* sorry to hear you have been having such a beastly time. It is wonderful that you have got through it again; you must have terrific staying power. I do hope you will hang on till they find the cure; you deserve to.

I have done a draft for a short book on the Faust of Marlowe, which had better come out by itself, I feel now (with my 'restoration' of the original text). But it is still very bad. Some of the recent reviews of my work have wondered why I am always so *facetious*, making it impossible to take what I say seriously; this author is probably a tragic clown, they say, staving off lunacy. Perhaps it comes from imitating Bertrand Russell. It is so, whether lunatic or not, that I can't bear to print a thing till I can read it over without feeling bored; if it feels boring, that proves it is wrong. Often only the order is wrong (as you pointed out about Mary Marvell). A lot of details get cleaned up from having to re-write, but it would be better to think clearly first.

Very good wishes
William Empson

George Watson

TO CHRISTOPHER RICKS

29 January 1979

Dear Ricks,

Thank you for your congratulations [on WE's knighthood]. Very glad to hear of your daughter.

We are having a small boasting party after the dubbing, from 6.30 on the 7th Feb. It would be nice if you could come, but it seems a lot to ask. Hetta is making the list bigger and bigger. Mog is now in San Francisco, 'on his way back' from Peking, and telephones to say he is enjoying it; and is to go to Peking again in March, so he is not sacked anyway. He is expected on the 7th. Hetta has a broken arm in plaster and is rather piano. She had much better stop fighting.

Love
William

TO CHRISTOPHER NORRIS

Studio House, 1 Hampstead Hill Gardens, NW3
15 March 1979

My dear Norris,

Thank you very much for a most pleasant week-end [in Cardiff, where WE gave a lecture], and for making me revive an interest in one of my interests; please pass on thanks to your patient lady too.

Two encyclopaedias told me that money began in Lydia in 700 BC, invented by Croesus no doubt. I think this a bit of the folk-lore of Victorian classical studies, indeed you found an earlier date yourself. But it does seem late, 1500 BC perhaps.

My return railway fare was £8. 6s. I showed the man my Old Age Voucher, so I suppose that is a reduction. With taxis in London one can say £10.

I made a mistake answering questions, and didn't think of it till I was back in Hampstead. A man in the front row asked why students need learn old meanings for English words, and I said with undue solemnity that they couldn't be prevented. But we were talking about VANITY in *Ecclesiastes*, and the sense 'pride, wanting to be admired' was already being used in the fourteenth century (NED). It was certainly part of the word for the Tudor translators, and would be obvious when the Preacher talks about being a king, in the first two chapters. Of course the Latin derivation is also at work, giving the equation 'Pride is empty, giving no solid satisfaction'. But this can be picked up from the text. The excuse for altering the old text was that it uses an out-of-date meaning, but the important meaning here is the familiar one. I wish you would tell the chap that, if you see him.

With very good wishes
William Empson.

TO PAUL ALPERS*

1 Hampstead Hill Gardens, London NW3
30 March 1979

Dear Mr Alpers,

Thank you for sending me the article.[1] It is very friendly, but hardly rude enough to teach me a lesson. I am glad you read Hugh Kingsmill on Shakespeare; he is at least a healthy influence.[2]

About saying there was probably real bad temper behind the writing of *King Lear*[3]—I can see now that this looks wilfully flippant, and I wish I hadn't alienated readers as I apparently did. But it is quite a serious line of thought, already present in Kingsmill.[4] Believing you have been wronged is a mental disease, and the effects are often crippling. Shakespeare was not the hero of a Revenge Play but he was very likely to feel, as the Victorians often said, that he was not properly appreciated and worked under bad conditions. Falstaff and Hamlet had been immense successes, but the rest of the Great Tragic Period was not so well received (I think this is clear from the Shakespeare Allusion Book, or did when I looked at it long ago)—*King Lear* is a very explosive work and the author needed to feel like Lear that his generosity had been taken advantage of. But he made a

---

[1] In 'Empson on Pastoral', *New Literary History*, 10: 1 (Autumn 1978, 101–23), Alpers notes (102) WE's 'obliqueness in argument, his casualness about the unity of the book, and his wit, colloquial ease and abruptness'.

[2] 'The Shakespeare critics he [WE] most admires are Bradley and Hugh Kingsmill, the author of *The Return of William Shakespeare* (1929), in which Shakespeare returns to life and tells a worshipful young critic what really lies behind and goes on in the plays. This extraordinary, witty invention wonderfully clears the air; like much Shakespeare criticism of its epoch (Wilde, Shaw, Frank Harris), it makes you think of Shakespeare as "a man speaking to men." Empson writes very much in the spirit of Kingsmill, whom he frequently invokes in order to puncture the pomposity of academic criticism' (118–19).

[3] 'But even in one of Empson's finest exercises in this vein,' writes Alpers, 'his devastating critique of the moralism of Robert Heilman's *This Great Stage*, Shakespeare is brought rather too much down to earth' (119). *This Great Stage* (1948) was reviewed by WE in *Kenyon Review* II (Spring 1949), where WE notes that 'the weight of suggestion about fundamental horrors that Shakespeare probably did not want to make definite (why should he?) did not I think make the immediate point of the play as he and his first audiences saw it . . . Lear is trying to get love and influence by a false renunciation; he is not holy enough for heaven and not practical enough for earth, so he falls between two stools. Naturally he thinks that nothing fits and the foundations of the world are all wrong. I do not say that this is what Shakespeare ultimately meant—no doubt that play released a lot of real bad temper in him—but that is how the thing could seem sensible to producers and actors at the time' (*SSS*, 54–5).

[4] See Kingsmill, *The Return of William Shakespeare* (1929), in *The Dawn's Delay* (1948), 295, 297: 'When Lear is separated both from the fool and Edgar, he abandons himself utterly to his ravings against the two enemies of the love he had struggled towards, lust, in which life is rooted, and hypocrisy, with which power veils its own filth in the interests of its security . . . After *Lear*, he was for a time worn out, and fell into the ill thoughts of Gloucester . . . For many reasons, I believe that Shakespeare pictured his own state when he wrote of Timon'.

splendid recovery, with no break in the yearly production of a masterpiece, so far as one can work out—the unfinished *Timon* and (also in 1607) *Coriolanus* are both therapeutic works, jeering at himself for imagining himself wronged, and in *Antony* he has begun preparing his soul for death.

Come now, surely that is unctuous enough.

With thanks and good wishes

William Empson

Christopher Norris

TO I. A. RICHARDS

1 Hampstead Hill Gardens NW3
25 April 1979

My dear Richards,

I am extremely pleased to hear you are going back to Peking, and that they have recovered their interest in English-teaching. It will be a grand scoop if you win all back after 42 years.

Earnest good wishes

William Empson

Magdalene

TO CHRISTOPHER RICKS

Studio House
25 April 1979

My dear Ricks,

Thank you for your kind words about my piece on Marvell [see *UB*, 3–27]. For once I am a jump ahead; I am praising yours in print, in a review of the York collection for the Cambridge magazine.[1] I thought you and [John] Carey were both very good, but you are in funny company, foreign Vandals and no mistake. However, the volume leaves stodgy old Hull at the post, I'm afraid.

I. A. Richards goes off to Peking, on the first of May, to establish Basic English there after all. It will be a splendid last-minute scoop if he brings it off. Perhaps you might telephone him with congratulations?

Yours

William Empson.

---

[1] 'The Love of Definition', in *A*, 264–72.

TO DAVID PIRIE

12 August 1979

Dear Pirie,

Thank you for sending me your Shakespeare piece. I enclose an old review, the last bit of writing I have printed on the subject; please let me have it back, but there is no hurry. I don't think you owe me any acknowledgement. I did say that the same property map would be used for *Lear* and *I Hen IV*, but in a long essay about staging which has remained unpublished; part of an eventual book I hope.

I am sure you are right to say they would be serious about politics in the first audiences, but they may have known more than you allowed for. To have several regional kings in England was not unknown in Lear's time, as they would know from Holinshed; one gathers from the play that there were no towns and no roads, so that government could not be much centralised. And men beyond eighty are usually encouraged to retire, in business for instance; they become a nuisance, as Lear has plainly become. Nobody tells them that they are neglecting their responsibilities when they consent to retire. Nobody told the Emperor Charles V that, either; if anything they said, rather absurdly, that it was very spiritual of him. It would be considered simply a misfortune for Lear that he had three daughters and no son; to prepare for his eventual death, and a very possible interlude of feeble-mindedness beforehand, was definitely a responsible thing to do. We all agree that it was not done well, but you do not suggest anything he had better have done, and I do not know that anyone else has.

There is one great bit of misteaching in modern Eng. Lit.; they are all taught a craving to scold. It would not be smart not to have one. You set out to praise 'the *ubiquitous* Edgar', who has not lost his sense of responsibility, and ends up as king; but it is obvious that this word means to jeer at somebody—if not Edgar, then his author. But Edgar does not arrange to be on the spot; he is simply put on the spot. He cannot refuse to help his blinded father, who still intends to kill him wherever he is found; and his father demands to be led to Cordelia in Dover. He then digs up a decisive betraying letter, which happens to be buried in sand nearby; but this is so unlikely that it asks to be regarded as a miracle. The only thing Edgar does of his own accord, until he fights the duel, is torment his father into repentance. I think that John Danby, who was usually too pious for my taste, said the right thing here: Shakespeare had repeatedly tried to imagine a good Machiavel, who could beat the politicians on their own ground; but in this play he admitted with despair that you couldn't have a good Machiavel—such a man could only arrange to keep alive and wait for the occasional divine help.

I marked some other points but none seem important. You say that Gloucester's 'exposing of Lear to the heath is equivocal'; it does not give you a direct licence to scold. Lear insists upon leaving his castle, and he returns from seeing him out saying 'The King is in high rage'. He does not consider himself exalted enough to stop the King from going out, nor even to disobey Cornwall, whom the King has made his overlord. When he does realise that the King is in serious need, he acts firmly. It is not equivocal at all, though of course he is a rather trivial man until he rises to this occasion. What is very odd or bad is that the King has no horse, let alone his private army of horsemen; the author should have given some excuse there, and perhaps once did.

'If you have poison for me I will drink it' is extremely unlike the way we usually talk to one another; it is arresting. You seem unable to feel that. The guilt-ridden Lear, you say, 'wrongly thinks that love from someone who is morally flawed cannot impress'. I do not see how this applies at all, but anyhow it feels shockingly mean-minded.

Edmund really did admire both sisters, and might easily have gained a throne by marrying one of them. He just got caught out. I do not see how you can imagine that you would have calculated better.

I will read your Wordsworth essay when I have time. I feel ashamed you had such a dull weekend.

TO JOHN HAFFENDEN

Studio House
11 October 1979

Dear Mr Haffenden,

I am afraid I can't be much use.[1] I liked Hayward and thought his judgement good. Anybody would have to admire the courage with which he carried on a lively social life in spite of his disease. But he was not a man who made jokes or epigrams; he had clear-cut opinions about matters of current literary discussion. His set-pieces to entertain a company were descriptions of some complicated social crisis at which he had been present; or he could make a good deal out of a visit to the ruins of the mansion of a millionaire. He was extremely loyal to Eliot, both before and

---

[1] JH had thought to write a critical biography of John Hayward (1905–65).

after the separation; he ascribed the suddenness of the blow to the extreme and comical embarrassment of Eliot at having to say anything about such a matter. I remember, when Eliot threatened to sue John Peter and E. in C. unless they withdrew any suggestion of homosexual love in *The Waste Land*,[2] Hayward rather laboured the point that poor old Tom, like any other business man, was the slave of his lawyer, and of course would not have behaved like that of his own accord. I did not much believe this at the time, and even less when I knew Eliot slightly better. But perhaps one need not regard it as a self-sacrificing bit of loyalty; to make Tom slightly funny was the most rewarding use that could be made of him in conversation. Conversation was of course a main part of Hayward's life, and he spoke with a perfection which was slightly thrilling to hear when you realised that he could not move his lips.

I did get a few brief notes from him, mostly invitations, but have not kept any. As to how I met him, he was then President of the Heretics Society, and I became (as a guess) the next President but one or two. Or was it Secretary? He could then just walk.

Elaine is a girl he was in love with. 'Quoniam tu es, mea luxe, magnus dismissa periculo' is a dedication after she had been ill.[3] It could not go on for ever; she married someone else.

Good luck.

William Empson.

TO ISAIAH BERLIN*

[n.d.: late 1979]

Dear Isaiah Berlin,

I am in a difficulty, and write to ask your advice. It may settle itself fairly soon, but more probably not, and I had better inquire beforehand.

I have been trying to make sense of the *Faust* of Marlowe, and it struck me that the extraordinary confusion of the text was likely to be a result of censorship. The clerical censorship which applied to books did not usually apply to plays, but in 1589 it did get a committee set up, ousting the Queen's man Tilney, who rather oddly survived it. This just suits the earlier possible date for Marlowe's play. (There is another strong case for crucial cuts in *The Spanish Tragedy*, and I hoped they would make one book,

---

[2] See John Peter, 'A New Interpretation of *The Waste Land* (1952)', *E in C* 19: 2 (1969), 140–75.
[3] 'Tu quoniam es, mea luxe, magno dismissa periclo'—from the poem 'Cynthia's Sickness' by Sextus Propertius (*Elegies* bk. ɪɪ), l. 25—is John Hayward's dedication to Elaine Binney in his anthology *Nineteenth Century Poetry* (Phoenix Library, 1932).

but it has become too long.) For this purpose one needs to know what is in the German Faust-book of 1587, and how much the English censor had altered the translation of it, from which Marlowe worked. It turned out that there has been no scholarly version, or indeed anything that could be called a translation, since the sixteenth century. I don't know German, and was very fortunate to find a man with the knowledge, skill and conscientiousness required to do one. The translation is complete, and so my own needs have been fully served; but he needs to get it published, and he needs a grant giving him leisure (as he has to earn his living) to mull over the original manuscripts and the expert German opinions, and in short to write his Preface. I have promised a Postscript on the English contemporary reactions to the Faust-book, which will need to be drastically shortened from my projected book on the subject, but will at least show that a translation was needed. I submit that the subject is sure to pay its way.

My colleagues in Eng. Lit. seem to have gone on pretending they could read the original for many years, whereas they couldn't. Two major surprises turn up. Faust does not go to bed with human women, as in the English version, but only with spirits who precisely imitate the women he has desired, a Queen seen in procession for example; but this can hardly apply to Helen of Troy, a demi-goddess (being a daughter of Jupiter) who bears him a son.[1] This is a heavy blow against the current theory that she was the first devil he had ever got to bed with, and that was his unforgivable sin. More important perhaps, Mephastophilus (as Marlowe spells him) has never been to Hell, but lives in the storm-clouds, and is pretty certainly a Middle Spirit, but might be one of the pacifist angels who took neither side in the War in Heaven ('non ragionem di lor')[2]; Faust is quite right to tell him not to talk nonsense when he claims to be suffering the pains of Hell even as he speaks.[3] The character of the English translator

---

[1] See also *FC*, 115–18.

[2] Dante has Virgil say of the pacifist angels, *non ragionam di lor, ma guarda e passa*: 'Let us not speak of these, but look and pass': *Inferno*, III. i. 51, trans. by Dorothy L. Sayers (1949). WE stresses, in *FC*, 88–9: 'They are very numerous ("I had not thought death had undone so many"), and may well be camping in the storm clouds, thinking they deserve forgiveness, though presumably they must wait till Judgement Day. However, there is no mention of this legend in the GFB . . . To be sure, Meph only once lets drop that "we spirits" can hope, but it comes at an important point, during his grand description of Hell. And he may be lying but if so why not follow up his lie, and make it plausible? . . . [T]here was a recent account of devils not living in Hell, without reference to this legend, which had excited resistance. Aquinas had spoken calmly about devils living in the storm clouds, but he appears to assume that they have been sent on particular missions from Hell, and will return there; whereas these recent ones are afraid of being sent to Hell.'

[3] See *FC*, 85 ff. John Henry Jones would later write in a draft letter to Richard Dutton: 'I have always felt that Empson's notion of Mephostophiles as a double-dealing Middle Spirit was

comes out plainly enough for us to feel sure that he would not have made these changes unless the English censor had demanded them. He is not likely to have kept his mouth shut either, and the play can often be found making jokes about these demands. It strikes me that most university Eng. Lit. Departments will find they need this translation.

My friend J. H. Jones has been rather a rolling stone, and I understand was researching at Heidelberg university on an area of inorganic chemistry which was almost entirely a German field, before he decided to become a writer. He is fully qualified for the work in knowledge of German and grasp of the philosophical problems concerned, also in his firm pursuit of the manuscript variants. There was a set-back when a draft of his first Part was offered to a university press and two Readers [one of them being Roma Gill] answered furiously that the style was vulgar. Well, as I understand, it really is as vulgar as the style of Luther himself, though also with passages of exaltation; that is one of the things a reader of a translation needs to realise. Dr Jones was quite ready to do it more moderately, and I hope he has not swung back too far, but anyhow the revision has been making the translation feel solid, and is now almost complete. But he plans also to revise the annotation and discussion.

At present the book has been provisionally accepted by the Athlone Press, the press of London University, on condition that they receive a grant from elsewhere. Dr Jones can get a grant (from someone else) if he has a firm acceptance. The Goethe Institute branch in London seems in favour but has to refer the decision to Bonn, and for a long time the Athlone has not heard from Bonn. It seems to me urgent that Jones should be enabled to get on with the work somehow.

One might expect that this was just what you had in view when you kindly urged me to join the British Academy committee on such grants, but I found on the occasion when I attended one that nobody was getting a

wrong-headed, largely because it trivialises the play; equally, it appeared to me highly improbable that the play could have intended to hint at Faustus escaping damnation. From the moment the pact is made, the drama consists in the tragic revelation of the inescapable consequence of Faustus's deed; it is the absolute mercilessness confronting the pitiful Faustus which ensures its intensity and its horrific impact.

'Why, then, did I edit a work [*FC*] so opposed to my view of the play, and promote its publication?—because I felt it was my duty to Empson, who had fully intended to publish his work (albeit doubtless after further revision). I am sorry that it should be regarded as any kind of "monument"—better to see it as a further late example of Empson at his most entertaining, without which our view of Empson is incomplete (the theme engaged him on-and-off for some fifteen years, so it cannot be regarded as a minor aspect of his thought). Sooner or later, someone would have edited his Faustus-papers for publication, and I seemed best fitted for the task, owing to my close association with him and with the background material. I do not believe I did him a disservice. Like it or not, he has become part of literary history and the more of his writing we know, the better.'

grant without very careful vetting, to such effect that he was always already receiving a salary for that kind of work, or at least had been for many years. I felt certain that Dr Jones was doing the work much better than any-one the committee would have appointed, but it seemed plainly hopeless for a newcomer to propose something totally at variance with its practice.

Perhaps you can suggest an American press which would be willing? I know they are having their own troubles. The Faust-book is quite short, about 60,000 words I think, but the edition needs quite a lot of extras to give it its scholarly due. After it is accepted, a text with fewer extras for students is the one which will bring in a regular turn-over for the publisher.

Yours with thanks

W. Empson

Houghton: carbon, bMS Eng 1401 (511)

TO RICHARD LUCKETT*

Studio House
4 January 1980

Dear Mr Luckett,

Sorry to be slow in answering.[1] I am bad at this kind of thing and thought I had best refuse, but one plan does seem possible. I could read the Hopkins sonnet *Earnest Earthless Equal* Etc., which would come as a refreshing contrast. When the book came out [*The Poems of Gerard Manley Hopkins* (1918, 1930)], with a rather dubious sponsoring by Bridges, Richards praised it heartily at once, with special attention to this sonnet. In those days he was a very pioneering literary critic, picking out the good things even when he might seem out of sympathy with them. It was one of the earliest bits of his criticism I read. Something to the effect should be said, and then the recital, and nothing after it.

Do you think this would do?

Yours

William Empson

---

[1] Richard Luckett had invited WE to speak at the memorial service for IAR in the Senate House on 2 Feb. 1980. WE's presentation was largely inaudible, and certain people came away with the impression that he had said something disobliging about IAR; and so WE would seek to explain to Dorothy Richards (5 Mar. 1980): 'I said that Richards' article on Hopkins had been my first introduction to his writing, and to Hopkins, and that in the twenties, when much good and novel work was coming out, he did valuable work in picking out the best ones. And he did it in a very large-minded way; one would not expect him to admire Hopkins, anyhow at that stage of his life.' (*Magdalene*)

TO CHRISTOPHER RICKS

Studio House
23 February [? March] 1980

My dear Ricks,

I have just got a welcome but rather surprising letter from the Cambridge University Press, saying that they are going to do a paper-back of *Milton's God*, and asking merely whether I approve of their blurb. The blurb describes it as a corrected edition but assumes I cannot want to make any further corrections after those of 1965.

Of course this won't do. The appendix needs re-writing, as you rightly pointed out at the time, but this I have largely done. There have also been a lot of rebuttals, most of which I have not seen. And here I do need to ask for help; you are so very well-informed that you can probably tell me at once, but if not please put me on to some Milton expert. I just want to know which books or articles are considered to have refuted me most completely, so that I can write brief answers to them. Not to pay that much attention would mean letting the case go by default.

I was lecturing in Oxford the other day and at question-time a child asked whether I minded having *Milton's God* refuted. I begged him to tell me who had refuted it, and he asked why I wanted to know. I explained that I wanted to answer them in the next edition; but I had no idea it was looming up. Do try to help quickly. On the other hand, it may be that there just isn't anything really worth answering. And yet, if everybody thinks it has been refuted, I ought at least to answer that. Sorry to be a nuisance but you are so tireless I expect you to take it in your stride.

I have just read Kermode's lecture on I A Richards, in the N. Y. and London review. It is extremely good, I think, going to the essentials and never putting a foot wrong. Please tell him I said so; I don't seem to know his college. (I didn't come to his lecture merely because I can't bear them).[1]

All the best

William Empson

The Only-Begotten Lady hasn't written to me, nor I to her; it seems

---

[1] See Frank Kermode, 'Educating the planet', *London Review of Books* 2: 5 (20 Mar. 1980), 1–4. Kermode recalled in a letter to JH (21 Feb. 1990): 'He came to the I. A. Richards Memorial thing, lunched at Magdalene but didn't feel up to the big affair that followed in the Senate House, where I gave an address. He read the address in *LRB* and wrote a word of congratulation, but not to me. Instead he wrote to Ricks, asking him to pass the message on and claiming not to know my college.'

useless by this time to try to change her mind.[2] But your appointing me to the lecture has shown me how un-made-up my mind is there. Of course I am sure there was a real woman involved (and a tendency of the [Emilia] Lanier to Women's Lib would be what made her so interesting and exasperating) but the other Sonnets needn't be all to the Earl. Wilson Knight said one often repeated, in a milder version in later life, a relationship which had formed a habit. But then, how did the papers get put together and in his mother's house? How unlikely we are to know.

WE

'That you were once unkind' was probably addressed to a fellow-actor, as Oscar Wilde said.[3] SYNCRETISM, I fear.

TO CHRISTOPHER RICKS

Studio House
22 June 1980

My dear Christopher,

Very glad to hear you are having another baby.[1] Give my respects to the son [David] who was doing classics, and told me how to pronounce NAUSICAA (but I forget how to).

I hope you are coming to London on 3 July to vote for Antony [*sic*] Blunt.[2] With Helen Gardner seconding for him there should be quite a

---

[2] S. C. Campbell, author of *Only Begotten Sonnets: A Reconstruction of Shakespeare's Sonnet Sequence* (1978 [1979]).

[3] Shakespeare's Sonnet no. 120, 'That you were once unkind befriends me now.'

[1] James Ricks was to be born on 1 Aug. 1980.

[2] Anthony Blunt (1907–83) was educated at Trinity College, Cambridge, where he took part 1 of the mathematical tripos before completing his degree in French and German. During the 1930s he gained a world-wide reputation as an art historian, and he would crown his career as Director of the Courtauld Institute of Art and Professor of the History of Art in the University of London, 1947–74. From 1947 he was also occupied as Surveyor of the King's (after 1952 the Queen's) Pictures, an appointment which he retained until 1972. He was knighted in 1952. Also during the 1930s, however, he had been recruited, through his friend Guy Burgess, as an agent of Russian intelligence, and throughout the Second World War, while he was working for MI5 in London, he was passing British secrets to the KGB. In the event, he was publicly unmasked on 15 Nov. 1979 by the Prime Minister, Margaret Thatcher—though it turned out that MI5 had known of his treachery since 1964 (when he had been granted immunity from prosecution in return for a confession). Following Thatcher's announcement in the House of Commons, Blunt was stripped of his knighthood; likewise, his honorary fellowship at Trinity College, Cambridge, was rescinded. At the British Academy, an unpleasant split was in the offing when the Fellows divided in their judgements; a vote at the annual general meeting was narrowly avoided, but Blunt anyway tendered his resignation. Mainly because he felt an inveterate sympathy for the poacher over the gamekeeper, WE was in favour of Blunt being allowed to retain his fellowship; equally, he felt that Thatcher's decision to name Blunt was a matter of political expediency rather than principle.

chance of keeping him in the beastly club. I am trying to polish a brief question from the floor asking 'when did Churchill start telling him what to say?'—but I am afraid most of them would not realise how plausible that is.

I was wondering whether to write to the TLS against that horrid lady who claimed me as a half-supporter, in the belief that Southampton was the Dark Lady.[3] It is shocking nonsense and ought not to be on any university-recommended list. I thought at first she considered the Earl to become a temptress (a 'vamp') when the Earl turned into a girl, but I see she interprets 'although thou steal thee all my poverty'[4] to mean the *Earl* was the Bard's poverty; not much, but at least usable, whereas the Bard had no use for a girl. Dragging in the sonnet ending 'Bear thine eyes straight though thy proud heart go wide'[5] (which would *only* be said to a woman) into a grand sequence written to the Earl, is enough to destroy her claims to give a good *order*.

Affectionately

William E.

It is more likely that Mr Darcy was liable to turn at night into the Rev. William Collins. They at least never appear together.

[*On envelope*] My piece about Milton is getting a bit better.[6] I can bear to read it over now.

---

[3] S. C. Campbell's *Only Begotten Sonnets: A Reconstruction of Shakespeare's Sonnet Sequence* (1978 [1979]), which integrates the Dark Lady sonnets into an earlier position in the sequence and discerns a single tenor throughout and a single addressee, argues that the Dark Lady was no lady but a disguise for the friend; she was really the Friend's female shadow-self. '[T]he poet's anger is really felt against a worst self who has supplanted a best self, a whore who has supplanted a friend within the same personality . . .' Campbell's study, and its companion volume, *Shakespeare's Sonnets, edited as a continuous sequence* (1978), were reviewed in the *TLS* (9 May 1980, 518) by Katherine Duncan-Jones: 'Despite S. C. Campbell's assertion that for many readers "the 1609 Quarto order . . . can be no better and no worse than any other", the 1609 order may well reflect Shakespeare's manuscript closely. No-one would seriously suggest changing the order of scenes in Volpone [published by Thomas Thorpe, who may have mangled Shakespeare's sonnet order] and I do not believe we have very much more warrant for rearranging Shakespeare's Sonnets.' S. C. Campbell revealed (*TLS*, 23 May 1980, 584): 'Sir William Empson has called my marginal re-ordering "very sensible" (he does not like my interpretation of it, but I readily agree that that is more subjective than the text itself).'

[4] Sonnet 40, l. 10.

[5] Sonnet 140, l. 14.

[6] 'Final Reflections', for the paperback edition of *MG* (Cambridge, 1981), 319–40.

TO GRAHAM HOUGH

1 Hampstead Hill Gardens, NW3
[n.d.: June 1980]

My dear Hough,[1]

I have been mulling over my Final Reflections on *Milton's God*, and feel I know of enough opponents to be representative, but am puzzled about the Milton section of your excellent essay 'An Eighth Ambiguity' [in Gill, 76–97]. You say that 'syncretism' was a settled practice, and led Milton in *Paradise Lost* to make classical comparisons and literary 'references', thus making the tone lighter and more humane; but no further explanation is required—he did not mean anything by it. I expect they all meant something by it, and I am sure Milton would; he does not accept conventions passively.

For example, you say that the manly exercises of the fallen angels in Hell lighten the tone very much, by recalling their source in Homer, and Milton intends this in that to bring in 'the whole variegated tapestry of pagan mythology is a necessary part of his plan'; but it comes 'where it is least convenient to the general design', making the society in Hell seem much better than that in Heaven. This effect was 'certainly unintended'.

Why [then] does Milton give [sheet torn] and at every opportunity? Because God thinks the good angels not nearly good enough, so that to secure the eventual good society he will have to put mankind through an extremely severe training and add the survivors to the brew, however cross it makes the good angels. So much for the story, but politically Milton wanted to offset the harm done by the Calvinists and soften Hell as much as he could without heresy. The characters in the Paradise of Fools are also having a remarkably mild kind of Hell, and I do not think this is syncretistic, however medieval.

What I have seen about early-Renaissance syncretism amounts to finding morals in myths, often silly ones. Was a principle about it ever formulated? Of course it might have to be kept secret, but then it could hardly affect Milton. One would expect Bentley to have heard of it, though with disapproval. But he seems to find Milton's treatment bleakly eccentric: 'Was the man bewitched?'

---

[1] In one of his notebooks, WE jotted: 'Hough said that the effect of disapproving Christianity would be to make one unable to appreciate Eng. Lit.—a drive at my professional competence. I don't think this usually true, but it does seem true about Herbert's *Sacrifice*. I now feel that he [Herbert] was an ass if he was ignorant of the ambiguities of the poem, and at best perverse if he wasn't. He ought not to have put up with such a disgusting doctrine—to this extent I agree with my opponents of a third of a century ago. Can one get further evidence from the manuscripts that he screwed up the ambiguity in later drafts? But what use would it be anyway?'

I wish I had asked this before. A treatise on the matter by return of post can hardly be expected, but perhaps you can tell me of a book I ought to have read.

Hope you are going on all right. I will be coming up for a College feast on 22 July, and would be glad if we can meet.

[William Empson]

Houghton: carbon, bMS Eng 1401 (581)

Professor Graham Hough replied on 19 June 1980: 'I think you underestimate the capacity of people for having it both ways. Theologically Milton is stuck with the conflict between absolute good and absolute evil. But his literary allegiance is to the world of classical epic—a conflict between two sets of honourable opponents, neither side enjoying the favour of *all* the gods. The theological viewpoint comes out in the main design, the literary in the detail. Surely this sort of thing is always happening. You begin with a firm overall purpose, which I would call the intention. But there are lots of interesting and attractive details that you want to get in as well, so you keep putting them in, without acknowledging or really noticing that they contradict the main design . . .'

See also WE's 'Final Reflections' in *MG* (1981), 336–7.

TO MR MONTAGUE

1 Hampstead Hill Gardens, London, N. W. 3.
26 October 1980

Dear Mr Montague,

Your script has just turned up again, and I hasten to answer it before it sinks into the sea of paper; I am trying to finish a book, and there is always much confusion.

Of course I am glad to be discussed, and in such a friendly way; I have no complaints really. But the method of making a large number of short quotations does strike me as actively misleading; you need to consider how they are connected up.

p. 2. I was described as Chinese Editor in the BBC; there was no propaganda department; we were all propagandists.

p. 3 You are lying when you praise my 'profound sense of inherited respect for Christianity' because I say that reverence ought to be aroused by the thought of Darwinian evolution, and that the religious figures who attacked it showed a great lack of genuine religious feeling. I do you credit when I assume that it was not merely gross misreading; it was an

intentional kindly complacency. But if an omnipotent God made animals
torture one another for thousands of millions of years only to produce you
at last, that does not say much for his benevolence. The Christians fought
like mad against evolution and are still telling lies against it.

You say 'Christianity has an undeniable hold upon us', and that Empson admits it when he says he found simpering coyness about the sex of
Jesus positively blasphemous [*MG*, 107]. But many people have resented
blasphemy for thousands of years before the cheat that a dead Jesus had
been the Creator was foisted upon a small area of the world. Many people
have continued to have religious feelings without perverting sex in the lush
Christian way. It is a lie to presume that they cannot.

You say that I 'see the effect of official beliefs such as Christianity upon
society as part and parcel of artistic creation', because I say that the
paradox of the artist is opposite to the paradox of Christianity—the artist
needs to be selfish, express his personal reaction, in order to say what his
society wanted to have said; he is like a dress-designer. [See *MG*, 317.] Of
course I had no idea of denying that all of us ought to be unselfish
sometimes, and that it is preferable to live under a settled society. The
worship of the Christian torture-monster has now been made falsely
tolerable by a long tradition of devoted and high-minded men, most of
whom suffered for their work, but in itself it is the worship of the Devil.
You smear this filth over me with an air of complacent charity.

Of course this language seems to you hardly sane, but only because you
have been given a very special education. The Creator (this is the basic
tenet of the religion) found that all mankind, though his own work,
deserved eternal torture, but the killing of his Son by torture was so pleasing to him that he could be bought off for it; he would redeem mankind in
exchange for this pleasure. But afterwards he ratted on the deal, and only
let off a tiny remnant of mankind; upon the unimaginable tortures of all
the rest of us he will still gloat for all eternity. The ones who are insane, I
suggest, are all you people who simper and pretend to take no notice of
the fundamental doctrine; which thus continues to be as harmful, as anyone would expect.

p. 4. It was the pious critic [J. S. Diekhoff] I was attacking who said that
God became a trustworthy witness [*MG*, 22]. Maybe I presume too much
that the reader has enough intelligence to recognise an implied quotation,
but this was a very obvious one; I think you merely shuffled through for
bits useful as quotes. I do not understand why you think this example
led me to rely upon intentionalism; the story and the feelings in the poetry
and the author's known character, obviously, have all to be considered.

p. 5. Ricks of course was right to say that the beauty of an insight is not enough, because authors are often nasty-minded, but I had given a series of examples to show that the intentions of the authors were unlikely to be so nasty as those of your many-legged neo-Christian torture-worshippers. I do not 'twist to my own advantage' a theory expounded by another critic that Shelley and others believed a moment of ecstasy to be eternal, so that whatever happens next 'they escape death by it'; the words given just before, 'is claimed', show that I am merely reporting this theory.

You say 'the reader is not excluded' when I say that a reader of Marvell's *Garden* is assumed to follow the sentiments of the poet. What on earth else can a poet assume? You must be nosing round for some theological advantage. And then you praise me for my bold freedom:

> The opening 'And' of the second sentence, in a sudden ungrammatical surge, emphasises Empson's imminent and . . .

What an appalling education it must be; terrified to use the most elementary resources of the language, and vowed to support any lie in favour of the torture-monster.

p. 6. You praise me for 'a brave demystification of the unconscious', and I am sorry to answer crossly, but millions of people are living in great misery from mental disease, and how can you conceivably imagine that I took some theological action in their favour? I was only recalling that the most familiar part of the unconscious mind had always been relied upon to go like clockwork. To call me brave for saying this is stinkingly unreal; I have to impute some bad purpose.

Then you accuse me of choosing quotations to fit my argument, as if anyone could do otherwise; and accuse me of ignoring the story in Marvell's *Garden*. I have printed my account of the story (in the Hull Centenary)[1] and cannot see that you offer any different account, only a holy tone.

We reach a real difference when you express shock at my vicious brutality; I suggest that Dryden went Catholic, in his old age, because that made him feel safer from Hell. Of course he had other reasons, such as his tiresome Catholic wife and her two fanatic sons, and after backing the Stuarts so far he would be much jeered at if he recanted; but he hated and despised priests, as you would realise if you read his poetry, and he did of course look at his prospects of eternal torment in a simple calculating manner. You feel it is beneath my high-minded stance to look at the matter

---

[1] 'Natural Magic and Populism in Marvell's Poetry', in *Andrew Marvell: Essays on the tercentenary of his death*, ed. R. L. Brett (1979), 36–61; revised in *UB*, 3–27.

so coarsely, because you assume that nobody ever believed in these doctrines, but only fooled about with them like you do. But Charles II received the priest at last because he was determined not to be caught out after all. Dryden's attitude is very down-to-earth, and he is good at saying so in his poetry. I am not concerned to rescue work for authors' reputations but in finding their real sentiments, and I cannot see why you find this 'disturbing', unless your reason is a bad one.

I hope you will show this, with my best regards, to Ricks.

Best wishes

William Empson

Christopher Ricks: photocopy of original typescript

TO CHRISTOPHER RICKS

1 Hampstead Hill Gardens NW3
[n.d.: 1980]

My dear Ricks,

Glad to find you are fighting the good fight [against the proponents of doctrinaire critical theory]. I will root for Ricks if you reach the Sunday papers. Roma Gill tells me that just the same thing is happening in Sheffield; the children are being made to learn nonsensical theories instead of getting on with their reading. It struck me in America that students there had made a more specific analysis; anything that shortened the amount of reading, they were pro; even plays were better than novels. Obviously vapouring about structure takes practically no prep. at all. So I am afraid democracy will favour the new deal.

Hoping to see you some time.

William Empson

TO JIN FA-SHEN

Studio House, 1 Hampstead Hill Gardens, London NW3.
6 February 1981

My dear chap,

I am delighted to hear from you, and to learn that you are now going on all right. My son Mogador, whom you last met when he was a child, is leaving for China on business tomorrow and will carry the books you ask for. I am shocked to hear that you have not even seen my book [*MG*], in which I acknowledge my debt to you. A paper-back is being brought out, and the hard-back is out of print, so Mogador is bringing you a Xerox. I am ashamed that you will find only a written correction of a mis-spelling of your name, which was made (somehow) long before this letter from you arrived, and it must be included in the corrected paper-back; but I have not demanded the change because I could not trace you and make sure the new version was correct. So you write just in time.

I am sure you are right to come back to literature, in almost any form. The philosophers nowadays seem plainly unable to make any further progress, though most conscientious and cleanly and devoted. I have always felt how terrible it would be to have to face a class regularly on that subject, always a fight to make the students interested. The literatures are interesting in themselves. By all means do a translation of Paradise Lost, but get away from Milton after; he is only interesting to China as a warning about the European mind.

Mogador is glad to hear he has an old friend in Wuhan, and will want you to help him see the sights there.

I am in good health, but of course I realise it has become a race against time to finish the books I want to write.

Yours
William Empson

TO CHRISTOPHER RICKS

Studio House
25 April 1981

My dear Christopher,

Thank you for a pleasure; I liked your piece about Theory; it could have been expressed more strongly, but then it would be liable to excite the intense American patriotic resistance.[1] I return their sentiments; what it amounts to is, they have invented their own English Literature, and never again may the English tell them they are wrong. But this freedom was won at the ghastly cost which you describe, of denying that there are any authors at all. Yale does seem to be the heart of the movement, or epidemic, but milder forms of it are widespread.

I liked [Geoffrey] Hartman when I met him, and wish we could have talked more, but I feel sure we could have done one another no

---

[1] CR's piece on Geoffrey Hartman and Stanley Fish appeared in *LRB*, 16 April–6 May 1981; it was revised for his collection *Essays in Appreciation*.

good.[2] He is a good man someone tricked into Yale, and now languishes there, Yaled for life. He really does, fairly often, know what an author felt or intended, but his principles forbid him to mention it. He has a very good passage on the Keats *Autumn*, insinuating that it is about death, and the peace that sometimes comes to men shortly before they die. That Keats was facing an early death he of course must not say, but he manages to overcome his rules, though very obscurely, as regards the general point; which would surely have been obvious to Horace or Vergil. But he was indignantly resistant when told so.[3]

The monstrous [Stanley] Fish I have heard in action; I happened to visit Princeton when he was holding a kind of discussion group there, and was kindly invited to join it.[4] He really does deny that one should admit an author to have existed: or at least give any consideration to his probable intentions. His besotted admirers (all young male dons) carried out the principle with sickening rigour, rejoicing to deny that any historical character had ever existed, or for that matter that anything existed outside their campus. I kept my mouth tight shut, and then Hetta and I discovered that a little train would take us at once to New York, where she was wanting to meet some left-wing high-minded friends. Of course it was rude to our hosts to skip their lunch without warning, but to answer their questions at all truthfully would have been much ruder.

More power to your elbow seems the right compliment.
William E.

Ricks; Houghton: carbon

---

[2] Geoffrey H. Hartman (b. 1929), German-born critic and editor, departed from his home country as a refugee on one of the *kindertransport*. After a while in England he migrated to the US in 1946 and studied at Queen's College, New York, and at Yale University (from where he graduated in 1953). He is best known for his studies in Romanticism, as a prominent mediator in the debate surrounding Jacques Derrida and the hermeneutics of indeterminacy, and for his questioning of the 'language-centredness' of literary criticism. For Hartman, criticism is a creative power, and must engage with literature, philosophy, politics, history, and religion. His works include *Wordsworth's Poetry, 1787–1814* (1964), *Beyond Formalism: Literary Essays, 1958–1970* (1970), *Saving the Text: Literature/Derrida/Philosophy* (1981), and *The Unremarkable Wordsworth* (1986). He taught successively at Yale, Chicago, Iowa, and Cornell, and in 1967 returned to Yale as Karl Young Professor of English and Comparative Literature. See also *The Yale Critics: Deconstruction in America*, ed. Jonathan Arac, Wlad Godzich, and Wallace Martin (1983).

[3] Hartman, 'Poem and Ideology: A Study of Keats's "To Autumn" ', in *Literary Theory and Structure: Essays in Honor of William K. Wimsatt*, ed. Frank Brady, John Palmer, and Martin Price (1973), 305–30.

[4] Stanley Fish (b. 1938), who is arguably best known for his advocacy of reader-response criticism, was teaching at the time of this letter at Johns Hopkins University, where he was forthwith to be elected Kenan Professor of English and Humanities, 1983–5. Educated at the University of Pennsylvania and at Yale, he began his career at the University of California at Berkeley. Since 1985 he has taught at Duke University. His works include *Surprised by Sin: The Reader in Paradise Lost* (1967), *Is There a Text in this Class?* (1980), *There's No Such Thing as Free Speech . . . And It's a Good Thing Too* (1994), and *How Milton Works* (2001).

TO D. P. WALKER*

[n.d.: ? August 1981]

Dear Professor Walker,

Thank you for sending me a copy of your new book [*Unclean Spirits: Possession and Exorcism in France and England in the Late Sixteenth and Early Seventeenth Centuries* (1981)], which has been much appreciated here. It is very cool and penetrating.

I ought long ago to have asked your advice on various points in my current book where I am deeply ignorant; of course I have no business to ask you to do research for me, but probably you will often know the answers at once. I told you, I think, that I am puzzling over Marlowe's *Faust*, and using David Jones's translation of the original German.

Around 1950 Sir Walter Greg decided that the love of Faust for Helen of Troy, near the end of the play, was a case of demoniality and ensured his damnation. This belief is now taken as gospel in all English Departments, often in the stronger form that sex with devils was 'the unforgivable sin', and that Faust 'must have known' he was loving a devil in disguise. This gives the play a kind of neurotic piety, like the 'Fleurs du Mal', very foreign to it I think. I want to ask whether there is *any* source of the belief reasonably available to Marlowe and his first audiences, or rather to Old Man, who denounces Faust here. Of course witches enjoyed devils at sabbats, but no one supposed this was their worst sin. The German authors of the Faust-book clearly did not believe it, as they make Faust enjoy devils as soon as he has signed the pact, and yet assume that he can still repent. The English version has the devil fetch him real women whom he has observed in the town (a Duchess in the procession at a state funeral, perhaps) instead of simulacra, and they never make any comment; this must be a demand of the censors. However, one result is to make Greg's theory just possible; Faust would be enjoying Helen as his first devil. But the literary effect, in both the Life and the play, is to make Helen extremely unlike both the devils that can be summoned; among other things, she will only appear if she has agreed to it beforehand. The students, who appear to be pious and sober-minded, accept her at once in language of grave liturgical beauty. And Old Man, who is supposed to denounce her as a devil, shows no sign of having observed her at all. Surely he could not be made to do this, if his belief that she is a devil was the real point at issue.

One reason why the scene is so impressive is that it presents two absolutely opposed moralities, with no room for discussion between them, so it is no use grumbling about vagueness; presumably Old Man thinks all sex outside marriage damnable, whether with women or devils. But maybe some of the first hearers would think sex with devils particularly damnable; all I maintain is that Marlowe did not agree with Old Man, and showed it by Old Man's hysteria in the 1604 version of his speech, carefully removed in the 1616 version. I would be glad to learn of any evidence for Greg's theory.

Also, a fairly strong reason is needed to explain why the English censor would not allow Faust to have sex with devils, at least till he loved Helen of Troy. (Needed for my theory, that it was done by a censor.) I thought it enough that the idea excited low jeering on a sacred subject, which is plain because Marlowe contrives to excite the jeering while obeying the censor's rule. Even Greg realises that some such jeering happens in the text, though he assumes it is added by some low-minded person. Goethe in the last scene of his complete *Faust* makes the devils lust after the angels, who scornfully reject them, and I had long assumed that Goethe would not risk his dignity here unless following a long tradition. But I was *producing* Marlowe when I read the passages so, though not eccentrically, merely as any modern producer would do. It has now occurred to me that I do not know any parallel sixteenth-century joke, not even in Scot's *Discovery [of Witchcraft*, 1584]. The theologians said that the devils, being pure spirit, were incapable of sexual pleasure and merely enjoyed the corruption of mankind when they pretended it. They had no difference of sex, because immortals must not breed. The common man was sure they had pleasure, but as a kind of sodomy, and the Elizabethan government did not want to have that subject bandied about. When Faust demands a wife, he is offered 'a devil dressed as a woman, with fireworks'; this stage-direction, in the older edition only, shows that devils were recognised as being sexless, but does not say what occurred to make Faust disgusted. I expect a particularly manly actor ogled Faust lustfully and raised a side of his farthingale to give a glimpse of his chief charm, a great hairy cloven hoof. When Lucifer arrives with his court he is toying with his current concubine, the monstrous torturer Beelzebub, who simpers. This is part of the plot because the apparent devils are Middle Spirits, playing a charade to help their friend Meph. Hence they can be still impressive though acted as parodies. Faust has promised to let Meph go to heaven, using his soul as a passport, and thus Faust can escape Hell, dying like a beast or a Middle Spirit.[1] He is

---

[1] Cf. *FC*, 96: 'Faust in his final lamentation says (GFB, chapter 66): "I could do without Heaven well enough, if only I could escape eternal punishment" [Sp. 215]. At some stage, the censor felt that the more tender lambs in the flock might be unsettled if they read this obvious remark; they must not hear that any man is not always yearning to be in Heaven . . . [P. F.] put

held to his promise by this deception, costing him years of terror, but at the last moment he dies in the arms of his false friend in an ecstasy of love and gratitude, because after all he has been saved from Hell. This was meant to be only understood by the wise few, but the audiences soon cottoned on to it and were enthusiastic; so the government found out, and there was an explosion. But the scandal was best outfaced by a complete closure (from 1590 to 94) and then a revival in doctored form, which survives with further elaborations in the 1616 edition. On this view, the use of the low fun about homosexual devils, welcome in itself, is to drive home how different they are in every way from the figure of Helen of Troy. Greek goddesses were a kind of Middle Spirit, and Helen was actually worshipped as one (Pausanias saw a shrine of hers in Sparta), so that Faust is now literally meeting her. This, if he can be sure of it, proves that his original calculation was right, and that by demanding to be made a 'spirit' he has become sure of death, safe from Hell.[2] For the whole sequence it is important to make the devils absurd, and any other case of jeering at their peculiar sex would be a help.

The third question of course is about the rejection of Middle Spirits in this period, and needs to be tied down into a specific form. Earlier in the century there seems to have been a wide readiness to accept them, as presented by Agrippa or Paracelsus, but before its end they were generally doubted, and this was independent of the stand against them made by Luther and Calvin, perhaps mainly because they agreed with Augustine (who had made the decisive attack on them) about the quite different question of free-will. Were there persecutions in Protestant Germany against believers in spirits, apart from witches? Perhaps the distinction merely vanished. The authors of the original Faust-book seem determined not to allow any mention of spirits, even when they seem demanded by the story, and yet they report the legend boldly. It had been first formed in a very different mental climate. They allow Helen to have a child by Faust, which a devil could not possibly have done.

(EFB, chapter 61): "ah that I could carry the heavens on my shoulders, so that there were time at last to quit me of this everlasting damnation" . . . This too, it has been confidently argued [by John Henry Jones], can be understood as a simple misreading of the German words. If so, it was clever of P. F. to discover the possibility.' For P. F.'s probable mistranslation, see Jones, 243, note to 2783 ff. Jones comments, in *FC* (96 note 34): 'Empson's suggestion that the mistranslation was deliberate is quite plausible.'

[2] *FC* (104) quotes Robert Kirk: 'they are far from Heaven, and safe from Hell' (*The Secret Commonwealth of Elves, Fauns and Fairies* (1933).

A tiresome letter, but I hope you will write down what occurs to you.
Yours very sincerely
[William Empson.]

Houghton: carbon, bMS Eng 1401 (675)

D. P. Walker's response (10 Aug. 1981) included: 'With regard to Faustus &
Helen, I can't see anything in favour of the Greg theory. Sex with demons is
certainly not "the unforgiveable sin", which was something quite different
(Mark, 3. 28–30). As you say, orgies at Sabbaths weren't regarded as specially wicked—and anyway English witches didn't go to Sabbaths or go in
for any kind of sex. Incubi & succubi only operated, I think, on sleeping
humans, who couldn't therefore be considered guilty.'

TO ROBERT VAS DIAS

On being asked whether his poem 'Let It Go' could be reprinted in the
periodical *Spectacular Diseases* (no. 6), as an epigraph to 'Omaggio a William
Empson, Il Miglior Fabbro'—a poem 'composed by systematic chance
methods' by Jackson MacLow—WE sent this curious response.

1 Hampstead Hill Gardens, NW3
1 December 1981

Dear Mr Vas Dias,
Reading that poem feels like baby-watching an imbecile child, oozing at
every hole and playing with itself incessantly, and trying to attract attention by untruthful cries of pain. A request from a hospital for such people,
with photographs, arrived by the same post. My poem had said 'You don't
want madhouse', and perhaps I deserve to get this eager reply 'O yes we
do. Like mad'.
Still, the poem is already a success in America, from what you say, so if I
say Yes I am not responsible for its appearance. I hope you won't imply, in
a preface for instance, that I think it anything but hopelessly bad. With that
understanding, it would seem fussy not to agree.
You also need to write to Chatto & Windus, the original publishers of
the poem, and they will probably demand a small fee.
Yours truly
W. Empson.

Houghton: carbon, bMS Eng 1401 (671)

TO JOHN HAFFENDEN

1 Hampstead Hill Gardens, NW3
21 March 1982

Dear Mr Haffenden,

I am sorry not to have answered your letters before; it is rude as well as inconvenient. There is a good excuse; I have had a long attack of back-ache, when I could do practically nothing but lie flat on my back reading old whodunits, all day and most of the night. It seemed to me that I actually could not compose sentences. Two Xrays concluded that I had not got either cancer or stone in the kidney, so it was merely what old men have to expect. I still have a bit of pain and cannot walk far without sitting down, but am in working order again. However, it has altered my view of the prospects; I have left the collection of unfinished work far too late, and so far as my part is concerned in your *Life* of me it had better be put off for two or three years. I hope you will still do it, certainly I do not want anyone else to do it; what I can't do is hunt around for 'papers in my possession'. I must refuse all distractions.

This may seem a fussy way to talk about collecting magazine articles, but I so often find I only discover the point of the thing in the final rewriting. The first book I am to do contains the article on *Ulysses*, for instance, and I [have] been finding more and more needs adding to that. Then I am contracted to do two for the Cambridge Press, one Shakespeare the other his colleagues, and both have to have a certain amount of new material. Then a book about Marlowe's *Faust*, with another man [John Henry Jones] doing a translation of the Faustbook, which would make my most important contribution if it is found credible (I lost my credibility with a bang when *Milton's God* came out, and need to supply ample references and suchlike in an effort to recover it). Then a final one giving the material on Donne and Coleridge, two very controversial ones where the different stages need collecting. Earlier I thought I was providing congenial employment for my old age, a kindness to it, but now I am afraid I will not stay the course.

Nearly all this stuff, you understand, is unavailable except for people with access to large libraries, and some not even for them. Surely a life of the author is much more likely to sell when two or three of the books are already out, and more in prospect. I realise that this is annoying for you; you need to go forward. But a good deal about the controversy over the books is available; I have found this enlarged bibliography[1] now, and can

---

[1] Frank Day, *Sir William Empson: An Annotated Bibliography* (1984).

post it on; but won't you probably be visiting London in the vacation? Posting documents about is always a worry. If you show that my work takes a coherent position, and is not just a series of pointless cooked-up shocks, you will be doing me a great service. The scraps of paper which I have not raised the energy to throw away, not being coherent at all, would be very tiresome to look through.

It seems a pity that your work on John Hayward should be wasted. His letters while he was living with Eliot would probably be the most interesting ones, and their absence would leave a prominent gap in your *Life*, but surely that is a way to twist the lady's [Mrs Valerie Eliot's] tail? Does she propose never to print them? You might remark in the book, with studied moderation, that Hayward was wittier than Eliot and had more social observation, though of course his remarks would be less profound. Probably she means to print letters to Eliot in a collected edition, so you would be free to print at any rate some of Hayward's in your second edition. Or damaging conjectures might be made about the reasons for secrecy. The ball is now in your court, and most of the work has already been done.

I have also your synopsis for the proposed life of me, and should have acknowledged it before. I must thank you most earnestly for your good wishes. But I cannot help thinking that my colleagues would find the account too saintly and inflated. *Total* consistency is a good deal to say of anyone; and my *public life* has consisted mainly of getting comfortable seats to observe the great events of our time. Many of us did that much, and some did a great deal more. I could say that my life has been fortunate, giving me opportunities to follow the line I was good at, and that I have at least been consistent in fluttering back, as insects often do, after being driven aside. You speak of me as learning from my experiences in the East, but this would be hard to document; it seems to me that I learned very little, and probably missed a great deal. Of course I learned a bit from the difficulties of students in my subject, but that could happen in England too. I was interested in Buddhism before I went East, if only because it comes in *The Waste Land*, but I think earlier than that; after all, the old [Thomas] Huxley had said it was a religion without a God. I did not 'prove' that Japan had no right to Manchuria, which no one needed me to do; I did sometimes advise students to keep out of trouble with the Government, but they seldom needed that either. I made no observation of the Japanese peasantry, except that they never had those hideous sticking-out teeth, familiar in cartoons, which really were prevalent among city desk-workers (as also among English debutantes if not made to wear plates when young; it is a nervous complaint). Perhaps it would be as well to put in that my Tokyo contract was for three years only; they did not want to have foreigners become senior in the hierarchy. The Chinese one was indefinite, but of course things were unsettled then. I learned very little indeed of either language. My wife was irritated by the piece you quote on learning Chinese, which was cooked up for a comic paper, and it had better not be used I think.[2]

You say I spent three months travelling in the USA while returning to England for the war, and thus realised the importance of propaganda. I had been robbed of my travel money in Chicago, but still had the tickets to go on to New York, where I managed to find the poet Auden. Of course no money could be sent from England, and Auden was presumably short, so it was plucky of him to lend the money, and I earned enough to return it before moving on. He said (not expecting any return) 'There are many things in the world to be afraid of, indeed we would be wrong not to be afraid of. But one can't be afraid of money too'. I admired him very much. I thought I had told this story before. It shows how much one needs to know the details before interpreting the dates.

So I would be willing—anxious, indeed, to read all the book as you proceed, and you do not need to follow my advice or even believe what I say; but I hope at least that the gossip-column part can be handled fairly coolly.

I have done very little theorising in my books, not enough perhaps, and I hope to get more by way of final reflections into these last ones; perhaps you might suggest places where you feel it to be needed.

Yours
William Empson.

TO JOHN PAUL RUSSO*

[? 23 March 1982]

Dear Dr Russo,

Thank you for showing me your article on I. A. Richards.[1] I think it is all true, but I am dubious about the practical deductions. His basic theory

---

[2] WE, 'Learning Chinese', *Night & Day*, 19 Aug. 1937.

[1] In 'Formalism and Humanism in America' (1979), John Paul Russo rehearses the debate between TSE, Irving Babbitt, and IAR with regard to standards of value. He favours IAR over TSE and Babbitt for remaining 'unwilling to yield full belief to any single body of myth, or science or philosophy, or tradition, or religion—any one system that claims authority for itself over the field of truth and value'. IAR's psychological theory of value is efficacious because it is concerned with equilibrium and integration: its goal is *completeness* or *wholeness*. In the concluding

is a defence against absolutisms; it is not a thing you can extract rules from. He would have liked it to, or at least to give useful advice, and when he arrived at these formulations was hoping that Psychology would show the way, but that hope soon became dim. That excellent little book full of reproductions and quotations [*The Fountains of Aesthetics* (1922)] which gives the eighteen definitions of Beauty—obviously one couldn't say anything about a scene of such variety. Of course I think there ought to be practical deductions, and [these] probably would be by now if his work had been better understood.

Your account often sounds to me like the principle of the Taoists:

All men are inherently on the Way; that is why the best men strive unceasingly to get onto it.

This seems clearly a good idea, and I have often tried to find a meaning for it; but I suspect now it is simply a rule of politeness.

But I hope I am wrong.

Yours with thanks,

William Empson

section of his essay, 'The Meaning of Humanism in the 1980's', Russo argues that IAR's thinking can help us to attain a humanistic standard of value. 'I attempt to seize upon the essential place of certain values in criticism—self-knowledge, imagination, sympathy, and perseverance—and to reassert their claims at a time when criticism is splintering into various formalisms and needs to be reminded of a fundamental, ethical, but non-dogmatic directive.' What we need in the 1980s is 'to find the right way to implement humanistic value in the service of mankind . . . The goal of this heroic humanism is the self perfected to the degree that it is made human and an expression of the deepest life of its people.' According to Russo, the 'most penetrating contemporary formulation' of a means to complete this process can be found in Aleksandr Solzhenitsyn's *The First Circle* (1969), in which the character Nerzhin strives to become 'both a self and a universal'. Russo cites the following passage as presenting 'most succinctly the direction for contemporary humanism':

Not by birth, not by the work of one's hands, not by the wings of education is one elected into the people.
But by one's inner self.
Everyone forges his inner self year after year.
One must try to temper, to cut, to polish one's soul so as to become *a human being*.
And thereby becomes a tiny particle of one's own people.

He concludes: 'One should study the self the way one studies a work of art. The work of art engages interest because its particulars lead on to a sense of universal import that is permanently valuable, toward a larger sense of relationship and hence of coherence. The universals are what integrate the particulars without annihilating them. Intelligence likewise discovers that the self has its deeper integration . . . The *telos* of criticism is knowledge of this condition, the attention and sympathies focused upon it, the energies engaged to foster what helps it, to impede or eradicate what detracts from it (*Quaderno* 13 (Univ. of Palermo), 1979, 13, 26–7, 29, 50–3).

TO JOHN HAFFENDEN

University of Miami, Coral Gables, Florida
4 April 1982

Dear Mr Haffenden,

Your letter of 20 Feb was posted just after I had left England for a term here, and arrived late, but I ought to have answered it earlier. I had thought you meant to write about my books, or discuss the theories in them, not write a biography; of course you say both, and I would not mind biography relevant to the criticism. But a sheer biography before I am dead seems a depressing idea, and I would be sure to disagree with it. Preparing one to be published after I am dead is quite usual, apparently, and I would be willing to help with that. But I have been thinking of writing some memoirs myself, if I can get various loads off my back, in the way of completing work I have already half-handled in magazine publication. My memory is very bad, and there would be plenty of correcting for you to do afterwards. But I do not see that the critical part of your work need wait for that.

I am booked to arrive home by Jumbo at the end of this month, and hope you will call round, as you suggest. Telephone 435/0977.

Yours
William Empson
I cannot recommend Miami. Friendly enough, though.

TO WILLIAM VESTERMAN*

William Vesterman, in 'Poldy's Potence Preserved' (*Essays in Literature* 10: 1 (Spring 1983), 111–18), sought to correct the many critics of Joyce's *Ulysses* who asserted, merely on account of a single reference in the section 'Ithaca' which refers to the sex life of Leopold and Molly Bloom as 'incomplete, without ejaculation of semen within the natural female organ', that the couple had not made love for ten years. The teasing term 'incomplete' need not mean that sexual intercourse was 'non-existent', Vesterman argued. For one crucial consideration, Molly never complains about the sex life the Blooms share, and she would be prompt to grumble if she had been given cause. After all, their sex might include *coitus interruptus*; and Bloom, as the novel makes clear, makes use on occasion of condoms. Sexual relations between the Blooms may have been 'incomplete' by the standards ordained for married love by the Catholic Church (which Joyce was always at pains to affront), but there is still plenty of textual evidence for an active sex life in the Bloom marriage. Vesterman accordingly suggests: 'Molly's adultery and

Bloom's flirtations must therefore be understood not as melodramatic surrenders to desires produced by a decade of deprivation, but as the much more commonplace explorations of tentative and ambiguous dissatisfactions' (116–17).

Vesterman admired WE's writings, including his articles on *Ulysses*, and in the autumn of 1982 sent WE a copy of his forthcoming piece. He was taken aback by WE's response, which ignored the main burden of 'Poldy's Potence Preserved' and was intent only on reiterating WE's own proposition that Joyce's ultimate purpose in the novel was to project a ménage à trois between the Blooms and Stephen Dedalus. Vesterman felt disappointed because his article had not even been concerned to vote for or against WE's argument. WE 'still thought Bloom "afraid of the vagina" and that idea must come in part from the Ithaca passage about incomplete intercourse. Condoms negate that evidence and I don't see that Poldy's love of the rump belies a love of the hump. The only meaning of Ithaca's evidence (for the Blooms) is that they didn't want pregnancy after Rudy's death. For Joyce's part, he also wanted to mock the narrowness of normal sex as defined by the Church. Kick the Pope was his constant amusement' (WV, letter to JH, 27 Feb. 2004).

1 Hampstead Hill Gardens, London NW3
19 November 1982

Dear Mr Vesterman,

Thank you for sending me your article about *Ulysses*. I had a long go at it in the *London Review of Books* for 19 August and 2 September 1982, and thought at first you were disagreeing with me about that, but evidently you haven't seen it. Your position seems to me rational but benighted, and only to be answered by my whole argument; if you tell me where I am wrong I will try to answer.

But a few points can be made. It is too normalizing to say that Bloom performs *coitus interruptus* with Molly in the contact briefly and obscurely described. He hugs her bottom and presumably if he felt stronger would go up her back passage, but has only a partial erection and tries not to trouble her with it—'a solicitous aversion'. He has a phobia against entering a vagina, perhaps his wife's perhaps any woman's—that does not need to be made clear. This specific phobia is what he needs to overcome so as to produce a son by his wife, and he could do it with the help of his voyeurism—by watching Stephen do it, wearing a condom, and then taking over without one. Such is the aim of the whole story, but it would be 'gross indecency' in the eye of the law, ample ground for suppressing the book. Joyce had reason to become frightened about this, in the last year before it was finished, and we know that he altered the Ithaca chapter for some 'plan'—making the story more obscure, presumably. I think the resulting muddle spoils it rather, and hope very much that the forthcoming Variorum edition will do something to recover the original.

Rudy wasn't a monster; the mistake only comes from misunderstanding a pious remark by the dear old midwife.

Yours

William Empson

Houghton, bMS Eng 1401 (672)

Vesterman's reply has not survived, but a draft includes these remarks:

> 'Your letter makes it seem as though we do disagree, alas. I am happy enough with your rating of "rational but benighted," but I do want to clear one thing up and to raise some questions. I did not intend to have suggested that coitus interruptus occurred in bed the night of the story, but Molly remembers his having "come on my bottom" two weeks earlier "the night Boylan gave my hand a great squeeze going along by the Tolka" (p. 740).
>
> 'I don't see that your point about the triangle need depend on complete absence of sexual intercourse. I try to show that Bloom has condoms, carries one (Molly says she's going to check to see that he still has it), is accused by Purfoy in the dream sequence of using them, and that they would satisfy the definition of "incomplete" intercourse in the passage I cite first and which seems the *only* evidence that he can not enter her vagina.'

TO ANTHONY HARWOOD (Chatto & Windus)

Studio House
14 August 1983

Dear Mr Harwood,

Mr [Andrew] Motion* has asked me to write to you answering his letter, while he is on holiday.[1] Please thank him for the enthusiastic praise in his blurbs, though I feel they need toning down a bit. I am glad to hear that the firm is willing to take *Using Biography*. What I chiefly want there is an estimate of length, and thence of price. I am anxious to have it as cheap as possible, and have an ignorant fancy that there are ceilings about price, so that a fairly short reduction of length might happen to yield a considerable

---

[1] Motion sent a conciliatory response on 24 Aug. 1983 (*Houghton*).

reduction of price. In that case I would struggle to meet the requirement, without removing any of the separate chapters. And I will need to go over the text again, adding details and making acknowledgements and suchlike; there is no carbon copy, so please do not send it back by post; if necessary I will come and collect it.

As to the photographic reprint of the *Poems*, this really cannot be made to appear a new edition, and I never promised to write a new Preface for it. I offered something different, which was rejected. When I am invited to read some of the poems I always talk a bit about each poem before reading it, giving the circumstances and what not, and would not expect them to swallow the naked text. I offered to write down a shortened version of this, preferably on the opposing page, but was assured that the plan would be impossibly expensive. I hope it may yet be done later on, perhaps soon after I am dead, when there is commonly a brief upsurge of interest; the text might be held in reserve till then. But I could, I thought, offer a snapshot of myself as a younger man, conveying a moment of illumination to an earnest but impassive don. Please understand, I think the snapshot is funny. I hoped my wife would be able to discover this object, and so she did. The poems, I think, had all been completed before this photo was taken, but I was still sometimes making attempts. Photos of the old buffer, respectably posed, are of course badly off the point.

I thought this would help out the paperback, and I would gladly write a few sentences about the occasion for taking it. They should come on the introductory page beginning 'This edition includes . . .'. But I can't write a new Preface full of general discussion; I haven't anything more to say. Or perhaps even that would be too expensive, and the photo will only be reproduced on the dustcover. Somehow I thought paperbacks didn't have dustcovers. But no, you only speak of the *cover* for the reprint of Ambiguity, which has been in paperback for many years. It doesn't need, anyhow, this recently dug up photo, which was meant as an encouragement for buyers of the poems. Surely, to use it for both would be to remove the point of it. There is another.

Please take out, from your Back Cover remarks, the phrase in brackets about Just a Smack at Auden. I entirely agreed with Auden, though I could not express the opinion nearly so well, that War II was coming, and that backing the People's Front was our only chance. I just thought that his hammering at it had become counter-productive, and by the time he read my joke he thought the hammering had become a boring duty. Later on I was praised for it by people who thought that we ought to have chosen to lose the war, just as a snub for Stalin. So, as it would be too costly for me to explain myself, the subject had better be dropped.

The account of my life gives me an eerie grandeur which would excite deep hatred in many readers. I did not 'travel widely'; I had jobs in Japan and China and could look at some of the early Buddhas there and while going there. I did not 'return to take up a Chair'; the British Council decided to leave China, withdrawing all its subsidies, and I was a year out of work in England, failing to get the job in Hull. Surely it is absurd to thank me for my kind permission to print a snapshot. But things I feel to deserve credit are slid over as almost beneath me. I suggest:

> William Empson was born in 1906 and studied at Cambridge. During the 1930s he held lectureships at national universities in Tokyo and Peking. Returning to England in 1939, he worked for the BBC, as Chinese Editor from 1942. In 1947 he returned to his post in Peking, and stayed there till 1952. In 1953 he was appointed to the Chair of English Literature at Sheffield University, which he held till his retirement in 1971. (rest as now)

I hope these remarks don't suggest that I am eager to do an edition of the poems with longer notes; I am committed to several books, collecting old essays and suchlike, and am eager to get on with them while I yet can.

Yours truly

William Empson.

I was called a Professor in Tokyo and Peking, but they don't mean much by it.

Reading; Houghton: carbon, bMS Eng 1401 (525)

TO JOSEPH NEEDHAM*

1 Hampstead Hill Gardens, London NW3
21 August 1983

Rhyming in Europe

Dear Needham,

I hope you are going on all right. The above subject is one I have long nursed an opinion about, and wanted to ask about from someone who knew, and it has only recently occurred to me that (of course) you are the right person to ask—probably you haven't bothered about it, but you will know who would know. The question is why Europe took to rhyming in poetry during the Dark Ages, and my answer is that they learned it from the Berbers; but this is merely for one historical reason, and I would not be distressed if the evidence led elsewhere. Still, the Berber theory got a leg-up just recently, when my wife Hetta took a trip to south-east Algeria, walking behind the camels, for a look at prehistoric paintings there; the camel-drivers were Touaregs, really very out of the world, and an old one was heard singing to himself.[1] He plainly rhymed. Of course he may have learned a very old translation of 'Yes, we have no bananas', but it did not sound like that.[2] You see how short of evidence we are.

Rhyming (around the Mediterranean) first appears in Latin hymns, around +200, and probably began a bit earlier, all in North Africa. These hymns would have a missionary purpose, trying to please those who might become converts; and perhaps the first ones were in the language of the people, who would not speak Latin, but dignified versions were made in the imperial language afterwards. All this happened fairly near Carthage, which of course had been colonised by Philistines, from the near east of the inland sea; but they had been thoroughly subdued by Rome, and were likely to have made themselves unpopular among the indigenes, and any-how would not have rhymed. The congregations who sang the first Christian hymns in rhyme were already accustomed to rhyming verse; I hope this obvious point is well known, but somehow I have never seen it in print.

Rhyming seems an obvious thing to invent, not like matches for instance, so that it probably occurred often. I agree that it is very likely to have occurred independently among the Berbers and the Chinese, for instance; but the origin needs to be isolated. Among non-rhyming groups it appears comically vulgar. Hercules in some play comes on the stage rhyming, and it proves he is drunk (Euripides?). For it to conquer an already self-confident culture it needs to act humbly at first; it is what the ignorant people like, which may be imitated by educated men at odds with their society, graduates without jobs, as a parody of the church services.

But this is to generalise from one case. I have looked at what collections I could find of South Sea Island poetry, Red Indian poetry, and suchlike, and the editors seem queerly unwilling to say whether rhyme is used or not, or even whether it is being used regularly when it occurs in a snippet of quotation. Maybe consistent rhyming occurs and disappears with

---

[1] The Tuareg, indigo-robed and veiled lords of the Sahara (the 'blue men'), are descended from north-African Berbers who moved south at the time of the eighth-century Arab invasions; they speak Tamashek.
[2] 'Yes! We have no bananas': a folk song by Frank Silver and Irving Cohn (1923).

casual ease among such groups, but it seems unlikely. The evidence ought surely to be assembled, and perhaps has been. I would be grateful to be informed.

However, in the present case, the broad fact is that there is a great block of non-rhyming peoples in the land mass, with rhyme used for poetry by China and Europe at the two ends, but only by Europe since the Roman Empire began to fail. I am told that much of the Koran is in rhyming prose, and that the Syriac liturgy follows it, or precedes it; but only the combination of rhyme and metre is suitable for marching or dancing. Could one say that all the songs which have called to a battle, and won the battle, have been in rhyme? As you have so amply shown, there are always many confusions to be handled before one can settle such a question. I expect the Berbers really did invent rhyme, but one can't say it did them much good.

With earnest admiration
William Empson

Joseph Needham; Houghton, bMS Eng 1401 (609)

Joseph Needham responded to Empson's 'interesting letter' on 9 Jan. 1984: 'the oldest rhyming dictionary in Chinese dates from the +3rd century.' (See *Science and Civilisation in China*, vol. vi, part 1.) 'This is just the sort of time when, as you say, the Christian Church was introducing rhyme into its Latin hymns. I have a recollection that Helen Waddell (whose books you will be very familiar with) once referred to rhyme as "the lyric Ariel hidden in the womb of the Greek metres".

'But it might be rather unwise to suppose that rhyming started in China at the time when the first rhyming dictionaries were written. After all, the language is monosyllabic, and lends itself very much to rhyme.'

LONDON REVIEW OF BOOKS, 5: 16 (1–14 September 1983), 4:
'Jacobean Sodomy'

'That Night at Farnham' [by Anne Barton][1] remarks, speaking of James I: 'The king and the labouring man both seem to have made the same extraordinary psychological separation between sodomy and what they themselves felt and did.' Sodomy has been defined, not long before, as

---

[1] Anne Barton, 'That Night at Farnham' (a review of Alan Bray, *Homosexuality in Renaissance England*; Linda Bamber, *Comic Women, Tragic Men: A Study of Gender and Genre in Shakespeare*; Lisa Jardine, *Still Harping on Daughters: Women and Drama in the Age of Shakespeare*), *LRB*, 5: 15 (18 Aug.– 31 Aug. 1983), 18–19.

'sexual relations between man and man (or man and beast)', and we are told that it was 'officially' regarded as so unnatural that it shocked even the devil, who was therefore not its patron. I think that the solution of the puzzle is obvious, though to explain how the confusion became so general might take a bit of psychology, or politics.

Anal penetration was what shocked even the devil, and many homosexuals can satisfy one another without it. Consider the 'labourer' (so-called) who was shocked and indignant at being accused of sodomy with his apprentice, who slept in the same bed, for want of another no doubt. If each of them was masturbating himself it would seem rude not to 'give a hand' to the other, a process undoubtedly not so unnatural as to shock the Devil. Of course there are stages between that and the accursed thing, but it is hard to get evidence about them. As to Shakespeare saying 'to my purpose nothing', he was always careful to boast of success with the girls, and might well feel it would be bad taste to express hope for success with an earl. The phrase is comical rather than sanctimonious. In general, a theatre with boys acting as girls must be expected to extract fun from the charm of boys; this was regarded as innocent, so long as it was remote from anal penetration.

I agree, however, that so widespread a confusion was not likely to survive against the intention of a Tudor or Stuart government, or even without its active support. The trick seems rather a healthy one. Young people are to grow up believing that there is one really dreadful thing about love between men, but if you keep right away from that it is good, as we are told by Christ and Plato. The penalty for the dreadful thing is death, but it never has to be inflicted in London, whatever the JPs in Somerset may get up to. One must expect so appalling a thing to be rare. In this way a decent moral tone may be preserved, without running into a great deal of public indecency, let alone the reprisals from important people which might be expected.

It was a civilised arrangement, and ought not to be regarded with blank astonishment, merely emphasised by an appeal to 'psychology', which presumes that they were all mad.

TO ANDREW MOTION*

[October 1983]

Dear Mr Motion,

Thank you for your letter. I cannot agree with your proposals at all.[1] It seems best to begin by repeating the point at issue, though I am sure you understand it. The photograph of me far off in the wood makes me look like a lost bunnyrabbit, hopeless but still plucky; an appeal to every mother's heart. This would be quite all right before *The Structure of Complex Words*, for example, where I seem confident and magisterial but really the theorizing is an adventure into the jungle. The snapshot I wanted for the poems, and asked my wife to hunt for (you and Carmen Callil were present), shows me argufying, and it has become quite unusual for a poet to argufy, so that a new reader needs to be told what to expect. Nowadays it is usual for a poet to present himself as a lost bunnyrabbit, so your Presentation Department thinks it will sell more copies by reassuring the reader that my verse is only a bad imitation of the usual, and nothing worse. This might increase the immediate sales a trifle but would be a trifle bad for the long-term ones, and the book has gone on selling moderately for a long time.

Your letter presumes that nothing can alter the decision of 'our design department', so I presume that it has the authority of a Sales Department. For you, the only question is whether I will write for it a sweet piece saying I am truly a lost bunnyrabbit. That is not the question for me. I think and hope that the firm has no right to reprint the book with additions considered by the author to be damaging, any more than it has to print rude comments in the margin. The firm has a right to reprint, which it has neglected for so long that maybe the right has been forfeited; but I am not keen to stand in the way of an unchanged reprint, so long as your own agreements about the blurb are accepted. Of course I would prefer to have what we first agreed upon, and if you remember I had made a larger proposal. These I might be able to get elsewhere, at any rate later on, when I am less busy; so I am quite willing for the firm to refuse to reprint.

Yours truly

W. Empson

Houghton, bMS Eng 1401 (525)

---

[1] Andrew Motion wrote on 28 Sept. 1983 quite reasonably to say that the photo of WE beside Charles Coffin, taken at Kenyon College in the 1940s—WE's preference for the cover of a new issue of *CP* (1984)—'has been inspected by our design department and judged less suitable for the design they have in mind than the one of you standing against a backdrop of trees . . . If you feel very strongly that you would rather have the one of you and Charles Coffin on the cover, please say, and we'll try and persuade the designers to change their minds.' (*Houghton*)

TO ROMA GILL

Studio House
15 December 1983

My dear Roma,

Now that I look at your letter again I see that it was disgraceful not to have answered it in 9. xi. but I was then refusing to do anything except struggle to finish a book [*UB*] with an unnecessary deadline. It is done now and I will have to try to improve it when I get the text back.

I am sure that Workshop merits ought to be eligible for the prize, pitiful when it left my hands but I gather made decent by other hands now, and hereby authorize the change in the terms.[1] Recently you sent me another small cheque, for the book which you edited about me. Surely by normal rule this goes to the editor, but if you refuse to receive it I cannot, so please pay it into the Empson Prize.

It is delightful to hear that you are well enough to be so active and to be planning so firmly ahead, but I do beg you to pause before advancing upon your Faustus volume. Consider how improbable it is that Marlowe wrote a play against all his own convictions, and that no record survives of all the hearty jeering at him which would follow. Almost all remarks of spies may be doubted, but when they say: 'in any company, he would tell them not to fear Hell', they presume something which would have to be well known; and it is at least consistent with his other published works. Consider too that he was at least a competent playwright; why would he have written a play with the appalling collapses of dramatic interest and relevance that run all through the play admired by Greg (I don't believe that Greg had ever even played charades). It seems plain that the text which remains to us has first been savagely cut by the clerical censorship and then been cockered up to recommend the opposite of what the author intended. If you allow yourself to recognise this, and the strong historical probability of it, you are free to consider how to handle the result; otherwise you join the simpering crew of apologisers. I wish you a better fate.

My family and I are going on all right. I hope we may meet again soon.

Yours very sincerely
William

---

[1] On his retirement in 1971, WE sponsored a student prize for drama.

GLOSSARY OF NAMES

Paul J. Alpers (b. 1932) is Emeritus Professor of English at the University of California at Berkeley. His writings include *The Poetry of 'The Faerie Queene'* (1967) and *What Is Pastoral?* (1996).

A. Alvarez (b. 1929) is a poet, critic, novelist, gambler, and mountain climber. Educated at Corpus Christi College, Oxford, he was a research scholar of Corpus Christi and of the Goldsmiths' Company in the early 1950s. He later held visiting fellowships at several American universities, and gave the Christian Gauss seminars at Princeton, 1957–8. In 1956–66 he was poetry critic of *The Observer*. His works include *The Shaping Spirit: Essays in Modern English and American Poets* (1958; published in USA as *Stewards of Excellence*), *The School of Donne* (1961); *The New Poetry* (ed., 1962), *The Savage God: A Study of Suicide* (1971), *The Biggest Game in Town* (1983), *Feeding the Rat: Profile of a Climber* (1988); and *Where Did It All Go Right?*, an autobiography (1999). He was advisory editor for the series Penguin Modern European Poets in Translation, 1966–78.

James Jesus Angleton (1917–87) was born in the USA and educated at Malvern School in England and at Yale University, 1937–41, where WE met him during a brief visit towards the close of 1939. Angleton worked on *Yale Lit*, and in 1939 founded the magazine *Furioso*, which—fuelled by Angleton's liking for WE—rushed out an essay by I. A. Richards, 'William Empson', *Furioso: A Special Note* (12 January 1940), as an unscheduled supplement to *Furioso* 1: 3 (Spring 1940). As a littérateur, he was friendly also with T. S. Eliot and with Ezra Pound (whom he visited at Rapallo in 1938). William H. Epstein argues in 'Counter-Intelligence: Cold-War Criticism and Eighteenth-Century Studies', *ELH* 57: 1 (1990), p. 84: 'Soon after receiving his B.A. in 1941, Angleton entered government intelligence work, where he remained for over thirty years, during which time he was to develop a theory and methodology of counter-intelligence more or less based on the formalist criticism of Richards and Empson.' During World War II Angleton was to join the US Office of Strategic Services (precursor of the CIA), and in 1943 he was sent to London to be trained by MI5 officers including Dick White and Harold A. R. (Kim) Philby. (Angleton came to know Philby during the latter's tour of duty in Washington, 1949–51; and Philby's defection to the USSR in 1963 may have aggravated Angleton's belief in a monolithic Communist conspiracy seeking to penetrate the intelligence services of the West.) Having won renown for his work in counter-intelligence, after 1949 Angleton was to turn into the psychotic chief of the CIA's Office of Special Operations, being in charge of the Agency's Counterintelligence Staff, until finally dismissed in 1974 by William Colby, Director of Central Intelligence. (He was officially disgraced for his involvement in illegal espionage activities.) He is thus best known for his obsessional quest to unmask 'moles' in the CIA and other intelligence services. See Tom Mangold, *James Jesus Angleton: The CIA's Master Spy Hunter* (1991).

DILIP KUMAR BARUA studied for a Ph.D. at Sheffield (1963–6), under W. H. G. Armytage (Head of the Department of Education) and E. D. Mackerness (Reader in English Literature), and submitted his thesis, *The Life and Work of Edward Carpenter in the light of intellectual, religious, political and literary movements of the later half of the Nineteenth Century*, in 1966; it was published as *Edward Carpenter 1844–1929: An Apostle of Freedom* (University of Burdwan, 1991).

ISAIAH BERLIN (1909–97), philosopher and historian of ideas, was born in Riga, Latvia, but brought to England with his family in 1920. He was educated at St Paul's School, London, and at Corpus Christi College, Oxford, where he gained a first in Greats and a second first in Philosophy, Politics and Economics; thereafter he won a prize fellowship at All Souls. He taught philosophy at New College until 1950. In 1957 he was appointed Chichele Professor of Social and Political Theory at Oxford; and in the same year he was elected to the British Academy, which he served in the capacity of both Vice-President (1959–61) and President (1974–8). He was appointed CBE in 1946 and knighted in 1957; and in 1971 he was appointed to the Order of Merit. From 1966 to 1975 he was founding President of Wolfson College, Oxford. His publications include *Karl Marx* (1939), *The Hedgehog and the Fox* (1953), and *The Roots of Romanticism* (1999).

FRANCIS BERRY (b. 1915) was educated at the University of London and the University of Exeter. After service in the British army, 1939–46, he taught from 1947 to 1970 at the University of Sheffield, where he became fast friends with WE. He crowned his career as Professor of English Language and Literature at Royal Holloway College, London, 1970–80. His publications include *Poets' Grammar: Person, Time and Mood in Poetry* (1958), *Poetry and the Physical Voice* (1962), and *The Shakespeare Inset: Word and Picture* (1965, rev. 1971), as well as poetry and translations. See also G. Wilson Knight, *Neglected Powers* (1971); and Philip Hobsbaum, *Tradition and Experiment in English Poetry* (1979).

MAX BLACK (1909–88) was born in Russia and studied at Queen's College, Cambridge, where he met WE (his brother Mischa designed the cover for the periodical *Experiment* that WE co-edited). After working at the Institute of Education, London, and at the University of Illinois, he joined Cornell University, where in 1954 he was to be elected Susan Linn Sage Professor of Philosophy and Humane Letters. In 1958 he served as President of the American Philosophical Association. His publications include *The Nature of Mathematics: A Critical Survey* (1933), *Critical Thinking: An Introduction to Logic and Scientific Method* (1946), *Problems of Analysis* (1954), *A Companion to Wittgenstein's Tractatus* (1964), and *The Labyrinth of Language* (1968).

ANTONY BRETT-JAMES (1920–84) worked for Chatto & Windus as reader, editor and publicity manager, 1952–8. He was later to become better-known as a military historian, and taught from 1961 at the Royal Military Academy, Sandhurst, where he was Head of War Studies and International Affairs, 1970–80. His works include a memoir, *Report My Signals* (1948), *Wellington at War 1794–1815* (1961), *The Hundred Days* (1964), and *Life in Wellington's Army* (1972).

CLEANTH BROOKS (1906–94) was Professor of English and Gray Professor of Rhetoric at Yale University, 1947–75. Educated at Vanderbilt and Tulane, and at Exeter College, Oxford (where his tutor was Nevil Coghill), he had previously taught at Louisiana State University. He edited (with Robert Penn Warren) *Southern Review*, 1939–42, and the textbook *Understanding Poetry: An Anthology for College Students* (also with Warren, 1938). *The Well-Wrought Urn: Studies in the Structure of Poetry* (1947) is a key text of the New Criticism. His other works include *Modern Poetry and the Tradition* (1939), *William Faulkner: The Yoknapatawpha Country* (1963), *The Hidden God: Studies in Hemingway, Faulkner, Yeats, Eliot, and Warren* (1963), *A Shaping Joy: Studies in the Writer's Craft* (1971), and *The Language of the American South* (1985).

MAURICE BRUCE (1913–88) was Director of Extramural Studies at the University of Sheffield, where he became a Professor, 1968–75. His works include *The Coming of the Welfare State* and *The Shaping of the Modern World: 1870–1939*.

ROBERT BURCHFIELD (1923–2004) was editor of *Supplement to the Oxford English Dictionary*, and Chief Editor of the Oxford English Dictionaries, 1971–84. A New Zealander by birth, he was educated at Wanganui Technical College and at Victoria University College, Wellington. War service in the Royal New Zealand Artillery interrupted his studies at Wellington, from where he graduated MA in 1948, winning a Rhodes Scholarship to Oxford in 1949. At Magdalen College he studied under C. S. Lewis and J. R. R. Tolkien; but C. T. Onions, who was then Magdalen's librarian, proposed him to Dan Davin as the most promising editor of the *Supplement*. He would in turn assist Onions on his *Oxford Dictionary of English Etymology* (1966). His work as editor of the *Supplement*—which he supplemented by lecturing in English Language first at Magdalen, then at Christ Church, and for many years at St Peter's College, where he was ultimately to become Senior Research Fellow, 1979–90—took more than 28 years to complete and finally appeared in four volumes (1972–86) adding up to 6,000 pages. His other publications include *The Spoken Word* (1981), *The English Language* (1985), *Studies in Lexicography* (1987), *Unlocking the English Language* (1991), the fifth volume of the *Cambridge History of the English Language: English in Britain and Overseas* (1994), and a comprehensive, and controversially descriptionist, revision of H. W. Fowler's prescriptionist *Modern English Usage* (1926)—informally known as *Burchfield's Fowler*—in 1998. He was a Member of the American Academy of Arts and Sciences, and was appointed CBE in 1975.

MARTIN BUXTON became in 1947 (aged 28) British Consul in Peiping. Though a shy intellectual by nature, he combined boyish good humour with upright imperturbability; he did not suffer fools gladly, and preferred to override etiquette in favour of practical activity. During the six-week siege of Peiping that commenced in December 1948 he proved to be equal to the very daunting task of ministering to the British community. 'One could quote many examples of his more than conscientious concern for individual British residents who found themselves in difficulties,' wrote Sybille van der Sprenkel, 'and a good number must have reason to remember with gratitude his generosity and resourcefulness.' WE too considered him 'much better value than most consuls'.

WILLIAM COOKSON (1939–2003) was educated at Westminster School and New College, Oxford. With the encouragement of Ezra Pound, whom he travelled to meet in Italy at the age of 16, he launched *Agenda* in the late 1950s (while still a teenager). A champion of Pound, Basil Bunting, Geoffrey Hill, David Jones, Robert Lowell, Kathleen Raine, W. D. Snodgrass, Derek Walcott and Louis Zukofsky, Cookson also published an anthology of Pound's work, *Selected Prose 1909–1965, A Guide to the Cantos of Ezra Pound*, and poetry pamphlets of his own. See memorial issue of *Agenda* 39: 4 (Summer 2003).

C. B. (BRIAN) COX (b. 1928) was John Edward Taylor Professor of English at Manchester University, 1976–93, where he also served as Dean of the Faculty of Arts, 1984–6, and Pro-Vice-Chancellor, 1987–91. He was a founder editor in 1959 of the literary periodical *Critical Quarterly*, which was launched to carry on the tradition of Leavis's *Scrutiny*. (*Critical Quarterly* helped to establish the reputations of a number of poets including Sylvia Plath, Philip Larkin, and Ted Hughes; and its circulation at its peak ran at around 5,000.) Well-known as an educational controversialist, Cox has served as Chair and later President of the National Council of Educational Standards, 1984–89; Chair of the National Curriculum English Working Group, 1988–89; and Chair of the Northwest Arts Board, 1994–2000. He co-edited the Black Papers on Education (1969–77); and *Cox on Cox: an English curriculum for the 1990s* (1991) was a best-seller. Other publications include *Collected Poems* (1993), volumes of literary criticism and anthologies, and *The Great Betrayal: Memoirs of a Life in Education* (1992).

BONAMY DOBRÉE (1891–1974) was Professor of English Literature at Leeds University, 1936–55. After early service in the army (he was twice mentioned in despatches and attained the rank of major), he read English at Christ's College, Cambridge, and taught briefly in London and Cairo. His publications include *Restoration Comedy* (1924), *Essays in Biography* (1925), *Restoration Tragedy, 1660–1720* (1929), *Alexander Pope* (1951), as well as editions and anthologies. He and WE liked one another, and WE gave talks and readings for Dobrée at Leeds.

FRANCIS DOHERTY (1932–93) read English at Sheffield and took a First in 1959. WE wrote of his performance as an undergraduate in the session 1957–8: 'A high-minded Catholic who praises Anglican devotional writers so warmly that one first thinks him an Anglican. An energetic mind, but so charitable in his tone of writing that it feels soft and almost bad grammar.' Doherty was to become Senior Lecturer in English Language and Literature at the University of Keele.

PENELOPE DOOB is Professor of English at York University, Toronto, where she specializes in poetry of the Early Modern period, 1500–1660. She has a BA from Harvard University, and an MA and Ph.D. from Stanford. Her works include *Nebuchadnezzar's Children: Conventions of Madness in Medieval Literature*, *The Idea of the Labyrinth from the Classical Period through the Middle Ages*, and *The Uses of Manuscripts in Literary Studies*. She has published articles on dance history and criticism, has developed more than twenty documentaries for the CBC Radio programme *The Dance*, and is cross-appointed to teach in the Department of Dance (serving as Chair, 2001–4). She has also been involved in strategic planning for several arts and academic organizations, and in the early 1990s was founding president of Reed MacFadden, a medical research company focusing on HIV/AIDS, where her work has included clinical trial design, fund-raising, statistical analysis and research into health-related quality of life.

ELSIE DUNCAN-JONES (1908–2003), née Phare, read English at Newnham College, Cambridge, where she was taught by I. A Richards, F. R. Leavis, and Enid Welsford; she took a starred First with Special Distinction in both parts of the Tripos. As President of the Newnham Literary Society, she invited Virginia Woolf (whom she found 'haughty') to give a talk in 1928 that would become *A Room of One's Own* (1929). She taught at Southampton University, 1931–34; at Birmingham University, 1936–75. She published one book, *The Poetry of Gerard Manley Hopkins: A Survey and Commentary* (1933), and articles on subjects including T. S. Eliot (1946); a British Academy Warton Lecture, 'A Great Master of Words: some aspects of Marvell's poems of praise and blame' (1976), and the third edition (with Pierre Legouis) of H. M. Margoliouth's *The Poems and Letters of Andrew Marvell* (2 vols., 1971). In 1933 she married Austin Duncan-Jones, a lecturer in Philosophy (who was to review *SCW* in *Mind*, 62 (1953), pp. 413–17).

ARTHUR EFRON (b. 1931) received his Ph.D. in 1964 from the University of Washington, Seattle (his dissertation led to a book entitled *Don Quixote and the Dulcineated World*, 1971), and was a Professor of English at Buffalo, 1964–2000. His research interests have included D. H. Lawrence, the body in literature, John Dewey's aesthetics and emotional wholeness in literature.

T. S. ELIOT (1888–1965), poet, critic and publisher, won his pre-eminent place in the world of letters with the publication both of his masterpiece *The Waste Land* (1922) and of an influential volume of criticism, *The Sacred Wood* (1920). In 1922 too he founded the international literary journal *The Criterion* (which ran until 1939). In 1925 he joined the young publishing firm of Faber & Gwyer (later Faber & Faber), of which he later became a director, and there he became the key figure in the publication of modern poetry. Brought up in the USA, he took British citizenship in 1927; the same year, he was baptized into the Church of England. His other verse collections include *Prufrock and Other Observations* (1917), *Poems, 1909–1925* (1925), *Ash-Wednesday* (1930), and *Four Quartets* (1943); and his plays include *The Rock* (1934), *The Family Reunion* (1939), and *The Cocktail Party* (1949). Critical volumes include *For Lancelot Andrewes* (1928), *The Use of Poetry and the Use of Criticism* (1933), *The Idea of a Christian Society* (1939), *Notes toward a Definition of Culture* (1948), and *On Poetry and Poets* (1957). In 1948 he was awarded both the Order of Merit and the Nobel Prize for Literature.

RICHARD ELLMANN (1918–87), biographer and critic, taught at Harvard, Northwestern and Yale before being appointed Goldsmiths' Professor of English Literature at Oxford, 1970–84, and a Fellow of New College. His publications include *Yeats: The Man and the Masks* (1948), *James Joyce* (1959, 1982), *Golden Codgers: Biographical Speculations* (1973), *The Consciousness of Joyce* (1977); and *Oscar Wilde* (1987), which won the Pulitzer Prize for Biography and the National Book Critics Circle Award for Biography/Autobiography. See also *Along the riverrun: Selected Essays* (1988), and *Omnium Gatherum: Essays for Richard Ellmann*, ed. Susan Dick (1989).

WILLIAM ELTON (b. 1921) was Professor of English at the University of California, Riverside, 1955–69, subsequently Professor of English at the City University of New York. See *Shakespeare's Universe: Renaissance Ideas and Conventions: Essays in Honour of W. R. Elton* (1996).

JACOB EMPSON (b. 1944), younger son of William and Hetta Empson, took his PhD at Sheffield University—on the effects on memory of depriving people of rapid eye movement (REM) sleep—and worked for many years at the University of Hull. His publications include *Human Brainwaves: The Psychological Significance of the Electroencephalogram* (1986) and *Sleep and Dreaming* (1989).

D(ENNIS) J(OSEPH) ENRIGHT (1920–2002), poet, novelist, and critic, was educated at Downing College, Cambridge. He taught English for 25 years, mainly in the East, and was Professor of English at the University of Singapore 1960–70 (see *Memoirs of a Mendicant Professor*, 1969). In addition to his own creative works he edited the anthologies: *Poets of the 1950s* (1955), *The Oxford Book of Contemporary Verse* (1980), and *The Oxford Book of Death* (1983).

LESLIE FIEDLER (1917–2003)—'an urban American Jew . . . influenced by Marxist ideas, communist and Trotskyist', as he called himself—was born in Newark, New Jersey, and educated at New York University; he took a Ph.D. in English and Comparative Studies at the University of Wisconsin. After the war, during which he learned Japanese and became a military cryptologist and translator (serving in Hawaii, Guam, Iwo Jima, China, and Okinawa), he served for 10 years on the faculty at Montana University before removing in 1964 to the State University of New York at Buffalo. In 1954–73 he was a Junior Fellow of the Indiana School of

Letters (where he met WE in 1954). He became known as an *enfant terrible* of American letters when he published in *Partisan Review* (1948) a ground-breaking essay, 'Come Back to the Raft Ag'in, Huck Honey', on the infantilistic and homo-erotic elements in Mark Twain's fiction; it was an iconoclastic argument he developed into *Love and Death in the American Novel* (1960), a psychosexual examin-ation of American literature from the beginnings to Hemingway and Faulkner which emphasizes the theme of male escapism from a female-dominated society. Later works include *An End to Innocence: Essays on Culture and Politics* (1955); *No! In Thunder: Essays on Myth and Literature* (1960); *Waiting for the End: The American Literary Scene from Hemingway to Baldwin* (1964)—the title being taken from WE's poem 'Just a Smack at Auden'—*The Return of the Vanishing American* (1967); and *Fiedler on the Roof* (1991). See Mark Royden Winchell, '*Too Good to be True*' (2002).

Boris Ford (1917–98), educationalist and literary critic, was education secretary at Cambridge University Press, 1958–9, and editor of *Universities Quarterly* (later *New Universities Quarterly*), 1955–83; it was in the latter capacity that he sent round the circular to which WE responded. From 1949 he was general editor of the *Pelican Guide to English Literature* (7 vols. 1954–61; revised, 1982–8). A sometime Director of the Bureau of Current Affairs, and Information Officer of the Tech-nical Assistance Board at UNESCO, in 1955–7 he was part-time secretary of Children's Play Activities and editor of the *Journal of Education*; and in 1957–58 he was the the first Head of School Broadcasting with the TV company Associated Rediffusion. In 1960 he was to become a colleague of WE's at Sheffield on being appointed Professor of Education and Director of the Institute of Education. In 1963 he moved to the University of Sussex, and in 1973 he became Professor of Education at Bristol University. His other works include *Changing Relationships between Universities and Teachers' Colleges* (1975) and the seven-volume *Cambridge Guide to the Arts in Britain* (1988–91).

Veronica Forrest-Thomson (1947–1975), critic and university teacher, was author of *Poetic artifice: A theory of twentieth-century poetry* (1978), which includes consideration of WE's poetry. See Alison Mark, *Veronica Forrest-Thomson and Lan-guage Poetry* (2001); *Jacket Magazine* 20 <http://jacketmagazine.com/20>

George Fraser (1915–80), poet and critic, was brought up in Glasgow and Aberdeen; graduating from St Andrews University, he worked as a newspaper-man before volunteering for wartime service in the Black Watch, serving mainly in North Africa. He was editor of the *Eritrean Daily News*, 1942–4. After the war, he was British cultural adviser in Tokyo, in succession to Edmund Blunden. For some years he lived in London as a freelance writer, earning his living as a reviewer for the *TLS* and other periodicals, before taking up an academic appointment at Leicester University, 1958–79, where he ultimately became Reader. His publications include *The Modern Writer and His World* (1953), *Essays on Twentieth-Century Poets* (1977), and *Poems of G. S. Fraser* (1981). WE greatly admired

Fraser's poem 'Letter to Anne Ridler' (see *A*, p. 171), and Fraser and WE were to become good friends after the end of the war.

MICHAEL FREEMAN (b. 1938) grew up in Stockton-on-Tees and took a Diploma in Education after reading English at Sheffield, 1956–9. From 1961 to 1981 he taught in comprehensive and grammar schools, and then lectured in teacher-education (Didsbury College, Manchester Polytechnic). In 1981 he became a publisher's reader, then an editor for Carcanet Press and *PN Review*; and since 1989 he has been a freelance editor and socialist activist. He is completing a book on Ralph Fox.

RINTARO FUKUHARA (b. 1894), essayist and critic, was WE's senior at the Tokyo University of Literature and Science. A graduate of the Tokyo Higher Normal School, he had also studied at London University. His publications include *A Bibliographical Study of Thomas Gray* (1933). See *Japan Biographical Encyclopedia and Who's Who*, 3rd edn. (1964–5). WE said of Fukuhara in *The Rising Generation*, 1 June 1981, p. 168: 'I admired Fukuhara very much. He was my boss when I was employed in Japan . . . and gave me much help and good advice.' See also Rintaro Fukuhara, 'Mr William Empson in Japan', in Gill, 21–33.

HELEN GARDNER (1908–86) was University Reader in Renaissance English Literature, and a Fellow of St Hilda's College, Oxford, where she taught from 1941 to 1966. She crowned her career as Merton Professor of English Literature at Oxford (1966–75)—the first woman to hold the Chair—with a Fellowship at Lady Margaret Hall. Her works include *The Art of T. S. Eliot* (1949), which won the poet's approval; *The Business of Criticism* (1959); *A Reading of 'Paradise Lost'* (1965); *The Composition of the 'Four Quartets'* (1977); and *In Defence of the Imagination* (1982); as well as editions of the works of John Donne, *The Divine Poems* (1952) and *The Elegies and the Songs and Sonnets* (1965)—to which WE was to take enraged exception—and two anthologies: *The Faber Book of Religious Verse* (1972), and *The New Oxford Book of English Verse, 1250–1950* (1972). She was appointed DBE in 1967; elected a Fellow of the British Academy (1958); and was twice winner of the Rosemary Crawshay Prize (1952, 1980).

ROMA GILL (1934–2001) studied English at New Hall, Cambridge, before taking a B. Litt. on the works of Philip Massinger under the supervision of Helen Gardner at Oxford. After teaching English for a few years at both Ripon and Kesteven Colleges of Education, in 1963 she was appointed by WE to his Department at Sheffield, where she was to remain until her early retirement in 1984 (she was becoming disabled by the symptoms of multiple sclerosis). She was promoted to Senior Lecturer in 1970 and Reader in 1979. She made her reputation as an authority on Christopher Marlowe with the New Mermaid edition of *Doctor Faustus* (1965), followed by a single-volume *The Complete Plays of Christopher Marlowe* (1971), two more editions for the New Mermaids, and twenty volumes for the Oxford School Shakespeare, a series which sold worldwide—the latter were 'ludicrously successful,' she declared (*Macbeth* sold 97,000 copies in one year). In 1994 she was awarded the OBE for her services to English Literature.

IAN HAMILTON (1938–2001) poet, critic and literary editor, was educated at Keble College, Oxford, and founded and edited *the Review*, 1962–72 (which ran a special issue on WE in 1963), and *The New Review*, 1974–79. He was also poetry and fiction editor for the *TLS*, 1965–73. His other publications include *The Visit* (1970), *The Little Magazines* (1976), *Robert Lowell* (1983), *Fifty Poems* (1988), *In Search of J. D. Salinger* (1988), *Writers in Hollywood, 1915–1951* (1990), *Keepers of the Flame: literary estates and the rise of biography* (1992), *Gazza Agonistes* (1998), and *Against Oblivion* (2002). See also *Another Round at the Pillars: Essays, Poems, and Reflections on Ian Hamilton*, ed. David Harsent (1999).

CHIYOKO HATAKEYAMA (1902–82) was a schoolteacher and poet with whom WE corresponded in the mid–1930s; they met just once, in Tokyo. See Peter Robinson, 'Very shrinking behaviour' *TLS*, 18 Jul. 2003, 13–15, and 'Ice cream with Empson' (a letter), *TLS*, 24 Oct. 2003, 19; along with Robinson, ' "*C. Hatakeyama* [Trans. W. E.]" ', *PN Review*, 31: 2 (Nov.–Dec. 2004), 55–60.

JOHN HAYWARD (1905–65), editor, scholar and critic, studied at King's College, Cambridge (where he came to know WE). Despite the early onset of muscular dystrophy, he rapidly became an eminent and prolific writer and editor, bringing out in quick succession highly respectable editions of the works of Rochester, Saint-Évremond, Jonathan Swift, Robert Herrick, and Samuel Johnson. Other publications included *Complete Poems and Selected Prose of John Donne* (1929), *Donne* (1950), *T. S. Eliot: Selected Prose* (1953), *The Penguin Book of English Verse* (1958), and *The Oxford Book of Nineteenth Century English Verse* (1964). Celebrated in addition as the learned and acerbic editor of *The Book Collector*, he was made a chevalier of the Légion d'honneur in 1952, a CBE in 1953. Writers including Graham Greene, Stevie Smith and T. S. Eliot valued his keen editorial counsel. See further Helen Gardner, *The Composition of 'Four Quartets'* (1978).

T. R. HENN (1901–74) was Fellow and then President of St Catharine's College, Cambridge, 1926–61; he was Judith Wilson Lecturer in Poetry and Drama, 1961–65. During World War II he rose to be a brigadier in the British Army, and was awarded the CBE (military) and the US Legion of Merit. His writings include *The Lonely Tower* (1950), *The Apple and the Spectroscope* (1950), *The Harvest of Tragedy* (1959), *Science in Writing* (1960), and *The Bible as Literature* (1970).

ROBERT HERRING (1903–75) was assistant editor of *The London Mercury*, 1925–34; editor of *Life and Letters*, 1935–50. See Meic Stephens, 'The Third Man: Robert Herring and *Life and Letters To-day*', *Welsh Writing in English: A Yearbook of Critical Essays* (1997), 157–69.

PHILIP HOBSBAUM (1932–2005) read English (BA, 1955; MA 1961) at Downing College, Cambridge (under F. R. Leavis), and worked for his doctorate under WE at Sheffield: his Ph.D. was finally awarded in 1968. In 1962–6 he taught at Queen's University, Belfast (where he encouraged Michael Longley, Derek Mahon, and Seamus Heaney); and in 1966 he became lecturer at Glasgow University, where he rose to be Professor of English Literature, 1985–97. He is credited with developing the writer's workshop known as 'The Group', first in Cambridge and London, later in Belfast and Glasgow: see *A Group Anthology* (1963), ed. Philip Hobsbaum and Edward Lucie-Smith. His works include *A Theory of Communication* (1970), *Tradition and Experiment in English Poetry* (1979), and *Essentials of Literary Criticism* (1983); and poetry including *The Place's Fault* (1964), *In Retreat* (1966), and *Coming Out Fighting* (1969). See also 'Empson as Teacher: The Sheffield Years', in *William Empson: The Critical Achievement*, ed. Christopher Norris and Nigel Mapp (1993); 'Empson as Critical Practitioner', in *Critical Essays on William Empson*, ed. John Constable (1993).

DAVID HOLBROOK (b. 1923), poet, novelist, and critic, was educated at Downing College, Cambridge. He has been a Fellow of King's College, Cambridge, 1961–5; lecturer in English at Jesus College, Cambridge; and Fellow and Director of English Studies at Downing College, 1981–8. His publications include *Dylan Thomas: The Code of Night* (1971) and *Sylvia Plath: Poetry and Existence* (1976). See also Edwin Webb, *Powers of Being: David Holbrook and His Work* (1995).

MICHAEL HOLROYD (b. 1935) is celebrated for his biographies of Hugh Kingsmill, Lytton Strachey, Augustus John, and Bernard Shaw. Other works include *Basil Street Blues* (1999) and *Works on Paper* (2002). He has been chair of the Society of Authors and the Book Trust, and president of English PEN; and he now chairs the Council of the Royal Society of Literature. He was awarded the CBE in 1989.

GRAHAM HOUGH (1908–90) was educated at Liverpool University and at Queen's College, Cambridge, and taught for most of the 1930s at Raffles College, Singapore. In 1942 he volunteered as a Gunner in the Singapore Royal Artillery, and was captured at the fall of Singapore and held prisoner of war until 1945. In 1946 he returned for a while to Raffles College as Professor of English. From 1955 he was Lecturer in English at Christ's College, Cambridge, where he ultimately became Professor of English, 1966–75, and a Fellow of Darwin College. His publications include *The Last Romantics* (1949), *The Romantic Poets* (1953), *Image and Experience: Studies in a Literary Revolution* (1960), *A Preface to 'The Faerie Queene'* (1962), *An Essay on Criticism* (1966), and *The Mystery Religion of W. B. Yeats* (1984). See also Hough on WE: 'An Eighth Type of Ambiguity', in Gill, 76–97; 'Graham Hough thinks about William Empson and his work', *London Review of Books*, 21 Jun.–4 Jul. 1984, 16; and Peter Schwendener, 'In Quest of Graham Hough', *American Scholar*, 67 (Winter 1998), 139–45.

STANLEY EDGAR HYMAN (1919–70) took his BA at Syracuse University (though no higher qualification) and then became a staff writer for the *New Yorker* in 1940.

From the mid–1940s he began teaching English at Bennington College, Vermont, where he ultimately rose to be a full professor. His first book was *The Armed Vision: A Study in the Methods of Literary Criticism* (1948), which drew on a fascination with modern social science—his heroes, like WE's, were Darwin, Freud, Marx and Frazer. It was followed by other volumes including *Poetry and Criticism* (1961), *The Tangled Bank* (1962), and *The Promised End* (1963).

Karunakar Jha teaches in the Department of English at Bhagalpur University, Bhagalpur, Bihar, India.

Jin Fa-shen was a student of WE's at Peking University in the late 1940s: his dissertation on *Paradise Lost* had a big influence upon WE in the writing of *MG*. In later years he taught in the Department of Philosophy at Wuhan University.

John Henry (David) Jones (1933–2001) studied chemistry at Bristol University (B.Sc. 1954, Ph.D., 1960), and pursued research at Heidelberg University (where he also learned German), 1957–58, and at Cambridge University, 1958–62. He was a lecturer at Cambridgeshire College of Arts and Technology, 1963–5, but in 1965 abandoned his academic career and removed to London to paint and write: he supported himself by translating German textbooks on chemistry. In the late 1960s he wrote plays (including *The Caveman Cometh*, broadcast on BBC Radio 3 in September 1968), and attempted a novel. In 1970 he was involved (as science editor, later editor) with Ted Hughes, Daniel Weissbort, and David Ross in their environmental quarterly, *Your Environment*. On first encountering Hughes (or so the story goes), he blurted out: 'Oh, the great lady-killer, I presume.' He met WE and collaborated with him on aspects of the Faust legend from 1975, when he became a lodger at Studio House; at WE's prompting he translated the full German Faust Book. In addition to editing WE's essay on the English Faust Book and Marlowe's *Doctor Faustus* (*Faustus and the Censor*), he published his own study *The English Faust-Book: A critical edition based on the text of 1592* (1994).

Hugh Kenner (1923–2003), Canadian critic, read English at the University of Toronto (BA, 1945; MA, 1946), where he studied under Marshall McLuhan; he gained his doctorate at Yale, where he was supervised by Cleanth Brooks. He taught for a while at Santa Barbara College (now the University of California, Santa Barbara); then at Johns Hopkins University, 1973–90; and finally at the University of Georgia, 1990–9. His works include *Paradox in Chesterton* (1947), *The Poetry of Ezra Pound* (1951), *Dublin's Joyce* (1956), *The Pound Era* (1971), *Ulysses* (1978), and *The Elsewhere Community* (1998); and non-literary writings including studies of Buckminster Fuller, Geodesic Maths, and Chuck Jones.

Frank Kermode (b. 1919) was educated at Liverpool University and served in the Royal Navy during World War II. He taught at the University of Durham, 1947–9; at Reading, 1949–58. He was Professor of English at Manchester, 1958–65; Winterstoke Professor of English at Bristol, 1965–7; Lord Northcliffe

Professor of Modern English Literature at University College, London, 1967–74; and King Edward VII Professor of English Literature at Cambridge, where he was a Fellow of King's College, 1974–82. His publications include *The Romantic Image* (1957), *The Sense of an Ending: Studies in the Theory of Fiction* (1967), *Shakespeare, Spenser, Donne: Renaissance Essays* (1971), *The Genesis of Secrecy: On the Interpretation of Narrative* (1979), *History and Value: The Clarendon Lectures and the Northcliffe Lectures, 1987* (1988), *An Appetite for Poetry* (1989), *The Uses of Error* (1991), *Not Entitled: A Memoir* (1995), *Shakespeare's Language* (1999), *Pleasing Myself: From Beowulf to Philip Roth* (2001), and *The Age of Shakespeare* (2004). He is a Fellow of the Royal Academy and of the Royal Society of Literature, an Honorary Member of the American Academy of Arts and Sciences and the American Academy of Arts and Letters, and an Officier de l'Ordre des Arts et des Sciences. He was knighted in 1991. 'You never really knew where you were with William Empson, except that you always knew you were in the presence of someone very distinguished,' he has said in interview. 'I would say . . . that in terms of pure intellectual capacity and force, Empson was the best critic of the twentieth century, in English. This is by no means to say that he didn't write an awful lot of nonsense in his time, because he did . . . He and I never really got on. That has to be said, and that's quite important, in a curious sense. There was a kind of mutual suspicion. Mine was only a reflection of his. He had got me down as a neo-Christian long before, and he could never really quite forgive me for being that, as he thought. As so often, the judgment was a totally prejudiced one' (Imre Salusinszky, *Criticism in Society* (1987), 110).

KIM JONG-GIL was born in Andong, Korea, in 1926, and read English Literature at Korea University, Seoul; he studied under WE at Sheffield in the 1950s.

L. C. KNIGHTS (1906–97) was WE's predecessor as Professor of English Literature at Sheffield, 1947–52. Thereafter he became Winterstoke Professor of English at Bristol, 1953–64, and King Edward VII Professor of English Literature, Cambridge, and Fellow of Queen's College, 1965–73. His publications include *How Many Children Had Lady Macbeth* (1933), *Drama and Society in the Age of Jonson* (1937), *Explorations: Essays in Criticism* (1946), *Some Shakespearean Themes* (1959), and *An Approach to Hamlet* (1960). WE and Knights first met while teaching at the Kenyon School of Letters at Bloomington, Indiana, in 1950.

DESMOND LEE (1908–93) studied at Corpus Christi College, Cambridge, where he became friends with WE (WE's series of smitten 'Letter' poems was written for Lee). Lee was one of Wittgenstein's favourite pupils during his second period at Cambridge (from 1929), and in 1930 he went to stay with the philosopher at his home in Austria. On 23 March 1935 he married Elizabeth Crockenden (the occasion is commemorated in WE's poem, 'Letter VI: A Marriage'), and he fathered a son and two daughters. After tutoring and lecturing in Classics at Cambridge, he became Headmaster of Clifton College, Bristol, 1948–54, and of

Winchester College, 1954–68 (serving as Chairman of the Headmaster's Conference for 1959–60 and 1967). He was later a Fellow of Wolfson College, Cambridge, 1968–73. He was knighted in 1961. His writings include translations of Aristotle and Plato, and *Wittgenstein's Lectures, 1930–1932* (co-edited, 1979).

PETER LEVI (1931–2000), poet, translator, and classicist, was educated at Beaumont College, Berkshire, and at Campion Hall, Oxford. He was for many years a member of the Society of Jesus but resigned his priesthood in 1977, when he married Cyril Connolly's widow, Deirdre. He lectured in Classics at Campion Hall and at Christ Church, and from 1977 he was a Fellow of St Catherine's College, Oxford. He was Professor of Poetry at Oxford, 1984–9. His writings include *Collected Poems* (1976), and translations of Pausanias, Yevtushenko, and Pavlopoulos, as well as the Psalms. Other works include *The Lightgarden of the Angel King* (1984), *The Hill of Kronos* (1980), *The Noise Made by Poems* (1975), *The Head in the Soup* (1979), and *The Flutes of Autumn* (autobiography, 1983).

ROBERT LOWELL (1917–77) is the foremost American poet of the mid-century. His works include *Lord Weary's Castle* (1946), which won a Pulitzer Prize; *The Mills of the Kavanaughs* (1951); *Life Studies* (1959), which won the National Book Award, 1960; *Imitations* (1960); *For the Union Dead* (1964), *Notebook* (1970), *History* (1973), *The Dolphin* (1973), *Day by Day* (1977), *Collected Prose* (1987), *Collected Poems* (2004), and *The Letters of Robert Lowell* (ed. Saskia Hamilton, 2005). WE met him in Cambridge, Mass., in 1939 but became much better acquainted with him while teaching summer school at Kenyon College, Ohio, in 1948. Lowell wrote to WE on 5 December 1966: 'Let me say again that ever since I first met you in 1939 I have loved and reverenced you as my friend and teacher, as the most important teacher in England, the greatest Englishman.'

RICHARD LUCKETT (b. 1945) is Pepys Librarian of Magdalene College, Cambridge. His publications include *The White Generals: an account of the White movement and the Russian Civil War* (1971) and *Handel's Messiah: A Celebration* (1992).

WILLIAM LYONS (1911–95) was Professor of French at the University of Sheffield (1970–76); he specialized in early medieval French language and literature.

HYAM MACCOBY (1924–2004), Orthodox Jew, biblical scholar, writer on early rabbinic Judaism, and polemicist, was educated at Balliol College, Oxford. After a career as a secondary schoolmaster, he was for nineteen years (1975–94) librarian of Leo Baeck College, London; then Visiting Professor in the Centre for Jewish Studies at Leeds University, 1998–99. His publications include *Revolution in Judaea: Jesus and the Jewish Resistance* (1973), *Judaism on Trial: Jewish-Christian Disputations in the Middle Ages* (1982), *The Sacred Executioner: Human Sacrifice and the Legacy of Guilt* (1982), *The Mythmaker: Paul and the Invention of Christianity* (1986), and *Judas Iscariot and the Myth of Jewish Evil* (1992; winner of the Wingate Prize). Maccoby researched the Jewish foundations of Christianity, and was controversial in his unremitting search for the roots and branches of anti-Judaism. Other writings include a play, *The Disputation* (1995).

CHARLES MADGE (1912–96), poet and sociologist, followed in WE's footsteps at Winchester College and Magdalene College, Cambridge. In the mid-1930s he worked as a reporter on the *Daily Mirror*: this was thanks to the help of T. S. Eliot (who also published his first volume of verse, *The Disappearing Castle*, in 1937). In 1937 he launched (with Tom Harrisson) the Mass-Observation project, in which WE played a role by helping to edit the anthology *May the Twelfth* in 1937. For a while from 1937 Madge was married to Kathleen Raine (who had formerly been married to Hugh Sykes Davies (1909–84)); but in 1939 he ran off with Stephen Spender's first wife, 'Inez' Pearn, whom he married in 1942. After the war he was the first Professor of Sociology at the University of Birmingham, 1920–70. See *Mass-Observation as Poetics and Science*, special issue of *new formations* 44 (Autumn 2001), ed. Nick Hubble, Margaretta Jolly, Laura Marcus.

NICK MALONE (b. 1947) was born in Warrington and read Sociology at Sheffield (where he came into touch with WE). He went on to do postgraduate work in Literature, gaining an MA with distinction from Queen Mary College, London. For a time he pursued an academic career, becoming Principal Lecturer in Humanities at the University of Luton, but he interrupted his career to take a degree in Fine Art at the University of Hertfordshire, 1987–92. In 1994–5 he was visiting professor in Modern Literature at the Aristotle University of Salonika, Greece; and in 1995–6 visiting professor in Contemporary Literature at the University of Wisconsin. In 1997 he left academic life to become a full-time artist: he has subsequently exhibited extensively, both in London and internationally.

W. D. MAXWELL-MAHON (d. 2002) was Professor of English at the University of South Africa, Pretoria. His writings include *South African Poetry: A Critical Anthology* (with D. R. Beeton, 1966), *Critical Texts: Plato to the Present Day* (ed., 1979), and *Creative Writing* (1984), and articles on Thornton Wilder and on WE.

EARL MINER (b. 1927) is author of many scholarly works on Japanese fiction, and on John Dryden. A professor of English at Princeton University, 1972–5, he had formerly taught for some years at the University of California, Los Angeles. His publications include *Dryden's Poetry* (1967), *A History of Japanese Literature* (1984), and three volumes in the standard edition of the works of John Dryden.

ANDREW MOTION (b. 1952), poet, biographer, novelist, was appointed Poet Laureate in 1999. After lecturing in English at the University of Hull, he was editor of *Poetry Review*, 1981–3; poetry editor at Chatto & Windus, 1983–9; and for some years Professor of Creative Writing at the University of East Anglia. His works include *Dangerous Play: Poems, 1974–1984* (1984), *The Lamberts: George, Constant, and Kit* (1987), *Philip Larkin: A Writer's Life* (1993), *Keats* (1998), *Wainewright the Poisoner* (2000), and *The Invention of Dr Cake* (2003).

JOSEPH NEEDHAM (1900–95), biochemist, historian of science and civilization in China, and Christian socialist, was educated at Gonville and Caius College, Cambridge (he remained a fellow for life, and served as Master of the college for ten years from 1966). His early writings included *The Sceptical Biologist* (1929) and *Chemical Embryology* (3 vols., 1931); but his major project—conceived during the Second World War when he established the Sino-British scientific cooperation office and served as scientific counsellor at the British Embassy in Chongqing—was a comprehensive history of Chinese science, technology, and medicine which was to absorb the second half of his life. A polymath and a pro-Chinese witness (he was for some years declared *persona non grata* by the USA), he was ultimately regaled with honours for his outstanding labours. In 1992 he was made a Companion of Honour; in 1994 he received the Einstein medal from UNESCO. WE (who reviewed the second volume of *Science and Civilisation in China* in 1956) profoundly admired his vast learning and his socialist principles.

CHRISTOPHER NORRIS (b. 1947), literary and cultural theorist, has taught since 1978 at the University of Wales Institute of Science and Technology, Cardiff. He was elected to a Personal Chair in English in 1987, but in 1994 switched disciplines to become Professor of Philosophy. His works include two studies of WE, *William Empson and the Philosophy of Literary Criticism* (1978), and *William Empson: The Critical Achievement* (ed. with Nigel Mapp, 1993); and many other works including *Deconstruction: Theory and Practice* (1982), *The Deconstructive Turn: Essays in the Rhetoric of Philosophy* (1983), *The Contest of Faculties: Philosophy and Theory after Deconstruction* (1985), *The Truth about Postmodernism* (1993), and *On the Limits of Anti-Realism: Truth, Meaning and Interpretation* (1996).

A. D. NUTTALL (b. 1937) taught for several years (1962–84) at the University of Sussex, where he became Professor of English. In 1984 he became a Fellow of New College, Oxford, where he has been Professor of English Literature since 1992. His publications include *Overheard by God: Fiction and Prayer in Herbert, Milton, Dante and St John* (1980), *A New Mimesis* (1983), *The Stoic in Love: Selected Essays on Literature and Ideas* (1989), *Openings: Narrative Beginnings from the Epic to the Novel* (1992), *Why Does Tragedy Give Pleasure?* (1996), *The Alternative Trinity: Gnostic Heresy in Marlowe, Milton and Blake* (1998), and *Dead from the Waist Down: Scholars and Scholarship in Literature and the Popular Imagination* (2003). He is a Fellow of the British Academy.

DARCY O'BRIEN (1939–98) was born in Los Angeles, the son of the movie stars George O'Brien and Marguerite Churchill. Educated at Princeton (from where he became a Fulbright scholar at Cambridge) and at the University of California, Berkeley, he taught English at Pomona College and then (from 1978) in the Faculty of English Language and Literature at the University of Tulsa. His publications include the best-selling novels *A Way of Life, Like Any Other* (1977), which won the PEN/Hemingway Award in 1978, and *Murder in Little Egypt* (1990); nonfiction works including *Power to Hurt*, which received the Edgar Allen Poe Award, and *The Hidden Pope* (1998), as well as two academic works: *The Conscience of James Joyce* and a critical study of Patrick Kavanagh.

C. K. OGDEN (1889–1957), psychologist, linguist, and polymath, founded *Cambridge Magazine* in 1912, co-founded (in 1911) the Heretics Society, and devised Basic English, 'an auxiliary international language' based on a vocabulary of just 850 words of English, which WE regarded as a practicable English teaching tool rather than as an international language. ('Basic' is an acronym for British American Scientific International Commercial.) He established the Orthological (Basic English) Institute in 1927. His publications include *Foundations of Aesthetics* (with I. A. Richards and James Wood, 1921), *The Meaning of Meaning* (with I. A. Richards, 1923), *Basic English* (1930), *The Basic Vocabulary* (1930), and *The System of Basic English* (1934); and with F. P. Ramsey he translated the *Logisch-Philosophische Abhandlung* of Ludwig Wittgenstein (1922). For many years he was editor of the psychological journal *Psyche*, and he planned and edited the major series 'The International Library of Psychology, Philosophy and Scientific Method' (which was a source of information and constant diversion for WE). See W. Terrence Gordon, *C. K. Ogden: A Bio-bibliographic Study* (1990), and *C. K. Ogden: A Collective Memoir*, ed. P. Sargant Florence and J. R. L. Anderson (1977), as well as the essays by WE collected as 'I. A. Richards and Basic English', in *A*, pp. 193–238.

GEORGE ORWELL (1903–50), novelist and essayist, was WE's colleague and friend in the Far Eastern section of the BBC (based at Oxford Street, London) between February 1941 and November 1943. Educated at Eton College, Orwell had worked for the Burma police, 1921–7, before resolving to endure long periods of slumming in London and Paris. His publications include *Down and Out in Paris and London* (1933), *The Clergyman's Daughter* (1935), *Keep the Aspidistra Flying* (1936), *The Road to Wigan Pier* (1937), *Homage to Catalonia* (the fruit of his engagement in the Republican cause in the Spanish Civil War, 1938), *Coming Up for Air* (1939), *Animal Farm* (1945), and *Nineteen Eighty-Four* (1949). See also *The Complete Works of George Orwell*, 20 vols., ed. Peter Davison (1986–98).

IAN PARSONS (1906–80), publisher, editor, and anthologist, was a close friend of WE's at Cambridge (where he edited *Cambridge Review* and acted in WE's play, *Three Stories*). Educated at Trinity College, he became a junior partner at Chatto & Windus in 1930, and Chairman and Managing Director, 1954–75. He was president of the Publishers' Association, 1957–9. His publications include *The Progress of Poetry: An Anthology of Verse from Hardy to the Present* (1936), *Men Who March Away* (1965), *The Collected Works of Isaac Rosenberg* (1979).

JOHN OLIVER PERRY (b. 1929), who was educated at Kenyon College, the University of Florida, and the University of California at Berkeley, was assistant professor of English at the State University of New York at Binghamton, 1958–64. His writings include *The Experience of Poems* (1972) and *Absent Authority: Issues in Contemporary Indian English Criticism* (1992).

JOHN PETER (b. 1921) was born and raised in South Africa. In 1961 he became a professor of English at the University of Victoria, British Columbia. His writings include *Vladimir's Carrot: Modern Drama and the Modern Imagination* (1987).

H. W. PIPER (b. 1915) was educated at the University of Adelaide and at Magdalen College, Oxford. He taught at the University of Adelaide, at the University of New England, Armidale, New South Wales, and from 1966 as Professor and Head of the School of English at Macquarie University, Sydney. His publications include *The Active Universe* (1962), *The Beginnings of Modern Poetry* (1967), and *The Singing of Mount Abora: Coleridge's Use of Biblical Imagery and National Symbolism in Poetry and Philosophy* (1987).

DAVID B. PIRIE (b. 1943) taught English at Manchester University and collaborated with WE in the demanding project of editing *Coleridge's Verse: A Selection* (1972); he also edited WE's posthumous *Essays on Shakespeare* (1986). His other publications include *William Wordsworth: the poetry of grandeur and of tenderness* (1982), *How To Write Critical Essays* (1985), and *Shelley* (1988).

F. T. PRINCE (1912–2003) was born in South Africa and educated at Wits University, Johannesburg, Balliol College, Oxford, and Princeton University. During the war he served in Army Intelligence. From 1946 he taught at the University of Southampton, where he was to become Professor of English, 1957–74; later at the University of the West Indies, Jamaica, 1975–78. He was President of the English Association, 1985–6, and a Visiting Fellow of All Souls College, Oxford, 1968–9. In 1973 he gave the Clark Lectures at Cambridge. His works include *Poems* (1938), *Soldiers Bathing and Other Poems* (1954), *The Italian Element in Milton's Verse* (1954), *Collected Poems* (1993); editions of Milton, and Shakespeare's *Poems* (New Arden, 1960). See *Dictionary of Literary Biography*, vol. 20 (1978); 'F. T. Prince: A Tribute', *PN Review* 29: 1 (Sept.–Oct. 2002), 26–38.

KATHLEEN RAINE (1908–2003), poet and scholar, read Natural Sciences and Psychology at Girton College, graduating in 1929. Briefly married in 1929 to Hugh Sykes Davies, she then married Charles Madge, though that marriage was almost as short-lived. She was a Research Fellow at Girton College, 1955–61; and Andrew Mellon Lecturer at the National Gallery of Art in Washington, DC, in 1962. Her early poetry was published by Tambimuttu (founder of *Poetry London*): her first volume was *Stone and Flower*, (1943), with illustrations by Barbara Hepworth; and other collections include *The Year One* (1952), *Collected Poems* (1956, 2000), and *The Hollow Hill* (1965). Her critical works include *Blake and Tradition* (2 vols., 1968–9)—'It makes all other studies of Blake obsolete,' said C. S. Lewis— *Thomas Taylor the Platonist: Selected Writings* (1969), *William Blake* (1970), *Yeats, The Tarot and The Golden Dawn* (1972), *From Blake to a Vision* (1979), and *Blake and the New Age* (1979); and she published four volumes of autobiography: *Farewell Happy Fields* (1972), *The Land Unknown* (1975), *The Lion's Mouth* (1977), *India Seen Afar* (1990). In 1968 she failed to win the Oxford Chair of Poetry (losing with a bad grace to Roy

Fuller—'he's no poet'); and in 1991 she turned down an invitation from the Royal Society of Literature to become one of its ten Companions of Literature. She won the W. H. Smith Literary Award (1972), the Queen's Gold Medal for Poetry (1992); and in 2000 she was appointed both CBE and Commandeur de l'Ordre des Arts et des Lettres. In 1980 she launched *Temenos* ('Sacred Enclosure'), a review 'devoted to the arts of the imagination' and stressing 'the intimate link between the arts and the sacred'; and in 1990, with patronage from the Prince of Wales, she founded the Temenos Academy of Integral Studies, which she styled a 'school of wisdom'.

HAROLD RAYMOND (1887–1975) was a partner in Chatto & Windus, 1919–53; chairman of Chatto & Windus Ltd., 1953–4. He is celebrated for inventing the Book Tokens scheme which was adopted by the British Book Trade in 1932.

I. A. RICHARDS (1893–1979), theorist of literature, education and communication studies, and poet and playwright, was WE's tutor for English in 1928–29 at Magdalene College, Cambridge (where Richards had been appointed college lecturer in English and moral sciences in 1922). He had initially studied History but switched to moral sciences, graduating BA from Magdalene in 1915. A vigorous, spell-binding educationalist, he was to the fore in the advancement of the English Tripos at Cambridge. His early studies—*The Foundations of Aesthetics* (with C. K. Ogden and James Wood, 1922), *The Meaning of Meaning* (also with Ogden, 1923), *Principles of Literary Criticism* (1924), *Science and Poetry* (1926), and *Practical Criticism: A Study of Literary Judgment* (1929)—are foundational texts in modern English literary studies; they stimulated much of WE's writing throughout the early years of his career. After teaching at National Tsing Hua University in Peking, 1929–30, Richards repaired for the remainder of his career to Harvard University, where he was made a university professor in 1944. His other works include *Basic Rules of Reason* (1933), *Basic in Teaching: East and West* (1935), *Mencius on the Mind* (1932), *Coleridge on Imagination* (1934), *The Philosophy of Rhetoric* (1936), *Interpretation in Teaching* (1938), *Internal Colloquies* (1971), and *Speculative Instruments* (1955), and translations from Plato and Homer. He was appointed CH in 1963, and awarded the Emerson-Thoreau medal of the American Academy of Arts and Sciences in 1970. Outside the teaching term, he enjoyed with his wife Dorothy Richards (1894–1986), whom he married in 1926, an active life of travel and mountain-climbing. Their shared passion is recounted in her *Climbing Days* (1935), a modern classic.

CHRISTOPHER RICKS (b. 1933) has been a Fellow of Worcester College, Oxford, 1958–68; Professor of English at Bristol, 1968–76; and Professor of English at Cambridge, 1975–86. Since 1986 he has taught at Boston University, where he is now a Director of the Editorial Institute. His works include *Milton's Grand Style* (1963), *The Poems of Tennyson* (ed., 1969), *Keats and Embarrassment* (1974), *The Force of Poetry* (1984), *The New Oxford Book of Victorian Verse* (ed., 1987), *Eliot and Prejudice*

(1988), *Beckett's Dying Words* (1993), T. S. Eliot, *Inventions of the March Hare: Poems 1909–1917* (ed., 1996), *The Oxford Book of English Verse* (ed., 1999), *Essays in Appreciation* (1999), and *Dylan's Visions of Sin* (2004).

LAURA RIDING (1901–91) was brought up in New York and studied at Cornell University. At Cornell she married in her second year a history tutor named Louis Gottschalk, though the marriage was to be dissolved in 1925; in 1941 she would marry Schuyler B. Jackson. For a while from 1924 she became associated with the Fugitive group of writers including John Crowe Ransom and Allen Tate (and was awarded the Nashville Prize in 1924); and for 14 years, from 1926 to 1939, she enjoyed a close relationship with Robert Graves. Riding and Graves co-authored both *A Survey of Modernist Poetry* (1927) and *A Pamphlet Against Anthologies* (1928); they also founded the Seizin Press. Her works include *The Close Chaplet* (published by the Hogarth Press, 1926), *Anarchism is Not Enough* (1928), *Collected Poems* (1938), *Selected Poems* (1970), and *The Telling* (1972).

(FRANCIS) WARREN ROBERTS (1916–98) was Director of the Harry Ransom Humanities Research Center at the University of Texas in Austin, 1962–78. Born in Texas, he studied at Southwestern University (BA, 1938) and at the University of Texas (Ph.D., 1956). He joined the faculty of the University in 1954, and became a well-reputed authority on the works of D. H. Lawrence. He edited (with Harry T. Moore) two studies—*D. H. Lawrence and His World* (1966) and *Phoenix II: Uncollected, Unpublished, and Other Prose Work by D. H. Lawrence* (1968)—and in 1977 he received a Fulbright–Hays fellowship to carry out research on 683 letters written by Lawrence between 1921 to 1924. He served as president of the South Central Modern Language Association, 1974–5, and he was a member of the Board of Trustees at Southwestern University, 1975–6.

MARK ROBERTS (b. 1923) was educated at Winchester and at Gonville & Caius College, Cambridge. After war service, he became Assistant Lecturer at King's College, London, and was a member of WE's department at Sheffield as Lecturer, then Senior Lecturer (1955–68). He was subsequently Professor of English, The Queen's University of Belfast 1968–75, and Professor of English Literature, University of Keele 1975–82. He contributed frequently to *Essays in Criticism*—provoking controversy with adversely critical pieces on such works as Helen Gardner's edition of Donne's *Songs and Sonnets* and Tolkien's *Lord of the Rings*—and he is author of *The Tradition of Romantic Morality* (1973), which has as its underlying theme the continuing and growing influence of the *moral* outlook of Romantic literature as opposed to the apparent decline of its *literary* influence.

MICHAEL ROBERTS (1902–48), critic, editor, and poet, was educated at King's College, London (where he read chemistry), and at Trinity College, Cambridge (mathematics). In the 1930s he worked as a schoolmaster (in London and at the Royal Grammar School in Newcastle upon Tyne). After the Second World War, during which he worked for the BBC European Service, he became Principal of the Church of England training college of St Mark and St John in Chelsea, London. In 1935 he married the critic and biographer Janet Adam Smith; the couple loved climbing mountains, and they went on a ski-ing holiday with WE— see Janet Adam Smith's engaging memoir, 'A is B at 8,000 feet', in *William Empson*, ed. Gill, pp. 34–40. Roberts edited the watershed anthologies *New Signatures* (1932) and *New Country* (1934); and *The Faber Book of Modern Verse* (1936). Other writings include *The Modern Mind* (1937), *T. E. Hulme* (1938), *The Recovery of the West* (1941), and *The Estate of Man* (1951). See also *A Portrait of Michael Roberts*, ed. T. W. Eason and R. Hamilton (College of S. Mark and S. John, 1949).

DEREK ROPER (b. 1930) was educated at the University of Durham and at Lincoln College, Oxford. In 1958 he was appointed (by WE) as a Lecturer in English Literature at the University of Sheffield, where he became Senior Lecturer, 1971–90. His works include *Reviewing before the 'Edinburgh', 1788–1802* (1978); and editions of Wordsworth and Coleridge, *Lyrical Ballads 1805* (1968); John Ford, *'Tis Pity She's a Whore* (1975); and (with Edward Chitham) *The Poems of Emily Bronte* (1995). For some years he worked on *The Annual Bibliography of English Language and Literature*: as general editor, 1975–7, and as UK editor, 1977–83.

S. P. ROSENBAUM (b. 1929) has taught at Cornell, Indiana, and Brown; and from 1964 he was a Professor of English at Erindale College, University of Toronto. A specialist in Bloomsbury, his publications include *The Early Literary History of the Bloomsbury Group* (1987), *Edwardian Bloomsbury* (1994), and *Aspects of Bloomsbury: Studies in Modern English Literary and Intellectual History* (1998).

A. L. ROWSE (1903–97), historian, was educated in Cornwall and at Christ Church, Oxford; in 1925 he was elected to a prize fellowship of All Souls College. His books include *Raleigh and the Throckmortons* (1961), *William Shakespeare: A Biography* (1963), two editions of Shakespeare's sonnets (1964, 1973), *Shakespeare the Man* (1973), *Simon Forman: Sex and Society in Shakespeare's Age* (1974), and *Discovering Shakespeare: A Chapter in Literary History* (1989).

ALAN RUDRUM (b. 1932), critic, editor, and university teacher, was educated in London and Nottingham, and taught at universities in Britain, Australia and the USA before being appointed Professor of English at Simon Fraser University in Canada, 1969–98. His major publications include *The Complete Poems of Henry Vaughan* (1976; rev. 1983, 1995), and *The Works of Thomas Vaughan* (1984).

JOHN PAUL RUSSO (b. 1944), who has taught at Harvard and Chicago, has been Professor of English at Rutgers University since 1977. His works include *Alexander Pope: Tradition and Identity* (1972), *Complementarities: I. A. Richards' Uncollected Essays* (1976), *I. A. Richards: His Life and Work* (1989),

ROGER SALE (b. 1932), educated at Swarthmore College and Cornell University, was from 1962 Professor of English at the University of Washington, Seattle. His works include *Modern Heroism: Essays on D. H. Lawrence, William Empson, and J. R. R.*

Tolkien (1973), *On Not Being Good Enough: Writings of a Working Critic* (1979), *Closer to Home: Writers and Places in England, 1780–1830* (1986).

MARTIN SEYMOUR-SMITH (1928–98), who was educated at St Edmund Hall, Oxford (BA, 1951), worked in Deya, Mallorca, as tutor to the son of Robert Graves, 1951–4. His publications include *Robert Graves: His Life and Work* (1982), *Rudyard Kipling* (1989), and *Hardy* (1994).

EDITH SITWELL (1887–1964), poet, biographer, anthologist, and novelist, praised WE's poetry, along with that of Ronald Bottrall and Dylan Thomas, in her Northcliffe Lecture, 'Three Eras of Modern Poetry' (which drew on her book *Aspects of Modern Poetry*), at the University of London in 1937 (see John Lehmann, *A Nest of Tigers: Edith, Osbert and Sacheverell Sitwell in their Times* (1968), 134–5). In June 1923 Sitwell's performance at the Aeolian Hall in London of her cycle of poems, *Façade*, with music by William Walton, placed her at the centre of modernistic experimentation. Her many other writings include *The Mother and Other Poems* (1915), *Gold Coast Customs* (1929), *Collected Poems* (1930), *Fanfare for Elizabeth* (1946), *The Queens and the Hive* (1962), and a tart autobiography, *Taken Care Of* (1965). She was appointed a DBE in 1954.

JANET ADAM SMITH (1905–99) read English at Somerville College, Oxford, and married the poet and editor Michael Roberts in 1935. She was assistant editor of the *Listener*, 1930–5; assistant literary editor, 1949–52, and literary editor, 1952–60, of the *New Statesman*. See her memoir of WE on skiing holidays, 'A is B at 8,000 feet', in Gill, 34–40. Her other publications include *Mountain Holidays* (1946), *John Buchan: A Biography* (1965), and *John Buchan and His World* (1979); as well as anthologies including *The Faber Book of Children's Verse* (1953).

JOHN SPARROW (1906–92) was so precocious as a scholar at Winchester College (where he was an exact contemporary of WE, though never his friend) that at the age of 16 he published an edition of John Donne's *Devotions upon Emergent Occasions* (1923). Educated after school at New College, Oxford, he was called to the Bar at the Middle Temple, 1931. From 1929 he was a Fellow of All Souls College, of which he became Warden, 1952–77. His writings include *Sense and Poetry: Essays on the Place of Meaning in Contemporary Verse* (1934), *Controversial Essays* (1966), *Mark Pattison and the Idea of a University* (1967).

STEPHEN SPENDER (1909–95), poet and critic, won a rapid reputation with a Faber & Faber collection, *Poems* (1933), following an appearance (alongside WE) in Michael Roberts's anthology *New Signatures* (1931). 'If Auden is the satirist of this poetical renascence,' wrote T. S. Eliot, 'Spender is the lyric poet.' Spender cultivated friendships with some of the foremost younger writers of the period, including W. H. Auden, Christopher Isherwood, John Lehmann, and J. R. Ackerley. With Cyril Connolly he set up the literary magazine *Horizon* in 1940. For a brief while in the 1930s he joined the Communist party and went to Spain to serve the republican cause. In the post-war years he was a visiting professor at a number of American universities, and he made international trips on behalf of the British Society for Cultural Freedom, the Congress for Cultural Freedom, and PEN. He served too as poetry consultant to the Library of Congress, 1965–6. For fourteen years from 1953 he was co-editor of the magazine *Encounter*, which—as it was ultimately proven—was from the start the beneficiary of funding from the CIA (just as many writers including WE had long suspected). Spender's other works include *The Destructive Element* (1935), *Vienna* (1934), *Forward from Liberalism* (1937), *The Still Centre* (1939), *World within World* (autobiography, 1951), *The Creative Element* (1953), *Collected Poems* (1955), *The Struggle of the Modern* (1963), *Love–Hate Relations* (1974); *The Thirties and After* (1978), *Journals, 1939–83* (1985), and the novels *The Backward Son* (1940) and *The Temple* (1989). He was instrumental in setting up *Index on Censorship* in 1971, and worked for five years (1970–5) as Professor of English at University College, London. He was awarded the CBE (1962), elected a Companion of Literature by the Royal Society of Literature (1977), and knighted in 1983.

Nikos (Nicolas) Stangos (1936–2004), poet and editor, was born in Greece and educated (from 1956) at colleges in the USA. In 1965 he came to London, where he was appointed by the aged Allen Lane to be poetry editor at Penguin Books, 1967–74; his productions included the Modern European Poets series and Art in Context. In 1967 he collaborated with David Hockney and Stephen Spender on an illustrated collection of translated poems by Constantine Cavafy (*Fourteen Poems*). From 1974 to 2003 he was editorial director of Thames & Hudson, where his most celebrated productions included beautiful studies of Francis Bacon, Lucian Freud, David Hockney, Frank Auerbach, and Howard Hodgkin.

Meary James Tambimuttu (1915–83), who was invariably known as 'Tambi', was the scion of a distinguished Ceylonese family. A flamboyant and charismatic poet and literary editor, the 'lion-waisted' Tambi descended upon London in 1938 and speedily got to know everyone of note in the artistic scene including T. S. Eliot, Kathleen Raine, Dylan Thomas, Louis MacNeice, Stephen Spender, David Gascoyne, and George Barker. He was celebrated for his editing of *Poetry London*, which he launched on a £5 shoestring budget in 1939 (it went broke on its second issue) and managed to keep going until 1951; Tambi was responsible for bringing out fourteen issues for the period ending in 1949. At its peak, the magazine had a circulation of 10,000. In 1948 he co-edited (with Richard March) *T. S. Eliot: A Symposium*. Of Eliot Tambi once said: 'He is really a wild man, like me!' In 1947 he left London for the USA (where in 1956 he launched *Poetry London—New York*), though he would return to London in 1968. See *Tambimuttu: Bridge between Two Worlds*, ed. by Jane Williams (1989).

E. M. W. Tillyard (1889–1962) was one of the examiners of the English Tripos when WE took his exams at Cambridge in the 1920s. His books include *The*

Elizabethan World Picture and *Studies in Milton.* See the obituary essay by Basil Willey, 'Eustace Mandeville Wetenhall Tillyard 1889–1962', *Proceedings of the British Academy* 49 (1963), 387–405. When WE put in for the Chair of English Literature at Sheffield in 1952, Tillyard was to apprise the Registrar: 'I shall never forget the brilliance of his papers. He has now an international reputation as critic and poet and in the eyes of the general literary world he would bring lustre on your English Chair in a way none of the other candidates could begin to do. He would command huge respect among the students. Unlike some modernists he has a catholic taste in Literature. He began as a scholar in mathematics and he has the logical penetration of the mathematician. In a certain kind of close literary analysis he has no equal. On the other hand his short flights are better than his long; and it was significant that his essay paper in the Tripos was ill-organized as a whole and much inferior to his other papers! And this brings me to my major doubt about him: whether he is suited to organizing and running an important department. Could he, I ask myself, really be bothered? For enthralling talk in the small hours he could be relied on, but I just don't know whether he would submit to the duty of running a department. I fear it will be most difficult to get evidence on this, his teaching posts having been in China. So I am compelled to end on this large doubt.' (*University of Sheffield*)

JULIAN TREVELYAN (1910–88)—son of the classical scholar and poet Robert Calverley Trevelyan, grandson of the Liberal politician and writer Sir George Otto Trevelyan, nephew of the historian George Macaulay Trevelyan—went up to Trinity College, Cambridge, to read English in 1928; like WE, he came to know Jacob Bronowski, Kathleen Raine and Humphrey Jennings. See his memories of WE in *Indigo Days* (1957). After training under Stanley William Hayter in the printmaking workshop at the 'Atelier Dix-Sept' in Paris, where he worked with Max Ernst, Oskar Kokoshka, Joan Miró, and Pablo Picasso, he took to Surrealism and exhibited at the *International Exhibition of Surrealism* in 1936. Also in 1936, he participated, with Tom Harrisson, Jennings and Charles Madge in the Mass-Observation project in Bolton, Lancashire. He was a founder member of the Printmaker's Council. In later years he specialized in etching and taught at the Chelsea College of Art and at the Royal College of Art (where he became Head of the Etching Department). In 1986 he was awarded a senior Fellowship of the Royal College of Art, and in 1987 he was elected an Academician of the Royal Academy of Arts. He was married first to Ursula Darwin (divorced 1950), and then to the painter Mary Fedden. See further *Julian Trevelyan: Catalogue raisonné of prints*, ed. Silvie Turner (London: Scolar and Bohun Gallery, 1999).

ROSEMOND TUVE (1903–64) taught English at Connecticut College, New London, from 1934 to 1962. In 1963 she was to become Professor of English at the University of Pennsylvania, Philadelphia. Her publications include *Elizabethan and Metaphysical Imagery: Renaissance Poetic and Twentieth-Century Critics* (1947), *A Reading of George Herbert* (1952), and *Essays by Rosemond Tuve: Spenser, Herbert, Milton,* ed. Thomas P. Roche, Jr (1970).

PETER URE (1919–69) taught at the University of Newcastle upon Tyne (1947–69), where he held the title of Joseph Cowen Professor of English Language and Literature. His publications include *Towards a Mythology: Studies in the Poetry of W. B. Yeats* (1946), *Yeats the Playwright* (1963), *Elizabethan and Jacobean Drama: Critical Essays* (1974), and the New Arden edition of *Richard II.*

WILLIAM VESTERMAN took his BA at Amherst College and his Ph.D. at Rutgers University, where he taught from 1969 in the English Department. He is author of *The Stylistic Life of Samuel Johnson* (1977) and of articles on English, American and Irish authors, incuding studies of time in twentieth-century fiction.

JOHN WAIN (1925–94), poet, critic, biographer, and novelist, was born in Stoke-on-Trent and educated at St John's College, Oxford (where he was friends with Kingsley Amis and Philip Larkin). He was Lecturer in English at the University of Reading, 1947–55, and thereafter a freelance writer (WE tried to dissuade him from giving up his academic post). He was Oxford Professor of Poetry in 1973–8. His works include *Hurry on Down* (1953), *Interpretations: Essays on Twelve English Poems* (ed., 1955), *Nuncle and Other Stories* (1960), *Sprightly Running: Part of an Autobiography* (1962), *Wildtrack: A Poem* (1965), *Samuel Johnson* (1974), which won the James Tait Black Memorial Prize and the Heinemann Award from the Royal Society of Literature, *Feng* (1975), and *Young Shoulders* (1982). See also David Gerard, *John Wain: A Biography* (1987); and Humphrey Carpenter, *The Angry Young Men: A Literary Comedy of the 1950s* (2002).

D. P. WALKER (1914–85) was Reader in Renaissance Studies at the Warburg Institute, University of London, 1961–75, and subsequently Professor of the History of the Classical Tradition. His works include *Spiritual and Demonic Magic: From Ficino to Campanella* (1958), *The Decline of Hell: seventeenth-century discussions of eternal torment* (1964), and *The Ancient Theology* (1972).

SYLVIA TOWNSEND WARNER (1893–1978) was a novelist and short story writer, and longtime companion of Valentine Ackland. Her novels include *Lolly Willowes* (1926), *Mr Fortune's Maggot* (1927), *The True Heart* (1929), *Summer Will Show* (1936); her non-fiction, *T. H. White: A Biography* (1967), *Scenes of Childhood* (1982), and *The Diaries of Sylvia Townsend Warner*, ed. Claire Harmon (1994). See also Claire Harman, *Sylvia Townsend Warner: A Biography* (1993). WE met her in London in 1930–1, and entertained her to an eccentric supper at his digs.

DAVID WILSON (b. 1944), was educated at Cambridge (where he read History) and Lancaster (MA in Linguistics), and taught for 25 years until his recent retirement at universities in England, Norway, and Finland. In-between academic appointments he spent eight years in Saudi Arabia: six years as a professional diver in the Red Sea while researching a study of the eighteenth-century marine biologist Petter Forsskal, and two years in the Asir Mountains, retracing the foot-steps of Wilfred Thesiger and St John Philby and collecting Himyaritic and Thamudic inscriptions. He also spent two years teaching Finnish Air Force pilots and mechanics how to comprehend the technical manuals of the F-18 Hornet. He has published mainly in the area of linguistics, but also articles on John Donne, e. e. cummings, and I. A. Richards. He has also co-edited an anthology, *Henceforth the Anglo-Saxon is the Brother of the Finn! Poems about Finland 1634–2000*.

G. WILSON KNIGHT (1897–1985) worked as a schoolmaster before being appointed Chancellors' Professor of English at the University of Toronto, 1931–40. In 1946 he was appointed Reader in English Literature at the University of Leeds, where he ultimately became Professor, 1955–62. His numerous publica-tions include *The Wheel of Fire: Essays on the Interpretation of Shakespeare's Sombre Tragedies* (1930), *The Imperial Theme: Further Interpretations of Shakespeare's Tragedies including the Roman Plays* (1931), *Principles of Shakespearian Production* (1936), *The Crown of Life: Essays in Interpretation of Shakespeare's Final Plays* (1947); and *Lord Byron's Marriage: The Evidence of the Asterisks* (1957).

RICHARD MIDDLEWOOD WILSON (1909–95) joined the University of Sheffield in 1946; he was Professor of English Language, 1955–73, and Dean of the Faculty of Arts, 1970–3. A graduate of the University of Leeds, he specialized in Middle English language and literature; his publications include *Early Middle English Litera-ture* (1939), *The Lost Literature of Medieval England* (1952), and an edition of the medieval text *The Equatorie of the Planetis* (with D. J. Prince, 1955).

ROBERT WINTER (1887–1987) was a flamboyant and gifted American academic. A native of Indiana, he studied at Wabash College—where his favourite teacher was Ezra Pound—and had lectured in English literature at Tsinghua University in Peking since the 1920s. His circle of friends included the writer Emily Hahn; and WE came to know him very well in Peking from the late 1940s. Winter was to write to a student, Wang Rujie, on 9 January 1982: 'In one of [Ezra Pound's] letters he said that I was the most civilised person in Crawfordsville . . . Without Pound I probably would now be an idiot crawling about in Crawfordsville. As it is, I am a belligerent atheist in China' (quoted in James J. Wilhelm, 'On the Trail of the "One" Crawfordsville Incident or, The Poet in Hoosierland', *Paideuma*, 13: 1 (Spring 1984), 25; also quoted in Herbert Stern, unpublished TS 'OIC III', p. 8; courtesy of Professor Stern). I. A. Richards, who met Winter in 1927, extolled him in the mid-1930s as an expert in Basic English—'a great increase in our strength . . . an excessively [*sic*] gifted man who seems to have almost been waiting for Basic to give him his proper work to do' (letter to David H. Stevens, Rockefel-ler Archive Center, RG1, series 601, box 48, folder 398); and he inscribed a copy of his collection *New and Selected Poems* (1978) to Winter as '*the* reader who knows my verse best.' Dorothy Richards was to recall, 'Winter's knowledge of China was deep, varied, and witty. He taught us much of old Chinese culture . . . He had a reputation for knowing the coolies' most uninhibited forms of swearing well beyond the average foreigner's range' (Stern, op. cit., 9). The *Daily Telegraph* noted in an obituary (27 Jan. 1987, 16): 'Prof. Robert Winter, who has died in Peking, aged 100, was an American academic who taught English and Shakespeare studies to Chinese for more than 60 years . . . He lectured at Wabash, Northwestern and Chicago universities before taking up his first Chinese post at Nanking in 1923.' See also David Finkelstein, '57 Years Inside China: An American's Odyssey', *ASIA*, 2: 5 (Jan./Feb. 1980), 10.

RICHARD WORDSWORTH (b. 1915), actor and great-great-grandson of William Wordsworth, organized the Wordsworth Conference at the poet's house in the Lake District which WE attended in 1972 and 1974.

SOLLY ZUCKERMAN (1904–93) published two authoritative studies of mammalian physiology and sociology, *The Social Life of Monkeys and Apes* (1932) and *Functional Affinities of Man, Monkeys, and Apes* (1933). Sands Cox Professor of Anatomy at the University of Birmingham, 1943–68; from 1974 he was President of the British Industrial Biological Research Association. In 1960–71 he was chief scientific adviser to the Ministry of Defence; President of the Zoological Society of London, 1977–84. Appointed to the Order of Merit in 1968, he was created a Life Peer in 1971. His other writings include *Nuclear Illusion and Reality* (1982).

INDEX

An asterisk following a surname indicates an entry in the Glossary of Names.

Abel, Karl 14
Adams, H. M. 613
Adams, J. C. 593
Adams, Robert Martin xxiv, 237–9, 464–7
Addison, Joseph 304
Aeschylus 397–8
Agenda 372; LETTER to 622–4
Agrippa, Cornelius 613–14, 669
Aiken, Conrad 369
Aldermaston March 339
Alexander, Peter 329
Allen, Walter 302
Alleyn, Edward 614
Alpers*, Paul LETTER to 649–50
Alvarez*, A. 257, 361–2, 372, 447; LETTER to 254–5
Ambler, Eric, *The Dark Frontier* 302
Amis, Kingsley 329
Amis, Martin 544–6
Angkor Wat 105–6
Angleton*, James Jesus 145; LETTERS to 125–9
Anglic spelling 54
Anthologies 89–90
Anti-Semitism 447–9
Aquinas, St Thomas 313, 528–9, 639, 644, 654
Arianism 282, 310–11, 325–6
Aristophanes 493
Aristotle 49, 560
Arnold, Matthew 24, 202, 551
Arrows 460; LETTER to 261–3
Arts Council 277
Athanasian Creed 416, 639
Athenaeum Club 224
Athlone Press, The 655
Auden, W. H. 51, 93–4, 105, 108, 298, 306–7, 320, 328, 331, 334, 426,
433, 460, 466, 597, 673; *Orators, The* 158; *Spain* 638
Augustine, St 669
Aurelius, Marcus 90
Austen, Jane 76, 122–5; *Mansfield Park* 124, 540–1
Authors Take Sides on the Civil War 460
Authors Take Sides on Vietnam 460–1

Bagby, Philip H. 253
Baker, Deborah 427–8
Bakhtin, Mikhail xxiii, xxx, xxxv
Bald, R. C., *John Donne: A Life* 535
Barclay, Christopher 302
Barker, George 144
Barnet, Sylvan xxvii
Barrett, Sylvia 141–3
Barton, Anne 681
Barua*, D. K. LETTERS to 384–5, 406–7
Basic Dictionary 132–3
Basic English 37–8, 43, 45–6, 53, 55, 66, 69–70, 72, 76–7, 84, 100, 112–13, 116, 132–4, 139–41, 155, 175–6, 185, 426; *see also* Ogden, C. K., and Richards, I. A.
Bate, Walter Jackson xlviii, 554
Bateson, F. W. xxiv, 202–12, 268–9
Baudelaire, Charles 392; *Fleurs du Mal* 667; 'L'Invitation au Voyage' 90
Bayley, John 206–7, 330, 589–91
BBC xix, 86–7, 126–9, 131, 134, 139–41, 144–5, 148–9, 155, 181, 186, 263, 537, 596–8, 625, 636–7, 661; WE in Monitoring Service of 127–9, 131; WE in Far Eastern Service of 134–5, 139–41, 144–5, 148–9; *see also* broadcasting
Beardsley, Monroe C., 'Intentional Fallacy, The', *see* Wimsatt, Jr., W. K.